CARSWELL

EVIDENCE
PRINCIPLES AND PROBLEMS

Twelfth Edition

by

Ronald Joseph Delisle
B.Sc., LL.B., LL.M.

Faculty of Law
Queen's University

Don Stuart
B.A., LL.B., Dip. Crim., D. Phil.

Faculty of Law
Queen's University

David M. Tanovich
B.A., M.A., LL.B., LL.M.

Faculty of Law
University of Windsor

Lisa Dufraimont
B.ArtsSc., J.D., LL.M., J.S.D.

Osgoode Hall Law School
York University

THOMSON REUTERS®

A cataloguing record for this publication is available from Library and Archives Canada.

ISBN 978-0-7798-8655-5

Printed in the United States by Thomson Reuters.

TELL US HOW WE'RE DOING
Scan the QR code to the right with your smartphone to send your comments regarding our products and services.
Free QR Code Readers are available from your mobile device app store.
You can also email us at feedback.legaltaxcanada@tr.com

 **THOMSON REUTERS**®

THOMSON REUTERS CANADA, A DIVISION OF THOMSON REUTERS CANADA LIMITED

One Corporate Plaza	**Customer Support**
2075 Kennedy Road	1-416-609-3800 (Toronto & International)
Toronto, Ontario	1-800-387-5164 (Toll Free Canada & U.S.)
M1T 3V4	Fax 1-416-298-5082 (Toronto)
	Fax 1-877-750-9041 (Toll Free Canada Only)
	Email CustomerSupport.LegalTaxCanada@TR.com

PREFACE TO TWELFTH EDITION

In 1984, in the first edition of this book, author Ron Delisle sought to depart from the usual casebook format of lengthy case extracts to teach evidence largely by narrative text and consideration of problems. The text throughout aimed to identify the principles of the law, their historical background, their inherent logic or lack of logic, ethical issues, and attempts at reform in Canada and other jurisdictions. Another major feature of the first edition was a reflection of the reality that in most trials evidence is allowed in rather than excluded. It was therefore important to address the positive part of the law of evidence regarding how evidence is adduced, rather than to view the law as a briar patch of exclusionary rules.

In 1989, the second edition included, at the urgings of fellow evidence teachers, a careful selection of extracts from leading evidence cases. From this time on the book became partly a text and partly a casebook. The struggle has always been to avoid overwhelming the original aim by including too many cases and too much detail.

The Law Reform Commission of Canada in the 1970s, for whom Ron was a major contributor on their Evidence Project, proposed that Parliament codify the principles of the law of evidence. This view was not well-received by the profession who seemed concerned that the new Code would give judges too much discretion. The irony is that, with reform left to the courts, the unremitting trend over the last 45 years has been to allow judges more discretion as to what evidence to admit and what evidence to exclude. The central issue is how best to provide guidelines for such discretion.

Evidence is a branch of jurisprudence in which lawyers, judges and those learning the law for the first time must carry a working knowledge in their heads. This can be a daunting challenge given that the principal source is ever-changing case law. We provide a detailed table of contents with many subheadings and the inclusion of the major cases to distinguish those in the text that are purely illustrative. To aid the reader we divide the law of evidence into just five broad chapters.

Chapter 1 starts by relating the law of evidence to the common law commitment to an adversarial system of fact adjudication and the roles of lawyers and judges. The reader is introduced to the sources of the laws of evidence. We consider views, such as those of Lisa Dufraimont, of whether the laws of evidence have a unifying purpose. We set out arguments in the controversial and ongoing debate as to whether rules of evidence should be codified. Finally we address their applicability to forums other than courts such as administrative tribunals and Aboriginal rights cases under s. 35 of the *Constitution Act, 1982*.

Chapter 2 considers burdens of proof in both criminal and civil cases. Special attention is given to the distinction between persuasive and evidentiary burdens, measures of proof, tests of sufficiency, and the thorny issue of presumptive devices including the presumption of innocence now entrenched in the *Canadian Charter of Rights and Freedoms*.

In Chapter 3 the central topics of relevance and discretion to exclude at common law and now under the *Charter* are considered in detail. We assess how courts in both criminal and civil cases have recognized a general discretion to exclude evidence where its probative value is exceeded by its prejudicial effect. We highlight reassertion of this principled approach in *Grant* in 2015 and *Hart* in 2014 and point to the recognition of a discretion to exclude if evidence does not meet a reliability threshold. We note the uncertain discretion the Supreme Court now recognizes under the *Charter* to exclude evidence to ensure a fair trial. We concentrate less on the *Charter* discretion in s. 24(2) to exclude evidence obtained in violation of a *Charter* right. Since one of the central considerations under s. 24(2) is the nature and seriousness of the *Charter* breach we are of the view that that topic is better considered in Criminal Procedure courses. See Stuart and Quigley, *Learning Canadian Criminal Procedure*, 12th ed. (Carswell, 2016). We do summarize the Supreme Court's bellwether 2009 rulings in *Grant* and *Harrison*, where the Court put in place a totally revised template of factors for the exercise of s. 24(2) discretion, and note the now robust exclusionary trend based on the seriousness of the *Charter* violation rather than the seriousness of the offence.

Chapter 4 considers the traditional common law canons of exclusion: A. Character, B. Hearsay, C. Voluntary Confession Rule, D. Opinion Evidence and Experts, and E. Privilege. In each of these diverse areas we explore how rigid traditions have mostly given way to discretionary approaches where it is essential to carefully identify the criteria to be used. The challenge for students and lawyers alike is that our courts remain active and often inconsistent.

Under Character we pay particular attention to the decisions of the Supreme Court in *Handy* and *Shearing* that similar fact evidence may exceptionally be admitted to show propensity. We focus on the impact of these decisions in the criminal and civil contexts. We explore the controversial topic of rape shield laws, including the Supreme Court's rulings in *Seaboyer* and *Darrach* and the difficulties of balancing the conflicting interests to determine admissibility on a case-by-case basis, especially where the evidence is of the complainant's prior sexual conduct *with the accused*.

The Hearsay materials focus on how to identify hearsay and the Supreme Court's principled approach now fully developed in *Khelawon, Baldree* and *Bradshaw* based on considerations of necessity and reliability.

The Voluntary Confession Rule material discusses the approach required by *Oickle* and the majority ruling in *Singh* that this rule has subsumed the pre-right to silence set out in *Hebert*. We address the approach of Justice Moldaver in *Hart* and *Mack* to confessions obtained by undercover agents resorting to the Mr. Big strategy. We question whether our laws respecting police interrogations are satisfactory.

In the section on the admissibility of Opinions we address the fundamental ruling in *Graat* that lay witnesses may express opinions based on personal knowledge. We fully explore the Supreme Court's "gatekeeper" approach to the admissibility of expert opinion through the new controlling authority of *White Burgess Langille Inman*, which largely adopts the approach of Justice Doherty for the Ontario Court of Appeal in 2009 in *Abbey*. We discuss how *White Burgess* was applied in the Ontario Court of Appeal in the 2017 case of *Abbey* and consider the admission of drug recognition experts in *Bingley*. We review the Court's approach to novel scientific evidence earlier set out in *J. (J.-L.)* and *Trochym*.

Under Privilege we discuss class privileges such as those of client/lawyer, litigation and marital privilege and the case-by-case privilege according to Wigmore's criteria. We conclude by examining the approach of the Supreme Court in *O'Connor* and *Mills*, and of Parliament, of balancing *Charter* rights of complainants in sexual assault cases on the issue of access to their therapeutic records. We compare the Court's controversial allowance of defence cross-examination on a diary in *Shearing*.

Chapter 5 addresses the positive side of the laws of evidence — how matters are proved by the admission of evidence. We first deal with situations where proof is not required: formal admissions of fact and the controversial and still-evolving doctrine of judicial notice. We focus consideration of the latter topic by comparing the broad views of Justice L'Heureux-Dubé with the more cautious views of Justice Binnie speaking for the Court in *Spence*. The section on real evidence considers practical topics such as how to file exhibits and how to authenticate, especially in the context of social media evidence. The section on demonstrative evidence reflects the growing use of such evidence by the courts, especially in civil cases. The lengthy section on witnesses now includes the current law as to the competency of young witnesses and adults with mental disabilities. We incorporate significant developments relating to the right to silence and the privilege against self-incrimination reinterpreted by Justice Moldaver speaking for the Supreme Court in *Nedelcu*. In the general section on cross-examination we include the Supreme Court of Canada's important ruling in *Lyttle* allowing cross-examination on unproven evidence subject to a requirement of good faith. Under the issue of cross-examination of prior inconsistent statements under ss. 10 and 11 of the *Canada Evidence Act* we include advocacy advice. This dimension is also evident in the section concerning cross-examination on declarations of adversity under ss. 9(1) and (2), using as a hard and recurring example the prosecution of domestic assault where the principal witness has recanted. The alternative is to rely on video-recorded evidence admitted as reliable hearsay under *B. (K.G.)* even where a witness has recanted.

In this twelfth edition the structure of this text and teaching book remain largely intact. We moved the Mechanics of Proof chapter to the end of the book because many teachers have found it better to first teach the canons of exclusion together, which we now do in Chapter 4. In Chapter 1 we focus more on the roles of lawyers, including Crown prosecutors and judges, and leave other ethics issues to other courses. In Chapter 5 we have removed the section on State privilege which focused on the right to confidentiality and is highly complex involving detailed statutory analysis. In an effort to decrease the overall length of the book we worked together to carefully re-edit throughout to remove footnotes, text, cases and problems that had grown out-of-date. We also added new problems and questions to test comprehension of the latest developments and to provoke discussion. We added the selected text of more than 20 new judgments. In our experience it is impossible to teach every topic and nuance of this case-driven subject in a four-hour-per-week semester course. The subject is too vast and complex so the teacher must be selective.

Although most of the leading decisions arise in the criminal context we continue to make a special effort to include leading civil cases and also rulings from various tribunals.

This edition considers the following major new rulings:

- *Villaroman* S.C.C. (circumstantial evidence; rule in Hodge's case)

- *Bradshaw* S.C.C. (corroboration for hearsay admissibility)

- *Bingley* S.C.C. (drug recognition experts)

- *Durham Regional Crime Stoppers* S.C.C. (informer privilege)

- *Barton* Alta. C.A. (sexual assault stereotypes and dated jury instructions)

- *Brissard* Ont. C.A. (motive in sexual assault cases)

- *Nero* Ont. C.A. (spousal privilege)

- *Hirsch* Sask. C.A. (Facebook messages)

- *Abbey* (2017) Ont. C.A. (expert evidence)

- *Falconer* N.S. C.A. (admissions)

- *MacIsaac* Ont. C.A. (collateral facts)

Attention is also given throughout to significant rulings by trial judges, including the sexual assault acquittal in *Ghomeshi* and Parliament's response in Bill C-51.

We thank Melissa Vieira of Carswell for her support. We are deeply indebted to Cheryl Finch, Thomson Reuters freelance editor, for her meticulous work in so carefully reviewing the production of this new edition.

Don Stuart
David M. Tanovich
Lisa Dufraimont
May 1, 2018

TABLE OF CONTENTS

Chapter 1

Introduction

The law of evidence provides lawyers with the rules and principles that govern the admissibility of material offered by them in an effort to prove or disprove the existence of a material fact. This material most often takes the form of testimony, documents or physical objects.

As the great evidence scholar Rupert Cross was so fond of saying, "evidence of a fact is that which tends to prove it". In most trials, evidence is admitted rather than excluded. However, the law of evidence is sometimes misleadingly viewed as a briar patch of exclusionary rules. Those exclusionary rules are now the subject of the fourth chapter of this book. The other chapters will deal with the positive aspects of the law of evidence, including how and on what criteria lawyers get evidence admitted.

This introductory chapter explores the nature and suitability of the adversarial model for fact adjudication, legal ethics, the sources of the law of evidence and the applicability of the rules in different adjudicative contexts.

1. THE ADVERSARY SYSTEM

(a) Not a Scientific Inquiry

A trial, civil or criminal, provides society with the final forum within which a dispute can be settled. Most disputes, civil or criminal, are settled by negotiation between the parties. It is only when they are unable to reach a settlement by themselves that they turn to the courts or administrative tribunals for help. Oftentimes the dispute centres around different appreciations of the applicable law. The parties are agreed as to what happened but cannot agree on the legal significance of those facts. The court or administrative tribunal, operating with agreed facts, provides a legal answer. More often, however, the dispute is caused by different interpretations as to what in fact occurred between the parties. When the parties cannot agree on the historical facts they turn to one of our institutions and ask a third party to make a determination so that the matter can be settled and the parties can get on with their lives. The method of fact determination that we in the Anglo-Canadian common law tradition have adopted is called the "adversary method".

The adversary method stands in contrast to the non-adversarial fact-finding method employed in civil law countries, which is sometimes called the "inquisitorial" method. A key distinction between the two methods is the role of the judge: in the civil law tradition, the judge actively investigates and conducts the inquiry, while the adversary judge remains relatively passive. She does not herself conduct the inquiry and she does not investigate. She presides over a contest between two parties and judges the merits of two positions that are put before her. The tradition in the English-speaking world is to regard the "over-speaking judge [as] no well-tuned cymbal".[1]

A frank description of our method of inquiry is seen in *Phillips v. Ford Motor Co.*[2] In *Phillips* the plaintiff sued for damages arising out of an automobile accident. The issue was whether the accident was caused by a defective brake mechanism or driver error. The trial judge appointed an expert pursuant to the rules of court, which then stated:

> The court may obtain the assistance of merchants, engineers, accountants, actuaries or scientific persons, in such way as it thinks fit, the better to enable it to determine any matter of fact in question in any cause or proceeding.

The parties had called their experts but so did the judge. The judge's expert did more than simply interpret the evidence of the other experts; he provided input of his own. The judge also involved himself very much in the conduct of the proceedings. The parties were Nathan Phillips, elderly and retired mayor of Toronto, and the Ford Motor Company. Might it be that the adversaries were seen by the trial judge to be not evenly balanced in resources? In ordering a new trial, Evans J.A. wrote:

> Our mode of trial procedure is based upon the adversary system in which the contestants seek to establish through relevant supporting evidence, before an impartial trier of facts, those events or happenings which form the bases of their allegations. This procedure assumes that the litigants, assisted by their counsel, will fully and diligently present all the material facts which have evidentiary value in support of their respective positions and that these disputed facts will receive from a trial Judge a dispassionate and impartial consideration in order to arrive at the truth of the matters in controversy. A trial is not intended to be a scientific exploration with the presiding Judge assuming the role of a research director; it is a forum established for the purpose of providing justice for the litigants. Undoubtedly a Court must be concerned with truth, in the sense that it accepts as true certain sworn evidence and rejects other testimony as unworthy of belief, but it cannot embark upon a quest for the "scientific" or "technological" truth when such an adventure does violence to the primary function of the Court, which has always been to do justice, according to law.

While it is true that our modern-day system of fact adjudication in criminal and civil trials is largely adversarial, there are inquisitorial elements at some stages of the process. For example, in cases where an accused has been found to be not criminally responsible by reason of mental disorder, the *Criminal Code* gives the court or Review Board the task of determining the appropriate disposition. In *Winko v. Forensic Psychiatric Institute,*[3] the Supreme Court of Canada described the procedure as follows:

> The regime's <u>departure</u> from the traditional adversarial model underscores the distinctive role that the provisions of Part XX.1 play within the criminal justice

---

1   Lord Chancellor Bacon, as quoted by Lord Denning in *Jones v. Nat. Coal Bd.*, [1957] 2 Q.B. 55 (C.A.) at 64.
2   (1971), 18 D.L.R. (3d) 641 (C.A.) at 661.
3   [1999] 2 S.C.R. 625, 135 C.C.C. (3d) 129, 25 C.R. (5th) 1 (S.C.C.) at para. 54.

system. The Crown may often not be present at the hearing. The NCR accused, while present and entitled to counsel, is assigned no burden. The system is inquisitorial. It places the burden of reviewing all relevant evidence on both sides of the case on the court or Review Board. The court or Review Board has a duty not only to search out and consider evidence favouring restricting NCR accused, but also to search out and consider evidence favouring his or her absolute discharge or release subject to the minimal necessary restraints, regardless of whether the NCR accused is even present. This is fair, given that the NCR accused may not be in a position to advance his or her own case. The legal and evidentiary burden of establishing that the NCR accused poses a significant threat to public safety and thereby justifying a restrictive disposition always remains with the court or Review Board. If the court or Review Board is uncertain, Part XX.1 provides for resolution by way of default in favour of the liberty of the individual.

Can you identify any other inquisitorial features in criminal or civil trials?

(b) Truth and Justice: Competing Goals?

Justice Evans appeared to strike the balance in the *Phillips* case in favour of justice over truth. Similarly, in *R. v. Stinchcombe*[4] the Supreme Court of Canada relied on fairness to mandate the Crown's obligation to make disclosure to the defence of all relevant information.

The judgment of the Court was delivered by Sopinka J.:

Production and discovery were foreign to the adversary process of adjudication in its earlier history when the element of surprise was one of the accepted weapons in the arsenal of the adversaries. This applied to both criminal and civil proceedings. Significantly, in civil proceedings this aspect of the adversary process has long since disappeared, and full discovery of documents and oral examination of parties and even witnesses are familiar features of the practice. This change resulted from acceptance of the principle that justice was better served when the element of surprise was eliminated from the trial and the parties were prepared to address issues on the basis of complete information of the case to be met. Surprisingly, in criminal cases in which the liberty of the subject is usually at stake, this aspect of the adversary system has lingered on. While the prosecution bar has generally co-operated in making disclosure on a voluntary basis, there has been considerable resistance to the enactment of comprehensive rules which would make the practice mandatory. This may be attributed to the fact that proposals for reform in this regard do not provide for reciprocal disclosure by the defence. . . .

It is difficult to justify the position which clings to the notion that the Crown has no legal duty to disclose all relevant information. The arguments against the existence of such a duty are groundless while those in favour, are, in my view, overwhelming. The suggestion that the duty should be reciprocal may deserve consideration by this Court in the future but is not a valid reason for absolving the Crown of its duty. . . .

---

4   [1991] 3 S.C.R. 326.

I would add that the fruits of the investigation which are in the possession of counsel for the Crown are not the property of the Crown for use in securing a conviction but the property of the public to be used to ensure that justice is done. In contrast, the defence has no obligation to assist the prosecution and is entitled to assume a purely adversarial role toward the prosecution. The absence of a duty to disclose can, therefore, be justified as being consistent with this role.[5]

In *R. v. Peruta*,[6] the Crown unsuccessfully maintained that he was entitled to discovery of prior statements of the defence witnesses just as he was obliged to provide prior statements of his witnesses. In denying the thought, Justice Proulx explained:

The discovery of evidence is a constitutional guarantee for the accused which tries fundamentally to balance the forces involved in the trial.[7] . . .

It would be presumptuous to assert that this balance has now been reached and that the two parties, as they do in a civil trial, can mutually claim the total disclosure of the evidence.[8]

Ought there to be reciprocity in disclosure in criminal cases?[9] As is clear from *Stinchcombe* and *Peruta*, procedural or constitutional rights and practices aimed at promoting justice or fairness may impede the search for the truth. In civil litigation, there are rights to full discovery and disclosure of the evidence relied on by your opponent. However, in criminal law the accused has a *Charter* right to disclosure of the Crown's case but the Crown cannot, generally speaking, force the accused to reveal its exculpatory evidence or potential defences.

While justice is often referred to as a goal of evidence, the Supreme Court has also held that the search for truth is arguably the primary goal of the law of evidence.

Consider *R. v. Levogiannis*.[10] There an attack was made on the constitutional validity of a *Criminal Code* provision, s. 486(2.1), which permits young complainants to testify behind a screen. The accused challenged the provision on the grounds that it violated his right to a fair trial guaranteed by ss. 7 and 11(d) of the *Canadian Charter of Rights and Freedoms*. In deciding that the provision was constitutional Justice L'Heureux-Dubé wrote for the Court. In the course of her judgment she wrote:

The examination of whether an accused's rights are infringed encompasses multifaceted considerations, such as the rights of witnesses, in this case children, the rights of accused and courts' duties to ascertain the truth. The goal of the court process is truth seeking and, to that end, the evidence of all those involved in judicial proceedings must be given in a way that is most favourable to

---

5   *Ibid.* at 332-333.
6   (1993), 78 C.C.C. (3d) 350 (Que. C.A.).
7   "For in criminal cases, the State has in the police, an agency for the discovery of evidence, superior to anything which even the wealthiest defendant could employ.": "Devlin Report on Evidence of Identification" (1976), H.C. 338, para. 1.17. [Proulx J.A.'s footnote.]
8   *Supra* note 6 at 370.
9   Compare Tanovich & Crocker, "Dancing with Stinchcombe's Ghost: A Modest Proposal for Reciprocal Defence Disclosure" (1994), 26 C.R. (4th) 333; and Davison, "Putting Ghosts to Rest: A Reply to the Modest Proposal for Defence Disclosure" (1995), 43 C.R. (4th) 105.
10   [1993] 4 S.C.R. 475.

eliciting the truth. . . . [O]ne cannot ignore the fact that, in many instances, the court process is failing children, especially those who have been victims of abuse, who are then subjected to further trauma as participants in the judicial process.[11]

In *R. v. Darrach*,[12] Gonthier J., for a unanimous Court, dealt with rape shield legislation designed to protect the complainants in sexual assault cases. The accused complained that the legislation was unconstitutional as it deprived him of his fair trial rights. Justice Gonthier wrote:

> The current version of s. 276 is carefully crafted to comport with the principles of fundamental justice. It protects the integrity of the judicial process while at the same time respecting the rights of the people involved. The complainant's privacy and dignity are protected by a procedure that also vindicates the accused's right to make full answer and defence. The procedure does not violate the accused's s. 7 *Charter* right to a fair trial nor his s. 11(c) right not to testify against himself or his s. 11(d) right to a fair hearing.
>
> . . .
>
> . . . while the right to make full answer and defence and the principle against self-incrimination are certainly core principles of fundamental justice, they can be respected without the accused being entitled to "the most favourable procedures that could possibly be imagined". Nor is the accused entitled to have procedures crafted that take only his interests into account. Still less is he entitled to procedures that would distort the truth-seeking function of a trial by permitting irrelevant and prejudicial material at trial. [Citations omitted.]

The Supreme Court of Canada has taken a similar approach to the purpose of the law of evidence in civil cases.

IMPERIAL OIL v. JACQUES
2014 SCC 66, [2014] 3 S.C.R. 287, 316 C.C.C. (3d) 1 (S.C.C.)

LEBEL and WAGNER JJ. —

[1] The question raised by the appeals before the Court is whether a party to a civil proceeding can request the disclosure of recordings of private communications intercepted by the state in the course of a criminal investigation.

. . .

[2] Nearly 20 years ago, Cory J. observed that "[t]he ultimate aim of any trial, criminal or civil, must be to seek and to ascertain the truth" (*R. v. Nikolovski*, [1996] 3 S.C.R. 1197, at para. 13). Although the parallel objectives of proportionality and efficiency have become increasingly important in the civil procedure context, seeking the truth remains the cardinal principle in civil proceedings . . . Informed by this objective, the rules of the law of evidence in civil matters allow judges "to find out the truth, and to do justice according to

---

[11]   *Ibid.* at 483.
[12]   [2000] 2 S.C.R. 443 at paras. 3, 24.

law" (*Frenette v. Metropolitan Life Insurance Co.*, [1992] 1 S.C.R. 647, at p. 666, quoting *Jones v. National Coal Board*, [1957] 2 Q.B. 55 (C.A.), at p. 63).

. . .

[24] Although the power of judges to intervene in the conduct of civil proceedings has become increasingly broad, judges generally do not play an active part in the search for truth . . . In an accusatory and adversarial system, the delicate task of bringing the truth to light falls first and foremost to the parties . . .

The adversary method has been justified over the years by many lawyers as capable of promoting the finest approximation to the truth. Jerome Frank noted:

> Many lawyers maintain that the best way for the court to discover the facts in a suit is to have each side strive as hard as it can, in a keenly partisan spirit, to bring to the court's attention the evidence favourable to that side. Macauley said that we obtain the fairest decision "when two men argue, as unfairly as possible, on opposite sides" for then "it is certain that no important consideration will altogether escape notice." [13]

Whether the adversary method will more closely approximate truth is certainly open to question. The lawyer is trained to seek success for her client, to win the game. Her goal is to present the best picture of her client's position and not the most complete picture at her disposal. Also, the adversary system presupposes for success some equality between the parties; when this is lacking, the "truth" becomes too often simply the view of the more powerful. Most judges will confess to the frequent temptation to reach out and "even the match" although the system cautions against such practice. Perhaps most importantly, while it is true that in deciding between the validity of two competing theories the decision-maker may be considerably aided by advocates on each side presenting their respective positions in the strongest arguments possible, it is certainly questionable whether such a technique is valuable in ensuring that all of the available evidence has been presented by the parties for examination. As Professor Peter Brett has noted:

> . . . observe the practice of scientists and historians in carrying out their investigations . . . a lengthy search will fail to reveal one competent practitioner in either discipline who will willingly and in advance confine himself, in deciding any question involving factual data, to a choice between two sets of existing data proffered to him by rival claimants. In short, the inquisitorial method is the one used by every genuine seeker of the truth in every walk of life (not merely scientific and historical investigations) with only one exception . . . the trial system in the common-law world. [14]

---

[13]   *Courts on Trial* (1949) at 80.
[14]   See Brett, "Legal Decision Making and Bias: A Critique of an 'Experiment'" (1973) 45 U. Col. L. Rev. 1 at 23.

And Jerome Frank expressed his concern:

> But frequently the partisanship of the opposing lawyers blocks the uncovering of
> vital evidence or leads to a presentation of vital testimony in a way that distorts it.
> We have allowed the fighting spirit to become dangerously excessive. . . . In
> short, the lawyer aims at victory, at winning in the fight, not at aiding the court to
> discover the facts. He does not want the trial court to reach a sound educated
> guess, if it is likely to be contrary to his client's interests. Our present trial method
> is thus the equivalent of throwing pepper in the eyes of a surgeon when he is
> performing an operation.[15]

A major impediment to our search for truth is that the facts to be
discovered by our courts are almost always past facts. Our method of
discovering them is normally through the oral testimony of witnesses who
have personal knowledge about what happened. This personal "knowledge"
might perhaps better be described as personal beliefs about what they now
remember of facts which they believe they observed. The trier of fact then
has regard to what the witness says, and based on her observations of what
the witness said and how he said it, she comes to her own belief as to
whether that is an honest belief. She can do no more. She cannot, as the
scientist might, duplicate in her laboratory the actual facts and test the
hypothesis proposed. Facts as found by the court are really then only
guesses about the actual facts. As an illustration:

> When Jack Spratt, as a witness, testifies to a fact, he is merely stating his belief
> or opinion about that past fact. When he says, "I saw McCarthy hit Schmidt," he
> means, "I believe that is what happened." When a trial judge or jury, after hearing
> that testimony, finds as a fact that McCarthy hit Schmidt, the finding means no
> more than the judge's or jury's belief that the belief of the witness Spratt is an
> honest belief, and that his belief accurately reflects what actually happened. A
> trial court's findings of fact is, then, at best, its belief or opinion about someone
> else's belief or opinion.[16]

Justice Haines in *R. v. Lalonde* described it this way:

> A trial is not a faithful reconstruction of the events as if recorded on some giant
> television screen. It is an historical recall of that part of the events to which
> witnesses may be found and presented in an intensely adversary system *where
> the object is quantum of proof.* Truth may be only incidental.[17]

Besides searching for a different truth than the scientist, our methods are
also circumscribed by other considerations, which require our fact-finding to
be done in a way which is acceptable to the parties and to society. Our courts
provide a forum for the purpose of resolving disputes between parties which
they themselves have been unable to resolve in any other way. Our modern
form of trial began simply as a substitute for private duels and feuds which
had later been dignified by the process of trial by battle. Resolution of conflict
now must be done in a way which ensures social tranquility generally, and
which is also acceptable to the individual parties. The parties should be able

---

[15]   *Courts on Trial* (1949) at 81, 85.
[16]   *Ibid.* at 22.
[17]   (1971), 15 C.R.N.S. 1 (Ont. S.C.) at 4 [emphasis added].

to leave the court feeling that they have had their say, that their case has been presented in the best possible light, and that they have been judged by an impartial trier.[18] In judging the efficacy of the legal system's method of fact-finding we must remember:

> A contested law suit is society's last line of defense in the indispensable effort to secure the peaceful settlement of social conflicts. . . . It is a last-ditch process in which something more is at stake than the truth only of the specific matter in contest. There is at stake also that confidence of the public generally in the impartiality and fairness of public settlement of disputes which is essential if the ditch is to be held and the settlements accepted peaceably.
>
> . . . While it is of course important that the court be right . . . a decision must be made now, one way or the other. . . . To require certainty . . . would be impracticable and undesirable. The law thus compromises.[19]

As we examine the material in the pages that follow, we should ask ourselves whether the compromises we have made are the best that we can do.

When the law of evidence speaks of the search for truth, it is, in effect, speaking of legal rather than factual truth. A verdict is the product of what can be proved in the confines of the adjudicative forum applying rules of proof and admissibility. So, for example, in criminal cases there are only two verdicts reached by the trier of fact: not guilty and guilty. A not guilty or acquittal is an example of legal as opposed to factual truth. It is not a verdict of innocence but only that the Crown has not been able to prove its case beyond a reasonable doubt. **Should there be a third verdict of innocence in criminal case?** The Ontario Court of Appeal addressed this issue in the following case involving a wrongful conviction.

R. v. MULLINS-JOHNSON
(2007), 50 C.R. (6th) 265, 228 C.C.C. (3d) 505 (Ont. C.A.)

BY THE COURT:

[1] The death of a child is always tragic. In this case, the tragedy of four-year-old Valin Johnson's death is compounded by the fact her uncle, William Mullins-Johnson, was wrongfully convicted of her murder and spent twelve years in prison. It is now clear that there is no evidence that Valin Johnson was assaulted or murdered, and no evidence that Mr. Mullins-Johnson was guilty of any crime in relation to her death.

. . .

---

[18]   See authorities described by Brooks, *The Judge and The Adversary System, The Canadian Judiciary* (A. Linden, ed., 1976) at 98 *et seq.*
[19]   Hart & McNaughton, *Evidence and Inference in the Law* (D. Lerner, ed.); "Evidence and Inference" (Hayden Colloquium, 1958) at 52-53.

THE DECLARATION OF INNOCENCE

[22] The fresh evidence shows that the appellant's conviction was the result of a rush to judgment based on flawed scientific opinion. With the entering of an acquittal, the appellant's legal innocence has been re-established. The fresh evidence is compelling in demonstrating that no crime was committed against Valin Johnson and that the appellant did not commit any crime. For that reason an acquittal is the proper result.

[23] There are not in Canadian law two kinds of acquittals: those based on the Crown having failed to prove its case beyond a reasonable doubt and those where the accused has been shown to be factually innocent. We adopt the comments of the former Chief Justice of Canada in *The Lamer Commission of Inquiry Pertaining to the Cases of: Ronald Dalton, Gregory Parsons, Randy Druken*, Annex 3, pp. 342:

> [A] criminal trial does not address "factual innocence". The criminal trial is to determine whether the Crown has proven its case beyond a reasonable doubt. If so, the accused is guilty. If not, the accused is found not guilty. There is no finding of factual innocence since it would not fall within the ambit or purpose of criminal law.

[24] Just as the criminal trial is not a vehicle for declarations of factual innocence, so an appeal court, which obtains its jurisdiction from statute, has no jurisdiction to make a formal legal declaration of factual innocence. The fact that we are hearing this case as a Reference under s. 696.3(3)(a)(ii) of the *Criminal Code* does not expand that jurisdiction. The terms of the Reference to this court are clear: we are hearing this case "as if it were an appeal". While we are entitled to express our reasons for the result in clear and strong terms, as we have done, we cannot make a formal legal declaration of the appellant's factual innocence.

[25] In addition to the jurisdictional issue, there are important policy reasons for not, in effect, recognizing a third verdict, other than "guilty" or "not guilty", of "factually innocent". The most compelling, and, in our view, conclusive reason is the impact it would have on other persons found not guilty by criminal courts. As Professor Kent Roach observed in a report he prepared for the *Commission of Inquiry into Certain Aspects of the Trial and Conviction of James Driskell*, "there is a genuine concern that determinations and declarations of wrongful convictions could degrade the meaning of the not guilty verdict" (p. 39). To recognize a third verdict in the criminal trial process would, in effect, create two classes of people: those found to be factually innocent and those who benefited from the presumption of innocence and the high standard of proof beyond a reasonable doubt.

[26] Nothing we have said in these reasons should be taken as somehow qualifying the impact of the fresh evidence. That evidence, together with the other evidence, shows beyond question that the appellant's conviction was

wrong and that he was the subject of a terrible miscarriage of justice. We conclude these reasons by paraphrasing what the president of the panel said to Mr. Mullins-Johnson at the conclusion of the oral argument after entering the verdict of acquittal: it is profoundly regrettable that as a result of what has been shown to be flawed pathological evidence Mr. Mullins-Johnson was wrongly convicted and has spent such a very long time in jail.

[27] We can only hope that these words, these reasons for judgment and the deep apology expressed by Ms. Fairburn on behalf of the Ministry of the Attorney General will provide solace to Mr. Mullins-Johnson, to his mother and to everyone who has been so terribly injured by these events.

DISPOSITION

[28] Accordingly, in accordance with the terms of the Reference and s. 696.3(3)(a)(ii) of the *Criminal Code,* we admit the fresh expert evidence, allow the appeal, quash the conviction for first degree murder and enter an acquittal.

. . .

Do you agree with the decision?[20]

In her article "Evidence Law and the Jury: A Reassessment"[21] Professor Lisa Dufraimont searches for the purpose of the laws of evidence. She identifies three rationales: fear that jurors may misconstrue evidence (although she finds that empirical evidence for this proposition is weak), to restrain excessive adversarial behaviour by lawyers, and to exclude perjured evidence. She concludes that the picture is complex and that none of these rationales can alone explain all the laws of evidence. She concludes that most lawyers, judges and scholars of the laws of evidence identify the jury system as the paradigmatic form of adjudication even though the jury system is in decline. Most trials, civil and criminal, are before judge alone:

> If asked to envision an ideal method for ferreting out the truth about past events, few would imagine a process encumbered by technicalities that conceal relevant information from fact-finders and seek to control their evaluation of the evidence they are allowed to see. But the law of evidence constitutes just such a set of encumbrances. And while some pursue other policies, frequently the rules are directed at serving the search for truth itself. Thus, evidence rules appear apt to impede the very fact-finding they are designed to promote.

> Why, then, does our law use evidence rules to advance the search for truth? The classic explanation points to the common law jury, which, it is argued, lacks competence to evaluate certain forms of proof. Unconstrained by evidentiary regulation, it is feared that lay juries would produce an unacceptably high level of error in adjudication. The extent to which the jury in fact accounts for evidence law, either historically or analytically, is a matter of ongoing debate. Other

---

[20]   See the discussion by Kent Roach, "Do We Need Innocence Hearings" in M.E. Beare, ed., *Honouring Social Justice: Honouring Dianne Martin* (Toronto: University of Toronto Press, 2008).

[21]   (2008) 53 McGill L.J. 199.

explanations have been offered, the most promising of which focus on two other elements of a common law trial: the adversary nature of the proceedings, and the ever-present risk of witness dishonesty. Like the jury, these trial features are said to explain how the search for historical truth can be facilitated rather than defeated by regulating evidence.

. . .

C. The Complex Picture

The debate over the explanatory principles of evidence law is largely a debate about whom to mistrust. Is our fear that juries may misconstrue the evidence, that adversaries may obscure the truth, or that witnesses may perjure themselves? Of whom are we afraid, and whom are we trying to control? It seems doubtful that these questions can ever be answered in any decisive way.

Certainly some authors identify one explanatory principle as the primary, underlying principle of evidence law. Thayer, among others, focused on the jury, while recently evidence scholars have suggested that the central rationale for evidence law lies elsewhere. Nance argues that the best evidence principle, which is concerned with advocate control, constitutes a superior explanatory principle to the traditional jury-centred rationale for evidence law. According to Imwinkelried, both of those explanatory principles are inferior to the dishonesty-control rationale, which he claims constitutes "the best explanatory hypothesis for the logical structure of Evidence law." The modern theorists admit forthrightly that no one principle explains the totality of evidence law, an admission that militates in favour of interpreting their claims modestly. But beyond arguing the explanatory power of the various rationales for evidence law, these scholars purport to choose the best, unifying theories, or even to explain the law's "logical structure". Such ambitious claims are difficult to defend.

The search for an "organizing principle" of evidence law is vain because evidence law is not organized around a principle. Given the ad hoc nature of evidentiary regulation, there is no reason to believe that the various possible rationales for evidence rules are mutually exclusive. A more tenable position is to recognize that various factors, including the trial features under consideration, play a role in explaining evidence law. The origins and justifications of evidentiary rules are best uncovered in specific doctrinal contexts. And one could easily add yet more layers of complexity to the picture. Issues that cannot entirely be disentangled from the explanatory principles include extrinsic policy considerations like fairness and due process, as well as concerns about the efficient conduct of the trial process, such as affordability, speed, and finality. [footnotes omitted]

(c) The Role of the Trial Judge

The diligence of the parties in searching out evidence favourable to their side and the vigour with which they attack their opponents' case are seen by many as finer guarantees of approximating the historical truth than giving the problem for resolution to some government official whose motivation can rarely be of the magnitude of the parties.[22] Also, it is believed that the bias of the decision-maker can be minimized if they play a much less active role than is demanded in the inquisitorial method.[23] The judge who conducts the examination of witnesses "descends into the arena and is liable to have his vision clouded by the dust of the conflict. Unconsciously he deprives himself of the advantage of calm and dispassionate observation."[24]

R. v. STUCKEY

2009 ONCA 151, 240 C.C.C. (3d) 141, 65 C.R. (6th) 46 (Ont. C.A.)

WEILER AND GILLESE JJ.A. (ARMSTRONG J.A. concurring):

[60] We agree that the trial judge's interventions at trial did undermine the appearance of fairness of the trial in that, at various times, the trial judge assumed the role of counsel for the Crown through his cross-examination of defence witnesses, including the accused, and appeared to pre-judge the credibility of the accused. Accordingly, for the reasons that follow, we would set aside the trial judgment, and order a new trial.

1) The role of a trial judge

[61] The role of a trial judge is often very demanding, owing not only to the inherent nature of the case, but also to the particular conduct of the litigants: *R. v. Brouillard*, 1985 CanLII 56 (SCC), [1985] 1 S.C.R. 39, at p. 42. In the case at bar, the trial lasted 69 days and involved the examination of multiple witnesses, including experts and the accused himself. Notwithstanding the length and complexity of a particular trial, a trial judge must exercise restraint and maintain impartiality so as to act within the scope of his or her neutral role. As cautioned by Lamer J. in *Brouillard*, at pp. 42-43:

> Like anyone, a judge may occasionally lose patience. He may then step down from his judge's bench and assume the role of counsel. When this happens, and, *a fortiori*, when this happens to the detriment of an accused, it is important that a new trial be ordered, even when the verdict of guilty is not unreasonable having regard to the evidence, and the judge has not erred with respect to the law applicable to the case and has not incorrectly assessed the facts.

> The reason for this is well-known. It is one of the most fundamental principles of our case law [citation omitted]

> . . .that justice should not only be done, but should manifestly and undoubtedly be seen to be done.

---

22   See Brooks, *supra* note 18.
23   See Lind, Thibault & Walker, "Cross-Cultural Comparison of the Effect of Adversary and Inquisitorial Processes on Bias in Legal Decision-Making" (1976) 62 Va. L. Rev. 271.
24   Lord Greene, M.R. in *Yuill v. Yuill*, [1945] 1 All E.R. 183 (C.A.) at 189.

[62] The principles that limit the permitted interventions by trial judges during the course of a trial and, specifically, during the examination-in-chief and cross-examination of witnesses, are well established. We review them below.

2) Permitted interventions by a trial judge

[63] In *Brouillard*, at p. 44, Lamer J. acknowledged that a trial judge may intervene to ask questions, and, where necessary, he or she has a duty to ask questions where justice requires it. However, at the same time, he expressly warned that there are definite limits on this right: *Brouillard* at p. 46. A trial judge "should confine himself as much as possible to his own responsibilities and leave to counsel. . .[his or her] function": *R. v. Torbiak and Campbell* (1974), 18 C.C.C. (2d) 229 (Ont. C.A.), at pp. 230-231.

[64] In *R. v. Valley* (1986), 26 C.C.C. (3d) 207 (Ont. C.A.), at p. 230, leave to appeal refused, [1986] 1 S.C.R. xiii, Martin J.A. set out three situations in which questions put by a trial judge to a witness may be justified, namely: to clear up ambiguities and call a witness to order; to explore some matter which the witnesses' answers have left vague; or, to put questions which should have been asked by counsel in order to bring out some relevant matter, but which were nonetheless omitted. He noted, however, that questions put by a trial judge to a witness should generally be put after counsel has completed his or her examination of the witness and, further, that the witness should not be cross-examined by the trial judge during examination-in-chief: *Valley* at p. 230. These comments provide guidance as to the timing and nature of interventions that a trial judge may make.

[65] The first two situations of permitted interventions by the trial judge set out in *Valley* are self-explanatory. The third situation in which a trial judge is permitted to intervene, namely, to ask questions that should have been asked by counsel, is not an open-ended invitation to the trial judge to usurp the role of Crown counsel. The judge cannot leave his or her position of neutrality as a fact-finder and become the cross-examiner: *R. v. W.(A.)* (1994), 1994 CanLII 218 (ON CA), 94 C.C.C. (3d) 441 (Ont. C.A.) Brooke J.A. in dissent, reversed for the reasons given by Brooke J.A., 1995 CanLII 83 (SCC), [1995] 4 S.C.R. 51.

[66] Where the appearance of fairness is not maintained at trial, the verdict reached cannot stand and a new trial must be ordered. In deciding whether or not the appearance of fairness has been compromised, one factor that warrants consideration is whether the trial judge gave counsel an opportunity to ask questions that arise out of the trial judge's questioning of a witness, in particular, the accused. An additional factor is whether counsel objected to the trial judge's questioning of a witness. The absence of an objection, however, is not in itself determinative.

[67] We turn now to the test for determining when this unfairness threshold is met.

3) The test for determining whether the trial judge's interventions have compromised the appearance of trial fairness

[68] The test is an objective one. As stated by Martin J.A. in *Valley*, at p. 232:

> The ultimate question to be answered is not whether the accused was in fact prejudiced by the interventions but whether he might reasonably consider that he had not had a fair trial or *whether a reasonably minded person who had been present throughout the trial would consider that the accused had not had a fair trial.* [Emphasis added.]

[69] The appearance of fairness and the trial judge's corresponding duty to exercise restraint and remain neutral is especially critical in the criminal context where the accused takes the stand: *Brouillard* at p. 48. Since a criminal trial is an adversarial process between the prosecution and defence, and not an investigation by the trial judge, the examination and cross-examination of witnesses is, for the most part, the responsibility of counsel: *Valley* at p. 231. Although the trial judge is justified in occasionally intervening for one of the legitimate purposes indicated above, the trial judge must be careful not to usurp the role of counsel because otherwise the overall impression created may be fatal to the appearance of trial fairness.

[70] The effect of interventions by the trial judge on the appearance of trial fairness in a given case must be assessed in relation to the unique facts and circumstances of the particular trial: *Valley* at p. 231, citing *Torbiak* at p. 231.

[71] In *Valley* at pp. 231-32, Martin J.A. listed types of interventions by trial judges which have resulted in the quashing of criminal convictions:

1. Questioning an accused or a defence witness to such an extent or in a manner which conveys the impression that the trial judge has placed the authority of his or her office on the side of the prosecution and conveys the impression that the trial judge disbelieves the accused or the witness;

2. Interventions which have effectively made it impossible for defence counsel to perform his or her duty in advancing the defence; and

3. Interventions which effectively preclude the accused from telling his or her story in his or her own way.

[72] Interventions by a trial judge which can reasonably be said to create the appearance of an unfair trial may be of more than one type, and trial fairness may be undermined by one or more types of interventions: *Valley* at p. 232. However, it is important to emphasize that no trial is perfect. Accordingly, the record must be assessed in its totality and the interventions complained of in a given case must be evaluated cumulatively, not as isolated occurrences, from

the perspective of a reasonable observer present throughout the trial. As stated by Doherty J.A. in *R. v. Stewart* (1991), 62 C.C.C. (3d) 289 (Ont. C.A.), at p. 320:

> It is a question of degree. At some point, incidents which, considered in isolation, may be excused as regrettable but of no consequence, combine to create an overall appearance which is incompatible with our standards of fairness.

Context is important in thinking about whether a trial judge's conduct has compromised trial fairness. In *R. v. L. (D.O.)*,[25] Justice L'Heureux-Dubé held:

> The final issue raised by the respondent is whether the trial judge may have acted in such a manner as to raise a reasonable apprehension of bias, as per *R. v. Brouillard*, [1985] 1 S.C.R. 39. In *Brouillard, supra*, Lamer J., for the court held that the judiciary should not be seen as "entering the ring" or acting on behalf of one of the parties. . .
>
> It is my view that, in the case at hand as well as in other cases involving fragile witnesses such as children, the trial judge has a responsibility to ensure that the child understands the questions being asked and that the evidence given by the child is clear and unambiguous. To accomplish this end, the trial judge may be required to clarify and rephrase questions asked by counsel and to ask subsequent questions to the child to clarify the child's responses. In order to ensure the appropriate conduct of the trial, the judge should provide a suitable atmosphere to ease the tension so that the child is relaxed and calm. The trial judge, in this case, did not prevent the mounting of a proper defence, nor did he demonstrate favouritism toward the witness in such a way as to preclude a fair trial. I find that the trial judge in this instance did nothing more than "intervene for justice to be done".[26]

In *Gordon v. Gordon*,[27] the Ontario Court of Appeal wrote:

> A custody case, where the best interest of the child is the only issue, is not the same as ordinary litigation and requires, in our view, that the person conducting the hearing take a more active role than he ordinarily would take in the conduct of a trial. Generally, he should do what he reasonably can to see to it that his decision will be based upon the most relevant and helpful information available.

Should the trial judge be able to comment on the evidence presented by the parties?

R. v. LAWES
(2006), 206 C.C.C. (3d) 15, 37 C.R. (6th) 301 (Ont. C.A.)

The accused was convicted of second degree murder arising out of a bank robbery in Brampton, Ontario. On appeal he argued that the trial judge's comments on the evidence violated his s. 11(f) right to be tried by a jury. His appeal was dismissed.

Rouleau J.A. (Moldaver and Feldman JJ.A. concurring): —

---

[25] (1994), 25 C.R. (4th) 285 (S.C.C.).
[26] *Ibid.* at 322-323.
[27] (1980), 23 R.F.L. (2d) 266 at 271.

(a)   The common law rule

Courts have long recognized that a trial judge is entitled to comment on the evidence while instructing the jury. The discretion to comment, however, is limited.

The Supreme Court of Canada has recently confirmed the principle that a trial judge is "entitled to give an opinion on a question of fact and express it as strongly as the circumstances permit, so long as it is made clear to the jury that the opinion is given as advice and not direction." [Footnote omitted]

There have been various formulations of guidelines to be used by appellate courts in deciding whether a trial judge has gone too far in expressing an opinion. In *R. v. Garofoli*, this court stated that an appellate court may find that the trial judge has crossed the boundary even though the jury was told that they were not bound by his views on the evidence if:

1)   the opinion expressed is far stronger than that facts warrant; or

2)   the opinion is expressed so strongly that there is a likelihood that the jury would be overawed by it. [Footnote omitted]

Somewhat different formulations of these guidelines appear in other decisions such as *R. v. Muckikekwanate* [Footnote omitted] and *R. v. Valentini*. What can be drawn from all of these cases is that, in this area, everything is a question of degree. The overarching principle is fairness. Within this principle of fairness is the recognition that the jury must remain the arbiter of the facts and that any comments made by the trial judge cannot amount to a rebuttal of the defence address to the jury or unfairly denigrate or undermine the position of the defence.

. . .

ii)   Does the common law rule contravene s. 11(f) of the Charter?

The appellant submits that considering the common law's limited "tolerance" of judicial comment in the context of the *Charter* guarantee leads to the conclusion that all judicial comment should be prohibited and, most certainly, that any comment that could influence the jury on a substantial contested factual issue would constitute a breach of the accused's right to a trial by jury.

The right to a trial by jury enshrined in s. 11(f) of the *Charter* was described by this court in *R. v. Finta* as follows:

> It is a basic tenet of our criminal law that in cases tried by a jury, it is the jury which must decide the guilt or innocence of the accused. Findings of facts which are germane to that task must be left to the jury . . . .. Any statutory or judge-made rule which transfers the fact-finding function as it relates to issues going to the culpability of the accused, from the jury to a judge is, at the very least, constitutionally suspect. [Footnote omitted]

The appellant submits that the proposed prohibition on the expression of opinion by trial judges is necessary because trial judges carry such authority and respect with the jury that juries will likely be swayed if a judge expresses any opinion on the facts. This would result in the trial judge usurping the fact finding role of the jury, thereby depriving the accused of the right to the "benefit of trial by jury".

Although I agree that a trial judge cannot usurp the function of the jury, I do not accept the proposition that every expression of opinion on factual issues by a trial judge, even on substantial, contested issues, will invariably lead to this result.

In view of their role, trial judges cannot avoid commenting on the evidence. These comments can be direct and either required or desirable at common law, such as *Vetrovec* warnings, advising a jury that certain previous convictions such as those involving dishonesty may be more important than others in deciding on credibility, or advising the jury of the risks of relying on eyewitness identification evidence. Comments can also be indirect in the sense that, in the charge, when trial judges deal with each element of the offence, they often select and summarize portions of the evidence that they consider relevant and of some significance. Trial judges will, however, take care to tell the jury that, despite any views or opinions on the evidence they may have expressed directly or indirectly and regardless of the cautions given, they, the jury, are the sole arbiters of the facts.

Beyond comments that are required or desirable, it is well recognized that a trial judge has a discretion to comment on evidence during the charge to help the jury focus on the critical issues. The exercise of this discretion is often uncontroversial, for example when, in the present case, the judge told the jury that there was little doubt that Lawes and Rowe formed an intention in common to carry out the unlawful purpose namely, armed robbery. What trial judges cannot do is: assess the evidence and make a determination that the Crown has proven one or more of the essential elements of the offence and to direct the jury accordingly. It does not matter how obvious the judge may believe the answer to be. Nor does it matter that the judge may be of the view that any other conclusion would be perverse. The trial judge may give an opinion on the matter when it is warranted, but never a direction. (*R. v. Gunning, supra*, at para. 31).

In my view, a prohibition on the expression of opinion by a trial judge is neither practical nor desirable and such a prohibition is neither explicitly nor implicitly provided for in the words of s. 11(f) of the *Charter*. To seek to limit the prohibition to substantial, contested factual issues is of little assistance. The concern at common law and as expressed in s. 11(f) of the *Charter* is that the trial judge not usurp the function of the jury. By allowing the trial judge to express views and opinions on the evidence "as strongly as the circumstances permit" provided that they do not have the effect of usurping the role of the jury by taking a contested issue away from them or by subverting their independence, the common law recognizes that comments are both a necessary and desirable part of the trial judge's role. The limit is set at the point where the comments interfere with the exercise of the jury's role. Although I firmly believe that judges should avoid unnecessary comments or opinions, the focus of the analysis on appeal is not whether an appellate court views the opinion given by the trial judge as having been necessary or even desirable, but rather whether it interfered with the jury's function or so undermined the defence position that it deprived the accused of a fair trial.

When considering whether a trial judge has gone beyond the limits, the basic assumption is that jurors will abide by their oaths and will accept and follow the judicial instructions they are given. It is assumed, therefore, that when so instructed, jurors will disregard any opinion or statement of the evidence made by the trial judge where it does not accord with their own assessment. This same presumption of juror competence is at the root of the constitutionally protected right to a trial by jury in s. 11(f).

In summary, therefore, the common law rule allows the trial judge to comment on the evidence provided it is made clear to the jury that they are not bound by the judge's views, that the judge's opinions are not stronger than the facts warrant and that the opinions are not overstated to the point where it is likely that the jury will be overawed by them. By setting the limit on judicial comment at the point where the comments might impermissibly erode or threaten the fact finding and ultimate arbiter role of the jury, the common law rule fosters rather than impedes the values underlying s. 11(f) of the *Charter*.

Do you agree with the decision?

(d) The Role of Lawyers

Notwithstanding the adversarial process and its emphasis on partisanship, zero sum gain and a "sporting theory of justice", we expect that counsel, as officers of the court, will be ethical in the preparation and presentation of their case.[28]

R. v. FELDERHOF
(2003), 180 C.C.C. (3d) 498, 17 C.R. (6th) 20, (Ont. C.A.)

ROSENBERG, J.A.:— The respondent to this appeal is facing eight counts of violating the Securities Act, R.S.O. 1990 c. S. 5 arising out of the affairs of Bre-X Minerals Ltd. The Ontario Securities Commission charged the respondent, a senior officer in Bre-X, with insider trading and authorizing or acquiescing in misleading press statements. After 70 days of trial, counsel for the prosecution took the unusual step of applying for prohibition and certiorari to halt the prosecution. Counsel for the Ontario Securities Commission, who are conducting the prosecution, seek to prohibit the continuation of the proceedings before Hryn J., to quash rulings he made and ask for an order that the trial begin anew before another judge of the Ontario Court of Justice. The prosecution alleges that the trial judge made a number of serious errors that have deprived him of jurisdiction to proceed and undermined the appellant's right to a fair trial. Fundamental to its position is the allegation that the trial judge has failed in his duty to curb the uncivil

---

[28]   For a detailed discussion of the ethical obligations of criminal lawyers (defence and Crown), see David M. Tanovich, "Chapter 8: Ethics and Criminal Law Practice" in Alice Woolley, Richard Devlin, Brent Cotter & John M. Law, *Lawyers' Ethics and Professional Regulation*, 3rd ed. (Toronto: Lexis Nexis, 2017).

conduct of the respondent's counsel. The prosecution also alleges that the trial judge has not made evidentiary rulings when he should have and which were necessary to the presentation of the prosecution case and has improperly interfered in the conduct of the prosecution case.

Campbell J. heard the application and in extensive and careful reasons he dismissed the application. He found no jurisdictional error. I agree with that conclusion. The respondent sought costs of the motion. Campbell J. dismissed that application and the respondent appeals from that order. I would dismiss that appeal.

. . .

. . . The application judge found that Mr. Groia made uncivil attacks on the prosecutors, especially Mr. Naster. He set out many of the comments in his reasons for judgment and I need not repeat them at length in these reasons. In summary, the comments fall within a number of categories. Mr. Groia frequently resorted to sarcasm. He belittled the efforts of the prosecutors to prepare their case and accused them of laziness. He suggested that the prosecutors had breached their promises and misled the judge. The trial judge rarely intervened to restrain counsel. On the other hand, counsel for the prosecution accused the defence of filing a misleading affidavit and wasting the court's time with its abuse of process motion.

. . .

3. Civility

In his reasons, the application judge has set out many examples of Mr. Groia's conduct in the trial. The application judge described this conduct in some of the following ways:

- "unrestrained invective" (at para. 34).
- "excessive rhetoric" (at para. 34).
- "The tone of Mr. Groia's submissions ... descended from legal argument to irony to sarcasm to petulant invective" (at para. 64).
- "Mr. Groia's theatrical excess reached new heights on day 58" (at para. 89).
- "Mr. Groia's conduct on this occasion more resembles guerilla theatre than advocacy in court" (at para. 91).
- "unrestrained repetition of ... sarcastic attacks" (at para. 271).
- "Mr. Groia's defence consists largely of attacks on the prosecution, including attacks on the prosecutor's integrity" (at para. 272).

As the application judge noted, the problem was not simply with Mr. Groia's conduct. His rhetoric was, in many cases, tied to a view about what constitutes improper prosecutorial conduct that was simply wrong. As the application judge pointed out (at para. 29), there is nothing wrong with a prosecutor seeking a conviction, yet "Mr. Groia constantly accused the prosecution of impropriety in doing the very thing it has the right to do". Mr. Groia accused the prosecution of unfairness for not introducing as part of its examination of Mr. Francisco, documents that it claimed favoured the defence and in objecting to the admissibility of such document in cross-examination. But, the prosecution is not duty bound to introduce all possible documents in examination of its witness and is not acting improperly in objecting to the admission of inadmissible evidence. It was wrong for Mr. Groia to accuse the prosecution of improperly attempting to secure a conviction because it was trying to apply the rules of evidence. As the application judge said (at para. 33), "it is inappropriate to attack a prosecutor for seeking a conviction. To do so, demonstrates a misunderstanding of the vital distinction between a prosecutor who improperly seeks nothing but a conviction and a prosecutor who properly seeks a conviction within the appropriate limits of fairness".

Mr. Groia's rhetoric was improper. The application judge so found and I agree. But, did the trial judge's response deprive him of jurisdiction to proceed with the trial? I agree with the test proposed by the application judge at para. 273 of his reasons.

Even if counsel's litigation style, as alleged by the prosecution, is abusive and sometimes personally nasty, the judge does not lose jurisdiction unless it prevents a fair trial. The trial judge, who takes the daily temperature of the trial in a case where both opposing counsel have a low threshold of moral outrage, has a wide discretion to decide whether the wounded feelings of one side prevent it from presenting its case adequately. . .

. . .

It is important that everyone, including the courts, encourage civility both inside and outside the courtroom. Professionalism is not inconsistent with vigorous and forceful advocacy on behalf of a client and is as important in the criminal and quasi-criminal context as in the civil context. Morden J.A. of this court expressed the matter this way in a 2001 address to the Call to the Bar: "Civility is not just a nice, desirable adornment to accompany the way lawyers conduct themselves, but, is a duty which is integral to the way lawyers do their work." Counsel are required to conduct themselves professionally as part of their duty to the court, to the administration of justice generally and to their clients. As Kara Anne Nagorney said in her article, "A Noble Profession? A Discussion of Civility Among Lawyers" (1999), 12 Georgetown Journal of Legal Ethics 815, at 816-17, "Civility within the legal system not only holds the profession together, but also contributes to the continuation of a just society. . . . Conduct that may be characterized as uncivil, abrasive, hostile, or obstructive necessarily impedes the goal of resolving conflicts rationally, peacefully, and efficiently, in turn delaying or even denying justice." Unfair and demeaning comments by counsel in the course of submissions to a court do not simply impact on the other counsel. Such conduct diminishes the public's respect for the court and for the administration of criminal justice and thereby undermines the legitimacy of the results of the adjudication.

Nothing said here is inconsistent with or would in any way impede counsel from the fierce and fearless pursuit of a client's interests in a criminal or quasi-criminal case. Zealous advocacy on behalf of a client, to advance the client's case and protect that client's rights, is a cornerstone of our adversary system. It is "a mark of professionalism for a lawyer to firmly protect and pursue the legitimate interests of his or her client". As G. Arthur Martin said, "The existence of a strong, vigorous and responsible Defence Bar is essential in a free

Society". Counsel have a responsibility to the administration of justice, and as officers of the court, they have a duty to act with integrity, a duty that requires civil conduct.

This was a complex case involving experienced counsel who took very different views about the role of the prosecutor and the rules of evidence. There is nothing in this record that shows that the trial judge was biased against the prosecution. The application judge has catalogued the attempts that the trial judge did make to keep the trial and defence counsel on track. The prosecution says he did not do enough but I think it difficult at this stage to second-guess a trial judge who was faced with what would be a very long and difficult case.

. . .

In *Marchand*, this court has commented upon the problems caused by incivility in the courtroom. In that case, the court noted that civility in the courtroom is not only the responsibility of counsel but also "very much the responsibility of the trial judge." The failure of counsel and the trial judge in that case to discharge their responsibilities "tarnished the reputation of the administration of justice". Crown counsel have special responsibilities as "ministers of justice". But, as officers of the court and as barristers and solicitors, defence counsel also have responsibilities to the court and to other counsel and they have a duty to uphold the standards of the profession. As I have said, defence counsel's obligation to his or her client to fearlessly raise every legitimate issue is not incompatible with these duties to the court, to fellow counsel and to the profession. See Arthur Maloney, Q.C., "The Role of the Independent Bar", 1979 Law Society of Upper Canada Special Lectures 49 at 63, and G. Arthur Martin, Q.C., "The Role and Responsibility of the Defence Advocate" (1970), 12 C.L.Q. 376 at 385.

Mr. Maloney and Mr. Martin both referred to the well-known passage from *Rondel v. Worsley*, [1969] 1 A.C. 191 at 227-8 where Lord Reid said, in part that, "[c]ounsel must not mislead the court, [and] he must not lend himself to casting aspersions on the other party or witnesses for which there is no sufficient basis in the information in his possession". As the application judge noted, in this case the core problem was that Mr. Groia did not seem to understand the role of the prosecutor. This led him to make his improper allegations against the prosecutor when the prosecutor simply objected to a question or an attempt to introduce a document. I assume Mr. Groia believed in the merit of these submissions and was not deliberately misleading the court and casting aspersions on counsel and the "government" for which there was no foundation; nevertheless, he was bound by the standards of the profession to keep his rhetoric within reasonable bounds. If he was unable to do so, the trial judge had the responsibility referred to in Marchand.

This has nothing to do with trials not being "tea parties". Every counsel and litigant has the right to expect that counsel will conduct themselves in accordance with The Law Society of Upper Canada, Rules of Professional Conduct. Those rules are crystal clear. Counsel are to treat witnesses, counsel and the court with fairness, courtesy and respect. See Rules 4 and 6 and Commentaries. I have set out what seems to have been the genesis for the acrimony between counsel in this case. Even if Mr. Groia honestly believed that the prosecution tactics were excessive and could amount to an abuse of process, this did not give him licence for the kind of submissions he made in this case. As the application judge said, "[a]buse of process and prosecutorial misconduct . . form part of the arsenal of defence tactics". But, motions based on abuse of process and prosecutorial misconduct can and should be conducted without the kind of rhetoric engaged in by defence counsel in this case.

In Felderhof's subsequent trial he was acquitted on all charges. However the Law Society of Upper Canada brought disciplinary proceedings against the defence counsel, Groia, on its own motion, alleging professional misconduct based on his uncivil behaviour during the trial. A three member panel of the Law Society Hearing Panel found G guilty of professional misconduct, suspended his licence to practice law for two months and ordered him to pay nearly $247,000 in costs. On appeal by G, the Law Society Appeal Panel also concluded that G was guilty of professional misconduct, but it reduced G's suspension to one month and decreased the costs award against him to $200,000. In its decision, the Appeal Panel developed a multi factorial, context specific approach for assessing whether in court incivility amounts to professional misconduct. The Divisional Court upheld the Appeal Panel's decision as reasonable. A majority of the Ontario Court of Appeal dismissed G's further appeal.

In a lengthy ruling in *Groia v. Law Society of Upper Canada*[29] Justice Moldaver for a 6-3 majority of the Supreme Court allowed Groia's appeal. The majority found that the Appeal Panel's finding of professional misconduct against G on the basis of incivility was unreasonable. Even though the Appeal Panel accepted that G's allegations of prosecutorial misconduct were made in good faith, it had wrongly used his honest but erroneous legal beliefs as to the disclosure and admissibility of documents to conclude that his allegations lacked a reasonable basis. G's legal errors, coupled with the OSC prosecutors' conduct, provided the reasonable basis for his allegations. Other contextual factors in this case could not reasonably support a finding of professional misconduct against G on the basis of incivility. The evolving abuse of process law at the time accounted, at least in part, for the frequency of G's allegations; the presiding judge took a passive approach in the face of G's allegations; and G's behaviour changed in response to the directions of the trial judge.

According to the three dissenting justices, Karakatsanis, Gascon and Rowe JJ., the majority should have deferred to the Law Society panel's finding of misconduct and had wrongly created a mistake of law defence for lawyers. The majority decision would invalidate improper conduct and threaten to undermine the administration of justice and the culture change the Supreme Court had called for in recent years.

Justice Moldaver recognized the importance of balancing the duty of civility with the duty of resolute advocacy especially in criminal cases:

---

[29]   2018 SCC 27.

[72] The importance of resolute advocacy cannot be understated. It is a vital ingredient in our adversarial justice system — a system premised on the idea that forceful partisan advocacy facilitates truth-seeking: see e.g. *Phillips v. Ford Motor Co.* (1971), 18 D.L.R. (3d) 641, at p. 661. Moreover, resolute advocacy is a key component of the lawyer's commitment to the client's cause, a principle of fundamental justice under s. 7 of the *Canadian Charter of Rights and Freedoms: Canada (Attorney General) v. Federation of Law Societies of Canada*, 2015 SCC 7, [2015] 1 S.C.R. 401, at paras. 83-84.

[73] Resolute advocacy requires lawyers to "raise fearlessly every issue, advance every argument and ask every question, however distasteful, that the lawyer thinks will help the client's case": Federation of Law Societies of Canada, *Model Code of Professional Conduct* (online), r. 5.1-1 commentary 1. This is no small order. Lawyers are regularly called on to make submissions on behalf of their clients that are unpopular and at times uncomfortable. These submissions can be met with harsh criticism — from the public, the bar, and even the court. Lawyers must stand resolute in the face of this adversity by continuing to advocate on their clients' behalf, despite popular opinion to the contrary.

[74] The duty of resolute advocacy takes on particular salience in the criminal law context. Criminal defence lawyers are the final frontier between the accused and the power of the state. As Cory J. noted in The Inquiry Regarding *Thomas Sophonow: The Investigation, Prosecution and Consideration of Entitlement to Compensation* (2001), at p. 53:

> It cannot be forgotten that it is often only the Defence Counsel who stands between the lynch mob and the accused. Defence Counsel must be courageous, not only in the face of an outraged and inflamed community, but also, on occasion, the apparent disapproval of the Court.

[75] For criminal defence lawyers, fearless advocacy extends beyond ethical obligations into the realm of constitutional imperatives. As the intervener the Criminal Lawyers' Association of Ontario ("CLAO") notes, defence lawyers advancing the accused's right to make full answer and defence "are frequently required to criticize the way state actors do their jobs": *Quebec (Director of Criminal and Penal Prosecutions) v. Jodoin*, 2017 SCC 26, [2017] 1 S.C.R. 478, at para. 32; *Doré*, at paras. 64-66. These criticisms range from routine Charter applications — alleging, for example, an unconstitutional search, detention, or arrest — to serious allegations of prosecutorial misconduct. Defence lawyers must have sufficient latitude to advance their clients' right to make full answer and defence by raising arguments about the propriety of state actors' conduct without fear of reprisal.

[76] In saying this, I should not be taken as endorsing incivility in the name of resolute advocacy. In this regard, I agree with both Cronk J.A. and Rosenberg J.A. that civility and resolute advocacy are not incompatible: see *Groia* ONCA, at paras. 131-39; *Felderhof ONCA*, at paras. 83 and 94. To the contrary, civility is often the most effective form of advocacy. Nevertheless, when defining incivility and assessing whether a lawyer's behaviour crosses the line, care must be taken to set a sufficiently high threshold that will not chill the kind of fearless advocacy that is at times necessary to advance a client's cause. The Appeal Panel recognized the need to develop an approach that would avoid such a chilling effect.

In its 2006 *Code of Professional Conduct*, the Canadian Bar Association included an Appendix entitled "Principles of Civility for Advocates". Part III addresses the conduct of lawyers at trial and offers advice on how to make an objection:

47. During trial, Counsel should not allude to any fact or matter which is not relevant or with respect to which no admissible evidence will be advanced.

48. Counsel should not engage in acrimonious exchanges with opposing Counsel or otherwise engage in undignified or discourteous conduct that is degrading to their profession and to the Court.

49. During trial, Counsel should not make any accusation of impropriety against opposing Counsel unless such accusation is well-founded and without first giving reasonable notice so that opposing Counsel has an adequate opportunity to respond.

50. Objections, requests and observations during trial should always be addressed to the Court, not to other Counsel.

51. Objections during trial are properly made as follows:

(1) Counsel rises and calmly states "Your Honour, I have an objection";

(2) When Counsel rises to make an objection or to address the Judge, other Counsel should be seated until the Judge asks for a response. Under no circumstances should two or more Counsel be addressing the Court at the same time;

(3) The basis for the objection should be briefly and clearly stated. Following a clear statement of the objection, Counsel should present argument in support of it and then sit down;

(4) Counsel opposing the objection shall in turn, or as directed by the Judge, rise and clearly state their position. They will then make their argument, if any, in support and sit down; and

(5) Usually, Counsel who made the objection will then be given an opportunity to reply. The reply should address only those points raised by opposing Counsel and avoid repetitious re-argument of the issues.

52. When the Court has made a ruling on a matter, Counsel should in no way attempt to re-argue the point or attempt to circumvent the effect of the ruling by other means.

53. In the absence of a jury, a question to a witness by Counsel should not be interrupted before the question is completed for the purposes of objection or otherwise, unless the question is patently inappropriate.

54. Counsel should never attempt to get before the Court evidence which is improper. If Counsel intends to lead evidence about which there may be some question of admissibility, then Counsel should alert opposing Counsel and the Court of that intention.

55. When addressed by the Judge in the courtroom, Counsel should rise. When one Counsel is speaking the other(s) should sit down until called upon.

Counsel should never remain with his or her back turned when the Judge is speaking.

56. Counsel cannot condone the use of perjured evidence and, if Counsel becomes aware of perjury at any time, they must immediately seek the client's consent to bring it to the attention of the Court. Failing that, the Counsel must withdraw. Nothing is more antithetical to the role of Counsel than to advance the client's case before the Court, directly or indirectly, on the basis of perjured evidence.

57. Counsel, or any member of their firm, should not give evidence relating to any contentious issue in a trial.

58. In trials where they are acting as Counsel, Counsel should not take part in any demonstrations or experiments in which their own person is involved except to illustrate what has already been admitted in evidence.

These civility principles apply to all lawyers. It is important to acknowledge that Crown prosecutors operate under distinct ethical requirements.

R. v. HILLIS
2016 ONSC 451, 26 C.R. (7th) 329 (Ont. S.C.J.)

POMERANCE J.:

[1] The accused's trial on charges of second degree murder and aggravated assault is about to begin. A jury has been selected. The central issue in the case is whether the accused was acting in self-defence when he killed John Jubenville and wounded Tanya Lapensee. The parties agree that Mr. Jubenville and Ms. Lapensee were the aggressors in the altercation, and that the accused used force in order to defend himself. The question for the jury is whether the actions taken by the accused to defend himself were reasonable.

. . .

[3] The Crown is no longer calling [certain witnesses] because they are in a position to offer exculpatory evidence. The Crown argues that this is a permissible strategy, so long as there has been full disclosure, and the witnesses are available to be called by the defence. The defence says that this is not a permissible Crown strategy; that it qualifies as an "oblique motive" and gives rise to an abuse of process.

[4] As a general rule, the Crown is entitled to choose the witnesses that it will and will not call. The prosecution is not required to assist the defence strategy. However, in exceptional cases, the court may direct that certain witnesses be called by the Crown.

[5] This is one of those exceptional cases. I will explain why in the reasons that follow.

. . .

[20] Is the Crown entitled to refrain from calling reliable evidence on the basis that it could assist the accused? I find that this is not a permissible Crown strategy. The desire to withhold reliable exculpatory evidence during the case for the Crown is inconsistent with the role of Crown counsel as a quasi-minister of justice, and custodian of the public interest. The Crown argues that the evidence is not concealed because there has been full disclosure to the defence. That may be so, but the effect of not calling the evidence is to conceal it from the jury unless the defence decides that it has to call it, thereby giving up procedural protections. The Crown may decide not to call a witness for any number of legitimate reasons. It should not omit reliable evidence from its case solely because it might help the accused.

. . .

[22] This is not a startling proposition. It flows quite naturally from the conception of the Crown as a quasi-minister of justice, and the implications of that role. The following passage from *R. v. Boucher*, 1954 CanLII 3 (SCC), [1955] S.C.R. 16, 110 C.C.C. 263, continues to govern the philosophy of prosecutorial decision making:

> It cannot be over-emphasized that the purpose of a criminal prosecution is not to obtain a conviction, it is to lay before a jury what the Crown considers to be credible evidence relevant to what is alleged to be a crime. Counsel have a duty to see that all available legal proof of the facts is presented: it should be done firmly and pressed to its legitimate strength but it must also be done fairly. The role of prosecutor excludes any notion 'of winning or losing; his function is a matter of public duty than which in civil life there can be none charged with greater personal responsibility. It is to be efficiently performed with an ingrained sense of the dignity, the seriousness and the justness of judicial proceedings.

. . .

[24] In other words, the Crown is not at liberty to curate the evidence, excising anything that might be exculpatory. To do so is to place too high a premium on "winning". It is to lose sight of the Crown's primary duty to present the case fairly, and in a manner that will secure a just result.

[25] This is not to say that Crown counsel is foreclosed from being a strong and vigorous advocate. That is expected in our adversarial system. It is only to say that Crown counsel cannot adopt a *purely* adversarial role toward the defence. As L'Heureux-Dubé observed at para. 21 in *R. v. Cook*:

> Nevertheless, while it is without question that the Crown performs a special function in ensuring that justice is served and cannot adopt a purely adversarial role towards the defence (*Boucher v. The Queen*, 1954 CanLII 3 (SCC), [1955] S.C.R. 16; *Power, supra*, at p. 616), it is well recognized that the adversarial process is an important part of our judicial system and an accepted tool in our search for the truth: see, for example, *R. v. Gruenke*, 1991 CanLII 40 (SCC), [1991] 3 S.C.R. 263, at p. 295, *per* L'Heureux-Dubé J. Nor should it be assumed that the Crown cannot act as a strong advocate within this adversarial process. In that regard, it is both permissible and desirable that it vigorously pursue a legitimate result to the

best of its ability. Indeed, this is a critical element of this country's criminal law mechanism: *R. v. Bain*, 1992 CanLII 111 (SCC), [1992] 1 S.C.R. 91; *R. v. Jones*, 1994 CanLII 85 (SCC), [1994] 2 S.C.R. 229; *Boucher, supra*. In this sense, within the boundaries outlined above, the Crown must be allowed to perform the function with which it has been entrusted; discretion in pursuing justice remains an important part of that function.

. . .

[29] Apart from the exculpating nature of the evidence, it is hard to imagine why else the Crown would decline to call these witnesses. Their evidence is directly relevant to the issues the jury must determine. The evidence purports to be reliable. Three of the witnesses are police officers. Two of them arrived at the scene just minutes after the 911 call was placed. The third is the blood spatter expert retained by the Crown and called by the Crown at the preliminary hearing. This is the very type of evidence that is ordinarily called by the Crown in a homicide prosecution. The Crown does not take issue with the accuracy of the evidence offered by these witnesses in this case.

. . .

[33] It is true that the defence has full disclosure of the witnesses' evidence, and could call them to testify at trial. However, this would disadvantage the defence. The defence cannot cross-examine its own witnesses, and by calling evidence it forfeits the right to address the jury last. These tactical disadvantages are a natural incident of the trial process, but should not be forced upon the defence by an unfair prosecution strategy.

. . .

[42] I am concerned that the Crown strategy in this case could adversely affect trial fairness. This justifies the court's intervention whether or not the conduct amounts to an abuse of process. The Crown proposes to call evidence of certain observations and events at the crime scene, but not others. The jurors will hear about certain things that happened during the case for the prosecution. But they will not hear Daniel Gobeil's evidence about the accused's statements at or around the time of the victim's death, in which he apologized and said he "didn't mean it". They will not hear PC Kettlewell's evidence that the accused was trying to staunch the victim's bleeding, by holding his neck when the police arrived (though this evidence might be available from PC D'Alimonte, which is being called by the Crown). They will not hear that the blood spatter evidence is consistent with the accused having been punched with significant impact. In short, the narrative will be missing several critical pieces.

. . .

[46] For the reasons discussed above, it is "essential in order to do justice in this case" that the jury hear from Daniel Gobeil, PC Stramacchia, PC Kettlewell, and PC Mollicone: see *Cook*, at para. 63. I direct that the Crown call these witnesses during the case for the prosecution. I leave it to the Crown to determine when it calls these witnesses and what, if any, evidence it chooses to elicit in-chief.

. . .

[49] For all of these reasons, the application by the defence to require that the Crown call the witnesses is allowed.

While the *Rules of Professional Conduct* may, by imposing ethical restrictions on the conduct of counsel, impact on what evidence is introduced by counsel and how it is used, courts have held that a violation of the *Rules of Professional Conduct* is not a basis to exclude evidence. In *Cowles v. Balac*,[30] Borins J.A. held:

> The Law Society passed the *Rules of Professional Conduct* to ensure that its members maintain the highest standards of professional conduct. Where a member's contravention of a rule is brought to the attention of the Law Society, in may result in the commencement of a disciplinary proceeding against the member. However, the *Rules of Professional Conduct* do not, and could not, affect the admissibility of relevant evidence in civil or criminal proceedings.

Why should a party be allowed to rely in court on evidence obtained through a lawyer's professional misconduct? How is this situation different from evidence obtained by police misconduct, which can ground exclusion in criminal cases?

2. SOURCES

The law of evidence is primarily judge-made. Numerous procedural reforms were accomplished by statute in England in the nineteenth century and these were largely copied in Canada. In Canada procedure in criminal matters is entrusted to the federal Parliament[31] and procedure in civil matters to the provincial legislatures.[32] Legislation enacted pursuant to these powers, the *Canada Evidence Act*[33] and the various provincial Evidence Acts, covers only a small portion of the law of evidence, and the bulk of it is still governed by the common law.

R. v. SALITURO
[1991] 3 S.C.R. 654, 9 C.R. (4th) 324, 68 C.C.C. (3d) 289

The accused was charged with using a forged document. He had signed his wife's name on a cheque payable to them jointly and cashed it. The accused's position was that he was acting under his wife's instructions. The accused's wife testified differently. On appeal the accused argued that his wife was incompetent to testify for the prosecution. The Crown asked the Supreme Court to alter the common law incompetence rule where the

---

[30]   (2006), 273 D.L.R. (4th) 596 (Ont. C.A.).
[31]   *Constitution Act, 1867*, s. 91(27).
[32]   *Ibid.*, s. 92(14).
[33]   Section 2 provides: "This part applies to all criminal proceedings and to all civil proceedings and other matters whatsoever respecting which Parliament has jurisdiction." Sometimes evidence rules, for example rape shield and intoxilyser provisions, are found in the *Criminal Code*.

spouses were separated at the time of the offence and there was no reasonable prospect of reconciliation.

IACOBUCCI J.: —

A. *What Are the Limits on the Power of Judges to Change the Common Law?*

(1) Introduction

At one time, it was accepted that it was the role of judges to discover the common law, not to change it. In Book One of his *Commentaries on the Laws of England* (4th ed. 1770), Sir William Blackstone propounded a view of the common law as fixed and unchanging, at p. 69:

> For it is an established rule to abide by former precedents, where the same points come again in litigation; as well to keep the scale of justice even and steady, and not liable to waver with every new judge's opinion; as also because the law in that case being solemnly declared and determined, what before was uncertain, and perhaps indifferent, is now become a permanent rule, which it is not in the best of any subsequent judge to alter or vary from, according to his private sentiments, he being sworn to determine, not according to his own private judgment, but according to the known laws and customs of the land; not delegated to pronounce a new law, but to maintain and expound the old one.

However, Blackstone's static model of the common law has gradually been supplanted by a more dynamic view. This Court is now willing, where there are compelling reasons for doing so, to overturn its own previous decisions. . . .

(2) Limits on the Power of the Courts to Change the Common Law

In keeping with these developments, this Court has signalled its willingness to adapt and develop common law rules to reflect changing circumstances in society at large. In four recent cases, *Ares v. Venner*, [1970] S.C.R. 608, *Watkins v. Olafson, supra, R. v. Khan*, [1990] 2 S.C.R. 531, and *R. v. Seaboyer*, [1991] 2 S.C.R. 577, this Court has laid down guidelines for the exercise of the power to develop the common law. The common theme of these cases is that, while complex changes to the law with uncertain ramifications should be left to the legislature, the courts can and should make incremental changes to the common law to bring legal rules into step with a changing society. However, a brief review of these cases is warranted.

The issue in *Ares, supra*, was whether it was appropriate to create a new exception to the hearsay rule for hospital records. Speaking for the Court, Hall J. adopted the reasons of Lord Donovan in *Myers v. Director of Public Prosecutions*, [1965] A.C. 1001, and accepted that the proposed new exception was required in consequence of changes in the business environment which could not have been foreseen at the time the hearsay rule was being developed. Hall J. rejected the argument that changes to the common law can only be made by Parliament. In support of his decision making hospital records admissible under a new exception to the hearsay rule, Hall J. quoted the following passage from the reasons of Lord Donovan in *Myers* at p. 1047:

The common law is moulded by the judges and it is still their province to adapt it from time to time so as to make it serve the interests of those it binds. Particularly is this so in the field of procedural law.

Hall J. followed the minority in *Myers, supra*. However, the majority in *Myers* was not of the opinion that the courts should never change common law rules, but only of the view that a change was not appropriate under the circumstances of the case. In the words of Lord Reid, at p. 1021:

> I have never taken a narrow view of the functions of this House as an appellate tribunal. The common law must be developed to meet changing economic conditions and habits of thought, and I would not be deterred by expressions of opinion in this House in old cases. But there are limits to what we can or should do. If we are to extend the law it must be by the development and application of fundamental principles. We cannot introduce arbitrary conditions or limitations: that must be left to legislation.
>
> . . .

(3) Conclusion

These cases reflect the flexible approach that this Court has taken to the development of the common law. Judges can and should adapt the common law to reflect the changing social, moral and economic fabric of the country. Judges should not be quick to perpetuate rules whose social foundation has long since disappeared. Nonetheless, there are significant constraints on the power of the judiciary to change the law. As McLachlin J. indicated in *Watkins, supra*, in a constitutional democracy such as ours it is the legislature and not the courts which has the major responsibility for law reform; and for any changes to the law which may have complex ramifications, however necessary or desirable such changes may be, they should be left to the legislature. The judiciary should confine itself to those incremental changes which are necessary to keep the common law in step with the dynamic and evolving fabric of our society.

The Court agreed to make the incremental change requested. **Was it really "incremental"?** Bill C-32 (*Victims Bill of Rights Act*), which received Royal Assent on April 23, 2015, abolished the spousal incompetence rule at issue in *Salituro*.

A further source of evidence law, and especially so in criminal law, is the entrenched *Charter of Rights and Freedoms*. We will in this course address in particular the rule against compellability of accused in s. 11(c), the principle against self-incrimination in s. 7, the right to a fair trial under ss. 7 and 11(d), the presumption of innocence in s. 11(d), the ability to exclude evidence in s. 24 and equality rights for complainants in sexual assault cases under s. 15.

3. CODIFICATION

There was an attempt at codification by the Law Reform Commission of Canada in 1975[34] but this was not well-received by the profession.[35] In 1977 the Federal/Provincial Task Force on Uniform Rules of Evidence was established[36] and its product, the proposed *Canada Evidence Act, 1986*, was much more comprehensive than existing legislation. No one has yet enacted this legislation.

In 1975 in the United States the Federal Rules of Evidence were legislated. This was a comprehensive scheme providing for the rules of evidence in federal courts. Since that time a majority of the states has enacted similar schemes patterned on the federal model. In 1995 the Australian Capital Territory enacted a similar comprehensive scheme. Within months Australia's largest state, New South Wales, copied them for use in its courts. Canada, which in the nineteenth century had adopted the English Draft Code to cover substantive criminal law and criminal procedure, does not appear ready for a similar venture into the area of evidence.

Arguments for a Comprehensive Statement

1. The main advantage of a comprehensive statement would be accessibility — bringing together into one document all the evidentiary rules. In Canada today the law of evidence is partly judge-made and partly made by legislation. A comprehensive legislated statement would bring it all together. Obviously this would be preferable to having some evidence rules regarding the use of evidence in judicial decisions while others appear in statutory form.

2. When an objection is made at trial the judge needs to make an immediate ruling. Wouldn't it be wonderful if we were all on the same page, aiming at the same target? At the very least the comprehensive statement would be, if not the definitive word, a good beginning to the argument. The Federal Rules of Evidence in the United States are available in a 4-inch by 5-inch pamphlet of about 50 pages. Based on our experience in the courtroom, the present rules are handled, to be kind, unevenly, and a comprehensive, ready-to-hand statement would necessarily improve the present situation. Both the evidentiary arguments and the results would be better based.

3. A comprehensive statement of the rules, written in terms of the underlying principles, would also create a better understanding of how the rules are meant to operate. This is particularly so if the rules were to be accompanied by explanatory notes. Such a rendition would minimize

---

[34] *Report on Evidence* (1975), Information Canada, Ottawa.
[35] See generally Brooks, "The Law Reform Commission of Canada's Evidence Code" (1978) 16 Osgoode Hall L.J. 241; Brooks, "The Common Law and the Evidence Code: Are They Compatible?" (1978) 27 U.N.B.L.J. 27; and Anderson, "A Criticism of the Evidence Code" (1976) 11 U.B.C. L. Rev. 163.
[36] See generally *Report of the Federal/Provincial Task Force on Uniform Rules of Evidence* (1982).

what some have referred to as "rampant conceptualism": the tendency of many lawyers to discuss the rules of evidence in terms of the meanings of the labels attached to them rather than in terms of their underlying rationale.

4. A comprehensive statement of the rules, written in terms of the underlying principles, would recognize a discretion in the judge in the application of the law of evidence, room for choice, room for judgment. The evidence rules are there to promote efficiency, fairness and the best approximation of the truth. Discretion in dealing with each particular case is necessary as it is inherent in the nature of the exercise. Recognizing that within each rule there must exist a fair amount of discretion, articulating the rule in principled terms thereby begins the process of describing the guidelines for a sound exercise of discretion. The simplicity of the process makes the law clearer and the discretion of the judge is better brought under control. Counsel then can make arguments based on principle rather than on technical interpretations of a mechanical rule, and the judge will similarly be obliged to make decisions based on principle. Indeed, once it is recognized that discretion already exists, and must necessarily exist, we make the law much more certain than it ever was before and the trial more fair.

5. Teaching the beginning student through an examination of a comprehensive statement would better prepare him or her for the world of practice.

6. Through a comprehensive statement the law becomes more accessible, not only because it is gathered together in one place, but also because it would tend to resolve many of the present ambiguities which give differing results depending on the individual judge. The law becomes more uniform. A comprehensive statement might also encourage uniformity among the various legislatures, easing the burden on the practitioner who goes back and forth between civil and criminal law encountering different pieces of legislation. If uniformity were achieved among the provincial and federal governments, we would all be further ahead as we generate judicial decisions and academic commentary regarding the rules, such writing coming from a common larger base.

7. Enacting a comprehensive statement of the rules would provide a forum within which reform of the law of evidence would be facilitated. It is true that much of the judge-made law can be reformed by judicial action but such reforms are by their nature piecemeal and also often resisted by the conservatism of the legal profession.

8. A comprehensive statement would also make the law of evidence more accessible to the citizenry. Bentham was moved in his calls for reform in the nineteenth century to better equip the ordinary person to understand. The present law of evidence is, for many, often unclear and difficult to ascertain. For those who see the rules as eight volumes of Wigmore with innumerable exceptions, the task is overly complex and daunting.

Success often goes to the advocate best equipped with a memory for precedent and the ability to articulate the mechanical rule with precision. For many looking on, the adversary system is seen as too much of a game with the outcome dependent on the skill of the adversaries. If, on the other hand, we recognize precedent as valuable only as a vehicle for the expression of principle and focus on understanding the principle, there will be a more genuine communication between counsel and the judge and a better appreciation by the onlooker as to why a particular piece of evidence was accepted or rejected. Resistance to a comprehensive statement might be partly attributed to the lawyers' self-interest in their wish to keep the law as complicated as possible and thus keep it to themselves.

Arguments Against a Comprehensive Statement

1. The present law of evidence is accessible and known to those who are willing to make the effort. The law of evidence is like any other body of law and can be discovered and learned. It is folly to think that the rules can be made so simple that a layperson would understand without the assistance of a lawyer. A suitable text can inform the profession and the judiciary as well as any legislated statement of the rules.

2. Enacting a comprehensive statute will produce years of extensive litigation with arguments as to whether the legislature intended to effect change in the area or intended to enact the *status quo*. While there may be some ambiguity in the existing rules, even a restatement will produce argument as to the meaning of the words chosen. Judicial interpretations will vary for a lengthy period of time and uniformity will be an elusive object.

3. A comprehensive statute, which is codification by another name, will freeze the law of evidence and the courts will no longer be vehicles for change. Judges will no longer be able to create a rule or an exception to do justice in an individual case but will be limited to interpreting the legislation. The limits on proper judicial statutory interpretation will straitjacket the judiciary. Changes will only be available by legislative action and delay will be the natural consequence. In addition, it is the judiciary and the litigation bar who are the experts in the law of evidence; it is they who actually know how the system works, and we ought not to forfeit their expertise.

4. Discretion in the trial judge equates, for many, to greater admissibility of evidence. The trial judge will no longer be as concerned with rejecting evidence as insufficiently reliable and will be moved to leave it to the trier of fact to assess worth given the totality of the evidence. Opponents who voice these concerns are normally found in those members of the bar who do not generally have the burden of proof. As their function is often seen to be preventing the admission of evidence, anything that increases admissibility is to be resisted.

5. A comprehensive legislative scheme runs the risk of being subject to political influence and this will particularly prejudice the accused in criminal cases. Prosecutors in the past, who have had difficulties in certain prosecutions, have been known to lobby, successfully, for changes in admissibility of evidence or changes with respect to the burdens of proof. Criminal lawyers believe that there is greater protection for an accused from a non-elected judge than from a legislator who feels he or she must give a fair hearing and respond to concerns of the community toward crime. Given the growing victims' rights movement, defence counsel are increasingly concerned about legislative action. They recognize that accused persons do not have a lobby in the legislature. If changes are to be made to the law of evidence by the legislature, as opposed to the judiciary, the criminal defence bar may feel, with some justification, that the accused's interests will not be well-served.

As we explore the laws of evidence you may wish to consider whether you accept this view that legislation is not necessary.[37]

Absent any legislative momentum to restate or reform the laws of evidence, it has fallen to the Supreme Court to be the major source of new law. The authors of McWilliams[38] have identified six major themes in the Supreme Court's approach to evidence:

- ensuring fairness in the evidence-gathering process;

- bestowing constitutional status to the organizing principles of the adversarial process;

- the development of a principled approach to admissibility;

- cleansing the law of evidence of stereotypes;

- a recognition of the relevance of social context; and

- protecting against wrongful convictions.

4. APPLICABILITY OF LAWS OF EVIDENCE

(a) Proceedings before Courts and Tribunals

The rules of evidence that we will be examining in this book are rules which cover court proceedings, civil and criminal. We will be examining the

---

[37] For more discussion on the value or not of a comprehensive statement see Delisle, "A Comprehensive Statement of Evidence Rules?" and Paciocco, "The Case Against Legislated Text in Matters of Proof", both pieces to be found in *Towards a Clear and Just Criminal Law: A Criminal Reports Forum* (Carswell, 1999) at 1-84. Emeritus Professor Marty Friedland, "Developing the Law of Evidence: a Proposal" (2011) 16 Can. Crim. L.R. 37, has recently called for comprehensive legislation to simplify the laws of evidence but he wants the effort controlled by judges not politicians.

[38] *Canadian Criminal Evidence*, 5th ed. (2015). See too Tanovich, "Starr Gazing: Looking into the Future of Hearsay in Canada" (2003) 28 Queen's L.J. 371 at 375-383.

rules as they are applied when insisted on by the parties to the litigation and when the proceedings are taking place in a courtroom.

In other forums, the rules are considerably relaxed. For example, labour arbitrators are not bound by the rules of evidence. The Ontario Court of Appeal held in *Toronto (City) v. C.U.P.E., Local 79*:[39]

> A decision by any board to refuse to admit evidence because it was not admissible in the Courts or because the board was bound by decisions of other labour arbitration boards would constitute an obvious error of law.

At the same time, arbitrators are entitled to consider the concerns underlying the rules of evidence, such as concerns about the reliability of hearsay evidence, when exercising their discretion over whether to receive evidence and how the evidence should be weighed.[40]

Even in the courtroom, the rules of evidence are sometimes relaxed: for example, in small claims court proceedings,[41] and in custody matters when the best interests of the child are being considered.[42] The sentencing stage in criminal matters is another example. In *R. v. Gardiner*,[43] Justice Dickson wrote the following on behalf of a majority of the Supreme Court of Canada:

> It is a commonplace that the strict rules which govern at trial do not apply at a sentencing hearing and it would be undesirable to have the formalities and technicalities characteristic of the normal adversary proceeding prevail. The hearsay rule does not govern the sentencing hearing. Hearsay evidence may be accepted where found to be credible and trustworthy. The judge traditionally has had wide latitude as to the sources and types of evidence upon which to base his sentence. He must have the fullest possible information concerning the background of the accused if he is to fit the sentence to the offender rather than to the crime. . . .

In criminal cases, the rules of evidence will also vary depending on who is the proponent. For example, given the concern for wrongful convictions, our courts have also slowly recognized that there is a need in some cases for a relaxation of the strict application of the rules of evidence in order to ensure that an accused can make full answer and defence. In *R. v. Brown*,[44] a case that we will examine later, Justice Major, for the majority, held:

> . . . [In *R. v. Williams*] Martin J.A. commented that "a court has a residual discretion to relax in favour of the accused a strict rule of evidence where it is necessary to prevent a miscarriage of justice and where the danger against which an exclusionary rule aims to safeguard does not exist" (p. 343 (emphasis added)). This suggests that, where there are some assurances of reliability and where necessary to avoid wrongful conviction, some rules of evidence may be applied with something less than their usual degree of rigour.

---

[39] (1982), 133 D.L.R. (3d) 94 (Ont. C.A.).
[40] See e.g. *Ontario Jockey Club v. Restaurant, Cafeteria & Tavern Employees' Union, Local 254* (1977), 15 L.A.C. (2d) 273 (Ont. Arb.) at 276.
[41] *Central Burner Service Inc. v. Texaco Canada Inc.* (1989), 36 O.A.C. 239 (Ont. Div. Ct.).
[42] See e.g. *Catholic Children's Aid Society of Toronto v. L. (J.)* (2003), 39 R.F.L. (5th) 54 (Ont. C.J.).
[43] [1982] 2 S.C.R. 368, 68 C.C.C. (2d) 477, 30 C.R. (3d) 289 (S.C.C.) at para. 109.
[44] (2002), 162 C.C.C. (3d) 257 (S.C.C.) at para. 42.

In a concurring opinion, Justice Arbour (Justice L'Heureux-Dubé concurring) noted:

> The idea that courts maintain the discretion to relax the rules of evidence when an accused's innocence is at stake has its roots in *Williams*. In that case, Martin J.A. held that an accused's right to make full answer and defence must comply with established rules respecting the admission of evidence (*Williams*, at p. 337; see also *Dersch v. Canada (Attorney General)*, [1990] 2 S.C.R. 1505 at p. 1515, 60 C.C.C. (3d) 132, 77 D.L.R. (4th) 473). Martin J.A. did, however, go on to state that the court had a residual discretion to relax strict rules of evidence in favour of the accused when necessary to prevent a miscarriage of justice (at p. 343). Support for this proposition, as expressed in *Williams*, is also found in the Ontario Court of Appeal decisions of *R. v. Rowbotham* (1988), 41 C.C.C. (3d) 1 at p. 57, and *R. v. Finta* (1992), 73 C.C.C. (3d) 65 at pp. 201-2, 92 D.L.R. (4th) 1, affirmed [1994] 1 S.C.R. 701, 88 C.C.C. (3d) 417, 112 D.L.R. (4th) 513, as well as in this Court's decision in *Finta*, at p. 854.[45]

There are, of course, a number of administrative tribunals functioning in Canada and each, by its enacting legislation and by general legislation referable to all administrative tribunals, must follow its own procedures. More often than not these tribunals are more liberal with respect to what evidence might be received.

For example, the *Statutory Powers Procedure Act*[46] of Ontario provides:

> 15. (1) Subject to subsections (2) and (3), a tribunal may admit as evidence at a hearing, whether or not given or proven under oath or affirmation or admissible as evidence in a court,
>
> > (a) any oral testimony; and
> >
> > (b) any document or other thing,
>
> relevant to the subject matter of the proceeding and may act on such evidence, but the tribunal may exclude anything unduly repetitious.
>
> > (2) Nothing is admissible in evidence at a hearing,
> >
> > > (a) that would be inadmissible in a court by reason of any privilege under the law of evidence; or
> > >
> > > (b) that is inadmissible by the statute under which the proceeding arises or any other statute.
> >
> > (3) Nothing in subsection (1) overrides the provisions of any Act expressly limiting the extent to or purposes for which any oral testimony, documents or things may be admitted or used in evidence in any proceeding.

Even though the rules of evidence are generally not directly applicable in administrative proceedings, understanding the basic rules applicable to the courts will assist in appreciating the process before other tribunals.

---

[45]   *Ibid.* at para. 116.
[46]   R.S.O. 1990, c. S.22.

(b) Aboriginal Rights Cases

In two decisions, the Supreme Court has provided guidance on the relationship between the rules of evidence and the use of oral histories in Aboriginal rights cases.

DELGAMUUKW v. BRITISH COLUMBIA
[1997] 3 S.C.R. 1010

The appellants, all Gitksan or Wet'suwet'en hereditary chiefs, claimed Aboriginal title over 58,000 square kilometres of territory in British Columbia. This landmark case which addressed issues including the content of Aboriginal title and how it is protected under s. 35(1) of the *Constitution Act, 1982*, also examined the trial judge's use of oral histories as part of his fact-finding mission. The Court held that the trial judge had erred in refusing to admit or give no independent weight to these histories. A new trial was ordered.

LAMER C.J. (CORY, MCLACHLIN and MAJOR JJ. concurring): —

This appeal requires us to . . . adapt the laws of evidence so that the aboriginal perspective on their practices, customs and traditions and on their relationship with the land, are given due weight by the courts. In practical terms, this requires the courts to come to terms with the oral histories of aboriginal societies, which, for many aboriginal nations, are the only record of their past. Given that the aboriginal rights recognized and affirmed by s. 35(1) are defined by reference to pre-contact practices or, as I will develop below, in the case of title, pre- sovereignty occupation, those histories play a crucial role in the litigation of aboriginal rights.

A useful and informative description of aboriginal oral history is provided by the Report of the Royal Commission on Aboriginal Peoples (1996), vol. 1 (Looking Forward, Looking Back), at p. 33:

> The Aboriginal tradition in the recording of history is neither linear nor steeped in the same notions of social progress and evolution [as in the non-Aboriginal tradition]. Nor is it usually human-centred in the same way as the western scientific tradition, for it does not assume that human beings are anything more than one—and not necessarily the most important—element of the natural order of the universe. Moreover, the Aboriginal historical tradition is an oral one, involving legends, stories and accounts handed down through the generations in oral form. It is less focused on establishing objective truth and assumes that the teller of the story is so much a part of the event being described that it would be arrogant to presume to classify or categorize the event exactly or for all time.

> In the Aboriginal tradition the purpose of repeating oral accounts from the past is broader than the role of written history in western societies. It may be to educate the listener, to communicate aspects of culture, to socialize people into a cultural tradition, or to validate the claims of a particular family to authority and prestige.

. . .

Oral accounts of the past include a good deal of subjective experience. They are not simply a detached recounting of factual events but, rather, are "facts enmeshed in the stories of a lifetime". They are also likely to be rooted in particular locations, making reference to particular families and communities. This contributes to a sense that there are many histories, each characterized in part by how a people see themselves, how they define their identity in relation to their environment, and how they express their uniqueness as a people.

Many features of oral histories would count against both their admissibility and their weight as evidence of prior events in a court that took a traditional approach to the rules of evidence. The most fundamental of these is their broad social role not only "as a repository of historical knowledge for a culture" but also as an expression of "the values and mores of [that] culture": Clay McLeod, "The Oral Histories of Canada's Northern People, Anglo-Canadian Evidence Law, and Canada's Fiduciary Duty to First Nations: Breaking Down the Barriers of the Past" (1992), 30 Alta. L. Rev. 1276, at p. 1279. Dickson J. (as he then was) recognized as much when he stated in *Kruger v. The Queen*, [1978] 1 S.C.R. 104, at p. 109, that "[c]laims to aboriginal title are woven with history, legend, politics and moral obligations." The difficulty with these features of oral histories is that they are tangential to the ultimate purpose of the fact-finding process at trial—the determination of the historical truth. Another feature of oral histories which creates difficulty is that they largely consist of out-of-court statements, passed on through an unbroken chain across the generations of a particular aboriginal nation to the present-day. These out-of-court statements are admitted for their truth and therefore conflict with the general rule against the admissibility of hearsay.

Notwithstanding the challenges created by the use of oral histories as proof of historical facts, the laws of evidence must be adapted in order that this type of evidence can be accommodated and placed on an equal footing with the types of historical evidence that courts are familiar with, which largely consists of historical documents. This is a long-standing practice in the interpretation of treaties between the Crown and aboriginal peoples: *Sioui, supra,* at p. 1068; *R. v. Taylor* (1981), 62 C.C.C. (2d) 227 (Ont. C.A.), at p. 232. To quote Dickson C.J., given that most aboriginal societies "did not keep written records", the failure to do so would "impose an impossible burden of proof" on aboriginal peoples, and "render nugatory" any rights that they have (*Simon v. The Queen*, [1985] 2 S.C.R. 387, at p. 408). This process must be undertaken on a case-by-case basis.[47]

---

[47]   See Napoleon, "*Delgamuukw*: A Legal Sraightjacket for Oral Histories?" (2005) 20:2 Can. J.L. & Soc'y 123.

MITCHELL v. MINISTER OF NATIONAL REVENUE
[2001] 1 S.C.R. 911

The respondent was a Mohawk of Akwesasne and a descendant of the Mohawk nation, one of the polities of the Iroquois Confederacy prior to the arrival of the Europeans. In 1988, he brought goods across the St. Lawrence River from the United States. He asserted that Aboriginal and treaty rights exempted him from paying duty. In concluding that the claimed Aboriginal right had not been established, the Supreme Court once again addressed the issue of evidence in Aboriginal rights cases.

MCLACHLIN C.J. (GONTHIER, IACOBUCCI, ARBOUR and LEBEL JJ. concurring): —

Courts render decisions on the basis of evidence. This fundamental principle applies to aboriginal claims as much as to any other claim. *Van der Peet* and *Delgamuukw* affirm the continued applicability of the rules of evidence, while cautioning that these rules must be applied flexibly, in a manner commensurate with the inherent difficulties posed by such claims and the promise of reconciliation embodied in s. 35(1). This flexible application of the rules of evidence permits, for example, the admissibility of evidence of post-contact activities to prove continuity with pre-contact practices, customs and traditions (*Van der Peet, supra*, at para. 62) and the meaningful consideration of various forms of oral history (*Delgamuukw, supra*).

The flexible adaptation of traditional rules of evidence to the challenge of doing justice in aboriginal claims is but an application of the time-honoured principle that the rules of evidence are not "cast in stone, nor are they enacted in a vacuum" (*R. v. Levogiannis*, [1993] 4 S.C.R. 475, at p. 487). Rather, they are animated by broad, flexible principles, applied purposively to promote truth-finding and fairness. The rules of evidence should facilitate justice, not stand in its way. Underlying the diverse rules on the admissibility of evidence are three simple ideas. First, the evidence must be useful in the sense of tending to prove a fact relevant to the issues in the case. Second, the evidence must be reasonably reliable; unreliable evidence may hinder the search for the truth more than help it. Third, even useful and reasonably reliable evidence may be excluded in the discretion of the trial judge if its probative value is overshadowed by its potential for prejudice.

In *Delgamuukw*, mindful of these principles, the majority of this Court held that the rules of evidence must be adapted to accommodate oral histories, but did not mandate the blanket admissibility of such evidence or the weight it should be accorded by the trier of fact; rather, it emphasized that admissibility must be determined on a case-by-case basis (para. 87). Oral histories are admissible as evidence where they are both useful and reasonably reliable, subject always to the exclusionary discretion of the trial judge.

Aboriginal oral histories may meet the test of usefulness on two grounds. First, they may offer evidence of ancestral practices and their significance that would not otherwise be available. No other means of obtaining the same evidence may exist, given the absence of contemporaneous records. Second, oral histories may provide the aboriginal perspective on the right claimed.

Without such evidence, it might be impossible to gain a true picture of the aboriginal practice relied on or its significance to the society in question. Determining what practices existed, and distinguishing central, defining features of a culture from traits that are marginal or peripheral, is no easy task at a remove of 400 years. Cultural identity is a subjective matter and not easily discerned: see R. L. Barsh and J. Y. Henderson, "The Supreme Court's Van der Peet Trilogy: Naive Imperialism and Ropes of Sand" (1997), 42 McGill L.J. 993, at p. 1000, and J. Woodward, Native Law (loose-leaf), at p. 137. Also see Sparrow, supra, at p. 1103; *Delgamuukw, supra*, at paras. 82-87, and J. Borrows, "The Trickster: Integral to a Distinctive Culture" (1997), 8 Constitutional Forum 27.

The second factor that must be considered in determining the admissibility of evidence in aboriginal cases is reliability: does the witness represent a reasonably reliable source of the particular people's history? The trial judge need not go so far as to find a special guarantee of reliability. However, inquiries as to the witness's ability to know and testify to orally transmitted aboriginal traditions and history may be appropriate both on the question of admissibility and the weight to be assigned the evidence if admitted.

In determining the usefulness and reliability of oral histories, judges must resist facile assumptions based on Eurocentric traditions of gathering and passing on historical facts and traditions. Oral histories reflect the distinctive perspectives and cultures of the communities from which they originate and should not be discounted simply because they do not conform to the expectations of the non- aboriginal perspective. Thus, *Delgamuukw* cautions against facilely rejecting oral histories simply because they do not convey "historical" truth, contain elements that may be classified as mythology, lack precise detail, embody material tangential to the judicial process, or are confined to the community whose history is being recounted.

In this case, the parties presented evidence from historians and archaeologists. The aboriginal perspective was supplied by oral histories of elders such as Grand Chief Mitchell. Grand Chief Mitchell's testimony, confirmed by archaeological and historical evidence, was especially useful because he was trained from an early age in the history of his community. The trial judge found his evidence credible and relied on it. He did not err in doing so and we may do the same.

The Supreme Court's acceptance of Indigenous oral histories makes *Mitchell* a significant decision. In addition, *Mitchell* can be understood as laying out a comprehensive theory of admissibility for the law of evidence. **What are the elements of that theory?**

Chapter 2

Burdens of Proof and Presumptions

1. BURDENS OF PROOF

(a) Terminology

To the confusion of both the student and the profession, the term "burden of proof" is used in the cases to signify different things. Sometimes the term is used to refer to the requirement of satisfying the trier of fact that a certain material proposition has been made out. If the party who has this burden of proof is unable to persuade the trier that his or her alleged version of the facts actually occurred, that party will lose the case. Sometimes the term is used to signify the obligation of ensuring that there is evidence in the case concerning an issue. Failing to satisfy this burden will prevent the issue from being considered by the trier.

Cases seeking to distinguish the two uses sometimes refer to the former the "persuasive burden", the "legal burden", the "ultimate burden", the "major burden", or the "primary burden", and to the latter as the "evidential burden", the "tactical burden", the "minor burden" or "secondary burden", or the "duty of going forward".

Chief Justice Dickson described the chaos and brought order to bear in *R. v. Schwartz*:[1]

> Judges and academics have used a variety of terms to try to capture the distinction between the two types of burdens. The burden of establishing a case has been referred to as the "major burden," the "primary burden," the "legal burden" and the "persuasive burden." The burden of putting an issue in play has been called the "minor burden," the "secondary burden," the "evidential burden," the "burden of going forward," and the "burden of adducing evidence." While any combination of phrases has its advantages and drawbacks, I prefer to use the terms "persuasive burden" to refer to the requirement of proving a case or disproving defences, and "evidential burden" to mean the requirement of putting an issue into play by reference to evidence before the court. The party who has the persuasive burden is required to persuade the trier of fact, to convince the trier of fact that a certain set of facts existed. Failure to persuade means that the party loses. The party with an evidential burden is not required to convince the trier of fact of anything, only to point out evidence which suggests that certain facts existed. The phrase "onus of proof" should be restricted to the persuasive burden, since an issue can be put into play without being proven. The phrases

---

[1]   [1988] 2 S.C.R. 443 (S.C.C.) at 466.

"burden of going forward" and "burden of adducing evidence" should not be used, as they imply that the party is required to produce his or her own evidence on an issue. As we have seen, in a criminal case the accused can rely on evidence produced by the Crown to argue for a reasonable doubt.

It is important not to identify the evidential burden solely with the accused. The Crown has the evidential burden of leading evidence which, if believed, would prove each element of the offence charged. If the Crown does not even meet this evidential requirement, the case never goes to the trier of fact; the accused has a right to a directed verdict of acquittal.

A leading case which illustrates the damage that can result from confusing the two burdens is *Woolmington v. Director of Public Prosecutions.*[2] The accused was convicted of murdering his bride. The accused admitted the shooting but testified that it was an accident. The trial judge charged the jury:

> If you come to the conclusion that she died in consequence of injuries from the gun which he was carrying, you are put by the law of this country into this position: The killing of a human being is homicide, however he may be killed, and all homicide is presumed to be malicious and murder, unless the contrary appears from circumstances of alleviation, excuse, or justification. "In every charge of murder, the fact of killing being first proved, all the circumstances of accident, necessity, or infirmity are to be satisfactorily proved by the prisoner, unless they arise out of the evidence produced against him; for the law will presume the fact to have been founded in malice, unless the contrary appeareth." That has been the law of this country for all time since we had law. Once it is shown to a jury that somebody has died through an act of another, that is presumed to be murder, unless the person who has been guilty of the act which causes the death can satisfy a jury that what happened was something less, something which might be alleviated, something which might be reduced to a charge of manslaughter, or was something which was accidental, or was something which could be justified.[3]

The Court of Appeal dismissed the accused's appeal as it recognized "ample authority for that statement of law".[4] The House of Lords traced the authority to Sir Michael Foster's text in 1762, written at a time when "the law of evidence was in a very fluid condition".[5] The Lords also noted that there had been many changes in procedure in the intervening two centuries, including the prisoner's right to give evidence, right to counsel, and right to an appeal. Viscount Sankey explained the true meaning of earlier authorities:

> All that is meant is that if it is proved that the conscious act of the prisoner killed a man and nothing else appears in the case, there is evidence upon which the jury may, not must, find him guilty of murder. It is difficult to conceive so bare and meagre a case, but that does not mean that the onus is not still on the prosecution.

---

[2]   [1935] A.C. 462 (H.L.).
[3]   *Ibid.* at 472-473.
[4]   *Ibid.* at 473.
[5]   *Ibid.* at 478.

. . . Just as there is evidence on behalf of the prosecution so there may be evidence on behalf of the prisoner which may cause a doubt as to his guilt. In either case, he is entitled to the benefit of the doubt. But while the prosecution must prove the guilt of the prisoner, there is no such burden laid on the prisoner to prove his innocence and it is sufficient for him to raise a doubt as to his guilt; he is not bound to satisfy the jury of his innocence.

. . . where intent is an ingredient of a crime there is no onus on the defendant to prove that the act alleged was accidental. Throughout the web of the English Criminal Law one golden thread is always to be seen, that it is the duty of the prosecution to prove the prisoner's guilt subject to what I have already said as to the defence of insanity and subject also to any statutory exception. If at the end of and on the whole of the case, there is a reasonable doubt, created by the evidence given by either the prosecution or the prisoner, as to whether the prisoner killed the deceased with a malicious intention, the prosecution has not made out the case and the prisoner is entitled to an acquittal. No matter what the charge or where the trial, the principle that the prosecution must prove the guilt of the prisoner is part of the common law of England and no attempt to whittle it down can be entertained. When dealing with a murder case the Crown must prove (a) death as the result of a voluntary act of the accused and (b) malice of the accused. It may prove malice either expressly or by implication. For malice may be implied where death occurs as the result of a voluntary act of the accused which is (i) intentional and (ii) unprovoked. When evidence of death and malice has been given (this is a question for the jury) the accused is entitled to show, by evidence or by examination of the circumstances adduced by the Crown that the act on his part which caused death was either unintentional or provoked. If the jury are either satisfied with his explanation or, upon a review of all the evidence, are left in reasonable doubt whether, even if his explanation be not accepted, the act was unintentional or provoked, the prisoner is entitled to be acquitted.[6]

(b) Allocation of Burdens

How do we decide the allocation of responsibility between the parties? Thayer believed we should have regard to the principles of pleading and in attending to these:

We shall sometimes find ourselves involved in an analysis of the substantive law of the particular case and perhaps in an inquiry into things obsolete, anomolous and forgotten. . .

Clearly one has no right to look to the law of evidence for a solution of such questions as these, and I am not proposing to answer them.[7]

Later commentators on the law of evidence have attempted to distill from the cases some general principles, but the furthest they have been able to take us is to note that problems of allocation involve "considerations of policy, fairness and probability".[8]

---

[6] *Ibid.* at 480-482.
[7] Thayer, *A Preliminary Treatise on Evidence at the Common Law* (1898) at 355.
[8] Cleary, "Presuming and Pleading: An Essay on Juristic Immaturity" (1959) 12 Stan. L. Rev. 5 at 11.

(i) *Civil Cases*

In civil cases the burden is normally on the person who asserts (e.g., the plaintiff in a negligence suit, the defendant on a defence of contributory negligence).

FONTAINE v. INSURANCE CORPORATION OF BRITISH COLUMBIA
[1998] 1 S.C.R. 424

The plaintiff claimed damages for negligence with respect to the death of her husband. His body and that of his hunting companion, which was still buckled in the driver's seat, were in the companion's badly damaged truck which had been washed along a flood-swollen creek flowing alongside a mountain highway. No one saw the accident and no one knew precisely when it occurred. A great deal of rain had fallen in the vicinity of the accident the weekend of the hunting trip. The trial judge found that negligence had not been proven against the driver and dismissed the plaintiff's case. An appeal to the Court of Appeal was dismissed.

MAJOR J. (for the court):—This appeal provides another opportunity to consider the so-called maxim of *res ipsa loquitur*. What is it? When does it arise? And what effect does its application have?

. . .

A. *When does res ipsa loquitur apply?*

Res ipsa loquitur, or "the thing speaks for itself", has been referred to in negligence cases for more than a century. In *Scott v. London and St. Katherine Docks Co.* (1865), 159 E.R. 665 . . . at p. 667 . . ., Erle C.J. defined what has since become known as *res ipsa loquitur* in the following terms:

> There must be reasonable evidence of negligence.

> But where the thing is shewn to be under the management of the defendant or his servants, and the accident is such as in the ordinary course of things does not happen if those who have the management use proper care, it affords reasonable evidence, in the absence of explanation by the defendants, that the accident arose from want of care.

. . .

For *res ipsa loquitur* to arise, the circumstances of the occurrence must permit an inference of negligence attributable to the defendant. The strength or weakness of that inference will depend on the factual circumstances of the case. As described in *Canadian Tort Law* (5th ed. 1993), by Allen M. Linden, at p. 233, "[t]here are situations where the facts merely whisper negligence, but there are other circumstances where they shout it aloud."

As the application of *res ipsa loquitur* is highly dependent upon the circumstances proved in evidence, it is not possible to identify in advance the types of situations in which *res ipsa loquitur* will arise. The application of *res ipsa loquitur* in previous decisions may provide some guidance as to when an inference of negligence may be drawn, but it does not serve to establish definitive categories of when *res ipsa loquitur* will apply. It has been held on numerous occasions that evidence of a vehicle leaving the roadway gives rise to an inference of negligence. Whether that will be so in any given case, however, can only be determined after considering the relevant circumstances of the particular case.

. . .

B.   *Effect of the application of res ipsa loquitur*

As in any negligence case, the plaintiff bears the burden of proving on a balance of probabilities that negligence on the part of the defendant caused the plaintiff's injuries. The invocation of *res ipsa loquitur* does not shift the burden of proof to the defendant. Rather, the effect of the application of *res ipsa loquitur* is as described in *The Law of Evidence in Canada* (1992), by John Sopinka, Sidney N. Lederman and Alan W. Bryant, at p. 81:

> *Res ipsa loquitur*, correctly understood, means that circumstantial evidence constitutes reasonable evidence of negligence. Accordingly, the plaintiff is able to overcome a motion for a non-suit and the trial judge is required to instruct the jury on the issue of negligence. The jury may, but need not, find negligence: a permissible fact inference. If, at the conclusion of the case, it would be equally reasonable to infer negligence or no negligence, the plaintiff will lose since he or she bears the legal burden on this issue. Under this construction, the maxim is superfluous. It can be treated simply as a case of circumstantial evidence.

Should the trier of fact choose to draw an inference of negligence from the circumstances, that will be a factor in the plaintiff's favour. Whether that will be sufficient for the plaintiff to succeed will depend on the strength of the inference drawn and any explanation offered by the defendant to negate that inference. If the defendant produces a reasonable explanation that is as consistent with no negligence as the *res ipsa loquitur* inference is with negligence, this will effectively neutralize the inference of negligence and the plaintiff's case must fail. Thus, the strength of the explanation that the defendant must provide will vary in accordance with the strength of the inference sought to be drawn by the plaintiff.

. . .

Whatever value *res ipsa loquitur* may have once provided is gone. Various attempts to apply the so-called doctrine have been more confusing than helpful. Its use has been restricted to cases where the facts permitted an inference of negligence and there was no other reasonable explanation for the accident. Given its limited use it is somewhat meaningless to refer to that use as a doctrine of law.

It would appear that the law would be better served if the maxim was treated as expired and no longer used as a separate component in negligence actions. After all, it was nothing more than an attempt to deal with circumstantial evidence. That evidence is more sensibly dealt with by the trier of fact, who should weigh the circumstantial evidence with the direct evidence, if any, to determine whether the plaintiff has established on a balance of probabilities a *prima facie* case of negligence against the defendant. Once the plaintiff has done so, the defendant must present evidence negating that of the plaintiff or necessarily the plaintiff will succeed.

C.   *Application to this case*

. . .

There are a number of reasons why the circumstantial evidence in this case does not discharge the plaintiff's onus. Many of the circumstances of the accident, including the date, time and precise location, are not known. Although this case has proceeded on the basis that the accident likely occurred during the weekend of November 9, 1990, that is only an assumption. There are minimal if any evidentiary foundations from which any inference of negligence could be drawn.

As well, there was evidence before the trial judge that a severe wind and rainstorm was raging at the presumed time of the accident. While it is true that such weather conditions impose a higher standard of care on drivers to take increased precautions, human experience confirms that severe weather conditions are more likely to produce situations where accidents occur and vehicles leave the roadway regardless of the degree of care taken. In these circumstances, it should not be concluded that the accident would ordinarily not have occurred in the absence of negligence.

. . . The trial judge's finding was not unreasonable and should not be interfered with on appeal.

. . .

The appellant submitted that an inference of negligence should be drawn whenever a vehicle leaves the roadway in a single-vehicle accident. This bald proposition ignores the fact that whether an inference of negligence can be drawn is highly dependent upon the circumstances of each case. . . The position advanced by the appellant would virtually subject the defendant to strict liability in cases such as the present one.

PEART v. PEEL (REGIONAL MUNICIPALITY)
POLICE SERVICES BOARD
(2006), 43 C.R. (6th) 175 (Ont. C.A.)

The plaintiffs launched a racial profiling lawsuit against two members of the Peel Regional Police Service. The officers, one of whom was African Canadian, decided to conduct a computer check on the plaintiffs' Honda Prelude. The plaintiffs were African Canadian. The officers testified that computer checks were routine especially at night and that, in addition, this model of vehicle was known to be easily stolen and that car theft was a prevalent problem in the area. They maintained surveillance on the vehicle until they received the results of the computer check. The officers began to follow the vehicle after it had left a gas station as now P was driving in excess of the speed limit. P saw the officers behind him. They had now turned on their lights and siren. He did not stop until he reached his home. He testified that, based on prior experiences with the police, he was afraid for his life.

Once he arrived home, he and G were subjected to a high-risk takedown, arrested and taken to the police station where they were strip-searched. Neither of the men were charged with any offence. The trial judge accepted that P had provided some information about a drug dealer he knew in exchange for not being charged with dangerous driving. The lawsuit was dismissed at trial. The plaintiffs appealed. The appeal was dismissed. One of the arguments raised was whether the onus of proof should be shifted to the police in racial profiling cases.

DOHERTY J.A. (GOUDGE and ROULEAU JJ.A. concurring): —

(e)   Should the burden of proof be reversed?

The ACLC submits that where racial profiling is alleged against the police in a civil proceeding, the police should bear the onus of demonstrating on a balance of probabilities that improper racial considerations were not a contributing factor to the state action that resulted in the interference with the liberty of a black plaintiff. In short, the ACLC would place the burden of persuasion on the defendant/police.

I do not understand the appellants to have raised the allocation of the burden of proof on the issue of racial profiling as a separate ground of appeal. Presumably, they did not do so because, as in most civil cases, the outcome of this trial did not turn on which party bore the onus of proof. As observed in John Sopinka, Sidney N. Lederman & Allan W. Bryant, *The Law of Evidence in Canada*, 2d ed. (Toronto: Butterworths, 1999) at 58:

> *In civil proceedings, the legal burden does not play a part in the decision-making process if the trier of fact can come to a determinate conclusion on the evidence.* If, however, the evidence leaves the trier of fact in a state of uncertainty, the legal burden is applied to determine the outcome. [Emphasis added.]

This trial judge was not left in any state of uncertainty by the evidence. He made factual findings on all of the contentious issues and from those findings concluded that the officers were not motivated by racial considerations.

I will, however, address the merits of the submission made by the ACLC. In civil proceedings, the burden of persuasion in respect of a fact in issue is generally on the party alleging that fact. The appellants claim that they were the victims of racial profiling at the hands of the police and demand compensation. Applying the normal rule, the appellants must bear the burden of proving racial profiling on the balance of probabilities: *Snell v. Farrell*, [1990] 2 S.C.R. 311 at 320; Kenneth S. Broun *et al.*, *McCormick on Evidence*, 6th ed. (St. Paul, Minn.: Thomson, 2006) vol. II at 473.

In the criminal context, on motions brought by an accused pursuant to s. 24(1) of the *Charter*, this court has followed the general rule and placed the burden on the accused to establish racial profiling on the balance of probabilities: *R. v. Brown, supra*, at para. 45; *R. v. Curry* (2005), 206 C.C.C. (3d) 100 at para. 24 (Ont. C.A.). Placing the onus on the accused to establish racial profiling on a *Charter* motion is consistent with the well established pleading principle that the onus of establishing a *Charter* breach is on the accused where the accused seeks relief under s. 24(1) of the *Charter*: see *R. v.*

Cobham (1994), 92 C.C.C. (3d) 333 at 340 (S.C.C.); *R. v. Collins* (1987), 33 C.C.C. (3d) 1 at 13-14 (S.C.C.).

The allocation of the legal burden of proof to the party alleging the fact in issue is not an immutable rule. For example, in some situations, the burden of persuasion will move to the Crown on a motion brought under s. 24(1) of the *Charter* if an accused establishes certain facts. This shifting of the legal burden occurs in cases where the accused alleges an unreasonable search or seizure. If the accused demonstrates that the search was not conducted pursuant to a prior judicial authorization, the burden of establishing the reasonableness of the search on the balance of probabilities moves to the Crown: *R. v. Collins*, *supra*.

The presumption that warrantless searches are unreasonable unless the Crown establishes that they are reasonable, is a reflection of the fundamental role that prior judicial authorizations have traditionally played in maintaining the delicate balance between state interests in the effective pursuit of criminal investigations and individual rights to personal privacy. At common law and by statute, state intrusion on personal privacy by way of searches or seizures has generally been acceptable only when sanctioned by a prior judicial authorization. Absence of that authorization renders a search or seizure presumptively unreasonable unless the Crown can demonstrate circumstances that overcome that presumption: *Hunter et al. v. Southam Inc.* (1984), 14 C.C.C. (3d) 97 at 109 (S.C.C.).

State interference with individual liberty whether by way of detention or arrest has never been seen as requiring prior judicial authorization. The varied and exigent circumstances in which the police must routinely resort to the use of their powers of detention or arrest defy any presumption that would require prior judicial authorization.

The ACLC does not submit that the onus should fall on the police to disprove racial profiling, because police detention without prior judicial authorization is presumptively unconstitutional. The ACLC makes a very different argument. It contends that the onus should fall on the police where the party who was subjected to detention or arrest is black. In effect, the ACLC submits that any arrest or detention of a black person by the police is as constitutionally suspect as a warrantless search and, therefore, merits the same rebuttable presumption of unconstitutionality.

This contention is based on the argument that racial profiling is so common that where it is alleged, placing the burden on the police to disprove racial profiling is more likely to achieve an accurate result than is leaving the onus on the party alleging racial profiling. As *McCormick*, supra, indicates at 475-76:

> Perhaps a more frequently significant consideration in the fixing of the burdens of proof is the judicial estimate of the probabilities of the situation. *The risk of failure of proof may be placed upon the party who contends that the more unusual event has occurred.* [Emphasis added.]

The reality of racial profiling cannot be denied. There is no way of knowing how common the practice is in any given community. I am not prepared to accept that racial profiling is the rule rather than the exception where the police detain black men. I do not mean to suggest that I am satisfied that it is indeed the exception, but only that I do not know.

In *R. v. Brown, supra,* at para. 45, this court rejected the argument, which was also advanced by the ACLC as intervenor, that the Crown should bear the onus of disproving racial profiling. The court held that a properly informed consideration of the relevant circumstantial evidence — indicators of racial profiling — combined with maintaining the traditional burden of proof on the party alleging racial profiling achieved a proper balancing of the respective interests of the parties. I see no reason to depart from the analysis in *R. v. Brown.* I would add that a sensitive appreciation of the relevant social context in which racial profiling claims must be assessed provides further protection against the failure of meritorious claims as a result of the allocation of the burden of proof.

The ACLC further submits that fairness considerations warrant placing the burden of disproving racial profiling on the police. The ACLC argues that the circumstances relevant to a racial profiling claim are better known to the police who also have better access to the information relevant to those claims. The ACLC submits that as the police are in a much better position to disprove racial profiling than the plaintiffs are to prove racial profiling, fairness dictates that the defendants should bear the legal burden.

Fairness may dictate a reversal of the usual legal burden of persuasion. It is not enough, however, for the party seeking to reverse the burden to demonstrate that the other party is in a better position to disprove the fact in issue. In many civil proceedings where the plaintiffs claim turns on the conduct or state of mind of the defendant, the defendant will be in a better position to prove or disprove the relevant facts. Fairness can justify a reversal of the legal burden in those relatively rare cases where the party who would normally bear the burden of proof has no reasonable prospect of being able to discharge that burden, and the opposing party is in a position to prove or disprove the relevant facts: see *Snell v. Farrell, supra,* at 326-30; *National Trust Co. v. Wong Aviation Ltd.,* [1969] S.C.R. 481 at 489-91.

A review of the caselaw demonstrates that racial profiling claims can and do succeed where the courts adhere to the traditional rule and place the onus of proof on the party alleging racial profiling: see e.g. *R. v. Peck,* [2001] O.J. No. 4581 (S.C.J.); *R. v. Kahn* (2004), 189 C.C.C. (3d) 49 (Ont. S.C.J.); *R. v. Campbell,* [2005] Q.J. No. 394 (Q. C.Q.); *R. v. Nguyen,* [2006] O.J. No. 272 (S.C.J.).

I would emphasize, however, that while the ultimate burden of persuasion remains on the appellants, in any given case there may well be a significant tactical burden on the defendant to introduce evidence negating the inference of racial profiling. In *Snell v. Farrell,* at 328-30, Sopinka J. described the tactical burden in the context of a causation issue in a medical malpractice case in these terms:

> *In many malpractice cases, the facts lie particularly within the knowledge of the defendant. In these circumstances, very little affirmative evidence on the part of the*

plaintiff will justify the drawing of an inference of causation in the absence of evidence to the contrary.

. . . .

It is not strictly accurate to speak of the burden shifting to the defendant when what is meant is that evidence adduced by the plaintiff may result in an inference being drawn adverse to the defendant. Whether an inference is or is not drawn is a matter of weighing evidence. *The defendant runs the risk of an adverse inference in the absence of evidence to the contrary.* This is sometimes referred to as imposing on the defendant a provisional or tactical burden. . . In my opinion, this is not a true burden of proof, and use of an additional label to describe what is an ordinary step in the fact-finding process is unwarranted. [Emphasis added.]

Do you think that Justice Doherty's reasoning is persuasive given the challenges posed when trying to prove systemic issues like unconscious racism?[9]

(ii) *Criminal Cases*

In the criminal law the presumption of innocence normally allocates the persuasive burden of proof to the Crown.

Since 1960, s. 2(f) of the *Canadian Bill of Rights* has guaranteed that a person charged with an offence will be "presumed innocent until proved guilty according to law in a fair and public hearing by an independent and impartial tribunal". An identical guarantee is contained in s. 11(d) of the *Charter of Rights and Freedoms*. The latter clearly operates irrespective of statutory wording to both federal and provincial legislation. It has long been clear that the *Woolmington* rule applies also to provincial offences.

What values underlie this presumption? The presumption of innocence characterizes most civilized systems of criminal law and is the cornerstone of ours. In the leading interpretation of s. 11(d), Chief Justice Dickson, for the Supreme Court of Canada in *R. v. Oakes*,[10] sees the presumption of innocence as embodying cardinal values lying at the very heart of criminal law which are protected expressly by s. 11(d) but are also integral to the general protection of life, liberty and security of the person in s. 7:

The presumption of innocence protects the fundamental liberty and human dignity of any and every person accused by the state of criminal conduct. An individual charged with a criminal offence faces grave social and personal consequences, including potential loss of physical liberty, subjection to social stigma and ostracism from the community, as well as other social, psychological and economic harms. In light of the gravity of these consequences, the presumption of innocence is crucial. It ensures that, until the state proves an accused's guilt beyond all reasonable doubt, he or she is innocent. This is essential in a society committed to fairness and social justice. The presumption

---

[9]   For an argument that there should be a reverse onus, see Tanovich, *The Colour of Justice: Policing Race in Canada* (Toronto: Irwin Law, 2006) at 144-147.

[10]   (1986), 50 C.R. (3d) 1 (S.C.C.) at 15.

of innocence confirms our faith in humankind; it reflects our belief that individuals are decent and law-abiding members of the community until proven otherwise.

Our complex and expensive system of police and prosecutors gives the State a powerful advantage against an accused. If we did not presume innocence, an elementary sense of fairness would require us to radically revise our system and give the accused an equivalent fact-finding capability. Before tampering with the presumption of innocence, the whole pattern of present evidential rules would have to be changed. The rules are interrelated. A trial is not just a relentless search for truth. We risk setting some of the guilty free for fear of convicting the innocent. Our universally high conviction rates indicate minimal risk.

Some view the presumption of innocence as legalistic nonsense. Common sense indicates a *de facto* presumption of guilt since the police usually get the right person. The presumption is unnatural. Our police must have reasonable grounds for their belief in guilt, yet the presumption of innocence requires fact-finders to ignore this and deduce nothing from the workings of the system which brought the accused to court. Brett offers a blunt and persuasive reply:

> Common sense has apparently overlooked that if the police do in fact bring only the guilty to the bar of justice, it may well be because they know that they will have to adduce proof beyond reasonable doubt. Whether they would continue to be so careful if the accused men had to prove their innocence is open to doubt. Moreover, common sense, in assuming that those found guilty are in fact guilty, overlooks the realities of plea bargaining, the cost of defending oneself, the imperfections of the trial process, and so on.[11]

Moreover, common sense is often wrong. Indeed, we are now learning that tunnel vision, a phenomenon whereby the police focus on one suspect and filter all information, including exculpatory evidence, through a lens of guilt is one of the leading causes of wrongful convictions.[12]

Expediency

Even in criminal cases, the allocation of burdens is impacted by matters of expediency. The insanity or mental disorder defence, as it is now known, is one such example. It is true that the judges in *M'Naghten's Case*[13] advised that every person shall be presumed sane until the contrary is proved, and the legislature has followed that lead.[14] Is there anything gained from the imposition of a persuasive burden on the accused that couldn't be equally gained by the lesser evidential burden? According to *Woolmington*, the accused in a murder case is entitled to an acquittal when the trier of fact has a reasonable doubt regarding his or her intent. Is it not inconsistent or illogical to foreclose an acquittal when the trier has a reasonable doubt regarding the

---

[11]   Brett, "Strict Responsibility: Possible Solutions" (1974) 37 Mod. L. Rev. 417.

[12]   See also Susan Bandes, "Loyalty to One's Convictions: The Prosecutor and Tunnel Vision" (2006) 49 Howard L.J. 475. See e.g. the discussion in "The Lamer Commission of Inquiry Pertaining to the Cases of: Ronald Dalton, Gregory Parsons, Randy Druken" (2005).

[13]   (1843), 8 E.R. 718 (H.L.).

[14]   *Criminal Code*, R.S.C. 1985, c. C-46, s. 16.

accused's capacity to form the necessary intent and to demand that the trier be satisfied that the accused was incapable? Harlan, J., in *Davis v. U.S.*,[15] rejected the idea that the presumption of sanity must be negatived by a preponderance of evidence in favour of a rule that the presumption simply called for evidence to be introduced to place the matter in issue:

> Upon whom then must rest the burden of proving that the accused, whose life it is sought to take under the forms of law, belongs to a class capable of committing crime? On principle, it must rest upon those who affirm that he has committed the crime for which he is indicted. That burden is not fully discharged, nor is there any legal right to take the life of the accused, until guilt is made to appear from all the evidence in the case. The plea of not guilty is unlike a special plea in a civil action, which, admitting the case averred, seeks to establish a substantive ground of defense by a preponderance of evidence. It is not in confession and avoidance, for it is a plea that controverts the existence of every fact essential to constitute the crime charged. Upon that plea the accused may stand, shielded by the presumption of his innocence, until it appears that he is guilty; and his guilt cannot in the very nature of things be regarded as proved, if the jury entertain a reasonable doubt from all the evidence whether he was legally capable of committing crime.

In *R. v. Chaulk*[16] it was argued that the presumption of sanity contained in s. 16(4) of the *Criminal Code*, placing the onus of proving the defence of insanity on the accused, was an unconstitutional violation of the presumption of innocence in s. 11(d). Chief Justice Lamer, writing for himself and four other judges, held that there had been a violation of s. 11(d) but it could be justified under s. 1. The objective of the presumption was to "avoid placing an impossible burden of proof on the Crown". Citing recent judgments of the Court indicating that Parliament was not required to adopt the absolutely least intrusive means, Chief Justice Lamer saw the issue as "whether a less intrusive means would achieve the same objective or would achieve the same objective as effectively". The Chief Justice concluded that the alternative of an evidentiary burden requiring that the accused merely raise a reasonable doubt would not be as effective, accepting arguments by Attorneys General that it would be very easy for accused persons to "fake" such a defence.

The sole dissent on this point in *Chaulk* was Madam Justice Wilson, who held that this was not a case for relaxing the minimum impairment test. This might be done where a legislature, mediating between competing groups of citizens or allocating scarce resources, had to compromise on the basis of conflicting evidence. But in *Chaulk* the State was acting as "singular antagonists" of a very basic legal right of an accused and the strict standard of review in *Oakes* should be applied. The government's objective could be quite readily met by a mere burden on the accused to adduce evidence that

---

[15]   160 U.S. 469 (1895) at 485-488. In *Leland v. Oregon*, 343 U.S. 790 (1952), the Supreme Court upheld *state* legislation which imposed a persuasive burden on the accused on the issue of insanity as not violative of due process and noted that the *Davis* case had announced a rule respecting federal cases as opposed to constitutional doctrine.

[16]   (1990), 2 C.R. (4th) 1 (S.C.C.).

made insanity "a live issue fit and proper to be left to the jury". Madam Justice Wilson noted the experience in the United States where an evidential burden was the order of the day, and believed the case for the imposition of a persuasive burden had not been made out.

Facts Peculiarly Within Knowledge of Accused

It is sometimes suggested that the burden of persuasion in a criminal case should be shifted to the accused in respect of facts that are particularly within the accused's knowledge. For example, in the classic case of *R. v. Turner*,[17] the accused was charged with having illegally hunted game in his possession. There were a number of exceptions in the statute that would have made his possession of the game legal. The Court held that the Crown was not required to bring evidence to prove than none of the exceptions applied. Rather, the burden was on the accused, who would have knowledge of any applicable exception, to prove that an exception applied.

Reported decisions have invoked this doctrine to place the persuasive burden on the accused to prove that the accused was not driving carelessly,[18] took due diligence in the case of regulatory offences,[19] or was relying on an officially induced error of law.[20]

The notion that an accused must prove matters peculiarly within his or her knowledge was part of the justification provided by Bastarache J. for a 5-4 majority in *R. v. Stone*[21] for requiring the accused to prove a defence of sane automatism on a balance of probabilities. The majority also asserted a so-called presumption of voluntariness.[22]

(c) Measure of Burden of Persuasion

(i) *Balance of Probabilities Standard for Civil Cases*

It is commonly said that the burden of persuasion in civil cases requires for satisfaction "a preponderance of evidence", or "proof on the balance of probability". Lord Denning expressed it as follows:

> That degree is well settled. It must carry a reasonable degree of probability, but not so high as is required in a criminal case. If the evidence is such that the tribunal can say: "We think it more probable than not," the burden is discharged, but, if the probabilities are equal, it is not.[23]

---

[17]   (1816), 105 E.R. 1026 (Eng. K.B.).

[18]   *R. v. McIver*, [1965] 2 O.R. 475 (C.A.), affirmed (1966), 48 C.R. 4 (S.C.C.).

[19]   *R. v. Sault Ste. Marie (City)*, [1978] 2 S.C.R. 1299 and *R. v. Wholesale Travel Group Inc.*, [1991] 3 S.C.R. 154.

[20]   *Lévis (Ville) c. Tétreault* (2006), 207 C.C.C. (3d) 1, 36 C.R. (6th) 215, [2006] 1 S.C.R. 420.

[21]   (1999), 24 C.R. (5th) 1 (S.C.C.).

[22]   For criticism see Delisle, "*Stone*: Judicial Activism Gone Awry to Presume Guilt" (1999), 24 C.R. (5th) 91; Editorial in (1999) 4 Can. Crim. L. Rev. 119; and Healy, "Automatism Confined" (2000) 45 McGill L.J. 87.

[23]   *Miller v. Min. of Pensions*, [1947] 2 All E.R. 372 (K.B.) at 374. See also Duff J. in *Clark v. R.* (1921), 61 S.C.R. 608 at 616: ". . . such a preponderance of evidence as to shew that the conclusion he seeks to establish is substantially the most probable of the possible views of the facts".

It is common then to contrast the civil standard with the criminal standard which requires the trier to be "satisfied beyond a reasonable doubt". This higher standard, according to Phipson,

> . . . dates from the end of the eighteenth century, [and] was due to the reaction then setting in, against the rigours of the penal code, and was originally applied *in favorem vitae* to capital cases only.[24]

F.H. v. MCDOUGALL
[2008] 3 S.C.R. 41, 61 C.R. (6th) 1 (S.C.C.)

The plaintiff was a resident of an Indian Residential School for some years. The school was operated by a religious organization (of which M was a member) and funded by the federal government. M was the junior and intermediate boys' supervisor during part of the time that H was a resident of the school. Years later, H brought a civil suit alleging that M had sexually assaulted him on four occasions in a washroom when children were brought one by one into the washroom to be inspected for cleanliness.

At trial, the trial judge found that H was a credible witness in spite of certain inconsistencies in his testimony. She held that M had anally raped H on four occasions and physically assaulted him on other occasions, and gave judgment for the plaintiff. The respondents appealed to the British Columbia Court of Appeal, which by a majority partially allowed the appeal and overturned the judgment in respect of the sexual assaults. According to the Court of Appeal, the trial judge had failed to consider serious inconsistencies in H's testimony, that closer scrutiny of the evidence was required in cases where moral blameworthiness was alleged, and that the standard of proof was required to be commensurate with the allegations. H appealed to the Supreme Court of Canada.

ROTHSTEIN J.:

. . .

III. Analysis

A. The Standard of Proof

(1) *Canadian Jurisprudence*

[26] Much has been written as judges have attempted to reconcile the tension between the civil standard of proof on a balance of probabilities and cases in which allegations made against a defendant are particularly grave. Such cases include allegations of fraud, professional misconduct, and criminal conduct, particularly sexual assault against minors. As explained by L. R. Rothstein, R. A. Centa, and E. Adams, in "Balancing Probabilities: The Overlooked

---

[24]   Phipson, *Evidence*, 9th ed. (1952) at 8. Wigmore seems to agree: 9 Wigmore, *Evidence* (Chad. Rev.), s. 2497 at 405. Compare, however, Thayer, *supra* note 7 at 558 suggesting the rule is an ancient one traceable to the *Corpus Juris* of the fourth century.

Complexity of the Civil Standard of Proof" in *Special Lectures of the Law Society of Upper Canada 2003: The Law of Evidence* (2003) 455, at p. 456:

> ... These types of allegations are considered unique because they carry a moral stigma that will continue to have an impact on the individual after the completion of the civil case.

[27] Courts in British Columbia have tended to follow the approach of Lord Denning in *Bater v. Bater*, [1950] 2 All E.R. 458 (C.A.). Lord Denning was of the view that within the civil standard of proof on a balance of probabilities "there may be degrees of probability within that standard" (p. 459), depending upon the subject matter. He stated at p. 459:

> It does not adopt so high a degree as a criminal court, even when it is considering a charge of a criminal nature, but still it does require a degree of probability which is commensurate with the occasion.

[28] In the present case the trial judge referred to *H.F. v. Canada (Attorney General)*, at para. 154, in which Neilson J. stated:

> The court is justified in imposing a higher degree of probability which is "commensurate with the occasion" ...

[29] In the constitutional context, Dickson C.J. adopted the *Bater* approach in *R. v. Oakes*, [1986] 1 S.C.R. 103. In his view a "very high degree of probability" required that the evidence be cogent and persuasive and make clear the consequences of the decision one way or the other. He wrote at p. 138:

> Having regard to the fact that s. 1 is being invoked for the purpose of justifying a violation of the constitutional rights and freedoms the *Charter* was designed to protect, a very high degree of probability will be, in the words of Lord Denning, "commensurate with the occasion". Where evidence is required in order to prove the constituent elements of a s. 1 inquiry and this will generally be the case, it should be cogent and persuasive and make clear to the Court the consequences of imposing or not imposing the limit.

[30] However, a "shifting standard" of probability has not been universally accepted. In *Continental Insurance Co. v. Dalton Cartage Co.*, [1982] 1 S.C.R. 164, Laskin C.J. rejected a "shifting standard". Rather, to take account of the seriousness of the allegation, he was of the view that a trial judge should scrutinize the evidence with "greater care". . .

[31] In Ontario Professional Discipline cases, the balance of probabilities requires that proof be "clear and convincing and based upon cogent evidence" (see *Heath v. College of Physicians & Surgeons (Ontario)* (1997), 6 Admin. L.R. (3d) 304 (Ont. Ct. (Gen. Div.), at para. 53).

(2) Recent United Kingdom Jurisprudence

[32] In the United Kingdom some decisions have indicated that depending upon the seriousness of the matters involved, even in civil cases, the criminal

standard of proof should apply. In *R (McCann) v. Crown Court at Manchester*, [2003] 1 A.C. 787, [2002] UKHL 39, Lord Steyn said at para. 37:

> . . . I agree that, given the seriousness of matters involved, at least some reference to the heightened civil standard would usually be necessary: In *re H (Minors) (Sexual Abuse: Standard of Proof)*, [1996] AC 563, 586 D H, per Lord Nicholls of Birkenhead. For essentially practical reasons, the Recorder of Manchester decided to apply the criminal standard. The Court of Appeal said that would usually be the right course to adopt. Lord Bingham of Cornhill has observed that the heightened civil standard and the criminal standard are virtually indistinguishable. I do not disagree with any of these views. But in my view pragmatism dictates that the task of magistrates should be made more straightforward by ruling that they must in all cases under section 1 apply the criminal standard.

[33] Yet another consideration, that of "inherent probability or improbability of an event" was discussed by Lord Nicholls in *In re H (Minors) (Sexual Abuse: Standard of Proof)*, [1996] A.C. 563 (H.L.), at p. 586:

> . . . the inherent probability or improbability of an event is itself a matter to be taken into account when weighing the probabilities and deciding whether, on balance, the event occurred. The more improbable the event, the stronger must be the evidence that it did occur before, on the balance of probability, its occurrence will be established.

[34] Most recently in *In re B (Children)*, [2008] 3 W.L.R. 1, [2008] UKHL 35, a June 11, 2008 decision, the U.K. House of Lords again canvassed the issue of standard of proof. Subsequent to the hearing of the appeal, Mr. Southey, counsel for the Attorney General of Canada, with no objection from other counsel, brought this case to the attention of the Court.

[35] Lord Hoffmann addressed the "confusion" in the United Kingdom courts over this issue. He stated at para. 5:

> Some confusion has however been caused by dicta which suggest that the standard of proof may vary with the gravity of the misconduct alleged or even the seriousness of the consequences for the person concerned. The cases in which such statements have been made fall into three categories. First, there are cases in which the court has for one purpose classified the proceedings as civil (for example, for the purposes of article 6 of the European Convention for the Protection of Human Rights and Fundamental Freedoms) but nevertheless thought that, because of the serious consequences of the proceedings, the criminal standard of proof or something like it should be applied. Secondly, there are cases in which it has been observed that when some event is inherently improbable, strong evidence may be needed to persuade a tribunal that it more probably happened than not. Thirdly, there are cases in which judges are simply confused about whether they are talking about the standard of proof or about the role of inherent probabilities in deciding whether the burden of proving a fact to a given standard has been discharged.

[36] The unanimous conclusion of the House of Lords was that there is only one civil standard of proof. At para. 13, Lord Hoffmann states:

> . . . I think that the time has come to say, once and for all, that there is only one civil standard of proof and that is proof that the fact in issue more probably occurred than not.

However, Lord Hoffmann did not disapprove of application of the criminal standard depending upon the issue involved. Following his very clear statement that there is only one civil standard of proof, he somewhat enigmatically wrote, still in para. 13:

> . . . I do not intend to disapprove any of the cases in what I have called the first category, but I agree with the observation of Lord Steyn in *McCann's* case, at p. 812, that clarity would be greatly enhanced if the courts said simply that although the proceedings were civil, the nature of the particular issue involved made it appropriate to apply the criminal standard.

[37] Lord Hoffmann went on to express the view that taking account of inherent probabilities was not a rule of law. At para. 15 he stated:

> I wish to lay some stress upon the words I have italicised ["to whatever extent is appropriate in the particular case"]. Lord Nicholls [In re H] was not laying down any rule of law. There is only one rule of law, namely that the occurrence of the fact in issue must be proved to have been more probable than not. Common sense, not law, requires that in deciding this question, regard should be had, to whatever extent appropriate, to inherent probabilities.

[38] In *re B* is a child case under the *United Kingdom Children Act 1989*. While her comments on standard of proof are confined to the 1989 Act, Baroness Hale explained that neither the seriousness of the allegation nor the seriousness of the consequences should make any difference to the standard of proof to be applied in determining the facts. At paras. 70-72, she stated:

> My Lords, for that reason I would go further and announce loud and clear that the standard of proof in finding the facts necessary to establish the threshold under section 31(2) or the welfare considerations in section 1 of the 1989 Act is the simple balance of probabilities, neither more nor less. Neither the seriousness of the allegation nor the seriousness of the consequences should make any difference to the standard of proof to be applied in determining the facts. The inherent probabilities are simply something to be taken into account, where relevant, in deciding where the truth lies.
>
> As to the seriousness of the consequences, they are serious either way. A child may find her relationship with her family seriously disrupted; or she may find herself still at risk of suffering serious harm. A parent may find his relationship with his child seriously disrupted; or he may find himself still at liberty to maltreat this or other children in the future.
>
> As to the seriousness of the allegation, there is no logical or necessary connection between seriousness and probability. Some seriously harmful behaviour, such as murder, is sufficiently rare to be inherently improbable in most circumstances. Even then there are circumstances, such as a body with its throat

cut and no weapon to hand, where it is not at all improbable. Other seriously harmful behaviour, such as alcohol or drug abuse, is regrettably all too common and not at all improbable.

(3) *Summary of Various Approaches*

[39] I summarize the various approaches in civil cases where criminal or morally blameworthy conduct is alleged as I understand them:

(1) The criminal standard of proof applies in civil cases depending upon the seriousness of the allegation;

(2) An intermediate standard of proof between the civil standard and the criminal standard commensurate with the occasion applies to civil cases;

(3) No heightened standard of proof applies in civil cases, but the evidence must be scrutinized with greater care where the allegation is serious;

(4) No heightened standard of proof applies in civil cases, but evidence must be clear, convincing and cogent; and

(5) No heightened standard of proof applies in civil cases, but the more improbable the event, the stronger the evidence is needed to meet the balance of probabilities test.

(4) *The Approach Canadian Courts Should Now Adopt*

[40] Like the House of Lords, I think it is time to say, once and for all in Canada, that there is only one civil standard of proof at common law and that is proof on a balance of probabilities. Of course, context is all important and a judge should not be unmindful, where appropriate, of inherent probabilities or improbabilities or the seriousness of the allegations or consequences. However, these considerations do not change the standard of proof. I am of the respectful opinion that the alternatives I have listed above should be rejected for the reasons that follow.

[41] Since *Hanes v. Wawanesa Mutual Insurance Co.*, [1963] S.C.R. 154, at pp. 158-64, it has been clear that the criminal standard is not to be applied to civil cases in Canada. The criminal standard of proof beyond a reasonable doubt is linked to the presumption of innocence in criminal trials.

[42] By contrast, in civil cases, there is no presumption of innocence. As explained by J. Sopinka, S. N. Lederman and A. W. Bryant, *The Law of Evidence* (2nd ed. 1999), at p. 154:

> . . . Since society is indifferent to whether the plaintiff or the defendant wins a particular civil suit, it is unnecessary to protect against an erroneous result by requiring a standard of proof higher than a balance of probabilities.

It is true that there may be serious consequences to a finding of liability in a civil case that continue past the end of the case. However, the civil case does not involve the government's power to penalize or take away the liberty of the individual.

[43] An intermediate standard of proof presents practical problems. As expressed by L. Rothstein et al., at p. 466:

> As well, suggesting that the standard of proof is "higher" than the "mere balance of probabilities" leads one inevitably to inquire what percentage of probability must be met? This is unhelpful because while the concept of "51% probability", or "more likely than not" can be understood by decision-makers, the concept of 60% or 70% probability cannot.

[44] Put another way, it would seem incongruous for a judge to conclude that it was more likely than not that an event occurred, but not sufficiently likely to some unspecified standard and therefore that it did not occur. As Lord Hoffmann explained in *In re B* at para. 2:

> If a legal rule requires a fact to be proved (a "fact in issue"), a judge or jury must decide whether or not it happened. There is no room for a finding that it might have happened. The law operates a binary system in which the only values are zero and one. The fact either happened or it did not. If the tribunal is left in doubt, the doubt is resolved by a rule that one party or the other carries the burden of proof.

> If the party who bears the burden of proof fails to discharge it, a value of zero is returned and the fact is treated as not having happened. If he does discharge it, a value of one is returned and the fact is treated as having happened.

In my view, the only practical way in which to reach a factual conclusion in a civil case is to decide whether it is more likely than not that the event occurred.

[45] To suggest that depending upon the seriousness, the evidence in the civil case must be scrutinized with greater care implies that in less serious cases the evidence need not be scrutinized with such care. I think it is inappropriate to say that there are legally recognized different levels of scrutiny of the evidence depending upon the seriousness of the case. There is only one legal rule and that is that in all cases, evidence must be scrutinized with care by the trial judge.

[46] Similarly, evidence must always be sufficiently clear, convincing and cogent to satisfy the balance of probabilities test. But again, there is no objective standard to measure sufficiency. In serious cases, like the present, judges may be faced with evidence of events that are alleged to have occurred many years before, where there is little other evidence than that of the plaintiff and defendant. As difficult as the task may be, the judge must make a decision. If a responsible judge finds for the plaintiff, it must be accepted that the evidence was sufficiently clear, convincing and cogent to that judge that the plaintiff satisfied the balance of probabilities test.

[47] Finally there may be cases in which there is an inherent improbability that an event occurred. Inherent improbability will always depend upon the circumstances. As Baroness Hale stated in *In re B* at para. 72:

> . . . Consider the famous example of the animal seen in Regent's Park. If it is seen outside the zoo on a stretch of greensward regularly used for walking dogs, then of course it is more likely to be a dog than a lion. If it is seen in the zoo next to the lions' enclosure when the door is open, then it may well be more likely to be a lion than a dog.

[48] Some alleged events may be highly improbable. Others less so. There can be no rule as to when and to what extent inherent improbability must be taken into account by a trial judge. As Lord Hoffmann observed at para. 15 of In re B:

> . . . Common sense, not law, requires that in deciding this question, regard should be had, to whatever extent appropriate, to inherent probabilities.

It will be for the trial judge to decide to what extent, if any, the circumstances suggest that an allegation is inherently improbable and where appropriate, that may be taken into account in the assessment of whether the evidence establishes that it is more likely than not that the event occurred. However, there can be no rule of law imposing such a formula.

(5) Conclusion on Standard of Proof

[49] In the result, I would reaffirm that in civil cases there is only one standard of proof and that is proof on a balance of probabilities. In all civil cases, the trial judge must scrutinize the relevant evidence with care to determine whether it is more likely than not that an alleged event occurred.

Appeal allowed; verdict for the plaintiff restored.

The Supreme Court achieves welcome clarity in holding that in all civil cases there is only the one standard of proof on a balance of probabilities and that in any case the trial judge must scrutinize the relevant evidence with care to determine whether it is more likely than not that an alleged event occurred [para. 40]. The level of scrutiny does not, it is held, depend on the seriousness of the case [para. 45]. The Court does say, borrowing an approach developed in professional malpractice cases, that in all civil cases evidence must be sufficiently clear, convincing and cogent to satisfy the balance of probabilities test [para. 46]. This is the new standard which all judges from now on will be presumed to know. **Does this in fact raise the standard of proof for all civil cases?**

The Court squarely rejects the often-quoted approach of Lord Denning in *Bater v. Bater*[25] that in civil cases the burden of proof must be "commensurate with the occasion" and within the standard of proof on a balance of probabilities "there may be degrees of probability within that standard depending on the subject matter". The Supreme Court does note that the Denning view was applied by Justice Dickson in *Oakes* to require a high degree of probability to demonstrably justify a *Charter* breach under s. 1. That particular standard has not been overruled. It was confusing for Lord

---

[25]   [1950] 2 All E.R. 458 (C.A.).

Denning to use a shifting standard of proof depending on the case. However, was Lord Denning not just being realistic rather than wrong-headed in suggesting that in both civil and criminal cases the degree of proof required is necessarily commensurate with the occasion? **Will triers of fact not require, as a practical matter, more proof to prove murder than cases of minor assault or shoplifting?**

(ii) *Reasonable Doubt Standard for Criminal Cases*

What does reasonable doubt mean? Should judges define it for juries?

R. v. LIFCHUS
[1997] 3 S.C.R. 320, 9 C.R. (5th) 1, 118 C.C.C. (3d) 1

The accused was charged with fraud. The trial judge told the jury in her charge on the burden of proof that she used the words "'proof beyond a reasonable doubt' . . . in their ordinary, natural everyday sense", and that the words "doubt" and "reasonable" are "ordinary, everyday words that . . . you understand". The accused was convicted of fraud. On appeal, he contended that the trial judge had erred in instructing the jury on the meaning of the expression "proof beyond a reasonable doubt". The Court of Appeal allowed the appeal and ordered a new trial. The Supreme Court dismissed the Crown's appeal.

CORY J. (LAMER C.J.C., and Sopinka, Mclachlin, Iacobucci and Major JJ. concurring):—

. . .

The phrase "beyond a reasonable doubt", is composed of words which are commonly used in everyday speech. Yet, these words have a specific meaning in the legal context. This special meaning of the words "reasonable doubt" may not correspond precisely to the meaning ordinarily attributed to them. In criminal proceedings, where the liberty of the subject is at stake, it is of fundamental importance that jurors fully understand the nature of the burden of proof that the law requires them to apply. An explanation of the meaning of proof beyond a reasonable doubt is an essential element of the instructions that must be given to a jury. That a definition is necessary can be readily deduced from the frequency with which juries ask for guidance with regard to its meaning. It is therefore essential that the trial judge provide the jury with an explanation of the expression.

. . .

Perhaps a brief summary of what the definition should and should not contain may be helpful. It should be explained that:

the standard of proof beyond a reasonable doubt is inextricably intertwined with that principle fundamental to all criminal trials, the presumption of innocence;

the burden of proof rests on the prosecution throughout the trial and never shifts to the accused; a reasonable doubt is not a doubt based upon sympathy or prejudice;

rather, it is based upon reason and common sense;

it is logically connected to the evidence or absence of evidence;

it does not involve proof to an absolute certainty; it is not proof beyond any doubt nor is it an imaginary or frivolous doubt; and

more is required than proof that the accused is probably guilty, a jury which concludes only that the accused is probably guilty must acquit.

On the other hand, certain references to the required standard of proof should be avoided. For example:

describing the term "reasonable doubt" as an ordinary expression which has no special meaning in the criminal law context;

inviting jurors to apply to the task before them the same standard of proof that they apply to important, or even the most important, decisions in their own lives;[26]

equating proof "beyond a reasonable doubt" to proof "to a moral certainty";

qualifying the word "doubt" with adjectives other than "reasonable", such as "serious", substantial" or "haunting", which may mislead the jury; and

instructing jurors that they may convict if they are "sure" that the accused is guilty, before providing them with a proper definition as to the meaning of the words "beyond a reasonable doubt".

A charge which is consistent with the principles set out in these reasons will suffice regardless of the particular words used by the trial judge. Nevertheless, it may be useful to set out a "model charge" which could provide the necessary instructions as to the meaning of the phrase beyond a reasonable doubt.

Suggested Charge

Instructions pertaining to the requisite standard of proof in a criminal trial of proof beyond a reasonable doubt might be given along these lines:

The accused enters these proceedings presumed to be innocent. That presumption of innocence remains throughout the case until such time as the Crown has on the evidence put before you satisfied you beyond a reasonable doubt that the accused is guilty.

What does the expression "beyond a reasonable doubt" mean? The term "beyond a reasonable doubt" has been used for a very long time and is a part of our history and traditions of justice. It is so engrained in our criminal law that some think it needs no explanation, yet something must be said regarding its meaning.

---

[26]   In *R. v. Bisson* (1998), 14 C.R. (5th) 1 (S.C.C.), a new trial was ordered in a first degree murder case because the trial judge had erred in giving an example of the everyday task of checking oil in a car as the degree of certainty required.

A reasonable doubt is not an imaginary or frivolous doubt. It must not be based upon sympathy or prejudice. Rather, it is based on reason and common sense. It is logically derived from the evidence or absence of evidence.

Even if you believe the accused is probably guilty or likely guilty, that is not sufficient. In those circumstances you must give the benefit of the doubt to the accused and acquit because the Crown has failed to satisfy you of the guilt of the accused beyond a reasonable doubt.

On the other hand you must remember that it is virtually impossible to prove anything to an absolute certainty and the Crown is not required to do so. Such a standard of proof is impossibly high.

In short if, based upon the evidence before the court, you are sure that the accused committed the offence you should convict since this demonstrates that you are satisfied of his guilt beyond a reasonable doubt.

This is not a magic incantation that needs to be repeated word for word. It is nothing more than a suggested form that would not be faulted if it were used .... Further, it is possible that an error in the instructions as to the standard of proof may not constitute a reversible error. It was observed in *R. v. W. (D.)*, [1991] 1 S.C.R. 742, at p. 758, that the verdict ought not be disturbed "if the charge, when read as a whole, makes it clear that the jury could not have been under any misapprehension as to the correct burden and standard of proof to apply." On the other hand, if the charge as a whole gives rise to the reasonable likelihood that the jury misapprehended the standard of proof, then as a general rule the verdict will have to be set aside and a new trial directed.

R. v. STARR
[2000] 2 S.C.R. 144, 36 C.R. (5th) 1, 147 C.C.C. (3d) 449

The accused had been convicted of two counts of first degree murder. The majority of the Court decided that the reasonable doubt instruction given in the case fell prey to many of the same difficulties outlined in *Lifchus*, and likely misled the jury as to the content of the criminal standard of proof. In allowing the accused's appeal they gave further advice.

IACOBUCCI J. (MAJOR, BINNIE, ARBOUR and LEBEL JJ. concurring): —

. . .

In the present case, the trial judge did refer to the Crown's onus and to the presumption of innocence, and he stated that the appellant should receive the benefit of any reasonable doubt. The error in the charge is that the jury was not told *how a reasonable doubt is to be defined*. As was emphasized repeatedly in *Lifchus* and again in *Bisson*, a jury *must* be instructed that the standard of proof in a criminal trial is higher than the probability standard used in making everyday decisions and in civil trials. Indeed, it is this very requirement to go beyond probability that meshes the standard of proof in criminal cases with the presumption of innocence and the Crown's onus. However, as Cory J. explained in these earlier decisions, it is generally inappropriate to define the meaning of the term "reasonable doubt" through examples from daily life, through the use of synonyms, or through analogy to moral choices. The criminal standard of proof has a special significance unique to the legal process. It is an exacting standard of proof rarely encountered in everyday life, and there is no universally intelligible illustration of the concept, such as the scales of justice with respect to the balance of probabilities standard. Unlike absolute certainty or the balance of probabilities, reasonable doubt is not an easily quantifiable standard. It cannot be measured or described by analogy. It must be explained. However, precisely because it is not quantifiable, it is difficult to explain.

In my view, an effective way to define the reasonable doubt standard for a jury is to explain that it falls much closer to absolute certainty than to proof on a balance of probabilities. As stated in *Lifchus*, a trial judge is required to explain that something less than absolute certainty is required, and that something more than probable guilt is required, in order for the jury to convict. Both of these alternative standards are fairly and easily comprehensible. It will be of great assistance for a jury if the trial judge situates the reasonable doubt standard appropriately between these two standards. The additional instructions to the jury set out in *Lifchus* as to the meaning and appropriate manner of determining the existence of a reasonable doubt serve to define the space between absolute certainty and proof beyond a reasonable doubt. In this regard, I am in agreement with Twaddle J.A. in the court below, when he said, at p. 177:

> If standards of proof were marked on a measure, proof "beyond reasonable doubt" would lie much closer to "absolute certainty" than to "a balance of probabilities". Just as a judge has a duty to instruct the jury that absolute certainty is not required, he or she has a duty, in my view, to instruct the jury that the criminal standard is more than a probability. The words he or she uses to convey this idea are of no significance, but the idea itself must be conveyed. . .[27]

By suggesting that proof beyond a reasonable doubt falls closer to absolute certainty than to balance of probabilities, has *Starr* moved us closer to thinking about quantifying reasonable doubt? Do you think this would be a good idea?[28]

(iii) *Choosing Between Competing Versions*

In being satisfied to the requisite standard the trier of fact does not "choose" between competing versions of the incident. The plaintiff or the prosecutor makes allegations, seeks to disturb the *status quo* and bears the burden of satisfying the trier. In *R. v. Nadeau*,[29] the accused was convicted of murder. The accused testified and his version of the incident differed from that of the prosecution's witness. The trial judge told the jury that they had to choose between the two versions. A new trial was ordered and Lamer, J. wrote:

---

[27]   See further Patrick Healy, "Direction and Guidance on Reasonable Doubt in the Charge to the Jury" (2001) 6 Can. Crim. L.R. 161.

[28]   See *United States v. Copeland*, 369 F.Supp.2d 275 (E.D.N.Y., 2005).

[29]   (1984), 42 C.R. (3d) 305 (S.C.C.).

With respect, this direction is in error. The accused benefits from any reasonable doubt at the outset, not merely if "the two versions are equally consistent with the evidence, are equally valid". Moreover, the jury does not have to choose between two versions. It is not because they would not believe the accused that they would then have to agree with Landry's version. The jurors cannot accept his version, or any part of it, unless they are satisfied beyond all reasonable doubt, having regard to all the evidence, that the events took place in this manner; otherwise, the accused is entitled, unless a fact has been established beyond a reasonable doubt, to the finding of fact the most favourable to him, provided of course that it is based on evidence in the record and not mere speculation.[30]

R. v. W. (D.)
[1991] 1 S.C.R. 742, 3 C.R. (4th) 302, 63 C.C.C. (3d) 347

The accused was convicted of sexual assault after a trial that pitted the credibility of the accused against that of the complainant. It was objected that the trial judge erred in his recharge in that he characterized the core issue to be determined by the jury as whether they believed the complainant or whether they believed the appellant.

CORY J.:—

A trial Judge might well instruct the jury on the question of credibility along these lines:

First, if you believe the evidence of the accused, obviously you must acquit.

Second, if you do not believe the testimony of the accused but you are left in reasonable doubt by it, you must acquit.

Third, even if you are not left in doubt by the evidence of the accused, you must ask yourself whether, on the basis of the evidence which you do accept, you are convinced beyond a reasonable doubt by that evidence of the guilt of the accused.

If that formula were followed, the oft-repeated error which appears in the recharge in this case would be avoided. The requirement that the Crown prove the guilt of the accused beyond a reasonable doubt is fundamental in our system of criminal law. Every effort should be made to avoid mistakes in charging the jury on this basic principle.[31]

The Supreme Court has recognized various criticisms of the W. (D.) approach and held that it should not be applied as a magical incantation:

---

30 *Ibid.* at 310.
31 *Ibid.* W. (D.) is one of the most frequently cited authorities. For different views as to its wisdom see Gans, (2000) 43 Crim. L.Q. 345 and Plaxton, (2000) 43 Crim. L.Q. 443. For a suggestion that judges are not properly applying W. (D.) see Tanovich, "Testing the Presumption that Trial Judges Know the Law: The Case of W. (D.)" (2001), 43 C.R. (5th) 298.

R. v. S. (J.H.)
[2008] 2 S.C.R. 152, 57 C.R. (6th) 79, 231 C.C.C. (3d) 302 (S.C.C.)

A stepfather was charged with sexual assault after the complainant alleged that he had sexually abused her over a number of years, starting when she was approximately four years old. She twice complained to her mother who did not believe her. When the complainant was 15 she went to the police. The accused denied all the allegations and suggested that they were falsely made after he threatened to send her to a Catholic school because of her uncontrollable behaviour. The issue at trial before judge and jury was whether the alleged events had ever happened. The complainant and the accused were the principal witnesses. The trial judge charged the jury on the credibility of the witnesses, instructing them that they had to consider all the evidence and that the trial was not a choice between two competing versions of events. The defence raised no objection to the charge. The jury returned a verdict of guilty.

A majority of the Nova Scotia Court of Appeal set aside the conviction and ordered a new trial. According to the Court of Appeal, the trial judge had insufficiently explained the principles of reasonable doubt as they applied to credibility. While the *W. (D.)* phrasing was not a magical incantation, the charge had failed to express the second *W. (D.)* principle that disbelief in the accused's testimony does not amount to proof of his or her guilt beyond a reasonable doubt. The dissenting judge found that the charge was sufficient.

BINNIE J. (for seven justices):

[8] A series of decisions over at least the past 20 years has affirmed and reaffirmed the proposition that where credibility is a central issue in a jury trial, the judge must explain the relationship between the assessment of credibility and the Crown's ultimate burden to prove the guilt of the accused to the criminal standard. A general instruction on reasonable doubt without adverting to its relationship to the credibility (or lack of credibility) of the witnesses leaves open too great a possibility of confusion or misunderstanding. The so-called *W. (D.)* instruction has long roots: *R. v. Challice* (1979), 45 C.C.C. (2d) 546 (Ont. C.A.), at p. 556; *R. v. Chan* (1989), 52 C.C.C. (3d) 184, (Alta. C.A.), at p. 186; *R. v. Morin*, [1988] 2 S.C.R. 345, at p. 362; *R. v. H. (C.W.)* (1991), 68 C.C.C. (3d) 146 (B.C. C.A.), at p. 155; *R. v. MacKenzie*, [1993] 1 S.C.R. 212, at pp. 219 and 239; *R. v. Levasseur*, [1994] 3 S.C.R. 518 (upholding Fish J.A.'s dissent reported at (1994), 89 C.C.C. (3d) 508 (Que. C.A.), at p. 534). *W. (D.)* has been cited by Canadian courts at all levels in no fewer than 3,743 subsequent reported cases. It has proven to be a fertile source of appellate review. For a recent application, see *R. v. C.L.Y.*, [2008] 1 S.C.R. 5, 2008 SCC 2.

[9] The passage from *W. (D.)* at issue in this case, as in so many others, is found at pp. 757-58, where Cory J. explained:

Ideally, appropriate instructions on the issue of credibility should be given, not only during the main charge, but on any recharge. A trial judge might well instruct the jury on the question of credibility along these lines:

> First, if you believe the evidence of the accused, obviously you must acquit.

> Second, if you do not believe the testimony of the accused but you are left in reasonable doubt by it, you must acquit.

> Third, even if you are not left in doubt by the evidence of the accused, you must ask yourself whether, on the basis of the evidence which you do accept, you are convinced beyond a reasonable doubt by that evidence of the guilt of the accused.

If that formula were followed, the oft repeated error which appears in the recharge in this case would be avoided. The requirement that the Crown prove the guilt of the accused beyond a reasonable doubt is fundamental in our system of criminal law. Every effort should be made to avoid mistakes in charging the jury on this basic principle.

Nonetheless, the failure to use such language is not fatal if the charge, when read as a whole, makes it clear that the jury could not have been under any misapprehension as to the correct burden and standard of proof to apply . . .

Essentially, *W. (D.)* simply unpacks for the benefit of the lay jury what reasonable doubt means in the context of evaluating conflicting testimonial accounts. It alerts the jury to the "credibility contest" error. It teaches that trial judges are required to impress on the jury that the burden never shifts from the Crown to prove every element of the offence beyond a reasonable doubt.

[10] The precise formulation of the *W. (D.)* questions has been criticized. As to the first question, the jury may believe inculpatory elements of the statements of an accused but reject the exculpatory explanation. In *R. v. Latimer*, [2001] 1 S.C.R. 3, 2001 SCC 1, the accused did not testify, but his description of the killing of his daughter was put into evidence by way of statements to the police. His description of the event itself was obviously believed. The exculpatory explanation did not amount to a defence at law. He was convicted. The principle that a jury may believe some, none, or all of the testimony of any witness, including that of an accused, suggests to some critics that the first *W. (D.)* question is something of an oversimplification.

[11] As to the second question, some jurors may wonder how, if they believe none of the evidence of the accused, such rejected evidence may nevertheless of itself raise a reasonable doubt. Of course, some elements of the evidence of an accused may raise a reasonable doubt, even though the bulk of it is rejected. Equally, the jury may simply conclude that they do not know whether to believe the accused's testimony or not. In either circumstance the accused is entitled to an acquittal.

[12] The third question, again, is taken by some critics as failing to contemplate a jury's acceptance of inculpatory bits of the evidence of an accused but not the

exculpatory elements. In light of these possible sources of difficulty, Wood J.A. in *H. (C.W.)* suggested an additional instruction:

> I would add one more instruction in such cases, which logically ought to be second in the order, namely: If, after a careful consideration of all the evidence, you are unable to decide whom to believe, you must acquit. [p. 155]

[13] In short the *W. (D.)* questions should not have attributed to them a level of sanctity or immutable perfection that their author never claimed for them. *W. (D.)*'s message that it must be made crystal clear to the jury that the burden never shifts from the Crown to prove every element of the offence beyond a reasonable doubt is of fundamental importance but its application should not result in a triumph of form over substance. In *R. v. S. (W.D.)*, [1994] 3 S.C.R. 521, Cory J. reiterated that the *W. (D.)* instructions need not be given "word for word as some magic incantation" (p. 533). In *R. v. Avetysan*, [2000] 2 S.C.R. 745, 2000 SCC 56, Major J. for the majority pointed out that in any case where credibility is important "[t]he question is really whether, in substance, the trial judge's instructions left the jury with the impression that it had to choose between the two versions of events" (para. 19). The main point is that lack of credibility on the part of the accused does not equate to proof of his or her guilt beyond a reasonable doubt.

[14] In the present case Oland J.A. agreed that the trial judge did not call upon the jury to simply decide which of the complainant or [the accused] it believed (para. 19). Nevertheless, in her view:

> The charge only instructed that probable guilt was not enough to meet the standard of proof beyond a reasonable doubt, that the appellant was to be given the benefit of the doubt, and they did not have to accept or reject all of the testimony of any witness including his, and that they were to consider all of the evidence. Nowhere did it provide any guidance as to how, in the event they were uncertain or unable to resolve the issue of credibility, they were to proceed with their deliberations. *The charge failed to direct that if the jury did not believe the testimony of the accused but were left in a reasonable doubt by that evidence, they must acquit.* [Emphasis added; para.20.]

In my view, with respect, the reasoning of the majority brushes uncomfortably close to the magic incantation error. At the end of the day, reading the charge as a whole, I believe the instruction to this jury satisfied the ultimate test formulated by Cory J. in *W. (D.)* as being whether the jury could not have been under any misapprehension as to the correct burden and standard of proof to apply (p. 758).

[15] Here the trial judge explained that any reasonable doubt must be resolved in favour of the accused. She also explained that even if they did not accept all of the accused's testimony, they could still accept some of it. She also explained to the jury that they should not see their task as that of deciding between two versions of events. She told them that they could not decide the case simply by choosing between the evidence of the complainant and that of the accused. She

reminded them, in that context, that they must consider all of the evidence when determining reasonable doubt. She stated:

> You do not decide whether something happened simply by comparing one version of events with another, or choosing one of them. You have to consider all the evidence and decide whether you have been satisfied beyond a reasonable doubt that the events that form the basis of the crime charged, in fact, took place. [A.R., at p. 54.]

. . .

> Again, you do not decide whether something happened simply by comparing one version of events with the other, or by choosing one of them. You have to consider all of the evidence and decide whether you have been satisfied beyond a reasonable doubt that the events that form the basis of the crimes charges, in fact, took place. [A.R., at p. 55.]

[16] In my view, the trial judge got across the point of the second *W. (D.)* question without leaving any realistic possibility of misunderstanding. As stated, she told the jury:

> It is for the Crown counsel to prove beyond a reasonable doubt that the events alleged in fact occurred. It is not for [the accused] to prove that these events never happened. If you have a reasonable doubt whether the events alleged ever took place, you *must* find him not guilty. [Emphasis added; A.R., at p. 54.]

[17] There was much discussion at the hearing about defence counsel's failure to object. In my view, he correctly ascertained that the jury had been adequately instructed on the relationship between the assessment of credibility and the ultimate determination of guilt beyond a reasonable doubt. Before the recharge was given he told the trial judge he would feel more comfortable if simply the wording that was read previously was re-read to the jury again (A.R., at p. 77). He discharged his duty to the respondent.

Appeal allowed; conviction restored.

Should the Supreme Court have expressly and clearly abandoned the *W. (D.)* approach? It has been responsible for many, many prolix appeals and orders of new trials. The main problem is that the second question is potentially confusing and/or too generous to the accused.[32]

In *S. (J.H.)*, Justice Binnie might have mentioned the remark of McLachlin J. dissenting in *R. v. S. (W.D.)*:[33]

---

[32] See especially the late Jack Gibson, "*R. v. W.D.* Revisited: Is Step Two a Misdirection?" (2003), 11 C.R. (6th) 323. His earlier article "The Liars' Defence" (1993), 20 C.R. (4th) 96 led to a spirited debate: see Alan Gold, "The 'Average, Nervous, Inadequate, Inarticulate in Short, Typical' Accused's Defence" (2003), 22 C.R. (4th) 253; Gibson, "Misquote Changes Meaning" (1994), 24 C.R. (4th) 395; and Gold, "Typo Does Not Change Anything" (1994), 24 C.R. (4th) 397. In *R. v. Edwards* (2012), 93 C.R. (6th) 387 (Ont. S.C.J), Justice Code held that "the so-called second branch of *W.D.* does not require a trier of fact to take evidence that has been completely rejected and use it as a basis for finding reasonable doubt" (para. 20).

[33] [1994] 3 S.C.R. 521.

Certainly if the jury rejected (as opposed to being merely undecided about) all of the evidence of the accused, it is difficult to see how that very evidence, having been rejected, could raise a reasonable doubt.

Should the Supreme Court have considered the disproportionate impact *W. (D.)* is having in sexual assault cases? Even the most cursory review of the cases reveals that the issue arises most frequently in sexual assault cases and that sexual assault convictions are being frequently reversed on appeal because of a *W. (D.)* error. Why is this happening?

Trial judges are at least now free to reject the complexity of *W. (D.)* as long as they make sure that the jury is warned of the Crown's burden of proof; that it is not just a choice between competing versions and that they may believe some, none or all of the testimony of any witness, including the accused. These principles, of course, apply equally to judge-alone trials.

R. v. G.W.

2017 ABPC 158, 39 C.R. (7th) 212 (Alta. Prov. Ct.)

LeGrandeur A.C.J.:

[25] The rule of reasonable doubt applies to the issue of credibility. This is explained by Cory J in the Supreme Court of Canada decision *R v W(D)*, 1991 CanLII 93 (SCC), [1991] 1 SCR 742 (also cited as *DW v Her Majesty the Queen*) where at pp.757-58 he explains:

> Ideally, appropriate instructions on the issue of credibility should be given, not only during the main charge but on any re-charge. A trial judge might well instruct a jury on the charge of credibility along these lines:
>
> > First, if you believe the evidence of the accused, obviously you must acquit.
> >
> > Second, if you do not believe the testimony of the accused, but you are left in reasonable doubt by it, you must acquit.
> >
> > Third, even if you are not left in doubt by the evidence of the accused, you must ask yourself whether, on the basis of the evidence which you do accept, you are convinced beyond a reasonable doubt by that evidence of the guilt of the accused.

[26] In the B.C. Court of Appeal case of *R v H(CW)* (1991), 1991 CanLII 3956 (BC CA), 68 CCC (3d) 146 Wood J.A. suggested an additional instruction be added to Cory J.'s direction:

> I would add one more instruction in such cases, which logically ought to be second in the order, namely: "If, after careful consideration of all the evidence you are unable to decide whom to believe, you must acquit." [p.155]

This added instruction appears to meet the approval of Binnie J in *R v JHS*, supra at para.12.

[27] In *R v Kramer* 2016 ABPC 293 (CanLII), Judge Fradsham, clearly and succinctly describes the focus of a *W(D)* analysis and the application of each part of the *W(D)* approach. At paragraph 273 of the judgment he makes the fundamental point:

> 273 All parts of the DW test are focused on the "beyond a reasonable doubt" standard of proof, and a proper understanding and application of the parts of the test is dependent upon making that focal point part of one's analysis and application.

[28] At paragraphs 270 and 271 he explains the first and second stages of *W(D)* and its application in an evidentiary situation:

> 270 The first part simply says that if the evidence of the accused sets out a version of events which contains a defence to the charge, and, if that version of events is believed (i.e., it is accepted as being the truth), then the accused must be acquitted because the Crown will not have proven the accused's guilt beyond a reasonable doubt.

> 271 The second part of the test takes into account the more difficult situation in which the overall version of events described in the accused's testimony is not believed. Often the situation is not that the trier of fact disbelieves the entirety of the accused's testimony, but rather the trier of fact concludes that he or she is not definitively satisfied that the accused's version is correct (as in the first part of the test), but, similarly, the trier of fact is not definitively satisfied as to what actually occurred. In other words, the trier of fact does not have a settled belief that the accused's version of events is accurate (therefore, we say that the tier of fact does not believe the accused's overall version of the events), but, concurrently, the trier of fact does not have a settled belief that the accused's evidence, when viewed within the totality of the evidence, should be rejected as being completely unreliable (therefore, we say the trier of fact, while not believing the accused's evidence, may find that the accused's evidence still leaves the trier of fact with a reasonable doubt).

[29] Essentially, if the trier of fact isn't sure that the exculpatory testimony of the accused is false, then he or she must still consider it in the second stage of the *W(D)* analysis.

[30] In *R v JHS*, supra Binnie J rationalized the second stage of *W(D)* as follows:

> As to the second question, some jurors may wonder how come, if they believe none of the evidence of the accused, such rejected evidence may nonetheless of itself raise a reasonable doubt. Of course, some elements of the evidence of an accused may raise a reasonable doubt even though the bulk of it is rejected. Equally, the jury may simply conclude that they do not know whether to believe the accused's testimony or not. In either circumstance, the accused is entitled to an acquittal.

[31] If I am reasonably left unsure that the exculpatory statement or exculpatory version offered by the accused as an accurate rendition of what happened, then I have a reasonable doubt about whether the allegation made

by the Crown is true. As Justice Blair stated in *R v D(B)*, 2011 ONCA 51 (CanLII), [2011] OJ No 198 (Ont CA):

> The trial judge must . . . [make] it clear to the jurors that it is not necessary for them to believe the defence evidence on a vital issue; rather it is sufficient if — in the context of all the evidence — the conflicting evidence leaves them in a state of reasonable doubt as to the accused's guilt. If so, they must acquit.

[32] With respect to the third stage, Judge Fradsham, paragraph 272 explains:

> 272 The third part of the test simply says that even if the accused's evidence on all essential points is rejected as being completely unreliable, it still falls to the Crown to prove beyond a reasonable doubt, on evidence which is believed by the Court, that the accused committed the offence with which he or she is charged.

[33] In *R v PSB* (2004), 2004 NSCA 25 (CanLII), 222 NSR (2d) 26, Cromwell JA (as he then was), explained the significance of Cory Js' *W(D)* instruction as follows:

> 56 *W(D)* is concerned with how a trier of fact should apply the burden of proof in a criminal case where the accused testifies. In brief, the trier must remember that the issue is not whether he or she believes the accused, but whether the evidence as a whole convinces the trier of fact of the accused's guilt beyond a reasonable doubt. If the trier of fact believes the exculpatory evidence of the accused, an acquittal must follow. However, even if the trier does not believe that evidence, the trier must ask him or herself if it nonetheless gives rise to a reasonable doubt. Finally, if the trier does not believe the accused and is not left in doubt on the basis of that evidence, the trier must still address and resolve the most critical, in fact the only question in every criminal case. Does the evidence as a whole convince the trier of guilt beyond a reasonable doubt?

[34] In a recent paper by Justice David M. Paciocco, entitled *Doubt about Doubt, Coping with R v W(D) and Credibility Assessment* found at (2017) 22 Can Crim L Rev 31. He summarizes the principles involved in the WD framework as follows:

1. Criminal trials cannot properly be resolved by deciding which conflicting version of events is preferred;

2. A criminal fact finder that believes evidence that is inconsistent with the guilt of the accused cannot convict the accused;

3. Even if a criminal fact finder does not entirely believe evidence inconsistent with guilt, if the fact finder cannot decide whether that evidence is true, there is a reasonable doubt and an acquittal must follow;

4. For even where the fact finder entirely disbelieves evidence inconsistent with guilt, the mere rejection of that evidence does not prove guilt;

5. Even when the fact finder entirely disbelieves evidence inconsistent with guilt, the accused should not be convicted unless the evidence that is given credit proves the accused guilty beyond a reasonable doubt.

[35] In addition, the fact that the trial judge may believe the complainant to be reliable does not mean that the accused must provide some explanation for the complainant's allegation. To require an explanation would be to shift the onus to the accused which is prohibited. This is explained by Hamilton J in *R v Liberatore* (2011), 262 CCC (3d) 559 (NSCA), para. 12, which articulates the principle as follows:

> 12 W.(D.) prohibits rejecting the appellant's evidence solely because it is inconsistent with the Crown's evidence, which he prefers, and making a finding of guilt without further consideration of reasonable doubt in light of the whole of the evidence — thus treating the standard of proof as a simple credibility contest.

[36] In *R v VY* (2010), 79 CR (6th) 321 at para.26, the Ontario Court of Appeal makes the point as well:

> 26 . . . A finding that the complainant was credible did not mean that the onus shifted to the appellant to show that he was not guilty. In other words, the appellant did not have an obligation to put forward a theory that would explain why the complainant would make a false complaint.

[37] Finally, in reviewing the credibility of the complainant, I am guided by the words of Madam Justice Rowles in the case *R v B(RW)* (1993), 24 BCCA 1, wherein at pp.9-10 she states:

> . . . Where, as here, the case for the Crown is wholly dependant upon the testimony of the complainant it is essential that the credibility and reliability of the complainant's evidence be tested in light of all the other evidence presented.

[38] It is with all these principles in mind that I move to consider the evidence before the Court to the ultimate determination of whether or not the Crown has proven its case against the accused beyond a reasonable doubt.

R. v. NYZNIK
2017 ONSC 4392, 350 C.C.C. (3d) 335, 40 C.R. (7th) 241 (Ont. S.C.J.)

Before acquitting three male police officers charged with sexual assault after engaging in sexual acts with a female complainant in an hotel room Justice Molloy said the following:

[14] It is not essential that the trial judge rigidly follow the three steps in the *W.(D.)* instruction. What is critical is for the judge to avoid turning the fact-finding exercise into a choice as to which is the more credible version of the events. This cannot be a credibility contest, with a conviction if the complainant wins the contest and an acquittal if the defendant does. To treat it as such would be to improperly shift the burden of proof. Rather, if the defence evidence, seen in the context of all the evidence, raises a reasonable doubt, then the trial judge cannot convict. Even in a situation where the trial judge completely rejects the defence evidence and has no reasonable doubt as a result of that evidence, he or she must then assess the evidence as a whole and

determine whether the Crown has discharged its burden of proving guilt beyond a reasonable doubt. In some cases, even without any evidence from the defence, it is not possible to be satisfied beyond a reasonable doubt based on the evidence of the complainant.

[15] Typically, the outcome of a sexual assault trial will depend on the reliability and credibility of the evidence given by the complainant. Reliability has to do with the accuracy of a witness' evidence — whether she has a good memory; whether she is able to recount the details of the event; and whether she is an accurate historian. Credibility has to do with whether the witness is telling the truth. A witness who is not telling the truth is by definition not providing reliable evidence. However, the reverse is not the case. Sometimes an honest witness will be trying her best to tell the truth and will fervently believe the truth of what she is relating, but nevertheless be mistaken in her recollection. Such witnesses will appear to be telling the truth and will be convinced they are right, but may still be proven wrong by incontrovertible extrinsic evidence. Although honest, their evidence is not reliable. Only evidence that is both reliable and credible can support a finding of guilt beyond a reasonable doubt.

[16] It is sometimes said that the application of these principles is unfair to complainants in sexual assault cases, that judges are improperly dubious of the testimony of complainants, and that the system is tilted in favour of the accused. In my opinion, those critics fail to understand the purpose of a sexual assault trial, which is to determine whether or not a criminal offence has been committed. It is essential that the rights of the complainant be respected in that process and that decisions not be based on outmoded or stereotypical ideas about how victims of assault will or will not behave. However, the focus of a criminal trial is not the vindication of the complainant. The focus must always be on whether or not the alleged offence has been proven beyond a reasonable doubt. In many cases, the only evidence implicating a person accused of sexual assault will be the testimony of the complainant. There will usually be no other eye-witnesses. There will often be no physical or other corroborative evidence. For that reason, a judge is frequently required to scrutinize the testimony of a complainant to determine whether, based on that evidence alone, the guilt of an accused has been proven beyond a reasonable doubt. That is a heavy burden, and one that is hard to discharge on the word of one person. However, the presumption of innocence, placing the burden of proof on the Crown, and the reasonable doubt standard are necessary protections to avoid wrongful convictions. While this may mean that <u>sometimes</u> a guilty person will be acquitted, that is the unavoidable consequence of ensuring that innocent people are <u>never</u> convicted.

[17] Although the slogan "Believe the victim" has become popularized of late, it has no place in a criminal trial. To approach a trial with the assumption that the complainant is telling the truth is the equivalent of imposing a presumption of guilt on the person accused of sexual assault and then placing a burden on

him to prove his innocence. That is antithetical to the fundamental principles of justice enshrined in our constitution and the values underlying our free and democratic society.

Despite the flexible approach advanced in *S. (J.H.)*, most courts of appeal,[34] and even the Supreme Court in *R. v. Y. (V.)*,[35] still seem to consider *W. (D.)* as the preferred direction in criminal cases.

In *F.H. v. McDougall* (see above) Justice Rothstein makes it crystal clear that in civil cases the complex *W. (D.)* approach is NOT an appropriate tool:

[85] The *W. (D.)* steps were developed as an aid to the determination of reasonable doubt in the criminal law context where a jury is faced with conflicting testimonial accounts. Lack of credibility on the part of an accused is not proof of guilt beyond a reasonable doubt.

[86] However, in civil cases in which there is conflicting testimony, the judge is deciding whether a fact occurred on a balance of probabilities. In such cases, provided the judge has not ignored evidence, finding the evidence of one party credible may well be conclusive of the result because that evidence is inconsistent with that of the other party. In such cases, believing one party will mean explicitly or implicitly that the other party was not believed on the important issue in the case. That may be especially true where a plaintiff makes allegations that are altogether denied by the defendant as in this case. *W. (D.)* is not an appropriate tool for evaluating evidence on the balance of probabilities in civil cases.

Do you find this reasoning persuasive? Why does it not equally apply in criminal cases?

A 4-3 majority of the Supreme Court held in *R. v. Y. (C.L.)*[36] that it was not reversible error that the trial judge had considered and weighed the evidence of the complainant before considering that of the accused. The minority held that this had reversed the onus of proof. Similarly, in *R. v. B. (H.S.)*[37] Chief Justice McLachlin, for the Court, affirmed the trial judge's reasons and noted:

[14] The trial judge had to determine whether the evidence as a whole proved the allegations beyond a reasonable doubt. This issue turned largely on the trial judge's findings with respect to the credibility of the complainant and the accused. It is clear from the trial judge's reasons for judgment that his verdict resulted from his acceptance of the complainant's evidence as to whether the incidents occurred, from his rejection of the accused's defence of lack of opportunity from his finding that the accused was not a credible witness and that the evidence as a whole did not leave him with a reasonable doubt. It is also clear that the trial judge found the frailties in the complainant's evidence to be an

---

[34] See however *R. v. Thiara*, (2010), 79 C.R. (6th) 259 (B.C. C.A.) and *R. v. Gray* (2012), 285 C.C.C. (3d) 539 (Alta. C.A.) favouring less complex directions. The Quebec Court of Appeal in *R. v. R. (J.)*, 2014 QCCA 869, 11 C.R. (7th) 409 (C.A. Que.) went out of its way to discourage the use of the *W. (D.)* formula.

[35] [2011] 2 S.C.R. 173, 84 C.R. (6th) 65, 269 C.C.C. (3d) 295 (S.C.C.). See too *R. v. Lepine*, 2014 CSC 65, 2014 SCC 65, [2014] 3 S.C.R. 285, 316 C.C.C. (3d) 313 (S.C.C.).

[36] [2008] 1 S.C.R. 5, 227 C.C.C. (3d) 129, 53 C.R. (6th) 207 (S.C.C.).

[37] [2008] 3 S.C.R. 32, 235 C.C.C. (3d) 312, 60 C.R. (6th) 21 (S.C.C.).

understandable result of trying to remember events that happened in childhood and were, in any case, related to peripheral, not core, issues.

PROBLEM

The accused was charged with murder. In his charge to the jury, the trial judge defined reasonable doubt in the following passages:

> In a criminal case, as I told you before, the accused is presumed to be innocent until the evidence put forth has proven his guilt to you beyond a reasonable doubt. It is not the responsibility of the accused to establish or demonstrate or prove his innocence, if the Crown fails to prove guilt beyond a reasonable doubt, you must acquit the accused. You must, therefore, be satisfied as to his guilt before you can convict and the standard that you use is proof beyond a reasonable doubt, so you have to be satisfied as to guilt and the standard that you use is proof beyond a reasonable doubt. Simply put, a reasonable doubt is just that, Supreme Court of Canada has made a pronouncement in recent—in the last number of months which says we should describe it as a reasonable doubt that is not an imaginary or frivolous doubt, nor is it one based on sympathy or prejudice. A reasonable doubt is a doubt based on reason and common sense which must logically be derived from the evidence or the absence of evidence.
>
> Now the accused gave evidence and he is to be judged as other witnesses in the same way. If you believe him that he did not kill the deceased, then you are to acquit him. If on considering all of the evidence, you are left in a state of reasonable doubt and you are not satisfied as to his guilt, it is your duty to acquit the accused. If, however, upon consideration of all of the evidence and the submissions of counsel, you are satisfied that the accused has been proven guilty beyond a reasonable doubt, it is your duty to convict the accused. I turn to the indictment again and as I've been telling you previously, the obligation and burden upon the Crown is to prove each and every element of the charge as stated in the indictment.

Is this charge in substantial compliance with *Starr* and *W. (D.)*?

New trials are sometimes ordered in sexual assault cases where it is determined that, in convicting, the trial judge placed too much emphasis on the demeanour of the accused or complainant,[38] intervened too much in defence cross-examination[39] or applied a different standard of scrutiny to the accused's evidence in assessing credibility.[40] In respect of the latter Laskin J.A. stated the following in *R. v. Aird*:[41]

> The "different standards of scrutiny" argument is a difficult argument to succeed on in an appellate court. It is difficult for two related reasons: credibility findings are the province of the trial judge and attract a very high degree of deference on

---

[38] See *R. v. Hemsworth*, 2016 ONCA 85, 334 C.C.C. (3d) 534, 26 C.R. (7th) 79 (Ont. C.A.); *R. v. Rhayel*, 2015 ONCA 377, 324 C.C.C. (3d) 362, 22 C.R. (7th) 78 (Ont. C.A.). The issue of using demeanour to assess credibility is fully considered in Chapter 5.

[39] *R. v. Churchill*, 2016 NLCA 29, 338 C.C.C. (3d) 145 (N.L. C.A.); *R. v. Bennett*, 2016 BCCA 406, 342 C.C.C. (3d) 150, 33 C.R. (7th) 216 (B.C. C.A.).

[40] *R. v. G. (B.G.)*, 2015 MBCA 76, 24 C.R. (7th) 44 (Man. C.A.); *Rhayel, supra* note 38.

[41] 2013 ONCA 447, 307 O.A.C. 183 (Ont. C.A.) at para. 39.

appeal; and appellate courts invariably view this argument with skepticism, seeing it as a veiled invitation to reassess the trial judge's credibility determinations. Thus, as Doherty J.A. said in *R. v. J.H.* (2005), 2005 CanLII 253 (ON CA), 192 C.C.C. (3d) 480 (Ont. C.A.), at para. 59: "[t]o succeed in this kind of argument, the appellant must point to something in the reasons of the trial judge or perhaps elsewhere in the record that make it clear that the trial judge had applied different standards in assessing the evidence of the appellant and the complainant."

(iv) *Considering Individual Pieces of Evidence*

Some types of evidence raise concerns either because of issues surrounding reliability (e.g., jailhouse informers) or because the evidence is especially incriminating (e.g., after-the-fact conduct). **Should the reasonable doubt standard apply to individual pieces of evidence?**

R. v. MORIN
[1988] 2 S.C.R. 345, 66 C.R. (3d) 1, 44 C.C.C. (3d) 193

The accused was acquitted on a charge of first degree murder. His position at trial was that he was not the killer, but in the alternative, if he was the killer he was not guilty by reason of insanity. On appeal it was found that the trial judge had misdirected the jury. The trial judge invited the jury to apply the criminal standard of proof beyond a reasonable doubt to individual pieces of evidence. The Court of Appeal allowed the Crown's appeal and directed a new trial. The accused appealed. The Supreme Court confirmed the order of a new trial.

SOPINKA J. (DICKSON C.J.C. and MCINTYRE and LA FOREST JJ. concurring):—

. . .

The appellant submits that the charge, when read as a whole, did not invite the jury to subject individual pieces of evidence to the criminal standard, but rather the effect of the charge was that during the "fact-finding" stage items of evidence were to be examined in relation to other evidence. The residuum resulting from this process constitutes the "whole of the evidence", from which the jury determines whether guilt has been proved beyond a reasonable doubt.

This argument raises two questions:

(i) Is the appellant's interpretation of the charge correct?

(ii) Assuming that it is, is it misdirection to instruct the jury to apply the criminal standard at two stages as submitted?

. . .

The following are the relevant excerpts from the charge to the jury set out in the order in which they occurred:

1. *Concerning Evidence*

You are not obliged to accept any part of the evidence of a witness just because there is no denial of it. If you have a reasonable doubt about any of the evidence, you will give the benefit of that doubt to the accused with respect to such evidence. *Having decided what evidence you consider worthy of belief, you will consider it as a whole, of course, in arriving at your verdict.* [emphasis added]

2. *Concerning Burden of Proof*

The accused is entitled to the benefit of reasonable doubt on the whole of the case and on each and every issue in the case.

Proof beyond a reasonable doubt does not apply to the individual items of evidence or the separate pieces of evidence in the case, but to the total body of evidence upon which the Crown relies to prove guilt. Before you can convict you must be satisfied beyond a reasonable doubt of his guilt.

3. *Concerning Hairs and Fibres*

It seems to me that this evidence does not go beyond proving that Christine could have been in the Honda motor vehicle and that the accused could have been at the scene of the killing, and of course that is not proof beyond a reasonable doubt.

4. *Concerning Appellant's Statements to Hobbs*

I was going to go on to say that, if you find that the evidence of the accused at trial here represents the correct interpretation of those tapes and transcripts, or parts of the tapes and transcripts, or if you have a reasonable doubt that that might be so, you will give him the benefit of the doubt as to those parts of the tapes or transcripts and adopt his interpretation.

5. *Concerning Appellant's Statement to Inmate May*

Now, as to that evidence, in relation to that part of the tape that I have just read, if you find the evidence of the accused at trial represents the correct interpretation of that exchange, or if you have a reasonable doubt that that may be so, you will give the benefit of the doubt to the accused and adopt his interpretation.

In my opinion, based on my reading of the charge as a whole, a jury would likely have concluded that in examining the evidence they were to give the accused the benefit of the doubt in respect of *any* evidence. This process of examination and elimination would occur during the so-called "fact-finding" stage, to use the appellant's phrase. The evidence as a whole to which the jury was to apply itself in order to determine guilt or innocence was the residuum after the "fact-finding" stage. There is no other way of reading the first excerpt from the charge.

. . .

The argument in favour of a two-stage application of the criminal standard has superficial appeal in theory but in my respectful opinion is wrong in principle and unworkable in practice. In principle it is wrong because the function of a standard of proof is not the weighing of individual items of evidence but the determination of ultimate issues. Furthermore, it would require the individual member of the jury to rely on the same facts in order to establish guilt. The law is clear that the members of the jury can arrive at a verdict by different routes and need not rely on the same facts. Indeed, the jurors need not agree on any single fact except the ultimate conclusion: see Wigmore on Evidence, Chadbourn revision, vol. 9 (1981), para. 2497, at pp. 412-14; *R. v. Lynch* (1978), 40 C.C.C. (2d) 7 at 19 (Ont. C.A.); *R. v. Bouvier*, supra, Ont. C.A. at pp. 264-65; *R. v. Moreau* (1986), 51 C.R. (3d) 209, 26 C.C.C. (3d) 359 at 389 (Ont. C.A.); *R. v. Agbim*, [1979] Crim. L. Rev. 171 (C.A.); *R. v. Thatcher*, supra, Sask. C.A. at p. 510, S.C.C. at p. 697.

The matter is summed up in Cross at p. 146:

> It has been held by the Court of Appeal that it is unnecessary for a judge to direct the jury that it must be unanimous with regard to even one item of evidence bearing upon a particular count before convicting on it. It seems to be enough that all members of the jury find the accused guilty upon the basis of some of the facts bearing upon that count.

In practice it is not practical, because the jury would have to agree on not only the same facts but what individual facts prove. Individual facts do not necessarily establish guilt, but are a link in the chain of ultimate proof. It is not possible, therefore, to require the jury to find facts proved beyond a reasonable doubt without identifying *what it is* that they prove beyond a reasonable doubt. Since the same fact may give rise to different inferences tending to establish guilt or innocence, the jury might discard such facts on the basis that there is doubt as to what they prove.

The concern which proponents of the two-stage process express is that facts which are doubtful will be used to establish guilt. The answer to this concern is that a chain is only as strong as its weakest link. If facts which are essential to a finding of guilt are still doubtful notwithstanding the support of other facts, this will produce a doubt in the mind of the jury that guilt has been proved beyond a reasonable doubt.

I conclude from the foregoing that the facts are for the jury to determine, subject to an instruction by the trial judge as to the law. While the charge may and often does include many helpful tips on the weighing of evidence, such as observing demeanour, taking into the account the interest of the witness and so forth, the law lays down only one basic requirement: during the process of deliberation the jury or other trier of fact must consider the evidence as a whole and determine whether guilt is established by the prosecution beyond a reasonable doubt. This of necessity requires that each element of the offence or issue be proved beyond a reasonable doubt. Beyond this injunction it is for the trier of fact to determine how to proceed. To intrude in this area is, as pointed out by North P., an intrusion into the province of the jury.

The reason we have juries is so that lay persons and not lawyers decide the facts. To inject into the process artificial legal rules with respect to the natural human activity of deliberation and decision would tend to detract from the value of the jury system. Accordingly, it is wrong for a trial judge to lay down additional rules for the weighing of the evidence. Indeed, it is unwise to attempt to elaborate on the basic requirement referred to above. I would make two exceptions. The jury should be told that the facts are not to be examined separately and in isolation with reference to the criminal standard. This instruction is a necessary corollary to the basic rule referred to above. Without it there is some danger that a jury might conclude that the requirement that each issue or element of the offence be proved beyond a reasonable doubt demands that individual items of evidence be so proved.

The second exception is that it is appropriate, where issues of credibility arise between the evidence for the prosecution and the defence, that the jury be charged as suggested by Morden J.A. in *Challice*, supra. There is a danger in such a situation that a jury might conclude that it is simply a matter as to which side they believe. The suggested charge alerts them to the fact that, if the defence evidence leaves them in a state of doubt after considering it in the context of the whole of the evidence, then they are to acquit.

Consequently, even if the appellant is correct in his interpretation of the charge to the jury, there was misdirection — although not as serious as the misdirection which I have found occurred.

Morin was convicted on the new trial but later exonerated by DNA evidence.[42]

(v) *Direct and Circumstantial Evidence*

In its discharge of the persuasive burden, the Crown can tender direct or circumstantial evidence.

In cases of circumstantial evidence, certain facts connected with the material fact are proved and the trier is asked to infer from those facts that the material fact exists. If reason and experience support the connection the evidence led is relevant. John Robinette described it:

> All that circumstantial evidence is, is that you are seeking to prove circumstances, subordinate circumstances, subordinate facts, from which a trial tribunal may draw the inference that a principal issue of fact vital to your case has been established. Therefore, as a matter of logic, if an inference may be drawn from a subordinate fact that the principal fact occurred then evidence is admissible to prove the subordinate fact and that is what is loosely called circumstantial evidence.[43]

R. v. MUNOZ
(2006), 38 C.R. (6th) 376, 205 C.C.C. (3d) 70 (Ont. S.C.J.)

The accused, M and F, were committed to stand trial on charges including conspiring to kill F's wife. All three men had been housed in the same unit at Maplehurst Detention Centre where the Crown alleged that the conspiracy was hatched. There was no direct evidence implicating the

---

[42]   See *R. v. Morin* (1995), 37 C.R. (4th) 395 (Ont. C.A.).
[43]   *Circumstantial Evidence*, [1955] L.S.U.C. Spec. Lect. 307. For the same author speaking in parables on the subject, see *Charge to the Jury in a Criminal Case*, [1959] L.S.U.C. Spec. Lect. 147 and 153.

accused. The Crown's sole witness at the preliminary inquiry testified that he and the accused discussed depositing $1,000 with the accused's lawyer. They did not discuss the conspiracy. M brought an application for *certiorari* to quash the decision. The application was granted.

DUCHARME J.: —

B. The Drawing of Inferences

While the jurisprudence is replete with references to the drawing of "reasonable inferences," there is comparatively little discussion about the process involved in drawing inferences from accepted facts. It must be emphasized that this does not involve deductive reasoning which, assuming the premises are accepted, necessarily results in a valid conclusion. This is because the conclusion is inherent in the relationship between the premises. Rather the process of inference drawing involves inductive reasoning which derives conclusions based on the uniformity of prior human experience. The conclusion is not inherent in the offered evidence, or premises, but flows from an interpretation of that evidence derived from experience. Consequently, an inductive conclusion necessarily lacks the same degree of inescapable validity as a deductive conclusion. Therefore, if the premises, or the primary facts, are accepted, the inductive conclusion follows with some degree of probability, but not of necessity. Also, unlike deductive reasoning, inductive reasoning is ampliative as it gives more information than what was contained in the premises themselves.

A good starting point for any discussion of inference drawing is the definition offered by Justice Watt:

> An *inference* is a deduction of fact which may logically and reasonably be drawn from another fact or group of facts found or otherwise established in the proceedings. It is a conclusion that *may*, not must be drawn in the circumstances.[44]

Equally important is Justice Watt's admonition that, "The boundary which separates permissible inference from impermissible speculation in relation to circumstantial evidence is often a very difficult one to locate."[45] The process of inference drawing was described by Doherty J.A. in *R. v. Morrissey* (1995), 97 C.C.C. (3d) 193 (Ont. C.A.) at p. 209, as follows:

> *A trier of fact may draw factual inferences from the evidence. The inferences must, however, be ones which can be reasonably and logically drawn from a fact or group of facts established by the evidence.* An inference which does not flow logically and reasonably from established facts cannot be made and is condemned as conjecture and speculation. As Chipman J.A. put it in *R. v. White* (1994), 89 C.C.C. (3d) 336 at p.351, 28 C.R. (4th) 160, 3 M.V.R. (3d) 283 (N.S.C.A.):

---

[44]   D. Watt, *Watt's Manual of Criminal Evidence* (Toronto: Carswell, 2005) at 108. (Italicized portions in original.) In this passage the phrase "deduction of fact" is not meant to suggest that the process involved is deductive reasoning. Rather, the word is simply used in the sense of a "factual conclusion".

[45]   *Ibid.*

These cases establish that there is a distinction between conjecture and speculation on the one hand and rational conclusions from the whole of the evidence on the other. [Emphasis added]

The highlighted sentence suggests that there are two ways in which inference drawing can become impermissible speculation and I will discuss each in turn.

The first step in inference drawing is that the primary facts, i.e. the facts that are said to provide the basis for the inference, must be established by the evidence. If the primary facts are not established, then any inferences purportedly drawn from them will be the product of impermissible speculation. The decision of Lord Wright in *Caswell v. Powell Duffryn Associated Collieries Ltd.*, [1940] A.C. 152 (H.L.) at 169-70, is often cited as authority for this long-standing principle:

> The Court therefore is left to inference or circumstantial evidence. Inference must be carefully distinguished from conjecture or speculation. *There can be no inference unless there are objective facts from which to infer the other facts which it is sought to establish.* In some cases the other facts can be inferred with as much practical certainty as if they had been actually observed. In other cases the inference does not go beyond reasonable probability. *But if there are no positive proved facts from which the inference can be made, the method of inference fails and what is left is mere speculation or conjecture.* [Emphasis added]

While the foregoing point may seem obvious, it can arise in subtle ways. Thus, in *R. v. Portillo* (2003), 176 C.C.C. (3d) 467 (Ont. C.A.), the Crown lead footwear evidence consisting of two primary facts: two partial shoeprints found at the scene were similar to impressions from two shoes found by the police in the course of their investigation, and the shoes were found in the vicinity of the appellant's apartment. The Crown did so in order to support the inference that the appellant had been at the scene of the homicide in close proximity to the body. That conclusion could be drawn only if it could reasonably be inferred that: (a) the shoes found by the police made the prints at the scene; and (b) that the shoes belonged to the appellant. The expert evidence called by the Crown, standing alone, could not support the first inference, and the fact that the shoes were found in the vicinity of the appellant's apartment, standing alone, could not support the second inference. While describing the Crown's argument as "seductive," after a careful analysis of the necessary underlying inferences, Doherty J.A. rejected the Crown's reasoning as circular, saying at 476-7:

> The "footwear" evidence could assist in proving either of the factual inferences needed to give the evidence relevance, only if the Crown could first prove the other factual inference for which the "footwear" evidence was offered.

> As indicated above, the evidence connecting Wilfredo Portillo to the homicide scene could not assist the jury in determining whether the shoes made the prints found at the scene unless other evidence established that the shoes belonged to Wilfredo Portillo. The only other evidence connecting Wilfredo Portillo to the shoes was the evidence that they were found in the vicinity of Wilfredo Portillo's apartment. *That fact alone could not reasonably support the inference that the shoes belonged to Wilfredo Portillo as opposed to the many other people who had equal access to that area.* Similarly, the evidence of the prints found at the scene could

only assist in identifying Wilfredo Portillo as the owner of the shoes if there was other evidence from which it could be inferred that the prints were made by those shoes. The only other evidence, was the expert's evidence that the treads on the shoes were similar to the partial prints found at the scene. *That evidence, standing alone, could not reasonably support the inference that those shoes made those prints.* This is particularly so given the expert's frank concession that he could not say how many shoes had the same tread pattern. His evidence amounted to no more than an assertion that the shoes found near Wilfredo Portillo's apartment were among an undetermined number of shoes that could have made the prints at the scene of the homicide.

The "footwear" evidence could not, *absent assumption of facts not proved, or speculation*, support either the inference that the shoes made the prints found at the scene or that the shoes belonged to Wilfredo Portillo. [Emphasis added]

Therefore Justice Doherty concluded that the evidence was not relevant and should have been excluded.

The second way in which inference drawing can become impermissible speculation occurs where the proposed inference cannot be reasonably and logically drawn from the established primary facts. This possibility stems precisely from the fact that an inductive conclusion is not necessarily valid. As McLachlin C.J.C. put it in *Arcuri* at 31-2:

[W]ith circumstantial evidence, there is, by definition, *an inferential gap between the evidence and the matter to be established*—that is, an inferential gap beyond the question of whether the evidence should be believed... The judge must therefore weigh the evidence, in the sense of assessing *whether it is reasonably capable of supporting the inferences that the Crown asks the jury to draw*. [Emphasis added]

Consequently, one can overreach and draw an inference that should not properly be drawn from the primary facts.

The courts have repeatedly cautioned against confusing a reasonable inference with mere speculation. Where an inferential gap exists, it can only be properly overcome by evidence. This point was powerfully made by Doherty J.A. in *United States of America v. Huynh* (2005), 200 C.C.C. (3d) 305 (Ont. C.A.). This case involved an appeal of the committal for extradition of an individual on charges of conspiracy and money laundering relating to the designated offence of trafficking in a controlled substance. The material relied on in support of the extradition justified the inference that the appellant had conspired with others to covertly transfer very large amounts of cash from the United States to Canada. He did so by concealing the money in a secret compartment fashioned in the gas tank of his vehicle. While there was no direct evidence as to the source of the cash, the Crown argued that it could be reasonably inferred that the cash was the proceeds of trafficking in a controlled substance based on: (a) the amount of cash involved; (b) the frequency with which cash was being transferred from the United States to Canada; (c) the manner of concealment of the cash suggesting a level of sophistication and a commercial operation; (d) the coded conversations of participants and their obvious concerns about surveillance; and (e) the anticipated evidence of a DEA officer that the modus operandi was consistent with the activities of drug dealers. In rejecting the Crown's contention, Doherty J.A. reasoned as follows:

The material identified by the respondent certainly permits the inference that the cash was the proceeds of some illicit activity. Drug trafficking comes readily to mind as one possible source. *The process of drawing inferences from evidence is not, however, the same as speculating even where the circumstances permit an educated guess. The gap between the inference that the cash was the proceeds of illicit activity and the further inference that the illicit activity was trafficking in a controlled substance can only be bridged by evidence.* The trier of fact will assess that evidence in the light of common sense and human experience, but neither are a substitute for evidence. The requesting state has not offered any evidence as to the source of the funds even though its material indicates that one of the parties to this conspiracy is cooperating with the police. ... *I do not think there is anything in the material that would reasonably permit a trier of fact to infer that the cash was the proceeds of drug trafficking and not some other illicit activity.*[46] [Emphasis added]

It is difficult, if not impossible, to define with any precision a bright line distinction between the drawing of reasonable inferences and mere speculation. However, in this regard I would adopt the language of Aldisert J. in *Tose v. First Pennsylvania Bank, N.A.*, 648 F.2d 879, 895 (3rd Cir.), cert. denied, 454 U.S. 893 (1981) at 895:

The line between a reasonable inference that may permissibly be drawn by a jury from basic facts in evidence and an impermissible speculation is not drawn by judicial idiosyncracies. The line is drawn by the laws of logic. If [page84] there is an experience of logical probability that an ultimate fact will follow a stated narrative or historical fact, then the jury is given the opportunity to draw a conclusion because there is a reasonable probability that the conclusion flows from the proven facts. As the Supreme Court has stated, "the essential requirement is that mere speculation be not allowed to do duty for probative facts after making due allowance for all reasonably possible inferences favoring the party whose case is attacked." *Galloway v. United States*, 319 U.S. 372, 395, 63 S. Ct. 1077, 1089, 87 L. Ed. 1458 (1943).[47]

However, it must be emphasized that this requirement of "logical probability" or "reasonable probability" does not mean that the only "reasonable" inferences that can be drawn are the most obvious or the most easily drawn.[48] This was explicitly rejected in *R. v. Katwaru, supra*, note 6 per Moldaver J.A. at 444:

[I]n the course of his instructions on the law relating to circumstantial evidence, the trial judge told the jury on numerous occasions that they could infer a fact from established facts but only if the inference flowed "easily and logically from [the] other established facts".

---

[46] In *Rodaro et. al. v. Royal Bank of Canada et. al.* (2002), 59 O.R. (3d) 74 (C.A.) at 94, Doherty J.A. applied the same distinction between legitimate inference drawing and speculation in a civil context.

[47] Although *Tose v. First Pennsylvania Bank, N.A.*, 648 F.2d 879, 895 (3rd Cir.), cert. denied, 454 U.S. 893 (1981) and *Galloway v. United States*, 319 U.S. 372 (1943) dealt with directed verdicts, this language is equally applicable to the assessment of the availability of inferences based on the evidence at a preliminary inquiry.

[48] This is especially true at a preliminary inquiry where the judge need only determine whether there is sufficient evidence to permit the trier of fact to draw the inferences necessary to convict.

The appellant submits, correctly in my view, that the trial judge erred by inserting the word "easily" into the equation. *In order to infer a fact from established facts, all that is required is that the inference be reasonable and logical. The fact that an inference may flow less than easily does not mean that it cannot be drawn. To hold otherwise would lead to the untenable conclusion that a difficult inference could never be reasonable and logical.* [Emphasis added]

Rather, the requirement of reasonable or logical probability is meant to underscore that the drawing of inferences is not a process of subjective imagination, but rather is one of rational explication. Supposition or conjecture is no substitute for evidence and cannot be relied upon as the basis for a reasonably drawn inference. Therefore, it is not enough simply to create a hypothetical narrative that, however speculative, could possibly link the primary fact or facts to the inference or inferences sought to be drawn. As Fairgrieve J. noted in *R. v. Ruiz*, [2000] O.J. No. 2713 (QL), 47 W.C.B. (2d) 66 (Ont. C.J.), at para. 3, "Simply because a possibility cannot be excluded does not necessarily mean that a reasonable trier could be justified in reaching such a conclusion on the evidence." The inference must be one that can be reasonably and logically drawn and, even where difficult; it cannot depend on speculation or conjecture, rather than evidence, to bridge any inferential gaps.

As Justice Ducharme highlights, the law of evidence is dominated by inductive reasoning. It is the process by which we draw a logical connection between proposed evidence and a material fact (i.e., the relevancy determination), when we decide what inferences to draw from circumstantial evidence and ultimately in deciding whether we find evidence credible.

One of the problems with inductive reasoning is that it is highly subjective and often grounded in erroneous assumptions about human behaviour.[49] This has been a particularly pronounced issue in homicide cases where the Crown has introduced how a suspect acts after the killing, such as not attending the funeral, not crying, or not assisting in the search for the body, as evidence of guilt.[50] The Supreme Court acknowledged the problem in the following case although they could not agree on the reasonableness of the inference urged by the Crown.

---

[49] See David M. Tanovich, "Regulating Inductive Reasoning in Sexual Assault Cases" in Ben Berger, Emma Cunliffe & James Stribopoulos, eds., *To Ensure that Justice is Done: Essays in Memory of Mark Rosenberg* (Toronto: Carswell, 2017).

[50] David Paciocco, "Simply Complex: Applying the Law of 'Post-Offence Conduct' Evidence" (2016) 63 Crim. L.Q. 275.

R. v. WHITE
2011 SCC 13, [2011] 1 S.C.R. 433, 82 C.R. (6th) 11,
267 C.C.C. (3d) 453 (S.C.C.)

ROTHSTEIN J. (LEBEL, ABELLA and CROMWELL JJ. concurring):—

I. Introduction

[1] In the early hours of December 3, 2005, Lee Matasi was killed by a gunshot to the heart. According to multiple eyewitnesses, he was shot by the appellant, Dennis Robert White. The two had been engaged in a physical altercation that began after Mr. Matasi made a disparaging remark to Mr. White, who was in possession of a loaded handgun. In the course of their struggle, the gun was fired into Mr. Matasi's chest, killing him instantly. Mr. White immediately fled the scene, but was later apprehended by the police.

[2] Mr. White was charged with second degree murder. Throughout the Crown's case, the identity of the shooter was a live issue. However, by trial's end, counsel for the defence had effectively (though not formally) conceded that Mr. White had shot Mr. Matasi unlawfully and was therefore guilty of manslaughter. Thus, the only live issue before the jury was whether Mr. White had the requisite intent for second degree murder. The jury found that he did and convicted him on that charge.

· · ·

[4] Mr. White's complaint centres on a piece of circumstantial evidence used by the Crown in its prosecution. At trial, counsel for the defence had developed a theory of the case according to which Mr. White had shot the victim accidentally as the two angrily grappled with one another. As a small part of its response to this theory, the Crown pointed out in its closing argument:

> Note as well that the accused ran immediately after the shooting. There is no hesitation here, no shock, no uncertainty on his part, just immediate flight. One would expect hesitancy if the shot was anything other than the intended action of Dennis White. [A.R., at p. 563]

[5] Counsel for the defence did not object to — or attempt to rebut — this line of argument, nor did he object to the way in which the trial judge presented the issue to the jury. Nevertheless, Mr. White appealed his conviction on the grounds that the trial judge erred in his instruction to the jury in relation to the relevance of the Crown's submission on this point.

[6] Relying on this Court's rulings in *R. v. Arcangioli*, 1994 CanLII 107 (SCC), [1994] 1 S.C.R. 129, and *R. v. White*, 1998 CanLII 789 (SCC), [1998] 2 S.C.R. 72 ("*White (1998)*"), Mr. White argued on appeal that the trial judge should have specifically instructed the jury that the evidence concerning the circumstances of his flight had no probative value in relation to the question before the jury. In his view, the evidence relied upon by the Crown was consistent with both manslaughter and second degree murder, and was therefore irrelevant to the only live issue in the case. Given the prejudicial

nature of such evidence, the trial judge's failure to provide a "no probative value" instruction was an error of law that irredeemably tainted the jury's verdict and warranted the ordering of a new trial.

. . .

[8] For the reasons set out below, I would dismiss the appeal. This case is distinguishable from *Arcangioli* on the facts, and in my view the jury charge was adequate. In any case, even assuming that the trial judge erred in his instructions to the jury, I believe the error to be harmless and would uphold the verdict under s. 686(1)(b)(iii) of the *Criminal Code*, R.S.C. 1985, c. C-46.

. . .

IV. Analysis

. . .

[28] The issue in this case is whether the trial judge ought to have given the jury a limiting instruction The purpose of a limiting instruction is to preclude the jury from considering certain evidence, either with respect to all the live issues in a case or with respect to one or more particular live issues.

[29] Similarly, finding an item of evidence inadmissible serves to preclude the jury from considering that evidence at all, with respect to the entire case. Issues of admissibility will arise over the course of the trial as evidence is tendered and evidence that is found to be inadmissible is not allowed on the record. Conversely, a limiting instruction is provided in directions to the jury. For an item of evidence to be subject to a limiting instruction, it must have been admitted in the first place. Still, it may be that an item of evidence that was admissible at trial must be removed from the jury's deliberations on some or all of the issues in the case. A limiting instruction will be necessary when, at the end of all the evidence and for the purposes of the charge to the jury, certain evidence that appeared unobjectionable when it was admitted should in fact be removed from the jury with respect to one or more of the issues in the case.

[30] The goal of excluding evidence as inadmissible or providing a limiting instruction is essentially the same: to prevent the jury from considering the evidence, either with respect to the entire case (for admissibility) or with respect to one or more issues (for a limiting instruction). Moreover, the same rules of evidence govern admissibility and the need for limiting instructions.

. . .

[33] Before I proceed, it is critical to bear in mind that removing evidence from the jury's consideration is not the only way of dealing with evidence associated with a heightened risk of jury error. It is also possible, and often appropriate, for the trial judge to warn the jury of the risks associated with certain types of evidence. The purpose of such a caution is to alert the jury to the danger, which has been recognized through judicial experience, but then to allow the properly informed jurors to evaluate the evidence with care.

[34] The terms "limiting instruction" and "caution" (or "warning") are not narrowly defined terms of art which courts have consistently treated as distinct. Nevertheless, there is a distinction between the following two types of jury instruction: one that tells the jury they must not consider the evidence for one or several purposes, and the other that leaves evidence for the jury to consider, but warns them to be careful with it. For ease of reference, I will refer to the first type of instruction as a limiting instruction and to the second type as a warning or caution.

. . .

[65] The Crown sought to convince the jury that Mr. White's conduct in the immediate aftermath of the gunshot was not reconcilable with the theory that the gun was fired accidentally. In Mr. White's view, this submission "breached the well-established rule that post-offence conduct, such as flight, is not admissible to determine an accused's level of culpability" (A.F., at para. 58). Relying on *Arcangioli*, and its successor cases, he argues that the Crown invited the jury to draw an impermissible inference of "consciousness of guilt" of second degree murder from his "immediate flight".

[66] However, this case is distinguished from *Arcangioli* on the facts. The conduct alluded to by the Crown is not the *flight itself*, but rather Mr. White's failure to hesitate after his gun was fired into Mr. Matasi's chest before he fled the scene. This is different from the question at issue in *Arcangioli*, which concerned the simple act of fleeing from the scene. In that case — as, indeed, in this one — the mere fact that the accused fled the scene did not provide any information as to whether he was guilty of the lesser or the greater charge. However, in this case, the fact that Mr. White failed to hesitate at the discharge of his firearm into another person's chest *does* potentially provide such information.

[67] As a matter of logic and human experience, one would expect an ordinary person to present some physical manifestation, such as hesitation, at a gun in their hand accidentally discharging into someone's chest, thereby killing them. It was open to the jury to infer that a failure to react in this way was incongruous with the theory, advanced by the defence, that the gun went off by accident as the two men struggled with each other. To use the language of *Arcangioli* and *White (1998)*, lack of hesitation was not "equally consistent with" or "equally explained by" accidentally as opposed to intentionally shooting the victim. It is less consistent with accident. Thus, the evidence that Mr. White did not hesitate when the gun was fired in response to this unexpected and calamitous turn of events supports an inference that he deliberately pulled the trigger.

[68] Again, this case is not simply a replay of *Arcangioli*. In my view, there is a meaningful difference between the following two questions:

> Would the accused have been *equally* likely to flee the scene whether he was guilty of murder or of manslaughter? (in *Arcangioli*)

Would the accused have been *equally* likely to hesitate before fleeing had he shot the victim intentionally or accidentally? (in this case)

[69] The two questions raise distinct sets of considerations. On the one hand, logic and human experience suggest that there is no reason to think that a person who has committed manslaughter would be more likely to stay at the scene of the crime than one who has committed murder. In both cases the person has committed a very serious offence by unlawfully killing someone and will be just as likely to flee. In both cases, the person may flee for a host of reasons, such as to avoid arrest, to minimize evidence of that person's connection with the crime, or to buy additional time. Indeed, flight is a response equally consistent with a wide range of much less serious offences, such as theft, vandalism, or common assault (as discussed in *Arcangioli*).

[70] On the other hand, logic and human experience suggest that people are more likely to show some outward sign, such as hesitation, before continuing on with their actions, when they do something accidentally than when they do it on purpose. This is all the more so when the accident involves a sharp physical effect on the person (the discharge of a gun in one's hand) and results in a terrible consequence, such as having killed another person. As I have discussed, lack of hesitation prior to flight, is less consistent with shooting and killing someone accidentally than it is with doing so intentionally. Thus, in the context of determining relevance, evidence of flight *per se* is different from evidence of lack of hesitation prior to flight.

. . .

[74] . . . A jury could legitimately infer that Mr. White's lack of hesitation after the gun was fired belied his claim that the shooting was accidental. Evidence of such a failure is thus relevant to the question of whether he had the requisite intent for second degree murder.

[75] This evidence was not tainted by the hallmark flaws associated with "demeanour evidence" so as to be irrelevant. Such hallmark flaws are generally associated with evidence in the form of a witness's impression of the accused's mental or emotional state (e.g. appeared calm or nervous), as inferred by the witness from the accused's outward appearance or behaviour. The accused's mental or emotional state is then submitted as suspect and probative of guilt (see *Nelles*; *R. v. Levert* (2001), 150 O.A.C. 208 at paras. 24-27; *R. v. Trotta* (2004), 191 O.A.C. 322 at paras. 40-43 (an appeal was allowed by this Court and a new trial was ordered, but solely on the basis of fresh evidence, 2007 SCC 49, [2007] 3 S.C.R. 453)).

[76] A problem with such evidence is that the inferential link between the witness's perception of the accused's behaviour and the accused's mental state can be tenuous (*Trotta*, at para. 40). The witness's assessment depends on a subjective impression and interpretation of the accused's behaviour (*Levert*, at para. 27). Moreover, it appears to involve an element of mind reading (*R. v. Anderson*, 2009 ABCA 67, 3 Alta. L.R. (5th) 29 at para. 51). Additionally, insofar as the witness is inferring the accused's state of mind from the accused's outward appearance, there may be a legitimate concern that this is inadmissible

lay opinion evidence. This is to be contrasted with evidence of objective conduct that allows the jury to draw its own inferences about the accused's state of mind.

[77] Lack of hesitation prior to flight is an objective fact, from which the finder of fact (and not the witness) is asked to draw an inference of no shock or surprise. This was not a case where the accused's outward behaviour was adduced to prove that an awareness of guilt was boiling under the surface. The evidence here is not analogous to a doctor's testimony that a nurse had "a very strange expression" and displayed no signs of grief when she was "writing up the final death note as part of her other difficult duties on the occasion of the death of a baby in her care" (*Nelles*, at p. 125, cited in Binnie J.'s reasons, at para. 142); nor is it analogous to testimony that the accused seemed "unusually quiet" in the area of a crime scene and turned his head away (*Anderson*, at para. 50, cited in Binnie J.'s reasons, at para. 143). Instead, the evidence was in the nature of the absence of an immediate reflex.

. . .

[86] In my view, Mr. White's lack of hesitation prior to fleeing the scene was relevant to the issue of his level of culpability. Accordingly, I consider that this evidence was properly left with the jury.

[87] Nevertheless, the evidence was not without its risks. There could have been explanations for Mr. White's failure to hesitate or evince any physical signs of surprise other than that he intentionally pulled the trigger. The notion that a person who accidentally shoots someone to death will normally have the immediate reaction of hesitating or showing some other sign of surprise is well founded. Still, there may be exceptional individuals who do not respond in the normal way. While the existence of other, less likely explanations does not render this evidence irrelevant, the possibility of other explanations might not have been immediately apparent to the jury. Thus, it was appropriate for the trial judge to warn the jury to be careful with this evidence and that it might not be of much assistance to them. So he did. This caution was adequate to alert the jury to the risk associated with this evidence and to allow them to properly weigh the evidence.

. . .

V. Conclusion

[103] In light of the forgoing, I would dismiss the appeal.

CHARRON J. (DESCHAMPS J. concurring):—

1. Introduction

[104] I have considered the reasons of Binnie J. and I am in substantial agreement with his analysis on the law concerning the use that may be made of evidence of post-offence conduct. However, I disagree with the significance he attaches to Crown counsel's reference in his closing address to the fact that Mr. White immediately fled the scene with "no hesitation here, no shock, no uncertainty". As I will explain, when considered in context, this comment

could only have been understood by the jury as a rhetorical observation by Crown counsel that there was no evidence to support the defence theory that the gun had gone off accidentally. I therefore agree with Rothstein J. that there is no reason to interfere with the jury's verdict.

. . .

[109] [T]he identity of the shooter was a very live issue in Mr. White's trial and the evidence of flight was highly relevant to the issue of identification. Further, it formed an inextricable part of the narrative as every witness to the event described the shooter, gun in hand, fleeing the scene. Therefore the evidence was admissible at trial and properly left for the jury's assessment. It is not open to Mr. White on appeal to rewrite the script of his trial. In addition, on the question of intention, the trial judge took care to instruct the jury that they should "be careful with" this evidence, as it may not tell them "much more than that for any number of reasons he would be in some kind of trouble if he stayed at the scene and it may not be of much assistance in assessing his precise state of mind at the time the gun was fired" (A.R., at p. 606). In the context of this trial, no more was required.

. . .

[126] In short, there was no evidence to speak of one way or the other about the shooter's demeanour as he immediately fled from the scene. To suggest that the Crown's comment about the *lack* of such evidence might have caused the jury to mistakenly leap from the evidence of demeanour to a finding of guilt, in my respectful view, has no air of reality on this record. In any event, even if there had been significant evidence about the look on the shooter's face immediately after the fatal shot was fired, I would see no basis for excluding it from the jury's consideration. Consider, for example, if the witnesses had indeed described the shooter looking surprised or shocked at the time the last shot went off, or stooping down to check on Mr. Matasi's condition and hesitated for a few seconds before taking off. The jury would be entitled to the benefit of these observations. Indeed, given the defence's strategy in this case, such evidence would have played a central role in the case for the defence. In my view, when considered in context, the Crown's comment that there was "no **hesitation** here, no shock, no uncertainty" could only have been understood by everyone present as a rhetorical observation that there was no evidence of this nature and hence that the *defence theory* that the gun had gone off accidentally should not be given any credence.

. . .

[132] BINNIE J. (McLachlin C.J. and Fish JJ concurring) (dissenting) — This appeal again raises the question of what guidance a judge should give to a jury concerning the use that may be made of evidence of post-offence conduct. Generally speaking, of course, evidence of what an accused did or said before, during and after the alleged offence, may all be potentially relevant to the issue of guilt or innocence. If admissible, it will be for the jury to determine what use to make of it in deciding about the facts. In this respect, evidence of post-offence conduct is treated as any other circumstantial evidence. It is not to be considered in isolation, but together with the rest of the evidence in its entirety.

[133] Yet experience has shown that prosecutors will occasionally put forward as evidence of guilt, post-offence conduct that is essentially equivocal — such as the accused's strange behaviour when first spoken to by the police or the fact he failed to render assistance to the victim. Even where considered of some slight probative value in relation to an issue in the case, its persuasive value in the hands of a skilled prosecutor may create unfair prejudice to an accused. Thus, in some situations, it has been found necessary to withdraw such evidence from the jury's consideration, or to give an instruction pointing out the danger and limiting the use that may be made of it.

[134] In this appeal, the appellant stands convicted of second degree murder. The dispute is whether the jury might have drawn an impermissible inference of guilt from the Crown's characterization of his flight from the scene of a Vancouver homicide with "no hesitation here, no shock, no uncertainty on his part" when it convicted him of murder instead of manslaughter. The defence responded that a quick flight was not surprising. The appellant knew that — accident or not — his illegal Glock handgun had been fired during a street fight with a stranger. The victim had crumpled to the street.

[135] In closing argument, the defence conceded that the appellant shot the victim, but eyewitness accounts of the street fight preceding the gunshot were conflicting. The appellant says the jury should have been told that the Crown's argument about his demeanour could not be used as a basis for inferring the *specific* intent necessary to support a murder conviction, because both his flight and his pre-flight demeanour were equally consistent with an accidental shooting and thus manslaughter. The trial judge did not rein in the Crown's approach. He told the jury in relation to the issue of murderous intent that "[y]ou may consider Mr. White's post-event conduct in fleeing the scene, but you should also be careful with it."

. . .

[181] In this case, my colleague Rothstein J. acknowledges as irrelevant the fact of flight but he supports the Crown's argument about the appellant's demeanour ("no hesitation here, no shock, no uncertainty on his part") as relevant and appropriate. This, in my view, invites the jury to draw a speculative and unreasonable inference of guilt of second degree murder. It seems to me every bit as plausible to conclude that a person in possession of an illegal handgun that has just shot a stranger — accidentally or otherwise — would run away as fast and far as he could without any hesitation at all.

[182] The bare fact of flight from the scene may be an objective fact. The same cannot be said of what a bystander interprets as a momentary lack of hesitation or absence of a demonstration of "shock" or "uncertainty". This type of evidence depends on the unspoken assumptions that hesitation is normal whereas an immediate reaction is abnormal, and that the conduct of the appellant fell below some assumed but unarticulated standard of procrastination (whatever the "standard" is). Moreover, this assumed departure from the assumed norm is said to give rise — potentially — to the further inference of murderous intent. The double inference is problematic, and

relies on the type of subjective after-the-fact evaluation which experience has shown to be unreliable. As stated in the Kaufman Report, "[p]urported evidence of the accused's 'demeanour' as circumstantial evidence of guilt can be overused and misused. . . The most innocent conduct and demeanour may appear suspicious to those predisposed by other events to view it that way" (pp. 1142-43).

. . .

[185] In summary, my view is that the courts should continue to draw on their experience with evidence of post-offence conduct — especially where it involves post-offence "demeanour evidence" — and instruct juries with this experience in mind, just as is done by judges with the evidence of jailhouse informants, criminal records, eyewitness identification and evidence of uncharged misconduct (i.e. similar fact evidence). Of course, every argument about the need (or not) of a limiting instruction turns on the facts of the case.

The principal disagreement between these judgments concerns whether or not the accused's manner of fleeing the scene could ground any legitimate inference about his intent. On several other key issues the full Court agreed. The law does not always require special warnings whenever evidence of the accused's post-offence conduct is admitted. Post-offence conduct evidence can be vulnerable to misuse and misinterpretation by juries, who may be tempted to conclude too easily that the accused's after-the-fact actions are those of a guilty person. Courts may control the risks associated with post-offence conduct by offering cautionary or limiting instructions, but the need for such instructions will depend on the facts of the case.

Post-offence conduct refers generally to evidence of an accused's behavior after an offence that may support an inference of guilt — fleeing the scene or fabricating an alibi, for example. The Supreme Court has dealt with the issue in several cases, of which the 2011 *White* case is only one example.[51] This kind of evidence was formerly labeled "consciousness of guilt" evidence, but the Supreme Court has expressed a preference for the more neutral term "post-offence conduct".[52]

The Supreme Court also addressed post-offence conduct evidence in *R. v. Rodgerson*.[53] Rodgerson was charged with the murder of Amber Young, who died in his apartment during an altercation. Rodgerson admitted that he caused Young's death but, among other defences, he claimed that he used moderate force and that he did not intend to kill or seriously injure her. The Crown relied on evidence of the accused's extensive efforts to clean his apartment after Young's death and to conceal her body in the backyard of his home. The trial judge instructed the jury that it could rely on this evidence of

---

[51]   See also *R. v. White*, (1998), 125 C.C.C. (3d) 385, 16 C.R. (5th) 199, [1998] 2 S.C.R. 72 (S.C.C.) and *R. v. Arcangioli*, [1994] 1 S.C.R. 129, 27 C.R. (4th) 1, 87 C.C.C. (3d) 289 (S.C.C.).

[52]   *White, ibid.*

[53]   2015 CSC 38, 2015 SCC 38, [2015] 2 S.C.R. 760, 327 C.C.C. (3d) 287, 21 C.R. (7th) 1 (S.C.C.).

concealment and clean-up in deciding whether the accused had the requisite intent for murder. The jury convicted the accused of second degree murder.

The Supreme Court held that the evidence of concealment and clean-up did have some probative value on the issue of the accused's intent, but that the trial judge did not adequately explain its limited relevance to the jury. This post-offence conduct evidence could support a broad common sense inference that the accused was trying to prevent discovery of an unlawful killing, but that broad inference was irrelevant to the question of intent for murder. The concealment and clean-up evidence was only relevant to intent through a narrower inference that the accused sought to conceal the nature and extent of the victim's injuries and the degree of force required to inflict them. The trial judge erred in failing to explain this narrow permissible inference to the jury, and, as a result, the Supreme Court quashed the conviction and ordered a new trial.

Do you think the required instruction is understandable and necessary? Did the trial judge's failure to offer this instruction warrant ordering a new trial? Contrast what the Supreme Court said about lack of hesitation in *White* with how the Ontario Court of Appeal treated the failure of Angelis, a trained nurse, to perform CPR on his wife:

R. v. ANGELIS
2013 ONCA 70, 296 C.C.C. (3d) 143, 99 C.R. (6th) 315 (Ont. C.A.)

LASKIN J.A.:

[56] In this case, the trial judge should not have invited the jury to use the appellant's post-offence conduct to infer the level of his culpability — to infer that he was guilty of murder, not manslaughter. As a matter of logic and human experience, the appellant's post-offence conduct could not support a rational inference of an intent to kill. That it could not do so is evident from the circumstances. The appellant and his wife had no history of violence or abuse in their relationship. Yet, they had just had a sudden and very physical altercation. The altercation occurred in front of their two children. It was brief. It left the appellant disoriented and bleeding profusely from his genitals. And when it was over he knew only two things: Lien was dead, and he had killed her.

[57] In these circumstances, logic and human experience suggest that the appellant's post-offence conduct was as consistent with a panicked reaction to Lien's sudden and unintended death, as it was with a panicked reaction to her sudden and intended death. Thus, the jury should not have been repeatedly instructed that they could use this evidence to decide whether the appellant had the intent for murder.

[58] Even if one were to focus on what was likely the most cogent of the appellant's post-offence conduct the first category, namely, his failure to administer CPR to Lien or to immediately call 911 — I am not persuaded that

his conduct could rationally support an inference of an intent to kill, rather than simply an inference of having done something wrong. Indeed, recent case law from this court suggests that an accused's failure to render assistance after learning the victim may be dead is not probative of an accused's level of culpability: see *R. v. Anthony*, 2007 ONCA 609 (CanLII), 228 O.A.C. 272, at paras. 52-58; *R. v. Cudjoe*, 2009 ONCA 543 (CanLII), 251 O.A.C. 163, at para. 88; *R. v. McIntyre*, 2012 ONCA 356 (CanLII), 291 O.A.C. 359, at para. 40.

Do you agree? For a critical commentary on this case, see David M. Tanovich, "*Angelis*: Inductive Reasoning, Post-Offence Conduct and Intimate Femicide" (2013), 99 C.R. (6th) 338-350.

If a witness is willing to testify that he or she saw the accused shoot the deceased, this is direct evidence of that fact. The trial judge will first ensure the witness' competence to speak, then the evidence may be evaluated according to the trier of fact's assessment of the witness' credibility and reliability. If a witness is willing to testify that he or she heard the deceased scream and moments later saw the accused standing over the body holding a smoking gun this is circumstantial evidence of the accused shooting the deceased. The trial judge will assess the relevance of the evidence led; if received the trier of fact will then assess its sufficiency.

Notice that in the case of direct evidence there is but one source of error. The person who describes a stabbing he or she witnessed might be mistaken or lying. The witness who says he or she only saw certain circumstances, the wounds and the blood-stained knife, may also be mistaken or lying about those circumstances, but also, even if he or she is accurate in his or her description, the inference that the prosecutor wants the trier to draw may not be the correct one. That is why we say that circumstantial evidence has two sources of error. **This leads some to conclude that circumstantial evidence is weaker than direct, but is it?**

R. v. JACK
2013 ONCA 80, 294 C.C.C. (3d) 163, 100 C.R. (6th) 164 (Ont. C.A.)

The accused was charged with two counts of robbery after a man entered a car rental establishment and robbed two men at gunpoint. The only issue at trial was the identity of the perpetrator, and the only evidence of identity was the eyewitness testimony from the two victims. Shortly after the robbery, each victim offered a general description of the assailant that did not mention any distinctive features. The accused had two permanent gold front teeth, a 7-inch scar on his jaw, and a 3.5 cm tattoo on his left hand. Both victims testified that they had briefly seen the assailant months before when he came to rent a car. When the police arrived after the robbery, the victim, who was also the owner of the establishment, found a copy of the accused's health card in his files and gave it to police on the basis that it identified the assailant. Both victims identified the accused as the perpetrator at trial.

EPSTEIN J.A.(JURIANSZ and WATT JJ.A. concurring): —

12 The jurisprudence is replete with guidance about how the jury should be instructed in cases where identity is the issue and where, as here, the Crown's ability to satisfy the jury that it was the accused who committed the crime depends on eyewitness identification.

13 The dangers inherent in eyewitness identification evidence and the risk of a miscarriage of justice through wrongful conviction have been the subject of much comment: see for example *R. v. Goran*, 2008 ONCA 195, 234 O.A.C. 283, at para. 19. Such evidence, being notoriously unreliable, calls for considerable caution by a trier of fact: *R. v. Nikolovski*, [1996] 3 S.C.R. 1197, at pp. 1209-10; *R. v. Bardales*, [1996] 2 S.C.R. 461, pp. at 461-62; *R. v. Burke*, [1996] 1 S.C.R. 474, at p. 498.

14 It is essential to recognize that it is generally the reliability, not the credibility, of the eyewitness' identification that must be established. The danger is an honest but inaccurate identification: *R. v. Alphonso*, 2008 ONCA 238, [2008] O.J. No. 1248, at para. 5; *Goran*, at paras. 26-27.

15 The jury must be instructed to take into account the frailties of eyewitness identification as they consider the evidence relating to the following areas of inquiry. Was the suspect known to the witness? What were the circumstances of the contact during the commission of the crime including whether the opportunity to see the suspect was lengthy or fleeting? *R. v. Carpenter*, [1998] O.J. No. 1819 (C.A.) at para. 1. Was the sighting by the witness in circumstances of stress? *Nikolovski*, at 1210; *R. v. Francis* (2002), 165 O.A.C. 131, at 132.

16 As well, the jury must be instructed to carefully scrutinize the witnesses' description of the assailant. Was it generic and vague, or was it a detailed description that includes reference to distinctive features of the suspect? *R. v. Ellis*, 2008 ONCA 77, [2008] O.J. No. 361, at paras. 5, 8; *R. v. F.A.* (2004), 184 O.A.C. 324, at para. 64; *R. v. Richards*, (2004), 70 O.R. (3d) 737, at para. 9. *R. v. Boucher*, 2007 ONCA 131, [2007] O.J. No. 722, at para. 21. In some cases, a failure to mention distinctive characteristics of a suspect is sufficiently important, especially where there is no other inculpatory evidence, to reduce the case from one of identification effectively to one of no identification.

17 Finally, the charge must caution the jury that an in-dock or in-court identification is to be given negligible, if any, weight: *R. v. Hibbert*, [2002] 2 S.C.R. 445, at pp. 468-69; *R. v. Tebo* (2003), 172 O.A.C. 148, at para. 19.

. . .

20 The trial judge addressed the frailties of the identification evidence as follows:

> The case against Mr. Jack depends entirely on eyewitness testimony. You must be
> very careful when relying on eyewitness testimony. In the past there have been

miscarriages of justice and persons have been wrongly convicted because eyewitnesses have made mistakes in identifying the person whom they saw committing a crime.

Eyewitness testimony is an expression by a witness of his or her belief or impression. It is quite possible for an honest witness to make a mistake in identification. Honest people do make mistakes. An apparently convincing witness can be mistaken.

21 The deficiencies in this instruction upon which the appellant relies focus on the trial judge's failure to adequately deal with the reasons why, on the evidence in this case, the identification evidence had to be scrutinized with considerable care. The most notable of these problems was that the victims' contact with the robber was brief and stressful and their descriptions of him were generic in nature, lacking any mention of any distinctive features. The appellant also relies on the trial judge's failure to provide any caution regarding the use of in-dock identification.

22 The Crown argues that the reliability of the identification evidence was strengthened by a number of factors. The Crown contends that this is a recognition case, not an identification case. The victims recognized the robber as someone with whom they had had contact—evidenced by their independent recollection and the fact that his health card was in AutoHire files. As well, the jury had Mr. Zuniga's testimony that the robber referred to him by his first name.

23 The Crown submits that while the charge was brief and perhaps not as tailored to the case as it could have been, there was evidence linking the appellant to the robbery. The jury did receive instructions that contained a caution about the identification evidence—instructions that came at the end of a short trial preceded by strong defence submissions. The Crown therefore maintains that the jury was adequately equipped to determine whether the prosecution had proven identity beyond a reasonable doubt.

24 As I will explain, I do not agree.

25 First, I do not see this as a recognition case. I see it as an identification case. The previous contacts between the victims and the appellant took place months earlier, were brief, and were in the normal course of business such that the men would have no particular reason to have made note of the appellant's features. The best evidence of this is that neither witness remembered observing anything distinctive about the man's face.

26 Furthermore, any impact from this previous contact became negligible in the light of the brief, stressful contact during the robbery. As Charron J.A. observed in *R. v. Miller* (1998), 116 O.A.C. 331, at pp. 338-39, despite the fact the complainant testified that she knew the accused "reasonably well", the "limited time" she had to observe the assailant diminished the reliability of her identification evidence.

27 Second, the charge did not provide the jury with adequate assistance on how to assess the reliability of the victims' description of the robber given that their descriptions were generic and did not contain any reference to the appellant's distinctive features—the gold teeth, the scar and the tattoo, features that would have been apparent given the proximity of the contact between the perpetrator and his victims.

28 Admittedly, the trial judge did instruct the jury to consider the victims' failure to notice the appellant's distinctive features. After summarizing the evidence relevant to this issue, including the fact that the arresting officer testified that he did not notice these features when he located the appellant several weeks after the robbery, the trial judge instructed the jury as follows:

> Are the gold teeth, facial scar, or hand tattoo something that the two eyewitnesses should have noticed if indeed the robber was Mr. Jack? Does the failure to do so raise a reasonable doubt about whether Mr. Jack was the robber? This is for you to decide.

29 However, I agree with the appellant that this instruction did not go far enough. As discussed in *R. v. Gonsalves* (2008), 56 C.R. (6th) 379 (Ont. S.C.J.), at para. 39, "eyewitness identification evidence has taught us to use discriminating scrutiny for badges of unreliability." One such "badge" is whether a witness' description of the suspect fails to include mention of "a distinctive feature of the accused": *Ellis*, at para. 5, 8; *F.A.*, at para. 64. The caution contained in the above paragraph simply advises the jury to consider the impact of the evidence that the victims did not notice the appellant's distinctive features. It does not caution them to take this factor into consideration together with the generic description they provided to the police in performing their critical analysis of assessing the reliability of the identification evidence upon which the Crown's case wholly depended.

30 Compounding the problems associated with the insufficient instruction about the reliability of the identification provided by the victims prior to the trial is the trial judge's failure to caution the jury about their use of the victims' in-court identification. The charge, in fact, contains no reference to this evidence at all let alone a warning about the inherent unreliability of such evidence, particularly a caution about the diminished correlation between a witness' confidence level and his or her accuracy.

31 The jury should specifically have been given what is known as a *Hibbert* instruction. The seeming persuasiveness of eyewitness identification can be misleading as there is a "very weak link between the confidence level of a witness and the accuracy of that witness": *Hibbert*, at p. 469. This was further discussed in *Richards*, at para. 33, in which this court noted that "certainty on the part of an honest identification witness is part of the reason that eyewitness identification evidence is dangerous."

32 The portion of the charge set out above does contain a caution that "[a]n apparently convincing witness can be mistaken", but this was in the context of a discussion of generic descriptions in eyewitness testimony in general and fell short of the requirements established in *Hibbert* and reinforced by many decisions that followed.

. . .

39 In my view, the deficiencies in the charge, deficiencies that can be described in a general fashion as a failure to connect the standard instruction on the frailties of eyewitness identification to the specific concerns raised by the evidence in this case, in a case devoid of other evidence linking the accused to the crime, amounts to a reversible error.

40 I would therefore give effect to this ground of appeal and allow the appeal. . .

43 Given my view that the verdicts are unreasonable, the appropriate order is an order quashing the convictions and entering an acquittal on each charge.

For further consideration of the unreliability of eyewitness identification and warning practices in Canada and the United States, see Lisa Dufraimont, "Regulating Unreliable Evidence: Can Evidence Rules Guide Juries and Prevent Wrongful Convictions?"[54]

R. v. HANEMAAYER
(2008), 234 C.C.C. (3d) 3 (Ont. C.A.)

ROSENBERG J.A.:

. . .

[2] Almost twenty years ago, on October 18, 1989, the appellant pleaded guilty to two criminal offences that he did not commit. The story of how that happened is an important cautionary tale for the administration of criminal justice in this province.

THE FACTS OF THE OFFENCES

[3] On September 29, 1987, at about 5:00 a.m., a man broke into a residence in Scarborough and went to the bedroom of the owner's 15-year-old daughter. He jumped on her back, put his hand over her mouth, threatened her, and told her that he had a knife. Fortunately, the homeowner was awakened by the noise in her daughter's room. Thinking that her daughter had fallen out of bed, she went into the hall and turned on the light. She saw a man sitting on her daughter. She yelled at him and he turned around so that she saw his face. She

---

[54]   (2008) 33 Queen's L.J. 361. See too Nick Kaschuk, "Toward a Proper and complete Instruction for Photo Lineups: Preserving the Probative Value of Identification Evidence" (2011) 16 Can. Crim. L. Rev. 2. See Lisa Dufraimont, "*R. v. Henry* and the Problem of the Weak Identification Case" (2011), 80 C.R. (6th) 84. Henry, convicted of a series of sexual assaults, unsuccessfully defended himself and served almost 27 years in penitentiary before being exonerated by the B.C. Court of Appeal.

would later testify that she studied the man's face very closely. The man then jumped off the bed and confronted the homeowner. He stood inches from her, raised his arms and "roared" at her. He then fled the house.

[4] The homeowner told police that she stared at the intruder for forty seconds to a minute and could identify him again. Her daughter testified that less than thirty seconds passed from the time her mother entered the bedroom to when the intruder fled. The homeowner provided a description of the intruder to the police as follows:

> 6'0", 170 lbs., slim build, 19 years of age with sandy brown, wavy hair, wearing a black leather jacket and blue jeans.

[5] Although the homeowner had never seen the man before she believed that she was particularly adept at remembering faces because her work as a teacher required her to put names to the faces of her students. She decided that the perpetrator must have been keeping watch on her daughter and on the house and likely was working on construction in the area. She drove around and looked at the various construction sites and then telephoned one of the companies working in the area. She provided her description to a woman in the personnel department and the woman gave her the appellant's name as someone who fit the description. She passed on the name to the police.

[6] In the same period of time, the homeowner helped with a composite drawing prepared by a police technician operating a computer. She also viewed about 100 photographs at the police station. She told the police that she remembered two particular characteristics of the man; he had very piercing eyes and small ears. She agreed that the composite sketch did not reflect the small ears but she testified this was because the computer could not get it right. Two months after the break-in, the police showed the homeowner a photo line-up and she picked out the appellant's photograph. The investigating officer told her she had picked out the appellant's picture.

[7] The line-up viewed by the homeowner is no longer available. However, she did testify in cross-examination that the appellant's photograph was the least sharp of all the pictures in the array.

[8] The appellant was arrested on December 18, 1987. He gave a signed statement to the police in which he denied knowing anything of the crime. He confirmed that he had been working on construction in the Scarborough area that summer. It appears that he stopped working with the company five days before the break-in.

THE ORIGINAL COURT PROCEEDINGS

[9] The appellant was originally released on bail but when he failed to appear for his scheduled preliminary inquiry, he was arrested and detained in custody until his trial. His preliminary inquiry was ultimately held in May 1989 and he

was committed for trial. His trial commenced on October 17, 1989 before Ferguson J.

[10] The complainant and the homeowner testified on the first day of the trial. On the second day of the trial, after the homeowner had completed her testimony, the appellant changed his plea to guilty. He pleaded guilty to break and enter and committing an assault and assault while threatening to use a weapon. He was convicted on the break and enter charge and the second charge was stayed pursuant to the *Kienapple* doctrine: *R. v. Kienapple* (1974), 15 C.C.C. (2d) 524 (S.C.C.). He was sentenced to two years less one day imprisonment in accordance with a joint submission. The appellant served more than eight months of the sentence before being released on parole.

[11] In an affidavit filed with this court, the appellant explained why he changed his plea. In short, he lost his nerve. He found the homeowner to be a very convincing witness and he could tell that his lawyer was not making any headway in convincing the judge otherwise. Further, since his wife had left him and wanted nothing more to do with him, he had no one to support his story that he was home at the time of the offence. He says that his lawyer told him he would almost certainly be convicted and would be sentenced to six years imprisonment or more. However, if he changed his plea, his lawyer said he could get less than two years and would not go to the penitentiary. The appellant agreed to accept the deal even though he was innocent and had told his lawyer throughout that he was innocent.

THE RE-INVESTIGATION

[12] On October 17, 2005, Paul Bernardo's lawyer sent an e-mail to a police officer with the Toronto Police Sex Crimes Unit listing 18 sexual assaults and other offences that he believed had not been solved. One of the crimes was the break-in to which the appellant had pleaded guilty.

[13] The police interviewed Bernardo in April 2006 and then conducted a further investigation. They are satisfied that Bernardo, not the appellant, committed the crime. At the time, Bernardo lived two blocks from the victim's home. He, of course, was the so-called "Scarborough rapist" and, after his conviction for murder, was convicted of a number of sexual assaults committed in the Scarborough area during this time period. For example, one of the rapes which Bernardo was known to have committed occurred two and one-half months after the attack on this victim and was committed only half a block from the victim's home. It is unnecessary to further detail why there is no doubt of Bernardo's guilt. The fresh evidence is absolutely compelling.

[14] In the course of the re-investigation, the police interviewed the appellant and the homeowner. The appellant reaffirmed his innocence. The homeowner told the investigators that she had been sure at the time that the perpetrator was not the Scarborough rapist because his method of operation was different.

She was also sure that the person she saw was not Bernardo. At the hearing of the appeal, counsel informed the court that the homeowner remains convinced that she identified the right person.

THE PROCEEDINGS IN THIS COURT

[15] With the consent of the Crown, the appellant was granted an extension of time to appeal his conviction. The Crown also agreed that fresh evidence in the form of the results of the police re-investigation and the appellant's affidavit should be admitted into evidence and that the appeal should be allowed.

. . .

(2) The Identification Evidence

[21] I wish to make a few comments about the identification evidence in this case. We now know that the homeowner was mistaken. No fault can be attributed to her. She honestly believed that she had identified the right person. What happened in this case is consistent with much of what is known about mistaken identification evidence and, in particular, that honest but mistaken witnesses make convincing witnesses. Even the appellant, who knew he was innocent, was convinced that the trier of fact would believe her. The research shows, however, that there is a very weak relationship between the witness' confidence level and the accuracy of the identification. The confidence level of the witness can have a "powerful effect on jurors": see Manitoba, *The Inquiry Regarding Thomas Sophonow: The Investigation, Prosecution and Consideration of Entitlement to Compensation* (Winnipeg: Manitoba Justice, 2001) at 28; see also *R. v. Hibbert* (2002), 163 C.C.C. (3d) 129 (S.C.C.) at 148.

[22] The homeowner's evidence also reveals a number of concerns that demonstrate the frailties of eyewitness identification. First, there was no circumstantial evidence connecting the appellant with this crime. The fact that he was working in the area around the time is not circumstantial evidence inculpating him, but may possibly explain why the homeowner was able to pick him out of the line-up. Research has shown that witnesses have a difficult time keeping track of where they have seen someone: see *The Inquiry Regarding Thomas Sophonow* at p. 28.

[23] Second, the photographic line-up itself was the kind then in use by the police, that is, presented as an array rather than sequentially. In his report, Commissioner Peter Cory referred at p. 28 to the expert evidence adduced before him that photo line-ups are a form of "multiple choice testing". As I understand it, the danger is that the witness may choose the picture from the array that is the best fit. The witness engages in a process of elimination rather than recognition. Commissioner Cory recommended that the photo pack be presented sequentially.

[24] Third, the appellant's picture was different than the other photographs in the array. In *Hill v. Hamilton-Wentworth Regional Police Services Board* (2005), 76 O.R. (3d) 481 (C.A.), aff'd [2007] 3 S.C.R. 129, Feldman and LaForme JJ.A., in their dissenting opinion, refer at para. 149 to the expert evidence of Professor Roderick Lindsay, adduced in that case concerning structural bias in the presentation of a photo line-up. As Professor Lindsay explained, structural bias results when one person in the line-up is visually distinct from the others in some way. This bias can cause misidentifications because the person who stands out is more likely to be picked by the identifying witness.

[25] Fourth, the officers conducting the line-up were involved in the investigation and knew the identity of the suspect. There is a danger that the investigating officer may, even if not consciously, convey information to the witness to cause her to select the suspect. Commissioner Cory recommended, at p. 32, that "it is essential that an officer who does not know who the suspect is and who is not involved in the investigation conducts the photo pack line-up".

[26] Fifth, the evidence discloses serious contamination by the investigating officers. They informed the homeowner that she had indeed identified the suspect. This could only serve to increase her confidence in the accuracy of the identification and thus make her a more convincing witness. As Commissioner Cory recommended at p. 32:

> Police officers should not speak to eyewitnesses after the line-ups regarding their identification or their inability to identify anyone. This can only cast suspicion on any identification made and raise concerns that it was reinforced.

[27] Sixth, no permanent record was made of the line-up procedure. Commissioner Cory recommended that the line-up process should be videotaped or at least audio taped. The taped record can provide valuable information for the trier of fact in evaluating the reliability of the identification.

[28] In making these comments, I do not intend any unfair criticism either of the witness or the police. As to the witness, as I have said, she honestly believed she had made a correct identification. That identification was made in difficult circumstances; she was naturally under considerable stress when she encountered the assailant; she only had a brief opportunity to make her observations and she was identifying a stranger. As to the police, they may have been following procedures that were in place at the time. Those procedures and standards have evolved in the last twenty years: see the Supreme Court of Canada's comments in *Hill v. Hamilton Wentworth Police Service* at paras. 78-80.

[29] However, this case represents an example of how flawed identification procedures can contribute to miscarriages of justice and the importance of taking great care in conducting those procedures. Mistaken eyewitness

identification is the overwhelming factor leading to wrongful convictions. A study in the United States of DNA exonerations shows that mistaken eyewitness identification was a factor in over 80 per cent of the cases: see *The Inquiry Regarding Thomas Sophonow* at p. 27.

CONCLUSION

[30] I would conclude by reiterating the court's thanks to Mr. Lockyer on behalf of the appellant and Mr. Leibovich on behalf of the Crown for the work they have done to expedite this matter and, so far as can be done, reverse this miscarriage of justice. I also repeat what we said to Mr. Hanemaayer at the conclusion of the hearing:

It is profoundly regrettable that errors in the justice system led to this miscarriage of justice and the devastating effect it has had on Mr. Hanemaayer and his family.

Was it ethical for defence counsel to plead his client guilty in these circumstances?[55]

(vi) *Hodge's Case*

HODGE'S CASE
Liverpool Sum. Assizes, 1838

(Where a charge depends upon circumstantial evidence, it ought not only to be consistent with the prisoner's guilt, but inconsistent with any other rational conclusion.)

The prisoner was charged with murder.

The case was one of circumstantial evidence altogether, and contained no one fact, which taken alone amounted to a presumption of guilt. The murdered party (a woman), who was also robbed, was returning from market with money in her pocket; but how much, or of what particular description of coin, could not be ascertained distinctly.

The prisoner was well acquainted with her, and had been seen near the spot (a lane), in or near which the murder was committed, very shortly before. There were also four other persons together in the same lane about the same period of time. The prisoner, also, was seen some hours after, and on the same day, but at a distance of some miles from the spot in question, burying something, which on the following day was taken up, and turned out to be money, and which corresponded generally as to amount with that which the murdered woman was supposed to have had in her possession when she set out on her return home from market, and of which she had been robbed.

---

[55]   See Tanovich, "*Taillefer*. Disclosure, Guilty Pleas and Ethics" (2004), 27 C.R. (6th) 149; and *R. v. K. (S.)* (1995), 99 C.C.C. (3d) 376 (Ont. C.A.).

Alderson, B., told the jury, that the case was made up of circumstances entirely; and that, before they could find the prisoner guilty, they must be satisfied, "not only that those circumstances were consistent with his having committed the act, but they must also be satisfied that the facts were such as to be inconsistent with any other rational conclusion than that the prisoner was the guilty person."

He then pointed out to them the proneness of the human mind to look for — and often slightly to distort the facts in order to establish such a proposition — forgetting that a single circumstance which is inconsistent with such a conclusion, is of more importance than all the rest, inasmuch as it destroys the hypothesis of guilt.

The learned Baron then summed up the facts of the case, and the jury returned a verdict of Not guilty.[56]

Would you have convicted based on the evidence presented in this case? How prophetic was Baron Alderson's concern about tunnel vision?[57]

R. v. VILLAROMAN
2016 SCC 33, [2016] 1 S.C.R. 1000, 338 C.C.C. (3d) 1, 30 C.R. (7th) 223
(S.C.C.)

V was having problems with his laptop computer, so he left it with a repair shop. The repair technician found child pornography on the laptop. He called the police, whose search of the laptop confirmed the presence of child pornography. V was charged with a number of pornography-related offences, including possession of child pornography. The trial judge found that the mainly circumstantial evidence against V proved guilt on the charge of possession of child pornography beyond a reasonable doubt. The trial judge also held that the police search of the laptop violated s. 8 of the *Canadian Charter of Rights and Freedoms*.

On V's appeal the Alberta Court of Appeal concluded that the judge had misstated the current law respecting circumstantial evidence and that the verdict of guilt based on that evidence was unreasonable. The Court found that the trial judge erred because he failed to consider reasonable inferences inconsistent with guilt that could have arisen from a lack of evidence and that by failing to give the accused the benefit of gaps in the evidence the trial judge had in effect put the burden of proof on the accused. It set aside the conviction and entered an acquittal. The Court of Appeal declined to consider the *Charter* issues because its acquittal of V made those issues academic.

Justice Cromwell for a unanimous Supreme Court allowed the appeal, set aside the acquittal and remanded the case to the Alberta Court of Appeal for hearing and disposition of the *Charter* ss. 8 and 24(2) issues.

---

[56]   (1838), 168 E.R. 1136.
[57]   See the discussion of this in Berger, "The Rule in *Hodge's Case*: Rumours of Its Death Are Greatly Exaggerated" (2005) 84 Can. Bar Rev. 47.

CROMWELL J.

[16] The Court of Appeal's concern with the trial judgment arises from some ongoing difficulties caused by the old rule in *Hodge's Case*. While that case was not mentioned by name, the principle that it enunciated cast a long shadow over the judgments at trial and on appeal. I will turn first to some of the troublesome aspects of the jurisprudence flowing from *Hodge's Case* and then return to the errors of law the trial judge is alleged to have committed.

(a) *The Current Status of the "Rule" in Hodge's Case*

[17] In *Hodge's Case*, the evidence of identification was made up entirely of circumstantial evidence: p. 1137. Baron Alderson, the trial judge, instructed the jury that in order to convict, they must be satisfied "not only that those circumstances were consistent with [the accused] having committed the act, but they must also be satisfied that the facts were such as to be inconsistent with any other rational conclusion than that the [accused] was the guilty person": p. 1137. This sort of jury instruction came to be required in circumstantial cases: see, e.g., *McLean v. The King*, [1933] S.C.R. 688.

[18] Over time, this requirement was relaxed: see, e.g., *R. v. Mitchell*, [1964] S.C.R. 471; *R. v. Cooper*, [1978] 1 S.C.R. 860. It is now settled that no particular form of instruction to the jury is required where the evidence on one or more elements of the offence is entirely or primarily circumstantial. As Charron J. writing for a majority of the Court put it in *R. v. Griffin*, 2009 SCC 28, [2009] 2 S.C.R. 42, at para. 33:

> We have long departed from any legal requirement for a "special instruction" on circumstantial evidence, even where the issue is one of identification: *R. v. Cooper*, [1978] 1 S.C.R. 860. The essential component of an instruction on circumstantial evidence is to instill in the jury that in order to convict, they must be satisfied beyond a reasonable doubt that the only rational inference that can be drawn from the circumstantial evidence is that the accused is guilty. Imparting the necessary message to the jury may be achieved in different ways: *R. v. Fleet* (1997), 120 C.C.C. (3d) 457 (Ont. C.A.), at para. 20. See also *R. v. Guiboche*, 2004 MBCA 16, 183 C.C.C. (3d) 361, at paras. 108-10; *R. v. Tombran* (2000), 142 C.C.C. (3d) 380 (Ont. C.A.), at para. 29. [Emphasis added.]

[19] There may be some tension between the first and the second sentence of this passage from *Griffin*: see, e.g., L. Dufraimont, "*R. v. Griffin* and the Legacy of *Hodge's Case*" (2009), 67 C.R. (6th) 74. While the first sentence states that there is no required special instruction, the second sentence makes it an "essential component" of a jury instruction to ensure that the jury understands that they must be persuaded beyond reasonable doubt that the only rational inference is guilt. However, the cases cited with approval by Charron J. in this passage and our subsequent decision in *R. v. Mayuran*, 2012 SCC 31, [2012] 2 S.C.R. 162, at para. 38, clear up any doubt about what was intended.

[20] In the above passage, Charron J. cited with approval *R. v. Fleet* (1997), 120 C.C.C. (3d) 457 (Ont. C.A.), at para. 20. It is worth quoting that paragraph at length as in my view it makes Charron J.'s meaning clear:

> It will be recalled that, in *Cooper*, Ritchie J. specifically rejected the necessity for any formula of words to be used in a case of circumstantial evidence of identity. In our view, he can hardly have intended to reject the mandatory recitation of one formula only to substitute another in its place. We read the object of both judgments in *Cooper* to be the eradication of any formulaic approach to such cases so long as the jury is clearly made aware of the necessity to find the guilt of the accused to be established beyond a reasonable doubt. This object may be achieved in more ways than one. Thus, the trial judge, reviewing the evidence and setting out the position of the defence and relating the substantial parts of the evidence to that position, may frame the requisite instruction in the manner he or she considers most appropriate in the circumstances, for example, by:
>
> (a) charging the jury in accordance with the traditional language of proof beyond a reasonable doubt (*per* Laskin C.J.C. in *Cooper*);
>
> (b) charging the jury in accordance with that language and pointing out to the jury the other inferences that the defence says should be drawn from the evidence and the necessity to acquit the accused if any of those inferences raises a reasonable doubt (as the trial judge did in *Cooper* in the final portion of his recharge); or
>
> (c) charging the jury that it must be satisfied beyond a reasonable doubt that the guilt of the accused is the only reasonable inference to be drawn from the proven facts (*per* Ritchie J. in *Cooper* and Dubin J.A. in *Elmosri*).

[21] Charron J. also cited with approval *R. v. Tombran* (2000), 142 C.C.C. (3d) 380 (Ont. C.A.), (a decision in which she participated as a member of the Ontario Court of Appeal), at para. 29. Once again, it is worth quoting that paragraph:

> The modern approach to the problem of circumstantial evidence, enunciated clearly in *Cooper*, *supra*, and reiterated and reinforced by *Fleet*, *supra*, is to reject a formulaic approach and to deal with all the evidence in terms of the general principles of reasonable doubt. Trial judges are given a degree of latitude to formulate the appropriate instruction as befits the circumstances of the case. Trial judges are not required to adopt any specific language or wording, provided the charge conveys to the jury in a clear fashion the central point, namely, the necessity to find the guilt of the accused beyond a reasonable doubt. In particular, trial judges are not required to deliver to the jury a general, abstract lecture on the nature of circumstantial evidence or on the steps of logic to be followed in assessing circumstantial as distinct from direct evidence. An academic exercise along those lines may well confuse rather than assist the jury. Trial judges are entitled to conclude that the essential message of the need to establish guilt beyond a reasonable doubt can be better conveyed in other ways.

[22] These paragraphs, quoted with approval in *Griffin*, are consistent with what Charron J. conveyed in her reasons. This reading of the judgment is confirmed by our subsequent decision in *Mayuran* in which the Court reiterated the statement from *Griffin* that "[w]e have long departed from any

legal requirement for a 'special instruction' on circumstantial evidence": per Abella J., writing for a unanimous Court, at para. 38. There is therefore no particular form of mandatory instruction. However, where proof of one or more elements of the offence depends solely or largely on circumstantial evidence, it may be helpful for the jury to receive instructions that will assist them to understand the nature of circumstantial evidence and the relationship between proof by circumstantial evidence and the requirement of proof beyond reasonable doubt. I will touch briefly on both of these aspects.

(i) An Explanation of the Difference Between Direct and Circumstantial Evidence

[23] An explanation of the difference between direct and circumstantial evidence is included in most criminal jury charges and rarely causes difficulty. One example of how this distinction may be conveyed to a jury is found in s. 10.2 of the *Model Jury Instructions* (online) prepared by the National Committee on Jury Instructions of the Canadian Judicial Council:

> [1] As I explained at the beginning of the trial, you may rely on direct evidence and on circumstantial evidence in reaching your verdict. Let me remind you what these terms mean.
>
> [2] Usually, witnesses tell us what they personally saw or heard. For example, a witness might say that he or she saw it raining outside. That is called direct evidence.
>
> [3] Sometimes, however, witnesses say things from which you are asked to draw certain inferences. For example, a witness might say that he or she had seen someone enter the courthouse lobby wearing a raincoat and carrying an umbrella, both dripping wet. If you believed that witness, you might infer that it was raining outside, even though the evidence was indirect. Indirect evidence is sometimes called circumstantial evidence.

[24] While there is no particular required form of explanation, something along these lines will usually be helpful when one or more elements of the Crown's case depends solely or mainly on circumstantial evidence.

(ii) The Relationship Between Circumstantial Evidence and Proof Beyond Reasonable Doubt

[25] The Court has generally described the rule in *Hodge's Case* as an elaboration of the reasonable doubt standard: *Mitchell*; *John v. The Queen*, [1971] S.C.R. 781, per Ritchie J., at pp. 791-92; *Cooper*; *Mezzo v. The Queen*, [1986] 1 S.C.R. 802, at p. 843. If that is all that *Hodge's Case* was concerned with, then any special instruction relating to circumstantial evidence could be seen as an unnecessary and potentially confusing addition to the reasonable doubt instruction.

[26] However, that is not all that *Hodge's Case* was concerned with. There is a special concern inherent in the inferential reasoning from circumstantial evidence. The concern is that the jury may unconsciously "fill in the blanks" or

bridge gaps in the evidence to support the inference that the Crown invites it to draw. Baron Alderson referred to this risk in *Hodge's Case*. He noted the jury may "look for — and often slightly . . . distort the facts" to make them fit the inference that they are invited to draw: p. 1137. Or, as his remarks are recorded in another report, the danger is that the mind may "take a pleasure in adapting circumstances to one another, and even straining them a little, if need be, to force them to form parts of one connected whole": W. Wills, *Wills' Principles of Circumstantial Evidence* (7th ed. 1937), at p. 45; cited by Laskin J. in *John*, dissenting but not on this point, at p. 813.

[27] While this 19th century language is not suitable for a contemporary jury instruction, the basic concern that Baron Alderson described — the danger of jumping to unwarranted conclusions in circumstantial cases — remains real. When the concern about circumstantial evidence is understood in this way, an instruction concerning the use of circumstantial evidence and the reasonable doubt instruction have different, although related, purposes: see B. L. Berger, "The Rule in Hodge's Case: Rumours of its Death are Greatly Exaggerated" (2005), 84 *Can. Bar Rev.* 47, at pp. 60-61.

[28] The reasonable doubt instruction describes a state of mind — the degree of persuasion that entitles and requires a juror to find an accused guilty: Berger, at p. 60. Reasonable doubt is not an inference or a finding of fact that needs support in the evidence presented at trial: see, e.g. *Schuldt v. The Queen*, [1985] 2 S.C.R. 592, at pp. 600-610. A reasonable doubt is a doubt based on "reason and common sense"; it is not "imaginary or frivolous"; it "does not involve proof to an absolute certainty"; and it is "logically connected to the evidence or absence of evidence": *Lifchus*, at para. 36. The reasonable doubt instructions are all directed to describing for the jurors how sure they must be of guilt in order to convict.

[29] An instruction about circumstantial evidence, in contrast, alerts the jury to the dangers of the path of reasoning involved in drawing inferences from circumstantial evidence: Berger, at p. 60. This is the danger to which Baron Alderson directed his comments. And the danger he identified so long ago — the risk that the jury will "fill in the blanks" or "jump to conclusions" — has more recently been confirmed by social science research: see Berger, at pp. 52-53. This Court on occasion has noted this cautionary purpose of a circumstantial evidence instruction: see, e.g., *Boucher v. The Queen*, [1955] S.C.R. 16, per Rand J., at p. 22; *John*, per Laskin J., dissenting but not on this point, at p. 813.

[30] It follows that in a case in which proof of one or more elements of the offence depends exclusively or largely on circumstantial evidence, it will generally be helpful to the jury to be cautioned about too readily drawing inferences of guilt. No particular language is required. Telling the jury that an inference of guilt drawn from circumstantial evidence should be the only reasonable inference that such evidence permits will often be a succinct and

accurate way of helping the jury to guard against the risk of "filling in the blanks" by too quickly overlooking reasonable alternative inferences. It may be helpful to illustrate the concern about jumping to conclusions with an example. If we look out the window and see that the road is wet, we may jump to the conclusion that it has been raining. But we may then notice that the sidewalks are dry or that there is a loud noise coming from the distance that could be street-cleaning equipment, and re-evaluate our premature conclusion. The observation that the road is wet, on its own, does not exclude other reasonable explanations than that it has been raining. The inferences that may be drawn from this observation must be considered in light of all of the evidence and the absence of evidence, assessed logically, and in light of human experience and common sense.

[31] I emphasize, however, that assistance to the jury about the risk of jumping to conclusions may be given in different ways and, as noted in *Fleet*, trial judges will provide this assistance in the manner they consider most appropriate in the circumstances: p. 549.

(iii) "Rational" v. "Reasonable" Inferences

[32] I have suggested the use of the word "reasonable" to describe the potential inferences rather than the word "rational" used by Baron Alderson in *Hodge's Case* and in many other cases including *Griffin*. Which of these words should be used was one of the issues touched on by the Court of Appeal (at para. 9) and I should explain why I think that the word "reasonable" is preferable. The following comments also apply to the adjective "*logique*", which has been frequently used in the French version of this Court's jurisprudence on this issue.

[33] The words "rational" and "reasonable" are virtually synonyms: "rational" means "of or based on reasoning or reason"; "reasonable" means "in accordance with reason": *Canadian Oxford Dictionary* (2nd ed. 2004). While some have argued that there is a significant difference, I do not find that position convincing: see, e.g., E. Scott, "Hodge's Case: A Reconsideration" (1965-66), 8 *C.L.Q.* 17, at p. 25; A. M. Gans, "Hodge's Case Revisited" (1972-73), 15 *C.L.Q.* 127, at p. 132. It seems that our jurisprudence has used the words "rational" and "reasonable" interchangeably with respect to inferences: see *McLean; Fraser v. The King*, [1936] S.C.R. 1, at p. 2; *Boucher*, at pp. 18, 22 and 29; *John*, at p. 792; *Cooper*, at p. 881; *Lizotte v. The King*, [1951] S.C.R. 115, at p. 132; *Mitchell*, at p. 478; *Griffin*, at para. 33. This, in addition to the dictionary definitions, suggests that there is no difference in substance between them.

[34] There is an advantage of using the word "reasonable". It avoids the risk of confusion that might arise from using the word "reasonable" in relation to "reasonable doubt" but referring to "rational" inferences or explanations when speaking about circumstantial evidence: see *John*, per Laskin J., dissenting but

not on this point, at p. 815. In saying this, I do not suggest that using the traditional term "rational" is an error: the Court has said repeatedly and recently that the necessary message may be imparted in different ways: see, e.g., *Griffin*, at para. 33.

(iv) <u>Whether the Inference Must Be Based on "Proven Facts"</u>

[35] At one time, it was said that in circumstantial cases, "conclusions alternative to the guilt of the accused must be rational conclusions based on inferences drawn from proven facts": see *R. v. McIver*, [1965] 2 O.R. 475 (C.A.), at p. 479, aff'd without discussion of this point [1966] S.C.R. 254. However, that view is no longer accepted. In assessing circumstantial evidence, inferences consistent with innocence do not have to arise from proven facts: *R. v. Khela*, 2009 SCC 4, [2009] 1 S.C.R. 104, at para. 58; see also *R. v. Defaveri*, 2014 BCCA 370, 361 B.C.A.C. 301, at para. 10; *R. v. Bui*, 2014 ONCA 614, 14 C.R. (7th) 149, at para. 28. Requiring proven facts to support explanations other than guilt wrongly puts an obligation on an accused to prove facts and is contrary to the rule that whether there is a reasonable doubt is assessed by considering all of the evidence. The issue with respect to circumstantial evidence is the range of reasonable inferences that can be drawn from it. If there are reasonable inferences other than guilt, the Crown's evidence does not meet the standard of proof beyond a reasonable doubt.

[36] I agree with the respondent's position that a reasonable doubt, or theory alternative to guilt, is not rendered "speculative" by the mere fact that it arises from a lack of evidence. As stated by this Court in *Lifchus*, a reasonable doubt "is a doubt based on reason and common sense which must be logically based upon the evidence <u>or lack of evidence</u>": para. 30 (emphasis added). A certain gap in the evidence may result in inferences other than guilt. But those inferences must be reasonable given the evidence and the absence of evidence, assessed logically, and in light of human experience and common sense.

[37] When assessing circumstantial evidence, the trier of fact should consider "other plausible theor[ies]" and "other reasonable possibilities" which are inconsistent with guilt: *R. v. Comba*, [1938] O.R. 200 (C.A.), at pp. 205 and 211, per Middleton J.A., aff'd [1938] S.C.R. 396; *R. v. Baigent*, 2013 BCCA 28, 335 B.C.A.C. 11, at para. 20; *R. v. Mitchell*, [2008] QCA 394 (AustLII), at para. 35. I agree with the appellant that the Crown thus may need to negative these *reasonable* possibilities, but certainly does not need to "negative every possible conjecture, no matter how irrational or fanciful, which might be consistent with the innocence of the accused": *R. v. Bagshaw*, [1972] S.C.R. 2, at p. 8. "Other plausible theories" or "other reasonable possibilities" must be based on logic and experience applied to the evidence or the absence of evidence, not on speculation.

[38] Of course, the line between a "plausible theory" and "speculation" is not always easy to draw. But the basic question is whether the circumstantial

evidence, viewed logically and in light of human experience, is reasonably capable of supporting an inference other than that the accused is guilty.

[39] I have found two particularly useful statements of this principle.

[40] The first is from an old Australian case, *Martin v. Osborne* (1936), 55 C.L.R. 367 (H.C.), at p. 375:

> In the inculpation of an accused person the evidentiary circumstances must bear no other reasonable explanation. This means that, according to the common course of human affairs, the degree of probability that the occurrence of the facts proved would be accompanied by the occurrence of the fact to be proved is so high that the contrary cannot reasonably be supposed. [Emphasis added.]

[41] While this language is not appropriate for a jury instruction, I find the idea expressed in this passage — that to justify a conviction, the circumstantial evidence, assessed in light of human experience, should be such that it excludes any other reasonable alternative — a helpful way of describing the line between plausible theories and speculation.

[42] The second is from *R. v. Dipnarine*, 2014 ABCA 328, 584 A.R. 138, at paras. 22 and 24-25. The court stated that "[c]ircumstantial evidence does not have to totally exclude other conceivable inferences"; that the trier of fact should not act on alternative interpretations of the circumstances that it considers to be unreasonable; and that alternative inferences must be reasonable, not just possible.

[43] Where the line is to be drawn between speculation and reasonable inferences in a particular case cannot be described with greater clarity than it is in these passages.

Turning to the facts, Cromwell J. held that the trial judge made no errors in his assessment of the circumstantial evidence and that the conviction was reasonable. It was speculative to consider that someone else might have downloaded the child pornography without the accused's knowledge.

The Supreme Court in *Villaroman* rejected the notion that instructions about circumstantial evidence are adequately dealt with by instructions on the meaning of reasonable doubt. So the Canadian position here differs from that approach, which is that of the House of Lords in *McGreevy v. Director of Public Prosecutions*[58] and the U.S. Supreme Court in *Holland v. United States*.[59] See too Elliot Herzig, "R. v. Villaroman: A Call for Simplicity" (2016), 27 C.R. (7th) 40, a comment on the Alberta Court of Appeal's decision.

Justice Cromwell is influenced by the position of Ben Berger, in "The Rule in Hodge's Case: Rumours of Its Death are Greatly Exaggerated" (2005) 84 Can. Bar Rev. 47, that it is important where evidence is circumstantial to instruct the jury as to the dangers of drawing inferences

---

[58]   [1973] 1 All E.R. 503 (U.K. H.L.).
[59]   348 U.S. 121 (U.S. Sup. Ct., 1954).

and the risk of "filling the blanks" by too quickly overlooking reasonable inferences other than guilt. He accepts the findings of two social science studies reviewed by Berger. Unlike Professor Berger, Justice Cromwell however avoids the position that such an instruction should be mandatory. Instead he writes that an instruction "may be helpful" [para. 22], that an instruction "will usually be helpful" [para. 24] and that "it will generally be helpful to the jury to be cautioned about too readily drawing inferences of guilt" [para. 30]. Furthermore, although Cromwell J. preferred the language of "reasonable" when speaking of inferences, he held that using the traditional term "rational" is not in error as the necessary message may be imparted in different ways [para. 34].

In his *Criminal Reports* comment on *Villaroman*, Don Stuart wrote:

> In my view it would have been preferable had the Supreme Court decided that jurors and judges always need to be instructed as to the difference between direct evidence, where the issue is only credibility, and circumstantial evidence, where there is an additional risk of having to draw reasonable inferences. In other contexts such as the test for committal the distinction is clearly crucial and always expressly in play (see *R. v. Arcuri* [2001] 2 S.C.R. 828]. As shown by Justice Cromwell's own analysis [see at paras. 23 and 30] such an instruction only requires a short explanation with a brief example rather than the complex lecture feared by Justice Sharpe in *R. v. Tombran* (2000) 142 C.C.C. (3d) 380 (Ont.C.A.) It is disappointing that the Supreme Court left it to the discretion of the trial judge as to whether to give any instruction at all and as to what language to use in any such instruction. With such uncontrolled discretion comes uncertainty, which risks the law having little meaning or effect. Under *Villaroman* it seems that a trial judge would not err in not mentioning the circumstantial issue or by just trotting out the much criticised formula of *Hodge'e case* of 178 years ago. Much of the careful analysis and wise best practice advice of Justice Cromwell for the Court should be followed. But it could be by-passed and this would be unreviewable on appeal. If that was the price of unanimity it was too high.

(vii) *Preliminary Findings of Fact*

The persuasive burden also applies where a party has to meet a legal standard in seeking to have evidence admitted (e.g., that a piece of real evidence is authentic or that a confession given to a person in authority is voluntary). What standard of proof applies in these circumstances?

R. v. EVANS
[1993] 3 S.C.R. 653, 25 C.R. (4th) 46, 85 C.C.C. (3d) 97

SOPINKA J.:

. . . The general rule is that preliminary questions which are a condition of admissibility are for the trial judge in his or her capacity as the judge of the law rather than as the trier of fact. See *R. v. B. (K.G.)*, *supra*, at pp. 783-84. If factual questions must be resolved, a *voir dire* may be required. The applicable standard of proof in both civil and criminal cases is on a balance of probabilities: *R. v. B.(K.G.)*, at p. 800.

R. v. ARP
[1998] 3 S.C.R. 339, 20 C.R. (5th) 1, 129 C.C.C. (3d) 321

CORY J.:

. . . However, the general rule that preliminary findings of fact may be determined on a balance of probabilities is departed from in those certainly rare occasions when admission of the evidence may itself have a conclusive effect with respect to guilt. For example, where the Crown adduces a statement of the accused made to a person in authority, the trial judge must be satisfied beyond a reasonable doubt of the voluntariness of the statement. That evidence may of itself, if accepted as true, provide conclusive proof of guilt. Since doubt about the statement's voluntariness also casts doubt on its reliability, proof beyond a reasonable doubt is warranted. See *Ward v. The Queen*, [1979] 2 S.C.R. 30. If this were not the rule, the jury would be permitted to rely on evidence which it could accept as extremely cogent even though the inherent reliability of that evidence was in doubt.

See further the discussion of this issue most recently in *R. v. H. (L.T.)*[60] where a majority of the Supreme Court held that the Crown must prove beyond a reasonable doubt that the police properly informed a young person of his or her legal rights in accordance with s. 146 of the *Youth Criminal Justice Act*.

(d) Measure of Evidential Burden

(i) *Criminal Cases*

The evidential burden signifies the duty of pointing to evidence to put an issue in play, either at the outset of the trial or during its course. The party who entertains the burden and fails in its discharge not only risks loss at the hands of the trier but also risks loss at the hands of the judge; the party who fails to produce evidence may not get past the judge and into the hands of the jury. While our system is predicated on the right to a jury's verdict, the system has always provided a role for the judge to confine the jury within the parameters of rationality.

Sometimes not meeting the evidential burden can have immediate legal consequences so the measure of the burden may be crucial. Examples are: where a trial judge rules that a defence has no air of reality and withdraws it from the jury; on a motion for a directed verdict (motion for non-suit); on whether to discharge or commit following a preliminary inquiry in a criminal trial; or on whether to extradite.

---

[60]   [2008] 2 S.C.R. 739, 234 C.C.C. (3d) 301, 59 C.R. (6th) 1 (S.C.C.).

U.S.A. v. SHEPHARD
[1977] 2 S.C.R. 1067, 34 C.R.N.S. 207, 30 C.C.C. (2d) 424

The case involved an application for extradition. The affidavit evidence filed on the hearing was that of an admitted drug dealer and alleged accomplice of Shephard who by his affidavit admitted that he was purchasing immunity for himself by offering his accusation of Shephard. The extradition judge, Hugessen, J., rejected this evidence as unworthy of belief and refused the extradition. The Supreme Court disagreed. For the 4-3 majority Ritchie J. stated:

> [The test for granting extradition] . . . is the same test which governs a trial Judge in deciding whether the evidence is sufficient to justify him in withdrawing the case from the jury, and this is to be determined according to whether or not there is any evidence upon which a reasonable jury properly instructed could return a verdict of guilty...[It] follows that credibility is not within his sphere....[The extradition judge overlooked] the well established rule that the weighing of evidence is always a matter for the jury.

The Supreme Court first applied its test in *Shephard* in *R. v. Mezzo*,[61] a case involving direct evidence. Justice McIntyre confirmed that the role of the reviewing judge is not to assess the quality of the evidence and held that the trial judge had erred in directing a verdict of acquittal because of his concerns about the reliability of the identification evidence.

R. v. ARCURI
[2001] 2 S.C.R. 828, 44 C.R. (5th) 213, 157 C.C.C. (3d) 21

The accused was charged with first degree murder. At the preliminary inquiry, the Crown's case was entirely circumstantial and the accused called two witnesses whose testimony was arguably exculpatory. The preliminary inquiry judge rejected the accused's contention that he must weigh the evidence and, after viewing the evidence as a whole, determined that the accused should be committed to trial for second degree murder. The accused's *certiorari* application was dismissed and that decision was affirmed by the Court of Appeal. The issue before the Supreme Court was whether the preliminary inquiry judge, in determining whether the evidence was sufficient to commit the accused to trial, erred in refusing to weigh the Crown's evidence against the allegedly exculpatory direct evidence adduced by the accused.

McLACHLIN C.J. (L'HEUREUX-DUBÉ, GONTHIER, IACOBUCCI, MAJOR, BASTARACHE, BINNIE, ARBOUR and LEBEL JJ. concurring): —

. . .

The question to be asked by a preliminary inquiry judge under s. 548(1) of the Criminal Code is the same as that asked by a trial judge considering a defence motion for a directed verdict, namely, "whether or not there is any evidence upon which a reasonable jury properly instructed could return a

---

[61]   (1986), 27 C.C.C. (3d) 97, 52 C.R. (3d) 113, [1986] 1 S.C.R. 802.

verdict of guilty": *Shephard, supra*, at p. 1080; see also *R. v. Monteleone*, [1987] 2 S.C.R. 154, at p. 160. Under this test, a preliminary inquiry judge must commit the accused to trial "in any case in which there is admissible evidence which could, if it were believed, result in a conviction": *Shephard, supra*, at p. 1080.

The test is the same whether the evidence is direct or circumstantial: see *R. v. Mezzo*, [1986] 1 S.C.R. 802, at p. 842—43; *Monteleone, supra*, at p. 161. The nature of the judge's task, however, varies according to the type of evidence that the Crown has advanced. Where the Crown's case is based entirely on direct evidence, the judge's task is straightforward. By definition, the only conclusion that needs to be reached in such a case is whether the evidence is true: see Watt's *Manual of Criminal Evidence* (1998), at §8.0 ("[d]irect evidence is evidence which, if believed, resolves a matter in issue"); McCormick *on Evidence* (5th ed. 1999), at p. 641; J. Sopinka, S. N. Lederman and A. W. Bryant, *The Law of Evidence in Canada* (2nd ed. 1999), at §2.74 (direct evidence is witness testimony as to "the precise fact which is the subject of the issue on trial"). It is for the jury to say whether and how far the evidence is to be believed: see *Shephard*, supra, at pp. 1086-87. Thus if the judge determines that the Crown has presented direct evidence as to every element of the offence charged, the judge's task is complete. If there is direct evidence as to every element of the offence, the accused must be committed to trial.

The judge's task is somewhat more complicated where the Crown has not presented direct evidence as to every element of the offence. The question then becomes whether the remaining elements of the offence — that is, those elements as to which the Crown has not advanced direct evidence — may reasonably be inferred from the circumstantial evidence. Answering this question inevitably requires the judge to engage in a limited weighing of the evidence because, with circumstantial evidence, there is, by definition, an inferential gap between the evidence and the matter to be established — that is, an inferential gap beyond the question of whether the evidence should be believed. . . The judge must therefore weigh the evidence, in the sense of assessing whether it is reasonably capable of supporting the inferences that the Crown asks the jury to draw. This weighing, however, is limited. The judge does not ask whether she herself would conclude that the accused is guilty. Nor does the judge draw factual inferences or assess credibility. The judge asks only whether the evidence, *if believed,* could reasonably support an inference of guilt.

. . .

Notwithstanding certain confusing language in *Mezzo* and *Monteleone* nothing in this Court's jurisprudence calls into question the continuing validity of the common law rule. . . In *Mezzo*, the issue was whether the Crown had proffered sufficient evidence as to identity. McIntyre J., writing for the majority, stated that a trial judge can direct an acquittal only if there is "no evidence" as to an essential element of the offence. . . He also stated that the judge has no authority to "weigh and consider the quality of the evidence and to remove it from the jury's consideration". . . Those statements, taken alone, might be understood to suggest that a preliminary inquiry judge must commit the accused to trial even if the Crown's evidence would not reasonably support an inference of guilt. However, as the dissent in *Charemski* . . . discusses, the remainder of McIntyre J.'s reasons make clear that by "no evidence" McIntyre J. meant "no evidence capable of supporting a conviction," and by "weighing" McIntyre J. was referring to the ultimate determination of guilt (a matter for the jury), as distinguished from the determination of whether the evidence can reasonably support an inference of guilt (a matter for the preliminary inquiry judge). His concern was to reject the argument that the judge must determine whether guilt is the only reasonable inference. His reasons cannot be read to call into question the traditional rule, namely, that the judge must determine whether the evidence can reasonably support an inference of guilt.

In *Monteleone*, the accused was charged with setting fire to his own clothing store. The evidence was entirely circumstantial. The question was whether the trial judge had erred in directing an acquittal on the grounds that the "cumulative effect [of the evidence] gives rise to suspicion only, and cannot justify the drawing of an inference of guilt". . . In ordering a new trial, McIntyre J. wrote that "[i]t is not the function of the trial judge to weigh the evidence, [or] . . . to draw inferences of fact from the evidence before him". . . Again, however, the remainder of the reasons make clear that by "weighing" McIntyre J. was referring to the final drawing of inferences from the facts (which task, again, is within the exclusive province of the jury), not to the task of assessing whether guilt could reasonably be inferred. Indeed, the reasons explicitly reaffirm the common law rule that the judge must determine whether "there is before the court any admissible evidence, . . . Whether direct or circumstantial, which, if believed by a properly charged jury acting reasonably, would justify a conviction". . .

Contrary to the appellant's contention, *Charemski* . . . did not evidence disagreement in this Court as to the proper approach. The appellant in *Charemski* . . . had been charged with the murder of his wife. The trial judge directed a verdict of acquittal, principally because the forensic evidence did not affirmatively suggest that the deceased had been murdered. The question in this Court was whether the Court of Appeal erred in setting aside the trial judge's directed verdict of acquittal. There was no disagreement between the majority and the dissent as to the test that the preliminary inquiry justice must apply. On the contrary, both the majority and the dissent clearly reaffirmed *Shephard* . . . and its progeny. . . Any disagreement concerned not the test for sufficiency but the question of whether sufficient evidence was led in that case. The majority conceded that forensic evidence had not affirmatively indicated that the deceased had been murdered, but reasoned that a properly instructed jury could reasonably infer guilt from the other evidence that the Crown had led. The dissent argued that, as it had not been established that the deceased had been murdered, it was meaningless to discuss identity and causation, two of the other essential elements of the offence. The dissent also argued that the accused's presence in the deceased's apartment could not reasonably be inferred from the accused's conceded presence in the lobby. The dissenting justices concluded that the circumstantial evidence could not reasonably support an inference of guilt.

. . .

The question that arises in the case at bar is whether the preliminary inquiry judge's task differs where the defence tenders exculpatory evidence, as is its prerogative under s. 541. In my view, the task is essentially the same, in situations where the defence calls exculpatory evidence, whether it be direct or circumstantial. Where the Crown adduces direct evidence on all the elements of the offence, the case must proceed to trial, regardless of the existence of defence evidence, as by definition the only conclusion that needs to be reached is whether the evidence is true. However, where the Crown's evidence consists of, or includes, circumstantial evidence, the judge must engage in a limited weighing of the whole of the evidence (i.e. including any defence evidence) to determine whether a reasonable jury properly instructed could return a verdict of guilty.

In performing the task of limited weighing, the preliminary inquiry judge does not draw inferences from facts. Nor does she assess credibility. Rather, the judge's task is to determine whether, *if the Crown's evidence is believed*, it would be reasonable for a properly instructed jury to infer guilt. Thus, this task of "limited weighing" never requires consideration of the inherent reliability of the evidence itself. It should be regarded, instead, as an assessment of the reasonableness of the inferences to be drawn from the circumstantial evidence.

. . .

With those principles in mind, I turn, then, to the question of whether Lampkin Prov. J. properly interpreted and applied the law in this case. . .

. . .

Notwithstanding . . . two reservations, I am not persuaded that Lampkin Prov. J. reached the wrong result. Before committing the appellant to trial, the preliminary inquiry justice thoroughly surveyed the circumstantial evidence that had been presented by the Crown. . . Only after considering "the evidence as a whole" did Lampkin Prov. J. commit the appellant to trial.

. . .

For the foregoing reasons, I conclude that the appeal should be dismissed.

Arcuri was acquitted at his trial.

The *Shephard* test emerged in the extradition context and was later applied to questions of sufficiency of evidence in criminal proceedings more broadly. In *R. v. Ferras*,[62] the Supreme Court adopted a new approach in extradition cases that grants the extradition judge discretion to refuse to extradite on the basis that the prosecution's evidence is unreliable. In coming to the conclusion that it was, Chief Justice McLachlin, for the Court, noted: "I

---

[62]   [2006] 2 S.C.R. 77. See now Lisa Dufraimont, "*M.M. v. United States of America* and the Continuing Evolution of the Shephard Test" (2016), 25 C.R. (7th) 238.

take it as axiomatic that a person could not be committed for trial for an offence in Canada if the evidence is so manifestly unreliable that it would be unsafe to rest a verdict upon it." The *Shephard* approach as explained in *Arcuri* continues to apply at preliminary inquiries and on motions for directed verdicts of acquittal.

On March 29, 2018, the Minister of Justice introduced the lengthy omnibus Bill C-75 which, among many amendments designed to reduce court delays, would limit preliminary inquiries to indictable offences carrying a life sentence. This reform would mean that sexual assault complainants would not bear the burden of having to testify twice. The amendment has been roundly criticized by defence counsel who argue preliminary inquiries are an important vehicle for testing credibility and allow for discharges to be entered at an early stage in weak cases.

In criminal cases the sufficiency of the Crown's case is tested before and during a trial. In cases where there is a preliminary inquiry, s. 548(1) of the *Criminal Code* mandates that there be sufficient evidence before the judge will commit the accused for trial. The defence can also challenge the sufficiency of the Crown's case at trial pursuant to the common law application for a directed verdict of acquittal after the close of the Crown's case. A trial judge must rule on the defence's application before the accused elects to call a defence.[63] If the defence successfully challenges the sufficiency of the Crown's case at a jury trial, the trial judge will now withdraw the case from the jury as opposed to directing them to acquit. The trial judge will then enter a verdict of acquittal.[64] Where the evidence is overwhelming and the trial judge is satisfied that the accused is guilty, the judge cannot, however, direct the jury to convict.[65] **Why not?**

PROBLEM

The accused is charged with second degree murder in the death of his estranged wife. The deceased was found in her bathtub in the early hours of Christmas Day. The deceased's head was near the faucets and there was evidence of hot-water scalding on her skin. Her lungs were heavy, which was consistent with drowning. There were no signs of strangulation. There was no evidence of foul play in her apartment. Everything was neat and in order. No fingerprints of the accused were found in the apartment. The forensic evidence failed to establish definitively that the deceased had died from natural causes, or as a result of accident, suicide or homicide. In support of its theory of homicide, the Crown relied on a number of pieces of circumstantial evidence including animus and motive. The accused and the deceased had a difficult marriage marked by periods of separation. During one such period, the deceased began a relationship with another man, which

---

[63]   See *R. v. Angelantoni*, (1975) C.R.N.S. 342 (Ont. C.A.); and *R. v. Boissonneault* (1986), 29 C.C.C. (3d) 345 (Ont. C.A.).

[64]   See *R. v. Rowbotham*, [1994] 2 S.C.R. 463.

[65]   See *R. v. Krieger* (2006), 41 C.R. (6th) 201 (S.C.C.) and Lisa Dufraimont, *"Krieger*: The Supreme Court's Guarded Endorsement of Jury Nullification" (2007), 41 C.R. (6th) 209; see also *R. v. Gunning* (2005), 29 C.R. (6th) 17 (S.C.C.).

the accused found "shameful" and which had made him feel like an "idiot". On one occasion, the deceased told her doctor that she was afraid of staying with her husband and wanted to move away from him. The deceased also once told a friend that the accused was verbally abusive and that she was afraid of him. There was also evidence of a $50,000 life insurance policy on the deceased. The accused admitted to the police that he was present at the deceased's apartment building on the night she died. He had travelled from Vancouver to London, Ontario. The accused also telephoned her. He asked her whether she was alone. The accused failed to account for the time between his arrival at the deceased's apartment building (11:00 pm) and the time he was picked up by a taxi and left for Toronto (12:30 am). The deceased died at some point between 11:00 pm and 1:00 am. The deceased's key to her apartment could not be found. Finally, three days after her death, the accused told the police that the deceased had complained about being short of money, being sick and forgetting things. He also volunteered, before the police had revealed the cause of death, that the deceased had complained to him about falling asleep in the bathtub sometimes for an hour or two and that she had almost drowned on a couple of occasions.

If you are the preliminary inquiry judge would you commit the accused to stand trial on this evidence? Would you convict? See *R. v. Charemski.*[66]

Lisa Dufraimont, "*R. v. Hay*: Enhanced Safeguards against Wrongful Conviction in Identification Cases"
(2014) 6 C.R. (7th) 246

In *R. v. Hay*,[67] the Supreme Court worked important changes in the law regarding eyewitness identification. All members of the Court agreed with Rothstein J. when he held as follows:

> Although the duty to assess the credibility and weight of an eyewitness' evidence sits with the jury and, in some circumstances, the testimony of one eyewitness will support a conviction, the jury should not be permitted to convict on the basis of eyewitness testimony that could not support an inference of guilt beyond a reasonable doubt. In other words, a jury should not be instructed that it may convict based on eyewitness testimony alone where that testimony, even if believed, would necessarily leave reasonable doubt in the mind of a reasonable juror; *R. v. Arcuri*, 2001 SCC 54, [2001] 2 S.C.R. 828, at paras. 21-25; *R. v. Reitsma*, [1998] 1 S.C.R. 769, rev'g (1997) 97 B.C.A.C. 303; *R. v. Zurowski*, 2004 SCC 72, [2004] 3 S.C.R. 509; *United States of America v. Shephard*, [1977] 2 S.C.R. 1067, at p. 1080. Indeed, where the Crown's case consists solely of eyewitness testimony that would necessarily leave reasonable doubt in the mind of a

---

[66]   [1998] 1 S.C.R. 679, 15 C.R. (5th) 1, 123 C.C.C. (3d) 225.
[67]   2013 SCC 61, [2013] 3 S.C.R. 694, 302 C.C.C. (3d) 147, 6 C.R. (7th) 215 (S.C.C.)

reasonable juror, the trial judge must direct an acquittal upon a motion for directed verdict (*Arcuri*, at para. 21).[68]

This passage holds a number of significant implications. First, it is now clearly open to trial judges to direct acquittals where the Crown presents only weak and unsupported eyewitness identification evidence against an accused. Second, since this holding is framed as an interpretation of the *Shephard* test for the sufficiency of evidence, which also applies at the preliminary inquiry, it now appears open to preliminary inquiry judges to discharge accused persons in weak eyewitness identification cases on the same grounds. Third, even where the Crown's case on identification is not limited to the eyewitness testimony, judges will be precluded from instructing juries that they may convict on weak eyewitness identification alone.

Each of these propositions breaks new ground and enhances the protections against wrongful conviction based on eyewitness mistake. In *R. v. Mezzo*,[69] the previous leading case on directed verdicts in identification cases, the Supreme Court held that the weight of eyewitness identification evidence was a matter reserved for the jury, and that it was not open to a trial judge to withdraw a case from the jury on the basis that the identification evidence was weak.[70] *Hay* has overturned *Mezzo* in this regard. *Hay* also calls into question the rule from *R. v. Arcuri*[71] (the leading case on applying the *Shephard* test in the context of the preliminary inquiry) that "[w]here the Crown adduces direct evidence on all the elements of the offence, the case must proceed to trial".[72] Eyewitness identification evidence is, by definition, direct evidence: it is witness testimony that, if believed, establishes a fact in issue.[73] Consequently, *Arcuri* implies that even weak eyewitness identification cases *must* proceed to trial.[74] As noted above, however, *Hay* seems to take the opposite view. Finally, by holding that judges should *not* instruct juries that they may convict on weak eyewitness identification alone, *Hay* qualifies significantly the long-established rule that a jury is free to convict on the basis of the testimony of one eyewitness.[75]

---

[68]   *Ibid.* at para. 41.

[69]   [1986] 1 S.C.R. 802, 27 C.C.C. (3d) 97, 52 C.R. (3d) 113 (S.C.C.).

[70]   *Ibid.* at paras. 61-63 (because "there was direct evidence of identification. . .[, the case] should have been left to the jury, with a proper caution. . ." at 63). See also Alan W. Bryant, Sidney N. Lederman & Michelle K. Fuerst, *Sopinka, Lederman & Bryant: The Law of Evidence in Canada*, 3rd ed. (Markham, Ont: LexisNexis, 2009) ("Although earlier Canadian authorities held that poor identification evidence could amount to 'no evidence' justifying a directed verdict of acquittal, it is now settled that a trial judge cannot withdraw a case from the jury on the ground of weak identification evidence" at para. 12.25 [footnotes omitted]).

[71]   2001 SCC 54, [2001] 2 S.C.R. 828, 157 C.C.C. (3d) 21, 44 C.R. (5th) 213 (S.C.C.).

[72]   *Ibid.* at para. 29.

[73]   *ibid.* at para. 22.

[74]   Even before *Hay*, a line of authority developed distinguishing frail eyewitness identifications from situations where the eyewitness was so equivocal that there was no positive identification at all (e.g., where the eyewitness said only that the accused resembled the perpetrator). In the latter cases, the eyewitness evidence arguably does not amount to direct evidence of identity, so the judge is not bound to commit the accused to trial. See *R. v. Herrera*, [2008] O.J. No. 3040 (Ont. S.C.J.) at paras. 27-29; *R. v. Vigneswaran* (2011), 270 C.C.C. (3d) 399, (Ont. C.J.).

[75]   See e.g. *R. v. Nikolovski*, [1996] 3 S.C.R. 1197, 111 C.C.C. (3d) 403, 3 C.R. (5th) 362 (S.C.C.) ("It is clear that a trier of fact may, despite all the potential frailties, find an accused guilty beyond a reasonable doubt on the basis of the testimony of a single eyewitness" at para. 23).

By now it is clear that *Hay* upsets settled authority in several respects. Yet, the language of Rothstein J. in the passage above offers no hint that he is changing the law. Even Fish J. in his concurring reasons seemed to understate the point when he noted that the law respecting eyewitness identification "is more certain now than it was at the time of trial".[76] In fact, the pre-existing law was not particularly uncertain as a matter of precedent; it was uncertain only to the extent that it cried out for reform as a matter of legal policy. Given that eyewitness misidentification is known to contribute greatly to the phenomenon of wrongful convictions,[77] the former law was unwise to prevent trial judges from throwing out the weakest identification cases without giving juries a chance to convict. Fortunately, in *Hay*, the Supreme Court has begun to rectify this problem by empowering judges to stop the prosecution of the weakest identification cases before the verdict stage.

Still, the circumstances of *Hay* demonstrate that the Court has not yet gone far enough. The Court unanimously ordered a new trial and made it clear that a directed verdict of acquittal would not be appropriate in the *Hay* case because the Crown's case on identity did not consist *solely* of the weak eyewitness identification evidence. Rather, there was of physical evidence — bullets and gunshot residue found in a hamper in the accused's bedroom and hair clipping evidence in the accused's bedroom and a nearby bathroom — that provided some support for the identification of the accused as the second shooter in the murder. However, these items of physical evidence could be easily explained away: the bullets and gunshot residue might have been placed in the hamper by the co-accused E., who was in the accused's home after the murder, and the uncontested forensic evidence demonstrated that the hair clippings were not (as argued by the trial Crown) indicative of the head shave that would account for the difference between the accused's short hair and the dreadlocks worn by the second shooter. Viewed fairly, the physical evidence amounted to lamentably weak evidence of identity. Consequently, the accused's fate inescapably depended (and will continue to depend, at any retrial) on the jury's view of the eyewitness identification evidence.

The problem, then, lies in the narrowness of Rothstein J.'s holding that "where the Crown's case consists *solely* of eyewitness testimony that would necessarily leave reasonable doubt in the mind of a reasonable juror, the trial judge must direct an acquittal upon a motion for directed verdict."[78] Regrettably, this holding leaves it open to the Crown to avoid a directed verdict of acquittal in a weak eyewitness identification case by pointing to some shred of corroborating evidence. One may hope that, in future, the Supreme Court will go one step further and decide that a directed verdict of acquittal should be ordered whenever the Crown's case *substantially depends* on eyewitness identification evidence that is incapable of amounting to proof of identity beyond a reasonable doubt.

---

[76]   *Hay, supra* note 67 at para. 82.
[77]   See e.g. *R. v. Hibbert*, [2002] 2 S.C.R. 445, 163 C.C.C. (3d) 129, 50 C.R. (5th) 209 (S.C.C.) ("The danger of wrongful conviction arising from faulty but apparently persuasive eyewitness identification has been well documented" at para. 51).
[78]   *Hay, supra* note 67 at para. 41 [emphasis added].

As noted earlier, in some cases there will be an evidential burden on the defence to ensure that there is sufficient evidence to put a defence in play.

R. v. CINOUS
[2002] 2 S.C.R. 3, 49 C.R. (5th) 209

The accused was charged with the first degree murder of a criminal accomplice, Mike. The accused testified that he and a friend had been involved in the theft and resale of computers along with Mike and another accomplice, Ice. About one month before the killing, he became convinced that Mike had stolen his gun. He told Mike and Ice that he wanted no more to do with them but they kept calling about doing thefts. He also testified that shortly after the gun went missing he began to hear rumours that Mike and Ice wanted to kill him, and that he was warned by a friend to watch out for them. One morning Mike and Ice called and asked the accused to participate in a computer theft. He agreed to meet with them that evening at his apartment. The accused testified that when they arrived, they kept their jackets on and whispered to one another as they sat in the living room. He saw Ice constantly placing his hand inside his coat. That made him suspect they were armed. The accused said he decided to participate in the theft to see if they really intended to kill him. They left the apartment and got into the accused's van to drive to the location of the theft. The accused said that he knew Mike and Ice wanted to kill him when he saw they had changed their gloves. Neither had changed to the black woollen gloves kept in the van compartment for computer thefts. Mike was wearing surgical latex gloves the accused associated with situations where bloodshed was expected. He had twice before seen them used on "burns" — attacks on criminals by other criminals. The accused drove. Ice sat next to him and Mike sat behind Ice. The accused testified Ice avoided making eye contact with him and kept touching his jacket as if he had a gun. He said he interpreted Ice's hand inside his jacket as a threat. The accused admitted that no other threats were made. The accused testified that he was sure that he was going to be killed and that the shot would more than likely come from behind — from Mike. Since he was driving, he could not get to his own gun quickly enough, were anything to happen. He felt trapped. He pulled into a populated and well-lit gas station to "release the pressure" and get himself out of this bad situation. He bought a bottle of windshield washer fluid after returning to the van to get money from Ice. He poured the fluid in under the hood and brought the bottle back around to the back of the van. He opened the back door, "saw the opportunity", pulled out his gun and shot Mike in the back of the head. The accused testified that this was an instinctive reaction to a situation of danger. It did not occur to him to run away or to call the police.

Per MCLACHLIN C.J.C. and BASTARACHE J. (L'HEUREUX-DUBÉ, GONTHIER, BINNIE, LEBEL JJ. concurring):—

Air of Reality

The key issue is whether there was an air of reality to the defence of self-defence in this case. It is our view that there is no air of reality to the defence: a properly instructed jury acting reasonably could not acquit the accused on the ground of self-defence, even if it accepted his testimonial evidence as true. Since the defence should never have been put to the jury, any errors made in the charge to the jury relating to that defence are irrelevant. The curative proviso of s. 686(1)(b)(iii) should be applied, and the conviction upheld. This Court has considered the air of reality test on numerous occasions. The core elements of the test, as well as its nature and purpose, have by now been clearly and authoritatively set out. See *R. v. Osolin*, [1993] 4 S.C.R. 595; *R. v. Park*, [1995] 2 S.C.R. 836; *R. v. Davis*, [1999] 3 S.C.R. 759. Nevertheless, a controversy has arisen in this case concerning the extent of a trial judge's discretion to keep from a jury defences that are fanciful or far-fetched. More narrowly, the contentious issue is the correct evidential standard to be applied in determining whether there is an air of reality to the defence of self-defence on the facts of this case. In our view, the controversy can be resolved on the basis of existing authority, which we consider to be decisive. The correct approach to the air of reality test is well established. The test is whether there is evidence on the record upon which a properly instructed jury acting reasonably could acquit. . . This long-standing formulation of the threshold question for putting defences to the jury accords with the nature and purpose of the air of reality test. We consider that there is nothing to be gained by altering the current state of the law, in which a single clearly-stated test applies to all defences. . . There is no need to invent a new test, to modify the current test, or to apply different tests to different classes of cases.

(1)   The Basic Features of the Air of Reality Test

The principle that a defence should be put to a jury if and only if there is an evidential foundation for it has long been recognized by the common law. This venerable rule reflects the practical concern that allowing a defence to go to the jury in the absence of an evidential foundation would invite verdicts not supported by the evidence, serving only to confuse the jury and get in the way of a fair trial and true verdict. Following Pappajohn . . . the inquiry into whether there is an evidential foundation for a defence is referred to as the air of reality test. . . The basic requirement of an evidential foundation for defences gives rise to two well-established principles. First, a trial judge must put to the jury all defences that arise on the facts, whether or not they have been specifically raised by an accused. Where there is an air of reality to a defence, it should go to the jury. Second, a trial judge has a positive duty to keep from the jury defences lacking an evidential foundation. A defence that lacks an air of reality should be kept from the jury. . . This is so even when the defence lacking an air of reality represents the accused's only chance for an acquittal, as illustrated by *R. v. Latimer*, [2001] 1 S.C.R. 3. It is trite law that the air of reality test imposes a burden on the accused that is merely evidential, rather than persuasive. Dickson C.J. drew attention to the distinction between these two types of burden in *R. v. Schwartz*, [1988] 2 S.C.R. 443. . . The air of reality test is concerned only with whether or not a putative defence should be "put in play", that is, submitted to the jury for consideration. This idea was crucial to the finding in *Osolin* that the air of reality test is consistent with the presumption of innocence guaranteed by s. 11(d) of the *Canadian Charter of Rights and Freedoms*. In applying the air of reality test, a trial judge considers the totality of the evidence, and assumes the evidence relied upon by the accused to be true. . . The evidential foundation can be indicated by evidence emanating from the examination-in-chief or cross-examination of the accused, of defence witnesses, or of Crown witnesses. It can also rest upon the factual circumstances of the case or from any other evidential source on the record. There is no requirement that the evidence be adduced by the accused. . . The threshold determination by the trial judge is not aimed at deciding the substantive merits of the defence. That question is reserved for the jury. . . The trial judge does not make determinations about the credibility of witnesses, weigh the evidence, make findings of fact, or draw determinate factual inferences. . . Nor is the air of reality test intended to assess whether the defence is likely, unlikely, somewhat likely, or very likely to succeed at the end of the day. The question for the trial judge is whether the evidence discloses a real issue to be decided by the jury, and not how the jury should ultimately decide the issue. Whether or not there is an air of reality to a defence is a question of law, subject to appellate review. It is an error of law to put to the jury a defence lacking an air of reality, just as it is an error of law to keep from the jury a defence that has an air of reality. See *Osolin*, supra; *Park*, supra; *Davis*, supra. The statements that "there is an air of reality" to a defence and that a defence "lacks an air of reality" express a legal conclusion about the presence or absence of an evidential foundation for a defence. The considerations discussed above have led this Court to reject unequivocally the argument that the air of reality test licenses an encroachment by trial judges on the jury's traditional function as arbiter of fact. As Cory J. stated in *Osolin*, supra, at p. 682-3:

> This is no more than an example of the basic division of tasks between judge and jury. . . The charge to the jury must be directed to the essential elements of the crime with which the accused is charged and defences to it. Speculative defences that are unfounded should not be presented to the jury. To do so would be wrong, confusing, and unnecessarily lengthen jury trials.

This Court has held on many occasions that a single air of reality test applies to all defences. The test has been applied uniformly to a wide range of defences over the years. These include the defence of honest but mistaken belief in consent in sexual assault cases (*Pappajohn..*; *Ewanchuk*, supra; *Davis*, supra), and other defences such as intoxication (*R. v. Robinson*, [1996] 1 S.C.R. 683. . ., necessity (*Latimer*, supra), duress (*R. v. Ruzic*, [2001] 1 S.C.R. 687), provocation (*R. v. Thibert*, [1996] 1 S.C.R. 37), and self-defence (*Brisson v. The Queen*, [1982] 2 S.C.R. 227 . . .). Adopting different evidential standards for different classes of cases would constitute a sharp break with the authorities.

BINNIE J.: —

I concur with the Chief Justice and Bastarache J., and with the reasons they have given, that the appeal should be allowed. I add these paragraphs on what I think is the decisive point.

My colleagues have mobilized considerable scholarship for and against all aspects of the issues. When the smoke clears, this appeal comes down to a simple proposition. A criminal code that permitted preemptive killings within a criminal organization on the bare assertion by the killer that no course of action was reasonably available to him while standing outside a motor vehicle other than to put a shot in the back of the head of another member sitting inside the parked vehicle at a well-lit and populated gas station is a criminal code that would fail in its most basic purpose of promoting public order.

The respondent says he did not consider going to the police, although he was outside the car and in a position to flee the scene. He said "I never called the police in my life". Even if the police unexpectedly got there before a shoot-out, they would ask for some information in return for protection. "That's how it works", he said. Accordingly, there was evidence that subjectively, as a self-styled criminal, he felt his only options were to kill or be killed. He wishes the jury to judge the reasonableness of his conduct by the rules of his criminal subculture, which is the antithesis of public order.

A trial judge should be very slow to take a defence away from a jury. We all agree on that. Here, however, the only way the defence could succeed is if the jury climbed into the skin of the respondent and accepted as reasonable a sociopathic view of appropriate dispute resolution.

In dissent Arbour J. (Iacobucci and Major JJ. concurring) sought to revise the approach of the Supreme Court, mainly on the Chief Justice's detailed analysis that the air of reality test developed in the context of the mistaken belief defence in sexual assault cases had departed from the common law "no evidence" test for withdrawal from the jury in favour of one of sufficiency of evidence which had usurped the fact-finding function of juries. The "no evidence" test should be adopted for defences such as self-defence especially where there were no special technical or policy considerations, no alternative defences and where it was the accused's only defence.[79]

In *R. c. Fontaine*[80] the Supreme Court of Canada confirmed that the air of reality test articulated in *Cinous* applies to all defences, even if the accused bears the persuasive burden of proving the defence.

---

[79] See comment by Stuart, "*Cinous*: The Air of Reality Test Requires Weak Defences to Be Withdrawn from Juries" (2002), 49 C.R. (5th) 392. The Supreme Court has since frequently relied on *Cinous* and its air of reality test to withdraw defences from juries: see e.g. Stuart, "The Supreme Court Strangles the Defence of Provocation" (2014), 5 C.R. (7th) 249.

[80] [2004] 1 S.C.R. 702, 18 C.R. (6th) 203, 183 C.C.C. (3d) 1 (S.C.C.).

(ii) *Civil Cases*

In civil cases, there are two stages at which the plaintiff's case is screened. Prior to trial, the defendant can bring a motion for summary judgment.

HRYNIAK v. MAULDIN
2014 CSC 7, 2014 SCC 7, [2014] 1 S.C.R. 87 (S.C.C.)

1 KARAKATSANIS J.:— Ensuring access to justice is the greatest challenge to the rule of law in Canada today. Trials have become increasingly expensive and protracted. Most Canadians cannot afford to sue when they are wronged or defend themselves when they are sued, and cannot afford to go to trial. Without an effective and accessible means of enforcing rights, the rule of law is threatened. Without public adjudication of civil cases, the development of the common law is stunted.

2 Increasingly, there is recognition that a culture shift is required in order to create an environment promoting timely and affordable access to the civil justice system. This shift entails simplifying pre-trial procedures and moving the emphasis away from the conventional trial in favour of proportional procedures tailored to the needs of the particular case. The balance between procedure and access struck by our justice system must come to reflect modern reality and recognize that new models of adjudication can be fair and just.

3 Summary judgment motions provide one such opportunity. Following the *Civil Justice Reform Project: Summary of Findings and Recommendations* (2007) (the Osborne Report), Ontario amended the *Rules of Civil Procedure*, R.R.O. 1990, Reg. 194 (*Ontario Rules* or Rules) to increase access to justice. This appeal, and its companion, *Bruno Appliance and Furniture, Inc. v. Hryniak*, 2014 SCC 8, address the proper interpretation of the amended Rule 20 (summary judgment motion).

4 In interpreting these provisions, the Ontario Court of Appeal placed too high a premium on the "full appreciation" of evidence that can be gained at a conventional trial, given that such a trial is not a realistic alternative for most litigants. In my view, a trial is not required if a summary judgment motion can achieve a fair and just adjudication, if it provides a process that allows the judge to make the necessary findings of fact, apply the law to those facts, and is a proportionate, more expeditious and less expensive means to achieve a just result than going to trial.

5 To that end, I conclude that summary judgment rules must be interpreted broadly, favouring proportionality and fair access to the affordable, timely and just adjudication of claims.

6 As the Court of Appeal observed, the inappropriate use of summary judgment motions creates its own costs and delays. However, judges can mitigate such risks by making use of their powers to manage and focus the process and, where possible, remain seized of the proceedings.

7 While I differ in part on the interpretation of Rule 20, I agree with the Court of Appeal's disposition of the matter and would dismiss the appeal.

. . .

IV.   Analysis

A.   *Access to Civil Justice: A Necessary Culture Shift*

23 This appeal concerns the values and choices underlying our civil justice system, and the ability of ordinary Canadians to access that justice. Our civil justice system is premised upon the value that the process of adjudication must be fair and just. This cannot be compromised.

24 However, undue process and protracted trials, with unnecessary expense and delay, can *prevent* the fair and just resolution of disputes. The full trial has become largely illusory because, except where government funding is available, ordinary Canadians cannot afford to access the adjudication of civil disputes. The cost and delay associated with the traditional process means that, as counsel for the intervener the Advocates' Society (in *Bruno Appliance*) stated at the hearing of this appeal, the trial process denies ordinary people the opportunity to have adjudication. And while going to trial has long been seen as a last resort, other dispute resolution mechanisms such as mediation and settlement are more likely to produce fair and just results when adjudication remains a realistic alternative.

25 Prompt judicial resolution of legal disputes allows individuals to get on with their lives. But, when court costs and delays become too great, people look for alternatives or simply give up on justice. Sometimes, they choose to represent themselves, often creating further problems due to their lack of familiarity with the law.

26 In some circles, private arbitration is increasingly seen as an alternative to a slow judicial process. But private arbitration is not the solution since, without an accessible public forum for the adjudication of disputes, the rule of law is threatened and the development of the common law undermined.

27 There is growing support for alternative adjudication of disputes and a developing consensus that the traditional balance struck by extensive pre-trial processes and the conventional trial no longer reflects the modern reality and needs to be re-adjusted. A proper balance requires simplified and proportionate procedures for adjudication, and impacts the role of counsel and judges. This balance must recognize that a process can be fair and just, without the expense and delay of a trial, and that alternative models of adjudication are no less legitimate than the conventional trial.

28 This requires a shift in culture. The principal goal remains the same: a fair process that results in a just adjudication of disputes. A fair and just process must permit a judge to find the facts necessary to resolve the dispute and to apply the relevant legal principles to the facts as found. However, that process is illusory unless it is also accessible—proportionate, timely and affordable.

The proportionality principle means that the best forum for resolving a dispute is not always that with the most painstaking procedure.

29 There is, of course, always some tension between accessibility and the truth-seeking function but, much as one would not expect a jury trial over a contested parking ticket, the procedures used to adjudicate civil disputes must fit the nature of the claim. If the process is disproportionate to the nature of the dispute and the interests involved, then it will not achieve a fair and just result.

. . .

32 This culture shift requires judges to actively manage the legal process in line with the principle of proportionality. While summary judgment motions can save time and resources, like most pre-trial procedures, they can also slow down the proceedings if used inappropriately. While judges can and should play a role in controlling such risks, counsel must, in accordance with the traditions of their profession, act in a way that facilitates rather than frustrates access to justice. Lawyers should consider their client's limited means and the nature of their case and fashion proportionate means to achieve a fair and just result.

33 A complex claim may involve an extensive record and a significant commitment of time and expense. However, proportionality is inevitably comparative; even slow and expensive procedures can be proportionate when they are the fastest and most efficient alternative. The question is whether the added expense and delay of fact finding at trial is necessary to a fair process and just adjudication.

B.   Summary Judgment Motions

34 The summary judgment motion is an important tool for enhancing access to justice because it can provide a cheaper, faster alternative to a full trial. With the exception of Quebec, all provinces feature a summary judgment mechanism in their respective rules of civil procedure. Generally, summary judgment is available where there is no genuine issue for trial.

35 Rule 20 is Ontario's summary judgment procedure, under which a party may move for summary judgment to grant or dismiss all or part of a claim. While, Ontario's Rule 20 in some ways goes further than other rules throughout the country, the values and principles underlying its interpretation are of general application.

36 Rule 20 was amended in 2010, following the recommendations of the Osborne Report, to improve access to justice. These reforms embody the evolution of summary judgment rules from highly restricted tools used to weed out clearly unmeritorious claims or defences to their current status as a legitimate alternative means for adjudicating and resolving legal disputes.

37 Early summary judgment rules were quite limited in scope and were available only to plaintiffs with claims based on debt or liquidated damages, where no real defence existed. Summary judgment existed to avoid the waste of a full trial in a clear case.

38 In 1985, the then new Rule 20 extended the availability of summary judgement to both plaintiffs and defendants and broadened the scope of cases that could be disposed of on such a motion. The rules were initially interpreted expansively, in line with the purposes of the rule changes. However, appellate jurisprudence limited the powers of judges and effectively narrowed the purpose of motions for summary judgment to merely ensuring that: "claims that have no chance of success [are] weeded out at an early stage".

. . .

42 Rule 20.04 now reads in part:

> **20.04** ...
>
> (2) [General] The court shall grant summary judgment if,
>
> > (a) the court is satisfied that there is no genuine issue requiring a trial with respect to a claim or defence; or
> >
> > (b) the parties agree to have all or part of the claim determined by a summary judgment and the court is satisfied that it is appropriate to grant summary judgment.
>
> (2.1) [Powers] In determining under clause (2) (a) whether there is a genuine issue requiring a trial, the court shall consider the evidence submitted by the parties and, if the determination is being made by a judge, the judge may exercise any of the following powers for the purpose, unless it is in the interest of justice for such powers to be exercised only at a trial:
>
> > 1. Weighing the evidence.
> >
> > 2. Evaluating the credibility of a deponent.
> >
> > 3. Drawing any reasonable inference from the evidence.
>
> (2.2) [Oral Evidence (Mini-Trial)] A judge may, for the purposes of exercising any of the powers set out in subrule (2.1), order that oral evidence be presented by one or more parties, with or without time limits on its presentation.

43 The Ontario amendments changed the test for summary judgment from asking whether the case presents "a genuine issue <u>for</u> trial" to asking whether there is a "genuine issue requiring a trial". The new rule, with its enhanced fact-finding powers, demonstrates that a trial is not the default procedure. Further, it eliminated the presumption of substantial indemnity costs against a party that brought an unsuccessful motion for summary judgment, in order to avoid deterring the use of the procedure.

44 The new powers in Rules 20.04(2.1) and (2.2) expand the number of cases in which there will be no genuine issue requiring a trial by permitting motion judges to weigh evidence, evaluate credibility and draw reasonable inferences.

45 These new fact-finding powers are discretionary and are presumptively available; they may be exercised *unless* it is in the interest of justice for them to be exercised only at a trial; Rule 20.04(2.1). Thus, the amendments are designed to transform Rule 20 from a means to weed out unmeritorious claims to a significant alternative model of adjudication.

46 I will first consider when summary judgment can be granted on the basis that there is "no genuine issue requiring a trial" (Rule 20.04(2)(a)). Second, I will discuss when it is against the "interest of justice" for the new fact-finding powers in Rule 20.04(2.1) to be used on a summary judgment motion. Third, I will consider the power to call oral evidence and, finally, I will lay out the process to be followed on a motion for summary judgment.

(1)   When is There no Genuine Issue Requiring a Trial?

47 Summary judgment motions must be granted whenever there is no genuine issue requiring a trial (Rule 20.04(2)(a)). In outlining how to determine whether there is such an issue, I focus on the goals and principles that underlie whether to grant motions for summary judgment. Such an approach allows the application of the rule to evolve organically, lest categories of cases be taken as rules or preconditions which may hinder the system's transformation by discouraging the use of summary judgment.

. . .

49 There will be no genuine issue requiring a trial when the judge is able to reach a fair and just determination on the merits on a motion for summary judgment. This will be the case when the process (1) allows the judge to make the necessary findings of fact, (2) allows the judge to apply the law to the facts, and (3) is a proportionate, more expeditious and less expensive means to achieve a just result.

50 These principles are interconnected and all speak to whether summary judgment will provide a fair and just adjudication. When a summary judgment motion allows the judge to find the necessary facts and resolve the dispute, proceeding to trial would generally not be proportionate, timely or cost effective. Similarly, a process that does not give a judge confidence in her conclusions can never be the proportionate way to resolve a dispute. It bears reiterating that the standard for fairness is not whether the procedure is as exhaustive as a trial, but whether it gives the judge confidence that she can find the necessary facts and apply the relevant legal principles so as to resolve the dispute.

51 Often, concerns about credibility or clarification of the evidence can be addressed by calling oral evidence on the motion itself. However, there may be cases where, given the nature of the issues and the evidence required, the judge cannot make the necessary findings of fact, or apply the legal principles to reach a just and fair determination.

. . .

(4)   The Roadmap/Approach to a Motion for Summary Judgment

66 On a motion for summary judgment under Rule 20.04, the judge should first determine if there is a genuine issue requiring trial based only on the evidence before her, *without* using the new fact-finding powers. There will be no genuine issue requiring a trial if the summary judgment process provides her with the evidence required to fairly and justly adjudicate the dispute and is a timely, affordable and proportionate procedure, under Rule 20.04(2)(a). If there appears to be a genuine issue requiring a trial, she should then determine if the need for a trial can be avoided by using the new powers under Rules 20.04(2.1) and (2.2). She may, at her discretion, use those powers, provided that their use is not against the interest of justice. Their use will not be against the interest of justice if they will lead to a fair and just result and will serve the goals of timeliness, affordability and proportionality in light of the litigation as a whole.

67 Inquiring first as to whether the use of the powers under Rule 20.04(2.1) will allow the dispute to be resolved by way of summary judgment, before asking whether the interest of justice requires that those powers be exercised only at trial, emphasizes that these powers are presumptively available, rather than exceptional, in line with the goal of proportionate, cost-effective and timely dispute resolution. As well, by first determining the consequences of using the new powers, the benefit of their use is clearer. This will assist in determining whether it is in the interest of justice that they be exercised only at trial.

68 While summary judgment *must* be granted if there is no genuine issue requiring a trial, the decision to use either the expanded fact-finding powers or to call oral evidence is discretionary. The discretionary nature of this power gives the judge some flexibility in deciding the appropriate course of action. This discretion can act as a safety valve in cases where the use of such powers would clearly be inappropriate. There is always the risk that clearly unmeritorious motions for summary judgment could be abused and used tactically to add time and expense. In such cases, the motion judge may choose to decline to exercise her discretion to use those powers and dismiss the motion for summary judgment, without engaging in the full inquiry delineated above.

A defendant can also bring a motion at trial for non-suit to challenge the sufficiency of the evidence submitted by the plaintiff.

FL RECEIVABLES TRUST v. COBRAND FOODS LTD.
2007 ONCA 425, 85 O.R. (3d) 561 (C.A.)

Laskin J.A. (Borins and Feldman JJ.A. concurring:—

. . .

[12] Before addressing Robert Laba's submission, I want to say a few words about non-suit motions in civil non-jury trials. The term "non-suit" refers to a motion brought by the defendant at the close of the plaintiff's evidence to dismiss the action on the ground that the plaintiff has failed to make out a case for the defendant to answer. Neither the *Courts of Justice Act*, R.S.O. 1990, c. C.43, nor the *Rules of Civil Procedure* specifically provides for non-suit motions, but judges continue to have a recognized jurisdiction to entertain these motions.

[13] Still, I question whether in this province a non-suit motion in a civil non-jury trial has much value. In Ontario, when a defendant moves for a non-suit, the defendant must elect whether to call evidence. See *Ontario v. Ontario Public Service Employees Union (OPSEU)* (1990), 37 O.A.C. 218 at para. 40 (Div. Ct.). If the defendant elects to call evidence, the judge reserves on the motion until the end of the case. If the defendant elects to call no evidence — as Robert Laba elected in this case — then the judge rules on the motion immediately after it has been made.

[14] A non-suit motion adds to the time and expense of a trial. And because of the election requirement, it has little practical value. Perhaps a defendant bringing the motion sees a tactical advantage in being able to argue first. To succeed on the motion, however, the defendant must show that the plaintiff has put forward no case to answer, in most lawsuits an onerous task. Why not simply take on the less onerous task of showing that the plaintiff's claim should fail? It is small wonder that most commentators consider that in civil judge alone trials, non-suit motions gain little and are becoming obsolete. See *Phipson on Evidence*, 16th ed. (London: Sweet & Maxwell, 2005) at 274, and John Sopinka, Donald B. Houston & Melanie Sopinka, *The Trial of an Action*, 2d ed. (Toronto: Butterworths Canada, 1999) at 151-52.

. . .

[35] On a non-suit motion, the trial judge undertakes a limited inquiry. Two relevant principles that guide this inquiry are these. First, if a plaintiff puts forward some evidence on all elements of its claim, the judge must dismiss the motion. Second, in assessing whether a plaintiff has made out a *prima facie* case, the judge must assume the evidence to be true and must assign "the most favourable meaning" to evidence capable of giving rise to competing inferences. This court discussed this latter principle in *Hall et al. v. Pemberton* (1974), 5 O.R. (2d) 438 at 438-9, quoting *Parfitt v. Lawless* (1872), 41 L.J.P. & M. 68 at 71-72:

> I conceive, therefore, that in judging whether there is in any case evidence for a jury the Judge must weigh the evidence given, must assign what he conceives to be the most favourable meaning which can reasonably be attributed to any ambiguous statements, and determine on the whole what tendency the evidence has to establish the issue.

> . . .

> From every fact that is proved, legitimate and reasonable inferences may of course be drawn, and all that is fairly deducible from the evidence is as much proved, for the purpose of a *prima facie* case, as if it had been proved directly. I conceive, therefore, that in discussing whether there is in any case evidence to go to the jury, what the Court has to consider is this, whether, assuming the evidence to be true, and adding to the direct proof all such inferences of fact as in the exercise of a reasonable intelligence the jury would be warranted in drawing from it, there is sufficient to support the issue.

[36] In other words, on a non-suit motion the trial judge should not determine whether the competing inferences available to the defendant on the evidence rebut the plaintiff's *prima facie* case. The trial judge should make that

determination at the end of the trial, not on the non-suit motion. See John Sopinka, Sidney N. Lederman & Alan W. Bryant, *The Law of Evidence in Canada*, 2d ed. (Toronto: Butterworths Canada, 1999) at 139.

As noted in *FL Receivables*, the defendant must elect not to call a defence if he or she wants an immediate ruling on his or her motion for non-suit. The same is true in cases before administrative tribunals. This is very different from the procedure in criminal cases. **Does it raise any concerns?**

The possibility of the motion for a non-suit being rendered redundant by the existing practice at civil law is bothersome. Although we do not speak of the defendant in a civil case having any right to silence, there seems to be some worth in his or her ability to have a judicial ruling as to whether the plaintiff has adduced sufficient evidence to warrant calling on the defence for a response. The plaintiff has made certain allegations in his or her statement of claim and seeks to disturb the *status quo*. The defendant should have the right to refuse to answer spurious claims.

The courts have evidently created their present practice out of concern that there may be unnecessary effort and expenses flowing from new trials when the trial judge rules incorrectly on a motion. If we posit the thought that trial judges are more often right than wrong, a change in the existing practice would be even more efficient. If there is no case to meet, the defendant is not put to the expense and effort of presenting a defence and the trial tribunal's time is not wasted. The procedure ought to be the same in civil and criminal cases and the plaintiff's claim vetted by a judicial officer before the defendant need determine whether he or she cares to answer.

2. PRESUMPTIONS

(a) Introduction

> Every writer of sufficient intelligence to appreciate the difficulties of the subject-matter has approached the topic of presumptions with a sense of hopelessness and has left it with a feeling of despair.[81]

Stanley presumed from certain basic facts that the man he was addressing was Dr. Livingstone. So, too, all presumptions in the law of evidence describe a process or a legal consequence whereby we infer the existence of a presumed fact when certain other basic facts have been established by evidence; the inference from the evidentiary fact is usually taken as a result of our own sense of logic or our own sense of experience but at times it may be statutorily or judicially directed to accommodate some extrinsic policy consideration.

The literature on the subject of presumptions is extensive and much of it is devoted to attempts to minimize the confusion by demonstrating the misuse or overuse of the term "presumption".[82]

---

[81]   Morgan, "Presumptions" (1937) 12 Wash. L. Rev. 255.
[82]   Among the classic expositions on the subject are Cleary, "Presuming and Pleading: An Essay

Professor Thayer, on whose thesis all other writers have built,[83] described presumptions as follows:

> Presumptions are aids to reasoning and argumentation, which assume the truth of certain matters for the purpose of some given inquiry. They may be grounded on general experience, or probability of any kind; or merely on policy and convenience. On whatever basis they rest, they operate in advance of argument or evidence, or irrespective of it, by taking something for granted; by assuming its existence. When the term is legitimately applied it designates a rule or a proposition which still leaves open to further inquiry the matter thus assumed. The exact scope and operation of these *prima facie* assumptions are to cast upon the party against whom they operate, the duty of going forward, in argument or evidence, on the particular point to which they relate. . . Presumption, assumption, taking for granted, are simply so many names for an act or process which aids and shortens inquiry and argument. . . Such is the nature of all rules to determine the legal effect of facts as contrasted with their logical effect. To prescribe and fix a certain legal equivalence of facts, is a very different thing from merely allowing that meaning to be given to them. A rule of presumption does not merely say that such and such a thing is a permissible and usual inference from other facts, but it goes on to say that this significance shall always, in the absence of other circumstances, be imputed to them, — sometimes passing first through the stage of saying that it *ought to be* imputed.[84]

Later writers interpreted the Thayerian view of presumptions as the "bursting bubble theory", meaning that the effect of any presumption was spent when the opponent led any evidence.[85] But Thayer never suggested that all presumptions should have this minimal effect, and he recognized that, depending on the need or purpose which gave rise to a recognition of the particular presumption, the onus on the opponent would vary. Later in his *Treatise* he wrote:

> How much evidence shall be required from the adversary to meet the presumption, or, as it is variously expressed, to overcome it or destroy it, is determined by no fixed rule. It may be merely enough to make it reasonable to require the other side to answer; it may be enough to make out a full *prima facie* case, and it may be a great weight of evidence, excluding all reasonable doubt. A mere presumption involves no rule as to the weight of evidence necessary to meet it. When a presumption is called a strong one, like the presumption of legitimacy, it means that it is accompanied by another rule relating to the weight of evidence to be brought in by him against whom it operates.[86]

on Juristic Immaturity" (1959) 12 Stan. L. Rev. 5; Stone, "Burden of Proof and the Judicial Process" (1944) 60 L.Q.R. 262; Morgan, "Some Observations Concerning Presumptions" (1931) 44 Harv. L. Rev. 906; McBaine, "Burden of Proof: Presumptions" (1955) 2 U.C.L.A. Law Rev. 13; Bohlen, "The Effect of Rebuttable Presumptions of Law Upon the Burden of Proof" (1920) 68 U. Pa. L. Rev. 307; Denning, "Presumptions and Burdens" (1945) 61 L.Q.R. 379. And see Helman, "Presumptions" (1944) 22 Can. Bar Rev. 117.

[83]   Interestingly, Wigmore refers to him simply as "the master in the law of evidence": 9 Wigmore, *Evidence* (Chad. Rev.), s. 2511 at 533.

[84]   Thayer, *supra* note 7 at 314-317.

[85]   Cleary points out that this was due to "tearing his statement from its context, and popularized by Wigmore": *supra* note 82 at 18. And see Helman, *supra* note 82 at 122.

[86]   Thayer, *supra* note 7 at 575-576.

From this framework we can profitably limit the use of the term presumption and so minimize the confusion.

(b) False Presumptions

Professor Thayer notes that the term "presumption" is legitimately used only when the matter presumed is left open to further inquiry. It is sometimes said that given certain facts other facts shall be "conclusively presumed". For example, at common law it was said that a child under seven years of age was conclusively presumed to be incapable of the commission of a crime; he was *doli incapax*.The *Criminal Code* provides that "a place that is found to be equipped with a slot machine shall be conclusively presumed to be a common gaming house".[87] In truth these are not presumptions apportioning burdens of proof, but rather rules of substantive law; a "conclusive presumption" is a contradiction in terms. On proof of the basic fact the so-called "presumed fact" in such a case is actually immaterial; if the prosecution proves that the place was equipped with a slot machine the substantive law provides for conviction and whether the place is a common gaming house or not is immaterial.[88] It would be best then, in our quest to minimize confusion, to discard the use of the term "conclusive presumption". The above section could simply be reworded to provide that "a place that is found to be equipped with a slot machine is a common gaming house".

At the other end of the scale, we note that Thayer would deny the use of the term presumption to describe simply the permissible inference which flows from the logical effect of certain facts. For him a presumption *demands* an effect unless the opponent does something. When a material fact *may* be inferred from basic facts proved, as opposed to *must*, it would be best to label such simply as a justifiable inference. The cases sometimes refer to this process as a presumption of fact as opposed to a presumption of law, or a permissive presumption as opposed to a compelling presumption, but this is misleading and can be dangerous. Let us take two examples: the presumption that persons intend the natural consequences of their acts, and the "doctrine" of recent possession.

When a criminal offence requires the mental element of intention, the prosecution will need to establish the same, barring a confession, by proof of the accused's actions, asking the jury to infer from such actions that the requisite state of mind existed. The best statement of the process is by Lord Goddard in *R. v. Steane*: [89]

> No doubt, if the prosecution prove an act, the natural consequence of which would be a certain result and no evidence or explanation is given, then a jury may, on a proper direction, find that the prisoner is guilty of doing the act with the intent alleged, but if on the totality of the evidence there is room for more than one view as to the intent of the prisoner, the jury should be directed that it is for the prosecution to prove the intent to the jury's satisfaction, and if, on a review of

---

[87]   Section 198(2).
[88]   See 9 Wigmore, *Evidence* (Chad. Rev.), s. 2492.
[89]   [1947] 1 K.B. 997 (C.C.A.) at 1004.

the whole evidence, they either think that the intent did not exist or they are left in doubt as to the intent, the prisoner is entitled to be acquitted.

To explain this to the jury, judges have occasionally advised them that persons are presumed to intend the natural consequences of their acts. Lord Denning explained, however:

> When people say that a man must be taken to intend the natural consequences of his acts, they fall into error: there is no "must" about it; it is only "may." The presumption of intention is not a proposition of law but a proposition of ordinary good sense. It means this: that, as a man is usually able to foresee what are the natural consequences of his acts, so it is, as a rule, reasonable to infer that he did foresee them and intend them. But, while that is an inference which may be drawn, it is not one which must be drawn. If on all the facts of the case it is not the correct inference, then it should not be drawn.[90]

In *R. v. Ortt*,[91] a murder prosecution, the trial judge instructed the jury in terms of the presumption and Jessup J.A., delivering the opinion of the Ontario Court of Appeal, wrote:

> It has been held by this Court that it is error in law to tell a jury it is a presumption of law that a person intends the natural consequences of his acts. . . Moreover the word "presumption" alone creates a difficulty in that it may suggest an onus on the accused. I agree with the comment of the authors of *Martin's Annual Criminal Code* (1968), p. 195:
>
> > The difficulty would not arise if the use of the word "presumption" were avoided. A presumption requires that a certain conclusion must be drawn, unless the accused takes steps to make that conclusion unwarranted. An inference, however, is no more than a matter of common sense and merely indicates that a certain conclusion may be drawn if warranted by the evidence. . .
>
> In my opinion, therefore, the word "presumption" is to be avoided in this context and juries simply told that generally it is a reasonable inference that a man intends the natural consequences of his acts so that when, for instance, a man points a gun at another and fires it the jury may reasonably infer that he meant either to cause his death or to cause him bodily harm that he knew was likely to cause death reckless of whether death ensued or not.[92]

In *Stapleton v. R.,*[93] Dixon C.J. of the Australian High Court was also critical of such a direction:

> The introduction of the maxim or statement that a man is presumed to intend the reasonable consequences of his act is seldom helpful and always dangerous. For it either does no more than state a self evident proposition of fact or it produces an illegitimate transfer of the burden of proof of a real issue of intent to the person denying the allegation.

The so-called legal doctrine of recent possession is also, on analysis, a matter of common sense and not of law.[94] An analysis of the early cases

---

90   *Hosegood v. Hosegood* (1950), 66 T.L.R. 735 (C.A.) at 738.
91   [1969] 1 O.R. 461 (C.A.).
92   *Ibid.* at 463. And see *R. v. Berger* (1975), 27 C.C.C. (2d) 357 (B.C. C.A.) at 383 per McIntyre J.A.
93   (1952), 86 C.L.R. 358 (H.C.) at 365.

involving charges of theft or possession of stolen goods shows the courts applying common sense to an evaluation of a piece of circumstantial evidence, namely, possession in the accused of the recently stolen goods. The early case of *Clement*[95] has no need for the language of presumption or doctrine. The entire report of the case reads:

> Prisoner was indicted for horse-stealing. The evidence was, that he had the horse in his possession in Kirkcudbright, three days after it had been stolen, in the county of Cumberland. Parke J. held this to be sufficient evidence of a stealing by the prisoner in Cumberland.

R. v. NICHOLL
(2004), 25 C.R. (6th) 192, 190 C.C.C. (3d) 549, (Ont. C.A.)

CRONK J.A. (LABROSSE and MACPHERSON JJ.A. concurring): —

The appellant was charged with seven offences on a single information: two counts of possession of stolen property, one count of break and enter, two counts of failing to comply with a probation order and two counts of failing to comply with an undertaking. He entered a plea of guilty to breach of an undertaking to inform the police of any change in his place of residence and not guilty to the remaining six charges.

On July 28, 2004, following a trial before Hachborn J. of the Ontario Court of Justice, the appellant was convicted on all counts and sentenced to one year imprisonment concurrent on all counts. He appeals his convictions on the first six counts and his sentence on all counts. If his appeal against conviction is dismissed, he seeks to have his overall sentence reduced to one of time served in light of the time that he has already served in custody.

The trial proceeded on the basis of an agreed statement of facts. No witnesses were called. The first six charges arose from the theft of a motor vehicle and a break and enter on the same day at a nearby high school where several cellos were stolen from the music department. Two weeks after the theft of the vehicle, municipal parking lot authorities reported the vehicle to the police as abandoned. When the police recovered the vehicle, the stolen cellos and a parking stub bearing a date five days after the date of the vehicles theft were inside the car. Three of the cellos were marked with the name of the high school from which the cellos had been stolen. The record does not establish whether the vehicle was locked or whether the windows of the vehicle were open or closed when the vehicle was recovered by the police.

At the time of the offences, the appellant was subject to probation and bail orders requiring that he keep the peace and abide by a curfew. He was also subject to an undertaking requiring that he notify the police of any change in his address.

Apart from the breach of undertaking charge to which the appellant pled guilty, the only evidence connecting the appellant to the offences was the

---

[94]   See *R. v. Smythe* (1980), 72 Cr. App. R. 8 (C.A.) at 11: "Nearly every reported case of recent possession is merely a decision of fact as an example of what is no more than a rule of evidence."

[95]   (1830), 168 E.R. 980.

presence of a single can of Coca Cola discovered by the police inside the stolen vehicle. The appellants thumb print was found on the can. The owner of the stolen vehicle confirmed that the pop can was not inside the vehicle prior to its theft.

The Crown asserted at trial that the doctrine of recent possession applied to the agreed facts and that, in the absence of any explanation from the appellant, the Crown had proven its case beyond a reasonable doubt based on the agreed facts. The Crown maintained that the presence of the pop can inside the stolen vehicle was sufficient to connect the appellant to the break and enter at the high school and the thefts of the cellos and the motor vehicle. In brief reasons, the trial judge accepted the Crown's argument and found the appellant guilty on all charges.

The appellant argues that the trial judge erred in relying on the doctrine of recent possession to convict him on the first six counts. I agree.

The unexplained recent possession of stolen goods permits, but does not require, an inference to be drawn that the possessor stole the goods: *R. v. Kowlyk*, [1988] 2 S.C.R. 59 at 71-72. Before such an inference may be drawn, however, the Crown must satisfy the trier of fact that: (i) the accused is in possession of the goods; (ii) the goods were stolen; and (iii) the theft was recent: *R. v. Cuming*, [2001] O.J. No. 3578 (C.A.). There is no question here that the motor vehicle and the cellos were stolen. The issue is whether the Crown met its burden to satisfy the remaining two prerequisites for invocation of the doctrine of recent possession.

Neither of these prerequisites was satisfied in this case. On the record before the trial judge, there was no evidence establishing that the appellant ever had possession of the vehicle or the cellos; nor was there any evidence to indicate when or how, during the two weeks that the car was missing, the pop can was placed inside the stolen car. As well, there was no demonstration that the appellant had been in recent possession of the coke can or how he had come to dispose of it. Importantly, the appellant's thumb print was found on the pop can — not on any of the stolen property.

. . .

In ... this case, the pop can bearing the respondent's thumb print was not discovered until two weeks after the theft of the vehicle. During that time, the pop can could have been placed in the vehicle by a variety of means. As well, the respondent's thumb print may have been placed on the pop can before or after the offences in question, or while the respondent was a passenger in the vehicle. In addition, the Crown failed to establish that the pop can had any connection with the theft of the motor vehicle or the cellos.

Thus, the evidence relied upon by the Crown as establishing the respondent's culpability was compatible with explanations other than those involving the respondent's guilt. The presence of the respondent's thumb print on the pop can establishes that he handled the pop can, but this does not prove possession of the stolen vehicle in which the can was found, or of the cellos contained in the vehicle: see *Poirier v. The Queen* (1971), 16 C.R.N.S. 174 (Que. C.A.) and *R. v. Sweezey* (1974), 20 C.C.C. (2d) 400 (Ont. C.A.).

In all the circumstances, there was an insufficient evidentiary footing at trial to support an inference of guilt based on the doctrine of recent possession. The appellant's convictions on counts one to six are unsustainable.

The appeal was allowed and acquittals were entered.[96]

(c) True Presumptions

If satisfied that the language of conclusive and permissive presumptions should be discarded, we can then examine the true presumptions: devices which leave open to inquiry the matters presumed but which demand a finding if the opponent does nothing.

A true presumption compels the trier of fact to find a fact, the presumed fact, to be proved against a party when another fact, the basic fact, is proved. The trier is compelled to find the presumed fact unless the party against whom the presumption operates does something. That "something" depends on the language of the particular presumptive device. It may be to ensure that there is evidence in the case contrary to the presumed fact or it may actually require the party to disprove the presumed fact. The former "something" imposes an evidential burden on the party and the latter a persuasive burden.

There are many true presumptions scattered throughout the cases and statutes created out of considerations of probabilities or substantive law policy. We will examine a few, as Professor Thayer cautioned that "any detailed consideration of the mass of legal presumptions [would be] an unprofitable and monstrous task".[97]

A good example of a presumptive device placing an evidential burden may be seen in the criminal case of *R. v. Proudlock.*[98] The accused was charged with break and enter with intent to commit an indictable offence contrary to what was then s. 306(1)(a) of the *Criminal Code.* The *Code* provided:

> 306. (2) For the purposes of proceedings under this section, evidence that an accused
>
> > (a) broke and entered a place is, in the absence of any evidence to the contrary, proof that he broke and entered with intent to commit an indictable offence therein.[99]

The crime charged required proof of an act and proof of an intention. An evidentiary assist was given to the prosecution with respect to the latter element. In *Proudlock,* the trial judge summarized the accused's evidence:

> When he testified, Proudlock said that he did not have an explanation and did not know what his motives had been. He acknowledged that it was "possible" he had told the janitor he was looking for soup, but said that would not have been

---

[96]   See also *R. v. Dionne* (2005), 198 C.C.C. (3d) 159, 29 C.R. (6th) 32, [2005] 1 S.C.R. 665.

[97]   Thayer, *supra* note 7 at 313.

[98]   (1979), 43 C.C.C. (2d) 321 (S.C.C.).

[99]   This presumption now appears in almost identical language in s. 348(2) of the *Criminal Code.* The language of "evidence to the contrary" also appears in a number of other sections of the *Code.*

a true statement of his purpose. He resolutely denied any intention to steal. . . I did not find Proudlock's evidence, when he was asked why he broke and entered the restaurant to be convincing in the least degree. To put the matter simply, I did not believe him. . .

In my opinion, Proudlock broke and entered the restaurant purposefully, and I do not believe that purpose has escaped his memory. . . I do not believe Proudlock.[100]

Nevertheless, the trial judge acquitted the accused. He reasoned that evidence to the contrary was present, the presumption of intent was rebutted, and as the prosecution led no evidence of intent a material ingredient of the crime had not been established. The Supreme Court of Canada held that "evidence disbelieved by the trier of fact is not 'evidence to the contrary' "[101] and Pigeon J. for the majority reasoned:

The accused does not have to "establish" a defence or an excuse, all he has to do is to raise a reasonable doubt. If there is nothing in the evidence adduced by the Crown from which a reasonable doubt can arise, then the accused will necessarily have the burden of adducing evidence if he is to escape conviction . . . The accused may remain silent, but, when there is a *prima facie* case against him and he is, as in the instant case, the only person who can give "evidence to the contrary" his choice really is to face *certain conviction* or to offer in testimony whatever explanation or excuse may be available to him. [Emphasis added.][102]

Since there had been no "evidence to the contrary" the accused had failed to discharge his evidential burden and the Supreme Court entered a conviction.

With respect to a prosecution for an over 80 offence, s. 258 enables the Crown to establish two facts by means of presumptions. The "presumption of identity" arising from s. 258(1)(c) is that the blood alcohol concentration of the accused at the time of driving is the same as that indicated by the Intoxilyzer tests. According to MacDonnell J. in *R. v. Snider*,[103] this presumption enables the Crown to bridge the temporal gap between the occurrence of the alleged offence and the administration of the breath tests without calling expert evidence. It presumes that in the interval between those two events nothing has changed in relation to the accused's blood alcohol concentration. The second "presumption of accuracy" in s. 258(1)(c) enables the Crown to establish is that the Intoxilyzer readings recorded in the certificate of a qualified technician are an accurate reflection of the accused's blood alcohol concentration at the time of the Intoxilyzer tests. Both presumptions are only available to the Crown in the absence of "evidence to the contrary". According to MacDonnell J. in *Snider*, where evidence to the contrary is offered in relation to the presumption of accuracy, a trial judge cannot take the breath test results into account in assessing the credibility of the evidence to the contrary. That would amount to circular reasoning. However, where the qualified technician gives evidence in relation to the breath tests results there

---

[100]   *Supra* note 98 at 329.
[101]   *Ibid.* at 323.
[102]   *Ibid.* at 325, 327. And see *R. v. Vanegas* (1987), 60 C.R. (3d) 169 (B.C. C.A.).
[103]   (2006) 37 C.R. (6th) 61 (C.J.)

is no presumption of accuracy. Whether the qualified technician's testimony is sufficient to establish the accused's blood alcohol concentration at the time of testing is simply an issue of fact to be resolved in the way all issues of fact are resolved. Here testimony of the qualified technician with respect to the blood alcohol concentrations revealed by the Intoxilyzer tests could be taken into account in assessing the credibility of the evidence of the accused and his friend and in determining whether the Crown has proved its case beyond a reasonable doubt.[104]

An example of a presumptive device placing an evidential burden on the opponent in a civil case is the presumption of testamentary capacity. Lord Dunedin, in *Robins v. National Trust*,[105] explained:

> Those who propound a will must show that the will of which probate is sought is the will of the testator, and that the testator was a person of testamentary capacity. In ordinary cases if there is no suggestion to the contrary any man who is shown to have executed a will in ordinary form will be presumed to have testamentary capacity, but the moment the capacity is called in question then at once the onus lies on those propounding the will to affirm positively the testamentary capacity.

As an example of a presumptive device shifting a persuasive burden on a material ingredient to the accused in a criminal case, consider the case of *R. v. Appleby*.[106] The accused was charged with having the care and control of a motor vehicle while his ability to drive was impaired by alcohol. There was no question of the accused's impairment, and the only question was whether he had care and control. The Crown relied on a statutory presumption which provided:

> 224A(1) [now s. 258(1)(a)] In any proceedings under section 222 or 224,
>
> > (a) where it is proved that the accused occupied the seat ordinarily occupied by the driver of a motor vehicle, he shall be deemed to have had the care or control of the vehicle unless he establishes that he did not enter or mount the vehicle for the purpose of setting it in motion.[107]

---

[104] Justice MacDonnell was interpreting a complex ruling of the Supreme Court in *R. v. Boucher*, [2005] 3 S.C.R. 499. See also *R. v. Gibson*, [2008] 1 S.C.R. 397, 230 C.C.C. (3d) 97, 55 C.R. (6th) 201 (S.C.C.), where the majority of the Supreme Court further narrows the "straddle the evidence" defence. In 2008, by amendment to ss. 258(1)(c) and (d) by s. 24 of the *Tackling Violent Crime Act*, S.C. 2008, c. 6, Parliament made the presumption of accuracy much harder to rebut, requiring evidence that the instrument malfunctioned or was improperly operated (s. 258(1)(c)). In *R. v. St.-Onge Lamoureux*, 2012 SCC 57, [2012] 3 S.C.R. 187, 294 C.C.C. (3d) 42, 96 C.R. (6th) 221 (S.C.C.), a 7-2 majority of the Supreme Court rejected several *Charter* challenges to s. 258(1)(c) but held that further requirements in ss. 258(1)(d.01) and (d.1) that the presumption could only be rebutted by proof that the malfunctioning or improper operation resulted in a wrong reading at the relevant time and that the true reading was lower than .08 violated the presumption of innocence in s. 11(d) and could not be saved under that section. The extra two requirements were declared inoperative.
[105] [1927] A.C. 515 (P.C.) at 519.
[106] (1971), 3 C.C.C. (2d) 354 (S.C.C.).
[107] *Ibid.* at 356.

The trial judge convicted though he did make the finding of fact:

> That the Defendant sought to rebut the presumption under Section 224A(1)(a) by testifying that he entered the driver's seat of the taxi to use the radio to summon a wrecker, rather than for the purpose of driving the vehicle and, although this evidence was unsupported by any other witness, it did raise a reasonable doubt in my mind.[108]

The conviction was entered then on the basis that the judge was not satisfied by a preponderance of evidence "that he did not enter or mount the motor vehicle for the purpose of setting it in motion". The British Columbia Court of Appeal found that the trial judge had erred and that the presumptive effect was to cast only an evidential burden on the accused. The Supreme Court of Canada reversed, and restored the conviction, holding that there had been an express enactment exceptionally[109] placing a persuasive burden on the accused. Ritchie J., for the majority, reasoned:

> With all respect, it appears to me that if the Court of Appeal of British Columbia were correct in holding that it is enough, to rebut the presumption created by the words "shall be deemed" as they occur in s. 224A(1)(a), for the accused to raise a reasonable doubt as to whether or not he entered the motor vehicle for the purpose of setting it in motion, then it would, in my view follow, that if the Crown has established the basis of the presumption beyond a reasonable doubt, it must also give similar proof of the facts which the statute deems to exist and expressly requires the accused to negate. This is exactly the burden which the Crown would have to discharge if the section had not been enacted, and in my view such a construction makes the statutory presumption ineffective and the section meaningless.[110]

Could the section have meaning by imposing an evidential burden? That is, by commanding a result if no contrary evidence was given?

An example of a presumptive device having the effect of shifting a persuasive burden to the opponent in a civil case is the presumption of legitimacy.[111] In *Welstead v. Brown*[112] the plaintiff was successful at trial in his claim for damages for criminal conversation. The wife had given birth to a child and blood tests indicated it was *impossible* for the husband to be the father. The Supreme Court of Canada decided that on such evidence the presumption of legitimacy could be rebutted. But Cartwright J. wrote:

> Had the doctors testified that the result of the tests indicated that it was in the highest degree improbable, but not impossible that the appellant be the father of

---

108   *Ibid.*

109   As to whether it is presently "exceptional" to place a persuasive burden on the accused in Canada, consider the fact that dozens of sections in the *Criminal Code* have language akin to that canvassed in *Appleby*.

110   *Appleby, supra* note 106 at 360.

111   Another presumption having such an effect in civil cases is the presumption of death of a person not heard of for seven years: *Middlemiss v. Middlemiss*, [1955] 4 D.L.R. 801 (B.C. C.A.); *Re Bell*, [1946] O.R. 854 (C.A.). And see Treitel, "The Presumption of Death" (1954) 17 Mod. L. Rev. 530. The adversary must also persuade on the balance of probabilities to rebut the presumption of advancement to show that no gift was intended: see *Dagle v. Dagle* (1990), 81 Nfld. & P.E.I.R. 245 (P.E.I. C.A.).

112   [1952] 1 D.L.R. 465 (S.C.C.).

the child it would, in my opinion, have been the duty of the trial Judge to direct the jury that as a matter of law such evidence could not avail against the presumption.[113]

And Kellock J. wrote:

In my view, a child born in lawful wedlock is still presumed to be a legitimate child, and *the presumption is to be overborne only by evidence excluding reasonable doubt.* [Emphasis added.][114]

(d) Presumption of Innocence and *Charter*

In the case of criminal law there is an important *Charter of Rights and Freedoms* dimension in the form of the *Charter* presumption of innocence set out in s. 11(d). In *R. v. Oakes*[115] the Court was called on to deal with the constitutionality of what was then s. 8 of the *Narcotic Control Act*. Where the charge was possession for the purposes of trafficking the Crown had first to prove possession beyond a reasonable doubt. Once possession was proven the section placed the onus on the accused of establishing that there was no purpose to traffic. Chief Justice Dickson held for the Court that requiring the accused to prove an essential element of intent on a balance of probabilities violated the presumption of innocence under s. 11(d) and could not be demonstrably justified under s. 1.

In *R. v. Whyte*,[116] the Court amplified on its reasons in *Oakes* and Dickson C.J. provided:

The distinction between elements of the offence and other aspects of the charge is irrelevant to the s. 11(*d*) inquiry. The real concern is not whether the accused must disprove an element or prove an excuse, but that an accused may be convicted while a reasonable doubt exists. When that possibility exists, there is a breach of the presumption of innocence. The exact characterization of a factor as an essential element, a collateral factor, an excuse, or a defence should not affect the analysis of the presumption of innocence. It is the final effect of a provision on the verdict that is decisive. If an accused is required to prove some fact on the balance of probabilities to avoid conviction, the provision violates the presumption of innocence because it permits a conviction in spite of a reasonable doubt in the mind of the trier of fact as to the guilt of the accused.

Section 16(4) of the *Criminal Code*, amended in 1991, formerly read:

16. (4) Every one shall, until the contrary is proved, be presumed to be and to have been sane.

---

[113]   *Ibid.* at 475-476.
[114]   *Ibid.* at 483.
[115]   [1986] 1 S.C.R. 103, 24 C.C.C. (3d) 321, 50 C.R. (3d) 1 (S.C.C.).
[116]   (1988), 64 C.R. (3d) 123 (S.C.C.) at 135-136.

R. v. CHAULK
[1990] 3 S.C.R. 1303, 2 C.R. (4th) 1, 62 C.C.C. (3d) 193

LAMER C.J. (DICKSON C.J.C., and LA FOREST and CORY JJ., concurring):—

. . .

In my view, the principles enunciated in *Whyte* are applicable to this case and establish that the presumption of sanity embodied in s. 16(4) violates the presumption of innocence. If an accused is found to have been insane at the time of the offence, he will **not** be found guilty; thus the "fact" of insanity precludes a verdict of guilty. Whether the claim of insanity is characterized as a denial of *mens rea*, an excusing defence or, more generally, as an exemption based on criminal incapacity, the fact remains that sanity is essential for guilt. Section 16(4) allows a factor which is essential for guilt to be <u>presumed</u>, rather than proven by the Crown beyond a reasonable doubt. Moreover, it requires an accused to disprove sanity (or prove insanity) on a balance of probabilities; it therefore violates the presumption of innocence because it permits a conviction in spite of a reasonable doubt in the mind of the trier of fact as to the guilt of the accused.

. . .

Is s. 16(4) a Reasonable Limit Under s. 1 of the Charter?

. . .

2. As Little as Possible

. . . In my view, the question to be addressed at this stage of the s. 1 inquiry is whether Parliament could reasonably have chosen an alternative means which would have achieved the identified objective as effectively.

Recent judgments of this Court (*R. v. Edwards Books and Art Ltd.*, [1986] 2 S.C.R. 713; *Irwin Toy Ltd. v. Quebec (Attorney General)*, [1989] 1 S.C.R. 927; and *Reference re ss. 193 and 195.1(1)(c) of the Criminal Code (Man.)*, [1990] 1 S.C.R. 1123) indicate that Parliament is **not** required to search out and to adopt the absolutely least intrusive means of attaining its objective. Furthermore, when assessing the alternative means which were available to Parliament, it is important to consider whether a less intrusive means would achieve the "same" objective or would achieve the same objective as effectively.

. . .

It is true that s. 16 will be seldom raised, given the substantial constraint on liberty which follows a successful insanity plea. Nonetheless, I have concluded that the objective of the current provision is "pressing and substantial", given the next to impossible burden which would be placed on the Crown if s. 16(4) did not exist. If insanity were easier for an accused to establish, the defence would be successfully invoked *more* often (even if, statistically, it is still infrequently raised). Thus, putting a lesser burden on the accused would *not* have achieved the objective which is achieved by s. 16(4).

. . .

WILSON J.:—

. . .

The issue under this part of the *Oakes* test is whether some other legislative provision could achieve the desired objective while impairing the *Charter* right "as little as possible". Lamer C.J. is of the view that Parliament is not required to seek and adopt "the absolutely least intrusive means of attaining its objective" (p. 1341). He indicates that he is unwilling to embark on a course of "second-guessing" the wisdom of Parliament's choice of legislative means and cites some recent decisions of this Court as authority for this deferential attitude. In my view, this is not a case for deference. In one of the cases on which the Chief Justice relies, *Irwin Toy Ltd. v. Quebec (Attorney General)*, [1989] 1 S.C.R. 927, this Court indicated that there might be exceptions to the stringent review called for under this part of the *Oakes* test. Whether or not such an exception was warranted would depend upon the role Parliament was fulfilling in enacting the impugned legislation.

As I understand this aspect of *Irwin Toy*, an exception may be made where the legislature mediating between the competing claims of groups of citizens or allocating scarce resources among them is forced to strike a compromise on the basis of conflicting evidence. In such cases there will be a substantial policy component to the choice of means selected by the legislature and that choice should be respected even if it cannot be said to represent the "least intrusive means". In my view, *Irwin Toy* does not stand for the proposition that in balancing the objective of government against the guaranteed right of the citizen under s. 1 different levels of scrutiny may be applied depending upon the nature of the right. The prerequisite for the exception to the minimal impairment test in *Oakes*, as I understand *Irwin Toy*, is that the guaranteed right of different groups of citizens cannot be fully respected; to respect to the full the right of one group will necessarily involve an infringement upon the right of the other. In such a circumstance *Irwin Toy* holds that it is appropriate for the government to fashion a compromise on the basis of policy considerations.

. . .

For these reasons, I am not persuaded that s. 16(4) impairs the accused's right to be presumed innocent as little as is reasonably possible. Rather, I am of the view that the government's objective could be quite readily met by imposing a purely evidentiary burden on the accused. The infringement on s. 11(*d*) of the *Charter* resulting from s. 16(4) is accordingly not saved by s. 1.

Justices Gonthier, McLachlin and L'Heureux-Dubé found the provision did not violate the presumption of innocence as s. 16 "should be read as relating to the fundamental precondition for the assignment of criminal responsibility rather than to the elements of an offence or to particular defences". Justice Sopinka dissented, but he agreed that s. 16(4) of the *Criminal Code* was valid for the reasons expressed by the Chief Justice.

In 1991, the *Code* was amended to provide:

16. (3) The burden of proof that an accused was suffering from a mental disorder so as to be exempt from criminal responsibility is on the party that raises the issue.

In *Re Boyle*,[117] the issue before the Ontario Court of Appeal concerned presumptions created by language of the *Criminal Code* "in the absence of any evidence to the contrary proof", a frequently used legislative device. The Court held that, although such presumptions can be displaced merely by evidence which raises a reasonable doubt rather than proof on a balance of probabilities, there was a common feature in the mandatory nature of the conclusion required to be drawn. The trier of fact must find the presumed fact; there was no may about it. The obligation on the accused required mandatory presumptions to also receive protection under the *Charter* presumption of innocence. In *Boyle*, the Court held that the presumption that arises under s. 354(2) on possession of a motor vehicle with an obliterated identification number, that the motor vehicle or part thereof was at some time obtained by the commission of an indictable offence, was entirely reasonable and constitutionally valid. However, the second presumption under s. 354(2), that the person found in possession knows that the vehicle or part thereof was obtained by the commission of an indictable offence, was not constitutionally valid, since it was arbitrary and hence unreasonable.

It has thus long been clear that any persuasive onus on the accused and any mandatory presumption violates s. 11(d) and the determinative issue is whether it amounts to a demonstrably justified reasonable limit under s. 1.[118] The Supreme Court has often decided that reverse onuses can be saved under s. 1, as in *Chaulk*, but has also read down a reverse onus to be a mandatory presumption.[119]

In contrast the Ontario Court of Appeal has been steadfast in holding that the appropriate *Charter* remedy for a reverse onus is simply to declare it inoperative. *R. v. Curtis*[120] concerned a charge under s. 215(2) of the *Criminal Code* of failing to provide necessaries of life. The section provides that everyone who commits an offence who, being under a legal duty within the meaning of s. 215(1) of the *Code*, fails without lawful excuse "the proof of which lies upon him" to perform that duty in certain specified circumstances. The Court struck down the reverse onus.

The *Criminal Code* has for years been replete with sections requiring an accused to prove a lawful excuse. Under Government Bill C-51 passed by the House of Commons on December 11, 2017 and omnibus Government Bill C-75 tabled on March 29, 2018, such reverse onuses would be expressly removed.

---

[117]   (1983), 35 C.R. (3d) 34 (Ont. C.A.). See too *R. v. Downey*, [1992] 2 S.C.R. 10, 72 C.C.C. (3d) 1, 13 C.R. (4th) 129 (S.C.C.).

[118]   For a full analysis see Stuart, *Charter Justice in Canadian Criminal Law*, 7th ed. (2018) at 23-37, 492-512.

[119]   *R. v. Laba*, [1994] 3 S.C.R. 965, 94 C.C.C. (3d) 385, 34 C.R. (4th) 360 (S.C.C.).

[120]   (1998), 123 C.C.C. (3d) 178, 14 C.R. (5th) 328 (Ont. C.A.).

Chapter 3

Relevance and Discretion to Exclude

1. RELEVANCE

(a) Tests

In 1898 Professor Thayer described the function and limitations of the law of evidence created by the English common law:

> There is a principle — not so much a rule of evidence as a presupposition involved in the very conception of a rational system of evidence, as contrasted with the old formal and mechanical system — which forbids receiving anything irrelevant, not logically probative. How are we to know what these forbidden things are? Not by any rule of law. The law furnishes no test of relevancy. For this, it tacitly refers to logic and general experience, — assuming that the principles of reasoning are known to its judges and ministers, just as a vast multitude of other things are assumed as already sufficiently known to them.[1]

Thayer later explained that by "logic" he was not referring to the deductive logic of the syllogism, but the inductive logic of knowledge or science. He noted that his book used:

> . . . the word relevancy merely as importing a logical relation, that is to say, a relation determined by the reasoning faculty. . . The law has no orders for the reasoning faculty, any more than the perceiving faculty, — for the eyes and ears.[2]

In *R. v. Watson*,[3] Doherty J.A. explained:

> Relevance . . . requires a determination of whether as a matter of human experience and logic the existence of "Fact A" makes the existence or non-existence of "Fact B" more probable than it would be without the existence of "Fact A." If it does then "Fact A" is relevant to "Fact B". As long as "Fact B" is itself a material fact in issue or is relevant to a material fact in issue in the litigation then "Fact A" is relevant and prima facie admissible.

Relevancy of evidence must be distinguished from sufficiency of evidence and we need to recognize that to be receivable as relevant the

---

[1]   Thayer, *Preliminary Treatise on Evidence at the Common Law* (1898) at 264-69 [footnotes omitted].

[2]   "Law and Logic" (1900), 14 Harv. L. Rev. 139 in reply to a criticism by Fox at p. 39 of the same volume. Interestingly, Thayer's earlier version of the material in his "Treatise in Presumptions and the Law of Evidence" (1889-1890), 3 Harv. L. Rev. 141 at 144 refers only to logic as the test rather than to logic and general experience.

[3]   (1996), 50 C.R. (4th) 245 (Ont. C.A.) at 257.

piece of evidence being tendered need not by itself be compelling. Also, evidence objected to as irrelevant may need to be received on counsel's undertaking to link up the same with other expected evidence and so later demonstrate relevance. The trier may need to be advised to disregard such evidence conditionally received if the connection fails to materialize.[4] McCormick explained:

> This is the distinction between relevancy and sufficiency. The test of relevancy, which is to be applied by the trial judge in determining whether a particular item or group of items of evidence is to be admitted is a different and less stringent one than the standard used at a later stage in deciding whether all the evidence of the party on an issue is sufficient to permit the issue to go to the jury. A brick is not a wall.
>
> What is the standard of relevance or probative quality which evidence must meet if it is to be admitted? We have said that it must "tend to establish" the inference for which it is offered. How strong must this tendency be? Some courts have announced tests, variously phrased, which seem to require that the evidence offered must render the inference for which it is offered more probable than the other possible inferences or hypotheses, that is, the chances must appear to preponderate that the inference claimed is the true one.
>
> . . .
>
> . . . It is believed that a more modest standard better reflects the actual practice of the courts, and that the most acceptable test of relevancy is the question, does the evidence offered render the desired inference *more probable than it would be without the evidence*?[5]

We know that evidence is relevant if it has any tendency to make the proposition for which it is tendered more probable than that proposition would be without the evidence. For evidence to have any value there must be a premise, a generalization that one makes, allowing the inference to be made. Borrowing from Professors Binder and Bergman,[6] evidence that roses were in bloom, when tendered to prove that it was then Springtime, has meaning only if we adopt the premise or generalization that roses usually bloom in the Spring. The tendency of evidence to prove a proposition, and hence its relevance, depends on the validity of the premise which links the evidence to the proposition. The probative worth of the relevant evidence depends on the accuracy of the premise which supports the inference. Sometimes the premise will be indisputable, sometimes always true, sometimes often true and sometimes only rarely true. But a premise there must be. The next time someone says to you that the evidence is *clearly* relevant ask the proponent of the evidence to articulate for you what premise he or she is relying on. If there is no premise the evidence is irrelevant. If there is a premise you can debate with him or her the validity of the premise. What experience does he

---

4   As noted in *R. v. Ward*, 2016 NBBR 2, 2016 NBQB 2, 28 C.R. (7th) 19 (N.B. Q.B.) at para. 31, "[i]n the event such latter testimony was not forthcoming what might have been conditionally relevant evidence led during cross-examination of a Crown witness or witnesses would likely be subject to a 'no probative value' final instruction to the jury".

5   McCormick, *Evidence*, 2nd ed. at 436-438.

6   *Fact Investigation* (West Publishing, 1984) at 82.

or she base it on? Is there contrary experience? Is the premise based on myth? Is the premise true always, sometimes or only rarely? These latter parameters do not affect relevance since relevance has a very low threshold, but may affect the probative worth which may cause rejection of the evidence if the probative value is outweighed by competing considerations. Approaching discussions of relevance in this way may yield a more intelligent discussion than the often typical exchange of conclusory opinions.

In *Morris v. R.*[7] the Supreme Court of Canada adopted the Thayerian view of relevance and rejected the Wigmore view that a piece of information must have a minimum probative value before it can be considered relevant.

MORRIS v. R.
[1983] 2 S.C.R. 190, 36 C.R. (3d) 1, 7 C.C.C. (3d) 97

McIntyre J. (Ritchie, Beetz and Estey JJ. concurring):—I have had the opportunity of reading the reasons for judgment prepared in this case [an appeal from (1982), 68 C.C.C. (2d) 115] by my brother Lamer. I agree with his observation on the subject of the relevancy of evidence. I also agree with his exposition of the reason for and the development of the exclusionary rule which applies to evidence in criminal cases dealing only with the question of disposition and character of the accused. I am unable, however, to agree with his characterization of the newspaper clipping in this case as evidence indicating only a disposition on the part of the appellant.

In my view, an inference could be drawn from the unexplained presence of the newspaper clipping among the possessions of the appellant that he had an interest in and had informed himself on the question of sources of supply of heroin, necessarily a subject of vital interest to one concerned with the importing of the narcotic.

. . .

I agree that the probative value of such evidence may be low, especially since the newspaper article here concerns the heroin trade in Pakistan rather than in Hong Kong, which was apparently the source of the heroin involved in this case. However, admissibility of evidence must not be confused with weight. If the article had concerned the heroin trade in Hong Kong, it would of course have had greater probative value. If the article had been a manual containing a step-by-step guide to importing heroin into Vancouver from Hong Kong, the probative value would have been still greater. The differences between these examples, however, and the facts at bar are differences in degree, not kind. In other words, the differences go to weight and not to admissibility.

The weight to be given to evidence is a question for the trier of fact, subject of course to the discretion of the trial judge to exclude evidence where the probative value is minimal and the prejudicial effect great: see *R. v. Wray*, [1971] S.C.R. 272. In the present case the trial judge did not consider that the evidence should be thus excluded. In my opinion it would not be proper in the

---

[7]   (1983), 7 C.C.C. (3d) 97 (S.C.C.) at 104, 106.

circumstances of this case for this court to substitute its view on this matter of discretion for that of the trial judge. In my opinion the trial judge made no error in law in admitting evidence of the newspaper clipping, and I would therefore dismiss the appeal.

LAMER J. (dissenting) (DICKSON and WILSON JJ. concurring):— The appellant, one Gary Robert Morris, was convicted in Vancouver, by a County Court Judge sitting without a jury, of having conspired with others to import and traffic heroin. He appealed from his conviction to the British Columbia Court of Appeal. His appeal was heard by a panel of three judges and was dismissed [(1982), 68 C.C.C. (2d) 115]. One of the judges, Anderson J.A., dissented and would have allowed the appeal and ordered a new trial on the following ground of law, namely:

> That the learned trial judge erred in admitting into evidence and in taking into consideration a newspaper clipping entitled, 'The Heroin Trade Moves to Pakistan', being Exhibit 26 at the Appellant's trial.

. . .

THE LAW

While I agree with Anderson J.A. that the clipping should not have been admitted in evidence, it is not because I believe the clipping irrelevant, but because it was, in my view, not admissible. His reference to the clipping as having "no probative value in proving the offence charged" is understandable given the language this court resorted to when dealing with analogous evidence in the case of *Cloutier*. Cloutier was charged with importing a narcotic into Canada, namely, 20 pounds of cannabis (marihuana). The evidence was that the merchandise was concealed in the false bottom of a dresser arriving from South America, which the appellant asked his mother to store in her home, and it was there that the police made the seizure.

One of the grounds of appeal in this court was that the trial judge refused to admit in evidence certificates of analysis to establish that the items seized at the accused's home, a cigarette butt, a pipe and a green substance, indicated that the accused was a user of marihuana.

Pratte J., writing for a majority of this court, stated the following, at p. 731:

> For one fact to be relevant to another, there must be a connection or nexus between the two which makes it possible to infer the existence of one from the existence of the other. One fact is not relevant to another if it does not have real probative value with respect to the latter (Cross, *On Evidence*, 4th ed. [1974], at p. 16).
>
> Thus, apart from certain exceptions which are not applicable here, evidence is not admissible if its only purpose is to prove that the accused is the type of man who is more likely to commit a crime of the kind with which he is charged; such evidence is viewed as having no real probative value with regard to the specific crime attributed to the accused: there is no sufficient logical connection between the one and the other.

It has been said that some might read in these comments (see Report of the Federal/Provincial Task Force on Uniform Rules of Evidence (1982), at p. 62

et seq.) a pronouncement by this court indicating a departure from Thayer's premise in A Preliminary Treatise on Evidence at the Common Law, of relevancy, logic and experience, and an adoption of Wigmore's concept of "legal relevancy" of which "the effect is to require a generally *higher degree of probative value for all evidence to be submitted to a jury*" and that "legal relevancy denotes, first of all, *something more than a minimum of probative value*. Each single piece of evidence must have a plus value.": Wigmore on Evidence, 3rd ed., vol. 1 (1940), para. 28, pp. 409-10. I do not think that it was intended by the majority in this court in *Cloutier*, supra, that such a departure be made. All agreed that the evidence could not be admitted to prove the accused's propensity, including the dissenting judges. In fact, the whole case, in my view, turned upon whether the evidence was relevant and admissible as tending to establish motive.

. . .

Thayer's statement of the law, which is still the law in Canada, was as follows (p. 530):

> (1) that nothing is to be received which is not logically probative of some matter requiring to be proved; and (2) that everything which is thus probative should come in, unless a clear ground of policy or law excludes it.

To this general statement should be added the discretionary power judges exercise to exclude logically relevant evidence (p. 266):

> . . . as being of too slight a significance, or as having too conjectural and remote a connection; others, as being dangerous, in their effect on the jury, and likely to be misused or overestimated by that body; others, as being impolitic, or unsafe on public grounds; others, on the bare ground of precedent. It is this sort of thing, as I said before, — the rejection on one or another practical ground, of what is really probative, — which is the characteristic thing in the law of evidence; stamping it as the child of the jury system.

It was through the exercise of this discretionary power that judges developed rules of exclusion. As said by Thayer at p. 265, when speaking of the rule of general admissibility of what is logically probative:

> . . . in an historical sense it has not been the fundamental thing, to which the different exclusions were exceptions. What has taken place, in fact, is the shutting out by the judges of one and another thing from time to time; and so, gradually, the recognition of this exclusion under a rule. These rules of exclusion have had their exceptions; and so the law has come into the shape of a set of primary rules of exclusion; and then a set of exceptions to these rules.

Thus came about, as a primary rule of exclusion, the following: disposition, i.e., the fact that the accused is the sort of person who would be likely to have committed the offence, though relevant, is not admissible. As a result, evidence adduced *solely* for the purpose of proving disposition is itself inadmissible, or, to put it otherwise, evidence the sole relevancy of which to the crime committed is through proof of disposition is inadmissible.

. . .

Now to consider the "clipping". The presence of the clipping in the room tends to prove that the accused either clipped it or received it and kept it for future reference. Had the article referred to movement of drugs in Hong Kong, to a laxity in that colony on the part of the customs officials, and so forth, it would have found its relevancy as proving the accused's participation in the conspiracies through his possession of a document that might have been instrumental to the commission of the crimes. But such is not the case. Its sole relevancy is through proof of the accused's disposition, the reasoning being as follows, that, because persons who are traffickers are more likely to keep such information than not, people who keep such information are more likely to be traffickers than people who do not, and that a person who traffics is more likely to have committed the alleged offence than a person who does not. The ultimate purpose of placing the accused in the first category (people who keep such information for future reference) is to put him in a category of people the character of which indicates a propensity to commit the offences of which he was charged. This is clearly inadmissible evidence.

. . .

I have read the evidence and agree with Anderson J.A. that this is not the proper case for the application of s. 613(1)(*b*)(iii). I cannot say, however, that, once the clipping and the answers of the accused when cross-examined as to the reasons for its presence in his room are excluded, there is left no evidence upon which a trier of fact might reasonably convict. As a result, I would allow the appeal, quash the conviction and order a new trial.

Appeal dismissed.

Are you satisfied with the way in which the majority articulated the relevance of the newspaper clipping? Do you think that Justice Lamer got it right when he concluded that its relevance was only in revealing the accused's disposition for criminality?

(b) Materiality

Not only must the evidence tendered be rationally probative of the fact sought to be thereby established; the fact sought to be established must concern a matter in issue between the parties (i.e., it must be material). Another way of saying this is that the evidence must be relevant to a legal issue in the case. With this concept as well the law of evidence does not dictate the parameters, but rather the same is set down by the substantive law and the pleadings.

In civil cases the statements of claim and defence narrow the issues between the parties. In criminal cases the prosecution sets out in the information or indictment what is intended to be established. In our system of fact-finding the parties select a particular slice of life to be litigated and test their rights in that context against their understanding of the substantive law; they do not litigate all of history.[8]

---

[8]   See 1 Wigmore, *Evidence* (3rd ed.), s. 2 at 6.

For example, an accused is charged with possession of undersized lobsters. Defence counsel tenders in evidence a witness who will testify that the accused didn't know that there were undersized lobsters in his catch. What do you, as prosecutor, say? "The evidence is immaterial".[9] Notice that by objecting that the evidence is immaterial the prosecutor is not arguing that the evidence would fail to rationally persuade a trier of fact regarding the accused's state of mind but rather that the accused's state of mind doesn't matter. It's immaterial. Our courts decided, as a matter of substantive law, that there is no *mens rea* requirement for the offence of possession of undersized lobsters; the offence was decided to be one of absolute liability. The evidence tendered was relevant to the matter sought to be established but what was sought to be established was beside the point; it was immaterial.

(c) Multiple Relevance

The same piece of evidence may be relevant to different matters. An awareness of the underlying policies for our rules will assist us in dealing with the problems that arise when the evidence has multiple relevance. We will then appreciate that though evidence may be inadmissible when tendered for one purpose as violative of a certain policy it may nevertheless be admissible when tendered for another purpose. For example, evidence of character may be relevant to both credibility and disposition; rules of evidence could exclude such evidence if tendered to prove that the person acted in conformity with that character on the occasion under review, but admit the same if tendered to impact the credibility of a witness. If we keep in mind the policy underlying the rule we should then be better able to judge whether the evidence ought to be received, with a limiting instruction to the trier of its limited utility, or rejected.

(d) Relevance and Social Context

The concept of relevancy is ordered by our present insistence on a rational method of fact-finding and its substance, we say, is dictated by our common sense and experience. The law furnishes no test for relevancy and therefore, in the final analysis, the decision rests with the individual judge to value the probabilities in the particular case.[10] While we cannot legally define relevance, and we, of necessity, must therefore leave it to the trial judge's sound exercise of discretion, subject to review, we need to recognize that "common sense and experience", and hence relevance, will vary depending on the judge's culture, age, sexual orientation, gender, racial or ethnic

---

[9]   See *R. v. Pierce Fisheries Ltd.*, [1970] C.C.C. 193 (S.C.C.).

[10]   In his classic article "Relevancy, Probability and the Law" (1941) 29 Cal. L. Rev. 689 at 696, Professor James explained that relevancy is a tendency to prove and commented:

This tendency to prove can be demonstrated only in terms of some general proposition, based most often on the practical experience of the judge and jurors as men, sometimes upon generalizations of science introduced into the trial to act as connecting links.

Professor McCormick wrote: "The answer must filter through the judge's experience, his judgment, and his knowledge of human conduct and motivation."

background, and socio-economic status. The judge's intuition that fact X frequently accompanies fact Y, making X's presence relevant to Y's, may not accord with another's and counsel may need to be provided with the opportunity to encourage the judge that the hunch is incorrect, and deserves to be rethought in light of the other's experience.[11]

In order to guard against this and to ensure a rational, fair and inclusive system of fact adjudication, should judges be able to use social context evidence, for example, evidence of the existence of systemic bias such as racism or sexism, in assessing relevance and later when engaging in fact-finding? Justice Doherty certainly thinks so. In *Peart v. Peel (Regional Municipality) Police Services Board,*[12] he noted:

> I do not pretend that the hypothetical, reasonable person is purely objective. The reasonable person is an analytical device that will inevitably reflect the world view of the judge applying that device: see Richard F. Devlin, "We Can't Go On Together With Suspicious Minds: Judicial Bias and Racialized Perspective in R. v. R.D.S." (1995), 18 Dal. L.J. 408 at 419-21. The realization that the hypothetical, reasonable person is to some degree reflective of the judge's own preconceptions is what makes an appreciation of social context so important. An understanding of how others legitimately view the circumstances serves to counteract the subjectivity of the judge's own view of the world.

R. v. LAVALLEE
[1990] 1 S.C.R. 852, 76 C.R. (3d) 329, 55 C.C.C. (3d) 97

The accused, a battered woman in a volatile common-law relationship, killed her partner late one night by shooting him in the back of the head as he left her room. A psychiatrist described the accused's terror and her inability to escape the relationship. The psychiatrist opined that the shooting was the final desperate act of a woman who sincerely believed that she would be killed that night. The accused was acquitted at trial. The Court had to decide whether the psychiatric evidence was properly received. Was the evidence relevant to a material issue?

WILSON J.:—

. . .

Expert evidence on the psychological effect of battering on wives and common law partners must, it seems to me, be both relevant and necessary in the context of the present case. How can the mental state of the appellant be appreciated without it? The average member of the public (or of the jury) can be forgiven for asking: Why would a woman put up with this kind of treatment? Why should she continue to live with such a man? How could she

---

[11]   See Weyrauch, "Law as Mask — Legal Ritual and Relevance" (1978) 66 Cal. L. Rev. 699; and Weinstein, "Some Difficulties in Devising Rules for Determining Truth in Judicial Trials" (1966) 66 Cal. L. Rev. 223. See also D.M. Tanovich, "Relevance, Social Context and Poverty" (2003), 9 C.R. (6th) 348; A. Mewett, "Secondary Facts, Prejudice and Stereotyping" (1999) 42 Crim. L.Q. 319; and M. MacCrimmon, "Developments in the Law of Evidence: The 1995-96 Term: Regulating Fact Determination and Common Sense Reasoning" (1997) 8 S.C.L.R. 367.

[12]   (2006), 43 C.R. (6th) 175 (C.A.).

love a partner who beat her to the point of requiring hospitalization? We would expect the woman to pack her bags and go. Where is her self-respect? Why does she not cut loose and make a new life for herself? Such is the reaction of the average person confronted with the so-called "battered wife syndrome". We need help to understand it and help is available from trained professionals.

. . .

The feature common to both s. 34(2)(*a*) and s. 34(2)(*b*) [the self-defence sections of the Criminal Code] is the imposition of an objective standard of reasonableness on the apprehension of death and the need to repel the assault with deadly force. . .

If it strains credulity to imagine what the "ordinary man" would do in the position of a battered spouse, it is probably because men do not typically find themselves in that situation. Some women do, however. The definition of what is reasonable must be adapted to circumstances which are, by and large, foreign to the world inhabited by the hypothetical "reasonable man".

. . .

It will be observed that subsection 34(2)(*a*) does not actually stipulate that the accused apprehend *imminent* danger when he or she acts. Case law has, however, read that requirement into the defence. . . The sense in which "imminent" is used conjures up the image of "an uplifted knife" or a pointed gun. The rationale for the imminence rule seems obvious. The law of self-defence is designed to ensure that the use of defensive force is really necessary. It justifies the act because the defender reasonably believed that he or she had no alternative but to take the attacker's life. If there is a significant time interval between the original unlawful assault and the accused's response, one tends to suspect that the accused was motivated by revenge rather than self-defence. In the paradigmatic case of a one-time bar room brawl between two men of equal size and strength, this inference makes sense. How can one feel endangered to the point of firing a gun at an unarmed man who utters a death threat, then turns his back and walks out of the room? One cannot be certain of the gravity of the threat or his capacity to carry it out. Besides, one can always take the opportunity to flee or to call the police. If he comes back and raises his fist, one can respond in kind if need be. These are the tacit assumptions that underlie the imminence rule.

All of these assumptions were brought to bear on the respondent in *R. v. Whynot* (1983), 37 C.R. (3d) 198 (C.A.).

. . .

Where evidence exists that an accused is in a battering relationship, expert testimony can assist the jury in determining whether the accused had a "reasonable" apprehension of death when she acted by explaining the heightened sensitivity of a battered woman to her partner's acts. Without such testimony I am skeptical that the average fact-finder would be capable of appreciating why her subjective fear may have been reasonable in the context of the relationship. After all, the hypothetical "reasonable man" observing only the final incident may have been unlikely to recognize the [batterer's] threat as potentially lethal. Using the case at bar as an example, the "reasonable man" might have thought, as the majority of the Court of Appeal seemed to, that it was unlikely that Rust would make good on his threat to kill the appellant that night because they had guests staying overnight.

Social context evidence can be admitted by taking judicial notice (discussed in Chapter 5) or by expert evidence (discussed in Chapter 4). The extent to which a judge may rely on social context evidence acquired from personal knowledge and judicial experience has proved highly controversial, and produced sharp divisions in *R. v. S. (R.D.)*.

R. v. S. (R.D.)
[1997] 3 S.C.R. 484, 10 C.R. (5th) 1, 118 C.C.C. (3d) 353

The accused was charged with a series of offences involving an encounter with a police officer. The relevant evidence is summarized, on behalf of the Court, by Justice Cory:

I. Facts

R.D.S. is an African-Canadian youth. When he was 15 years of age he was charged with three offences: unlawfully assaulting Constable Donald Stienburg; unlawfully assaulting Constable Stienburg with the intention of preventing the arrest of N.R.; and unlawfully resisting Constable Stienburg in the lawful execution of his duty.The Crown proceeded with the charges by way of summary conviction. There were only two witnesses at the trial: R.D.S. himself and Constable Stienburg. Their accounts of the relevant events differed widely. The credibility of these witnesses would determine the outcome of the charges.

A. Constable Stienburg's Evidence

Constable Stienburg testified that he was in his police cruiser with his partner when a radio transmission alerted them that other officers were in pursuit of a stolen van. In the car was a "ride-along", Leslie Lane, who was unable to testify at the trial. The occupants of the stolen van were described as "non-white" youths. When Constable Stienburg and his partner arrived at the designated area they saw two black youths running across the street in front of them. Constable Stienburg detained one of the individuals, N.R., while his partner pursued the other. He testified that there were a number of other people standing around at the time.

N.R. was detained outside the police car since the "ride-along" was in the back seat. While Constable Stienburg was standing by the side of the road with N.R., the accused, R.D.S., came towards Constable Stienburg on his bicycle. Constable Stienburg testified that R.D.S. ran into his legs, and while still on the bicycle, yelled at him and pushed him. R.D.S. was then arrested for interfering with the arrest of N.R., and Constable Stienburg called for back-up. Constable Stienburg stated that he put both R.D.S. and N.R. in "a neck restraint". When R.D.S. was finally brought to the police station, he was read his rights, and charged with the three offences.

In cross-examination, it was suggested to Constable Stienburg that R.D.S. had been overcharged. It was pointed out that R.D.S. had no prior record and it was suggested, although not particularly clearly, that R.D.S. had been singled out because he was black.

B. Testimony of R.D.S.

R.D.S. testified that he remembered that the weather on the particular day was misty and humid. While riding his bike from his grandmother's to his mother's house he saw the police car and the crowd standing beside it. A friend told him that his cousin N.R. had been arrested. R.D.S. approached the crowd, and stopped his bike when he saw N.R. and the officer. R.D.S. then tried to talk to N.R. to ask him what had happened and to find out if he should tell N.R.'s mother. Constable Stienburg told him: "Shut up, shut up, or you'll be under arrest too". When R.D.S. continued to ask N.R. if he should call his mother, Constable Stienburg arrested R.D.S. and put him in a choke hold. R.D.S. indicated that he could not breathe, and that he heard a woman tell the officer to "Let that kid go . . ." He also heard her ask for his phone number. He could not talk so N.R. gave the number to her. R.D.S. indicated that the crowd standing around were all "little kids" under the age of 12. He denied that he ran into anyone or that he intended to run into anyone on his bike. He also testified that his hands remained on the handlebars, and he did not push the officer. In cross-examination, he indicated that the reason he approached the crowd was because he was "being nosey". He remembered that N.R. was handcuffed when he arrived. Both R.D.S. and N.R. were placed in a choke hold at the same time. He repeated his denial that he touched the officer either with his bicycle or his hands. He also denied that he said anything to Constable Stienburg prior to his arrest. He indicated that all his questions were directed to N.R.

The trial judge weighed the evidence and determined that the accused should be acquitted. Her reasons are described by Justice Cory as follows:

> In her oral reasons, Judge Sparks reviewed the details of Constable Stienburg's testimony, and noted that R.D.S.'s evidence was directly opposed to it. In describing R.D.S.'s testimony, she observed that she was impressed with his clear recollection of the weather conditions on that day, and his candour in pointing out that he was simply being nosey in approaching the crowd. She also noted that his description of being placed in the choke hold was vivid. R.D.S. stated clearly that when he was placed in the choke hold, he could not speak and had difficulty breathing. In fact, he was unable to respond when a woman asked him for his phone number so she could notify his mother.
>
> The Youth Court Judge paid particular attention to R.D.S.'s testimony that N.R. was handcuffed when R.D.S. arrived on the scene. This aspect of R.D.S.'s

testimony suggested that N.R. was not a threat to the officer. Significantly, Constable Stienburg did not mention that N.R. was handcuffed, and gave the Court the distinct impression that he had difficulty restraining N.R. In Judge Sparks' view, R.D.S.'s testimony that N.R. was handcuffed had "a ring of truth" to it, which raised questions in her mind about the divergence between R.D.S.'s evidence and the evidence of Constable Stienburg on this point.

In general, Judge Sparks described R.D.S's demeanour as "positive", even though he was not particularly articulate. She found him to be a "rather honest young boy". In particular, she was struck by his openness in acknowledging his own "nosiness" and by his surprise at the hostility of the police officer. Judge Sparks indicated that she was not saying that she accepted everything that R.D.S. said, but noted that "certainly he has raised a doubt in my mind". She still had queries about "what actually transpired on the afternoon of October the 17th". As a result, she concluded that the Crown had not discharged its evidentiary burden to prove all the elements of the offence beyond a reasonable doubt.

At the end of her reasons, the trial judge, who is African-Canadian, remarked:

The Crown says, well, why would the officer say that events occurred the way in which he has relayed them to the Court this morning? I am not saying that the Constable has misled the court, although police officers have been known to do that in the past. I am not saying that the officer overreacted, but certainly police officers do overreact, particularly when they are dealing with non-white groups. That to me indicates a state of mind right there that is questionable. I believe that probably the situation in this particular case is the case of a young police officer who overreacted. I do accept the evidence of [R.D.S.] that he was told to shut up or he would be under arrest. It seems to be in keeping with the prevalent attitude of the day. At any rate, based upon my comments and based upon all the evidence before the court I have no other choice but to acquit.

In her later written reasons for judgment, Justice Sparks also observed:

On cross-examination by defence counsel the police officer admitted that his police department routinely refers to African-Canadian persons, at least back in October 1993, the date of these alleged offences, as "non-white." At this point in his viva voce evidence, the officer became ruffled; and in my view became tense. The line of questioning by defence counsel was that this labelling of "non-white" was a pejorative categorization of African-Canadians. As well, on cross-examination, the witness admitted that the accused had no police record. Generally the court observed that this witness appeared nervous when he commenced giving evidence. It was not unnoticed by the Court that this may have been due to the racial configuration in the court which consisted of the accused, the defence counsel, the court reporter and the judge all being of African-Canadian ancestry. . .

Apart from the above, the general demeanour of the accused was pleasant, honest and forthright. Here the Court notes that the police officer is a full bodied man while the young person is slight and slender and was probably lighter in weight when the incident occurred as the incident happened over one year ago. The Court questioned the necessity of choke-holding a young person of such a slight and slender build.

Also, in my mind, was the fact that, from other proceedings, it is not routine for a police officer to place a 15 year old youngster in a choke-hold.[13]

On appeal, the Crown challenged these comments as revealing an actual "racial bias" and "bias" against the police. Chief Justice Glube of the Summary Conviction Appeal Court concluded that Justice Sparks' oral reasons revealed an apprehension of bias and ordered a new trial. Her decision was affirmed by the Nova Scotia Court of Appeal. The accused appealed further. The Supreme Court of Canada first concluded that Justice Sparks' supplementary written reasons could not be considered on the bias issue because they had been produced after the Crown had filed their notice of appeal. **Do you agree that these reasons should not have been considered?** The Supreme Court went on to determine whether the oral reasons raised a reasonable apprehension of bias.

A 6-3 majority of the Supreme Court held that there was no reasonable apprehension of bias in this case, allowed the appeals and restored the acquittals. The division in the Court on the law is complex. **What is the majority ratio of the decision for future cases?**

CORY J. (Iacobucci J. concurring):—

. . .

In some circumstances it may be acceptable for a judge to acknowledge that racism in society might be, for example, the motive for the overreaction of a police officer. This may be necessary in order to refute a submission that invites the judge as trier of fact to presume truthfulness or untruthfulness of a category of witnesses, or to adopt some other form of stereotypical thinking. Yet it would not be acceptable for a judge to go further and suggest that all police officers should therefore not be believed or should be viewed with suspicion where they are dealing with accused persons who are members of a different race. Similarly, it is dangerous for a judge to suggest that a particular person overreacted because of racism unless there is evidence adduced to sustain this finding. It would be equally inappropriate to suggest that female complainants, in sexual assault cases, ought to be believed more readily than male accused persons solely because of the history of sexual violence by men against women.

If there is no evidence linking the generalization to the particular witness, these situations might leave the judge open to allegations of bias on the basis that the credibility of the individual witness was prejudged according to stereotypical generalizations. This does not mean that the particular generalization — that police officers have historically discriminated against visible minorities or that women have historically been abused by men —-is not true, or is without foundation. The difficulty is that reasonable and informed people may perceive that the judge has used this information as a basis for assessing credibility instead of making a genuine evaluation of the evidence of the particular witness' credibility. As a general rule, judges should avoid placing themselves in this position.

. . .

---

[13]   *R. v. S. (R.D.)*, [1994] N.S.J. No. 629 (Fam. Ct.). Justice Sparks' oral reasons were delivered on December 2, 1994. The Crown filed its Notice of Appeal on December 22, 1994. These written reasons were released January 13, 1995.

The Crown contended that the real problem arising from Judge Sparks' remarks was the inability of the Crown and Constable Stienburg to respond to the remarks. In other words, the Crown attempted to put forward an argument that the trial was rendered unfair for failure to comply with "natural justice". This cannot be accepted. Neither Constable Stienburg nor the Crown was on trial. Rather, it is essential to consider whether the remarks of Judge Sparks gave rise to a reasonable apprehension of bias. This is the only basis on which this trial could be considered unfair.

. . .

However, there was no evidence before Judge Sparks that would suggest that anti-black bias influenced this particular police officer's reactions. Thus, although it may be incontrovertible that there is a history of racial tension between police officers and visible minorities, there was no evidence to link that generalization to the actions of Constable Stienburg. The reference to the fact that police officers may overreact in dealing with non-white groups may therefore be perfectly supportable, but it is nonetheless unfortunate in the circumstances of this case because of its potential to associate Judge Sparks' findings with the generalization, rather than the specific evidence. This effect is reinforced by the statement "[t]hat to me indicates a state of mind right there that is questionable" which immediately follows her observation.

There is a further troubling comment. After accepting R.D.S.'s evidence that he was told to shut up, Judge Sparks added that "[i]t seems to be in keeping with the prevalent attitude of the day". Again, this comment may create a perception that the findings of credibility have been made on the basis of generalizations, rather than the conduct of the particular police officer. Indeed these comments standing alone come very close to indicating that Judge Sparks predetermined the issue of credibility of Constable Stienburg on the basis of her general perception of racist police attitudes, rather than on the basis of his demeanour and the substance of his testimony.

The remarks are worrisome and come very close to the line. Yet, however troubling these comments are when read individually, it is vital to note that the comments were not made in isolation. It is necessary to read all of the comments in the context of the whole proceeding, with an awareness of all the circumstances that a reasonable observer would be deemed to know.

The reasonable and informed observer at the trial would be aware that the Crown had made the submission to Judge Sparks that "there's absolutely no reason to attack the credibility of the officer". She had already made a finding that she preferred the evidence of R.D.S. to that of Constable Stienburg. She gave reasons for these findings that could appropriately be made based on the evidence adduced. A reasonable and informed person hearing her subsequent remarks would conclude that she was exploring the possible reasons why Constable Stienburg had a different perception of events than R.D.S. Specifically, she was rebutting the unfounded suggestion of the Crown that a police officer by virtue of his occupation should be more readily believed than the accused. Although her remarks were inappropriate they did not give rise to a reasonable apprehension of bias.

. . .

A high standard must be met before a finding of reasonable apprehension of bias can be made. Troubling as Judge Sparks' remarks may be, the Crown has not satisfied its onus to provide the cogent evidence needed to impugn the impartiality of Judge Sparks. Although her comments, viewed in isolation, were unfortunate and unnecessary, a reasonable, informed person, aware of all the circumstances, would not conclude that they gave rise to a reasonable apprehension of bias. Her remarks, viewed in their context, do not give rise to a perception that she prejudged the issue of credibility on the basis of generalizations, and they do not taint her earlier findings of credibility.

. . .

I must add that since writing these reasons I have had the opportunity of reading those of Major J. It is readily apparent that we are in agreement as to the nature of bias and the test to be applied in order to determine whether the words or actions of a trial judge raise a reasonable apprehension of bias. The differences in our reasons lies in the application of the principles and test we both rely upon to the words of the trial judge in this case. The principles and the test we have both put forward and relied upon are different from and incompatible with those set out by Justices L'Heureux-Dubé and McLachlin.

MAJOR J. (LAMER C.J.C. and SOPINKA J. concurring):— The trial judge stated that "police officers have been known to [mislead the court] in the past" and that "police officers do overreact, particularly when they are dealing with non-white groups" and went on to say "[t]hat to me indicates a state of mind right there that is questionable." She in effect was saying, "sometimes police lie and overreact in dealing with non-whites, therefore I have a suspicion that this police officer may have lied and overreacted in dealing with this non-white accused." This was stereotyping all police officers as liars and racists, and applied this stereotype to the police officer in the present case. The trial judge might be perceived as assigning less weight to the police officer's evidence because he is testifying in the prosecution of an accused who is of a different race. Whether racism exists in our society is not the issue. The issue is whether there was evidence before the court upon which to base a finding that this particular police officer's actions were motivated by racism. There was no evidence of this presented at the trial.

. . .

Trial judges have to base their findings on the evidence before them. It was open to the appellant to introduce evidence that this police officer was racist and that racism motivated his actions or that he lied. This was not done. For the trial judge to infer that based on her general view of the police or society is an error of law. For this reason there should be a new trial.

. . .

The life experience of this trial judge, as with all trial judges, is an important ingredient in the ability to understand human behaviour, to weigh the evidence, and to determine credibility. It helps in making a myriad of decisions arising during the course of most trials. It is of no value, however, in reaching conclusions for which there is no evidence. The fact that on some other occasions police officers have lied or overreacted is irrelevant. Life experience is not a substitute for evidence. There was no evidence before the trial judge to support the conclusions she reached.

. . .

Canadian courts have, in recent years, criticized the stereotyping of people into what is said to be predictable behaviour patterns. If a judge in a sexual assault case instructed the jury or him or herself that because the complainant was a prostitute he or she probably consented, or that prostitutes are likely to lie about such things as sexual assault, that decision would be reversed. Such presumptions have no place in a system of justice that treats all witnesses equally. Our jurisprudence prohibits tying credibility to something as irrelevant as gender, occupation or perceived group predisposition. . . It can hardly be seen as progress to stereotype police officer witnesses as likely to lie when dealing with non-whites. This would return us to a time in the history of the Canadian justice system that many thought had past. This reasoning, with respect to police officers, is no more legitimate than the stereotyping of women, children or minorities.

. . .

I agree with the approach taken by Cory J. with respect to the nature of bias and the test to be used to determine if the words or actions of a judge give rise to apprehension of bias. However, I come to a different conclusion in the application of the test to the words of the trial judge in this case. It follows that I disagree with the approach to reasonable apprehension of bias put forward by Justices L'Heureux-Dubé and McLachlin.

L'HEUREUX-DUBÉ J. (MCLACHLIN J. concurring):—

. . .

In our view, the test for reasonable apprehension of bias established in the jurisprudence is reflective of the reality that while judges can never be neutral, in the sense of purely objective, they can and must strive for impartiality. It therefore recognizes as inevitable and appropriate that the differing experiences of judges assist them in their decision-making process and will be reflected in their judgments, so long as those experiences are relevant to the cases, are not based on inappropriate stereotypes, and do not prevent a fair and just determination of the cases based on the facts in evidence. We find that on the basis of these principles, there is no reasonable apprehension of bias in the case at bar. Like Cory J. we would, therefore, overturn the findings by the Nova Scotia Supreme Court (Trial Division) and the majority of the Nova Scotia Court of Appeal that a reasonable apprehension of bias arises in this case, and restore the acquittal of R.D.S. This said, we disagree with Cory J.'s position that the comments of Judge Sparks were unfortunate, unnecessary, or close to the line. Rather, we find them to reflect an entirely appropriate recognition of the facts in evidence in this case and of the context within which this case arose — a context known to Judge Sparks and to any well-informed member of the community.

. . .

Cardozo recognized that objectivity was an impossibility because judges, like all other humans, operate from their own perspectives. As the Canadian Judicial Council noted in Commentaries on Judicial Conduct (1991), at p. 12, "[t]here is no human being who is not the product of every social experience, every process of education, and every human contact". What is possible and desirable, they note, is impartiality:

> The wisdom required of a judge is to recognize, consciously allow for, and perhaps to question, all the baggage of past attitudes and sympathies that fellow citizens are free to carry, untested, to the grave.

> True impartiality does not require that the judge have no sympathies or opinions; it requires that the judge nevertheless be free to entertain and act upon different points of view with an open mind.

. . .

As discussed above, judges in a bilingual, multiracial and multicultural society will undoubtedly approach the task of judging from their varied perspectives. They will certainly have been shaped by, and have gained insight from, their different experiences, and cannot be expected to divorce themselves from these experiences on the occasion of their appointment to the bench. In fact, such a transformation would deny society the benefit of the valuable knowledge gained by the judiciary while they were members of the Bar. As well, it would preclude the achievement of a diversity of backgrounds in the judiciary. The reasonable person does not expect that judges will function as neutral ciphers; however, the reasonable person does demand that judges achieve impartiality in their judging.

. . .

An understanding of the context or background essential to judging may be gained from testimony from expert witnesses in order to put the case in context: *R. v. Lavallee, R. v. Parks*, and *Moge v. Moge*, from academic studies properly placed before the Court; and from the judge's personal understanding and experience of the society in which the judge lives and works. This process of enlargement is not only consistent with impartiality; it may also be seen as its essential precondition. A reasonable person far from being troubled by this process, would see it as an important aid to judicial impartiality.

. . .

It is important to note that having already found R.D.S. to be credible, and having accepted a sufficient portion of his evidence to leave her with a reasonable doubt as to his guilt, Judge Sparks necessarily disbelieved at least a portion of the conflicting evidence of Constable Stienburg. At that point, Judge Sparks made reference to the submissions of the Crown that "there's absolutely no reason to attack the credibility of the officer", and then addressed herself to why there might, in fact, be a reason to attack the credibility of the officer in this case. It is in this context that Judge Sparks made the statements which have prompted this appeal. [The trial judge's] remarks do not support the conclusion that Judge Sparks found Constable Stienburg to have lied. In fact, Judge Sparks did quite the opposite. She noted firstly, that she was not saying Constable Stienburg had misled the court, although that could be an explanation for his evidence. She then went on to remark that she was not saying that Constable Stienburg had overreacted, though she was alive to that possibility given that it had happened with police officers in the past, and in particular, it had happened when police officers were dealing with non-white groups. Finally, Judge Sparks concluded that, though she was not willing to say that Constable Stienburg did overreact, it was her belief that he probably overreacted. And, in support of that finding, she noted that she accepted the evidence of R.D.S. that "he was told to shut up or he would be under arrest".

At no time did Judge Sparks rule that the probable overreaction by Constable Stienburg was motivated by racism. Rather, she tied her finding of probable overreaction to the evidence that Constable Stienburg had threatened to arrest the appellant R.D.S. for speaking to his cousin. At the same time, there was evidence capable of supporting a finding of racially motivated overreaction. At an earlier point in the proceedings, she had accepted the evidence that the other youth arrested that day, was handcuffed and thus secured when R.D.S. approached. This constitutes evidence which could lead one to question why it was necessary for both boys to be placed in choke holds by Constable Stienburg, purportedly to secure them. In the face of such evidence, we respectfully disagree with the views of our colleagues Cory and Major JJ. that there was no evidence on which Judge Sparks could have found "racially motivated" overreaction by the police officer.

. . .

While it seems clear that Judge Sparks did not in fact relate the officer's probable overreaction to the race of the appellant R.D.S., it should be noted that if Judge Sparks had chosen to attribute the behaviour of Constable Stienburg to the racial dynamics of the situation, she would not necessarily have erred. As a member of the community, it was open to her to take into account the well-known presence of racism in that community and to evaluate the evidence as to what occurred against that background. That Judge Sparks recognized that police officers sometimes overreact when dealing with non-white groups simply demonstrates that in making her determination in this case, she was alive to the well-known racial dynamics that may exist in interactions between police officers and visible minorities.

. . .

Judge Sparks' oral reasons show that she approached the case with an open mind, used her experience and knowledge of the community to achieve an understanding of the reality of the case, and applied the fundamental principle of proof beyond a reasonable doubt. Her comments were based entirely on the case before her, were made after a consideration of the conflicting testimony of the two witnesses and in response to the Crown's submissions, and were entirely supported by the evidence. In alerting herself to the racial dynamic in the case, she was simply engaging in the process of contextualized judging which, in our view, was entirely proper and conducive to a fair and just resolution of the case before her.

Gonthier J. (La Forest J. concurring):—I agree with Cory J. and L'Heureux-Dubé and McLachlin JJ. as to the disposition of the appeal and with their exposition of the law on bias and impartiality and the relevance of context. However, I am in agreement with and adopt the joint reasons of L'Heureux-Dubé and McLachlin JJ. in their treatment of social context and the manner in which it may appropriately enter the decision-making process as well as their assessment of the trial judge's reasons and comments in the present case.

***

If we accept that we must rely on informed generalizations to draw links between two facts in order to conclude that a fact is relevant or when assessing credibility, how is what Justice Sparks did in S. (R.D.) different from a trier of fact who concludes that a witness is not credible because he or she has a criminal record or has provided inconsistent statements, or that a witness' flight from the scene is evidence of a guilty mind?[14]

Professor Connie Backhouse, "Bias in Canadian Law: A Lopsided Precipice",[15] observes:

> . . . the initial finding of apprehension of bias against Canada's first African-Canadian judge, Corrine Sparks, is far from anomalous. An all-white bench of the Ontario Divisional Court had removed African-Canadian adjudicator, Frederica Douglas, from the tri-partite Ontario Police Complaints Board in 1994, also on the basis of reasonable apprehension of bias. The complaint involved a case in which an African-Canadian woman had alleged that she had been strip-searched by white police officers. The African-Canadian vice-president of the Toronto chapter of the Congress of Black Women had commented publicly to the media about the case. Douglas was removed from the board because she was the president of the Mississauga chapter of the same organization. Derrick Bell, an outstanding African American scholar of critical race issues, describes the phenomenon as "a widespread assumption that blacks, unlike whites, cannot be objective on racial issues and will favor their own no matter what." Bell notes that in the American context: "Black judges hearing racial cases are eyed suspiciously and sometimes asked to recuse themselves in favor of a white judge — without those making the request even being aware of the paradox in their motions.
>
> Since there are still very few judges who are drawn from racially distinct groups, it is useful to expand this analysis to encompass female adjudicators

---

[14] For competing views on *S. (R.D.)*, see Archibald, "The Lessons of the Sphinx: Avoiding Apprehensions of Judicial Bias in a Multi-racial, Multi-cultural Society" (1998), 10 C.R. (5th) 54 and Delisle, "An Annotation to *S. (R.D.)*" (1998), 10 C.R. (5th) 7. See also David M. Paciocco, "The Promise of *R.D.S.*: Integrating the Law of Judicial Notice and Apprehension of Bias" (1998) 3 Can. Crim. L. Rev. 319; R.F. Devlin, "We Can't Go On Together With Suspicious Minds: Judicial Bias and Racialized Perspective in *R. v. R.D.S.*" (1995) 18 Dal. L.J. 408; C.A. Alyward, "Take The Long Way Home: *R.D.S. v. R.* The Journey" (1998) 47 U.N.B.L.J. 249.

[15] (1997) 10 C.J.W.L. 170.

who have been challenged on the basis of gender bias. Here, too, it is noteworthy how many challenges of bias have emerged against a numerically small group of female adjudicators. The Honourable Maryka Omatsu has outlined the allegations of bias made against Ontario law professor Mary Jane Mossman, feminist litigators Mary Eberts, Lillian Pan, and Mayo Moran, and myself in an earlier issue of the *Canadian Women and the Law*. The thrust of these allegations seems to have been aimed at our reputations as feminist advocates. In addition, in *Great Atlantic & Pacific Co. of Canada v. Ontario* . . . the Ontario Court General Division concluded that the fact that I was one of 121 female law students, law professors, and lawyers who maintained an outstanding human rights complaint against Osgoode Hall Law School and York University was sufficient to disqualify me from adjudicating on "the same issues."

In *R. v. Hamilton*,[16] Doherty J.A. held as follows:

R. v. S.(R.D.) draws a distinction between findings of fact based exclusively on personal judicial experience and judicial perceptions of social context and findings of fact based on evidence viewed through the lens of personal judicial experience and social context. The latter is proper; the former is not.

2. DISCRETION AND LAW OF EVIDENCE

(a) Introduction

Recognizing a discretion in the trial judge recognizes room for choice, room for judgment. It's inherent in the nature of the exercise. We should not fear it nor should we insist on certainty in all our rules of evidence. The so-called "rules" of evidence were designed largely by trial judges seeking justice in their individual cases and were not meant to be a calculus rigidly applied. The best that we can do is to catalogue factors which are important to the sound exercise of discretion. Nor should discretion be feared as some form of palm-tree justice which is unreviewable. Protection against a trial judge's abuse of discretion should always be available by appeal.[17] Appellate court judges at the same time should recognize, however,

. . . the vantage point of the trial judge, the superiority of his position. It's not that he knows more. It's that he sees more, and sometimes smells more.[18]

What do we mean by "discretion"? Consider these contrasting views:

The discretion of a Judge is the Law of Tyrants; it is always unknown; it is different in different men; it is casual and depends on constitution, temper and passion. In the best it is often times caprice, in the worst it is every vice, folly and passion to which human nature is liable.[19]

Discretion when applied to a court of justice means sound discretion guided by law. It must be governed by rule not by humour; it must not be arbitrary, vague and fanciful, but legal and regular.[20]

---

[16]   (2004), 186 C.C.C. (3d) 129, 22 C.R. (6th) 1 (Ont. C.A.) at para. 126.
[17]   See e.g. *R. v. B. (C.R.)* (1990), 55 C.C.C. (3d) 1, 76 C.R. (3d) 1, [1990] 1 S.C.R. 717 at 23-24 [C.C.C.] (similar fact evidence)
[18]   Rosenberg, "Judicial Discretion" (1965) 38 The Ohio Bar 819.
[19]   Lord Camden in *Doe d. Hindson v. Kersey* (1765).
[20]   Lord Mansfield in *R. v. Wilkes* (1770), 4 Burr 2527 (H.L.) at 2539.

No one would speak in favour of the former type of discretion; no one however can deny the necessity of the latter. Discretion is endemic to the law of evidence and essential to any model of adjudication. There is a need to recognize that fact and to get on with the task of articulating the guidelines necessary to exercise the judicial function.

It is somewhat odd to see resistance to discretion in the application of the rules of evidence when we remind ourselves that in bench trials we regularly equip the trial judge with the ultimate discretion of finding guilt or innocence. When a judge seeks to reach a conclusion of fact from the evidence of witnesses, he or she discriminates as to weight and cogency. Jerome Frank referred to this exercise as "fact discretion".[21] A witness describes a past event. On analysis, the witness is stating his present recall of what he believes he then saw. The trier of fact observes the demeanour of the witness, sees him tested on cross-examination, and expresses her opinion regarding the correctness of the witness' belief. We have "subjectivity piled on subjectivity"; guesses upon guesses.[22] In this exercise, which is the best we can do, we trust in the judge to exercise her discretion in a sound manner and to discriminate wisely.[23]

A sound exercise of discretion is absolutely essential to the proper application of the rules of evidence and recognition of that fact will likely produce greater actual certainty at the sacrifice only of apparent certainty. In answer to those who fear discretion, listen to Professor Rosenberg:

> Discretion need not be, as Lord Camden said, a synonym for lawlessness or tyranny, if those who created it wield it and review its use are sensitive to the risks and responsibilities it raises, and if they play fair with the system; for the difference between government of law and government of man is not that the lawyers decide cases in one and fools in the other. Men, that is the judges, always decide. The difference is in whether judges are aware of their power, sensitive to their responsibilities and true to the tradition of the common law.[24]

We, properly, trust our judges to make all manner of preliminary and final decisions affecting the outcome of a case. It would be incongruous then to deny them the right to exercise discretion in judging how and what evidence will be heard by the trier of fact. We should always then be conscious of the policy on which the rule is based, so that we may gauge whether that policy is actually being advanced in the particular application of the rule and whether the policy that gave birth to the rule continues as a viable support.

In the proposed *Code of Evidence*,[25] the most important sections, indeed the *Code*'s heart and soul, were:

> 4. (1) All relevant evidence is admissible except as provided in this Code or any other Act.

---

21   *Courts on Trial* (1949) at 57.
22   *Ibid.*, Ch. III, Facts are Guesses.
23   See H.L. Krongold, "A Comparative Perspective on the Exclusion of Relevant Evidence: Common Law and Civil Law Jurisdictions" (2003) 12 Dal. J. Leg. Studies.
24   Rosenberg, *supra* note 18 at 826.
25   Law Reform Commission of Canada, 1975.

(2) "Relevant evidence" means evidence that has any tendency in reason to prove a fact in issue in a proceeding.

5. Evidence may be excluded if its probative value is substantially outweighed by the danger of undue prejudice, confusing the issues, misleading the jury, or undue consumption of time.

The *Code* was not accepted by the profession. The profession expressed great concern with equipping trial judges with discretion in the application of the law of evidence. Antonio Lamer was the Vice-Chairman of the Law Reform Commission at the time and G.V. La Forest was the Commissioner in charge of the Evidence Project. We shall discover that the Supreme Court was able to effectively establish judicially what these two jurists were unable to accomplish legislatively.

(b) Discretion to Exclude

Even though evidence is relevant to a legal issue in the case and therefore admissible, we will discover that the courts have over the past 30 years developed various forms of discretions to exclude. Sometimes exclusion occurs because of a canon of exclusion, such as the Hearsay Rule (to which there are a number of exceptions), where judicial tradition has been established favouring exclusion.

Here we consider the more general discretions available to judges to exclude otherwise admissible evidence. We will discover that:

1. In criminal cases, a discretion to exclude can be read into a statute.

2. In civil and criminal cases, there is now a discretion, at common law, to exclude where probative value is exceeded by prejudicial effect. Probative value refers to the strength of the inference that can be drawn.[26] By prejudicial effect, the concern is not that the evidence is unfavourable to the party's case but that the evidence will generate unfairness either by its misuse, the undue consumption of time or the confusion it creates.[27]

3. In criminal cases where evidence is tendered by the accused, the evidence may only be excluded where the probative value is substantially exceeded by its prejudicial effect (see especially *R. v. Seaboyer*, below).

4. In criminal cases there is also an uncertain discretion developed under the *Charter* to exclude evidence to ensure a fair trial.

5. In criminal cases, s. 24(2) gives courts discretion to exclude evidence obtained in violation of the *Charter* where admission would bring the administration of justice into disrepute (see *R. v. Grant*, below).

---

[26]   See *R. v. B. (L.)* (1997), 35 O.R. (3d) 35, 9 C.R. (5th) 38, 116 C.C.C. (3d) 481 (C.A.) at 46 [C.R.] per Charron J.A.

[27]   See Delisle, "Three Recent Decisions of the Supreme Court of Canada Affecting the Law of Similar Fact Evidence" (1992) 16 Prov. Judges J. 13 at 15 as cited by Justice Charron in *B. (L.)*, *ibid.* at para. 22.

(i) *Discretion to Exclude Read In to a Statute under the Charter*

CORBETT v. R.
[1988] 1 S.C.R. 670, 64 C.R. (3d) 1, 41 C.C.C. (3d) 385

The accused was convicted of murder. He appealed, arguing that he was deprived of his right to a fair hearing by reason of the introduction of evidence of his earlier conviction of another murder. The accused had sought a ruling that, if he was called as a witness, s. 12 of the *Canada Evidence Act* would not apply to him because of s. 11(d) of the *Charter* and he could not be cross-examined as to his prior criminal record. Under s. 12 "a witness may be cross-examined as to whether the witness has been convicted of any offence. . . .". The evidence of his previous conviction was elicited after a negative ruling by the trial judge. When the matter reached the Supreme Court, the Court was divided. The Court held 4-2 that a discretion should be read into s. 12 to make it constitutional. The four majority judges (see below) further divided 3-1 on the correct application of the discretion to the facts of the case. The sole dissent of La Forest on the facts was however accepted as properly stating the factors relevant to the exercise of the discretion.

DICKSON C.J.C. (Lamer J. concurring and Beetz J. concurring separately):—

. . .

I agree with La Forest J. that there is a discretion to exclude evidence of prior convictions of an accused. However, as I take a different view as to the manner in which the trial judge's discretion should have been exercised, it will be necessary for me to deal with the constitutional validity of s. 12 of the Canada Evidence Act.

Facts

Corbett was charged with the first-degree murder of Réal Pinsonneault, who was shot and killed in Vancouver on December 2, 1982. Corbett and Pinsonneault were involved in the cocaine trade. Corbett was financing Pinsonneault in the purchase of illegal drugs. At the time of the killing, Pinsonneault owed Corbett $27,000. Corbett travelled from Victoria to Vancouver on December 1, 1982, the day before the murder, with a female companion, Colleen Allan. At the time, he was on parole from a life sentence imposed in 1971 after his conviction on a charge of non-capital murder, upheld by this Court: *Corbett v. The Queen*, [1975] 2 S.C.R. 275. One of the conditions of his parole was that he had to stay within a 25-mile radius of the city of Victoria unless he had permission to leave the area. He had no such permission. The purpose of Corbett's trip to Vancouver was to collect the money Pinsonneault owed him. Corbett and Allan registered in the Sands Motor Hotel under the assumed name of "Baxter". Corbett testified that the reason for using an assumed name was that his trip to Vancouver constituted a violation of his parole conditions.

Pinsonneault shared an apartment with Michèle Marcoux (also known as Smith) and Gilles Bergeron, a few blocks away from the Sands Motor Hotel. On the evening of December 1, 1982, Corbett and Allan had dinner at the hotel and after much drinking, a prolonged argument ensued in their hotel room. The hotel clerk called at 12:30 a.m. to complain about the noise. An occupant in the next room of the hotel testified that he heard Corbett leaving the room and that he heard Allan try to persuade Corbett to return. He then heard Allan make a telephone call asking the other party if she could come over.

The following facts are taken from the judgment of Craig J.A. (at p.139):

> Marcoux and Bergeron testified that about 1:30 a.m. on December 2, 1982, Allan whom they knew from their association with Corbett, came to their apartment. Allan had an injury or cut near one of her eyes. A few minutes later, Corbett arrived. Pinsonneault let him into the apartment. After saying something to Allan, Corbett told Pinsonneault and Bergeron to sit down. When Pinsonneault protested, Corbett took out a gun and fired several shots, killing Pinsonneault instantly and wounding Bergeron. Marcoux escaped from the apartment.

Colleen Allan was not called by the Crown at the trial but was presented for cross-examination only. She had sworn at the preliminary hearing that neither she nor Corbett had left the hotel on the night in question. At the trial, however, she admitted that many of the statements she had made at the preliminary hearing, including that she had not seen the shooting of Pinsonneault, were untrue.

Bergeron had a serious criminal record. Marcoux also had a criminal record, although less serious than that of Bergeron. In the stories they gave to the police shortly after the shooting of Pinsonneault, neither Bergeron nor Marcoux identified Corbett as Pinsonneault's killer. At trial, Corbett's counsel forcefully cross-examined both witnesses, whom he later described in his address to the jury as "unmitigated liars". Both witnesses admitted their criminal records during examination-in-chief by Crown counsel.

Before calling any evidence, Corbett's counsel sought a ruling that, if the accused were called, s. 12 of the Canada Evidence Act would not apply to him because of s. 11(d) of the Charter, and therefore that Corbett could not be cross-examined as to his prior criminal record. The trial judge ruled against Corbett on this issue, following the decision of the British Columbia Supreme Court in R. v. Jarosz (1982), 3 C.R.R. 333. The accused was then called, and in order "to soften the blow" his own counsel put to him his criminal record, which Corbett admitted. The record is as follows:

— 23 April 1954 armed robbery, receiving stolen property, breaking, entering and theft (four counts)

— 12 May 1954 escaping custody

— 6 Dec. 1954 theft of auto, breaking and entering

— 8 Nov. 1971 non-capital murder

In his evidence, Corbett denied shooting Pinsonneault and swore that he left his hotel room only once during the night, to get some liquor and cigarettes from his car, the hotel clerk having testified that he had let Corbett back into the hotel at 3:10 a.m.

In charging the jury, the trial judge stated as follows with regard to the relevance of Corbett's criminal record:

> There was evidence tendered by the accused that he was previously convicted of a number of Criminal Code offences, including the offence of non-capital murder, which conviction was registered on November 8th 1971. Evidence of previous convictions is admissible only in respect to the credibility of the witness. It can only be used to assess the credibility of the accused, and for no other purpose. Because the accused was previously convicted of murder, it must not be used by you, the jury, as evidence to prove that the accused person committed the murder of which he stands charged. You, the jury, must not take the person's previous convictions into account in your deliberations when determining whether the Crown has proven beyond a reasonable doubt that the accused committed the murder with which he is charged.

This warning could hardly have been more explicit. Then, later in his direction, the trial judge reiterated his earlier instruction:

> Once again, Mr. Foreman and Members of the jury, I tell you that that type of evidence only goes to credibility, that is his previous criminal record.

The trial judge returned to the matter a third time and stated as follows:

> I have already told you that you must not use the criminal record of the Accused for any purpose other than credibility. You must not, under any circumstances, come to the conclusion that, because he has a criminal record, he would be more inclined or predisposed to commit this particular offence.

The case clearly turned on credibility and on whether the jury believed Bergeron and Marcoux or the accused. After deliberating for some 27 hours, the jury returned a verdict of guilty of second degree murder.

. . .

It is my view that on the facts of the present case a serious imbalance would have arisen had the jury not been apprised of Corbett's criminal record. Counsel for Corbett vigorously attacked the credibility of the Crown witnesses and much was made of the prior criminal records of Marcoux and Bergeron. What impression would the jury have had if Corbett had given his evidence under a regime whereby the Crown was precluded from bringing to the jury's attention the fact that Corbett had a serious criminal record? It would be impossible to explain to the jury that one set of rules applies to ordinary witnesses, while another applies to the accused, for the very fact of such an explanation would undermine the purpose of the exclusionary rule. Had Corbett's criminal record not been revealed, the jury would have been left with the quite incorrect impression that, while all the Crown witnesses were hardened criminals, the accused had an unblemished past. It cannot be the case that nothing short of this entirely misleading situation is required to satisfy the accused's right to a fair trial.

There is perhaps a risk that, if told of the fact that the accused has a criminal record, the jury will make more than it should of that fact. But concealing the prior criminal record of an accused who testifies deprives the jury of information relevant to credibility, and creates a serious risk that the jury will be presented with a misleading picture.

In my view, the best way to balance and alleviate these risks is to give the jury all the information, but at the same time give a clear direction as to the limited use they are to make of such information. Rules which put blinders over the eyes of the trier of fact should be avoided except as a last resort. It is preferable to trust the good sense of the jury and to give the jury all relevant information, so long as it is accompanied by a clear instruction in law from the trial judge regarding the extent of its probative value. . .

In my view, it would be quite wrong to make too much of the risk that the jury *might* use the evidence for an improper purpose. This line of thinking could seriously undermine the entire jury system. The very strength of the jury is that the ultimate issue of guilt or innocence is determined by a group of ordinary citizens who are not legal specialists and who bring to the legal process a healthy measure of common sense. The jury is, of course, bound to follow the law as it is explained by the trial judge. Jury directions are often long and difficult, but the experience of trial judges is that juries do perform their duty according to the law. We should regard with grave suspicion arguments which assert that depriving the jury of all relevant information is preferable to giving them everything, with a careful explanation as to any limitations on the use to which they may put that information. So long as the jury is given a clear instruction as to how it may and how it may not use evidence of prior convictions put to an accused on cross-examination, it can be argued that the risk of improper use is outweighed by the much more serious risk of error should the jury be forced to decide the issue in the dark. . .

I agree with La Forest J. that the trial judge has a discretion to exclude prejudicial evidence of previous convictions in an appropriate case.

However, I respectfully disagree with my colleague La Forest J. that this discretion should have been exercised in favour of the appellant in the circumstances of the present case. In his reasons, La Forest J. provides a useful catalogue of factors to which reference may be had in determining how this discretion is to be exercised. In my view, however, my colleague gives too little weight to the fact that in this case the accused appellant made a deliberate attack on the credibility of Crown witnesses, largely based upon their prior records.

LA FOREST J. (dissenting):—

. . .

GENERAL PRINCIPLES

As is true with respect to the resolution of most, if not all, issues relating to the law of evidence, resort must be had first and foremost to its animating or first principles, for it is only with reference to these that the more specific rules of evidence can be understood and evaluated. Failure to so reference discussion often results in the unhappy divorce of legal reasoning from common sense, with the consequence that rules of evidence are apt to be viewed as both self-sustaining and self-justifying. The present case further illustrates that statutory rules of evidence must also be interpreted in light of these guiding principles.

The organizing principles of the law of evidence may be simply stated. All relevant evidence is admissible, subject to a discretion to exclude matters that may unduly prejudice, mislead or confuse the trier of fact, take up too much time, or should otherwise be excluded on clear grounds of law or policy. Questions of relevancy and exclusion are, of course, matters for the trial judge, but over the years many specific exclusionary rules have been developed for the guidance of the trial judge, so much so that the law of evidence may superficially appear to consist simply of a series of exceptions to the rules of admissibility, with exceptions to the exceptions, and their sub-exceptions. . .

I agree with Professor Friedland that the law's sedulously fostered position, that the character of an accused may not be considered unless he first raises the issue or unless the Crown meets the criteria of similar fact evidence, ought not to easily yield to what a Law Reform Commission of Canada paper has described as "the fallacy [in s. 12] that it is rational to treat the accused like an ordinary non-party witness" (Evidence Study Paper 3, Credibility (1972), at p. 8). Furthermore, I think it self-evident that the law cannot profess to learn from common sense and experience and yet selectively ignore such lessons. I also think it significant that I have not unearthed any academic or empirical evidence tending to undermine these observations. Indeed, quite the contrary is true: see Wissler and Saks, "On the Inefficacy of Limiting Instructions: When Jurors Use Prior Conviction Evidence to Decide on Guilt" (1985), 9 L. & Human Behavior 37; also Ratushny and Friedland.

. . .

Having satisfied myself that the risk of prejudice is by no means speculative or illusory, I now turn to the question whether s. 12 admits of a discretion in the trial judge to prevent such prejudice materializing.

[Having found that there was a discretion, he continued.]

It is impossible to provide an exhaustive catalogue of the factors that are relevant in assessing the probative value or potential prejudice of such evidence, but among the most important are the nature of the previous conviction and its remoteness or nearness to the present charge.

. . .

. . . [T]he more similar the offence to which the previous conviction relates to the conduct for which the accused is on trial, the greater the prejudice harboured by its admission.

. . .

I think that a court should be very chary of admitting evidence of a previous conviction for a similar crime, especially when the rationale for the stringent test for admitting "similar fact" evidence is kept in mind. . .

. . .

As I indicated in my earlier comments respecting the admission into evidence of previous convictions for offences similar to that for which the accused is on trial, I think it self-evident that the prejudicial potential harboured by the admission at a trial for murder of a previous conviction for non-capital murder is manifestly profound. Furthermore, the probative value of this item of evidence in relation to credibility (which is the only use to which it legitimately could be put) is, at best, trifling, certainly in this case. The foregoing alone appears to satisfy a narrow reading of the test in *Wray*.

However, as I mentioned earlier, discretion cannot be judicially exercised in a vacuum; it is only with reference to the circumstances of the case that its exercise becomes meaningful. The circumstances of the present case, however, rather than "indicat[ing] strong reasons for disclosure" (*Gordon*, supra, at p. 940), militate strenuously for exclusion. It is true that the appellant had assailed the credibility of Crown witnesses, and indeed that credibility was the vital issue at trial. However, the circumstances of the case itself, indicating a violation by the appellant of his parole conditions, and the substance of the appellant's defence, indicating clearly the appellant's involvement in cocaine transactions, would have served to bring home to the jury the unsavoury criminal character of the appellant and, on the theory that such evidence affects credibility, this objective would have been fulfilled. This, along with the evidence of the appellant's previous convictions for theft and breaking and entering, amply served the purpose of impeaching his credibility. Indeed, the convictions for theft and breaking and entering, though quite remote in time, would appear far more probative of a disposition for dishonesty than a conviction for murder. The latter, in the circumstances of the case, added very little, if anything, to the jury's perception of the appellant's character for veracity; on the other hand, in the words of Hutcheon J.A. in the court below [p. 230], "it might well be that the fact that he had been convicted some years before of a similar offence might have been the last ounce which turned the scales against him". The jury's actions at trial in this case in no way diminish this possibility.

CONCLUSION

I conclude, therefore, that s. 12 of the Canada Evidence Act, when read in conjunction with the salutary common law discretion to exclude prejudicial evidence, does not violate an accused's right to a fair trial or deprive him of his liberty except in accordance with the principles of fundamental justice. Here, the trial judge erred in law in failing to recognize the existence of the exclusionary discretion described above, and consequently in admitting into evidence the previous conviction for murder. Given my belief that the introduction of this evidence was, in the circumstances of the case, unjustifiably prejudicial to the fairness of the appellant's trial, I am unable to conclude that no substantial wrong or miscarriage of justice was occasioned thereby. I would therefore allow the appeal, quash the conviction and order a new trial pursuant to s. 613(2)(*b*) of the Criminal Code. I would answer the first constitutional question in the negative, and consequently find it unnecessary to answer the second constitutional question.

Appeal dismissed.[28]

Where cross-examination of an accused under s. 12 is allowed the Supreme Court in *Corbett* requires a warning to the jury that the evidence can only be used to assess credibility rather than to show the accused is the type of bad character likely to have committed this crime. **Can the jury make and act on such a distinction?**[29] Jury instructions permitting evidence to be used for one purpose while prohibiting its use for some other purpose are known as "limiting instructions". Despite reasonable doubts about their effectiveness, limiting instructions are routinely used in Canadian jury trials to address a variety of evidence problems.[30]

In *R. v. Potvin* [31] the Supreme Court had to deal with the admissibility at trial of former testimony. The accused and two others, D. and T., were charged with murder. The Crown proceeded against the accused first, and called D. as a witness. Although D. had testified at the preliminary inquiry, he refused to testify at the trial. The transcript of D.'s testimony at the preliminary inquiry was received into evidence at trial pursuant to s. 643 [now s. 715] of the *Criminal Code*, and the accused was convicted. An appeal from his conviction was dismissed, and the accused appealed further. The Supreme Court allowed the appeal and ordered a new trial. The Court decided that the statutory provision did not violate s. 7 or s. 11(d) of the *Charter*. All five judges concluded, however, that a trial judge has a discretion to exclude former testimony, even though the statutory conditions have been met, and determined that the trial judge in this case had failed to exercise that discretion. Madam Justice Wilson, Justices Lamer and Sopinka concurring, wrote:

> . . . In my view there are two main types of mischief at which the discretion might be aimed. First, the discretion could be aimed at situations in which there has been unfairness in the manner in which the evidence was obtained. . . An example of unfairness in obtaining the testimony might be a case in which, although the witness was temporarily absent from Canada, the Crown could have obtained the witness's attendance at trial with a minimal degree of effort. Another example might be a case in which the Crown was aware at the time when the evidence was initially taken that the witness would not be available to testify at the trial but did not inform the accused of this fact so that he could make best use of the opportunity to cross-examine the witness at the earlier proceeding. . .

---

[28] See generally Delisle, "Case Note to *Corbett v. R.*" (1988) 67 Can. Bar Rev. 706.

[29] See Knazan, "Putting Evidence Out of Your Mind" (1999) 42 Crim. L.Q. 501. For how the discretion under s. 12 of the *Canada Evidence Act* has been exercised, see Chapter 5 C.3(c) Character of the Witness.

[30] See generally Lisa Dufraimont, "Limited Admissibility and Its Limitations" (2013) 46 U.B.C. L. Rev. 241.

[31] (1989), 68 C.R. (3d) 193 (S.C.C.).

A different concern at which the discretion might have been aimed is the effect of the admission of the previously-taken evidence on the fairness of the trial itself. This concern flows from the principle of the law of evidence that evidence may be excluded if it is highly prejudicial to the accused and of only modest probative value.

. . .

In my view,. . . s. 643(1) of the Code should be construed as conferring a discretion on the trial judge broader than the traditional evidentiary principle that evidence should be excluded if its prejudicial effect exceeds its probative value.[32]

Madam Justice Wilson stressed that even evidence of high probative value could be excluded if admission would render the trial unfair. She noted that the credibility of the witness in this case was critical, the jury had no opportunity to observe the witness' demeanour, and the trial judge had failed to consider this possible lack of fairness.[33]

Similar discretionary treatment was accorded the reception of videotaped interviews under s. 715.1 in the *Criminal Code*. In *R. v. L. (D.O.)*[34] the Supreme Court dealt with the admissibility of videotaped statements of young complainants in sexual assault cases pursuant to s. 715.1 of the *Criminal Code*. The question was whether the statutory provision was consistent with principles of fundamental justice. The Court of Appeal had held that s. 715.1 contravened ss. 7 and 11(d) of the *Charter* and could not be sustained under s. 1. The Supreme Court decided that the statutory provision did not violate the *Charter* as there was discretion in the trial judge in the application of the section. Lamer, C.J., La Forest, Sopinka, Cory, McLachlin and Iacobucci JJ., concurring, wrote:

[T]he incorporation of judicial discretion into s. 715.1, which permits a trial judge to edit or refuse to admit videotaped evidence where its prejudicial effect outweighs its probative value, ensures that s. 715.1 is consistent with fundamental principles of justice and the right to a fair trial protected by ss. 7 and 11(*d*) of the *Charter*.[35]

L'Heureux-Dubé J. (Gonthier J. concurring), wrote:

[T]he wording of s. 715.1 itself supports the interpretation that such a provision accommodates traditional rules of evidence and judicial discretion. Thus, in addition to the power to expunge or edit statements where necessary, the trial judge has discretion to refuse to admit the videotape in evidence if its prejudicial effect outweighs its probative value. Properly used, this discretion to exclude admissible evidence ensures the validity of s. 715.1 and is conversant with fundamental principles of justice necessary to safeguard the right to a fair trial enshrined in the *Charter*.[36]

---

[32]   *Ibid.* at 236-237.
[33]   See *R. v. Lewis*, 2009 ONCA 874, 249 C.C.C. (3d) 265 (Ont. C.A.) for an application of *Potvin* in the context of the non-disclosure of evidence prior to the testimony of a witness at the preliminary inquiry.
[34]   [1993] 4 S.C.R. 419.
[35]   *Ibid.* at 429.
[36]   *Ibid.* at 461.

Notice that in both *Potvin* and *L. (D.O.)* the statutory provisions say nothing about discretion in the trial judge. The judges in the Supreme Court of Canada, to ensure a fair trial, read the requirement in.

(ii) *Balancing Probative Value and Prejudicial Effect*

R. v. SEABOYER
[1991] 2 S.C.R. 577, 7 C.R. (4th) 117, 66 C.C.C. (3d) 321

The accused were charged with sexual assault. They argued that s. 276 of the *Criminal Code*, commonly known as the "rape shield provision", was unconstitutional because it deprived them of the ability to introduce relevant evidence. We will address the constitutional arguments in the next chapter. In this part of the judgment, the Supreme Court overruled its earlier decision in *R. v. Wray*[37] on the scope of a trial judge's discretion to exclude evidence. It also established a narrower discretion for defence evidence.

McLACHLIN J. (LAMER C.J.C., LA FOREST, SOPINKA, CORY, STEVENSON and IACOBUCCI JJ. concurring): —

. . . The precept that the innocent must not be convicted is basic to our concept of justice. One has only to think of the public revulsion felt at the improper conviction of Donald Marshall in this country or the Birmingham Six in the United Kingdom to appreciate how deeply held is this tenet of justice. Lamer J. (as he then was) put it this way in *Re B.C. Motor Vehicle Act*, *supra*, at p. 513:

> It has from time immemorial been part of our system of laws that the innocent not be punished. This principle has long been recognized as an essential element of a system for the administration of justice which is founded upon a belief in the dignity and worth of the human person and on the rule of law.

> . . .

The right of the innocent not to be convicted is dependent on the right to present full answer and defence. This, in turn, depends on being able to call the evidence necessary to establish a defence and to challenge the evidence called by the prosecution. As one writer has put it:

> If the evidentiary bricks needed to build a defence are denied the accused, then for that accused the defence has been abrogated as surely as it would be if the defence itself was held to be unavailable to him. (Doherty, supra, at p. 67).

> . . .

It is fundamental to our system of justice that the rules of evidence should permit the judge and jury to get at the truth and properly determine the issues. This goal is reflected in the basic tenet of relevance which underlies all our rules of evidence: see *Morris v. The Queen*, [1983] 2 S.C.R. 190, and *R. v. Corbett*, [1988] 1 S.C.R. 670. In general, nothing is to be received which is not logically probative of some matter requiring to be proved and everything which is

---

[37] (1970), 4 C.C.C. 1, 11 C.R.N.S. 235, [1971] S.C.R. 272.

probative should be received, unless its exclusion can be justified on some other ground. A law which prevents the trier of fact from getting at the truth by excluding relevant evidence in the absence of a clear ground of policy or law justifying the exclusion runs afoul of our fundamental conceptions of justice and what constitutes a fair trial.

The problem which arises is that a trial is a complex affair, raising many different issues. Relevance must be determined not in a vacuum, but in relation to some issue in the trial. Evidence which may be relevant to one issue may be irrelevant to another issue. What is worse, it may actually mislead the trier of fact on the second issue. Thus the same piece of evidence may have value to the trial process but bring with it the danger that it may prejudice the fact-finding process on another issue.

The law of evidence deals with this problem by giving the trial judge the task of balancing the value of the evidence against its potential prejudice. Virtually all common law jurisdictions recognize a power in the trial judge to exclude evidence on the basis that its probative value is outweighed by the prejudice which may flow from it.

Professor McCormick, in McCormick's Handbook of the Law of Evidence (2nd ed. 1972), put this principle, sometimes referred to as the concept of "legal relevancy", as follows at pp. 438-40:

> Relevant evidence, then, is evidence that in some degree advances the inquiry, and thus has probative value, and is prima facie admissible. But relevance is not always enough. There may remain the question, is its value worth what it costs? There are several counterbalancing factors which may move the court to exclude relevant evidence if they outweigh its probative value. In order of their importance, they are these. First, the danger that the facts offered may unduly arouse the jury's emotions of prejudice, hostility or sympathy. Second, the probability that the proof and the answering evidence that it provokes may create a side issue that will unduly distract the jury from the main issues. Third, the likelihood that the evidence offered and the counter proof will consume an undue amount of time. Fourth, the danger of unfair surprise to the opponent when, having no reasonable ground to anticipate this development of the proof, he would be unprepared to meet it. Often, of course, several of these dangers such as distraction and time consumption, or prejudice and surprise, emerge from a particular offer of evidence. This balancing of intangibles—probative values against probative dangers—is so much a matter where wise judges in particular situations may differ that a leeway of discretion is generally recognized.

This Court has affirmed the trial judges' power to exclude Crown evidence the prejudicial effect of which outweighs its probative value in a criminal case, but a narrower formula than that articulated by McCormick has emerged. In *Wray*, *supra*, at p. 293, the Court stated that the judge may exclude only "evidence gravely prejudicial to the accused, the admissibility of which is tenuous, and whose probative force in relation to the main issue before the court is trifling". More recently, in *Sweitzer v. The Queen*, [1982] 1 S.C.R. 949, at p. 953, an appeal involving a particularly difficult brand of circumstantial evidence offered by the Crown, the Court said that "admissibility will depend upon the probative effect of the evidence balanced against the prejudice caused to the accused by its admission". In *Morris, supra*, at p. 193, the Court without mentioning *Sweitzer* cited the narrower *Wray* formula. But in *R. v. Potvin*, [1989] 1 S.C.R. 525, La Forest J. (Dickson C.J. concurring) affirmed in general terms "the rule that the trial judge may exclude admissible evidence if its prejudicial effect substantially outweighs its probative value" (p. 531).

I am of the view that the more appropriate description of the general power of a judge to exclude relevant evidence on the ground of prejudice is that articulated in *Sweitzer* and generally accepted throughout the common law world. It may be noted that the English case from which the *Wray* formula was adopted has been superseded by more expansive formulae substantially in the language of *Sweitzer*.

The Canadian cases cited above all pertain to evidence tendered by the Crown against the accused. The question arises whether the same power to exclude exists with respect to defence evidence. Canadian courts, like courts in most common law jurisdictions, have been extremely cautious in restricting the power of the accused to call evidence in his or her defence, a reluctance founded in the fundamental tenet of our judicial system that an innocent person must not be convicted. It follows from this that the prejudice must substantially outweigh the value of the evidence before a judge can exclude evidence relevant to a defence allowed by law.

These principles and procedures are familiar to all who practise in our criminal courts. They are common sense rules based on basic notions of fairness, and as such properly lie at the heart of our trial process. In short, they form part of the principles of fundamental justice enshrined in s. 7 of the *Charter*. They may be circumscribed in some cases by other rules of evidence, but as will be discussed in more detail below, the circumstances where truly relevant and reliable evidence is excluded are few, particularly where the evidence goes to the defence. In most cases, the exclusion of relevant evidence can be justified on the ground that the potential prejudice to the trial process of admitting the evidence clearly outweighs its value.

R. v. GRANT
2015 SCC 9, [2015] 1 S.C.R. 475, 321 C.C.C. (3d) 27, 17 C.R. (7th) 229 (S.C.C.)

The accused was charged in 2007 with first degree murder of a 13-year-old girl, C.D., who died almost 23 years earlier. C.D. went missing after leaving school one afternoon and her body was found several weeks later tied up in a shed in an industrial yard. The accused sought to lead evidence suggesting that an unknown third party committed the murder. The third-party suspect evidence related to the alleged abduction of a 12-year-old girl, P.W., after she left school several months after the C.D. murder. The defence argued that the *modus operandi* and other physical evidence indicated that the same person abducted both girls. The accused was in custody on an unrelated matter at the time P.W. was allegedly abducted. The trial judge excluded the evidence related to P.W.

The jury found the accused guilty of second degree murder. The Manitoba Court of Appeal allowed the appeal, quashed the conviction and ordered a new trial. The Supreme Court of Canada dismissed the Crown's appeal.

KARAKATSANIS J.:—. . .

18 The truth-seeking function of the trial creates a starting premise that all relevant evidence is admissible (R. v. L. (D.O.), [1993] 4 S.C.R. 419; R. v. Corbett, [1988] 1 S.C.R. 670). Evidence is logically relevant where it has any tendency to prove or disprove a fact in issue (Corbett, at p. 715).

19 However, not all relevant evidence is admissible. The trial judge must also balance the probative value of the evidence against the prejudicial effects of its admission (R. v. Noël, 2002 SCC 67, [2002] 3 S.C.R. 433; Corbett; Sweitzer v. The Queen, [1982] 1 S.C.R. 949; Seaboyer; R. v. Harrer, [1995] 3 S.C.R. 562). Evidence led by the Crown will be excluded where its prejudicial effects outweigh its probative value (Seaboyer). The presumption of the accused's innocence leads us to strike a different balance where defence-led evidence is concerned. As this Court explained in Seaboyer, "the prejudice must substantially outweigh the value of the evidence before a judge can exclude evidence relevant to a defence allowed by law" (p. 611; see also R. v. Shearing, 2002 SCC 58, [2002] 3 S.C.R. 33; R. v. Arcangioli, [1994] 1 S.C.R. 129).

20 In order for the judge to put a defence to the jury, the accused must point to evidence on the record that gives the defence an air of reality (R. v. Cinous, 2002 SCC 29, [2002] 2 S.C.R. 3). The trial judge must determine whether there is some evidence that is "reasonably capable of supporting the inferences required for the defence to succeed" (ibid, at para. 83). The air of reality test applies to all defences, and acts as a threshold to ensure that "fanciful or far-fetched" defences are not put before the trier of fact (ibid, at para. 84). When applying this test, the trial judge must take the evidence to be true and must not assess credibility or make other findings of fact (Cinous, at para. 54).

21 These principles are distinct, but may be interrelated. In most cases, where the defence evidence relates to the facts underlying the offence charged, the logical relevance and the admissibility of the evidence will be obvious. However, where the evidence refers to a factual matrix beyond the offence charged, its relevance to a fact in issue or an available defence may be less clear. In such circumstances, the gate-keeping role of the trial judge may require her to determine whether the evidence is logically relevant and connected to a defence that has an air of reality. For example, while the degree of similarity may be logically relevant to whether the same person committed the offence, it will not relate to a fact in issue at trial unless the defence has an air of reality. In this case, the unknown third party suspect defence will not have an air of reality unless there is evidence that the accused could not have committed the other offence. Thus, logical relevance will sometimes be assessed with reference to whether the defence for which the evidence is tendered is available. That said, the air of reality test set out in Cinous does not displace the Seaboyer

admissibility test. The air of reality test and the Seaboyer admissibility test remain two distinct inquiries.

22 These principles are firmly established in this Court's jurisprudence and are not generally challenged by the parties to this appeal. Instead, the dispute concerns their proper application to evidence concerning an unknown third party suspect.

. . .

37 In my view, the admissibility of evidence concerning an unknown third party suspect is best determined in accordance with the broader, principled approach to the admission of evidence found in Seaboyer. Evaluating the admissibility of this evidence under Seaboyer, rather than under disparate tests not designed for its particularities, allows the trial judge to tailor her evaluation and weighing of the probative value and prejudicial effects of the evidence to the specific facts presented. In accordance with Seaboyer, once the evidence has been found to be relevant, unknown third party suspect evidence will be admitted unless its prejudicial effects substantially outweigh its probative value.

38 As noted above, there are two components to the Seaboyer analysis. First, in applying Seaboyer, the trial judge must assess the potential probative value of the evidence. Where the evidence relates to an unknown third party suspect, probative value will depend in part on the strength of the connection or nexus between the two events—that is, the degree of similarity between the indicted crime and the allegedly similar incident. As the Supreme Court of Wisconsin noted in Scheidell, "the greater the similarity, complexity, and distinctiveness of the events, as well as the relative frequency of the event, the stronger the case for admission": (para. 41, citing State v. Sullivan, 216 Wis.2d 768 (1998), at para. 54).

39 Second, the Seaboyer test is concerned with the potential prejudicial effects of the evidence. Unknown third party suspect evidence, like Crown-led similar fact evidence, poses a particular risk of reasoning prejudice. Introducing evidence of other crimes that are sufficiently similar to the crime charged may risk "the distraction of members of the jury from their proper focus on the charge itself aggravated by the consumption of time" (Handy, at para. 144).

40 However, these significant prejudicial effects must nonetheless be evaluated in accordance with the fundamental principles governing criminal proceedings. In giving constitutional protection to the accused's rights to make full answer and defence and to be presumed innocent until proven guilty, we must accept a certain amount of complexity, length, and distraction from the Crown's case as a necessary concession to the actualization of those rights. (See, for example Scheidell, at para. 65, per Abrahamson C.J., dissenting in the result.)

41 Contrary to the Crown's submissions, applying Seaboyer does not "[make] the test for admissibility turn on whether or not the third party is named" (A.F., at para. 44). Known third party suspect evidence is already subject to the Seaboyer admissibility test: do the prejudicial effects substantially outweigh the probative value? (See, for example R. v. Murphy, 2012 ONCA 573, 295 O.A.C. 281 (third party suspect evidence); R. v. Underwood, 2002 ABCA 310, 170 C.C.C. (3d) 500 (hearsay evidence of a third party suspect).) Indeed, defence-led evidence is generally subject to Seaboyer (Shearing (defence cross-examination of a complainant); R. v. Clarke (1998), 129 C.C.C. (3d) 1 (complainant's credibility); R. v. Jackson, 2013 ONCA 632, 301 C.C.C. (3d) 358, aff'd 2014 SCC 30, [2014] 1 S.C.R. 672 (deceased victim's criminal convictions); R. v. C. (T.) (2004), 189 C.C.C. (3d) 473 (Ont. C.A.) (third party records in the possession of the accused); Pollock (character evidence of a co-accused); R. v. Humaid (2006), 37 C.R. (6th) 347 (Ont. C.A.) (defence hearsay evidence); Hamilton (bad character evidence of the deceased)). Thus, while the principles in Seaboyer will always apply, they play out differently in different situations.

42 As this discussion demonstrates, many of the concerns animating the specific tests governing the admissibility of known third party suspect and similar fact evidence are also addressed in the Seaboyer analysis. In all cases, the evidence must be beyond mere speculation and conjecture. The value of the evidence must be balanced against the risks posed to the integrity of the trial when a party seeks to expand the ambit of the trial to individuals or events not directly related to the crime indicted.

. . .

45 The trial judge must determine whether the evidence is logically relevant to an available defence—one that can be put to the jury. The air of reality test requires the trial judge, taking the proposed evidence at its greatest strength, to determine whether the record would contain "a sufficient factual foundation for a properly instructed jury to give effect to the defence" (R. v. Buzizi, 2013 SCC 27, [2013] 2 S.C.R. 248, at para. 16). Where the defence's theory is that an unknown third party committed the indicted crime, this factual foundation will be established by a sufficient connection between the crime for which the accused is charged and the allegedly similar incident(s), coupled with the impossibility that the accused committed the other offence.

46 The trial judge must also assess and balance the extent of the probative value and prejudicial effects of the evidence in accordance with Seaboyer. Like the 'air of reality' test, the Seaboyer admissibility test does not permit the trial judge to decide how much weight to give the evidence or to make findings of fact. Doing so would usurp the role of the jury and would place a persuasive burden on the accused inconsistent with the presumption of innocence.

. . .

53 To summarize, any elevated risks of prejudice that arise when an accused seeks to introduce evidence of an unknown third party suspect do not require

the accused to satisfy a higher admissibility threshold or require the judge to engage in an enhanced evaluation of the evidence. Existing rules achieve the appropriate balance of maintaining the integrity of the trial process while protecting the right of an accused to make full answer and defence to the charges against her.

54 Thus, defence evidence is admissible where (1) the evidence is relevant to a fact in issue; and (2) the probative value of the evidence is not substantially outweighed by its prejudicial effects. Where the connection between the evidence and a fact in issue at trial is not obvious, the air of reality test may help a trial judge in determining if the evidence tends to prove a defence that may become available. Relevant evidence concerning an unknown third party suspect will only be excluded where its prejudicial effects substantially outweigh its probative value.

Application to the Facts

. . .

57 The Court of Appeal concluded that the evidence was "very relevant" and that its probative value arose from the marked similarities between the alleged abduction of P.W. and the crime for which Mr. Grant is charged. In each case, the victim was of a similar age. Both victims left school at the same time of day, on the same day of the week, nine months apart. Both were left in unlocked shed-like premises in the same industrial area of Winnipeg, 2.6 kilometres apart. Both victims were found abandoned with their hands and feet tied with similar knots. In neither case was there evidence of physical or sexual assault. The same type of gum wrapper was found at both scenes (although, in the crime charged, it was found in the deceased's pocket, suggesting it may have been hers).

. . .

59 The Court of Appeal was entitled to conclude that there was evidence upon which the jury could find that the subsequent crime had occurred and, having regard to the similarities, that it had been committed by the same person who killed Candace Derksen. In light of the evidence that the accused could not have committed the other offence, there was some evidence capable of giving the unknown third party suspect defence an air of reality.

. . .

65 The appeal is dismissed, and the Manitoba Court of Appeal's decision to order a new trial is upheld.

A trial judge's discretion to exclude evidence on the basis that its prejudicial effect outweighs its probative value is well-established but its scope remains uncertain. One long-standing question has been whether a trial judge may exclude evidence because it is unreliable. Historically, the tradition in Canadian law has been to consider questions of reliability as going only to the weight and not to the admissibility of evidence.[38] This traditional view was expressed in *R. v. Hodgson*,[39] where the Supreme Court held that "the quality, weight or reliability of evidence is a matter for the jury, and that the admission of evidence which may be unreliable does not per se render a trial unfair". In recent years, however, courts have increasingly recognized that reliability concerns can go to admissibility.

For example, in *Mitchell v. Minister of National Revenue*,[40] a case about Aboriginal rights discussed earlier in Chapter 1, the Supreme Court of Canada described the law of evidence in a way that seems to put reliability at the centre of the question of admissibility:

> The flexible adaptation of traditional rules of evidence to the challenge of doing justice in aboriginal claims is but an application of the time-honoured principle that the rules of evidence are not "cast in stone, nor are they enacted in a vacuum" (*R. v. Levogiannis*, [1993] 4 S.C.R. 475, at p. 487). Rather, they are animated by broad, flexible principles, applied purposively to promote truth-finding and fairness. The rules of evidence should facilitate justice, not stand in its way. Underlying the diverse rules on the admissibility of evidence are three simple ideas. First, the evidence must be useful in the sense of tending to prove a fact relevant to the issues in the case. Second, the evidence must be reasonably reliable; unreliable evidence may hinder the search for the truth more than help it. Third, even useful and reasonably reliable evidence may be excluded in the discretion of the trial judge if its probative value is overshadowed by its potential for prejudice.

More recently, the Supreme Court decided *R. v. Hart*, a case that turned on the admissibility of confessions obtained from a suspect during an undercover Mr. Big operation. *Hart* will be examined in detail in the discussion of confessions in Chapter 4. At this point, it is useful to examine the part of the judgment discussing the role of reliability in weighing probative value against prejudicial effect:

R. v. HART
2014 SCC 52, [2014] 2 S.C.R. 2014 CSC 52, 544, 312 C.C.C. (3d) 250, 12 C.R. (7th) 221 (S.C.C.)

MOLDAVER J.:

94 Determining whether the probative value of an item of evidence outweighs its prejudicial effect requires engaging in a "cost benefit analysis" (*R. v. Mohan*, [1994] 2 S.C.R. 9, at p. 21). That is, trial judges must assess "whether [the evidence's] value is worth what it costs" (*ibid.*). The first step in conducting this exercise, then, is to assess the value of the proposed evidence.

95 How are trial judges to assess the value of evidence? This requires more than asking whether the evidence is logically relevant; it necessitates some weighing

---

[38]   See e.g. *R. v. Buric* (1997), 106 C.C.C. (3d) 97, 48 C.R. (4th) 149 (Ont. C.A.), affirmed [1997] 1 S.C.R. 535, 114 C.C.C. (3d) 95 (S.C.C.); *R. v. Duguay* (2007), 50 C.R. (6th) 378 (N.B. C.A.).

[39]   [1998] 2 S.C.R. 449, 127 C.C.C. (3d) 449, 18 C.R. (5th) 135 (S.C.C.) at para. 21.

[40]   [2001] 1 S.C.R. 911 (S.C.C.) at para. 30.

of the evidence. After all, probative means "tending to prove an issue" and "questionable evidence will have less of that tendency" (*R. v. McIntyre*, 1993 CanLII 1488 (Ont. C.A.), at p. 2). It would be "artificial" and "self-defeating" for trial judges to ignore defects in the evidence during the assessment of its value (D. M. Paciocco and L. Stuesser, *The Law of Evidence* (6th ed. 2011, at p.38)). Generally, what this weighing exercise requires will vary depending on the specific inferences sought to be drawn from a piece of evidence.

96 As one example, trial judges are routinely called upon to determine the admissibility of expert evidence. Part of the admissibility inquiry involves taking stock of the probative value of the proposed evidence. This requires weighing the evidence and assessing its reliability:

> When one looks to potential probative value, one must consider the reliability of the evidence. Reliability concerns reach not only the subject matter of the evidence, but also the methodology used by the proposed expert in arriving at his or her opinion, the expert's expertise and the extent to which the expert is shown to be impartial and objective.

(*R. v. Abbey*, 2009 ONCA 624, 97 O.R. (3d) 330, 87, *per* Doherty J.A.)

97 Similarly, in *R. v. Humaid* (2006), 81 O.R. (3d) 456 (C.A.), Doherty J.A. held that otherwise admissible hearsay evidence may be excluded on the basis that its prejudicial effect outweighs its probative value. This can occur in circumstances where "the credibility or reliability of the narrator of the out-of-court statement is so deficient that it robs the out-of-court statement of any potential probative value" (para. 57). This Court endorsed that approach in *R. v. Blackman*, 2008 SCC 37, [2008] 2 S.C.R. 298, at para. 51.

98 Undoubtedly, weighing evidence in this way thrusts trial judges into a domain that is typically reserved for the jury. The jury, as the trier of fact, is ultimately responsible for weighing evidence and drawing conclusions from it. The overlap of roles cannot be avoided, but this is not problematic as long as the respective functions of the trial judge, as gatekeeper, and the jury, as finder of fact, are fundamentally respected. In conducting this weighing exercise, the trial judge is only deciding the threshold question of "whether the evidence is worthy of being heard by the jury" and not "the ultimate question of whether the evidence should be accepted and acted upon" (*Abbey*, at para. 89; see also Paciocco and Stuesser, at p. 38).

99 Returning to Mr. Big confessions, their probative value derives from their reliability. A confession provides powerful evidence of guilt, but only if it is true. A confession of questionable reliability carries less probative force, and in deciding whether the probative value of a Mr. Big confession outweighs the prejudicial effect of the character evidence that accompanies it, trial judges must examine its reliability.

Assuming *Hart* can be applied outside the narrow context of Mr. Big confessions, it provides strong support for the view that judges are empowered to exclude evidence on the ground that it is unreliable. In a commentary on *Hart*, David Tanovich put it this way:

> *Hart* is now the most explicit and highest authority on point. It has returned the law of evidence to first principles. The search for truth and justice are impeded by unreliable evidence and *Hart* and *Mitchell* make it clear that trial judges have an obligation to be the gatekeeper and regulate its admission. It now seems clear that where there is reason to be concerned about the reliability of a particular type of evidence, a trial judge must now ensure that there is sufficient threshold reliability in the particular case to give the evidence the necessary probative value to warrant its admission.[41]

Empowering trial judges to exclude evidence on reliability grounds has the potential to protect innocent people from being wrongly convicted on the basis of unreliable prosecution evidence.[42] Given the acknowledged problem of wrongful convictions in the Canadian criminal justice system, this potential to protect the innocent is probably the most important benefit to be gained by bringing reliability concerns within the ambit of the trial judge's discretion to exclude.

R. v. HUNTER
(2001), 155 C.C.C. (3d) 225, 45 C.R. (5th) 345 (Ont. C.A.)

The accused was charged with attempted murder of a police officer. At trial, the Crown sought to call Lorenzo DiCecco whose evidence was that on the day of the accused's preliminary hearing he was walking past the accused and his lawyer who were standing together in an open area of the Old City Hall. Mr. DiCecco said that he overhead the accused say: "I had a gun, but I didn't point it." He acknowledged that he just caught that part of the conversation. He agreed that there might have been conversation between the accused and his lawyer both before and after the overheard utterance. He could not give the Court the context of the utterance. After a *voir dire* the trial judge held this evidence to be admissible.

GOUDGE J.A. (MOLDAVER and ROSENBERG JJ.A. concurring):—

The appellant's first ground of appeal is that the trial judge erred in admitting the evidence of the appellant's utterance overheard by Mr. DiCecco. Relying on *R. v. Ferris* (1994), 34 C.R. (4th) 26 (S.C.C.) affirming (1993), 27 C.R. (4th) 141 (Alta. C.A.), the appellant argued that the utterance cannot

---

[41]   David M. Tanovich, "*Hart*: A Welcome New Emphasis on Reliability and Admissibility" (2014), 12 C.R. (7th) 298 at 302-303. See too Nikos Harris, "Justice for All: The Implications of *Hart* and *Hay* for Vetrovec Witnesses" (2015), 22 C.R. (7th) 105.

[42]   Kent Roach, "Unreliable Evidence and Wrongful Convictions: The Case for Excluding Tainted Identification Evidence and Jailhouse and Coerced Confessions" (2007) 52 Crim. L.Q. 210; Lisa Dufraimont, "Regulating Unreliable Evidence: Can Evidence Rules Guide Juries and Prevent Wrongful Convictions" (2008) 33 Queen's L.J. 261.

meet the threshold of relevance required for admissibility because its meaning cannot be determined without its context or alternatively its meaning is so speculative that it ought to have been excluded because its prejudicial effect outweighed its tenuous probative value. I agree.

The facts in *Ferris* closely parallel this case. The accused was arrested for murder and taken into police custody. He was permitted to telephone his father from the police station. A police officer walked past the accused on two occasions while he was on the phone. On the first occasion the accused was overheard to say "I've been arrested" and on the second occasion, shortly thereafter, "I killed David". The police officer heard the appellant talking before, after and in between the two sets of words but, apart from the quoted utterances, he could not tell what was said. The trial judge ruled that the officer could give evidence of the two overheard utterances.

Conrad J.A., writing for the majority in the Alberta Court of Appeal, turned first to whether, in the circumstances, it was possible to ascertain the meaning of these words so that they could be said to meet the relevance requirement for admissibility. She pointed out that the only possible relevance of these words was if they could be found to constitute an admission by the accused that he killed David. However, the Crown had no evidence of the words preceding or following the overheard phrases and Conrad J.A. cited examples of possible surrounding words that would make the full statement innocuous rather than an admission of guilt and hence not probative of any fact in issue. Given that there was a verbal context for the overheard phrases but no evidence of what that context was, Conrad J.A. found that a properly instructed jury could not determine from the fragmented utterance which was overheard the meaning either of the whole thought or of the overheard words themselves. Hence she concluded that these words could not be said to be probative of a fact in issue and were therefore irrelevant and inadmissible.

Conrad J.A. went on to find that since the utterance "I killed David" had no probative value (given that the court did not know the words surrounding it) and since the utterance was extremely prejudicial its exclusion must be favoured. On this basis as well she found that the overheard words should not have been admitted.

The Supreme Court of Canada dismissed the appeal from this judgment. The reasons of the court by Sopinka J. are as follows:

> In our opinion, with respect to the evidence that the respondent was overheard to say "I killed David", if it had any relevance, by reason of the circumstances fully outlined by Conrad J.A. [reported at (1994), 27 C.R. (4th) 141 (Alta. C.A.)], its meaning was so speculative and its probative value so tenuous that the trial judge ought to have excluded it on the ground its prejudicial effect overbore its probative value.

> The appeal is therefore dismissed.

In my view, Sopinka J.'s reasoning is anchored in the important role that context can play in giving meaning to spoken words. Where an overheard utterance is known to have a verbal context, but that context is itself unknown, it may be impossible to know the meaning of the overheard words or to otherwise conclude that those words represent a complete thought regardless of context. Even if the overheard words can be said to have any relevance, where their meaning is speculative and their probative value therefore tenuous yet their prejudicial effect substantial, the overheard words should be excluded.

When the principles derived from *Ferris* are applied to this case, I think the evidence must be excluded as it was in *Ferris.* The only possible relevance of the overheard utterance is if it could be found to constitute an admission by the appellant that he had a gun. Here, as in *Ferris,* the trial judge found that the overheard utterance had a verbal context, which is unknown and that it was part of a fuller statement. That statement may have been a statement such as "I could say I had a gun, but I didn't point it, but I won't because it is not true" or "What if the jury finds I had a gun but I didn't point it —— is that aggravated assault?" Neither would constitute an admission. Indeed, given the reasoning of the trial judge, had these possibilities been pointed out to him he might well have reached a different conclusion.

In my view, without the surrounding words, it would be impossible for a properly instructed jury to conclude that the overheard utterance was an admission or perhaps even what it meant. Clearly its meaning remains highly speculative. The trier of fact would have to guess at the words that came before and after to fix on a meaning. Since its meaning is highly speculative, its probative value is correspondingly tenuous. However, the substantial prejudicial effect is obvious. This balance clearly favours exclusion of the overheard utterance and, as in *Ferris,* that should have been the result.

ANDERSON v. MAPLE RIDGE (DISTRICT)
(1992), [1993] 1 W.W.R. 172 (B.C. C.A.)

The negligence alleged against the defendant municipality had to do with the placement of a stop sign and the nature of road markings at an intersection within its corporate limits; these were said to have contributed to the cause of a motor vehicle accident in which Anderson was seriously injured. Some months after the accident, the municipality moved the stop sign in question to a different location. A local resident, who testified to a frequency of accidents at that intersection before the sign was moved, was said to be able to give evidence that there had been no accidents since it was moved. The trial judge refused to admit any evidence relating to either the relocation of the sign or its apparent consequences. The plaintiff appealed.

Per WOOD J.A. (SOUTHIN and LEGG JJ.A. concurring):—

. . .

I begin with the fundamental proposition that evidence which is relevant, and which is not excluded by any rule of evidence, is admissible.

(a)   Was the evidence relevant?

Evidence is relevant if it is logically probative of either a fact in issue or a fact which itself is probative of a fact in issue. Evidence which tends to make the existence of a fact in issue either more or less probable is logically probative of that fact. . . Here, as an essential first step in his case, the appellant had to establish that the stop sign facing east bound traffic on Chigwell Street approaching Princess Street was, at the time, of the accident, positioned so as to be either difficult to see or easily overlooked by the very traffic it was meant to serve. Without proof of that there was no point moving on to consider what duty of care, if any, was owed by the municipality to the plaintiff, or whether that duty was breached.

In support of that essential fact the plaintiff offered the evidence of his expert, and the evidence of the police constable who attended at the scene of the accident. Mr. Arcand's evidence of the accident history of the intersection in question before the appellant's accident, and the evidence which he would have given if permitted, of what happened after the stop sign was moved, was offered for the same purpose. In my view that evidence would have been logically probative of the fact sought to be proved, in the sense that it could reasonably support the inference the sign was less visible to east bound drivers on Chigwell Street in its pre-accident location than it was after it was moved. Thus I am satisfied that the evidence which the trial judge excluded was relevant.

(b)   Was the evidence inadmissible by virtue of any exclusionary rule?

At different times throughout the course of argument, both in the court below and in this Court, at least two different "rules" were relied upon by the defendant as a basis. The first was that to which reference has already been made, namely the policy, which Wigmore discusses at para. 283 of Vol II of the Chadbourn Revision, which is said to exclude evidence of acts of "repair" or "improvement" undertaken by a defendant subsequent to the occurrence giving rise to the cause of action.

This policy is said by Wigmore to have two distinct rationales. The first is the fact that such acts of repair or improvement, by themselves, will most often support nothing more than an inference that the owner believed the prior condition was capable of causing injury such as that alleged, a state of mind which is equally consistent with a belief that the injury was in fact caused in some other way. Thus there is no "probable" inference to draw from such acts and they should be excluded. The other rationale is that evidence of such acts would likely be overemphasized by juries, thus inhibiting all owners, the careful as well as the negligent, from undertaking repairs or improvements which would enure to the benefit of all. While the learned editor concedes that the first rationale is theoretically weak, it is suggested that when combined with the second "policy" rationale, the impropriety of admitting such evidence is clear.

With respect I do not agree with the first rationale. In my view it is the product of Wigmore's concept of "legal relevance" which requires that "[e]ach single piece of evidence must have a plus value" before it can be received in evidence. But as Lamer, J. (as he then was) made clear in *Morris v. The Queen*, [1983] 2 S.C.R. 190, at pp.199-201, the law in Canada has never adopted that supercharged view of relevance. Instead, we have adhered to Thayer's analysis which applies principles of logic and common sense to determine relevance, and which, subject to recognized exclusionary rules, admits all evidence logically probative of a fact in issue, reserving for the court only a narrow discretion to exclude for reasons of policy or fairness.

As for the second rationale described by Wigmore, Seaton, J.A. in *Cominco Ltd. v. Westinghouse Canada Limited et al* (1979), 11 B.C.L.R. 142 noted the following at p. 157:

> No case binding on us supports an exclusionary rule based on policy and I am not inclined to introduce such a rule. In my view a defendant will not expose other persons to injury and himself to further lawsuits in order to avoid the rather tenuous argument that because he has changed something he has admitted fault.

The fact is that the argument advanced by the respondent goes further than even Wigmore would attempt to take the exclusionary rule which he describes, for after reviewing several authorities, the following appears in para. 283 in the latter's work at p. 185:

> Accordingly, it is conceded by almost all courts that no act in the nature of repairs, improvements, substitution, or the like, done after the occurrence of an injury, is receivable as evidence of a consciousness (or an "implied admission"), on the part of the owner, of his negligence, connivance, or other culpability in causing the injury.

The learned editor then goes on to point out:

> There may of course be other evidential purposes for which the acts in question may be relevant; in that event they are to be received, subject to a caution restricting their use to a specific proper purpose.

As I have noted, the evidence at issue in this case, as it was described in argument, was relevant to the question whether the pre-accident location of the stop sign made it difficult to see. The exclusionary rule described in Wigmore does not purport to limit its admissibility for that purpose, so long as the Jury are instructed that standing by itself the evidence can not be taken as an admission of liability.

The other "exclusionary rule" relied upon by the respondent, both here and in the court below, was a general discretion which a trial Judge is said to have, in a civil case, to exclude evidence the relevance of which is overshadowed by its prejudicial effect. This was, in fact, the "rule" relied upon by the trial judge when he held the evidence to be inadmissible.

There is no doubt that a Judge trying a civil case in Canada has a discretion to exclude relevant evidence on the ground that its prejudicial effect outweighs its probative value; *Draper v. Jacklyn et al*, [1970] S.C.R. 92, per Spence, J. What is less clear is under what circumstances that discretion should be exercised. There is a paucity of jurisprudence on the subject. Counsel did refer us to a 1975 English Court of Appeal decision in *Mood Music Publishing Co. Ltd. v. De Wolfe Ltd.*, [1976] 1 All E.R. 763, where Lord Denning, M.R. said this at p. 766 in connection with the admissibility of similar fact evidence in that case:

> The admissibility of evidence as to 'similar facts' has been much considered in the criminal law. Some of them have reached the highest tribunal, the latest of them being *Boardman v. Director of Public Prosecutions*. The criminal courts have been

very careful not to admit such evidence unless its probative value is so strong that it should be received in the interests of Justice: and its admission will not operate unfairly to the accused. In civil cases the courts have followed a similar line but have not been so chary of admitting it. In civil cases the courts will admit evidence of similar fact evidence if it is logically probative, that is if it is logically relevant in determining the matter which is in issue; provided that it is not oppressive or unfair to the other side; and also that the other side has fair notice of it and is able to deal with it.

To the extent that this passage suggests there is a more narrow discretion to exclude prejudicial evidence in civil cases than exists in criminal cases, it would appear to be at odds with the situation in this country where the broad scope of the discretion suggested by Spence, J. in *Draper v. Jacklyn et al.*, stands in contrast to the very narrow discretion to exclude described in the decision of the Supreme Court of Canada a year later in *Regina v. Wray*, [1971] S.C.R. 272.

The exact scope of the discretion of the court trying a civil case, to exclude otherwise relevant evidence because of its prejudicial effect, is a complex question that can be left for another day. I am satisfied that whatever that scope may be, it was exceeded in this case. The only potential prejudice to the defendant, resulting from the admission of the evidence in question, was that already discussed, namely that the jury might improperly draw the inference that by changing the position of the stop sign the municipality was admitting negligence. But the jury could, and should, have been told that standing alone the evidence could not be used for that purpose, and I have every confidence that if such instruction had been given it would have been followed. In my view, in the absence of evidence to suggest that it would be impossible for a reasonable jury to follow such an instruction, there could be no basis for the exercise of the discretion to exclude otherwise relevant evidence.

In the result, I am of the view that the trial judge erred when he excluded the evidence that the stop sign in question was moved by the defendant municipality some months after the appellant's accident, and that, so far as Mr. Arcand knew, no further accidents had occurred at that intersection since that date.

Subsequent civil cases have identified the discretion broadly. For example, in *Landolfi v. Fargione*,[43] the trial judge excluded video surveillance evidence relied on by the defendant to impeach the plaintiff on the extent of his injuries. Justice Cronk held that the trial judge had erred in exercising his exclusionary discretion:

> I conclude that while the probative value of the video evidence may not have been high, it was not trifling. Nor did the potential prejudicial effect of the videos outweigh their probative value. It was for the jury, as the trier of fact, to determine what weight, if any, should attach to the evidence of Landolfi and his medical experts elicited through cross-examination on the videos. Although this court will not lightly interfere with the discretionary decision by a trial judge to exclude

---

[43]   (2006), 79 O.R. (3d) 767 (Ont. C.A.) at para. 66.

potentially prejudicial evidence, the exclusion of the videos in this case was based on the application of the wrong legal test for admissibility and a flawed analysis of their prejudicial effect.

However, in *Homolka v. Harris*,[44] Justice Saunders observed that "the extent to which evidence in a civil case will be excluded on the basis of prejudice may not coincide always with the experience in criminal cases, an issue which is unresolved as Mr. Justice Wood pointed out in *Anderson v. Erickson*..." **Should the discretion in civil cases be narrower than in criminal cases? What policy arguments support such an argument?**

(iii) *Assessing Trial Fairness*

R. v. HARRER
[1995] 3 S.C.R. 562, 42 C.R. (4th) 269, 101 C.C.C. (3d) 193

The accused's boyfriend escaped from custody in Vancouver while awaiting extradition to the United States. The United States immigration officers began an investigation which led them to the accused. The accused was herself suspected of being illegally in the United States. The accused was arrested and she was given the "Miranda" warning against self-incrimination. She was later taken to a State Police post. The immigration officers left her with U.S. Marshals and advised that the Marshals wanted to question her. At some point the interview shifted to the accused's alleged criminal participation in her boyfriend's escape, but she was not given another warning as would be required under the *Canadian Charter of Rights*. American law does not require a second warning. The accused was returned to Canada, the Marshals forwarded her statements to police in Vancouver, and she was charged with assisting in an escape from custody, contrary to s. 147(a) of the *Criminal Code*. At trial, the Crown attempted to adduce the statement to the United States Marshals but the judge ruled that the interrogation violated s. 10(b) of the *Charter*, which guarantees the right of a person arrested or detained to retain and instruct counsel without delay. The evidence was rejected on the basis that its admission would bring the administration of justice into disrepute. Accordingly, the accused was acquitted. On appeal to the British Columbia Court of Appeal, a new trial was ordered on the ground that the *Charter* has no application to interrogations conducted in the United States. The accused appealed to the Supreme Court of Canada. The appeal was dismissed. The Supreme Court decided that the rights flowing from s. 10(b) to persons arrested or detained had no application in this case. The *Charter* applied when the Canadian police began proceedings against the accused. If the admission of crucial evidence, such as the out-of-court self-incriminatory statement, would violate the principles of fundamental justice, the trial would not be fair. The Supreme Court held that there was no unfairness in the manner in which the

---

[44]   (2002), 100 B.C.L.R. (3d) 218, [2002] 6 W.W.R. 432 (C.A.).

evidence was obtained. Although *dicta*, the following excerpt emphasizes the trial judge's role in conducting a fair trial.

LA FOREST J. (LAMER C.J.C., L'HEUREUX-DUBÉ, SOPINKA, GONTHIER, CORY and IACOBUCCI JJ. concurring):—

. . .

Would, then, the admission of the impugned evidence result in an unfair trial? In approaching this issue, I do not think one can automatically assume that the evidence was unfairly obtained or that its admission would be unfair (which may not be precisely the same question) simply because it was obtained in a manner that would in this country violate a Charter guarantee. As in other cases involving broad concepts like "fairness" and "principles of fundamental justice", one is not engaged in absolute or immutable requirements; these concepts vary with the context in which they are invoked; see *Lyons*, at p. 361. Specifically here, one is engaged in a delicate balancing to achieve a just accommodation between the interests of the individual and those of the state in providing a fair and workable system of justice; see my remarks in *Thomson Newspapers Ltd. v. Canada (Director of Investigation and Research, Restrictive Trade Practices Commission)*, [1990] 1 S.C.R. 425, at p. 539. On the same page in that case, it is recognized that different balances may be achieved in different countries, all of which are fair or, to put it in s. 7 terminology, "in accordance with the principles of fundamental justice". I add that this Court has also stated that "s. 7 of the *Charter* entitles the appellant to a fair hearing; it does not entitle him to the most favourable procedures that could possibly be imagined"; see *Lyons, supra*, at p. 362. It follows that, in the present context, evidence may be obtained in circumstances that would not meet the rigorous standards of the *Charter* and yet, if admitted in evidence, would not result in the trial being unfair.

Looking specifically at the present situation, it is obvious that Canada cannot impose its procedural requirements in proceedings undertaken by other states in their own territories. And I see no reason why evidence obtained in other countries in a manner that does not conform to our procedures should be rejected if, in the particular context, its admission would not make the trial unfair. For us to insist that foreign authorities have followed our internal procedures in obtaining evidence as a condition of its admission in evidence in Canada would frustrate the necessary cooperation between the police and prosecutorial authorities among the various states of the world. Moreover, we must be mindful that a constitutional rule may be adopted to ensure that our system of obtaining evidence is so devised as to ensure that a guaranteed right is respected as a matter of course. Thus there may well be cases where in an objective sense there may be no unfairness where a second warning is not given to a suspect when an investigation moves to a more serious offence, but by imposing the rule we encourage a type of police practice that ensures the individual's right to counsel is respected. The rule is not geared to the individual case alone, but to ensuring the fairness of the system and general respect for this country's constitutional values. We have no systemic concern of this kind in relation to the actions of foreign police abroad. We are concerned solely with whether the admission of evidence in the particular case will affect the fairness of the trial.

On the other hand, Canada is not bound by the law of other countries in conducting trials in this country. We must, in determining whether evidence should be admitted into evidence, be guided by our sense of fairness as informed by the underlying principles of our own legal system as it applies to the specific context of the case. The fact that the evidence was obtained in another country in accordance with the law of that country may be a factor in assessing fairness. Its legality at the place in question will necessarily affect all participants, including the police and the individual accused. More specifically, conformity with the law of a country with a legal system similar to our own has even more weight, for we know that a number of different balances between conflicting principles can be fair; see *Thomson Newspapers, supra*, at p. 539.

But the foreign law is not governing in trials in this country. For example, it may happen that the evidence was obtained in a manner that conformed with the law of the country where it was obtained, but which a court in this country would find in the circumstances of the case would result in unfairness if admitted at trial. On the other hand, the procedural requirements for obtaining evidence imposed in one country may be more onerous than ours. Or they may simply have rules that are different from ours but are not unfair. Or again we may not find in the particular circumstances that the manner in which the evidence was obtained was sufficiently objectionable as to require its rejection. In coming to a decision, the court is bound to consider the whole context.

At the end of the day, a court is left with a principled but fact-driven decision. Thus far, there have been few, if any other cases on the issue. As the number of cases increases, more precise legal principles or guidelines may, of course, develop. In the United States, for example, the law seems to be to admit evidence obtained in a foreign country unless the manner of its obtention shocks the conscience; see *United States v. Toscanino*, 500 F.2d 267 (2d Cir. 1974), at p. 276; *United States of America v. Hensel*, 509 F.Supp. 1364 (1981), at p. 1372. I agree that one should not be overly fastidious or adopt a chauvinistic attitude in assessing practices followed in other countries but, given the few cases on the matter, I am not at this stage prepared to accept that the unfairness must be such as to shock the conscience to warrant rejection. Simply, what we seek is a fair trial in the specific context, and I am by no means sure this requirement can be satisfied by the rejection of foreign evidence only in the most egregious circumstances. It is right to add, however, that this issue does not arise here because I am satisfied that there was no unfairness in the circumstances of this case.

. . .

I would be inclined to think that evidence obtained following a *Miranda* warning should ordinarily be admitted in evidence at a trial unless in the light of other circumstances the court has reason to think the admission of the evidence would make the trial unfair.

There were no such circumstances here — quite the opposite. As I mentioned, not only was the *Miranda* warning given at the outset of the questioning by the Immigration agents; it was also later recalled to the appellant when the police began their questioning. As well, before the relevant statements were made, the interrogating Marshal impressed upon the appellant the seriousness of her situation and his knowledge that she was involved in the escape. On a reading of the judge's findings, it is abundantly clear that the appellant (whom the trial judge, despite her age, described as a "cagey witness" and as "a street wise and sophisticated young woman" intimately associated with a fugitive sought on charges of high level cocaine trafficking) knew full well that she was being questioned in relation to the very matter in respect of which it is argued a second warning should have been given. Under these circumstances, I am at a loss to understand how these statements would, if admitted, result in the trial being unfair.

I should add that, had the circumstances been such that the admission of the evidence would lead to an unfair trial, I would have had no difficulty rejecting the evidence by virtue of the *Charter*. I would not take this step under s. 24(2), which is addressed to the rejection of evidence that has been wrongfully obtained. Nor would I rely on s. 24(1), under which a judge of competent jurisdiction has the power to grant such remedy to a person who has suffered a *Charter* breach as the court considers just and appropriate. Rather, I would reject the evidence on the basis of the trial judge's duty, now constitutionalized by the enshrinement of a fair trial in the *Charter*, to exercise properly his or her judicial discretion to exclude evidence that would result in an unfair trial.

I shall, however, attempt to put more flesh on this approach because the argument was strongly advanced that since there was no breach of the *Charter* in obtaining the evidence, a prerequisite to the power to exclude evidence under s. 24(2) of the *Charter*, there was no *Charter* based jurisdiction to exclude evidence. The difficulty with this contention is that it fails to appreciate the full nature of a fair trial. As I mentioned, while s. 24(2) is directed to the exclusion of evidence obtained in a manner that infringed a *Charter* right, it does not operate until there is a *Charter* breach. What we are concerned with here is not the remedy for a breach but with the manner in which a trial must be conducted if it is to be fair.

The law of evidence has developed many specific rules to prevent the admission of evidence that would cause a trial to be unfair, but the general principle that an accused is entitled to a fair trial cannot be entirely reduced to specific rules. In *R. v. Corbett*, [1988] 1 S.C.R. 670, a majority of this court made it clear that a judge has a discretion to exclude evidence that would, if admitted, undermine a fair trial; see also *R. v. Potvin*, [1989] 1 S.C.R. 525. . . In *Thomson Newspapers*, supra, I attempted to explain that this approach is a necessary adjunct to a fair trial as guaranteed by s. 11(*d*) of the Charter in the following passage:

> There can really be no breach of the *Charter* until unfair evidence is admitted. Until that happens, there is no violation of the principles of fundamental justice and no denial of a fair trial. Since the proper admission or rejection of derivative evidence does not admit of a general rule, a flexible mechanism must be found to deal with the issue contextually. That can only be done by the trial judge.

I went on to further explain, as I had in *Corbett*, supra, that the common law principle had now been constitutionalized by the *Charter's* guarantee of a fair trial under s. 11(*d*) of the *Charter*. I continued:

> The fact that this discretion to exclude evidence is grounded in the right to a fair trial has obvious constitutional implications. The right of an accused to a fair hearing is constitutionalized by s. 11(*d*), a right that would in any event be protected under s. 7 as an aspect of the principles of fundamental justice.

The effect of s. 11(*d*), then, is to transform this high duty of the judge at common law to a constitutional imperative. As I noted in *Thomson Newspapers*, judges must, as guardians of the Constitution, exercise this discretion where necessary to give effect to the *Charter's* guarantee of a fair trial. In a word, there is no need to resort to s. 24(2), or s. 24(1) for that matter. In such circumstances, the evidence is excluded to conform to the constitutional mandate guaranteeing a fair trial, i.e., to prevent a trial from being unfair at the outset.

McLACHLIN J. (MAJOR J. concurring):—

. . .

[T]he argument [is] that the conduct of the American police prior to the taking of the statement requires its exclusion from evidence to preserve a fair trial in Canada. The argument is simply put. Every person charged in Canada has a right to a fair trial. The Canadian courts are bound to provide this fair trial, and to this end may exclude evidence which would render a trial unfair. Admission of Harrer's second statement would render her trial unfair. Therefore the trial judge correctly excluded it.

The first premise of this argument does not permit of dissent. Every person tried in Canada is entitled to a fair trial. The right to a fair trial is the foundation upon which our criminal justice system rests. It can neither be denied nor compromised. The common law has for centuries proclaimed it, and the Canadian Charter confirms it. Section 11(d) provides that "Any person charged with an offence has the right . . . to be presumed innocent until proven guilty according to law in a fair and public hearing by an independent and impartial tribunal". The right to a fair trial is also a "principle of fundamental justice" which s. 7 of the Charter requires to be observed where the liberty of the subject is at stake.

The second premise of the argument, that judges have the power to exclude evidence where its admission would render the trial unfair, while less obvious, is readily resolved. At common law, a trial judge has a discretion to exclude evidence "if the strict rules of admissibility would operate unfairly against the accused": *Kuruma v. The Queen*. Similarly, in Canada, the discretion allows exclusion of evidence that "would undermine the right to a fair trial": *R. v. Corbett*, considering s. 12 of the Canada Evidence Act. . .

In addition to the common law exclusionary power, the Charter guarantees the right to a fair trial (s. 11(d)) and provides new remedies for breaches of the legal rights accorded to an accused person. Evidence obtained in breach of the Charter may only be excluded under s. 24(2): *R. v. Therens*,

[1985] 1 S.C.R. 613. Evidence not obtained in breach of the Charter but the admission of which may undermine the right to a fair trial may be excluded under s. 24(1), which provides for "such remedy as the court considers appropriate and just in the circumstances" for Charter breaches. Section 24(1) applies to prospective breaches, although its wording refers to "infringe" and "deny" in the past tense: *Operation Dismantle Inc. v. The Queen*, [1985] 1 S.C.R. 441. It follows that s. 24(1) permits a court to exclude evidence which has not been obtained in violation of the Charter, but which would render the trial unfair contrary to s. 11(d) of the Charter.

. . .

Whether a particular piece of evidence would render a trial unfair is often a matter of some difficulty. A distinction must be made at the outset between unfairness in the way a statement was obtained and an unfair process or trial. The situation in which police take evidence is complex. Even where every effort is made to comply with the law, aspects of the process may, in hindsight, be argued to have been less than fair. Sometimes the unfairness is minor or rendered insignificant by other developments (for example, that the police would probably have obtained the evidence anyway) or by other aspects of the case (for example, that the accused waived or acquiesced in the unfairness). Sometimes the unfairness is more serious. The point is simply this: unfairness in the way evidence is taken may affect the fairness of the admission of that evidence at trial, but does not necessarily do so. This is true for *Charter* breaches; not every breach of the *Charter* creates an unfairness at trial which requires exclusion of the evidence thereby obtained: *R. v. Collins*, [1987] 1 S.C.R. 265, at p. 284. It must also be true for irregularities that do not constitute *Charter* breaches.

At base, a fair trial is a trial that appears fair, both from the perspective of the accused and the perspective of the community. A fair trial must not be confused with the most advantageous trial possible from the accused's point of view: *R. v. Lyons*, [1987] 2 S.C.R. 309, at p. 362, per La Forest J. Nor must it be conflated with the perfect trial; in the real world, perfection is seldom attained. A fair trial is one which satisfies the public interest in getting at the truth, while preserving basic procedural fairness to the accused.

Evidence may render a trial unfair for a variety of reasons. The way in which it was taken may render it unreliable. Its potential for misleading the trier of fact may outweigh such minimal value it might possess. Again, the police may have acted in such an abusive fashion that the court concludes the admission of the evidence would irremediably taint the fairness of the trial itself. In the case at bar, police abuse or unfairness is the only ground raised, and hence the only one with which we need concern ourselves.

. . .

The question is whether the failure of the foreign police to comply with the procedures required under the Charter in Canada so taints the evidence that its admission would result in an unfair trial. In my view, it does not. This is because the police conduct of which Harrer complains was, viewed in all the circumstances of this case, including the expectations of Harrer in the place where the evidence was taken, neither unfair or abusive. Since the police conduct was not unfair, it follows necessarily that its admission cannot render the trial unfair.

In *R. v. White*,[45] a majority of the Supreme Court held that the trial judge's discretion to exclude evidence, the admission of which would render the trial unfair, can indeed be grounded in s. 24(1) of the *Charter*.

(iv) *Bringing Administration of Justice into Disrepute (Charter, s. 24(2))*

In addition to the discretion witnessed above we should recognize of course that there is given in the *Charter* an express discretion to exclude evidence obtained in violation of an accused's rights. Section 24 provides:

> 24. (1) Anyone whose rights or freedoms, as guaranteed by this Charter, have been infringed or denied may apply to a court of competent jurisdiction to obtain such remedy as the court considers appropriate and just in the circumstances.

> (2) Where, in proceedings under subsection (1), a court concludes that evidence was obtained in a manner that infringed or denied any rights or freedoms guaranteed by this Charter, the evidence shall be excluded if it is established that, having regard to all the circumstances, the admission of it in the proceedings would bring the administration of justice into disrepute.

Under s. 24(2), the focus is on whether admission of the evidence at trial will bring the administration of justice into disrepute, but the decision will depend on "all the circumstances". As we explain in the Preface, this topic is better explored in Criminal Procedure courses since one of the main factors is the seriousness of the *Charter* violation and this requires a full assessment of each *Charter* right. What follows here is a brief discussion of major Supreme Court rulings on s. 24(2).

In *R. v. Collins*,[46] Chief Justice Lamer identified as a "matter of personal taste" three groups of factors to be considered. Under the first grouping, where an accused had been conscripted against himself or herself, the trial would be rendered unfair and the evidence should generally be excluded. The second factor was the seriousness of the breach and the third, the effect of admission or exclusion on the administration of justice. Ten years later Justice Cory, speaking for a 5-4 majority in *R. v. Stillman*,[47] refused to change course and held that conscriptive evidence is generally inadmissible — because of its presumed impact on trial fairness — unless it would have been independently discovered. For several years the effect of *Stillman* was the drawing of a bright line: conscripted evidence was almost always excluded and non-conscripted evidence almost always included. A

---

45   [1999] 2 S.C.R. 417, 135 C.C.C. (3d) 257, 24 C.R. (5th) 201 (S.C.C.).
46   [1987] 1 S.C.R. 265 at para. 36.
47   [1997] 1 S.C.R. 607 at para. 80.

satisfactory definition of conscription also proved elusive. In *Stillman*, Justice Cory described conscription broadly as a process in which the accused is "compelled to participate in the creation or discovery of the evidence", and also as a narrow category approach of compelled incrimination "by means of a statement, the use of the body or the production of bodily samples". Courts tended to rely on the category test when defining conscription, which sometimes led to strange results.

The approach to s. 24(2) changed with the bellwether rulings of the Canadian Supreme Court in *R. v. Grant*[48] and *R. v. Harrison*.[49] In *Grant* a 6-1 majority rejected the *Collins/Stillman* conscripted/non-conscripted dichotomy as too rigid for a discretionary power, hard to apply and yielding inconsistent results. It asserted a discretionary approach with revised criteria and emphasis. The Court arrived at a revised discretionary approach to s. 24(2) free of rigid rules but placing special emphasis on the factor of the seriousness of the breach rather than the seriousness of the offence or the reliability of the evidence. The same criteria are to be applied to all cases of *Charter* breach. Furthermore, the Court emphasized that where the trial judge has considered the proper factors, appellate courts should accord considerable deference to his or her ultimate determination.

In a joint judgment, Chief Justice McLachlin and Justice Charron (Binnie, LeBel, Fish and Abella JJ. concurring) settled on the following revised template:

> When faced with an application for exclusion under s. 24(2), a court must assess and balance the effect of admitting the evidence on society's confidence in the justice system having regard to:
>
> (1) the seriousness of the Charter-infringing state conduct (admission may send the message the justice system condones serious state misconduct),
>
> (2) the impact of the breach on the Charter-protected interests of the accused (admission may send the message that individual rights count for little), and
>
> (3) society's interest in the adjudication of the case on its merits.
>
> The court's role on a s. 24(2) application is to balance the assessments under each of these lines of inquiry to determine whether, considering all the circumstances, admission of the evidence would bring the administration of justice into disrepute.[50]

According to the Chief Justice and Justice Charron, the words of s. 24(2) capture its purpose: to maintain the good repute of the administration of justice. Viewed broadly, the term "administration of justice" embraces maintaining the rule of law and upholding *Charter* rights in the justice system as a whole. The phrase "bring the administration of justice into

---

48   [2009] 2 S.C.R. 353, 245 C.C.C. (3d) 1, 66 C.R. (6th) 1 (S.C.C.). The Court built on the earlier analysis of Arbour J. in *R. v. Buhay*, [2003] 1 S.C.R. 631, 174 C.C.C. (3d) 97, 10 C.R. (6th) 205 (S.C.C.) respecting the exclusion of non-conscripted evidence.

49   [2009] 2 S.C.R. 494, 245 C.C.C. (3d) 86, 66 C.R. (6th) 105 (S.C.C.).

50   *Grant, supra* note 48 at para. 71.

disrepute" must be understood in the long-term sense of maintaining the integrity of, and public confidence in, the justice system. The inquiry is objective. It asks whether a reasonable person, informed of all relevant circumstances and the values underlying the *Charter*, would conclude that the admission of the evidence would bring the administration of justice into disrepute. Deterring police misconduct is not the aim, although it could be a happy windfall.[51]

In *R. v. Côté*[52] an 8-1 majority of the Supreme Court strongly reasserts the approach to s. 24(2) it declared in *Grant* and *Harrison*. Faced with an exclusion decision for multiple *Charter* violations in an investigation of a domestic murder case, the Quebec Court of Appeal arrived at a compromise along the lines of the now-rejected *Collins/Stillman* dichotomy: the conscripted evidence of statements should be excluded but the non-conscripted reliable evidence, here forensic evidence found in a warrantless search contrary to s. 8, was to be admitted as the murder offence was serious. According to Justice Cromwell for the Supreme Court majority, the Quebec Court of Appeal had firstly erred in intervening on the basis that the police had not deliberately acted in an abusive manner. The Court had exceeded its role by its recharacterization of the evidence, which departed from express findings by the trial judge of deliberate and systemic police misconduct not tainted by any clear and determinative error. The Court of Appeal had also erred in interfering with the trial judge's s. 24(2) determination by assigning greater importance to the seriousness of the offence. Justice Cromwell powerfully reasserts that once there has been a determination on the first and second *Grant* factors that the *Charter* violation or violations were serious, the factors of the seriousness of the offence, the reliability of the evidence and the importance of the evidence to the Crown's case are not determinative and should not lead to admission.

Most Canadian academics have welcomed the abandonment of the dichotomy between conscripted and non-conscripted evidence.[53] The abandonment of the *Collins/Stillman* trial fairness yardstick has admittedly set up an inconsistency with the separate discretion to exclude under s. 11(d) to ensure a fair trial, which the Court recognized in *R. v. Harrer*.[54] This rarely exercised discretion is mostly applied in trials in Canada where the *Charter*

---

51   *Ibid.* at para. 73. Compare the pro-State view of the majority of the U.S. Supreme Court that the exclusionary remedy in that jurisdiction requires evidence that exclusion will deter this type of police conduct in the future (*Herring v. U.S.*, 129 S.Ct. 695 (U.S. Sup. Ct., 2009)).

52   [2011] 3 S.C.R. 215, 87 C.R. (6th) 1, 276 C.C.C. (3d) 42 (S.C.C.). See too the majority ruling in *R. v. Paterson*, 2017 SCC 15, [2017] 1 S.C.R. 202, 347 C.C.C. (3d) 280, 35 C.R. (7th) 229 (S.C.C.) and Doherty J.A. in *R. v. McGuffie*, 2016 ONCA 365, 336 C.C.C. (3d) 486, 28 C.R. (7th) 243 (Ont. C.A.).

53   See Stuart, *Charter Justice in Canadian Criminal Law*, 7th ed. (2018) at 690-709 and authors there cited. See too Penney, Rondinelli & Stribopoulos, *Criminal Procedure in Canada* (LexisNexis, 2011) at 557-573. David Paciocco, "Section 24(2): Lottery or Law — The Appreciable Limits of Purposive Reasoning" (2011) 58 Crim. L.Q. 1 is, however, less enthusiastic about the new regime and expresses concerns *inter alia* about too much discretion for trial judges and the discounting of the factor of seriousness of the offence.

54   [1995] 3 S.C.R. 562, 101 C.C.C. (3d) 193, 42 C.R. (4th) 269 (S.C.C.). See further Paciocco, *supra* note 53 at 22-23, 39-43.

breach occurred outside our borders. The *Harrer* jurisprudence needs to be reconsidered and made consistent with *Grant*.

There can be no doubt now that *Grant* has put in place a robust discretionary exclusion remedy for s. 24(2). Surveys now indicate that across the country trial judges are likely to exclude for *Charter* violations in roughly two out of every three cases for all types of *Charter* breaches, whatever the type of evidence.[55] Appeal courts are less likely to exclude. Of course the discrepancy between trial and appeal courts may be explained by the reality that courts of appeal are more likely to be confronted by selective Crown appeals against exclusion decisions by trial judges based on unreasonable errors. And *Côté* sends an unmistakable message that absent errors, appeal courts should defer to rulings by trial judges.

The importance of this reality should not be exaggerated. In the vast majority of criminal trials across the country, *Charter* issues are not even raised and often, where they are, *Charter* violations are not found. But it is the reality that in hundreds of rulings each year where *Charter* violations are found, the s. 24(2) remedy of exclusion is now regularly invoked. In s. 24(2) cases it is clear that trial judges are to be concerned not only about truth concerning guilt or innocence, but also about the truth that police officers are often proved to be deliberately flouting, careless or ignorant about *Charter* standards. If there is a concern about exclusion of highly probative evidence the question should be directed against the apparently lax and ineffective training of police officers respecting *Charter* standards, even where they are clearly established. If the police learned to apply *Charter* standards there would be no possibility of exclusion. The police disregard for the *Charter* in *Côté*, a serious but routine domestic assault investigation, is shocking and an affront to the rule of law, as found by the trial judge, Justice Cournoyer.

In *Hudson v. U.S.*[56] Justice Scalia, writing for a 5-4 majority, refused to apply the exclusionary rule to a violation of the Fourth Amendment "knock-and-announce" rule. He suggested that the exclusion remedy may no longer be necessary because of the increasing professionalism of police forces, with wide-ranging reforms in education, training and supervision, better internal discipline, and various forms of citizen review.

Policing and review standards have improved in Canada as well. However, those preferring alternative remedies, such as civil suits and police complaints procedures, now bear a heavy burden of demonstrating their comparative efficacy. In Canada they have thus far generally proved to be a poor and low-visibility response to systemic problems of police abuse or ignorance of their powers under an entrenched *Charter*. Police are rarely, if ever, disciplined for *Charter* breaches. Civil litigation is expensive, uncertain in outcome, and, if successful, likely to be subject to confidentiality

---

[55]   See Mike Madden "Empirical Data on Section 24(2) under *Grant*" (2010), 78 C.R. (6th) 278 (and see also in (2011) 14 Can. Crim. L. Rev. 229) and, for a similar Quebec survey, see Thierry Nadon in (2011), 86 C.R. (6th) 33. The most comprehensive survey is that of Ariane Asselin, "Trends for Exclusion of Evidence in 2012" (2013), 1 C.R. (7th) 74, which reports the major findings of her LL.M. thesis at Queen's: "The Exclusionary Rule in Canada: Trends and Future Directions", online: <http://hdl.handle.net/1974/8244>.

[56]   547 U.S. 586 (U.S. Mich., 2006).

agreements. Civil litigation is also highly unlikely where the plaintiff is in prison. In *Ward v. City of Vancouver*[57] the Supreme Court recently recognized a new right to sue civilly for compensation for a *Charter* breach but pragmatically restricted the remedy to superior courts.[58]

Thankfully our Supreme Court in *Grant* and *Harrison* saw the need for a vigorous remedy of exclusion for serious *Charter* breaches, however serious the crime (35 kilograms of cocaine were excluded in *Harrison,* found in a vehicle search held to violate search and seizure and arbitrary detention rights in ss. 8 and 9). In this area as in others, our Supreme Court, mindful of its role as guardian of our Constitution, has given our criminal justice system a welcome balance against law and order expediency. In considering exclusion remedies courts must be especially concerned with the long-term integrity of the justice system if *Charter* standards for the accused are ignored and/or operate unequally against vulnerable groups, such as Indigenous people and racialized youth.[59]

PROBLEMS

Problem 1

In a civil suit for negligent injury arising out of a motor vehicle collision, counsel wants the jury to see pictures of the plaintiff's injuries soon after her emergency surgery. Her face is bruised and disfigured with bones showing and also medical pins to hold her fractured skull together. **Relevant? Receivable? Does it matter that the photographs are in colour? What if counsel for the plaintiff wants to wheel in the plaintiff in her hospital bed where she has been confined for a year? Relevant? Receivable?** See *Draper v. Jacklyn*, [1970] S.C.R. 92 and compare *R. v. Wade* (1994), 18 O.R. (3d) 33 (C.A.), *R. v. S. (J.)* (2008), 236 C.C.C. (3d) 486 (Ont. S.C.J.) and *R. v. Teerhuis-Moar* (2009) 65 C.R. (6th) 335 (Man. Q.B.). See too *R. v. Patrick* (2007), 46 C.R. (6th) 187 (Ont. S.C.J.) and *R. v. S. (C.L.)* (2009), 266 C.C.C. (3d) 344 (Man. Q.B.).

Problem 2

In a prosecution for assault causing bodily harm the accused argued self-defence. The incident occurred at Joe's Bar. The accused wants to lead evidence that the alleged victim had a reputation as a bully, that the alleged victim regularly beat on newcomers to the bar. **Relevant? Receivable? Does it matter whether the accused was aware of the alleged victim's reputation prior to the incident? Why? If you say the evidence is**

---

[57]   [2010] 2 S.C.R. 28, 76 C.R. (6th) 207 (S.C.C.).

[58]   The justifications the Court gave for this new civil remedy, such as the need for deterrence and stress on a functional approach, are inconsistent with the rationales the Court relied on for s. 24(2) exclusion in *Grant*. See further Paciocco, *supra* note 53 at 20-27.

[59]   In developing standards for strip searches the majority of the Court in *R. v. Golden*, [2001] 3 S.C.R. 679, 47 C.R. (5th) 1, 159 C.C.C. (3d) 449 (S.C.C.) at para. 83 took into account Commission findings of overrepresentation of African-Canadians and Indigenous people in the Canadian criminal justice system and likely disproportionality in arrests and searches.

relevant, what is the premise that rationally connects the evidence offered with the proposition sought to be established? Is that premise indisputable? Usually true? Sometimes true? Rarely true?

Problem 3

The accused was charged with speeding. He allegedly travelled 30 K.P.H. in a school zone that prescribed a limit of 20 k.p.h. The prosecutor wants to call a witness who will testify that he saw the accused, a block away from the school zone, travelling at 40 k.p.h. in a 30 k.p.h. zone. **Relevant? Why? Premise? Always or sometimes true? Suppose the observation was made three blocks away? A mile away?** The accused wants to tender evidence that the police officer who gave him the speeding ticket had been told by his superior that week that if he didn't issue his quota of speeding tickets he'd be suspended. **Relevant? Prejudicial? Receivable?**

Problem 4

The accused is charged with the theft of a rare stamp. The Crown wants to lead evidence that the accused is a stamp collector. **Relevant? Premise? Receivable?**

Problem 5

Smith sues Jones for damages arising out of a motor vehicle accident. Jones earlier pleaded guilty to a charge of dangerous driving arising out of the same incident and Smith seeks to tender this fact in evidence. Relevant? Receivable? See *Pollard v. Simon*, [2009] B.C.J. No. 1258 (B.C. Prov. Ct.). **If Jones had pleaded not guilty would that fact be relevant? Receivable when tendered by Jones? If he was acquitted would that fact be receivable? If convicted?** See *Toronto (City) v. C.U.P.E., Local 79*, [2003] 3 S.C.R. 77. **What if the trial judge in the criminal case concluded that not only was there reasonable doubt but she was satisfied that Jones was innocent?** See *Polgrain Estate v. Toronto East General Hospital* (2008), 60 C.R. (6th) 67 (Ont. C.A.).

Problem 6

The accused is charged with possession of a weapon for a purpose dangerous to the public peace. In his bedroom the police found a loaded .25 calibre pistol. From a kitchen cupboard they seized notes handwritten in Italian. The notes have been translated and an expert has testified that they are a constitution of a secret Italian criminal organization related to the Mafia and that anyone in possession of them almost certainly had to belong to the organization. **Are the notes relevant? Receivable?** Compare *R. v. Caccamo* (1975), 29 C.R.N.S. 78 (S.C.C.).

Problem 7

The plaintiff sues the sues defendant bus company for personal injuries sustained as the result of negligent operation of a bus claimed to belong to the defendant. On the facts presented the defendant concedes that the evidence warranted the submission to the jury of the question of the operator's negligence in the management of the bus. The accident occurred on Main Street at 1:00 a.m. and the only description of the bus came from the plaintiff who was able to describe the bus simply as "a great big, long, wide affair". Records at City Hall indicate that the defendant bus company was the only bus company licensed to operate on that street. The defendant's timetable shows its buses scheduled to leave North Square for South Square via Main Street at 12:15 a.m., 12:45 a.m., 1:15 a.m., and 1:45 a.m. **Are these records relevant? Receivable? Sufficient?** Compare *Smith v. Rapid Transit Inc.*, 58 N.E. 2d 754 (Mass. Sup. Ct., 1945). See also *People v. Collins*, 438 P. 2d 33 (Cal. Sup. Ct., 1968).

Problem 8

In a civil suit for negligence the plaintiff seeks to tender evidence that the defendant is insured. **Relevant?** The plaintiff argues that it is rational to infer that a person who is insured is less apt to careful, as he is fully protected against loss, and to then infer that he was careless on the particular occasion under review. The defendant argues that being insured marks him as one of those careful and wise individuals who take all appropriate precautions against risk. **If the evidence is relevant ought it to be received?** See *Hamstra v. BC Rugby Union*, [1997] 1 S.C.R. 1092.

Problem 9

The accused is charged with the murder of his wife. Following the discovery of the body and upon informing his children that their mother was dead, the accused unsuccessfully tried to take his own life. **Is the evidence admissible? On what basis? Is the strength of the Crown's case relevant to the question of admissibility?** See *R. v. Sodhi* (2003), 179 C.C.C. (3d) 60 (Ont. C.A.).

Problem 10

The accused was arrested at Pearson International Airport after returning to Toronto following a trip to Ghana. Customs officers discovered 1.038 kilograms of heroin secreted in the insoles of three pairs of shoes that were found in his possession. The only disputed issue at trial was knowledge. The accused testified that a former girlfriend who lives in Ghana gave him the shoes and that he was not aware that they contained heroin. Apart from the evidence relating to the discovery of the heroin, the Crown relied on evidence of its value and of the accused's poor financial situation in an effort to demonstrate a motive to import narcotics into Canada. **Was the evidence as to the accused's financial status relevant? Was it admissible?** See *R. v. Mensah* (2003), 9 C.R. (6th) 339 (Ont. C.A.).

See comments by Michael C. Plaxton, "Poverty and Motive" (2003), 9 C.R. (6th) 345 and David Tanovich, "Relevance, Social Context and Poverty" (2003), 9 C.R. (6th) 348. See further *R. v. Phillips*, 2008 ONCA 726 (Ont. C.A.).

Problem 11

A police officer shot to death a man stopped as a robbery suspect. The officer testified that he did so because the victim made a quick movement with his hand to his coat as if going for a gun. The officer was sued for a civil rights violation. The jury found against the officer and awarded $1.6 million in damages. The officer appeals on the basis that the trial judge erred in placing before the jury that the victim was in fact unarmed. **Relevant? Premise? Receivable?** See *Sherrod v. Berry*, 856 F.2d 002 (U.S. 7th Cir., 1988).

Problem 12

The accused was charged with murder after his 22-year-old girlfriend, a student at the Scarborough campus of the University of Toronto, disappeared in circumstances suggesting foul play. The victim's body was never found. The accused was convicted of the murder in 1992, but the Court of Appeal quashed the conviction and ordered a new trial in 2004.

At the opening of the second trial, the accused applied to introduce third-party suspect evidence suggesting that the victim may have been murdered by Paul Bernardo. The proffered evidence was of two kinds. First, there was evidence of Bernardo's proven crimes of sexual assault and murder. Second, there was other evidence linking Bernardo to the victim's murder, including evidence that Bernardo had met the victim, evidence that the victim had been seen with a man matching Bernardo's general description, evidence that Bernardo was seen acting suspiciously on the Scarborough campus around the time of the victim's disappearance, and evidence of other crimes admitted by Bernardo but not established by independent investigation. **How would you rule?**

Compare *R. v. Baltovich* (2008), 56 C.R. (6th) 369 (Ont. S.C.J.).

Problem 13

The accused was charged with three counts of sexual assault. The female complainant claimed that the accused attacked her on three occasions while the accused claimed the sexual activity was consensual. At trial, defence counsel seeks to use a visual prop during his closing address to the jury: a medieval painting by Sandro Botticelli entitled "Calumny of Apelles". The painting depicted a young man being falsely accused, with female figures representing slander, ignorance, suspicion, fraud, conspiracy and repentance. Defence counsel planned to use the painting as a memorable tool of persuasion to show that the theme of false accusation was not invented by defence lawyers but has been depicted in historical works of art and literature. **How would you rule on admissibility?**

See *R. v. Muvunga*, 2013 ONSC 3076, 3 C.R. (7th) 292 (Ont. S.C.J.).

Problem 14

The accused was charged with first degree murder of an Indigenous woman, C.G. The Crown alleges that C.G. was a prostitute who bled to death in the bathtub of the accused's hotel room as a result of an 11 cm cut to her vaginal wall. A Crown expert is called to testify that this wound was caused by a sharp object. He wants to tender evidence of a preserved part of the vaginal tissue. The Crown argued that the tissue was real evidence, relevant and material to an issue at trial, not subject to any exclusionary rule, and its probative value exceeded any prejudicial effect on the accused. The defence opposed the motion, arguing it was unnecessary and duplicative of the Crown expert's oral evidence following the autopsy and there were photographs of the pelvic region to show the jury. There was little probative value of showing the tissue which was significantly outweighed by its prejudicial effect. **Are there other factors that should be considered in making the ruling? What ruling would you make?**

See *R. v. Barton*, 2015 ABQB 159, 19 C.R. (7th) 1 (Alta. Q.B.). See further Lisa Kerr and Elin Sigurdson: <http://www.pivotlegal.org/the dignity of cindy gladue>.

Problem 15

A young black accused is charged with first degree murder. The theory of the Crown is that the killing was gang-related. The Crown alleges that the accused was a member of a street gang "MOB Klick" and that the deceased was a member of a rival gang. It brings a motion to introduce rap videos posted by the accused on YouTube. The rap lyrics involve references to drugs, violence, guns and "MOB Klick". **What factors should the trial judge take into account when assessing probative value and prejudicial effect?** See *R. v. Williams*, 2013 ONSC 1076 (Ont. S.C.J.) and *R. v. Campbell* (2015), 24 C.R. (7th) 1, 2015 ONSC 6199 (Ont. S.C.J.). See David Tanovich "*R. v. Campbell*. Rethinking the Admissibility of Rap Lyrics in Criminal Cases" (2016), 24 C.R. (7th) 27.

Problem 16

The accused is charged with murder in the stabbing of the deceased. The Crown seeks to introduce the following poem written by the accused:

Crazy thoughts pass through my head. Now I've killed a life it's dead. I drained his blood with my knife. How stupid am I to take his life. He had done nothing wrong. But I took his life and how he's gone. Why, why did I do it. How, How could I.

How would you rule on its admissibility? See *R. v. Terry*, [1996] 2 S.C.R. 207, 106 C.C.C. (3d) 508, 48 C.R. (4th) 137 (S.C.C.). See further *R. v. Parsons* (1996), 146 Nfld. & P.E.I.R. 210 (Nfld. C.A.) and *R. v. Williams*, 2013 ONSC 3100, 300 C.C.C. (3d) 240 (Ont. S.C.J.).

Chapter 4

Exclusionary Canons

As discussed in the previous chapter, not all relevant evidence is admissible and judges have several forms of discretion to exclude evidence. In addition, the law of evidence contains a number of general rules or principles that make certain types of evidence inadmissible or make evidence inadmissible for certain inferential purposes. These general rules and principles can be called canons of exclusion, and they are the subject of this chapter. Historically, exclusionary rules were relatively strict and absolute, and were subject to rigidly defined exceptions. Over time, these exclusionary canons have become more flexible. Currently, the exclusionary canons recognized in Canadian law allow for a significant degree of judicial discretion in their application.

A. CHARACTER EVIDENCE

1. HABIT

Evidence of how a person acted on another occasion is evidence of a circumstance from which we ask the trier of fact to infer that the person acted in a similar fashion on the occasion being litigated.[1] If the evidence is that the person always, invariably, acted in a certain way, the circumstantial evidence is very probative and deserves to be received. We label this as evidence of habit but see it for what it is — a piece of circumstantial evidence, more specific than evidence of the person's general character but differing only in degree and not in kind. If the circumstantial evidence indicates invariable habit the evidence is very powerful. If the evidence is that the person normally acted in that way the circumstantial evidence is less powerful. If the evidence is that he or she acted in that way occasionally the court may have concerns that the time necessary to hear the evidence may not be justified given the low probative value. If the evidence is of the person's general character or personality trait, the court recognizes that, even though the person's character or trait has relevance, the probative value may be outweighed by competing considerations and should be excluded. The court recognizes that even so-called "good people" sometimes do bad things and "bad people" do good things. Plumbing the depths of their character may not be worth the time and trouble. Determining receivability is thus seen to be a matter for the trial judge's discretion where he or she weighs probative value

---

[1] For a review of the Canadian law on character evidence, see L. Dufraimont, "Justice Marc Rosenberg and the Development of a Principled Approach to Character Evidence" in B.L. Berger, E. Cunliffe & J. Stribopoulos, *To Ensure that Justice is Done: Essays in Memory of Marc Rosenberg* (Toronto: Thomson Reuters, 2017) at 53.

against the dangers of consumption of time, confusion of the issues and prejudice to the proper outcome of the trial.

McCormick distinguished between habit and character:

> Although the courts frown on evidence of traits of character when introduced to prove how a person or organization acted on a given occasion, they are more receptive to evidence of personal habits or of the customary behaviour of organizations. To understand this difference one must appreciate the distinction between habit and character. The two are easily confused. People sometimes speak of a habit for care, a habit for promptness, or a habit of forgetfulness. They may say that an individual has a bad habit of stealing or lying. Evidence of these "habits" would be identical to the kind of evidence that is the target of the general rule against character evidence. Character is a generalized description of a person's disposition, or of the disposition in respect to a general trait, such as honesty, temperance or peacefulness. Habit, in the present context, is more specific. It denotes one's regular response to a repeated situation. If we speak of a character for care, we think of the person's tendency to act prudently in all the varying situations of life — in business, at home, in handling automobiles and in walking across the street. A habit, on the other hand, is the person's regular practice of responding to a particular kind of situation with a specific type of conduct. Thus, a person may be in the habit of bounding down a certain stairway two or three steps at a time, of patronizing a particular pub after each day's work, or of driving his automobile without using a seatbelt. The doing of the habitual act may become semi-automatic, as with a driver who invariably signals before changing lanes.
>
> Evidence of habits that come within this definition has greater probative value than does evidence of general traits of character. Furthermore, the potential for prejudice is substantially less. By and large, the detailed patterns of situation-specific behaviour that constitute habits are unlikely to provoke such sympathy or antipathy as would distort the process of evaluating the evidence.
>
> As a result, many jurisdictions accept the proposition that evidence of habit is admissible to show an act. These courts only reject the evidence categorically if the putative habit is not sufficiently regular or uniform, or if the circumstances are not sufficiently similar to outweigh the dangers of prejudice, distraction and time-consumption.[2]

BELKNAP v. MEAKES
(1989), 64 D.L.R. (4th) 452 (B.C. C.A.)

The Court allowed an appeal from a finding of negligence.

SEATON J.A. (HUTCHEON and WALLACE JJ.A. concurring):—

. . .

The defence had a difficult time putting its case. Dr. Meakes was prevented from saying what he did before the operation. He could not specifically remember it. That is understandable. Nearly three years elapsed between the operation and the trial, and two and one-half years elapsed between the operation and the time the allegation of negligent blood pressure

---

2   McCormick, *Evidence*, 5th ed. (1999) at 686-690.

management was raised. Dr. Meakes said that his "pre-operative assessment is a very standard part of my practice" and that he could say what had happened "because this is a habit from which I do not waiver". The trial judge said that he did not think the evidence was admissible unless the witness could "remember what he said to Mr. Belknap" and that if the evidence of Dr. Meakes's practice from which he did not waiver was admitted it carried so little weight that it would be "not much help to me at all"

If a person can say of something he regularly does in his professional life that he invariably does it in a certain way, that surely is evidence and possibly convincing evidence that he did it in that way on the day in question.

Wigmore on Evidence, vol. IA (Tillers rev. 1983), states that there is no reason why habit should not be used as evidence either of negligent action or of careful action (para. 97), and that habit should be admissible as a substitute for present recollection. *Phipson on Evidence*, 13th ed. (1982), paras. 9-22, reaches a similar conclusion.

Similar reasoning admits evidence of a general course of business, a question dealt with by the New Brunswick Court of Appeal in *Medical Arts Ltd. v. Minister of Municipal Affairs* (1977), 17 N.B.R. (2d) 147 at p. 152:

> The evidence adduced on behalf of the Minister of the usual course of business in the district office together with the certificate of the post office employee date stamped September 3, 1974 were admissible to prove the sending to the respondent of the documents referred to in s. 25(4) of the Act. *Phipson on Evidence*, 7th ed. states at p. 102:
>
>> To prove that an act has been done, it is admissible to prove any general course of business or office, whether public or private, according to which it would ordinarily have been done; there being a probability that the general course will be followed in the particular case.

R. v. WATSON
(1996), 50 C.R. (4th) 245, 108 C.C.C. (3d) 310 (Ont. C.A.)

The accused was charged with murder. The Crown took the position that the accused, with Headley and Cain, went to the deceased's premises, armed, with the intention of killing the deceased. The deceased went to the rear of the premises while the accused remained near the front office. The Crown took the position that the accused remained on guard in the front area and was guilty as an aider and abetter. The accused took the position that the shooting was the result of a dispute which arose in the context of a private drug transaction between the deceased and Headley. According to the accused, the deceased was hit five times by Headley, and the deceased shot Cain, who was standing some distance away, unarmed. The accused claimed to have panicked, then fled the scene with Headley and Cain.

The accused wanted to introduce the evidence of Mair, a good friend of the deceased, to demonstrate that the deceased had a habit of carrying a gun. In a statement to the police, Mair had said that the deceased always carried a gun; in fact, the gun was like a credit card for the deceased, since he never left home without it. The trial judge found that this evidence was irrelevant. He concluded that there was no viable issue of self-defence, that there was no evidence that the deceased had a gun on the day in question, and that there was no evidence that he fired a gun, if he did have a gun in his possession on that date.

The accused was convicted of manslaughter and successfully appealed.

DOHERTY J.A. (MORDEN A.C.J.O. and ARBOUR J.A. concurring):—

. . .

Where a person's conduct in given circumstances is in issue, evidence that the person repeatedly acted in a certain way when those circumstances arose in the past has been received as circumstantial evidence that the person acted in conformity with past practice on the occasion in question: *Cross and Tapper on Evidence*, 8th ed. (1995) at pp. 25-26; *Wigmore on Evidence*:Tillers Rev. (1983) Vol. 1A, pp. 1607-1610; R. Delisle, *Evidence Principles and Problems,* 4th ed. (1996) at p. 38; *McCormick on Evidence*, 4th ed. (1992), Vol. I, pp. 825-830. For example, in *McCormick* at p. 826 it is said:

> Surely any sensible person in investigating whether a given individual did a particular act would be greatly helped in his inquiry by evidence as to whether that individual was in the habit of doing it.

The position taken in these authorities is, in my opinion, consistent with human experience and logic. The fact that a person is in the habit of doing a certain thing in a given situation suggests that on a specific occasion in which those circumstances arose the person acted in accordance with established practice. It makes the conclusion that the person acted in a particular way more likely than it would be without the evidence of habit. Evidence of habit is therefore properly viewed as circumstantial evidence that a person acted in a certain way on the occasion in issue.

Evidence of habit is closely akin to, but not identical to, evidence of disposition. Evidence of habit involves an inference of conduct on a given occasion based on an established pattern of past conduct. It is an inference of conduct from conduct. Evidence of disposition involves an inference of the existence of a state of mind (disposition) from a person's conduct on one or more previous occasions and a further inference of conduct on the specific occasion based on the existence of that state of mind. Evidence of habit proceeds on the basis that repeated conduct in a given situation is a reliable predictor of conduct in that situation. Evidence of disposition is premised on the belief that a person's disposition is a reliable predictor of conduct in a given situation.

The distinction between evidence of habit and evidence of disposition is demonstrated by a comparison of this case and the facts in *Scopelliti.* Here the defence wanted to show that the deceased habitually carried a gun in the past and to invite the jury to infer from that prior conduct that he had a gun when he was shot. In *Scopelliti*, the defence wanted to show that the deceased had on occasions in the past been the aggressor in physical confrontations with others and to invite the jury to infer, first that the deceased was a physically aggressive person (his disposition), and second that the deceased's actions at the relevant time were in keeping with his physically aggressive nature. Like evidence of habit, evidence of disposition can constitute circumstantial evidence of conduct on a specific occasion. The inferences necessary to render disposition evidence relevant to prove conduct on a specific occasion may be more difficult to draw than those required where evidence of habit is tendered.

The recognition that evidence of habit is relevant to prove conduct on a specific occasion begs the more fundamental question — what is a habit? *McCormick* at p. 826 decribes habit as:

> the person's regular practice of responding to a particular kind of situation with a specific type of conduct.

Habit therefore involves a repeated and specific response to a particular situation.

Mair's graphic assertion that the deceased carried a gun "like a credit card. He never left home without it" strongly suggests repeated and specific conduct. Mair's statement does not suggest that the deceased's possession of a weapon was limited to any particular situation. To the contrary, Mair indicated that the deceased always carried a gun. The general nature of the habit described by Mair does not affect the relevance of the evidence, but would, along with other aspects of the evidence (e.g., the duration and regularity of the habit), go to the weight to be given to the evidence by the jury.

Having concluded that evidence that the deceased always carried a gun was relevant to the question of whether he had a gun when he was shot, I turn to the second level of the relevance inquiry. Mair's evidence may put the deceased in possession of a gun at the material time, but standing alone it cannot support the inference that he fired the gun at that time. In fact, Mair's evidence did not suggest that the deceased had ever used his gun. The further inference from possession to use of the weapon is essential to make Mair's evidence relevant to any issue in the trial. The availability of that inference requires a consideration of the rest of the evidence.

There were at most three people at the back of the warehouse. The deceased and Cain were shot and the evidence does not suggest that Cain shot himself. He must have been shot by either Headley or the deceased. Headley definitely shot the deceased and at least two of the bullets which hit the deceased came from a different gun than the one used to shoot Cain. There were, therefore, two possibilities. Either Cain was shot by the deceased or Headley fired two different guns hitting the deceased with one and Cain with the other. In my opinion, a jury, having concluded that the deceased was armed, could have inferred that Cain was shot not by his friend Headley, but by the deceased who was the target of Headley's assault.

I am further satisfied, had the jury inferred that the deceased was armed and fired a weapon, that those inferences could logically have influenced the jury's conclusion as to the origins of the shooting. If the deceased was unarmed, the circumstances strongly suggest a preconceived plan to shoot the deceased. If the deceased was armed and used his weapon, then the possibility that the shooting was a result of a spontaneous confrontation between Headley and the deceased, both of whom were armed, becomes a viable one. If the shooting was the product of an armed confrontation between the two men it could reasonably be inferred that the confrontation arose during the discussion involving Headley and the deceased. If the confrontation arose in this manner, it offered strong support for the appellant's contention that he was not party to any plan to kill or do harm to the deceased. Therefore, evidence supporting the inferences that the deceased was armed and used a weapon during the confrontation made the defence position as to the appellant's non-involvement in any plan to kill or do harm to the deceased more viable than it would have been if those inferences were not available. Mair's proposed evidence, which provided the basis for those inferences, was, therefore, relevant to a material fact in issue. In so concluding, I do not pass on the cogency of the inferences relied on by the defence or attempt to measure the effect of the proposed evidence on the jury's assessment of the appellant's liability. I limit myself to the inquiry demanded by our concept of relevancy.[3]

New trial ordered.

How many occurrences are necessary to infer habit?

DEVGAN v. COLLEGE OF PHYSICIANS & SURGEONS (ONTARIO)
(2005), 193 O.A.C. 357 (Ont. Div. Ct.)

Dr. Devgan was charged with professional misconduct in his treatment of three terminally ill cancer patients. The Discipline Committee of the College of Physicians and Surgeons concluded that he charged exorbitant fees for the treatments and failed to fairly and accurately explain the likelihood of success. On appeal, Devgan argued that the Committee had erred in excluding evidence of what he told other cancer patients about a cure as this was relevant to the issue of what he told these three patients. The appeal was dismissed.

THEN J. (GRAVELY and WHALEN JJ. concurring):—

. . . [T]he exclusion of the evidence of the representations made by the Appellant to other cancer patients is more problematic if, as the Appellant submits, the excluded evidence was admissible as evidence of habit or routine. Although counsel for either parties had not supplied the court nor the Committee with any authority on this issue, evidence of habit or routine has been ruled to be admissible both in a criminal and civil context.

[The Court discusses *R. v. Watson.*]

It is also useful to refer to the observations of Professors Delisle and Stuart in Evidence. Principles and Problems, 6th edition, Carswell, where they explain with their customary clarity the basis of admissibility and the probative value of evidence of habit at p. 125:

---

[3]   *Watson* was applied in *R. v. Pilon* (2009), 64 C.R. (6th) 356, 243 C.C.C. (3d) 109 (Ont. C.A.). For a view that *Watson* should be reconsidered on the basis that evidence of habit is nothing other than a kind of disposition evidence see Michael Plaxton, "Dissolving the Boundaries Between Habit and Disposition" (2011), 85 C.R (6th) 237.

Evidence of how a person acted on another occasion is evidence of a circumstance from which we ask the trier of fact to infer that the person acted in a similar fashion on the occasion being litigated. If the evidence is that the person always, invariably, acted in a certain way, the circumstantial evidence is very probative and deserves to be received. We label this as evidence of Habit but see it for what it is - a piece of circumstantial evidence, more specific than evidence of the person's general character but differing only in degree and not in kind. If the circumstantial evidence indicates invariable habit the evidence is very powerful. If the evidence is that the person normally acted in that way the circumstantial evidence is less powerful. If the evidence is that he acted in that way occasionally the court may have concerns that the time necessary to hear the evidence may not be justified given the low probative value.

In the civil context, the decision of the British Columbia Court of Appeal in *Belknap v. Meakes* (1980) 64 D.L.R. (4th) 452 is instructive as there is some factual similarity to the instant case.

[The Court quotes from the decision.]

In the instant case there was no issue as to the admissibility of the evidence of the Appellant as to the representations he routinely claimed to have made to all of his cancer patients. It is of some importance to consider the Appellant's own evidence of what he routinely told his patients before considering the admissibility of the proffered evidence of the 3 or 4 other cancer patients as to what the Appellant represented to them. The Appellant's evidence was that he never told any patient that his treatments would cure them because to do so was improper. What he did tell them was that he could not promise a cure but that only God could do that. He told them that his treatments would not harm them but would help them feel better and to become stronger to fight the cancer and might prolong life and that while his treatments had helped some patients his treatments did not help all patients.

In my view, the terse outline by counsel of the proffered evidence of the 3 or 4 other cancer patients simply amounts to this: 1) the Appellant did not say anything about a cure; 2) the Appellant did say that his treatment did "work" on other patients. In the context of the Appellant seeing four to five cancer patients a week over a number of years the proffered evidence that he did not mention a cure on 3 or 4 specific occasions which are not even identified by means of a timeline does not amount to evidence of any habit or routine on the part of the Appellant to never mention a cure within any of the authorities to which I have referred or have been able to find. In my view, at its highest this evidence may be minimally supportive of the credibility of the Appellant that he never mentioned a cure to his cancer patients. Even if the evidence could have been used for that limited purpose its probative value is so slight that it was properly excluded in the exercise of its discretion by the Committee.

In *McCormick on Evidence* (5th ed.) Practitioner Treatise Series Vol. 1 (1999) West Group, the authors state that there must be enough instances to permit the finding of habit and provide a helpful example to demonstrate how evidence of specific instances may result in admissibility of evidence of routine conduct or exclusion at the discretion of the court. At p. 690 in footnote 22 the authors state:

22. See, e.g., *Strauss v. Douglass Aircraft Co.*, 404 F.2d 1152, 1158 (2d Cir. 1968); *Wilson v. Volkswagen of America*, 561 F.2d 494, 511-12 (4th Cir. 1977); *Coats & Clark, Inc. v. Gay*, 755 F.2d 1506, 1511 (11th Cir. 1985) ("the methods employed by a single warehouser at a single location are not sufficiently probative of the custom of the warehouse industry generally"); *State v. Mary*, 368 N.W.2d 166, 168-169 (Iowa 1985) (10-12 observations of nurse drawing blood samples adequate to show habitual features of her procedure); *Weisenberger v. Senger*, 381 N.W.2d 187, 191 (N.D. 1986) (insufficient number of observations to establish habit of driving on extreme right of narrow country roads); *Steinberg v. Arcilla*, 535 N.W.2d 444 (Wis.Ct.App.1995) (anesthesiologist's regular response of positioning arms of patients in certain way during each of 65 to 70 cases per month); *Lewan*, supra note 574; Mode Code Evid. R. 307(3) ("many instances"); supra note 583.

And footnote 24 contains the following example:

See supra ss. 185. Thus, citing illustrations to the Model Code of Evidence Rule 307, the Federal Advisory Committee mentions the possibility of admitting testimony by W that on numerous occasions he had been with X when X crossed a railroad track and that on each occasion X had first stopped and looked in both directions, but that offers of ten witnesses, each testifying to a different occasion, might be excluded in the discretion of the court. Note to Fed.R.Evid. 406(b).

It will be evident that in this case evidence of 3 or 4 witnesses who can testify only that the Appellant did not mention anything about a cure but do not purport to testify about anything the Appellant states he routinely or habitually did tell his patients about a cure does not rise to the probative value of the evidence mentioned in the example. In my view, the Committee was not unreasonable in excluding this evidence in its discretion nor was the Appellant deprived of natural justice or unfairly impeded in establishing his defence.

In considering whether the bad character exclusionary rule applies in criminal cases, what matters is not whether the evidence can be characterized as habit but whether it is discreditable.

R. v. B. (L.)
(1997), 116 C.C.C. (3d) 481, 9 C.R. (5th) 38 (Ont. C.A.)

CHARRON J.A. (MCMURTRY C.J. and DOHERTY J.A. concurring):—

. . . Where the Crown seeks to introduce evidence of the conduct of an accused other than which forms the subject-matter of the charge, it is the adverse reflection that this evidence may have on the accused's character that signals the need for further investigation. One should ask, is the prior conduct discreditable? If it is not, the rationale underlying the similar fact evidence rule will not apply. Unless the proposed evidence, which does not discredit the accused, triggers the application of some other exclusionary rule of evidence, it is admissible. However, where the other conduct is sufficiently discreditable that it may prejudice the trier of fact against the accused, the similar fact evidence rule does apply and its probative value must outweigh its prejudicial effect before it will be admitted.

Professors Paciocco and Stuesser set out an example that distinguishes will between discreditable conduct and other conduct which does not discredit the accused:

> So, evidence that the accused was in the habit of carrying a concealed, illegal weapon should be inadmissible unless it conforms to the similar fact evidence rule. By contrast, the similar fact evidence rule does not apply to evidence that the accused was in the habit of smoking a particular brand of cigarette that was found at the scene of a crime. . .

The authors in fact start off by saying that "[i]t is important in applying these rules to distinguish between 'character' and 'habit'." (Other authors have drawn such a distinction as well: see, for example, Strong, ed., McCormick on Evidence, 4th ed., vol. 1 (1992), at pp. 825-30.) However, Paciocco and Stuesser, in explaining why the distinction must be made, identify discreditability as the distinguishing feature that will trigger the application of the similar fact evidence rule, regardless of whether the evidence can be categorized as character or habit. I agree with that conclusion.

2. CHARACTER OR DISPOSITION

(a) Admissible as Directly Relevant to Material Issue

Before examining the evidence rules concerning character we need to recognize that character evidence may be relevant in different ways. A person's conduct or reputation previous to the event being litigated may be relevant to a material issue in the case without the necessity of the trier of fact inferring that the person acted in conformity with his or her previous conduct or reputation on the occasion under review. For example, in a case of assault, a claim of self-defence might be founded on the accused's belief, based on his or her understanding of the victim's previous conduct or reputation, that the victim had a disposition towards violent behaviour; such a belief, if honestly held, could cause the accused to view the victim's conduct with apprehension and so cause the accused to strike out at the victim. The chain of reasoning which we ask the trier of fact to follow in these cases does not involve the necessity of inferring that the person acted in conformity with his or her character. The evidence of character is led, and the trier is asked simply to infer from it that the accused's belief was genuine.

Occasionally the character of a person is not just relevant to a fact in issue but rather is itself a material point in the case; an operative fact which dictates rights and liabilities. For example, in an action for defamation in which justification is pleaded, the plaintiff's reputation or character is the determining matter. An action for wrongful dismissal might include as a material issue the lack of fitness or competency of the employee.

When the character of a person is relevant to a fact in issue other than by inferring from the character to the conduct of the person, or when the substantive law makes the character material as the very core of the inquiry, evidence of it should, generally speaking, be admitted. For example the Ontario Court of Appeal in *R. v. Kruger*[4] admitted evidence of threats and spying by the accused on a former girlfriend as character evidence of motive directly at issue where he was charged with her murder.[5] In such cases courts have usually[6] held that there need be no warning as to the limited use to be made of character evidence.

Consider the broad approach to admissibility in the following endorsement judgment:

R. v. W. (L.)

(2004), 191 O.A.C. 22 (Ont. C.A.)

THE COURT (LABROSSE, MACPHERSON and CRONK JJ.A.):

1   The appellant appeals his conviction for sexual assault by Byers J. of the Superior Court of Justice.

2   The complainant met the appellant over the telephone in December 2000. . . . She sponsored the appellant to join her in Canada and he arrived in August 2002. Thereafter, the complainant alleged that their previously good relationship changed and the appellant became extremely domineering and controlling. Over the next few months, she alleged that he assaulted her, both physically and sexually, on several occasions. The appellant was convicted of assault in March 2003, but the couple got back together after he vowed to change his ways.

3   The complainant alleged that he began to abuse her again and, in June 2003, he was charged with assault and sexual assault. . . .

4   At the trial, the appellant challenged the complainant's allegations, suggesting that she had a motive to fabricate the offences and that the sex between them was consensual. The appellant did not testify. He was acquitted of the assault charge and convicted of sexual assault.

. . .

6   In our view, the circumstances of the present case support the admissibility of the . . . prior discreditable conduct evidence. This evidence related to the history of domestic abuse in the relationship between the appellant and the complainant and it had probative value regarding the material issues in the prosecution.

7   The evidence demonstrated how the relationship had progressed from the appellant lecturing about his strict rules to abusive conduct. It also

---

[4]   (2000), 31 C.R. (5th) 314 (Ont. C.A.).

[5]   See too *R. v. Escobar-Benavidez*, 200 C.C.C. (3d) 287, [2005] 3 S.C.R. 386; *R. v. G. (S.G.)* (1997), 8 C.R. (5th) 198 (S.C.C.); *R. v. Merz* (1999), 140 C.C.C. (3d) 259 (Ont. C.A.); *R. v. Sandhu*, (2009), 63 C.R. (6th) 1, 242 C.C.C. (3d) 262 (Ont. C.A.); and *R. v. D. (D.)* (2005), 203 C.C.C. (3d) 6 (B.C. C.A.) (criminal harassment to establish context as to whether complainant fearful or accused reckless).

[6]   See *Sandhu, supra* note 5 and *R. v. Stubbs*, 2013 ONCA 514, 300 C.C.C. (3d) 181 (Ont. C.A.). However, sometimes courts require a warning against use to show general propensity (e.g., *D. (D.), supra* note 5; *R. v. Rodrigues* (2007), 223 C.C.C. (3d) 53 (Yuk. C.A.); and *R. v. Seck* (2007), 52 C.R. (6th) 300 (Que. C.A.)).

demonstrated the appellant's domineering and possessive behaviour in his attempt to control the complainant.

8   The evidence was admissible as part of the narrative, as evidence of motive or animus and it was relevant in assessing the complainant's credibility, particularly on the questions why she did not leave the relationship or disclose the abuse earlier. Its probative value outweighed its prejudicial effect.

9   It is important to keep in mind that the risk of prejudice was much reduced because of the fact that this was a trial by judge alone. When the trial judge decided to admit the evidence, he noted that this was not a jury case and when the complainant's testimony extended past her relationship with the appellant, he immediately stopped Crown counsel. The trial judge saw the prior discreditable conduct as relevant to the relationship between the appellant and the complainant and used it to assist him in understanding and explaining the actions of the parties.

. . .

15 Accordingly, the appeal is dismissed.

Was this evidence really directly relevant to a material fact in issue or was it really admitted to show the accused's bad disposition, which evidence we shall see below is normally excluded? Some see resort to words such as animus, motive, context or part of the narrative as glib devices to avoid the exclusionary rule.[7] If this is true, does this matter? Do you agree that such evidence should be admitted?

Notice that the Court of Appeal indicated they were less concerned about the prejudicial effect of the evidence because this was a judge-alone trial.[8] Do you agree?

The Ontario Court of Appeal further considered the issue of motive and character in the following two decisions:

R. v. JOHNSON
(2010), 80 C.R. (6th) 145, 262 C.C.C. (3d) 404 (Ont. C.A.)

ROULEAU J.A. (ROSENBERG and EPSTEIN JJ.A. concurring:—

[97] Where the matter at issue is proof of a motive, a somewhat different analysis is required. Evidence of an accused's motive is relevant, as it can impact questions of identity and intent: *Lewis v. The Queen*, [1979] 2 S.C.R. 821, at p. 833; *R. v. Griffin*, [2009] 2 S.C.R. 42, at para. 60. Consequently, evidence establishing motive is normally admissible. However, where, as in the present case, the evidence of motive arises from discreditable conduct, the evidence's admissibility must still be gauged. In these circumstances, motive evidence is not automatically admissible. The trial judge must still balance

---

[7]   See Stuart, Annotation to *Sandhu* (2009), 63 C.R. (6th) 3 and Nowlin, "Narrative Evidence: A Wolf in Sheep's Clothing" (2006) 51 Crim. L.Q. 238 and 271.

[8]   See also *R. v. B. (T.)* (2009), 243 C.C.C. (3d) 158, 63 C.R. (6th) 197 (Ont. C.A.), and comment by Lisa Dufraimont, discussed below under similar fact evidence.

probative value versus prejudicial effect: *R. v. Chapman* (2006), 204 C.C.C. (3d) 449 (Ont. C.A.), at para. 27.

. . .

[99] It is not sufficient for the Crown to identify some past conflict between an accused and a victim, and then speculate that it establishes animus and therefore motive. The Supreme Court in *R. v. Barbour*, [1938] S.C.R. 465, at p. 469, warned that "it is rather important that the court should not slip into a habit of admitting evidence which, reasonably viewed, cannot tend to prove motive or explain the acts charged merely because it discloses some incident in the history of the relations of the parties."

[100] Thus, evidence of past misconduct that is woven into a speculative theory of motive does nothing more than bring in the bad character of the accused, and ought to be excluded on the basis that its prejudicial value exceeds any small probative value it might have: see, e.g. *R. v. Smith*, [1992] 2 S.C.R. 915, at pp. 938-941.

[101] On the other hand, evidence that provides the trier of fact with real insight into the background and relationship between the accused and the victim, and which genuinely helps to establish a *bona fide* theory of motive is highly probative, even in the absence of similarity with the charged offence: see, e.g. *R. v. Moo* (2009), 247 C.C.C. (3d) 109 (Ont. C.A.), at paras. 70-109.

R. v. BRISSARD
2017 ONCA 891, 356 C.C.C. (3d) 494, 42 C.R. (7th) 174 (Ont. C.A.)

The accused was charged with sexual assault of a 12-year-old girl, his neighbour. The charge related to sexual touching including intercourse that was alleged to have occurred at the accused's home late one night. The trial judge admitted evidence that, on previous occasions, the accused had engaged in "play fighting" with the complainant, which involved him grinding his pelvis against her buttocks. On appeal, the defence argued that the evidence of the accused's prior conduct should not have been admitted.

PARDU J.A.:

[1] Timothy Dominic Brissard appeals his conviction for the sexual assault of a 12 year old girl under s. 271 of the *Criminal Code*, R.S.C. 1985, c. C-46. The Crown appeals the trial judge's refusal to designate Mr. Brissard a dangerous offender pursuant to s. 753 of the *Criminal Code*.

[2] For the reasons that follow, I would dismiss both appeals.

. . .

[5] M.W., the complainant, was 12 years old at the time of the offences in December 2010. She was friends with her next door neighbour, N.A., and babysat for her from time to time. Mr. Brissard was 26 years old at the time and lived with N.A.

. . .

[10] At trial, N.A. testified that she first met the complainant in August 2010 when N.A. moved into a house beside the complainant's. N.A. stated that she quickly became friends with the complainant, saw the complainant almost every day, and that the complainant would come over to babysit about twice a month.

[11] N.A. further testified that she saw Mr. Brissard "play fight" with the complainant "pretty much every time [the complainant] came over" beginning in August 2010. N.A. also described how Mr. Brissard would bend the complainant over, grab her waist, and touch her buttocks with his groin.

[12] This behaviour was also noticed by another witness, Armand Cummings, who lived in N.A.'s house from late October 2010 until early December 2010. He testified that he saw Mr. Brissard grinding his pelvis against the complainant's buttocks and that he found it to be disturbing.

[13] Mr. Cummings testified that he mentioned what he saw to N.A. before he moved out. For her part, N.A. testified that although she did not notice the impropriety of the touching before Mr. Cummings brought it up, she thought that Mr. Brissard was "feeling [the complainant] up" in retrospect.

Trial judge's use of the evidence of prior conduct

[14] At para. 22 of his reasons, the trial judge accepted the Crown's theory that the appellant was "exhibiting a prior sexual interest in M.W" and that this explained "objectively why he would take the occasion, when his own girlfriend was intoxicated to the point of passing out, to take his sexual interest in M.W. to a more significant level." He used this evidence of prior conduct to support the complainant's credibility and stated at para. 31 of his reasons:

> I also find that M.W.'s evidence that she was assaulted is made more credible by the evidence of prior sexual interest demonstrated by Mr. Brissard. To the extent that both N.A. and Mr. Cummings noticed prior incidents of inappropriate contact between Mr. Brissard and M.W., I am assisted in assessing M.W.'s evidence as credible. Also N.A.'s evidence concerning the argument that occurred in the morning of December 23rd, and her evidence concerning M.W.'s avoidance of Mr. Brissard corroborates her evidence of being assaulted. Accordingly I find that Timothy Brissard intentionally applied force to M.W. by touching her in a sexual nature using both his penis and his hands.

[15] No one objected to the admission of this prior conduct evidence or suggested that a *voir dire* was required at trial.

Analysis

[16] Mr. Brissard submits that the trial judge erred by admitting the evidence of prior conduct because it was similar fact evidence that should have been

subject to a *voir dire* and the analysis set out by the Supreme Court of Canada in *R. v. Handy*, 2002 SCC 56 (CanLII), [2002] 2 S.C.R. 908. The Crown, on the other hand, submits that the prior conduct evidence was used to illustrate Mr. Brissard's state of mind and sexual interest in the complainant. As such, the Crown argues that the prior conduct was admissible as evidence of motive and that its probative value outweighed its prejudicial effect.

Is the evidence relevant?

[17] Motive is a state of mind, a specific inclination to do the very act charged in relation to a particular victim. Evidence of a mental state, or motive, may be relevant to prove the accused did the act constituting the offence or it may be relevant to prove his or her intention or other mental state.

[18] As this court explained in *R. v. Jackson* (1980), 57 C.C.C. (2d) 154 at 167 (Ont. C.A.), [1980] O.J. No. 1468, at para. 37, evidence of motive may include evidence of relevant emotions or desires:

> Motive, in the sense of an emotion or feeling such as anger, fear, jealousy and desire, which are likely to lead to the doing of an act, is a relevant circumstance to prove the doing of an act as well as the intent with which an act is done. The relevant emotion may be evidenced by
>
> (a) conduct or utterances expressing the emotion,
>
> (b) external circumstances which have probative value to show the probable excitement of the relevant emotion, and
>
> (c) by its prior or subsequent existence (if sufficiently proximate): see Wigmore On Evidence, 3rd ed., Vol. I, pp. 557-61; Vol. II, pp. 328-29.
>
> [Emphasis added.]

[19] Here the prior conduct tends to establish that the accused had a sexual interest in a twelve year-old girl. It was proximate in time and location, occurring repeatedly between August and December 2010 within the same home where the offence was alleged to have taken place. Importantly, the prior conduct directly involved and was aimed at the complainant.

[20] Evidence that the accused had a sexual interest in the complainant logically tends to support the position that he acted on that interest on December 23, 2010, the date of the offence alleged in the indictment. Accordingly, the evidence is relevant.

Does the prior conduct cast the accused in a disreputable light?

[21] The prior conduct ascribed to the accused is outside the time period described in the indictment. It tends to show that he committed other sexual acts against the complainant at earlier times. There can be no doubt that these earlier acts would be viewed as disreputable by a reasonable person.

[22] As such, this evidence is presumptively inadmissible. Once these two elements are present, even where the evidence is tendered as proof of motive, it is not admissible unless a trial judge first concludes that the probative value outweighs its prejudicial effect: *R. v. Johnson*, 2010 ONCA 646 (CanLII), at paras. 92 and 97 *per* Rouleau J.A.

[23] The procedural rules of the Superior Court of Justice applicable to criminal proceedings recognize this presumptive inadmissibility. Rule 30.01 of the Criminal Proceedings Rules for the Superior Court of Justice (Ontario), SI/2012-7 provides that a party who wishes to tender evidence that is presumptively inadmissible, including "evidence of disreputable conduct by an accused, other than the conduct charged in the indictment" must serve an application asking for that relief 30 days before trial or the date set for pre-trial motions. The application must include a "precise, case-specific statement of the basis and grounds upon which the evidence is said to be admissible.

Does the probative value of the evidence outweigh the potential prejudice associated with admission of this evidence?

[24] I would conclude that this evidence was admissible. It was relevant. The risk of prejudice was low in this judge alone trial. The prior conduct was much less serious than the offence covered by the indictment.

[25] Each assessment of the balance of probative value and potential prejudice depends on the facts of a particular case and the purpose for which the evidence is tendered. The evidence here is not general bad character evidence as, for example, use of child pornography, or writings expressing a desire to sexually assault children generally. It is more akin to evidence that an accused shot and missed the victim who was ultimately killed in a shooting shortly thereafter. Or, for example, writings that express an intention to commit a sexual assault on the very person ultimately targeted: *R. v. Byers*, 2017 ONCA 639 (CanLII). The proximity in time and location, and the identity of the victim enhance the probative value of this evidence. The probative value of this evidence outweighed the potential for prejudice from misuse of the evidence.

[26] The appellant relies on *R. v. J.H.* (2006), 2006 CanLII 40664 (ON CA), 215 C.C.C. (3d) 233 (Ont. C.A.), [2006] O.J. No. 4832 in support of his argument that the prior conduct evidence should have been excluded. However, that case is very different from the present one. In *R. v. J.H.*, a man was accused of forced sexual intercourse with a step-sibling some 20 years earlier when they were both underage. The Crown attempted to introduce evidence of sexual activity between them at least four years before the incident giving rise to the charge. There was no temporal connection between those previous activities and the offence at bar. As a result, this court held that the evidence of the accused's prior conduct was more in the nature of general propensity rather than motive. Sexual contact four years before an alleged assault has little probative value in relation to motive to commit the alleged assault. The trial

judge in that case, therefore, erred in admitting the evidence and using it to support a finding of guilt.

Did the trial judge misuse the evidence?

[27] The trial judge did not misuse the evidence. He did not reason that the accused was a person of bad character who was therefore likely to have committed the offence. According to the trial judge, the appellant's sexual interest in the victim made it more likely that he acted on that interest. That interest supported the complainant's credibility.

Guidance for trial judges

[28] Despite the presumptive inadmissibility of bad character evidence, this court has frequently held that motive evidence is admissible — even if it tends to show bad conduct: *R. v. Chenier* (2006), 2006 CanLII 3560 (ON CA), 205 C.C.C. (3d) 333 at 362-65 (Ont. C.A.), [2006] O.J. No. 489, at paras. 80-86; and *R. v. Carroll*, 2014 ONCA 2 (CanLII), 304 C.C.C. (3d) 252, at paras. 121-27. Evidence of prior familial violence is frequently admitted where an accused is charged with the homicide of a domestic partner. Evidence of sexual grooming to facilitate commission of a sexual assault on a child is frequently admitted, even where the conduct is outside the time frame defined by the indictment. Both are evidence of motive.

[29] This court has held that prior conduct evidencing motive does not require a cautionary jury instruction against propensity reasoning even where that conduct amounts to disreputable behaviour: *R. v. Pasqualino*, 2008 ONCA 554 (CanLII), 233 C.C.C. (3d) 319, at para. 65; *R. v. Moo*, 2009 ONCA 645 (CanLII), 247 C.C.C. (3d) 34, at para. 100; *R. v. Carroll*, at para. 123; and *R. v. Salah*, 2015 ONCA 23 (CanLII), at para. 88.

[30] This does not mean, however, that a court can disregard the need for an admissibility inquiry in relation to this evidence. In some cases, evidence suggesting motive may be tenuous, or remote, and where it amounts to bad character evidence, the probative value may be outweighed by the risk of prejudice, particularly in a jury trial.

[31] On the other hand, in this post *R. v. Jordan*, 2016 SCC 27 (CanLII), [2016] 1 S.C.R. 631 era, trial judges should not be required to embark on unnecessary evidentiary hearings. In many cases where admissibility is evident, and there is no opposition to admission of the evidence, trial judges should note that agreement on the record, or a prehearing judge should record that agreement, so that the consensus is clear, and no lengthy evidentiary hearing will be necessary.

[32] In this case, questions posed to the complainant did not clearly elicit evidence about whether the prior disreputable conduct took place. Defence counsel expressly consented to the Crown asking N.A. about the prior

improper touching by way of re-opening its examination in chief. Defence counsel's theory was that the complainant's repeated visits to N.A.'s home were inconsistent with her allegations of the sexual assaults. All participants at trial proceeded on the assumption that the prior conduct evidence was admissible. It was appropriate for the trial judge to rely on the position expressed by defence counsel.

This part of the chapter is concerned with the canons of exclusion which the law of evidence has created for the reception of character as circumstantial evidence of how a person acted during the material incident; character evidence of this sort is seen to be relevant on the premise that character reflects disposition and a person's disposition to act, think or feel in a particular way is evidence from which it might be inferred that he or she behaved in conformity with that character on the particular occasion.

(b) Underlying Assumptions Grounding Character Evidence

The common law assumes that character evidence is predictive of behaviour; that a person's behaviour is governed by personality traits. The common law assumes, for example, that if there is evidence that the accused has behaved aggressively in the past, that evidence has probative worth in determining if he or she committed the assault with which he or she is now charged. Some disagree:

> Empirical research, however, has not only failed to validate trait theory but has generally rejected it. As Walter Mischel notes: "The initial assumptions of trait-state theory were logical, inherently plausible, and also consistent with common sense and intuitive impressions about personality. Their real limitation turned out to be empirical — they simply have not been supported adequately." Instead, the research shows that behaviour is largely shaped by specific situational determinants that do not lend themselves easily to predictions about individual behaviour. . . From this psychological perspective, evidence that a witness has been convicted of a felony involving dishonesty or has cheated on his taxes may or may not tell us anything about whether he was truthful on the stand. Likewise, evidence that the accused was engaged in an altercation after a New Year's Eve party may tell us nothing about his behaviour during a peace demonstration. These findings threaten the common law's basic assumptions about the probative value of character evidence.[9]

While empirical findings may threaten, the common law nevertheless continues with its assumptions.

---

[9]   Mendez, "California's New Law on Character Evidence: The Impact of Recent Psychological Studies" (1984) 31 U.C.L.A. L. Rev. 1003 at 1052.

R. v. CLARKE
(1998), 18 C.R. (5th) 219, 129 C.C.C. (3d) 1 (Ont. C.A.)

The issue concerned the admissibility of evidence of a witness' reputation for veracity. It was resolved that questions could be put to an impeaching witness concerning a witness' reputation, or character, for truth-telling. In the course of approving such evidence the Court offered the following advice.

ROSENBERG J.A. (MCMURTRY C.J.O. and LABROSSE J.A. concurring):—

The theory upon which the admissibility of this evidence is based, the "trait or generality theory" has been criticized. It has been argued that there is no such thing as stable personality traits from which one could reasonably predict how a person would act in a given situation. To the contrary, it is argued that a theory of "situationism" provides a more reasonable basis for predicting behaviour. According to this theory, behaviour is determined almost exclusively by environmental factors, by the situation in which the actors find themselves. However, even this theory has been found to be flawed and trait theory has come back into its own. Susan M. Davies describes the understanding of social scientists, S.M. Davies, "Evidence of Character to Prove Conduct: A Reassessment of Relevancy" (1991), 27 Crim. L.B. 504 at 516-17:

> Using improved methodology, trait theorists are now able to demonstrate the existence in individuals of consistent behavioral tendencies over a sample of situations, and to predict average behaviour accurately. In fact, the usefulness of trait information in predicting behaviour is no longer controverted by members of the psychology community. The most outspoken critic of trait theory has conceded that traits exist and that trait theorists 'can predict many things about people at levels of confidence that are reasonable for various goals and purposes.' Even more significant for the forensic consideration of character is the fact that most psychologists now recognize that, as a general matter, a lay person, given information about a subject's past behaviour, can predict the subject's future behaviour with a significant degree of accuracy.

(c) Character of Parties in Civil Cases

Generally speaking, the character of the plaintiff or defendant in a civil case is not receivable for the purpose of proving that the litigant acted in conformity therewith on the occasion under review. In the old case of *A.G. v. Radloff*,[10] Baron Martin "reasoned":

> In criminal cases evidence of the good character of the accused is most properly and with good reason admissible in evidence, because there is a fair and just presumption that a person of good character would not commit a crime; but in civil cases such evidence is with equal good reason not admitted, because no presumption would fairly arise, in the very great proportion of such cases, from the good character of the defendant, that he did not commit the breach of contract or of civil duty alleged against him.

---

[10]   (1854), 156 E.R. 366 at 371.

This reasoning seems strained. If character is relevant in one context, can it really be said that it is not relevant in the other? Perhaps the distinction is to be justified on the basis that, in a criminal case, with the disparity in resources between the litigants and the consequences for the accused, the accused is entitled to lead any evidence that could possibly affect the result. In civil cases, the court may be more concerned that the probative value of the character evidence, whether it be good or bad character, is outweighed by the prejudice it causes by confusing the issues, prolonging the proceedings or unfairly surprising the opposing litigants.

As you read the following cases, are you satisfied with how the court deals with the character evidence?

In *McArthur v. Prudential Insurance Co. of America*[11] a widow was suing on a life insurance policy following her husband's death. The insurance company would not pay on the basis that he had misled the company as to his state of health. The plaintiff wanted to lead evidence as to his reputation for honesty. The evidence was disallowed. **Defensible?**

RAWDAH v. EVANS
(February 1, 1995), Clarke J., [1994] O.J. No. 3322 (Ont. Gen. Div.)

CLARKE J.:—

In this action before judge and jury for damages arising from a motor vehicle accident, liability was admitted. The plaintiff moved to call three friends to testify with respect to his general reputation in the community for honesty. The motion raised the issue of character evidence in a civil proceeding. . . .

. . . [C]ounsel for the defendant ... cross-examined the plaintiff on his lack of candour, with respect to pre-accident history and also attempted to demonstrate that he was exaggerating pain and disability ... I find such evidence of good character has little probative value here. No compelling inference could be drawn from it that the plaintiff was not deliberately exaggerating injuries and disability for secondary economic gain because other rational explanations exist, apart from dishonesty, to explain the shortcomings of the plaintiff's testimony. The plaintiff claimed memory loss related to the accident for his faulty disclosure. Further, it is widely recognized that where as here there is scant objective pathology to support injuries, litigants often entertain sincere, but mistaken beliefs as their gravity and cause. . . .

. . . [E]xcept in restricted circumstances where character is directly in issue, the law holds that evidence of a litigant's character is inadmissible.

> The exclusionary rule prevails also in civil cases, where there is no exception in favour of one party. Thus, where a will was impeached for fraud, the defendant was not allowed to prove his good character in answer, nor, in divorce cases, can a husband, in disproof of a particular act of cruelty, tender evidence of his general character for humanity. So, to rebut a charge of cowardice on a particular

---

[11]   (1969), 6 D.L.R. (3d) 477 (Ont. H.C.).

occasion, both general evidence of courage and specific acts of bravery on other occasions are inadmissible." (Phipson on Evidence, 12ed, p. 217.)

This is not a civil assault or defamation case where the character of one of the parties for peacefulness or violence or some other moral quality may be germane. Nor is this a case where the reputation of a third party is at stake. The sole issues here are the extent of the plaintiff's injuries and the compensation to which he is entitled. In sum general evidence of good character is irrelevant.

For these reasons, the plaintiff's motion is dismissed.

PLESTER v. WAWANESA MUTUAL INSURANCE CO.
(2006), 269 D.L.R. (4th) 624 (Ont. C.A.), varied (2006), 275 D.L.R. (4th) 552 (Ont. C.A.)

1 ARMSTRONG J.A.:— Terry Plester and his wife, Cecile Plester, owned and operated a furniture store, The Oak House Furniture Company, in Ingersoll Ontario. Terry Plester's father, Norman Plester, operated an antique furniture business under the name of The Oak House Importing Company from the premises of the furniture store. Terry and Cecile Plester insured their building and business with Wawanesa Mutual Insurance Company ("Wawanesa"). Norman Plester also insured his business under a separate insurance policy with Wawanesa.

2 In the early morning hours of March 14, 1997, the furniture store and much of its contents were damaged by fire. Terry and Cecile Plester submitted a claim for their losses to Wawanesa, as did Norman Plester. Wawanesa denied each of the claims on the basis that Terry, Cecile or Norman Plester, or all of them, set the fire or caused someone to set it on their behalf.

3 . . . After a trial of both actions before Justice W.A. Jenkins of the Superior Court of Justice and a jury, judgment was rendered in favour of the Plesters . . .

. . .

Did the trial judge err in permitting the Plesters to call evidence of good character?

41 In ruling that character evidence was admissible, the trial judge recognized that such evidence in civil cases is generally excluded on grounds of irrelevance: see *Deep v. Wood* (1983), 143 D.L.R. (3d) 246 (Ont. C.A.) at 250. However, he noted that there are some exceptions, such as defamation cases where the good character of a plaintiff may be put in issue by the defendant.

42 The trial judge concluded his ruling on the admissibility of this evidence as follows:

Evidence of good character is routinely admitted in criminal cases and since the defendant is alleging that the plaintiffs in these actions committed criminal acts I see no reason why they should not be permitted to call evidence of their general reputation in the community. I therefore order that the plaintiffs be permitted to call such evidence at the trial of these actions.

43 In my view, the trial judge did not err in admitting character evidence in this case. Once the appellant alleged arson against the Plesters, it was permissible for them to respond with the kind of evidence that would be available to them in a criminal court.

44 The appellant also takes issue with the trial judge's charge to the jury on the use that it could make of the character evidence. The trial judge told the jury:

> Evidence of good character, such as honesty and reliability in their business or personal dealings, may be of assistance to you in deciding this case. Good character by itself is not evidence that the Plesters did not set this fire, but it may make it less likely that they were involved in the fire. So you should consider the character evidence in the same way that you consider the rest of the evidence in deciding whether Wawanesa has proved on a balance of probabilities that the Plesters set this fire.

I do not find fault in the trial judge's charge on the use that could be made of the character evidence.

We shall see later that bad character evidence is sometimes admitted in civil cases under the head of similar fact evidence.

(d) Character of Accused in Criminal Cases[12]

(i) Good Character Evidence

Shortly stated, the accused is entitled to lead evidence of his or her own good character but, generally speaking, the prosecution is not entitled to lead evidence of the accused's bad character.

Martin J.A., in *R. v. Tarrant*,[13] wrote:

> Evidence of good character is evidence which has a bearing on the improbability of the accused committing the offence and also is relevant to his credibility. The effect of the charge by the learned trial Judge was to deprive character evidence of any use unless the jury was in doubt or the scales were evenly balanced. It need scarcely be pointed out that if the jury were in doubt or if the scales were equally balanced it would be their duty to acquit whether or not there was evidence of good character. The evidence of good character may, along with all the other evidence, create or result in the jury having a reasonable doubt.

How probative is good character evidence in sexual assault cases?

---

[12]   See generally Matthew Shuber, "Evidence of the Accused's Character: A Road Map for Young Counsel" (2000) 43 Crim. L.Q. 489.

[13]   (1982), 63 C.C.C. (2d) 385 (Ont. C.A.) at 388.

R. v. PROFIT
(1992), 16 C.R. (4th) 332, 85 C.C.C. (3d) 232 (Ont. C.A.)

The accused, a school principal, was convicted of sexual offences involving students. The accused appealed.

GOODMAN J.A. (BLAIR J.A. concurring):—

. . .

Twenty-two character witnesses testified on behalf of the appellant. Fifteen were colleagues or school board employees who had worked either for or with the appellant. Three were associated with the appellant through volunteer or church organizations. Two were independent businessmen from the appellant's community and two were personal friends. Some of them had, as children, attended camps where the appellant was a director and in later years had acted as counsellors in the camp under the appellant's supervision. All of these witnesses had seemingly impeccable backgrounds and were well qualified to give evidence with respect to the reputation of the appellant in the community with respect to honesty, integrity and morality.

A fair résumé of their evidence with respect to their personal knowledge was that they had never seen the appellant conduct himself in a sexually inappropriate manner, nor had they ever heard the appellant make a statement that they would consider sexually inappropriate. None of them had ever received a complaint about the appellant's conduct.

. . .

The trial judge, however, made no reference whatsoever to the use of character evidence as a basis of an inference that the appellant was unlikely to have committed the crime charged.

. . .

[W]here the character witnesses have given evidence as to the moral behaviour of an accused with respect to children in cases alleging sexual offences against children and have given evidence with respect to the general reputation of an accused for not only honesty and integrity but also morality, in the broader sense, such evidence has the same degree of relevance and weight to establish the improbability that the accused committed the offence, as evidence of general reputation with respect to honesty has in the case of an alleged offence involving a theft or a fraudulent transaction. In each case it is only one part of the evidence to be considered by the finder of fact along with all other evidence in determining the culpability of an accused and its weight will no doubt vary with the circumstances of each case. .... [T]he character evidence in the case at bar dealt specifically with the appellant's behaviour with his students and his general reputation with respect to morality.

. . .

Accordingly, I would allow the appeal and quash the convictions.

GRIFFITHS J.A. (dissenting):—

. . .

[W]hile such evidence may be relevant in cases involving crimes of commercial dishonesty, it has little probative value in cases involving sexual misconduct against children by persons in positions of trust or control.

Recently there have been a number of cases involving persons who enjoyed impeccable reputations in the community for honesty, integrity and morality, such as teachers, scout leaders, priests and others who, in breach of their positions of trust, have committed acts of sexual assault. In these cases, the sexual assaults were generally shrouded in secrecy, and the flaw in the character of the offender frequently did not come to light until he had been charged and convicted.

R. v. PROFIT
[1993] 3 S.C.R. 637, 24 C.R. (4th) 279, 85 C.C.C. (3d) 232

SOPINKA J.:—We agree with the conclusion of Griffiths J.A. in his dissenting reasons. When the reasons of the trial judge are considered as a whole, we are satisfied that he dealt with the character evidence tendered in this case adequately. The reasons of the trial judge must be viewed in light of the fact that as a matter of common sense, but not as a principle of law, a trial judge may take into account that in sexual assault cases involving children, sexual misconduct occurs in private and in most cases will not be reflected in the reputation in the community of the accused for morality. As a matter of weight, the trial judge is entitled to find that the propensity value of character evidence as to morality is diminished in such cases.

Accordingly, the appeal is allowed and the convictions restored.

With whom do you agree on this issue?

(ii) *Bad Character Evidence*

Just as good character is relevant, so too evidence of the accused's bad character is relevant to whether he or she committed the complained of act. We might rationally infer that on the occasion under review the accused may have acted in conformity with his or her character, his or her disposition. While it is relevant, the law has created a canon of exclusion lest the trier of fact give it more probative force than it warrants or be diverted from judging the action to judging the person. In the leading case of *R. v. Rowton*[14] Willes J. wrote of character evidence:

> It is strictly relevant to the issue; but such evidence is not admissible upon the part of the prosecution . . . because if the prosecution were allowed to go into such evidence we should have the whole life of the prisoner ripped up, and as has been witnessed in the proceedings of jurisdictions where such evidence is admissible upon a charge preferred, you might begin by showing that when a boy at school he had robbed an orchard and so read the rest of his conduct and

---

[14]   (1865), 10 Cox. C.C. 25 at 38. See the description of French trials where character evidence was freely used.

the whole of his life; and the result would be that a man on his trial would be overwhelmed by prejudice instead of being convicted on affirmative evidence, which the law of this country requires. The prosecution is prevented from giving such evidence for reasons rather of policy and humanity than because proof that the prisoner was a bad character is not relevant to the issue, — it is relevant to the issue, but it is expedient for the sake of letting in all the evidence which might possibly throw light upon the subject; you might arrive at justice in one case and you might do injustice in ninety-nine.

And Baron Parke in *Attorney General v. Hitchcock*:[15]

We cannot enter into a collateral question as to the man's having committed a crime on some former occasion, one reason being, that it would lead to complicated issues and long inquiries; and another, that a party cannot be expected to be prepared to defend the whole of the actions of his life.

R. v. HANDY
[2002] 2 S.C.R. 908, 1 C.R. (6th) 203, 164 C.C.C. (3d) 481 (S.C.C.)

BINNIE J., for the Court:—

B. *The General Exclusionary Rule*

31 The respondent is clearly correct in saying that evidence of misconduct beyond what is alleged in the indictment which does no more than blacken his character is inadmissible. Nobody is charged with having a "general" disposition or propensity for theft or violence or whatever. The exclusion thus generally prohibits character evidence to be used as circumstantial proof of conduct, i.e., to allow an inference from the "similar facts" that the accused has the propensity or disposition to do the type of acts charged and is therefore guilty of the offence. The danger is that the jury might be confused by the multiplicity of incidents and put more weight than is logically justified . . . ("reasoning prejudice") or by convicting based on bad personhood ("moral prejudice"): Great Britain Law Commission, Consultation Paper No. 141, *Evidence in Criminal Proceedings: Previous Misconduct of a Defendant* (1996), at § 7.2.

32 This is a very old rule of the common law. Reference may be made to seventeenth-century trials in which the prosecution was scolded for raising prior felonious conduct, as for example to Lord Holt C.J. in *Harrison's Trial* (1692), 12 How. St. Tr. 833 (Old Bailey (London)), at p. 864: "Are you going to arraign his whole life? Away, Away, that ought not to be; that is nothing to the matter."

33 Subsequently, and most famously, the general exclusionary rule was laid down by Lord Herschell L.C. *Makin v. Attorney-General for New South Wales*, [1894] A.C. 57 (P.C.), in these terms, at p. 65:

It is undoubtedly not competent for the prosecution to adduce evidence tending to shew that the accused has been guilty of criminal acts other than those covered by

---

[15]   (1847), 1 Ex. 91.

the indictment, for the purpose of leading to the conclusion that the accused is a person likely from his criminal conduct or character to have committed the offence for which he is being tried.

. . .

35 The dangers of propensity reasoning are well recognized. Not only can people change their ways but they are not robotic. While juries in fourteenth-century England were expected to determine facts based on their personal knowledge of the character of the participants, it is now said that to infer guilt from a knowledge of the mere character of the accused is a "forbidden type of reasoning": *Boardman, supra*, at p. 453, *per* Lord Hailsham.

36 The exclusion of evidence of general propensity or disposition has been repeatedly affirmed in this Court and is not controversial. See *Morris v. The Queen*, [1983] 2 S.C.R. 190; *R. v. Morin*, [1988] 2 S.C.R. 345; *R. v. B. (C.R.)*, [1990] 1 S.C.R. 717; *R. v. Arp*, [1998] 3 S.C.R. 339.

Policy Basis for the Exclusion

37 . . . Its potential for prejudice, distraction and time consumption is very great and these disadvantages will almost always outweigh its probative value. It ought, in general, to form no part of the case which the accused is called on to answer. It is excluded notwithstanding the general rule that all relevant evidence is admissible: *Arp, supra*, at para. 38; *Robertson, supra*, at p. 941; *Morris, supra*, at pp. 201-2; *R. v. Seaboyer*, [1991] 2 S.C.R. 577, at p. 613.

38 If propensity evidence were routinely admitted, it might encourage the police simply to "round up the usual suspects" instead of making a proper unblinkered investigation of each particular case. One of the objectives of the criminal justice system is the rehabilitation of offenders. Achievement of this objective is undermined to the extent the law doubts the "usual suspects" are capable of turning the page and starting a new life.

39 It is, of course, common human experience that people generally act consistently with their known character. We make everyday judgments about the reliability or honesty of particular individuals based on what we know of their track record. If the jurors in this case had been the respondent's inquisitive neighbours, instead of sitting in judgment in a court of law, they would undoubtedly have wanted to know everything bout his character and related activities.... [A]s pointed out by Sopinka J. in *B. (C.R.), supra*, at p. 744:

> The principal reason for the exclusionary rule relating to propensity is that there is a natural human tendency to judge a person's action on the basis of character. Particularly with juries there would be a strong inclination to conclude that a thief has stolen, a violent man has assaulted and a pedophile has engaged in pedophilic acts. Yet the policy of the law is wholly against this process of reasoning.

40 The policy of the law recognizes the difficulty of containing the effects of such information which, once dropped like poison in the juror's ear, "swift as

quicksilver it courses through the natural gates and alleys of the body":
Hamlet, Act I, Scene v, ll. 66-67.

There are a number of exceptions to the general rule that the
prosecution cannot lead evidence of bad character as disposition
evidence. They include where:

1. the accused puts his or her character in issue (discussed in the next
   section);

2. the evidence constitutes similar act evidence (see *R. v. Handy*,
   below); and,

3. the accused leads propensity evidence to suggest that a third party
   committed the offence (see section on Character of Third Party/Co-
   Accused below).

(iii) *When Does an Accused Put His or Her Character in Issue?*

When does the accused put his or her character into issue and thereby
open the door for the prosecution to rebut? In *R. v. Shrimpton*[16] the accused
maintained that he had not given evidence of good character as he had not
called witnesses to that fact but rather elicited the same in cross-examination
of a prosecution witness. It was held:

> If, either by calling witnesses on his part, or by cross-examination of the
> witnesses for the Crown, the prisoner relies upon his good character, it is lawful
> for the prosecutor to give the previous conviction in evidence.

At that time, of course, the accused was incapable of giving evidence. When
he now takes the stand and denies the charge, does he open the door to
character evidence being led by the prosecution? Let us compare three
cases.

In *R. v. McFadden*[17] the accused was charged with first degree murder.
The Crown's theory was that the accused had killed the deceased in the
course of an indecent assault. In cross-examination of the accused it was
suggested that he had gone to the deceased's place to satisfy his sexual
urge and that he had stabbed her when she resisted. The accused replied: "I
have the most beautiful wife in the world. I worship the ground that girl walks
on." The British Columbia Court of Appeal held that the accused had thereby
placed his character for sexual morality in issue because he meant to convey
that he would not get sexually involved with any other woman. Craig J.A.
said:

> The purpose of evidence of good character is to show the accused is a person
> who is not likely to have committed the act with which he is charged and, also, to
> enhance his credibility. An accused may adduce evidence of good character (1)
> by calling witnesses; (2) by cross-examining Crown witnesses on the subject; (3)
> by giving testimony. Normally, he may lead evidence of good character by

---

[16]   (1851), 5 Cox. C.C. 387.
[17]   (1981), 65 C.C.C. (2d) 9 (B.C. C.A.).

adducing evidence only of his general reputation, not by adducing evidence of specific acts which might tend to establish his character. The Crown may call evidence of bad character in rebuttal, but such evidence, also, must relate only to general reputation: *R. v. Rowton* (1865), 169 E.R. 1497. An accused may put his character in issue in the course of giving his testimony, not by giving evidence of his general reputation, but by making assertions which tend to show that he is a person of good character, particularly with regard to the aspect of his character which is in issue. Obviously, the Crown may rebut this testimony by calling evidence of bad character, but may the Crown call evidence only of general reputation or may the Crown call evidence other than the evidence of general reputation? In some circumstances, the Crown may call evidence of specific incidents in rebutting evidence of good character. For example, under the provisions of s. 593 of the *Criminal Code*, the Crown could prove previous convictions as evidence of bad character. The Crown may, also, adduce similar fact evidence to rebut evidence of good character: *Guay v. The Queen* (1979), 42 C.C.C. (2d) 536, [1979] 1 S.C.R. 18.[18]

R. v. McNamara[19] was a prosecution of a number of companies and individuals for conspiracy to defraud by agreeing on who should make the successful bid on dredging contracts. A principal Crown witness, Rindress, was the president of two companies, J.P. Porter and Richelieu, which were part of a corporate structure of which the accused Jean Simard was a director. Rindress testified that he assumed he had a mandate from Simard to bid-rig. In Simard's examination-in-chief he was asked as to the mandate he had given Rindress:

Q. Mr. Rindress in giving his evidence has told us that what he considered his mandate was in connection with the operation of the Porter Company and the Richelieu Company, what did you consider was the mandate of Mr. Rindress in connection with operating the company?

A. The mandate that Mr. Rindress had is to run the company like a company should be run, legally.

Q. I am sorry?

A. Like any company should be run, legally.

The trial judge ruled that the accused had put his character into issue, and the Crown was permitted to cross-examine Simard with respect to an otherwise unrelated building transaction which inpugned Simard's character for honesty. The Ontario Court of Appeal held:

Manifestly, an accused does not put his character in issue by denying his guilt and repudiating the allegations made against him, nor by giving an explanation of matters which are essential to his defence. An accused is not entitled, however, under the guise of repudiating the allegations against him to assert expressly or impliedly that he would not have done the things alleged against him because he is a person of good character; if he does, he puts his character in issue.

The difficult question is whether the appellant crossed over the line of permissible repudiation of the charge and asserted that he was an honest man...

18   *Ibid.* at 13.
19   (1981), 56 C.C.C. (2d) 193 (Ont. C.A.) at 343.

The appellant Jean Simard in response to his counsel's question as to the scope of Rindress' mandate did not confine himself to saying that the mandate was to run the company legally. The appellant said that Rindress' mandate was to run the company like a company should be run, legally. He followed that answer by repeating that Rindress' mandate was to run the company "like any company should be run, legally". The appellant's evidence is consistent only with his intention to assert that he would not knowingly permit a Simard company to be operated other than legally. If there were any doubt whether the appellant, by these answers, intended to project the image of a law-abiding citizen, these answers, when taken together with his subsequent evidence, make it clear that the appellant intended to project the image of a man of integrity and of an ethical businessman.[20]

In *R. v. Shortreed*[21] the accused was charged with a number of sexual assaults. He testified in chief that he never sexually assaulted anyone. The accused later explained that what he meant by that was that he had not attacked any of the victims in this case. The Court held that the accused had not placed his character in issue and the Crown should not therefore have been permitted to cross-examine the accused as to facts underlying a prior conviction for wounding:

> Having regard to the qualification of his general statement when he was asked in-chief to explain its meaning, it is apparent that the appellant was not attempting to rely on his non-violent nature, but merely intended to deny having assaulted any of the five complainants. He was not adducing evidence of good character within the meaning of s. 666 of the *Criminal Code*. . . .
>
> . . .
>
> An accused person does not place his character in issue by denying his guilt and repudiating the allegations made against him. Neither do the introductory routine questions as to education, marital status, religious affiliation have the effect of rendering the accused's character relevant.[22]

Do you agree with the Court of Appeal that questions about education, marital status and religious affiliation do not put character in issue? If not, what is their relevance?

---

20   *Ibid.* at 346-347.
21   (1990), 54 C.C.C. (3d) 292 (Ont. C.A.).
22   *Ibid.* at 307. In *R. v. Farrant*, 4 C.C.C. (3d) 354, [1983] 1 S.C.R. 124, 32 C.R. (3d) 289, the accused put his character in issue when he testified that "It's not my character to be violent." An opposite conclusion was reached in *R. v. Turpin*, 2005 BCSC 490 (S.C.) where the accused testified that "It's not my style to kill people." The trial judge distinguished *Farrant* on the basis that the testimony was elicited during the Crown's cross-examination and the accused seemed to regret the fact that he had made the utterance.

R. v. P. (N.A.)
(2002), 171 C.C.C. (3d) 70, 8 C.R. (6th) 186 (Ont. C.A.)

The accused was charged with offences of violence against his wife and daughter.

DOHERTY J.A. (AUSTIN and ARMSTRONG JJ.A. concurring):—

The vexing question of when an accused can be said to put his or her character in issue through his answers during examination-in-chief was considered by this court in *R. v. McNamara (No. 1), supra*, at p. 346:

> Manifestly, an accused does not put his character in issue by denying his guilt and repudiating the allegations made against him, nor by giving an explanation of matters which are essential to his defence. An accused is not entitled, however, under the guise of repudiating the allegations against him to assert expressly or impliedly that he would not have done the things alleged against him because he is a person of good character; if he does, he puts his character in issue. The difficult question is whether the appellant crossed over the line of permissible repudiation of the charge and asserted that he was an honest man.

The line between permissible repudiation of the Crown's case and putting one's character in issue can be particularly difficult to draw in cases where the prosecution is allowed to lead evidence of a lengthy marital and family relationship so as to provide a proper context in which the jury can assess the specific allegations made against an accused. The importance of context and background in this kind of case is beyond doubt: *R. v. F. (D.S.)* (1999), 132 C.C.C. (3d) 97 (Ont. C.A.) at 106-107. In my view, however, the accused must be able to repudiate the charges by presenting his or her version of that context without suffering the disadvantage of putting character in issue. For example, where the Crown is allowed to lead evidence to demonstrate that an accused was a controlling and dominating spouse in order to give context to the allegations, I do not think that an accused should be said to have put his character in issue when he describes himself as a loving and caring spouse.

That is not to say that where the Crown is allowed to introduce evidence of the dynamics within a family to provide context or narrative, an accused has free rein and can never be said to put his character in issue during examination-in-chief. In *R. v. W. (L.K.), supra*, the accused was charged with having assaulted five of his children on many occasions over many years. The Crown led evidence that throughout those many years, the accused systematically abused and intimidated his wife and children. After reviewing the substance of the accused's examination-in-chief, Moldaver J.A. said at pp. 465-66:

> Having reviewed the appellant's examination-in-chief, I have no doubt that he placed his character in issue, thereby opening the door to being questioned about prior acts of discreditable conduct, including the details surrounding the 1956 assault upon his sister. Throughout his examination-in-chief, the appellant availed himself of every opportunity to extol his moral and ethical virtues in an effort to portray himself as the kind of person who would not abuse anyone physically or sexually, let alone those people, such as his immediate family members, whom he cared for and loved. Having adopted that posture, he placed his character in issue.
> . . . . Once the appellant placed his character in issue, the Crown was entitled to

lead evidence designed to level the playing field and provide the jury with a yardstick against which to measure the clear and unmistakable impression that the appellant sought to convey, namely, that he was not the type of person to commit the offences in question.

Drawing the line between repudiation of the Crown's case and putting character in issue requires that an evaluation of the accused's evidence-in-chief be informed by the nature of the case he or she had to meet. .. A review of the Crown's evidence demonstrates that a large part of the Crown's case consisted of a detailed description of the relationship between M.P. and the respondent. He was entitled to give his version of that relationship during his examination-in-chief without being said to have put his character in issue. . . .

The Crown chose to make the entire family history and the relationships within the family the focal point of its case against the respondent. In so commenting, I do not suggest any criticism of Crown counsel. The Crown, quite properly, took the position that the charges could only be properly understood in the context of the marital and family relationships involving the respondent, M.P., N.P., and the rest of her family. On the Crown's evidence, the family picture was not a pretty one. In that picture, the respondent was painted as a terrible husband and father. To repudiate this part of the Crown's case, the respondent had to put forward his version of those relationships. Given the scope of the evidence led by the Crown, repudiation of that case extended to a description of the respondent's relationship with M.P., N.P. and his other children. To the extent that the respondent's evidence adopted a moral tone, it was directly responsive to the many allegations of immorality made against him during the Crown's case.

. . .

I do not think that the respondent put his character in issue. Section 666 was not engaged.

Will the accused be deemed to have put his or her character in issue when the evidence emerges from a Crown cross-examination of a defence witness?

R. v. A. (W.A.)
(1996), 3 C.R. (5th) 388, 112 C.C.C. (3d) 83 (Man. C.A.)

The accused was charged with sexually assaulting his stepdaughter. At trial, the stepdaughter's long cross-examination attacked her character and truthfulness. The accused's wife, who was the stepdaughter's natural mother, gave evidence for the accused as to her daughter's bad behaviour, and the accused's lack of opportunity to commit the crime. During the Crown's cross-examination as to why she considered her daughter a liar, the wife said, "I know my husband." The trial judge then let the Crown cross-examine the wife as to the family's dynamics. Under further cross-examination, the wife admitted that the accused had once assaulted her, that he had committed himself to a mental health centre, and that he had had an angry meeting with the stepdaughter's teacher. The trial judge cautioned the members of the jury that the cross-examination evidence was useful only to give them a balanced insight into the accused's temperament and that it was not relevant as to the accused's propensity to commit the offence charged. The accused was convicted, and he appealed.

SCOTT C.J.M. (HUBAND and MONNIN JJ.A. concurring):—

. . .

In my opinion, the accused did not put his "character" in issue through answers given by Mrs. A. during cross-examination by Crown counsel. The line of questioning pursued by Crown counsel that led Mrs. A. to make the response "I know my husband" was directly attributable to Crown counsel's persistence in cross-examination in querying why she was supportive of the accused and not her daughter, the complainant.

In any event there is clear authority that, while the accused may put his own character in issue by introducing such evidence himself, when dealing with defence witnesses it is only through their examination-in-chief that an accused's character may be put in issue. . . In my opinion, limiting the ways of putting character in issue through defence witnesses to evidence-in-chief makes eminent good sense as illustrated by the very facts of this case where the approbation by Mrs. A. of her husband's "character" was not volunteered, but was elicited as a direct response to a line of questioning only pursued during cross-examination. If it were otherwise, the Crown could put the accused's character in issue through clever cross-examination of defence witnesses and thus frustrate the rule against it.

The evidence brought out during the cross-examination of Mrs. A. is simply incapable of constituting character evidence introduced by or on behalf of the accused. Indeed, the point is so obvious that I have not been able to find any authorities directly on point. See, for example, *R. v. Valeanu* (1995), 97 C.C.C. (3d) 338 (Ont. C.A.), where the Crown conceded on appeal that questioning such as occurred here was clearly improper cross-examination.

Since it is not now strictly necessary to review the scope of character evidence once the accused has put it in issue, I simply note that authorities of many years' standing make it clear that it ordinarily refers to evidence of reputation and not to evidence of disposition. This is normally attested to by evidence as to the accused's general reputation within the community. Thus the evidence brought out during cross-examination is not character evidence in the traditional sense since it deals with specific incidents involving the accused and members of his household during the period relevant to the indictment.

(iv) *How Character May be Proved*

Having examined *when* the character of the accused may be evidenced, we turn now to the separate question of *how* that character may be shown. Three methods suggest themselves as rational: first, by reports of the accused's reputation in the community for the pertinent character trait; second, by the opinion of one who knows the accused's character; and, finally, by description of specific acts of conduct or misconduct from which his or her general disposition or character might be inferred. The last method was viewed by the courts as of little probative value and carried the danger of multiplicity of issues and unfair surprise. Willes J. explained:

> You exclude particular facts on the part of the prisoner because a person who is a robber may do an act or acts of generosity, and the proof of such acts are, therefore, irrelevant to the question whether he was likely to have committed the particular act of robbery or not; and, on the one hand, I agree that particular acts must be excluded on the part of the prosecution partly for the reason that excludes them in the first instance, and partly for the reason that no notice has been given to the prisoner that you are going into an inquiry as to particular facts.[23]

Prior to the landmark decision of *Rowton* the normal technique of informing the trier of the accused's character was by the opinions of those who knew him or her, bolstered at times by their reports of his or her reputation. Curiously, this practice was there suddenly reversed.[24] Rowton was charged with having committed an indecent assault upon a 14-year-old boy. The accused called several witnesses who gave him an excellent character as a moral and well-conducted man. The prosecution called in reply a witness who knew the accused and when asked:

> What is the defendant's general character for decency and morality of conduct?

He replied:

> I know nothing of the neighbourhood's opinion, because I was only a boy at school when I knew him; but my own opinion, and the opinion of my brothers who were also pupils of his, is, that his character is that of a man capable of the grossest indecency and the most flagrant immorality.

This evidence was received over the objections of the accused, the accused was convicted, and the question was reserved for the opinion of 12 judges. The majority[25] held this to be error and the conviction was quashed. Since that time evidence of character has usually been limited to evidence of reputation, and character witnesses are commanded that they are not to speak from their own experience of the accused but rather to report on the rumours in the community. As Wurtele J. later summarized:

> In criminal prosecutions evidence respecting the general character of the defendant is admissible for the purpose of raising a presumption of innocence or of guilt, but the party who tenders such evidence must restrict himself to evidence of mere general reputation, and the question to be put to a witness to character is: What is the defendant's reputation for honesty, morality or humanity? as the case may be. The Crown has no right, however, in making out its case to put in evidence of bad character, but, on the other hand, the defendant is at liberty to give evidence of his general good character; and then the counsel for the Crown can cross-examine the witnesses as to particular or

---

[23] *R. v. Rowton* (1865), 10 Cox. C.C. 25 at 39.
[24] See 7 Wigmore, *Evidence* (3rd ed.), s. 1981 at 210 for a description of how *Rowton* surprised the legal profession.
[25] Willes J. and Erle C.J. dissented.

isolated facts and as to the ground of their belief, and may also call witnesses to prove the general bad reputation of the defendant, and thus to contradict his witnesses.[26]

The character witness must have knowledge of the person's reputation in the community. Our jurisprudence reflects the fact, however, that the nature of the community changes with the times.

R. v. LEVASSEUR
(1987), 56 C.R. (3d) 335, 35 C.C.C. (3d) 136 (Alta. C.A.)

The accused was charged with break, enter and theft. The defence sought to introduce evidence of the accused's good character through testimony of her employer, who had discussed the accused's general reputation with 15 of their business acquaintances. The trial judge ruled the evidence was inadmissible because the evidence was not of her reputation in the community in which she lived.

HARRADENCE J.A.:—

. . .

Scrutiny by a modern appellate court can only result in the conclusion that the neighbourhood requirement is no longer justifiable. While it may have been appropriate in the days of the redoubtable Duke of Wellington, who regretted the advent of the British railroad system because it would allow the lower classes to move about, it is not appropriate to a society which has supersonic transport available to it.

The laws of evidence must not continue to reflect this parochial attitude; as Lord Ellenborough pointed out, "The rules of evidence must expand according to the exigencies of society" (*Pritt v. Fairclough* (1812), 170 E.R. 1391 at 1392).

. . .

Credibility is crucial to the issue of whether the appellant committed the offence of breaking and entering. The appellant claims that she was told to remove the vehicles from the warehouse bay and therefore had colour of right. Had the jurors heard evidence of her good character, their conclusion might have differed.

[A new trial was ordered.]

Levasseur was applied in *R. v. Clarke*[27] where Justice Rosenberg held that:

> ... I should point out that, in my view, the trial judge was in error in holding that the character witnesses could only give evidence about reputation if they were aware of the accused's or complainant's reputation in a particular city or town where they lived, such as Trenton. With the increasing urbanization of society, a

---

[26] *R. v. Barsalou* (1901), 4 C.C.C. 347 (Que. K.B.) at 348. And see *Michelson v. U.S.*, 335 U.S. 469 (1948). See also *R. v. Grosse* (1983), 9 C.C.C. (3d) 465 (N.S.C.A.).

[27] (1998), 129 C.C.C. (3d) 1, 18 C.R. (5th) 219 (Ont. C.A.) at 10 [C.C.C.].

person's community will not necessarily coincide with a particular geographic location. Thus, in this case, it would seem to me that it was open to the defence to lead evidence of the respondent's reputation in the Caribbean community in the area.[28]

An accused can, generally speaking, lead good character evidence in one of three ways:

1.   Cross-examining witnesses called by the Crown;

2.   Calling defence witnesses;

3.   Testifying himself or herself as to his or her character.

While the first two are limited to general reputation evidence, the accused can testify about specific acts that reveal his or her good character (see *R. v. Brown*, below).

In responding to an accused's good character evidence, the Crown is also, generally speaking, limited to general reputation evidence. There are, however, exceptions to this general rule. Where the defence puts the accused's character in issue and the accused testifies, the Crown can cross-examine the accused on specific bad acts.

Another exception to the general rule forbidding the evidencing of character by specific acts of the accused was created by the legislature in England[29] and now finds itself exampled in s. 666 of the *Criminal Code*, which provides:

> Where, at a trial, the accused adduces evidence of his good character, the prosecutor may, in answer thereto, before a verdict is returned, adduce evidence of the previous conviction of the accused for any offences, including any previous conviction by reason of which a greater punishment may be imposed.

The legislation was enacted

> . . . to defeat the scandalous attempt often made by persons, who had been repeatedly convicted of felony, bringing witnesses, or cross-examining the witnesses for the prosecution, to prove that the prisoner had previously borne a good character for honesty.[30]

Note that the legislation allows for proof of specific acts to be called in reply only when the act resulted in a conviction.

Note that s. 666 only applies where the accused puts his or her character in issue. Recall that s. 12 of the *Canada Evidence Act* allows any witness including the accused to be cross-examined on a criminal record whether or not the accused has put his or her character in issue. This evidence can only

---

[28]   See further *R. v. Soikie*, [2004] O.J. No. 2902 (S.C.J.).

[29]   See *An Act to Prevent the Fact of a Previous Conviction being given on Evidence to the Jury*, 1836 (6 & 7 Will. 4, c. 111), and *An Act for the Better Prevention of Offences, 1851* (14 & 15 Vict., c. 19), s. 9. See also *R. v. Nealy* (1987), 17 O.A.C. 164 (C.A.).

[30]   *R. v. Shrimpton* (1851), 5 Cox. C.C. 387. Consider the legislative history of s. 666 as prior to the 1955 revision. It apparently was limited to prosecutions for offences which called for a greater penalty on a second conviction.

be used to assess credibility. Under *Corbett* we have seen that there is a discretion to prevent such cross-examination in the case of the accused.

In *R. v. P. (N.A.)*,[31] it was observed that:

> If an accused puts his or her character in issue during examination-in-chief, the scope of cross-examination on the criminal record permitted by s. 666 goes beyond that allowed under s. 12 of the *Canada Evidence Act*. Since the cross-examination under s. 666 is predicated on the accused having put his or her character in issue, the accused may also be questioned about the specifics underlying the criminal convictions: *R. v. W. (L.K.)* (1999), 138 C.C.C. (3d) 449 (Ont. C.A.) at 465, leave to appeal to S.C.C. refused [2000] S.C.C.A. No. 383 (QL) [148 C.C.C. (3d) vi]; *R. v. Deyardin* (1997), 119 C.C.C. (3d) 365 (Que. C.A.) at 375-77. The wide ambit of cross-examination contemplated by s. 666 could have been significant in this case. If cross-examination had been allowed, the jury would have heard not only about the respondent's conviction for attempted murder but also that it involved a brutal beating administered in the course of a robbery.

Where an accused has put his or her character in issue, the Ontario Court of Appeal has recognized a discretion to allow evidence of specific acts, apart from s. 666, to level the playing field.

R. v. BROWN
(1999), 27 C.R. (5th) 151, 137 C.C.C. (3d) 400 (Ont. C.A.)

The accused was charged with aggravated assault. The Crown case was that he had violently shaken a 14-month-old baby causing him severe brain injury. The accused, who was unrepresented, denied the shaking and called witnesses to testify as to his good character. He testified himself that he had never abused a child in his life. After the accused closed his case, the Crown called one of the accused's sons who testified that as a child he was assaulted on many occasions by the accused. The accused was convicted. The Ontario Court of Appeal allowed the appeal and ordered a new trial.

ROSENBERG J.A.:—

In my view, the trial judge erred in permitting Stewart to give evidence of specific bad acts by the appellant.

In this case, the appellant put his character in issue by calling a character witness. He also put his character in issue by asserting in his own testimony that he had never abused a child and, indeed, that he had rescued children on prior occasions. By testifying in this way, the appellant was attempting to show that he was not the type of person who would have abused the infant.

Where an accused puts his character in issue, as this appellant clearly did, he may be cross-examined on prior specific acts of misconduct: *R. v. McNamara et al. (No. 1)* (1981), 56 C.C.C. (2d) 193 (Ont. C.A.) at 346-49; *R. v. Farrant*, [1983] 1 S.C.R. 124 at 145. Thus, it would have been open to Crown counsel to cross-examine the appellant on the specific acts of misconduct by the appellant against Stewart and his brother. Crown counsel

---

[31]   (2002), 171 C.C.C. (3d) 70, 8 C.R. (6th) 186 (Ont. C.A.) at 83 [C.C.C.].

did not do so in this case. Rather, she chose to put these allegations before the trial judge by calling Stewart in reply.

The law as it has developed to date is that where the Crown proposes to call extrinsic evidence in reply, solely to rebut evidence of the accused's good character, the Crown may not lead evidence of specific acts of bad conduct. The only established exception to this rule is for acts that would also constitute evidence of similar facts. Otherwise, the Crown is limited to leading evidence of general reputation, the accused's criminal record pursuant to s. 666 of the Criminal Code, or s. 12 of the Canada Evidence Act if the accused testifies, or possibly expert evidence of disposition. *See R. v. McNamara et al.* (No. 1) at 348-49; *R. v. Tierney* (1982), 70 C.C.C. (2d) 481 (Ont. C.A.) at 485-86; *R. v. Donovan* (1991), 65 C.C.C. (3d) 511 (Ont. C.A.) at 534-5.

In my view, Stewart's evidence does not come within the exception that permits evidence of good character to be rebutted by similar fact evidence. The incidents to which Stewart testified bore no resemblance to the allegation in this case. . .

A more difficult question is whether the appellant in this case, by not asserting simply that he was a person of good character, but by expressly stating in direct examination that he had never abused a child and — implicitly — that he had never abused his own children and grandchildren, should be open to contradiction on that point. . . .

[I]n a proper case the trial judge does have a discretion to permit contradiction of the type of sweeping claim the appellant made in this case. The discretion to admit such evidence is necessary as a matter of fairness to prevent the accused from manipulating the rules of evidence to present a wholly distorted picture to the trier of fact. . . .

In my view, similarly, where an accused does not simply lead evidence of his good character generally, but relies upon specific acts that bear a direct relationship to the offence charged, he or she should be open to contradiction on those narrow points to avoid permitting the accused to leave the trier of fact with a distorted picture. However, because of the potentially prejudicial nature of the evidence when called in reply, before the Crown would be entitled to lead such evidence, it should have to demonstrate that resort to the traditional rules of evidence will not suffice to prevent a distorted picture. That did not occur here. Under the established rules of evidence, the Crown was entitled to cross-examine the appellant on prior acts of misconduct, but did not do so. It might be that such cross-examination would have been sufficient to prevent a distorted picture being placed before the court and, at the same time, cross-examination would have provided the appellant with a timely opportunity to present his version of the events involving his children. A rule requiring the Crown to first confront the accused with the allegations promotes the interests of fairness and trial economy: *R. v. P. (G.)*, 112 C.C.C. (3d) 263, 4 C.R. (5th) 36 (Ont. C.A.) at 280 [C.C.C.]. In view of Crown counsel's failure to confront the appellant with the allegations by Stewart, I would hold that she was precluded from leading that evidence in reply.

. . .

Moreover, even if Stewart's evidence was otherwise admissible, a careful balancing was required to ensure that the rebuttal evidence did not "overcompensate for the imbalance sought to be offset" Or, put another way, the trial judge was required to exercise his discretion carefully to ensure that the prejudicial effect of the evidence did not outweigh its probative value.

. . .

Moreover, I also have some concern that the trial judge may have misused that evidence. Where the Crown is permitted to adduce evidence of bad character, to rebut evidence of good character, and that evidence does not constitute similar fact evidence, the reply evidence can only be used to neutralize the evidence of good character and to assess the accused's credibility. This court held in *R. v. McNamara et al.* No. (1), supra, at pp. 352-53, that it cannot be used as affirmative evidence of the accused's disposition to commit the offence charged.

(v) *Warnings to Jury*

Where character evidence is admitted courts usually insist on a warning to the jury as to the permissible use of the evidence. In the case of good character evidence the jury must be advised that they can use the evidence to show that the accused was unlikely to have committed the crime (see, e.g., *R. v. Millar,*[32] below). However in the case of bad character evidence the jury must be warned that the jury cannot use the evidence merely to show the accused was the type of person to commit the crime. For example in *R. v. Dunn*[33] a new trial was ordered on an appeal against a conviction for living off the avails of prostitution because the jury were not warned that they could not infer from evidence that the accused was a drug dealer that he was the type of person who was likely to exploit a prostitute.[34]

Do these warnings make sense?

PROBLEMS

Problem 1

The accused is charged with manslaughter in the death of his wife. The defence is accident. He does not testify but his statement to the police is introduced by the Crown. In it, he states that he is a loving husband and father and that he is not a violent person. **Will the Crown be permitted to introduce evidence of the accused's criminal record for assault? What if he had testified that his wife had assaulted him in the past and threatened him with a gun before she was killed?** He further testifies that the gun went off accidentally when he tried to grab it from his wife. See *R. v.*

---

[32]   (1989), 71 C.R. (3d) 78 (Ont. C.A.). See also *R. v. McNamara* (1981), 56 C.C.C. (2d) 193 (Ont. C.A.), affirmed 45 C.R. (3d) 289, 19 C.C.C. (3d) 1, [1985] 1 S.C.R. 662 (S.C.C.).
[33]   (1993), 22 C.R. (4th) 344 (Ont. C.A.).
[34]   See also *R. v. N. (R.K.)* (1996), 114 C.C.C. (3d) 40 (Ont. C.A.).

Wilson (1999), 136 C.C.C. (3d) 252 (Man. C.A.) at 265-269 and *R. v. Truscott* (2006), 213 C.C.C. (3d) 183 (Ont. C.A.) at 192.

Problem 2

A nurse is charged with three counts of sexual assault arising out of the course of his duties at Toronto East General Hospital. In his examination-in-chief, the accused testified that "he had never been involved with the police". **How would you rule as to whether he has put his character in issue?** See *R. v. Cocchio*, [2003] O.J. No. 780, and *R. v. Morris* (1978), 43 C.C.C. (2d) 129, [1979] 1 S.C.R. 405, 6 C.R. (3d) 36 (S.C.C.) at 157-158 [C.C.C.].

Problem 3

The accused is on trial for perjury and threatening death. The charges relate to false statements made on a Legal Aid application and a phone call to the Area Director in which he said "I'm going to knock you off". The accused has a lengthy criminal record including convictions for making threatening or harassing phone calls. During his examination-in-chief, the accused admitted that he had a criminal record but not the details. During cross-examination, the accused stated that he believed in honesty and fairness. The trial judge concluded that he put his character in issue:

> In so far as the issue of character, I think it has been put in issue on the basis of your direct examination. You indicated, and got an affirmative answer from the accused, that he had a criminal record and I believe the issue of character evidence is germane to what is before the court. I think having indicated that he is a firm believer in honesty and forthrightness, he has put his character on the line, and on that basis I am prepared to hear further evidence as it relates to the record.

Is there a basis to appeal? See *R. v. Bricker* (1994), 90 C.C.C. (3d) 268 (Ont. C.A.).

Problem 4

The accused is charged with first degree murder. The only issue is identity. The theory of the Crown is that the accused killed the victim because of an unpaid drug debt. The defence is alibi. The defence also vigorously challenged the integrity of the police investigation including the failure to investigate other potential suspects. To respond, the Crown wants to lead evidence of the accused's involvement in the drug trade. **Admissible? Has the accused put his character in issue?** See *R. v. Dhillon* (2002), 166 C.C.C. (3d) 262, 5 C.R. (6th) 317 (Ont. C.A.). But see: *R. v. Truscott* (2006), 213 C.C.C. (3d) 183 (Ont. C.A.).

Problem 5

The accused was charged with sexual offences against the 15-year-old daughter of his common-law spouse. The complainant testified that one afternoon when she and the accused were alone at home, he started to watch pornography and masturbate in her presence. According to the complainant, the accused asked her to come over, which she did, whereupon the accused used her hand to masturbate, rubbed her thigh and ejaculated. The accused testified and denied that this event ever occurred. The Crown elicited evidence from the complainant and her mother that the accused frequently watched and recorded televised pornography and used phone-sex lines. Under cross-examination, the accused admitted using pornography and engaging in phone sex but insisted that his involvement in these activities was not as frequent as suggested by the Crown. In his reasons, the trial judge stated that the accused's attempts to downplay his interest in pornography gave the trial judge a negative impression of his truthfulness as a witness. The accused was convicted of sexual interference and invitation to sexual touching, and appealed. **Should the evidence of prior use of pornography and phone-sex lines have been admitted? Should there be a new trial ordered?** Compare *R. v. J. (C.)* (2011), 87 C.R. (6th) 386, 276 C.C.C. (3d) 454 (N.S. C.A.) and see C.R. annotation by Lisa Dufraimont.

(e) Similar Facts

So far, we have seen that disposition evidence led by the Crown is most commonly admissible as an exception to the bad character exclusionary rule when the Crown is responding to something the defence has done, such as putting the accused's character in issue. In other words, it is largely rebuttal evidence which can only be used to rebut propensity evidence led by the accused. We now come to the controversial case of similar fact evidence. Here, the Crown is permitted to go on the offensive and lead propensity evidence to prove the commission of the offence. You will see as you read the cases that it is only recently that courts accepted this view of similar fact evidence. Courts for many years in England and Canada would only admit similar fact evidence if it was relevant to some issue other than propensity.

The classic and oft-repeated statement of the rule regarding the reception in evidence of similar facts was that of Lord Herschell L.C. in *Makin v. Attorney-General for New South Wales*:[35]

> It is undoubtedly not competent for the prosecution to adduce evidence tending to shew that the accused has been guilty of criminal acts other than those covered by the indictment, for the purpose of leading to the conclusion that the accused is a person likely from his criminal conduct or character to have committed the offence for which he is being tried. On the other hand, the mere fact that the evidence adduced tends to shew the commission of other crimes does not render it inadmissible if it be relevant to an issue before the jury, and it may be so relevant if it bears upon the question whether the acts alleged to constitute the crime charged in the indictment were designed or accidental, or to rebut a defence which would otherwise be open to the accused. The statement of these general principles is easy, but it is obvious that it may often be very difficult to draw the line and to decide whether a particular piece of evidence is on the one side or the other.

---

[35] [1894] A.C. 57 at 65.

This statement, however, has been the cause of considerable confusion and difficulty both for the law student and the courts as it seeks to distinguish between different kinds of relevance. If the evidence is relevant only as showing the accused to be by his or her nature or disposition a person likely to commit the crime alleged, the evidence is inadmissible. If, on the other hand, the evidence is relevant in some other way to an issue before the jury, it is admissible. This approach led to the judicial creation over the years of categories of relevance[36] which would admit similar facts if the evidence "rebutted the defence of accident", "rebutted a defence of legitimate association for honest purpose", "demonstrated system", "went to identity", and so on. While this pigeon-hole method of analysis can be used to explain most of the similar fact cases, some cases continued to be troubling[37] and after repeated attempts at resolution the House of Lords opted for a quite different approach.

In *R. v. Boardman*[38] the accused was charged and convicted of buggery and incitement to commit buggery. The victims, pupils at the accused's school, testified concerning the particular acts committed on each, and the trial judge ruled that the evidence of each could be taken as corroborative of the other as the acts were similar. The Court of Appeal dismissed the accused's appeal but certified the following question of law:

> Whether, on a charge involving an allegation of homosexual conduct there is evidence that the accused person is a man whose homosexual proclivities take a particular form, that evidence is thereby admissible although it tends to show that the accused has been guilty of criminal acts other than those charged.[39]

In answering that question, the House of Lords were unanimous in declining to create, or recognize, a "category of relevance" giving "automatic admissibility to evidence where proclivities take a particular form".[40] Rather the approach was to be based on principle and the trial judge in each case was to assess the probative worth of the evidence compared to the possibilities of prejudice and confusion of issues.

Lord Wilberforce in *Boardman* wrote:

> The basic principle must be that the admission of similar fact evidence (of the kind now in question) is exceptional and requires a strong degree of probative force. This probative force is derived, if at all, from the circumstance that the facts testified to by the several witnesses bear to each other such a striking similarity that they must, when judged by experience and common sense, either all be true, or have arisen from a cause common to the witnesses or from pure

---

36   See the numerous categories detailed in Cross, *Evidence*, 5th ed. at 378-393. See the pigeon-hole approach in *Leblanc v. R.*, [1977] 1 S.C.R. 339.

37   Cases such as *R. v. Straffen*, [1952] 2 Q.B. 911 (C.C.A.); *Thompson v. R.*, [1918] A.C. 221; and *R. v. Ball*, [1911] A.C. 47 (C.C.A.); the opinions profess to follow *Makin*, but on analysis the only relevance of the similar facts lies in showing the accused to be one "likely from his criminal conduct or character to have committed the offence for which he is being tried". See analysis by Hoffman, "Similar Facts after Boardman" (1975) 91 L.Q. R. 193.

38   [1975] A.C. 421 (H.L.).

39   *Ibid.* at 437.

40   *Ibid.* at 441 per Lord Morris of Borth-y-Gest.

coincidence. The jury may, therefore, properly be asked to judge whether the right conclusion is that all are true, so that each story is supported by the other(s).[41]

Lord Cross agreed:

the reason for this general rule is not that the law regards such evidence as inherently irrelevant but that it is believed that if it were generally admitted jurors would in many cases think that it was more relevant than it was, so that, as it is put, its prejudicial effect would outweigh its probative value. Circumstances, however, may arise in which such evidence is so very relevant that to exclude it would be an affront to common sense. Take, for example, *Reg. v. Straffen* [1952] 2 Q.B. 911. There a young girl was found strangled. It was a most unusual murder for there had been no attempt to assault her sexually or to conceal the body though this might easily have been done. The accused, who had just escaped from Broadmoor and was in the neighbourhood at the time of the crime, had previously committed two murders of young girls, each of which had the same peculiar features. It would, indeed, have been a most extraordinary coincidence if this third murder had been committed by someone else and though an ultra-cautious jury might still have acquitted him it would have been absurd for the law to have prevented the evidence of the other murders being put before them although it was simply evidence to show that Straffen was a man likely to commit a murder of that particular kind. . . The question must always be whether the similar fact evidence taken together with the other evidence would do no more than raise or strengthen a suspicion that the accused committed the offence with which he is charged or would point so strongly to his guilt that only an ultra-cautious jury, if they accepted it as true, would acquit in face of it. In the end — although the admissibility of such evidence is a question of law, not of discretion — the question as I see it must be one of degree.[42]

Viewed in this way, the so-called similar fact evidence rule may be stated in terms of its underlying rationale. Previous misconduct of the accused which is similar to the activity presently charged is relevant thereto but in our concern for a fair trial we erect a canon of exclusion lest the accused be prejudiced by its reception. Prejudice in this context does not mean that the evidence might increase the chances of conviction but rather that the evidence may be improperly used by the trier of fact. The trier who learns of the accused's previous misconduct may then view the accused as a bad person, one who deserves punishment regardless of his or her guilt of the instant offence and may be less critical of the evidence presently marshalled against him or her. The only true relevance of the previous activity follows a chain of reasoning through the accused's disposition and the law recognizes that frequently such chain is tenuous in its nature as people can change and dispositions vary. The law then erects a canon of exclusion for similar fact evidence which is tenuous in nature when viewed against the possibility of prejudice. If, however, the similar fact evidence is *not* tenuous in nature, if it has sufficient relevance, if it has genuine probative worth when taken together with the other evidence and is not then outweighed by

---

[41]   *Ibid.* at 444.
[42]   *Ibid.* at 456.

considerations of prejudice, the reason for the canon of exclusion disappears. The first principle of rational fact-finding, that all relevant evidence should be received, then controls.

Whether similar fact act evidence can be admitted in some cases to show propensity as in *Boardman* or whether some other purpose must be found as in *Makin* has been one of the most hotly contested issues in the Canadian law of evidence.

(i) *Need for Connection Between Previous Acts and Accused*

Before similar facts can be considered as evidence in the case there must be seen to be a connection between the previous acts and the accused. If the previous acts cannot be tied to the accused they have no relevance at all. The Supreme Court of Canada explained in *R. v. Sweitzer*:[43]

> Before evidence may be admitted as evidence of similar facts, there must be a link between the allegedly similar facts and the accused. In other words there must be some evidence upon which the trier of fact can make a proper finding that the similar facts to be relied upon were in fact the acts of the accused. . . .

R. v. MILLAR
(1989), 71 C.R. (3d) 78, 49 C.C.C. (3d) 193 (Ont. C.A.)

The accused was charged with manslaughter. The victim was his 9-week-old son. The cause of death was subdural haemorrhage as a result of the child having been shaken by the accused. It was the theory of the Crown that the accused had shaken the baby excessively using more force than was necessary to assist the infant, or that he shook the infant in anger. The defence maintained that the accused shook the infant because he had stopped breathing. The Crown adduced evidence of a number of other injuries including fractures to the child's ribs. These injuries had occurred some weeks before. On appeal, objection was taken to the admissibility of the evidence of other injuries to the child. This ground of appeal failed. The appeal was allowed on the basis that the trial judge had not properly directed the jury as to the proper use of the evidence of these other injuries and as to expert evidence suggesting that they pointed to abuse. A new trial was ordered.

MORDEN J.A. (GRIFFITH and CARTHY JJ. concurring):—

. . .

2. The admission of the evidence of other injuries

The appellant's basic submission with respect to this evidence is that it was inadmissible because it had little probative value and strong prejudicial effect. The appellant concedes that evidence of other injuries to the victim is potentially relevant.... Evidence of this kind is potentially relevant to the state of mind with which the accused person kills the victim and, where relevant, to

---

[43]   [1982] 1 S.C.R. 949, 68 C.C.C. (2d) 193, 29 C.R. (3d) 97 (S.C.C.) at para. 9.

the fact that he killed him. The appellant, however, submits that notwithstanding its potential relevance this evidence should have been excluded because it was incapable of supporting two inferences:

(1) that the injuries were not the result of mere accident, but were the consequence of aggression towards the victim; and

(2) that the injuries were inflicted by the appellant.

With respect to (1), although there was evidence to the contrary — that is, that the other injuries could have been the result of accidents — it is clear that there was evidence sufficient for consideration by the jury that the injuries were not the result of accidents but were intentionally inflicted.

With respect to (2), there is, however, more difficulty. Because there was no objection to the admissibility of this evidence at the trial we do not have the benefit of the trial judge's consideration of this issue. It is clear that there must, at least, be some evidence capable of reasonably supporting a finding that the appellant was implicated in the other injuries.

. . .

The only evidential basis for considering that the appellant was implicated in the earlier injuries is that the deceased was in the appellant's custody for the whole of his short life. This was not, however, exclusive custody. No doubt he spent more time alone with his mother than with the appellant alone. There is really no evidence of the deceased's being in the care of anyone else apart from the appellant's sister for one night at the Millar residence and Mrs. Chouinard, the grandmother, from time to time at the campsite. Both of these persons gave evidence and I do not think it could be said from a reading of the record as a whole that there was a reasonable possibility that either of these persons caused the injuries. Mrs. Millar testified that after Michael had been with his grandmother there never was any indication that he could have been hurt and, further, that she never saw any mishap when other people were holding the child that could have caused the injuries.

When the Crown had completed its case I do not think that there was any basis on which the jury could more reasonably conclude, assuming that the injuries were intentionally caused, that it was the appellant rather than Mrs. Millar who had caused the injuries. When, however, all of the evidence at the trial had been given I think that the picture changed.

Mrs. Millar gave evidence that she had been charged with manslaughter with respect to the death of the child. Although it is not stated clearly in the record it may be inferred that she was discharged following the preliminary inquiry. Mrs. Millar was never asked point blank whether she had caused the injuries. However, at more than one point in her evidence she testified that she had had no idea of the injuries that Michael was subsequently discovered to have suffered. She speculated in her evidence that the rib injuries could have occurred during birth, and also that the injuries could have occurred on the two occasions when Sean carried the baby or when the baby had apparently fallen out of bed. She also referred to the occasion when the baby fell out of the appellant's arms.

Although, certainly, there is no positive suggestion in Mrs. Millar's evidence that the appellant caused the injuries, if the jury accepted her evidence that she was ignorant of the injuries before August 1st and rejected the appellant's evidence that he had not caused the injuries, then there was an evidentiary basis which could reasonably support a finding that the appellant had caused the other injuries.

The Crown, at the end of the case, was entitled to rely upon all of the evidence in the record. Accordingly, I think that this ground of appeal should fail.

. . .

It should be emphasized that the evidence of the other injuries was before the jury solely on the issue of the accused's state of mind at the time he shook the baby; it could not be used to support a general inference that the appellant was the sort of person likely to have committed the crime in question: *Makin v. A.-G. N.S.W.*, [1894] A.C. 57 at p. 65 (P.C.).

We will return to this difficult issue of linkage when we later consider the Supreme Court's judgment in *R. v. Arp.*

(ii) *How are Similar Facts Relevant?*

R. v. B. (C.R.)
[1990] 1 S.C.R. 717, 76 C.R. (3d) 1, 55 C.C.C. (3d) 1

The accused was charged with sexual offences against a young child, his natural daughter. The daughter testified that the acts of sexual misconduct by the accused began in 1981 when she was 11 years old and continued for almost two years. In support of the child's testimony, the Crown sought to introduce evidence that the accused had had sexual relations in 1975 with a 15-year-old girl, the daughter of his common law wife, with whom he had enjoyed a father-daughter relationship. The trial judge admitted the evidence and convicted the accused. The majority of the Court of Appeal held that the similar fact evidence was properly admitted and upheld the conviction. The accused appealed further.

McLACHLIN J. (DICKSON C.J.C. and WILSON, L'HEUREUX-DUBÉ and GONTHIER JJ. concurring):—

. . .

The common law has traditionally taken a strict view of similar fact evidence, regarding it with suspicion. In recent years, the courts have moved to loosen the formalistic strictures which had come to encumber the rule. The old category approach determining what types of similar fact evidence is admissible has given way to a more general test which balances the probative value of the evidence against its prejudice.

Despite the apparent simplicity of the modern rule for the admission of similar fact evidence, the rule remains one of considerable difficulty in application. The problems stem in part from a tendency to view the modern formulation of the rule in isolation from the historical context from whence it springs. While the contemporary formulation may permit a more flexible, less restricted analysis, the dangers which it addresses and the principles upon which it rests remain unchanged.

. . .

Problems with the category approach to similar fact evidence became increasingly apparent in the less formalistic 20th century. On the one hand, the effect of the categories and the frequently referred to requirement of "striking similarity" was that similar fact evidence, which from the point of view of common sense had great relevance, might be excluded — a result which provoked one judge to declaim (*R. v. Hall* (1987), 5 N.Z.L.R. 93 at 108-10 (C.A)):

> Viewed in the light of science ... or common sense, there is without doubt a nexus . . . The common law must often result in what the public may regard as a failure of justice. That is really not our concern.

Other judges reacted to the tendency of the rule to exclude probative evidence by drawing distinctions that were fundamentally unworkable or imaginary in order to admit evidence which common sense told them should be admitted. On the other hand, the rule sometimes permitted reception of evidence of doubtful worth. Provided it fell within one of the accepted categories, evidence of prior misconduct or inclination might be admitted even though its relevance was suspect.

From the point of view of theory too, the category approach associated with *Makin* was subject to criticism. The categories focussed attention on the *purpose* for which the similar fact evidence was adduced, rather than the real question — its *relevance*: see J.A. Andrews and M. Hirst, Criminal Evidence (1987), para. 15.34. As Sklar stated ("Similar Fact Evidence — Catchwords and Cartwheels" (1977), 23 McGill L.J. 60 at 62), "Whether the evidence was really *relevant* to the issue by whatever the rationale and whether, if it was, it was *relevant enough* to justify its reception despite its nearly uncontrollable tendency to damn the accused in the minds of the jury, was lost in the shuffle" (emphasis added in original). If the evidence fell within a recognizable category, it was admitted even if its relevance may have been suspect. Moreover, the emphasis on the need for the evidence to relate to an issue other than disposition was arguably artificial. As Professor Andrews and Mr. Hirst have commented at pp. 342-43:

> 15.37 Although the courts made a great show of relying on the categories of relevance and of avoiding the forbidden chain of reasoning [guilt from propensity], their whole approach was really based upon a fundamental misconception. In reality, similar fact evidence can hardly ever show design or rebut a defence except by encouraging the court or jury to utilise the forbidden chain of reasoning. Whether the judges realised this or not, the undeniable fact is that in many of the leading cases evidence was admitted where it could only have been relevant because it showed disposition or propensity.

Provided some element, however small, other than disposition could be found to which the evidence related, it went in, although the effect might be almost entirely related to disposition.

Difficulties such as these led the House of Lords to readdress the question of similar fact evidence in *D.P.P. v. Boardman*, [1975] A.C. 421. On its face, *Boardman* constitutes no great departure from *Makin*, with three of the five Law Lords (Lords Morris, Hailsham and Salmon) expressly affirming the validity of *Makin*. However, all five judges rejected the category approach that had become associated with *Makin*, emphasizing that similar fact evidence is not automatically admissible merely because it fits into a prescribed category. The admissibility of similar fact evidence was to be based on general principle, not categories and catch phrases. That general principle was relevance.

While the five separate and sometimes conflicting opinions delivered in *Boardman* may not provide a comprehensive picture of the various ways in which cogency may be found, the ratio decidendi of the case is clear: the admissibility of similar fact evidence depends on its bearing a very high degree of probative value — sufficient to outweigh the inherent prejudice likely to flow from its reception.

. . .

The Canadian jurisprudence since *Boardman* is generally consistent with the approach advocated in that case. It has followed *Boardman* in rejecting the category approach to the admission of similar fact evidence. At the same time, cases in Canada have on the whole maintained an emphasis on the general rule that evidence of mere propensity is inadmissible, and have continued to emphasize the necessity that such evidence possess high probative value in relation to its potential prejudice.

. . .

While our courts have affirmed the general exclusionary rule for evidence of disposition and propensity, they have for the most part cast it in terms of *Boardman* rather than *Makin*. It is no longer necessary to hang the evidence tendered on the peg of some issue other than disposition. While the language of some of the assertions of the exclusionary rule admittedly might be taken to suggest that mere disposition evidence can *never* be admissible, the preponderant view prevailing in Canada is the view taken by the majority in *Boardman* — evidence of propensity, while generally inadmissible, may exceptionally be admitted where the probative value of the evidence in relation to an issue in question is so high that it displaces the heavy prejudice which will inevitably inure to the accused where evidence of prior immoral or illegal acts is presented to the jury.

. . .

Catchwords have gone the same way as categories. Just as English courts have expressed doubts about the necessity of showing "striking similarity" . . . , so in *Robertson* Wilson J. rejected the validity of this phrase as a legal test.

A third feature of this court's treatment of the similar fact rule since *Boardman* is the tendency to accord a high degree of respect to the decision of the trial judge, who is charged with the delicate process of balancing the probative value of the evidence against its prejudicial effect. . . This deference to the trial judge may in part be seen as a function of the broader, more discretionary nature of the modern rule at the stage where the probative value of the evidence must be weighed against its prejudicial effect.

. . .

. . . In a case such as the present, where the similar fact evidence sought to be adduced is prosecution evidence of a morally repugnant act committed by the accused, the potential prejudice is great and the probative value of the evidence must be high indeed to permit its reception. The judge must consider such factors as the degree of distinctiveness or uniqueness between the similar fact evidence and the offences alleged against the accused, as well as the connection, if any, of the evidence to issues other than propensity, to the end of determining whether, in the context of the case before him, the probative value of the evidence outweighs its potential prejudice and justifies its reception.

Against this background, I turn to the facts in this case and the ruling of the trial judge.

. . .

The main similarity is that in each case the accused, shortly after establishing a father-daughter relationship with the victim, is alleged to have engaged her in a sexual relationship. Additionally, the trial judge detailed similarities relating to the place and manner in which the relations occurred in the two situations. The age of the girls was different; one was sexually mature, the other only a child when the acts began. One girl was a blood relation, the other was not. . .

That said, it cannot be concluded that the evidence necessarily fails the test indicated by the authorities to which I earlier referred. The fact that in each case the accused established a father-daughter relationship with the girl before the sexual violations began might be argued to go to showing, if not a system or design, a pattern of similar behaviour suggesting that the complainant's story is true. The question then is whether the probative value of the evidence outweighs its prejudicial effect. While I may have found this case to have been a borderline case of admissibility if I had been the trial judge, I am not prepared to interfere with the conclusion of the trial judge, who was charged with the task of weighing the probative value of the evidence against its prejudicial effect in the context of the case as a whole.

I would dismiss the appeal and affirm the conviction.

SOPINKA J. (LAMER J. concurring), dissenting:—

. . .

There is no special rule with relation to similar fact evidence in sexual offences. . . There is no support in the cases in our court for the theory that the rule has special application in sexual offences. Accordingly, evidence that the accused has a propensity to molest children or his or her own children is never admissible solely for that purpose.

. . .

To have probative value the evidence must be susceptible of an inference relevant to the issues in the case other than the inference that the accused committed the offence because he or she has a disposition to the type of conduct charged: *Morris v. R.*, supra, . . . As in the case of relevance, evidence can be logically probative but not legally probative. When the term "probative value" is employed in the cases, reference is made to legally probative value.

The principal reason for the exclusionary rule relating to propensity is that there is a natural human tendency to judge a person's action on the basis of character. Particularly with juries there would be a strong inclination to conclude that a thief has stolen, a violent man has assaulted and a pedophile has engaged in pedophilic acts. Yet the policy of the law is wholly against this process of reasoning. This policy is reflected not only in similar acts cases, but as well in the rule excluding evidence of the character of the accused unless placed in issue by him. The stronger the evidence of propensity, the more likely it is that the forbidden inference will be drawn and, therefore, the greater the prejudice.

I am unable therefore to subscribe to the theory that in exceptional cases propensity alone can be the basis for admissibility. To say that propensity may have probative value in a sufficiently high degree to be admissible is a contradiction in terms. It is tantamount to saying that when the danger of the application of the forbidden line of reasoning is the strongest, the evidence can go in. The view has been expressed that this change in the principles outlined above was made in *Boardman*, supra (see Hoffmann, "Similar Facts after *Boardman*" (1975), 91 L.Q. Rev. 193 at 202).

The suggestion that *Boardman* effected a radical change in the law is not borne out by an analysis of the respective speeches in the House of Lords. . .

. . .

In considering the admissibility of the evidence in this case, I observe that no attempt appears to have been made to negative the possibility of collaboration. No questions were directed to Crown witnesses to determine whether this possibility existed. The Crown, who must persuade the trial judge that the evidence has probative value, has the burden of proof. . . In my view, the Crown must negative conspiracy or collaboration in accordance with the criminal standard. This is a requirement that applies whenever a preliminary finding of fact is a precondition to the admissibility of evidence tendered by the Crown. . . .

There is then the further question of coincidence. Are the common characteristics in the evidence of the two girls so unusual that it would be against common sense to conclude that they are not both telling the truth? In this connection, the observation of Lord Cross in *Boardman*, quoted above, is helpful. We have only two instances and should proceed with caution. They are separated by a considerable passage of time and as well there are material differences which are detailed in the reasons of Harradence J.A. in the Court of Appeal. McLachlin J. stresses that in each case the appellant established a father relationship. As her statement of the facts indicates, the appellant was the father of one child and he enjoyed a father-daughter relationship with the other. These are not unusual facts and indeed are neutral. In any case, where it is alleged that a father has had an incestuous relationship with two of his children, this fact will be common to both. If one or both girls are not telling the truth, is it unlikely that they would both have said that the appellant established a father relationship with them? Obviously not, because that happened irrespective of whether the balance of their evidence is true.

. . .

. . . I am unable to say what would have occurred if the similar fact evidence had been rejected by the trial judge. Accordingly, I would direct a new trial. The appeal is therefore allowed and a new trial directed.[44]

Why has, as Justice McLachlin writes, the common law "traditionally taken a strict view of similar fact evidence, regarding it with suspicion"?

Do you think that this concern is linked to the nature of the offences where similar act evidence is most likely to be tendered by the Crown?[45]

R. v. ARP
[1998] 3 S.C.R. 339, 20 C.R. (5th) 1, 129 C.C.C. (3d) 321

Two women, U and B, were murdered some two and one-half years apart in the same city and in similar circumstances. The accused was charged with first degree murder of both women. Defence counsel unsuccessfully applied to sever the two murder counts in the indictment. The Crown opposed the application and asserted that even in the case of severance, it would seek to adduce the evidence of each offence in the other trial as similar fact evidence. The Crown conceded that unless the evidence concerning the one murder was admissible to establish that the accused committed the other murder, there should be a severance of the two counts. However, the Crown argued that there were many similarities between the two events indicative of pattern and design.

The trial judge charged the jury that, if they concluded both counts were likely committed by the same person, they could use the evidence on each count to assist in deciding the accused's guilt on both counts. He stated that the evidence on the B killing was admissible in proving the guilt of the accused for the U killing and vice versa. When examining the evidence on both counts, they were instructed not to conclude that the appellant was a person whose character or disposition was such that he likely committed the offences. The trial judge stated that they could infer from the evidence, although they were not required to do so, that the incident mentioned in the B count and the incident mentioned in the U count had characteristics in

---

[44] For several years after *B. (C.R.)*, the Supreme Court and courts below vacillated between the focus on propensity and that requiring a purpose other than propensity: see analysis by R.J. Delisle, "The Direct Approach to Similar Fact Evidence" (1996), 50 C.R. (4th) 286.

[45] See Hanson, "Sexual Assault and the Similar Fact Rule" (1993) 27 U.B.C. L. Rev. 51.

common that were so strikingly similar that it was likely that they were committed by one person.

The trial judge reviewed the evidence related to the murder of U. The trial judge noted that the Crown submitted the crimes were similar in that the victims were young single females who were vulnerable and who were without funds or transportation in the early morning hours; there was evidence that each was picked up by the accused in a grey pickup truck; the U case clearly involved sexual intercourse, while in the B murder a sexual purpose could be inferred; the victims were left in isolated but accessible areas outside Prince George; the victims' clothes were found discarded nearby; there was evidence that in both cases a sharp-edged instrument, such as a knife, was used.

The accused was convicted and his appeal dismissed.

CORY J. (LAMER C.J. and L'HEUREUX-DUBÉ, GONTHIER, MCLACHLIN, IACOBUCCI, MAJOR, BASTARACHE and BINNIE JJ. concurring):—

. . .

[W]here identity is at issue in a criminal case and the accused is shown to have committed acts which bear a striking similarity to the alleged crime, the jury is not asked to infer from the accused's habits or disposition that *he is the type of person* who would commit the crime. Instead, the jury is asked to infer from the degree of distinctiveness or uniqueness that exists between the commission of the crime and the similar act that *the accused is the very person* who committed the crime. This inference is made possible only if the high degree of similarity between the acts renders the likelihood of coincidence objectively improbable. See *Hoch v. The Queen* (1988), 165 C.L.R. 292 (Aust. H.C.). That is, there is always a possibility that by coincidence the perpetrator of the crime and the accused share certain predilections or that the accused may become implicated in crimes for which he is not responsible. However, where the evidence shows a distinct pattern to the acts in question, the possibility that the accused would repeatedly be implicated in strikingly similar offences purely as a matter of coincidence is greatly reduced.

. . .

[A] principled approach to the admission of similar fact evidence will in all cases rest on the finding that the accused's involvement in the alleged similar acts or counts is unlikely to be the product of coincidence. This conclusion ensures that the evidence has sufficient probative force to be admitted, and will involve different considerations in different contexts. Where, as here, similar fact evidence is adduced on the issue of identity, there must be a high degree of similarity between the acts for the evidence to be admitted. For example, a unique trademark or signature will automatically render the alleged acts "strikingly similar" and therefore highly probative and admissible. In the same way, a number of significant similarities, taken together, may be such that by their cumulative effect, they warrant admission of the evidence. Where identity is at issue ordinarily, the trial judge should review the manner in which the similar acts were committed — that is to say, whether the similar acts involve a unique trademark or reveal a number of significant similarities. This review will enable him or her to decide whether the alleged similar acts were all committed by the same person. This preliminary determination establishes the objective improbability that the accused's involvement in the alleged acts is the product of coincidence and thereby gives the evidence the requisite probative force. Thus, where the similar fact evidence is adduced to prove identity, once this preliminary determination is made, the evidence related to the similar act (or count, in a multi-count indictment) may be admitted to prove the commission of another act (or count).

. . .

In summary, in considering the admissibility of similar fact evidence, the basic rule is that the trial judge must first determine whether the probative value of the evidence outweighs its prejudicial effect. In most cases where similar fact evidence is adduced to prove identity it might be helpful for the trial judge to consider the following suggestions in deciding whether to admit the evidence:

(1)   Generally where similar fact evidence is adduced to prove identity a high degree of similarity between the acts is required in order to ensure that the similar fact evidence has the requisite probative value of outweighing its prejudicial effect to be admissible. The similarity between the acts may consist of a unique trademark or signature on a series of significant similarities.

(2)   In assessing the similarity of the acts, the trial judge should only consider the manner in which the acts were committed and not the evidence as to the accused's involvement in each act.

(3)   There may well be exceptions but as a general rule if there is such a degree of similarity between the acts that it is likely that they were committed by the same person then the similar fact evidence will ordinarily have sufficient probative force to outweigh its prejudicial effect and may be admitted.

(4)   The jury will then be able to consider all the evidence related to the alleged similar acts in determining the accused's guilt for any one act.

Once again these are put forward not as rigid rules but simply as suggestions that may assist trial judges in their approach to similar fact evidence.

. . .

Link to the Accused

Where the similar fact evidence adduced to prove identity suggests that the same person committed the similar acts, then logically this finding makes the evidence linking the accused to each similar act relevant to the issue of identity for the offence being tried. Similarly, in a multi-count indictment, the link between the accused and any one count will be relevant to the issue of identity on the other counts which disclose a striking similarity in the manner in which those offences were committed.

A link between the accused and the alleged similar acts is, however, also a precondition to admissibility. This requirement was set forth in *R. v. Sweitzer*, [1982] 1 S.C.R. 949, at p. 954. . .

. . .

Should the trial judge be required to conclude *not only* that the evidence suggests that the acts are the work of one person with sufficient force to outweigh the prejudicial effect of the evidence, but that they also are likely the acts of the accused? This is the approach advocated by Professor R. Mahoney in "Similar Fact Evidence and the Standard of Proof", [1993] Crim. L. Rev. 185, at pp. 196-97, and is implicitly favoured by those courts which have endorsed the "anchor" or "sequential" approach to similar fact evidence. See, e.g., *R. v. Ross*, [1980] 5 W.W.R. 261 (B.C. C.A.); *R. v. J.T.S.*, [1997] A.J. No. 125 (C.A.).

The suggestion that the evidence linking the accused to the similar acts must also link the acts to the accused goes too far. Once the trial judge has concluded that the similar acts were likely the work of one person and that there is some evidence linking the accused to the alleged similar acts, it is not necessary to conclude that the similar acts were likely committed by the accused. The answer to this question may well determine guilt or innocence. This is the very question which the trier of fact must determine on the basis of all the evidence related to the similar acts, including of course the accused's involvement in each act. The standard set out in *Sweitzer* should be maintained. This only requires that the trial judge be satisfied that there is some evidence which links the accused to the similar acts.[46]

. . .

The general principles enunciated in these cases indicate that the jury should determine, on a balance of the probabilities, whether the similarities between the acts establishes that the two counts were committed by the same person. If that threshold is met, the jury can then consider all the evidence relating to the similar acts in determining whether, beyond a reasonable doubt, the accused is guilty.

However, the general rule that preliminary findings of fact may be determined on a balance of probabilities is departed from in those certainly rare occasions when admission of the evidence may itself have a conclusive effect with respect to guilt. For example, where the Crown adduces a statement of the accused made to a person in authority, the trial judge must be satisfied beyond a reasonable doubt of the voluntariness of the statement. That evidence may of itself, if accepted as true, provide conclusive proof of guilt. Since doubt about the statement's voluntariness also casts doubt on its reliability, proof beyond a reasonable doubt is warranted. See *Ward v. The Queen*, [1979] 2 S.C.R. 30. If this were not the rule, the jury would be permitted to rely on evidence which it could accept as extremely cogent even though the inherent reliability of that evidence was in doubt.

---

[46]   For a recent discussion of the linkage requirement see *R. v. MacCormack* (2009), 241 C.C.C. (3d) 516, 64 C.R. (6th) 137 (Ont. C.A.) and annotation by Lisa Dufraimont.

Similar fact evidence, on the other hand, as circumstantial evidence, must be characterized differently, since, by its nature, it does not carry the potential to be conclusive of guilt. It is just one item of evidence to be considered as part of the Crown's overall case. Its probative value lies in its ability to support, through the improbability of coincidence, other inculpatory evidence. As with all circumstantial evidence, the jury will decide what weight to attribute to it. The mere fact that in a particular case, similar fact evidence might be assigned a high degree of weight by the trier is entirely different from the concept that, by its very nature, the evidence has the potential to be decisive of guilt.

One of the curiosities of *Arp* is that it would appear that there was no need for similar facts evidence to establish identity. At the time of the first murder, the accused was released by police because hair samples could not be linked to the accused. However, two and one-half years later, DNA evidence linked the accused to cigarette samples and semen found at the second murder scene and also to the hair samples seized in the earlier case.

Cory J. emphasized that where similar fact evidence is admitted to prove identity in a multi-count indictment the jury must be warned

> that they are not to use the evidence on one count to infer that the accused is a person whose character or disposition is such that he or she is likely to have committed the offence or offences charged in the other count or counts" (para. 80).

In *Arp*, Cory J. also remarks in *obiter* that normally a prior acquittal cannot be relied on for similar fact evidence in a subsequent trial of the same accused. He speaks of a fundamental principle that an accused not repeatedly defend himself or herself against the same allegations (para. 31). The House of Lords in *R. v. Z.*[47] specifically rejected this aspect of *Arp*. However, the Supreme Court of Canada recently endorsed this aspect of *Arp*.[48] **With whom do you agree?**[49]

R. v. HANDY
[2002] 2 S.C.R. 908, 1 C.R. (6th) 203, 164 C.C.C. (3d) 481

The accused was charged with sexual assault. His defence was that the sex was consensual. The complainant's position was that she had consented to vaginal sex but not hurtful or anal sex. The Crown sought to introduce similar fact evidence from the accused's former wife to the effect that the accused had a propensity to inflict painful sex, including anal sex, and when aroused would not take no for an answer. The similar fact evidence concerned seven alleged prior incidents. The accused denied committing

---

[47]   [2002] 1 A.C. 483.

[48]   See *R. v. Mahalingan*, [2008] 3 S.C.R. 316, 237 C.C.C. (3d) 417, 61 C.R. (6th) 207 (S.C.C.) at paras. 66-69.

[49]   For differing views to this question see Lee Stuesser, "Admitting Acquittals as Similar Fact Evidence" (2002) 45 Crim. L.Q. 488 and Richard Mahoney, "Acquittals as Similar Fact Evidence: Another View" (2003) 47 Crim. L.Q. 265. See also *R. v. Akins* (2002), 5 C.R. (6th) 400 (Ont. C.A.) and *R. v. Mahalingan* (2006), 208 C.C.C. (3d) 515 (Ont. C.A.).

any of the alleged assaults on his ex-wife. The trial judge admitted the similar fact evidence.

The ex-wife testified that she had met the complainant a few months before the alleged sexual assault took place. She had told the complainant at that time about the accused's criminal record and her allegations of his abuse of her during their marriage. The ex-wife told the complainant that she had received $16,500 from the Criminal Injuries Compensation Board and agreed when it was put to her in cross-examination that all she had to do to get the money was say that she had been abused. The trial judge ruled that it was not for him to resolve the possibility of collusion between the complainant and the ex-wife.

The jury convicted. The Court of Appeal held that the former wife's testimony had been wrongly admitted and ordered a new trial.

The appeal was dismissed.

Per BINNIE, J. (MCLACHLIN C.J. and L'HEUREUX-DUBÉ, GONTHIER, Iacobucci, MAJOR, BASTARACHE, ARBOUR and LEBEL JJ. concurring):

. . .

I. Facts

The complainant's evidence was that on the evening of December 6, 1996, she went out drinking with some friends. The respondent, whom she had met six months earlier, was also at the bar. The two spent the evening drinking and flirting with one another. After leaving the bar, they went to the home of one of the complainant's friends to smoke marijuana. The respondent and the complainant left the house together and drove to a nearby motel intending to have sex. In the course of vaginal intercourse, she became upset because the respondent was hurting her, forcing himself into her. She told him that it was painful but he continued. He then brusquely switched to anal intercourse. She said, "Stop that, it hurts". She tried to get him off her or to make him stop but he would not. She slapped his face. She says he hit her on the chest, he grabbed her arms, squeezed her stomach and choked her, and he punched her. She says she was pleading and crying. She had consented to vaginal sex but she did not consent to and did not want anal sex. After the incident, she told the respondent that he had made [page 915] her bleed. He allegedly responded to her by saying, "What the hell am I doing here? Why does this keep happening to me?"

A number of witnesses testified that they had seen bruises on her throat, chest and arms in the days following the incident. The complainant was diagnosed with post-traumatic stress.

A. The Similar Fact Evidence

The respondent's defence was that the sex was consensual. The issue thus came down to credibility on the consent issue. The Crown sought to introduce similar fact evidence from the respondent's former wife to the effect that the respondent has a propensity to inflict painful sex and when aroused will not take no for an answer. It was thus tendered to explain why the complainant should be believed when she testified that the assault proceeded despite her protest.

(1)   Incident One

In March 1990, a few weeks after their first child was born, the ex-wife says the respondent wanted to have sexual intercourse with her to "see what it would feel like". She did not want to do so because she thought that it would be painful. The respondent insisted that they have vaginal intercourse. Once they started she told the respondent that she was in pain but he did not stop.

(2)   Incident Two

Five or six months later she and the respondent visited her sister and brother-in-law in their mobile trailer. After everyone went to bed, the respondent wanted to have sexual intercourse. She told the respondent that she did not want to have sex because her sister and her husband were at the other end of the trailer. She tried to move away from him. The respondent told her to shut up and had vaginal intercourse with her anyway.

(3)   Incident Three

She returned home one day to find that the respondent had invited a number of people to their apartment for a party. After seeing the respondent tickle two women on the couch, she got angry and told everyone to leave. After most of the guests departed, she went into the bedroom. The respondent followed her. He was upset that she had broken up his party. He tried to have intercourse with her. She tried to get away but he blocked the door with a dresser. She then attempted to flee through the second floor bedroom window, but he pulled her back in. He then forced her to have vaginal intercourse and passed out.

(4)   Incident Four

Sometime early in 1992, the respondent came home drunk and wanted to have anal intercourse. She told him that she did not want to do so because it had hurt her on previous occasions. The respondent initiated anal intercourse nonetheless. She kept moving and tried to get away. Eventually, he grabbed a bottle of baby oil from underneath the bed and applied the oil to his penis and her anus. He initiated anal intercourse. They were interrupted by a crying baby, and she used the distraction to escape to the basement but the respondent followed her. He told her that if she did not stop running, he would tie her up with a rope. She ran naked from the house and over to the neighbour's house. The police were called but she did not lay charges.

(5)   Incident Five

The respondent was imprisoned from 1992 until 1995 for sexual assaults on two other women (although the fact they were "other" women was withheld from the jury by agreement of counsel). In that period he placed a threatening phone call to his then wife, which precipitated their divorce. They resumed living together soon after he was released. Shortly thereafter, she became upset because the respondent had gone out with a woman he had once dated. The respondent became angry, grabbed her by the throat, threw her around, pinned her against the wall and broke their glass coffee table. He did not, however, sexually assault her on that occasion.

(6)   Incident Six

One night during the summer of 1996, she and the respondent were returning home after dropping off their friends. The respondent told her that instead of going home, they were going to a gravel pit where she "was going to get it up the ass". She testified that he had forced her to have sex with him at the gravel pit in the past. She told him that she was willing to do anything other than anal intercourse because it hurt too much. The respondent, however, insisted on anal intercourse. Once at the gravel pit he attempted anal intercourse, but was unsuccessful because there was insufficient room in the back seat of the car. The respondent took her out of his car and put her face down on the hood. He attempted anal intercourse again. He eventually turned her over onto her back and had vaginal intercourse.

(7)   Incident Seven

In October 1996, her grandfather passed away. She and the respondent were alone in her mother's home. She was crying and upset. She testified that her crying "turned [the respondent] on" and that he wanted to have sexual intercourse on her mother's new couch. She told him that she did not want to. The respondent put her on the couch and commenced vaginal intercourse. She cried. While they were having intercourse, he punched her a number of times in the stomach to make her cry louder.

B.   The Respondent's Testimony

The respondent denied committing any of the alleged assaults on his ex-wife. With respect to the complainant's allegations, he testified that he met her at the bar, that they were both intoxicated and that they left the bar together. Eventually they went to a motel room. He testified that once inside the room, the complainant straddled him while he lay on his back and they engaged in approximately 15 to 20 minutes of vaginal intercourse. He denied that she had complained or told him to stop. He also denied hitting her and choking her. He testified that she drove him home at approximately 6:40 a.m. He did not see her again.

C.   The Evidence of Collusion

The ex-wife testified that she had met the complainant a few months before the alleged sexual assault took place. She had told the complainant at that time about the respondent's criminal record and her allegations of his abuse of her during their marriage. The ex-wife told the complainant that she had received $16,500 from the Criminal Injuries Compensation Board and agreed when it was put to her in cross-examination that "[a]ll you had to do [to get the money] was say that you were abused". The ex-wife's cross-examination was, in part, as follows:

Q. You knew [the complainant]?

A. Yes, I did.

Q. You had met her in the summer of '96?

A. That's correct.

Q. She had come over and visited with you, right?

A. That's correct.

Q. At one point, she actually said to you that she thought that [the respondent] loved you very much?

A. Yes, she did.

Q. And you straightened her out?

A. That's correct.

Q. And you told her that he had been to jail?

A. Yes, I did.

Q. You told her that he abused you?

A. Yes, I did.

Q. And you told her that you collected $16,500 from the government. All you had to do was say that you were abused.

A. Yes.

Q. So she knew all of that before December of 1996?

A. Yes. [Emphasis added.]

Subsequently, on December 6, 1996, the complainant met up with the respondent at the bar and, after sharing some marijuana, agreed to accompany him to a motel for sex.

. . .

A.   The Disputed Inferences

The ex-wife's testimony related to incidents removed in time, place and circumstances from the charge. It was thus only circumstantial evidence of the matters the jury was called on to decide and, as with any circumstantial evidence, its usefulness rests entirely on the validity of the inferences it is said to support with respect to the matters in issue. The argument for admitting this circumstantial evidence is that the jury may infer firstly that the accused is an individual who derives pleasure from sex that is painful to his partner, and will not take no for an answer, and secondly, that his character or propensity thus established gives rise to the further inference that he proceeded wilfully in this case knowing the complainant did not consent.

. . .

B.   The General Exclusionary Rule

The respondent is clearly correct in saying that evidence of misconduct beyond what is alleged in the indictment which does no more than blacken the accused's character is inadmissible. . . .

C.   The Narrow Exception of Admissibilty

While emphasizing the general rule of exclusion, courts have recognized that an issue may arise in the trial of the offence charged to which evidence of previous misconduct may be so highly relevant and cogent that its probative value in the search for truth outweighs any potential for misuse. . .

The "common sense" condemnation of exclusion of what may be seen as highly relevant evidence has prompted much judicial agonizing, particularly in cases of alleged sexual abuse of children and adolescents, whose word was sometimes unfairly discounted when opposed to that of ostensibly upstanding adults. The denial of the adult, misleadingly persuasive on first impression, would melt under the history of so many prior incidents as to defy innocent explanation. That said, there is no special rule for sexual abuse cases. In any case, the strength of the similar fact evidence must be such as to outweigh "reasoning prejudice" and "moral prejudice". The inferences sought to be drawn must accord with common sense, intuitive notions of probability and the unlikelihood of coincidence. Although an element of "moral prejudice" may be introduced, it must be concluded by the trial judge on a balance of probabilities that the probative value of the sound inferences exceeds any prejudice likely to be created.

. . .

Canadian case law recognizes that as the "similar facts" become more focussed and specific to circumstances similar to the charge (i.e., more situation specific), the probative value of propensity, thus circumscribed, becomes more cogent. As the differences and variables that distinguish the earlier "similar facts" from the subject matter of the charge in this type of case are reduced, the cogency of the desired inferences is thought to increase. Ultimately the policy premise of the general exclusionary rule (prejudice exceeds probative value) ceases to be true.

D.   The Test of Admissibilty

. . .

Although evidence relating solely to the accused's disposition will generally be excluded, exceptions to this rule will arise when the probative value of the evidence outweighs its prejudicial effect. . . Evidence classified as "disposition" or "propensity" evidence is, exceptionally, admissible. . . Similar fact evidence is thus presumptively inadmissible. The onus is on the prosecution to satisfy the trial judge on a balance of probabilities that in the context of the particular case the probative value of the evidence in relation to a particular issue outweighs its potential prejudice and thereby justifies its reception.

E.   Difficulties in the Application of the Test

. . .

It is one thing to talk about so general a test as balancing probative value against prejudice, and a different and much more difficult thing to apply the test in a practical way. In an attempt to provide more precise guidance. . . Canadian appellate courts have from time to time advocated, amongst others, a "categories" approach, a multi-step "purpose" approach and a "conclusiveness" approach. Each of these attempts, helpful as they were in practice, were ultimately thought to obfuscate and detract from the principled approach eventually adopted.

(1)   Propensity Evidence by Any Other Name Is Still Propensity Evidence

. . .

While identification of the issue defines the precise purpose for which the evidence is proffered, it does not, and cannot, change the inherent nature of the propensity evidence, which must be recognized for what it is. By affirming its true character the Court keeps front and centre its dangerous potential.

(2)   Identification of the "Issue in Question" is an Important Control

. . .

Whether or not probative value exceeds prejudicial effect can only be determined in light of the purpose for which the evidence is proffered. . . The requirement to identify the material issue in question, i.e., the purpose for which the similar fact evidence is proffered, does not detract from the probative value/prejudice balance, but is in fact essential to it. Probative value cannot be assessed in the abstract. The utility of the evidence lies precisely in its ability to advance or refute a live issue pending before the trier of fact. . . It is therefore incumbent on the Crown to identify the live issue in the trial to which the evidence of disposition is said to relate. . . The relative importance of the issue in the particular trial may also have a bearing on the weighing up of factors for and against admissibility. Similar fact evidence that is virtually conclusive of a minor issue may still be excluded for reasons of overall prejudice. The "issues in question" are not however, categories of admissibility. Their identification is simply an element of the admissibility analysis which turns on weighing probative value against prejudice.

(3)   Identification of the Required Degree of Similarity

The principal driver of probative value in a case such as this is the connectedness or nexus that is established between the similar fact evidence and the offence alleged. . . The issue in the present case is not identification but the actus reus of the offence. The point is not that the degree of similarity in such a case must be higher or lower than in an identification case. The point is that the issue is different, and the drivers of cogency in relation to the desired inferences will therefore not be the same. . . If, for example, the complainant in this case had not been able to identify the accused as the perpetrator of the alleged offence, the conduct described by the ex-wife was not so particular and distinctive as to amount to a signature that would safely differentiate him from other possible assailants. On the other hand, in a case where the issue is the animus of the accused towards the deceased, a prior incident of the accused stabbing the victim may be admissible even though the victim was ultimately shot, the accused says accidentally. The acts could be said to be dissimilar but the inference on the issue in question would nonetheless be compelling.

(4)   Identification of Connecting Factors

The decided cases suggest the need to pay close attention to similarities in character, proximity in time and frequency of occurrence. . . The trial judge was called on to consider the cogency of the proffered similar fact evidence in relation to the inferences sought to be drawn, as well as the strength of the proof of the similar facts themselves. . . On the other hand, countervailing factors which have been found helpful in assessing prejudice include the inflammatory nature of the similar acts and whether the Crown can prove its point with less prejudicial evidence. In addition the court was required to take into account the potential distraction of the trier of fact from its proper focus on the facts charged and the potential for undue time consumption. These may be collectively described as moral prejudice and reasoning prejudice.

(5)   Differentiating Admissible from Inadmissible Propensity Evidence

Part of the conceptual problem with similar fact evidence is that words like "disposition" or "propensity" are apt to describe a whole spectrum of human character and behaviour of varying degrees of potential relevance. At the vague end of the spectrum, it might be said that the respondent has a general disposition or propensity "for violence". . . At a more specific level, it is alleged here that the propensity to violence emerges in this accused in a desire for hurtful sex. This formulation provides more context, but the definition of so general a propensity is still of little real use. . . Cogency increases as the fact situation moves further to the specific end of the spectrum. . .. References to "calling cards" or "signatures" or "hallmarks" or "fingerprints" similarly describe propensity at the admissible end of the spectrum precisely because the pattern of circumstances in which an accused is disposed to act in a certain way are so clearly linked to the offence charged that the possibility of mere coincidence, or mistaken identity or a mistake in the character of the act, is so slight as to justify consideration of the similar fact evidence by the trier of fact.

The issue at that stage is no longer "pure" propensity or "general disposition" but repeated conduct in a particular and highly specific type of situation. At that point, the evidence of similar facts provides a compelling inference that may fill a remaining gap in the jigsaw puzzle of proof, depending on the view ultimately taken by the jury.

. . .

(6)   Similar Fact Evidence Need Not Be Conclusive

Some authorities urge adoption of a further refinement that has been accepted in some common law jurisdictions in the balancing of prejudice against probative value, namely that similar fact evidence should only be admitted if its probative value is so great as to be virtually conclusive of guilt . . . (But) we are dealing here with admissibility, not adjudication. The conclusiveness test does not sit well with the balancing model set out in *B. (C.R.)*. If the evidence were truly "conclusive", its probative value would ex hypothesi outweigh prejudice.

Application of the Test to the Facts of this Case

(1)   The Probative Value of the Evidence

The issue at this stage is to determine whether the similar fact evidence is indeed strong enough to be capable of properly raising in the eyes of the jury the double inferences contended for by the Crown.

(a)   The Potential for Collusion

If collusion is present, it destroys the foundation on which admissibility is sought, namely that the events described by the ex-wife and the complainant, testifying independently of one another, are too similar to be credibly explained by coincidence. . . The trial judge cannot assess "the objective improbability of coincidence" without addressing the issue of whether the apparent coincidence is in fact the product of collusion. Admissibility is a question of law for the judge alone. . . The trial judge held that he ought not to reach even a preliminary view of the likelihood of collusion. . . If the evidence amounts to no more than opportunity, it will usually best be left to the jury. Here there is something more. It is the whiff of profit. The ex-wife acknowledged that she had told the complainant of the $16,500 she received from the Criminal Injuries Compensation Board on the basis that all you had to do was say that you were abused. A few days later the complainant, armed with this information, met the respondent and went off with him to have sex in a motel room. Where, as here, there is some evidence of actual collusion, or at least an air of reality to the allegations, the Crown is required to satisfy the trial judge, on a balance of probabilities, that the evidence of similar facts is not tainted with collusion. That much would gain admission. It would then be for the jury to make the ultimate determination of its worth. The trial judge erred in law in deferring the whole issue of collusion to the jury.

(b)   Identification of the Issue in Question

The Crown says the issue generally is "the credibility of the complainant" and more specifically "that the accused has a strong disposition to do the very act alleged in the charges against him", but this requires some refinement. Care must be taken not to allow too broad a gateway for the admission of propensity evidence or, as it is sometimes put, to allow it to bear too much of the burden of the Crown's case (Sopinka, Lederman and Bryant, supra, at s. 11.26). Credibility is an issue that pervades most trials, and at its broadest may amount to a decision on guilt or innocence.

Anything that blackens the character of an accused may, as a by-product, enhance the credibility of a complainant. Identification of credibility as the "issue in question" may, unless circumscribed, risk the admission of evidence of nothing more than general disposition ("bad personhood").

. . .

If the jury could legitimately infer sexual intransigence in closely comparable circumstances from the accused's past behaviour and refusal to take his wife's no for an answer, the present complainant's testimony that intercourse occurred despite her lack of consent gains in credibility. The issue broadly framed is credibility, but more accurately and precisely framed, the issue in question in this trial was the consent component of the actus reus and in relation to that issue the accused's alleged propensity to refuse to take no for an answer.

(c)   Similarities and Dissimilarities Between the Facts Charged and the Similar Fact Evidence-The Connecting Factors

(i)   Proximity in Time of the Similar Acts

The charge against the accused relates to December 6, 1996. The ex-wife's seven alleged incidents occurred between March 1990 and October 1996. The evidence of the accused's inability to take no for an answer gains cogency both from its repetition over many years and its most recent manifestation a couple of months before the offence charged.

(ii)   Extent to Which the Other Acts Are Similar in Detail to the Charged Conduct

The learned trial judge paid insufficient attention to the dissimilarities. . . None of the incidents described by the ex-wife began as consensual, then allegedly became non-consensual. Each of the incidents recounted by the ex-wife were bound up with the intimacy of a long-term relationship. The dynamic of these situations is not the same as the motel scene. . . The search for similarities is a question of degree. Sexual activity may not show much diversity or distinctiveness. Not every dissimilarity is fatal, but for the reasons already mentioned, substantial dissimilarities may dilute probative strength and, by compounding the confusion and distraction, aggravate the prejudice.

(iii)   Number of Occurrences of the Similar Acts

An alleged pattern of conduct may gain strength in the number of instances that compose it . . . The ex-wife's evidence here, if believed, established a pattern over many years that the jury might think showed that the respondent's pleasure in not taking no for an answer in sexual encounters was a predictable characteristic of general application.

(iv)   Circumstances Surrounding or Relating to the Similar Acts

Perhaps the most important dissimilarity lies not in the acts themselves but in the broader context. The "similar fact" evidence occurred in the course of a long-term dysfunctional marriage whereas the charge relates to a one-night stand following a chance meeting of casual acquaintances in a bar.

(v)   Any Distinctive Feature(s) Unifying the Incidents

It is not alleged that the sex acts themselves or the surrounding circumstances were highly distinctive. Cogency was said to derive from repetition rather than distinctiveness.

(vi)   Intervening Events

If the similar facts were sufficient to raise the inferences suggested by the Crown, there were no intervening events as such to undermine their probative value.

(d)   Strength of the Evidence that the Similar Acts Actually Occurred

The respondent did not admit the prior misconduct, and, "quite apart from the issue of collusion", a vigorous attack was made in cross-examination on the ex-wife's credibility. . . In the usual course, frailties in the evidence would be left to the trier of fact, in this case the jury. However, where admissibility is bound up with, and dependent upon, probative value, the credibility of the similar fact evidence is a factor that the trial judge, exercising his or her gatekeeper function is entitled to take into consideration. Where the ultimate assessment of credibility was for the jury and not the judge to make, this evidence was potentially too prejudicial to be admitted unless the judge was of the view that it met the threshold of being reasonably capable of belief.

(2)   Assessment of the Prejudice

(a)   Moral Prejudice

Prejudice in this context is not the risk of conviction. It is, more properly, the risk of an unfocussed trial and a wrongful conviction. The forbidden chain of reasoning is to infer guilt from general disposition or propensity. The evidence, if believed, shows that an accused has discreditable tendencies. In the end, the verdict may be based on prejudice rather than proof, thereby undermining the presumption of innocence.

The inflammatory nature of the ex-wife's evidence in this case cannot be doubted. It is, to the extent these things can be ranked, more reprehensible than the actual charge before the court. The jury would likely be more appalled by the pattern of domestic sexual abuse than by the alleged misconduct of an inebriated lout in a motel room on an isolated occasion. . . This evidence has a serious potential for moral prejudice.

(b)   Reasoning Prejudice

The major issue here is the distraction of members of the jury from their proper focus on the charge itself aggravated by the consumption of time in dealing with allegations of multiple incidents involving two victims in divergent circumstances rather than the single offence charged. Distraction can take different forms. In *R. v. D. (L.E.)*, McLachlin, J. observed that the similar facts may induce in the minds of the jury sentiments of revulsion and condemnation which might well deflect them from the rational, dispassionate analysis upon which the criminal process should rest.

Further, there is a risk, evident in this case, that where the similar facts are denied by the accused, the court will be caught in a conflict between seeking to admit what appears to be cogent evidence bearing on a material issue and the need to avoid unfairness to the right of the accused to respond. The accused has a limited opportunity to respond. Logistical problems may be compounded by the lapse of time, surprise, and the collateral issue rule, which will prevent trials within trials on the similar facts. Nor is the accused allowed to counter evidence of discreditable conduct with similar fact evidence in support of his or her credibility. Thus the practical realities of the trial process reinforce the prejudice inherent in the poisonous nature of the propensity evidence itself.

(3)   Weighing Up Probative Value Versus Prejudice

As probative value advances, prejudice does not necessarily recede. On the contrary, the two weighing pans on the scales of justice may rise and fall together. Nevertheless, probative value and prejudice pull in opposite directions on the admissibility issue and their conflicting demands must be resolved. . . . Justice is achieved when relevant evidence whose prejudice outweighs any probative value is excluded and where evidence whose probative value exceeds its prejudice, albeit an exceptional circumstance, is admitted. Justice includes society's interest in getting to the truth of the charges as well as the interest of both society and the accused in a fair process. A criminal justice system that has suffered some serious wrongful convictions in part because of misconceived notions of character and propensity should not, and does not, take lightly the dangers of misapplied propensity evidence.

In this case, the similar fact evidence was prima facie inadmissible and the Crown did not discharge the onus of establishing on a balance of probabilities that its probative value outweighed its undoubted prejudice. The probative value of the evidence, especially with respect to potential collusion, was not properly evaluated. The potential of such evidence for distraction and prejudice was understated. The threshold for admission of this sort of evidence was set too low.

. . .

A trial judge's decision to admit similar fact evidence is entitled to substantial deference. In this case, however, quite apart from the other frailties of the similar fact evidence, the trial judge's refusal to resolve the issue of collusion as a condition precedent to admissibility was an error of law. A new trial is required.

The Crown decided subsequently not to re-prosecute.

We now have a unanimous nine-person decision of our highest court clearly stating that the test for the admissibility of similar fact evidence is assessing probative value against the possibility of prejudice and that reasoning through propensity is, exceptionally, permissible, if specific and not just general disposition. The test is now easier to articulate. The Court also spells out various factors that trial judges need to take into account. The principled approach adopted and the clear statement of values deserves our applause. What had been a most confusing area in the law of evidence is now clearer. The approach taken in *Handy* now applies to the admissibility of all character evidence not just similar fact evidence.[50]

On *Handy* it is not necessary to find a purpose other than propensity, as appeared to be the approach of Justice Sopinka in judgments such as that in *D. (L.E.)*. The Court has expressly returned to the position of McLachlin J. in *B. (C.R.)* This is a very welcome development and one long-preferred by the Ontario Court of Appeal.[51]

Are you satisfied with the manner in which the Court applied the test to the facts of the case? Did the Court apply too narrow a view about sexual assault in distinguishing between marital and date rape?

It is not clear whether *Handy* has resulted in more or less exclusion of similar fact evidence. The Supreme Court in *Handy* rejects the Australian limit that the evidence must be "conclusive" (para. 93). On the other hand, less favourable to admission, the Court stands firmly against general propensity evidence and expressly indicates that propensity evidence is presumptively inadmissible (para. 55).

It also rules that the issue in question cannot be framed as broadly as "credibility" (paras. 115-116), which has often in the past been the basis for the admission of similar fact evidence.[52] Consider the following two cases identifying credibility as the issue in question.

---

[50]   See *R. v. Kirk* (2004), 188 C.C.C. (3d) 329, 22 C.R. 13 (6th) 231 (Ont. C.A.) and *R. v. S. (P.)* (2007), 221 C.C.C. (3d) 56 (Ont. C.A.).

[51]   See its leading pronouncements in *R. v. B. (L.)* (1997), 9 C.R. (5th) 38 (Ont. C.A.) (giving practical advice on how to weigh probative value and prejudicial effect) and *R. v. Batte* (2000), 145 C.C.C. (3d) 498, 34 C.R. (5th) 263 (Ont. C.A.) (where Doherty J.A. adopts the general/ specific propensity distinction adopted in *Handy*).

[52]   See also, generally, Hamish Stewart, "Rationalizing Similar Facts: A Comment on *R. v. Handy*" (2003) 8 Can. Crim. L. Rev. 113 and Mahoney, "Similar Fact Evidence" (2009) 55 Crim. L.Q. 22 (applauding *Handy* for its cautious approach to similar fact evidence, in contrast to a trend of admission in New Zealand, Australia, the U.K. and the United States).

R. v. BLAKE
(2003), 68 O.R. (3d) 75, 181 C.C.C. (3d) 169 (Ont. C.A.)

The accused was charged with sexual assault and sexual interference alleging touching of the vagina of an 8-year-old girl in a bedroom. The trial judge admitted as similar fact evidence details of the accused's two previous convictions involving genital touching of a girl aged 10 and a boy aged 8. In both cases the accused had lured them to a private space. The jury returned a verdict of guilty. Noting that the decision was pre-*Handy*, the majority of the Ontario Court of Appeal ordered a new trial on the basis that the similar fact evidence ought not to have been admitted.

SIMMONS J.A. (ARMSTRONG JJ.A.) (concurring):—

. . . the cumulative effect of five aspects of the trial judge's reasoning led her to set the threshold for admissibility of the discreditable conduct evidence too low:

i)   she framed the issue in question too widely allowing too broad "a gateway" for the admission of discreditable conduct evidence;

ii)   she did not identify the degree of connection to the alleged offence required to make the discreditable conduct evidence admissible;

iii) in assessing the cogency of the discreditable conduct evidence, she relied primarily on generic similarities between it and the evidence of the complainant;

iv)   in assessing the cogency of the discreditable conduct evidence, she did not identify the features of proposed evidence that distinguished it from the evidence of the complainant; and

v)   she failed to recognize the significant moral prejudice arising from the generic quality of the similarities she identified.

[On the issue of framing the issue, the majority held that the trial judge had relied too heavily on the issue of credibility.]

ii. Identification of the Issue in Question

Initially, the trial judge framed the issue in question as "whether the incident alleged by T.D. occurred". However, she later found that the discreditable conduct evidence was probative of several issues "other than [the appellant's] propensity to sexually assault young children". Those issues were the credibility of the complainant, the credibility of the allegations, B.'s credibility and character, a pattern of behaviour on the part of B., and rebuttal of the defence of innocent association.

As noted by my colleague, at paras. 116 and 117 of *Handy*, Binnie J. cautioned that framing "the issue in question" as credibility may result in "too broad a gateway for the admission of propensity evidence" therefore "risk[ing] the admission of evidence of nothing more than general disposition ("bad personhood")". In particular, he noted that when the issue in question is framed as the complainant's credibility, "anything that blackens the character of the accused" tends to enhance the credibility of the complainant.

In dissent Abella J.A. (as she then was) expressed the opinion that although this was not a "clear-cut" case for admissibility, strong deference should be paid to the trial judge. The further appeal to the Supreme Court was dismissed in a brief oral judgment expressing agreement with the majority in the Court below.[53]

A different approach was taken by the British Columbia Court of Appeal in *R. v. Titmus*.

R. v. TITMUS
(2004), 27 C.R. (6th) 77, 191 C.C.C. (3d) 468 (B.C. C.A.)

1. Identifying the Issue

The Crown tendered the similar fact evidence as relevant to the *actus reus* of the offences (para. 98) and the trial judge treated the evidence of both complainants concerning the shower incidents as admissible on that issue (para. 105). In the case of each complainant, the only evidence of the acts alleged against the appellant came from their own testimony. So the credibility of each complainant was central to the Crown's case, and the similar fact evidence was therefore relevant to their credibility, as well as to the *actus reus* of the offences alleged.

The trial judge held that the similar fact evidence enhanced the credibility of both complainants and tipped the scales beyond a balance of probability in establishing the *actus reus* of the shower incidents (paras. 140-141). I see no error by the trial judge in her identification of the issues to which the similar fact evidence was relevant.

As in this case, where it is the conduct element of the *actus reus* and not the accused's identity that is in issue, "similar fact evidence may be admitted to prove that the accused committed the offence or offences in question": *R. v. Arp*, [1998] 3 S.C.R. 339, 129 C.C.C. (3d) 321, at para. 48, see also *R. v. P.*, [1991] 3 All E.R. 337 (H.L), cited at para. 44 of *Arp*, supra, and *R. v. Handy*, supra, at paras. 78, 118-120. For sexual assault cases in particular, Madam Justice McLachlin (as she then was) said that where identity is not an issue, the credibility of a complainant is an issue in which similar fact evidence might be received: *B. (C.R.)*, *supra*, at paras. 38-41 [p. 27]. In *Handy, supra*, while warning against the admissibility of similar fact evidence on the issue of credibility because of the risk that the evidence might go only to the appellant's general disposition or propensity, Mr. Justice Binnie said that where the similar fact evidence is relevant to an element of the *actus reus*, the fact that it is also relevant to the complainants' credibility will not render the evidence inadmissible.

In the case at bar the issue of both complainants' credibility was inextricably tied to proof of the *actus reus*. In my view, in admitting the similar

---

[53]   (2004) 23 C.R. (6th) 63, [2004] 3 S.C.R. 503, 188 C.C.C. (3d) 428.

fact evidence as relevant to both credibility and to the *actus reus*, the trial judge made no error of law.

Which approach do you prefer?[54]

Should there be a special rule in sexual assault cases for the admission of similar fact evidence?[55] **How would you articulate and justify such a rule? Would such an approach create a slippery slope for admission of other types of bad character evidence?**

In *Handy*, the Court also makes it clear that admission should not occur where there is an air of reality to the issue of collusion amongst witnesses.[56] **Are you satisfied with the Court's conclusion that there was collusion in *Handy*?**

The issue of collusion was further addressed by Binnie J. in *Shearing* where he applied his *Handy* approach to admit similar fact evidence.

R. v. SHEARING
[2002] 3 S.C.R. 33, 165 C.C.C. (3d) 225, 2 C.R. (6th) 213

The accused was charged with 20 counts of sexual offences alleged to have occurred between 1965 and 1989. The accused was the leader of a cult. He preached that sexual experience was a way to progress to higher levels of consciousness and that he, as cult leader, could be instrumental in enabling young girls to reach these higher levels. Two of the complainants were sisters who lived in a group home while the others, adherents to the cult, did not. The counts were tried together and each was admitted as similar fact evidence for the others. We consider here the unanimous ruling that the similar fact evidence had been properly admitted. We will consider later another controversial aspect of *Shearing* in which the majority of the Supreme Court decided that the trial judge ought to have allowed cross-examination of a complainant as to the absence of mention of abuse in her diary.

BINNIE J.:—

. . .

As the test of admissibility weighs probative value against prejudice, a question that quickly emerges is whether the Crown is able to lead cogent evidence of the alleged similar acts. In this case, the similar acts are all the subject of distinct charges. They are therefore, in any event, before the jury for a verdict. Apart from the usual issues of credibility, the appellant says there is evidence of collusion.

---

[54]   See Tanovich, "Annotation" (2004), 27 C.R. (6th) 78. See also *R. v. C. (T.)* (2005), 27 C.R. (6th) 94 (Ont. C.A.).

[55]   See Tanovich, "An Equality Oriented Approach to the Admissibility of Similar Fact Evidence in Sexual Assault Cases" in Sheehy, ed., *Sexual Assault Law, Practice & Activism in a Post-Jane Doe Era* (Ottawa: University of Ottawa Press, 2012).

[56]   For commentary on this aspect of the case, see Schreck, "*Handy*: Raising the Threshold for the Admission of Similar Fact Evidence" (2002), 1 C.R. (6th) 245 and Morris, "The Possibility of Collusion as a Bar to the Admissibility of Similar Fact Evidence" (2003), 11 C.R. (6th) 181.

The theory of similar fact evidence turns largely on the improbability of coincidence. Collusion, by offering an alternative explanation for the "coincidence" of evidence emanating from different witnesses, destroys its probative value, and therefore the basis for its admissibility.

In *Handy* we held that where there is an air of reality to the allegation of collusion, the trial judge, in assessing the admissibility of the similar fact evidence, must be satisfied on a balance of probabilities that the evidence is not the product of concoction. This is inherent in deciding whether, as a matter of law, the evidence has sufficient probative value to overcome the prejudice.

If this threshold test is passed, the jury must determine for itself what weight, if any, to assign to the similar fact evidence.

There was evidence of some communication among the complainants. With respect to the G sisters, this was almost inevitable. They had also kept in touch with JV. Other complainants were in touch with each other prior to trial. Civil proceedings had been commenced by the G sisters for compensation and to close down the Kabalarians. KWG expressed the hope that the appellant would "rot in Hell".

The evidence here is far more speculative than in *Handy*. In that case, there was consultation between the complainant and the similar fact witness prior to the alleged offence about the prospect of financial profit. Here, there is some evidence of opportunity for collusion or collaboration and motive, but nothing sufficiently persuasive to trigger the trial judge's gatekeeper function. There is no reason here to interfere with the trial judge's decision to let the collusion issue go to the jury. He instructed the jury to consider "all of the circumstances which affect the reliability of that evidence including the possibility of collusion or collaboration between the complainants". He defined collusion as the possibility that the complainants, in sharing their stories with one another, intentionally or accidentally allowed themselves to change or modify their stories in order that their testimony would seem more similar or more convincing. It was for the jury to make the ultimate determination whether the evidence was "reliable despite the opportunity for collaboration" or that "less weight or no weight should be given to evidence which may have been influenced by the sharing of information".

While the trial judge did not specifically link the potential of collusion to the issue of admissibility, he appears to have thought collusion (as distinguished from contact) was not a serious danger. The evidence supports his decision. He was justified in letting the collusion issue go to the jury with an appropriate warning.

. . .

The cogency of the similar fact evidence in this case is said to arise from the repetitive and predictable nature of the appellant's conduct in closely defined circumstances. There must therefore be shown a persuasive degree of connection between the similar fact evidence and the offence charged in order to be capable of raising the double inferences. The degree of required similarity is assessed in relation to the issue sought to be established and must be evaluated in relation to the other evidence in the case. If the cumulative result is simply to paint the appellant as a "bad person", it is inadmissible.

The Crown's position is that the appellant utilized a distinctively bizarre modus operandi which runs like a common thread through the incidents charged.

While the sexual acts themselves were not particularly distinctive, the underlying unity lies in the alleged abuse of a cult leader's authority. It is the fantastic sales pitch and rationale developed by the appellant that could be considered "particular and distinctive" *Handy, supra*, at paras. 77-79). While it is not necessary to reach for these epithets or insert catch words into the test—as explained in *B. (C.R.)*—such distinctiveness enhances probative value.

. . .

Similarity does not lie in the physical sexual acts themselves (the G counts are far more serious). The incidents occurred in private places on Kabalarian premises and sexual touching began in the majority of cases when the complainants were under 18. . . The similarities really lay in the *modus operandi* employed by the appellant to create sexual opportunities. . .

The surrounding circumstances are united by the allegation of gross abuse of power by a cult leader. The spiritual theme is more dominant in the non-G counts because "spiritualism" was the source of the appellant's power over the complainants who did not live under his roof. Nevertheless, the "spiritual" theme surfaced in the testimony of KWG ("removing disembodied planes of mind") and SG (being made an "instrument"). . . .

The combination of spiritualist imagery (achieving higher states of awareness) and horror stories (invasion of young girls by disembodied minds), and the supposed prophylactic power of the appellant's sexual touching to ward off these horrific threats is, to say the least, distinctive.

. . .

In my view, the similar act evidence has significant potential to create moral prejudice. The appellant's defence to the non-G complainants (religiously inspired consent) becomes more delicate when the jury is told that he also had sexual relations with two sisters from the age of 13 who were not Kabalarian disciples but simply residents of his Kabalarian household. The atmosphere of the case is redolent of quack spiritualism and this would clearly disturb a Canadian jury. Similarly, the appellant's denial of abuse of the G sisters may lose much of its force in light of the admitted sexual touching of other adolescent girls, to which the only defence is consent (vitiated, so the jury must have found, by the abuse of authority).

. . .

In the weighing up of probative value versus prejudice, a good deal of deference is inevitably paid to the view of the trial judge: B. (C.R.), supra, at p. 733. This does not mean that the trial judge has a discretion to admit similar fact evidence whose prejudicial effect outweighs its probative value, but it does mean that the Court recognizes the trial judge's advantage of being able to assess on the spot the dynamics of the trial and the likely impact of the evidence on the jurors. These are evidentiary issues on which reasonable judges may differ and, absent error in principle, the decision should rest where it was allocated, to the trial judge. In this case the trial judge's view has been endorsed by a unanimous Court of Appeal.

The trial judge concluded that both the prejudicial effect and the probative value of the similar fact evidence were "significant", but that in the end the probative value prevailed. I see no reason to interfere with that conclusion.

Once the Court in *Handy* agreed that propensity is the true basis for the admission of similar fact evidence it seemed to follow, as it did for Doherty J.A. in *R. v. Batte*,[57] that the jury need not be warned that they cannot use this to show that the accused was the type of person who could have committed the crime. Yet the Supreme Court has persisted with the need for a warning, as it did in *Arp* and *Shearing*.

This seems unfortunate as the lack of a warning has often necessitated a new trial and seems superfluous if the jury can indeed rely on propensity. Furthermore warnings have often been so tortuous as to be arguably perverse. In *R. v. Peterffy*,[58] for example, evidence by several witnesses as to acts of prior physical abuse by a husband to his common-law wife were held to have been properly admitted in a murder case to show a violent and threatening attitude, a motive of anger at the deceased's taunting and disobedience and the type of relationship. However the Court confirmed that this was only so because the trial judge had properly warned the jury that they could not conclude from the bad character evidence that he was the sort of person likely to have committed the murder!

In *R. v. B. (C.)*,[59] a case alleging sexual assault against a daughter and a granddaughter, the judge had admitted, as similar fact evidence, evidence of sexual conduct with other daughters. One of the reasons for ordering a new trial and as a violation of the *Handy* approach was an improper warning. Although the judge warned the jury not to use the evidence of prior sexual conduct with other daughters to show the accused was a bad character such that they could infer that he was more likely to have committed the offences charged, there had not been a direction as to the distinction between general and specific propensity. The Court was also concerned about the issue of collusion.[60]

However, in *R. v. B. (R.T.)*,[61] where the accused was charged with several sexual offences against his two teenaged stepnieces, the Court held

---

[57] (2000), 34 C.R. (5th) 197 (Ont. C.A.). See, however, concerns expressed by Michael Plaxton & Glen Luther, "Limiting Instructions and Similar Facts" (2009), 63 C.R. (6th) 12.

[58] (2000), 30 C.R. (5th) 297 (B.C. C.A.).

[59] (2003), 7 C.R. (6th) 3 (Ont. C.A.).

[60] See further N. Harris, "Limiting Instructions: Preventing Wrongful Conviction or Causing Juror Confusion?" (2004), 20 C.R. 6th 117. See also *R. v. Thomas* (2004), 26 C.R. (6th) 274, 190 C.C.C. (3d) 31 (Ont. C.A.).

[61] 243 C.C.C. (3d) 158, 63 C.R. (6th) 197 (Ont. C.A.); and see earlier *R. v. Vrdoljak* (2002), 1 C.R. (6th) 250 (Ont. C.J.).

that the trial judge had erred in dismissing the Crown's application to have evidence across counts considered as similar fact evidence. Justice Borins reasoned that this was a judge-alone trial and moral prejudice was not a significant risk. In her Criminal Reports annotation, Lisa Dufraimont has severely criticized this assumption. She argues that this view overlooks the key danger identified in *Handy* from reasoning from general propensity to guilt. She concludes as follows:

> If one focuses on this general propensity reasoning, it is far from clear that trial judges are invulnerable to moral prejudice. To be sure, courts frequently state that jurors are especially prone to this type of faulty reasoning; for example, in *B. (C.R.)*, [1990] 1 S.C.R. 717, Sopinka J. identified "a natural human tendency to judge a person's action on the basis of character. Particularly with juries there would be a strong inclination to conclude that a thief has stolen, a violent man has assaulted and a pedophile has engaged in pedophilic acts" (at 744, cited in *Handy, supra* at para. 39). Of course, judges have an advantage over lay jurors because their training and experience help them achieve an accurate understanding of which inferences are permitted, and which forbidden, in the context of similar fact evidence. On the other hand, there is little basis for any confident assertion that judges are immune to the "natural human tendency" Sopinka J. described. Psychological research suggests that people have difficulty mentally cabining off information and using it only for limited purposes (see, *e.g.*, Owen M. Rees, "The Jury's Propensity for Prohibited Reasoning: *Corbett* Revisited" (2002) 7 Can. Crim. L. Rev. 333, 344-47; Roselle L. Wissler & Michael J. Saks (1985) "On the Inefficacy of Limiting Instructions" 9 Law & Hum. Behav. 37, 43-47). No doubt judges, like juries, can be affected by moral prejudice when they hear evidence of the accused's bad character (see Mirjan R. Damaska, *Evidence Law Adrift* (New Haven: Yale University Press, 1997) at 31-32).
>
> To recognize that judges may be vulnerable to moral prejudice arising from similar fact evidence is not to deny that the potential for prejudice is typically unavoidable. Often, as in *B. (R.T.)*, the similar facts relate to the various counts of a multi-count indictment, and in even in cases where the similar facts alleged lie outside the indictment, the trial judge will normally hear the evidence in order to determine its admissibility. Thus, as Borins J.A. points out in *B. (R.T.)*, the potential for prejudice that flows from the fact finder's exposure to evidence of the accused's bad character exists whether or not the evidence is ruled admissible. Trial judges are routinely asked to do what may well be impossible: to remain unaffected by the prejudicial material they hear. What the Court of Appeal may have overlooked in *B. (R.T.)* is the way in which the admissibility inquiry surrounding similar fact evidence can help judges rise to this challenge. Surely a judge who has grappled with the prejudicial effect of similar fact evidence and perhaps even ruled it inadmissible on that basis is more likely to resist the influence of moral prejudice than one who relies on the easy assumption that moral prejudice is not an issue in bench trials.

Where there is more than one count and evidence on one count is not admissible as similar fact evidence on other counts, the jury must be instructed to consider each charge separately and not to use evidence relating to one count as evidence on any other count.[62]

---

[62]   *R. v. Farler* (2006), 131 C.C.C. (3d) 134 (N.S. C.A.) (per Cromwell J.A., in ordering a new trial).

In *R. v. B. (M.)*[63] the Court ordered a new trial respecting charges of sexual offences against three children on the basis that where multiple children make simultaneous disclosures of sexual abuse the jury must be warned of the possibility of innocent collusion.

In *R. v. Perrier*[64] the Supreme Court announced a special, very complex approach to similar fact evidence in gang trials.

PROBLEMS

Problem 1

A is charged with the murder of B, a woman with whom he was then living. The cause of B's death was arsenical poisoning. The prosecution seeks to tender evidence that A's wife died of arsenical poisoning two years earlier. **Relevant? Receivable?** Compare *Noor Mohammed v. R.*, [1949] A.C. 182 (P.C.).

Problem 2

The accused is charged with sexual assault. The victim, a 12-year-old girl, was sleeping in an Eastern Ontario campsite in a small pup tent. She was with her brother while her parents slept in a larger tent nearby. After midnight, a man entered her tent by cutting it and attempted to fondle her. She fought him off by biting him and he ran off. Identification is an issue at trial because she only saw him for seconds and it was dark. She did not identify him until more than two years after the attack, from police photographs. The Crown seeks to enter similar act evidence from six years earlier. In the dark of night, the accused unzipped the small pup tent of a 12-year-old girl in a different Eastern Ontario campsite where she was sleeping with a group of Girl Guides. Adult supervisors were sleeping near by. The offense also involved fondling. A number of other tents were slashed that night. The accused pled guilty to sexual assault in relation to that incident. **Would you admit the evidence applying *Handy*?** See *R. v. Harvey* (2001) 48 C.R. (5th) 247, 160 C.C.C. (3d) 52 (Ont. C.A.), affirmed 7 C.R. (6th) 1, 169 C.C.C. (3d) 576, [2002] 4 S.C.R. 311.

Problem 3

The accused is charged with second degree murder in the death of his former girlfriend. She was found dead in her bedroom with a cord wrapped around her neck. A detached part of the cord was wrapped around the outside bedroom doorknob. A kitchen chair was found nearby. The defence position was that the death was a suicide. The theory of the Crown was that

---

[63]   (2011), 267 C.C.C. (3d) 72, 83 C.R. (6th) 153 (Ont. C.A.). See too *R. v. Dorsey* (2012), 288 C.C.C. (3d) 62, 93 C.R. (6th) 65 (Ont. C.A.). In *R. v. Dueck* (2011), 88 C.R. (6th) 150 (Sask. C.A.) it was held that no warning was required where the trial judge concluded on a balance of probabilities that the evidence was not tainted by collusion.

[64]   [2004] 3 S.C.R. 228, 22 C.R. (6th) 209, 188 C.C.C. (3d) 1 (S.C.C.) and see C.R. comment by Lou Strezos.

the accused could not accept that the relationship was over and, as had happened in the past, he became violent. The Crown wants to introduce evidence from the accused's former girlfriend. She will testify that the accused could not accept that she wanted to end the relationship, and during an argument the accused bound her hands with a telephone cord and then wrapped it around a doorknob and then around a bannister. **Admissible?** See *R. v. Watkins* (2003), 181 C.C.C. (3d) 78 (Ont. C.A.) and *R. v. Trochym*, 43 C.R. (6th) 217, 216 C.C.C. (3d) 225, [2007] 1 S.C.R. 239 (S.C.C.).

Problem 4

The accused is charged with murder. The victim was one of his children, aged three, and there is no doubt from the evidence that the child died as the result of external violence. Two prosecution witnesses have testified in graphic detail to the manner in which the accused allegedly beat the child into unconsciousness. The defence is an outright denial. The prosecution wishes to tender in evidence descriptions of other occasions on which the accused beat the child. **Relevant? Receivable?** Of other occasions when the accused beat the other children. Of occasions when he abused the family dog. **Relevant? Receivable?** Compare *R. v. Drysdale*, [1969] 2 C.C.C. 141 (Man. C.A., 1968), *R. v. Roud* (1981), 58 C.C.C. (2d) 226 (Ont. C.A.), *R. v. Speid* (1985), 46 C.R. (3d) 22 (Ont. C.A.), and *R. v. Gottschall* (1983), 10 C.C.C. (3d) 447 (N.S. C.A.).

Problem 5

The accused is charged with several counts of assault causing bodily harm and sexual assault of S, his male common-law partner. The allegation is that the accused one particular night came home somewhat drunk and in a grumpy mood. After a fight over washing the dishes the accused beat S twice with a broom and chased him up to the bedroom where he had anal sexual intercourse with S despite S's protests that he did not want that.

The Crown seeks to tender evidence of the accused's violent relationship towards two previous male common-law partners. In both cases the evidence will be that the accused was often moody and quick-tempered and often accused them of sleeping with others. Each former partner will detail incidents when this jealousy lead to the accused attacking them with his fists, causing bruises. **With reference to appropriate authority, consider whether this evidence is admissible.**

Compare *R. v. K. (C.P.)* (2002), 7 C.R. (6th) 16 (Ont. C.A.).

Problem 6

The accused was charged with several sexual offences on the basis of allegations by his niece that he repeatedly abused her when she was between 8 and 10 years of age. The allegations ranged from vaginal touching to oral and anal sex. The trial proceeded without a jury. The trial judge admitted, as similar fact evidence, evidence relating to the accused's conviction for sexual assault on another 8-year-old girl. In that instance the accused touched the girl's vaginal area underneath her clothes twice on a single day. The trial judge assessed the weight to be assigned to the similar fact evidence as high and convicted the accused on all counts. **Should this evidence of one prior sexual assault have been admitted?**

Compare *R. v. M. (T.L.)*, [2012] 1 S.C.R. 233, 90 C.R. (6th) 1, 281 C.C.C. (3d) 289 (S.C.C.). See too *R. v. Jesse*, 2012 SCC 21, [2012] 1 S.C.R. 716, 281 C.C.C. (3d) 145, 92 C.R. (6th) 268 (S.C.C.), but see *R. v. Bent*, 2016 ONCA 651, 342 C.C.C. (3d) 343, 32 C.R. (7th) 437 (Ont. C.A.), additional reasons 2016 ONCA 722 (Ont. C.A.).

(iii) *Civil Cases*

There are far fewer reported civil cases involving the problem of similar facts than criminal cases.

JOHNSON v. BUGERA
(1999), 172 D.L.R. (4th) 535 (B.C. C.A.)

Statton, Johnson and Robertson were involved in a single car accident. The accident resulted in Robertson's death, and left Statton in a coma for several weeks. Statton had virtually no recall of the events several days before the accident and several weeks thereafter. Statton appealed against the trial judge's determination that he was the driver of the vehicle at the time of the accident. Although he was thrown from the vehicle as a result of the accident, Johnson did not suffer any major injuries, and he said that he had a clear memory of the events. The vehicle involved in the accident was owned by Statton's common-law wife, Bugera. Johnson claimed that Statton was driving at the time of the accident. It was determined that the accident occurred as a result of the vehicle being driven at a very high rate of speed. While Johnson had a remarkable record for speeding, this was not taken into account by the trial judge.

Per HALL J.A. (GOLDIE and DONALD JJ.A. concurring):

. . .

In his reasons for judgment His Lordship said this concerning the respondent Johnson:

His prior driving record was tendered in regard to his credibility. It is not suggested there is any basis for a similar act analysis and indeed there is none.

With respect, it seems to me that there does exist a very substantial basis for a similar act analysis on the facts of this case.

It must be remembered that what was at the heart of this case and the issue being litigated was the question of who, on a balance of probabilities, was the driver of the car that was involved in the fatal accident. In other words, the central issue was a question of identity. "Similar facts" or "similar acts" is a much discussed principle in the law of evidence, particularly in its application in the criminal law. A case often referred to as a starting point in such an analysis is *Makin v. Attorney-General for New South Wales*, [1894] A.C. 57. Although Makin, often referred to as the baby farming case, is perhaps the most well known and a leading case in the area, the principle upon which it is based is older and lies much deeper in the law. One starts with the proposition that all relevant evidence is admissible. Of course, some "relevant evidence" may be rather marginal and such evidence can also be highly prejudicial. The rule of evidence preventing rebuttal of collateral fact evidence is one device employed by courts to avoid the admission of evidence that may be tangentially relevant but would lead to a great expansion of time taken in trials. The courts have also exercised a jurisdiction to avoid the introduction of highly prejudicial but marginally probative evidence, especially in jury trials, in order to prevent the misuse of evidence by the trier of fact.

But I return to the proposition that evidence is adduced in a trial to prove a fact or facts in issue. In assessing the admissibility of evidence, lawyers and judges ask themselves the question, is this evidence probative of a fact in issue and hence relevant? Subject to other exclusionary rules like the hearsay rule, if those queries be answered in the affirmative, then the evidence is prima facie admissible at a trial.

. . .

I doubt that there is any difference between admissibility of evidence in civil and criminal cases, with the possible exception that in the latter class of case, particularly cases tried before a jury, there may be a heightened concern that potentially prejudicial evidence not be placed before the trier of fact unless it has significant probative value.

. . .

In this case, a combination of speeding infractions admitted by the respondent Johnson in cross-examination at trial coupled with a transcript of his driving record that was filed establish that he had amassed a great number of speeding convictions between 1989 and 1997. As I counted them, there are over 25 of these infractions. The great majority of these occurred between 1989 and 1994. A large number of the offences involved highway speeding. As noted by the trial judge, Johnson was under a driving suspension at the time of the accident. This accident occurred as a result of a vehicle being driven at a very excessive rate of speed. The respondent Johnson has a remarkable record for this sort of conduct. I do not overlook the fact that Statton had some speeding convictions as well but his record is of a different order entirely from that of Johnson. It seems to me that it could justly be said that this very substantial history of speeding on the part of Johnson could be found to have probative force and be a highly relevant matter for a trier of fact to assess in deciding the question at issue in this case, namely, who was the driver of the Dodge car at the time of the accident? I find it impossible to say as a matter of logic that this would not be a matter potentially probative on this matter. While the record is one arguably demonstrating "bad conduct" of Johnson as a driver, it also could be reckoned to be highly probative of the fact that he was more probably the driver of the Dodge at the relevant time. I believe that a trial judge could and should undertake a similar act analysis in deciding this case. . . .

. . .

New trial ordered.

S. (R.C.M.) v. K. (G.M.)
(2005), 266 Sask. R. 31 (Sask. Q.B.)

This was an application for custody. One of the issues was the admissibility of evidence that the father was abusive in a previous relationship.

RYAN-FROSLIE J.:—

When family relationships break down, children are hurt. This is particularly true when parents, obsessed with their own battles, lose sight of the needs and interests of their children. It is against such a backdrop that this Court must determine the appropriate parenting arrangements for two young girls. Their mother, Jane, wants sole custody with no, or limited, access to their father. Their father, John, wants joint custody with specified parenting time. The only thing these two parents appear to agree upon is that their relationship is an acrimonious one and the only thing they appear to have in common is love for their daughters.

. . .

During the course of the trial, counsel for Jane proffered as a witness the former common-law spouse of John who testified that during her relationship with John she was subjected to physical and emotional abuse. Counsel for John objected to the admission of this evidence, arguing that it is evidence of bad character, that it is extremely prejudicial and irrelevant to the issues before this Court. Counsel for Jane argued the evidence is relevant, that domestic violence and spousal abuse are matters that relate directly to an individual's ability to parent and that the evidence proffered corroborates Jane's claims of spousal abuse and thus bolsters her credibility. After a voir dire, this Court ruled the evidence was admissible. What follows are the reasons for that decision.

The leading case on similar fact evidence is the Supreme Court of Canada in *R. v. Handy*, [2002] 2 S.C.R. 908, 2002 SCC 56. As a general rule, similar fact evidence is inadmissible. The rationale is that individuals should not be judged on past conduct but rather on conduct that is in issue. People can and do change. If they are judged on past conduct, no allowance is made for that ability. The exception to the rule is when the probative value of the evidence tendered outweighs its prejudicial effect. The Supreme Court of Canada in *R. v. Handy* set out the framework within which a court could make that determination. The court must look at a number of factors including whether the evidence is relevant to an issue before the court, the similarity of the evidence in time and circumstance to the case in issue and whether there is prejudice to the party against who the evidence was tendered.

Section 16(9) of the *Divorce Act* provides that in making orders with regard to custody and access ". . . the court shall not take into consideration the past conduct of any person unless the conduct is relevant to the ability of that person to act as a parent of a child."

Abuse is conduct that is relevant to a person's ability to act as a parent. This is so for a number of reasons. The negative effect on children who witness domestic violence is well-documented. Moreover, spousal abuse affects the dynamics of decision-making as it relates to the children and the milieu in which exchanges of the children occur. It is also an important consideration in determining parenting arrangements — whether sole or joint custody is appropriate, where the child should reside, whether the parenting time should be supervised or unsupervised, flexible or inflexible. Issues of abuse may directly impact the psychological and emotional needs of the children as well as their physical safety. It also relates to the type of "role model" a parent is for a child. Whether John abused Jane during their relationship is therefore relevant to his ability to parent.

Jane also alleges John sexually abused her and the parties' daughter, Sally. An individual's sexual appetites or proclivities may or may not be relevant to parenting. If an individual is discreet and they do not act inappropriately in the children's presence, what they do behind closed doors may very well have no bearing on ability to parent. The only way a court can make this determination, however, is to hear the evidence.

How does a victim of spousal abuse prove that abuse when they and their spouse and/or their infant children are the only witnesses to the altercations? Spousal abuse is a pattern of conduct. Human experience tells us that generally people act consistently. Counsel for Jane put forward the evidence in issue to show that John was abusive in the spousal relationship he had immediately prior the relationship with Jane and that, true to form, he continued that abuse with Jane.

The evidence in issue relates to circumstances which are removed in time and place from the spousal abuse alleged by Jane. As such, it is only circumstantial evidence. Its usefulness rests in the validity of the inference it is said to support, that is, that John engaged in spousal abuse in the relationship he had immediately prior to his relationship with Jane and thus Jane's evidence that he abused her is more credible.

The rules relating to the admissibility of similar fact evidence apply in civil cases but as Lord Denning pointed out in *Mood Music Publishing Co. Ltd. v. De Wolfe Ltd.*, [1976] 1 All E.R. 763 (C.A.), the rule in civil cases is not as rigidly applied as in criminal ones.

> ... The criminal courts have been very careful not to admit [similar fact] evidence unless its probative value is so strong that it should be received in the interests of justice; and its admission will not operate unfairly to the accused. In civil cases the courts have followed a similar line but have not been so chary of admitting it. In civil cases the courts will admit evidence of similar facts if it is logically probative, that is if it is logically relevant in determining the matter which is in issue; provided that it is not oppressive or unfair to the other side; and also that the other side has fair notice of it and is able to deal with it. . .

This Court has examined the differences between the criminal standard and the civil standard in the recent cases of *C.M. v. A.G. (Canada)*, 2004

SKQB 174, (2004), 248 Sask.R. 1 (Q.B.) and *K.M. v. A.G.* (Canada), 2004 SKQB 287, (2004), 251 Sask.R. 12 (Q.B.). Both those cases indicate the bar for the admission of similar fact evidence in civil cases is lower than in criminal cases. They both found similar fact evidence relating to credibility admissible.

While the fact John may have been abusive in a prior spousal relationship does not necessarily mean he was abusive to Jane, it does support her credibility on this issue. There are strong similarities between the evidence of John's former common-law spouse and Jane. Both of them had spousal relationships with John. Both of them testified that during their relationships John was controlling and that he was emotionally, physically and sexually abusive to them. While the extent of the abuse does vary, for example John's former common-law spouse testified that John ground his open hand into her face, while Jane testified he hit her with his fist, there is sufficient similarity in the conduct to form the necessary nexus. In addition, there is considerable similarity in the emotional abuse alleged - the name-calling and control. The evidence proffered is relevant as it relates to spousal abuse, an important factor in determining parenting arrangements. It is of sufficient probative value to warrant its admission.

The admission of this evidence does not unduly prejudice John. While he had no prior notice that this evidence was to be tendered, the fact that this Court adjourned for a considerable length of time afforded him the opportunity to examine and fully meet the evidence presented.

The judge granted sole custody to the mother and specified parenting time to the father. She was satisfied that while the father had physically abused the mother, including in front of the children, he had never physically or sexually assaulted his children.

PROBLEM

Two individuals entered into a franchise agreement for the sale of flowers under the plaintiff's name. The relationship broke down after less than two years. The plaintiff alleges that the defendant breached the agreement by purchasing flowers from non-authorized suppliers. The defendant did not dispute this but responded that the flowers provided by the plaintiff were of such low quality that this deprived the defendant of the benefit of the agreement. The defendant wanted to call three franchisees to testify that they experienced similar problems with the product they received from the plaintiff. **Is this evidence admissible? On what theory of relevance?** See *Jardin Direct Inc. v. Floradin Florists Ltd.* (2006), 258 Nfld. & P.E.I.R. 197 (Nfld. T.D.).

(f) Character of Third Party/Co-Accused

An accused is entitled to lead bad character evidence of a third party to suggest, for example, that the third party's propensity for violence makes it more likely that he committed the offence. There is a requirement, however, that there be some evidence of a link between the third party and the offence: see most recently the discussion in *R. v. Grandinetti*.[65] Once the defence leads this evidence, it opens the door for the Crown to rebut by calling propensity evidence in relation to the accused.

In *R. v. Parsons*[66] Finlayson J.A. addressed the propriety of propensity evidence by the Crown to counter a defence raised by the accused based on the alleged propensity of another person.

> In my opinion, Mercier J. was correct in ruling that if the evidence relating to Miller's propensity to commit robberies was introduced into evidence, fairness dictated that the very similar evidence that the Crown possessed relating to the appellant could also be introduced. *I would go further and suggest that if the appellant chose to throw sticks at Miller, the Crown should be able to counter this evidence with any similar evidence relating to the propensity to commit robbery, not only of the appellant, but of the other suspects arrested with the appellant....To rule otherwise would leave the jury with the highly misleading impression that Miller alone of those arrested had a propensity to commit robberies, whereas in truth he was part of a gang that committed robberies and the appellant was part of that gang* [emphasis added].[67]

In addition to fairness concerns, courts have held that when third-party propensity evidence is called, the accused impliedly puts his or her own character in issue.[68]

The Ontario Court of Appeal limited the "tit for tat" principle to cases where it is general propensity evidence led by the accused. In *R. v. Vanezis*,[69] the defence wanted to call evidence of a third party's threats to kill the victim and assaults directed at her. Justice Moldaver held that the trial judge had erred in concluding that this opened the door for the Crown to lead evidence of the accused's propensity for violence towards third parties. As he put it, this evidence was "not being led to show that he was the kind of person likely to have killed her but that he was in fact the person who killed her".

An accused can also lead bad character evidence in relation to a co-accused: see *R. v. Suzack*.[70] However, in *R. v. Pollock*,[71] Justice Rosenberg recognized that "there must be some evidentiary foundation to support" the assertion that the evidence is necessary to make full answer and defence. When admitted, a trial judge has the difficult task of providing a careful limiting instruction, namely that this evidence cannot be used as part of the Crown's case against the co-accused.

---

[65]   191 C.C.C. (3d) 449, [2005] 1 S.C.R. 27, 25 C.R. (6th) 1.

[66]   (1993), 84 C.C.C. (3d) 226, 24 C.R. (4th) 112 (Ont. C.A.).

[67]   *Ibid.* at 237-238 [C.C.C.]. See also *R. v. Dhillon* (2002), 166 C.C.C. (3d) 262, 5 C.R. (6th) 317 (Ont. C.A.) at 277 [C.C.C.]; *R. v. Woodcock* (2003), 177 C.C.C. (3d) 346, 14 C.R. (6th) 155 (Ont. C.A.) at 381-382 [C.C.C.]; *R. v. Rodgers* (2000), 144 C.C.C. (3d) 568 (Ont. C.A.); *R. v. B. (C.)* (1997), 118 C.C.C. (3d) 43 (Ont. C.A.) at 56-57; *R. v. McMillan* (1975), 23 C.C.C. (2d) 160, 29 C.R.N.S. 191 (Ont. C.A.), affirmed 33 C.C.C. (2d) 360, [1977] 2 S.C.R. 824.

[68]   See the discussion in *R. v. Truscott* (2006), 213 C.C.C. (3d) 183 (Ont. C.A.) and *R. v. M. (M.)* (2003), [2003] O.J. No. 5949 (S.C.J.).

[69]   (2006), 213 C.C.C. (3d) 449, 43 C.R. (6th) 116 (Ont. C.A.).

[70]   (2002), 141 C.C.C. (3d) 449 (Ont. C.A.).

[71]   (2004), 187 C.C.C. (3d) 213, 23 C.R. (6th) 98 (Ont. C.A.), applied in *R. v. Earhart* (2010), 81 C.R. (6th) 148, 272 C.C.C. (3d) 475 (Ont. C.A.) at 165 [C.R.].

R. v. KHAN
(2004), 189 C.C.C. (3d) 49, 24 C.R. (6th) 48 (Ont. S.C.J.)

The accused was charged with possession of one kilogram of cocaine for the purpose of trafficking. The police found the drugs in a vehicle being driven by the accused. The accused alleged that he was the victim of racial profiling. He was African-Canadian and the vehicle was a Mercedes. The accused wanted to rely on evidence of another individual who had been stopped by the same officer as similar act evidence of racial profiling.

MOLLOY J.:—

. . .

(ii)   Similar Fact Evidence and Racial Profiling

On the other hand, if as Mr. Khan alleges, he was targeted by these officers because of racial profiling, this would constitute an improper purpose and would invalidate the stop, and everything that flowed from the stop. A finding that a police officer was motivated by racism, whether consciously or unconsciously, is a serious matter. It ought not to be made lightly. Knowledge of the existence of racial profiling by police of young black males driving expensive cars, even knowledge that such profiling exists in Metro Toronto, is not sufficient to establish that it actually occurred in this particular case. It would be improper to infer racist motivation in the absence of evidence that the particular officer or officers involved actually had that intent: *R. v. S. (R.D.)*, [1997] 3 S.C.R. 484.

In *R. v. Brown* (2003), 173 C.C.C. (3d) 23 (Ont. C.A.) the Court of Appeal noted that racial profiling will rarely be proven by direct evidence, as officers are not likely to admit their motivation was overtly racist. The Court held that one way racial profiling can be proven is by circumstantial evidence where: (a) the circumstances relating to the detention correspond to the phenomenon of racial profiling (as is the case here); and (b) the circumstances provide a basis for the court to infer that the police officer is lying about why the police officer singled out the accused person for attention: *R. v. Brown* at paras. 44 and 45.

As I noted in my earlier ruling on the production motion in this case [reported at [2004] O.J. No. 3811 (S.C.J.)], that is only one of the ways in which racial profiling may be proven. I ruled that an accused could also rely on evidence that the officer in question had acted in a similar manner in the past or on evidence of bias. In the case before me, evidence was called by the defence with respect to the detention and arrest of Sheldon Jackson by these same two officers in March 2001 (about 7 months before Mr. Khan's arrest). The officers testified they were driving along St. Clair Avenue and passed Mr. Jackson who was driving in the opposite direction in an expensive BMW. Mr. Jackson is also a young black male. Officer Asselin noticed that when Mr. Jackson saw the police, he gave a strange look, as if he looked guilty. The officers made a U-turn and followed Mr. Jackson's vehicle which, they testified, was being driven in an erratic manner suggestive of an attempt to avoid the police. A CPIC check disclosed the owner of the vehicle was a suspended driver. The officers pulled Mr. Jackson over. As Officer Asselin was approaching the car, he said he could see Mr. Jackson frantically trying to put a white powdered substance wrapped in clear plastic into a hand-held single bottle beer cooler with a zipper on it. Mr. Jackson was asked to step out of the car and he accompanied Officer James to the police cruiser. Officer Asselin then went to Mr. Jackson's car and retrieved the beer cooler, which did in fact turn out to have cocaine in it.

Mr. Jackson's version of events was quite different. He said he was driving along St. Clair Avenue going toward a restaurant to meet a friend. He did not notice the police car on St. Clair and did not make eye contact with the officers. He turned off St. Clair and travelled a number of one-way side streets to find a parking spot. He then noticed the police lights and siren behind him and pulled over. He was asked to step out of the car, which he did. He was also asked to unlock the doors, which he also did. Officer James then took him back to the police cruiser while Officer Asselin proceeded to search his car. Mr. Jackson acknowledged there were drugs in the car and that they were inside a zipped up red single-bottle beer cooler. However, he said he put the drugs in the bottle cooler earlier that day, and then hid it in a space at the back of his headrest, which, he said, is where Officer Asselin actually found it.

As I have already ruled, evidence of discreditable conduct, bad character or bias is admissible against a mere witness in a trial even in circumstances where it might not be admissible against an accused. The strictures surrounding the admission into evidence of similar fact evidence against an accused do not apply with the same rigour against a non-accused witness. That said, many of the same considerations apply to the weight that can be given to the similar fact evidence and its degree of probative value.

In *R. v. Handy* (2002), 164 C.C.C. (3d) 481 at paras. 102-136, the Supreme Court of Canada held that in assessing the probative value of similar fact evidence it is relevant to consider: (a) the potential for collusion; (b) identification of the issue in question; (c) the degree of similarity or dissimilarity between the allegations in the case and the similar fact evidence (otherwise referred to as "connecting factors"); and (d) the strength of the evidence that the similar acts actually occurred. Within category (c), the trial judge should consider any factor connecting the similar facts to the circumstances being alleged, including:

(i)   proximity in time of the similar acts;

(ii)   extent to which the other acts are similar in detail to the conduct alleged;

(iii)   number of occurrences of the similar acts;

(iv)   circumstances surrounding or relating to the similar acts;

(v)   any distinctive features unifying the incidents;

(vi)   intervening events;

(vii)   any other factor which would tend to support or rebut the underlying unity of the similar events.

(*R. v. Handy* at para. 82)

As a preliminary matter, I am satisfied that collusion between Mr. Jackson and Mr. Khan can be ruled out. They did not know each other. Each, coincidentally, happened to retain the same criminal defence counsel and it was their lawyer who noted the similarity between the two arrests and the fact that the same two officers were involved.

Other factors enhancing the probative value of the similar fact evidence in this case are their proximity in time and the degree of similarity between them. In both situations, the targeted individuals were young black men driving expensive vehicles. The officers' initial reasons for curiosity were slightly different in each case. Mr. Khan was staring straight ahead, and he failed to take the right-of-way; Mr. Jackson had a look of guilt on his face. However, both Mr. Khan and Mr. Jackson allege that the police followed them for no reason and then pulled them over without there having been any traffic infraction. In both cases, the police allege a traffic infraction in full view of the police as an initial reason for the stop. In both cases, the police allege that as they approached the stopped vehicle they could see the driver attempting to hide something. Both Mr. Khan and Mr. Jackson allege that they were first removed from their cars and detained by Officer James while Officer Asselin searched their vehicles and that they were not arrested until his search turned up drugs.

There are also dissimilarities between the two events, as one would expect. Further, the circumstances in which the incidents arose (a routine traffic stop) are so similar that there will almost inevitably be some degree of similarity between the two events. For example, when police pull over any vehicle for an alleged traffic violation and then find drugs, it is not uncommon for the driver to deny the traffic violation. There will always be some similarities between cases of this nature.

I do not propose to dwell at length on these and other connecting factors because in my opinion there are two critical factors that completely undermine the probative value of the similar fact evidence. The first, and lesser in importance, is the fact that there is only one incident. That is not necessarily fatal. However, the fact that a person has done something once before is not nearly as compelling as the fact he has done it, say, twenty times before. If there is only one other similar incident, its probative strength in other areas would need to be greater. For example, I would be less concerned about attaching weight to one prior incident if it was so similar in detail as to be almost a "fingerprint." Conversely, in the absence of striking similarity, I would be reluctant to conclude that one prior incident was a coincidence so compelling as to be highly probative.

The second, and most persuasive, negative factor is the strength of the evidence that the similar act actually occurred. Sheldon Jackson is not the most credible of witnesses. He is an admitted drug dealer. He has a criminal record, including a drug-related offence. He was a suspended driver, but was driving. He was using a fabricated driver's license with false identification, and had used it with success in the past. He attempted to flee the scene. He had a motive to fabricate, as he is himself facing charges of possession for the purposes of trafficking in relation to that same event. Of course, none of this means he is not telling the truth about this particular incident. However, since proof that this incident occurred depends entirely on Mr. Jackson's credibility, I am driven to the conclusion that this evidence is frail, at best, and possibly unproven.

I have a discretion in determining the weight and admissibility of evidence of this nature. Having heard the evidence, I am of the view that its probative value is too weak to attach any weight to it. That means, as is undoubtedly often the case, Mr. Khan is in the difficult position of having to prove racial profiling by showing that the police have lied.

The trial judge ultimately found that the officers had lied about the reason they stopped the accused and that he was the victim of racial profiling. Khan was acquitted. The charges against Mr. Jackson were ultimately stayed.

(g) Character of Victim

Chief Justice Cardozo sought to justify a difference in treatment of character evidence depending on whether it was of the accused or the victim:

> In a very real sense a defendant starts his life afresh when he stands before a jury, a prisoner at the bar. There has been a homicide in a public place. The killer admits the killing, but urges self-defence and sudden impulse. Inflexibly the law has set its face against the endeavour to fasten guilt upon him by proof of character or experience predisposing to an act of crime. At times, when the issue has been self-defence, testimony has been admitted as to the murderous propensity of the deceased, the victim of the homicide, but never of such a propensity on the part of the killer. The principle back of the exclusion is one, not of logic, but of policy. There may be cogency in the argument that a quarrelsome defendant is more likely to start a quarrel than one of a milder type, a man of dangerous mode of life more likely than a shy recluse. The law is not blind to this, but equally it is not blind to the peril of the innocent if character is accepted as probative of crime. "The natural and inevitable tendency of the tribunal — whether judge or jury — is to give excessive weight to the vicious record of crime thus exhibited, and either to allow it to bear too strongly on the present charge, or to take the proof of it as justifying a condemnation irrespective of guilt of the present charge."[72]

Are you satisfied with this justification?

(i) Self-defence

The accused is charged with murder and he offers self-defence as a justification. The accused testifies that he viewed the deceased's actions as threatening since he believed him to be a violent man. The accused offers in evidence the deceased's character, his reputation and his violent acts to support his defence.

Earlier in this chapter we discussed character evidence as admissible for a non-character purpose. We used this example to show that the evidence

---

[72]   *People v. Zackowitz*, 172 N.E. 466 (1930). The quotation in this excerpt is from 1 Wigmore, *Evidence*, s. 194.

would be relevant not to establish that the deceased is a violent person but instead for the purpose of assessing the reasonableness of the accused's state of mind.

Suppose, however, that in the manslaughter case the deceased's character or disposition towards violence was not known to the accused at the time of the incident.

In this case we ask the trier to infer that the persons acted in conformity with their character. Since here we are offering the character evidence as circumstantial evidence from which we ask the trier of fact to infer that the victim acted in conformity with his character, a problem of relevance arises. The law provides no answer to such a problem. Rather, we must rely on our common sense and experience to guide us.

In *R. v. Scopelliti* [73] the accused was charged with two counts of murder. The principal defence was self-defence. The accused testified to his apprehension caused by the deceased's actions. The trial judge allowed the defence to introduce evidence of three prior acts of violence or threats of violence, *not known to the accused*, committed by the deceased and directed at other persons. On appeal from the acquittal the Ontario Court of Appeal, presented with no authorities on the issue, reasoned from basic principles:

> ... the admission of such evidence accords in principle with the view expressed by this Court that the disposition of a person to do a certain act is relevant to indicate the probability of his having done or not having done the act. The law prohibits the prosecution from introducing evidence for the purpose of showing that the *accused* is a person who by reason of his criminal character (disposition) is likely to have committed the crime charged, on policy grounds, not because of lack of relevance. There is, however, no rule of policy which excludes evidence of the disposition of a third person for violence where that disposition has probative value on some issue before the jury. [74]

Interestingly, the Court, following Wigmore, [75] saw "no substantial reason against evidencing the character by particular instances of violent or quarrelsome conduct". While not necessary to its decision, the Court went on to hold that in a case such as this the Crown would be entitled to rebut the defence evidence by character evidence showing the deceased to be of a peaceable disposition. [76]

---

[73] (1981), 63 C.C.C. (2d) 481 (Ont. C.A.). *Scopelliti* has been frequently followed: see e.g. *R. v. Hamilton*, 2003 BCCA 490, 180 C.C.C. (3d) 80 (B.C. C.A.) and *R. v. Varga* (2001), 159 C.C.C. (3d) 502, 48 C.R. (5th) 387 (Ont. C.A.). In *R. v. Borden*, 2017 NSCA 45, 349 C.C.C. (3d) 162, 37 C.R. (7th) 430 (N.S. C.A.), the Court affirmed the principles in *Scopelliti* and held that in a self-defence case involving an assault short of a homicide, the accused has an automatic right to cross-examine the complainant on his or her violent antecedents.

[74] *Scopelliti, ibid.* at 493.

[75] 1 Wigmore, *Evidence* (3rd ed.), s. 198.

[76] See the discussion of this issue, including whether evidence of a victim's peaceable disposition is admissible in self-defence cases not involving an attack on the victim's character, in cases such as *R. v. Diu* (2000), 144 C.C.C. (3d) 481, 33 C.R. (5th) 203 (Ont. C.A.) at 498-503 [C.C.C.] and *R. v. Dejong* (1998), 125 C.C.C. (3d) 302, 16 C.R. (5th) 372 (B.C. C.A.) at 323-326 [C.C.C.]. See too, Uniform Law Conference of Canada, *Report of the Federal/Provincial Task Force on Uniform Rules of Evidence* (Toronto: Carswell, 1982) at 91 and Nate Jackson, "*Scopelleti* Applications and Trial Fairness: A Comment on *R. v. Jackson*" (2014) 18 Can. Crim. L.R. 331.

Recognizing that evidence of the victim's character for violence is relevant to whether he or she was the aggressor on the occasion under review, is there any policy presented that might argue for exclusion?

In *Scopelliti* the Court recognized the need for a weighing by the trial judge of the probative worth of the evidence against the possibility of an irrational decision by the jury:

> Since evidence of prior acts of violence by the deceased is likely to arouse feelings of hostility against the deceased, there must inevitably be some element of discretion in the determination whether the proferred evidence has sufficient probative value for the purpose for which it is tendered to justify its admission.[77]

(ii) *Sexual Assault*

When dealing with evidence of the alleged victim's character in sexual assault cases there are hazards. Professor Estrich describes the difficulties of teaching in this area.[78] She writes:

> I know many students, and even a few professors, who believe that the women are always right and the men are always wrong; that if she didn't consent fully and voluntarily, it is rape, no matter what she said or did, or what he did or did not realize. Everything about his past should be admitted, and nothing about hers. And that's what they want to hear in class.
>
> This kind of orthodoxy is not only bad educationally but, in the case of rape, it also misses the point. Society is not so orthodox in its views. There is a debate going on in courthouses and prosecutors' offices, and around coffee machines and dinner tables, about whether Mike Tyson was guilty or not, and whether William Kennedy Smith ever should have been prosecuted; about when women should be believed, and what counts as consent. There's a debate going on in America as to what is reasonable when it comes to sex. Turn on the radio and you will hear it. To silence that debate in the classroom is to remove the classroom from reality, and to make ourselves irrelevant. It may be hard for some students, but ultimately the only way to change things — and that's usually the goal of those who find the discussions most difficult — is to confront the issues squarely, not to pretend that they don't exist. Besides, the purpose of education, in my classes anyway, is to prepare our students to participate in the controversies that animate the law, not to provide them with a shelter from reality.
>
> . . .
>
> Judges and juries these days are less inclined to accept male conduct that only a few years ago was tolerated as understandably macho. I don't find as many students in my classes these days who believe that a man has the right to ignore the fact that a woman is saying no. And I don't think the reason for this change is that feminists have defined what is "politically correct" in the classroom; I think instead that most of my students, male and female, actually believe that a man should listen to a woman's words, and take her at her word.
>
> This shift in our thinking about the elements of culpability leaves credibility as the only defense game in town. After all, rapes rarely take place in front of witnesses. If no doesn't mean yes, if bruises aren't necessary, and if no unusual

---

77   *Scopelliti, supra* note 73 at 496. See also *R. v. Yaeck* (1991), 10 C.R. (4th) 1, 23 (Ont. C.A.).
78   Susan Estrich, "Teaching Rape Law" (1992) Yale L.J. 509. See also Tomkovicx, "On Teaching Rape: Reasons, Risks and Rewards" (1992) Yale L.J. 481.

force is required, then in many cases there's not going to be much physical evidence to rely on. She gives her version and he gives his. If you are the defense attorney, your job is to convince the jury not to believe what she says — which means that the only way to defend may be to destroy the credibility of the victim.

The key question in many acquaintance rape cases today thus becomes not what counts as rape but rather what we need to know about the victim, and the defendant, in order to decide who is telling the truth.

. . .

It is one thing to exclude evidence of a woman's sexual past or of psychiatric treatment when she has been beaten and burned; it is easy to argue there that admitting such evidence does almost nothing except to deter legitimate prosecutions and to victimize the victim. But it is surely a harder case when there have been no weapons and no bruises, and when the man's liberty depends on convincing a jury not to believe a woman who appears at least superficially credible.

Many of the traditional rules of rape liability were premised on the notion that women lie; Wigmore went so far as to view rape complainants as fundamentally deranged. I don't buy that for a moment nor, I expect, do most of my students. Yet even if only one of a hundred men, or one of a thousand, is falsely accused, the question is still how we can protect that man's right to disprove his guilt. Assume for a moment, I tell my students, that it was you, or your brother, or your boyfriend or your son, who was accused of rape by a casual date with a history of psychiatric problems, or by a woman he met in a bar who had a history of one-night stands. Would you exclude that evidence? What else can the man do to avoid a felony conviction and a ruined life? Where do you draw the line? But if you don't exclude the evidence, will some women as a result become unrapable, at least as a matter of law? That is, will women who have histories of mental instability or of "promiscuity" ever be able to convince juries who know those histories that they really were raped?

Similar issues arise with respect to the man's credibility. The first question many people asked when Anita Hill charged that Clarence Thomas had harassed her was whether there were other women who had been similarly mistreated. The first significant ruling in the Smith case, indeed the decisive ruling, was the judge's pretrial decision to exclude the testimony of three other women who claimed that they had been sexually abused by the defendant. If the testimony of only one woman cannot be believed — unless she is a Sunday school teacher, camera in hand, as Desiree Washington was, and the defendant is a black man who has made a host of inconsistent statements, as Mike Tyson did — is it fair to exclude the testimony of the other women? And if the testimony is not excluded, do we risk convicting a defendant for being a bad man, indeed being a rapist, rather than committing the particular act charged?

One answer is to say that we need symmetry: exclude all the evidence about both of them. That's the approach the judge followed in the William Kennedy Smith case. On the surface, it is neat and appealing. The only problem is that it's a false symmetry that is being enforced. After all, evidence that a man has abused other women is much more probative of rape than evidence that a woman has had consensual sex with other men is probative of consent. Most women have had sexual experiences, and unless those experiences fall into some kind of unusual pattern, the mere fact that a woman has had lovers tells us almost nothing about whether she consented on the particular occasion that she is charging as rape. But won't we all look at a defendant differently if three other women have also come forward to say they were abused? The danger with such evidence is not that it proves so little, but that it may prove too much. Symmetry won't get you out of this hole, at least not in my classroom.

Thus, even if most students can agree these days that no means no, and that force can be established if you push a woman down, there's very little agreement about what we need to know about her or him before deciding whether she in fact said yes or no, and whether he actually pushed her down or just lay down with her. The consensus on what counts as rape is more apparent than real. These days, society's continued ambivalence towards acquaintance rape is increasingly being expressed in evidentiary rules and standards of credibility rather than in the definitions of force and consent. The questions have shifted; answering them is no easier.[79]

Historically, prior sexual history was characterized as character evidence because, as we will see in the next section, triers of fact were invited to use it to make an evaluative or moral judgment about the complainant. Is it still appropriate today to refer to prior sexual history as character evidence? If so, would other human functions such as sleeping or eating be classified as character evidence? **Is it now more appropriate to refer to prior sexual history evidence as conduct or circumstantial evidence from which relevant inferences may possibly be drawn?**

Common Law

The position at common law regarding evidence of the character of the alleged victim in sexual assault cases was summarized by the English Court of Appeal in *R. v. Krausz*:[80]

It is settled law that she who complains of rape or attempted rape can be cross-examined about (1) her general reputation and moral character, (2) sexual intercourse between herself and the defendant on other occasions, and (3) sexual intercourse between herself and other men; and that evidence can be called to contradict her on (1) and (2) but that no evidence can be called to contradict her denials of (3).

The common law regarded evidence of (1) and (2) as relevant to the material issue of consent[81] but evidence of (3) as irrelevant to the issue of consent but relevant to credit. As (3) was only relevant to credit the matter was collateral and the witness could not be contradicted. Osler J.A. in the Ontario Court of Appeal remarked:

---

[79]   Estrich, *ibid.* at 515-520.

[80]   (1973), 57 Cr. App. R. 466 at 472. See *R. v. Finnessey* (1906), 11 O.L.R. 338 (C.A.) at 341 for a similar outline of the common law. And see *R. v. Basken* (1974), 21 C.C.C. (2d) 321 (Sask. C.A.) at 337, approving this description. See also *Gross v. Brodrecht* (1897), 24 O.A.R. 687 (C.A.).

[81]   For examples of cases where evidence of the complainant's reputation and general habits for promiscuity was received, see *R. v. Krausz* (1973), 57 Cr. App. R. 466; *R. v. Barker* (1829), 172 E.R. 558 (N.P.); and *R. v. Bashir*, [1969] 3 All E.R. 692 (Q.B.).

. . . she may be asked, but, inasmuch as the question is one going strictly to her credit, she is not generally compellable to answer whether she has had connection with persons other than the prisoner. This seems to rest to some extent in the discretion of the trial Judge. Whether, however, she answers it or not that is an end of the matter, otherwise as many collateral, and therefore irrelevant issues might be raised as there were specific charges of immorality suggested, and the prosecutrix could not be expected to come prepared to meet them, though she might well be prepared to repel an attack upon her general character for chastity.[82]

While most of the older authorities state that sexual history with persons other than the accused is irrelevant to the issue of consent, can it be argued that on our understanding of the meaning of the term "relevant" (i.e., "does the evidence offered render the desired inference more probable than it would be without the evidence?"), the evidence may, in exceptional cases, be relevant? Though relevant the evidence could nevertheless still be excluded because of considerations of fairness to the victim-witness and because of prejudice to the outcome of the trial through improper use of the evidence. Cardozo J. deplored the existence of the inflexible rule based on "irrelevancy" and argued for a discretion in the trial judge, who could assess probative worth against the dangers in his or her particular case.[83]

Arguments have been advanced, however, that prior sexual history with others is not relevant to the issue of consent. In a speech given on sexual harassment, Professor Catherine MacKinnon stated:

> The question of prior sexual history is one area in which the issue of sexual credibility is directly posed. Evidence of the defendant's sexual harassment of other women in the same institutional relation or setting is increasingly being considered admissible, and it should be. The other side of the question is whether evidence of a victim's prior sexual history should be discoverable or admissible, and it seems to me it should not be. Perpetrators often seek out victims with common qualities or circumstances or situations — we are fungible to them so long as we are similarly accessible — but victims do not seek out victimization at all, and their nonvictimized sexual behavior is no more relevant to an allegation of sexual force than is the perpetrator's consensual sex life, such as it may be.
>
> So far the leading case, consistent with the direction of rape law, has found that the victim's sexual history with other individuals is not relevant, although consensual history with the individual perpetrator may be.[84]

Professor Christine Boyle has argued:[85]

---

[82] In *R. v. Finnessey*, *supra* note 80 at 341. The historical development of the common law position is concisely presented in Julie Taylor, "Rape and Women's Credibility: Problems of Recantations and False Accusations Echoed in the Case of Cathleen Crowell Webb and Gary Dotson" (1987) 10 Harvard Women's L.J. 59 at 74-81.

[83] Cardozo, *The Nature of the Judicial Process* (1921) at 156. Wigmore argued for admissibility of the particular acts: 1 Wigmore, *Evidence* (3rd ed.), s. 200. See also Scutt, "Admissibility of Sexual History Evidence and Allegations in Rape Cases" (1979) 53 Aust. L.J. 817 and Bohmer Blumberg, "Twice Traumatized: The Rape Victim and the Court" (1975) 58 Judicature 391.

[84] MacKinnon, *Feminism Unmodified: Discourses on Life and Law* (1987) at 113.

[85] *Sexual Assault* (1984) at 137.

The tendency in this area has been, unfortunately, simply to assert or deny the relevance of the sexual activity of the complainant. One can appreciate the reluctance of those concerned about the abuse of such evidence in the past to concede its relevance in any context, but the problems have arisen with respect to the introduction of the evidence to suggest consent or to undermine the credibility of the complainant. Its use for these purposes is unjustifiable since the tests of relevance, common sense and human experience, suggest that people exercise choice over each sexual partner. Moreover, there is no evidence to suggest that sexual activity has any link with credibility.

An intermediate approach to this issue focuses on the assumptions underlying findings of relevance of the victim's prior sexual history. The position advanced is that, although evidence of prior sexual acts may be relevant in certain limited circumstances, the identification of those circumstances must be based on a re-evaluation of the assumptions upon which findings of relevance have traditionally been based.

Professor Adler explains the premise upon which the intermediate approach is based:

> According to one authority on evidence, "relevant" means that "any two facts to which it is applied are so related to each other that according to the common course of events one either taken by itself or in connection with other facts proves or renders probable the past, present or future existence or non-existence of another." Thus, if one "fact" is the complainant's sexual experience, and the other, her consent to intercourse on the occasion of the alleged rape, there must be a link of some sort between the two for evidence of the former to be relevant and hence admissible in court. In practice, such a link almost invariably involves some alleged or actual aspect of the complainant's past sexual behaviour which is argued to bear some similarity to the incident involved in the trial. The similarity may be in the mere fact of her having had sexual intercourse in the past, or additional factors inherent in the situation may be drawn upon to imply greater relevance.
>
> The main question currently open to judicial interpretation concerns the nature, logic and strength of such links. Few would wish to argue that a woman's past experience of consensual intercourse with her husband makes her more likely to have consented to another defendant. But where the line is to be drawn is far from clear, and without explicit guidelines, decisions in individual cases remain diverse and uneven.[86]

Professor Adler notes that one difficulty with leaving determinations of relevance of previous sexual history to the discretion of the trial judge is the subjectivity inherent in the exercise of discretion.

Compare the remarks of Susan Brownmiller in *Against Our Will:*[87]

> Not only is the victim's response during the act measured and weighed, her past sexual history is scrutinized under the theory that it relates to her "tendency to consent," or that it reflects on her credibility, her veracity, her predisposition to tell the truth or to lie. Or so the law says. As it works out in practice, juries

---

[86]   Adler, "The Relevance of Sexual History Evidence in Rape: Problems of Subjective Interpretation" (1985) Crim. L. Rev. 769 at 772.

[87]   (New York: Simon & Schuster, 1975) at 385-386.

presented with evidence concerning a woman's past sexual history make use of such information to form a moral judgment on her character, and here all the old myths of rape are brought into play, for the feeling persists that a virtuous woman either cannot get raped or does not get into situations that leave her open to assault. Thus the questions in the jury room become "Was she or wasn't she asking for it?"; "If she had been a decent woman, wouldn't she have fought to death to defend her 'treasure'?"; and "Is this bimbo worth the ruination of a man's career and reputation?"

The crime of rape must be totally separated from all traditional concepts of chastity, for the very meaning of chastity presupposes that it is a woman's duty (but not a man's) to refrain from sex outside the matrimonial union. That sexual activity renders a woman "unchaste" is a totally male view of the female as *his* pure vessel. The phrase "prior chastity" as well as the concept must be stricken from the legal lexicon, along with "prosecutrix," as inflammatory and prejudicial to a complainant's case.

A history of sexual activity with many partners may be indicative of a female's healthy interest in sex, or it may be indicative of a chronic history of victimization and exploitation in which she could not assert her own inclinations; it may be indicative of a spirit of adventure, a spirit of rebellion, a spirit of curiosity, a spirit of joy or a spirit of defeat. Whatever the reasons, and there are many, prior consensual intercourse between a rape complainant and other partners of her choosing should not be scrutinized as an indicator of purity or impurity of mind or body, not in this day and age at any rate, and it has no place in jury room deliberation as to whether or not, in the specific instance in question, an act of forcible sex took place. Prior consensual intercourse between the complainant and *the defendant* does have some relevance and such information probably should not be barred.

An overhaul of present laws and a fresh approach to sexual assault legislation must go hand in hand with a fresh approach to enforcing the law. The question of who interprets and who enforces the statutes is as important as the contents of the law itself. At present, female victims of sexual crimes of violence who seek legal justice must rely on a series of male authority figures whose masculine orientation, values and fears place them securely in the offender's camp.

Charter of Rights

R. v. SEABOYER
[1991] 2 S.C.R. 577, 7 C.R. (4th) 117, 66 C.C.C. (3d) 321

The accused were each charged with sexual assault. At their preliminary hearings they sought to cross-examine the respective complainants with respect to their previous sexual conduct. In each case the judge ruled that such cross-examination was foreclosed by the *Criminal Code*. Each accused applied to the Supreme Court for an order quashing their committals for trial on the ground that the judge, in enforcing the then-existing ss. 276 and 277 of the *Criminal Code*, had exceeded his jurisdiction and deprived the accused of his right to make full answer and defence. The orders were granted on the ground that ss. 276 and 277 violated the *Charter of Rights and Freedoms*.

The cases were remitted to the preliminary inquiry judges for a ruling on the evidentiary issues unhampered by the statutory provisions. An appeal to the Court of Appeal was allowed on the ground that the preliminary inquiry judges lacked the jurisdiction to determine the constitutional validity of the impugned sections and accordingly had not erred in applying the sections. The Court of Appeal went on however to consider the constitutional validity of the sections. The majority of the Court held that s. 276 was capable of contravening an accused's rights under the *Charter* in some circumstances. The majority held that the section would generally be operative and the appropriate course was for the trial judge to decline to apply it in those limited and rare instances where it could lead to a *Charter* breach. The accused appealed. On the appeal, constitutional questions were stated putting in issue the constitutional validity of ss. 276 and 277.

McLACHLIN J. (LAMER C.J.C., LA FOREST, SOPINKA, CORY, STEVENSON and IACOBUCCI JJ. concurring):—

. . .

These cases raise the issue of the constitutionality of ss. 276 and 277 of the *Criminal Code*, . . . commonly known as the "rape-shield" provisions. The provisions restrict the right of the defence on a trial for a sexual offence to cross-examine and lead evidence of a complainant's sexual conduct on other occasions. The question is whether these restrictions offend the guarantees accorded to an accused person by the *Canadian Charter of Rights and Freedoms*.

My conclusion is that one of the sections in issue, s. 276, offends the *Charter*. While its purpose—the abolition of outmoded, sexist-based use of sexual conduct evidence—is laudable, its effect goes beyond what is required or justified by that purpose. At the same time, striking down s. 276 does not imply reversion to the old common law rules, which permitted evidence of the complainant's sexual conduct even though it might have no probative value to the issues on the case and, on the contrary, might mislead the jury. Instead, relying on the basic principles that actuate our law of evidence, the courts must seek a middle way that offers the maximum protection to the complainant compatible with the maintenance of the accused's fundamental right to a fair trial.

. . .

I deal first with *Seaboyer*. The accused was charged with sexual assault of a woman with whom he had been drinking in a bar. On the preliminary inquiry the judge refused to allow the accused to cross-examine the complainant on her sexual conduct on other occasions. The appellant contends that he should have been permitted to cross-examine as to other acts of sexual intercourse which may have caused bruises and other aspects of the complainant's condition which the Crown had put in evidence. While the theory of the defence has not been detailed at this early stage, such evidence might arguably be relevant to consent, since it might provide other explanations for the physical evidence tendered by the Crown in support of the use of force against the complainant.

The *Gayme* case arose in different circumstances. The complainant was 15, the appellant 18. They were friends. The Crown alleges that the appellant sexually assaulted her at his school. The defence, relying on the defences of consent and honest belief in consent, contends that there was no assault and that the complainant was the sexual aggressor. In pursuance of this defence, the appellant at the preliminary inquiry sought to cross-examine and present evidence of prior and subsequent sexual conduct of the complainant. . .

. . .

It should be noted that the admissibility of the evidence sought to be tendered in the two cases is not at issue. In neither case did the preliminary inquiry judge consider whether the evidence would have been relevant or admissible in the absence of ss. 276 or 277 of the *Criminal Code*.

Relevant Legislation

Criminal Code, s. 276:

276. (1) In proceedings in respect of an offence under section 271, 272 or 273, no evidence shall be adduced by or on behalf of the accused concerning the sexual activity of the complainant with any person other than the accused unless

(*a*) it is evidence that rebuts evidence of the complainant's sexual activity or absence thereof that was previously adduced by the prosecution;

(*b*) it is evidence of specific instances of the complainant's sexual activity tending to establish the identity of the person who had sexual contact with the complainant on the occasion set out in the charge; or

(*c*) it is evidence of sexual activity that took place on the same occasion as the sexual activity that forms the subject-matter of the charge, where that evidence relates to the consent that the accused alleges he believed was given by the complainant.

(2) No evidence is admissible under paragraph (1)(*c*) unless

(*a*) reasonable notice in writing has been given to the prosecutor by or on behalf of the accused of his intention to adduce the evidence together with particulars of the evidence sought to be adduced; and

(*b*) a copy of the notice has been filed with the clerk of the court.

(3) No evidence is admissible under subsection (1) unless the judge, provincial court judge or justice, after holding a hearing in which the jury and the members of the public are excluded and in which the complainant is not a compellable witness, is satisfied that the requirements of this section are met.

Criminal Code, s. 277:

277. In proceedings in respect of an offence under section 271, 272 or 273, evidence of sexual reputation, whether general or specific, is not admissible for the purpose of challenging or supporting the credibility of the complainant.

. . .

Everyone, under s. 7 of the *Charter*, has the right to life, liberty and security of person and the right not to be deprived thereof except in accordance with the principles of fundamental justice.

. . .

The real issue under s. 7 is whether the potential for deprivation of liberty flowing from ss. 276 and 277 takes place in a manner that conforms to the principles of fundamental justice.

. . .

All the parties agree that the right to a fair trial—one which permits the trier of fact to get at the truth and properly and fairly dispose of the case—is a principle of fundamental justice. Nor is there any dispute that encouraging reporting of sexual offences and protection of the complainant's privacy are legitimate goals provided they do not interfere with the primary objective of a fair trial. Where the parties part company is on the issue of whether ss. 276 and 277 of the *Criminal Code* in fact infringe the right to a fair trial. The supporters of the legislation urge that it furthers the right to a fair trial by eliminating evidence of little or no worth and considerable prejudice. The appellants, on the other hand, say that the legislation goes too far and in fact eliminates relevant evidence which should be admitted notwithstanding the possibility of prejudice.

. . .

[Here the Supreme Court set out the scope of a trial judge's discretion to exclude evidence including defence evidence. In the latter case, the prejudicial effect of the evidence must substantially outweigh its probative value. This was reviewed in Chapter 3.]

. . .

Section 277 excludes evidence of sexual reputation for the purpose of challenging or supporting the credibility of the plaintiff. The idea that a complainant's credibility might be affected by whether she has had other sexual experience is today universally discredited. There is no logical or practical link between a woman's sexual reputation and whether she is a truthful witness. It follows that the evidence excluded by s. 277 can serve no legitimate purpose in the trial. Section 277, by limiting the exclusion to a purpose which is clearly illegitimate, does not touch evidence which may be tendered for valid purposes, and hence does not infringe the right to a fair trial.

I turn then to s. 276. Section 276, unlike s. 277, does not condition exclusion on use of the evidence for an illegitimate purpose. Rather, it constitutes a blanket exclusion, subject to three exceptions—rebuttal evidence, evidence going to identity, and evidence relating to consent to sexual activity on the same occasion as the trial incident. The question is whether this may exclude evidence which is relevant to the defence and the probative value of which is not substantially outweighed by the potential prejudice to the trial process. To put the matter another way, can it be said *a priori*, as the Attorney General for Ontario contends, that any and all evidence excluded by s. 276 will necessarily be of such trifling weight in relation to the prejudicial effect of the evidence that it may fairly be excluded?

In my view, the answer to this question must be negative. The Canadian and American jurisprudence affords numerous examples of evidence of sexual conduct which would be excluded by s. 276 but which clearly should be received in the interests of a fair trial, notwithstanding the possibility that it may divert a jury by tempting it to improperly infer consent or lack of credibility in the complainant.

Consider the defence of honest belief. It rests on the concept that the accused may honestly but mistakenly (and not necessarily reasonably) have believed that the complainant was consenting to the sexual act. If the accused can raise a reasonable doubt as to his intention on the basis that he honestly held such a belief, he is not guilty under our law and is entitled to an acquittal. The basis of the accused's honest belief in the complainant's consent may be sexual acts performed by the complainant at some other time or place. Yet section 276 would preclude the accused leading such evidence.

Another category of evidence eliminated by s. 276 relates to the right of the defence to attack the credibility of the complainant on the ground that the complainant was biased or had motive to fabricate the evidence. In *State v. Jalo*, 557 P.2d 1359 (Or. Ct. App. 1976), a father accused of sexual acts with his young daughter sought to present evidence that the source of the accusation was his earlier discovery of the fact that the girl and her brother were engaged in intimate relations. The defence contended that when the father stopped the relationship, the daughter, out of animus toward him, accused him of the act. The father sought to lead this evidence in support of his defence that the charges were a concoction motivated by animus. Notwithstanding its clear relevance, this evidence would be excluded by s. 276. The respondent submits that the damage caused by its exclusion would not be great, because all that would be forbidden would be evidence of the sexual activities of the children, and the father could still testify that his daughter was angry with him. But surely the father's chance of convincing the jury of the validity of his defence would be greatly diminished if he were reduced to saying, in effect, "My daughter was angry with me, but I can't say why or produce any corroborating evidence." As noted above, to deny a defendant the building blocks of his defence is often to deny him the defence itself.

Other examples abound. Evidence of sexual activity excluded by s. 276 may be relevant to explain the physical conditions on which the Crown relies to establish intercourse or the use of force, such as semen, pregnancy, injury or disease—evidence which may go to consent:. . . In the case of young complainants where there may be a tendency to believe their story on the ground that the detail of their account must have come from the alleged encounter, it may be relevant to show other activity which provides an explanation for the knowledge: . . .

Even evidence as to pattern of conduct may on occasion be relevant. Since this use of evidence of prior sexual conduct draws upon the inference that prior conduct infers similar subsequent conduct, it closely resembles the prohibited use of the evidence and must be carefully scrutinized: . . . Yet such evidence might be admissible in non-sexual cases under the similar fact rule. Is it fair then to deny it to an accused, merely because the trial relates to a sexual offence? . . .

. . .

These examples leave little doubt that s. 276 has the potential to exclude evidence of critical relevance to the defence. Can it honestly be said, as the Attorney General for Ontario contends, that the value of such evidence will always be trifling when compared with its potential to mislead the jury? I think not. The examples show that the evidence may well be of great importance to getting at the truth and determining whether the accused is guilty or innocent under the law—the ultimate aim of the trial process. They demonstrate that s. 276, enacted for the purpose of helping judges and juries arrive at the proper and just verdict in the particular case, overshoots the mark, with the result that it may have the opposite effect of impeding them in discovering the truth.

. . .

2. *Is s. 276 Saved by s. 1 of the Charter?*

Is s. 276 of the *Criminal Code* justified in a free and democratic society, notwithstanding the fact that it may lead to infringements of the *Charter*?

The first step under s. 1 is to consider whether the legislation addresses a pressing and substantial objective: . . .

The second requirement under s. 1 is that the infringement of rights be proportionate to the pressing objective. . . In creating exceptions to the exclusion of evidence of the sexual activity of the complainant on other occasions, Parliament correctly recognized that justice requires a measured approach, one which admits evidence which is truly relevant to the defence notwithstanding potential prejudicial effect. Yet Parliament at the same time excluded other evidence of sexual conduct which might be equally relevant to a legitimate defence and which appears to pose no greater danger of prejudice than the exceptions it recognizes. To the extent the section excludes relevant defence evidence whose value is not clearly outweighed by the danger it presents, the section is overbroad.

I turn finally to the third aspect of the proportionality requirement — the balance between the importance of the objective and the injurious effect of the legislation. The objective of the legislation, as discussed above, is to eradicate the erroneous inferences from evidence of other sexual encounters that the complainant is more likely to have consented to the sexual act in issue or less likely to be telling the truth. The subsidiary aims are to promote fairer trials and increased reporting of sexual offences and to minimize the invasion of the complainant's privacy. In this way the personal security of women and their right to equal benefit and protection of the law are enhanced. The effect of the legislation, on the other hand, is to exclude relevant defence evidence, the value of which outweighs its potential prejudice. As indicated in the discussion of s. 7, all parties agree that a provision which rules out probative defence evidence which is not clearly outweighed by the prejudice it may cause to the trial strikes the wrong balance between the rights of complainants and the rights of the accused. The line must be drawn short of the point where it results in an unfair trial and the possible conviction of an innocent person. Section 276 fails this test.

I conclude that s. 276 is not saved by s. 1 of the Charter.

. . .

4. *What Follows From Striking Down s. 276?*

The first question is whether the striking down of s. 276 revives the old common law rules of evidence permitting liberal and often inappropriate reception of evidence of the complainant's sexual conduct. . .

The answer to this question is no. The rules in question are common law rules. Like other common law rules of evidence, they must be adapted to conform to current reality. As all counsel on these appeals accepted, the reality in 1991 is that evidence of sexual conduct and reputation in itself cannot be regarded as logically probative of either the complainant's credibility or consent. Although they still may inform the thinking of many, the twin myths which s. 276 sought to eradicate are just that—myths—and have no place in a rational and just system of law. It follows that the old rules which permitted evidence of sexual conduct and condoned invalid inferences from it solely for these purposes have no place in our law.

The inquiry as to what the law is in the absence of s. 276 of the *Code* is thus remitted to consideration of the fundamental principles governing the trial process and the reception of evidence. Harking back to Thayer's maxim, relevant evidence should be admitted, and irrelevant evidence excluded, subject to the qualification that the value of the evidence must outweigh its potential prejudice to the conduct of a fair trial. Moreover, the focus must be not on the evidence itself, but on the use to which it is put. As Professor Galvin puts it, our aim is "to abolish the outmoded, sexist-based use of sexual conduct evidence while permitting other uses of such evidence to remain": *supra*, at p. 809.

This definition of the problem suggests an approach which abolishes illegitimate uses and inferences, while preserving legitimate uses. There is wide agreement that the approach of a general exclusion supplemented by categories of exceptions is bound to fail because of the impossibility of predicting in advance what evidence may be relevant in a particular case: see Galvin, *supra*, Doherty, *supra*, and Elliott, *supra*. On the other hand, judges are not free to act on whim. As Professor Vivian Berger puts it in her article "Man's Trial, Woman's Tribulation:Rape Cases in the Courtroom" (1977), 77 *Colum. L. Rev.* 1, at p. 69:

> The problem is to chart a course between inflexible legislative rules and wholly untrammelled judicial discretion: The former threatens the rights of defendants; the latter may ignore the needs of complainants.

. . .

Galvin's proposal, with some modification, reflects an appropriate response to the problem of avoiding illegitimate inferences from evidence of the complainant's sexual conduct, while preserving the general right to a fair trial. It is, moreover, a response which is open to trial judges in the absence of legislation. It reflects, in essence, an application of the fundamental common law notions which govern the reception of evidence on trials. The general prohibition on improper use of evidence of sexual conduct reflects the fact that it is always open to a judge to warn against using a particular piece of evidence for an inference on an issue for which that evidence has no probative force. Similarly, the mandate to the judge to determine when the evidence may be properly receivable is a reflection of the basic function of the trial judge of determining the relevance of evidence and whether it should be received, bearing in mind the balance between its probative value and its potential prejudice.

As for the procedures which should govern the determination of whether the sexual conduct evidence should be admitted, Galvin proposes a written motion followed by an in camera hearing. The devices of a preliminary affidavit and an in camera hearing are designed to minimize the invasion of the complainant's privacy. If the affidavit does not show the evidence to be relevant, it will not be heard at all. Where this threshold is met, the evidence will be heard in camera so that, in the event the judge finds its value is outweighed by its potential prejudice, it will not enter the public domain. Such procedures do not require legislation. It has always been open to the Courts to devise such procedures as may be necessary to ensure a fair trial. The requirements of a voir dire before a confession can be admitted, for example, is judge-made law.

While accepting the premise and the general thrust of Galvin's proposal, I suggest certain modifications. There seems little purpose in having separate rules for the use of sexual conduct evidence for illegitimate inferences of consent and credibility in the Canadian context. Again, I question whether evidence of other sexual conduct with the accused should automatically be admissible in all cases; sometimes the value of such evidence might be little or none. The word "complainant" is more compatible with the presumption of innocence of the accused than the word "victim". Professor Galvin's reference to the defence of reasonable belief in consent must be adapted to meet Canadian law, which does not require reasonableness. And the need to warn the jury clearly against improper uses of the evidence should be emphasized, in my view.

In the absence of legislation, it is open to this Court to suggest guidelines for the reception and use of sexual conduct evidence. Such guidelines should be seen for what they are—an attempt to describe the consequences of the application of the general rules of evidence governing relevance and the reception of evidence—and not as judicial legislation cast in stone.

In my view the trial judge under this new regime shoulders a dual responsibility. First, the judge must assess with a high degree of sensitivity whether the evidence proffered by the defence meets the test of demonstrating a degree of relevance which outweighs the damages and disadvantages presented by the admission of such evidence. The examples presented earlier suggest that while cases where such evidence will carry sufficient probative value will exist, they will be exceptional. The trial judge must ensure that evidence is tendered for a legitimate purpose, and that it logically supports a defence. The fishing expeditions which unfortunately did occur in the past should not be permitted. The trial judge's discretion must be exercised to ensure that neither the *in camera* procedure nor the trial become forums for demeaning and abusive conduct by defence counsel.

The trial judge's second responsibility will be to take special care to ensure that, in the exceptional case where circumstances demand that such evidence be permitted, the jury is fully and properly instructed as to its appropriate use. The jurors must be cautioned that they should not draw impermissible inferences from evidence of previous sexual activity. While such evidence may be tendered for a purpose logically probative of the defence to be presented, it may be important to remind jurors that they not allow the allegations of past sexual activity to lead them to the view that the complainant is less worthy of belief, or was more likely to have consented for that reason. It is hoped that a sensitive and responsive exercise of discretion by the judiciary will reduce and even eliminate the concerns which provoked legislation such as s. 276, while at the same time preserving the right of an accused to a fair trial.

I would summarize the applicable principles as follows:

1. On a trial for a sexual offence, evidence that the complainant has engaged in consensual sexual conduct on other occasions (including past sexual conduct with the accused) is not admissible solely to support the inference that the complainant is by reason of such conduct:

    (*a*) more likely to have consented to the sexual conduct at issue in the trial;

    (*b*) less worthy of belief as a witness.

2. Evidence of consensual sexual conduct on the part of the complainant may be admissible for purposes other than an inference relating to the consent or credibility of the complainant where it possesses probative value on an issue in the trial and where that probative value is not substantially outweighed by the danger of unfair prejudice flowing from the evidence.

    By way of illustration only, and not by way of limitation, the following are examples of admissible evidence:

    (A) Evidence of specific instances of sexual conduct tending to prove that a person other than the accused caused the physical consequences of the rape alleged by the prosecution;

    (B) Evidence of sexual conduct tending to prove bias or motive to fabricate on the part of the complainant;

    (C) Evidence of prior sexual conduct, known to the accused at the time of the act charged, tending to prove that the accused believed that the complainant was consenting to the act charged (without laying down absolute rules, normally one would expect some proximity in time between the conduct that is alleged to have given rise to an honest belief and the conduct charged);

    (D) Evidence of prior sexual conduct which meets the requirements for the reception of similar act evidence, bearing in mind that such evidence cannot be used illegitimately merely to show that the complainant consented or is an unreliable witness;

(E) Evidence tending to rebut proof introduced by the prosecution regarding the complainant's sexual conduct.

3. Before evidence of consensual sexual conduct on the part of a victim is received, it must be established on a *voir dire* (which may be held *in camera*) by affidavit or the testimony of the accused or third parties, that the proposed use of the evidence of other sexual conduct is legitimate.

4. Where evidence that the complainant has engaged in sexual conduct on other occasions is admitted on a jury trial, the judge should warn the jury against inferring from the evidence of the conduct itself, either that the complainant might have consented to the act alleged, or that the complainant is less worthy of credit.

[L'Heureux-Dubé J., Gonthier J. concurring, decided that s. 276 did not violate ss. 7 or 11(d) and, if it did, it would be saved by s. 1.]

L'HEUREUX-DUBÉ J. (GONTHIER J. concurring), dissenting in part:—

. . .

Sexual assault is not like any other crime. In the vast majority of cases the target is a woman and the perpetrator is a man. . . Unlike other crimes of a violent nature, it is for the most part unreported. Yet, by all accounts, women are victimized at an alarming rate and there is some evidence that an already frighteningly high rate of sexual assault is on the increase. The prosecution and conviction rates for sexual assault are among the lowest for all violent crimes. Perhaps more than any other crime, the fear and constant reality of sexual assault affects how women conduct their lives and how they define their relationship with the larger society. Sexual assault is not like any other crime.

. . .

There are a number of reasons why women may not report their victimization: fear of reprisal, fear of a continuation of their trauma at the hands of the police and the criminal justice system, fear of a perceived loss of status and lack of desire to report due to the typical effects of sexual assault such as depression, self-blame or loss of self-esteem. Although all of the reasons for failing to report are significant and important, more relevant to the present inquiry are the numbers of victims who choose not to bring their victimization to the attention of the authorities due to their perception that the institutions with which they would have to become involved will view their victimization in a stereotypical and biased fashion. . .

. . .

The woman who comes to the attention of the authorities has her victimization measured against the current rape mythologies, i.e., who she should be in order to be recognized as having been, in the eyes of the law, raped; who her attacker must be in order to be recognized, in the eyes of the law, as a potential rapist; and how injured she must be in order to be believed. If her victimization does not fit the myths, it is unlikely that an arrest will be made or a conviction obtained. As prosecutors and police often suggest, in an attempt to excuse their application of stereotype, there is no point in directing cases toward the justice system if juries and judges will acquit on the basis of their stereotypical perceptions of the "supposed victim" and her "supposed" victimization. . .

. . .

More specifically, police rely in large measure upon popular conceptions of sexual assault in order to classify incoming cases as "founded" or "unfounded". It would appear as though most forces have developed a convenient shorthand regarding their decisions to proceed in any given case. This shorthand is composed of popular myth regarding rapists (distinguishing them from men as a whole), and stereotype about women's character and sexuality. Holmstrom and Burgess, *supra*, at pp. 174-99, conveniently set out and explain the most common of these myths and stereotypes:

> 1. *Struggle and Force:Woman As Defender of Her Honor*. There is a myth that a woman cannot be raped against her will, that if she really wants to prevent a rape she can.
>
> The prosecution attempts to show that she did struggle, or had no opportunity to do so, while the defence attempts to show that she did not.

Women know that there is no response on their part that will assure their safety. The experience and knowledge of women is borne out by the *Canadian Urban Victimization Survey: Female Victims of Crime* (1985). At page 7 of the report the authors note:

> Sixty percent of those who tried reasoning with their attackers, and 60% of those who resisted actively by fighting or using weapon [*sic*] were injured. Every sexual assault incident is unique and so many factors are unknown (physical size of victims and offenders, verbal or physical threats, etc.) that no single course of action can be recommended unqualifiedly.
>
> 2. *Knowing the Defendant: The Rapist As a Stranger*. There is a myth that rapists are strangers who leap out of bushes to attack their victims. . . the view that interaction between friends or between relatives does not result in rape is prevalent.

The defence uses the existence of a relationship between the parties to blame the victim. . .

> 3. *Sexual Reputation: The Madonna-Whore Complex.* . . . women . . . are categorized into one-dimensional types. They are maternal or they are sexy. They are good or they are bad. They are madonnas or they are whores.

The legal rules use these distinctions.

> 4. *General Character: Anything Not 100 Percent Proper and Respectable.* . . . Being on welfare or drinking or drug use could be used to discredit anyone, but where women are involved, these issues are used to imply that the woman consented to sex with the defendant or that she contracted to have sex for money.
>
> 5. *Emotionality of Females*. Females are assumed to be 'more emotional' than males. The expectation is that if a woman is raped, she will get hysterical during

the event and she will be visibly upset afterward. If she is able to 'retain her cool,' then people assume that "nothing happened". . .

6. *Reporting Rape.* Two conflicting expectations exist concerning the reporting of rape. One is that if a woman is raped she will be too upset and ashamed to report it, and hence most of the time this crime goes unreported. The other is that if a woman is raped she will be so upset that she will report it. Both expectations exist simultaneously.

7. *Woman as Fickle and Full of Spite.* Another stereotype is that the feminine character is especially filled with malice. Woman is seen as fickle and as seeking revenge on past lovers.

8. *The Female Under Surveillance: Is the Victim Trying to Escape Punishment?* . . . It is assumed that the female's sexual behavior, depending on her age, is under the surveillance of her parents or her husband, and also more generally of the community. Thus, the defense argues, if a woman says she was raped it must be because she consented to sex that she was not supposed to have. She got caught, and now she wants to get back in the good graces of whomever's surveillance she is under.

9. *Disputing That Sex Occurred.* That females fantasize rape is another common stereotype. Females are assumed to make up stories that sex occurred when in fact nothing happened. . . Similarly, women are thought to fabricate the sexual activity not as part of a fantasy life, but out of spite.

10. *Stereotype of the Rapist.* One stereotype of the rapist is that of a stranger who leaps out of the bushes to attack his victim and later abruptly leaves her. . . stereotypes of the rapist can be used to blame the victim. She tells what he did. And because it often does not match what jurors think rapists do, his behavior is held against her.

. . .

This list of stereotypical conceptions about women and sexual assault is by no means exhaustive. Like most stereotypes, they operate as a way, however flawed, of understanding the world and, like most such constructs, operate at a level of consciousness that makes it difficult to root them out and confront them directly. This mythology finds its way into the decisions of the police regarding their "founded"/"unfounded" categorization, operates in the mind of the Crown when deciding whether or not to prosecute, influences a judge's or juror's perception of guilt or innocence of the accused and the "goodness" or "badness" of the victim, and finally, has carved out a niche in both the evidentiary and substantive law governing the trial of the matter.

. . .

Absolutely pivotal to an understanding of the nature and purpose of the provisions and constitutional questions at issue in this case is the realization of how widespread the stereotypes and myths about rape are, notwithstanding their inaccuracy.

The appellants argue that we, as a society, have become more enlightened, that prosecutors, police, judges and jurors can be trusted to perform their tasks without recourse to discriminatory views about women manifested through rape myth. Unfortunately, social science evidence suggests otherwise. Rape myths still present formidable obstacles for complainants in their dealings with the very system charged with discovering the truth. Their experience in this regard is illustrated by the following remarks of surprisingly recent vintage:

> Women who say no do not always mean no. It is not just a question of saying no, it is a question of how she says it, how she shows and makes it clear. If she doesn't want it she has only to keep her legs shut and she would not get it without force and there would be marks of force being used. (Judge David Wild, Cambridge Crown Court, 1982, quoted in Elizabeth Sheehy, "Canadian Judges and the Law of Rape: Should the Charter Insulate Bias?" (1989), 21 *Ottawa L. Rev.* 741, at p. 741.)

> Unless you have no worldly experience at all, you'll agree that women occasionally resist at first but later give in to either persuasion or their own instincts. (Judge Frank Allen, Manitoba Provincial Court, 1984, quoted in Sheehy, *supra*, at p. 741.)

> . . . it is easy for a man intent upon his own desires to mistake the intentions of a woman or girl who may herself be in two minds about what to do. Even if he makes no mistake it is not unknown for a woman afterwards either to take fright or for some other reason to regret what has happened and seek to justify herself retrospectively by accusing the man of rape. (Howard, *Criminal Law* (3rd ed. 1977), at p. 149.)

> Modern psychiatrists have amply studied the behavior of errant young girls and women coming before the courts in all sorts of cases. Their psychic complexes are multifarious, distorted partly by inherent defects, partly by diseased derangements or abnormal instincts, partly by bad social environment, partly by temporary physiological or emotional conditions. One form taken by these complexes is that of contriving false charges of sexual offenses by men. (Wigmore, *Evidence in Trials at Common Law*, vol. 3A (1970), at p. 736.)

Regrettably, these remarks demonstrate that many in society hold inappropriate stereotypical beliefs and apply them when the opportunity presents itself.

. . .

Traditional definitions of what is relevant include "whatever accords with common sense" (McWilliams, *Canadian Criminal Evidence* (3rd ed. 1990), at p. 3-5); " 'relevant' means that any two facts to which it is applied are so related to each other that according to the common course of events one either taken by itself or in connection with other facts proves or renders probable the past, present or future existence or non-existence of the other" (Stephens, *A Digest of the Law of Evidence* (12th ed. 1946), art. 1), and finally Thayer's "logically probative" test with relevance as an affair of logic and not of law, a test adopted by this Court in *Morris, infra.*

Whatever the test, be it one of experience, common sense or logic, it is a decision particularly vulnerable to the application of private beliefs. Regardless of the definition used, the content of any relevancy decision will be filled by the particular judge's experience, common sense and/or logic. For the most part there will be general agreement as to that which is relevant and the determination will not be problematic. However, there are certain areas of inquiry where experience, common sense and logic are informed by stereotype and myth. As I have made clear, this area of the law has been particularly prone to the utilization of stereotype in determinations of relevance and again, as was demonstrated earlier, this appears to be the unfortunate concomitant of a society which, to a large measure, holds these beliefs. It would also appear that recognition of the large role that stereotype may play in such determinations has had surprisingly little impact in this area of the law. . .

. . .

Once the mythical bases of relevancy determinations in this area of the law are revealed (discussed at greater length later in these reasons), the irrelevance of most evidence of prior sexual history is clear. Nevertheless, Parliament has provided broad avenues for its admissibility in the setting out of the exceptions to the general rule in s. 246.6 (now s. 276). Moreover, <u>all</u> evidence of the complainant's previous sexual history with the accused is *prima facie* admissible under those provisions. Evidence that is excluded by these provisions is simply, in a myth- and stereotype-free decision-making context, irrelevant.[88]

Most would agree that receiving evidence of the complainant's previous sexual history on a trial of sexual assault will so prejudice the trial that the same should rarely be admitted. **Did the Court draw the proper line?**

While striking down the complainant's statutory protection, the Court recognized the possibility that the then-existing common law rules could permit the inappropriate reception of evidence of the complainant's sexual conduct and the majority therefore changed the common law. The majority said it was suggesting "guidelines for the reception of sexual conduct evidence" and these were not to be seen as "judicial legislation cast in stone". Rather they were "an attempt to describe the consequences of the application of the general rules of evidence governing relevance and the reception of evidence". While the majority wrote that it was not legislating but only offering "guidelines", if the "guidelines" are the Supreme Court of Canada's thoughts on the common law of today, their expression differs little from the exercise of legislating. There will surely be no different result waiting for the trial judge who decides not to follow the guidelines.

The regime announced in *Seaboyer* offered greater protection to the complainant than did the legislative provision that was struck down. The old s. 276 forbade the introduction of evidence "concerning the sexual activity of the complainant with any person other than the accused". The common law had always recognized that previous sexual conduct with the accused was relevant to the issue of whether the complainant consented on the occasion under review. The majority's opinion "question[ed] whether evidence of other

---

[88] For comments on *Seaboyer* see Christine Boyle & Marilyn MacCrimmon, "*R. v. Seaboyer:* A Lost Cause?" (1992), 7 C.R. (4th) 225 and a reply by Anthony Allman in (1992), 10 C.R. (4th) 153. See too Paciocco, "Techniques for Eviscerating the Concept of Relevance" (1995), 33 C.R. (4th) 365.

sexual conduct with the accused should automatically be admissible in all cases; sometimes the value of such evidence might be little or none".

The majority in *Seaboyer* cited frequently and quoted heavily from Professor Galvin's article, "Shielding Rape Victims in the State and Federal Courts: A Proposal for the Second Decade". Galvin's proposed rape shield law, however, was confined to the exclusion of evidence of sexual conduct with persons other than the accused. The majority in *Seaboyer* wrote "Galvin's proposal, with some modification, reflects an appropriate response to the problem . . ." One "modification" eliminates the distinction regarding sexual conduct with the accused. This is a major modification. Professor Galvin wrote:

> Even the most ardent reformers acknowledged the high probative value of past sexual conduct in at least two instances. The first is when the defendant claims consent and establishes prior consensual relations between himself and the complainant. . . Although the evidence is offered to prove consent, its probative value rests on the nature of the complainant's specific mindset toward the accused rather than on her general unchaste character. . . All 25 statutes adopting the Michigan approach (to rape shield laws) allow the accused to introduce evidence of prior sexual conduct between himself and the complainant. The high probative value and minimal prejudicial effect of this evidence have been discussed.

But see research which suggests that "as the sexual intimacy of the couple increases, people are more likely to be focussed on the behaviour of the woman and question the validity of her claim".[89]

Another article quoted by the majority in *Seaboyer* is Professor Vivian Berger's "Man's Trial, Woman's Tribulation". Professor Berger justified the reception of evidence of sexual conduct with the accused in this way:

> The inference from past to present behaviour does not, as in cases of third party acts, rest on highly dubious beliefs about "women who do and women who don't" but rather relies on common sense and practical psychology. Admission of the proof supplies the accused with a circumstance making it probable that he did not obtain by violence what he might have secured by persuasion.

Another major modification to Galvin's proposal is with respect to so-called similar fact evidence. Galvin proposed that "evidence of a pattern of sexual conduct so distinctive and so closely resembling the accused's version of the alleged encounter with the victim as to tend to prove that the victim consented to the act charged" could be received. The majority in *Seaboyer* wrote that "similar fact evidence cannot be used illegitimately merely to show that the complainant consented", and where evidence of sexual conduct on other occasions is admitted the trial judge should warn the jury against this prohibited use. Why? This major modification of Galvin's proposal is not explained unless we are to take it as a given that previous sexual conduct of the complainant can never be indicative of a specific

---

[89]   Schuller & Klippenstine, "The Impact of Complaint Sexual History Evidence on Juror's Decisions: Considerations for a Psychological Perspective" (2004) 10 Psych. Pub. Pol. & Law 321.

propensity to have sexual intercourse, from which a trier could infer that she acted in conformity with that character.

Suppose the evidence is that the accused and complainant met in Sam's Bar one Saturday night and left to go to her apartment. It's agreed that sexual intercourse occurred but the parties disagree on the issue of consent. The accused's evidence is that he was sitting at the bar when the complainant approached him, offered him a drink and propositioned him. Should the accused be able to call Sam to testify that every Saturday night for the previous four weeks the complainant came into his bar, offered a stranger a drink, propositioned him and left in his company? Should Sam be permitted to testify that the complainant had been picking up these men because she is a working prostitute? He knows because he is her pimp and has been receiving a portion of her fees.

On the issue of receiving similar fact evidence tendered by the accused, Professor Berger wrote:

> What if the accused were offering to show that the victim habitually goes to bars on Saturday nights, picks up strangers and takes them home to bed with her, and that over the past 12 months she has done so on more than 20 occasions. Now could one assert with assurance that this particular sexual record does not substantially reinforce the defendant's version of the night's events? And if it does, should he not be permitted as a matter of constitutional right to place this evidence before the jury?

New Legislation — Bill C-49

Seaboyer produced an immediate outcry on the basis that it would mean that women and children would be even less likely to pursue charges of sexual assault given that there would be unrestricted cross-examination of their prior sexual history. Such comments were quite unfair to the majority of the Supreme Court of Canada. For the majority, Madam Justice McLachlin had been quite alive to the dangers of leaving this crucial issue to unfettered judicial discretion and had crafted what she considered to be careful guidelines as to the admissibility of such evidence. She had also extended the protection to prior sexual conduct with the accused. One of the sources of the vehement reaction was that the majority took but a line to hold that, although victims might have equality rights, these had to give way to the accused's right to make full answer and defence.

The response from the Minister of Justice, the Honourable Kim Campbell, was swift. She announced that Parliament would better respond to protect women and children. She called a meeting of national and regional women's groups and thereafter worked very closely with them in drafting and revising a Bill. The coalition of some 60 women's groups reached unanimity at each point and agreed to oppose any attempt to water down the Bill.

Bill C-49 was tabled on December 12, 1991. It was referred to committee after second reading on April 16, 1992. It quickly passed through the House of Commons and Senate and received Royal Assent on June 23, 1992. Bill C-49 was proclaimed to be in force on August 15, 1992.[90] The new s. 276, regarding the admissibility of evidence of the complainant's sexual activity, provides:

276. (1) In proceedings in respect of an offence under section 151, 152, 153, 155 or 159, subsection 160(2) or (3) or section 170, 171, 172, 173, 271, 272 or 273, evidence that the complainant has engaged in sexual activity, whether with the accused or with any other person, is not admissible to support an inference that, by reason of the sexual nature of that activity, the complainant

(a) is more likely to have consented to the sexual activity that forms the subject-matter of the charge; or

(b) is less worthy of belief.

(2) In proceedings in respect of an offence referred to in subsection (1), no evidence shall be adduced by or on behalf of the accused that the complainant has engaged in sexual activity other than the sexual activity that forms the subject-matter of the charge, whether with the accused or with any other person, unless the judge, provincial court judge or justice determines, in accordance with the procedures set out in sections 276.1 and 276.2, that the evidence

(a) is of specific instances of sexual activity;

(b) is relevant to an issue at trial; and

(c) has significant probative value that is not substantially outweighed by the danger of prejudice to the proper administration of justice.

(3) In determining whether evidence is admissible under subsection (2), the judge, provincial court judge or justice shall take into account

(a) the interests of justice, including the right of the accused to make a full answer and defence;

(b) society's interest in encouraging the reporting of sexual assault offences;

(c) whether there is a reasonable prospect that the evidence will assist in arriving at a just determination in the case;

(d) the need to remove from the fact-finding process any discriminatory belief or bias;

(e) the risk that the evidence may unduly arouse sentiments of prejudice, sympathy or hostility in the jury;

(f) the potential prejudice to the complainant's personal dignity and right of privacy;

(g) the right of the complainant and of every individual to personal security and to the full protection and benefit of the law; and

---

[90] See Sheila McIntyre, "Redefining Reformism: The Consultations that Shaped Bill C-49" in J. Roberts & R. Mohr, eds., *Confronting Sexual Assault. A Decade of Legal and Social Change* (1994) ch. 12.

(h) any other factor that the judge, provincial court judge or justice considers relevant.

The new s. 276.1 imposes a requirement of written notice for a hearing to determine admissibility under s. 276(2). Section 276.2 provides for the exclusion of the public at the hearing and the non-compellability of the complainant at the hearing. The new s. 276.4 requires the trial judge to instruct the jury as to the proper use of the evidence received.

Does the new legislation give more or less discretion to judges than did *Seaboyer*? What are the differences?

At the time Parliament enacted these revised rape shield provisions, it also imposed limits to the defence that the accused mistakenly believed that the complainant consented. Under s. 273.2(a) there is no defence of the belief arising from self-induced drunkenness, recklessness or wilful blindness. The most significant new limit under s. 273.2(b) is that there is no defence if the accused "did not take reasonable steps, in the circumstances known to the accused at the time, to ascertain that the complainant was consenting". Later in *R. v. Ewanchuk*,[91] the Supreme Court imposed further common law limits on the mistaken belief defence. These include that there must be belief that consent was communicated, that belief that silence, ambiguity or passivity constitutes consent is a mistake of law and will not excuse, and finally that proceeding after a "no" is reckless conduct. The practical effect of these developments is that the defence of mistaken belief will very seldom pass the air of reality test and will rarely succeed.

The Court in *Ewanchuk* also decided that consent is to be determined subjectively. In determining whether the complainant consented, the Court held that there was no such thing as implied consent to sexual assault but the Court did say that consent may be inferred from words or conduct.

Given the above substantive law, as a practical matter the admissibility of prior sexual history will often relate to the issue of consent. Sometimes the issue will be whether the Crown has charged the right accused.

R. v. CROSBY
[1995] 2 S.C.R. 912, 39 C.R. (4th) 315, 98 C.C.C. (3d) 225

The accused was charged with sexual assault. The complainant testified that she had been attacked by the accused and another man and forced to engage in non-consensual sexual acts with both. The accused testified that the complainant had consented throughout. In a *voir dire* before the commencement of the trial, the defence sought permission from the trial judge to lead evidence or cross-examine the complainant on certain statements which referred in some way to sexual activity other than that which formed the subject matter of the charge. This application triggered s. 276 scrutiny.

---

91   [1999] 1 S.C.R. 330, 131 C.C.C. (3d) 481, 22 C.R. (5th) 1.

In her original statement to police, the complainant admitted to having engaged in consensual sexual intercourse with the accused three days before the alleged assault. She also admitted that when she visited the accused on the day of the alleged assault she did so with the intention of having sexual intercourse with him again. At the preliminary hearing, the complainant testified that she did not visit the accused with the intention of having sex with him. The material inconsistency was inextricably linked in the police questioning to a reference to the earlier, consensual sexual contact between the complainant and the accused. Relying upon s. 276 of the *Code*, the trial judge prohibited defence counsel from cross-examining the complainant on her original statement made to police. The accused was convicted of sexual assault. He appealed on the basis that the trial judge erred in excluding the evidence of the statements. The majority in the Court of Appeal upheld his conviction.

Held: Appeal allowed; new trial ordered.

L'HEUREUX-DUBÉ J. (LAMER C.J., LA FOREST, and GONTHIER JJ. concurring):—

. . .

In her original statement to police, the complainant admitted to having engaged in consensual sexual intercourse with Crosby on November 1, 1991, three days before the alleged assault. She also admitted that when she visited Crosby on November 4, she did so with the intention of having sexual intercourse with him again:

Q. Have you had sex with Scott before?

A: The Friday night before I did.

Q: Is that the reason you went there on Monday?

A: Yup.

Q: Why did you change your mind?

A: Because I didn't feel right with John there and I didn't want to have to have sex with him.

By contrast, at the preliminary hearing, the complainant testified that she did not visit Crosby on November 4, 1991 with the intention of having sex with him:

Q: O.K. Were you hoping to have sex with Scott again that night?

A: No.

There was an apparent inconsistency between these two statements.

Ordinarily, nothing would prevent defence counsel from cross-examining the complainant on an inconsistency which related to her intentions in going to the accused's house on the day of the alleged assault. Material inconsistencies are relevant to the complainant's credibility. Unfortunately for the accused in this case, however, the material inconsistency was inextricably linked in the police questioning to a reference to the earlier, consensual sexual contact between the complainant and the accused. Defence counsel (and apparently the trial judge) thought that it was necessary to place into evidence the actual excerpts from the interview between the complainant and the police.

This created a dilemma. If the actual questions and answers were placed before the jury, then the jury would also have been alerted to the prior sexual activity between the complainant and Crosby on November 1. Relying upon s. 276 of the Code, the trial judge therefore prohibited defence counsel from cross-examining the complainant on this entire portion of her original statement made to police. When the complainant was cross-examined at trial, the following exchange occurred between defence counsel and the complainant:

Q: Now when you went to Mr. Crosby's home on November 7th, did you want to have sex with Mr. Crosby?

A: November 7th?

Q: Or sorry, November 4th, the day this happened with you and Rines...

A: No.

Q: You didn't?

A: No.

As a result of the s. 276 ruling, counsel for the appellant was precluded from pursuing this inconsistency between the complainant's trial testimony and her original statement to the police.

With respect, the trial judge erred in excluding this statement, and therefore in preventing defence counsel from cross-examining the complainant on this material inconsistency in her statements.

Where the defence of honest but mistaken belief is not realistically advanced by the accused at trial, then evidence of prior, unrelated sexual activity between the complainant and the accused will seldom be relevant to an issue at trial. . . However, although the defence of honest but mistaken belief in consent was not realistically at issue in the present case, the circumstances were nonetheless somewhat exceptional. In particular, it appears from the transcripts that the only reason the unrelated sexual activity of November 1 was at all implicated was because it was directly referred to *by police* while posing a question which did, indeed, bear on the sexual activity which formed the subject matter of the charge. The effect of the trial judge's invocation of s. 276 in this case was therefore to exclude otherwise admissible evidence (the complainant's prior statement as to her original intention in going to Crosby's house) by piggybacking it atop otherwise *prima facie* inadmissible evidence (the evidence of the unrelated sexual activity). In my view, it would be unfair for an accused person to be denied access to evidence which is otherwise admissible and relevant to his defence if the prejudice related to admitting that evidence is uniquely attributable to the authorities' conduct. I do not believe that s. 276 was ever designed or intended to be employed to prevent cross-examination in a situation such as this.

. . . Section 276 cannot be interpreted so as to deprive a person of a fair defence. This is not its purpose. This does not mean, of course, that the accused is entitled to the most beneficial procedures possible. . . Rather, it is evident from the majority's remarks in *Seaboyer* and from the criteria enumerated in s. 276(3) that judges must undertake a balancing exercise under s. 276 that is sensitive to many differing, and potentially conflicting, interests.

In the present case, however, consideration of those factors favoured admission of the complainant's earlier statement. The versions told by the complainant and the accused were diametrically opposed in every material respect, and credibility was consequently the central issue at trial. An inconsistency on a material and pertinent issue is highly relevant in such circumstances. The interests of justice, including the right of the accused to make full answer and defence, therefore militated in favour of admitting the evidence (s. 276(3)(*a*)). So, too, did the fact that there was a reasonable prospect that the evidence would have assisted the jury in arriving at a just determination in the case (section 276(3)(*c*)).

[Sopinka J., Iacobucci and Major JJ. concurring, agreed with the reasons for judgment of Justice L'Heureux-Dubé with respect to the admissibility of the complainant's statement to the police.]

In *Crosby* all the justices agreed that evidence of the statement to the police should have been admitted as it was necessary to ensure a fair trial for the accused. This was despite the fact that the first statement referred to previous sexual activity with the accused. The Court read a discretion into s. 276.

Section 276(1) seems to contain an express blanket prohibition on what is commonly referred to as the "twin myths" reasoning. It prohibits the use of prior sexual history of the complainant on the issue of consent or to show that the complainant was less worthy of belief. This seemed to make it unconstitutional because *Seaboyer* had called for discretion.[92]

However, Professor David Paciocco[93] suggested that the legislation could be read down. Section 276(1) only prohibited general stereotypical inferences. Evidence of prior sexual history with the accused could be admitted under s. 276(2) where the defence could establish that a specific inference can be drawn from such evidence to an issue relevant in the trial. In *Charter* challenges in lower courts the Paciocco position carried the day and was increasingly relied on as the proper interpretation.[94]

When the Supreme Court finally considered the constitutionality of the "new" statutory scheme in *Darrach* a unanimous Court had little difficulty in declaring the "new" rape shield provisions constitutional.

---

[92] See Delisle, "Potential *Charter* Challenges to the New Rape Shield Law" (1992), 13 C.R. (4th) 390.

[93] "The New Rape Shield Provisions in Section 276 Should Survive *Charter* Challenge" (1993), 21 C.R. (4th) 223.

[94] See e.g. *R. v. Ecker* (1995), 96 C.C.C. (3d) 161 (Sask. C.A.) and *R. v. Darrach* (1998), 122 C.C.C. (3d) 225 (Ont. C.A.).

R. v. DARRACH
[2000] 2 S.C.R. 443, 36 C.R. (5th) 223, 148 C.C.C. (3d) 97

The accused was charged with sexual assault and, at his trial, attempted to introduce evidence of the complainant's sexual history. He unsuccessfully challenged the constitutionality of s. 276.1 (2)(a) of the *Criminal Code* (which requires that the affidavit contain "detailed particulars" about the evidence), ss. 276(1) and 276(2)(c) (which govern the admissibility of sexual conduct evidence generally), and s. 276.2(2) (which provides that the complainant is not a compellable witness at the hearing determining the admissibility of evidence of prior sexual activity). After a *voir dire*, the trial judge refused to allow the accused to adduce the evidence of the complainant's sexual history. The accused was convicted and the Court of Appeal dismissed the accused's appeal, concluding that the impugned provisions did not violate the accused's right to make full answer and defence, his right not to be compelled to testify against himself or his right to a fair trial as protected by ss. 7, 11(c) and 11(d) of the *Canadian Charter of Rights and Freedoms*. Here we consider the accused's argument that s. 276(1) was unconstitutional.

GONTHIER J. (McLACHLIN C.J.C., L'HEUREUX-DUBÉ , IACOBUCCI, MAJOR, BASTARACHE, BINNIE, ARBOUR and LEBEL JJ. concurring):—

. . .

The current s. 276 categorically prohibits evidence of a complainant's sexual history only when it is used to support one of two general inferences. These are that a person is more likely to have consented to the alleged assault and that she is less credible as a witness by virtue of her prior sexual experience. Evidence of sexual activity may be admissible, however, to substantiate other inferences. . .

. . .

The current version of s. 276 is in essence a codification by Parliament of the Court's guidelines in *Seaboyer*.

. . .

[T]he Court's jurisprudence . . . has consistently held that the principles of fundamental justice enshrined in s. 7 protect more than the rights of the accused. . . One of the implications of this analysis is that while the right to make full answer and defence and the principle against self-incrimination are certainly core principles of fundamental justice, they can be respected without the accused being entitled to "the most favourable procedures that could possibly be imagined" (*R. v. Lyons*, [1987] 2 S.C.R. 309, at p. 362; cited in *Mills, supra*, at para. 72). Nor is the accused entitled to have procedures crafted that take only his interests into account. Still less is he entitled to procedures that would distort the truth-seeking function of a trial by permitting irrelevant and prejudicial material at trial.

In *Seaboyer,* the Court found that the principles of fundamental justice include the three purposes of s. 276 identified above: protecting the integrity of the trial by excluding evidence that is misleading, protecting the rights of the accused, as well as encouraging the reporting of sexual violence and protecting "the security and privacy of the witnesses" (p. 606). This was affirmed in *Mills, supra*, at para. 72. The Court crafted its guidelines in *Seaboyer* in accordance with these principles, and it is in relation to these principles that the effects of s. 276 on the accused must be evaluated.

The Court in *Mills* upheld the constitutionality of the provisions in the Criminal Code that control the use of personal and therapeutic records in trials of sexual offences. The use of these records in evidence is analogous in many ways to the use of evidence of prior sexual activity, and the protections in the Criminal Code surrounding the use of records at trial are motivated by similar policy considerations. L'Heureux-Dubé J. has warned that therapeutic records should not become a tool for circumventing s. 276: "[w]e must not allow the defence to do indirectly what it cannot do directly" (*R. v. O'Connor*, [1995] 4 S.C.R. 411, at para. 122, and *R. v. Osolin*, [1993] 4 S.C.R. 595, at p. 624). Academic commentators have observed that the use of therapeutic records increased with the enactment of s. 276 nonetheless (see K. D. Kelly, "'You must be crazy if you think you were raped': Reflections on the Use of Complainants' Personal and Therapy Records in Sexual Assault Trials" (1997), 9 C.J.W.L. 178, at p. 181).

. . .

(T)he test for admissibility in s. 276(2) requires not only that the evidence be relevant but also that it be more probative than prejudicial. *Mills* dealt with a conflict among the same three Charter principles that are in issue in the case at bar: full answer and defence, privacy and equality (at para. 61). The Court defined these rights relationally: "the scope of the right to make full answer and defence must be determined in light of privacy and equality rights of complainants and witnesses" (paras. 62-66 and 94). The exclusionary rule was upheld. The privacy and equality concerns involved in protecting the records justified interpreting the right to make full answer and defence in a way that did not include a right to all relevant evidence.

. . .

In the case at bar, I affirm the reasons in *Seaboyer* and find that none of the accused's rights are infringed by s. 276 as he alleges. *Seaboyer* provides a basic justification for the legislative scheme in s. 276, including the determination of relevance as well as the prejudicial and probative value of the evidence. *Mills* and *White* show how the impact of s. 276 on the principles of fundamental justice relied on by the accused should be assessed in light of the other principles of fundamental justice that s. 276 was designed to protect. The reasons in *Mills* are apposite because they demonstrate how the same principles of equality, privacy and fairness can be reconciled. I shall show below how the procedure created by s. 276 to protect the trial process from distortion and to protect complainants is consistent with the principles of fundamental justice. It is fair to the accused and properly reconciles the divergent interests at play, as the Court suggested in *Seaboyer*.

. . .

Section 276(1) — The Exclusionary Rule

The accused objects to the exclusionary rule itself in s. 276(1) on the grounds that it is a "blanket exclusion" that prevents him from adducing evidence necessary to make full answer and defence, as guaranteed by ss. 7 and 11(d) of the Charter. He is mistaken in his characterization of the rule. Far from being a "blanket exclusion", s. 276(1) only prohibits the use of evidence of past sexual activity when it is offered to support two specific, illegitimate inferences. These are known as the "twin myths", namely that a complainant is more likely to have consented or that she is less worthy of belief "by reason of the sexual nature of the activity" she once engaged in.

This section gives effect to McLachlin J.'s finding in *Seaboyer* that the "twin myths" are simply not relevant at trial. They are not probative of consent or credibility and can severely distort the trial process. Section 276(1) also clarifies *Seaboyer* in several respects. Section 276 applies to all sexual activity, whether with the accused or with someone else. It also applies to non-consensual as well as consensual sexual activity, as this Court found implicitly in *R. v. Crosby*, [1995] 2 S.C.R. 912, at para. 17. Although the *Seaboyer* guidelines referred to "consensual sexual conduct" (pp. 634-35), Parliament enacted the new version of s. 276 without the word "consensual". Evidence of non-consensual sexual acts can equally defeat the purposes of s. 276 by distorting the trial process when it is used to evoke stereotypes such as that women who have been assaulted must have deserved it and that they are unreliable witnesses, as well as by deterring people from reporting assault by humiliating them in court. The admissibility of evidence of non-consensual sexual activity is determined by the procedures in s. 276. Section 276 also settles any ambiguity about whether the "twin myths" are limited to inferences about "unchaste" women in particular; they are not (as discussed by C. Boyle and M. MacCrimmon, "The Constitutionality of Bill C-49: Analyzing Sexual Assault As If Equality Really Mattered" (1999), 41 Crim. L.Q. 198, at pp. 231-32).

The Criminal Code excludes all discriminatory generalizations about a complainant's disposition to consent or about her credibility based on the *sexual nature* of her past sexual activity on the grounds that these are improper lines of reasoning. This was the import of the Court's findings in *Seaboyer* about how sexist beliefs about women distort the trial process. The text of the exclusionary rule in s. 276(1) diverges very little from the guidelines in *Seaboyer*. The mere fact that the wording differs between the Court's guidelines and Parliament's enactment is itself immaterial. In *Mills, supra,* the Court affirmed that "[t]o insist on slavish conformity" by Parliament to judicial pronouncements "would belie the mutual respect that underpins the relationship" between the two institutions (para. 55). In this case, the legislation follows the Court's suggestions very closely.

The phrase "by reason of the sexual nature of that activity" in s. 276 is a clarification by Parliament that it is inferences from the *sexual nature* of the activity, as opposed to inferences from other potentially relevant features of the activity, that are prohibited. If evidence of sexual activity is proffered for its non-sexual features, such as to show a pattern of conduct or a prior inconsistent statement, it may be permitted. The phrase "by reason of the sexual nature of that activity" has the same effect as the qualification "solely to support the inference" in *Seaboyer* in that it limits the exclusion of evidence to that used to invoke the "twin myths" (p. 635).

. . .

An accused has never had a right to adduce irrelevant evidence. Nor does he have the right to adduce misleading evidence to support illegitimate inferences: "the accused is not permitted to distort the truth-seeking function of the trial process" (*Mills, supra*, at para. 74). Because s. 276(1) is an evidentiary rule that only excludes material that is not relevant, it cannot infringe the accused's right to make full answer and defence. Section 276(2) is more complicated, and I turn to it now.

Section 276(2)(c) — "Significant Probative Value"

If evidence is not barred by s. 276(1) because it is tendered to support a permitted inference, the judge must still weigh its probative value against its prejudicial effect to determine its admissibility. This essentially mirrors the common law guidelines in *Seaboyer* which contained this balancing test (at p. 635). The accused takes issue with the fact that s. 276(2)(c) specifically requires that the evidence have "significant probative value". The word "significant" was added by Parliament but it does not render the provision unconstitutional by raising the threshold for the admissibility of evidence to the point that it is unfair to the accused.

. . .

The context of the word "significant" in the provision in which it occurs substantiates this interpretation. Section 276(2)(c) allows a judge to admit evidence of "*significant* probative value that is not *substantially* outweighed by the danger of prejudice to the proper administration of justice" (emphasis added). The adverb "substantially" serves to protect the accused by raising the standard for the judge to exclude evidence once the accused has shown it to have significant probative value. In a sense, both sides of the equation are heightened in this test, which serves to direct judges to the serious ramifications of the use of evidence of prior sexual activity for all parties in these cases.

In light of the purposes of s. 276, the use of the word "significant" is consistent with both the majority and the minority reasons in *Seaboyer*. Section 276 is designed to prevent the use of evidence of prior sexual activity for improper purposes. The requirement of "significant probative value" serves to exclude evidence of trifling relevance that, even though not used to support the two forbidden inferences, would still endanger the "proper administration of justice". The Court has recognized that there are inherent "damages and disadvantages presented by the admission of such evidence" (*Seaboyer, supra*, at p. 634). As Morden A.C.J.O. puts it, evidence of sexual activity must be significantly probative if it is to overcome its prejudicial effect. The Criminal Code codifies this reality.

By excluding misleading evidence while allowing the accused to adduce evidence that meets the criteria of s. 276(2), s. 276 enhances the fairness of trials of sexual offences. Section 11(d) guarantees a fair trial. Fairness under s. 11(d) is determined in the context of the trial process as a whole (*R. v. Stoddart* (1987), 37 C.C.C. (3d) 351 (Ont. C.A.), at pp. 365-66). As L'Heureux-Dubé J. wrote in *Crosby, supra*, at para. 11, "[s]ection 276 cannot be interpreted so as to deprive a person of a fair defence." At the same time, the accused's right to make full answer and defence, as was held in *Mills, supra*, at para. 75, is not "automatically breached where he or she is deprived of relevant information". Nor is it necessarily breached when the accused is not permitted to adduce relevant information that is not "significantly" probative, under a rule of evidence that protects the trial from the distorting effects of evidence of prior sexual activity.

. . .

Thus the threshold criteria that evidence be of "significant" probative value does not prevent an accused from making full answer and defence to the charges against him. Consequently his Charter rights under ss. 7 and 11(d) are not infringed by s. 276(2)(c).

The Procedural Sections to Determine Relevance: The Affidavit and Voir Dire

The constitutionality of the procedure that must be followed to introduce evidence of prior sexual activity has also been challenged. It requires that whoever seeks to introduce it "by or on behalf of the accused" must present an affidavit and establish on a voir dire that the evidence is admissible in accordance with the criteria in the Criminal Code.

[The Court determined that the procedural provisions were not violative of the accused's constitutional rights. In the course of its analysis the Court later commented on relevance and probative value of evidence of previous sexual activity.]

———

Although the Supreme Court has determined the issue of constitutionality, it seems very likely that *Darrach* has not resolved the question of the proper application of ss. 276(1) and (2), especially in the context of prior sexual history with the accused where the issue is consent. The Court does not refer to the views of David Paciocco. **Has the Court implicitly accepted his approach?** We have seen that the Court in *Darrach* at one point says that such evidence is not relevant, then in the next breath it says it may be admitted. Towards the end of the judgment this is put in yet another way:

> Evidence of prior sexual activity will rarely be relevant to support a denial that sexual activity took place or to establish consent (C.R., para. 58).

That judges have different views on the issue of the relevance and probative value of evidence of prior sexual history with the accused on the issue of consent is reflected in the views of the Ontario Court of Appeal in the court below in *Darrach*, which were not addressed in the Supreme Court. According to Morden, A.C.J.O.[95] for the Court:

It will likely be that evidence of previous sexual activity with the accused will satisfy the requirements of admissibility in s. 276(2) more often than that relating to sexual activity with others. This does not mean that this evidence should always be admissible.

In *R. v. A.*,[96] the House of Lords referred to both *Seaboyer* and *Darrach* before deciding that a U.K. rape shield law did not operate to exclude the complainant's prior sexual history with the accused. The Court concluded that excluding such evidence would be incompatible with the accused's fair trial rights under the European Convention on Human Rights. One of the Lords, Lord Steyn, wrote as follows:

> As a matter of common sense, a prior sexual relationship between the complainant and the accused may, depending on the circumstances, be relevant to the issue of consent. It is a species of prospectant evidence which may throw light on the complainant's state of mind. It cannot, of course, prove that she consented on the occasion in question. Relevance and sufficiency of proof are different things. The fact that the accused a week before an alleged murder threatened to kill the deceased does not prove an intent to kill on the day in question. But it is logically relevant to that issue. After all, to be relevant the evidence need merely have some tendency in logic and common sense to advance the proposition in issue. It is true that each decision to engage in sexual activity is always made afresh. On the other hand, the mind does not usually blot out all memories. What one has been engaged on in the past may influence what choice one makes on a future occasion. Accordingly, a prior relationship between a complainant and an accused may sometimes be relevant to what decision was made on a particular occasion.
>
> . . .
>
> Following *R v Seaboyer* section 276 of the Criminal Code was amended. Subsequently the Supreme Court held that section 276 as amended was valid. As amended it was not viewed as a blanket exclusion: *R v Darrach* (2000) 191 DLR (4th) 539. Unfortunately, the Secretary of State's understanding of the Canadian position was flawed. *R v Seaboyer* is largely concerned with the irrelevance of sexual experience between the complainant and third parties. In her leading judgment McLachlin J placed general reliance upon an article of Galvin, who emphasises the probative value of prior sexual conduct between a complainant and an accused to the issue of consent: "Shielding Rape Victims in the State and Federal Courts: A Proposal for the Second Decade" (1986) 70 Minn L Rev 763. Moreover, McLachlin J made a telling comment on prior sexual history with the accused. It is to the following effect, at 83 DLR (4th) 193, 280D:

> > I question whether evidence of other sexual conduct with the accused should automatically be admissible in all cases; sometimes the value of such evidence might be little or none.

> *R v Seaboyer* does not justify the breadth of the exclusionary provisions of section 41 in respect of previous sexual experience between a complainant and a defendant.

---

[95]   (1998), 13 C.R. (5th) 283, 122 C.C.C. (3d) 225 (Ont. C.A.) at 299 [C.R.] (Osborne and Doherty JJ.A. concurring).

[96]   [2001] UKHL 25, [2001] 3 All E.R. 1 (U.K. H.L.) at para. 31.

There is a line of authority, especially in the Ontario Superior Court (reviewed in *R. v. Strickland*),[97] to admit prior evidence of sexual conduct with the accused to show "context". Other courts apply the twin myths rigorously to exclude such evidence.[98] **What do you think of the analysis in the following case?**

R. v. TEMERTZOGLOU
(2002), 11 C.R. (6th) 179 (S.C.J.)

After spending an evening in a motel room with a young woman, C, the accused, aged 40, was charged with sexual assault. It was alleged that he had sexual intercourse with her without her consent. Following a preliminary inquiry the accused was committed for trial. He re-elected to be tried by judge without a jury. His defence counsel brought an application under s. 276 of the *Criminal Code*, to adduce evidence of the complainant's prior consensual sexual activity with the accused. According to the accused he had met three times with the complainant and they had engaged in sexual touching. They had spoken about going to a motel. She had indicated that she was allergic to latex condoms. That is why he had brought a lambskin condom to the motel. The judge granted the defence an *in camera* hearing pursuant to s. 276.2. On the hearing, defence called the *viva voce* evidence of the accused and a detective who gave evidence about statements made to him by C which appeared inconsistent with her videotaped statement to police and her testimony at the preliminary inquiry.

FUERST J.:—

Subsection 276(2) provides that in a prosecution for, inter alia, sexual assault, no evidence shall be adduced by or on behalf of the accused that the complainant has engaged in sexual activity other than that forming the subject-matter of the charge, whether with the accused or with any other person, unless the judge determines in accordance with the specified procedure that the evidence

(a) is of specific instances of sexual activity;

(b) is relevant to an issue at trial; and

(c) has significant probative value that is not substantially outweighed by the danger of prejudice to the proper administration of justice.

---

[97]   (2007), 45 C.R. (6th) 183 (Ont. S.C.J.) See criticism of Senem Ozkin, "Balancing of Interests: Admission of Private Sexual History under Section 276" (2011) 57 Crim. L.Q. 327. See too *R. v. T. (M.)* (2012), 289 C.C.C. (3d) 115, 95 C.R. (6th) 223 (Ont. C.A.) and *R. v. Beilhartz*, 2013 ONSC 5670, 6 C.R. (7th) 79 (Ont. S.C.J.).

[98]   See cases reviewed by Ozkin. See earlier Christine Boyle & Marilyn MacCrimmon, "The Constitutionality of Bill C-49: Analysing Sexual Assault as if Equality Really Mattered" (2011) 57 Crim. L.Q. 327; Sue Chapman, "Section 276 of the *Criminal Code* and the Admissibility of Sexual Activity Evidence" (1998) 41 Crim. L.Q. 188; and Gotell, "When Privacy is Not Enough: Sexual Assault Complainants, Sexual History Evidence and Disclosure of Personal Records" (2006) 43 Alta. L. Rev. 743.

Subsection 276(1) specifies that evidence of other sexual activity is not admissible to support an inference that, by reason of the sexual nature of that activity, the complainant is more likely to have consented to the sexual activity that forms the subject-matter of the charge, or is less worthy of belief. These illegitimate inferences have been referred to as the "twin myths".

Subsection 276(3) requires that in determining the admissibility of evidence of other sexual activity, the trial judge must take into account eight enumerated factors.

In *R. v. Darrach*, [2000] 2 S.C.R. 443 the Supreme Court of Canada held that s. 276 does not function as a blanket exclusion of evidence of other sexual activity, but prohibits the admission of such evidence solely to support the inference that a complainant is more likely to have consented, or is less worthy of belief, by virtue of that other sexual activity. The exclusion of evidence is limited under ss. 276(1) to that used to invoke the twin myths, and under ss. 276(2)(c), to relevant information that is more prejudicial to the administration of justice than it is probative.... The Supreme Court of Canada agreed with the interpretation given to the term "significant" in ss. 276(2)(c), by the Ontario Court of Appeal. It means that the evidence is not to be so trifling as to be incapable, in the context of all the evidence, of raising a reasonable doubt, but it is not necessary for the defence to demonstrate strong and compelling reasons for admission of the evidence.

The principle was stated by Cory J. in *R. v. Osolin*, *supra*, as follows: "Generally a complainant may be cross-examined for the purpose of eliciting evidence relating to consent and pertaining to credibility when the probative value of that evidence is not substantially outweighed by the danger of unfair prejudice which might flow from it. Cross-examination for the purposes of showing consent or impugning credibility which relies upon "rape myths" will always be more prejudicial than probative. Such evidence can fulfil no legitimate purpose and would therefor be inadmissible to go to consent or credibility".

In *R. v. Seaboyer* (1991), 66 C.C.C. (3d) 321 (S.C.C.) McLachlin J. gave as an example of admissible evidence, prior sexual conduct known to the accused at the time of the alleged offence, tending to prove that the accused believed that the complainant was consenting to the act charged. In *R. v. Crosby*, [1995] 2 S.C.R. 912 (S.C.C.) evidence of other sexual activity was held to be admissible where the complainant's credibility was the central issue at trial, and she had made a prior inconsistent statement to the police that was inextricably linked to an admission of prior sexual activity with the accused. The Ontario Court of Appeal held in *R. v. Harris*, [1997] O.J. No. 3560 that where the complainant testified in examination-in-chief that she was shocked when the accused asked her if they were going to have sex, because prior to that there had been nothing sexual between them, evidence of their prior sexual activity became admissible to contradict her. The court pointed out that the jury otherwise was left with the misleading impression that the relationship had been platonic, and could not fairly assess the conduct of the parties and the believability of their respective positions on the issue of consent. The court was aware that the complainant would have denied the accused's version of their prior contact. In *R. v. M. (M.)*, [1999] O.J. No. 3943 (Ont. Sup. Ct.) evidence of prior sexual activity between the parties was admitted because the development of the relationship between the parties was necessary to provide context, without which the alleged sexual assault would be assessed in a vacuum and the testimony of the accused in support of his position that the contact was consensual would appear improbable. . .

I am satisfied that the preconditions set out in ss. 276(2) have been met. The evidence the defence seeks to adduce is evidence of specific instances of sexual activity.

Further, as the Supreme Court of Canada pointed out in *R. v. Ewanchuk*, once the complainant asserts that she did not consent, it will be open to the defence to raise a reasonable doubt about that element of the offence, by adducing relevant evidence. In that sense, consent and Ms. M.C.'s credibility will be issues at the trial. I am satisfied that the evidence of other sexual activity is relevant to those issues, in particular ways that do not involve twin myth reasoning. The inferences to be drawn from the evidence are not the general inferences that solely by reason of the other sexual activity, Ms. M.C. is more likely to have consented on November 24, or should not be believed. Specifically, the evidence of other sexual activity has relevance in that it shows the development of a relationship between the parties which is more than platonic, notwithstanding an age difference that might otherwise engender a presumption against the defence; it provides necessary context to the motel visit on November 24, without which aspects of Mr. Temertzoglou's account such as the obtaining of lambskin condoms would be untenable; it is necessary in order to make sense of prior inconsistent statements that will be put to Ms. M.C., which can impact on her credibility; and it demonstrates the complainant's involvement in planning the evening of November 24, which tends to support the defence position.

I also find that the evidence of other sexual activity has significant probative value that is not substantially outweighed by the danger of prejudice to the proper administration of justice.

In determining whether the evidence of other sexual activity is admissible, I have considered all of the factors in ss. 276(3). The evidence bears on Mr. Temertzoglou's right to make full answer and defence to a very serious allegation that he had forcible sexual intercourse with a teenaged girl. There is a reasonable prospect that the evidence will assist in arriving at a just determination of the case, given its relevance to the issues. It is not in the interests of justice that Mr. Temertzoglou be prevented from making full answer and defence, or that I as the trier of fact not receive relevant evidence that will assist in arriving at a just determination. The evidence cannot and will not be used to support illegitimate inferences. This is not a case where discriminatory belief or bias will form part of the fact-finding process. There is no jury involved, and there is no risk that sentiments of prejudice, sympathy or hostility will be unduly aroused by the evidence. Any potential prejudice to Ms. M.C.'s personal dignity and right of privacy is minimized, given that the nature of the other sexual activity is less intrusive than the acts involved in the offence alleged, and given that she spoke to the police about some of this other activity in her videotaped interview. Further, her anonymity can be achieved through a publication ban concerning her identity. Society's interest in encouraging the reporting of sexual assault offences cannot prohibit an accused from making full answer and defence by adducing relevant evidence that has significant probative value. The right of Ms. M.C. and of every individual to personal security and to the full protection and benefit of the law is not infringed in the circumstances of this case, where the evidence to be adduced is limited to that of her prior contact with Mr. Temertzoglou on occasions proximate in time to the alleged offence, and does not involve an intrusion into other aspects of her life.

In *R. v. S. (L.R.)*[99] the trial judge admitted evidence of post-charge sexual conduct between the parties but instructed the jury that this could not be used to assess credibility. The New Brunswick Court of Appeal ordered a new trial. They held that the jury ought to have been instructed that the evidence could have been used to assess the complainant's credibility in relation to the specific events charged but not to support the inference that by reason of the sexual nature of the later incident she was more likely to have consented or was less worthy of belief. **How is the evidence relevant to credibility?**[100]

R. v. L.S.

2017 ONCA 685, 354 C.C.C. (3d) 71, 40 C.R. (7th) 351 (Ont. C.A.)

The accused and the complainant, E.K., lived in a spousal relationship from 2007-2012. After the relationship broke down, E.K. reported to police that the accused had assaulted her physically and sexually. The accused was charged with offences including one count of sexual assault. The complainant testified that the accused had non-consensual sexual intercourse with her on one occasion in 2009. The accused testified and denied that the assault occurred. The accused was convicted by a jury. On appeal, the issue was whether the trial judge should have permitted the defence to lead evidence that the sexual relationship between the accused and the complainant continued after the alleged sexual assault.

DOHERTY J.A.:

75 It was clear from the evidence adduced at the preliminary inquiry that the jury would hear evidence that E.K. and the appellant were in a spousal relationship of some length before and after the alleged sexual assault. It was equally clear that the jury would hear evidence from which it could readily conclude that the relationship included consensual sexual activity, both before and after the alleged assault. The defence wanted to make that inference explicit by adducing evidence that before and after the alleged assault, E.K. and the appellant, as part of their spousal relationship, regularly engaged in consensual sexual intercourse.

---

[99] (2005) 40 C.R. (6th) 180 (N.B. C.A.).

[100] For differing views on this case see C.R. annotations by Janine Benedet and Don Stuart.

76 This submission raises two questions — does s. 276(2) apply to "relationship" evidence and, if so, should the evidence have been admitted in this case?

(iii) Does s. 276(2) apply?

77 In R. v. C. (A.R.), the judge was asked to admit evidence that between and before the two alleged sexual assaults, the accused and the complainant had been involved in an intimate relationship involving consensual sexual activity. The trial judge held that the exclusionary rule in s. 276(2) did not apply to evidence describing the nature of the relationship. He reasoned that since s. 276(2)(a) required, as a precondition to admissibility, that the evidence refer to "specific instances of sexual activity", the exclusionary rule did not reach evidence that was not evidence of "specific instances of sexual activity". The trial judge went on to consider the admissibility of the evidence under the generally applicable rules of evidence.

78 The analysis in R. v. C. (A.R.) produces an interpretation of s. 276(2) that is inconsistent with the purpose of the statute and its plain language. On the approach adopted in R. v. C. (A.R.), the language in s. 276(2)(a) — "specific instances of sexual activity" — intended to create a precondition to admissibility, becomes a basis upon which one kind of evidence about sexual activity is entirely exempted from the exclusionary rule in s. 276(2). A provision clearly designed to limit the admissibility of evidence of other sexual activity would instead limit the scope of the exclusionary rule.

79 The purpose behind the enactment of ss. 276(1) and (2) is well-understood. Evidence of other sexual activity can be important to an accused's ability to make full answer and defence. At the same time, however, that evidence has historically been misused to blacken the character of the complainant, distort the trial process, and undermine the ability of the criminal justice system to effectively and fairly try sexual allegations. Sections 276(1) and (2) are designed to create an evidentiary filter, which separates evidence of other sexual activity that is germane to an accused's ability to make full answer and defence, from evidence of other sexual activity that will prejudice the proper conduct of the trial.

80 Evidence referring to other sexual activity of a complainant in general terms as part of the description of a relationship between the complainant and an accused carries the potential to distort the trial process and unfairly disparage the complainant, as does more detailed evidence of specific sexual activity. While the latter perhaps carries greater risk than the former, the risk exists when either kind of evidence is tendered. The purpose driving ss. 276(1) and (2) is best served by subjecting all evidence of other sexual activity, whether specific or general, to the exclusionary rule in s. 276(1), and the test for admissibility in s. 276(2).

81 The plain meaning of the words of ss. 276(1) and (2) is consistent with the purpose of those sections. The phrase "sexual activity" is not qualified in either section. Evidence that two people were in a relationship involving regular consensual sexual intercourse is clearly evidence that those two people were "engaged in sexual activity". As the plain meaning of the words promotes the purpose underlying the sections, I see no reason to depart from the plain reading. R. v. C. (A.R.) was wrongly decided on this point. Section 276(2) applies to "relationship" evidence of sexual activity.

(iv) Was the "relationship" evidence admissible?

82 As outlined above, there are three preconditions to the admissibility of evidence under s. 276(2). The first, found in 276(2)(a), requires that the evidence refer to "specific instances of sexual activity". This provision is designed to ensure that the nature of the proposed evidence is properly identified so that the criteria for admissibility in s. 276(2) can be accurately applied. The provision also serves to ensure that the Crown has full notice of the evidence to be adduced and that the complainant's legitimate interests can be properly safeguarded: R. v. B. (B.), [2009] O.J. No. 862 (Ont. Sup. Ct.), at para. 16.

83 The phrase "specific instances" modifies the phrase "sexual activity". The degree of specificity required to meet s. 276(2) (a) depends to a large extent on the nature of the sexual activity that the accused seeks to adduce: see R. v. Aziga, [2008] O.J. No. 4669, at paras. 21-22 (S.C.). If an accused wants to lead evidence of a specific incident of sexual activity, the details must identify that specific incident. If, however, the accused seeks to adduce evidence of a general nature, describing the relationship between himself and the complainant, the specificity requirement speaks to factors relevant to identifying the relationship and its nature and not to details of specific sexual encounters. Insofar as relationship evidence is concerned, the required specifics would include reference to the parties to the relationship, the relevant time period, and the nature of the relationship.

84 The appellant gave notice that he sought to introduce evidence that during the currency of his spousal relationship with E.K., both before and after the alleged assault, he and E.K. regularly engaged in consensual sexual intercourse. The appellant identified the sexual activity by reference to the parties, the time period, and the general nature of the activity.

85 Having regard to the nature of the evidence the appellant sought to adduce, the description of the evidence provided permitted the trial judge to properly determine its admissibility under s. 276(2) and, if admitted, to fully protect E.K. against questioning that was unfair, irrelevant or unnecessarily intrusive. I am satisfied that the appellant adequately identified the sexual activity in respect of which he sought to adduce evidence.

86 The second admissibility requirement, common to all evidence, requires that the evidence of other sexual activity be "relevant to an issue at trial" (s. 276(2)(b)). Relevance is fact-specific. It depends on the material facts in issue, the evidence adduced, and the positions of the parties. The appellant was charged with sexual assault, arising out of a specific incident described by the complainant as occurring in early May 2009. On E.K.'s evidence, the appellant raped her over her clear objections. On the appellant's evidence, the incident never happened. As the trial judge told the jury, their verdict turned on whether the Crown had proved that the incident described by E.K. occurred.

87 On the evidence heard by the jury, the appellant and E.K. had a spousal relationship that began sometime before the alleged sexual assault and carried on long after the alleged sexual assault. In her evidence, E.K. acknowledged that after the sexual assault, she and the appellant carried on as if nothing had happened. It was the defence position that in fact nothing had happened.

88 I think that evidence that the relationship between E.K. and the appellant, including the sexual component of the relationship, carried on as it had before the alleged assault was relevant to whether the assault occurred. The defence could argue that evidence that the sexual component of the relationship carried on as before, supported the defence position that the parties carried on as if nothing had happened because nothing had in fact happened.

89 I do not suggest that evidence that E.K. and the appellant continued a relationship that included consensual sexual intercourse after the alleged assault demonstrated that the assault did not occur. Different people will react differently to the same event. However, to acknowledge that evidence that the relationship continued as before was far from determinative of whether the assault occurred, is not the same as holding that the evidence is irrelevant. Evidence does not have to establish or refute a fact in issue to be relevant; it need only, as a matter of common sense and human experience, have some tendency to make the existence or non-existence of that material fact more or less likely. There is a big difference between evidence that is relevant and evidence that is determinative: see R. v. A. (No. 2), [2001] 2 W.L.R. 1546, at para. 31 (H.C.). This evidence was relevant.

90 The third and final condition to admissibility is found in s. 276(2)(c). The accused must demonstrate that the evidence has "significant probative value", and that the probative value "is not substantially outweighed by the danger of prejudice to the proper administration of justice". Evidence of "significant probative value" is evidence that has more than "trifling relevance" and is capable in the context of all of the evidence of leaving the jury with a reasonable doubt: R. v. Darrach, at paras. 39-41.

91 Evidence that a consensual sexual relationship existed between E.K. and the appellant before the alleged assault and that it continued after the alleged assault had probative value that was more than trifling. A jury could

reasonably, by considering and comparing the nature of the relationship between the two before and after the alleged assault, be assisted in deciding whether the assault described by E.K. had happened.

92 The potential probative value can be demonstrated by considering the effect of evidence that the relationship had ended immediately after the alleged assault. Had the evidence been that the relationship ended, the Crown could have argued that the termination of the relationship was consistent with E.K.'s testimony that she had been raped by the appellant. The same logic applies to defence use of the evidence based on the absence of any change in the relationship, although evidence of absence of any change in the relationship may have less potential probative value than evidence that E.K. immediately terminated the relationship after the alleged assault.

93 Turning to the prejudice side of the balance sheet, I see virtually no risk of any prejudice flowing from the admission of this evidence. The evidence the jury heard strongly indicated that the relationship between E.K. and the appellant, both before and after the alleged assault included consensual sexual intercourse. E.K. candidly acknowledged that the relationship carried on after the assault just as it had been before the assault. She specifically agreed that she and the appellant continued to share the same bed. I think it highly probable that the jury inferred from this evidence that the appellant and E.K. continued to engage in consensual sexual intercourse after the alleged assault. Express evidence to that effect would only have made explicit that which was strongly implied by the evidence the jury heard.

94 No one suggests that the jury should not have heard the evidence that it did hear about the nature of the relationship between E.K. and the appellant, both before and after the alleged assault. Considered in the context of that evidence, there is no risk that additional evidence simply confirming the strong inference available from that evidence the jury heard, could have prejudiced "the proper administration of justice": s. 276(2)(c).

95 I also do not agree with the trial judge that the risk that the jury would misuse the evidence by reasoning that "once a willing participant, always a willing participant" justified the exclusion of the evidence. There is always a risk that jurors will misuse evidence. The risk can be high when the accused is charged with sexual assault and the evidence in issue relates to other sexual activity.

96 The risk of juror misuse of evidence of other sexual activity is taken into account by the scheme established under s. 276. Section 276.4 requires that when a trial judge admits evidence of other sexual activity, she must "instruct the jury as to the uses that the jury may and may not make of the evidence". Any consideration of the potential prejudice under s. 276(2) (c) premised on the potential misuse of the evidence by the jurors must take into account that the jurors will be properly instructed in compliance with s. 276.4.

97 I am confident that the trial judge could have effectively explained to the jury that evidence that there was no change in the relationship between E.K. and the appellant, including the sexual component of that relationship, after the alleged assault, was evidence to be considered, along with the other relevant evidence, in deciding whether the Crown had proved beyond a reasonable doubt that the incident described by E.K. had in fact occurred. I am equally confident that the trial judge could have made it clear to the jury that if, after considering all of the relevant evidence, the jury was satisfied beyond a reasonable doubt that the incident described by E.K. had occurred, evidence that E.K. and the appellant had engaged in consensual sexual intercourse on other occasions had no relevance to, and was of no assistance in, determining whether E.K. had consented to sexual intercourse on the occasion in issue.

98 I have full confidence that a jury having received the proper instructions would have followed those instructions. The jury's verdict on the sexual assault charge justifies that confidence. The jury convicted the appellant in the face of evidence that left little doubt that he and E.K. engaged in consensual sexual intercourse, before and after the alleged assault. The jury's verdict demonstrates that it did not reason "once a willing participant, always a willing participant", even without the benefit of an instruction telling them they could not use that line of reasoning.

99 In summary, having regard to the evidence the jury actually heard and taking into account the instruction the jury would have received had the evidence been admitted, I see no risk of prejudice to "the proper administration of justice" flowing from admitting evidence that the relationship between E.K. and the appellant, before and after the alleged assault, included consensual sexual intercourse. The evidence was admissible under s. 276(2).

100 I am, however, satisfied that the error caused no substantial wrong or miscarriage of justice. As explained above, the jury would inevitably have understood from the evidence it did hear that E.K. and the appellant were in a relationship that included consensual sexual intercourse, both before and after the alleged assault. While the jury was not expressly instructed as to the use it could make of that evidence in deciding whether the Crown had proved that the alleged incident occurred, I think it would have been obvious to the jury that the evidence was capable of supporting the appellant's claim that the relationship carried on as if nothing had happened between E.K. and the appellant, because nothing had happened. The real risk inherent in the failure to give a more explicit instruction on the use of the relationship evidence lay in the danger that the jury would misuse the evidence in favour of the appellant on the issue of consent. The verdict shows that the jury did not make that error.

101 The improper exclusion of the "relationship" evidence effectively kept nothing of substance from the jury, but did assist the appellant in the sense that

the jury did not hear the limiting instruction it would have heard had the evidence been admitted under s. 276(2) as it should have been.

102 I would dismiss the conviction appeal.

A broader question underlying *L.S.* is what inferences can legitimately be drawn from a complainant's conduct after an alleged sexual assault. The issue attracted some attention in *R. v. Ghomeshi*,[101] in which each of the three sexual assault complainants continued to socialize with the accused, including dating and sending him flirtatious correspondence, after the alleged assaults. Ghomeshi was acquitted on all charges primarily because of inconsistencies and untruths in the complainants' testimony, but the trial judge also put some weight on the complainants' after-the-fact conduct, which he described as "out of harmony with the assaultive behaviour" alleged.[102] While this line of reasoning is arguably permissible in Canadian law, it raises a danger that trial judges may rely on myths and stereotypes in assessing whether the complainant's after-the-fact conduct is consistent with the conduct of a "real" victim. The Supreme Court of Canada has warned against reliance on myths and stereotypes about sexual assault complainants[103] and has held that "there is no inviolable rule on how people who are the victims of trauma like a sexual assault will behave".[104]

In *R. v. A.R.J.D.*,[105] the trial judge had acquitted the accused of sexual offences against his teenaged stepdaughter because there was no evidence that the complainant avoided the accused. The trial judge reasoned:

> I do not discount the complainant's credibility because she delayed complaint or because she did not cry out or search out help from her mother or other family members. To judge her credibility against those myths of appropriate behaviour is not helpful. The supposed expected behaviour of the usual victim tells me nothing about this particular victim.

> Having said all of that, however, given the length of time that these events occurred over, and the fact that the most serious event occurred months before [the complainant] complained, I would have expected some evidence of avoidance either conscious or unconscious. There was no such evidence. As a matter of logic and common sense, one would expect that a victim of sexual abuse would demonstrate behaviours consistent with that abuse or at least some change of behaviour such as avoiding the perpetrator. While I recognize that everyone does not react in the same way, the evidence suggests that despite these alleged events the relationship between the accused and the complainant was an otherwise normal parent/child relationship. That incongruity is significant enough to leave me in doubt about these allegations.[106]

---

[101]   2016 ONCJ 155, 27 C.R. (7th) 17 (Ont. C.J.). For critical perspectives on *Ghomeshi*, see C.R. comments by Janine Benedet and Don Stuart.

[102]   *Ghomeshi, ibid.* at para. 136.

[103]   See e.g. *Seaboyer*, above, and *R. v. Find*, 2001 SCC 32, [2001] 1 S.C.R. 863, 154 C.C.C. (3d) 97, 42 C.R. (5th) 1 (S.C.C.) at para. 101.

[104]   *R. v. D. (D.)*, 2000 SCC 43, [2000] 2 S.C.R. 275, 148 C.C.C. (3d) 41, 36 C.R. (5th) 261 (S.C.C.) at para. 65.

[105]   2018 CSC 6, 2018 SCC 6, 43 C.R. (7th) 207 (S.C.C.), affirming 2017 ABCA 237, 353 C.C.C. (3d) 1, 40 C.R. (7th) 306 (Alta. C.A.).

The Alberta Court of Appeal set aside the acquittal and ordered a new trial, a decision that was affirmed on appeal at the Supreme Court. In brief reasons, the Supreme Court held that the trial judge erred in law when he "judged the complainant's credibility based solely on the correspondence between her behaviour and the expected behaviour of the stereotypical victim of sexual assault".

Admitting evidence of a complainant's sexual history without an application and hearing under s. 276 is an error of law. Such an error was part of the basis for the Alberta Court of Appeal's decision to set aside an acquittal on a charge of first degree murder in the following case.

R. v. BARTON
2017 ABCA 216, 354 C.C.C. (3d) 245, 38 C.R. (7th) 316 (Alta. C.A.)

Barton was charged with the murder of Cindy Gladue, who died from an injury she sustained during sexual activity with the accused. The Crown's theory was that the accused intentionally inflicted the fatal injury, or alternatively that the force that caused the injury was applied without consent. The defence contended that the injury was caused accidentally in the course of consensual sexual activity. During the trial, Gladue was frequently referred to as a "native prostitute" and evidence of an instance of sexual activity between Barton and Gladue the night before was admitted without any proceedings under s. 276 of the *Code*. The Court of Appeal set aside the acquittal.[107]

The Court (Fraser C.J.A., Watson and Martin JJ.A.):

[119] To those who would immediately say, "of course it is relevant that she was a prostitute", our answer is this. A decision that sexual conduct evidence is admissible requires compliance with s. 276. Parliament has called for a careful consideration of underlying assumptions according to a set of stated factors. Given the limits of s. 276 in its current form, it is open to an accused to apply to introduce evidence of a complainant's prostitution. This is so notwithstanding that, as early as *Seaboyer*, L'Heureux-Dubé J (in dissent but not on this point) observed that "[e]vidence of prior acts of prostitution or allegations of prostitution . . . is never relevant and, besides its irrelevance, is hugely prejudicial." However, whether an accused will succeed in opening this generally prejudicial door is another question: *R v Nepinak* (2010), 82 CR (6th) 362; *R v Ingman* (2004), 246 Sask R 305; *R v Roper* (1997), 98 OAC 225, 32 OR (3d) 204 (CA).

[120] Section 276 was intended to replace quick conclusions based on false logic and discriminatory thinking about who consents, who tells the truth and what is relevant with a careful and structured analytical process designed to balance

---

[106]   *Ibid.*; trial judge's reasons quoted at para. 82 [(C.A.)].
[107]   Leave to appeal allowed [2017] S.C.C.A. No. 387 (S.C.C.).

evidence in the search for the truth, notably by excluding misleading evidence in support of illegitimate inferences. Everyone in Canada, including sex trade workers, is entitled to that protection.

. . .

[122] Expressly referring to Gladue as a prostitute conveyed that she was a female sex trade worker who made her living by routinely and habitually performing sexual activities for money. Prostitution is largely a gendered practice. Most prostitutes are female; most buyers are male. Calling someone a prostitute is a form of sexual conduct evidence caught by s. 276 if advanced by the defence, and governed by *Seaboyer* if advanced by the Crown. Since it is not evidence of a specific instance of sexual activity as required under s 276(2)(a), it is, by itself, inadmissible. It also amounts to evidence of sexual reputation which is separately prohibited under s 277, regardless of who seeks to tender it.

[123] This one word — prostitute — had the effect of ushering in Gladue's prior sexual conduct with all the others, real or imaginary, who may have paid her for sex. Gladue was referred to as a prostitute at least 25 times during the trial. Where a participant in sexual activity is a prostitute, a litany of unjust stereotypes about autonomy and consent persist in our society. That is so regardless of the label used to describe the person who sells sex for money. At the top of the list is that a prostitute will consent to anything for money. Linked to this is another improper belief, namely that once a prostitute has agreed to sell sex for money, the prostitute has given "implied consent" to any and all sexual acts to which the prostitute is then subjected. And perhaps worse yet, labelling someone a prostitute signals to the jurors that the prostitute is "deserving" of harm sustained on the job because prostitutes "choose" to engage in a risky profession: *Bedford, supra* at para 80.

[124] To compound this problem, the jurors were repeatedly told that Gladue was a "Native girl" or "Native woman". In particular, she was referred to as "Native" approximately 26 times throughout the trial by witnesses, defence counsel and Crown counsel. In one instance, the witness was directly asked to describe Gladue's ethnicity. In other circumstances, witnesses introduced and used the term "Native" or "Native woman" as a descriptor of Gladue and defence counsel, and Crown counsel continued to use that descriptor while questioning the witness.

[125] The defence argued there was no evidence before this Court to support the Interveners' submission that widespread racism against Aboriginal peoples was likely to negatively influence jurors. It suggested a commission of inquiry or parliamentary committee would be required to properly evaluate the Interveners' submission. We reject this argument.

[126] Courts in this country have long recognized that the potential for racial prejudice against visible minorities in the justice system is a notorious social

fact not capable of reasonable dispute: *R v Spence*, at para 5, [2005] 3 SCR 458 [*Spence*]. Jurors may consciously or subconsciously consider certain people less worthy and this bias can shape the information received during the trial to conform with the bias: see *R v Parks* (1993), 84 CCC (3d) 353 at 372 (Ont CA); *Spence* (inter-racial crime); *R v Find*, [2001] 1 SCR 863 (nature of the charges); and *R v Kokopenace*, [2015] 2 SCR 398 (representativeness in juries and impartiality). Hence, beginning almost two decades ago in *R v Williams*, [1998] 1 SCR 1128 [*Williams*], Canadian courts moved from a "hands-off" approach to the recognition that courts could, *and should*, take proactive steps to prevent racism from compromising trials.

[127] In this case, the trial judge ought to have addressed the repeated references to Gladue as a "Native" girl and "prostitute" to overcome the real risk of reasoning prejudice. And yet, the only caution given to this jury was this limited generic one typically offered in every jury trial:

> When examining the evidence, you must do so without sympathy or prejudice for or against anyone involved in these proceedings. That means you must now make good on your promise to put aside whatever biases or prejudices you may hold or feel. It also means that sympathy can have no place in your deliberations.

[128] This standard caution in the final instructions was not wrong in itself. But it was inadequate to counter the stigma and potential bias and prejudice that arose from the repeated references to Gladue as a "prostitute", "Native girl" and "Native woman". Those references implicitly invited the jury to bring to the fact-finding process discriminatory beliefs or biases about the sexual availability of Indigenous women and especially those who engage in sexual activity for payment. What was at play here, given the way in which the evidence unfolded, was the intersection of assumptions based on gender (woman), race (Aboriginal) and class (sex trade worker). We emphasize that we are not suggesting that counsel or the trial judge sought to insinuate improper thinking into the minds of this jury. Nevertheless, without a sufficient direction to the jury, the risk that this jury might simply have assumed that Barton's money bought Gladue's consent to whatever he wanted to do was very real, indeed inescapable. Add to this the likely risk that because Gladue was labelled a "Native" prostitute — who was significantly intoxicated — the jury would believe she was even more likely to have consented to whatever Barton did and was even less worthy of the law's protection. This is the very type of thinking that s 276 was introduced to eradicate.

[129] Prior consent to sexual activity is not a blanket authorization, or for that matter, any authorization, for future sexual activity. Decades ago, Parliament jettisoned the marital rape exception to rape and the idea that a wife was legally obliged to submit to sexual activity at the behest of her husband. Today, we recognize that each person's entitlement to human autonomy, especially in sexual matters, is essential to the bodily integrity and security of that person. Our law does not abide discriminating against sex trade workers by depriving them of the rights accorded to every citizen in this country merely because they

are sex trade workers. Juries need to understand this as a matter of law. Just as it is improper to impose "implied consent" to sexual activity on a spouse or person in an intimate relationship, a jury needs to be told that a sex trade worker does not give her "implied consent" to whatever sexual acts the client decides to do and still less to whatever degree of force the client inflicts upon her incidental to the sexual acts. Canadian law does not recognize "implied consent" to sexual activity, and this protection extends to everyone in our society.

[130] The jury charge here was further skewed by the trial judge's acting on a defence request to warn the jury that they could draw no negative inference *against Barton* for being the type of person who used prostitutes. That such a caution was requested and considered necessary clearly shows that the trial judge accepted the defence position that Gladue's being a prostitute would likely have a negative impact on the jury's thinking. The sting of this warning was that if Barton's actions were somehow viewed as discrediting Barton, it was because prostitutes, including Gladue, should be regarded as discreditable. That was the message left with this jury. It was false and prejudicial. To caution the jury on the stigma and potential prejudice only from the perspective of Barton's character and reputation did not counter the stigma and potential prejudice to Gladue's rights to equality and privacy and the state's interests in a fair trial from Gladue's being labelled a prostitute.

[131] One very real consequence of not conducting the analysis required under s. 276 is that the trial judge never addressed whether prostitution generally, or the alleged sexual activity between Gladue and Barton the prior night, was relevant to any issue in the trial. Nor did the trial judge address the further question whether the evidence had significant probative value that was not substantially outweighed by its prejudicial effect. Most important, had s 276 been followed, the trial judge would have been obligated to set out in the required ruling what use the jury could — and could not — make of the admissible evidence. The trial judge's failure to reflect on the scope of admissibility of this evidence may well have influenced other contents of his charge to the jury as well.

[132] Finally, even if it were determined that the commercial context of the sexual relationship between Barton and Gladue on the night she died was relevant for certain purposes, that would not require repeatedly labelling Gladue a prostitute, and still less a Native prostitute, any more than it would require labelling Barton a john.

For differing views on *Barton* see Stuart, "*Barton*: Assault Trials Must be Fair Not Fixed" (2017), 38 C.R. (7th) 438 and Janine Benedet, "*Barton*. 'She knew what she was coming for'. Sexual Assault, Prostitution and the Meaning of Consent" (2017) 38 C.R. (7th) 445.

On June 6, 2017, Canada's Minister of Justice introduced Bill C-51, *An Act to amend the Criminal Code and the Department of Justice Act and to make consequential amendments to another Act*. The Act would make some changes to the rape shield provisions in s. 276 of the *Code*. Importantly, the legislation would bring communications of a sexual nature within the ambit of the rape shield provisions. The proposed s. 276(4) provides: "For the purpose of this section, sexual activity includes any communication made for a sexual purpose or whose content is of a sexual nature." This change would appear to bring sexual communications within the scope of the rape shield provisions irrespective of their timing or whether they were directed at the accused. It would seem to cover certain communications sent by the complainants to the accused in *Ghomeshi*,[108] for example. In that case, the complainants sent various electronic communications to the accused after the alleged assaults, including communications suggesting a desire to engage in sexual activity with him. The proposed expansion would also seem to cover communications of a sexual nature sent to the accused before an alleged assault. For instance, in another high-profile case, *R. v. Ururyar*,[109] there was evidence that, a few hours before the alleged sexual assault at the accused's apartment, the complainant texted the accused from a bar where a group of mutual friends was socializing, saying "Come drink and then we can have hot sex". **Should the accused have to bring a s. 276 application to establish the admissibility of this evidence?**

Bill C-51 would also create a process whereby the defence could apply to admit evidence of records relating to the complainant that are in the hands of the accused (see the proposed s. 278.92). To this point, assuming relevance, records in the hands of the accused have been generally admissible. If the proposed changes are adopted, where the defence holds records relating to the complainant in which there is a reasonable expectation of privacy, the defence will be required to bring an application in writing setting out detailed particulars of the proposed evidence and its relevance. The private records covered by this proposed scheme would clearly include the medical and therapeutic records of the complainant when these are legitimately in the hands of the accused, and may even extend to emails and social media messages sent to the accused. Many of the communications used to cross-examine the complainants in the *Ghomeshi* case, even those not of a sexual nature, might fall into this broad category of private records relating to the complainant in the hands of the accused.

The proposed law further provides that, both in relation to private records and sexual history evidence, the complainant has a right to appear and to be represented by counsel at the admissibility hearing. Some have argued that these changes mandate a form of "defence disclosure" that will impair the ability of the defence to cross-examine sexual assault complainants. In *Ghomeshi*, for example, the defence confronted the complainants with their communications with the accused to contradict their claims in police

---

[108]   *Ghomeshi, supra* note 101.
[109]   2017 ONSC 4428 (Ont. S.C.J.).

statements and in direct examination that they cut off or limited contact with the accused after the alleged assaults. This cross-examination strategy might have been less effective if the communications held by the defence had been disclosed to the Crown and to the complainants in advance of their direct examination. **Should the defence be required to reveal to the Crown and to the complainant the evidence on which it plans to rely?**

PROBLEMS

Problem 1

The accused was convicted of two counts of indecent assault, which incidents occurred some 20 years before. On appeal he argued that the trial judge had erred in not permitting his counsel to cross-examine the complainant with respect to other alleged sexual assaults committed upon her by other male persons in the small community in which she lived during the same period of time and with respect to which she had made complaints. The complainant had made statements to the police officer investigating the matter that seven men, including the accused, had sexually assaulted her while she was in her sub-teens and teens. Counsel at trial had received copies of the statements made by the complainant to the police during the police investigation of the matter and the allegations made in each of these statements were, according to counsel, strikingly similar to the allegations made against the accused. Counsel submitted that it was highly improbable that the seven individuals would have committed strikingly similar offences against the same complainant and that he should be permitted to cross-examine the complainant with respect to these similar acts because the similarity of these statements reflected on the complainant's credibility. **Should the evidence have been allowed?** *See R. v. Anstey* (2002), 2 C.R. (6th) 203 (Nfld. C.A.); *R. v. G. (S.)* (2007), 219 C.C.C. (3d) 549 (Ont. S.C.J.); and *R. v. G. (A.)*, 2015 ONSC 923, 17 C.R. (7th) 319 (Ont. S.C.J.); but see *R. v. Riley* (1992), 11 O.R. (3d) 151 (C.A.) and *R. v. B. (A.R.)* (1998), 128 C.C.C. (3d) 457 (Ont. C.A.), affirmed (2000), 146 C.C.C. (3d) 191 (S.C.C.).

Problem 2

The accused is charged with sexual assault. His defence is consent and the defence counsel wants to lead evidence that the act occurred in the course of the complainant's work as a prostitute. **Admissible? What if the defence is that the charge was laid because the complainant was a prostitute attempting to extort more money by laying a false charge?**

See *R. v. Sauve* (1997), 13 C.R. (5th) 391 (B.C. C.A.) and Boyle and MacCrimmon, above at note 88 and *R. v. Nepinak* (2010), 82 C.R. (6th) 362 (B.C. S.C.); but see *R. v. Quesnelle* (2010) 76 C.R. (6th) 146 (Ont. S.C.J.).

Problem 3

The accused is charged with sexual assault based on allegations of hurtful sadomasochistic acts. The defence counsel wishes to introduce email messages to the accused from the complainant prior to the day in question in which the complainant indicates her desire for, and experience in, participating in sadomasochistic sexual acts. **How would you rule?**

People v. Jovanovic, 263 A.D.2d 182 (U.S. N.Y.A.D. 1st Dept.) (discussed in (2001) 51 Syracuse L. Rev. at 529-530).

Problem 4

The accused is charged with sexual assault. The complainant indicates that she never consented as by this time she had developed an exclusive preference for sexual relations with women.

The defence wants:

(a) to call a man to testify he had sexual relations with the complainant before and after the day is question; and

(b) to call another man to testify that she had him charged with sexual assault but the charged was determined to be false.

How would you rule as to the admissibility of this testimony.

See *R. v. Morden* (1991), 9 C.R. (4th) 315, 69 C.C.C. (3d) 123 (B.C. C.A.).

Problem 5

The accused was charged with sexual assault and forcible confinement against a female patron at an adult entertainment club where the accused worked as a male dancer. On the day of the offence the complainant gave a statement to the police that she had been practising abstinence from sex for the preceding six or seven months. At the preliminary inquiry she disagreed with the proposition that she had told the accused on the day of the alleged assaults that she had not had sex in months. At trial the accused applied under s. 276.2 to cross-examine the complainant on the issue to challenge her credibility, to support the defence of consent and to demonstrate her motive to fabricate. **Should this evidence be ruled admissible?**

See *R. v. Antonelli* (2011), 280 C.C.C. (3d) 96 (Ont. S.C.J.).

Problem 6

The accused and the complainant were members of the armed forces residing in the same barracks. He was charged with sexual assault. The defence was consent or mistaken belief in consent. The accused knew that the complainant had a girlfriend and identified herself as lesbian. The accused sought to introduce evidence that earlier that day she told him she had been sexually intimate with men before but that had been a long time ago. **How would you rule? What if the prosecutor cross-examines the accused on his knowledge of the complainant's sexual orientation and girlfriend apparently to bolster the argument that the accused was wilfully blind as to consent?**

Compare *R. v. LeBlanc* (2011), 89 C.R. (6th) 306 (Can. Ct. Martial App. Ct.) and see C.R. annotation by Janine Benedet.

Problem 7

B appealed his conviction for sexually assaulting a 16-year-old acquaintance based on the trial judge's refusal to admit evidence of the complainant's sexual activity after the alleged assault. The complainant had been kicked out of her parents' home and planned to stay at B's apartment, where her boyfriend had also recently been living. On the night of the assault, she was drinking with her boyfriend, the accused, B, and another male friend, M. The complainant became ill and vomited twice. She was upset and crying. She alleged that the accused followed her into the bedroom and forced her to have intercourse with him. The accused claimed the intercourse was consensual. The complainant later returned to the living room in an upset state and then went for a walk with M. In her statement to police she stated that she had consensual intercourse with M in a stairwell while they were absent from the apartment. **Should there be a new trial?**

See *R. v. Butts* (2012), 285 C.C.C. (3d) 569, 91 C.R. (6th) 424 (Ont. C.A.) and C.R. annotation by Janine Benedet.

Problem 8

The accused was charged with several sexual offences against his niece, who was 8 years old at the time of the alleged abuse and 12 years old at the time of trial. The Crown alleged that the accused repeatedly sexually abused the complainant in his home while he was babysitting her and when she was visiting his family. The accused denied the allegations. The accused and his wife and son all testified that the accused was never alone with the complainant.

At trial, the defence applied under s. 276 of the *Criminal Code* to cross-examine the complainant about an allegation she had made that she had been sexually abused by her biological father before the time period in which the accused's alleged abuse began. The trial judge refused to permit the cross-examination.

Both the complainant and her mother testified about the complainant's initial disclosure of the abuse to her mother when the complainant was 10 years of age. The trial judge did not offer any limiting instruction to the jury about the use they could make of the evidence related to the complainant's initial disclosure.

In her testimony, the complainant recounted an incident in which the accused assaulted her brother, who ended up with a goose egg on his head. The trial judge did not offer any limiting instruction to the jury about the use they could make of the evidence of this alleged assault.

In his charge to the jury, the trial judge reviewed the evidence of the accused's son that the accused was never alone with the complainant. He instructed the jury that it was for them to determine whether this evidence was a reliable expression of the son's recollection or "whether it was, for example, the scripted result of an interest in the outcome".

The accused was convicted. **Should the Court of Appeal find errors sufficient to order a new trial?**

Compare *R. v. T. (M.)* (2012) 289 C.C.C. (3d) 115, 95 C.R. (6th) 223 (Ont. C.A.).

Problem 9

The accused, who was charged with sexual assault, applied to cross-examine the complainant with regard to her past sexual activity with the accused, pursuant to the provisions of s. 276 of the *Criminal Code*. The accused sought to cross-examine the complainant about: (i) a statement she allegedly made to the accused that she had been raped by her ex-husband; (ii) that the complainant and the accused had cuddled and held each other while watching television; (iii) that the complainant had once put the accused's hand on her breast; and (iv) a nude photo of herself she had sent the accused.

The accused's position was that the sexual intercourse with the complainant giving rise to the charge was consensual or that he honestly believed that the complainant was consenting. **How would you rule on admissibility?**

See *R. v. Beilhartz*, 2013 ONSC 5670, 6 C.R. (7th) 79 (Ont. S.C.J.) and critical C.R. annotation by Janine Benedet.

Problem 10

The accused was charged with sexually assaulting his wife. He applied under s. 276 of the *Criminal Code* to introduce evidence of prior sexual activity between himself and the complainant. The complainant and the accused were married two months after they met. A few weeks into the marriage, the complainant alleged that the accused pushed her and ripped her underwear off in an attempt to force intercourse on her. He later pushed his penis in her face and she bit him slightly to get him to stop. The accused eventually left the home and the complainant called police.

The accused acknowledged the sexual activity but took the position that the complainant consented. He sought to introduce evidence that on one prior occasion they had engaged in consensual sexual activity in which the complainant bit him on the penis and scratched him. He argued that the evidence was relevant to the credibility of the complainant's claim that she did not consent. The Crown opposed the application on the ground that the accused was arguing that the complainant ought not to be believed because she had sex like that before. **Was the evidence admissible?**

See *R. v. G. (G.)*, 2015 ONSC 5321, 22 C.R. (7th) 415 (Ont. S.C.J.) and C.R. comment by Janine Benedet.

Problem 11

The 18-year-old accused was charged with sexual interference against the complainant, who was 11 or 12 years old when the two instances of sexual intercourse took place. Both the accused and the complainant were Indigenous. The accused brought an application under s. 276 of the *Criminal Code* to cross-examine the complainant on statements she made to a social worker that she had engaged in oral and digital sexual contact with a girl who was around four years older than her sometime prior to the sexual intercourse with the accused, and may also have had some sexual contact with a second girl.

Defence counsel argued that the cross-examination was relevant to the complainant's credibility, since she had testified at the preliminary inquiry that her activity with the accused was "the first time ever having sex with somebody" and also that the accused had asked her age during their first sexual encounter and that she had told him she was 11 or 12 years old. He also claimed that the evidence would be relevant to the accused's defence that he honestly believed that the complainant was 14 or 15 years old and thus that he was less than 5 years older than her when the sexual intercourse took place. In such circumstances, he could raise her consent as a defence. **Was the evidence of the complainant's prior sexual experience admissible?**

See *R. v. Ward*, 2016 NBBR 2, 2016 NBQB 2, 28 C.R. (7th) 19 (N.B. Q.B.) and C.R. comment by Janine Benedet.

Problem 12

The male accused was charged with offences including sexual assault against the female complainant, his wife at the time. The sexual assault charge involved an alleged incident of non-consensual anal sex. In her statement to police, the complainant stated that anal sex was not her preference but that she often went along with it because it was what the accused wanted. The defence tendered evidence of a sex video made by the accused and the complainant in which the complainant called herself a "slut" and engaged in anal sex with the accused with apparent eagerness. **Is the video admissible?**

See *R. v. B. (S.)*, 2016 NLCA 20, 336 C.C.C. (3d) 38, 30 C.R. (7th) 61 (N.L. C.A.), reversed 2017 CSC 16, 2017 SCC 16, [2017] 1 S.C.R. 248, 346 C.C.C. (3d) 459, 36 C.R. (7th) 25 (S.C.C.).

B. HEARSAY

A picture of the hearsay rule with its exceptions would resemble an old-fashioned crazy quilt made of patches cut from a group of paintings by cubists, futurists and surrealists.[110]

---

[110]   Morgan & Maguire, "Looking Backward and Forward at Evidence" (1937) 50 Harv. L.R. 909 at 921.

1. THE RULE

(a) History

The hearsay rule was described by Professor Wigmore as "that most characteristic rule of the Anglo-American law of evidence — a rule which may be esteemed, next to jury trial, the greatest contribution of that eminently practical legal system to the world's methods of procedure".[111] It was not always thus, and it may assist our understanding of the rule's present-day workings and justifications if we have some regard for its origin.[112]

The jury initially was not to decide issues on the basis of evidence produced in open court; its members were selected because they had knowledge of the facts. Insofar as their knowledge was imperfect it was their function to investigate and gather information from those who were knowledgeable. The members of the jury were witnesses from the community, selected by a public official, who then tried the case.[113]

> We must not think of them as coming into court ignorant, like their modern successors, of the cases about which they will have to speak. . . . Some of the verdicts that are given must be founded on hearsay and floating tradition. Indeed, it is the duty of the jurors, so soon as they have been summoned, to make inquiries about the facts of which they will have to speak when they come before the court. They must collect testimony; they must weigh it and state the net result in a verdict. . . . At the least a fortnight had been given them in which to "certify themselves" of the facts. We know of no rule of law which prevented them from listening during this interval to the tale of the litigants; indeed it was their duty to discover the truth. . . . Separately or collectively, in court or out of court, they have listened to somebody's story and believed it. . . . We may say, if we will, that the old jurors were witnesses; but even in the early years of the thirteenth century they were not, and were hardly supposed to be, eye-witnesses.[114]

Witnesses had been called before the jury during the thirteenth and fourteenth centuries but these were pre-appointed witnesses; witnesses who had agreed at the time of the transaction to support its credit if later called upon, for example, attesting witnesses to a deed. These witnesses joined with the jurors and conferred privately to make a finding; they did not, until the middle of the fourteenth century,[115] testify in open court, but rather assisted the jury members with their particular knowledge. Professor Thayer described it:

> In the earlier cases these witnesses sometimes appear to have been conceived of as a constituent part of the jury; it was a combination of business witnesses and community witnesses who tried the case, the former supplying to others their more exact information. . . . But in time the jury and the witnesses came to be

---

[111]   5 Wigmore, *Evidence* (Chad. Rev.) at 28.

[112]   A full account is provided in 5 Wigmore, *Evidence* (Chad. Rev.) at 1364. And see Morgan, "History and Theory of the Hearsay Rule" in *Some Problems of Proof under the Anglo-American System of Litigation* (New York: Columbia University Press, 1956) at 106-140.

[113]   See generally Thayer, "Trial by Jury and Its Development" in *A Preliminary Treatise on Evidence at the Common Law* (1898) ch. 3.

[114]   Pollock & Maitland, *The History of English Law*, 2nd ed. (1898) vol. 2 at 621-628.

[115]   See Thayer, *supra* note 113 at 125.

sharply discriminated. . . . The charge to the jury is to tell the truth to the best of their knowledge, while that to the witnesses is to tell the truth and loyally inform the inquest, without saying anything about their knowledge; "for the witnesses," says Thorpe, C.J. in 1349, "should say nothing but what they know as certain, i.e., what they see and hear."

It was not until the latter part of the fifteenth century that ordinary witnesses as we know them today, casual witnesses as Bentham called them, began to testify in open court about disputed facts. The earlier prohibition against the pre-appointed witnesses speaking to second-hand information may have caused litigants and judges to be skeptical about the value of hearsay from these new witnesses, and while it was being received there was constant worrying over its worth, and agitation for reform.

In 1552 the first statutory attempt at reform took place.[116] Although it was confined to treason trials, it demanded the production of the accusers, if then alive, to confront the accused at the trial and maintain their earlier depositions. This requirement was a marked departure from the then-normal criminal trial process wherein previously sworn depositions were routinely filed. The celebrated case of Sir Walter Raleigh's prosecution on an indictment for conspiracy to commit various treasons[117] illustrates the practice of the time, the narrow judicial construction given the statutory efforts at reform, and the arguments then being made for change. When Raleigh demanded his statutory right to be confronted with his accuser, Lord Cobham, he was refused:

Raleigh:	The Proof of the Common Law is by witness and jury: let Cobham be here, let him speak it. Call my accuser before my face, and I have done. . . . All this is but one Accusation of Cobham's, I hear no other thing; to which accusation he never subscribed nor avouched it. I beseech you, my lords, let Cobham be sent for, charge him on his soul, on his allegiance to the King; if he affirm it, I am guilty. . . . By the rigour and cruelty of the law (the Accusation) may be a forcible evidence.
Popham, L.C.J.:	That is not the rigour of the law, but the justice of the law; else when a man hath made a plain Accusation, by practice he might be brought to retract it again.
Raleigh:	Oh my lord, you may use equity.
L.C.J.:	That is from the King; you are to have justice from us. . . . This thing cannot be granted, for then a number of Treasons should flourish: the Accuser may be drawn by practise, whilst he is in person.

---

[116]   5 & 6 Edw. VI, c. 11, s. 12. "Which said accusers at the time of the arraignment of the party accused, if they be then living, shall be brought in person before the party so accused, and avow and maintain that which they have to say to prove him guilty." And, in (1554), 1 & 2 Phil. & Mar., c. 10, s. 11: Upon arraignment for treason the persons "or two of them at the least", who shall declare any thing against the accused "shall, if living and within the realm, be brought forth in person before the party arraigned if he require the same, and object and say openly in his hearing what they or any of them can against him".

[117]   *Sir Walter Raleigh's Trial* (1603), 2 Howell's State Trials 1 at 15-19.

Gawdy, J.:	The Statute you speak of concerning two Witnesses in case of Treason, is found to be inconvenient, therefore by another law it was taken away.
Raleigh:	The common Trial of England is by Jury and Witnesses.
Warburton, J.:	I marvel, Sir Walter, that you being of such experience and wit, should stand on this point; for so many horse-stealers may escape, if they may not be condemned without witnesses. . . . My Lord Cobham hath, perhaps, been labored withal; and to save you, his old friend, it may be that he will deny all that which he hath said.
Raleigh:	I know not how you conceive the Law.
L.C.J.:	Nay, we do not conceive the Law, but we know the Law.
Raleigh:	Indeed, where the Accuser is not to be had conveniently, I agree with you; but here my Accuser may; he is alive, and in the house. Susanna had been condemned, if Daniel had not cried out, "Will you condemn an innocent Israelite, without examination or knowledge of the truth?" Remember, it is absolutely the Commandment of God: If a false witness rise up, you shall cause him to be brought before the Judges; if he be found false, he shall have the punishment which the accused should have had. It is very sure, for my lord to accuse me is my certain danger, and it may be a means to excuse himself. . . . Good my lords, let my Accuser come face to face, and be deposed.
L.C.J.:	You have no law for it.

Common law courts disapproved of hearsay evidence with increasing frequency throughout the seventeenth and eighteenth centuries. By the end of the eighteenth century, this disapproval hardened into an exclusionary rule in both civil and criminal practice.[118] As the parties took greater control over what evidence would be presented, and challenged the worth of evidence presented by their opponent, the adversary system and the peculiarly English technique of cross-examination was fashioned. With these developments, the hearsay rule was born as a natural counterpart. Juries were to be informed by witnesses with personal knowledge, speaking on oath, publicly, in their presence and in the presence of the parties, and were to be open to cross-examination when they expressed themselves; if the evidence was otherwise it was to be excluded as hearsay.

Against this background, observe two cases which display the early stated reasons for the hearsay rule. In the trial of Braddon and Speke[119] in 1684, the accused seeks to lead evidence:

Jeffries, L.C.J.:	Does she know anything of her own knowledge?
Braddon:	She can tell what she heard, my lord.

---

[118]   See Langebin, *The Origins of Adversary Criminal Trial* (New York: Oxford University Press, 2003) at 242.

[119]   *Re Braddon and Speke* (1684), 9 Howell's State Trials 1127 at 1188-1189.

L.C.J.:   'Tis no evidence. . . . Where is the woman that told her? Why is not she brought?

Counsel for   They say, she is so big with child she can't come.
Braddon:

L.C.J.:   Why, if that woman were here herself, if she did say it, and would not swear it, we could not hear her; how then can her saying be an evidence before us? I wonder to hear any man that wears a gown, to make a doubt of it.

The rule is now settled law, and became a source of pride to the English lawyer, as we read in a note from 1730:

The excellency therefore of our laws above others, I take chiefly to consist in that part of them, which regards Criminal Prosecutions: here indeed it may with great truth and justice be said, that we have by far the better of our neighbours, and are deservedly their admiration and envy.

This might be made to appear in many particulars. In other Countries . . . the Witnesses are examined in private, and in the Prisoner's absence; with us they are produced face to face, and deliver their Evidence in open court, the prisoner himself being present, and at liberty to cross-examine them.[120]

(b) Reason for Rule

In Hawkins' *Pleas of the Crown* we read:

It seems agreed, that what a Stranger has been heard to say is in Strictness no manner of Evidence either for or against a Prisoner, not only because it is not upon Oath but also because the other Side hath no opportunity of a cross-examination.[121]

While it is sometimes said[122] that the hearsay rule was fashioned out of a distrust for the lay juror's capacity to properly assess the worth of the evidence, the history noted above confirms Professor Morgan's view that the reasons for the rule given at the time by judges and commentators:

. . . have to do with the credulity not of jurors but of witnesses. . . . Not one of them even suggests a peculiar incapacity of jurors to evaluate such evidence, and so long as jurors could properly rely upon what they learned by inquiry or otherwise outside the presence of the court, any such suggestion would have bordered on absurdity.[123]

Nevertheless, distrust for the jury's capacity to adequately assess hearsay becomes an after-the-fact added justification. The trier of fact will be more assured of accuracy in his or her decision if descriptions of events are given in open court rather than through an intermediary. Trustworthiness of

---

[120] Emlyn's Preface to the Second Edition of the State Trials, 1 Howell's State Trials, XXV.
[121] Hawkins, *Pleas of the Crown* (1716), Book II, c. 46, s. 14 as noted by Morgan, *supra* note 112 at 111.
[122] See e.g. Ewaschuk, "Hearsay Evidence" (1978) Osgoode Hall L.J. 407.
[123] Morgan, *supra* note 112 at 112.

decision-making is enhanced for a number of reasons which may be grouped under two heads. First, the witness who speaks in open court is subject to a perjury prosecution should he or she lie; this witness who speaks in open court is encouraged to speak honestly and without exaggeration by the solemnity of the occasion and by the presence of the party against whose interests he or she speaks; the witness' manner of speaking, his or her demeanour, will be available for review by the trier of fact, who will thus be better able to evaluate his or her credibility. The second group of reasons resides in our adversary system and in the faith we repose in "the greatest legal engine ever invented for the discovery of truth"[124] — cross-examination. The description of a past event by a witness has resident within it the possibility of error due to at least four dangers.[125] The description may be defective because first, the witness did not perceive the incident accurately; second, the witness does not now remember the incident accurately; third, the witness' language describing the incident may be ambiguous or otherwise defective and the communication of his or her thoughts may therefore be misunderstood; fourth, the witness may be presently insincere in his or her account and wish to deliberately mislead the trier of fact. These four dangers may be guarded against by canvassing their existence through cross-examination which, of course, is only possible when the individual with the personal knowledge is present in the witness stand; the adversary may be greatly prejudiced if the description comes in through the relation of another who has no ability to aid in exposing possible defects in the declarant's perception, memory, communication or sincerity.

If we keep this background of history and reason in mind, we will be better able to deal with the ever-recurring problem of identifying whether a particular piece of evidence is hearsay, and we should also be better able to construct arguments for and against the receivability of hearsay evidence in a particular case.

(c) Identifying Hearsay

Professor McCormick defined hearsay:

Hearsay evidence is testimony in court, or written evidence, of a statement made out of court, the statement being offered as an assertion to show the truth of matters asserted therein, and thus resting for its value upon the credibility of the out-of-court asserter.[126]

Notice particularly the closing lines of that definition, "resting for its value upon the credibility of the out-of-court asserter". Why is that a requirement? Because, as we discussed above, the principal reasons for excluding hearsay evidence are the lack of the protective safeguards of oath and cross-

---

[124]   5 Wigmore, *Evidence* (Chad. Rev.), c. 1367 at 32.
[125]   See the classic exposition by Morgan, "Hearsay Dangers and the Application of the Hearsay Concept" (1948) 62 Harv. L. Rev. 177.
[126]   McCormick, *Evidence*, 2nd ed. (1972) at 584.

examination, safeguards which are only necessary when the value of the evidence depends on the credibility of the asserter.

A sues B for failure to deliver lumber in accordance with their contract; B defends, denying the existence of any contract. A calls X to testify that he heard B unequivocally and unambiguously agreeing to deliver lumber to A on a certain date for a certain price. Clearly this is not hearsay, as we care not whether B was sincere in expressing his intention to accept the terms. The legal consequences of a valid contract are produced by the fact that B spoke the words, and the value of the words does not rest on the credibility of the out-of-court asserter.[127] Similarly, proof of statements constituting defamation would not offend the hearsay rule; the proponent of the evidence is obviously not attempting to prove the truth asserted within the statements.[128] Words accompanying actions often characterize the same, and if the substantive law has an objective test of intention, the words are receivable.[129] Statements made by suspects which are established as false during the course of a police investigation may be received as non-hearsay evidencing a consciousness of guilt.[130] The list of situations of relevant non-hearsay statements, and their variety, is limitless, and their identification is only eased when the purpose of the hearsay rule is kept in the forefront.

Identifying whether an out-of-court statement is hearsay or not is seen by many as a difficult exercise and various formulae of words have been used for the purpose. The best way to begin is to ask:

1. Who is the declarant? (i.e., who uttered the out-of-court statement?)
2. What does the statement assert?
3. What is the purpose of tendering the assertion?
4. If it is to prove the truth of the assertion, there is a hearsay problem.

One popular formula of words is problematic. Ask whether the statement is being tendered for its truth or tendered for the fact that the statement was made. Although this is perhaps a fair description, the formula frequently produces circumlocutions that confound. It is not unusual for counsel to seek an end run around the hearsay rule by insisting that he or she is not tendering the evidence for the purpose of establishing its truth but rather only for the purpose of establishing that the statement was in fact made. When counsel offers such in justification, the adversary should ask the proponent of the evidence to precisely articulate the relevance in the case resident in the fact that the statement was made. It will often be seen that the only relevance that can be found will reside in accepting the speaker's belief concerning an external event as accurate; the statement will be seen to be of value only if we assume its truth. The statement on close analysis will often be seen to be hearsay.

---

[127]   See *Creaghe v. Iowa Home Mut. Casualty Co.*, 323 F. 2d 981 (10th Cir., 1963).
[128]   See *Dalrymple v. Sun Life Assur. Co.*, [1966] 2 O.R. 227 (C.A.), affirmed (1967), 60 D.L.R. (2d) 192n (S.C.C.).
[129]   See *Leeson v. Leeson*, [1936] 2 K.B. 156 (C.A.).
[130]   See *Mawaz Khan v. R.*, [1967] 1 A.C. 454 (P.C.).

A better analytical technique for determining whether a statement is hearsay would be framed in terms of the underlying concern of the rule. As with the proper application of all rules of evidence, it is wise to always keep in mind the purpose of the rule. Given the basis for the hearsay rule — the adversary's inability to cross-examine the person with knowledge of the event — we can then construct an analytical tool for identifying hearsay. If there are relevant, meaningful questions that the adversary might wish to ask of the person who made the out-of-court statement, then the out-of-court statement is hearsay; if there are no meaningful questions that can be put, the statement is not hearsay. To properly identify whether or not an out-of-court statement is hearsay keep in mind the reason for the rule.

An example from the cases might assist. In *Subramaniam v. Public Prosecutor*,[131] the accused had been convicted of unlawfully possessing ammunition contrary to Emergency Regulations in Malaya and was sentenced to death. His defence had been duress and he sought to relate conversations he had had with the terrorists who had threatened him; the trial court ruled this evidence was hearsay, and not admissible unless the terrorists were called. The Privy Council held that the trial judge was in error and noted:

> Evidence of a statement made to a witness by a person who is not himself called as a witness may or may not be hearsay. It is hearsay and inadmissible when the object of the evidence is to establish the truth of what is contained in the statement. It is not hearsay and is admissible when it is proposed to establish by the evidence, not the truth of the statement, but the fact that it was made. The fact that the statement was made, quite apart from its truth, is frequently relevant in considering the mental state and conduct thereafter of the witness or of some other person in whose presence the statement was made.

The Privy Council then noted that the value of the impugned evidence in this case did not rest on the credibility of the out-of-court asserter; the value of the evidence was in the fact of the statement having been made, since if believed by the accused it would support his defence of duress. The trier of fact would not be misled, nor the adversary prejudiced, by the absence from the witness stand of the terrorist-declarant. If the terrorist were called as a witness, what questions would the adversary ask? Could the adversary ask the terrorist if he was sincere when he treatened the accused? If he intended to communicate a threat? Surely these questions would be properly objected to as immaterial since the issue before the Court was not the terrorist's state of mind but rather the accused's. Since it was the fact of the statement having been made that was relevant, the adversary would be protected and trustworthiness guarded by allowing the accused to testify; the accused is on oath and may be cross-examined regarding his sincerity, perception and memory concerning whether the statement was in fact made.

---

[131] [1956] 1 W.L.R. 965, 970 (P.C.). Compare *R. v. Bencardino* (1973), 15 C.C.C. (2d) 342 (Ont. C.A.): a witness had denied being threatened and the Court held that another might be called to testify that the same witness had earlier told him he had been threatened "because the evidence will be received not to prove the fact of intimidation but rather to prove [witness'] state of mind of fear". The Court relied on *Subramanian*. Do you agree?

A more modern example may be seen in the case of *R. v. Dunn*.[132] On a charge of threatening, the Crown needed to establish that the interception of the telecommunication containing the threat was lawfully made. The wiretap provisions of the *Criminal Code*[133] provide that an intercept is lawfully made if the recipient of the communication has consented to the interception. The prosecution sought to lead evidence of conversations between the police officer and the victim, by then deceased, in which the victim, the recipient of the telecommunication, had given her consent to the interception. The defence objected to this evidence as hearsay, the Court agreed, and the evidence was ruled inadmissible. Fortunately, the Court found the necessary consent by implication from other evidence, and later confessed its error in identifying the evidence as hearsay. The Court had initially failed to recognize that the value of the evidence did not rest on the credibility of the out-of-court asserter. The police officer had been tendered to testify to an objective fact which he had observed, consent given, the relevance of which resided simply in its happening. The adversary was not prejudiced in being unable to cross-examine the complainant regarding what she meant by the words she uttered and the trier of fact could equally well decide, without her presence, whether the words uttered amounted to a valid consent.[134]

Understanding the purpose of the rule is essential to avoid errors in identification of out-of-court statements. Justice MacDonald described it very well:

> Essentially it is not the form of the statement that gives it its hearsay or non-hearsay characteristics but the use to which it is put. Whenever a witness testifies that someone said something, immediately one should then ask, "what is the relevance of the fact that someone said something". If, therefore, the relevance of the statement lies in the fact that it was made, it is the making of the statement that is the evidence — the truth or falsity of the statement is of no consequence: if the relevance of the statement lies in the fact that it contains an assertion which is, itself, a relevant fact, then it is the truth or falsity of the statement that is in issue. The former is not hearsay, the latter is.[135]

R. v. KHELAWON
[2006] 2 S.C.R. 787, 42 C.R. (6th) 1, 215 C.C.C. (3d) 161 (S.C.C.)

CHARRON J. (MCLACHLIN C.J., BINNIE, LEBEL, DESCHAMPS, FISH, and ABELLA JJ. concurring): —

---

[132] (1975), 28 C.C.C. (2d) 538 (N.S. Co. Ct.).
[133] Section 189.
[134] On the same point the Ontario Court of Appeal properly noted that "consent was an issue of fact in these proceedings and could be proved like any other fact in issue": *R. v. Cremascoli and Goldman* (1977), 38 C.C.C. (2d) 212 at 217, per Brooke, J.A. Curiously the Supreme Court of Canada was less than emphatic in its approval: "While I am inclined to agree with that statement, I do not consider it necessary to deal with the point." (1979), 51 C.C.C. (2d) 1 at 25, per McIntyre, J.
[135] *R. v. Baltzer* (1974), 27 C.C.C. (2d) 118 (N.C. C.A.) at 143.

Definition of Hearsay

At the outset, it is important to determine what is and what is not hearsay. The difficulties in defining hearsay encountered by courts and learned authors have been canvassed before and need not be repeated here: see *R. v. Abbey*, [1982] 2 S.C.R. 24, at pp. 40-41, *per* Dickson J. It is sufficient to note, as this Court did in *Starr*, at para. 159, that the more recent definitions of hearsay are focussed on the central concern underlying the hearsay rule: the difficulty of testing the reliability of the declarant's assertion. See, for example, *R. v. O'Brien*, [1978] 1 S.C.R. 591, at pp. 593-94. Our adversary system puts a premium on the calling of witnesses, who testify under oath or solemn affirmation, whose demeanour can be observed by the trier of fact, and whose testimony can be tested by cross-examination. We regard this process as the optimal way of testing testimonial evidence. Because hearsay evidence comes in a different form, it raises particular concerns. The general exclusionary rule is a recognition of the difficulty for a trier of fact to assess what weight, if any, is to be given to a statement made by a person who has not been seen or heard, and who has not been subject to the test of cross-examination. The fear is that untested hearsay evidence may be afforded more weight than it deserves. The essential defining features of hearsay are therefore the following: (1) the fact that the statement is adduced to prove the truth of its contents and (2) the absence of a contemporaneous opportunity to cross-examine the declarant. I will deal with each defining feature in turn.

Statements Adduced for Their Truth

The purpose for which the out-of-court statement is tendered matters in defining what constitutes hearsay because it is only when the evidence is tendered to prove the truth of its contents that the need to test its reliability arises. Consider the following example. At an accused's trial on a charge for impaired driving, a police officer testifies that he stopped the accused's car because he received information from an unidentified caller that the car was driven by a person who had just left a local tavern in a "very drunk" condition. If the statement about the inebriated condition of the driver is introduced for the sole purpose of establishing the police officer's grounds for stopping the vehicle, it does not matter whether the unidentified caller's statement was accurate, exaggerated, or even false. Even if the statement is totally unfounded, that fact does not take away from the officer's explanation of his actions. If, on the other hand, the statement is tendered as proof that the accused was in fact impaired, the trier of fact's inability to test the reliability of the statement raises real concerns. Hence, only in the latter circumstance is the evidence about the caller's statement defined as hearsay and subject to the general exclusionary rule.

Absence of Contemporaneous Cross-Examination

The previous example, namely where the witness tells the court what A told him, is the more obvious form of hearsay evidence. A is not before the court to be seen, heard and cross-examined. However, the traditional law of hearsay also extends to out-of-court statements made by the witness who does testify in court when that out-of-court statement is tendered to prove the truth of its contents. This extended definition of hearsay has been adopted in Canada: *R. v. B. (K.G.)*, [1993] 1 S.C.R. 740, at pp. 763-64; *Starr*, at para. 158. It is important to understand the rationale for treating a witness's out-of-court statements as hearsay.

When the witness repeats or adopts an earlier out-of-court statement, in court, under oath or solemn affirmation, of course no hearsay issue arises. The statement itself is not evidence, the testimony is the evidence and it can be tested in the usual way by observing the witness and subjecting him or her to cross-examination. The hearsay issue does arise, however, when the witness does not repeat or adopt the information contained in the out-of-court statement and the statement itself is tendered for the truth of its contents. Consider the following example to illustrate the concerns raised by this evidence.

In an out-of-court statement, W identifies the accused as her assailant. At the trial of the accused on a charge of assault, W testifies that the accused is *not* her assailant. The Crown seeks to tender the out-of-court statement as proof of the fact that the accused did assault W. In these circumstances, the trier of fact is asked to accept the out-of-court statement over the sworn testimony of the witness. Given the usual premium placed on the value of in-court testimonial evidence, a serious issue arises as to whether it is at all necessary to introduce the statement. In addition, the reliability of that statement becomes crucial. How trustworthy is it? In what circumstances did W make that statement? Was it made casually to friends at a social function, or rather, to the police as a formal complaint? Was W aware of the potential consequences of making that statement, did she intend that it be acted upon? Did she have a motive to lie? In what condition was W at the time she made the statement? Many more questions can come to mind on matters that relate to the reliability of that out-of-court statement. When the trier of fact is asked to consider the out-of-court statement as proof that the accused in fact assaulted W, assessing its reliability may prove to be difficult.

Concerns over the reliability of the statement also arise where W does not recant the out-of-court statement but testifies that she has no memory of making the statement, or worse still, no memory of the assault itself. The trier of fact does not see or hear the witness making the statement and, because there is no opportunity to cross-examine the witness *contemporaneously* with the making of the statement, there may be limited opportunity for a meaningful testing of its truth. In addition, an issue may arise as to whether the prior statement is fully and accurately reproduced.

Hence, although the underlying rationale for the general exclusionary rule may not be as obvious when the declarant is available to testify, it is the same — the difficulty of testing the reliability of the out-of-court statement. The difficulty of assessing W's out-of-court statement is the reason why it falls within the definition of hearsay and is subject to the general exclusionary rule. As one may readily appreciate, however, the degree of difficulty may be substantially alleviated in cases where the declarant is available for cross-examination on the earlier statement, particularly where an accurate record of the statement can be tendered in evidence. I will come back to that point later. My point here is simply to explain why, by definition, hearsay extends to out-of-court statements tendered for their truth even when the declarant is before the court.

R. v. BALDREE
2013 SCC 35, [2013] 2 S.C.R. 520, 298 C.C.C. (3d) 425, 3 C.R. (7th) 10 (S.C.C.)

The accused was charged with possessing marijuana and cocaine for the purposes of trafficking. When the accused was arrested, police seized his cell phone, and shortly thereafter a police officer answered a call to the cell phone from a person who wanted to buy marijuana. The caller identified the accused by his first and last name, and specified an amount of marijuana and the price the accused usually charged. The caller provided an address for delivery but the police did not visit that address or try to find the caller. The trial judge admitted the call as circumstantial evidence that the accused was engaged in drug trafficking and convicted the accused. The accused appealed and the Ontario Court of Appeal allowed the appeal, quashed the conviction and ordered a new trial. The Crown appealed to the Supreme Court of Canada

The Crown's appeal was dismissed and the order for a new trial was affirmed. The Court held that the call to the accused's phone should have been excluded. At this point we consider the Court's ruling that assertions implied in verbal statements are properly considered hearsay.

FISH J. (MCLACHLIN C.J., LEBEL, ABELLA, ROTHSTEIN, CROMWELL, KARAKATSANIS, WAGNER JJ., concurring):

1 An out-of-court statement by a person not called as a witness in the proceedings is properly characterized as hearsay where it is tendered in evidence to make proof of the truth of its contents.

2 It is undisputed on this appeal that hearsay evidence is presumptively inadmissible as a matter of law.

3 The sole issue is whether this exclusionary rule applies to "express hearsay" only, or to "implied hearsay" as well. As a matter of logic and of principle, I am satisfied that it does.

4 In both instances, the relevance of the out-of-court statement is not *that the statement was made*, but rather *what the content of the statement purports to prove*. And, in both instances, what the statement purports to prove is the truth of what the person not called as a witness is alleged to have asserted—expressly or by implication.

5 With respect to their logical relevance, there is thus no substantive distinction between express and implied hearsay. The principled reasons for their presumptive inadmissibility apply equally to both.

. . .

IV

30 The defining features of hearsay are (1) the fact that the statement is adduced to prove the truth of its contents and (2) the absence of a contemporaneous opportunity to cross-examine the declarant: *R. v. Khelawon*, 2006 SCC 57, [2006] 2 S.C.R. 787, at para. 56. As Justice Charron explained in *Khelawon*, at para. 35, the hearsay rule reflects the value our criminal justice system places on live, in-court testimony:

> Our adversary system puts a premium on the calling of witnesses, who testify under oath or solemn affirmation, whose demeanour can be observed by the trier of fact, and whose testimony can be tested by cross-examination. We regard this process as the optimal way of testing testimonial evidence. Because hearsay evidence comes in a different form, it raises particular concerns. The general exclusionary rule is a recognition of the difficulty for a trier of fact to assess what weight, if any, is to be given to a statement made by a person who has not been seen or heard, and who has not been subject to the test of cross-examination. The fear is that untested hearsay evidence may be afforded more weight than it deserves.

31 In short, hearsay evidence is presumptively inadmissible because of the difficulties inherent in testing the reliability of the declarant's assertion. Apart from the inability of the trier of fact to assess the declarant's demeanour in making the assertion, courts and commentators have identified four specific concerns. They relate to the declarant's perception, memory, narration, and sincerity: *Khelawon*, at para. 2; *R. v. Starr*, 2000 SCC 40, [2000] 2 S.C.R. 144, at para. 159.

32 First, the declarant may have *misperceived* the facts to which the hearsay statement relates; second, even if correctly perceived, the relevant facts may have been *wrongly remembered*; third, the declarant may have narrated the relevant facts in an *unintentionally misleading manner*; and finally, the declarant may have *knowingly made a false assertion*. The opportunity to fully probe these potential sources of error arises only if the declarant is present in court and subject to cross-examination.

. . .

35 The hearsay rule, like many others, is easier to state than to apply.

36 No evidence is hearsay on its face. As mentioned at the outset, its admissibility depends on the *purpose* for which it is sought to be admitted. Evidence is hearsay - and presumptively inadmissible - if it is tendered to make proof of the truth of its contents.

V

37 Plainly, in this case, the Crown adduced Sgt. Martelle's evidence as proof of the truth of its contents. Since the declarant was not called to testify, Sgt.

Martelle's testimony constituted hearsay and was therefore presumptively inadmissible. Accordingly, in my view, the trial judge erred in failing to subject the evidence to a principled analysis.

38 Sergeant Martelle testified, it will be recalled, that someone claiming to be a resident of 327 Guy Street called the cell phone which Sgt. Martelle had seized from Chris Baldree, asked for Mr. Baldree, and requested an ounce of marijuana for the price of $150.

39 I agree with Feldman J.A. that the Crown did not offer this testimony as circumstantial evidence that the respondent was engaged in drug trafficking. Rather, the Crown asked the trier of fact to conclude, based on Sgt. Martelle's testimony, that the unknown caller intended to purchase marijuana from the respondent *because he believed the respondent to be a drug dealer*. The relevance of the statement thus hinges on the truth of the declarant's underlying belief. Any inference that can be drawn from the statement necessarily assumes its veracity.

40 Had the caller stated that he wanted to buy drugs from Mr. Baldree because *Mr. Baldree sells drugs*, this would have amounted to an express assertion that Mr. Baldree is a drug dealer. Thus framed, the caller's assertion would doubtless have constituted hearsay.

41 But the caller stated instead that he was calling because he wished to *purchase drugs from Mr. Baldree*. His assertion that Mr. Baldree is a drug dealer was no less manifest in substance, though implicit rather than explicit in form. In the Crown's submission, implied assertions are not caught by the hearsay rule and the telephone conversation was presumptively admissible for that reason.

42 In my view, the hearsay nature of this evidence cannot be made to depend on how the declarant framed his request. Such a formalistic analysis disregards the purposive approach to the hearsay rule adopted by this Court. Indeed, "it seems absurd that anything should turn on the grammatical form of the declarant's assertions": L. Dufraimont, Annotation to *R. v. Baldree* (2012), 92 C.R. (6th)331, at p. 334.

43 There is no principled or meaningful distinction between (a) "I am calling Mr. Baldree because I want to purchase drugs from him" and (b) "I am calling Mr. Baldree because he sells drugs". In either form, this out-of-court statement is being offered for an identical purpose: to prove the truth of the declarant's assertion that Mr. Baldree sells drugs. No trier of fact would need to be a grammarian in order to understand the import of this evidence.

44 The need for a functional approach to implied assertions is readily apparent, bearing in mind the core hearsay dangers of perception, memory, narration, and sincerity.

45 It has been argued that the danger of lack of sincerity is sometimes diminished for implied assertions. This is because "[i]f a declarant possesses no intention of asserting anything, it would seem to follow that he also possesses no intention of misrepresenting anything": P. R. Rice, "Should Unintended Implications of Speech be Considered Nonhearsay? The Assertive/ Nonassertive Distinction Under Rule 801(a) of the Federal Rules of Evidence" (1992), 65 *Temp. L. Rev.* 529, at p. 531.

46 But the other hearsay dangers clearly remain operative, and may in fact increase when an individual "states" something by implication:

> Looked at from the point of view of the four hearsay dangers, there is a much reduced risk of lies if the declarant did not intend to convey that which his statement is relied upon to prove, particularly if he it [*sic*] was not his purpose to make a representation of fact at all. But the other hearsay dangers remain, that is, the risk of misperception, false memory (unless the implied assertion concerns the declarant's own state of mind) and ambiguity. Indeed the last danger may be magnified. When X says: "Is Z in there?" does this imply that Z is not with X and nothing more, or that Z is not with X and X wants Z, or Z is in danger, or X wants to know where Z is? *The upshot is that in many situations implied assertions depend for their value on the reliability of the declarant just as much as express assertions.* [Emphasis added.]

(H. M. Malek et al., eds., *Phipson on Evidence* (17th ed. 2010), at p. 889)

Moreover, even insincerity remains a concern with implied assertions:

> If the justification for the assertive/nonassertive distinction is the absence of the insincerity problem, and through that guarantee of sincerity a reduced level of perception, memory, and ambiguity problems, this justification cannot be applied to implied statements from speech. Speech is a mechanism of communication; it is virtually always used for the purpose of communicating something to someone. It is illogical to conclude that the question of sincerity is eliminated and that the problem of unreliability is reduced for unintended implications of speech if that speech might have been insincere in the first instance, relative to the direct message intentionally communicated. If potential insincerity is injected into the utterance of words that form the basis for the implied communication, the implication from the speech is as untrustworthy as the utterance upon which it is based. [Rice, at p. 534]

47 In short, "if the standard for comparing express and implied assertions is the quantity of dangers each entails, they are indistinguishable": T. Finman, "Implied Assertions as Hearsay: Some Criticisms of the Uniform Rules of Evidence" (1962), 14 Stan. L. Rev. 682, at p. 689.

48 Accordingly, there is no principled reason, in determining their admissibility, to distinguish between express and implied assertions adduced for the truth of their contents. Both function in precisely the same way. And the benefits of cross-examining the declarant are not appreciably different when dealing with one form of testimony than the other. If an out-of-court statement implicates the traditional hearsay dangers, it constitutes hearsay and must be dealt with accordingly.

49 In the present matter, the trial judge and the dissenting judge in the Court of Appeal both found that this Court had decided otherwise in *Ly*. With respect, I disagree.

50 *Ly* concerned the admissibility of a telephone conversation between a police officer who had called a suspected "dial-a-dope" operation and the person who answered his call. The officer had called to arrange for the purchase and delivery of drugs. And the appellant, drugs in hand, later showed up at the agreed-upon time and place - where he was promptly arrested and charged with possession of drugs for the purpose of trafficking.

51 The trial judge characterized as hearsay, and excluded for that reason, evidence of the police officer's conversation with the person who had answered his call. On an appeal by the Crown, the Alberta Court of Appeal disagreed. It found that the impugned conversation was admissible as "part of the narrative", since "[i]t was impossible to understand the development of the later events without the evidence of the telephone conversation which preceded them" ((1996), 193 A.R. 149, at para. 3).

52 In brief oral reasons, this Court agreed with the Court of Appeal that evidence of the conversation was improperly excluded at trial. The Court noted that the conversation was tendered to explain why the appellant appeared at the designated time and place in possession of the drugs - and not, as in the case that concerns us here, for the truth of its contents: *Ly*, at para. 3.

53 I see nothing in *Ly* to suggest - let alone decide - that an implied assertion tendered for the truth of its contents stands on a different footing, with respect to the hearsay rule, than an explicit assertion to the same effect. Unlike *Ly*, that is the issue here.

54 And the issue now comes before us for the first time, though it has for at least half a century divided lower courts in several provinces: see, for example, *R. v. Fialkow*, [1963] 2 C.C.C. 42 (Ont. C.A.); *Edwards*; *Wilson*; *R. v. Lucia*, 2010 ONCA 533 (CanLII); *R. v. Cook* (1978), 10 B.C.L.R. 84 (C.A.); *R. v. Nguyen*, 2003 BCCA 556, 188 B.C.A.C. 218; *R. v. Parchment*, 2004 BCSC 1806 (CanLII); *R. v. Williams*, 2009 BCCA 284, [page538] 273 B.C.A.C. 86; *R. v. Graham*, 2013 BCCA 75 (CanLII); *R. v. Ramsum*, 2003 ABQB 45, 329 A.R. 370.

VI

55 The highest courts of England and Wales, and Australia, have likewise concluded that the hearsay rule governs implied assertions, only to have these decisions reversed by statute: see *Kearley*; *R. v. Bannon* (1995), 132 A.L.R. 87

(H.C.); *Criminal Justice Act 2003* (U.K.), 2003, c. 44, s. 115; *Evidence Act 1995* (Aust.), No. 2, s. 59(1).

56 In Canada, Parliament has not found it necessary or appropriate to adopt legislation classifying implied assertions as non-hearsay. This is, of course, entirely understandable in view of our principled and more flexible approach to exclusion.

57 As noted by Feldman J.A., the facts in *Kearley*, the leading British decision, were similar to the facts in this case. In *Kearley*, the police raided the home of the accused on suspicion that he was selling drugs. Drugs were found, but in insufficient quantities to support an inference of drug trafficking. While the police were present at the accused's residence, they intercepted ten telephone calls from callers asking to purchase drugs from him. Seven people also came to the apartment seeking to buy narcotics.

58 The majority of the House of Lords concluded that the drug purchase calls and the in-person statements were inadmissible hearsay. Because they were phrased as requests for drugs, the statements did not directly assert but instead implied that the accused was a drug dealer. However, whether stated expressly or impliedly, their Lordships found the information communicated to be the same. In Lord Ackner's words:

> ... if the inquirer had said in the course of making his request, "I would like my usual supply of amphetamine at the price which I paid you last week" ..., the hearsay rule prevents the prosecution from calling police officers to recount the conversation which I have described...

> If [however] the simple request or requests for drugs to be supplied by the appellant, as recounted by the police, contains in substance, but only by implication, the same assertion, then I can find neither authority nor principle to suggest that the hearsay rule should not be equally applicable and exclude such evidence. What is sought to be done is to use the oral assertion, even though it may be an implied assertion, as evidence of the truth of the proposition asserted. That the proposition is asserted by way of necessary implication rather than expressly cannot, to my mind, make any difference. [pp. 363-64]

59 Two main reasons have been urged against applying the hearsay rule to implied assertions.

60 First, as Watt. J.A. states (at para. 83) and as the Crown argues, excluding implied assertions as hearsay has the potential of broadening the exclusionary rule, given that "[v]irtually every human action is based on some set of assumptions implicitly accepted and, on this approach, 'asserted' by the actor" (A.F., at para. 62, quoting *McWilliams' Canadian Criminal Evidence* (4th ed. (loose-leaf)), at p. 7-21).

61 Second, as critics of *Kearley* have pointed out, applying the hearsay rule to implied assertions such as drug purchase calls has the potential to deprive the trier of fact of reliable evidence and thereby impede the truth-finding process:

see, for example, D. Birch, "Criminal Justice Act 2003 (4) Hearsay: Same Old Story, Same Old Song?", [2004] *Crim. L.R.* 556, at pp. 564-65.

62 The short answer to the first argument is that we are not concerned on this appeal with the application of the hearsay rule to assertions implied [page540] through non-verbal conduct. Our concern, rather, is with a quintessentially *verbal* statement.

63 The issue of the applicability of the hearsay rule to inferences that can be drawn from non-verbal conduct is best left for another day. For present purposes, I find it sufficient to say that "one can engage in conduct without ever intending to communicate *anything* to *anyone* [but] the same is not true of speech or a combination of speech and conduct (for example, placing a bet) because the sole purpose of speech is communication": Rice, at p. 536 (emphasis in original).

64 The second concern mentioned above is greatly attenuated, I again emphasize, by Canada's principled approach to hearsay.

65 In *Kearley*, having found the evidence in that case to be hearsay, it was automatically excluded because it did not fall within a traditional exception to the hearsay rule.

66 The Canadian approach suffers from no such inflexibility. Under our law, hearsay evidence that is not admissible under a traditional exception may nonetheless be admitted pursuant to a principled analysis of its necessity and reliability. This "sensible scheme" recognizes that "some implied assertions, like some express assertions, will be highly reliable even in the absence of cross-examination": Finman, at p. 693. Pursuant to its terms, implied assertions that are necessary and reliable may be admitted while those that are unreliable or unnecessary will be excluded.

PROBLEMS

Problem 1

For some reason the material issue is whether the plaintiff could speak on March 4, 1993. A witness is prepared to testify that on March 4, 1993, he heard the plaintiff say, "I can speak."

Hearsay?

Problem 2

The plaintiff claims that he entered into a contract with the defendant who agreed to sell his old car to the plaintiff for $500. The plaintiff wants to call a witness to testify that he heard the defendant say to the plaintiff, "I offer to sell you my old car for $500."

Hearsay? See *R. v. Cook*, [1986] 1 S.C.R. 144, 50 C.R. (3d) 96.

Problem 3

The witness is being examined in chief:

Q.: Did you see the accident?

A.: Yes.

Q.: Who had the green light?

A.: I can't remember. But I did tell my husband when I got home that day. He reminded me this morning.

Q.: What did you tell him?

Hearsay?

Problem 4

The accused claims that he was still suffering the effects of provocation when he attacked the victim, Tom Jones. The accused wants to testify that his wife said to him, "Tom Jones assaulted me."

Hearsay?

Problem 5

In a paternity suit, the plaintiff offers evidence that the defendant sent the child a birthday card addressed "To my darling son."

Hearsay?

Problem 6

A witness to an accident observes the plate number of the offending vehicle, makes a note of it, and communicates the number to another, who in turn records it. At the trial the witness no longer has his note and cannot recall the number, but the other person is prepared to testify to the number related. **What result?** Compare *R. v. Davey* (1969), 6 C.R.N.S. 288; and *R. v. Schantz* (1983), 34 C.R. (3d) 370 (Ont. Co. Ct.).

Problem 7

Defendant, a power tool manufacturer, was displaying his wares at a hardware exhibition. Plaintiff, a potential customer, while operating defendant's table saw, suffered the loss of two fingers for which he now brings suit. Defendant resists plaintiff's claim and maintains he was contributorily negligent. Defendant offers his employee to testify that shortly before plaintiff screamed the employee heard defendant shout "Put the guard down before operating the saw!" **Objectionable? Could employee testify that defendant told him "I told that nitwit to put the guard down before operating the saw!" Could defendant testify "I told that nitwit to put the guard down before operating the saw!"**

(d) Approaches to Hearsay

For many years courts in England and Canada were content to limit the admission of hearsay to slowly developed pigeon-hole exceptions which changed little over time. We shall see that Canadian courts have now developed a broad principled approach to admitting hearsay through criteria of reasonable necessity and circumstantial guarantees of reliability.

In *Myers v. D.P.P.*,[136] the majority of the House of Lords refused to create a new exception to the hearsay rule as there had not been a new exception created for some 90 years.[137] The accused had been prosecuted for conspiracy to receive stolen cars and it was necessary to establish that numbers on the cylinder blocks of the seized cars were the same numbers as on the blocks in the stolen cars. The prosecution sought to do this by introducing the business records of the manufacturer. The common law then recognized an exception to the hearsay rule for declarations made in the course of duty provided the declarant was deceased. The prosecution was unable to satisfy this condition as they were unable to identify the declarant who was but a single worker on a mass production assembly line. They tried to justify reception of the evidence on the basis of unavailability of the declarant, the consequent necessity of using the best evidence available, and assurances of trustworthiness arising from the circumstances in which the record was made. The majority insisted that the rule had become so fixed that only the legislature could create new exceptions to meet society's new needs and conditions.[138]

The law regarding hearsay can produce absurd results if it is slavishly and mechanically applied. As with any rule of evidence, we should always keep in mind the reason for the rule. If the reason for the rule is otherwise satisfied by the circumstances of a particular case the rule need not operate to exclude relevant evidence. The classic Canadian exposition of common sense in this area is seen in one of the first Supreme Court of Canada opinions choosing not to follow the House of Lords' lead.

In *Ares v. Venner*,[139] the Supreme Court of Canada faced the same question of deciding on the proper approach to hearsay. The plaintiff had suffered a broken leg while skiing. At the hospital Dr. Venner attended, reduced the fracture and applied a full-leg plaster cast. However, he later had to amputate the right leg and this led to a negligence suit. The trial judge received in evidence notes which had been made by the attending nurses. These notes described the plaintiff's toes as "blue", "bluish pink", "cool", and "cold", and were relevant to the issue of the doctor's negligence, as the trial court made the crucial finding that:

> The classic signs of circulatory impairment manifested themselves clearly and early.

---

[136]   [1965] A.C. 1001.
[137]   See *Sugden v. Lord St. Leonard's* (1876), 1 P.D. 154 (C.A.).
[138]   See the English response in the *Civil Evidence Act*, 1968, c. 64. And see Newark & Samuels, "Comment" (1968) 31 Mod. L. Rev. 668.
[139]   (1970), 14 D.L.R. (3d) 4 (S.C.C.).

The trial court described the usual medical practice in response to such signs and observed that the defendant had not followed such practice. The trial judge relied on a passage from Wigmore,[140] which argued for the admissibility of hospital records as an exception to the hearsay rule based on grounds of necessity and circumstantial guarantees of trustworthiness. Professor Wigmore had found the grounds of necessity in the "serious interference with convenience of hospital management", and the circumstances guaranteeing trustworthiness in the fact that they are made and relied on in affairs of life and death. The Alberta Court of Appeal ordered a new trial on the basis that the nurses' notes contained not just numerical data but observations expressed in opinions which would be fruitful areas of cross-examination. It also noted that one of Professor Wigmore's requirements for admissibility, grounds of necessity, was not satisfied here since the nurses had been subpoenaed by the plaintiff and were present throughout the trial. The Supreme Court of Canada restored the trial judgment.

Speaking for a unanimous Court, Hall J. noted that there had been a long-felt need for a restatement of the hearsay rule and that there were two schools of thought regarding how the change should come about — by legislative action or judicial action. He noted that in *Myers v. D.P.P.*, the learned Law Lords had split on the question of approach, with the majority agreeing to the need for reform but deciding it must be left to the legislature. Hall J. decided:

> I am of opinion that this Court should adopt and follow the minority view rather than resort to saying in effect: "This judge-made law needs to be restated to meet modern conditions, but we must leave it to Parliament and the ten legislatures to do the job."[141]

The Court in *Ares v. Venner* recognized that the adversary was not prejudiced by the reception of the nurses' notes. If the nurses were in fact called they would have been allowed to "refresh their memory" by having regard to their notes and little would be gained by their attendance as they would ordinarily add little or nothing to the information furnished by the record. The notes were made by trained observers and that should satisfy any concerns regarding the hearsay danger of perception. The notes were made contemporaneously with the observation and so concern for the memory danger should be stilled. Sincerity of the declarant should not be a concern as the nurses were under a duty to record their observations accurately and discipline could flow from any mistakes. The Court displayed a common sense, principled approach. The Court was aware of the reason for the rule and why that reason was not applicable to the particular factual situation before it.

For 20 years courts balked at applying *Ares v. Venner* in criminal cases. Then came *Khan*.

---

[140] 6 Wigmore, *Evidence* (Chad. Rev.), s. 1707.
[141] *Supra* note 139 at 16.

R. v. KHAN
[1990] 2 S.C.R. 531, 79 C.R. (3d) 1, 59 C.C.C. (3d) 92

The accused was charged with sexual assault. The alleged victim was three-and-a-half years old at the time of the assault. She attended with her mother at the office of the family doctor for a general examination of the mother and a routine examination of the child. The child was in the doctor's office, alone with the doctor, for five to seven minutes, while the mother undressed and put on a hospital gown. When the mother rejoined her child she noticed the child picking at a wet spot on her sleeve. The spot on the sleeve was determined to have been produced by a deposit of semen and, in some areas, a mixture of semen and saliva that had soaked through the fabric before it dried. The concentration of the mixture suggested to the forensic biologist that the substances were probably mixed before they were applied to the material. Fifteen minutes after they left the doctor's office, the mother and daughter had essentially the following conversation:

MRS. O.: So you were talking to Dr. Khan, were you? What did he say?

T.: He asked me if I wanted a candy. I said "Yes". And do you know what?

MRS. O.: What?

T.: He said, "Open your mouth". And do you know what? He put his birdie in my mouth, shook it and peed in my mouth.

MRS. O.: Are you sure?

T.: Yes.

MRS. O.: You're not lying to me, are you?

T.: No. He put his birdie in my mouth. And he never did give me my candy.

The mother testified that the word "birdie" meant penis to T. At the trial, T. was called as a witness. She was four years and eight months old. The trial judge ruled that she could not give evidence, sworn or unsworn. The trial judge also ruled that the child's statement to her mother was inadmissible hearsay and could not be adduced. The Ontario Court of Appeal held that the trial judge was wrong in not allowing the child to give unsworn evidence. The Court also held that the statement to the mother should have been received as falling within the exception for spontaneous declarations. In the Supreme Court it was decided that the Court of Appeal was right in their determination of error regarding the child's right to testify but, while agreeing that the child's statement deserved to be received, the Court decided the spontaneous declaration exception was not the appropriate route. Rejecting the Court of Appeal's approach, Madam Justice McLachlin, writing for the Court, noted, regarding

statements made by children to others about sexual abuse. Insofar as they are tied to the exception to the hearsay rule of spontaneous declarations . . . they suffer from certain defects. There is no requirement [of necessity].[142]

---

[142]   (1991), 79 C.R. (3d) 1 (S.C.C.) at 11.

The Court decided it would be more appropriate to adopt the more flexible and principled approach of *Ares v. Venner.* Madam Justice McLachlin, writing for the Court, decided that where there were grounds of necessity and circumstances surrounding the making of the statement, the hearsay could come in.

McLACHLIN J.:—

. . .

The hearsay rule has traditionally been regarded as an absolute rule, subject to various categories of exceptions, such as admissions, dying declarations, declarations against interest and spontaneous declarations. While this approach has provided a degree of certainty to the law on hearsay, it has frequently proved unduly inflexible in dealing with new situations and new needs in the law. This has resulted in courts in recent years on occasion adopting a more flexible approach, rooted in the principle and the policy underlying the hearsay rule rather than the strictures of traditional exceptions.

This Court took such an approach in *Ares v. Venner.* . . .

. . .

[There are] two general requirements: necessity and reliability. The child's statement to the mother in this case meets both these general requirements. Necessity was present, other evidence of the event, as the trial judge found, being inadmissible. . . . The evidence also bore strong indicia of reliability. T. was disinterested, in the sense that her declaration was not made in favour of her interest. She made the declaration before any suggestion of litigation. And beyond doubt she possessed peculiar means of knowledge of the event of which she told her mother. Moreover, the evidence of a child of tender years on such matters may bear its own special stamp of reliability.

. . .

These developments underline the need for increased flexibility in the interpretation of the hearsay rule to permit the admission in evidence of statements made by children to others about sexual abuse. Insofar as they are tied to the exception to the hearsay rule of spontaneous declarations, however, they suffer from certain defects. There is no requirement that resort to the hearsay evidence be necessary. Even where the evidence of the child might easily be obtained without undue trauma, the Crown would be able to use hearsay evidence. Nor is there any requirement that the reliability of the evidence in the particular be established; hence inherently unreliable evidence might be admitted. Finally, the rule being of an absolute "in-or-out" character, there is no means by which a trial judge could attach conditions on the reception of a particular statement which the judge might deem prudent in a particular case, as, for example, the right to cross-examine the deponent referred to in *Ares v. Venner*, supra. In addition to these objections, it can be argued that to extend the spontaneous declaration rule as far as these cases would extend it is to deform it beyond recognition and is conceptually undesirable.

In Canada too, courts have been moving to more flexibility in the reception of the hearsay evidence of children, although not under the aegis of the spontaneous declaration exception to the hearsay rule.

. . .

These cases point the way in the correct direction. Despite the need for caution, hearsay evidence of a child's statement may be received where the requirements of *Ares v. Venner* are met. The general approach is summed up in the comment of Wilson J. in *R. v. B. (G.)*, [1990] 2 S.C.R. 30 at 55 [Sask.]:

> In recent years we have adopted a much more benign attitude to children's evidence, lessening the strict standards of oath taking and corroboration, and I believe that this is a desirable development.

The first question should be whether reception of the hearsay statement is necessary. Necessity for these purposes must be interpreted as "reasonably necessary". The inadmissibility of the child's evidence might be one basis for a finding of necessity. But sound evidence based on psychological assessments that testimony in court might be traumatic for the child or harm the child might also serve. There may be other examples of circumstances which could establish the requirement of necessity.

The next question should be whether the evidence is reliable. Many considerations, such as timing, demeanour, the personality of the child, the intelligence and understanding of the child, and the absence of any reason to expect fabrication in the statement, may be relevant on the issue of reliability. I would not wish to draw up a strict list of considerations for reliability or to suggest that certain categories of evidence (for example the evidence of young children on sexual encounters) should be always regarded as reliable. The matters relevant to reliability will vary with the child and with the circumstances, and are best left to the trial judge.

In determining the admissibility of the evidence, the judge must have regard to the need to safeguard the interests of the accused. In most cases a right of cross-examination, such as that alluded to in *Ares v. Venner*, would not be available. If the child's direct evidence in chief is not admissible, it follows that his or her cross-examination would not be admissible either. Where trauma to the child is at issue, there would be little point in sparing the child the need to testify in chief only to have him or her grilled in cross-examination. While there may be cases where, as a condition of admission, the trial judge thinks it possible and fair in all the circumstances to permit cross-examination of the child as the condition of the reception of a hearsay statement, in most cases the concerns of the accused as to credibility will remain to be addressed by submissions as to the weight to be accorded to the evidence and submissions as to the quality of any corroborating evidence.

I add that I do not understand *Ares v. Venner* to hold that the hearsay evidence there at issue was admissible where necessity and reliability are established only where cross-examination is available. First, the court adopted the views of the dissenting judges in *Myers v. D.P.P.*, supra, which do not make admissibility dependent on the right to cross-examine. Second, the cross-examination referred to in *Ares v. Venner* was of limited value. The nurses were present in court at the trial, but, in the absence of some way of connecting particular nurses with particular entries, meaningful cross-examination on the accuracy of specific observations would have been difficult indeed.

I conclude that hearsay evidence of a child's statement on crimes committed against the child should be received, provided that the guarantees of necessity and reliability are met, subject to such safeguards as the judge may consider necessary and subject always to considerations affecting the weight that should be accorded to such evidence. This does not make out-of-court statements by children generally admissible; in particular, the requirement of necessity will probably mean that in most cases children will still be called to give viva voce evidence.

I conclude that the mother's statement in the case at bar should have been received. It was necessary, the child's viva voce evidence having been rejected. It was also reliable. The child had no motive to falsify her story, which emerged naturally and without prompting. Moreover, the fact that she could not be expected to have knowledge of such sexual acts imbues her statement with its own peculiar stamp of reliability. Finally, her statement was corroborated by real evidence. Having said this, I note that it may not be necessary to enter the statement on a new trial, if the child's viva voce evidence can be received as suggested in the first part of my reasons.

CONCLUSION

I would dismiss the appeal and direct a new trial.

In *Khan v. College of Physicians & Surgeons (Ontario)*,[143] the Ontario Divisional Court reviewed the decision of the College to revoke Dr. Khan's licence to practice. It was four years later and the child was now seven-and-a-half years old. At the hearing by a panel of the Discipline Committee, T. testified and her mother was permitted to give the statement attributed to T. That hearing was after the Court of Appeal's judgment in the criminal prosecution and before the decision of the Supreme Court of Canada. Writing for the majority, O'Driscoll J. noted:

> [T]he precondition of "necessity" was absent and, therefore, the out-of-court statement by Tanya to her mother did not qualify as an exception to the rule against hearsay. . . . [C]ounsel for the respondent College submitted that because Tanya, in her evidence before the Discipline Committee, could not recall anything about "ejaculation", it was "necessary" to allow the mother to give the hearsay statement as truth of the facts contained therein. . . .
>
> Whatever may be the outside limit of the meaning of "necessity", in my view, it does not include shoring up and/or filling in aspects of the evidence of Tanya.[144]

The Court of Appeal disagreed. In *Khan v. College of Physicians and Surgeons (Ontario)*[145] Doherty J.A. decided:

---

[143] (1990), 43 O.A.C. 130 (Ont. Div. Ct.).
[144] *Ibid.* at 137.
[145] (1992), 9 O.R. (3d) 641 (C.A.).

The fact that the child testifies will clearly impact on the necessity of receiving his or her out-of-court statement. Necessity cannot, however, be equated with unavailability. In *Khan*, McLachlin J. instructs us that necessary means "reasonably necessary" (at p. 546 S.C.R., p. 104 C.C.C.). In the context of cases involving an alleged sexual assault on a child, reasonable necessity refers to the need to have the child's version of events pertaining to the alleged assault before the tribunal charged with the responsibility of determining whether the assault occurred. In my view, if that tribunal is satisfied that despite the *viva voce* evidence of the child, it is still "reasonably necessary" to admit the out-of-court statement in order to obtain an accurate and frank rendition of the child's version of the relevant events, then the necessity criterion set down in *Khan* is satisfied: see Anne McGillivray, "*R. v. Laramee*: Forgetting Children, Forgetting Truth" (1991), 6 C.R. (4th) 325 at pp. 335-41.

In *R. v. Khan*,[146] the retrial following the Supreme Court's dismissal of the accused's appeal, the child T., now aged nine, testified. The Crown was invited to argue necessity but declined. She was cross-examined and discrepancies were pointed out between her evidence at the disciplinary hearing and her evidence at the trial. At the trial, for example, T. testified to the accused putting his penis in her mouth and the accused then wiping her chest with a kleenex. She had not mentioned the ejaculation at the disciplinary hearing. Pointing to this and other discrepancies, defence counsel submitted that it would be dangerous to convict upon T.'s evidence, relying on the rule of practice in *Kendall v. R.*[147] that it is dangerous to convict on the evidence of a child even when the child had been sworn. The mother, while testifying at the trial about matters that she herself had witnessed, did not relate what T. had told her soon after leaving the doctor's office. The accused was convicted and sentenced to four years.

What of recanted out-of-court statements? At common law we have seen that they are only admissible for credibility and can only be admitted to prove the truth if the recanting declarant now expressly adopts the contents as true. This all changed with *B. (K.G.)*.

R. v. B. (K.G.)
[1993] 1 S.C.R. 740, 19 C.R. (4th) 1, 79 C.C.C. (3d) 257

The accused and three other young men were involved in a fight with two others. In the course of the fight, one of the four young men pulled a knife and stabbed one of the men in the chest and killed him. The four young men then fled the scene. About two weeks later, the accused's friends were interviewed separately by the police. With the youths' consent the interviews were videotaped. In their statements, they told the police that the accused had made statements to them in which he acknowledged that he had caused the death of the victim. The accused was charged with second

---

[146]   [1991] O.J. No. 637.
[147]   (1962), 132 C.C.C. 216 (S.C.C.).

degree murder. At trial, the three youths recanted their earlier statements. They said they had lied to the police to exculpate themselves from any possible involvement. The trial judge held that the witnesses' prior inconsistent statements could not be tendered as proof that the accused actually made the admissions. They were, per the orthodox rule, hearsay. They could only be used to impeach the witnesses' credibility by proving that on an earlier occasion the witnesses had in fact made statements inconsistent with their present testimony. In the absence of other sufficient identification evidence, the trial judge acquitted. The Court of Appeal upheld the acquittal.

LAMER C.J. (SOPINKA, GONTHIER, MCLACHLIN and IACOBUCCI JJ. concurring): —

. . .

The orthodox rule has been almost universally criticized by academic commentators. Their criticisms can be distilled into the assertion that the hearsay dangers on which the orthodox rule is based are ill-founded or non-existent in the case of prior inconsistent statements. Respecting the oath, commentators discount the significance of the oath in modern society. Stuesser, is representative in arguing that "[t]he unfortunate reality in our modern society is that the power of an oath must be discounted as a means of ensuring reliability for a statement." . . . However, I note that while the witness faces the legal consequences of violating an oath or solemn affirmation at trial, in most cases there is less incentive to be truthful when the statement is made, leading to a natural preference for the testimony at trial if the alternative is unsworn or unaffirmed testimony.

Critics also claim that the lack of opportunity for the trier of fact to observe the demeanour of the witness at the time the statement was made, and thus to assess credibility based on that demeanour, is overstated in its significance. They argue that the opportunity to observe the witness as he or she denies or professes not to remember making the statement can give the trier insight into the truthfulness of the recantation, and therefore also the truthfulness of the prior statement which is denied. This does not obviate the problem of ensuring that the witness's prior statement is fully and accurately reproduced for the trier of fact. Of course, both of these criticisms of the orthodox rule are reinforced when, as in this case, the prior statement is videotaped, allowing the trier of fact to observe the witnesses' demeanour and ensuring that an accurate record of the statement is tendered as evidence.

. . .

The lack of cross-examination is the most important of the hearsay dangers, but perhaps also the most overstated in the context of prior inconsistent statements. By definition, commentators argue, the maker of the statement is present in court and amenable to vigorous cross-examination respecting his or her recollection, testimonial capacity and bias at the time of the making of the prior statement. As it is argued in McCormick on Evidence, supra, at p. 120:

The witness who has told one story aforetime and another today has opened the gates to all the vistas of truth which the common law practice of cross-examination and re-examination was invented to explore. The reasons for the change of face, whether forgetfulness, carelessness, pity, terror, or greed, may be explored by the two questioners in the presence of the trier of fact, under oath, casting light on which is the true story and which the false.

. . .

Furthermore, commentators observe, the witness's recantation has accomplished all that the opponent's cross-examination could hope to: the witness now testifies under oath that the prior statement was a lie, or claims to have no recollection of the matters in the statement, thus undermining its credibility as much as cross-examination could have.

. . .

Finally, it is clear that the orthodox rule, in so far as it is based on the hearsay rule, has been undermined by the decisions of this Court in *Khan* and *Smith*. In *Smith*, I stated that the decision in *Khan* "should be understood as the triumph of a principled analysis over a set of ossified judicially created categories", and that that decision:

> . . . signalled an end to the old categorical approach to the admission of hearsay evidence. Hearsay evidence is now admissible on a principled basis, the governing principles being the reliability of the evidence, and its necessity.

I will return to *Smith* and the principled approach to the hearsay rule as it applies in the particular case of prior inconsistent statements, but it is important to note that any erosion of the categorical approach to the hearsay rule must influence the Court's consideration of the orthodox rule as one instance of that rule.

[The Court then examined the role of *stare decisis* and decided: "The existing rule has been attenuated by developments in the law of hearsay and is somewhat, if not overly, technical, and reforming the rule would not directly expand the scope of criminal liability."]

. . .

I am of the view that evidence of prior inconsistent statements of a witness other than an accused should be substantively admissible on a principled basis, following this Court's decisions in *Khan* and *Smith*. However, it is clear that the factors identified in those cases — reliability and necessity — must be adapted and refined in this particular context, given the particular problems raised by the nature of such statements. Furthermore, there must be a *voir dire* before such statements are put before the jury as substantive evidence, in which the trial judge satisfies him or herself that the statement was made in circumstances which do not negate its reliability.

. . .

(1) Reliability

(i) The oath

It is undeniable that the significance of the oath has drastically changed since its introduction. Originally the oath was grounded upon a belief that divine retribution would visit those who lied under oath. Accordingly, witnesses were required to believe in this retribution if they were to be properly sworn and their evidence admissible. . . .

We no longer require this belief in divine retribution; in *Reference re Truscott*, [1967] S.C.R. 309, at p. 368, this Court stated in the context of child witnesses that the witness need only understand "the moral obligation of telling the truth". In this sense the oath can be said to have a changed significance, and if critics of the oath suggest only that its original supernatural force has disappeared, I agree with that observation.

. . .

However, there remain compelling reasons to prefer statements made under oath, solemn affirmation or solemn declaration. While the oath will not motivate all witnesses to tell the truth . . . its administration may serve to impress on more honest witnesses the seriousness and significance of their statements, especially where they incriminate another person in a criminal investigation.

In addition to this positive effect on the declarant, the presence of an oath, solemn affirmation or solemn declaration will increase the evidentiary value of the statement when it is admitted at trial. First, it will mean that the trier of fact will not be asked to accept unsworn testimony over sworn testimony; instead, the trier will have the opportunity to choose between two sworn statements, and the trier's ultimate decision will not be made on the basis of unsworn or unaffirmed testimony. Similarly, should the prior statement be decisive, there is no danger of the accused being convicted solely on the basis of unsworn testimony.

Second, the presence of the oath during the making of the prior statement eliminates the explanation offered by many recanting witnesses, including one of the witnesses in this case: when confronted with the prior inconsistent statement, witnesses explain that it was not made under oath, and assert that the oath they took at trial persuaded them to tell the truth. This naturally privileges the trial testimony in the mind of the trier of fact. If both statements were made under oath, such an explanation can no longer be employed. Furthermore, since both statements cannot be true, the trier of fact has an indication of the low regard in which the witness holds the oath. Therefore, while it is true that the oath in itself has no power to ensure truthfulness in some witnesses, the fact that both statements were made under oath removes resort to the absence of an oath as an indicium of the alleged unreliability of the prior inconsistent statement.

The presence of an oath, solemn affirmation or solemn declaration will have yet another positive effect on the declarant's truthfulness and the administration of justice. A sworn prior statement will be highly persuasive evidence in any prosecution against the declarant related to false testimony (whether in the statement or at trial), and the knowledge that this evidence exists for this purpose should weigh heavily on the mind of one who considers lying in a statement, or recanting his or her prior statement to lie at trial.

Of course, the incentives provided by the declarant's exposure to prosecution under ss. 137, 139 and 140 in relation to the first statement, and his or her fear of a perjury prosecution in relation to testimony given at trial, will only be effective if these sanctions are made known to the declarant. For this reason, the witness should be warned by the person taking the statement that the statement may be used as evidence at a subsequent trial if the witness recants (thereby engaging s. 137), and also that severe criminal sanctions will accompany the making of a false statement. This warning should refer specifically to ss. 137, 139 and 140 of the Criminal Code, and repeat the elements of and sanctions for those offences. As does the formal swearing of the witness in the trial process, this warning and the administration of the oath should serve to bring home to the witness the gravity of the situation and his duty to tell the truth.

. . .

However, I do not wish to create technical categorical requirements duplicating those of the old approach to hearsay evidence. It follows from *Smith* that there may be situations in which the trial judge concludes that an appropriate substitute for the oath is established and that notwithstanding the absence of an oath the statement is reliable. Other circumstances may serve to impress upon the witness the importance of telling the truth, and in so doing provide a high degree of reliability to the statement. While these occasions may not be frequent, I do not foreclose the possibility that they might arise under the principled approach to hearsay evidence.

(ii) Presence

Proponents of the orthodox rule emphasize the many verbal and non-verbal cues which triers of fact rely upon in order to assess credibility. When the witness is on the stand, the trier can observe the witness's reaction to questions, hesitation, degree of commitment to the statement being made, etc. Most importantly, and subsuming all of these factors, the trier can assess the relationship between the interviewer and the witness to observe the extent to which the testimony of the witness is the product of the investigator's questioning. Such subtle observations and cues cannot be gleaned from a transcript, read in court in counsel's monotone, where the atmosphere of the exchange is entirely lost.

All of these indicia of credibility, and therefore reliability, are available to the trier of fact when the witness's prior statement is videotaped. During the course of the hearing, counsel for the appellant screened a brief excerpt from the videotape of one of the interviews. In the main portion of the television screen is a medium-length shot of the witness facing the camera and seated across a table from the interviewing officer, showing the physical relationship between the two people. In one upper corner is a close-up of the witness's face as he or she speaks, capturing nuances of expression lost in the main view.

Along the bottom of the screen is a line showing the date and a time counter, with the seconds ticking off, ensuring that the continuity and integrity of the record is maintained. The audio-visual medium captures other elements of the statement lost in a transcript, such as actions or distinctive motions which the witness demonstrates (as in this case), or answers given by nodding or shaking the head. In other words, the experience of being in the room with the witness and the interviewing officer is recreated as fully as possible for the viewer. Not only does the trier of fact have access to the full range of non-verbal indicia of credibility, but there is also a reproduction of the statement which is fully accurate, eliminating the danger of inaccurate recounting which motivates the rule against hearsay evidence. In a very real sense, the evidence ceases to be hearsay in this important respect, since the hearsay declarant is brought before the trier of fact.

Of course, the police would not resort to this precaution in every case; it may well be reserved for cases such as this, where a major crime such as murder is being investigated, the testimony of the witnesses is important to the Crown's case, and the character of the witnesses suggests that such precautions would be advisable. It is quite possible that such equipment would be available to police of given forces at a central location, and that such crucial though unstable witnesses will be taken to such locations to make their statements, or, where the statements have already been made, to repeat them in a form which may be substantively admissible should the witness recant.

In addition to an oath or solemn affirmation and warning, then, a complete videotape record of the type described above, or one which duplicates the experience of observing a witness in the courtroom to the same extent, is another important indicium of reliability which will satisfy the principled basis for the admission of hearsay evidence.

Again, it may be possible that the testimony of an independent third party who observes the making of the statement in its entirety could, in exceptional circumstances, also provide the requisite reliability with respect to demeanour evidence. I would only note at this point that there are many persons who could serve this function: police stations will have justices of the peace present or available, the witness may have his or her own lawyer present, and ss. 56(2)(c) and 56(2)(d) of the Young Offenders Act, R.S.C., 1985, c. Y-1, provide that a young person making a statement has a right of access to counsel, parents, or adult relatives. It will be a matter for the trial judge to determine whether or not a sufficient substitute for a videotape record has been provided to allow the trier of fact access to sufficient demeanour evidence to make the statement admissible.

(iii) Cross-examination

The final hearsay danger is the lack of contemporaneous cross-examination when the statement is made. The appellant is correct to concede that this is the most important of the hearsay dangers. However, in the case of prior inconsistent statements, it is also the most easily remedied by the opportunity to cross-examine at trial. This is a feature of prior inconsistent statements that conclusively distinguishes them from other forms of hearsay. . . .

Furthermore, unlike the oath and presence, it is the hearsay danger which is impossible to address outside of judicial or quasi-judicial processes. Whereas the police can easily administer a warning and oath, and videotape a statement in the course of a witness interview, it would restrict the operation of a reformed rule to judicial or quasi-judicial proceedings to require contemporaneous cross-examination, and thereby severely restrict the impact of a reformed rule. Consider the facts of the present case: when the three witnesses were interviewed by the police, no one had yet been charged with an offence. Who could have cross-examined the witnesses at that point? How could cross-examination have been effective before the case to be met was known? These and other practical difficulties in requiring contemporaneous cross-examination tip the balance in favour of allowing cross-examination at trial to serve as a substitute. Again, we must remember that the question is not whether it would have been preferable to have had the benefit of contemporaneous cross-examination, but whether the absence of such cross-examination is a sufficient reason to keep the statement from the jury as substantive evidence. Given the other guarantees of trustworthiness, I do not think that it should be allowed to be a barrier to substantive admissibility. Of course, it will be an important consideration for the trier of fact in deciding what weight to attach to the prior inconsistent statement, and it is likely that opposing counsel will stress the absence of such cross-examination to the trier of fact.

Therefore, the requirement of reliability will be satisfied when the circumstances in which the prior statement was made provide sufficient guarantees of its trustworthiness with respect to the two hearsay dangers a reformed rule can realistically address: if (i) the statement is made under oath or solemn affirmation following a warning as to the existence of sanctions and the significance of the oath or affirmation, (ii) the statement is videotaped in its entirety, and (iii) the opposing party, whether the Crown or the defence, has a full opportunity to cross-examine the witness respecting the statement, there will be sufficient circumstantial guarantees of reliability to allow the jury to make substantive use of the statement. Alternatively, other circumstantial guarantees of reliability may suffice to render such statements substantively admissible, provided that the judge is satisfied that the circumstances provide adequate assurances of reliability in place of those which the hearsay rule traditionally requires.

(2) Necessity

Prior inconsistent statements present vexing problems for the necessity criterion. The necessity criterion has usually been satisfied by the unavailable witness: in *Khan*, the child declarant who could not be sworn, and in *Smith*, the dead declarant. By definition, the declarant in the case of prior inconsistent statements is available at trial; it is his or her prior statement that is unavailable because of the recantation.

However, it is important to remember that the necessity criterion "must be given a flexible definition, capable of encompassing diverse situations" [see

Smith]. Wigmore, vol. 5 (Chadbourn rev. 1974), § 1421, at p. 253, referred to two classes of necessity:

> (1) The person whose assertion is offered may now be *dead*, or out of the jurisdiction, or insane, or *otherwise unavailable* for the purpose of testing. This is the commoner and more palpable reason.
>
> . . .
>
> (2) The assertion may be such that we cannot expect, again, or at this time, to get *evidence of the same value* from the same or other sources. . . . The necessity is not so great; perhaps hardly a necessity, only an expediency or convenience, can be predicated. But the principle is the same. [Emphasis in original.]
>
> . . .

The precise limits of the necessity criterion remain to be established in the context of specific cases. It may be that in some circumstances, the availability of the witness will mean that hearsay evidence of that witness's prior *consistent* (the kind of statement at issue in *Khan*) statements will not be admissible. However, I am not prepared, at this point, to adhere to a strict interpretation that makes unavailability an indispensable condition of necessity.

In the case of prior *inconsistent* statements, it is patent that we cannot expect to get evidence of the same value from the recanting witness or other sources: as counsel for the appellant claimed, the recanting witness holds the prior statement, and thus the relevant evidence, "hostage". The different "value" of the evidence is found in the fact that something has radically changed between the time when the statement was made and the trial and, assuming that there is a sufficient degree of reliability established under the first criterion, the trier of fact should be allowed to weigh both statements in light of the witness's explanation of the change.

[The Court then described the process that should be followed on the *voir dire* determining necessity and reliability.]

. . .

Even where there has been a warning and oath administered, and the statement videotaped, or sufficient substitutes established, the trial judge will still have the discretion to refuse to allow the jury to make substantive use of the statement. Prior statements share many characteristics with confessions, especially where police investigators are involved. Proponents of the orthodox rule voice the concern that malign influences on the witness by police may precede the making of the statement and shape its content, in the same way that confessions may be suspect if coerced by police investigators. That is, it still may be the case that the oath and videotape, and the acknowledgement of the warning, were made under circumstances that make them suspect. For this reason, the test developed by this court for the admission of confessions is well suited to making a threshold determination of whether the circumstances under which the statement was made undermine the veracity of the indicia of reliability. . . . I would apply this test to prior statements. The trial judge must satisfy him or herself (again, in the majority of cases on the balance of probabilities) on the *voir dire* that the statement was not the product of coercion of any form, whether it involves threats, promises, excessively leading questions by the investigator or other person in a position of authority, or other forms of investigatory misconduct. I would add another element to the trial judge's inquiry to address situations where the first factor might be satisfied, but there are other aspects of police conduct which militate against rewarding that conduct by admitting the evidence. In *R. v. Rothman* (1981), 59 C.C.C. (2d) 30 at p. 74, 121 D.L.R. (3d) 578, [1981] 1 S.C.R. 640, I wrote that even if the *Ibrahim* test was satisfied to make a confession admissible, such a confession "shall nevertheless be excluded if its use in the proceedings would, as a result of what was said or done by any person in authority in eliciting the statement, bring the administration of justice into disrepute".

It must be stressed that the trial judge is not making a determination on the *voir dire* as to the ultimate reliability and credibility of the statement. As I have indicated, that is a matter for the trier of fact. The trial judge need not be satisfied that the prior statement was true and should be believed in preference to the witness's current testimony. This distinction is also derived from the law relating to confessions.[148]

New trial ordered.

In *R. v. U. (F.J.)*,[149] the Supreme Court considered the admissibility of the police statement of a 13-year-old girl who reported in the statement that her father had been having sexual intercourse with her on a regular basis and that the last time it occurred was the previous night. The officer subsequently interviewed the accused, who admitted that he had had intercourse with his daughter many times and had done so the previous night. The accused's statement to police was clearly admissible against him. However, at trial, the daughter recanted, stating that the allegations in her police statement were untrue. The Supreme Court determined that the daughter's recanted police statement was admissible for the truth of its contents under *B. (K.G.)*. While the statement was not made under the ideal conditions laid out in *B. (K.G.)* — there was no oath or video recording — the unusual circumstances provided adequate assurances of reliability. The daughter's statement to police was "strikingly similar" to a statement that was clearly admissible against the accused and, given that collusion was not an issue and the daughter could be cross-examined at trial, that was enough to make the recanted statement admissible for the truth of its contents.

In *R. v. Chappell*,[150] the accused appealed from his conviction on charges of assault causing bodily harm. Police had been called to Chappell's residence after a neighbour complained. They broke down the door when they heard struggling and fighting inside. Upon finding Chappell's wife in the bedroom, visibly injured, and noting broken glass on the floor, the officers arrested Chappell. The officers testified that the wife told them that Chappell

---

[148] For an excellent comment see Rosenberg, "*B. (K.G.)* — Necessity and Reliability: the New Pigeonholes" (1993), 19 C.R. (4th) 69. For general concerns with the approach see Rollie Thompson, "The Supreme Court Goes Hunting and Nearly Catches a Hearsay Woozle" (1995), 37 C.R. (4th) 282 and Robert Currie, "The Evolution of the Law of Evidence: Plus ça Change. . .?" (2011) 15 Can. Crim. L. Rev. 213.

[149] [1995] 3 S.C.R. 764, 101 C.C.C. (3d) 97, 42 C.R. (4th) 133 (S.C.C.).

[150] (2003), 172 C.C.C. (3d) 539, 15 C.R. (6th) 350 (Ont. C.A.).

had been beating her for several hours. They claimed that she was visibly frightened and did not want to cooperate in the laying of charges. She was taken to hospital, where she claimed that she had fallen down and that Chappell had not assaulted her. At trial, she testified to this effect. The Crown sought leave to admit the evidence of her initial statements to the officer as evidence of its truth. The trial judge allowed the evidence. The officer used notes to testify about her statements, as they had not been recorded. The trial judge found that this evidence, along with other circumstantial evidence, was sufficient to convict.

The Court of Appeal allowed the appeal, ruling that the complainant's prior inconsistent statements should not have been admitted solely on the basis that she was available for cross-examination. Writing for the Court, Rosenberg J.A. cautioned against opening the door too wide to admit prior inconsistent statements for the truth of their contents. He wrote that while "*R. v. U. (F.J.)* illustrates the flexibility of the principled approach as applied to prior inconsistent statements, it also shows the unusual circumstances that must exist before the *R. v. B. (K.G.)* requirements can be wholly disregarded".

R. v. DEVINE
(2008), 232 C.C.C. (3d) 1, 57 C.R. (6th) 1, [2008] 2 S.C.R. 283 (S.C.C.)

The accused was charged with robbery and assault causing bodily harm. The complainant (S) was allegedly assaulted by the accused a second time. S and P, a witness, refused to give a statement after the first assault but agreed following the second one, and both identified the accused as S's assailant. At trial, they recanted their identification. The trial judge admitted P's statement under the principled approach and convicted the accused (the Crown did not seek to introduce the complainant's statement because it was not videotaped). The Court of Appeal dismissed the appeal. The accused appealed to the Supreme Court.

CHARRON J. (for the Court):—

. . .

[25] Here, there was no contemporaneous cross-examination as in *R. v. Hawkins*, [1996] 3 S.C.R. 1043, but the *K.G.B.* requirements were found by the trial judge to have been complied with:

the statement was videotaped and recorded, and before Ms. Pawliw gave her statement, a police officer explained the seriousness of making the statement, the possible consequences of giving a false statement, and administered a form of oath. These factors were identified in *K.G.B.* as the general attributes of in-court testimony that provide the usual safeguards of reliability (pp. 795-96).

In the words of *K.G.B.*, together with the availability of the declarant for cross-examination, these attributes bring "the prior statement to a comparable standard of reliability" such that the statement can be "admitted as substantive evidence" (p. 787).

[26] It is important to note that the availability of the declarant to be cross-examined will not necessarily tip the scales in favour of admissibility. In order for this factor to weigh in favour of admission, there must be a "full opportunity to cross-examine the witness" at trial (*K.G.B.*, at p. 796). As this Court explained in *R. v. U. (F.J.)*, [1995] 3 S.C.R. 764, at para. 46:

> The first factor contributing to reliability is the cross-examination of the witness. If the witness provides an explanation for changing his or her story, the trier of fact will be able to assess both versions of the story, as well as the explanation. However, where a witness does not recall making an earlier statement, or refuses to answer questions, the trial judge should take into account that this may impede the jury's ability to assess the ultimate reliability of the statement.

[27] For example, in *R. v. Post* (2007), 217 C.C.C. (3d) 225, 2007 BCCA 123, the accused pointed to the trial judge's finding that the *K.G.B.* factors were all present to support his argument that the witness's police statement should be admitted under the principled approach to hearsay. A unanimous Court of Appeal rejected this argument, noting that "it is clear that the most important of these three, namely the opportunity for cross-examination, existed only notionally because while Malloway was present in the courtroom, there was no real opportunity to test her account because of her inability to recall what she saw, or to say that what she had said previously was true" (para. 65). A similar conclusion was reached in *R. v. N. (T.G.)* (2007), 216 C.C.C. (3d) 329, 2007 BCCA 2. The Court of Appeal in that case concluded (at para. 17):

> In this case, any "full opportunity to cross-examine" was completely frustrated. There was no meaningful comparison between different accounts because Mason denied any knowledge of the facts, apart from a grudging concession that he had given a statement to the police, which he asserted was completely false.

[28] Here, although Ms. Pawliw recanted her identification of Mr. Devine at trial, there was a meaningful opportunity to test her evidence through cross-examination. Ms. Pawliw testified under oath that at the time she gave her statement, she was aware of the seriousness of the statement and told the truth to the best of her ability. The trial judge was able to assess the witness's demeanour, and gave a detailed account of her evasiveness and reluctance to identify Mr. Devine in the courtroom. He concluded by stating as follows (at para. 41):

> I have reviewed the manner of Ms. Pawliw giving evidence on the stand and compared it to the straightforward manner in which she described the incident, and Mr. Devine's involvement, when she gave the KGB statement to the police. I conclude that she was trying to avoid identifying the accused from the witness stand and is trying to distance herself on the witness stand from any identification of the accused.

There is no reason to disturb the trial judge's finding in this regard.[151]

---

[151]   See John McInnes, "*Devine* and *Blackman*: Back to the Future or Ahead to the Past" (2008), 57 C.R. (6th) 31 for criticism of some of the reasoning in these rulings.

. . .

Appeal dismissed.

R. v. KHELAWON
[2006] 2 S.C.R. 787, 42 C.R. (6th) 1, 215 C.C.C. (3d) 161 (S.C.C.)

In 1999, C, a cook at a retirement home, found S, an 81-year-old resident of the home, badly bruised in his room. S told C that the accused, the manager of the home, had repeatedly punched him in the face and ribs the previous evening, had packed his belongings in garbage bags and had threatened to kill him if he did not leave the home by noon the next day. C took S to her apartment and cared for him for a few days. He later agreed to be seen by a doctor. The doctor testified that he found three fractured ribs and bruises consistent with S's allegation of assault but which also could have resulted from a fall. The next day, C took S to the police and S gave a videotaped statement repeating the allegation he had been beaten and threatened. The statement was not under oath but S answered "yes" when asked if he understood it was important to tell the truth and that he could be charged if he did not tell the truth. Medical records seized from the retirement home described S as depressed, aggressive, angry and paranoid, and revealed that he had been treated for paranoid psychosis and depression. A psychiatrist testified that S understood that it was important to tell the truth and had the capacity to communicate evidence. The defence argued that C had influenced S to complain out of spite because the accused had earlier terminated C's employment.

After the police arrested the accused they obtained further statements from other residents alleging assaults by the accused. The accused was charged with various counts of assaults against five complainants but, by the time of the trial, four complainants, including S and D, had died of causes unrelated to the alleged assaults and the fifth was no longer competent to testify. Only one complainant had testified at the preliminary inquiry. The central issue at trial was whether the complainants' hearsay statements should be received in evidence. The trial judge admitted some of the hearsay based in large part on the striking similarity between the statements. The trial judge ultimately found videotaped statements given by S and D to the police sufficiently credible to found convictions for aggravated assault and uttering a death threat in respect of S, as well as assault causing bodily harm and assault with a weapon in respect of D. The accused was acquitted on the remaining counts.

On appeal, a majority of the Ontario Court of Appeal excluded all of the hearsay statements and acquitted the accused on all charges. The dissenting judge would have upheld the convictions in respect of S. The Crown appealed as of right from the acquittals in respect of S and was denied leave to appeal from the acquittals in respect of D.

CHARRON J. (MCLACHLIN C.J., BINNIE, LEBEL, DESCHAMPS, FISH, and ABELLA JJ. concurring):—

Hearsay Exceptions: A Principled Approach

It has long been recognized that a rigid application of the exclusionary rule would result in the unwarranted loss of much valuable evidence. The hearsay statement, because of the way in which it came about, may be inherently reliable, or there may be sufficient means of testing it despite its hearsay form. Hence, a number of common law exceptions were gradually created. A rigid application of these exceptions, in turn, proved problematic leading to the needless exclusion of evidence in some cases, or its unwarranted admission in others. Wigmore urged greater flexibility in the application of the rule based on the two guiding principles that underlie the traditional common law exceptions: necessity and reliability (*Wigmore on Evidence* (2nd ed. 1923), vol. III, 1420, at p. 153). This Court first accepted this approach in *Khan* and later recognized its primacy in *Starr*. The governing framework, based on *Starr*, was recently summarized in *R. v. Mapara*, [2005] 1 S.C.R. 358, 2005 SCC 23, at para. 15:

(a) Hearsay evidence is presumptively inadmissible unless it falls under an exception to the hearsay rule. The traditional exceptions to the hearsay rule remain presumptively in place.

(b) A hearsay exception can be challenged to determine whether it is supported by indicia of necessity and reliability, required by the principled approach. The exception can be modified as necessary to bring it into compliance.

(c) In "rare cases", evidence falling within an existing exception may be excluded because the indicia of necessity and reliability are lacking in the particular circumstances of the case.

(d) If hearsay evidence does not fall under a hearsay exception, it may still be admitted if indicia of reliability and necessity are established on a *voir dire*.

. . .

Constitutional Dimension: Trial Fairness

Prior to admitting hearsay statements under the principled exception to the hearsay rule, the trial judge must determine on a *voir dire* that necessity and reliability have been established. The onus is on the person who seeks to adduce the evidence to establish these criteria on a balance of probabilities. In a criminal context, the inquiry may take on a constitutional dimension, because difficulties in testing the evidence, or conversely the inability to present reliable evidence, may impact on an accused's ability to make full answer and defence, a right protected by s. 7 of the *Canadian Charter of Rights and Freedoms*: *Dersch v. Canada (Attorney General)*, [1990] 2 S.C.R. 1505. The right to make full answer and defence in turn is linked to another principle of fundamental justice, the right to a fair trial: *R. v. Rose*, [1998] 3 S.C.R. 262. The concern over trial fairness is one of the paramount reasons for rationalizing the traditional hearsay exceptions in accordance with the principled approach. As stated by Iacobucci J. in *Starr*, at para. 200, in respect of Crown evidence: "It would compromise trial fairness, and raise the spectre of wrongful convictions, if the Crown is allowed to introduce unreliable hearsay against the accused, regardless of whether it happens to fall within an existing exception."

As indicated earlier, our adversary system is based on the assumption that sources of untrustworthiness or inaccuracy can best be brought to light under the test of cross-examination. It is mainly because of the inability to put hearsay evidence to that test, that it is presumptively inadmissible. However, the constitutional right guaranteed under s. 7 of the *Charter* is not the right to confront or cross-examine adverse witnesses in itself. The adversarial trial process, which includes cross-examination, is but the means to achieve the end. Trial fairness, as a principle of fundamental justice, is the end that must be achieved. Trial fairness embraces more than the rights of the accused. While it undoubtedly includes the right to make full answer and defence, the fairness of the trial must also be assessed in the light of broader societal concerns: see *R. v. Mills*, [1999] 3 S.C.R. 668, at paras. 69-76. In the context of an admissibility inquiry, society's interest in having the trial process arrive at the truth is one such concern.

The broader spectrum of interests encompassed in trial fairness is reflected in the twin principles of necessity and reliability. The criterion of necessity is founded on society's interest in getting at the truth. Because it is not always possible to meet the optimal test of contemporaneous cross-examination, rather than simply losing the value of the evidence, it becomes necessary in the interests of justice to consider whether it should nonetheless be admitted in its hearsay form. The criterion of reliability is about ensuring the integrity of the trial process. The evidence, although needed, is not admissible unless it is sufficiently reliable to overcome the dangers arising from the difficulty of testing it. As we shall see, the reliability requirement will generally be met on the basis of two different grounds, neither of which excludes consideration of the other. In some cases, because of the circumstances in which it came about, the contents of the hearsay statement may be so reliable that contemporaneous cross-examination of the declarant would add little if anything to the process. In other cases, the evidence may not be so cogent but the circumstances will allow for sufficient testing of evidence by means other than contemporaneous cross-examination. In these circumstances, the admission of the evidence will rarely undermine trial fairness. However, because trial fairness may encompass factors beyond the strict inquiry into necessity and reliability, even if the two criteria are met, the trial judge has the discretion to exclude hearsay evidence where its probative value is outweighed by its prejudicial effect.

The Admissibility Inquiry

Distinction Between Threshold and Ultimate Reliability: A Source of Confusion

As stated earlier, the trial judge only decides whether hearsay evidence is admissible. Whether the hearsay statement will or will not be ultimately relied upon in deciding the issues in the case is a matter for the trier of fact to determine at the conclusion of the trial based on a consideration of the statement in the context of the entirety of the evidence. It is important that the trier of fact's domain not be encroached upon at the admissibility stage. If the trial is before a judge and jury, it is crucial that questions of ultimate reliability be left for the jury — in a criminal trial, it is constitutionally imperative. If the judge sits without a jury, it is equally important that he or she not prejudge the ultimate reliability of the evidence before having heard all of the evidence in the case. Hence, a distinction must be made between "ultimate reliability" and "threshold reliability". Only the latter is inquired into on the admissibility *voir dire*.

The distinction between threshold and ultimate reliability has been made in a number of cases (see, for example, *B. (K.G.)* and *R. v. Hawkins*, [1996] 3 S.C.R. 1043), but we are mainly concerned here with the elaboration of this principle in *Starr*. In particular, the following excerpt from the Court's analysis has been the subject of much of the discussion and commentary (at paras. 215 and 217):

> In this connection, it is important when examining the reliability of a statement under the principled approach to distinguish between threshold and ultimate reliability. Only the former is relevant to admissibility: see *Hawkins, supra*, at p. 1084. Again, it is not appropriate in the circumstances of this appeal to provide an exhaustive catalogue of the factors that may influence threshold reliability. However, our jurisprudence does provide some guidance on this subject. Threshold reliability is concerned not with whether the statement is true or not; that is a question of ultimate reliability. Instead, it is concerned with whether or not the circumstances surrounding the statement itself provide *circumstantial* guarantees of trustworthiness. This could be because the declarant had no motive to lie (see *Khan, supra*; *Smith*, supra), or because there were safeguards in place such that a lie could be discovered (see *Hawkins, supra*; *U. (F.J.), supra*; *B. (K.G.), supra*).
>
> . . .
>
> At the stage of hearsay admissibility the trial judge should not consider the declarant's general reputation for truthfulness, nor any prior or subsequent statements, consistent or not. These factors do not concern the circumstances of the statement itself. Similarly, I would not consider the presence of corroborating or conflicting evidence. On this point, I agree with the Ontario Court of Appeal's decision in *R. v. C. (B.)* (1993), 12 O.R. (3d) 608; see also *Idaho v. Wright*, 497 U.S. 805 (1990). In summary, under the principled approach a court must not invade the province of the trier of fact and condition admissibility of hearsay on whether the evidence is ultimately reliable. However, it will need to examine whether the circumstances in which the statement was made lend sufficient credibility to allow a finding of threshold reliability. [Underlining added.]

The Court's statement that "threshold reliability is concerned not with whether the statement is true or not" has created some uncertainty. While it is clear that the trial judge does not determine whether the statement will ultimately be relied upon as true, it is not so clear that in every case threshold reliability is *not* concerned with whether the statement is true or not. Indeed, in *U. (F.J.)*, the rationale for admitting the complainant's hearsay statement was based on the fact that "the only likely explanation" for its striking similarity with the independent statement of the accused was that "they were both telling the truth" (para. 40).

Further, it is not easy to discern what is or is not a circumstance "surrounding the statement itself". For example, in *Smith*, the fact that the deceased may have had a motive to lie was considered by the Court in determining threshold admissibility. As both Rosenberg J.A. and Blair J.A. point out in their respective reasons, "in determining whether the declarant had a motive to lie, the judge will necessarily be driven to consider factors outside the statement itself or the immediately surrounding circumstances" (para. 97).

Much of the confusion in this area of the law has arisen from this attempt to categorically label some factors as going only to ultimate reliability. The bar against considering "corroborating or conflicting evidence", because it is only relevant to the question of ultimate reliability, is a further example. Quite clearly, the corroborative nature of the semen stain in *Khan* played an important part in establishing the threshold reliability of the child's hearsay statement in that case.

This part of the analysis in *Starr* therefore requires clarification and, in some respects, reconsideration. I will explain how the relevant factors to be considered on an admissibility inquiry cannot invariably be categorized as relating either to threshold or ultimate reliability. Rather, the relevance of any particular factor will depend on the particular dangers arising from the hearsay nature of the statement and the available means, if any, of overcoming them. I will then return to the impugned passage in *Starr*, dealing more specifically with the question of supporting evidence since that reference appears to have raised the most controversy.

Identifying the Relevant Factors: A Functional Approach

Recognizing Hearsay

The first matter to determine before embarking on a hearsay admissibility inquiry, of course, is whether the proposed evidence is hearsay. This may seem to be a rather obvious matter, but it is an important first step. Misguided objections to the admissibility of an out-of-court statement based on a misunderstanding of what constitutes hearsay are not uncommon. As discussed earlier, not all out-of-court statements will constitute hearsay. Recall the defining features of hearsay. An out-of-court statement will be hearsay when: (1) it is adduced to prove the truth of its contents *and* (2) there is no opportunity for a contemporaneous cross-examination of the declarant.

Putting one's mind to the defining features of hearsay at the outset serves to better focus the admissibility inquiry. As we have seen, the first identifying feature of hearsay calls for an inquiry into the purpose for which it is adduced. Only when the evidence is being tendered for its truth will it constitute hearsay. The fact that the out-of-court statement is adduced for its *truth* should be considered in the context of the issues in the case so that the court may better assess the potential impact of introducing the evidence in its hearsay form.

Second, by putting one's mind, at the outset, to the second defining feature of hearsay — the absence of an opportunity for contemporaneous cross-examination of the declarant, the admissibility inquiry is immediately focussed on the dangers of admitting hearsay evidence. Iacobucci J. in *Starr* identified the inability to test the evidence as the "central concern" underlying the hearsay rule. Lamer C.J. in *U. (F.J.)* expressed the same view but put it more directly by stating: "Hearsay is inadmissible as evidence because its reliability cannot be tested" (para. 22).

Presumptive Inadmissibility of Hearsay Evidence

Once the proposed evidence is identified as hearsay, it is presumptively *inadmissible*. I stress the nature of the hearsay rule as a general exclusionary rule because the increased flexibility introduced in the Canadian law of evidence in the past few decades has sometimes tended to blur the distinction between admissibility and weight. Modifications have been made to a number of rules, including the rule against hearsay, to bring them up to date and to ensure that they facilitate rather than impede the goals of truth seeking, judicial efficiency and fairness in the adversarial process. However, the traditional rules of evidence reflect considerable wisdom and judicial experience. The modern approach has built upon their underlying rationale, not discarded it. In *Starr* itself, where this Court recognized the primacy of the principled approach to hearsay exceptions, the presumptive exclusion of hearsay evidence was reaffirmed in strong terms. Iacobucci J. stated as follows (at para. 199):

> By excluding evidence that might produce unfair verdicts, and by ensuring that litigants will generally have the opportunity to confront adverse witnesses, the hearsay rule serves as a cornerstone of a fair justice system.

Traditional Exceptions

The Court in *Starr* also reaffirmed the continuing relevance of the traditional exceptions to the hearsay rule. More recently, this Court in *Mapara* reiterated the continued application of the traditional exceptions in setting out the governing analytical framework, as noted in para. 42 above. Therefore, if the trial judge determines that the evidence falls within one of the traditional common law exceptions, this finding is conclusive and the evidence is ruled admissible, unless, in a rare case, the exception itself is challenged as described in both those decisions.

Principled Approach: Overcoming the Hearsay Dangers

Since the central underlying concern is the inability to test hearsay evidence, it follows that under the principled approach the reliability requirement is aimed at identifying those cases where this difficulty is sufficiently overcome to justify receiving the evidence as an exception to the general exclusionary rule. As some courts and commentators have expressly noted, the reliability requirement is usually met in two different ways: see, for example, *R. v. Wilcox* (2001), 152 C.C.C. (3d) 157, 2001 NSCA 45; *R. v. Czibulka* (2004), 189 C.C.C. (3d) 199 (Ont. C.A.); D. M. Paciocco, "The Hearsay Exceptions: A Game of 'Rock, Paper, Scissors'", in *Special Lectures of the Law Society of Upper Canada 2003: The Law of Evidence* (2004), 17, at p. 29.

One way is to show that there is no real concern about whether the statement is true or not because of the circumstances in which it came about. Common sense dictates that if we can put sufficient trust in the truth and accuracy of the statement, it should be considered by the fact finder regardless of its hearsay form. Wigmore explained it this way:

> There are many situations in which it can be easily seen that such a required test [i.e., cross-examination] would add little as a security, because its purposes had been already substantially accomplished. If a statement has been made under such circumstances that even a sceptical caution would look upon it as trustworthy (in the ordinary instance), in a high degree of probability, it would be pedantic to insist on a test whose chief object is already secured. [&1420, p. 154]

Another way of fulfilling the reliability requirement is to show that no real concern arises from the fact that the statement is presented in hearsay form because, in the circumstances, its truth and accuracy can nonetheless be sufficiently tested. Recall that the optimal way of testing evidence adopted by our adversarial system is to have the declarant state the evidence in court, under oath, and under the scrutiny of contemporaneous cross-examination. This preferred method is not just a vestige of past traditions. It remains a tried and true method, particularly when credibility issues must be resolved. It is one thing for a person to make a damaging statement about another in a context where it may not really matter. It is quite another for that person to repeat the statement in the course of formal proceedings where he or she must commit to its truth and accuracy, be observed and heard, and be called upon to explain or defend it. The latter situation, in addition to providing an accurate record of what was actually said by the witness, gives us a much higher degree of comfort in the statement's trustworthiness. However, in some cases it is not possible to put the evidence to the optimal test, but the circumstances are such that the trier of fact will nonetheless be able to sufficiently test its truth and accuracy. Again, common sense tells us that we should not lose the benefit of the evidence when there are adequate substitutes for testing the evidence.

These two principal ways of satisfying the reliability requirement can also be discerned in respect of the traditional exceptions to the hearsay rule. Iacobucci J. notes this distinction in *Starr*, stating as follows:

> For example, testimony in former proceedings is admitted, at least in part, because many of the traditional dangers associated with hearsay are not present. As pointed out in Sopinka, Lederman and Bryant, *supra*, at pp. 278-79:
>
> > . . .a statement which was earlier made under oath, subjected to cross-examination and admitted as testimony at a former proceeding is received in a subsequent trial *because the dangers underlying hearsay evidence are absent.*
>
> Other exceptions are based not on negating traditional hearsay dangers, but on the fact that the statement provides circumstantial guarantees of reliability. This approach is embodied in recognized exceptions such as dying declarations, spontaneous utterances, and statements against pecuniary interest. [Emphasis in original; para. 212.]

Some of the traditional exceptions stand on a different footing, such as admissions from parties (confessions in the criminal context) and co-conspirators' statements: see *Mapara*, at para. 21. In those cases, concerns about reliability are based on considerations other than the party's inability to test the accuracy of his or her own statement or that of his or her co-

conspirators. Hence, the criteria for admissibility are not established in the same way. However, in cases where the exclusionary rule is based on the usual hearsay dangers, this distinction between the two principal ways of satisfying the reliability requirement, although not by any means one that creates mutually exclusive categories, may assist in identifying what factors need to be considered on the admissibility inquiry.

Khan is an example where the reliability requirement was met because the circumstances in which the statement came about provided sufficient comfort in its truth and accuracy. Similarly in *Smith*, the focus of the admissibility inquiry was also on those circumstances that tended to show that the statement was true. On the other hand, the admissibility of the hearsay statement in *B. (K.G.)* and *Hawkins* was based on the presence of adequate substitutes for testing the evidence. As we shall see, the availability of the declarant for cross-examination goes a long way to satisfying the requirement for adequate substitutes. In *U. (F.J.)*, the Court considered both those circumstances tending to show that the statement was true and the presence of adequate substitutes for testing the evidence. *U. (F.J.)* underscores the heightened concern over reliability in the case of prior inconsistent statements where the trier of fact is invited to accept an out-of-court statement over the sworn testimony from the same declarant. I will briefly review how the analysis of the Court in each of those cases was focussed on overcoming the particular hearsay dangers raised by the evidence.

. . .

Revisiting paras. 215 and 217 in Starr

As I trust it has become apparent from the preceding discussion, whether certain factors will go only to ultimate reliability will depend on the context. Hence, some of the comments at paras. 215 and 217 in *Starr* should no longer be followed. Relevant factors should not be categorized in terms of threshold and ultimate reliability. Rather, the court should adopt a more functional approach as discussed above and focus on the particular dangers raised by the hearsay evidence sought to be introduced and on those attributes or circumstances relied upon by the proponent to overcome those dangers. In addition, the trial judge must remain mindful of the limited role that he or she plays in determining admissibility — it is crucial to the integrity of the fact-finding process that the question of ultimate reliability not be pre-determined on the admissibility *voir dire*.

I want to say a few words on one factor identified in *Starr*, namely "the presence of corroborating or conflicting evidence" since it is that comment that appears to have raised the most controversy. I repeat it here for convenience:

> Similarly, I would not consider the presence of corroborating or conflicting evidence. On this point, I agree with the Ontario Court of Appeal's decision in *R. v. C. (B.)* (1993), 12 O.R. (3d) 608; see also *Idaho v. Wright*, 497 U.S. 805 (1990). [para. 217]

I will briefly review the two cases relied upon in support of this statement. The first does not really provide assistance on this question and the second, in my respectful view, should not be followed.

. . .

Idaho v. Wright, 497 U.S. 805 (1990), is more on point. In that case, five of the nine justices of the United States Supreme Court were not persuaded that "evidence corroborating the truth of a hearsay statement may properly support a finding that the statement bears 'particularized guarantees of trustworthiness'" (p. 822). In the majority's view, the use of corroborating evidence for that purpose "would permit admission of a presumptively unreliable statement by bootstrapping on the trustworthiness of other evidence at trial, a result we think at odds with the requirement that hearsay evidence admitted under the Confrontation Clause be so trustworthy that cross-examination of the declarant would be of marginal utility" (p. 823). By way of example, the majority observed that a statement made under duress may happen to be true, but evidence tending to corroborate the truth of the statement would be no substitute for cross-examination of the declarant at trial. The majority also raised the concern, arising mostly in child sexual abuse cases, that a jury may rely on the partial corroboration provided by medical evidence to mistakenly infer the trustworthiness of the entire allegation.

In his dissenting opinion, Kennedy J., with whom the remaining three justices concurred, strongly disagreed with the position of the majority on the potential use of supporting or conflicting evidence. In my view, his reasons echo much of the criticism that has been voiced about this Court's position in *Starr*. He said the following:

> I see no constitutional justification for this decision to prescind corroborating evidence from consideration of the question whether a child's statements are reliable. It is a matter of common sense for most people that one of the best ways to determine whether what someone says is trustworthy is to see if it is corroborated by other evidence. In the context of child abuse, for example, if part of the child's hearsay statement is that the assailant tied her wrists or had a scar on his lower abdomen, and there is physical evidence or testimony to corroborate the child's statement, evidence which the child could not have fabricated, we are more likely to believe that what the child says is true. Conversely, one can imagine a situation in which a child makes a statement which is spontaneous or is otherwise made under circumstances indicating that it is reliable, but which also contains undisputed factual inaccuracies so great that the credibility of the child's statements is substantially undermined. Under the Court's analysis, the statement would satisfy the requirements of the Confrontation Clause despite substantial doubt about its reliability. [pp. 828-29]

Kennedy J. also strongly disagreed with the majority's view that only circumstances surrounding the making of the statement should be considered:

> The [majority] does not offer any justification for barring the consideration of corroborating evidence, other than the suggestion that corroborating evidence does not bolster the "inherent trustworthiness" of the statements. But for purposes of determining the reliability of the statements, I can discern no difference between the factors that the Court believes indicate "inherent trustworthiness" and those,

like corroborating evidence, that apparently do not. Even the factors endorsed by the Court will involve consideration of the very evidence the Court purports to exclude from the reliability analysis. The Court notes that one test of reliability is whether the child "use[d] . . . terminology unexpected of a child of similar age." But making this determination requires consideration of the child's vocabulary skills and past opportunity, or lack thereof, to learn the terminology at issue. And, when all of the extrinsic circumstances of a case are considered, it may be shown that use of a particular word or vocabulary in fact supports the inference of prolonged contact with the defendant, who was known to use the vocabulary in question. As a further example, the Court notes that motive to fabricate is an index of reliability. But if the suspect charges that a third person concocted a false case against him and coached the child, surely it is relevant to show that the third person had no contact with the child or no opportunity to suggest false testimony. Given the contradictions inherent in the Court's test when measured against its own examples, I expect its holding will soon prove to be as unworkable as it is illogical.

The short of the matter is that both the circumstances existing at the time the child makes the statements and the existence of corroborating evidence indicate, to a greater or lesser degree, whether the statements are reliable. If the Court means to suggest that the circumstances surrounding the making of a statement are the best indicators of reliability, I doubt this is so in every instance. And, if it were true in a particular case, that does not warrant ignoring other indicators of reliability such as corroborating evidence, absent some other reason for excluding it. If anything, I should think that corroborating evidence in the form of testimony or physical evidence, apart from the narrow circumstances in which the statement was made, would be a preferred means of determining a statement's reliability for purposes of the Confrontation Clause, for the simple reason that, unlike other indicators of trustworthiness, corroborating evidence can be addressed by the defendant and assessed by the trial court in an objective and critical way. [References omitted; pp. 833-34.]

In my view, the opinion of Kennedy J. better reflects the Canadian experience on this question. It has proven difficult and at times counterintuitive to limit the inquiry to the circumstances surrounding the making of the statement. This Court itself has not always followed this restrictive approach. Further, I do not find the majority's concern over the "bootstrapping" nature of corroborating evidence convincing. On this point, I agree with Professor Paciocco who commented on the reasoning of the majority in *Idaho v. Wright* as follows (at p. 36):

The final rationale offered is that it would involve "bootstrapping" to admit evidence simply because it is shown by other evidence to be reliable. In fact, the "bootstrapping" label is usually reserved to circular arguments in which a questionable piece of evidence "picks itself up by its own bootstraps" to fit within an exception. For example, a party claims it can rely on a hearsay statement because the statement was made under such pressure or involvement that the prospect of concoction can fairly be disregarded, but then relies on the contents of the hearsay statement to prove the existence of that pressure or involvement: *Ratten v. The Queen*, [1972] A.C. 378. Or, a party claims it can rely on the truth of the contents of a statement because it was a statement made by an opposing party litigant, but then relies on the contents of the statement to prove it was made by an opposing party litigant: see *R. v. Evans*, [1991] 1 S.C.R. 869. Looking to *other* evidence to confirm the reliability of evidence, the thing *Idaho v. Wright* purports to prevent, is the very antithesis of "bootstrapping."

Turning to the case at bar, the Court decided that S's videotaped statement to the police was inadmissible. Although S's death before trial made his hearsay statement necessary, the statement did not meet concerns as to reliability. Since S had died before the trial, he was no longer available to be seen, heard and cross-examined in court. There was no opportunity for contemporaneous cross-examination. Nor had there been an opportunity for cross-examination at any other hearing. Although S was elderly and frail at the time he made the allegations, there is no evidence that the Crown attempted to preserve his evidence by application under ss. 709 to 714 of the *Criminal Code*. He did not testify at the preliminary hearing.

Obviously, there was no case to be made here on the presence of adequate substitutes for testing the evidence. There were no adequate substitutes here for testing the evidence. There was the police video — nothing more. There was also no case to be made on the inherent trustworthiness of the statement. S was elderly and frail. His mental capacity was at issue. There was also the possibility that his injuries were caused by a fall rather than an assault. The evidence of the garbage bags filled with S's possessions provided little assistance in assessing the likely truth of his statement — he could have filled those bags himself. C's obvious motive to discredit the accused presented further difficulties. The extent to which S may have been influenced in making his statement by this disgruntled employee was a live issue. S had issues of his own with the way the retirement home was managed. This was apparent from his rambling complaints on the police video itself. The absence of an oath and the simple "yes" in answer to the police officer's question as to whether he understood that it was important to tell the truth did not give much insight into whether he truly understood the consequences for the accused of making his statement. In these circumstances, S's unavailability for cross-examination posed significant limitations on the accused's ability to test the evidence and, in turn, on the trier of fact's ability to properly assess its worth.

The crux of the trial judge's finding that the evidence was sufficiently trustworthy was based on the "striking similarities" between the statements of the five complainants. The possibility of the presence of a striking similarity between statements from different complainants could well provide sufficient cogency to warrant the admission of hearsay evidence in an appropriate case. However, the statements made by the other complainants in this case posed even greater difficulties and could not be substantively admitted to assist in assessing the reliability of S's allegations.

This judgment on the hearsay rule is a tour de force. Justice Charron provides a detailed and instructive review of the current law of hearsay and in particular of the Court's principled approach which requires proof of necessity and reliability before hearsay evidence can be admitted. She takes us all back to first principles in rehearsing how hearsay should be identified and why judges should be mindful about admitting presumptively inadmissible hearsay.

In identifying a "functional" approach she emphasizes the need for flexibility in the approach to the factor of reliability. She finds this largely reflected in the Supreme Court's jurisprudence, which she fully reviews. The most important change in the law comes at the end of this lengthy judgment when the Court expressly reverses *R. v. Starr* to the extent that it divided factors into categories relevant to threshold and those relevant to ultimate reliability and forbade consideration of evidence extrinsic to the making of the statement. As the Court recognizes, without providing citations, most judges and commentators have found no wisdom in those quick and restrictive *obiter*. Laurie Lacelle in "The Role of Corroborating Evidence in Assessing the Reliability of Hearsay Statements for Substantive Purposes"[152] long ago pointed out that not allowing consideration of extrinsic evidence such as medical evidence of bruises would have a detrimental and undesirable effect on the prosecution of domestic assault cases where, for example, the complainant's out-of-court statement speaks of assault causing bruises but the complainant has now recanted.

Of course, as the ruling in *Khelawon* on the facts demonstrates, the existence of corroborating physical evidence will not necessarily be determinative on the issue of sufficient reliability. So too the Court stresses in its ruling on the facts that just because there are striking similarities in other statements there is to be no "rigid pigeon hole" admission.[153] The catchword is case-by-case flexibility looking to all the facts. For those concerned by the length of pre-trial *voir dires*, it is noteworthy that in *Khelawon* itself it was agreed that the *voir dire* on the statements would determine the result at trial.

In passing, the Court confirms the ruling in *R. v. Mapara*,[154] on the relationship between traditional exceptions and the principled approach. *Starr* seemed to promise that there would be a thorough review of each existing exception to see whether the principled requirements of necessity and reliability were met. Here, the Court again accepts the *Mapara* ruling that traditional exceptions are presumptively valid. With the Court's own acceptance of the wide co-conspirator's exception in *Mapara*, there seems little likelihood that existing exceptions will be reconfigured. The only change so far has been with respect to the present intention exception in *Starr*. On the other hand, where the exception is narrow, the principled approach may be available as an avenue to admission in an appropriate case.[155]

---

152   (1999), 19 C.R. (5th) 376.
153   See [2006] 2 S.C.R. 787 expressly at para. 45.
154   [2005] 1 S.C.R. 358, 195 C.C.C. (3d) 225, 28 C.R. (6th) 1.
155   See e.g. Hill J. in *R. v. West* (2001), 45 C.R. (5th) 307 (Ont. S.C.) who avoided the rigours of statutory business records requirements by going straight to the principled approach to admit a forensic report from an expert who was now deceased. See similarly Romilly J. in *R. v. Larsen* (2001), 42 C.R. (5th) 49 (B.C. S.C.) respecting hospital records.

R. v. BRADSHAW
2017 CSC 35, 2017 SCC 35, [2017] 1 S.C.R. 865, 349 C.C.C. (3d) 429,
38 C.R. (7th) 1 (S.C.C.)

The accused was charged with two counts of first degree murder after two people were shot to death five days apart. Police ran a Mr. Big operation against T., who they suspected was involved in both murders. In the course of that operation, both T. and the accused were recorded making self-incriminating statements. After T. was arrested and police revealed he had been the subject of a Mr. Big investigation, T. made additional statements to police including a lengthy video-recorded re-enactment of the killings in which T. implicated the accused in both murders. T. pled guilty to second degree murder before the accused's trial. T. was called as a Crown witness at the accused's trial but refused to be sworn of give testimony. The Crown sought to admit part of T.'s video re-enactment as a hearsay statement. The trial judge admitted the video re-enactment into evidence and instructed the jury on its use. The jury found the accused guilty on both counts of first degree murder. The British Columbia Court of Appeal found that the re-enactment was improperly admitted, set aside the convictions and ordered a new trial. The Crown appealed to the Supreme Court of Canada.

In a lengthy judgment a 5-2 majority of the Supreme Court dismissed the appeal. According to the majority, the trial judge erred in admitting the re-enactment evidence because the evidence was hearsay and inadmissible under the principled approach. The evidence met the necessity criterion because T. refused to testify, but the evidence did not meet the threshold reliability criterion. The majority gave guidance on determining whether corroborative evidence can assist in establishing threshold reliability.

KARAKATSANIS J (MCLACHLIN C.J. and ABELLA, WAGNER and BROWN JJ. concurring):

[27] The hearsay dangers can be overcome and threshold reliability can be established by showing that (1) there are adequate substitutes for testing truth and accuracy (procedural reliability) or (2) there are sufficient circumstantial or evidentiary guarantees that the statement is inherently trustworthy (substantive reliability) (*Khelawon*, at paras. 61-63; *Youvarajah*, at para. 30).

[28] *Procedural* reliability is established when "there are adequate substitutes for testing the evidence", given that the declarant has not "state[d] the evidence in court, under oath, and under the scrutiny of contemporaneous cross-examination" (*Khelawon*, at para. 63). These substitutes must provide a satisfactory basis for the trier of fact to rationally evaluate the truth and accuracy of the hearsay statement (*Khelawon*, at para. 76; *Hawkins*, at para. 75; *Youvarajah*, at para. 36). Substitutes for traditional safeguards include a video recording of the statement, the presence of an oath, and a warning about the consequences of lying (*B. (K.G.)*, at pp. 795-96). However, some form of cross-examination of the declarant, such as preliminary inquiry testimony (Hawkins) or cross-examination of a recanting witness at trial (*B. (K.G.)*; *R. v. U. (F.J.)*,

[1995] 3 S.C.R. 764), is usually required (*R. v. Couture*, 2007 SCC 28, [2007] 2 S.C.R. 517, at paras. 92 and 95). . .

. . .

[30] A hearsay statement is also admissible if *substantive* reliability is established, that is, if the statement is inherently trustworthy (*Youvarajah*, at para. 30; *R. v. Smith*, [1992] 2 S.C.R. 915, at p. 929). To determine whether the statement is inherently trustworthy, the trial judge can consider the circumstances in which it was made and evidence (if any) that corroborates or conflicts with the statement (*Khelawon*, at paras. 4, 62 and 94-100; *R. v. Blackman*, 2008 SCC 37, [2008] 2 S.C.R. 298, at para. 55).

[31] While the standard for substantive reliability is high, guarantee "as the word is used in the phrase 'circumstantial guarantee of trustworthiness', does not require that reliability be established with absolute certainty" (*Smith*, at p. 930). Rather, the trial judge must be satisfied that the statement is "so reliable that contemporaneous cross-examination of the declarant would add little if anything to the process" (*Khelawon*, at para. 49). The level of certainty required has been articulated in different ways throughout this Court's jurisprudence. Substantive reliability is established when the statement "is made under circumstances which substantially negate the possibility that the declarant was untruthful or mistaken" (*Smith*, at p. 933); "under such circumstances that even a sceptical caution would look upon it as trustworthy" (*Khelawon*, at para. 62, citing Wigmore, at p. 154); when the statement is so reliable that it is "unlikely to change under cross-examination" (*Khelawon*, at para. 107; *Smith*, at p. 937); when "there is no real concern about whether the statement is true or not because of the circumstances in which it came about" (*Khelawon*, at para. 62); when the only likely explanation is that the statement is true (*U. (F.J.)*, at para. 40).

[32] These two approaches to establishing threshold reliability may work in tandem. Procedural reliability and substantive reliability are not mutually exclusive (*Khelawon*, at para. 65) and "factors relevant to one can complement the other" (*Couture*, at para. 80). That said, the threshold reliability standard always remains high — the statement must be sufficiently reliable to overcome the specific hearsay dangers it presents (*Khelawon*, at para. 49). For example, in *U. (F.J.)*, where the Court drew on elements of substantive and procedural reliability to justify the admission of a hearsay statement, both cross-examination of the recanting witness and corroborative evidence were required to meet threshold reliability, though neither on its own would have sufficed (see also *Blackman*, at paras. 37-52). I know of no other example from this Court's jurisprudence of substantive and procedural reliability complementing each other to justify the admission of a hearsay statement. Great care must be taken to ensure that this combined approach does not lead to the admission of statements despite insufficient procedural safeguards and guarantees of inherent trustworthiness to overcome the hearsay dangers.

. . .

[39] The distinction between threshold and ultimate reliability, while "a source of confusion", is crucial (*Khelawon*, at para. 50). Threshold reliability concerns admissibility, whereas ultimate reliability concerns reliance (*Khelawon*, at para. 3). When threshold reliability is based on the inherent trustworthiness of the statement, the trial judge and the trier of fact may both assess the trustworthiness of the hearsay statement. However, they do so for different purposes (*Khelawon*, at paras. 3 and 50). In assessing ultimate reliability, the trier of fact determines whether, and to what degree, the statement should be believed, and thus relied on to decide issues in the case (*Khelawon*, at para. 50; D. M. Paciocco and L. Stuesser, *The Law of Evidence* (7th ed. 2015), at pp. 35-36). This determination is made "in the context of the entirety of the evidence" including evidence that corroborates the accused's guilt or the declarant's overall credibility (*Khelawon*, at para. 3).

[40] In contrast, in assessing threshold reliability, the trial judge's preoccupation is whether in-court, contemporaneous cross-examination of the hearsay declarant would add anything to the trial process (*Khelawon*, at para. 49; see also H. Stewart, "*Khelawon*: The Principled Approach to Hearsay Revisited" (2008), 12 *Can. Crim. L.R.* 95, at p. 106). At the threshold stage, the trial judge must decide on the *availability* of competing explanations (substantive reliability) and whether the trier of fact will be in a position to choose between them by means of adequate substitutes for contemporaneous cross-examination (procedural reliability). For this reason, where procedural reliability is concerned with whether there is a satisfactory basis to rationally *evaluate* the statement, substantive reliability is concerned with whether the circumstances, and any corroborative evidence, provide a rational basis to *reject* alternative explanations for the statement, other than the declarant's truthfulness or accuracy.

[41] In short, in the hearsay context, the difference between threshold and ultimate reliability is qualitative, and not a matter of degree, because the trial judge's inquiry serves a distinct purpose. In assessing substantive reliability, the trial judge does not usurp the trier of fact's role. Only the trier of fact assesses whether the hearsay statement should ultimately be relied on and its probative value.

[42] To preserve the distinction between threshold and ultimate reliability and to prevent the *voir dire* from overtaking the trial, "[t]here must be a distinction between evidence that is admissible on the *voir dire* to determine necessity and reliability, and the evidence that is admissible in the main trial" (Stewart, at p. 111; see also L. Lacelle, "The Role of Corroborating Evidence in Assessing the Reliability of Hearsay Statements for Substantive Purposes" (1999), 19 C.R. (5th) 376; *Blackman*, at paras. 54-57). As Charron J. explained in *Khelawon*, "the trial judge must remain mindful of the limited role that he or she plays in determining admissibility — it is crucial to the integrity of the fact-finding process that the question of ultimate reliability not be pre-determined on the admissibility *voir dire*" (para. 93). Similarly, she noted in *Blackman*: "The

admissibility *voir dire* must remain focused on the hearsay evidence in question. It is not intended, and cannot be allowed by trial judges, to become a full trial on the merits" (para. 57). Limiting the use of corroborative evidence as a basis for admitting hearsay also mitigates the risk that inculpatory hearsay will be admitted simply because evidence of the accused's guilt is strong. The stronger the case against the accused, the easier it would be to admit flawed and unreliable hearsay against him. The limited inquiry into corroborative evidence flows from the fact that, at the threshold reliability stage, corroborative evidence is used in a manner that is qualitatively distinct from the manner in which the trier of fact uses it to assess the statement's ultimate reliability. As Lederman, Bryant and Fuerst explain, at the threshold reliability stage,

> [t]he use of corroborative evidence should be directed to the reliability of the hearsay. Certain items of evidence can take on a corroborative character and be supportive of the Crown's theory when considered in the context of the evidence as a whole. Such evidence relates to the merits of the case rather than to the limited focus of the *voir dire* in assessing the trustworthiness of the statement and is properly left to the ultimate trier of fact.

(S. N. Lederman, A. W. Bryant and M. K. Fuerst, *The Law of Evidence in Canada* (4th ed. 2014), at §6.140)

. . .

[44] In my view, the rationale for the rule against hearsay and the jurisprudence of this Court make clear that not all evidence that corroborates the declarant's credibility, the accused's guilt, or one party's theory of the case, is of assistance in assessing threshold reliability. A trial judge can only rely on corroborative evidence to establish threshold reliability if it shows, when considered as a whole and in the circumstances of the case, that the only likely explanation for the hearsay statement is the declarant's truthfulness about, or the accuracy of, the material aspects of the statement. If the hearsay danger relates to the declarant's sincerity, truthfulness will be the issue. If the hearsay danger is memory, narration, or perception, accuracy will be the issue.

[45] First, corroborative evidence must go to the truthfulness or accuracy of the *material aspects* of the hearsay statement (see *Couture*, at paras. 83-84; *Blackman*, at para. 57). Hearsay is tendered for the truth of its contents and corroborative evidence must go to the truthfulness or accuracy of the content of the hearsay statement that the moving party seeks to rely on. Because threshold reliability is about admissibility of evidence, the focus must be on the aspect of the statement that is tendered for its truth. The function of corroborative evidence at the threshold reliability stage is to mitigate the need for cross-examination, not generally, but *on the point* that the hearsay is tendered to prove.

. . .

[47] Second, at the threshold reliability stage, corroborative evidence must work in conjunction with the circumstances to overcome the *specific hearsay*

dangers raised by the tendered statement. When assessing the admissibility of hearsay evidence, "the scope of the inquiry must be tailored to the particular dangers presented by the evidence and limited to determining the evidentiary question of admissibility" (*Khelawon*, at para. 4). Thus, to overcome the hearsay dangers and establish substantive reliability, corroborative evidence must show that the material aspects of the statement are unlikely to change under cross-examination (*Khelawon*, at para. 107; *Smith*, at p. 937). Corroborative evidence does so if its combined effect, when considered in the circumstances of the case, shows that the *only likely explanation* for the hearsay statement is the declarant's truthfulness about, or the accuracy of, the material aspects of the statement (see *U. (F.J.)*, at para. 40). Otherwise, alternative explanations for the statement that could have been elicited or probed through cross-examination, and the hearsay dangers, persist.

[48] In assessing substantive reliability, the trial judge must therefore identify alternative, even speculative, explanations for the hearsay statement (*Smith*, at pp. 936-37). Corroborative evidence is of assistance in establishing substantive reliability if it shows that these alternative explanations are unavailable, if it "eliminate[s] the hypotheses that cause suspicion" (S. Akhtar, "Hearsay: The Denial of Confirmation" (2005), 26 C.R. (6th) 46, at p. 56 (emphasis deleted)). In contrast, corroborative evidence that is "equally consistent" with the truthfulness and accuracy of the statement as well as another hypothesis is of no assistance (*R. v. R. (D.)*, [1996] 2 S.C.R. 291, at paras. 34-35). Adding evidence that is supportive of the truth of the statement, but that is also consistent with alternative explanations, does not add to the statement's inherent trustworthiness.

[49] While the declarant's truthfulness or accuracy must be more likely than any of the alternative explanations, this is not sufficient. Rather, the fact that the threshold reliability analysis takes place on a balance of probabilities means that, based on the circumstances and any evidence led on *voir dire*, the trial judge must be able to rule out any plausible alternative explanations on a balance of probabilities.

[50] To be relied on for the purpose of rejecting alternative hypotheses for the statement, corroborative evidence must itself be trustworthy. Untrustworthy corroborative evidence is therefore not relevant to the substantive reliability inquiry (see *Khelawon*, at para. 108). Trustworthiness concerns are particularly acute when the corroborative evidence is a statement, rather than physical evidence (see Lacelle, at p. 390).

. . .

[56] Clarifying when corroborative evidence can be relied on to establish substantive reliability is not a departure from the functional approach to the admissibility of hearsay. There is no bright-line rule restricting the type of corroborative evidence that a trial judge can rely on to determine that substantive reliability is established. In all cases, the trial judge must consider

the specific hearsay dangers raised by the statement, the corroborative evidence as a whole, and the circumstances of the case, to determine whether the corroborative evidence (if any) can be relied on to establish substantive reliability.

[57] In sum, to determine whether corroborative evidence is of assistance in the substantive reliability inquiry, a trial judge should

1.   identify the material aspects of the hearsay statement that are tendered for their truth;
2.   identify the specific hearsay dangers raised by those aspects of the statement in the particular circumstances of the case;
3.   based on the circumstances and these dangers, consider alternative, even speculative, explanations for the statement; and
4.   determine whether, given the circumstances of the case, the corroborative evidence led at the *voir dire* rules out these alternative explanations such that the only remaining likely explanation for the statement is the declarant's truthfulness about, or the accuracy of, the material aspects of the statement.

Applying this new framework to the facts of the case, the majority found that the trial judge erred in admitting T.'s video re-enactment for the truth of its contents. The trial judge relied on corroborative evidence, including forensic evidence that corroborated T.'s detailed description of the murders and self-incriminating statements by the accused. Justice Karakatsanis concluded that this corroborative evidence could not properly be relied on to establish the threshold reliability of T.'s video re-enactment. The purpose of admitting the video re-enactment was to show that the accused participated in the murders, and corroborative evidence could only assist in establishing threshold reliability if it supported that aspect of the statement. The hearsay danger in the circumstances related to sincerity: there was a concern that T. might have been lying in the video re-enactment when he implicated the accused.

The corroborative evidence could only assist in establishing the threshold reliability of the re-enactment if it showed, considered in all the circumstances, that the only likely explanation was that T. was telling the truth when he implicated the accused. None of the corroborative evidence met this standard. Some of it did not implicate the accused in the murders at all. For example, the forensic evidence corroborating T.'s account of certain details of the murders could be explained by T.'s known presence at the scene. Some other items of corroborative evidence, including the accused's self-incriminating statements, were probative of the accused's involvement in the murders. However, none of this evidence effectively ruled out an alternative explanation: that T. lied about the accused's involvement. Moreover, the accused's self-incriminating statements were themselves untrustworthy, and for that reason they could not be relied on to establish the threshold reliability of the video re-enactment.

Bradshaw sets a new high bar for the use of corroboration in the hearsay *voir dire*, and it qualifies significantly the previous flexible approach to threshold reliability. As Moldaver J. pointed out in dissent, strict limits on the use of corroborative evidence seem particularly difficult to reconcile with the holding in *Khelawon* that factors indicating substantive and procedural reliability are not mutually exclusive and can be taken together to establish threshold reliability (*Bradshaw* at para. 121; *Khelawon* at paras. 65-66). It is clear that the approach to corroborative evidence on the hearsay *voir dire* has changed. What remains to be seen is whether *Bradshaw* signals a more fundamental shift away from the open-ended approach to threshold reliability.

Motive to lie has played a central role in determinations of threshold reliability and will continue so after *Khelawon*.

R. v. BLACKMAN

232 C.C.C. (3d) 233, [2008] 2 S.C.R. 298, 57 C.R. (6th) 12 (S.C.C.)

The accused was charged with first degree murder of E. The Crown's theory was that the shooting was in revenge for E having earlier stabbed the accused. The Crown also alleged that in the months before the shooting, the accused and two other men unsuccessfully tried to kill E. Before the fatal shooting, E allegedly told his mother about the stabbing and attempt on his life. The trial judge admitted E's statement to his mother under the principled approach. The accused was convicted. The Court of Appeal dismissed his appeal. Justice Simmons dissented and would have ordered a new trial. The accused appealed to the Supreme Court. One of the issues before the Court was the relevance of an apparent absence of motive for E to lie to his mother.

CHARRON J. (for the Court):-

. . .

5.2.2 The Question of Motive

[39] Simmons J.A. was of the view that, much as in *Czibulka*, "the trial judge erred by founding his implicit conclusion that Ellison had no motive to fabricate on an absence of evidence of a motive to fabricate" (para. 106). In *Czibulka*, the Court of Appeal for Ontario overturned the accused's conviction for second degree murder based on the trial judge's failure to distinguish between an absence of evidence of motive and evidence of an absence of motive in his assessment of threshold reliability. Rosenberg J.A., in writing for the court, explained the distinction between the two concepts as follows (at para. 35):

> It seems to me that it was fundamental to the trial judge's conclusion about reliability that the deceased had "no apparent motive to lie". In my view, however, since there was little or no evidence of the circumstances under which the letter was written, the trial judge had no evidence that the deceased had no motive to lie. The trial judge appeared to approach the question of fabrication by using the absence of evidence of fabrication to find that there was no evidence of a motive to

fabricate. There was nothing in the circumstances to justify this approach. This was not a case like *Khan*, for example, where it was apparent from the circumstances as related by the mother that the declarant child had no motive to accuse the accused falsely. <u>The absence of evidence of motive to fabricate is not the same as evidence of the absence of motive to fabricate. In fact, what evidence exists tells against the deceased having no motive to fabricate.</u> [Emphasis added.]

[40] The court in *Czibulka* added that where there is no evidence of a motive to lie, motive "is in effect a neutral consideration" (para. 43).

[41] The distinction between an "absence of evidence of motive to fabricate" and "evidence of absence of motive to fabricate", if taken out of context, can be rather elusive. It is therefore important to consider the Court of Appeal's decision in *Czibulka* in context. First, there was "little or no evidence" before the court about the circumstances surrounding the writing of the letter by the deceased. In addition, the Court of Appeal was of the view that what evidence did exist supported the *opposite* conclusion on the question of motive. Therefore, the trial judge's finding that there was no motive to fabricate was held to be unreasonable and unsupported by the evidence. Second, the trial judge's decision on threshold reliability essentially *turned* on the finding that the deceased had no motive to lie in her letter about the accused's alleged abusive conduct. Therefore, since the decision on threshold reliability was without support in the evidence, the trial judge's error on motive was decisive on appeal.

[42] There is no doubt that the presence or absence of a motive to lie is a relevant consideration in assessing whether the circumstances in which the statements came about provide sufficient comfort in their truth and accuracy to warrant admission. It is important to keep in mind, however, that motive is but one factor to consider in the determining of threshold reliability, albeit one which may be significant depending on the circumstances. The focus of the admissibility inquiry in all cases must be, not on the presence or absence of motive, but on the particular dangers arising from the hearsay nature of the evidence. In *Czibulka*, the question of motive, in the circumstances of that case, was a very significant factor. If the deceased had a motive to lie about the accused abusing her, the contents of her letter could not be relied on for their truth. In other cases, motive may not feature so prominently.

[43] Here, the majority of the Court of Appeal concluded that, unlike in *Czibulka*, there was circumstantial evidence to support the inference that Mr. Ellison had no motive to lie to Ms. Freckleton. I agree with the majority's conclusion that, the trial judge considered the relevant factors in determining whether Mr. Ellison had a motive to fabricate, including the nature of the relationship between Mr. Ellison and his mother and the context in which the statements were made. Among other factors, the trial judge noted that this was a case of a "shot and wounded" son telling his mother about the circumstances surrounding the shooting, an incident she already knew about from independent sources. Mr. Ellison had nothing to gain by telling this story

falsely to his mother. As the trial judge put it, "[i]f he wanted to mislead her the easiest thing would be to say it was a stranger who shot him, thereby minimizing his own blameworthiness from the stabbing." Also, if he wanted to lie to his mother in order to alleviate her fears, linking his shooting to his own stabbing would achieve the opposite. Hence, this was "hardly a factor that suggests unreliability and perhaps a factor that suggest[s] the opposite to some degree." The trial judge was further of the view that the statements were "contemporaneous enough, having regard to the unusual and attention-focusing nature of the event . . . to provide some measure of reliability." Finally, the trial judge held that "[h]aving regard to the code of silence testified to by Detective Prisor, there is an inherent plausibility and logical consistency in telling his mother more about the identity of the shooters than he told the police." In my respectful view, Simmons J.A. placed too much emphasis on the distinction drawn in *Czibulka*, a distinction which has no application on the facts here.

[44] In distinguishing *Czibulka*, the majority also noted that there were other indicia of reliability present including, as noted by the trial judge, that the statements were against Mr. Ellison's interest. In my view, it cannot be said that the statements were against interest in the hearsay sense of the term. The statements would not satisfy the criteria of the traditional hearsay exception for declarations against interest. There is also no suggestion in the evidence that Ms.Freckleton was inclined to go to the police and report that her son had stabbed someone the summer before. That being said, however, I am not persuaded that the mischaracterization of this factor had any significant bearing on the trial judge's ruling.

. . .

Appeal dismissed.

In *R. v. Pasqualino*,[156] LaForme J.A. (Laskin and Rosenberg JJ.A. concurring) refused to declare a broad rule that hearsay statements uttered during the course of marital difficulties or imminent divorce proceedings are presumptively unreliable under the principled exception. The existence of a motive to lie was just one factor to consider when determining threshold reliability. There should be no broad rule of presumptive exclusion.

R. v. BALDREE
2013 SCC 35, [2013] 2 S.C.R. 520, 298 C.C.C. (3d) 425, 3 C.R. (7th) 10 (S.C.C.)

See earlier for facts and ruling on implied assertions being hearsay. Here we consider the ruling to exclude evidence of the drug-purchase call to the accused's phone.

FISH J. (MCLACHLIN C.J., LEBEL, ABELLA, ROTHSTEIN, CROMWELL, KARAKATSANIS, WAGNER JJ., concurring):

---

[156]   (2008), 233 C.C.C. (3d) 319 (Ont. C.A.).

67 On the facts of this case, no traditional exception applies and the impugned evidence withers on a principled analysis. It satisfies neither the requirement of necessity nor the requirement of reliability.

68 In *Khelawon*, necessity was conceded. Justice Charron nonetheless took care to note that

> in an appropriate case, the court in deciding the question of necessity may well question whether the proponent of the evidence made all reasonable efforts to secure the evidence of the declarant in a manner that also preserves the rights of the other party. [para. 104]

This is the kind of "appropriate case" contemplated by *Khelawon*. And the answer is that the police *made no effort at all* to secure the evidence of the declarant: they never sought to interview or even find him, though *he gave them his address*. Moreover, there was no explanation offered as to why no efforts were made to locate the declarant.

69 Nor is the single telephone call in this case sufficiently reliable. As Feldman J.A. found in the court below, "[t]here was no basis to say that the caller's belief was reliable without testing the basis for that belief by cross-examination" (para. 146). Indeed, this is not a situation "in which it can be easily seen that such a required test [i.e., cross-examination] would add little as a security, because its purposes had been already substantially accomplished": *Khelawon*, at para. 62, quoting *Wigmore on Evidence*, at s.1420.

70 In concluding as I have, I take care not to be understood to have proposed a categorical rule for drug purchase calls. Although the call at issue here does not withstand scrutiny under the principled approach, this need not always be the case.

71 For example, where the police intercept not one but several drug purchase calls, the quantity of the calls might well suffice in some circumstances to establish reliability — indeed, while "[o]ne or two might [be] mistaken, or might even have conspired to frame the defendant as a dealer", it would "def[y] belief that all the callers had made the same error or were all party to the same conspiracy": I. H. Dennis, *The Law of Evidence* (4th ed. 2010), at p. 708.

72 Moreover, the number of callers could also inform necessity. The Crown cannot be expected, where there are numerous declarants, to locate and convince most or all to testify at trial, even in the unlikely event that they have supplied their addresses - as in this case. And it is important to remember that the criteria of necessity and reliability work in tandem: if the reliability of the evidence is sufficiently established, the necessity requirement can be relaxed: see *Khelawon*, at para. 86, citing *R. v. B. (K.G.)*, [1993] 1 S.C.R. 740, and *R. v. U. (F.J.)*, [1995] 3 S.C.R. 764.

73 Here, we are presented with a single drug purchase call of uncertain reliability. The caller gave his address. No effort was made to find and interview him, still less to call him as a witness - where the assertion imputed to him could have been evaluated by the trier of fact in the light of cross-examination and the benefit of observing his demeanour.

VIII

74 Manifestly, the curative proviso of s. 686(1)(*b*)(iii) of the *Criminal Code* can have no application in this case, since it cannot be said that there is no reasonable possibility that the verdict would have been different had the impugned telephone call not been admitted: *R. v. Bevan*, [1993] 2 S.C.R. 599, at p. 617.

Justice Moldaver concurred with the majority but expressed reservations about the majority's discussion of the principled requirement of necessity. Necessity should not be understood as a box that must invariably be checked off before evidence of a drug-purchase call can be admitted. Rather, reliability should be the focus. The necessity criterion is linked to the reliability requirement such that a high degree of reliability can render it necessary to admit the evidence in the pursuit of truth. In this case, the necessity analysis should not turn on the fact that the police did not try to find the individual who placed the drug-purchase call. Police should not be required, in the name of necessity, to track down unknown and unknowable declarants who are unlikely to be found and unlikely to cooperate. The necessity criterion is met where, as here, there is little chance of finding the declarant and little chance that, if found, he or she will be forthcoming and provide the police with evidence in a better form than the drug-purchase call itself.

While the necessity requirement was met in this case, the drug-purchase call evidence failed to meet the threshold reliability requirement. There was nothing in the record or in the caller's statements themselves to raise suspicions about the sincerity of the caller's belief that the accused was a drug dealer. However, even assuming the caller was sincere, it is impossible to examine the basis for that belief and to determine whether that belief was in fact true. In a future case involving multiple calls or even a single drug-purchase call, different circumstances might permit a finding of threshold reliability to be made.

In 2014 several provincial courts of appeal applied *Baldree* but found grounds for admitting the evidence.

In. *R. v. Belyk*[157] the Saskatchewan Court of Appeal considered the admissibility of a series of drug-related text messages implicating the accused. The admissibility of the text messages was not challenged at trial and the Court found that applying *Baldree* suggested at most a *possibility*

---

[157]   2014 SKCA 24, 9 C.R. (7th) 400 (Sask. C.A.).

that the text messages might have been excluded if challenged. The Court emphasized the possible grounds for distinguishing two cases: *Belyk* involved a whole series of text messages, while in *Baldree* the issue was the admissibility of a "single call alone".[158]

In *R. v. Wilcox*[159] the British Columbia Court of Appeal considered the admissibility against the accused of evidence of a telephone call between a third party and the co-accused to whom the accused was alleged to have delivered a large quantity of cocaine. The third-party caller allegedly asked the co-accused to come to a meeting and take the cocaine. The Court held that the trial judge properly admitted the evidence as narrative to explain why the co-accused went out and met with the accused. The Court rejected the suggestion that the trial judge had relied on the call for the improper hearsay purpose of showing that the co-accused in fact received the drugs from the accused.

Finally, in its lengthy ruling in *R. v. Badgerow*[160] the Ontario Court of Appeal applied the principled approach to hearsay to admit evidence of an assertion unintentionally implied in conduct. A few days after a murder in the early 1980s, a 911 caller gave details of the murder that suggested the caller might be the perpetrator. The telephone company traced the call but with the lapse of time there was no direct evidence of the trace. There was, however, evidence that within minutes of the call police were dispatched to secure a particular pay phone in the accused's workplace. The Court held that even if the police response was properly construed as an implied assertion by conduct that the call had been traced to that phone, that evidence met the requirements of the principled approach and should be admitted.

Taken together, these cases indicate that even though the evidence of the drug-purchase call in *Baldree* was excluded, applying the *Baldree* analysis can lead to admission of similar evidence on a number of grounds. In some cases, the requirements of necessity and reliability that failed in *Baldree* may be met in different circumstances, such as where the number of drug-purchase communications is higher (as in *Belyk*) or where the implied hearsay assertion is supported by circumstances and corroborative evidence strongly suggesting reliability (as in *Badgerow*). In other cases, the evidence may be admitted for a non-hearsay purpose (as in *Wilcox*).

PROBLEMS

Problem 1

The accused is charged with sexual assault against his biological daughter when she was three years old. The Crown seeks to admit unsworn statements she made to her foster parents and to police when she was four. At that time she was unable to give a coherent statement to the police as to what it means to tell the truth. At the time of the trial she is 11 and has no

---

[158]   *Ibid.* at para. 24.
[159]   2014 BCCA 65, 9 C.R. (7th) 414 (B.C. C.A), additional reasons 2014 BCCA 357 (B.C. C.A.).
[160]   2014 ONCA 272, 311 C.C.C. (3d) 26 (Ont. C.A.).

recollection of making the statements or of the abuse. **Are the child's out-of-court statements admissible?**

See *R. v. G. (P.)* (2012), 292 C.C.C. (3d) 569, 99 C.R. (6th) 401 (Ont. C.A.).

Problem 2

The accused is charged with first degree murder in a shooting death that arose from a drug deal gone wrong. The victim was shot by a young person, D.S., but the Crown alleged that the accused arranged the shooting. D.S. pleaded guilty in youth court to second degree murder. D.S. signed an agreed statement of facts that was drafted by Crown counsel with input from defence counsel. The agreed statement of facts indicated that the accused was involved in the shooting in that he gave D.S. the handgun that was used, he instructed D.S. to shoot the victim during the drug deal, and he demanded that D.S. return the handgun shortly after the shooting. The presentation of the agreed statement of facts was neither videotaped nor preceded by oath or affirmation.

At the accused's trial, the Crown calls D.S. as a witness. Contrary to the account given in the agreed statement of facts, D.S. testifies that no one gave him the gun, that he shot the accused for his own reasons, and that he later threw the weapon in a river. In light of D.S.'s recantation of his earlier account, the Crown applies to have the agreed statement of facts from D.S.'s plea proceeding admitted for the truth of its contents in the accused's trial. **Is it admissible?**

See *R. v. Youvarajah*, 2013 SCC 41, [2013] 2 S.C.R. 720, 300 C.C.C. (3d) 1, 3 C.R. (7th) 40 (S.C.C.).

Problem 3

The accused and four other men are charged with various offences related to a fraudulent credit and debit card scheme. The four other men, V, S, I and R, pled guilty to various offences based on agreed statements of facts that implicated the accused. The accused pleads not guilty. The Crown's case rests on the testimony of the four co-accused. However, at the accused's trial, all four men recant some of their earlier statements implicating the accused, including portions of the agreed statements of facts underlying their guilty pleas and, in two cases, statements made in testimony at the accused's preliminary inquiry. In light of these recantations, Crown counsel brings a *B. (K.G.)* application. **Should the application succeed?**

See *R. v. Kanagalingam*, 2014 ONCA 727, 315 C.C.C. (3d) 199, 15 C.R. (7th) 340 (Ont. C.A.).

Problem 4

The accused is charged with fraud. She took most of the life savings of an elderly woman who died before trial. The accused was the complainant's caregiver and power of attorney. The accused had a bank card issued for herself on the complainant's savings account and over a period of less than two years the accused emptied the account of over $127,000, which she used for her own needs. The defence claims that the accused acted with the consent of the complainant. The Crown contends that the accused acted without the knowledge or consent of the complainant, and in support of that position the Crown tenders a detailed video statement to that effect given under oath to police by the complainant before her death. **Is the statement admissible?**

See *R. v. Taylor* (2012), 294 C.C.C. (3d) 483, 99 C.R. (6th) 166 (Ont. C.A.).

Problem 5

The accused was charged with sexual assault causing bodily harm and related offences. The complainant was a 32-year-old woman with intellectual disabilities and schizophrenia. She arrived at her mother's workplace injured and in distress. The complainant's mother took her to the police where the complainant recounted being violently attacked first on the street and then in her apartment. Many details of the statement were bizarre or impossible. The complainant said that she was under the influence of drugs at the time of the assault and when she gave the statement. The statement was videotaped but not given under oath although the complainant's mother told her that she should tell the truth. A doctor gave evidence that the complainant's injuries were not consistent with consensual sex. **Is the video statement admissible?**

See *R. v. Threefingers*, 2016 ABCA 225, 340 C.C.C. (3d) 301, 32 C.R. (7th) 31 (Alta. C.A.). See also Janine Benedet, "The Evidence of Mentally Disabled Complainants in Sexual Assault Cases: Some Key Issues" (2016), 32 C.R. (7th) 8.

(e) Establishing Necessity

One early and influential explanation of the necessity criterion was offered by the Supreme Court of Canada in *R. v. Smith*:[161]

> The . . . criterion of "necessity" refers to the necessity of the hearsay evidence to prove a fact in issue. Thus, in *Khan*, the infant complainant was found by the trial judge not to be competent to testify herself. In this sense, hearsay evidence of her statements was necessary, in that what she said to her mother could not be adduced through her. It was her inability to testify that governed the situation.

> The criterion of necessity, however, does not have the sense of "necessary to the prosecution's case". If this were the case, uncorroborated hearsay evidence which satisfied the criterion of reliability would be admissible if uncorroborated, but might no longer be "necessary" to the prosecution's case if corroborated by other independent evidence. Such an interpretation of the criterion of "necessity" would thus produce the illogical result that uncorroborated hearsay evidence

---

[161]   [1992] 2 S.C.R. 915, 75 C.C.C. (3d) 257, 15 C.R. (4th) 133 (S.C.C.) at 933-934 [S.C.R.].

would be admissible, but could become inadmissible if corroborated. This is not what was intended by this Court's decision in *Khan*.

As indicated above, the criterion of necessity must be given a flexible definition, capable of encompassing diverse situations. What these situations will have in common is that the relevant direct evidence is not, for a variety of reasons, available. Necessity of this nature may arise in a number of situations. Wigmore, while not attempting an exhaustive enumeration, suggested at s. 1421 the following categories:

> (1) The person whose assertion is offered may now be dead, or out of the jurisdiction, or insane, or otherwise unavailable for the purpose of testing [by cross-examination]. This is the commoner and more palpable reason . . .

> (2) The assertion may be such that we cannot expect, again or at this time, to get evidence of the same value from the same or other sources . . . . The necessity is not so great; perhaps hardly a necessity, only an expediency or convenience, can be predicated. But the principle is the same.

Clearly the categories of necessity are not closed. In *Khan*, for instance, this Court recognized the necessity of receiving hearsay evidence of a child's statements when the child was not herself a competent witness. We also suggested that such hearsay evidence might become necessary when the emotional trauma that would result to the child if forced to give viva voce testimony would be great. Whether a necessity of this kind arises, however, is a question of law for determination by the trial judge.

The Supreme Court offered further guidance on the necessity criterion in the following case:

R. v. PARROTT
[2001] 1 S.C.R. 178, 39 C.R. (5th) 255, 150 C.C.C. (3d) 449

A mature woman with a mental disability was seen being put into the accused's car parked outside the psychiatric hospital where the woman resided. After conducting a search which lasted over seven hours, the police located the car, with the woman and the accused, in a remote area. Her shorts and underwear were in disarray. She had bruises and scratches on her body. The woman made out-of-court statements to the police constable who found her and to the doctor who first examined her. Pointing to her injuries, she communicated that the man in the car had done it. The accused was charged with kidnapping and sexual assault. The out-of-court statements were admitted. The accused was convicted of kidnapping, acquitted of sexual assault, but convicted of assault causing bodily harm. The majority of the Court of Appeal held that the trial judge erred in admitting the hearsay evidence when the complainant herself was available to testify and there was no expert suggestion that she would suffer any trauma or adverse effect by appearing in court. The curative proviso of the *Criminal Code* was applied to maintain the conviction with respect to kidnapping but the conviction with respect to assault causing bodily harm was quashed and a new trial was ordered. The Crown appealed against the setting aside of the assault verdict.

BINNIE J. (MAJOR, BASTARACHE, and ARBOUR JJ. concurring): —

This appeal tests the limits of the principled hearsay exception that allows the Crown in exceptional circumstances to lead the out-of-court evidence of a complainant at a criminal trial without having him or her present in court and available for cross-examination by the defence.

In this case, the complainant in a kidnapping and sexual assault case was a mature woman who had suffered since birth from Down's Syndrome. She was considered mildly to moderately retarded and had been in institutional care for almost 20 years. Expert evidence was called to establish that her mental development was equivalent to that of a three- or four-year-old child and that her memory of events was poor. Her response to even the simplest questions was said to be not very coherent. The complainant herself was never called into the presence of the trial judge so that these attributes could be verified even though she was available and there was no suggestion that she would suffer any trauma or other adverse effect by appearing in court. Instead the court received evidence of out-of-court statements that she had earlier made to the police and to a doctor.

. . .

About 7:00 p.m. on July 15, 1994, the respondent drove to the Waterford hospital, a psychiatric hospital in St. John's, and was seen talking to a female resident of the hospital who then brought the complainant to his car. James Barry, a psychiatric nursing assistant at the hospital observed these events from a distance of about 200 feet. He shouted at the respondent and the female resident but neither of them acknowledged the shouts. Mr. Barry testified he saw the female resident grip the complainant, seat her in the car and lift her knees and shut the door. He saw the respondent reach over the seat and lock the door. The respondent was observed giving the female resident $20. Mr. Barry reported the incident to his supervisors who called the police. Despite a search effort it took over seven hours to find the complainant. When she was found, both she and the respondent were still in the same car, now located in a remote coastal area at about 2:35 the next morning.

. . .

The complainant made statements to police at the time of her being found, as well as to the doctor who first examined her. She repeatedly pointed to her injuries and stated "Man did it, bad man, man in car, patient". Police also conducted a videotaped interview the following day. She was questioned for 15 minutes in the presence of two nurses who had known and worked with her. She was asked about the marks on her hands, arm and face to which, in halting broken sentences, she replied that a man "in handcuffs" did it and that he should be "put in jail". She said that it happened "last night" and that he was wearing glasses and a black hat. She also communicated the facts that he scratched her in the car and that he smacked her.

. . .

Analysis

While in this country an accused does not have an absolute right to confront his or her accuser in the course of a criminal trial, the right to full answer and defence generally produces this result. In this case, unusually, the Crown precipitated an inquiry under s. 16 of the Canada Evidence Act not for the purpose of establishing the testimonial competence of "a proposed witness", namely the complainant, but to lay an evidentiary basis to keep her out of the witness box. Having satisfied the trial judge entirely through expert evidence that the complainant neither understood the nature of an oath nor could communicate her evidence, the Crown used the *voir dire* as a springboard to establish the admissibility of hearsay evidence of her out-of-court statements under the principles established in *Khan*.

. . .

This procedure raises two distinct though related issues, firstly the admissibility of the expert evidence at the voir dire, and secondly the admissibility of the complainant's out-of-court statements at the trial. In my view, these issues ought to have been resolved in favour of the respondent, as held by the majority judgment of the Newfoundland Court of Appeal, for the following reasons:

1. The expert evidence was improperly admitted at the voir dire. Trial judges are eminently qualified to assess the testimonial competence of a witness. The trial judge, after all, was to be at the receiving end of the complainant's communication, and could have determined whether or not she was able to communicate her evidence to him. If she had been called and it became evident that the trial judge required expert assistance to draw appropriate inferences from what he had heard her say (or not say), or if either the defence or the Crown had wished to pursue the issue of requiring an oath or solemn affirmation, expert evidence might then have become admissible to assist the judge. At the time the expert testimony was called, it had not been shown that expert evidence as such was necessary, and the testimony of Drs. Gillespie, Morley and Parsons was therefore inadmissible: *R. v. Mohan*, [1994] 2 S.C.R. 9.

2. Consequently, the trial judge erred in ruling at the conclusion of the *voir dire* that the complainant's out-of-court statements would be admissible at trial. Having dispensed with hearing from the complainant, and the expert medical testimony having been improperly admitted, the trial judge had no admissible evidence on which to exercise a discretion to admit the complainant's out-of-court statements.

3. Even if the expert medical evidence were to be admitted, and accepting the trial judge's conclusion that the out-of-court statements were "reliable" under the first branch of the *Khan* requirements, the trial judge still erred in the circumstances of this case in finding the admission of out-of-court statements to be "necessary" without first hearing from the complainant.

. . .

Whether a complainant "is able to communicate the evidence" in this broad sense is a matter on which a trial judge can (and invariably does) form his or her own opinion. It is not a matter "outside the experience and knowledge of a judge or jury" (*Mohan*, supra, at p. 23). It is the very meat and potatoes of a trial court's existence.

Necessity

In *Rockey*, supra, Sopinka J. (for the majority) held that because the evidence regarding the child witness' competence to testify was equivocal, the out-of-court statements were not admissible on this basis. However, he further found that there was uncontroverted evidence that the child would be traumatized by giving evidence and decided that the out-of-court statements were necessary for that reason.

The complainant in this case could have been examined before the trial judge in a format that would have attempted to put her at ease. The trial judge could have ensured that nothing, including questions put to her by opposing counsel, would be used to demean or embarrass her. It is possible that, as anticipated by Dr. Gillespie, the complainant might have been incoherent or otherwise unable to communicate whatever she recalled of the events in question. On the other hand, it is also possible that she might, as suggested by Dr. Morley, have been able to give "some account of what happened to her". In the absence of any suggestion of potential trauma or other exceptional circumstances, I think the respondent was entitled to have this issue determined on the basis of the evidence of the complainant rather than on the conflicting opinions, however learned, of her various doctors.

I accept that it was kinder to the complainant to excuse her from appearing at the trial. It is possible, as my colleague LeBel J. suggests at para. 12, that her appearance "would have served no real purpose". But we do not know this. What we do know is that there were very serious accusations made against the respondent. He was confronted with evidence of her out-of-court statements taken in his absence and on which, of course, he could not cross-examine. As a result of the trial, he was sentenced to three years and nine months in jail in addition to the time already served. Compassion for the complainant must be balanced against fairness to the respondent.

While the concept of necessity "must be given a flexible definition capable of encompassing diverse situations" (*R. v. B. (K.G.)*, [1993] 1 S.C.R. 740, at p. 796), it must nevertheless be established on the facts of each particular case. Wells C.J.N., in dissent, observed that the phrase "to communicate the evidence" in s. 16(1)(b) requires exploration of whether the witness is capable of perceiving events, remembering events and communicating events to the court. This is so, but absent special circumstances, the exploration should include hearing from the witness herself.

The *Khan* principles of necessity and reliability were recently applied by a divided Court in *F. (W.J.)*, [1999] 3 S.C.R. 569, where the hearsay evidence of a child complainant was admitted but not until after the child herself had entered the witness box and demonstrated an inability to answer questions about the events surrounding the sexual assault. Even at that, Lamer C.J. dissented on the basis that the trial court had not adequately pursued the reasons why the child appeared unable to provide her recollection of events.

In this case, we are asked to take *F. (W.J.)* one step further. There was no attempt to seek the evidence directly from the witness/complainant even though there was no suggestion that she would suffer adverse effects from appearing in the witness box. No other explanation was given for her non-appearance. The Crown simply decided to relieve the trial judge of the burden of making his own decision, and left him to pick among the competing versions of her testimonial competence offered up by the medical experts.

In my view, if the witness is physically available and there is no suggestion that he or she would suffer trauma by attempting to give evidence, that evidence should generally not be pre-empted by hearsay unless the trial judge has first had an opportunity to hear the potential witness and form his or her own opinion as to testimonial competence. I say generally because there may arise exceptional circumstances where a witness is available and not called and the out-of-court statements may be nevertheless admitted. The Court was careful not to close the door to this possibility in *R. v. Hawkins*, [1996] 3 S.C.R. 1043, at paras. 71-72; *B. (K.G.)*, supra, at pp. 798-99; and *Rockey*, supra, per McLachlin J., concurring in the result, at para. 23. Green J.A. recognized that possibility in the majority judgment in this case (p. 111). The point is that there are no circumstances put in evidence here that would justify such an exceptional procedure.

The Crown in written and oral argument makes several points in justification of the procedure that was followed. It says, first of all, that while there was no evidence that the complainant would suffer trauma, nevertheless the Court can infer the likelihood of something approaching trauma from the video and the nature of the events she was to be asked about. Her otherwise reclusive existence in the Waterford Hospital suggests an inability to cope with the outside world. The Crown submits that "it would have been simply a bit of a circus and a bit of a farce to have gone through the procedure of calling her as a witness simply to be complete in relation to form", and "[i]t would have been, in effect, almost marking her as an exhibit simply for the purpose of bringing her into the Court and showing her to all sides".

Few complainants can welcome a courtroom appearance in a sexual assault charge, but there is no reason to think this complainant was more vulnerable than others on this account. If there was an issue about trauma, it ought not to have been left to inference. Psychiatric evidence was called specifically to address the necessity of having the complainant testify in person, and none of the doctors raised the issue of potential trauma. The onus was on the Crown to meet the *Khan* criteria for the hearsay exception. It was clear that trauma to a potentially vulnerable witness is an important consideration. No such evidence was called.

Further, as Green J.A. pointed out, the Court should not be quick to leap to the assumption that a person with mental disabilities is not competent to give useful testimony. Trauma should not be presumed, not only because such a presumption would deprive the accused of the ability to observe and cross-examine the witness, but also because stereotypical assumptions about persons with disabilities should be avoided. For the same reason, I disagree with my colleague LeBel J. that we should assume that the complainant's appearance in the witness box would be demeaning or an "infringement . . . of her dignity and integrity" (para. 22). Persons with disabilities should not be underestimated.

. . .

For these reasons the judgment of the Newfoundland Court of Appeal should be affirmed and the Crown's appeal dismissed.

LeBel J. (L'Heureux-Dubé and Gonthier JJ. concurring) dissenting: —

. . .

A hallmark of the principled approach to hearsay is flexibility. In moving away from the categorical approach of the past to hearsay exceptions, the Court signalled in the last decade an intention to render the rules governing the reception of hearsay evidence more responsive to individual situations. . . . When dealing with young children or people with mental disabilities, this approach seeks to address the necessity and reliability required for the admission of the evidence while at the same time safeguarding the dignity and integrity of the complainants or witnesses.

. . .

We are far from the strict approach to hearsay which prevailed in the past. Perhaps the most important aspect of the broad account of necessity quoted above is the fact that "the categories of necessity are not closed". Trial judges now have a much broader discretion to admit evidence which would otherwise be considered as hearsay. This court should not attempt to confine this discretion into limited categories, but should rather content itself with stating broad principles to guide judges in the exercise of their discretion.

. . .

In this context, the ruling of the trial judge was not a narrow one limited to the application of a test of mental competence as in s. 16 of the Canada Evidence Act, R.S.C. 1985, c. C-5. The trial judge's inquiry was much broader. It sought to examine the whole of the complainant's condition as mandated by our principled approach to hearsay and necessity as discussed above. In that regard, the trial judge did not simply express a preference for the views of one of the experts heard, Dr. Gillespie. Barry J.'s decision examined more broadly the victim's childlike mental condition or mental retardation and its impact on her potential testimony. This careful consideration of the condition of the complainant led the judge to decide that she was incapable (as opposed to the more narrow concept of "incompetence") of testifying. He then decided that the out-of-court statements in the video should be received into evidence, because they met the reliability and necessity tests.

. . .

This Court has without exception assumed a posture of deference toward a trial judge's assessment of testimonial capacity. As McLachlin J. admonished in *Marquard*, "[m]eticulous second-guessing on appeal is to be eschewed." The majority of the Court of Appeal engaged in just such a re-evaluation of the record and interfered too readily with the trial judge's findings. The trial judge was in a superior position to assess the expert testimony, which obviously confirmed his own observation of the complainant's abilities during her interview with Sergeant Ryan. In my view, the trial judge's decision to admit the hearsay evidence manifests no palpable error.

I would accordingly allow the appeal and restore the respondent's conviction.

PROBLEM

The accused is charged with second degree murder. At the time of the homicide the accused was living with his girlfriend and her 21-year-old son. At trial the son testifies he has no memory of what the accused said when he returned home shortly after the time of the killing. The Crown seeks to tender a sworn videotaped statement of the son telling the police that the accused told him he had followed a man who owed him money and had broken down his door and beat him badly. **Is the statement admissible?**

See *R. v. Chretien,* 2014 ONCA 403, 309 C.C.C. (3d) 418 (Ont. C.A.).

Once admitted, a trial judge must provide a careful warning to the jury on the use it can make of a hearsay statement. In *R. v. Pasqualino* the Ontario Court of Appeal held:[162]

> 62 This court has also held that with regard to hearsay evidence admitted for the purpose of proving the truth of its contents under the principled exception, the trial judge's jury instructions must explain the increased risk that such statements may be unreliable, as well as the jury's obligation to determine the reliability and weight it will attribute to such evidence: see *R. v. Blackman* (2006), 215 C.C.C. (3d) 524 at para. 85, aff'd 2008 S.C.C. 37; *R. v. Warner* (1994), 94 C.C.C. (3d) 540 at 551; *R. v. A. (S.)* (1992), 76 C.C.C. (3d) 522 at 527-29. In *Blackman,* Justice Cronk stated, at para. 85, that instructions concerning hearsay admitted under the principled exception are adequate so long as they make clear to the jury "the need to determine whether the [s]tatements were made and, if made, the nature of their contents, as well as the imperative to evaluate the evidence of the [s]tatements carefully and in the light of all the other evidence at trial."

There is authority for a more relaxed approach to admitting hearsay in civil cases, which started in *Ares v. Venner.*

DODGE v. KANEFF HOMES INC.
[2001] O.J. No. 1141 (Ont. S.C.J.)

Kaneff Homes had agreed that Dodge would act as the real estate broker for the sale of a subdivision. The parties agreed on the payment of commission. Dodge's estate alleged that the vice president of Kaneff entered into an oral agreement with Dodge prior to his death that the commission payable to Dodge would be increased. The estate proposed to introduce evidence from Dodge's wife, and the ex-wife of the vice-president of Kaneff and others, to support the existence of the oral agreement.

---

[162]   *Supra* note 156.

Per Pitt J.:—

. . .

The plaintiffs allege that on or about July 18, 1996, Raymond Dodge struck an oral agreement with Andy Berzins, whereby the commission rate payable to the Plaintiff Corporation would be increased from 2% to 4%. Raymond Dodge, the spouse of the plaintiff Susan Dodge, died suddenly and unexpectedly of a heart attack on December 24, 1996. It is the plaintiffs' position that certain notes made by Raymond Dodge, conversations he had with family members and friends in the months preceding his death, and an allegation by the former spouse of Andy Berzins of a conversation she had with Andy Berzins, all confirmatory of Raymond Dodge's recollection of the agreement, ought not to be excluded simply because Raymond Dodge is not available to testify at trial.

. . .

Counsel quickly conceded that the real issue emanating from the application of the "principled approach", . . . is the issue of reliability, since in the present case necessity is obvious.

. . .

The defendants contend that the absence of an opportunity for meaningful, contemporaneous, sworn cross-examination of the out-of-court declarant (the deceased) regarding the truth of the specific statement sought to be admitted—which is the rationale for the exclusion of hearsay evidence—will cause them irreparable harm. . . . The defendants accordingly argue that a hearsay statement may be admitted only if it "is made under circumstances which substantially negate the possibility that the declarant was untruthful or mistaken."

The defendants further allege that not only have the plaintiffs failed to adduce the evidence necessary to meet their burden of establishing reliability, by not providing the surrounding circumstances in which the alleged statements were made, but that the record contains undisputed facts which by themselves render the hearsay statement unreliable. They offer as examples:

    (a) The deceased's failure to refer to the alleged agreement in communications with the defendants;

    (b) The deceased's failure to increase the price of homes before his death, such increases having been a part of the alleged agreement and the basis for sustaining the increased commission rates;

    (c) The very allegation that the deceased had promised to increase the price of the houses, since real-estate agents in the normal course of events do not determine the price of homes.

    (d) The apparent lack of consideration for the alleged increase in the commission rate.

The defendants are particularly concerned about the circumstances under which the deceased is alleged to have told his spouse of the agreement to increase the rates. Susan Dodge will testify that on the morning after the agreement was made, the deceased's first words to her were "I got my deal."

He then indicated the difficulty he had had in the negotiation, and the negotiating strategy he used, from which inferences may be drawn about Ray Berzins' response and his final agreement. The defendants argue that the attempt to provide testimony about what Berzins said is a form of double hearsay and therefore should require a higher level of reliability.

. . .

Another important issue raised by the defendant's falls under the rubric of the interest or lack thereof of the declarant. It emanates from a passage in *Khan, supra*, in the judgment of McLachlin J. at p. 541. Her Ladyship referred to *Ares v. Venner*, [1970] S.C.R. 608 at 624, a seminal case on the hearsay exception for business records. Hall J. quoted from the reasons of Lord Pearce's dissent in *Myers v. Director of Public Prosecutions*, [1965] A.C. 1001 at pp. 1040-41:

> I find it impossible to accept that there is any "dangerous uncertainty" caused by obvious and sensible improvements in the means by which the court arrives at the truth. One is entitled to choose between the individual conflicting obiter dicta of two great judges and I prefer that of Jessel M.R. His dictum was as follows, 1 P.D. 154, 241: "Now I take it the principle which underlies all these exceptions is the same. In the first place, the case must be one in which it is difficult to obtain other evidence, for no doubt the ground for admitting the exceptions was that very difficulty. In the next place the declarant must be disinterested: that is, disinterested in the sense that the declaration was not made in favour of his interest. And, thirdly, the declaration must be made before dispute or litigation, so that it was made without bias on account of the existence of a dispute or litigation which the declarant might be supposed to favour."

I respectfully suggest that since Raymond Dodge could not have predicted his demise, he may fairly be viewed as a disinterested party, since his assertion that there was an amended agreement could not have been made with a view to advance his interest.

. . .

Of the plaintiffs' arguments, I find two particularly persuasive. The first is that at this stage, I am concerned only with threshold reliability, as ultimate reliability and the weight attached to it are to be decided later. . . . The second argument, even more important in my view, is that courts have held there is some flexibility with respect to the admissibility of hearsay evidence in civil proceedings, where the ultimate burden of proof is only on a balance of possibilities.

As I said at the outset, the main purpose of this proceeding is the plaintiffs' desire to determine whether the hearsay evidence is admissible so that they can decide whether they should devote scarce resources to a full-scale trial. A passage from Sopinka, supra at p. 195 may be appropriately quoted here:

> Accordingly, there may be instances where the necessity is so great—such as where the declarant is dead — that some elasticity on the issue of reliability may be given. . .

Is the standard of proof to establish admissibility less in civil cases, where the ultimate burden of proof is only on a balance of probabilities and other considerations such as expediency and the crippling costs of litigation come into question? Adams J., in *Clark v. Horizon Holidays Ltd. [supra]* in considering a wrongful dismissal case, had regard to the general flexibility in respect to the admission of hearsay evidence in the determination of such disputes as follows:

> This is a wrongful dismissal case where alternative dispute resolution systems abound. All of these forums freely admit hearsay evidence in the name of informality, expediency and the reduction of cost. Indeed, those systems have arisen in reaction to the austere formalism of courts. In my view, Khan and Smith signal willingness in the judiciary to design procedures and evidentiary rules to enhance the accessibility, and therefore, the relevance of our courts.

On balance, it is my view that Raymond Dodge's death should not by itself completely deprive his estate of an opportunity to vindicate a contractual right he may have had. I am also mindful that, apart from the notes, in each instance one of the parties to the discussions will be available for cross-examination.

After careful consideration of the defendants' concerns, I am nonetheless prepared to admit the proffered evidence, except for the typed notes and the testimony of the son-in-law.

2. EXCEPTIONS

Professor Wigmore[163] sought to provide us with a theory which would explain the various existing exceptions to the hearsay rule and to generate a principled approach to the creation of new exceptions. Having eliminated from the hearsay category admissions and former testimony, he finds first, that with each of the other exceptions there are circumstances surrounding the making of the statement which guarantee its trustworthiness and so dispense with the need for an oath and cross-examination, and second, that some grounds of necessity exist resident in the unavailability of the declarant or the inconvenience in requiring his or her attendance.[164] But his teacher, Professor Thayer, in his historical researches, suggests no single theory to explain the various exceptions. He notes,[165] rather, that along with the development of the hearsay rule in the late seventeenth century:

> There came a large and miscellaneous number of so-called "exceptions." Some of these, in reality, were quite independent rules, whose operation was rather that of qualifications and abatements to the generality of this other doctrine; rules which were coeval with the doctrine itself or much older. . . . a number of the so-called "exceptions" to the hearsay prohibition came in under the head of written entries or declarations; they came in, or rather, so to speak, stayed in, simply

---

[163] 5 Wigmore, *Evidence* (Chad. Rev.), s. 1420.

[164] See the criticism by Morgan that if this demonstration of the law of hearsay seems rational and consistent, it is only a "seeming", and that Wigmore's theory has sadly encouraged piecemeal rather than fundamental reform: *Some Problems of Proof under the Anglo-American System of Litigation* (New York: Columbia University Press, 1956) at 167-168.

[165] *Preliminary Treatise on Evidence* (1898) at 519-522.

because they had always been received, and no rule against hearsay had ever been formulated or interpreted as applying to them. Such things, continuing at the present day, are, e.g., the admission of old entries and writings in proof of ancient matters, written declarations of deceased persons against interest, and in the course of duty or business; and, to a limited extent, a merchant's own account books to prove his own case. So also of regular entries in public books, a matter probably never even doubted to be admissible in evidence.

Nevertheless, Professor Wigmore's justification of the exceptions has become accepted by many as a useful tool for evaluating the creation of new exceptions.[166] The exact number of existing exceptions is unclear and the subject of some debate in the writings. Clearly all are not of equal importance and it is sufficient if the student is simply generally aware of their existence; those exceptions which regularly occur will need some exploration.

(a) Admissions

(i) Generally

The orthodox view is to treat admissions as an exception to the hearsay rule although they do not share the normal attributes, necessity and circumstantial guarantees of trustworthiness, possessed by the others. This fact has led some to suggest that, though admissible, they would be better characterized as non-hearsay.[167] An admission is, very simply, a statement made by a party tendered by the opposing party. For this purpose a party is the plaintiff or defendant in civil cases and the accused in a criminal case (but not the complainant).

A number of theories have been suggested to justify the reception of admissions.[168] For this exception only, grounds of necessity obviously do not exist and trustworthiness is not always present, as there is no requirement that the declarant have personal first-hand knowledge.

The various theories advanced to justify reception are grounded in ideas of fairness, responsibility and the adversarial nature of our system. Professor Morgan has offered:

> The admissibility of an admission made by the party himself rests not upon any notion that the circumstances in which it was made furnish the trier means of evaluating it fairly, but upon the adversary theory of litigation. A party can hardly object that he had no opportunity to cross-examine himself or that he is unworthy of credence save when speaking under sanction of an oath.[169]

Lower courts have differed as to whether admissions of parties should also be subject to the necessity and reliability determination.[170] In *Khelawon*,

---

[166] See e.g. *Ares v. Venner*, [1970] S.C.R. 608 and s. 45(3) of the *Uniform Evidence Bill*.
[167] See Federal Rules of Evidence, Rule 801, 28 U.S.C.A. and Advisory Committee Note; see also McCormick, *supra* note 126 at 629; 4 Wigmore, *Evidence* (Chad. Rev.), s. 1048; and Strahorn, "A Reconsideration of the Hearsay Rule and Admissions" (1937) 85 U. Pa. L. Rev. 564.
[168] See their examination in Pickard, "Statements of Parties" (1978) 41 Mod. L. Rev. 124 together with his own suggested theory.
[169] Morgan, *Basic Problems of Evidence* (1962) at 266.
[170] See e.g. *R. v. Osmar* (2007), 217 C.C.C. (3d) 174, 44 C.R. (6th) 276 (C.A.); *R. v. Terrico*

Justice Charron makes an enigmatic comment that seems to suggest that such an inquiry should not occur:

> Some of the traditional exceptions stand on a different footing, such as admissions from parties (confessions in the criminal context) and co-conspirators' statements: see *Mapara*, at para. 21. In those cases, concerns about reliability are based on considerations other than the party's inability to test the accuracy of his or her own statement or that of his or her co-conspirators. Hence, the criteria for admissibility are not established in the same way. [par. 63]

In all fairness, if the adversary chooses to introduce a statement by the party-opponent he or she must introduce all of the statement and not just the portion which favours him or her. As noted in *Capital Trust Co. v. Fowler:*[171]

> The law seems quite settled that, if an admission is used by one party, it must be used in its entirety, that is, everything must be read that is necessary to the understanding and appreciation of the meaning and extent of the admission. It is also equally established that, if a party uses an admission, he makes it evidence in the cause both as to himself and as to the opposition party in the litigation as well; but, if he desires to contradict or qualify any statement in it, he may do so. He can therefore give other evidence so to contradict or qualify it, but, if he does not see fit to do so, the whole of the admission remains as evidence in the cause for the benefit of both parties.

While a party may have the right to insist that his or her adversary introduce the entirety of a single narrative, this governing principle does not, of course, demand that adversary must introduce all statements or none. As Kaufman, J. said:

> A word of warning may be in order. The fact that the prosecution is obliged, where it chooses to offer in evidence a declaration made by the accused, to introduce the whole, and not just parts, does not mean that an accused can create self-serving evidence by writing out a statement and handing it to the police.[172]

R. v. PHILLIPS
[1995] O.J. No. 2985 (Ont. Gen. Div.)

McISAAC J.:—

The accused, Lenard Roy Phillips, is charged with the murder of Provincial Constable Eric Nystedt as a result of a stabbing incident which took place in the early morning hours of July 3, 1993 in a relatively isolated cottage area near Furnace Falls, in the County of Haliburton. Mr. Phillips fled the scene and was not arrested until noon of the same day. At that time, he was located hiding in a ditch off Highway #503 several kilometres from the scene of the stabbing. The arresting officers, P.C. DeVoss and P.C. McMaster initially

---

(2005), 199 C.C.C. (3d) 126, 31 C.R. (6th) 161 (B.C. C.A.); *R. v. Connolly* (2003), 176 C.C.C. (3d) 292 (N.S. C.A.); and *R. v. Foreman* (2002), 6 C.R. (6th) 201, 169 C.C.C. (3d) 489 (Ont. C.A.).

[171] (1921), 64 D.L.R. 289 (Ont. C.A.) at 292.

[172] Kaufman, *The Admissibility of Confessions* (1979) at 287. See the adoption of this caution in *R. v. Jackson* (1980), 57 C.C.C. (2d) 154 (Ont. C.A.).

advised him at gunpoint that he was being arrested for stabbing a peace officer. That advice was shortly changed to include the killing of an officer. His response at that time was "I guess I really did it this time." He was immediately advised of his rights to counsel and he received the standard primary and secondary cautions. The defence waives the voluntariness of these statements.

When he was placed into the police cruiser, he asked the arresting officers "So who's the guy I murdered?" P.C. McMaster advised him that he should not say anything further when he said "Can I ask another question?" He did not speak further to these officers other than advising them that he wished to call his mother once they arrived at the Coboconk O.P.P. detachment at 12:34 p.m. At that time, he was asked if he wanted to call a lawyer. That led to his speaking to counsel before he was turned over to the investigating officers at 1:16 p.m. During that interview which lasted until 2:55 p.m., Mr. Phillips advanced several theories that either justified his actions by way of mistaken self-defence or partially excused his actions due to the consumption of alcohol or drugs. He claimed amnesia for the stabbing of P.C. Nystedt, but admitted taking a swing at "someone."

Counsel for Mr. Phillips submits that the utterances shortly after noon and the answers given in the interview that took place between 1:16 p.m. and 2:55 p.m. constitute one entire statement and if the former part goes before the jury then they must hear the second part as well. On the other hand, the Crown suggests that the doctrine of severability applies and the second interview should be excluded on the principle that it is self-serving and is in no way explanatory of the statements made to the arresting officers.

In *Wigmore on Evidence* (Chadbourn Rev.), v. VII, at p. 670, the following comments from *Steward v. Sherman* 5 Conn. 244, 245 (1824) are presented as authoritative on the issue:

> The past and future cannot thus be brought together in order to form an artificial identity. The law never intends that a party may make evidence for himself from his own declarations, but merely that the meaning of a conversation shall not be perverted by proof of a part of it only.

My review of the Canadian jurisprudence with these observations of Hosmer, C.J. As one can easily see, the opportunity for reflection militates against the admissibility of such self-serving evidence.

. . .

In this case, the statement by the accused to the investigating officers took place at least one hour after his initial contact with the arresting officers. In fact, the recorded interview did not begin until 1:33 p.m. It is clear that not only was Mr. Phillips speaking to completely different police personnel, but he had also had ample time for reflection on what he was going to say. Most importantly, he had had the benefit of legal advice in the interim. In my opinion, this is sufficient in itself to destroy any nexus between the two statements. I am not satisfied that anything said to P.C. Harvey and P.C. Bowen was an "amplification, qualification or explanation" of what he had said to P.C. DeVoss and P.C. McMaster at the time of his arrest.

The statement made or adopted by the party is admissible against that party, and in a joint trial an admission is only evidence against the party who made it and the trier of fact must be warned of its limited utility.[173] There remains a large danger that the jury will not follow the limiting instruction when the confession of the co-accused implicates the other. Indeed the limiting instruction has been referred to as a "placebo", a "medicinal lie", and "a kind of judicial lie",[174] as it is practically impossible to follow.

Sometimes admissions are characterized as "declarations against interest". This phrasing is confusing as there is no requirement that the statement be "against interest" when made, and with respect to it being "against interest" when tendered, Professor Wigmore has noted:

> . . . in effect and broadly, *anything said by the party-opponent may be used against him as an admission*, provided it exhibits the quality of inconsistency with the facts now asserted by him in pleadings or in testimony. (This proviso never needs to be enforced, because no party offers thus his opponent's statement unless it does appear to be inconsistent.) [Emphasis added.][175]

R. v. STREU
[1989] 1 S.C.R. 1521, 70 C.R. (3d) 1, 48 C.C.C. (3d) 321

The accused was convicted of possession of stolen property having a value in excess of $200. He sold the property to a police officer, who had posed as a purchaser, for $125. The officer testified that the accused, during conversation leading to the sale, had admitted that the tires and rims belonged to a friend who had "ripped them off". In the absence of the accused's statement there would not be evidence, sufficient to meet the criminal standard of proof, that the items were in fact stolen.

SOPINKA J.: —

. . .

---

[173] It is "an advisable practice" that the jury be immediately warned when a confession is received in a joint trial that it is not evidence against a co-accused: see *Schmidt v. R.*, [1945] S.C.R. 438; *Chote v. Rowan*, [1943] O.W.N. 646 (C.A.). See too *R. v. Parberry* (2005), 202 C.C.C. (3d) 337 (Ont. C.A.).

[174] Remarks attributed to Learned Hand J. and Jerome Frank J. in *Bruton v. U.S.*, 391 U.S. 123 (1968); in that case the U.S. Supreme Court held that a limiting instruction was not sufficient in such a case as the accused was denied his Sixth Amendment right to confront witnesses. Generally speaking, then, in the U.S. the prosecution must proceed in separate trials or not tender the confession. It is interesting to note another solution which appears to have been the law in England until 1830: see *R. v. Hearne* (1830), 172 E.R. 676 and *R. v. Clewes* (1830), 172 E.R. 678. In a reporter's note to the latter case we read: "The practice has been, in reading confessions, to omit the names of other accused parties, and where they are used to say 'another person' 'a third person' & etc." In the above two cases Littledale, J. ordered the witnesses to use the names mentioned in the confession of the co-accused as it was seen necessary that the whole be repeated; he later noted that he would "take care to make such observations to the Jury, as will prevent its having any injurious effect against the other prisoners; and I shall tell the jury that they ought not to pay the slightest attention to this letter, except so far as it goes to affect the person who wrote it." *R. v. Fletcher* (1830), 172 E.R. 691.

[175] 4 Wigmore, *Evidence* (Chad. Rev.), s. 1048(1)(b).

The evidence at trial indicated that the appellant attempted to sell four tires and rims to a police officer who posed as a purchaser. The police officer testified to the following conversation with the appellant:

> I ask him, referring to the wheels: What are these off of? And he replies: A Volkswagen Rabbit. And I ask: Oh, yeah. From the City here? And he replies: I don't know. My friend ripped them off. I ask: Well, where's the other ones? Harv replies:

> They're in my house. I reply: Oh, I see. Well, I'll give you twenty bucks apiece. And he replies: I can't let them go for that, they are my friend's wheels. I ask: How much did he want. And Harv replies: He priced them out at one hundred and thirty apiece. That's for the rims. I reply: I'm not paying that much. Just yesterday I bought a 1984 Datsun for $180.

> . . .

> Harv replies: Well, I know they're hot and all but they're his tires. I reply: Let me talk to your friend then. Harv replies: I know he'll be mad at me if I only get that much.

The appellant and the police officer proceeded to a garage at the end of a lane near the appellant's home to complete the sale. The appellant expressed concern that they not be observed. The police officer further testified that he paid the appellant $125 for the tires and rims.

. . .

In *R. v. O'Neill* (1976), 13 C.R. (3d) 193 (Ont. C.A.), the only evidence against the accused regarding the theft of a stereo and turntable — the subjects of the charge against her of unlawful possession — was her statement to the police. In response to the question of whether she knew that the items were stolen the accused replied "yes". She then added that she had been given the items by a male friend.

The Court of Appeal followed *R. v. Porter*, [1976] Crim. L.R. 58, in finding that the hearsay statement of the accused was not proof that the items were stolen. The Court, at p.194, cited the editorial commentary following *R. v. Porter* with approval:

> It is one thing for the accused to admit facts of which he has personal knowledge and for an inference to be drawn from those facts that the goods are stolen. It is another thing for the accused to 'admit' facts of which he has no personal knowledge.

In *R. v. Rydzanicz* (1979), 13 C.R. (3d) 190 (Ont. C.A.), the accused was charged with having in his possession a quantity of stolen cigarettes. The accused stated to the police that he saw his friend Mike enter the shopping centre and come out with a whole shopping cart full of cartons of cigarettes. The accused added that he helped Mike put the cigarettes in the back of the truck. The accused also stated that he knew that the cigarettes were stolen when he saw Mike come out of the shopping centre.

The accused was acquitted at trial on the strength of *R. v. O'Neill, supra*. The Court of Appeal overturned the acquittal because the trial judge had overlooked the fact that the accused stated that he saw Mike go into the store and come out with a shopping cart full of cigarettes. The Court of Appeal, at p. 192, held that:

> That admission was based on the personal knowledge of the respondent, and constituted evidence of relevant fact in a chain of circumstances in support of an inference that the cigarettes were stolen.

Aside from the accused's stated belief, sufficient circumstantial evidence existed to support a finding that the goods were stolen. The Court of Appeal added that it is a question of fact whether the inference that the goods were stolen should be drawn by the trier of fact.

In *R. v. Elliott* (1984), 15 C.C.C. (3d) 195 (Alta. C.A.), the accused was charged with possession of certain roof panels, the property of person or persons unknown, knowing them to "have been obtained by the commission in Canada of theft" contrary to s. 312 of the *Criminal Code*. The items involved were worth approximately $1,300 although the accused testified that he paid $150 for them, having purchased them from an unknown person in a bar. He did not receive a sales slip for the goods and the police testified that the accused told them that because of the low price he paid he realized they were "hot". There was no evidence as to where the goods had been obtained or who their owner was. On appeal by the accused from his conviction, the appeal was allowed and an acquittal entered.

The majority held that it was clear that the element of theft can be proved by circumstantial evidence. In this case, the circumstantial evidence was not strong enough to support the inference that the goods were stolen:

> Here the only evidence of theft is proof of purchase for far below value, at a bar, from a stranger, without a bill of sale. Certainly, this gives rise to the suspicion that the goods which are being sold were stolen. Certainly in a civil case a court could prove on a balance of probabilities that a theft had occurred but I am of the opinion that proof of theft beyond all reasonable doubt has not been established by these facts alone. There has to be more. [p. 201]

> . . .

Although they do not always make it clear, some of these authorities deal with the question relating to the use to be made of an admission based on hearsay as a matter of weight, and others, as a matter of admissibility. In deciding which position is correct, account must be taken of the decision of this Court in *R. v. Schmidt*, [1948] S.C.R. 333, a case that apparently was not drawn to the attention of the Court of Appeal and is not referred to in the factum of either party in this Court. . . .

. . .

The rationale underlying the exclusion of hearsay evidence is primarily the inherent untrustworthiness of an extra-judicial statement which has been tendered without affording an opportunity to the party against whom it is adduced to cross-examine the declarant. This rationale applies equally in both criminal and civil cases. It loses its force when the party has chosen to rely on the hearsay statement in making an admission. Presumably in so doing, the party making the admission has satisfied himself or herself as to the reliability of the statement or at least had the opportunity to do so. The significance of this factor is evident in the decision of this Court in *Ares v. Venner*, [1970] S.C.R. 608, in which evidence was admitted as an exception to the hearsay rule where the party against whom the evidence was tendered had the opportunity to test the accuracy of the evidence.

I agree with the following statement in *Kitchen v. Robbins*, 29 Ga. 713 (1860), cited by 4 *Wigmore, Evidence*, s. 1053 (Chadbourn rev. 1972) for which I am indebted to McWilliams, *Canadian Criminal Evidence* (2nd ed. 1984), at p. 428:

> Are no admissions good against a party, unless founded on his personal knowledge? The admissions would not be made except on evidence which satisfies the party who is making them against his own interest, that they are true, and that is evidence to the jury that they are true.

Accordingly, once it is established that the admission was in fact made, there is no reason in principle for treating it any differently than the same statement would be treated had it been made in the witness box. In the latter case, if a party indicates a belief in or acceptance of a hearsay statement, that is some evidence of the truth of its contents. The weight to be given to that evidence is for the trier of fact. On the other hand, if the party simply reports a hearsay statement without either adopting it or indicating a belief in the truth of its contents, the statement is not admissible as proof of the truth of the contents.

. . .

Turning to the admission in question in this appeal, it is impossible to read it as merely reporting a hearsay statement without more. Clearly the appellant was relying on the hearsay statement as being true. Either he accepted it as being true or at least believed it to be true.

. . . Any evidentiary weakness in the information on which the admission was based was a matter of weight and not admissibility. This was a matter for the trial judge who considered the statement along with other evidence and concluded that the accused was guilty beyond a reasonable doubt.

Appeal dismissed.

(ii) *Confessions*

At common law, all statements made by an accused to a person in authority (i.e., a confession) are inadmissible unless the Crown can prove voluntariness beyond a reasonable doubt. The voluntary confessions rule is addressed separately in the next section **(C. Voluntary Confession Rule).**

(iii) *Implied Admissions*

R. v. SCOTT
2013 MBCA 7, 296 C.C.C. (3d) 311, 99 C.R. (6th) 282 (Man. C.A.)

CHARTIER J.A.:—

2 In certain circumstances, when an accused remains silent or fails to refute a statement made by another person in his or her presence, it can be said that the accused implicitly adopted it, and the statement will become an admission by the accused of the facts contained in the statement. Admissions of this sort have been referred to as implied admissions, adopted or adoptive admissions, and admissions by silence.

3 In the present case, a jury found the accused guilty of second degree murder. He now appeals against conviction. . . . [T]he determinative issue on this appeal is whether the trial judge erred by concluding that, on the facts of this case, there was sufficient evidence from which a jury might reasonably draw the inference that the accused adopted a statement by his silence. . . .

. . .

6 For the purposes of this appeal, it is only necessary to convey those facts which relate to the adopted or implied admissions issue. Identical twin sisters Arabella Garson (Arabella) and Fanney Garson (Fanney) attended to the house trailer of the accused for an evening of drinking. Other than the three, no one else was present. During the evening, the accused was flirting with Arabella. She made it clear that she had no interest in pursuing a relationship with him. At around midnight, Fanney went to lie down on the couch. The other two continued to drink. At one point Fanney heard Arabella say: "Help me Fanney." Fanney got up and saw her sister seated in a chair in the kitchen. Blood was coming from her sister's chest. Fanney tried to staunch the flow of blood with paper towels. The accused was standing about a foot behind Arabella. Fanney instructed the accused to apply pressure to her sister's chest and not to move her. He complied. As there was no telephone in the accused's trailer, she obtained the keys to the accused's truck and drove to the house of a neighbour.

7 A short time later, Fanney returned with the neighbour, only to find the trailer door locked. After several unsuccessful attempts to gain entrance (by repeated knocking and yelling and then obtaining and trying a spare key), Fanney and the neighbour kicked the door down. They found Arabella lying on her back. Fanney unsuccessfully tried to revive her. The neighbour saw that the accused was in the washroom. He described him as being all "cleaned up" and "like a guy going to a wedding." The neighbour confronted the accused who denied any wrongdoing and who repeatedly said "I have no blood on me. It can't be me."

8 Upon hearing the accused's response, Fanney asked him: "What did you do." He did not reply. She struck the accused twice in the jaw causing him to fall down and then flipped over the kitchen table. She told the accused to "stay down." He responded by saying "I didn't do it." When a paramedic arrived a short time later, Fanney told him, while pointing to the accused, "He did it." The accused, who was sitting 20 feet away, never replied. Later on, the accused told the paramedic: "She's not dead, wake her up."

9 It turned out Arabella was indeed deceased. The autopsy revealed that the cause of death was a left shoulder stab wound that penetrated the chest cavity. It also disclosed three stabs wounds in the deceased's back and a defensive type injury to her right hand. A knife was found on a chair in the accused's trailer. It had the deceased's DNA on it. Diluted blood was located on the side of the washroom sink. DNA analysis revealed that this blood contained DNA from two individuals, one of which was male. No blood sample was ever taken from the accused. Fanney testified at trial and said she did not kill her sister. The accused did not testify.

10 Surprisingly, I am unaware of any decisions from this court on the issue of adopted or implied admissions and, while other appellate courts have considered this issue, the Supreme Court of Canada has said very little on it since *Stein v. The King*, [1928] S.C.R. 553, and *Chapdelaine v. The King*, [1935] S.C.R. 53.

11 The fundamental principles surrounding the law of adopted or implied admissions, and approved in the two above-referenced Supreme Court of Canada decisions, originally came from the House of Lords in *Rex v. Christie*, [1914] A.C. 545. In *Christie*, the House of Lords generally discussed when statements made in the presence of an accused will be admissible against the accused, and the procedure a court should follow when faced with such evidence. Lord Atkinson stated as follows (at pp. 554-55):

> . . . [T]he rule of law undoubtedly is that a statement made in the presence of an accused person, even upon an occasion which should be expected reasonably to call for some explanation or denial from him, is not evidence against him of the facts stated save so far as he accepts the statement, so as to make it, in effect, his own. .... He may accept the statement <u>by word or conduct, action or demeanour,</u> and it is the function of the jury which tries the case to determine whether his words, action, conduct, or demeanour at the time when a statement was made amounts to an acceptance of it in whole or in part. It by no means follows, I think, that a mere denial by the accused of the facts mentioned in the statement necessarily renders the statement inadmissible, because he may deny the statement in such a manner and under such circumstances as may lead a jury to disbelieve him, and constitute evidence from which an acknowledgement may be inferred by them.

> . . .

18 While most of the *Christie* principles have been consistently applied by appellate courts, there is some inconsistency with respect to the issue of how the silence of accused persons is to be regarded. Some suggest that an accused's mere silence may be sufficient to render the accusatory statement made in his or her presence evidence of its truth, if the circumstances are such that a response could reasonably have been expected. See for example *R. v. Eden,* [1970] 2 O.R. 161 at 164 (C.A.); *R. v. Baron and Wertman* (1976), 14 O.R. (2d) 173 (C.A.) at 186; *R. v. Warner (J.R.)* (1994), 75 O.A.C. 288 at para. 21; and *R. v. J.F.,* 2011 ONCA 220 at para. 46, 276 O.A.C. 292. This last case is pending before the Supreme Court of Canada, [2011] S.C.C.A. No. 291.

19 In my respectful view, these decisions do not quite accord with the principles set out in *Christie, Stein* and *Chapdelaine,* which indicate that a statement made in the presence of an accused, "even upon an occasion which should be expected reasonably to call for some explanation or denial from him, is not evidence" (*Chapdelaine* at p. 55) of the facts stated, unless he or she accepts the statement as his or her own. Put another way, mere silence, even where it would be reasonable to expect a denial in the face of an accusation, will not constitute an admission. There must be something more in the circumstances than the mere silence of the accused and an expectation that he or she would have said something. In essence, these three decisions stand for the proposition that, when the accused's own silence is the only evidence that the accusatory statement was adopted, the statement is to be excluded because its prejudicial effect outweighs its probative value.

. . .

21 In summary, the authorities make it clear that great caution should be exercised when considering a question of adopted or implied admission by silence as there may be other reasons for an accused's silence. A statement made in the accused's presence is not evidence of the facts contained therein, even if it is reasonable to expect an explanation or denial, unless the accused accepts or adopts the statement, either expressly or by inference, as his or her own.

22 A trial judge has a gatekeeper function and must be satisfied that the accused had the state of mind to hear and comprehend the accusatory statement and adopted it in some verbal or non-verbal way. A trial judge should hold a *voir dire* to determine the admissibility of the statement as an adopted admission. The decision on admissibility entails a consideration of all of the circumstances under which the statement was made and possibly adopted by the accused. On the *voir dire*, the trial judge must determine whether there is sufficient evidence from which a jury might reasonably draw the inference that the accused adopted the statement. Even when there is sufficient evidence, the trial judge should balance the probative value and the prejudicial effect before determining whether to allow the statement to go to the jury.

23 The Supreme Court of Canada authorities also establish that the mere silence of the accused, after hearing a statement made in his or her presence, will not permit an inference that the accused adopted the statement as his or her own. More is needed. It is only when an accused by "word or conduct, action or demeanour" (*Christie* at p. 554) has accepted the truth of the statement made by another person in his or her presence that the statement can have evidentiary value against the accused as to its truth. In the absence of any such acceptance by the accused of the truth of the statement made in his or her presence, the jury should be told that the statement has no evidentiary value as to its truth, and should be entirely disregarded.

24 Finally, if there is sufficient evidence from which a jury could infer that the accused adopted the statement made in his presence, notwithstanding the failure to hold a *voir dire*, there will be no error involved in admitting the evidence. In other words, if the trial judge would inevitably have admitted the evidence had a *voir dire* been held, no harm would result. However, where there is a lack of evidence, the failure to hold a *voir dire* will constitute a serious procedural error.

. . .

44 In all of the circumstances, I am of the view that the trial judge erred in law by allowing the jury to consider that the accused's silence could be an adopted or implied admission that "he did [cause the death]." Through no fault of the trial judge, the evidence surrounding a possible adopted or implied admission was before the jury without a *voir dire* having been held. Had one been held, to carefully examine the admissibility of the evidence on this issue, it is my opinion that rather than instructing on adopted or implied admissions, he would have instructed the jury to completely disregard the accusatory statement and the accused's subsequent silence as evidence of its truth against the accused.

. . .

57 I would set the conviction aside and order a new trial.

Under s. 7 of the *Charter* an accused has a pre-trial right to silence in detention and that right is violated if adverse inferences were to be drawn from its exercise in response to an accusation made by the police.[176]

Given that oral statements in the presence of the party may be adopted by silence, does the same hold true for written statements? Is it "reasonable to infer" that the recipient by his or her silence admits the truth of the statement?[177]

There are certain relationships where there has been mutual correspondence over a period of time which would make it "reasonable to infer" that failing to reply was an admission of the truthful nature of the communication, and each situation must be evaluated according to its own circumstances. For example, it has been noted:

> When a tradesman makes out his statement of account for goods against, and sends it to, a person, and that person takes no objection thereto, such

---

[176]   *R. v. Chambers*, [1990] 2 S.C.R. 1293 (S.C.C.) and *R. v. Turcotte*, [2005] 2 S.C.R. 519 (S.C.C.).

[177]   Compare *Bessela v. Stern* (1877), 46 L.J.C.P. 467 (C.A.) with *Wiedeman v. Walpole* (1890), 24 Q.B.D. 537.

statement and the failure to object are some evidence that the goods were furnished for the credit of that person . . .

. . .

In mercantile matters where an account is rendered it was said as far back as 1741 in *Willis v. Jernegan:* "There is no absolute necessity that it should be signed by the parties who have mutual dealings . . . it is not the signing which will make it a stated account but the person to whom it is sent, keeping it by him any length of time . . . which shall bind him."[178]

(iv) *Statements Authorized by Party*

In *R. v. Strand Electric Ltd.,*[179] the Court held that a statement made by an agent of a party to the litigation is admissible against that party as long as the agent was within the scope of his or her authority in making the statement.

To receive vicarious admissions is consistent with the philosophy which underlies the subject as a whole: fairness, responsibility and the adversarial nature of our system. Scope of authority is key. As recited in a U.S. decision:

> The test of admissibility should not rest on whether the principal gave the agent authority to make declarations. No sensible employer would authorize his employee to make damaging statements. The right to speak on a given topic must arise out of the nature of the employee's duties. The errand boy should not be able to bind the corporation with a statement about the issuance of treasury stock, but a truck driver should be able to bind his employer with an admission regarding his careless driving. Similarly, an usher should be able to commit his employer with an observation about a slippery spot on the lobby floor.[180]

Having agreed that scope of authority governs, it is perhaps sufficient to agree with Professor Wigmore that:

> Upon the application of the principle to specific instances, it would be useless here to enter, for only the rules of the substantive law of agency are involved.[181]

One particular form of agency does deserve mention. In a partnership each partner, when acting within the scope of the partnership, is an agent for the other partners and for the partnership. Applying the above principle, then, statements made by a partner while conducting the firm's business are receivable as admissions against the partnership if the existence of the firm is independently established.

(v) *Statements of Person with Common Purpose*

A particular form of partnership, of course, is conspiracy, civil or criminal. Responsibility underlies the receipt of statements of co-conspirators, as

---

[178] *Sarbit v. Hanson & Booth Fisheries (Canada) Co.,* [1951] 2 D.L.R. 108 (Man. C.A.) at 112.
[179] (1968), [1969] 2 C.C.C. 264 (Ont. C.A.).
[180] *Rudzinski v. Warner Theatres Inc.,* 114 N.W. 2d 466 (Wisc., 1962) at 471.
[181] 4 Wigmore, *Evidence* (Chad. Rev.), s. 1078 at 170. As an example of common sense, see *Tesco Supermarkets Ltd. v. Nattrass,* [1972] A.C. 153 (H.L.) restricting company's vicarious liability to acts of senior management.

the basal reason for admitting the evidence of the acts or words of one against the other is that the combination or preconcert to commit the crime is considered as implying an authority to each to act or speak in furtherance of the common purpose on behalf of the others.[182]

Professor Wigmore notes:

> A conspiracy makes each conspirator liable under the criminal law for the acts of every other conspirator done in pursuance of the conspiracy. Consequently . . . the admissions of a co-conspirator may be used to affect the proof against the others, on the same conditions as his acts when used to create their legal liability.[183]

The statements to be received must then have been statements made during the term of the conspiracy and in furtherance of it, and not simply a narrative describing it.[184] This preliminary condition of admissibility presents a problem, as it coincides with the very fact sought to be established. When this concurrence exists[185] it seems reasonable that the statements be received if there is *some* other evidence of a conspiracy and indeed the trial judge in his or her discretion may even have to relax that requirement.[186]

The leading case on the co-conspirators' exception to the hearsay rule is *R. v. Carter*,[187] a case involving a conspiracy to import marijuana into Canada from the United States. The test set out in *Carter* was summarized by the Supreme Court in *R. v. Barrow*[188] as follows:

1. The trier of fact must first be satisfied beyond reasonable doubt that the alleged conspiracy in fact existed.

2. If the alleged conspiracy is found to exist then the trier of fact must review all the evidence that is directly admissible against the accused and decide on a balance of probabilities whether or not he is a member of the conspiracy.

3. If the trier of fact concludes on a balance of probabilities that the accused is a member of the conspiracy then he or they must go on and decide whether the Crown has established such membership beyond reasonable doubt. In this last step, only the trier of fact can apply the hearsay exception and consider evidence of acts and declarations of co-conspirators done in furtherance of the object of the conspiracy as evidence against the accused on the issue of his guilt.

The Court also explained that in taking the first step the jury would not necessarily have to be satisfied beyond a reasonable doubt as to the identity of the persons involved in the conspiracy. It is entirely possible, and not uncommon, to be satisfied beyond a reasonable doubt on all the evidence that a conspiracy for the purposes alleged in the indictment existed while still

---

[182]   *Tripodi v. R.* (1961), 104 C.L.R. 1 (Aust. H.C.) at 7.
[183]   4 Wigmore, *Evidence* (Chad. Rev.), s. 1079 at 180.
[184]   See *R. v. Miller* (1975), 63 D.L.R. (3d) 193 (B.C.C.A.) at 217-221 and *R. v. Lynch* (1978), 40 C.C.C. (2d) 7 (Ont. C.A.) at 24 re: the distinction.
[185]   See generally on this point Cross, *Evidence*, 5th ed. at 69-71.
[186]   See 4 Wigmore, *Evidence* (Chad. Rev.), s. 1079 at 187.
[187]   [1982] 1 S.C.R. 938.
[188]   (2003), 12 C.R. (6th) 185, 174 C.C.C. (3d) 301 (B.C. C.A.).

being uncertain as to the identity of all the conspirators. The hearsay exception would have no application at this stage but could certainly be useful at the third stage, if reached, in satisfying the trier that the accused was a member of the alleged conspiracy. This exception is not confined, of course, to cases where the offence charged is conspiracy, but rather the underlying principle makes it applicable to any offence which has been committed pursuant to some common design.[189]

R. v. MAPARA
28 C.R. (6th) 1, [2005] 1 S.C.R. 358, 195 C.C.C. (3d) 225

The accused and C were charged with first degree murder. The victim was shot seven times in a car lot of a business owned by the accused. The Crown alleged a conspiracy to murder consisting of five people including the accused, C, B and W. The accused was alleged to have lured the victim to the parking lot. Following trial by judge and jury, the accused and C were convicted.

On appeal the main issue was whether the trial judge had wrongly admitted evidence of B that he had met with W at a gas station where W had told him that "the little guy", understood to be the accused, had a job for him. The issue was whether the Court should revisit the co-conspirators' exception to the hearsay rule set out in *R. v. Carter* in light of the principled approach to the hearsay rule set out in *R. v. Starr.*

McLACHLIN C.J.C. (BASTARACHE, BINNIE, ABELLA and CHARRON JJ. concurring): —

I first address the appellant's main argument - the co-conspirators' exception to the hearsay rule does not reflect the necessary indicia of necessity and reliability. In *R. v. Chang* (2003), 173 C.C.C. (3d) 397, the Ontario Court of Appeal, per O'Connor A.C.J.O. and Armstrong J.A., rejected this argument. The criterion of necessity poses little difficulty. As stated in Chang, "necessity will arise from the combined effect of the non-compellability of a co-accused declarant, the undesirability of trying alleged co-conspirators separately, and the evidentiary value of contemporaneous declarations made in furtherance of an alleged conspiracy" (para. 105).

The criterion of reliability requires closer scrutiny. The appellant raises the concern that co-conspirators' statements tend to be inherently unreliable because of the character of the declarants and the suspicious activities in which they are engaged.

A preliminary issue arises at this stage. The federal Crown argues that the co-conspirators' exception is not grounded in a concern for reliability, but rests rather on the reasoning that once it is established that the people concerned were involved in the same conspiracy, then the statements of one are admissions against all. Thus, "the rationale for the rule in Canada was grounded in principles governing admissions by party litigants": *Chang*, at

---

[189]   See cases cited in *R. v. Parrot* (1979), 51 C.C.C. (2d) 539 (Ont. C.A.).

para. 82. This exception is grounded in "a different basis than other exceptions to the hearsay rule. Indeed, it is open to dispute whether the evidence is hearsay at all": *R. v. Evans*, [1993] 3 S.C.R. 653, 85 C.C.C. (3d) 97, 108 D.L.R. (4th) 32, per Sopinka J., at p. 664. Sopinka J. went on to suggest that circumstantial guarantees of trustworthiness are irrelevant to the party admissions exception to the hearsay rule:

> The practical effect of this doctrinal distinction is that in lieu of seeking independent circumstantial guarantees of trustworthiness, it is sufficient that the evidence is tendered against a party. Its admissibility rests on the theory of the adversary system that what a party has previously stated can be admitted against the party in whose mouth it does not lie to complain of the unreliability of his or her own statements.

It follows on this reasoning that if the appellant was a co-conspirator with the witness, Binahmad, the appellant cannot be heard to complain that what he said to Binahmad was unreliable. Similarly, it is argued, he cannot complain about the unreliability of what a third co-conspirator, Wasfi, said to Binahmad. They were all plotting together, and what each says can be used against the other. Having entered into a criminal conspiracy, the accused cannot in his defence rely on its very criminality and the unreliability of his co-conspirators.

The unique doctrinal roots of the co-conspirators' exception to the hearsay rule cannot be denied. However, as noted in *Chang*, "the fact that the co-conspirators' rule is grounded in those principles does not alter the fact that a statement that becomes admissible under the *Carter* process is hearsay and concerns about unreliability are very real" (para. 85). In this sense, the directive of *Starr* that the traditional exceptions should be examined for conformity with necessity and reliability remains pertinent.

I return, therefore, to the question of whether the co-conspirators' exception to the hearsay rule possesses sufficient circumstantial indicators of reliability. The *Carter* process allows the jury to consider a hearsay statement by a co-conspirator in furtherance of the conspiracy only after it has found (1) that the conspiracy existed beyond a reasonable doubt and (2) that the accused was probably a member of the conspiracy, by virtue only of direct evidence against him.

The appellant argues that *Carter* cannot satisfy the reliability requirement because it amounts to using corroborating evidence to bolster the reliability of hearsay declarations against the accused, contrary to *Starr*, per Iacobucci J., at para. 217.

I do not agree. The question is whether the first two stages of the *Carter* process provide circumstantial indicators of reliability that do not amount to simply corroborating the statements in issue. In my view, they do. Proof that a conspiracy existed beyond a reasonable doubt and that the accused probably participated in it does not merely corroborate the statement in issue. Rather, it attests to a common enterprise that enhances the general reliability of what was said in the course of pursuing that enterprise. It is similar in its effect to the res gestae exception to the hearsay rule, where surrounding context furnishes circumstantial indicators of reliability. The concern is not with whether a particular statement is corroborated, but rather with circumstantial indicators of reliability.

The evidence under the first two stages of *Carter* is not inherently corroborative of the hearsay statement, in the sense of confirming the truth of its contents. Indeed the evidence establishing the conspiracy and the accused's probable participation may conflict with the hearsay evidence subsequently adduced. More often than not, the trier of fact will find corroboration, rather than conflict, in the direct evidence implicating the accused. However, this ultimate use of the evidence should not be confused with its initial role in establishing threshold reliability. Here it is relevant with respect to the context of the hearsay evidence, and not to its contents. The use of the *Carter* approach in the present inquiry thus stays within the boundaries of threshold reliability, as explained in *Starr*.

In addition to these preliminary conditions, the final *Carter* requirement, i.e., only those hearsay statements made in furtherance of the conspiracy can be considered, provides guarantees of reliability in the more immediate circumstances under which the statement is made. "In furtherance" statements "have the reliability-enhancing qualities of spontaneity and contemporaneity to the events to which they relate" (*Chang*, at paras. 122-23). They have res gestae type qualities, being "the very acts by which the conspiracy is formulated or implemented and are made in the course of the commission of the offence" (*Chang*, at para. 123). This "minimizes the motive and opportunity for contrivance" (*Chang*, at para. 124). The characters' doubtful reputation for veracity is not a factor at this stage of the analysis. Rather, it is to be taken into account by the jury when assessing the ultimate reliability of such characters' statements.

In sum, the conditions of the *Carter* rule provide sufficient circumstantial guarantees of trustworthiness necessary to permit the evidence to be received.

This conclusion makes practical sense. First, the rule does not operate unfairly to accused persons. Indicia of reliability exist. In this way, unreliable evidence that is likely to mislead the jury can be excluded. It remains open to the accused to cross-examine the deponent, call contrary evidence, and argue the unreliability of the co-conspirators' evidence before the jury. Moreover, it is not unfair to expect people who enter into criminal conspiracies to accept that if they are charged, the evidence of their co-conspirators about what they said in furtherance of the conspiracy may be used against them. Finally, the hearsay rule is supplemented by the discretion of the trial judge to exclude evidence where its prejudicial effect outweighs its probative value, discussed below.

Second, the rule allows the Crown to effectively prosecute criminal conspiracies. It would become difficult and in many cases impossible to marshal the evidence of criminal conspiracy without the ability to use co-conspirators' statements of what was said in furtherance of the conspiracy against each other. To deprive the Crown of the right to use double hearsay evidence of co-conspirators as to what they variously said in furtherance of the conspiracy would mean that serious criminal conspiracies would often go unpunished.

Finally, to modify the *Carter* rule would increase delay and difficulties in trial procedure. Any approach that requires the trial judge to scrutinize the necessity and reliability of particular pieces of hearsay evidence in deciding its admissibility would undermine the efficiency of the traditional categories of exceptions to the hearsay rule and increase the number of voir dire. As stated in *Chang*:

> We are concerned that conspiracy trials, many of which are already complicated, may become more so if every time the Crown seeks to introduce co-conspirators' declarations, the trial judge is required to hold a *voir dire* to determine if there is compliance with the principled approach. We do not anticipate that will be the case. A *voir dire* addressing the principled approach should be the exception. It will only be required when an accused is able to point to evidence raising serious and real concerns about reliability emerging from the circumstances in which a declaration was made, which concerns will not be adequately addressed by use of the *Carter* approach. As a general rule, the presumption that evidence that meets the *Carter* requirements also meets the principled approach should obviate the need for a voir dire. [para. 132]

The appellant suggests simply that we make the *Carter* rule inapplicable to double hearsay evidence. However, the underlying rationale for doing so is that all hearsay evidence, even if it falls under an established exception, must be rejected if that particular piece of evidence does not meet the concerns of necessity and reliability. This implies a case-by-case vetting more resembling the ultimate reliability inquiry that is for the jury, than the threshold reliability inquiry relevant to admissibility.

I conclude that the co-conspirators' exception to the hearsay rule meets the requirements of the principled approach to the hearsay rule and should be affirmed.

The appellant also asks us to change the *Carter* rule to require the first two elements to be determined by the trial judge, rather than the jury, on the ground that allowing the jury to decide these elements renders the exception operationally unfair. While courts may adjust common law rules incrementally to avoid apparent injustice, they do so only where there is clear indication of a need to change the rule in the interests of justice. That is not established in this case. Indeed, the appellant's suggestion was considered and rejected in *Carter* precisely because of the danger that the jury might confuse the direct and the hearsay evidence against the accused and rely on the latter to convict the accused. The Court concluded that the three-stage approach was better suited to bring home to the jury the need to find independent evidence of the accused's participation in conspiracy. I would not accede to this request.

I conclude that the *Carter* rule stands and that the evidence in question was not excluded by the hearsay rule.

This leaves for consideration the argument that even if the co-conspirators' exception to the hearsay rule satisfies the need for indicia of necessity and reliability, this is one of those rare cases where evidence falling within a valid exception to the hearsay rule should nevertheless not be admitted because the required indicia of necessity and reliability are lacking in the particular circumstances of the case. The same considerations that lead to the conclusion that the co-conspirators' exception to the hearsay rule satisfies the requirements for indicia of necessity and reliability, are applicable here. Necessity is established, in the absence of direct evidence from the co-accused declarants. Indicia of reliability are found in the requirements of the *Carter* rule for a conspiracy proved beyond a reasonable doubt, membership of the accused in it on a balance of probability, and the rule that only statements made in furtherance of the conspiracy are admitted. It therefore becomes difficult to conclude that evidence falling under the *Carter* rule would lack the indicia of reliability and necessity required for the admission of hearsay evidence on the principled approach. In all but the most exceptional cases the argument is spent at the point where an exception to the hearsay rule is found to comply with the principled approach to the hearsay rule.

Is this such a case? Certainly there are frailties in the evidence of the co-conspirator. Wasfi arguably had a motive to lie, namely a desire to falsely implicate the appellant, so Binahmad would think the appellant's money would be used in the killing. According to the appellant, Wasfi had his own reasons to have Chand killed, namely to obtain vengeance for the alleged rape of his girlfriend and to eliminate a debt. He implicated the appellant because Binahmad knew he himself could not finance the contract killing. Finally, the evidence showed that Wasfi was in jail at the time when Binahmad testified that the discussion took place.

These concerns, with the exception of the discrepancy as to the date of the conversation, do not go beyond concerns already addressed in the analysis of whether the co-conspirators' exception complies with the principled approach to the hearsay rule. They are characteristic of any conspiracy. Any weaknesses go to the ultimate weight of the evidence, which is for the jury to decide. Nor does Binahmad's error on when the conversation took place merit rejection of the evidence. This problem is one of ultimate reliability that the jury can decide. The trial judge reminded the jury in his charge about this difficulty, in the context of highlighting the defence position that both Wasfi and Binahmad were completely unreliable characters.

It follows that the appellant has not established that the evidence to which he objects constitutes one of those "rare cases" where evidence falling within a valid exception to the hearsay rule fails, in the peculiar circumstances of the case, to satisfy the indicia of necessity and reliability necessary for the admission of hearsay evidence.

. . .

I would dismiss the appeal and affirm the decision of the Court of Appeal.

LeBel J. (Fish J. concurring) delivered a concurring opinion.

The bottom line of *Mapara* is that the co-conspirators' exception and the *Carter* rules remain unaffected by *Starr*.

The minority's difference of opinion with the majority turns out to be limited to the majority's view that the trial judge should only intervene to assess necessity and reliability in highly exceptional cases. According to the minority, this set the bar too high. An inquiry should rather occur when the circumstances in which the evidence was obtained or given raise real and serious concerns as to reliability or necessity. In such cases, the trial judge should be required to scrutinize the evidence to ensure that it meets the criteria of the principled approach. However even the minority judges emphasize that a *voir dire* to assess the hearsay evidence will remain the exception.

When the majority in *Starr* called for existing hearsay exceptions to be reviewed according to the requirements of necessity and reliability, many writers, as the minority acknowledge, suggested that the complex and inherently circular co-conspirator's exception was a prime candidate for review and reform. The major problem is that it seems more consistent with *Starr* to have the issues of threshold liability and necessity determined by a trial judge at a *voir dire* before the jury hears the evidence.[190] David Layton, for example, points out that the co-conspirator exception has been applied in many contexts other than conspiracy and is best named the joint venture exception. He addresses concerns about rationale, reliability and necessity, the issue of corroboration inherent in the rule, the lack of a *voir dire* and the reality of the doctrine's dangerous reliance on conditional relevancy. Layton notes that some trial judges have decided on the compromise approach of allowing the statements to be conditionally admissible during the Crown's case, with the trial judge making a final decision as to admissibility at the close of the Crown's case[191] or holding that statements not in furtherance of the alleged common design are not admissible at stage one of the *Carter* test.[192]

These concerns and solutions were not directly confronted by the Supreme Court and are now water under the bridge. The trumping consideration for the majority is the need to ensure that conspiracy trials are "effective" and not unduly complicated by hearsay *voir dires*. That seems at odds with the concern of the majority in *Starr* to ensure that necessity and reliability criteria are taken seriously before the admission of any hearsay. Chief Justice McLachlin was a dissenter in *Starr* and appears to have found a new majority much more accepting of the *status quo* of existing categories of exception to the hearsay rule, including this one sometimes known as "the prosecutor's darling". In her comprehensive review of *Mapara* and critics of the co-conspirators' rule, Lisa Dufraimont concludes, however, that "the co-conspirators' exception, . . . for all its flaws offers a stable and workable response to a problem that admits of no perfect solution".[193]

---

[190] See especially the detailed analysis of David Layton, "*R. v. Pilarinos*: Evaluating the Co-conspirators or Joint Venture Exception to the Hearsay Rule" (2002), 2 C.R. (6th) 293.

[191] See especially *R. v. Duncan* (2002), 1 C.R. (6th) 265 (Man. Prov. Ct.).

[192] See *R. v. Pilarinos* (2002), 167 C.C.C. (3d) 97 (B.C. S.C.). See too Marvin Bloos & Michael Plaxton, "A Co-conspirators' Exception to the Standing Rule Keeping Out Hearsay in Gang Trials" (2003) 47 Crim. L.Q. 286.

In *R. v. Simpson*[194] a new trial was ordered because the trial judge erred in admitting co-conspirator hearsay where necessity was not met because the declarant was available to testify and reliability was not met because of the manner of recording the statements. Lisa Dufraimont[195] suggests this ruling is more in keeping with the minority view in *Mapara*.

(b) Exceptions where Declarant or Testimony Unavailable

We will consider four common law exceptions under this heading: declarations against interest, dying declarations, declarations in course of duty and former testimony. At common law the declarant in each case needed to be deceased.

(i) *Declarations Against Interest*

The common law recognized an exception for a declaration made by a person concerning a matter within his or her personal knowledge which declaration when made was to the declarant's own prejudice. The "standard" requirements of a hearsay exception are satisfied by this definition. There are clearly grounds of necessity, as the declarant is unavailable, and there are circumstances guaranteeing trustworthiness resident in the thought that a person is unlikely to intentionally misstate a situation against his or her own position. The hearsay danger of insincerity is guarded against though the dangers in perception, memory and communications are not eliminated. Commenting on the basis for the exception, Hamilton, L.J. noted:

> The ground is that it is very unlikely that a man would say falsely something as to which he knows the truth, if his statement tends to his own pecuniary disadvantage. As a reason this seems sordid and unconvincing. Men lie for so many reasons and some for no reason at all; and some tell the truth without thinking or even in spite of thinking about their pockets, but it is too late to question this piece of eighteenth century philosophy.[196]

It seemed to be early settled that the interest affected must be a pecuniary or proprietary interest[197] but there have always been arguments for expanding the nature of the interest to include exposure to criminal liability.

---

[193]   See "*R. v. Mapara*: Preserving the Co-conspirators' Exception to the Hearsay Rule" (2006) 51 Crim. L.Q. 169 at 197-198.

[194]   (2007) 53 C.R. (6th) 1 (Ont. C.A.). For other applications of *Mapara* see *R. v. Wang*, 2013 BCCA 311, 299 C.C.C. (3d) 419 (B.C. C.A.) and *R. v. Puddicombe*, 2013 ONCA 506, 299 C.C.C. (3d) 534, 5 C.R. (7th) 31 (Ont. C.A.).

[195]   C.R. annotation.

[196]   See *Lloyd v. Powell Duffryn Steam Coal Co.*, [1913] 2 K.B. 130 at 138, reversed on other grounds [1914] A.C. 733 (H.L.).

[197]   *Sussex Peerage Case* (1844), 8 E.R. 1034 (H.L.). See *Watt v. Miller*, [1950] 2 W.W.R. 1144 (B.C. S.C.), holding that a declaration admitting tortious liability is a declaration against pecuniary interest.

R. v. DEMETER

[1978] 1 S.C.R. 538, 38 C.R.N.S. 317, 34 C.C.C. (2d) 137

Accused was charged with murder. The Crown case was that accused had procured some unknown person to kill his wife. Accused sought to introduce evidence that a person unconnected with him had confessed to the murder of the wife.

MARTLAND J. (JUDSON, RITCHIE, PIGEON, DICKSON, BEETZ and DE GRANDPRÉ JJ. concurring):—

. . .

The appellant sought to introduce evidence through the witness Dinardo that one Eper, who was apparently unconnected with the appellant, had confessed to the murder of the appellant's wife. Eper was an escaped convict, who had been serving a sentence for life at the time of his escape, and who had died prior to the trial. Dinardo was his friend and testified that he would not have given evidence implicating Eper in this murder if Eper had still been alive. The trial judge excluded the alleged confession as being hearsay evidence.

. . .

It has generally been accepted as the law of England since *The Sussex Peerage* case that the exception to the rule excluding hearsay evidence in respect of declarations made against interest is confined to statements made against pecuniary or proprietary interest and does not permit evidence of a statement by a deceased person against his penal interest.

The Court of Appeal . . . . held that, even if a declaration against penal interest was not necessarily inadmissible, the confession of Eper in question here was not a declaration against penal interest. The reason for so holding is stated as follows:

. . .

> At the time of both the alleged declarations in question in this case Eper was an escaped convict under sentence of life imprisonment. In the result, he could not be sentenced to a consecutive sentence so that there could be no penal consequence for the crime admitted to which he was vulnerable. The completely uncertain effect on his prospects of parole in the event of another conviction is too remote and uncertain to be regarded as a penal consequence. In addition, at the time of the declaration to Dinardo he and Eper had been accomplices in crimes for many years and Dinardo, on his evidence, was acting as an accessory after the fact in assisting concealment of evidence of the crime declared. Dinardo testified he would not have given his evidence if Eper were alive.

The Court of Appeal enunciated a number of principles which would have to be applied in determining whether a declaration is against penal interest which, in its view, would have to be applied in addition to those applicable in determining whether a declaration is against pecuniary or proprietary interest. They are as follows:

1. The declaration would have to be made to such a person and in such circumstances that the declarant should have apprehended a vulnerability to penal consequences as a result.

2. The vulnerability to penal consequences would have to be not remote.

3. The declaration sought to be given in evidence must be considered in its totality. If upon the whole tenor the weight is in favour of the declarant, it is not against his interest.

4. In a doubtful case a Court might properly consider whether or not there are other circumstances connecting the declarant with the crime and whether or not there is any connection between the declarant and the accused.

5. The declarant would have to be unavailable by reason of death, insanity, grave illness which prevents the giving of testimony even from a bed, or absence in a jurisdiction to which none of the processes of the Court extends. A declarant would not be unavailable in the circumstances that existed in *R. v. Agawa*.

These furnish a valuable guide for consideration in the event that this Court should determine that a declaration against penal interest is not to be held inadmissible under the rule against the reception of hearsay evidence.

Finally, in *R. v. O'Brien*,[198] the Supreme Court of Canada agreed:

> The distinction is arbitrary and tenuous. There is little or no reason why declarations against penal interest and those against pecuniary or proprietary interest should not stand on the same footing. A person is as likely to speak the truth in a matter affecting his liberty as in a matter affecting his pocketbook.[199]

R. v. LUCIER
65 C.C.C. (2d) 150, [1982] 1 S.C.R. 28

The accused was charged with arson as a result of the destruction of his house by fire. The fire was actually set by a friend of the accused who was badly burned in the fire. He was interviewed in hospital by the police and admitted setting the fire and stated that he did so for the accused for $500. The accused's friend died shortly after this and the Crown sought to introduce his statements to the police as declarations against penal interest. The statements were admitted. An appeal by the accused from his conviction was dismissed by the Manitoba Court of Appeal. On further appeal by the accused to the Supreme Court of Canada, held, the appeal should be allowed and a new trial ordered.

RITCHIE J.: —

---

[198] (1977), 76 D.L.R. (3d) 513 (S.C.C.).
[199] *Ibid.* at 518; the Court, however, applying the requirements of the exception outlined by Hamilton, L.J. in *Lloyd v. Powell, supra* note 196, held that the instant declaration was not knowingly made against the declarant's interest.

Having regard to the judgment of this Court in the Demeter and O'Brien cases, it must now be recognized that in a proper case statements tendered on behalf of the accused and made by an unavailable person may be admitted at trial if they can be shown to have been made against the penal interest of the person making them; but neither the two cases to which I have just referred nor any of the wealth of authorities cited in the Courts below apply such a rule to statements which have an inculpatory effect on the accused. On the contrary, wherever such statements have been admitted it will be found that they have an exculpatory effect. The difference is a very real one because a statement implicating the accused in the crime with which he is charged emanating from the lips of one who is no longer available to give evidence robs the accused of the invaluable weapon of cross-examination which has always been one of the mainstays of fairness in our Courts. In the present case the statements made by Dumont which were tendered by the prosecutor are obviously inculpatory of the appellant and in my opinion this is not a "proper case" for admitting them so that the learned trial Judge did err in permitting their introduction into evidence and I would accordingly allow this appeal on the first ground specified in the notice of appeal, quash the conviction and direct a new trial in accordance with the alternative relief sought by the appellant.

(ii) *Dying Declarations*

At common law a deceased's declaration regarding the cause of his death was receivable in a prosecution for his or her death provided there was evidence that when he or she made the declaration he or she entertained a hopeless expectation of death.[200] The ground for this exception was detailed very early in the development of the rules of evidence:

> . . . the general principle on which this species of evidence is admitted is, that they are declarations made in extremity, when the party is at the point of death, and when every hope of this world is gone; when every motive to falsehood is silenced, and the mind is induced by the most powerful considerations to speak the truth; a situation so solemn, and so awful, is considered by the law as creating an obligation equal to that which is imposed by a positive oath administered in a Court of Justice.[201]

The assurance of trustworthiness from the circumstances will only flow if the declarant was aware of his or her state and the statement would be competent evidence by him or her in the stand. Chief Justice Duff in the Supreme Court of Canada described the duty of the trial judge:

> First of all, he must determine the question whether or not the declarant at the time of the declaration entertained a settled, hopeless expectation that he was about to die almost immediately. Then, he must consider whether or not the statement would be evidence if the person making it were a witness. . . . a declaration which is a mere accusation against the accused, or a mere

---

[200]   Compare Cross, *Evidence*, 5th ed. at 564.

[201]   *R. v. Woodcock* (1789), 168 E.R. 352 at 353, per Eyre, C.B.

expression of opinion, not founded on personal knowledge, as distinguished from a statement of fact, cannot be received.[202]

Courts have traditionally held that the dying declarations exceptions to the hearsay rule apply only in homicide cases where the victim is the declarant. Given the assurances or trustworthiness resident in the requirements of the exception, it is difficult to see why the law does not go further and allow reception with respect to *any* charge arising out of the transaction. Indeed it is worth noting that the common law restriction to the use of dying declarations only in homicide cases was the result, as unfortunately is the case with many of our rules of evidence, of an historical accident. Until the nineteenth century, the exception operated both in civil and criminal cases. The source of the restriction appears to be a statement by East in his chapter on Homicide; in that chapter he noted that dying declarations were receivable in homicide prosecutions. By the next generation this statement had been interpreted to mean that dying declarations were *only* receivable in homicide prosecutions.[203] Limiting receipt of the dying declaration to those cases where it concerns the *declarant's* death or injuries was described by Wigmore as an "irrational and pitiful absurdity of this feat of legal cerebration".[204]

R. v. AZIGA
(2006), 42 C.R. (6th) 42

Ontario Superior Court of Justice

1 T.R. LOFCHIK J.:— This is an Application by the Crown concerning the admission of evidence at the trial of the charges against the accused respondent. The accused was committed to trial on two counts of first-degree murder and 13 counts of aggravated sexual assault. He is alleged to have had sex with 13 complainants without first disclosing that he was HIV Positive, a fact of which he was aware at the relevant time.

2 Sylvia Barnes and Heather Cook are alleged to have died as a result of being infected with HIV by the respondent. This Application by the Crown is to allow the Crown to tender the video statements and transcripts of the statements (which may have to be edited) made by Sylvia Barnes and Heather Cook, as their dying declarations during the Crown's case in-chief, or, in the alternative, for an Order allowing the Crown to tender the said materials as Khan, [1990] 2 S.C.R. 531, statements.

3 Sylvia Barnes gave a sworn videotaped dying declaration and KGB, [1993] 1 S.C.R. 740, statement at her cousin's home in Barrie on November 19th, 2003. She was hospitalized at the Princess Margaret Hospital for palliative care on

---

[202] *Chapdelaine v. R.*, [1935] 2 D.L.R. 132 (S.C.C.) at 136.
[203] See 5 Wigmore, *Evidence* (Chad. Rev.), s. 1431.
[204] 5 Wigmore, *Evidence* (Chad. Rev.), s. 1433.

November 21st, 2003, where she remained until her death, 18 days later on December 7th, 2003. She was 51 years of age.

4 Heather Cook met with Detective Troy Ashbaugh, of the Hamilton Police Service, on August 11th, 2003, at the Offices of the Toronto Public Health Unit and gave a KGB statement, recorded on audiotape, describing her relationship with the accused.

5 On May 18th, 2004, Ms. Cook provided a videotaped, sworn, dying declaration and KGB statement to police. She died approximately 18 hours later, on May 19th, 2004, at the Princess Margaret Hospital in Toronto. She was 49 years of age.

. . .

DYING DECLARATIONS

12 The nature and basis for the dying declaration exception to the rule against the reception of hearsay is succinctly reviewed by Paciocco and Stuesser in The Law of Evidence (2d):

> In a criminal case, a dying declaration of a deceased person is admissible . . . when
>
> - The deceased had a settled, hopeless expectation of almost immediate death;
>
> - The statement was about the circumstances of the death;
>
> - The statement would have been admissible if the deceased had been able to testify; and
>
> - The offence involved is the homicide of the deceased.

The Law of Evidence (2d) at 109

13 According to Paciocco and Stuesser the exception is a principled one. There is necessity. The witness is dead. Reliability derives from the belief that a person who knows that he or she is about to die, will be motivated to speak truthfully.

. . .

Sylvia Barnes

26 The basis of the argument that Sylvia Barnes' statement is not a dying declaration is based on a passage that appears at page 25 of the transcript of her interview as follows:

> The lymphoma has progressed to a point where . . . I will no longer have a life pretty soon because it is terminal. And I'm not quite sure how long that's going to be. Hopefully a long time . . .

27 Counsel for the accused focuses on the words "and I'm not quite sure how long that is going to be. Hopefully a long time . . ." as a basis for the argument that Barnes has failed to acknowledge that death is imminent and that therefore the statement does not qualify as a dying declaration. This argument ignores the immediately preceding sentence "The lymphoma has progressed to a point where I will no longer have a life pretty soon because it is terminal" and the part of the caution put to her by Detective Ashbaugh where he says, "The disease has progressed to a point, where you are terminal with no hope of recovery and that your succumbing to the disease is imminent." and she acknowledges that to be accurate.

28 Looking at the circumstances as a whole, I am satisfied that Sylvia Barnes was . . . aware at the time that her impending death in the immediate future was a certainty. At best, the sentence relied upon by counsel for Aziga was an expression of hope. The following passage from Sopinka, Lederman and Bryant, The Law of Evidence in Canada (1992) at pp. 268 and 269 appears applicable:

> The feeling to be possessed is not merely fear that the declarant may succumb to death, but that in fact the declarant has a solemn conviction that he or she will soon die and there is no hope whatsoever of recovery. The fact that death does not take place until some time thereafter will not affect the admissibility of the statement so long as it occurs within a certain proximity of the making of the statement.

29 In light of all the circumstances I am satisfied that Ms. Barnes, when she made the statement, had a settled, hopeless expectation of death and that the statement meets the requirements of a dying declaration.

. . .

Heather Cook

39 The dying declaration of Heather Cook was taken on May 18th, 2004, at a time when she could not speak. It was a combination of asking her questions to which she responded by nodding or shaking her head for "yes" or "no" and the playing to her of an audiotape of an interview she gave on August 11th, 2003, and having her confirm by nodding or shaking her head that the contents of the interview were true and accurate.

40 So far as the playing of the tape of the August 11th, 2003, interview is concerned, counsel for the accused argues that it was made a considerable time before the May 18th, 2004, interview and that the declarant could not remember it all so that it cannot be said to be a dying declaration. He further argues that being unable to speak, Ms. Cook could not express any concerns she might have or add anything to what was on the tape.

41 In assessing that argument it must be borne in mind that Ms. Cook appears to be "in extremis" at the time of the interview and, after being cautioned and

sworn to tell the truth, she adopts as true, the contents of the earlier interview. In my view, under the circumstances, the adopting by her of the August 11th, 2003, interview qualifies it as a dying declaration. So far as the portions played and acknowledged by her are concerned, if she disagreed with anything, she could have shaken her head "no" to so indicate. In fact, on one occasion she does this at page 10 of the transcript when asked if she remembers Ginette, a nurse from the Toronto Public Health Unit, being present at the August interview, she shakes her head "no".

. . .

46 I find that the August 11th, 2003, statement, as adopted by Heather Cook in her interview of May 18th, 2004, qualifies as a dying declaration. I also find that the test of reliability is met and the statements are admissible, both as dying declarations and under the principled approach.

47 In the result, the Crown's Application is allowed and the evidence of both Sylvia Barnes and Heather Cook is admissible at trial subject to the editing out of some portions which may be inadmissible on other grounds.

(iii) *Declarations in Course of Duty*

General

Common law declarations of a deceased person were receivable as exceptions to the hearsay rule if they described the deceased's own activities, were made contemporaneously therewith and the deceased was then under a duty to record the same.[205] This common law exception is no longer as important as it once was, as the federal government and most of the provincial governments have enacted statutory provisions regarding business records; the exception operates with respect to oral and written statements while the statutory provisions deal only with the latter. The exception has, been considerably broadened by the Supreme Court of Canada in *Ares v. Venner.*[206] The unanimous opinion of the Court, delivered by Hall, J., concluded:

> Hospital records, including nurses' notes, made contemporaneously by someone having a personal knowledge of the matters then being recorded and under a duty to make the entry or record should be received in evidence as *prima facie* proof of the facts stated therein.[207]

The exception now does not demand that the declarant be deceased; indeed in this case the declarants, the nurses, were present in the courtroom but

---

[205] See Ewart, "Admissibility at Common Law of Records" (1981) Can. Bar Rev. 52.
[206] [1970] S.C.R. 608. Accepted as authoritatively stating the common law position in Ontario in *R. v. Laverty (No. 2)* (1979), 47 C.C.C. (2d) 60 (Ont. C.A.) at 64, per Zuber, J.A.: ". . . a declaration in the course of a business duty either in its classic form or as enlarged by *Ares v. Venner . . .*" and in *Setak Computer Services Corp. v. Burroughs Business Machines Ltd.* (1977), 15 O.R. (2d) 750 (H.C.) at 755, per Griffiths, J.: "that case settles the common law in Ontario." But *contra* see *Exhibitors Inc. v. Allen* (1989), 70 O.R. (2d) 103 (Ont. H.C.) per Arbour, J.
[207] *Ares v. Venner, supra* note 206 at 626.

neither side wished to call them as their own witnesses. The common law exception required the declarant to be under a duty to do the act and under a duty to record it; in this case the nurses were under a duty to observe and to record their observations, and therefore their observations, clearly opinions, were receivable. The Alberta Court of Appeal in *Ares v. Venner* had seen these opinions as providing "fruitful areas for cross-examination",[208] but despite that truth the Court ordered them received. It is true that Hall, J. continued:

> This should, in no way, preclude a party wishing to challenge the accuracy of the records or entries from doing so. Had the respondent here wanted to challenge the accuracy of the nurses' notes, the nurses were present in court and available to be called as witnesses if the respondent had so wished.[209]

It is difficult to imagine, however, that the bold direction towards reform of the hearsay rule described by the Court was only to be applicable when the declarants were present in the Court. In the Court's decision in *R. v. Khan*, above, that position was specifically disavowed:

> I add that I do not understand *Ares v. Venner* to hold that the hearsay evidence there at issue was admissible where necessity and reliability are established only where cross-examination is available. First, the Court adopted the views of the dissenting judges in *Myers v. D.P.P.* which do not make admissibility dependent on the right to cross-examine. Second, the cross-examination referred to in *Ares v. Venner* was of limited value. The nurses were present in court at the trial, but in the absence of some way of connecting particular nurses with particular entries, meaningful cross-examination would have been difficult indeed.[210]

R. v. LARSEN
(2001), 42 C.R. (5th) 49 (S.C.)

The accused was charged with first degree murder. The Crown applied for a ruling that an autopsy report and supplemental report were admissible in evidence. The initial report was prepared in 1978 and the pathologist who made it had died. He had deferred his decision on cause of death for 14 months, at which later time, in a supplemental report, he declared that the victim had died of asphyxiation. His conclusions accorded with at least two observations made by the pathologist at the scene. The accused contended that the evidence was inadmissible hearsay. The Crown contended that the reports were admissible as declarations made in the course of duty and in the alternative under the principled approach to the hearsay rule.

ROMILLY J.: —

. . .

Before addressing admissibility under the principled approach, I shall first address the issue of whether the autopsy and supplemental reports were declarations made in the course of duty. As recently noted by the Nova Scotia

---

[208]   (1969), 70 W.W.R. 96 (Alta. C.A.) at 105.
[209]   *Supra* note 206 at 626.
[210]   (1990), 79 C.R. (3d) 1 (S.C.C.) at 14.

Court of Appeal in *R. v. Wilcox*, [2001] N.S.J. No. 85, 2001 NSCA 45, this is a prudent approach because, among other reasons, the analysis of admissibility under a traditional exception will assist in the application of the principled approach.

Are the autopsy report and supplemental report admissible as declarations made in the course of duty?

In *R. v. Wilcox, supra*, at para. 49, the Nova Scotia Court of Appeal accepted the following passage from *R. v. Monkhouse*, [1988] 1 W.W.R. 725 (Alta. C.A.) as an accurate statement of the requirements for admissibility under the common law exception of declarations made in the course of duty:

> In his useful book, *Documentary Evidence in Canada* (Carswell Co., 1984), Mr. J.D. Ewart summarizes the common law rule after the decision in *Ares v. Venner* as follows at p. 54:
>
> > . . . the modern rule can be said to make admissible a record containing (i) an original entry (ii) made contemporaneously (iii) in the routine (iv) of business (v) by a recorder with personal knowledge of the thing recorded as a result of having done or observed or formulated it (vi) who had a duty to make the record and (vii) who had no motive to misrepresent.

The rationale for admissibility of such documents at common law was that the routine nature of their creation, the fact they are relied upon for business purposes and the absence of any motive to misrepresent the information recorded all provide circumstantial guarantees of trustworthiness: *R. v. Wilcox, supra*, at para. 67. A duty to create or maintain the document was also considered to provide a circumstantial guarantee of trustworthiness "based upon the assumption that a declarant would fear censure and dismissal should an employer discover an inaccuracy in the statement": Sopinka, Lederman and Bryant, *The Law of Evidence in Canada*, 2d (Toronto: Butterworths, 1999) at pp. 211-12.

. . .

On the basis of the above, I conclude the autopsy report dated October 20, 1978, is admissible under the common law exception of declarations made in the course of duty. Dr. Sturrock prepared the autopsy report shortly after conducting the autopsy and he had personal knowledge of the information in the report, having conducted the autopsy himself. Further, Dr. Sturrock was under a duty to make the record having been directed to conduct a post-mortem examination of the deceased by the coroner in accordance with the Coroners Act, S.B.C. 1975, c. 15. The making of an autopsy report is a routine procedure conducted by the medical practitioner who performs an autopsy. Further, Dr. Sturrock had no motive to misrepresent.

However, I conclude that the supplemental report dated December 19, 1979, is inadmissible under the common law exception of declarations made in the course of duty. I make this finding because the supplemental report, dated 14 months following the performance of the autopsy, fails the requirement of contemporaneousness.

In *R. v. Starr*, *supra*, at para. 155, the Supreme Court of Canada held that where a traditional exception to the hearsay rule conflicts with the principled approach, the principled analysis of necessity and reliability should prevail.

. . .

In my view, this is not one of those rare cases where a traditional exception to the hearsay rule, specifically declarations made in the course of duty, fails the test of reliability and necessity under the new principled approach to the hearsay rule. . . . I therefore turn to consider whether the autopsy report and the supplement report are admissible under the principled exception to the hearsay rule.

. . .

On the basis of the evidence adduced on the voir dire, I am satisfied the Crown has met the onus of establishing the threshold reliability of both the autopsy report and the supplemental report.

I am satisfied the circumstances surrounding the making of both the autopsy report and the supplemental report provide sufficient circumstantial guarantees of trustworthiness. I conclude that Dr. Sturrock had no motive to misrepresent the information recorded in either report. I also find that the duty of Dr. Sturrock to prepare both reports provides a circumstantial guarantee of trustworthiness. Finally, the testimony of Dr. Harris, in that it corroborated aspects of Dr. Sturrock's reports, also suggests the reports are reliable.

The autopsy report of Dr. Sturrock is admissible both under the common law exception of declarations made in the course of duty and under the principled approach to hearsay. The supplemental report, while not meeting the requirements for admission as a declaration in the course of duty, does meet the requirements of necessity and reliability and thus is admissible under the principled approach to hearsay.

Business Records

The common law exception for declarations in the course of duty had been fashioned in the nineteenth century and, if narrowly interpreted, was clearly inappropriate to the business methods which had evolved by the middle of the 20th. The decisions in *Myers v. D.P.P.*[211] caused the legislature to act, both in England[212] and in Canada. In Ontario, for example, the McRuer-Common Committee reported that

> the absurdity of the common law is forcibly exposed in *Myers v. D.P.P.* . . . the law of evidence with respect to the proof of the contents of records kept in the ordinary course of business is quite unrelated to modern scientific developments in the making and the keeping of records.[213]

---

[211] [1965] A.C. 1001 (H.L.). On the topic of business records see generally Ewart, "Documentary Evidence: The Admissibility of Documents under Sec. 30 of the Canada Evidence Act" [1979-80] Crim. L.Q. 189.

[212] See *Criminal Evidence Act*, 1965, c. 20 and *Civil Evidence Act, 1968*, c. 64.

[213] *Report of the Committee on Medical Evidence in Civil Cases* (1965) at 64, 77.

At the federal level, the then-Minister of Justice regretted the fact that Canadian courts were following the *Myers* decision and noted:

> It is therefore apparent that the law in this country has fallen far behind the major changes which the computer age has brought to business methods. Frequently records are kept either entirely or almost entirely by mechanical means, and in such cases it may be difficult and perhaps impossible to produce a witness to testify to the facts of a particular case, as distinct from testifying about the mechanical system under which transactions or events are recorded. Even in the case of records kept manually it is frequently impossible to trace the person, assuming he is still alive, who made the entries originally in the business records. A useful source of evidence is thereby excluded from the courts. It is little wonder that intelligent laymen conclude that, far from being blind, the goddess of justice is looking the wrong way.[214]

Various provinces and the federal government brought in statutory provisions during the late 1960s to ease the introduction of business records as evidence. These statutory provisions were to some extent rendered redundant shortly after their enactment when the Supreme Court of Canada decided to follow the dissenting opinion in *Myers* and reform judicially the hearsay rule to expand the admissibility of declarations in the course of duty at common law.[215]

Despite the overlap with the common law, the legislation remains in place and provides one route to admissibility for business records. For example, the *Ontario Evidence Act* provides:

> 35. (1) In this section,
>
>> "business" includes every kind of business, profession, occupation, calling, operation or activity, whether carried on for profit or otherwise;
>
>> "record" includes any information that is recorded or stored by means of any device.
>
> (2) Any writing or record made of any act, transaction, occurrence or event is admissible as evidence of such act, transaction, occurrence or event if made in the usual and ordinary course of any business and if it was in the usual and ordinary course of such business to make such writing or record at the time of such act, transaction, occurrence or event or within a reasonable time thereafter.
>
> (3) Subsection (2) does not apply unless the party tendering the writing or record has given at least seven days notice of the party's intention to all other parties in the action, and any party to the action is entitled to obtain from the person who has possession thereof production for inspection of the writing or record within five days after giving notice to produce the same.
>
> (4) The circumstances of the making of such a writing or record, including lack of personal knowledge by the maker, may be shown to affect its weight, but such circumstances do not affect its admissibility.

---

[214] Hansard, Jan. 20, 1969 at 4496.

[215] *Ares v. Venner, supra* note 206, discussed above. Alberta, the birthplace of the *Ares* decision, did not enact business records legislation, seemingly content with the judicial creation.

(5) Nothing in this section affects the admissibility of any evidence that would be admissible apart from this section or makes admissible any writing or record that is privileged.

The *Canada Evidence Act* provides:

30. (1) Where oral evidence in respect of a matter would be admissible in a legal proceeding, a record made in the usual and ordinary course of business that contains information in respect of that matter is admissible in evidence under this section in the legal proceeding on production of the record.

. . .

(12) In this section,

"business" means any business, profession, trade, calling, manufacture or undertaking of any kind carried on in Canada or elsewhere whether for profit or otherwise, including any activity or operation carried on or performed in Canada or elsewhere by any government, by any department, branch, board, commission or agency of any government, by any court or other tribunal or by any other body or authority performing a function of government;

. . .

"record" includes the whole or any part of any book, document, paper, card, tape or other thing on or in which information is written, recorded, stored or reproduced. . .

There is apparent conflict between the statutory provisions. The provincial legislation specifically makes lack of personal knowledge by the maker a factor which does not affect admissibility but only weight. The federal legislation has, as a precondition, the requirement that oral evidence of the matter recorded be admissible.

Does this mean that the maker of the record must have had personal knowledge of the event recorded? Or does it simply mean that the record must have relevance to the matters in issue and that if *any* witness would be permitted to describe the matter recorded, the record, though double hearsay, is receivable?[216]

R. v. MARTIN
(1997), 8 C.R. (5th) 246 (Sask. C.A.)

The accused was charged with six counts of defrauding the Wheat Board. The Crown's theory was that the accused dishonestly overstated the amount of wheat and barley he had on hand, causing the Canadian Wheat Board to advance him more money than it would otherwise have done and depriving it of the difference. The Crown sought to introduce evidence of average crop yields for the municipalities where the accused farmed. The Crown called the Director of the Statistics Branch at the Saskatchewan

---

[216] Sometimes courts resort to the common law exception to avoid these technicalities: see *R. v. Crate* (2012), 285 C.C.C. (3d) 431 (Alta. C.A.); *R. v. Keats*, 2016 NSCA 94, 345 C.C.C. (3d) 139, 35 C.R. (7th) 392 (N.S. C.A.); and *R. v. Clarke*, 2016 ONSC 575, 28 C.R. (7th) 211 (Ont. S.C.J.) (payroll records)

Department of Agriculture and Food. Through him, the Crown sought to present to the jury tables of estimated crop yield averages produced by the Statistics Branch from data gathered by Statistics Canada from Saskatchewan farmers. The tables pertained to the rural municipalities where the accused farmed. The trial judge refused to admit the tables because they relied on hearsay information collected by Statistics Canada and no witness could testify as to its accuracy.

JACKSON J.A. (CAMERON and SHERSTOBITOFF JJ.A. concurring):—

. . .

Subsection 30(1) of the Canada Evidence Act increased the likelihood of a Court admitting a business record without testimony as to the source of the information contained in the record. It puts forward only two qualifications for admission: (i) the evidence tendered must be "a record made in the usual and ordinary course of business;" and (ii) it must contain the same information "where oral evidence in respect of a matter would be admissible in a legal proceeding." But vestiges of the old law, which resisted the admissibility of documents except under strict circumstances, remained.

The principal issue concerned "double hearsay", i.e., information contained in a record which was given to the record keeper who has no knowledge of its accuracy.

Many of the provincial equivalents of s. 30(1) specifically require a court to overlook double hearsay. For example, s. 31(3) of The Saskatchewan Evidence Act, R.S.S. 1978, c. S-16 provides "[t]he circumstances of the making of a writing or record mentioned in subsection (2), including lack of personal knowledge by the maker, may be shown to affect its weight, but such circumstances do not affect its admissibility." The difference between the provincial and federal legislation appears to lessen the effectiveness of the latter.

Added to this, s. 30(6) of the Canada Evidence Act provides that a court may consider the circumstances in which the information was written to determine whether an provision of s. 30 applies. This lends further weight to the proposition that Parliament intended courts to exclude documents containing double hearsay.

Mr. Ewart (*Documentary Evidence in Canada*, Carswell, 1984) indicated early academic opinion leaned toward the view that s. 30 did preclude the admissibility of records containing double hearsay but the courts did not share that view. In fact, early cases held double hearsay documents to be admissible, as long as they met the twin requirements of s. 30(1), with little comment.

In *R. v. Anthes Business Forms Ltd.* (1975), 19 C.C.C. (2d) 394, aff'd 26 C.C.C. (2d) 349, aff'd 32 C.C.C. (2d) 207 (S.C.C.) the Ontario Court of Appeal considered the admissibility of corporate files which contained third party records showing details of certain transactions. As in the case at bar, the corporate files were developed from information received from someone who in turn had received it from yet another. Houlden J.A., speaking for the Court, said the files were admissible because they were records "made in the usual and ordinary course of business by the persons who prepared them, and oral evidence in respect of the matters contained in them would have been admissible" (see p. 369). Although the Supreme Court of Canada's brief reasons may represent concurrence with the result rather than with the reasons, Houlden J.A.'s statement is significant in that it focused only on the twin requirements of s. 30(1).

Similarly, in *R. v. Penno* (1977), 35 C.C.C. (2d) 266 the British Columbia Court of Appeal also admitted a written record of inventory numbers prepared by one person based on the information of another. The Court relied on *Ares v. Venner* and s. 30(1) of the Canada Evidence Act.

In *R. v. Grimba* (1978), 38 C.C.C. (2d) 469 (Ont. Co. Ct.), the Crown tendered expert fingerprint evidence to demonstrate that the fingerprints taken from the accused were the same as those on a fingerprint record obtained from the United States Federal Bureau of Investigation. The expert had not made the record and had no personal knowledge of its accuracy, but had been with the FBI for eleven years and described the FBI as serving as a repository for fingerprint records. The Court interpreted s. 30(1) to allow the admission of the records even though they contained double hearsay. Callaghan Co. Ct. J. stated (at p. 471):

> It would appear that the rationale behind [s. 30(1)] for admitting a form of hearsay evidence is the inherent circumstantial guarantee of accuracy which one would find in a business context from records which are relied upon in the day to day affairs of individual businesses, and which are subject to frequent testing and cross-checking. Records thus systematically stored, produced and regularly relied upon should, it would appear under s. 30, not be barred from this Court's consideration.

This passage characterizes s. 30(1) as providing a clear exception to the hearsay rules.

In *R. v. Biasi* (1982), 62 C.C.C. (2d) 304 (B.C.S.C.) Justice Paris had to decide whether a telephone company's "circuit card security documents" were admissible. Some of the information contained in the cards was provided by the RCMP to the telephone company who then prepared them. With respect to their admissibility Paris J. ruled:

> Nor does the fact that when the record was made up the information was received from another party make the record inadmissible as being hearsay. The provisions of the Canada Evidence Act provide for the admissibility of such records as proof of the facts contained in them even if the record maker received his information from another party, as long as the facts recorded on the document would themselves be admissible in evidence.

Since the Ewart text was published, the Alberta Court of Appeal in *R. v. Boles* (1985), 57 A.R. 232 considered the admissibility of hotel records which confirmed the presence of some of the principal conspirators in India. Admissibility was questioned on the basis that the records contained double hearsay, i.e., presumably the information was given to the hotel management by its employees. Relying on each of the above authorities, the Court concluded that s. 30(1) renders admissible a document made in the ordinary course of business notwithstanding that it contains double hearsay. (See also *R. v. Ross* (1992), 92 Nfld. & P.E.I.R. 51 (Nfld. S.C.) where the Court confirmed the admissibility under s. 30 of written records prepared by a manager with information given to him by other employees.)

Turning to apply these authorities to the case at bar, the trial judge ought to have admitted the tables pursuant to s. 30 of the Canada Evidence Act. As Houlden J.A. said in Anthes, s. 30 makes admissible records made in the usual and ordinary course of business where oral evidence in respect of a matter would be admissible in a legal proceeding. The tables in this case were made in the usual and ordinary course of business of Sask. Agriculture and Food. Section 6 of The Department of Agriculture Act mandates the gathering of the statistics which are then used in the department's regular business of administering agricultural programs. Oral evidence would be admissible, but at some considerable cost and inconvenience. To call every farmer who had farmed for the applicable 15 year period in the two rural municipalities would be impossible. In this case, but for the ability to admit these tables, the information they contained would be lost to the court as occurred in this case. The Crown's witness was prepared to testify that the department used these statistics in its work and relied upon them. As Callaghan Co. Ct. J. said in Grimba, "records thus systematically stored, produced and regularly relied upon should not be barred from the courts' consideration."

The opening words of s. 30(6) appear to permit a consideration of weight to be made when the court considers admissibility. But if this means a court must reject a record because it contains double hearsay, it places documents prepared in the ordinary course of business in a fundamentally different category than documents admitted pursuant to the common law business duty exception. As indicated in Ares, weight is an issue to be addressed after the document is accepted as evidence. The circumstances in which the information was gathered or the record produced, or the lack of such evidence, may affect the weight to be given to it by the trier of fact, but it does not affect its admissibility.

As a general rule, documents made in the ordinary course of business are admitted to avoid the cost and inconvenience of calling the record keeper and the maker. As a matter of necessity the document is admitted. Proof that a document is made in the ordinary course of business prima facie fulfils the qualification that in order for hearsay to be admitted it must be trustworthy.

Section 30 would have accomplished little if the author of the data contained in a business record had to be called to testify. The complexity of modern business demands that most records will be composed of information gleaned by the maker from others.

R. v. L. (C.)
(1999), 138 C.C.C. (3d) 356 (C.A.)

The accused was charged with three historical sexual offences in relation to his wife's sister who alleged that she became pregnant as a result of sexual intercourse with the accused when she was 13 years of age, and that she had an abortion. The Crown entered medical records as an exhibit at trial. These had not previously been disclosed to the defence and defence counsel did not read the contents of the medical records which included a letter from a doctor which stated that the complainant's pregnancy resulted from a relationship with a 15-year-old male. The trial judge instructed the jury that this statement was hearsay and should be ignored. The complainant testified at trial that when she told the hospital staff that the accused was responsible for the pregnancy, she was told to leave the room while her mother remained.

The accused argued on his appeal that he had been denied effective representation. In support of this argument, the accused introduced evidence from the doctor who signed the letter, who explained that attendance at the teen clinic for an abortion would have involved multiple interviews by nurses and a doctor and that the complainant would have been separated from any accompanying adult in order to get at the truth of the matter. The doctor did not recall whether she had direct dealings with the complainant or whether she relied on notes made in the records by the professional interviewers for the purposes of her letter. The doctor also advised that if the complainant had in any interview mentioned the accused as being the father, there would have been a duty upon the interviewer to report it to the appropriate authorities including the police.

BY THE COURT:—

We are of the view that the hospital records, including Dr. Cowell's letter, were admissible as business records made in the ordinary course of the hospital's business by those charged with the responsibility for making such records: see s. 30 Canada Evidence Act, R.S.C. 1985, c. C-5. See also *R. v. Monkhouse* (1987), 61 C.R. (3d) 343 (Alta. C.A.) where the Court stated at pp. 350-51:

> An even earlier modification of the common law rules may be seen in a decision in the Supreme Court of Canada in *Can. Atl. Ry. Co. v. Moxley* (1888), 15 S.C.R. 145 [Ont.]. That case held that the person originally recording the event need not himself have direct personal knowledge of the event recorded. It was held to be sufficient if the person who has a duty to do and record the act "causes" a record to be made by an agent. This case, too, was cited by Mr. Justice Hall in *Ares v. Venner*.
>
> . . .
>
> These hearsay records are not to be accepted in evidence merely to avoid the inconvenience of identifying a witness or because many witnesses would be involved, or even because otherwise no evidence would be available. Rather, they can be admitted only if they have come into existence under circumstances which make them inherently trustworthy. Where an established system in a business or other organization produces records which are regarded as reliable and customarily accepted by those affected by them, they should be admitted as prima facie evidence.

Given the evidence of Dr. Cowell in cross-examination on her affidavit, it appears reasonable to conclude that it would be likely that the complainant would have been interviewed separately from her mother as to the identify of the father, especially when the interviewers were under a duty to report a case of this nature if the father were not indicated to be a 15-year-old youth. The separate interview was corroborated by the complainant in her 1998 police interview. However, it is unfortunate there is no longer available the original notes on which Dr. Cowell relied to make her statement that the complainant's "pregnancy result[ed] from a relationship with a 15 year old male of two years duration". Even if Dr. Cowell's letter is not regarded as a business record, hearsay evidence is admissible if the criteria of necessity and reliability have been met: See *R. v. Khan* (1990), 59 C.C.C. (3d) 92 (S.C.C.); *R. v. Smith* (1992), 75 C.C.C. (3d) 257 (S.C.C.); *R. v. Hawkins* (1996), 111 C.C.C. (3d) 129 (S.C.C.); *R. v. B. (K.G.)* (1993), 19 C.R. (4th) 1, 79 C.C.C. (3d) 257 (S.C.C.). We are of the view that it would be unrealistic to expect hospital personnel to recall the specific event in question, given that they would deal with teenage pregnancies and abortion requests on a daily basis and therefore the criterion of necessity is met. As a result of interviews, it appears that it was recorded (as distilled by Dr. Cowell in her ordinary course of business procedure in reviewing such records to provide the responsible committee at the performing hospital with the background information and reasons in support of the abortion) that a 15-year-old boyfriend had been the father. No one on the interview team would have any reason not to faithfully record what had been said; further no reason for anything contrary to that was conjectured. Falsely recorded information would be cause for disciplinary action and even possible criminal compliant. It would appear to us that the distillation of those records into a "one-liner", given Dr. Cowell's responsibilities in writing such a letter, would be reliable.

We are of the view that if appellant's trial counsel had been alert to the contents of Dr. Cowell's letter which would be of exculpatory assistance to the appellant, then counsel would have been justified in requesting an adjournment to interview Dr. Cowell and to obtain further information of the sort now sought to be introduced as fresh evidence. That he did not do so appears to be pure inadvertence as opposed to any tactical decision on the part of the defence. This difficulty was compounded by the trial Crown not giving disclosure of this letter well prior to trial and in fact by her merely putting it in as an exhibit with other hospital records at trial, plus the trial judge, without any debate by counsel, declaring to the jury that "some factual statement" in the letter was hearsay and should be ignored. While the trial judge appropriately drew the jury's attention to: "The issue is who fathered the fetus and that is what we are here to decide today" she closed off a material avenue of exploration. It appears that she ignored what a valuable tool that letter and its reference to the pregnancy being as a result of an extended relationship with a mid-teenager would be for the defence not only as a base for effective cross-examination but for the searching out of cogent evidence of clinic procedures to present the basis of a reasonable doubt. Given the nature of the charges and their apparent interrelationship, together with the effect pro (without the letter and other evidence) and con (with such evidence) upon the complainant's credibility and vice versa for the appellant's credibility, we are of the view that the appellant was prejudiced on all three counts by lack of effective counsel. Under these circumstances, while ordinarily the fresh evidence would have been available for the appellant to make use of at trial, his lack of effective counsel prevented that end. We are therefore of the view that the fresh evidence may be introduced as it is relevant to the issues at trial. This fresh evidence, when taken with the evidence available but deemed inadmissible at trial, could reasonably be expected to have affected the result when credibility was obviously the main issue at trial.

Appeal allowed; new trial ordered.

(iv) *Former Testimony*

At common law:

> Where a witness has given his testimony under oath in a judicial proceeding, in which the adverse litigant had the power to cross-examine, the testimony so given will, if the witness himself cannot be called, be admitted in any subsequent suit between the same parties, or those claiming under them, provided it relate to the same subject or substantially involve the same material questions.[217]

Grounds of necessity reside in the declarant's unavailability, and circumstantial guarantees of trustworthiness in the fact that the statement was given under oath and subject to cross-examination. Indeed, Professor Wigmore[218] would say that "if it has been already subjected to proper cross-examination, it has satisfied the rule and needs no exception in its favour". Nevertheless, the orthodox treatment is to characterize it as an exception, as the trier does not have the advantage of observing the evidence being given and tested on cross-examination.

In criminal cases a statutory embodiment of the common law rule presently appears in the *Criminal Code*:

> 715. (1) Where, at the trial of an accused, a person whose evidence was given at a previous trial on the same charge, or whose evidence was taken in the investigation of the charge against the accused or on the preliminary inquiry into the charge, refuses to be sworn or to give evidence, or if facts are proved on oath from which it can be inferred reasonably that the person
>
> (a) is dead,
>
> (b) has since become and is insane,
>
> (c) is so ill that he is unable to travel or testify, or
>
> (d) is absent from Canada,
>
> and where it is proved that the evidence was taken in the presence of the accused, it may be admitted as evidence in the proceedings without further proof, unless the accused proves that the accused did not have full opportunity to cross-examine the witness.
>
> (2) Evidence that has been taken on the preliminary inquiry or other investigation of a charge against an accused may be admitted as evidence in the prosecution of the accused for any other offence on the same proof and in the same manner

---

[217] Taylor, *Evidence*, s. 464, as adopted in *Town of Walkerton v. Erdman* (1894), 23 S.C.R. 352.

[218] 5 Wigmore, *Evidence* (Chad. Rev.), s. 1370. See *R. v. Speid* (1988), 63 C.R. (3d) 253 (Ont. C.A.).

in all respects, as it might, according to law, be admitted as evidence in the prosecution of the offence with which the accused was charged when the evidence was taken.

R. v. POTVIN
[1989] 1 S.C.R. 525, 68 C.R. (3d) 193, 47 C.C.C. (3d) 289

The accused was charged with murder. The Crown called a witness who was alleged to have been an accomplice in the commission of the offence. The witness had testified at the preliminary inquiry and was cross-examined by counsel for the accused. He refused to testify at the accused's trial. The trial judge held that since the conditions set out in then s. 643 of the *Criminal Code* had been met the evidence should be admitted. The accused was convicted and his appeal dismissed. He appealed further.

WILSON J. (LAMER and SOPINKA JJ. concurring):—

The main issue on this appeal is whether the admission at trial of previously taken evidence under s. 643(1) [now section 715(1)] of the *Criminal Code*, R.S.C. 1970, c. C-34, as amended, . . . violates an accused's rights under ss. 7 or 11(*d*) of the *Canadian Charter of Rights and Freedoms.* . . .

. . .

What rights then does an accused have under s. 7 of the Charter with respect to the admission of previous testimony? It is, in my view, basic to our system of justice that the accused have had a full opportunity to cross-examine the witness when the previous testimony was taken if a transcript of such testimony is to be introduced as evidence in a criminal trial for the purpose of convicting the accused. This is in accord with the traditional view that it is the opportunity to cross-examine and not the fact of cross-examination which is crucial if the accused is to be treated fairly. As Professor Delisle has noted: Annotation (1986), 50 C.R. (3d) 195 at p. 196: "If the opposing party has had an opportunity to fully cross-examine he ought not to be justified in7 any later complaint if he did not fully exercise that right". . . .

. . .

With respect to the appellant's submission that he was deprived of a fair trial under s. 11(*d*) of the Charter, I would conclude, for the reasons given above in reviewing his s. 7 claim, that this claim must also fail if his constitutional right to have had a full opportunity to cross-examine the witness on the earlier occasion was respected. . . .

. . .

It is my view that the word "may" in s. 643(1) is directed not to the parties but to the trial judge. I believe it confers on him or her a discretion not to allow the previous testimony to be admitted in circumstances where its admission would operate unfairly to the accused. . . .

. . .

What then is the nature and purpose of the discretion conferred in s. 643(1) which enables the trial judge not to allow the evidence in at trial even in cases in which the requirements of the section have been met? In my view, there are two main types of mischief at which the discretion might be aimed. First, the discretion could be aimed at situations in which there has been unfairness in the manner in which the evidence was obtained. Although Parliament has set out in the section specific conditions as to how the previous testimony has to have been obtained if it is to be admitted under s. 643(1) (the most important, of course, being that the accused was afforded full opportunity to cross-examine the witness), Parliament could have intended the judge to have a discretion in those rare cases in which compliance with the requirements of s. 643(1) gave no guarantee that the evidence was obtained in a manner fair to the accused. This would, of course, represent a departure from the traditional common law approach that the manner in which evidence is obtained, with a few well-established exceptions such as the confessions rule, is not relevant to the question of its admissibility but it would be consistent with the contemporary approach to the expanded requirements of adjudicative fairness. An example of unfairness in obtaining the testimony might be a case in which, although the witness was temporarily absent from Canada, the Crown could have obtained the witness's attendance at trial with a minimal degree of effort. Another example might be a case in which the Crown was aware at the time the evidence was initially taken that the witness would not be available to testify at the trial but did not inform the accused of this fact so that he could make best use of the opportunity to cross-examine the witness at the earlier proceeding. These kinds of circumstances related to the obtaining of the evidence on the earlier occasion might have been in the mind of the legislator as triggering the judge's discretion with respect to its admission at the trial.

A different concern at which the discretion might have been aimed is the effect of the admission of the previously taken evidence on the fairness of the trial itself. This concern flows from the principle of the law of evidence that evidence may be excluded if it is highly prejudicial to the accused and of only modest probative value. . . . How the evidence was obtained might be irrelevant under this principle.

. . .

In my view, once it is accepted that s. 643(1) gives the trial judge a statutory discretion to depart from the purely mechanical application of the section, the discretion should be construed as sufficiently broad to deal with both kinds of situations, namely where the testimony was obtained in a manner which was unfair to the accused or where, even although the manner of obtaining the evidence was fair to the accused, its admission at his or her trial would not be fair to the accused. I would stress that in both situations the discretion should only be exercised after weighing what I have referred to as the "two competing and frequently conflicting concerns" of fair treatment of the accused and society's interest in the admission of probative evidence in order to get at the truth of the matter in issue. . . . Having regard to the reservations that have been expressed over the restrictive formulation of the common law discretion in *Wray, supra,* . . . I believe there is no need or justification for importing a similar restriction into the statutorily conferred discretion in s. 643(1). The protection of the accused from unfairness rather than the admission of probative evidence "without too much regard for the fairness of the adjudicative process" . . . should be the focus of the trial judge's concern.

It will follow that I cannot accept the hard and fast rule approach to this issue taken by the Manitoba Court of Appeal in *Sophonow, supra*. That court seems to suggest that the very importance of the evidence requires it to be excluded. . . .I believe that this proposition is at odds with the purpose of s. 643(1) in ensuring that evidence, even important and highly probative evidence, is not lost because of the unavailability of a witness at trial. . . .

In the case at bar I am of the view that the trial judge did not instruct himself properly as to the nature and scope of his discretion under s. 643(1). He stressed the high probative value of the evidence of someone who had been in the victim's home at the time the events occurred but failed, in my view, to give adequate consideration to possible unfairness to the accused arising from either the manner in which the evidence was obtained or the effect of its admission on the fairness of the trial. The Court of Appeal proceeded on the basis that the trial judge had no discretion other than the restrictive common law formulation in *Wray*. Neither court applied its mind to the question whether in the circumstances of this case the trial judge should have exercised his statutory discretion in s. 643(1) to exclude the evidence.

There can be no doubt about the fact that the decision whether or not to exercise the statutory discretion in this case would not have been an easy one. In favour of the admission of the evidence is the absence of any allegation that the manner in which Deschênes' testimony was obtained was unfair to the appellant. Moreover, the appellant's counsel exercised his right to cross-examine Deschênes at the preliminary inquiry and there was some cross-examination. There was also a measure of corroboration of Deschênes' testimony (so far as it purported Potvin as the culprit) by the testimony of Thibault at trial. Also favouring admission of Deschênes' testimony was the factor emphasized by the trial judge, namely its high probative value. The testimony purported to be an eyewitness account of the appellant beating and killing the victim. On the other hand, given the appellant's defence that he was a passive observer and that it was Deschênes, the unavailable witness, who did the actual beating and killing, the issue of Deschênes' credibility was obviously critical to the trier of fact's decision whether to accept or reject Deschênes' version of the events. Yet the jury had no opportunity to observe Deschênes' demeanour as an aid in assessing that witness's credibility.

This is not, however, a matter for this court to decide but rather a matter to be referred back to a trial judge properly instructed as to the nature and scope of his or her statutory discretion under s. 643(1).

. . .

La Forest J. (Dickson C.J.C. concurring):— I have had the advantage of reading the reasons of my colleague, Wilson J. I agree with her conclusion and, apart from what follows, her reasoning as well. However, I take a different view of s. 643(1) of the *Criminal Code* and, in consequence, of the source of the discretion to exclude the evidence permitted to be adduced under that provision.

As I read s. 643, it is not directly addressed to the prosecution or the judge, although it has, of course, implications for how they perform their duties. The provision is directed at a certain type of evidence. It makes it admissible. The parties to a trial may, therefore, invoke the provision if they wish. But the provision does not provide that the evidence previously taken shall be accepted; it provides, rather, that it may be read as evidence. This leaves room for the operation of the ordinary principles of the law of evidence, including the rule that the trial judge may exclude admissible evidence if its prejudicial effect substantially outweighs its probative value: see *R. v. Corbett*. . . . The case most frequently cited for the discretion to exclude is *R. v. Wray*, . . . where it is referred to in a dictum by Martland J., but it is simply one of the fundamental postulates of the law of evidence.

As my colleague notes, some have interpreted Martland J.'s dictum as limiting the discretion solely to situations where the evidence is highly prejudicial to the accused and is only of modest probative value. I do not accept this restrictive approach to the discretion. As I noted in *Corbett, supra*, at pp. 433-6 C.C.C., pp. 736-40 S.C.R., this narrow view, which can be traced from a statement by Lord du Parcq in *Noor Mohamed v. The King*, [1949] A.C. 182 at p. 192, has now been rejected by the House of Lords: *R. v. Sang*, [1980] A.C. 402 (H.L.). That case, and others there referred to, make it clear that under English law, a judge in a criminal trial always has a discretion to exclude evidence if, in the judge's opinion, its prejudicial effect substantially outweighs its probative value. . . .

. . . As their Lordships make clear, the discretion is grounded in the judge's duty to ensure a fair trial. . . . I am in accord with their view of the nature of the discretion.

. . . [I]t is evident that the trial judge failed to properly instruct himself either about the existence of the discretion or, more likely, about its nature. He repeatedly stresses the relevance of the evidence without any consideration of its prejudicial character. This smacks of the restricted view of the discretion I have rejected. In my view, therefore, the trial judge failed to exercise the discretion which was incumbent upon him to ensure a fair trial.

The Manitoba Court of Appeal had decided in *R. v. Sophonow* [219] that there was a discretion in the trial judge to exclude previous testimony, as the statutory provision

> was never intended to apply to a crucial witness whose evidence could work an injustice to the accused if the jury were deprived of seeing his demeanour and his reaction to cross-examination.[220]

PROBLEM

At a sexual assault trial the accused was unrepresented. He was permitted to cross-examine the complainant for two days. The accused was

---

[219]   (1986), 50 C.R. (3d) 193.
[220]   *Ibid.* at 209.

convicted but on appeal the Quebec Court of Appeal ordered a new trial. At the new trial the complainant refused to testify on the basis the experience of the first trial had lead to depression and a suicide attempt. The Crown applies to have the evidence of the complainant at the first trial admitted to prove the truth. **Would you as the judge admit the evidence? On what basis? Do different considerations apply to admitting the transcript as distinct from the audio recording?** See *R. v. Dégarie, No. 1* (June 28, 2001) (C.Q.) and *R. v. Dégarie, No. 2* (June 29, 2001) (C.Q.).

(c) Exceptions Not Dependent on Availability of Declarant

(i) *Declarations as to Physical Sensation*

In *Gilbey v. Great Western Railway* [221] it was alleged that the deceased had suffered his injury on the job and that compensation from his employer was forthcoming. The trial court received in evidence statements made by the deceased to his wife not merely of his sensations but as to the cause of the injury. On appeal it was held, by Cozens-Hardy, M.R.:

> I do not doubt at all that statements made by a workman to his wife of his sensations at the time, about the pain in the side or his head, or what not — whether those statements were made by groans or by actions or were verbal statements — would be admissible to prove the existence of those sensations. But to hold that those statements ought to go further and be admitted as evidence of the facts deposed to is, I think, open to doubt; such a contention is contrary to all authority.

There have never been grounds of necessity, such as death or insanity of the declarant, attached to this exception but it is believed that there is "a fair necessity, in the sense that there is no other equally satisfactory source of evidence either from the same person or elsewhere".[222] Given these grounds of necessity the evidence

> is not to be extended beyond the necessity on which the rule is founded. Anything in the nature of narration or statement is to be carefully excluded, and the testimony is to be confined strictly to such complaints, exclamations, and expressions as usually and naturally accompany and furnish evidence of a present existing pain or malady.[223]

Circumstantial guarantees of trustworthiness are resident in the fact that the declarant, if anyone, should be able to perceive his or her own sensations or feelings; his or her declaration is of the moment and defects in memory are absent. Arising from the spontaneity of the declaration and lack of opportunity to fabricate there is some assurance of sincerity, though it is recognized that fabrication can occur. Though the statements under review need not be

---

[221] (1910), 102 L.T. 202 (C.A.); cited with approval by Middleton, J. in *Youlden v. London Guar. Co.* (1912), 4 D.L.R. 721 (Ont. H.C.), affirmed 12 D.L.R. 433 (Ont. C.A.).

[222] 6 Wigmore, *Evidence* (Chad. Rev.), s. 1714 at 90. It is believed that his spontaneous declaration would be superior to his later recounting of the condition in the witness stand.

[223] Per Bigelow, J. in *Bacon v. Charlton* (1851), 7 Cush. 586, as quoted in 6 Wigmore, *Evidence* (Chad. Rev.), s. 1718.

made to a physician, such declarations would carry the further assurance that the declarant is unlikely to mislead the person from whom he or she seeks assistance.

(ii) *Declarations as to Mental or Emotional State*

When a person's mental or emotional state is a material issue in the trial, then that person's statements evidencing the same may be received, and for the same reasons as recounted above justifying declarations as to physical sensation. If at trial X's domicile is material, his earlier statement, "I plan to make Canada my home" is receivable to prove his intent, as we see that the hearsay dangers of communication, memory and perception are absent; in a suit for alienation of affections the wife-declarant's earlier statement of "I don't love you anymore" would similarly be receivable under this exception. Notice that these statements will be received though they were made before or after the moment that the state of mind was material; if the trier determines that a certain state of mind existed on Day 1 he will be able to reason that the same state of mind continued to exist to Day 5.

In a prosecution for murder, statements of the accused, "I am going to kill him", "I hate him", would also be receivable under this exception as evidence of intent, but since they also constitute admissions, and are receivable under that head, this exception is seldom canvassed. Of course, admissions are only received when tendered *against* the accused. If statements of the accused, "I never meant to do him harm", "I loved him", are tendered under this exception they would be met with the rebuke that they are self-serving and inadmissible on that ground. Self-serving evidence is excluded because of the danger that an accused might manufacture evidence; but to assume the falsity of the evidence is to beg the question. Professor Wigmore comments:

> Because [we say] this accused person *might* be guilty and therefore *might* have contrived these false utterances, therefore we shall exclude them, although without this assumption they indicate feelings wholly inconsistent with guilt, and although, if he is innocent, their exclusion is a cruel deprivation of a most natural and effective sort of evidence. To hold that every expression of hatred, malice and bravado is to be received, while no expression of fear, goodwill, friendship, or the like, can be considered, is to exhibit ourselves the victims of a narrow whimsicality, which might be expected in the tribunal of Jeffreys, going down from London to Taunton with a list of his intended victims already in his pocket, or on a bench "condemning" to order, as Zola said of Dreyfus's military judges.

> . . . There is no reason why a declaration of an existing state of mind, if it would be admissible against the accused, should not also be admissible in his favour, except so far as the circumstances indicate plainly a motive to deceive.[224]

In the above instances, the statements are tendered as evidence when state of mind is a material issue. A larger problem develops if the statements are tendered to evidence an existing state of mind which is not itself material

---

[224]   6 Wigmore, *Evidence* (Chad. Rev.), s. 1732 at 160.

but is relevant to a material issue: for example, in a murder prosecution, evidence of the deceased's statement "I want it all to end" indicating her intention to commit suicide as evidence that later she did perform the act; evidence of the deceased's statement that "I'm going to see Joe tonight and have it out with him" as evidence against Joe that the two fought later that evening. The authorities on this point are meagre and in conflict.[225] The classic "textbook" case in this area is *Mutual Life Insurance Co. v. Hillmon.*[226] The plaintiff sought to recover the proceeds from an insurance policy on her deceased husband. The insurance company resisted on the ground that the body found in Crooked Creek, Kansas was not that of Hillmon but that of his travelling companion, Walters. The disputed evidence consisted of letters written by Walters to his fiancée that he intended to go with Hillmon to Crooked Creek. The Court held that the letters should have been received:

> The existence of a particular intention in a certain person at a certain time being a material fact to be proved, evidence that he expressed that intention at that time is as direct evidence of that fact as his own testimony that he then had that intention would be. After his death there can hardly be any other way of proving it, and while he is still alive his own memory of his state of mind at a former time is no more likely to be clear and true than a bystander's recollection of what he then said, and is less trustworthy than letters written by him at the very time and under circumstances precluding a suspicion of misrepresentation. The letters in question were competent . . . evidence that . . . he had the intention of going, and of going with Hillmon, which made it more probable both that he did go and that he went with Hillmon than if there had been no proof of such intention.[227]

The hearsay analysis is faultless; the hearsay dangers are minimized. True it is that "it was only a statement of intention which might or might not have been carried out"[228] but the problem that the declarant might not follow through with his intention is not a hearsay problem but rather a problem of relevance.

Suppose however that the declaration of mental state is a statement of belief in the declarant as evidence of some past act.[229] In *Shepard v. U.S.*,[230] a murder prosecution, the statement of the deceased was received as a dying declaration: "Dr. Shepard has poisoned me". On appeal, the conditions of that exception were found not to have been met and the prosecution sought to justify the evidence as indicating the deceased's state of mind which was then inconsistent with the defence of suicide. Cardozo J. wrote:

> There are times when a state of mind, if relevant, may be proved by contemporaneous declarations of feeling or intent. Mutual Life Ins. Co. v. Hillmon. . . . (other examples are then given) . . . The ruling in that case marks the

---

[225] Contrast *R. v. Buckley* (1873), 13 Cox C.C. 293 and *R. v. Wainwright* (1875), 13 Cox C.C. 171.
[226] 145 U.S. 285 (1892).
[227] *Ibid.* at 295.
[228] The reason given by Cockburn, C.J. in *R. v. Wainwright, supra* note 225 at 172, for rejecting such a statement.
[229] The problem is canvassed in Seligman, "An Exception to the Hearsay Rule" (1912-13) 26 Harv. L. Rev. 146; and see Maguire, "The *Hillmon* Case — Thirty-three Years After" (1925) 38 Harv. L. Rev. 709.
[230] 290 U.S. 96 (1933).

high-water line beyond which courts have been unwilling to go. . . . Declarations of intention, casting light upon the future, have been sharply distinguished from declarations of memory, pointing backwards to the past. There would be an end, or nearly that, to the rule against hearsay if the distinction were ignored.[231]

R. v. STARR
[2000] 2 S.C.R. 144, 36 C.R. (5th) 1, 147 C.C.C. (3d) 449

The accused was charged with two counts of first degree murder. He was accused of shooting C and W by the side of a highway. C and W had been drinking with the accused in a hotel. C and W drove to a gas station. The accused also drove to that station. There G, a sometime girlfriend of C, angry with C because he was out with W rather than her, confronted C. G asked C why he would not come home with her. According to G, C replied that he had to "go and do an Autopac scam with Robert". She understood "Robert" to be the accused. The Crown's theory was that the killing was a gang-related execution perpetrated by the accused. W was an unfortunate witness who was killed simply because she was in the wrong place at the wrong time. The theory was that the accused had used an Autopac scam as a pretext to get C out into the countryside. The trial judge found that G's anticipated testimony regarding the scam was admissible under the "present intentions" or "state of mind" exception to the hearsay rule. The Court of Appeal, in a majority decision, upheld the accused's convictions.

IACOBUCCI J. (MAJOR, BINNIE, ARBOUR and LEBEL JJ. concurring): —

. . .

The theory of the Crown at trial was that the killing of Cook was a gang-related execution perpetrated by the appellant. Weselowski was an unfortunate witness who was killed simply because she was in the wrong place at the wrong time. The theory was that the appellant had used an Autopac scam as a pretext to get Cook out into the countryside. Outside the Turskis' home, Cook got into the smaller car and drove it into the ditch, hitting telephone poles in an effort to damage the car. The appellant shot Weselowski twice in the head, then drove Weselowski's station wagon up the road to where Cook had stopped the smaller car in the ditch. When Cook entered the station wagon on the passenger side, the appellant shot him from the driver's seat three times in the head and three times in the chest. He then pushed Cook's body out of the vehicle and drove away, parking near his brother's house, where the appellant abandoned the station wagon.

. . .

The Crown argued that the "state of mind" or "present intentions" exception to the hearsay rule applied to render Cook's statement to Giesbrecht admissible. This exception was most recently discussed in detail by this Court in *Smith*, supra, where it was recognized that an "exception to the hearsay rule arises when the declarant's statement is adduced in order to demonstrate the

---

[231]   *Ibid.* at 104. But compare *People v. Merkouris*, 344 P. 2d 1 (Cal. S.C., 1959); cert. den. 361 U.S. 943 (1960).

intentions, or state of mind, of the declarant at the time when the statement was made". Wigmore has argued that the present intentions exception also includes a requirement that a statement "be of a present existing state of mind, and must appear to have been made in a natural manner and not under circumstances of suspicion": *Wigmore on Evidence*, vol. 6 (Chadbourn rev. 1976), at para. 1725, p. 129. L'Heureux-Dubé J., at para. 63 of her reasons, denies that Wigmore's suggestion has ever been adopted in our jurisprudence. As I will discuss below, regardless of whether the present intentions requirement ever had such a requirement, the principled approach demands that it must have it now. I will therefore examine the admissibility of Cook's statement under the present intentions exception in light of that understanding.

. . .

It is important to emphasize that even in "cases where the act was a joint one involving the deceased and another person", the hearsay is not generally admissible to show the intentions of a third party. I draw this conclusion for two reasons. First, I can find no support in Canadian jurisprudence for the proposition that statements of intention are admissible against someone other than the declarant, apart from the one comment by Doherty J. noted above. . . . Second, there are very good reasons behind the rule against allowing statements of present intention to be used to prove the state of mind of someone other than the declarant. As noted above, the central concern with hearsay is the inability of the trier of fact to test the reliability of the declarant's assertion. When the statement is tendered to prove the intentions of a third party, this danger is multiplied. If a declarant makes a statement about the intentions of a third party, there are three possible bases for this statement: first, it could be based on a prior conversation with the accused; second, it could be based on a prior conversation with a fourth party, who indicated the third party's intentions to the declarant; or third, it could be based on pure speculation on the part of the declarant. Under the first scenario, the statement is double hearsay. Since each level of double hearsay must fall within an exception, or be admissible under the principled approach, the mere fact that the declarant is making a statement of present intention is insufficient to render it admissible. The second level of hearsay must also be admissible.

The other two scenarios also clearly require exclusion. If the statement about joint acts is based on a conversation with a fourth party, then the statement is triple hearsay, or worse. If, on the other hand, it is based on pure speculation, then it clearly is unreliable and does not fit within the rationale underlying the present intentions exception. In conclusion then, a statement of intention cannot be admitted to prove the intentions of someone other than the declarant, unless a hearsay exception can be established for each level of hearsay. One way to establish this would obviously be the co-conspirator exception: see *R. v. Carter*, [1982] 1 S.C.R. 938; Sopinka, Lederman and Bryant, supra, at pp. 303-7. This is no doubt what Doherty J. was referring to in *P. (R.)*, supra, when he spoke of "cases where the act was a joint one involving the deceased and another person". Barring the applicability of this or some other exception to each level of hearsay involved, statements of joint intention are only admissible to prove the declarant's intentions.

. . .

With great respect to the Court of Appeal, I conclude that the trial judge erred in admitting Cook's statement to Giesbrecht under the present intentions exception and, having admitted it, in not limiting its use by the jury, for three reasons. First, the statement contained no indicia of reliability since it was made under circumstances of suspicion; second, the trial judge failed to instruct the jury that the statement was only admissible as evidence regarding the intentions of Cook, not the appellant; and third, even if it had been properly limited, the evidence was more prejudicial than probative.

Turning first to the circumstances of suspicion, I agree with Twaddle J.A. that the statement lacked circumstantial guarantees of trustworthiness. As Twaddle J.A. noted, Cook and Giesbrecht had been romantically involved for almost two years. Cook had lived with Giesbrecht and her mother for a time, and had spent the night before his murder with Giesbrecht, after getting out of jail. Then, in the early morning hours of August 21, 1994, Giesbrecht observed Cook in the car of another woman, Darlene Weselowski. Giesbrecht testified that she thought Cook might try to "take off on her" if he saw Giesbrecht approaching the car, and she endeavoured not to be seen by Cook until she was close enough to talk to him. After an initial confrontation, Giesbrecht walked away into an alley behind the gas station, where Cook followed her. Their conversation ended in an argument because Cook was with Weselowski. She was angry at Cook for being with another woman, and asked him expressly why Cook would not come home with her rather than remain with Weselowski. It was at this point, and in this heated context, that Cook said he was going to engage in an Autopac scam with the appellant, who was sitting in a car nearby. Giesbrecht testified that it was unusual for Cook to discuss such business matters with her.

Twaddle J.A. found that the circumstances surrounding the making of the statement cast serious doubt upon the reliability of the statement. The possibility that Cook was untruthful could not be said to have been substantially negated. Twaddle J.A. relied, in particular, upon the fact that Cook may have had a motive to lie in order to make it seem that he was not romantically involved with Weselowski, and upon the ease with which Cook could point to the appellant, who was sitting nearby in a car but out of earshot, as being the person with whom he was going to do a scam. In my view, Twaddle J.A. was correct in finding that these circumstances bring the reliability of Cook's statement into doubt. The statement was made under "circumstances of suspicion", and therefore does not fall within the present intentions exception. The statement should have been excluded.

. . .

Finally, I would exclude Cook's statement as more prejudicial than probative. The trial judge did not make a finding on the issue of reliability. His focus was upon the impermissible inferences that the jury might draw from otherwise admissible hearsay, and he regarded the primary prejudice to the appellant to be that the jury might infer that he was the type of person likely to commit insurance fraud. However, as noted above, this was not the primary source of prejudice. The trial judge erred by not considering whether "the prejudicial effect of the prohibited use of the evidence [i.e., the appellant's intentions] overbears its probative value on the permitted use [i.e., Cook's intentions]": *Watt's Manual of Criminal Evidence* (1999). The impermissible inferences that the jury might well have drawn from Cook's statement are that the appellant was in the car that followed Cook, that the appellant was alone in the car (since Cook referred only to the appellant), and that the appellant went with Cook as part of a plan to lure Cook to a secluded area and kill him. These were the specific impermissible inferences that the jury might have drawn in this regard — indeed, they are inferences that the Crown specifically invited the jury to draw — quite apart from the inferences that they might have drawn regarding his general criminality. In my view, Twaddle J.A. was correct in finding that the prejudicial effect of the admission of Cook's statement accordingly outweighed the statement's probative value. The statement ought to have been excluded on this basis as well.

PROBLEM

You are the trial judge in the trial of Jack, who is charged with first degree murder of K. K's body was found by the police in a shallow grave on the farm Jack managed and occupied.

At trial you have admitted into evidence a voluntary statement by the accused to the police, soon after the police found the body. Admissibility of this statement is not in issue. In the statement Jack admitted he was at the farm when K was shot but maintained that the shooting was by a neighbour, who has since left the country. In the statement the accused also admitted that he helped bury the corpse.

The Crown's case is that the accused persuaded K to come to the farm with $50,000 cash to do a drug transaction with a third party but that this was just a ruse to get him to the farm to rob and kill him. A number of evidentiary rulings arise during the course of the trial. **With reference to appropriate authority, rule on the admissibility of the following evidence tendered by the Crown:**

(a) A statement made by K to a friend shortly before K disappeared that "I am collecting a large sum of money to go to the farm where Jack and I are going to make a big-time drug score".

(b) A recorded 911 call by the accused's wife, Jill, to police on the night of the killing, "Come quickly I think my husband is going to shoot someone". The police answered the call to the farm within 10 minutes. Everything seemed calm and Jack assured them all was well. Jill denied that she had called the police. The next day the police found the body in the shallow grave. The voice on the 911 call is now identified to be that of Jill.

Compare *R. v. Harrison* (2001), 44 C.R. (5th) 120 (B.C. C.A.).

(iii) *Spontaneous Statements (Excited Utterances)*

Discretion in this area there must be, but it is best to have guidelines articulated for its exercise; when the guidelines are spelled out in terms of the exception's justification, we are even further advanced. The chief justification lies in the fact that the danger of insincerity is minimized as there has been no opportunity for the declarant to fabricate, and the memory danger is eliminated since the declaration is contemporaneous with the event. A difficulty, of course, remains in the danger of misperception, and deserves stressing when evaluating the worth of the statement: how often have we exclaimed about a situation and found ourselves later saying, "on second thought. . . ." The very fact that the event was startling and caused the viewer to be excited can impair his or her perceptual abilities.[232]

Establishing the preliminary condition of admissibility, that the declaration was in response to a startling event, can produce a problem. Can we look at the statement itself to determine the relationship? While it appears as a bootstrap operation it appears to be the better view that the statement can be regarded, in the discretion of the trial judge, along with other matters.[233]

R. v. BEDINGFIELD
(1879), 14 Cox C.C. 341

The accused was charged with murder. The accused was present with the deceased in the deceased's house. The deceased came suddenly out of the house with her throat cut. She said something, pointing backwards to the house. In a few minutes she was dead. In the course of the opening speech on the part of the prosecution it was proposed to state what she said. It was objected on the part of the prisoner that it was not admissible.

Cockburn C.J. said he had carefully considered the question and was clear that it could not be admitted and therefore ought not to be stated, as it might have a fatal effect. I regret, he said, that according to the law of England, any statement made by the deceased should not be admissible. Then could it be admissible having been made in the absence of the prisoner, as part of the res gestae but it is not so admissible for it was not part of anything done, or something said while something was being done, but something said after something done. Anything, he said, uttered by the deceased at the time the act was being done would be admissible, as, for instance, if she had been heard to say something, as "Don't, Harry!". But here it was something stated by her after it was all over, whatever it was, and after the act was completed.

It was submitted, on the part of the prosecution, that the statement was admissible as a dying declaration, the case to be proved being that the woman's throat was cut completely and the artery severed, so that she was dying, and

---

[232]   See Hutchins & Slesinger, "Some Observations on the Law of Evidence" (1928) 28 Col. L. Rev. 432; Stewart, "Perception Memory and Hearsay" [1970] Utah L. Rev. 1 at 28; and Marshall, *Law and Psychology in Conflict* (1969) at 19-20.

[233]   *Ratten v. R.*, [1971] 3 All E.R. 801 (P.C.), discussed below in *R. v. Clark.*

was actually dead in a few minutes; but Cockburn C.J. said the statement was not admissible as a dying declaration, because it did not appear that the woman was aware that she was dying.

It was urged that the woman must have known it as she was actually dying at the time, but Cockburn C.J. said that though she might have known it if she had had time for reflection, here that was not so, for at the time she made the statement she had no time to consider and reflect that she was dying; there is no evidence to show that she knew it, and I cannot presume it. There is nothing to show that she was under the sense of impending death, so the statement is not admissible as a dying declaration.

[The statement was later reported to be "See what Harry has done!" In the result the jury nevertheless found him guilty based on the other evidence.]

R. v. CLARK

(1983), 35 C.R. (3d) 357, 7 C.C.C. (3d) 46 (Ont. C.A.)

On the accused's trial for murder, spontaneous utterances by the deceased made shortly after she had been injured by the accused when the accused in fact was still present, including the words "Help, I've been murdered, I've been stabbed", were admitted as evidence of the truth of the facts stated. On appeal it was argued that the statements were improperly admitted.

DUBIN J.A. (MACKINNON A.C.J.O and CORY J.A. concurring): —

. . .

The appellant married Mr. Ade in January, 1977. Their marriage was a somewhat stormy and unusual one, and they separated in November, 1977. The appellant testified that she was still very much in love with her husband and during the period of their separation frequently attended upon him with a view apparently of winning him back. The marriage was annulled in April, 1978, and shortly after Mr. Ade began to see the deceased Beverly Ade. The appellant was devastated when he became involved with another woman. She telephoned his office with such frequency that Mr. Ade asked the switchboard operator to stop passing on her calls to him although some calls did get through. She waited outside his place of work, would follow him to the bank, to the parking-lot or to the cafeteria where he was having lunch.

In December, 1978, Mr. Ade married the deceased. The appellant was observed on many occasions loitering in the area of the residence of Mr. Ade and the deceased. She continued to telephone and visited his office and scouted his premises and the area in which he lived.

. . .

On the morning of July 7th she attended at the residence of the deceased. The appellant testified that she did so to recover two lawn chairs which had been left in Mr. Ade's garage and which, unbeknownst to her, had been given away by him prior to July 7th. . . . It was during that visit that Beverly Ade came to her death as a result of penetrating stab wounds to her heart, admittedly at the hands of the appellant. The deceased had one superficial wound to the back, one to the right side, ten front torso wounds and four wounds to her hands. . . . The appellant's left hand was cut in three places.

The defence was self-defence and/or provocation. The appellant testified that she knocked on the door of the deceased's premises and told the deceased that she wanted the two lawn chairs. They attended at the garage but could not find the chairs. According to the appellant, the deceased said, "Howard's been over you a long time, just don't make anymore excuses." The appellant replied, "Don't be too sure." The appellant testified that as they came out of the garage the deceased gave the appellant a push and said "not to come around anymore". She stated that she then stood with her back to the garage door and with her eyes closed. When she heard footsteps, she opened her eyes and saw the deceased quite close holding a knife. The appellant was startled and afraid. She testified that she grabbed the knife with her left hand and pushed the deceased with the other. The deceased fell. As the appellant tried to run away, she tripped over the deceased and fell down. She was not sure whether she had hit the deceased but saw that her own hand was bleeding. She said that the deceased then grabbed her, and she felt that she was hanging on to the deceased near a chair which was near the garage entrance. She testified that she did not know that she had injured the deceased who was at that time sitting on the chair.

. . .

Spontaneous exclamations

It was submitted that the learned trial judge erred in admitting certain of the evidence to be found in the testimony of Fawn Pitcher. On July 7, 1980, Miss Pitcher was staying with her aunt who resided across the street from the Ade residence. . . . In order to appreciate the evidentiary issues raised as well as to indicate the over-all importance of her testimony in this case, I set out hereunder in some detail the relevant portions of Miss Pitcher's testimony:

> Q. Okay, just take it slowly and tell the jury please what it was that you heard please.

> A. Okay, I was in the back kitchen making my breakfast. It was around ten o'clock and I heard somebody calling for help. First I thought it was kids fooling around a pool. I was sort of annoyed at it and it kept up and I thought no, so I went outside and I realized it wasn't a child in a pool. I went out the back gate and I realized where the cries were coming from, across the road.

> Q. Fawn, could you tell me then what you saw and heard as you went across the street to find out what was going on?

> A. Okay, as I came out the back gate to my aunt's place and up her side lawn I saw a woman standing at the top of the driveway in the picture shown and she was yelling: "Help, help I've been murdered. I've been stabbed." And I didn't see anyone else around. I walked across the road, down through their ditch and up into the lawn and I saw the accused sort of agitated going back and forth towards the deceased. . . .

Q. All right. Now, where was the accused lady when you first saw her?

A. She was on the grass.

Q. Yes.

A. Near a clump of trees or tree and she was moving back and forth towards the deceased and then back on to the lawn again.

Q. Okay. Did you see the accused lady right away?

A. Not right away. Not when I first came out I only saw the deceased.

. . .

Q. You were then approaching and the jury has seen the angle that you were approaching on, just tell me what happened then as you approached?

A. Okay, as I approached, I saw only the deceased and she was yelling, "Help I've been murdered, I've been stabbed." I crossed the road, went up onto the lawn of the other house and she seemed to see me then and she said, "Go call the police, go call an ambulance."

Q. All right, now, what can you tell me about the appearance of the deceased lady at this time when she was saying these things to you?

A. She seem to be very distressed. I couldn't see at first that there was any injury apparent until I crossed up into her lawn and as I got closer I saw a red circle on the right shoulder and just below her right shoulder.

. . .

It was the submission by counsel for the appellant that the words spoken by the deceased, "Help I've been murdered, I've been stabbed" were inadmissible hearsay. No objection was taken by counsel at trial to the admissibility of that evidence, but if the evidence was in fact inadmissible and highly prejudicial, the failure to object is not fatal.

[The Court then reviewed *Bedingfield* and English and Canadian cases that had followed it over the years.]

It is to be noted that the admissibility of the statements under consideration in the foregoing cases was dependent upon whether they could be said to be part of the res gestae, a Latin phrase much criticized in *Wigmore on Evidence*, which will be presently commented upon. In order to fit into a res gestae test, the statement had to form part of the transaction or event and if not immediately contemporaneous was held to be outside the otherwise permissible exception to the hearsay rule.

The basis for the admissibility of a spontaneous exclamation, the label assigned by Wigmore to such statements, was considered and expanded upon in *Ratten v. Reginam*, [1971] 3 All E.R. 801. Ratten was charged with the murder of his wife. Her death had been caused by a wound from a shot-gun held by the appellant. His explanation was that the discharge was accidental and had occurred while he was cleaning his gun in the kitchen of his house. He was unable to explain how the gun from which the shot was fired had come to be loaded. He testified that he immediately telephoned for an ambulance and, shortly after, the police had telephoned him, at which time he asked them to come immediately. At about 1:15 p.m. on the day of the alleged offence, a telephone call was made from their premises. The telephone operator who answered had stated in evidence at trial:

> I plugged into a number [the appellant's number] . . . and . . . I opened the speak key and I said to the person, "Number please" and the reply I got was "Get me the police please".

The person on the telephone gave her address and hung up. The telephone operator testified that the person on the telephone was in a hysterical state and later added that the person on the telephone sobbed. The telephone operator advised the police of the call. The police telephoned the Ratten house and spoke to the accused. By this time the deceased had been shot.

Objection was taken to the admissibility of the evidence of the telephone operator on the ground that it was hearsay and that it did not come within any of the recognized exceptions to the rule against hearsay, but the objection was overruled. The issue was again raised on appeal on the premise that the trial judge properly instructed the jury that on the evidence they might find the telephone call was made by the deceased woman.

The Privy Council first held that the evidence of the telephone operator was not hearsay evidence but was admissible as evidence of a fact relevant to an issue.

Lord Wilberforce stated at p. 805:

> The mere fact that evidence of a witness includes evidence as to words spoken by another person who is not called is no objection to its admissibility. Words spoken are facts just as much as any other action by a human being. If the speaking of the words is a relevant fact, a witness may give evidence that they were spoken. A question of hearsay only arises when the words spoken are relied on 'testimonially', i.e., as establishing some fact narrated by the words. Authority is hardly needed for this proposition, but their Lordships will restate what was said in the judgment of the Board in *Subramaniam v. Public Prosecutor*, [1956] 1 W.L.R. 965 at 970:
>
> > Evidence of a statement made to a witness by a person who is not himself called as a witness may or may not be hearsay. It is hearsay and inadmissible when the object of the evidence is to establish the truth of what is contained in the statement. It is not hearsay and is admissible when it is proposed to establish by the evidence, not the truth of the statement but the fact that it was made.

He then proceeded, however, to deal with the admissibility of the evidence on the premise that it was put forth as evidence of the truth of the facts asserted by the statement, and on that premise concluded at pp. 806-7 as follows:

> Their Lordships, as already stated, do not consider that there is any hearsay element in the evidence, nor in their opinion was it so presented by the trial judge, but they think it right to deal with the appellant's submission on the assumption that there is, i.e. that the words said to have been used involve an assertion of the truth of some facts stated in them and that they may have been so understood by the jury. The Crown defended the admissibility of the words as part of the "res gestae", a contention which led to the citation of numerous authorities.

The expression "res gestae", like many Latin phrases, is often used to cover situations insufficiently analysed in clear English terms.

. . .

The possibility of concoction, or fabrication, where it exists, is on the other hand an entirely valid reason for exclusion, and is probably the real test which judges in fact apply. In their Lordships' opinion this should be recognised and applied directly as the relevant test: the test should be not the uncertain one whether the making of the statement was in some sense part of the event or transaction. This may often be difficult to establish: such external matters as the time which elapses between the events and the speaking of the words (or vice versa), and differences in location being relevant factors but not, taken by themselves, decisive criteria. As regards statements made after the event it must be for the judge, by preliminary ruling, to satisfy himself that the statement was so clearly made in circumstances of spontaneity or involvement in the event that the possibility of concoction can be disregarded. Conversely, if he considers that the statement was made by way of narrative of a detached prior event so that the speaker was so disengaged from it as to be able to construct or adapt his account, he should exclude it. And the same must in principle be true of statements made before the event. The test should be not the uncertain one, whether the making of the statement should be regarded as part of the event or transaction. This may often be difficult to show. But if the drama, leading up to the climax, has commenced and assumed such intensity and pressure that the utterance can safely be regarded as a true reflection of what was unrolling or actually happening, it ought to be received. The expression "res gestae" may conveniently sum up these criteria, but the reality of them must always be kept in mind: it is this that lies behind the best reasoned of the judges' rulings.

And at p. 808:

These authorities show that there is ample support for the principle that hearsay evidence may be admitted if the statement providing it is made in such conditions (always being those of approximate but not exact contemporaneity) of involvement or pressure as to exclude the possibility of concoction or distortion to the advantage of the maker or the disadvantage of the accused.

It is clear in this case that the challenged evidence was tendered as evidence of the truth of that which was stated, and, thus, if admissible, as a true exception to the hearsay rule.

. . .

[A]lthough what was stated by Chief Justice Robertson in *R. v. Leland*, [1951] O.R. 12, 98 C.C.C. 337, 11 C.R. 152, [one of the Canadian cases that followed the contemporaneity requirement of *Bedingfield*] appears to have been consistent with the then state of the authorities, it cannot, in my respectful opinion, now be viewed as an authoritative statement of the law. This case can, of course, be readily distinguishable from *Leland*, in that, it is apparent from the evidence of Miss Pitcher that the words attributed by her as having been spoken by the deceased were spoken while the event was still transpiring and, thus, contemporaneous with the unfolding events. But I would prefer to rest my judgment on a broader base as it is now apparent from the foregoing that the narrow test of exact contemporaneity should no longer be followed.

The circumstances, as outlined by Miss Pitcher, under which the words were said to have been spoken by the deceased were such as to exclude the possibility of concoction or distortion, and if Miss Pitcher's evidence were accepted by the jury, the words spoken, "Help I've been murdered, I've been stabbed" were evidence of the belief of the deceased as to what had occurred and evidence as to the truth of the facts stated by her as a true exception to the hearsay rule. . . . The words, "Go call the police, go call an ambulance", to which no exception was taken on appeal, were, of course, admissible as a verbal act and not as an exception to the hearsay rule.

For these reasons, I would reject the submission made by counsel for the appellant on this issue.

In *R. v. Andrews*,[234] the Law Lords decided, following *Ratten*, that *R. v. Bedingfield* "would not be so decided today".

R. v. SHEA
(2011), 279 C.C.C. (3d) 511 (N.S. C.A.)

In the course of a violent home invasion a victim told his brother over the phone that the two accused were "strapped", meaning that they carried firearms. The victim did not testify at trial. The conversation had been intercepted by a police wiretap. It was admitted at the forcible confinement and extortion trial. The accused argued on appeal that the conversation was inadmissible hearsay.

FERRAR J.A.

61 R. v. Ratten was cited with approval by this Court in R. v. Magloir, 2003 NSCA 74 (& 27).

62 In R. v. Hamilton, 2004 CarswellOnt 6424 (Sup. Ct. J.) one of the accused attempted to introduce disposition evidence through intercepts that also constituted hearsay. The moving defendant, Davis, wanted to show that a third party, Webb, was a viable murder suspect, in part through the violent disposition of Webb revealed on the recorded intercepts. The application judge rejected the admissibility of the evidence on the basis of propensity but made comments regarding hearsay and the *res gestae* exception as it relates to intercepted communications:

> 34. . . . First, the intercepts of December 7, 2001, indicate the recording of criminal activity during the recording and may well be admissible as part of the res gestae of the crimes talked about during the recordings.

The trial judge rejected the evidence on the basis they did not implicate Webb in the crime before the court (& 35).

---

[234]   [1987] A.C. 281.

63 In R. v. MacInnes, [2010] O.J. No. 4639 (Q.L.) (Sup. Ct. J.) the accused was charged with kidnapping, assault, and extortion of Paul Aubry. Aubry later committed suicide before trial. Family members were going to testify to unrecorded phone conversations with the victim *during his confinement*. There was clear evidence that Aubry sounded scared on the phone (& 21-22). The trial judge held that the statements were part of the *res gestae* and admissible:

> 30 In my opinion the telephone calls to Andre Vezina and Beryl Aubry on July 17 constitute compelling and substantively spontaneous statements with respect to Mr. Aubry's state of mind on the date in question. In both cases there are circumstantial guarantees of trustworthiness in the circumstances surrounding the making of the statements. I can divine no motive for Aubry to lie to Andre Vezina and his sister given the dire predicament in which he found himself. ...

> 31 In any event, in my view, the statements constitute part of the res gestae because they occurred during the course of the unlawful confinement of Paul Aubry. To that extent the statements would be admissible as part of the circumstances of the offences themselves. In *R. v. Khan* (1988), 42 C.C.C. (3d) 197 (O.C.A.) at p. 207, the Court stated:

> . . .

> 32 In my view the statements by Paul Aubry to his brother-in-law Andre Vezina and his sister Beryl Aubry should be admitted under the rubric of res gestae in that the stress or pressure of the events can safely discount the possibility of concoction or deception on the part of Paul Aubry. The statements may also be admitted under the principled exception to the rule against hearsay, as they meet the twin criteria of necessity and threshold reliability.

64 A review of the case law shows that the key elements of this test are a statement that is spontaneously declared under shock or pressure sufficient to ensure the declaration's reliability and remove any suspicion of concoction or fabrication, and made under circumstances of relative contemporaneity to the traumatic event.

65 Given the violent, threatening, menacing or stressful nature inherent in the crime of extortion and unlawful confinement, and given the ability of wiretap intercepts to capture a crime in progress, intercepts of victims to extortion as in the present case would seem to be a text-book case for the application for the *res gestae* exception to the hearsay rule. R. v. Hamilton, supra and R. v. MacInnes, supra reflect this.

66 I am satisfied that the trial judge did not err in admitting the conversation between Joel and Luke Hersey into evidence as part of the *res gestae*. As stated previously, the statement was made at a time Luke Hersey was being held against his will, he did not know he was being recorded and had no reason or motive to fabricate. As such, it can be regarded as a true reflection of the situation as it unfolded and was properly introduced in evidence for the truth of its contents.

67 Even if I found the trial judge erred in admitting the statement as part of the *res gestae*, I would find it admissible on the principled approach to the exception to the hearsay rule.

R. v. BROWN
2015 ONSC 4121, 22 C.R. (7th) 118 (Ont. S.C.J.)

The accused was charged with three counts of robbery. The Crown alleged that she was the getaway driver in a series of robberies committed at gunpoint by a male accomplice about 30 minutes apart at different bus shelters. The alleged victim of the third robbery, B.S., called 911 at 11:29 p.m. on the night in question. He claimed that he had just been robbed at gunpoint by a man who then fled in a minivan driven by a woman. B.S. gave the licence plate number to the 911 operator and police identified the vehicle as a minivan belonging to the accused. The vehicle was located within hours of the 911 call on the street outside the accused's residence, and when it was searched it was found to contain items stolen from the second robbery victim. Despite extensive efforts by police to try to locate him, B.S. could not be found to testify at trial. As an alternative to his viva voce evidence, the Crown sought to introduce evidence of B.S.'s 911 call.

FAIRBURN J.:

[34] 911 calls have been repeatedly admitted under the *res gestae* exception to the hearsay rule. Chief Justice Fraser and Picard J.A. recently catalogued a number of these judgments in *Sylvain* at paragraph 34. As for the Ontario Court of Appeal, in *R. v. Nicholas*, 2004 CanLII 13008 (ON CA), [2004] O.J. No. 725, 184 O.A.C. 139 [*Nicholas*], Abella J.A. (as she then was) endorsed the view that a 911 call could be categorized as falling within the *res gestae* exception. In the circumstances of *Nicholas*, the call had been made within ten minutes of the attack and there was no suggestion of motive for misrepresentation of what happened: *Nicholas* at paras. 88-90.

[35] While not in the context of a 911 call, the Court of Appeal for Ontario has recently dealt with spontaneous utterances in *R. v. Nguyen*, 2015 ONCA 278 (CanLII) at para. 145, where Gillese J.A., for the majority, reinforced this "established exception to the hearsay rule", resting on the understanding that statements made "under pressure and emotional intensity give the guarantee of reliability upon which the rule has traditionally rested".

. . .

[38] I conclude that the 911 call made by Mr. Singh falls within the long-established *res gestae* exception to the hearsay rule. I am satisfied that Mr. Singh made the call right on the heels of having been robbed and the getaway car having left. I make this determination for a few reasons.

[39] First, I find that Mr. Singh's voice, captured on the 911 tape, that I have had the opportunity to listen to, is clearly one of a man who is still suffering

from the shock of what has just happened to him. While he was able to communicate, he was clearly concerned and anxious on the phone. In short, his tone of voice sounds like someone who had just been robbed. Indeed, he used the word "just" on a few occasions during the call. For instance, he told the operator that he was "just standing at the bus stop to go" home when he was attacked. He also made the call from the Pizza Nova, at the spot where he said the vehicle driven by the woman had been parked.

[40] I find that when Mr. Singh told the police during his statement that he had been robbed between 10:20 and 10:25 p.m., he merely misspoke. I note that earlier in his statement he said that it was 11:15 p.m. when he crossed the intersection. When later asked to clarify, likely still under extreme stress (a fact that he confirmed for the officer), he got the time wrong. Under oath at the preliminary inquiry, he confirmed that the time was 11:20 p.m.

[41] I find as a fact that Mr. Singh was robbed after 11:15 p.m. When he told the police that it was between 10:20 and 10:25 p.m., this was nothing more than a slip of the tongue. I find that he made the 911 call almost immediately after the robbery. I find that he was under stress when he made the call and there was no possibility of concoction or fabrication. I find that the 911 call falls squarely within the *res gestae* exception to the hearsay rule and is admissible on this basis.

[42] I also find that the 911 call is admissible under the principled approach to the hearsay rule. The statement is necessary in light of the fact that the declarant is not available for trial.

[43] As for threshold reliability, for the very same reasons that the *res gestae* exception exists, because of the absence of opportunity to concoct, fabricate or invent, I find threshold reliability is met. In addition, I consider the fact that Mr. Singh's statement has external markers of reliability. For instance, the licence plate number that he provided to the 911 operator came back to a vehicle that contained items taken from the second robbery victim, Ms. Dhingra. This fact strengthens my confidence in the threshold reliability of Mr. Singh's statement to the 911 operator.

[44] As for the position that Mr. Singh was inconsistent as between the information he provided in the 911 call and his statement to the police and his preliminary inquiry evidence, I find that to the extent there are inconsistencies, they are minor and of little concern. For instance, while he told the 911 operator that the woman driving the car was 25 to 30 years of age, read in context, I am not at all confident that he was referring to the female driver, as this sentence is followed by reference to the male: "the girl was like, uh, between 25 to 30. And he was wearing the cap and a chain. . . . he was wearing, wearing black, uh . . . black t-shirt." English was not Mr. Singh's first language and he was in a state of shock, as confirmed during the police interview, when

he made the 911 call. Getting a pronoun wrong is perfectly understandable in the circumstances.

[45] Another inconsistency relied upon by counsel was the fact that during the call Mr. Singh said he could not see any other identifying features of the female driver, but during the interview he said that she had shoulder length hair. Again, this is a minor inconsistency that is entirely understandable when taken in context.

[46] The defence ask that I exclude the statement under my residual powers to protect the fairness of the trial: *Khelawon* at para. 49; *R. v. Whittaker*, 2003 CanLII 64249 (ON SC), [2003] O.J. No. 5617, 21 C.R. (6th) 273 (Sup. Ct.) at para. 11. The defence argued that, as Mr. Singh's first language was not English, there was confusion about the timing of the 911 call relative to the robbery and some confusion about answers given to questions put by the operator, such that I should exclude the statement.

[47] I find that the defence argument for exclusion is an argument that goes to ultimate reliability. These are certainly matters to take into account when determining whether Mr. Singh's 911 call is to be relied upon and, if so, what weight should be attributed to the statement. The residual discretion to exclude a hearsay statement, despite it falling within the principled approach, is one that rests largely on assessing the probative value of the statement and whether it is outstripped by its prejudicial impact: *Khelawon* at para. 49. These are the considerations that trial fairness concerns rest on. I find that these concerns are not operative here.

Conclusion

[48] I find that the 911 call is captured by the *res gestae* exception to the hearsay rule. To the extent necessary, I also find that its admission is necessary and that threshold reliability has been met, pursuant to the requirements of admissibility under the principled exception. The call is admissible.

C. VOLUNTARY CONFESSION RULE

1. COMMON LAW PRE-*OICKLE*

In the middle of the sixteenth century, statutes were enacted[235] requiring justices of the peace to take depositions from all witnesses to felony, including the accused. The results of the inquisitorial examination of the accused were transmitted to the judge, and his deposition was read to the jury at the outset of the trial. At the trial as well the accused was frequently questioned by the judge. The practice of questioning an accused at trial

---

[235]   (1554), 1 & 2 Phil. & Mar., c. 13, s. 4; (1555), 2 & 3 Phil. & Mar., c. 10, s. 2. See 1 Stephen, *History of The Criminal Law of England* (1883) at 237-238; and 4 Holdsworth, *History of the English Law*, 3rd. ed. (1945) at 529.

diminished during the seventeenth century, and questioning pre-trial diminished during the eighteenth century. By 1700 questioning at trial had ceased and by the early nineteenth century the pre-trial examination by the justices was limited to the recording of any statements which the accused volunteered. This new practice of preliminary examination was embodied in statute form in 1848,[236] giving us the form of preliminary inquiry now provided for by the Canadian *Criminal Code*:

> Having heard the evidence, do you wish to say anything in answer to the charge? You are not bound to say anything, but whatever you do say will be taken down in writing and may be given in evidence against you at your trial. You must clearly understand that you have nothing to hope from any promise of favour and nothing to fear from any threat that may have been held out to you to induce you to make any admission or confession of guilt, but whatever you now say may be given in evidence against you at your trial notwithstanding the promise or threat.

Two reasons appear to account for the fall-off of judicial questioning. First, the development and growth of professional police which lessened the need for an investigative role by the judicial officers,[237] and, second, the growth of the concept known as the privilege against self-incrimination.

Statements of accused obtained by police interrogation were freely admissible at trial as the admissions of a party. Until the late eighteenth century there does not appear to be any judicial rule foreclosing their receipt.[238] The courts, however, perhaps mindful of the conclusive nature of these admissions and the heavy consequences of a finding of guilt, erected a barrier to their reception, and demanded that admissions of accused persons have an additional assurance of trustworthiness: to be receivable in a criminal prosecution a confession had to be proved voluntary. In 1783 in *R. v. Warickshall*,[239] the accused was charged with possession of stolen goods. She had made a full confession of her guilt, and as a result the goods were found under her bed. The confession had been obtained by promises of favour and the Court refused to admit it. Her counsel then argued

> that as the fact of finding the stolen property in her custody had been obtained through the means of an inadmissible confession, the proof of that fact ought also to be rejected; for otherwise the faith which the prosecutor had pledged would be violated, and the prisoner made the deluded instrument of her own conviction.[240]

But the Court held:

> It is a mistaken notion, that the evidence of confessions and facts which have been obtained from prisoners by promises or threats, is to be rejected from a regard to public faith: no such rule ever prevailed. The idea is novel in theory, and would be as dangerous in practice as it is repugnant to the general principles of criminal law. Confessions are received in evidence, or rejected as

---

[236]   *Jervis's Act*, 11 & 12 Vict., c. 42. See now *Criminal Code*, s. 541.
[237]   See 1 Stephen, *History of Criminal Law, supra* note 235 at 194-200.
[238]   See generally regarding the history of confessions, 3 Wigmore, *Evidence* (Chad. Rev.), s. 817.
[239]   168 E.R. 234 (Crown Cases).
[240]   *Ibid.* at 234.

inadmissible, under a consideration whether they are or are not entitled to credit. A free and voluntary confession is deserving of the highest credit, because it is presumed to flow from the strongest sense of guilt, and therefore it is admitted as proof of the crime to which it refers; but a confession forced from the mind by the flattery of hope, or by the torture of fear, comes in so questionable a shape when it is to be considered as the evidence of guilt, that no credit ought to be given to it; and therefore it is rejected. This principle respecting confessions has no application whatever as to the admission or rejection of facts, whether the knowledge of them be obtained in consequence of an extorted confession, or whether it arises from any other source; for a fact, if it exist at all, must exist invariably in the same manner, whether the confession from which it is derived be in other respects true or false. Facts thus obtained, however, must be fully and satisfactorily proved, without calling in the aid of any part of the confession from which they may have been derived; and the impossibility of admitting any part of the confession as a proof of the fact, clearly shews that the fact may be admitted on other evidence; for as no part of an improper confession can be heard, it can never be legally known whether the fact was derived through the means of such confession or not.[241]

During the nineteenth century, the judicial attitude toward confessions hardened and a great prejudice against them led to the general exclusion of confessions whenever the slightest hope of advantage or fear of prejudice had been held out. For example, in *R. v. Drew,*[242] it was held to be an inducement, rendering the confession inadmissible, to advise the accused:

> . . . not to say anything to prejudice himself, as what he said I should take down, and it would be used for him or against him at his trial,

as, per Coleridge J.:

> I cannot conceive a more direct inducement to a man to make a confession, than telling him that what he says may be used in his favour at the trial.

A few years later in *R. v. Harris,*[243] the accused is advised

> that whatever he said would be . . . used against him,

but the confession was rejected, as, per Maule J.:

> The prisoner was told that *whatever* he said would be taken down and used against him. I cannot say that that did not induce him to say something which he thought might be favourable to him.

The courts began to develop an attitude that *all* police questioning of accused persons, after they had been taken into custody, was wrong. In *R. v. Mick,*[244] Mellor, J. grudgingly received the accused's statement, given following a proper caution, but admonished the police superintendent:

> I think the course you pursued in questioning the prisoner was exceedingly improper. I have considered the matter very much: many Judges would not

---

[241] *Ibid.* at 234-235.
[242] (1837), 173 E.R. 433 (N.P.).
[243] (1844), 1 Cox C.C. 106, and see *R. v. Furley* (1844), 1 Cox C.C. 76. But *contra* see *R. v. Baldry* (1852), 169 E.R. 568 (C.A.).
[244] (1863), 176 E.R. 376.

receive such evidence. The law does not intend you, as a policeman, to investigate cases in that way. I entirely disapprove of the system of police officers examining prisoners. The law has surrounded prisoners with great precautions to prevent confessions being extorted from them, and the magistrates are not allowed to question prisoners, or to ask them what they have to say; and it is not for policemen to do these things. It is assuming the functions of the magistrate without those precautions which the magistrates are required by the law to use, and assuming functions which are entrusted to the magistrates and to them only. The evidence is admissible, but I entirely disapprove of this way of obtaining it.

In *R. v. Gavin*,[245] Smith J. prevented the receipt of one accused's statement against other accused with the statement:

When a prisoner is in custody the police have no right to ask him questions. . . . A prisoner's mouth is closed after he is once given in charge, and he ought not to be asked anything.

The early English decisions in the nineteenth century were by no means unanimous, however, and the courts appear uncertain as to whether the exclusion of confessions is based solely on considerations of reliability, or whether there is an ability to exclude when the questioning is viewed as improper because of a perceived conflict with the accused's privilege against self-incrimination. As late as 1914 in *Ibrahim v. R.*,[246] we see the House of Lords still struggling with the question. The accused in that case, a soldier in the Indian army, was charged with murder. Evidence was admitted at his trial that within 10 or 15 minutes of the murder, the accused, being in custody of the guard, was addressed by his commanding officer: "Why have you done such a senseless act?" to which the accused replied "some three or four days he had been abusing me; without a doubt I killed him". Lord Sumner recognized the oft-quoted classic formula:

It has long been established as a positive rule of English criminal law, that no statement by an accused is admissible in evidence against him unless it is shewn by the prosecution to have been a voluntary statement, in the sense that it has not been obtained from him either by fear of prejudice or hope of advantage exercised or held out by a person in authority. The principle is as old as Lord Hale.[247]

He noted that it was common ground between the parties that in the circumstances receipt of the statement did not breach the rule, but felt it necessary to consider the objection that receipt was foreclosed simply because the prisoner's answer was preceded by and made in answer to a question, and that the question was put by a person in authority and the answer given by a man in his custody. Lord Sumner reviewed the authorities and concluded:

The English law is still unsettled, strange as it may seem, since the point is one that constantly occurs in criminal trials. Many judges, in their discretion, exclude such evidence, for they fear that nothing less than the exclusion of all such

---

[245]   (1885), 15 Cox C.C. 656.
[246]   [1914] A.C. 599 (P.C.).
[247]   *Ibid.* at 609.

statements can prevent improper questioning of prisoners by removing the inducement to resort to it. This consideration does not arise in the present case. Others, less tender to the prisoner or more mindful of the balance of decided authority, would admit such statements, nor would the Court of Criminal Appeal quash the conviction thereafter obtained, if no substantial miscarriage of justice had occurred. If, then, a learned judge, after anxious consideration of the authorities, decides in accordance with what is at any rate a "probable opinion" of the present law, if it is not actually the better opinion, it appears to their Lordships that his conduct is the very reverse of that "violation of the principles of natural justice" which has been said to be the ground for advising His Majesty's interference in a criminal matter. If, as appears even on the line of authorities which the trial judge did not follow, the matter is one for the judge's discretion, depending largely on his view of the impropriety of the questioner's conduct and the general circumstances of the case, their Lordships think, as will hereafter be seen, that in the circumstances of this case his discretion is not shewn to have been exercised improperly.

Having regard to the particular position in which their Lordships stand to criminal proceedings, they do not propose to intimate what they think the rule of English law ought to be, much as it is to be desired that the point should be settled by authority, so far as a general rule can be laid down where circumstances must so greatly vary. That must be left to a Court which exercises, as their Lordships do not, the revising functions of a general Court of Criminal Appeal.[248]

In 1966 in *Commissioners of Customs v. Harz*,[249] Lord Reid reviewed the authorities and concluded:

I do not think that it is possible to reconcile all the very numerous judicial statements on rejection of confessions but two lines of thought appear to underlie them: first, that a statement made in response to a threat or promise may be untrue or at least untrustworthy: and, secondly, that *nemo tenetur seipsum prodere*. It is true that many of the so-called inducements have been so vague that no reasonable man would have been influenced by them, but one must remember that not all accused are reasonable men or women: they may be very ignorant and terrified by the predicament in which they find themselves. So it may have been right to err on the safe side.

The question was squarely put to the Supreme Court of Canada in *R. v. Wray*.[250] The accused was charged with murder. The accused gave a statement to the police which ended as follows:

Q. What happened to the gun?

A. I threw it in the swamp.

Q. Where?

A. Near Omemee.

Q. Will you try and show us the spot?

---

[248] *Ibid.* at 614.
[249] [1967] 1 A.C. 760 (H.L.) at 820.
[250] (1970), 11 D.L.R. (3d) 673 (S.C.C.) at 677.

A. Yes.

Q. Is there anything else you wish to add to this John?

A. Not now thank you.

The accused directed the police to the area where the rifle was found and ballistic evidence matched the bullet from the victim's body to the gun. After a lengthy *voir dire* the trial judge ruled the accused's statement was involuntary and hence legally inadmissible.[251] The prosecution then wished to introduce into evidence the accused's involvement in finding the murder weapon and relied on *R. v. St. Lawrence* where McRuer C.J.H.C. had said:

> Where the discovery of the fact confirms the confession — that is, where the confession must be taken to be true by reason of the discovery of the fact — then that part of the confession that is confirmed by the discovery of the fact is admissible, but further than that no part of the confession is admissible.[252]

The trial judge in *Wray* purported to exercise a discretion to disallow this evidence and directed a verdict of acquittal. The Ontario Court of Appeal, while recognizing the validity of the *St. Lawrence* rule, declined to disturb his decision, saying:

> In our view, a trial Judge has a discretion to reject evidence, even of substantial weight, if he considers that its admission would be unjust or unfair to the accused or calculated to bring the administration of justice into disrepute, the exercise of such discretion, of course, to depend upon the particular facts before him. Cases where to admit certain evidence would be calculated to bring the administration of justice into disrepute will be rare, but we think the discretion of a trial Judge extends to such cases.[253]

The Supreme Court of Canada reversed and directed a new trial. Martland J. reasoned:

> This development of the idea of a general discretion to exclude admissible evidence is not warranted by the authority on which it purports to be based. . . . the exercise of a discretion by the trial Judge arises only if the admission of the evidence would operate unfairly. The allowance of admissible evidence relevant to the issue before the Court and of substantial probative value may operate unfortunately for the accused, but not unfairly. It is only the allowance of evidence gravely prejudicial to the accused, the admissibility of which is tenuous, and whose probative force in relation to the main issue before the Court is trifling, which can be said to operate unfairly.[254]

In a separate concurring opinion, Judson J. wrote:

> I agree . . . that we ought not to overrule *R. v. St. Lawrence*. This case reviews the law which has stood since *R. v. Warwickshall*, to the effect that even if a confession is inadmissible in evidence, nevertheless facts which become known by means of this confession may be proved on behalf of the prosecution. . . .

---

[251] For a detailed description of how the confession was obtained see Ontario L.R.C. *Report on Evidence* (1976) at 74-90.

[252] [1949] O.R. 215 (H.C.) at 228. Approved in *R. v. Myrby* (1975), 28 C.C.C. (2d) 395 (Alta. C.A.).

[253] [1970] 2 O.R. 3 (Ont. C.A.) at 4.

[254] *Supra* note 250 at 689-690.

The theory for the rejection of confessions is that if they are obtained under certain conditions, they are untrustworthy. This theory has no application whatever to incontrovertible facts, such as the finding of articles. . . .

How are the facts relating to the discovery of the weapon to be put before the jury? The minimum in this case is the account of Wray's trip from Toronto in the company of police officers to a swamp 15 miles west of the scene of the crime and the search for and the discovery of the weapon under the direction of the accused.[255]

The Supreme Court here appears then to regard the policy underlying the confession rule as rooted solely in concern for trustworthiness; if the confession is confirmed as true by tangible evidence, there is no need to exclude.

The "rule" forecloses receipt of confessions unless they are "voluntary". What is the meaning of "voluntary"? The *Shorter Oxford Dictionary* defines voluntary as

(a) Of feelings, etc.: Arising or developing in the mind without external constraint; purely spontaneous.

(b) Of actions: Performed or done of one's own free will, impulse, or choice, not constrained, prompted, or suggested by another.

Clearly the courts are not using the word in this sense. In *Boudreau v. R.,*[256] Rand J. had written:

. . . the rule is directed against the danger of improperly instigated or induced or coerced admissions. It is the doubt cast on the truth of the statement arising from the circumstances in which it is made that gives rise to the rule. What the statement should be is that of a man free in volition from the compulsions or inducements of authority and what is sought is assurance that that is the case. The underlying and controlling question then remains: Is the statement freely and voluntarily made?

In *R. v. Fitton,*[257] Pickup C.J.O. interpreted this passage:

In my opinion, the Crown does not discharge the onus resting upon it by merely adducing oral testimony showing that an incriminating statement made by an accused person was not induced by a promise or by fear of prejudice or hope of advantage. That statement of the rule of law is too narrow. The admissions must not have been "improperly instigated or induced or coerced": per Rand J. in *Boudreau v. The King, supra*. The admissions must be self-impelled, and the statement must be the statement of a man "free in volition from the compulsions or inducements of authority". The statement must be "freely and voluntarily made".

---

[255] *Ibid.* at 692, 695 [citations omitted]. Compare the attitude of the Court in *R. v. Warickshall* (1783), 168 E.R. 234 regarding evidence of accused's involvement in the finding of facts.

[256] [1949] 3 D.L.R. 81 (S.C.C.) at 88.

[257] [1956] O.R. 696 (C.A.) at 714.

R. v. SWEENEY
(2000), 36 C.R. (5th) 198, 148 C.C.C. (3d) 247 (Ont. C.A.)

The accused was charged with robbery, assault with a weapon, possession of a weapon for a purpose dangerous to the public peace and possession of a restricted weapon. The police had prepared a warrant to search the accused's family's home. A police officer told the accused that the police would "trash" his mother's home if he did not tell them where the weapon was located. The accused told the officer that the weapon was in a box in his mother's closet and drew a diagram. The police executed the warrant and found the weapon in the location indicated on the diagram. The trial judge held that the accused's statements to the police officer were induced and involuntary, but admissible on the authority of the rule in *R. v. St. Lawrence*. The accused was convicted and appealed.

ROSENBERG J.A.:

. . .

I have reached the following conclusions concerning the appellant's appeal from conviction:

(a) Admitting the involuntary confession in accordance with the common law St. Lawrence rule violated the appellant's rights under s. 7 of the Charter.

(b) In view of the violation of the appellant's s. 7 rights, the entire confession should have been excluded under s. 24(2) of the Charter.

(c) The common law St. Lawrence rule must be modified in light of subsequent decisions of the Supreme Court of Canada to give the trial judge a discretion to exclude those parts of the confession confirmed by the finding of the evidence.

(d) It would only be in the most exceptional circumstances that a trial judge would be entitled to exercise a discretion in favour of admitting the involuntary confession and such circumstances do not exist in this case.

(e) Without the appellant's confession there is no evidence upon which a properly instructed jury could convict and the appeal must be allowed, the convictions quashed and acquittals entered.

What is the definition of "person in authority"?

R. v. HODGSON
(1998), 127 C.C.C. (3d) 449, 18 C.R. (5th) 135, [1998] 2 S.C.R. 449

The accused was charged with acts of sexual assault, alleged to have occurred when he babysat the complainant. The complainant did not tell anyone about the incidents for several years. When the allegations were revealed, the complainant, her mother, her father and her stepfather went to the accused's place of employment and confronted him. They all testified that the accused confessed to having sexually assaulted the complainant on several occasions, that the accused said he was sorry, and that he said he knew it would catch up to him. The complainant's mother went to call the police, and when she returned she struck the accused. At some point, the complainant's father held a knife to the accused's back in order to prevent the accused from leaving before the police arrived. The accused testified that he was stunned, shocked and upset by the confrontation, but that he was neither frightened nor threatened. The accused raised no objection to the admission of the confession evidence at trial.

The trial judge relied on this evidence and convicted the accused. The Ontario Court of Appeal dismissed the accused's appeal.

CORY J., (LAMER C.J.C., GONTHIER, MCLACHLIN, IACOBUCCI, MAJOR and BINNIE JJ. concurring):—

. . .

The basic issue in this appeal is whether the trial judge erred in failing to hold a *voir dire* of his own motion to test the voluntariness of certain out-of-court statements made by the accused before admitting them. In order to resolve this issue, it is appropriate to consider whether the confessions rule should continue to apply only to statements made to persons in authority, or whether it should be expanded so as to capture the out-of-court statements made by the accused in this case. It will therefore be helpful to begin by examining the history of the confessions rule generally, and the person in authority requirement in particular, in order to understand the purpose and function of the rule in the criminal law.

A.   The Confessions Rule and its Relation to the Person in Authority Requirement

Evidence of a confession has always been accorded great weight by triers of fact. This is a natural manifestation of human experience. It is because of the tremendous significance attributed to confessions and the innate realization that they could be obtained by improper means that the circumstances surrounding a confession have for centuries been carefully scrutinized to determine whether it should be admitted. A confession is not excluded, however, simply because of the risk that a conviction may result, but because of the greater risk that the conviction will be unfairly obtained and unjust. The unfairness of admitting a confession has historically been addressed by a consideration of two factors. First, the voluntariness of the statement; and second, the status of the receiver of the statement, that is to say, whether the receiver was a person in authority.

. . .

The person in authority requirement generally refers to anyone formally engaged in "the arrest, detention, examination or prosecution of the accused". This definition may be enlarged to encompass persons who are deemed to be persons in authority as a result of the circumstances surrounding the making of the statement. For the moment, however, let us consider the purpose of each of these factors as they pertain to the admissibility of statements of the accused.

. . .

The person in authority requirement is properly seen as an integral component of the confessions rule. The emphasis on voluntariness has two main effects: it both avoids the unfairness of a conviction based on a confession that might be unreliable, and has a deterrent effect on the use of coercive tactics. This deterrent effect is properly focused upon the prosecutorial authority of the state, not the personal authority of private individuals. It cannot be forgotten that it is the nature of the authority exerted by the state that might prompt an involuntary statement. As Estey J. stated in Rothman, supra, at pp. 650-51, "their very authority might, by promise or threat, express or implied, produce a statement whether or not the accused was truly willing to speak". In other words, it is the fear of reprisal or hope of leniency that persons in authority may hold out and which is associated with their official status that may render a statement involuntary. The rule is generally not concerned with conversations between private citizens that might indicate guilt, as these conversations would not be influenced or affected by the coercive power of the state. This limitation is appropriate since most criminal investigations are undertaken by the state, and it is then that an accused is most vulnerable to state coercion.

On a practical level, the Crown would obviously face an overwhelming burden if it had to establish the voluntariness of every statement against interest made by an accused to any person. See the Law Reform Commission of Canada, Report on Evidence (1975), at p. 62. In particular, as the intervener the Attorney General of Canada notes, the elimination of the person in authority requirement would have serious consequences for undercover police work and for the admissibility of wiretap evidence, where the identity of the receiver of the accused's statement is often unknown. For example, if the Crown were to intercept a phone call between an accused and a confederate who is senior to him in a criminal hierarchy, the Crown would obviously have difficulty tendering the requisite evidence if it were forced to prove beyond a reasonable doubt that the statements were made "without fear of prejudice or hope of advantage". Moreover, all statements to undercover police officers would become subject to the confessions rule, even though the accused was completely unaware of their status and, at the time he made the statement, would never have considered the undercover officers to be persons in authority.

Practical considerations alone lead to the conclusion that the person in authority requirement should remain a part of the confessions rule. Yet there can be no doubt that there may well be great unfairness suffered by the accused when an involuntary confession obtained as a result of violence or credible threats of imminent violence by a private individual is admitted into evidence. . . . However, it is the sort of change which should be studied by Parliament and remedied by enactment. . . . Because of the very real possibility of a resulting miscarriage of justice and the fundamental unfairness of admitting statements coerced by the violence of private individuals, I would hope that the study will not be long postponed.

I would suggest that in circumstances where a statement of the accused is obtained by a person who is not a person in authority by means of degrading treatment such as violence or threats of violence, a clear direction should be given to the jury as to the dangers of relying upon it. The direction might include words such as these: "A statement obtained as a result of inhuman or degrading treatment or the use of violence or threats of violence may not be the manifestation of the exercise of a free will to confess. Rather, it may result solely from the oppressive treatment or or fear of such treatment. If it does, the statement may very well be either unreliable or untrue. Therefore if you conclude that the statement was obtained by such oppression very little if any weight should be attached to it." However, if a private individual resorts to violence or threatens violence after the statement has been made, this conduct will not as a general rule be a factor affecting the voluntariness of the statement and the suggested direction will not be needed.

B.   Limits of the Person in Authority Requirement

31 It has been seen that the person in authority requirement is grounded in the underlying rationales for the confessions rule, and as a result it should remain part of the rule. Consideration must now be given as to who should come within the designation "person in authority".

32 "Person in authority" typically refers to those persons formally engaged in the arrest, detention, examination or prosecution of the accused: see *A.B.*, *supra*, at p. 26. However, it may take on a broader meaning. Canadian courts first considered the meaning of "person in authority" in *R. v. Todd* (1901), 4 C.C.C. 514 (Man. K.B.). In that case, the accused made a statement to two men he believed to be fellow prisoners, but who were in fact acting as agents of the police. It was held, at pp. 526-27, that:

> A person in authority means, generally speaking, anyone who has authority or control over the accused or over the proceedings or the prosecution against him. . . . [T]he authority that the accused knows such persons to possess may well be supposed in the majority of instances both to animate his hopes of favour on the one hand and on the other to inspire him with awe, and so in some degree to overcome the powers of his mind. . . . [Emphasis added.]

Thus, from its earliest inception in Canadian law, the question as to who should be considered as a person in authority depended on the extent to which the accused believed the person could influence or control the proceedings against him or her. The question is therefore approached from the viewpoint of the accused. See also *R. v. Roadhouse* (1933), 61 C.C.C. 191 (B.C. C.A.), at p. 192.

33 The subjective approach to the person in authority requirement has been adopted in this Court. See *Rothman, supra*, at p. 663. The approach adopted by McIntyre J.A. (as he then was) in *R. v. Berger* (1975), 27 C.C.C. (2d) 357 (B.C.C.A.), at pp. 385-86 is, in my view, a clear statement of the law:

> The law is settled that a person in authority is a person concerned with the prosecution who, in the opinion of the accused, can influence the course of the

prosecution. The test to be applied in deciding whether statements made to persons connected in such a way with the prosecution are voluntary is subjective. In other words what did the accused think? Whom did he think he was talking to? . . . Was he under the impression that the failure to speak to this person, because of his power to influence the prosecution, would result in prejudice or did he think that a statement would draw some benefit or reward? If his mind was free of such impressions the person receiving this statement would not be considered a person in authority and the statement would be admissible.

34 However, to this statement I would add that the accused's belief that he is speaking to a person in authority must also be reasonable, in the context of the circumstances surrounding the making of the statement. If the accused were delusional or had no reasonable basis for the belief that the receiver of the statement could affect the course of the prosecution against him, the receiver should not be considered a person in authority. Since the person in authority requirement is aimed at controlling coercive state conduct, the test for a person in authority should not include those whom the accused unreasonably believes to be acting on behalf of the state. Thus, where the accused speaks out of fear of reprisal or hope of advantage because he reasonably believes the person receiving the statement is acting as an agent of the police or prosecuting authorities and could therefore influence or control the proceedings against him or her, then the receiver of the statement is properly considered a person in authority. In other words, the evidence must disclose not only that the accused subjectively believed the receiver of the statement to be in a position to control the proceedings against the accused, but must also establish an objectively reasonable basis for that belief. For example, if the evidence discloses a relationship of agency or close collaboration between the receiver of the statement and the police or prosecution, and that relationship was known to the accused, the receiver of the statement may be considered a person in authority. In those circumstances the Crown must prove beyond a reasonable doubt that the statement was made voluntarily.

35 Over the years, the courts have determined when and in what circumstances a person will be deemed a person in authority for the purposes of the confessions rule. See, e.g., *R. v. Trenholme* (1920), 35 C.C.C. 341 (Que. K.B.) (complainant's father was held to be a person in authority where he has control over the prosecution of the accused); *R. v. Wilband*, [1967] S.C.R. 14 (psychiatrist is not a person in authority where he cannot control or influence the course of the proceedings); *R. v. Downey* (1976), 32 C.C.C. (2d) 511 (N.S.S.C.A.D.) (victim is a person in authority if the accused believed that the victim had control over the proceedings); *A.B., supra* (a parent is not, in law, a person in authority if there is no close connection between the decision to call the authorities and the inducement to a child to make a statement); *R. v. Sweryda* (1987), 34 C.C.C. (3d) 325 (Alta. C.A.)(a social worker is a person in authority if the accused knew the social worker was investigating allegations of child abuse and believed it could lead to his arrest). These cases have not departed from the governing rule that defines a person in authority in relation to the accused's perception of the receiver's involvement with the investigation

or prosecution of the crime nor have these decisions defined a person in authority solely in terms of the personal authority that a person might wield in relation to the accused. Moreover, in concluding that the receiver of the statement was a person in authority, the courts have consistently found the accused believed the receiver was allied with the state authorities and could influence the investigation or prosecution against the accused.

36 The important factor to note in all of these cases is that there is no catalogue of persons, beyond a peace officer or prison guard, who are automatically considered a person in authority solely by virtue of their status. A parent, doctor, teacher or employer all may be found to be a person in authority if the circumstances warrant, but their status, or the mere fact that they may wield some personal authority over the accused, is not sufficient to establish them as persons in authority for the purposes of the confessions rule. As the intervener the Attorney General of Canada observed, the person in authority requirement has evolved in a manner that avoids a formalistic or legalistic approach to the interactions between ordinary citizens. Instead, it requires a case-by-case consideration of the accused's belief as to the ability of the receiver of the statement to influence the prosecution or investigation of the crime. That is to say, the trial judge must determine whether the accused reasonably believed the receiver of the statement was acting on behalf of the police or prosecuting authorities. This view of the person in authority requirement remains unchanged.

37 Finally, something must be said about the respective burdens which must be borne by the accused and the Crown on a *voir dire* to determine whether a statement of the accused to a person in authority should be admitted. The Crown, of course, bears the burden of proving beyond a reasonable doubt that the statement was made voluntarily. However, in relation to the person in authority requirement, the evidence required to establish whether or not a person should be deemed a person in authority will often lie primarily with the accused. The accused therefore must bear some burden in relation to this aspect of the confessions rule. The burden should be an evidential and not a persuasive one. See, e.g., *R. v. Scott* (1984), 1 O.A.C. 397, at p. 399. John Sopinka, Sidney N. Lederman and Alan W. Bryant, in *The Law of Evidence in Canada* (1992), at pp. 56-57, explain the difference between the two burdens:

> The term evidential burden means that a party has the responsibility to insure that there is sufficient evidence of the existence or non-existence of a fact or of an issue on the record to pass the threshold test for that particular fact or issue. . . . In contrast, the term legal burden of proof means that a party has an obligation to prove or disprove a fact or issue to the criminal or civil standard. The failure to convince the trier of fact to the appropriate standard means that party will lose on that issue.

The evidential burden on an accused in a criminal case is described as follows (at p. 138):

Where an evidential burden for an issue rests on the defendant in a criminal case, for example self-defence, the accused has the obligation to ensure that there is some evidence on the record to make it a live issue. The evidence necessary to satisfy an evidential burden may arise in the case for the Crown or the defence.

38 In the vast majority of cases, the accused will meet this evidential burden by showing the accused's knowledge of the relationship between the receiver of the statement and the police or prosecuting authorities. For example, the fact that the statement was made to a police officer who was in uniform or identified himself or herself as a peace officer will satisfy the accused's evidential burden in relation to the person in authority requirement. See, e.g., *Morris v. The Queen*, [1979] 2 S.C.R. 1041, at p. 1066. Once the accused satisfies this evidential burden, the ultimate burden of proof rests with the Crown. See R. *v. McKenzie*, [1965] 3 C.C.C. 6 (Alta. S.C.A.D.), at p. 28. In *R. v. Postman* (1977), 3 A.R. 524, at p. 542, the Alberta Supreme Court, Appellate Division held, correctly in my view, that where a witness is not prima facie a person in authority (in that case, a doctor), "it is open to defence counsel to challenge the prima facie case and require evidence to be given to determine the facts of the matter". Thus, once the defence discharges its burden and establishes that there is an evidential basis to the claim that the receiver of a statement made by the accused is a person in authority, the burden shifts to the Crown to establish beyond a reasonable doubt either that the receiver is not a person in authority, or, if this burden cannot be discharged, that the statement was made voluntarily.

39 The receiver's status as a person in authority arises only if the accused had knowledge of that status. If the accused cannot show that he or she had knowledge of the receiver's status (as, for example, in the case of an undercover police officer) or close relationship to the authorities (as in the case of persons acting on behalf of the state), the inquiry pertaining to the receiver as a person in authority must end. It is therefore appropriate to consider at the outset the reasonable belief of the accused. It may not be useful to have the trial judge undertake a full analysis of the objective relationship between the receiver of the statement and the authorities, as Justice L'Heureux-Dubé suggests (para. 83), only to have those findings vitiated if the accused is later found to have no knowledge of this relationship. In addition, it is important to recognize that focusing the trial judge's inquiry on the reasonable belief of the accused accords with the allocation of the burden of proof on the voir dire.

[Justice Cory then addressed the issue of when a trial judge is obligated to hold a *voir dire* where defence counsel does not object to the admissibility of the accused's statement.]

IV. Summary

48 Perhaps it may be of some assistance to set out in summary form the applicable principles pertaining to the admission of statements made by the accused to persons in authority and some of the factors to be taken into consideration with regard to them.

1. The rule which is still applicable in determining the admissibility of a statement made by an accused to a person in authority is that it must have been made voluntarily and must be the product of an operating mind.

2. The rule is based upon two fundamentally important concepts: the need to ensure the reliability of the statement and the need to ensure fairness by guarding against improper coercion by the state. This results in the requirement that the admission must not be obtained by either threats or inducements.

3. The rule is applicable when the accused makes a statement to a person in authority. Though no absolute definition of "person in authority" is necessary or desirable, it typically refers to those formally engaged in the arrest, detention, examination or prosecution of the accused. Thus, it would apply to person such as police officers and prison officials or guards. When the statement of the accused is made to a police officer or prison guard a *voir dire* should be held to determine its admissibility as a voluntary statement, unless the *voir dire* is waived by counsel for the accused.

4. Those persons whom the accused reasonably believes are acting on behalf of the police or prosecuting authorities and could therefore influence or control the proceedings against him or her may also be persons in authority. That question will have to be determined on a case-by-case basis.

5. The issue as to who is a person in authority must be resolved by considering it subjectively from the viewpoint of the accused. There must, however, be a reasonable basis for the accused's belief that the person hearing the statement was a person in authority.

6. The issue will not normally arise in relation to undercover police officers. This is because the issue must be approached from the viewpoint of the accused. On that basis, undercover police officers will not usually be viewed by the accused as persons in authority.

7. If it is contended that the recipient of the statement was a person in authority in the eyes of the accused then the defence must raise the issue with the trial judge. This is appropriate for it is only the accused who can know that the statement was made to someone regarded by the accused as a person in authority.

8. On the ensuing *voir dire* the accused will have the evidential burden of demonstrating that there is a valid issue for consideration. If the accused meets the burden, the Crown will then have the persuasive burden of demonstrating beyond a reasonable doubt that the receiver of the statement was not a person in authority or if it is found that he or she was a person in authority, that the statement of the accused was made voluntarily.

9. In extremely rare cases the evidence adduced during a trial may be such that it should alert the trial judge that the issue as to whether the receiver of a statement made by an accused was a person in authority should be explored by way of voir dire. In those cases, which must be extremely rare in light of the obligation of the accused to raise the issue, the trial judge must of his or her own motion direct a voir dire, subject, of course, to waiver of the *voir dire* by counsel for the accused.

10. The duty of the trial judge to hold a *voir dire* of his or her own motion will only arise in those rare cases where the evidence, viewed objectively, is sufficient to alert the trial judge of the need to hold a *voir dire* to determine if the receiver of the statement of the accused was, in the circumstances, a person in authority.

11. If the trial judge is satisfied that the receiver of the statement was not a person in authority but that the statement of the accused was obtained by reprehensible coercive tactics, such as violence or credible threats of violence, then a direction should be given to the jury. The jury should be instructed that if they conclude that the statement was obtained by coercion, they should be cautious about accepting it, and that little if any weight should be attached to it.

Justice Cory then held that there was no evidence in the case that the family members of the complainant were persons in authority so as to trigger the trial judge's obligation to hold a *voir dire*:

V. Application to this Appeal

49 The appellant contends that the fact that the confession was made to the complainant and her immediate family should have alerted the trial judge to the need for a *voir dire* since they are capable of being persons in authority for the purpose of the confessions rule. It is true the complainant and her family members are capable of being persons in authority. Indeed, anyone is capable of being a person in authority where a person becomes sufficiently involved with the arrest, detention, examination or prosecution of an accused, and the accused believes that the person may influence the process against him or her. It does not follow that simply because it has been held, in the circumstances presented in other cases, that a family member was a person in authority, that the trial judge should have been alerted to the need for a voir dire. Virtually any category of person—parents of the accused, parents of the complainant, teachers, psychiatrists, physicians—may, in light of the particular evidence adduced, be considered to be a person in authority. As the respondent observed, to hold that the trial judge committed an error on the basis that the receiver of the confession is merely capable of being a person in authority is to require a *voir dire* (or waiver) for every statement against interest made by every accused person to anyone. It cannot be forgotten that it is the accused who is in the best position to demonstrate that the receiver of the statement was in his or her eyes a person in authority.

50 In this case, the evidence at trial did not disclose any evidence that was sufficient to trigger the trial judge's obligation to hold a voir dire. The confrontation at the appellant's workplace was first described by the complainant. She testified as to the events leading up to the confrontation. She stated (1) that her mother questioned her about whether she was pregnant and whether she had had intercourse; (2) that in the course of that conversation, she told her mother that the appellant had sexually assaulted her; (3) that her mother telephoned her father; (4) that she and her mother visited a walk-in clinic in Mississauga where it was confirmed that the complainant was pregnant (her boyfriend at the time was the father); (5) that the complainant, together with her mother, father, stepfather and cousin went to confront the appellant. The complainant then related, without objection by the defence, the statements made by the appellant. Thus, when the statements were admitted into evidence, there was nothing to suggest that the complainant or her family members had spoken to the police or anyone else in authority or were even considering making a complaint. Similarly, there was nothing to suggest that the appellant subjectively believed the complainant's family to have control over criminal proceedings. In those circumstances, the trial judge cannot be said to have committed an error by failing to hold a *voir dire* on his own motion.

Appeal dismissed.

Parliament has not acted on Justice Cory's recommendation. See also *R. v. Wells*[258] where the Court recognized a power to exclude a confession by an accused to a person not in authority obtained by oppression and violence.

2. REVISED APROACH IN *R. v. OICKLE*

R. v. OICKLE
[2000] 2 S.C.R. 3, 36 C.R. (5th) 129, 147 C.C.C. (3d) 321

During a police investigation into a series of fires, the accused agreed to submit to a polygraph. The test was audiotaped. The fires, which appeared to be deliberately set, involved four buildings and a car (which belonged to Oickle's fiancée). He was a member of the local volunteer fire department and had responded to each of the fires. At 3:00 p.m., the accused was informed of his right to silence his rights, to counsel, and his ability to leave at any time. He was also informed that while the interpretation of the polygraph results was not admissible, anything he said was admissible. At the end of the test, about 5:00 p.m., the officer conducting the test informed the accused that he had failed. The accused was reminded of his rights and questioned for one hour. At 6:30 p.m., a second officer questioned the accused and, after 30 to 40 minutes, the accused confessed to setting fire to his fiancée's car

---

[258]   (2003), 12 C.R. (6th) 185, 174 C.C.C. (3d) 301 (B.C. C.A.).

and provided the police with a statement. He appeared emotionally distraught at this time. The accused was arrested and warned of his rights. At the police station, he was placed in an interview room equipped with videotaping facilities where he was questioned about the other fires. Around 8:30 p.m. and 9:15 p.m., the accused indicated that he was tired and wanted to go home. He was informed that he was under arrest and he could call a lawyer but that he could not go home. A third officer took over the interrogation at 9:52 p.m. He questioned the accused until about 11:00 p.m., at which time the accused confessed to setting seven of the eight fires. The accused was then seen crying with his head in his hands. The police then took a written statement from the accused. He was placed in a cell to sleep at 2:45 a.m. At 6:00 a.m., a police officer noticed that the accused was awake and asked whether he would agree to a re-enactment. On the tape of the re-enactment, the accused was informed of his rights and was advised that he could stop the re-enactment at any time. The police drove the accused to the various fire scenes, where he described how he had set each fire. The accused was charged with seven counts of arson. The trial judge ruled on a *voir dire* that the accused's statements, including the video re-enactment, were voluntary and admissible, and subsequently convicted him on all counts. The Nova Scotia Court of Appeal (per Cromwell J.A.) excluded the confessions and entered an acquittal.

IACOBUCCI J. (L'HEUREUX-DUBÉ, MCLACHLIN, MAJOR, BASTARACHE and BINNIE JJ. concurring): —

This appeal requires this Court to rule on the common law limits on police interrogation. Specifically, we are asked to decide whether the police improperly induced the respondent's confessions through threats or promises, an atmosphere of oppression, or any other tactics that could raise a reasonable doubt as to the voluntariness of his confessions. I conclude that they did not. The trial judge's determination that the confessions at stake in this appeal were voluntarily given should not have been disturbed on appeal, and accordingly the appeal should be allowed.

In this case, the police conducted a proper interrogation. Their questioning, while persistent and often accusatorial, was never hostile, aggressive, or intimidating. They repeatedly offered the accused food and drink. They allowed him to use the bathroom upon request. Before his first confession and subsequent arrest, they repeatedly told him that he could leave at any time. In this context, the alleged inducements offered by the police do not raise a reasonable doubt as to the confessions' voluntariness. Nor do I find any fault with the role played by the polygraph test in this case. While the police admittedly exaggerated the reliability of such devices, the tactic of inflating the reliability of incriminating evidence is a common, and generally unobjectionable one. Whether standing alone, or in combination with the other mild inducements used in this appeal, it does not render the confessions involuntary.

. . .

Two Elements of the Rule

As indicated by McLachlin J. . . . in *R. v. Hebert*, [1990] 2 S.C.R. 151, there are two main strands to this Court's jurisprudence under the confessions rule. One approach is narrow, excluding statements only where the police held out explicit threats or promises to the accused. The definitive statement of this approach came in *Ibrahim v. The King*, [1914] A.C. 599 (P.C.), at p. 609:

> It has long been established as a positive rule of English criminal law, that no statement by an accused is admissible in evidence against him unless it is shewn by the prosecution to have been a voluntary statement, in the sense that it has not been obtained from him either by fear of prejudice or hope of advantage exercised or held out by a person in authority.

This Court adopted the "*Ibrahim* rule" in *Prosko v. The King* (1922), 63 S.C.R. 226, and subsequently applied it in cases like *Boudreau v. The King*, [1949] S.C.R. 262, *Fitton*, supra, *R. v. Wray*, [1971] S.C.R. 272, and *Rothman v. The Queen*, [1981] 1 S.C.R. 640.

The *Ibrahim* rule gives the accused only "a negative right — the right not to be tortured or coerced into making a statement by threats or promises held out by a person who is and whom he subjectively believes to be a person in authority": *Hebert*, supra, at p. 165. However, *Hebert* also recognized a second, "much broader" approach, according to which "[t]he absence of violence, threats and promises by the authorities does not necessarily mean that the resulting statement is voluntary, if the necessary mental element of deciding between alternatives is absent". . . .

While not always followed, McLachlin J. noted . . . that this aspect of the confessions rule "persists as part of our fundamental notion of procedural fairness". This approach is most evident in the so-called "operating mind" doctrine, developed by this Court in *Ward*, supra, *Horvath v. The Queen*, [1979] 2 S.C.R. 376, and *R. v. Whittle*, [1994] 2 S.C.R. 914. In those cases the Court made "a further investigation of whether the statements were freely and voluntarily made even if no hope of advantage or fear of prejudice could be found": *Ward*, supra, at p. 40. The "operating mind" doctrine dispelled once and for all the notion that the confessions rule is concerned solely with whether or not the confession was induced by any threats or promises.

These cases focused not just on reliability, but on voluntariness conceived more broadly. None of the reasons in *Ward* or *Horvath* ever expressed any doubts about the reliability of the confessions in issue. Instead, they focused on the lack of voluntariness, whether the cause was shock (*Ward*), hypnosis (*Horvath*), or "complete emotional disintegration" (*Horvath*). Similarly, in *Hobbins v. The Queen*, [1982] 1 S.C.R. 553, at pp. 556-57, Laskin C.J. noted that in determining the voluntariness of a confession, courts should be alert to the coercive effect of an "atmosphere of oppression", even though there was "no inducement held out of hope of advantage or fear of prejudice, and absent any threats of violence or actual violence"; see also *R. v. Liew*, [1999] 3 S.C.R. 227, at para. 37. Clearly, the confessions rule embraces more than the narrow *Ibrahim* formulation; instead, it is concerned with voluntariness, broadly understood.

The Charter Era

The Charter constitutionalized a new set of protections for accused persons, contained principally in ss. 7 to 14 thereof. The entrenchment of these rights answered certain questions that had once been asked under the aegis of the confessions rule. For example, while the confessions rule did not exclude statements elicited by undercover officers in jail cells (*Rothman*, supra), such confessions can violate the Charter: see *Hebert*, supra, and *R. v. Broyles*, [1991] 3 S.C.R. 595.

In *Hebert*, McLachlin J. interpreted the right to silence in light of existing common law protections, such as the confessions rule. However, given the focus of that decision on defining constitutional rights, it did not decide the inverse question: namely, the scope of the common law rules in light of the Charter. One possible view is that the Charter subsumes the common law rules.

But I do not believe that this view is correct, for several reasons. First, the confessions rule has a broader scope than the Charter. For example, the protections of s. 10 only apply "on arrest or detention". By contrast, the confessions rule applies whenever a person in authority questions a suspect. Second, the Charter applies a different burden and standard of proof from that under the confessions rule. Under the former, the burden is on the accused to show, on a balance of probabilities, a violation of constitutional rights. Under the latter, the burden is on the prosecution to show beyond a reasonable doubt that the confession was voluntary. Finally, the remedies are different. The Charter excludes evidence obtained in violation of its provisions under s. 24(2) only if admitting the evidence would bring the administration of justice into disrepute: see *R. v. Stillman*, [1997] 1 S.C.R. 607, *R. v. Collins*, [1987] 1 S.C.R. 265, and the related jurisprudence. By contrast, a violation of the confessions rule always warrants exclusion.

These various differences illustrate that the Charter is not an exhaustive catalogue of rights. Instead, it represents a bare minimum below which the law must not fall. A necessary corollary of this statement is that the law, whether by statute or common law, can offer protections beyond those guaranteed by the Charter. The common law confessions rule is one such doctrine, and it would be a mistake to confuse it with the protections given by the Charter. While obviously it may be appropriate, as in *Hebert*, to interpret one in light of the other, it would be a mistake to assume one subsumes the other entirely.

The Confessions Rule Today

As previously mentioned, this Court has not recently addressed the precise scope of the confessions rule. Instead, we have refined several elements of the rule, without ever integrating them into a coherent whole. I believe it is important to restate the rule for two reasons. First is the continuing diversity of approaches as evidenced by the courts below in this appeal. Second, and perhaps more important, is our growing understanding of the problem of false confessions. As I will discuss below, the confessions rule is concerned with voluntariness, broadly defined. One of the predominant reasons for this concern is that involuntary confessions are more likely to be unreliable. The confessions rule should recognize which interrogation techniques commonly produce false confessions so as to avoid miscarriages of justice.

In defining the confessions rule, it is important to keep in mind its twin goals of protecting the rights of the accused without unduly limiting society's need to investigate and solve crimes. Martin J.A. accurately delineated this tension in *R. v. Precourt* (1976), 18 O.R. (2d) 714 (C.A.), at p. 721:

> Although improper police questioning may in some circumstances infringe the governing [confessions] rule it is essential to bear in mind that the police are unable to investigate crime without putting questions to persons, whether or not such persons are suspected of having committed the crime being investigated. Properly conducted police questioning is a legitimate and effective aid to criminal investigation . . . . On the other hand, statements made as the result of intimidating questions, or questioning which is oppressive and calculated to overcome the freedom of will of the suspect for the purpose of extracting a confession are inadmissible. . . .

All who are involved in the administration of justice, but particularly courts applying the confessions rule, must never lose sight of either of these objectives.

The Problem of False Confessions

The history of police interrogations is not without its unsavoury chapters. Physical abuse, if not routine, was certainly not unknown. Today such practices are much less common. In this context, it may seem counterintuitive that people would confess to a crime that they did not commit. And indeed, research with mock juries indicates that people find it difficult to believe that someone would confess falsely. See S. M. Kassin and L. S. Wrightsman, "Coerced Confessions, Judicial Instructions, and Mock Juror Verdicts" (1981), 11 *J. Applied Soc. Psychol.* 489.

However, this intuition is not always correct. A large body of literature has developed documenting hundreds of cases where confessions have been proven false by DNA evidence, subsequent confessions by the true perpetrator, and other such independent sources of evidence. See, e.g., R. A. Leo and R. J. Ofshe, "The Consequences of False Confessions: Deprivations of Liberty and Miscarriages of Justice in the Age of Psychological Interrogation" (1998), 88 *J. Crim. L. & Criminology* 429 (hereinafter Leo & Ofshe (1998)); R. J. Ofshe and R. A. Leo, "The Social Psychology of Police Interrogation: The Theory and Classification of True and False Confessions" (1997), 16 *Stud. L. Pol. & Soc.* 189 (hereinafter Ofshe & Leo (1997)); R. J. Ofshe and R. A. Leo, "The Decision to Confess Falsely: Rational Choice and Irrational Action" (1997), 74 *Denv. U. L. Rev.* 979 (hereinafter Ofshe & Leo (1997a)); W. S. White, "False Confessions and the Constitution: Safeguards Against Untrustworthy Confessions" (1997), 32 *Harv. C.R.-C.L. L. Rev.* 105; G. H. Gudjonsson and J. A. C. MacKeith, "A Proven Case of False Confession: Psychological Aspects of the Coerced-Compliant Type" (1990), 30 *Med. Sci. & L.* 329 (hereinafter Gudjonsson & MacKeith (1990)); G. Gudjonsson and J. A. C. MacKeith, "Retracted Confessions: Legal, Psychological and Psychiatric Aspects" (1988), 28 *Med. Sci. & L.* 187 (hereinafter Gudjonsson &

MacKeith (1988)); H. A. Bedau and M. L. Radelet, "Miscarriages of Justice in Potentially Capital Cases" (1987), 40 *Stan. L. Rev.* 21.

One of the overriding concerns of the criminal justice system is that the innocent must not be convicted: see, e.g., *R. v. Mills*, [1999] 3 S.C.R. 668, at para. 71; *R. v. Leipert*, [1997] 1 S.C.R. 281, at para. 4. Given the important role of false confessions in convicting the innocent, the confessions rule must understand why false confessions occur. Without suggesting that any confession involving elements discussed below should automatically be excluded, I hope to provide a background for my synthesis of the confessions rule in the next section.

Ofshe & Leo (1997), *supra*, at p. 210, provide a useful taxonomy of false confessions. They suggest that there are five basic kinds: voluntary, stress-compliant, coerced-compliant, non-coerced-persuaded, and coerced-persuaded. Voluntary confessions *ex hypothesi* are not the product of police interrogation. It is therefore the other four types of false confessions that are of interest.

According to Ofshe & Leo (1997), *supra*, at p. 211, stress-compliant confessions occur "when the aversive interpersonal pressures of interrogation become so intolerable that [suspects] comply in order to terminate questioning". They are elicited by "exceptionally strong use of the aversive stressors typically present in interrogations", and are "given knowingly *in order to escape* the punishing experience of interrogation" (emphasis in original). See also Gudjonsson & MacKeith (1990), *supra*. Another important factor is confronting the suspect with fabricated evidence in order to convince him that protestations of innocence are futile: see *ibid.*; Ofshe & Leo (1997a), *supra*, at p. 1040.

Somewhat different are coerced-compliant confessions. These confessions are the product of "the classically coercive influence techniques (e.g., threats and promises)", with which the *Ibrahim* rule is concerned: Ofshe & Leo (1997), *supra*, at p.214. As Gudjonsson & MacKeith (1988), *supra*, suggest at p. 191, "most cases of false confession that come before the courts are of the compliant-coerced type". See also White, *supra*, at p. 131.

A third kind of false confession is the non-coerced-persuaded confession. In this scenario, police tactics cause the innocent person to "become confused, doubt his memory, be temporarily persuaded of his guilt and confess to a crime he did not commit": Ofshe & Leo (1997), *supra*, at p. 215. For an example, see *Reilly v. State*, 355 A.2d 324 (Conn. Super. Ct. 1976); Ofshe & Leo (1997), *supra*, at pp. 231-34. The use of fabricated evidence can also help convince an innocent suspect of his or her own guilt.

A final type of false confession is the coerced-persuaded confession. This is like the non-coerced-persuaded, except that the interrogation also involves the classically coercive aspects of the coerced-compliant confession: see Ofshe & Leo (1997), *supra*, at p. 219.

From this discussion, several themes emerge. One is the need to be sensitive to the particularities of the individual suspect. For example, White, *supra*, at p. 120, notes the following:

> False confessions are particularly likely when the police interrogate particular types of suspects, including suspects who are especially vulnerable as a result of their background, special characteristics, or situation, suspects who have compliant personalities, and, in rare instances, suspects whose personalities make them prone to accept and believe police suggestions made during the course of the interrogation.

. . .

Another theme is the danger of using non-existent evidence. Presenting a suspect with entirely fabricated evidence has the potential either to persuade the susceptible suspect that he did indeed commit the crime, or at least to convince the suspect that any protestations of innocence are futile.

Finally, the literature bears out the common law confessions rule's emphasis on threats and promises. Coerced-compliant confessions are the most common type of false confessions. These are classically the product of threats or promises that convince a suspect that in spite of the long-term ramifications, it is in his or her best interest in the short - and intermediate - term to confess.

Fortunately, false confessions are rarely the product of proper police techniques. As Leo & Ofshe (1998), *supra*, point out at p. 492, false confession cases almost always involve "shoddy police practice and/or police criminality". Similarly, in Ofshe & Leo (1997), *supra*, at pp. 193-96, they argue that in most cases, "eliciting a false confession takes strong incentives, intense pressure and prolonged questioning. . . . Only under the rarest of circumstances do an interrogator's ploys persuade an innocent suspect that he is in fact guilty and has been caught."

Before turning to how the confessions rule responds to these dangers, I would like to comment briefly on the growing practice of recording police interrogations, preferably by videotape. As pointed out by J. J. Furedy and J. Liss in "Countering Confessions Induced by the Polygraph: Of Confessionals and Psychological Rubber Hoses" (1986), 29 *Crim. L.Q.* 91, at p. 104, even if "notes were accurate concerning the *content* of what was said . . ., the notes cannot reflect the *tone* of what was said and any body language that may have been employed" (emphasis in original). White, *supra*, at pp. 153-54, similarly offers four reasons why videotaping is important:

First, it provides a means by which courts can monitor interrogation practices and thereby enforce the other safeguards. Second, it deters the police from employing interrogation methods likely to lead to untrustworthy confessions. Third, it enables courts to make more informed judgments about whether interrogation practices were likely to lead to an untrustworthy confession. Finally, mandating this safeguard accords with sound public policy because the safeguard will have additional salutary effects besides reducing untrustworthy confessions, including more net benefits for law enforcement.

This is not to suggest that non-recorded interrogations are inherently suspect; it is simply to make the obvious point that when a recording is made, it can greatly assist the trier of fact in assessing the confession.

The common law confessions rule is well-suited to protect against false confessions. While its overriding concern is with voluntariness, this concept overlaps with reliability. A confession that is not voluntary will often (though not always) be unreliable. The application of the rule will by necessity be contextual. Hard and fast rules simply cannot account for the variety of circumstances that vitiate the voluntariness of a confession, and would inevitably result in a rule that would be both over- and under-inclusive. A trial judge should therefore consider all the relevant factors when reviewing a confession.

(a) Threats or Promises

This is of course the core of the confessions rule from *Ibrahim*, supra. It is therefore important to define precisely what types of threats or promises will raise a reasonable doubt as to the voluntariness of a confession. While obviously imminent threats of torture will render a confession inadmissible, most cases will not be so clear.

As noted above, in *Ibrahim* the Privy Council ruled that statements would be inadmissible if they were the result of "fear of prejudice or hope of advantage". The classic "hope of advantage" is the prospect of leniency from the courts. It is improper for a person in authority to suggest to a suspect that he or she will take steps to procure a reduced charge or sentence if the suspect confesses. Therefore in *Nugent*, supra, the court excluded the statement of a suspect who was told that if he confessed, the charge could be reduced from murder to manslaughter. . . . Another type of inducement relevant to this appeal is an offer of psychiatric assistance or other counselling for the suspect in exchange for a confession. While this is clearly an inducement, it is not as strong as an offer of leniency and regard must be had to the entirety of the circumstances. . . . Threats or promises need not be aimed directly at the suspect for them to have a coercive effect. In *R. v. Jackson* (1977), 34 C.C.C. (2d) 35 (B.C. C.A.), McIntyre J.A. . . . offered, as examples of improper inducements, telling a mother that her daughter would not be charged with shoplifting if the mother confessed to a similar offence (see *Commissioners of Customs and Excise v. Harz* , [1967] 1 A.C. 760 (H.L.), at p. 821), or a sergeant-major keeping a company on parade until he learned who was responsible for a stabbing (see *R. v. Smith*, [1959] 2 Q.B. 35.

The *Ibrahim* rule speaks not only of "hope of advantage", but also of "fear of prejudice". Obviously, any confession that is the product of outright violence is involuntary and unreliable, and therefore inadmissible. More common, and more challenging judicially, are the more subtle, veiled threats that can be used against suspects. The Honourable Fred Kaufman, in the third edition of *The Admissibility of Confessions* (1979), at p. 230, provides a useful starting point:

> Threats come in all shapes and sizes. Among the most common are words to the effect that "it would be better" to tell, implying thereby that dire consequences might flow from a refusal to talk. Maule J. recognized this fact, and said that "there can be no doubt that such words, if spoken by a competent person, have been held to exclude a confession at least 500 times" (*R. v. Garner* (1848), 3 Cox C.C. 175, at p. 177).

Courts have accordingly excluded confessions made in response to police suggestions that it would be better if they confessed. However, phrases like "it would be better if you told the truth" should not automatically require exclusion. Instead, as in all cases, the trial judge must examine the entire context of the confession, and ask whether there is a reasonable doubt that the resulting confession was involuntary. . . . I agree that "it would be better" comments require exclusion only where the circumstances reveal an implicit threat or promise.

A final threat or promise relevant to this appeal is the use of moral or spiritual inducements. These inducements will generally not produce an involuntary confession, for the very simple reason that the inducement offered is not in the control of the police officers. If a police officer says "If you don't confess, you'll spend the rest of your life in jail. Tell me what happened and I can get you a lighter sentence", then clearly there is a strong, and improper, inducement for the suspect to confess. The officer is offering a quid pro quo, and it raises the possibility that the suspect is confessing not because of any internal desire to confess, but merely in order to gain the benefit offered by the interrogator. By contrast, with most spiritual inducements the interrogator has no control over the suggested benefit. If a police officer convinces a suspect that he will feel better if he confesses, the officer has not offered anything.

. . .

In summary, courts must remember that the police may often offer some kind of inducement to the suspect to obtain a confession. Few suspects will spontaneously confess to a crime. In the vast majority of cases, the police will have to somehow convince the suspect that it is in his or her best interests to confess. This becomes improper only when the inducements, whether standing alone or in combination with other factors, are strong enough to raise a reasonable doubt about whether the will of the subject has been overborne. On this point I found the following passage from *R. v. Rennie* (1981), 74 Cr. App. R. 207 (C.A.), at p. 212, particularly apt

> Very few confessions are inspired solely by remorse. Often the motives of an accused are mixed and include a hope that an early admission may lead to an earlier release or a lighter sentence. If it were the law that the mere presence of such a motive, even if promoted by something said or done by a person in authority, led inexorably to the exclusion of a confession, nearly every confession would be rendered inadmissible. This is not the law. In some cases the hope may be self-generated. If so, it is irrelevant, even if it provides the dominant motive for making the confession.

> In such a case the confession will not have been obtained by anything said or done by a person in authority. More commonly the presence of such a hope will, in part at least, owe its origin to something said or done by such a person. There can be few prisoners who are being firmly but fairly questioned in a police station to whom it does not occur that they might be able to bring both their interrogation and their detention to an earlier end by confession.

The most important consideration in all cases is to look for a quid pro quo offer by interrogators, regardless of whether it comes in the form of a threat or a promise.

(b) Oppression

There was much debate among the parties, interveners, and courts below over the relevance of "oppression" to the confessions rule. Oppression clearly has the potential to produce false confessions. If the police create conditions distasteful enough, it should be no surprise that the suspect would make a stress-compliant confession to escape those conditions. Alternately, oppressive circumstances could overbear the suspect's will to the point that he or she comes to doubt his or her own memory, believes the relentless accusations made by the police, and gives an induced confession.

A compelling example of oppression comes from the Ontario Court of Appeal's recent decision in *R. v. Hoilett* (1999), 136 C.C.C. (3d) 449. The accused, charged with sexual assault, was arrested at 11:25 p.m. while under the influence of crack cocaine and alcohol. After two hours in a cell, two officers removed his clothes for forensic testing. He was left naked in a cold cell containing only a metal bunk to sit on. The bunk was so cold he had to stand up. One and one-half hours later, he was provided with some light clothes, but no underwear and ill-fitting shoes. Shortly thereafter, at about 3:00 a.m., he was awakened for the purpose of interviewing. In the course of the interrogation, the accused nodded off to sleep at least five times. He requested warmer clothes and a tissue to wipe his nose, both of which were refused. While he admitted knowing that he did not have to talk, and that the officers had made no explicit threats or promises, he hoped that if he talked to the police they would give him some warm clothes and cease the interrogation. Under these circumstances, it is no surprise that the Court of Appeal concluded the statement was involuntary. Under inhumane conditions, one can hardly be surprised if a suspect confesses purely out of a desire to escape those conditions. Such a confession is not voluntary. . . . Without trying to indicate all the factors that can create an atmosphere of oppression, such factors include depriving the suspect of food, clothing, water, sleep, or medical attention; denying access to counsel; and excessively aggressive, intimidating questioning for a prolonged period of time.

A final possible source of oppressive conditions is the police use of non-existent evidence. As the discussion of false confessions, supra, revealed, this ploy is very dangerous. The use of false evidence is often crucial in convincing the suspect that protestations of innocence, even if true, are futile. I do not mean to suggest in any way that, standing alone, confronting the suspect with inadmissible or even fabricated evidence is necessarily grounds for excluding a statement. However, when combined with other factors, it is certainly a relevant consideration in determining on a *voir dire* whether a confession was voluntary.

(c) Operating Mind

This Court recently addressed this aspect of the confessions rule in *Whittle*, supra, and I need not repeat that exercise here. Briefly stated, Sopinka J. explained that the operating mind requirement "does not imply a higher degree of awareness than knowledge of what the accused is saying and that he is saying it to police officers who can use it to his detriment". I agree, and would simply add that, like oppression, the operating mind doctrine should not be understood as a discrete inquiry completely divorced from the rest of the confessions rule. . . . [T]he operating mind doctrine is just one application of the general rule that involuntary confessions are inadmissible.

(d) Other Police Trickery

A final consideration in determining whether a confession is voluntary or not is the police use of trickery to obtain a confession. Unlike the previous three headings, this doctrine is a distinct inquiry. While it is still related to voluntariness, its more specific objective is maintaining the integrity of the criminal justice system. Lamer J.'s concurrence in *Rothman*, supra, introduced this inquiry. In that case, the Court admitted a suspect's statement to an undercover police officer who had been placed in a cell with the accused. In concurring reasons, Lamer J. emphasized that reliability was not the only concern of the confessions rule; otherwise the rule would not be concerned with whether the inducement was given by a person in authority. He summarized the correct approach . . .:

> [A] statement before being left to the trier of fact for consideration of its probative value should be the objectof a *voir dire* in order to determine, not whether the statement is or is not reliable, but whether the authorities have done or said anything that could have induced the accused to make a statement which was or might be untrue. It is of the utmost importance to keep in mind that the inquiry is not concerned with reliability but with the authorities' conduct as regards reliability.

Lamer J. was also quick to point out that courts should be wary not to unduly limit police discretion (at p. 697):

> [T]he investigation of crime and the detection of criminals is not a game to be governed by the Marquess of Queensbury rules. The authorities, in dealing with shrewd and often sophisticated criminals, must sometimes of necessity resort to tricks or other forms of deceit and should not through the rule be hampered in their work. What should be repressed vigorously is conduct on their part that shocks the community. [Emphasis added.]

As examples of what might "shock the community", Lamer J. suggested a police officer pretending to be a chaplain or a legal aid lawyer, or injecting truth serum into a diabetic under the pretense that it was insulin.

In *Hebert*, supra, this Court overruled the result in *Rothman* based on the Charter's right to silence. However, I do not believe that this renders the "shocks the community" rule redundant. There may be situations in which police trickery, though neither violating the right to silence nor undermining voluntariness per se, is so appalling as to shock the community. I therefore believe that the test enunciated by Lamer J. in *Rothman* is still an important part of the confessions rule.

(e) *Summary*

While the foregoing might suggest that the confessions rule involves a panoply of different considerations and tests, in reality the basic idea is quite simple. First of all, because of the criminal justice system's overriding concern not to convict the innocent, a confession will not be admissible if it is made under circumstances that raise a reasonable doubt as to voluntariness. Both the traditional, narrow *Ibrahim* rule and the oppression doctrine recognize this danger. If the police interrogators subject the suspect to utterly intolerable conditions, or if they offer inducements strong enough to produce an unreliable confession, the trial judge should exclude it. Between these two extremes, oppressive conditions and inducements can operate together to exclude confessions. Trial judges must be alert to the entire circumstances surrounding a confession in making this decision.

The doctrines of oppression and inducements are primarily concerned with reliability. However, as the operating mind doctrine and Lamer J.'s concurrence in *Rothman*, *supra*, both demonstrate, the confessions rule also extends to protect a broader conception of voluntariness "that focuses on the protection of the accused's rights and fairness in the criminal process": J. Sopinka, S. N. Lederman and A. W. Bryant, *The Law of Evidence in Canada* (2nd ed. 1999), at p. 339. Voluntariness is the touchstone of the confessions rule. Whether the concern is threats or promises, the lack of an operating mind, or police trickery that unfairly denies the accused's right to silence, this Court's jurisprudence has consistently protected the accused from having involuntary confessions introduced into evidence. If a confession is involuntary for any of these reasons, it is inadmissible.

Wigmore perhaps summed up the point best when he said that voluntariness is "shorthand for a complex of values": *Wigmore on Evidence* (Chadbourn rev. 1970), vol. 3, § 826, at p. 351. I also agree with Warren C.J. of the United States Supreme Court, who made a similar point in *Blackburn v. Alabama*, 361 U.S. 199 (U.S. Ala. S.C., 1960) at p. 207:

> [N]either the likelihood that the confession is untrue nor the preservation of the individual's freedom of will is the sole interest at stake. As we said just last Term, "The abhorrence of society to the use of involuntary confessions . . . also turns on the deep-rooted feeling that the police must obey the law while enforcing the law; that in the end life and liberty can be as much endangered from illegal methods used to convict those thought to be criminals as from the actual criminals themselves." . . . Thus a complex of values underlies the stricture against use by the state of confessions which, by way of convenient shorthand, this Court terms involuntary, and the role played by each in any situation varies according to the particular circumstances of the case.

See *Hebert*, *supra*. While the "complex of values" relevant to voluntariness in Canada is obviously not identical to that in the United States, I agree with Warren C.J. that "voluntariness" is a useful term to describe the various rationales underlying the confessions rule that I have addressed above.

Again, I would also like to emphasize that the analysis under the confessions rule must be a contextual one. In the past, courts have excluded confessions made as a result of relatively minor inducements. At the same time, the law ignored intolerable police conduct if it did not give rise to an "inducement" as it was understood by the narrow *Ibrahim* formulation. Both results are incorrect. Instead, a court should strive to understand the circumstances surrounding the confession and ask if it gives rise to a reasonable doubt as to the confession's voluntariness, taking into account all the aspects of the rule discussed above. Therefore a relatively minor inducement, such as a tissue to wipe one's nose and warmer clothes, may amount to an impermissible inducement if the suspect is deprived of sleep, heat, and clothes for several hours in the middle of the night during an interrogation: see *Hoilett, supra*. On the other hand, where the suspect is treated properly, it will take a stronger inducement to render the confession involuntary. If a trial court properly considers all the relevant circumstances, then a finding regarding voluntariness is essentially a factual one, and should only be overturned for "some palpable and overriding error which affected [the trial judge's] assessment of the facts": *Schwartz v. R.*, [1996] 1 S.C.R. 254 (S.C.C.) at p. 279 [S.C.R.] (quoting *Stein v. "Kathy K" (The)* (1975), [1976] 2 S.C.R. 802 (S.C.C.) at p. 808 [S.C.R.]) (emphasis in *Schwartz*).

Application to the Present Appeal

Applying the foregoing law to the facts of this appeal, and having viewed the relevant video- and audiotapes, I find no fault with the trial judge's conclusion that the respondent's confession was voluntary and reliable. The respondent was fully apprised of his rights at all times; he was never subjected to harsh, aggressive, or overbearing interrogation; he was not deprived of sleep, food, or drink; and he was never offered any improper inducements that undermined the reliability of the confessions. As the Court of Appeal reached a contrary conclusion with respect to a number of these issues, I will address them in turn.

[The Court then analyzed the fact situation under a variety of heads: 1. Minimizing the Seriousness of the Crimes. 2. Offers of Psychiatric Help. 3. "It Would Be Better". 4. Alleged Threats Against the Respondent's Fiancée. 5. Abuse of Trust. 6. Atmosphere of Oppression. And finally, 7. The Use of the Polygraph Test.]

. . .

Summary on Voluntariness

In summary, there were several aspects of the police's interrogation of the respondent that could potentially be relevant to the voluntariness of his confessions. These include the comments regarding Ms. Kilcup; the suggestions that "it would be better" for the respondent to confess; and the exaggeration of the polygraph's accuracy. These are certainly relevant considerations when determining voluntariness. However, I agree with the trial judge that neither standing alone, nor in combination with each other and the rest of the circumstances surrounding the respondent's confessions, do these factors raise a reasonable doubt about the voluntariness of the respondent's confessions. The respondent was never mistreated, he was questioned in an extremely friendly, benign tone, and he was not offered any inducements strong enough to raise a reasonable doubt as to voluntariness in the absence of any mistreatment or oppression. As I find no error in the trial judge's reasons, the Court of Appeal should not have disturbed her findings.

ARBOUR J.: —

I have had the benefit of the reasons of my colleague, Justice Iacobucci, on this appeal. With respect, I believe that there were improper inducements held out by the police officers who interrogated the respondent and that these inducements, considered cumulatively and contextually in light of the "failed" polygraph test, require the exclusion of the respondent's statements. Moreover, in my view the proximity and the causal connection between the "failed" polygraph test and the confession also compels this result. Accordingly, I would dismiss the appeal, set aside the convictions and enter acquittals on all counts. . . . Properly understood, this case involves two confessions obtained by the police following the "failure" of a polygraph test and a skillful interrogation which lasted nearly six hours. Repeated threats and promises were made. They were often subtle but in my view, against the backdrop of the polygraph procedure, they overwhelmed the free will of the respondent. These seemingly mild pressures make this case a difficult one in which to apply the confessions rule and demand an attentive appreciation of the full context in which the alleged voluntary, incriminating statements were made. I fully agree with the summary of the applicable law provided by Justice Iacobucci. . . . However, I take a different view of the proper legal characterization of what happened in the course of the many hours during which the respondent was interrogated and of the voluntary quality of his incriminating statements.

[Justice Arbour then analyzed admissibility under the heads of The Administration of the Polygraph Test, The Post-Polygraph Interrogation, Promise of Psychiatric Help, Minimization of the Seriousness of the Crimes, Threat to Interrogate the Accused's Girlfriend, and finally, as another basis for exclusion, Fair Trial Considerations.]

For these reasons I would dismiss the appeal, set aside the convictions and enter acquittals on all counts.

Academic comment on *Oickle* has been critical.[259]

In *R. v. Spencer*,[260] the majority ruling of the Supreme Court confirms that police are to be given considerable leeway to offer inducements to obtain confessions without rendering the statement involuntary. The accused was arrested in connection with a series of robberies. His girlfriend was also arrested in connection with one of the robberies. Throughout an eight-hour

---

[259] See Stuart, "*Oickle*: The Supreme Court's Recipe for Coercive Interrogation" (2001), 36 C.R. (5th) 188; Lisa Dufraimont, "The Common Law Confessions Rule in the *Charter* Era: Current Law and Future Directions" (2008) 40 Supr. Crt. L. Rev. 250; Dale Ives, "Preventing False Confessions: Is *Oickle* Up to the Task" (2007) San Diego L. Rev. 1; and Edmund Thomas, "Lowering the Standard: *R. v. Oickle* and the Confessions Rule in Canada" (2005) 10 Can. Crim. L. Rev. 69. See too Stuart, *Charter Justice in Canadian Criminal Law*, 7th ed. (2018).

[260] [2007] 1 S.C.R. 500, 217 C.C.C. (3d) 353, 44 C.R. (6th) 199 (S.C.C.).

interview, the accused repeatedly attempted to obtain lenient treatment for his girlfriend in exchange for his own confession. He also requested to visit his girlfriend but the police told him he could not visit her until he "cleaned his slate". He confessed to one of the robberies and was then allowed to visit his girlfriend. The majority of the Supreme Court upheld the trial judge's ruling that the accused's statements were voluntary. Withholding the visit until the accused confessed did amount to an inducement but it was not strong enough to raise a reasonable doubt that the accused's will was overborne. Writing for the majority, Deschamps J. held that "it is the strength of the alleged inducement that must be considered in the overall contextual inquiry into voluntariness".

A strong dissent was authored by Fish J., who read the transcript of the interview as revealing an implied threat to charge the girlfriend unless the accused confessed. The police did not claim to have authority to offer leniency to his girlfriend but they did indicate they would speak to the Crown if he confessed.

Spencer and *Oickle* may well encourage police to exploit emotions about possible prosecution against partners. *Oickle* says police may use polygraphs and lie about their accuracy. **Do you think that *Oickle* has resulted in too few judicial controls on interrogation?**

The community shock test is a very high hurdle for accused and does not apply to the s. 24(2) remedy of exclusion for *Charter* breaches. In the U.K., judges under s. 76(2) of the *Evidence Act of 1984* have a discretion to exclude a confession where police interrogation methods are considered oppressive and not just where they shock the community. Under s. 76(5) oppression "includes torture, inhuman or degrading treatment or the use or threatened use of violence (whether or not amounting to torture)".

Trial judges who have relied on *Oickle* to exclude confessions have often done so by giving a very wide meaning to the category of oppression resulting in involuntariness. Regulation of police interrogation is one area where Parliament may have achieved a better balance than the courts. Under s. 269.1 of the *Criminal Code*, torture is an indictable offence punishable to a maximum of 14 years. Torture is widely defined in s. 269.1(2) as:

> any act or omission by which severe pain or suffering, whether physical or mental, is intentionally inflicted on a person.

Further, under subsection (4), a statement obtained by torture is inadmissible in any proceedings over which Parliament has jurisdiction.[261] This may be a vehicle for further judicial checks on police interrogation.

---

[261]   See generally Donald Macdougall, "Torture in Canadian Criminal Law" (2005), 24 C.R. (6th) 74.

3. THE PRE-TRIAL RIGHT TO SILENCE AND INTERROGATION

The issue in *R. v. Hebert*[262] was the admissibility of a statement by an accused who had been arrested on a charge of robbery. He gave the statement to an undercover police officer placed in his cell after he had indicated that he did not wish to speak to the police. The Supreme Court of Canada unanimously decided that the statement had been obtained in violation of a breach of the right to silence under s. 7 and had been properly excluded under s. 24(2).

McLachlin J. delivered the majority judgment, with six justices concurring.[263] She found in the common law voluntary confession rule and in the privilege against self-incrimination, which granted the accused immunity from incriminating himself at trial, the essence of the right to silence:

> [T]he person whose freedom is placed in question by the judicial process must be given the choice of whether to speak to the authorities or not.

Consideration of other *Charter* rights suggested that the right to silence of detained persons under s. 7 had to be broad enough to accord that person a free choice on the matter of whether to speak to the authorities. The most important function of the right to counsel was to ensure that the accused understood his or her rights, chief among which was his or her right to silence. The privilege against self-incrimination enshrined in ss. 11(c) and 13 of the *Charter* would be diminished if a person were to be compelled to make statements at the pretrial stage. The right of a detained person to silence under s. 7 had to be viewed as broader in scope than the confession rule existing in Canada at the time of the adoption of the *Charter*. The right had to reflect the *Charter*'s concern for individual freedom and the integrity of the judicial process, and permit the exclusion of evidence offensive to those values. On a "purposive approach" to the right to silence, the scope of the right had to be extended to exclude police tricks which would effectively deprive the suspect of the choice of remaining silent:

> To permit the authorities to trick the suspect into making a confession to them after he or she has exercised the right of conferring with counsel and declined to make a statement, is to permit the authorities to do indirectly what the Charter does not permit them to do directly. This cannot be in accordance with the purpose of the Charter.

McLachlin J. had earlier pointed out that *Rothman* had been decided after the majority ruling in *Wray* that a court had no power to exclude admissible and relevant evidence on the basis that the administration of justice would be brought into disrepute. Distinguished scholars and judges had criticized this approach and it could no longer be maintained under the *Charter*.

Justice McLachlin further determined that her approach was not one of an "absolute right to silence in the accused, capable of being discharged only

---

[262]   (1990), 77 C.R. (3d) 145 (S.C.C.).
[263]   Dickson C.J., Lamer, La Forest, L'Heureux-Dubé, Gonthier and Cory JJ. Wilson and Sopinka JJ. gave separate concurring reasons.

by waiver". On the subjective approach to waiver defined in R. v. Clarkson[264] all statements made by detainees not knowingly made to a police officer would be excluded because the Crown could not establish waiver. The majority decided that the scope of the right to silence should not be extended this far.[265]

Madam Justice McLachlin further identified four limits to this newly recognized constitutional right to silence:

1. The police may question the accused in the absence of counsel after the accused has retained counsel:

    Presumably, counsel will inform the accused of the right to remain silent. If the police are not posing as undercover officers and the accused chooses to volunteer information, there will be no violation of the Charter. Police persuasion, short of denying the suspect the right to choose or depriving him of an operating mind, does not breach the right to silence.

2. The right to silence applies only after detention:

    In an undercover operation prior to detention, the individual from whom information is sought is not in the control of the state. There is no need to protect him from the greater power of the state. After detention, the situation is quite different; the state takes control and assumes the responsibility of ensuring that the detainee's rights are respected.

3. The right to silence does not affect voluntary statements to a cellmate provided that person is not acting as a police informant or an undercover police officer.

4. The right to silence is not violated where undercover agents observe the suspect and do not "actively elicit information in violation of the suspect's choice to remain silent".

Provincial courts proved reluctant to extend the *Hebert* pre-trial right to silence to situations where the officer is identified. It has been held that non-coercive questioning prior to detention is no violation.[266] In *R. v. Smith*,[267] Mr. Justice Doherty for the Ontario Court of Appeal confirmed that a detained person has no absolute right to remain silent. The police are not absolutely prohibited from questioning a detained person and do not have to advise as to the right to remain silent. Where there is no s. 10(b) right to counsel, as in the case of a motorist asked to perform sobriety tests under the *Highway Traffic Act*, the s. 7 right to make an informed choice as to whether to speak to police requires only that the police do not engage in conduct that effectively and unfairly deprives the detainee of the right to choose whether to speak. The Court held that s. 7 had not been violated by two simple questions as to whether the motorist had been drinking and as to the quantity.

---

[264] [1986] 1 S.C.R. 383.
[265] Both Sopinka and Wilson JJ. would have applied the accepted waiver standard.
[266] *R. v. Hicks* (1988), 64 C.R. (3d) 68 (Ont. C.A.), affirmed (1990), 54 C.C.C. (3d) 575 (S.C.C.). See too *R. v. Imeson* (1992), 13 C.R. (4th) 322 (Ont. Gen. Div.).
[267] (1996), 46 C.R. (4th) 229 (Ont. C.A.).

In *R. v. Orbanski,*[268] a 5-2 majority of the Supreme Court chose not to confront the right to silence issues in deciding that a motorist detained and asked questions as to alcohol consumption or asked to perform sobriety tests was not entitled to the right to counsel under s. 10(b) of the *Charter.*

Some interpretations of the right to silence in the context of police questioning after the accused has been afforded an opportunity to consult counsel have turned on the following passage of McLachlin, J. in *Hebert*:

> [The] Charter requires that the suspect be informed of his or her right to counsel and be permitted to consult counsel without delay. If the suspect chooses to make a statement, the suspect may do so. But if the suspect chooses not to, the state is not entitled to use its superior power to override the suspect's will and negate his or her choice.[269]

The B.C. Court of Appeal determined in *R. v. K. (H.W.)*[270] that the s. 7 right to silence was not breached by overriding the accused's choice not to speak where police asked the accused in a murder case whether he wished to take a breathalyzer, after assuring the lawyer they would not be interviewing him. Because of the agreement with the lawyer, McEachern C.J.B.C., for the Court, found this case close to the line between "fair and unfair treatment" but noted that the accused had chosen freely and voluntarily to say far more than was necessary to answer the question.[271] So too the B.C. Court held there was no right to silence violation in *R. v. Ekman.*[272] The accused had indicated that he was only willing to answer questions with his lawyer present, but did so without his lawyer when the police advised him he had no right to the presence of a lawyer and the choice was his. There had been no confusion in the accused's mind as to his rights.

However, in *R. v. Otis,*[273] the Quebec Court of Appeal decided that the right to silence should be more meaningful. Although the Court decided that the accused had sufficient, though limited, cognitive capacity to make choices, Justice Proulx for the Court decided that the continued police questioning, after he had asked them to stop four times, violated s. 7. The police were not entitled to use their superior power to totally disregard the accused's desires and undermine his choice to remain silent. Once an accused has clearly stated he or she wishes to remain silent, the police cannot act as if there has been a waiver.

In *R. v. Roy*[274] the accused was convicted of a murder of an 11-year-old girl lured from her home. On his conviction appeal the Ontario Court of Appeal dismissed the argument that his confession following an eight-hour interrogation had breached his s. 7 pre-trial right to silence. The Court held that he had not chosen not to speak as he had a game plan to answer some

---

268 (2005), 29 C.R. (6th) 205, 196 C.C.C. (3d) 481, [2005] 2 S.C.R. 3.
269 *Hebert, supra* note 262 at para. 80.
270 (2000), 32 C.R. (5th) 359 (B.C. C.A.).
271 *Ibid.* at para. 18.
272 (2000), 146 C.C.C. (3d) 346 (B.C. C.A.).
273 (2000), 37 C.R. (5th) 320 (Que. C.A.). See Guy Cournoyer, "*Otis*: The Quebec Court of Appeal Asserts a Meaningful Right to Silence Where a Suspect Says No to Interrogation" (2000), 37 C.R. (5th) 342.
274 (2004), 15 C.R. (6th) 282 (Ont. C.A.).

not all questions. For the Court, Doherty J.A. (Feldman and Macpherson JJ.A. concurring) however added *obiter*:

> [The] repeated assertion by a detained person during a lengthy interview that he does not want to speak to the police any further will provide strong and sometimes conclusive evidence that any subsequent statement was not the product of a free exercise of the detainee's right to choose whether to speak. The question is, however, a factual question to be decided on a case by case basis by the trial judge (at 187).[275]

Otis and *Roy* were not followed in the surprising and controversial ruling of a 5-4 majority of the Supreme Court in *R. v. Singh* that in the context of interrogation by police the s. 7 pre-trial right to silence has been subsumed by the voluntary confession rule.

R. v. SINGH

(2007), 51 C.R. (6th) 199, 225 C.C.C. (3d) 103, [2007] 3 S.C.R. 405

The accused was charged with second degree murder after an altercation outside a pub resulted in a man's death. Several shots were fired and an innocent bystander was fatally shot by a stray bullet. There was no physical evidence linking the accused to the shooting, but the doorman and another eyewitness implicated the accused as the shooter.

The accused was arrested, properly cautioned and advised of his right to counsel, and he privately consulted with counsel. The accused was subsequently interviewed twice by a police officer while in detention. During these interviews, which were videotaped, the accused stated on numerous occasions that he did not want to talk about the incident, that he knew nothing about it, and that he wished to return to his cell. On each occasion, the officer either affirmed that the accused did not have to say anything or explained that he, the officer, had a duty or desire to place the evidence before the accused. In all cases the officer persisted in questioning the accused and confronting the accused with incriminating evidence. The officer testified that he intended to put the police case before the accused in an attempt to get him to confess, no matter what.

During the first interview, the accused did not confess but made incriminating statements, admitting that he had been in the pub on the night of the shooting and identifying himself in pictures taken from video surveillance inside the pub in question and another pub. The accused had asserted his right to silence 18 times before making these admissions.

At trial, the accused challenged the admissibility of the statements, arguing that they were involuntary and that they were obtained in violation of the accused's pre-trial right to silence under s. 7 of the *Charter*. The trial judge admitted the statements and the accused was convicted. The accused's appeal to the British Columbia Court of Appeal was dismissed. The accused appealed to the Supreme Court on the s. 7 issue.

A 5-4 majority dismissed the appeal.

---

[275]   See annotation by Guy Cournoyer in (2004), 15 C.R. (6th) 284.

Per CHARRON J. (MCLACHLIN C.J., BASTARACHE, DESCHAMPS, ROTHSTEIN JJ. concurring):

. . .

Mr. Singh contends that trial and appellate courts, including the courts below, have generally misinterpreted the holding in Hebert as an authoritative statement which permits the police to ignore a detainee's expressed wish to remain silent and to use "legitimate means of persuasion" to break that silence (p. 177). He contends that the British Columbia Court of Appeal in the case at bar went even further and effectively extinguished the s. 7 right to silence when it questioned the utility of conducting "a double-barrelled test of admissibility", stating that "[i]n the context of an investigatory interview with an obvious person in authority " the expansive view of the common law confessions rule adopted in Oickle "may leave little additional room" for a separate s. 7 Charter inquiry (para. 19). Mr. Singh therefore submits that the Court of Appeal proceeded on the basis of erroneous legal principles when it affirmed the trial judge's dismissal of his s. 7 Charter application.

Further, Mr. Singh invites this Court to enhance the protection afforded to detainees under s. 7 by adopting a new approach that would require police officers to inform the detainee of his or her right to silence and, absent a signed waiver, to refrain from questioning any detainee who states that he or she does not wish to speak to the police.

First, I reject the appellant's contention that this Court should change the law relating to the pre-trial Charter right to silence. The new approach advocated by the appellant ignores the critical balancing of state and individual interests which lies at the heart of this Court's decision in Hebert and of subsequent s. 7 decisions. I see no reason to depart from these established principles.

Second, I find no error in law in the approach adopted by the courts below. The Court of Appeal's impugned comment on the interplay between the confessions rule and s. 7 of the Charter merely reflects the fact that, in the context of a police interrogation of a person in detention, where the detainee knows he or she is speaking to a person in authority, the two tests are functionally equivalent. It follows that, where a statement has survived a thorough inquiry into voluntariness, the accused's Charter application alleging that the statement was obtained in violation of the pre-trial right to silence under s. 7 cannot succeed. Conversely, if circumstances are such that the accused can show on a balance of probabilities that the statement was obtained in violation of his or her constitutional right to remain silent, the Crown will be unable to prove voluntariness beyond a reasonable doubt. As I will explain, however, this does not mean that the residual protection afforded to the right to silence under s. 7 of the Charter does not supplement the common law in other contexts.

Finally, I see no basis for interfering with the trial judge's factual determinations concerning Sgt. Attew's conduct and its effect on the appellant's freedom to choose whether to speak to the police. I would therefore dismiss the appeal.

. . .

Although historically the confessions rule was more concerned with the reliability of confessions than the protection against self-incrimination, this no longer holds true in the post-Charter era. Both the confessions rule and the constitutional right to silence are manifestations of the principle against self-incrimination. The principle against self-incrimination is a broad concept which has been usefully described by Lamer C.J. as "a general organizing principle of criminal law" from which a number of rules can be derived.

. . .

What the common law recognizes is the individual's right to remain silent. This does not mean, however, that a person has the right not to be spoken to by state authorities. The importance of police questioning in the fulfilment of their investigative role cannot be doubted. One can readily appreciate that the police could hardly investigate crime without putting questions to persons from whom it is thought that useful information may be obtained. The person suspected of having committed the crime being investigated is no exception. Indeed, if the suspect in fact committed the crime, he or she is likely the person who has the most information to offer about the incident. Therefore, the common law also recognizes the importance of police interrogation in the investigation of crime.

Of course, the information obtained from a suspect is only useful in the elucidation of crime if it can be relied upon for its truth — hence the primary reason for the confessions rule, the concern about the reliability of confessions. The common law confessions rule is largely informed by the problem of false confessions. As noted in *Oickle*, "[t]he history of police interrogations is not without its unsavoury chapters" (para. 34). The parameters of the rule are very much tailored to counter the dangers created by improper interrogation techniques that commonly produce false confessions: see *Oickle*, at paras. 32-46. Further, a confession is a very powerful item of evidence against an accused which, in and of itself, can ground a conviction. One of the overriding concerns of the criminal justice system is that the innocent must not be convicted. Because it is recognized that involuntary confessions are more likely to be unreliable, the confessions rule requires proof beyond a reasonable doubt of the voluntariness of any statement obtained from an accused by a person in authority before it may be admitted in evidence, so to avoid miscarriages of justice.

Of course, not every involuntary confession is false. While the confession rule's primary concern is with reliability, it is well established that voluntariness is a broader concept. As this Court stated in *Oickle* (at para. 70): "Wigmore perhaps summed up the point best when he said that voluntariness is 'shorthand for a complex of values': *Wigmore on Evidence* (Chadbourn rev. 1970), vol. 3, § 826, at p. 351." These values include respect for the individual's freedom of will, the need for law enforcement officers themselves to obey the law, and the overall fairness of the criminal justice system: see *Oickle*, at paras. 69-70, citing *Blackburn v. Alabama*, 361 U.S. 199 (1960), at p. 207.

Therefore, the notion of voluntariness is broad-based and has long included the common law principle that a person is not obliged to give information to the police or to answer questions. This component of the voluntariness rule is reflected in the usual police caution given to a suspect and the importance attached (even before the advent of the Charter) to the presence of a caution as a factor in determining the voluntariness of a statement made by a person under arrest or detention: see *Boudreau v. The King*, [1949] S.C.R. 262; *R. v. Fitton*, [1956] S.C.R. 958; and *R. v. Esposito* (1985), 24 C.C.C. (3d) 88 (Ont. C.A.). A common form of the police caution given to a person who has been charged with an offence is the following: "You are charged with. . . Do you wish to say anything in answer to the charge? You are not obliged to say anything but whatever you do say may be given in evidence." Therefore, the police caution, in plain language, informs the suspect of his right to remain silent. Its importance as a factor on the question of voluntariness was noted by this Court as early as 1949 in *Boudreau*:

> The fundamental question is whether a confession of an accused offered in evidence is voluntary. There mere fact that a warning was given is not necessarily decisive in favour of admissibility but, on the other hand, the absence of a warning should not bind the hands of the Court so as to compel it to rule out a statement. All the surrounding circumstances must be investigated and, if upon their review the Court is not satisfied of the voluntary nature of the admission, the statement will be rejected. Accordingly, the presence or absence of a warning will be a factor and, in many cases, an important one.

Although the confessions rule applies whether or not the suspect is in detention, the common law recognized, also long before the advent of the *Charter*, that the suspect's situation is much different after detention. (As we shall see, the residual protection afforded to the right to silence under s. 7 of the *Charter* is only triggered upon detention.) After detention, the state authorities are in control and the detainee, who cannot simply walk away, is in a more vulnerable position. There is a greater risk of abuse of power by the police. The fact of detention alone can have a significant impact on the suspect and cause him or her to feel compelled to give a statement. The importance of reaffirming the individual's right to choose whether to speak to the authorities after he or she is detained is reflected in the jurisprudence concerning the timing of the police caution. Rene Marin, in his text *Admissibility of Statements* (9th ed. (looseleaf)), at pp. 2-24.2 and 2-24.3, provides a useful yardstick for the police on when they should caution a suspect:

> The warning should be given when there are reasonable grounds to suspect that the person being interviewed has committed an offence. An easy yardstick to determine when the warning should be given is for a police officer to consider the question of what he or she would do if the person attempted to leave the questioning room or leave the presence of the officer where a communication or exchange is taking place. If the answer is arrest (or detain) the person, then the warning should be given.

These words of advice are sound. Even if the suspect has not formally been arrested and is not obviously under detention, police officers are well advised to give the police caution in the circumstances described by Marin. Of course, with the advent of the Charter, the s. 10 right to counsel is triggered upon arrest or detention. The right to counsel has both an informational and an implementational component. It seeks to ensure that persons who become subject to the coercive power of the state will know about their right to counsel and will be given the opportunity to exercise it so they can make an informed choice whether to participate in the investigation against them. Therefore, if the detainee has exercised his s. 10 Charter right to counsel, he will presumably have been informed of his right to remain silent, and the overall significance of the caution may be somewhat diminished. Where the suspect has not consulted with counsel, however, the police caution becomes all the more important as a factor in answering the ultimate question of voluntariness.

· · ·

On the question of voluntariness, as under any distinct s. 7 review based on an alleged breach of the right to silence, the focus is on the conduct of the police and its effect on the suspect's ability to exercise his or her free will. The test is an objective one. However, the individual characteristics of the accused are obviously relevant considerations in applying this objective test.

Therefore, voluntariness, as it is understood today, requires that the court scrutinize whether the accused was denied his or her right to silence. The right to silence is defined in accordance with constitutional principles. A finding of voluntariness will therefore be determinative of the s. 7 issue. In other words, if the Crown proves voluntariness beyond a reasonable doubt, there can be no finding of a Charter violation of the right to silence in respect of the same statement. The converse holds true as well. If the circumstances are such that an accused is able to show on a balance of probabilities a breach of his or her right to silence, the Crown will not be in a position to meet the voluntariness test. . . .

Mr. Singh takes particular issue with the leeway afforded to the police in questioning the detainee, even after he has retained counsel and has asserted his choice to remain silent. He submits that courts have erroneously interpreted the underlined passage above as permitting the police to ignore a detainee's expressed wish to remain silent and to use "legitimate means of persuasion". I say two things in response to this argument. First, the use of legitimate means of persuasion is indeed permitted under the present rule — it was expressly endorsed by this Court in Hebert. This approach is part of the critical balance that must be maintained between individual and societal interests. Second, the law as it stands does not permit the police to ignore the detainee's freedom to choose whether to speak or not, as contended. Under both common law and Charter rules, police persistence in continuing the interview, despite repeated assertions by the detainee that he wishes to remain silent, may well raise a strong argument that any subsequently obtained statement was not the product of a free will to speak to the authorities. As we shall see, the trial judge in this case was very much alive to the risk that the statement may be involuntary when a police officer engages in such conduct.

· · ·

Despite Sgt. Attew's admitted intention to put parts of the police case against Mr. Singh before him in an effort to get him to confess, "no matter what", his conduct of the interview as evidenced on the videotape shows that in so describing his method his bark is much worse than his bite. In my respectful view, the trial judge's ultimate judgment call on this issue is supported by the record and is entitled to deference. Therefore, I see no reason to interfere with his ruling on admissibility.

It must again be emphasized that such situations are highly fact-specific and trial judges must take into account all the relevant factors in determining whether or not the Crown has established that the accused's confession is voluntary. In some circumstances, the evidence will support a finding that continued questioning by the police in the face of the accused's repeated assertions of the right to silence denied the accused a meaningful choice whether to speak or to remain silent: see Otis. The number of times the accused asserts his or her right to silence is part of the assessment of all of the circumstances, but is not in itself determinative. The ultimate question is whether the accused exercised free will by choosing to make a statement: *Otis*, at paras. 50 and 54.

Per FISH J. (BINNIE, LeBEL, ABELLA JJ. concurring) (dissenting):

The question on this appeal is whether "no" means "yes" where a police interrogator refuses to take "no" for an answer from a detainee under his total control. As a matter of constitutional principle, I would answer that question in the negative, allow the appeal and order a new trial.

. . .

What is at stake, rather, is the Court's duty to ensure that a detainee's right to silence will be respected by interrogators once it has been unequivocally asserted, and not disregarded or insidiously undermined as an investigative "stratagem" (the trial judge's own word in this case).

The appellant, Jagrup Singh, asserted his right to silence unequivocally — not once, but eighteen times. Throughout his interrogation, Mr. Singh was imprisoned in a police lock-up. In the trial judge's words, he was "totally under the control of the police authorities", "[did] not have freedom of unescorted movement" and "relie[d] totally on his jailers for the necessaries of life" (Ruling on the voir dire, [2003] B.C.J. No. 3174 (QL), 2003 BCSC 2013, at para. 8). Powerless to end his interrogation, Mr. Singh asked, repeatedly, to be returned to his cell. Yet he was not permitted to do so until he capitulated and made the incriminating statements impugned on this appeal.

Mr. Singh's interrogator understood very well that Mr. Singh had chosen not to speak with the police. The interrogator nonetheless disregarded Mr. Singh's repeated assertions of his right to silence. It is undisputed that he did so "an effort to get [Mr. Singh] to confess, no matter what" (Ruling on the voir dire, at para. 34. . .).

In his relentless pursuit of this objective, the interrogator urged Mr. Singh, subtly but unmistakeably, to forsake his counsel's advice. I find this aspect of the interrogation particularly disturbing.

To the officer's knowledge, Mr. Singh had been advised by his lawyer to exercise his right to silence. The officer, with irony if not cynicism, discounted this "absolutely great advice" (his words) as something he too would say if he were Mr. Singh's lawyer. And he then pressed Mr. Singh to instead answer his questions — "to confess, no matter what".

Mr. Singh was thus deprived not only of his right to silence, but also, collaterally, of the intended benefit of his right to counsel. These rights are close companions, like glove and hand.

. . .

At the very least, the interrogator's conduct in this case "unfairly frustrated [Mr. Singh's] decision on the question of whether to make a statement to the authorities" (*Hebert*, at p. 186). Accordingly, the impugned statements, in the words of s. 24(2) of the *Charter*, were "obtained in a manner that infringed or denied" Mr. Singh's constitutional right to silence. And I am satisfied that authorizing their admission in the circumstances of this case would bring the administration of justice into disrepute. They should therefore have been excluded at trial.

In the trial judge's view, Mr. Singh's repeated assertions of his right to silence signify that "Mr. Singh successfully invoked his right to silence" (para. 36). . .

Where continued resistance has been made to appear futile to one person under the dominance or control of another, as it was in this case, ultimate submission proves neither true consent nor valid waiver. It proves the failure, not the success, of the disregarded assertions of the right of the powerless and the vulnerable to say "no".

. . .

I take care not to be understood to have held that eighteen (a significant number in other contexts) is of any importance at all in determining whether a detainee's right of silence has been effectively undermined. On the contrary, I favour a purposive approach and find it unnecessary to decide whether eighteen times is too many or once is too few. Constitutional rights do not have to be asserted or invoked a pre-determined number of times before the state and its agents are bound to permit them to be exercised freely and effectively. A right that need not be respected after it has been firmly and unequivocally asserted any number of times is a constitutional promise that has not been kept.

Nothing in *Hebert*, or in any other decision of this Court, permits the police to press detainees to waive the *Charter* rights they have firmly and unequivocally asserted, or to deliberately frustrate their effective exercise. This is true of the right to counsel and true as well of the right to silence.

Justice Charron agrees with the British Columbia Court of Appeal that "[i]n the context of an investigatory interview with an obvious person in authority, the expansive view of the confession rule in *Oickle* may leave little additional room for s. 7" ((2006), 38 C.R. (6th) 217 (B.C. C.A.), at para. 19). With respect, I am of a different view.

The rationale of the enhanced confessions rule adopted in *R. v. Oickle*, [2000] 2 S.C.R. 3, 2000 SCC 38, like the rationale of its narrower predecessor, is distinct from the purposes served by the Charter. A confession may be "voluntary" under the common law rule and yet be obtained by state action that infringes s. 7 of the *Charter*. And s. 7 will be infringed where, as in this case, a police interrogator has undermined a detainee's "freedom to choose whether to make a statement or not" (*Hebert*, at p. 176). Flagrantly disregarded in this way, the detainee's "positive right to make a free choice" (*Hebert*, at p. 177), is neither "positive" nor "free".

. . .

Justice Charron finds that the expansion of the confessions rule in *Oickle* leaves no additional room for the operation of s. 7 in the context of an "investigatory interview" (paras. 8, 25). I agree with her that there is considerable overlap between the *Charter* protection of the right to silence and the common law confessions rule. Given their different purposes, however, they should remain distinct doctrines: To overlap is not to overtake.

Even under its broader formulation in *Oickle*, the common law rule remains principally concerned with the reliability of confessions and the integrity of the criminal justice system. The purpose of the Charter, on the other hand, is "to constrain government action in conformity with certain individual rights and freedoms, the preservation of which are essential to the continuation of a democratic, functioning society in which the basic dignity of all is recognized" (*Canadian Egg Marketing Agency v. Richardson*, [1998] 3 S.C.R. 157, at para. 57).

As this case illustrates, a purposive approach makes plain that the right to pre-trial silence under s. 7 of the *Charter* is not eclipsed by the common law confessions rule under *Oickle*. This asymmetry should not surprise. The Court has consistently held that the two doctrines are distinct. Lower courts have continued to apply them separately. And even upon expanding the common law rule in *Oickle*, the Court took care to explain that neither rule "subsumes the other" (at para. 31).

Justice Charron finds the reasons of Proulx J.A. in *Otis* "particularly instructive" on the issue that concerns us here. I agree. In Justice Proulx's words: [Translation] "The refusal of the investigator to respect the respondent's specific insistent request to end the interrogation constitutes a violation of the right to remain silent": *R. v. Otis* (2000), 151 C.C.C. (3d) 416 (Que. C.A.), at para. 43. And I think it especially instructive that Justice Proulx [Translation] "ruled that the confession should be excluded due to the breach of a right guaranteed by the Charter" (para. 57) rather than under the common law confessions rule — even though, in the particular circumstances of *Otis* (notably the "emotional disintegration" of the accused), he would have excluded the accused's statement under the confessions rule as well.

The Court held in *Hebert*, as we have seen, that the s. 7 right to silence "must be interpreted in a manner which secures to the detained person the right to make a free and meaningful choice as to whether to speak to the authorities or to remain silent" (p. 181). Under the *Oickle* test, as noted earlier, a statement is admissible at common law where the detainee had an operating mind and the confession did not result from inducements, oppression, or police trickery that would shock the community. Clearly, however, a confession that meets these common law standards does not invariably represent a "free and meaningful choice" for the purposes of the *Charter*. A choice that has been disregarded, and "unfairly frustrated" (*Hebert*, at p. 186) by relentless interrogation "an effort to get a detainee to confess, no matter what", is, once again, neither "free" nor "meaningful". And it is a choice not born of "legitimate means of persuasion" within the meaning of *Hebert* (at p. 177).

. . .

With respect, I am troubled by Justice Charron's suggestion that the ability of the police to investigate crime in Canada would be unduly impaired by the effective exercise of the pre-trial right to silence. In a similar vein, the respondent warns against its "massive and far-reaching consequences in the arena of police investigations" and the federal Director of Public Prosecutions, an intervener, submits that it would have "a devastating impact on criminal justice in Canada".

. . .

Potential witnesses are rightfully expected, as a matter of civic duty, to assist the police by answering their questions. As a matter of law, however, they may refuse to answer, and go on home. Prisoners and detainees, on the other hand, are by definition not free to leave as they please. They are powerless to end their interrogation. As explained in *Hebert*, this is why they have been given the right to counsel and its close relative, the right to silence.

Neither of these rights has been given constitutional protection on the condition that it not be exercised, lest the investigation of crime be brought to a standstill. On the contrary, the policy of the law is to facilitate, and not to frustrate, the effective exercise of both rights by those whom they are intended to protect. They are *Charter* rights, not constitutional placebos.

Moreover, we have no evidence to support the proposition that requiring the police to respect a detainee's right of silence, once it has been unequivocally asserted, would have a "devastating impact" on criminal investigations anywhere in this country.

For more than 40 years, it has been the law in the United States that where a suspect "indicates in any manner, at any time prior to or during questioning, that he wishes to remain silent, the interrogation must cease": *Miranda v. Arizona*, 384 U.S. 436 (1966), at pp. 473-74. And yet, as Wharton puts it, "[n]umerous studies in the years following this decision have concluded that *Miranda* had little impact on the ability of the police to obtain statements": Wharton's *Criminal Procedure* (14th ed. looseleaf), at p. 19-9.

. . .

Not everyone will agree with Wharton that *Miranda* appears to have had little effect on the ability of the police to obtain statements. There are, of course, conflicting assessments of the evidence as to its impact, but *Miranda* can hardly be said to have paralysed criminal investigations in the United

States. And there is no evidentiary basis for suggesting that it would do so in Canada.

In any event, the success of this appeal does not depend on the importation of the *Miranda* rule into Canada. And I take care not to be misunderstood to suggest that *Miranda* either is now, or ought to be made, the law in Canada. Here, the right to silence, once asserted, is not a barrier to the admissibility of any subsequent pre-trial statement of a detainee or prisoner. Nor is there any requirement that interrogators obtain a signed waiver from detainees, as the appellant suggests there ought to be. On the other hand, in the words of Professors Delisle, Stuart and Tanovich, "once an accused has clearly stated he wishes to remain silent, the police cannot act as if there has been a waiver" (R. Delisle, D. Stuart and D. Tanovich, *Evidence: Principles and Problems* (8th ed. 2007), at p. 489).

In short, detainees who have asserted their right to silence are entitled to change their minds. As I have stated elsewhere, "[a]n initial refusal can later give way to a crisis of conscience, to an 'unconscious compulsion to confess' — or, simply, to a genuine change of heart": *R. v. Timm* (1998), 131 C.C.C. (3d) 306 (Que. C.A.), at para. 145. But they cannot be compelled to do so by the persistent disregard of that choice. As mentioned earlier, that is what happened here.

Finally, even in the absence of the required evidentiary foundation, I am prepared for present purposes to recognize that the work of the police would be made easier (and less challenging) if police interrogators were permitted to undermine the constitutionally protected rights of detainees, including the right to counsel and the right to silence — either by pressing detainees to waive them, or by "unfairly frustrat[ing]" their exercise (*Hebert* at p. 186). More draconian initiatives might prove more effective still.

Nonetheless and without hesitation, I much prefer a system of justice that permits the effective exercise by detainees of the constitutional and procedural rights guaranteed to them by the law of the land. The right to silence, like the right to counsel, is in my view a constitutional promise that must be kept. . . .

In her comment on *Singh*, Professor Lisa Dufraimont writes in part:

Arguably, *Singh* provides insufficient protection for the right to silence. As long as the Charter protects the pre-trial right to silence, there is something unseemly about the Supreme Court jealously guarding the power of police interrogators to undermine a suspect's choice to remain silent. At the same time, the majority in *Singh* recognizes that persistent questioning of suspects who repeatedly assert their right to silence can result in the exclusion of the resulting statements under the voluntariness rule. Such a statement will be involuntary, and exclusion automatic, where it was not the product of the suspect's free will to speak to the authorities.

Ultimately, then, there may be less separating the majority and the minority in *Singh* that one might initially suppose. Certainly the majority rejects the dissenters' suggestion that the police are obliged to stop questioning a detainee who clearly asserts the right to silence. However, the full court agrees that persistent questioning in the face of repeated assertions of the right to silence can render a statement inadmissible. The question whether the exclusionary remedy arises from the confessions rule or the s. 7 pre-trial right to silence is less important than the availability of the remedy itself.

The problem is that even *Oickle* is not just about voluntariness. Under *Oickle,* there is a freestanding discretion to exclude confessions obtained by tricks that shock the community. Why wasn't such a sustained effort by the police to override an assertion of the right to silence shocking? Justice Abella held for the Supreme Court in *R. v. Turcotte* that adverse inferences should not be drawn against someone who is silent at the pre-trial stage as it would be a "snare and delusion" to advise about the right to silence and then to turn around and use silence as a sign of guilt. Why isn't it a snare and delusion to say a suspect has the right to silence but allow police to ignore its exercise? *Singh* has suddenly reduced this very little s. 7 right to one that an undercover agent cannot elicit statements from a detainee by the functional equivalent of an interrogation. Certainly in *Singh* there is no mention of any s. 7 right to be advised of the right to silence where police are not undercover. Whether the accused received advice from the police or a lawyer (if there was one) is just a factor to be considered on the voluntariness inquiry. With the changed composition of the Court one can only hope that *Singh* will be reconsidered.[276]

In *R. v. Sinclair*[277] the Court found that the s. 10(b) right to retain and instruct counsel without delay does not, in contrast to the law in the United States, mandate the presence of defence counsel during custodial interrogation. The real heat of the very strong divisions in the Court stems from the further decision of the 5-4 majority that the right to counsel normally ends with the initial consultation with counsel. The majority decide that in most cases an initial warning, coupled with a reasonable opportunity to consult counsel or duty counsel when the detainee invokes the right, satisfies s. 10(b). However, the police must give the detainee an additional opportunity to receive advice from counsel where developments in the course of the investigation make this necessary to serve the purpose underlying s. 10(b) of providing the detainee with legal advice relevant to his or her s. 7 right to choose whether to cooperate with the police interrogation. The majority recognizes existing jurisprudence that a second consultation should occur when there is a change of circumstance such as a new procedure for the detainee (such as an identification parade), a new jeopardy as where the victim dies and where the "detainee may not have understood the initial advice".

---

[276]   For further critical comments on *Singh* see Timothy Moore & Karina Gagnier, "'You can talk if you want to': Is the Police Caution on the 'Right to Silence' Understandable?" (2008), 51 C.R. (6th) 233, and Dale Ives & Christopher Sherrin, "*R. v. Singh* — A Meaningless Right to Silence with Dangerous Consequences" (2008), 51 C.R. (6th) 250, but see, however, strong support from Suhail Akhtar, "Whatever Happened to The Right to Silence?" (2009), 62 C.R. (6th) 73.

[277]   [2010] 2 S.C.R. 310, 77 C.R. (6th) 203, 259 C.C.C. (3d) 443 (S.C.C.). See critical comments by Don Stuart, "*Sinclair* Regrettably Completes the *Oickle* and *Singh* Manual for Coercive and Lawless Interrogation" (2010), 77 C.R. (6th) 303 and Christine Boyle, "*R. v. Sinclair:* A Comparatively Disappointing Decision on the Right to Counsel" (2010), 77 C.R. (6th) 310.

The vehemence of the protests of the dissenters is palpable. Justice Binnie fires the most direct salvo:

> What now appears to be licenced as a result of the "interrogation trilogy" — Oickle, Singh, and [now Sinclair] — is that an individual (presumed innocent) may be detained and isolated for questioning by the police for at least five or six hours without reasonable recourse to a lawyer, during which time the officers can brush aside assertions of the right to silence or demands to be returned to his or her cell, in an endurance contest in which the police interrogators, taking turns with one another, hold all the important legal cards [para. 98].

> When the decisions are read together the resulting latitude allowed to the police to deal with a detainee, who is to be presumed innocent, disproportionately favours the interests of the state in the investigation of crime over the rights of the individual in a free society [para. 77]

According to Lebel and Fish JJ (with Abella J. concurring) the suggestion of the majority

> that our residual concerns can be meaningfully addressed by way of the confessions rule thus ignores what we have learned about the dynamics of custodial interrogations and renders pathetically anaemic the entrenched constitutional rights to counsel and to silence [para. 184]

In the view of these three dissenters the majority opinions in both *Singh* and *Sinclair* project a view of the right to silence that hinges too closely on the voluntariness of a detainee's inculpatory statement. This approach ignores the fact that the right to silence can be breached in a manner other than the taking by the police of an involuntary statement. The majority's conclusion in *Singh* that a detainee cannot use the s. 7 right to silence to cease a custodial interview, and the majority view in this case that a detainee cannot use s. 10(b) in this same fashion, in effect creates a new right on the part of the police to the unfettered and continuing access to the detainee, for the purposes of conducting a custodial interview to the point of confession. The clear result is that custodial detainees cannot exercise their constitutional rights in order to prevent their participation in the investigation against them. These dissenters added that none of the majority's justifications based on law enforcement concerns were put through the rigour of a s. 1 analysis, and they were based on nothing more than speculation rather than empirical evidence, for example, as to the effect of the Miranda rules in the United States.

McLachlin C.J. and Charron J. fire back for the majority (Deschamps, Rothstein and Cromwell JJ. concurring):

> Our colleagues LeBel and Fish JJ. also assert that our approach is such that the detainee is effectively forced to participate in the police investigation. The suggestion is that the questioning of a suspect, in and of itself, runs counter to the presumption of innocence and the protection against self-incrimination. This is clearly contrary to settled authority and practice. In our view, in defining the contours of the s. 7 right to silence and related Charter rights, consideration must be given not only to the protection of the rights of the accused but also to the societal interest in the investigation and solving of crimes. The police are

charged with the duty to investigate alleged crimes and, in performing this duty, they necessarily have to make inquiries from relevant sources of information, including persons suspected of, or even charged with, committing the alleged crime. While the police must be respectful of an individual's Charter rights, a rule that would require the police to automatically retreat upon a detainee stating that he or she has nothing to say, in our respectful view, would not strike the proper balance between the public interest in the investigation of crimes and the suspect's interest in being left alone.[278]

Prior to *Oickle*, Justice Ketchum in *R. v. S. (M.J.)*[279] excluded a confession in part because a videotape revealed the use of the Reid method of psychological interrogation pioneered in the United States which was seen to be an oppressive and brainwashing technique which should not be accepted in Canada. The Reid method involves a nine-step procedure of sustained confrontation with allegations of guilt and minimization of the consequences of confession:

> It is a two-stage process. The first stage, encompassing steps one through four is designed to reduce the suspect's self-confidence in surviving the interrogation by convincing them that there exists incontrovertible evidence of their guilt, that no reasonable person could come to any other conclusion and that there is no way out of their situation other than to confess. Once the suspect has accepted that they are powerless to change their situation, the investigator moves to the second stage, steps five through nine, wherein inducements are offered, by way of alternative reasons for the crime, that are designed to persuade the suspect that confessing is in their best interest psychologically, materially and legally.[280]

Since *Oickle*, the Reid technique has been adopted by police training and practice in most parts of the country and has been seen by most courts as consistent with *Oickle*.[281] However, social psychologists have increasingly pointed to the danger that the Reid method risks, and has lead to, false confessions in the United States and in Canada.[282]

In the case of undercover officers, the small *Hebert* right to silence is generally thought to have no application to undercover activities in the field as there is no detention nor is the voluntary confession rule applicable given

---

[278] *Sinclair, supra* note 277 at para. 12.

[279] (2000), 32 C.R. (5th) 378 (Alta. P.C.).

[280] Nadia Klein, "Forensic Psychology and the Reid Technique of Interrogation: How an Innocent can be Psychologically Coerced into Confession" (2016) 63 Crim. L.Q. 504 at 513 (footnotes omitted).

[281] See Thierry Nadon, "The Reid Interrogation Technique: Effective, For Some Controversial and Legal" (2012), 91 C.R. (6th) 359, but see recently *R. v. Chapple*, 2012 ABPC 229 (Alta. Prov. Ct.). There has been a call from a Newfoundland psychology professor and a police inspector to abandon the Reid method in favour of the less accusatorial PEACE method use in the U.K.: Brent Snook & John House, "An Alternative Interviewing Method, All We Are Saying Is Give PEACE A Chance" Blue Line Magazine, November 2008, and Brent Snook, Joseph Eastwood & Todd Barron, "The Next Stage in the Evolution of Interrogations: The PEACE Model" (2014) 2 Can. Crim. L.R. 221.

[282] See especially Tim Moore & Lindsay Fitzsimmons, "Justice Imperiled: False Confessions and the Reid Technique" (2011) 57 Crim. L.Q. 509 and CBC *The National*'s special report "Truth, Lies and Confessions", June 24, 2012 (see the CBC website for a wealth of material and videotapes of interrogations).

that there is no known person in authority. There seem to be few, if any, legal controls on such undercover tactics.

4. CONFESSIONS IN UNDERCOVER OPERATIONS

In 2014, the Supreme Court released two important judgments regarding confessions obtained through the use of a controversial undercover investigation technique known as the Mr. Big strategy.

R. v. HART
2014 CSC 52, 2014 SCC 52, [2014] 2 S.C.R. 544, 312 C.C.C. (3d) 250, 12 C.R. (7th) 221 (S.C.C.)

The accused was charged with the first degree murder of his twin three-year-old daughters who drowned in a lake while under his care. The accused had taken the girls to a lakeside park by car. When questioned by police on the day of the drownings, he claimed that one of his daughters fell into the water and he panicked and drove home to get his wife, leaving his other daughter on the dock. First responders found both girls floating in the lake but it was too late to save their lives. The accused told the same story when interrogated by police about a month later.

Two weeks later, the accused contacted police and volunteered that his previous account of events was untruthful. He explained that he had a seizure at the park after removing his daughters from the car. When he came to and saw one of his daughters in the water, his only thought was to drive home to his wife. The accused explained that he lied in his earlier statements to police because he did not want to lose his driver's licence. The accused suffers from epilepsy and his licence has been suspended in the past because of that condition.

Police were convinced that the accused had murdered his daughters but they did not have sufficient evidence to charge him. More than two years after the girls' deaths, police decided to mount a Mr. Big operation by luring the accused into a fictitious criminal organization and trying to get him to confess to the boss. The operation began with several weeks of lifestyle surveillance which revealed that the accused rarely left home and did so only when accompanied by his wife. The accused was then befriended by two undercover officers who hired the accused as a driver. Several weeks into the accused's employment, the officers told the accused that they were part of a criminal organization headed by a boss. From that point, the accused participated in simulated criminal activity including delivering smuggled alcohol and stolen credit cards.

The accused was paid $4,470 for his work in the first two months of the operation, and the officers also paid for his travel, hotel rooms and frequent dinners. After two months, the accused was fully immersed in his new fictitious life and would tell the undercover officers that he loved them and that they were brothers. At this point, according to one of the officers, the accused spontaneously offered what can be described as his first confession, stating that he had planned to murder his daughters and had carried it out. This admission came in response to the officer claiming to have assaulted a prostitute and explaining that sometimes bad things had to be done for the organization. The admission was not recorded and the accused denied that it occurred.

The operation continued for two more months, during which time the officers constantly emphasized the importance of trust, honesty and loyalty within the organization, indicating that the untrustworthy were met with violence. The accused was told that there was a big deal coming in the future and that if he participated the accused could be paid up to $25,000. The accused was told that he would only be allowed to participate in the deal if Mr. Big approved, and that Mr. Big had checked into him and found a problem that would have to be resolved before he could continue to work for the organization.

The accused met with the undercover officer posing as Mr. Big. The accused expressed his gratitude to Mr. Big, telling him that his life had turned around since he started working for the organization. Mr. Big raised the topic of the accused's daughters and asked why the accused had killed them. The accused stated that he had had a seizure, implying that their deaths were accidental. Mr. Big rejected this explanation and told the accused not to lie. After further probing by Mr. Big, the accused gave his second confession, saying that he had killed his daughters because he feared child welfare authorities would remove them from his home. On being pressed for details of their deaths, the accused said he struck his daughters with his shoulder, which caused them to fall in the water.

Two days later, the accused returned with an undercover officer to the scene of the drownings to re-enact the event. In this context the accused gave a third confession. The officer knelt down to play the role of one of the girls and the accused demonstrated how he pushed his daughters into the water by nudging the officer with his knee. Shortly thereafter, the accused was arrested and charged with two counts of first degree murder.

By the time of his arrest, the accused had participated in 63 "scenarios" with the undercover officers, had been paid $15,720 for his work, and had travelled to Halifax, Montreal, Ottawa, Toronto and Vancouver, and stayed in hotels and dined in fine restaurants. The total cost of the operation was $413,268.

Evidence of the accused's self-incriminating statements during the Mr. Big operation was admitted at trial. The jury found the accused guilty on both counts of first degree murder. The accused appealed. The Newfoundland and Labrador Court of Appeal, by a majority, allowed the appeal, quashed the convictions and ordered a new trial. The Crown appealed to the Supreme Court of Canada.

MOLDAVER J (MCLACHLIN C.J. and LEBEL, ABELLA, and WAGNER JJ. concurring):

V. Analysis

. . .

B. The Admissibility of the Mr. Big Confessions

Mr. Big Operations in Canada

56 The Mr. Big technique is a Canadian invention. Although a version of the technique appears to have been used by the police as far back as 1901, its modern use began in the 1990s and has continued since then (see R. v. Todd (1901), 4 C.C.C. 514 (Man. K.B.), at p. 523). According to the B.C. RCMP, the technique has been used across Canada on more than 350 occasions as of 2008.

57 The technique tends to follow a similar script in each case. Undercover officers conduct surveillance on a suspect in order to gather information about his or her habits and circumstances. Next, they approach the suspect and attempt to cultivate a relationship. The suspect and the undercover officers socialize and begin to work together, and the suspect is introduced to the idea that the officers work for a criminal organization that is run by their boss—"Mr. Big". The suspect works for the criminal organization and is assigned simple and apparently illegal tasks—serving as a lookout, delivering packages, or counting large sums of money are common examples. As occurred in this case, this stage of the operation can last for several months. See T. E. Moore, P. Copeland and R. A. Schuller, "Deceit, Betrayal and the Search for Truth: Legal and Psychological Perspectives on the 'Mr. Big' Strategy" (2009), 55 Crim. L.Q. 348, at pp. 351-52; K. T. Keenan and J. Brockman, Mr. Big: Exposing Undercover Investigations in Canada (2010), at p. 19.

58 As the operation wears on, the suspect is offered increasing responsibility and financial rewards. By flying the suspect across the country, putting him up in hotels, and taking him to expensive restaurants, undercover officers show the suspect that working with the group provides a life of luxury and close friendships. All the while, the suspect is constantly reminded that his or her ultimate acceptance into the group depends on Mr. Big's approval (see Keenan and Brockman, at p. 20).

59 Throughout the operation, the suspect is also told that the organization demands honesty, trust and loyalty from its members. An aura of violence is cultivated to reinforce these values. Officers teach the suspect that those who betray the trust of the organization are met with violence. They do this by telling the suspect that the organization kills "rats," or by exposing him to simulated acts of violence perpetrated by members of the organization against other undercover officers as punishment for imagined betrayals (see, e.g., Moore, Copeland and Schuller, at pp. 356-57). R. v. Hathaway, 2007 SKQB 48, 292 Sask. R. 7, provides a stark example. In that case, undercover officers simulated an assault on a woman who had crossed the criminal organization. During the beating, officers threatened to kill the woman, her husband, and

her infant child. The accused watched as undercover officers threw the bloodied woman into the trunk of a car.

60 Once the stage is set, the operation culminates in a meeting, akin to a job interview, between the suspect and Mr. Big. Invariably during these meetings, Mr. Big expresses concern about the suspect's criminal past and the particular crime under investigation by the police. As the meeting unfolds, it becomes clear that confessing to the crime provides a ticket into the criminal organization and safety from the police. Suspects may be told that Mr. Big has conclusive evidence of their guilt and that denying the offence will be seen as proof of a lack of trustworthiness. In another variation, suspects are told that Mr. Big has learned from contacts within the police that a prosecution for the offence is imminent based on new evidence. The organization offers to protect the target through a variety of means—by offering to eliminate a witness or by having someone else confess to the crime—if the suspect confesses to Mr. Big. Throughout the interrogation, any denials of guilt are dismissed as lies, and Mr. Big presses for a confession (see, e.g., C.L.A. factum, at paras. 7-8; Keenan and Brockman, at pp. 19-21).

61 As indicated, the technique has proved valuable and has been used to secure convictions in hundreds of cases (see, e.g., R. v. Copeland, 1999 BCCA 744, 131 B.C.A.C. 264, where a confession elicited through a Mr. Big operation led the police to the victim's previously undiscovered body).

62 To date, there are no established wrongful convictions stemming from its use. However, in 1992, Kyle Unger was convicted of murder based in part on a confession elicited through a Mr. Big operation, as well as forensic evidence found at the scene of the crime. In 2004, the forensic evidence was called into question by a review committee. The Minister of Justice ordered a review of the conviction, and the Crown ultimately withdrew the charges after determining it did not have sufficient evidence to proceed with a new trial (see also R. v. Bates, 2009 ABQB 379, 468 A.R. 158, where an accused, though properly convicted of manslaughter, overstated his involvement by falsely confessing to Mr. Big that he was the person who shot a rival drug dealer).

Do We Need a Test for Determining the Admissibility of Mr. Big Confessions?

63 In cases where the Mr. Big technique has been used, the ensuing confessions have typically been received at trial. Under the existing case law, they have been admitted under the party admissions exception to the hearsay rule (see R. v. Evans, [1993] 3 S.C.R. 653, at p. 664; R. v. Osmar, 2007 ONCA 50, 84 O.R. (3d) 321, at para. 53). The admissibility of party admissions flows from the adversarial nature of our trial system, and the belief that "what a party has previously stated can be admitted against the party in whose mouth it does not lie to complain of the unreliability of his or her own statements" (Evans, at p. 664).

64 Attempts to extend existing legal protections to Mr. Big operations have failed. This Court has held that Mr. Big operations do not engage the right to silence because the accused is not detained by the police at the time he or she confesses (see R. v. McIntyre, [1994] 2 S.C.R. 480; R. v. Hebert, [1990] 2 S.C.R. 151). And the confessions rule—which requires the Crown to prove an accused's statement to a person in authority is "voluntary"—is inoperative because the accused does not know that Mr. Big is a police officer when he confesses (see R. v. Grandinetti, 2005 SCC 5, [2005] 1 S.C.R. 27).

. . .

67 . . .In my view, the law as it stands today provides insufficient protection to accused persons who confess during Mr. Big operations. Three concerns lead me to this conclusion.

The Danger of Unreliable Confessions

68 First, because of the nature of Mr. Big operations, concerns arise as to the reliability of the confessions they produce. The purpose of these operations is to induce confessions, and they are carefully calibrated to achieve that end. Over a period of weeks or months, suspects are made to believe that the fictitious criminal organization for which they work can provide them with financial security, social acceptance, and friendship. Suspects also come to learn that violence is a necessary part of the organization's business model, and that a past history of violence is a boast-worthy accomplishment. And during the final meeting with Mr. Big—which involves a skillful interrogation conducted by an experienced police officer—suspects learn that confessing to the crime under investigation provides a consequence-free ticket into the organization and all of the rewards it provides.

69 It seems a matter of common sense that the potential for a false confession increases in proportion to the nature and extent of the inducements held out to the accused. Unsurprisingly, this view is supported by academic literature (see R. v. Oickle, 2000 SCC 38, [2000] 2 S.C.R. 3, at paras. 39 and 44; S. M. Kassin, et al. "Police-Induced Confessions: Risk Factors and Recommendations" (2010), 34 Law. & Hum. Behav. 3, at pp. 14-15).

70 The common law confessions rule serves to illustrate the importance of a trial judge's role in assessing reliability. The confessions rule has long concerned itself with the dangers posed by unreliable confessions (see, e.g., G. A. Martin, "The Admissibility of Confessions and Statements" (1963), 5 Crim. L.Q. 35, at p. 35). Under the confessions rule, we recognize that unreliable confessions made by an accused pose particular dangers, as juries often attach great weight to the accused's own words. When an accused falsely confesses to a crime, the risk of a wrongful conviction becomes acute. This Court recognized as much in Oickle, when it noted that false confessions have played an "important role" in cases where wrongful convictions have occurred (para. 36). Subsequent research has confirmed that risk. In 40 of the first 250 DNA exonerations in the United States, for example, the accused was found to

have falsely confessed to the crime (see B. L. Garrett, "The Substance of False Confessions", (2010), 62 Stan. L. Rev. 1051).

71 The confessions rule thus guards against the danger of unreliable confessions by requiring the Crown to prove to a judge beyond a reasonable doubt that an accused's statement was voluntarily made. Where the Crown is unable to do so, the accused's statement is rendered inadmissible.

72 But as the law stands today, unlike our approach with the confessions rule, we have failed to adopt a consistent approach to assessing the reliability of Mr. Big confessions before they go to the jury. This is so despite the obvious nature of the inducements these operations create. In my view, it would be dangerous and unwise to assume that we do not need to be concerned about the reliability of Mr. Big confessions simply because the suspect does not know that the person pressuring him to confess is a police officer. And although it will be easier for a jury to understand why an accused would falsely confess to Mr. Big than to the police during a conventional interrogation (because of the more obvious nature of the inducements and the accused's belief that it is in his self-interest to confess), this does not provide a complete answer to the reliability concerns raised by these confessions. Under the confessions rule, we do not abandon our concern for reliability in cases where a confession is the product of clear threats or inducements, on the assumption that the jury will have an easier time understanding why it is unreliable.

The Prejudicial Effect of Mr. Big Confessions

73 The second concern with Mr. Big confessions—and one that distinguishes them from confessions made in other contexts—is that they are invariably accompanied by prejudicial facts regarding the accused's character. Putting these confessions into evidence requires showing the jury that the accused wanted to join a criminal organization and that he participated in "simulated" crimes that he believed were real. The absence of a consistent approach in assessing the admissibility of these confessions sits uneasily with the general rule that bad character evidence is presumptively inadmissible for the Crown. This centuries-old rule prohibits the Crown from leading evidence of misconduct engaged in by the accused that is unrelated to the charges before the court, unless it can demonstrate that its probative value outweighs its prejudicial effect (see R. v. Handy, 2002 SCC 56, [2002] 2 S.C.R. 908).

74 Bad character evidence causes two kinds of prejudice. It causes "moral prejudice" by marring the character of the accused in the eyes of the jury, thereby creating a risk that the jury will reason from the accused's general disposition to the conclusion that he is guilty of the crime charged, or that he is deserving of punishment in any event (Handy, at para. 31). And it causes "reasoning prejudice" by distracting the jury's focus away from the offence charged, toward the accused's extraneous acts of misconduct (ibid.). As this

Court held in Handy, the "poisonous potential" of bad character evidence cannot be doubted (para. 138).

75 When a Mr. Big confession is admitted, the character evidence that accompanies it places the accused in a difficult situation. In these cases, the accused is often obliged, as a tactical necessity, to testify in order to explain why he falsely confessed to Mr Big. The character evidence that has already been admitted is damaging in this context because it shrouds the accused with an aura of distrust before he or she steps into the witness box. This distrust is compounded when the accused asks the jury to disregard his confession because he was lying when he gave it. And all of this furnishes the Crown with ample fodder for a forceful attack on the accused's credibility in cross-examination.

76 Despite the well-established presumption that bad character evidence is inadmissible, it is routinely admitted in Mr. Big cases because it provides the relevant context needed to understand how the accused's pivotal confession came about. Indeed, even the accused comes to depend on this evidence in order to show the nature of the inducements he faced and the reason his confession should not be believed.

77 In my view, the prejudicial effect of Mr. Big confessions is a substantial concern, especially since these confessions may also be unreliable. Putting evidence before a jury that is both unreliable and prejudicial invites a miscarriage of justice. The law must respond to these dangers. The fact that there are no proven wrongful convictions in cases involving Mr. Big confessions provides little comfort. The criminal justice system cannot afford to wait for miscarriages of justice before taking reasonable steps to prevent them.

Police Misconduct

78 Finally, Mr. Big operations create a risk that the police will resort to unacceptable tactics in their pursuit of a confession. As mentioned, in conducting these operations, undercover officers often cultivate an aura of violence in order to stress the importance of trust and loyalty within the organization. This can involve—as it did in this case—threats or acts of violence perpetrated in the presence of the accused. In these circumstances, it is easy to see a risk that the police will go too far, resorting to tactics which may impact on the reliability of a confession, or in some instances amount to an abuse of process.

79 At present, however, these operations are conducted in a legal vacuum. The legal protections afforded to accused persons, which are often intended at least in part to place limits on the conduct of the police in their investigation and interrogation of accused people, have no application to Mr. Big operations. The confessions rule, for example, is intended not only to guard against the risk

of unreliable confessions, but also to prevent abusive state conduct (see R. v. Hodgson, [1998] 2 S.C.R. 449, at para. 20). Yet its protection does not apply because the accused does not know the person he is speaking to is a person in authority. Other protections—like the right to counsel under s. 10(b) of the Charter—are rendered inapplicable because the accused is not "det[ained]" by the police while the operation is ongoing. And the doctrine of abuse of process—intended to protect against abusive state conduct—appears to be somewhat of a paper tiger. To date, it has never operated to exclude a Mr. Big confession, nor has it ever led to the stay of charges arising from one of these operations.

80 In my view, the lack of an effective mechanism for monitoring the conduct of the undercover officers who engage in these operations is problematic. The law must enable trial judges to respond effectively to police misconduct in this context.

How Should the Law Respond to the Problems Posed by Mr. Big Confessions?

. . .

83 In searching for a response to the concerns these operations raise, we must proceed cautiously. To be sure, Mr. Big operations can become abusive, and they can produce confessions that are unreliable and prejudicial. We must seek a legal framework that protects accused persons, and the justice system as a whole, against these dangers. On the other hand, Mr. Big operations are not necessarily abusive, and are capable of producing valuable evidence, the admission of which furthers the interests of justice. We ought not forget that the Mr. Big technique is almost always used in cold cases involving the most serious crimes. Put simply, in responding to the dangers posed by Mr. Big confessions, we should be wary about allowing serious crimes to go unpunished.

Summary of a Proposed Solution

84 In this section, I propose a solution that, in my view, strikes the best balance between guarding against the dangers posed by Mr. Big operations, while ensuring the police have the tools they need to investigate serious crime. This solution involves a two-pronged approach that (1) recognizes a new common law rule of evidence, and (2) relies on a more robust conception of the doctrine of abuse of process to deal with the problem of police misconduct.

85 The first prong recognizes a new common law rule of evidence for assessing the admissibility of these confessions. The rule operates as follows. Where the state recruits an accused into a fictitious criminal organization of its own making and seeks to elicit a confession from him, any confession made by the accused to the state during the operation should be treated as presumptively inadmissible. This presumption of inadmissibility is overcome where the Crown can establish, on a balance of probabilities, that the probative value of the confession outweighs its prejudicial effect. In this context, the confession's

probative value turns on an assessment of its reliability. Its prejudicial effect flows from the bad character evidence that must be admitted in order to put the operation and the confession in context. If the Crown is unable to demonstrate that the accused's confession is admissible, the rest of the evidence surrounding the Mr. Big operation becomes irrelevant and thus inadmissible. This rule, like the confessions rule in the case of conventional police interrogations, operates as a specific qualification to the party admissions exception to the hearsay rule.[283]

86 Second, I would rely on the doctrine of abuse of process to deal with the problem of police misconduct. I recognize that the doctrine has thus far proved less than effective in this context. While the problem is not an easy one, I propose to provide some guidance on how to determine if a Mr. Big operation crosses the line from skillful police work to an abuse of process.

87 The purposes of this two-pronged approach are to protect an accused's right to a fair trial under the Charter, and to preserve the integrity of the justice system. Those are the ends that must ultimately be achieved. This approach strives to reach them by ensuring that only those confessions that are more probative than prejudicial, and which do not result from abuse, are admitted into evidence.

88 However, it must be remembered that trial judges always retain a discretion to exclude evidence where its admission would compromise trial fairness (see R. v. Harrer, [1995] 3 S.C.R. 562). This is because "the general principle that an accused is entitled to a fair trial cannot be entirely reduced to specific rules" (ibid., at para. 23). It is impossible to predict every factual scenario that could present itself. As such, I do not foreclose the possibility that, in an exceptional case, trial fairness may require that a Mr. Big confession be excluded even where the specific rules I have proposed would see the confession admitted.

89 In practice, this two-pronged approach will necessitate that a voir dire be held to determine the admissibility of Mr. Big confessions. The Crown will bear the burden of establishing that, on balance, the probative value of the confession outweighs its prejudicial effect, and it will be for the defence to establish an abuse of process. Trial judges may prefer to begin their analysis by assessing whether there has been an abuse of process. A finding of abuse makes weighing the probative value and prejudicial effect of the evidence unnecessary.

90 Against this backdrop, I will now elaborate on the main features of this two-pronged solution.

---

[283] This rule targets Mr. Big operations in their present form. A change in the way the police use undercover operations to elicit confessions may escape the scope of this rule. However, it is not for this Court to anticipate potential developments in policing. To do so would be speculative. Time will tell whether, in a future case, the principles that underlie this rule warrant extending its application to another context.

Why Does the Crown Bear the Onus of Establishing that the Probative Value of a Mr. Big Confession Outweighs its Prejudicial Effect?

91 The common law rule of evidence I have proposed creates a presumption that Mr. Big confessions are inadmissible, and places the onus of demonstrating that they ought to be received on the Crown. The onus is justified because of the central role played by the state in creating these confessions. It is the state that designs and implements these operations, expending significant resources and acting as puppeteer in the production of the accused's ultimate confession. The state creates the potent mix of a potentially unreliable confession accompanied by prejudicial character evidence. Given its pivotal role, the state should bear the responsibility of showing that the confession it has orchestrated and produced warrants admission into evidence.

92 Placing the onus on the Crown also works to address concerns with abusive state conduct. Confronted by the reality that the Crown will ultimately bear the burden of justifying reception of a Mr. Big confession, the state will be strongly encouraged to tread carefully in how it conducts these operations. As I will explain, the conduct of the police is a factor to be taken into account in assessing the reliability of a Mr. Big confession. This creates a strong incentive for the state to conduct these operations with restraint.

93 The onus has the added benefit of encouraging the creation of a more thorough record of the operation. At present, many of the key interactions between undercover officers and the accused are unrecorded. This is problematic. Where it is logistically feasible and would not jeopardize the operation itself or the safety of the undercover officers, the police would do well to record their conversations with the accused. With the onus of demonstrating reliability placed on the Crown, gaps in the record may undermine the case for admissibility, which will encourage better record keeping.[284]

How is Probative Value Assessed?

. . .

99 Returning to Mr. Big confessions, their probative value derives from their reliability. A confession provides powerful evidence of guilt, but only if it is true. A confession of questionable reliability carries less probative force, and in deciding whether the probative value of a Mr. Big confession outweighs the prejudicial effect of the character evidence that accompanies it, trial judges must examine its reliability.

---

[284]   It appears that the RCMP have already adopted the practice of recording a substantial number of the interactions between the accused and undercover officers in British Columbia (see W. E. Dawson, "The Use of 'Mr. Big' in Undercover Operations", in Criminal Law: Special Issues (2011), Paper 5.2, at p. 5.2.44).

100 What factors are relevant in assessing the reliability of a Mr. Big confession? A parallel can perhaps be drawn between the assessment of "threshold reliability" that occurs under the principled approach to hearsay. Under the principled approach, hearsay becomes admissible where it is both necessary and reliable. Reliability can generally be established in one of two ways: by showing that the statement is trustworthy, or by establishing that its reliability can be sufficiently tested at trial (R. v. Khelawon, 2006 SCC 57, [2006] 2 S.C.R. 787, at paras. 61-63). The latter route to reliability is often met through an opportunity to cross-examine the hearsay declarant, but this has no application in the present context because the accused is not a compellable witness.

101 However, the factors used to demonstrate the trustworthiness of a hearsay statement are apposite. In assessing the trustworthiness of a hearsay statement, courts look to the circumstances in which the statement was made, and whether there is any confirmatory evidence (Khelawon, at paras. 62 and 100).

102 Confessions derive their persuasive force from the fact that they are against the accused's self-interest. People do not normally confess to crimes they have not committed (Hodgson, at para. 60). But the circumstances in which Mr. Big confessions are elicited can undermine that supposition. Thus, the first step in assessing the reliability of a Mr. Big confession is to examine those circumstances and assess the extent to which they call into question the reliability of the confession. These circumstances include—but are not strictly limited to—the length of the operation, the number of interactions between the police and the accused, the nature of the relationship between the undercover officers and the accused, the nature and extent of the inducements offered, the presence of any threats, the conduct of the interrogation itself, and the personality of the accused, including his or her age, sophistication, and mental health.

103 Special note should be taken of the mental health and age of the accused. In the United States, where empirical data on false confessions is more plentiful, researchers have found that those with mental illnesses or disabilities, and youth, present a much greater risk of falsely confessing (Garrett, at p. 1064). A confession arising from a Mr. Big operation that comes from a young person or someone suffering from a mental illness or disability will raise greater reliability concerns.

104 In listing these factors, I do not mean to suggest that trial judges are to consider them mechanically and check a box when they apply. That is not the purpose of the exercise. Instead, trial judges must examine all the circumstances leading to and surrounding the making of the confession—with these factors in mind—and assess whether and to what extent the reliability of the confession is called into doubt.

105 After considering the circumstances in which the confession was made, the court should look to the confession itself for markers of reliability. Trial judges should consider the level of detail contained in the confession, whether it leads to the discovery of additional evidence, whether it identifies any elements of the crime that had not been made public (e.g., the murder weapon), or whether it accurately describes mundane details of the crime the accused would not likely have known had he not committed it (e.g., the presence or absence of particular objects at the crime scene). Confirmatory evidence is not a hard and fast requirement, but where it exists, it can provide a powerful guarantee of reliability. The greater the concerns raised by the circumstances in which the confession was made, the more important it will be to find markers of reliability in the confession itself or the surrounding evidence.

How is Prejudicial Effect Measured?

106 Weighing the prejudicial effect of a Mr. Big confession is a more straightforward and familiar exercise. Trial judges must be aware of the dangers presented by these confessions. Admitting these confessions raises the spectre of moral and reasoning prejudice. Commencing with moral prejudice, the jury learns that the accused wanted to join a criminal organization and committed a host of "simulated crimes" that he believed were real. In the end, the accused is forced to argue to the jury that he lied to Mr. Big when he boasted about committing a very serious crime because his desire to join the gang was so strong. Moral prejudice may increase with operations that involve the accused in simulated crimes of violence, or that demonstrate the accused has a past history of violence. As for reasoning prejudice—defined as the risk that the jury's focus will be distracted away from the charges before the court—it too can pose a problem depending on the length of the operation, the amount of time that must be spent detailing it, and any controversy as to whether a particular event or conversation occurred.

107 On the other hand, the risk of prejudice can be mitigated by excluding certain pieces of particularly prejudicial evidence that are unessential to the narrative. Moreover, trial judges must bear in mind that limiting instructions to the jury may be capable of attenuating the prejudicial effect of this evidence.

How are Probative Value and Prejudicial Effect Compared?

108 In the end, trial judges must weigh the probative value and the prejudicial effect of the confession at issue and decide whether the Crown has met its burden. In practice, the potential for prejudice is a fairly constant variable in this context. Mr. Big operations are cut from the same cloth, and the concerns about prejudice are likely to be similar from case to case. As a result, trial judges will expend much of their analytical energy assessing the reliability of the confessions these operations generate.

109 Determining when the probative value of a Mr. Big confession surpasses its potential for prejudice will never be an exact science. As Justice Binnie observed in Handy, probative value and prejudicial effect are two variables which "do not operate on the same plane" (para. 148). Probative value is concerned with "proof of an issue", while prejudicial effect is concerned with "the fairness of the trial" (ibid.). To be sure, there will be easy cases at the margins. But more common will be the difficult cases that fall in between. In such cases, trial judges will have to lean on their judicial experience to decide whether the value of a confession exceeds its cost.

110 Despite the inexactness of the exercise, it is one for which our trial judges are well prepared. Trial judges routinely weigh the probative value and prejudicial effect of evidence. And as mentioned, they are already asked to examine the reliability of evidence in a number of different contexts, as well as the prejudicial effect of bad character evidence. They are well positioned to do the same here. Because trial judges, after assessing the evidence before them, are in the best position to weigh the probative value and prejudicial effect of the evidence, their decision to admit or exclude a Mr. Big confession will be afforded deference on appeal.

What is the Role of the Doctrine of Abuse of Process?

111 The rule of evidence I have proposed goes a long way toward addressing all three of the concerns raised by Mr. Big operations. It squarely tackles the problems they raise with reliability and prejudice. And it takes significant account of the concern regarding police misconduct both by placing the admissibility onus on the Crown, and by factoring the conduct of the police into the assessment of a Mr. Big confession's probative value.

112 I should not, however, be taken as suggesting that police misconduct will be forgiven so long as a demonstrably reliable confession is ultimately secured. That state of affairs would be unacceptable, as this Court has long recognized that there are "inherent limits" on the power of the state to "manipulate people and events for the purpose of . . . obtaining convictions" (R. v. Mack, [1988] 2 S.C.R. 903, at p. 941).

113 In my view, this is where the doctrine of abuse of process must serve its purpose. After all, the doctrine is intended to guard against state conduct that society finds unacceptable, and which threatens the integrity of the justice system (R. v. Babos, 2014 SCC 16, at para. 35). Moreover, the doctrine provides trial judges with a wide discretion to issue a remedy—including the exclusion of evidence or a stay of proceedings—where doing so is necessary to preserve the integrity of the justice system or the fairness of the trial (ibid., at para. 32). The onus lies on the accused to establish that an abuse of process has occurred.

114 I acknowledge that, thus far, the doctrine has provided little protection in the context of Mr. Big operations. This may be due in part to this Court's decision in R. v. Fliss, 2002 SCC 16, [2002] 1 S.C.R. 535, where Binnie J., writing for the majority, described the Mr. Big technique as "skillful police work" (para. 21). But the solution, in my view, is to reinvigorate the doctrine in this context, not to search for an alternative framework to guard against the very same problem. The first step toward restoring the doctrine as an effective guard against police misconduct in this context is to remind trial judges that these operations can become abusive, and that they must carefully scrutinize how the police conduct them.

115 It is of course impossible to set out a precise formula for determining when a Mr. Big operation will become abusive. These operations are too varied for a bright-line rule to apply. But there is one guideline that can be suggested. Mr. Big operations are designed to induce confessions. The mere presence of inducements is not problematic (Oickle, para. 57). But police conduct, including inducements and threats, becomes problematic in this context when it approximates coercion. In conducting these operations, the police cannot be permitted to overcome the will of the accused and coerce a confession. This would almost certainly amount to an abuse of process.

116 Physical violence or threats of violence provide examples of coercive police tactics. A confession derived from physical violence or threats of violence against an accused will not be admissible—no matter how reliable—because this, quite simply, is something the community will not tolerate (see, e.g., R. v. Singh, 2013 ONCA 750, 118 O.R. (3d) 253).

117 Violence and threats of violence are two forms of unacceptable coercion. But Mr. Big operations can become coercive in other ways as well. Operations that prey on an accused's vulnerabilities—like mental health problems, substance addictions, or youthfulness—are also highly problematic (see Mack, at p. 963). Taking advantage of these vulnerabilities threatens trial fairness and the integrity of the justice system. As this Court has said on many occasions, misconduct that offends the community's sense of fair play and decency will amount to an abuse of process and warrant the exclusion of the statement.

118 While coercion is an important factor to consider, I do not foreclose the possibility that Mr. Big operations can become abusive in other ways. The factors that I have outlined, while not identical, are similar to those outlined in Mack, with which trial judges are well-familiar (p. 966). At the end of the day, there is only so much guidance that can be provided. Our trial judges have long been entrusted with the task of identifying abuses of process and I have no reason to doubt their ability to do the same in this context.

Why Use This Two-Pronged Approach?

119 As we have seen, Mr. Big operations raise three interrelated concerns—reliability, prejudice, and police misconduct. I have proposed two separate tests that, taken together, address all three.

120 The reason for this lies in the analytically distinct problems that the three concerns raise. Reliability and prejudice are fundamentally evidentiary issues. They are concerned with the quality of the evidence these operations produce. Indeed, they do not emerge as problems at all until a Mr. Big confession is admitted at trial. The concern that the police may engage in misconduct, by contrast, is focused on the behaviour of the state in eliciting the evidence. To be sure, there is significant overlap between the concerns. Police misconduct is more likely to produce an unreliable confession. But the overlap is not perfect. For example, a confession elicited during a Mr. Big operation where there has been no misconduct may still turn out to be unreliable and prejudicial. Similarly, a confession that is the product of misconduct may turn out to be reliable. Thus, in order to take complete account of both issues, two legal tools are required—one that looks directly at the evidence, and one that serves as a check on the conduct of the police.

121 I have turned to a common law rule of evidence to address the concerns these confessions raise with reliability and prejudice. Without question, unreliable and prejudicial evidence implicate rights under the Charter, including the right to a fair trial and the presumption of innocence. But our common law rules of evidence are, and must be, capable of protecting the constitutional rights of the accused. It is axiomatic that the common law must be developed in a manner consistent with the fundamental values enshrined in the Charter (see RWDSU v. Dolphin Delivery Ltd., [1986] 2 S.C.R. 573, at p. 603). Our rules of evidence have embraced this constitutional imperative and have evolved into principled, flexible tools that are "highly sensitive to the due process interests of the accused" (D. Paciocco, "Charter Tracks: Twenty-Five Years of Constitutional Influence on the Criminal Trial Process and Rules of Evidence" (2008), S.C.L.R. (2d) 309, at p. 311). The common law rule of evidence I have proposed fits comfortably with this Court's approach in the post-Charter era.

122 To deal with the concern regarding police misconduct, I have turned to the doctrine of abuse of process. Doing so makes good sense because, as mentioned, the doctrine is intended to guard against state misconduct that threatens the integrity of the justice system and the fairness of trials. Moreover, a form of abuse of process has long provided a residual protection against unfair police tactics in the context of conventional police interrogations (see Oickle, at paras. 65-67; Rothman v. The Queen, [1981] 1 S.C.R. 640, at p. 697). The doctrine is therefore well suited to providing a check against police misconduct in this context.

123 The two-pronged approach I have articulated is also consistent with the demands of the principle against self-incrimination. The principle against self-incrimination has two purposes: protecting against abusive state conduct, and guarding against unreliable confessions (Hebert, at p. 175; R. v. Jones, [1994] 2 S.C.R. 229, at p. 250). These protections flow from "the value placed by Canadian society upon individual privacy, personal autonomy and dignity" (White, at para. 43). However, the principle does not act as a free-standing legal protection. Rather, the principle is a "general organizing principle of criminal law from which particular rules can be derived" (Jones, at p. 249). Where its underlying rationale suggests that legal protection is needed in a specific context, but the law provides for none, the principle can be used to fashion a "contextually-sensitive" new rule to address the gap in the law (White, at para. 45). In my view, the common law rule of evidence I have proposed acts, along with the abuse doctrine, as yet another specific legal protection that derives from the general principle and its underlying rationale. . .

Application to the Facts

The Admissibility of the Respondent's Confessions

126 During the Mr. Big operation, the respondent confessed on three separate occasions: on April 10, June 9, and June 11, 2005. These confessions—and in particular the June 9 and 11 confessions—were the heart of the Crown's case against the respondent at trial. Guided by the legal framework I have proposed, I must decide whether these confessions were properly admitted into evidence.

The June 9 and June 11, 2005 Confessions

131 The June 9 confession was elicited by Mr. Big during his meeting with the respondent. The June 11 confession is a brief re-enactment of how the drowning occurred. As mentioned, these confessions were critical to the Crown's case against the respondent. Because the re-enactment followed from the respondent's confession to Mr. Big, these confessions are intertwined, and I will consider their admissibility together.

132 The first step is to take stock of the probative value of these confessions, which hinges on an assessment of their reliability. This requires considering the circumstances in which the confessions were made, and whether the confessions contain any markers of reliability.

133 Turning first to the circumstances in which these confessions were made, I am of the view that the circumstances cast serious doubt on the reliability of the respondent's confessions. At the time the Mr. Big operation began, the respondent was socially isolated, unemployed, and living on welfare. Over the next four months, the Mr. Big operation transformed the respondent's life, becoming its focal point. The respondent participated in 63 "scenarios" in which he worked with undercover officers. He also had near daily phone

contact with two of these officers, Jim and Paul, who became his closest friends. Even when the respondent was not working with the undercover officers, much of his time was devoted to the work doled out to him by the fictitious organization. He spent long hours driving across Newfoundland, spending nights in hotels, as he delivered mysterious packages and cargo. By all accounts, this was a lengthy and intense operation.

134 With this transformation of the respondent's life came powerful inducements. Financially, the Mr. Big operation lifted the respondent out of poverty. Undercover officers paid the respondent over $15,000 in cash for his work. And they promised him much greater financial rewards in the future if he was admitted into the organization; the undercover officers had him count hundreds of thousands of dollars in cash, and told him a $25,000 pay day was coming if he was allowed to participate in an upcoming "big job". There was a corresponding change in the respondent's lifestyle. Dinners at expensive restaurants became common. Paul bought the respondent new clothes to wear, and the respondent relied on Paul to teach him how to behave during their dinners, as dining at expensive restaurants was "all new to him" and he often felt uncomfortable.

135 The respondent attested to the powerful impact of these financial inducements at the outset of his meeting with Mr. Big, telling the crime boss that his life had been "really rough" before he started working for the organization, and that he had been unable to afford even a bed to sleep on. He told Mr. Big that he had come from having "nothing", that working for the organization had lifted him out of those dire circumstances, and that he would "never ever forget" how good they had been to him.

136 At least as enticing as the financial inducements held out to the respondent was the promise of friendship that came with working for the criminal organization. The undercover officers—aware of the respondent's social isolation—sought to become his "best friend". At the outset of the operation, the officers plotted to separate the respondent from his wife, telling him that she was not allowed to accompany him as he traveled across the country working for the organization.

137 With remarkable ease, the officers quickly and deeply engrained themselves in the respondent's life. By early April, less than two full months into the operation, the respondent told Jim and Paul that they were like brothers to him and that he loved them—a sentiment he would repeat throughout the rest of the operation. Indeed, the respondent preached that loyalty to this "family" was more important to him than money.

138 The depth of the respondent's commitment to the organization and the undercover officers can hardly be exaggerated. The respondent would constantly call his friends—Jim and Paul—looking for work, and he would anxiously await their planned meetings. He told the officers he was planning to

leave Newfoundland so he could work for the organization full time. He even purported a willingness to leave his wife if that is what it would take to join the organization. And when he was finally arrested on June 13, the respondent's first call for help was naturally placed to Jim.

139 It was in these circumstances that the respondent confessed to Mr. Big and participated in the re-enactment. When he entered their June 9 meeting, the respondent knew that his ticket out of poverty and social isolation was at stake. Jim implored him to be "honest" with the boss. Early on in the interrogation, Mr. Big drove home the importance of honesty, telling the respondent that "the minute the trust is gone ... everything is gone". The conversation quickly turned to the death of the respondent's daughters, and Mr. Big immediately asserted that the respondent had killed them. When the respondent denied it and claimed to have had a seizure, Mr. Big perfunctorily dismissed this explanation as a lie: "[n]o don't lie to me ... don't go with the seizure stuff ... [y]ou're lying to me on this okay ...".

140 The circumstances left the respondent with a stark choice: confess to Mr. Big or be deemed a liar by the man in charge of the organization he so desperately wanted to join. In my view, these circumstances, considered as a whole, presented the respondent with an overwhelming incentive to confess—either truthfully or falsely.

141 Having determined that the circumstances in which these confessions were made cast serious doubt on the reliability of the respondent's confessions, the next question is whether these confessions contain any indicators of reliability. In my view, they do not.

142 In the first place, the respondent's description of how the crime was committed is somewhat inconsistent. In his meeting with Mr. Big, the respondent started off by denying that he killed his daughters. Later, he said that they "fell" into the water. After further pressing by Mr. Big, the respondent claimed that he pushed his daughters into the water by striking them with his shoulder. But when he participated in the re-enactment with Jim two days later, his explanation changed again. When Jim knelt down next to the respondent and asked him to demonstrate how he pushed his daughters, the respondent nudged him with his knee. He had to use his knee because Jim, kneeling down, was not tall enough for the respondent to shove with his shoulder. The same would undoubtedly have been true for his small children.

143 More important than these inconsistencies is the complete lack of confirmatory evidence. Given the peculiar circumstances of the case, this is unsurprising. The issue has always been whether the respondent's daughters drowned accidentally or were murdered. There was never any question that the respondent was present when his daughters entered the water. All of the objectively verifiable details of the respondent's confession (e.g. his knowledge

of the location of the drowning) flow from his acknowledged presence at the time the drowning occurred.

144 When the circumstances in which the respondent's confessions were made are considered alongside their internal inconsistencies and the lack of any confirmatory evidence, their reliability is left in serious doubt, and I am forced to conclude that their probative value is low.

145 On the other hand, these confessions—like all Mr. Big confessions—carried with them an obvious potential for prejudice. The jury heard extensive evidence that—for four months—the respondent devoted his entire life to trying to join a criminal gang. They heard that he repeatedly participated in what he thought were criminal acts, including transporting stolen property and smuggling alcohol. On one occasion, he and Jim, wearing balaclavas, broke into a car to steal a package from it. The jury was repeatedly told that the respondent had described himself as having "no limits," and that he would do anything "as long as the trust was there". And it is easy to see how the jury could come to view the respondent with disdain. Here was a man who bragged about killing his three-year-old daughters to gain the approval of a group of criminals. The potential for moral prejudice in these circumstances was significant.

146 Comparing the probative value and prejudicial effect of these confessions leads me to conclude that their limited probative value is outweighed by their prejudicial effect. Put simply, these confessions are not worth the risk they pose. In my view, it would be unsafe to rest a conviction on this evidence.

The April 10 Confession

147 I reach the same conclusion with respect to the respondent's alleged April 10 confession. This confession also suffers from serious reliability concerns. Although unprompted, it came about during a conversation in which the respondent and Jim were bragging about their willingness to engage in violence. By this time, the respondent was already under the spell of powerful financial and social inducements. The confession came after two months and more than 30 scenarios with undercover officers, at a time when the respondent had already begun professing his love for Jim and Paul. Importantly, the confession itself contains no details—it amounts to a bald assertion by the respondent that he killed his daughters and that he "planned it". Finally, the confession was not recorded and the respondent denies making it, which only makes it harder to assess its probative value. On the other hand, admitting this confession into evidence carries with it all of the attendant prejudice I have already discussed. In my view, the probative value of this confession does not outweigh its prejudicial effect.

Abuse of Process

148 Given my conclusion that the respondent's confessions must be excluded under the common law, it is not necessary to consider whether the police conduct in this case amounted to an abuse of process. But there is no denying that this was an extremely intensive Mr. Big operation, and one that preyed upon the respondent's poverty and social isolation. In addition, the respondent had a seizure in front of an undercover officer. The respondent's past seizures had caused his licence to be suspended to protect against the risk that a seizure would cause him to have an accident while driving. However, the operation continued after this seizure, and undercover officers continued to send the respondent long distances over public roads in order to make deliveries for the fictitious criminal organization. The respondent submits that this placed his and the public's safety at risk, and that this conduct warrants excluding the confessions.

149 Without question, the police conduct in this case raises significant concerns, and might well amount to an abuse of process. However, this is not how the issue was presented at trial. At trial, the respondent took issue with the threatening and intimidating conduct of the officers, and the trial judge rejected those arguments. Given this, and the fact that there is no need to decide the matter, I do not believe this is an appropriate case to decide whether an abuse of process has been established.

VI. Disposition

150 The Court of Appeal excluded the respondent's June 9 and 11 confessions and quashed his convictions. It ordered a new trial on the basis that the respondent's April 10 confession was admissible, and that it provided a "sliver" of evidence upon which a jury could convict the respondent of murder (para. 258).

151 I have concluded that the April 10 confession must also be excluded. As such, it is doubtful whether any admissible evidence remains upon which a jury, properly instructed and acting reasonably, could convict. However, the final decision on how to proceed rests with the Crown. In the result, I would dismiss the appeal.

Appeal dismissed.

Separate concurring reasons were delivered by Cromwell J. and Karakatsanis J.

R. v. MACK
2014 CSC 58, 2014 SCC 58, [2014] 3 S.C.R. 3, 315 C.C.C. (3d) 315,
13 C.R. (7th) 225 (S.C.C.)

The accused was charged with the first degree murder of his roommate. The victim disappeared and, about a month later, a friend of the accused reported to police that the accused had confessed to killing the victim and burning his body. Police mounted a Mr. Big operation targeting the accused. The operation began when the accused was introduced to an undercover officer, B., at a nightclub where the accused was working. The accused soon learned that B. was involved in criminal activity and worked for an organization headed by a man named L. The accused did several jobs for the organization over the next few months.

Early on, in a conversation with B., the accused described the victim as a crackhead and a drug addict who had stolen from his son's piggy bank. Two months into the operation, the accused met with L., who attempted to question the accused about his missing roommate. The accused asked if he could decline to speak about the victim. L. indicated that it was his choice but that refusing to speak would mean the accused would remain on the organization's third line. L. told the accused that talking about his roommate was the only way to advance to the organization's first line. During that meeting, the accused continued to refuse to discuss the victim.

Three weeks later, the accused met with B. and said he was willing to do what it took to work for the organization. When B. asked why the accused had killed his roommate, the accused responded that the victim was a liar, a thief and a drug dealer. The accused told B. that he shot the victim five times before burning his body. The accused offered to show B. where he had burned the victim's body and took B. to the fire pit on his father's property. The accused claimed that he had taken the ashes out of the fire pit and that there was nothing left of the victim.

A few days later, the accused again met with L. He described the victim as a crackhead who had stolen from his son's piggy bank, and claimed to have shot the victim five times before burning his body on the accused's father's property. Shortly after this second meeting with L., the accused was arrested and charged with first degree murder. Police searched the father's property and found the victim's remains and shell casings in the fire pit. The Mr. Big operation lasted four months and the accused participated in 30 scenarios with undercover officers. He was paid approximately $5,000 plus expenses for his work with the organization.

The accused's statements in the Mr. Big operation were admitted in evidence against him. The jury found the accused guilty and his appeal to the Alberta Court of Appeal was dismissed. The accused appealed to the Supreme Court of Canada.

MOLDAVER J. (McLACHLIN C.J. & LeBel, ABELLA, CROMWELL, KARAKATSANIS and WAGNER JJ. concurring):

. . .

32 Neither the courts below nor the parties before this Court have considered whether the appellant's confessions would be admissible under the two-pronged framework set out in *Hart*. In my view, however, this poses no difficulty as these confessions would clearly be admissible under that framework.

33 To begin with, the probative value of the appellant's confessions is high. The inducements provided by the undercover officers were modest—the appellant was paid approximately $5,000 over a four-month period, at a time when well-paying, legitimate work was readily available to him. He was not threatened by the officers. And he was told, in his first meeting with Liam, that he could decline to say anything and remain on the organization's "third line"—an option he initially accepted.

34 Moreover, there was an abundance of evidence that was potentially confirmatory. First, the appellant's purported confessions to Mr. Argueta and Mr. Love described the same motive for killing Mr. Levoir as his confessions to the undercover officers. They also made reference to burning Mr. Levoir's body. Second, immediately after confessing to Ben, the appellant led him to the firepit in which Mr. Levoir's remains lay undiscovered. And third, shell casings fired from a gun found in the appellant's apartment were found in the same firepit. All of this made for a confession that was highly probative.

35 On the other hand, while the confessions were accompanied by bad character evidence, the prejudice was limited. The appellant was not involved in any scenarios that involved violence, nor did the operation reveal prejudicial facts about the appellant's past history. The appellant's involvement with the organization was primarily limited to assisting with repossessing vehicles and delivering packages. In my view, any prejudicial effect arising from the Mr. Big confessions is easily outweighed by their probative value.

36 Nor did the undercover officers engage in any improper conduct which could ground an application for abuse of process. The appellant was not presented with overwhelming inducements. He had prospects for legitimate work that would have paid even more than the undercover officers were offering. Nor did the officers threaten the appellant with violence if he would not confess. The most that can be said is that the officers created an air of intimidation by referring to violent acts committed by members of the organization. But the appellant was not coerced into confessing. This much is evidenced by the appellant's initial refusal to speak with Ben and Liam about Mr. Levoir's disappearance. Indeed, the undercover officers explicitly made clear to the appellant that he did not have to speak with them about Mr. Levoir, and that he could remain in his current role within the organization. None of the undercover officers' conduct approaches abuse.

. . .

43 In *Hart*, this Court identified two evidentiary concerns with confessions that are the product of a Mr. Big operation. The first is that the confessions may be unreliable. Mr. Big operations are intended to induce confessions, and the inducements offered to a suspect may incentivize the suspect to falsely confess. Second, Mr. Big confessions are invariably accompanied by bad character evidence in which the accused has shown a willingness to commit crimes to gain entry into a criminal organization (see *Hart*, at paras. 68-77).

44 The common law rule of evidence that was set out in *Hart* was intended to respond to the evidentiary concerns raised by Mr. Big operations. However, while this rule responds to these two evidentiary concerns, it does not erase them. The focus of the rule is to determine whether a Mr. Big confession should be admitted into evidence. It does not decide the ultimate question of whether the confession is reliable, nor does it eliminate the prejudicial character evidence that accompanies its admission. Thus, even in cases where Mr. Big confessions are admitted into evidence, concerns with their reliability and prejudice will persist. It then falls to the trial judge to adequately instruct the jury on how to approach these confessions in light of these concerns.

. . .

50 . . .[T]here is no magical incantation that must be read to juries by trial judges in all Mr. Big cases. Instead, trial judges are required to provide juries with the tools they need to address the concerns about reliability and prejudice that arise from these confessions. The nature and extent of the instructions required will vary from case to case.

51 However, there is some guidance—short of a prescriptive formula—that can be provided to trial judges who must instruct juries in cases where a Mr. Big confession has been admitted into evidence.

52 With respect to the reliability concerns raised by a Mr. Big confession, the trial judge should tell the jury that the reliability of the accused's confession is a question for them. The trial judge should then review with the jury the factors relevant to the confessions and the evidence surrounding it. As explained in *Hart*, the reliability of a Mr. Big confession is affected by the circumstances in which the confession was made and by the details contained in the confession itself. Thus, the trial judge should alert the jury to "the length of the operation, the number of interactions between the police and the accused, the nature of the relationship between the undercover officers and the accused, the nature and extent of the inducements offered, the presence of any threats, the conduct of the interrogation itself, and the personality of the accused"—all of which play a role in assessing the confession's reliability (see *Hart*, at para. 102).

53 Moreover, the trial judge should discuss the fact that the confession itself may contain markers of reliability (or unreliability). Jurors should be told to consider the level of detail in the confession, whether it led to the discovery of additional evidence, whether it identified any elements of the crime that had not been made public, or whether it accurately described mundane details of the crime the accused would not likely have known had he not committed it (see *Hart*, at para. 105).

54 This is not to suggest that trial judges are required to provide a detailed catalogue of every piece of evidence that might bear on the reliability of the confession. The task is simply to alert the jury to the concern about the reliability of the confession, and to highlight the factors relevant to assessing it.

55 With respect to the bad character evidence that accompanies a Mr. Big confession, the challenge is a more familiar one. The trial judge must instruct the jury that this sort of evidence has been admitted for the limited purpose of providing context for the confession. The jury should be instructed that it cannot rely on that evidence in determining whether the accused is guilty. Moreover, the trial judge should remind the jury that the simulated criminal activity—even that which the accused may have eagerly participated in—was fabricated and encouraged by agents of the state.

56 In this case, the trial judge addressed the concerns about reliability and prejudice in his charge to the jury. The trial judge told the jury that it had to "carefully consider whether the themes of violence and the level of inducement may reasonably have compromised the reliability" of the appellant's confessions. He specifically instructed the jury that it had to "assess the environment, the themes of easy money, violence, the importance of honesty and integrity, any offers of exit points, and any threats or intimidation". Ultimately, the trial judge left the final assessment of the reliability of the appellant's confessions to the jury:

> Overall, it's your responsibility to decide whether the statements attributed to Mr. Mack are reliable in whole or in part, bearing in mind Mr. Mack's testimony that he was given pep talks every day ... that he felt indebted ... and very insecure, especially after he heard about the day of reckoning for the ice pick attack. Also that Mr. Mack felt out of his league, and whenever he started a story he felt pushed in a direction that he had done it.
>
> When a statement may have arisen partly out of fear and partly from an inducement to easy money, it's important to assess carefully how reliable it is, if at all. You need to assess that against all of the evidence in order to decide not only what was said, but whether what was said was truthful. [Emphasis added.]

57 With respect to the bad character evidence that was admitted along with the Mr. Big confessions, although the trial judge did not address it specifically, he provided the jury with a standard limiting instruction on the use that could be made of any evidence that bore on the accused's character:

> You'll recall in my opening remarks I alerted you that we would likely hear evidence that does not reflect Mr. Mack in a positive light, including views and conducts which are unfavourable to him. You have now heard some evidence of that type, and I remind you not to rely upon or use that evidence to conclude that

Mr. Mack is guilty or even that he is more likely to be guilty of the crime with which he is charged based on that evidence.

In Canada people are not prosecuted or judged as guilty because they have certain beliefs or values. Evidence about things Mr. Mack may have said or acts he may have committed which you find objectionable, it has been provided to you for the very limited purpose of ensuring that you know the context for the other things that are said or done that relate directly to the offence with which he is charged. Background evidence, which we sometimes refer to as the narrative, is provided to you so you understand more accurately the overall circumstances and can then better assess what and whom to believe.

So I also repeat that you're not to decide this case based on your personal views of what you might consider to be Mr. Mack's value system or his opinions or even whether he might have committed some other wrongful acts or offences. We are concerned with only one charge: the murder of Robert Levoir. [Emphasis added.]

58 When these instructions regarding reliability and bad character evidence are viewed through a functional lens, I am satisfied that they reveal no error. The trial judge plainly addressed the two concerns raised by the appellant's confessions to undercover officers. He directed the jury to "assess carefully" how reliable the appellant's confessions were, and pointed specifically to the police deception, the level of inducements, the "themes of easy money", and the presence of any threats or intimidation. During the trial and in his final instructions, the trial judge directed the jury to disregard the prejudicial character evidence that had been admitted in reaching a verdict.

59 Undoubtedly, more could have been said by the trial judge in his discussion of the reliability of the Mr. Big confession. The trial judge, for example, could have specifically reviewed the payments received by the appellant during the operation, or the encouragements to confess that were provided by Ben and Liam. Equally, however, the trial judge could have detailed the evidence that was capable of supporting the reliability of the appellant's confessions, including the fact that the appellant had gainful employment available to him at the time the cash inducements were offered to him, that he correctly pointed out the location of Mr. Levoir's remains during his confession to Ben, and that shell casings fired by a rifle found in the appellant's apartment were discovered in the firepit. The trial judge did not do so, but this does not mean his charge was deficient. A failure to say all that could have been said does not amount to a legal error. . . :

61 In my view, the trial judge's charge left the jury equipped to deal with the concerns of reliability and prejudice that emerged from the Mr. Big confessions. No error has been shown. Accordingly, I would reject this ground of appeal.

Appeal dismissed.

There has been an unmistakeable general trend since *Hart* and *Mack* to admit Mr. Big evidence subject to a cautionary jury instruction.[285] In most decisions courts have little difficulty deciding that the Mr. Big strategy in issue is less coercive than those used in *Hart*, that the accused was not as vulnerable and/or that the confession did not have reliability dangers.

Most courts do not even consider the prong of abuse of process, or dismiss it. There is only one stay entered for a Mr. Big sting case. In *R. c. LaFlamme*[286] the Quebec Court of Appeal stayed a murder case where the accused had confessed to murdering his wife after 23 years. The Court held that the police had exceeded the *Hart* line by exposing the accused to acts of violence.[287]

Several writers suggest that the Supreme Court did not do enough to control or prohibit these highly coercive and costly Mr. Big operations.[288] It seems clear that *Hart* and this subsequent trend to distinguish will not discourage police Mr. Big operations but rather advise police as to how to legitimate them by avoiding violence, being careful of use against vulnerable victims, keeping notes and recordings where possible and, above all, ensuring reliability by obtaining corroborative evidence. In the U.K. or the United States, principles against the admission of coerced statements apply equally to confessions to known persons in authority AND to undercover agents.[289] We have seen that our own voluntary confession rule does not overlook police threats to persons other than the accused nor does it have a corroboration route to admission. Many view the Mr. Big regime as a pro-State anomaly in which the end is seen to justify the means.[290]

In a development more favourable to accused there are two acquittal rulings based on the invigorated abuse of process doctrine referred to in *Hart* respecting undercover operations not amounting to a full Mr. Big sting. In *R. v. Derbyshire*,[291] a woman was charged with being an accessory after the fact to murder. Undercover officers posing as members of an outlaw motorcycle gang and associates of her boyfriend, the murder suspect, accosted her in a parking garage. They aggressively ordered her back into her car and threatened her to clean up the mess as they were concerned she was a rat in the organization. She testified she was terrified and confessed immediately. In contrast, *R. v. Nuttall*[292] involved a lengthy and complex

---

[285]   See e.g. *R. v. Allgood*, 2015 SKCA 88, 327 C.C.C. (3d) 196, 23 C.R. (7th) 86 (Sask. C.A.); *R. v. West*, 2015 BCCA 379, 329 C.C.C. (3d) 97, 23 C.R. (7th) 107 (B.C. C.A.); *R. v. Johnston*, 2016 BCCA 3, 333 C.C.C. (3d) 555, 26 C.R. (7th) 147 (B.C. C.A.); and *R. v. Yakimchuk*, 2017 ABCA 101, 352 C.C.C. (3d) 434 (Alta. C.A.). But see *R. v. Buckley*, 2018 NSSC 1 (N.S. S.C.).

[286]   (2015), 2015 QCCA 1517, 23 C.R. (7th) 137 (C.A. Que.).

[287]   See comment by Jason MacLean & Frances Chapman, "Au Revoir, Monsieur Big? Confessions, Coercion and the Courts" (2015), 23 C.R. (7th) 184 at 195-198.

[288]   MacLean & Chapman, *supra* note 287; Adelina Iftene, "The Hart of the (Mr.) Big Problem" (2016) 63 Crim. L.Q. 178; Archie Kaiser, "Hart: More Positive Steps Needed to Rein in Mr. Big Undercover Operations" (2014), 12 C.R. (7th) 304; and Adriana Popoz, "Motive to Lie? A Critical Look at the 'Mr. Big' Investigative Technique" (2015) 19 Can. Crim. L. Rev. 231.

[289]   See Chris Hunt & Micah Rankin, "*R. v. Hart*: A New Common Law Confession Rule for Undercover Operations" (2015) 14 Oxford University Commonwealth Law Journal 322. The authors urge that the new Canadian Mr. Big model not be followed in other jurisdictions.

[290]   MacLean & Chapman, *supra* note 287, point to data that the RCMP alone has used Mr. Big 350 times with a 75% success rate and a 95% conviction rate.

[291]   2016 NSCA 67, 340 C.C.C. (3d) 1, 31 C.R. (7th) 263 (N.S. C.A.).

[292]   2016 BCSC 1404, 339 C.C.C. (3d) 1 (B.C. S.C.).

operation that included extensive manipulation of a married couple found guilty by a jury of terrorism. They had planted three explosive devices made from pressure cookers on the grounds of the B.C. Legislature. The devices were inert and had been constructed mainly by the police, who had tried hard to get the Muslim couple, who were heroin addicts and socially isolated and had voiced fanciful jihadist ideas, to come up with a workable terrorist plot. The Court stayed the proceedings on the basis that the police conduct amounted to an abuse of process. Entrapment was an alternative basis for the stay. These two decisions confirm that the invigorated doctrine of abuse of process does apply to undercover operations beyond the context of Mr. Big operations and may be used to control some truly abusive undercover tactics even worse than Mr. Big techniques.[293]

PROBLEMS

Problem 1

The accused was charged with arson. At 5 a.m. the Calgary Fire Department responded to a fire at an up/down duplex. They found the accused on a couch in the basement apartment, roused him and carried him out. He was taken to hospital. His nose hair, eyebrows, eyelashes and hair were singed and he had soot in his mouth. He was alert and could answer all questions. Further investigation revealed that the cause of the fire was tampering with the gas supply. The police found a bag in garbage containers in the back alley which contained two wrenches and torn pieces of mail addressed to the accused. The accused was arrested on his release from hospital a day later.

Shortly after the arrest, after he had been read his *Charter* rights and had consulted his lawyer, the accused agreed to be interviewed by detectives. During the next two hours of interrogation, which were recorded, detectives suggested that his daughter would be caused mental anguish if the explanation was attempted suicide. The detectives tricked the accused in two ways: falsely telling the accused that they had found his prints on the circuitbreakers and that this was highly incriminating, and fabricating that a neighbour had seen him place the tools in the garbage can. They also left the impression, which was false, that the neighbour was conspiring with the police to unfairly put fabricated evidence to the court. The accused finally made several incriminating statements. **Should these statements be admitted under the *Oickle* tests?**

Compare *R. v. Wiegand* (2003), 11 C.R. (6th) 356 (Alta. Q.B.).

---

[293] See further Lisa Dufraimont, "*R. v. Nuttall* and *R. v. Derbyshire*: Abuse of Process and Undercover Operations" (2016), 31 C.R. (7th) 315 and Adrien Iafrate, "Unleashing the Paper Tiger: How the Abuse of Process Doctrine Can Overcome *Charter* Limitations" (2017) 64 Crim. L.Q. 147.

Problem 2

The accused, Pinnock and Robinson, were charged with first degree murder. During the investigation the police employed an undercover officer to pretend to be an Obeahman, a spiritual advisor in some Caribbean cultures. The officer befriended the mother of one of the accused and thereby arranged to meet with the two accused numerous times and persuade them that, in accordance with the religious practices of Obeah, they needed to confide to him what they knew about the death of the victim. In this manner, he elicited inculpatory statements from the accused as well as investigatively helpful information. All of the meetings were audio- and videotaped, and the Crown sought to admit the tapes into evidence. The accused sought the exclusion of the evidence on the basis that there was a violation of their freedom of religion rights, that the police tactic was a dirty trick, that there was a violation of their equality rights, and that the communications were privileged. **How would you rule?**

Compare *R. v. Welsh* (2007), 51 C.R. (6th) 33 (Ont. S.C.), and see annotation by Stephen Coughlan, C.R. *ibid.* at 35 and *R. v. Welsh*, 2013 ONCA 190, 296 C.C.C. (3d) 483, 2 C.R. (7th) 137 (Ont. C.A.).

Problem 3

The accused was charged with second degree murder after a man was fatally attacked in the street outside the accused's apartment. The attack took place in the early morning hours, soon after intruders robbed and pistol-whipped the accused and his friends in the accused's apartment. When the accused was arrested soon after these events, his left hand was injured so seriously that he required surgery. In hospital after the events, an officer who was seizing clothing heard the accused comment that he felt like he was going to jail. This comment was not in the context of any conversation or in response to any question.

The accused was taken to the police station later the same day. That night, police interrogated the accused for four hours but the accused made no admissions concerning the victim's death. The accused was then left in his cell for several hours, but he got little sleep before being interrogated for a further two hours early the next morning. The accused was 20 years old and had little experience with the law. In six hours of interrogation, he asked to be returned to his cell to sleep and asserted his right to silence many times. Although he was in the police station for most of the day, the accused was not brought before a court within 24 hours of his detention, as required under the *Criminal Code*. In questioning the accused, the police made numerous inflammatory and unfounded accusations, including that the accused was an evil monster, a killer, a racist and that he had tortured the victim. During the second interview, the accused made several equivocal statements that might be considered admissions or confessions.

The Crown applied to have the statements admitted as evidence against the accused. **How would you rule?**

Compare *R. v. Taylor* (2008), 63 C.R. (6th) 142 (N.B. Q.B.) and see C.R. annotation by Lisa Dufraimont.

Problem 4

The accused was charged with several offences in connection with a home invasion. He was interrogated by an RCMP officer after his arrest. The interrogation was video-recorded and resulted in a confession. The interrogation was a well-planned, well-orchestrated exercise. Prior to the interview, police prepared extensive briefing notes on, among other things, the props to be used and the moral themes to be developed during the interrogation. The interviewing officer went into the interrogation familiar with the alleged offences and believing the accused guilty. The interrogation lasted 2 hours 51 minutes, and the accused was allowed two bathroom breaks. The interviewing officer maintained a conversational tone and conducted the interrogation in a skilful and professional manner.

The accused was alert and willing to participate in the interrogation to some extent. However, in the course of the interview, he expressed a wish to remain silent more than 40 times. On 19 such occasions, the interviewing officer responded that he was happy to hear the accused's comment because it indicated that the accused was aware of his right to silence, whereupon the officer immediately continued the interrogation. The accused's express exercise of his right to silence became increasingly persistent throughout the interrogation but was always ignored. For a substantial period near the end of the interview, the accused said nothing other than repeatedly expressing his refusal to talk.

The Crown applies to have the record of the interrogation admitted into evidence. **Admissible?**

Compare *R. v. Reader* (2007), 49 C.R. (6th) 301 (Man. Q.B.).

5. VIDEOTAPING OF INTERROGATIONS

Should Confessions be Videotaped?

R. v. MOORE-McFARLANE
(2001), 47 C.R. (5th) 203, 160 C.C.C. (3d) 493 (Ont. C.A.)

The accused M and B were charged with robbery and other offences arising out of the armed robbery of a convenience store. M denied any involvement in the robbery. He testified that the police approached him in the vicinity of the robbery, drove him to the spot where they later claimed to have apprehended him, and arrested him for robbery. On a *voir dire* to determine the voluntariness of inculpatory statements allegedly made by M, M testified that he was hit in the jaw with a walkie-talkie by the police on the way to the station. When they arrived, the police waited in the car for 30 minutes before bringing M into the station. That delay was unexplained. The trial judge did not permit counsel for M to ask questions relating to the events prior to the actual interview. Counsel did not correct the trial judge's assumption that those events were not relevant to the issue of voluntariness. M also testified that he gave three audiotaped statements during the interrogation, although the police said that only one was made. He stated that his confession was false, that he had been coerced into giving the statement after being assaulted during the interrogation by members of the hold-up squad and that he was questioned while naked. M's statement was not videotaped, nor was the first half-hour of his interrogation by the police audiotaped. The trial judge ruled that the statements were voluntary. B also testified on the *voir dire* and denied any involvement in the robbery. He was pepper-sprayed by the police prior to his arrest at the scene of the robbery. The arresting officer testified that he advised the accused of his right to counsel and asked him if he wanted to contact a lawyer, to which B replied, "No, because my eyes are killing me." The arresting officer continued to question B while taking him to the hospital to get his eyes washed out. B responded to the questions and continued to complain about the effects of the pepper spray in his eyes. B testified that he was struck in the face after being placed in the police cruiser. The officer in charge at the police station testified that B had a cut lip when he arrived. Counsel for B began to cross-examine that officer on the issue of lost records of arrest, but the trial judge cut off that line of questioning. B was interrogated by two members of the hold-up squad. One of those officers testified that B stated, "You got us and the gun. I'm fucked. You know what you need to know." The interrogation was not videotaped. Counsel for B sought to cross-examine this officer on his knowledge of recent remarks by the judiciary, primarily directed at the hold-up squad, concerning the need to videotape interrogations. The trial judge interrupted counsel mid-sentence and instructed the officer that he did not need to answer that question. When counsel submitted that it was relevant to his cross-examination, the trial judge ruled that it was a matter for argument before him and not for the witness to answer. The officer confirmed that B was not given an opportunity to check the notes of the conversation for accuracy and that he was not asked to initial them. The trial judge ruled that the statements made by B and M were both admissible. The accused were convicted and appealed.

CHARRON J.A. (SHARPE and SIMMONS JJ.A. concurring): —

In my view, the evidence adduced on the *voir dire* with respect to the voluntariness of the statements allegedly made by each accused cannot reasonably support the trial judge's conclusion that the statements were voluntary except for one spontaneous utterance allegedly made by McFarlane upon his arrest with respect to lottery tickets found in his coat. All other statements should have been excluded. Since I am not satisfied that this is an appropriate case to apply the curative proviso, I would order a new trial.

. . .

It is clear from the discussion in *Oickle* that both elements of the modern confessions rule, the absence of threats or promises and the principles related to the "operating mind", are closely related to the predominant concern for reliability. Since voluntary confessions are admitted as an exception to the hearsay rule, it should come as no surprise that concerns over the reliability of the evidence are at the root of the confessions rule. In turn, the reliability of the evidence is intrinsically connected to trial fairness, the second rationale for the confessions rule. . . .

. . .

One of the main issues raised on these appeals is the police officers' failure to record the statements allegedly made by either appellant. Counsel for the appellants submit that there should be both a common-law and a constitutional obligation on the police to create a record, preferably by videotape, of all custodial interrogations and waivers of the s. 10(b) right to counsel. The appellants have noted some of the numerous decisions in Ontario where courts have either excluded confessions where the failure to videotape was deliberate or have strongly urged the recording of interrogations. [Citations omitted.]

The Crown submits that there should be no firm rule on the issue of recording. Crown counsel submits that the Supreme Court of Canada in *Oickle*, while commenting on the desirability of video records, was clearly reluctant to go further and impose an obligation on the police to make such records. . . . Crown counsel submits further that the appellants have confused issues of weight with issues of admissibility. Since it is for the trier of fact to determine the ultimate reliability of the statement, including whether it was in fact made, and the weight that should be attached to it, it is submitted that a failure to accurately or completely record an accused's statement should not render the statement inadmissible. I agree that there is no absolute rule requiring the recording of statements. It is clear from the analysis in both *Hodgson* and *Oickle* that the inquiry into voluntariness is contextual in nature and that all relevant circumstances must be considered. . . . However, the Crown bears the onus of establishing a sufficient record of the interaction between the suspect and the police. That onus may be readily satisfied by the use of audio, or better still, video recording. Indeed, it is my view that where the suspect is in custody, recording facilities are readily available, and the police deliberately set out to interrogate the suspect without giving any thought to the making of a reliable record, the context inevitably makes the resulting non-recorded interrogation suspect. In such cases, it will be a matter for the trial judge on the *voir dire* to determine whether or not a sufficient substitute for an audio or video tape record has been provided to satisfy the heavy onus on the Crown to prove voluntariness beyond a reasonable doubt.

The sufficiency of the record does not go exclusively to the question of ultimate reliability and weight as contended by the Crown. . . . And, in my view, the completeness, accuracy and reliability of the record have everything to do with the court's inquiry into and scrutiny of the circumstances surrounding the taking of the statement. Indeed, it is difficult to see how the Crown could discharge its heavy onus of proving voluntariness beyond a reasonable doubt where proper recording procedures are not followed. It is clear that, while determining the legal test of voluntariness is a question of law, its application to the evidence is a question of fact or of mixed law and fact. A trial judge's finding of voluntariness is entitled to deference in this court and should not be interfered with in the absence of legal error in determining the test, or overriding and palpable error with respect to the facts.

. . .

The police officers' allegation that their notes contained a complete, albeit not verbatim, account of the conversation and of the events that transpired during the first part of the interview with McFarlane, between 11:50 p.m. and 12:22 a.m., raised a serious issue of credibility given the short conversation that was noted. The concern over the reliability of the record was further heightened by McFarlane's allegation that he had given three statements on tape, the third one alone finding its way into court because he had finally got it right. Finally, the officers' decision not to videotape the interview or audiotape the first part of the interview was a very important factor to consider. The mysterious loss of the arrest records that purportedly would have confirmed each appellant's waiver of his right to counsel raised another concern. The significance of this evidence was heightened in the circumstances of this case where little, if any, effort was made to create a reliable record.

. . .

In the usual case, the new trial would include a *voir dire* to determine the admissibility of any alleged confession. However, in this case, it is my view that the evidence falls far short of meeting the test of voluntariness. Quite apart from any question of credibility of the appellants' testimony and the police officers' evidence on the *voir dire* on issues related to voluntariness, a matter that would require a determination by a trial judge, it is my view that the Crown cannot meet its heavy onus of proving voluntariness based on the evidence adduced in this case. The serious deficiencies alone in the overall recording by the police authorities of the events that transpired while the two appellants were in police custody on the evening in question militate against any reasonable finding that the statements were voluntary. I would therefore give effect to this ground of appeal, declare that the statements allegedly made by each appellant are inadmissible (with the exception of McFarlane's alleged utterance to May at the scene of the crime as noted earlier) and order a new trial.

R. v. WILSON
(2006), 210 C.C.C. (3d) 23, 39 C.R. (6th) 345 (C.A.)

The accused was convicted of importing cocaine into Canada. He made an inculpatory statement to the arresting officer that was not audio- or videotaped. The accused denied making the admission. On appeal, it was argued that the trial judge had erred in not warning the jury that the failure of the police to record the confession was an important factor in determining whether it was, in fact, made.

ROSENBERG J.A. (ARMSTRONG and ROULEAU JJ.A. concurring): —

In pre-charge discussions, trial counsel for the appellant asked that the trial judge instruct the jury in accordance with this court's decision in *R. v.*

Moore-McFarlane (2001), 160 C.C.C. (3d) 493 at para. 65 that where "the police deliberately set out to interrogate the suspect without giving any thought to the making of a reliable record, the context inevitably makes the resulting non-recorded interrogation suspect". The trial judge held that *Moore-McFarlane* applies only at the admissibility stage and since she had held that the statement was admissible, the special instruction was not required. Unfortunately, the trial judge did not have the benefit of this court's later decision in *R. v. Swanek* (2005), 28 C.R. (6th) 93, which I will discuss later.

In the result, the trial judge gave the following instruction concerning the reliability of the appellant's statement to the police:

> When Constable Mitchell says what Rohan Wilson said to him, you have to decide whether you believe Rohan Wilson made the statement or any part of it. Regardless of who the witness is, it is still up to you to decide whether you believe him. In deciding whether Rohan Wilson actually said these things or any of them, you should use your common sense. Take into account the condition of Mr. Wilson and of Constable Mitchell at the time of the interview. Consider the circumstances in which the interview took place. Bear in mind anything else that may make Constable Mitchell's story more or less reliable.

> Whether a witness has recorded a conversation or taken notes about it does not itself determine how reliable that witness' testimony may be. It is, however, one of the things that you may consider in deciding whether or how much of the witness' testimony to believe.

> Unless you decide that Rohan Wilson made a particular remark or statement, you must not consider it in deciding this case. Some or all of the statements may help Mr. Wilson in his defence. You must consider those remarks that may help Mr. Wilson along with all of the other evidence unless you are satisfied that he did not make them. In other words, you must consider all the remarks that might help Mr. Wilson even if you cannot decide whether he said them.

In my view, for the following reasons, this was not an adequate instruction. This court briefly dealt with this issue in *R. v. Swanek*. In that case, the accused argued, for the first time on appeal, that the trial judge should have directed the jury that it was dangerous to rely upon an unrecorded inculpatory statement that was not confirmed by other evidence. Doherty J.A. at para. 12, noted the concern with unrecorded oral statements:

> Counsel makes the valid point that while those who are regularly involved in the criminal process are familiar with the historical unreliability of oral confessions attributed to persons in custody, a jury may well not appreciate that unreliability.

Thus, he held at para. 13 that in a proper case a special instruction should be given to the jury:

> If the police failure to make a proper recording of an alleged inculpatory statement is in issue at trial, I think a trial judge should tell the jury that the failure to make a proper recording is an important factor for the jury to consider in deciding whether to rely on the police version of the alleged statement.

In *Swanek*, the court held that there was no error in failing to give the instruction since the failure to make a proper recording was not an issue at trial and no special instruction had been requested by the accused. That is not the case here: defence counsel raised the failure to videotape in his examination of the officers and asked the trial judge to give a special instruction. I note that in *Swanek* the concern was with an oral statement that was not signed by the accused and only reduced to writing in the officers' notebooks. However, given the uncontested evidence that the appellant was all but illiterate, nothing turns on the fact the statement in this case was signed. The point remains that because of the failure to audio or video record the circumstances or manner of obtaining the statement cannot be objectively assessed.

Most of the cases that have considered the issue of videotaping of statements have been concerned with the impact of the failure to videotape on admissibility. However, in my view, and for the reasons set out in *Swanek*, in appropriate circumstances, a special instruction should be given to the jury where the accused contests the accuracy of the non-recorded statement. Over a decade ago, Carthy J.A. in his concurring reasons in *R. v. Barrett* (1993), 82 C.C.C. (3d) 266 (Ont. C.A.) at 270, noted the central feature a confession can play in a criminal case and the importance of having an accurate record of what occurred: and he said this: "On this determinative issue of conviction the police force has, by its own choice in this case, denied the court the opportunity of an undeniable record of what led to the "conviction". Given the modest cost of videotape equipment, such critical evidence should not, in fairness, be restricted to sworn recollection of two contesting individuals as to what occurred in stressful conditions months or years ago. The evidence is admissible under our present rules, but everyone involved in the criminal justice system should make reasonable efforts to better serve its ultimate ends."

These concerns do not relate solely to voluntariness; they also relate to the jury's task in attempting to decide whether the accused confessed as alleged by the police. *Barrett* was overturned on appeal to the Supreme Court of Canada (1995), 96 C.C.C. (3d) 319, on the basis that the failure of the trial judge to give reasons for admitting the statement did not amount to an error of law. That decision does not take away from the common sense identified by Carthy J.A.'s reasons.

In *R. v. Oickle* (2000), 147 C.C.C. (3d) 321 (S.C.C.) at para. 46, Iacobucci J. held that a video or audio recording "can greatly assist the trier of fact in assessing the confession". The trier of fact, of course is concerned not solely with voluntariness but whether the statement was made and the truth of the contents of the statement. It must also be said that at the present time the failure to electronically record the statement does not itself render the statement inherently suspect. Iacobucci J. made that clear in *Oickle* at para. 46. To the same effect is the decision of the Manitoba Court of Appeal in *R. v. Ducharme* (2004), 182 C.C.C. (3d) 243 at para. 46:

> The difficulty is that until either the Supreme Court articulates or Parliament legislates the duties of the police and lays out a protocol to be followed, the common law definition of voluntariness will remain in effect. That being the case, it cannot be said that the failure to videotape or electronically record will automatically mean the exclusion of the evidence on a voir dire. [Footnote omitted]

Thus, there must be other circumstances before a trial judge would be entitled to give the special instruction sought in this case. One set of circumstances was identified in *R. v Moore-McFarlane* at para. 65: "where the suspect is in custody, recording facilities are readily available, and the police deliberately set out to interrogate the suspect without giving any thought to the making of a reliable record, the context inevitably makes the resulting non-recorded interrogation suspect". Admittedly, in that case, Charron J.A. was concerned with voluntariness, but for the reasons set out above the concern for accuracy that arises at the voluntariness stage also applies at the guilt or innocence stage.

In my view, it was open to the jury to find that the police deliberately set out to interrogate the appellant without giving any thought to the making of a reliable video or audio record. The jury should therefore have been instructed along the lines suggested in *R. v. Swanek* that this was an important factor to consider in deciding whether to rely on the officer's version of the statement.

The respondent submits that the jury would have understood the concern with the reliability of the written statement because both counsel in their jury addresses acknowledged the problem stemming from the lack of an audio or video recording. I do not accept that position. While defence counsel in his address did review the circumstances of the taking of the statement and pointed out that Constable Mitchell could have used the pocket recorder, he expressly told the jury that the legal effect of those circumstances would be explained by the trial judge:

> So he's in a room specifically designed to audio and video-record a confession or a statement generally and he chose not to use that. Now, why is that important? Now, Her Honour will suggest what the law says about that but the logical reason why, over time, we've moved from having them written to having them video, doesn't take a lawyer to explain that. Obviously a video statement is much more trustworthy than having to take someone's word for how this all happened and that wasn't utilized.

Unfortunately, after the jury addresses, the trial judge ruled that she would not give this special instruction. While Crown counsel also gave a fair recitation of the facts in her jury address, she invited the jury to draw the inference that had there been a recording it would simply have confirmed Constable Mitchell's version:

> It is trite to say that given the accused's version of events, it would be very nice at this trial to have a perfect video or audio record. Obviously we may not even have been here.

In any event, counsel's views on the law are no substitute for a proper legal direction from the trial judge. Given the central role played by the statement, I cannot be satisfied that the absence of a proper instruction did not prejudice the appellant's defence.

6. MIXED INCULPATORY AND EXCULPATORY STATEMENTS

Recall earlier the discussion of the requirement of the Crown to lead the entire statement including any exculpatory parts. How is the trial judge to instruct the jury on the weight to be given the inculpatory and exculpatory portions? U.K. courts favour a so-called *Duncan* instruction to the jury that

> the incriminating parts are likely to be true (otherwise why say them?), whereas the excuses do not have the same weight.

The Supreme Court has recently decided that such a direction would be dangerous and was not required.

R. v. ROJAS

[2008] 3 S.C.R. 111, 236 C.C.C. (3d) 153, 60 C.R. (6th) 271 (S.C.C.)

CHARRON J.:—

. . .

36 Exculpatory out-of-court statements made by an accused are also subject to the general exclusionary rule against hearsay. Where the accused testifies, such statements are generally inadmissible because they are viewed as self-serving and lacking in probative value. Where the accused does not testify, there is an additional rationale for excluding such statements. McIntyre J. explained it in *R. v. Simpson*, [1988] 1 S.C.R. 3, as follows (at p. 22):

> As a general rule, the statements of an accused person made outside court - subject to a finding of voluntariness where the statement is made to one in authority - are receivable in evidence against him but not for him. This rule is based on the sound proposition that an accused person should not be free to make an unsworn statement and compel its admission into evidence through other witnesses and thus put his defence before the jury without being put on oath and being subjected, as well, to cross-examination.

37 Of course, the general rule that excludes out-of-court exculpatory statements is not without exceptions. One such exception is relevant here - the mixed statement exception. Just as in England, it has long been established that where the Crown seeks to tender an accused's out-of-court statement which contains both inculpatory and exculpatory parts, it must tender the entire statement, and the exculpatory portions are substantively admissible in favour of the accused: *R. v. Hughes*, [1942] S.C.R. 517, at p. 521. Fairness to the accused is the obvious rationale for the mixed statement exception. The exception is also based on the more pragmatic consideration that it is often difficult to determine which parts of a statement are inculpatory and which parts are exculpatory.

38 In recognizing both the basis for admitting inculpatory statements and the exceptional admissibility of an accused's untested statements, the *Duncan* instruction, as such, accurately reflects the state of the law. In England, the

instruction is also perceived as achieving the "right balance", as the House of Lords explained in *Aziz* (at p. 485):

> Moreover, I would reject the suggestion that the law as stated in *Sharp* is unduly balanced in favour of the defendants who do not testify. On the contrary, as was emphasised in *Duncan* and *Sharp*, a judge is entitled to comment adversely on the quality of the exculpatory parts of a mixed statement which has not been tested by cross-examination. The right balance has been found. [Emphasis added.]

Judges in Canada, as in England, are also entitled to comment on the evidence so long as they make it clear that factual issues are for the jury to decide: *R. v. Gunning*, [2005] 1 S.C.R. 627, 2005 SCC 27, at para. 27. The Crown therefore urges this Court to adopt the *Duncan* instruction in Canada.

39 With respect to the contrary position adopted by our English colleagues, I would not accede to the Crown's argument. In certain circumstances, it may be useful to explain to the jury why the law permits them to hear a particular piece of evidence where such instruction will assist them with their task. This may be the case, for example, where evidence is admitted for a limited purpose only. The jury may be more likely to comply with the limiting instruction if they understand the underlying rationale for the rule. In most circumstances, however, expounding the rationale for an evidentiary rule may only serve to confuse the jury unnecessarily or risk encroaching unduly upon their role as fact finders. For example, I can think of no principled reason to explain to a jury that they are hearing the accused's confession because the court is satisfied beyond a reasonable doubt that it was voluntarily made. Likewise, it would only risk encroaching unduly on the jury's domain to tell them that they are hearing a piece of similar fact evidence because, in the judge's view, the similarities with the offence are such that they "defy coincidence".

40 In the same way, I see little advantage in expounding for the jury the underlying rationale for the mixed statement exception. If only for the pragmatic reason that it is often very difficult to differentiate between admissions and excuses, I . . . conclude—- as did . . .the court below, that it is dangerous for the judge to instruct the jury in a manner that suggests that inculpatory and exculpatory statements ought to be weighed differently. Such "common sense" comments are better left to the advocacy of counsel (David, at para. 42). Therefore, I conclude that the *Duncan* instruction should not be adopted by Canadian trial courts.

. . .

47 When viewed in context, I am satisfied that the *Duncan* instruction could not have misled the jury. It was clear from the charge that the burden of proof did not shift to Hugo or Miguel, that any exculpatory statement need only raise a reasonable doubt, and that the accused were entitled to the benefit of any such doubt. In commenting on the relative weight that may be attributed to the statements, the trial judge did not exceed his function. It was clear that the assessment of the reliability of the statements was left entirely with the jury.

Accordingly, I agree with the Court of Appeal below that the *Duncan* instruction did not constitute reversible error in the context of this case.

48 Accordingly, for these reasons, I would dismiss the appeals.

D. OPINION EVIDENCE AND EXPERTS

1. OPINION RULE

The common law has long upheld a general rule that witnesses who are not testifying as experts should speak to the material facts and not offer opinions. At the same time, it is widely recognized that the distinction between facts and opinion can be difficult to maintain. The English and Canadian courts have not applied the exclusionary rule strictly.   As suggested by Cowen & Carter:[294]

> The opinion rule has appeared to work in England only because it has been laxly applied.

The true scope of an opinion rule in the law of evidence can be properly appreciated only with an awareness of the historical development in this area. The early eighteenth-century announcements of English courts, that witnesses must speak to facts and not to opinion, when read in the context of that age, forbade quite different testimony than is presently thought to be foreclosed by the opinion rule. Samuel Johnson's Dictionary (1st ed., 1755) defined opinion as "Persuasion of the mind without proof of certain knowledge . . . Sentiments, Judgment, Notion," and never referred to "opinion" in the sense of a reasoned conclusion from facts observed.[295] Prior to the close of the eighteenth century there was no opinion rule, as we know it today[296] and statements made at the time such as "it is mere opinion, which is not evidence"[297] were statements condemning testimony by witnesses who had no personal knowledge of the event and so suffered from the same lack of testimonial qualification as the witness who repeated hearsay. What was being forbidden then were notions, guesses, conjectures; as phrased by Professor Wigmore, they were statements demanding that "the witness must speak as a knower, not merely a guesser".[298]

While judges and writers in Canada still mouth expressions that lay witnesses cannot give their opinions but must state facts, the intrinsic impossibility of the requirement has led in actual practice to the reception of opinion testimony from witnesses who have personal knowledge.

---

[294] Cowen & Carter, *Essays on the Law of Evidence* (1956) at 164.
[295] See King & Pillinger, *Opinion Evidence in Illinois* (1942) at 8.
[296] See *Phipson on Evidence*, 11th ed. (1970) at 504, noting that *Gilbert's Evidence* of 1726 and Buller's *Nisi Prius* of 1767 make no mention of such rule with the first appearance of the same apparently in *Peake on Evidence* in 1801.
[297] Lord Mansfield in *Carter v. Boehm* (1766), 97 E.R. 1162 at 1168.
[298] 7 Wigmore, *Evidence* (Chad. Rev.), s. 1917.

GRAAT v. R.
[1982] 2 S.C.R. 819, 31 C.R. (3d) 289, 2 C.C.C. (3d) 365

21st December 1982. The judgment of the court was delivered by

DICKSON J.:—

This appeal [from 17 C.R. (3d) 55] raises the issue whether on a charge of driving while impaired the court may admit opinion evidence on the very question to be decided, namely, Was the accused's ability to drive impaired by alcohol at the time and place stated in the charge?

. . .

At approximately 2:15 a.m. on the date in question, Constables Case and McMullen of the London City Police observed Mr. Graat's vehicle travelling at a high rate of speed. The constables followed for several blocks. They observed Mr. Graat's car weaving in the southbound lane, crossing the centre line on two occasions and driving on to the shoulder of the road on another occasion. When the vehicle turned left it straddled the centre line.

Both constables testified they noticed the smell of alcohol on the appellant's breath; both said Mr. Graat was unsteady on his feet, he staggered as he walked and had bloodshot eyes. At the police station Mr. Graat was observed by a Sergeant Spoelstra. The sergeant testified he smelled alcohol on the appellant's breath, the top part of his body was swaying and his walk was "kind of wavy".

Mr. Graat complained of chest pains. He told the police he suffered from a heart condition and asked to be taken to a hospital. The police complied. By the time Mr. Graat returned to the police station it was too late to take two breath samples because the two-hour time-limit for the taking of such samples had expired or was about to expire.

Mr. Graat testified he had had two drinks of gin between the hours of 3:00 p.m. and 7:00 p.m., and two glasses of wine with his dinner about 11:00 p.m. He said he and two friends, George Wilson and Vincent O'Donovan, were returning from a sailing party; he became tired. Wilson drove the car while he dozed in the back seat. The appellant resumed driving after Wilson had driven O'Donovan and himself home. Wilson testified that if he had thought Mr. Graat was not in a fit condition to drive he would have asked him to stay at his, Wilson's, house.

At trial Constable Case was asked the following questions and gave the following answers:

Q. All right, now what, if any, opinion having made those observations, what if any opinion did you form regarding the accused man's ability to drive a motor vehicle?

A. I formed the opinion that the accused's ability was impaired.

Q. By?

A. By alcohol.

Q. You said the accused man's ability to what?

A.   To drive a motor vehicle was impaired by alcohol.

Constable McMullen was asked the following question:

Q.   Now officer when you were at the scene and having made the observations of the driving of the accused man, having observed him, having smelled the alcoholic beverage on his breath and observed him walk and observed him standing, observed him speaking to you what, if any, conclusion did you come to regarding his ability to drive a motor vehicle?

A.   It was in my opinion that the accused's ability to operate a motor vehicle was impaired by alcohol beverage.

Sergeant Spoelstra, the desk sergeant, gave similar evidence:

Q.   You saw him standing and you saw him walking. What, if any opinion, did you form regarding his ability to drive a motor vehicle?

A.   In my opinion the accused's ability was impaired by the use of alcohol to drive a motor vehicle.

. . .

The trial judge preferred the evidence of the police witnesses to the evidence of Mr. Graat and Mr. Wilson. In particular, the judge relied on the evidence of Constable McMullen and Sergeant Spoelstra, policemen for 8 and 17 years respectively. Constable Case had only been a police officer for a few months, and had only charged two or three persons with impaired driving. The judge said he accepted the opinions of Officers McMullen and Spoelstra in reaching his conclusion that the accused's ability to drive was impaired: I'm of the view that I'm entitled to accept and I do accept the opinions of those two police officers on the issue of impairment as part of the totality of the evidence.

III

THE ONTARIO COURT OF APPEAL

The appellant sought leave to appeal to the Court of Appeal of Ontario and at that time the question was raised as to whether the trial judge had erred in law in relying on the opinion evidence of the two police officers that the appellant's ability to drive a motor vehicle had been impaired by alcohol.

The court dismissed the appeal, saying [p. 442] that the evidence was admissible under the exception to the rule excluding opinion evidence:

. . . that permits non-expert opinion evidence where the primary facts and the inferences to be drawn from them are so closely associated that the opinion is really a compendious way of giving evidence as to certain facts — in this case the condition of the appellant.

This echoes the words of Parke B. in *Wright v. Tatham* (1838), 4 Bing. N.C. 489 at 543-44 (H.L.):

. . . and though the opinion of a witness upon oath, as to that fact [testamentary capacity], might be asked, it would only be a compendious mode of ascertaining the result of the actual observation of the witness, from acts done, as to the habits and demeanour of the deceased.

. . .

CONCLUSION

I have attempted in the foregoing to highlight the opposing points of view as reflected in some of the cases, texts, and reports of the law reform commissions.

We start with the reality that the law of evidence is burdened with a large number of cumbersome rules, with exclusions, and exceptions to the exclusions, and exceptions to the exceptions. The list of subjects upon which the non-expert witness is allowed to give opinion evidence is a lengthy one. The list mentioned in *Sherrard v. Jacob*, supra, is by no means exhaustive: (i) the identification of handwriting, persons and things; (ii) apparent age; (iii) the bodily plight or condition of a person, including death and illness; (iv) the emotional state of a person, e.g., whether distressed, angry, aggressive, affectionate or depressed; (v) the condition of things, e.g., worn, shabby, used or new; (vi) certain questions of value; and (vii) estimates of speed and distance. . . .

Except for the sake of convenience there is little, if any, virtue in any distinction resting on the tenuous and frequently false antithesis between fact and opinion. The line between "fact" and "opinion" is not clear.

To resolve the question before the court I would like to return to broad principles. Admissibility is determined, first, by asking whether the evidence sought to be admitted is relevant. This is a matter of applying logic and experience to the circumstances of the particular case. The question which must then be asked is whether, though probative, the evidence must be excluded by a clear ground of policy or of law.

There is a direct and logical relevance between (i) the evidence offered here, namely, the opinion of a police officer (based on perceived facts as to the manner of driving and indicia of intoxication of the driver) that the person's ability to drive was impaired by alcohol, and (ii) the ultimate probandum in the case. The probative value of the evidence is not outweighed by such policy considerations as danger of confusing the issues or misleading the jury. It does not unfairly surprise a party who had not had reasonable ground to anticipate that such evidence will be offered, and the adducing of the evidence does not necessitate undue consumption of time. As for other considerations, such as "usurping the functions of the jury" and, to the extent that it may be regarded as a separate consideration, "opinion on the very issue before the jury", Wigmore has gone a long way toward establishing that rejection of opinion evidence on either of these grounds is unsound historically and in principle. If the court is being told that which it is in itself entirely equipped to determine without the aid of the witness on the point then of course the evidence is supererogatory and unnecessary. It would be a waste of time listening to superfluous testimony.

The judge in the instant case was not in as good a position as the police officers or Mr. Wilson to determine the degree of Mr. Graat's impairment or his ability to drive a motor vehicle. The witnesses had an opportunity for personal observation. They were in a position to give the court real help. They were not settling the dispute. They were not deciding the matter the court had to decide, the ultimate issue. The judge could accept all or part or none of their evidence. In the end he accepted the evidence of two of the police officers and paid little heed to the evidence of the third officer or of Mr. Wilson.

. . .

A non-expert witness cannot, of course, give opinion evidence on a legal issue as, for example, whether or not a person was negligent. That is because such an opinion would not qualify as an abbreviated version of the witness's factual observations. An opinion that someone was negligent is partly factual, but it also involves the application of legal standards. On the other hand, whether a person's ability to drive is impaired by alcohol is a question of fact, not of law. It does not involve the application of any legal standard. It is akin to an opinion that someone is too drunk to climb a ladder or to go swimming, and the fact that a witness's opinion, as here, may be expressed in the exact words of the Criminal Code does not change a factual matter into a question of law. It only reflects the fact that the draftsmen of the Code employed the ordinary English phrase: "his ability to drive . . . is impaired by alcohol" (s. 234).

In short, I know of no clear ground of policy or of law which would require the exclusion of opinion evidence tendered by the Crown or the defence as to Mr. Graat's impairment.

I conclude with two caveats. First, in every case, in determining whether an opinion is admissible, the trial judge must necessarily exercise a large measure of discretion. Second, there may be a tendency for judges and juries to let the opinion of police witnesses overwhelm the opinion evidence of other witnesses. Since the opinion is admitted under the "compendious statement of facts" exception rather than under the "expert witness" exception, there is no special reason for preferring the police evidence over the "opinion" of other witnesses. As always, the trier of fact must decide in each case what weight to give what evidence. The "opinion" of the police officer is entitled to no special regard. Ordinary people with ordinary experience are able to know as a matter of fact that someone is too drunk to perform certain tasks, such as driving a car. If the witness lacks the relevant experience, or is otherwise limited in his testimonial capacity, or if the witness is not sure whether the person was intoxicated to the point of impairment, that can be brought out in cross-examination. But the fact that a police witness has seen more impaired drivers than a non-police witness is not a reason in itself to prefer the evidence of the police officer. Constables McMullen and Spoelstra were not testifying as experts based on their extensive experience as police officers.

There was some confusion about this matter in this case as appears from the following cross-examination of Mr. Wilson:

Q.   . . . And of course you've not and never have been a police officer. Do you agree or disagree with me?

A.   No. No.

Q. You have never been a police officer?

A. No.

Q. And you're not in the habit of checking people as to the amount of alcohol that is consumed in order to make him impaired. Do you agree or disagree with me?

A. I have to agree with you?

Q. Yes. So you're really not in a position to tell us whether or not he was impaired or not impaired by alcohol. Do you agree or disagree with me?

A. I was only . . .

Q. . . But of course you were in no position to judge as to whether or not he was impaired. Do you agree or disagree with me?

A. I don't have any qualifications in that regard, I guess.

Mr. Wilson does not need any special qualifications. Nor were the police officers relying on any special qualifications when they gave their opinions. Both police and non-police witnesses are merely giving a compendious statement of facts that are too subtle and too complicated to be narrated separately and distinctly. Trial judges should bear in mind that this is non-expert opinion evidence, and that the opinion of police officers is not entitled to preference just because they may have extensive experience with impaired drivers. The credit and accuracy of the police must be viewed in the same manner as that of other witnesses and in the light of all the evidence in the case. If the police and traffic officers have been closely associated with the prosecution, such association may affect the weight to be given to such evidence.

The trial judge was correct in admitting the opinions of the three police officers and Mr. Wilson.

For the foregoing reasons, as well as for the reasons given by Howland C.J.O., I would dismiss the appeal.

Appeal dismissed.

Is the analysis in the following case consistent with *Graat*?

R. v. B. (H.)
2016 ONCA 953, 345 C.C.C. (3d) 206, 34 C.R. (7th) 422 (Ont. C.A.)

GILLESE J.A. (ROULEAU J.A., concurring):

1 Following a jury trial, H.B. (the "appellant") was convicted of sexual assault, sexual interference and invitation to sexual touching for incidents involving his step-daughter ("T" or the "complainant"). The offences were alleged to have occurred between 2008 and 2012, when T was between 11 and 14 years of age and living with her mother ("L"), her sister, and the appellant. The appellant was sentenced to four and a half years in prison.

2 He appeals against conviction alone.

. . .

24 A CAS worker and two police officers — one of whom was PC Kimens — went to the home to pick up T for questioning at the police station. The appellant, L, a family friend and the two children were at the home. PC Kimens spoke to L privately about T's allegations. In examination in chief, he testified:

> A. I explained to [L] briefly about the allegation that we had received from CAS about [the appellant] inappropriately touching [T]. Her reaction was, was not surprise.
>
> Q. What do you mean? Please explain that.
>
> A. There was no real change in her demeanour, protesting, or, facial expressions, and, in my experience, as a police officer...

25 At that point, defence counsel objected and submissions were made in the absence of the jury and the witness. . . .

. . .

27 The trial judge allowed the question to be answered.

28 When the jury returned, PC Kimens was asked to continue with his answer. He said:

> Based on my experience, as a police officer, when telling others of allegations of this nature there's usually a reaction, whether it be rage, denial, um, but, again, what I noticed was, was the fact that there was no real surprised look, and that struck me as odd.

29 PC Kimens then testified that he explained to L the role of the police when they receive information of this kind and the steps that would follow — both children would be taken that evening to the York Regional Police building in Aurora because that facility enabled the police to videotape conversations and interviews. He told L the location of the police building and that she was free to attend if she wished.

30 PC Kimens testified that L asked if the children would be returning and he told her that he was not able to answer that but he could tell her that they would be going with the CAS. The next question and answer were as follows:

> Q. Did [L's] demeanour change at all during the course of this interaction that you had with her?
>
> A. No. And, again, in, in harkening to my experience, in that, there weren't a lot of questions. Normally, when an allegation of that nature is brought out, people have a lot of questions in terms of the specifics and what next.

. . .

33 Defence counsel cross-examined PC Kimens extensively on his demeanour observations. The officer admitted that he had no special training, education or expertise in psychology, human conduct or facial expressions, and he readily agreed with the suggestion that people react to shocking news in different ways.

34 In her closing submissions, Crown counsel referred to PC Kimens's testimony that when he told L of T's allegations, L had no change in her facial expression and that her lack of reaction to being told that her partner was abusing her daughter struck him as odd. She said:

> I would submit that Officer Kimens'[s] evidence is significant, as it suggests that [L's] purpose, throughout the police investigation, was to conceal the truth, and to prevent the authorities from learning the truth. Her conduct on January 4th to January 7th of 2013, in my respectful submission, is consistent with [T's] evidence surrounding [L's] words and actions throughout the years that [T] describes having been abused, years that her mother knew about the ongoing abuse.
>
> . . .
>
> I submit to you, that the only logical conclusion that you can draw from the evidence you have heard is that [L] already knew about the abuse, because [T] had told her.

. . .

74 In my view, in determining whether the trial judge erred in admitting the demeanour evidence, this court need not go further than to refer to the list in *Graat*, reproduced above. That list sets out accepted categories upon which lay witnesses are allowed to express opinions. Item (iv) of that list is evidence of "the emotional state of a person — *e.g.* whether [a person was] distressed, angry, aggressive, affectionate or depressed".

75 The demeanour evidence in this case was PC Kimens's opinion of L's observable emotional state on being told of the allegations T had made against the appellant. Because the demeanour evidence falls squarely within list item (iv) in *Graat*, it was admissible.

. . .

103 *Graat* . . . does provide assistance in determining whether the trial judge erred in permitting PC Kimens to offer his opinion on L's demeanour. As we have seen, in *Graat*, the Supreme Court explained that the admissibility of lay opinion evidence must be determined using appropriate legal principles:

> Admissibility is determined, first, by asking whether the evidence sought to be admitted is relevant. This is a matter of applying logic and experience to the circumstances of the particular case. The question which must then be asked is whether, though probative, the evidence must be excluded by a clear ground of policy or of law.

104 In accordance with *Graat*, in my view, the trial judge should have determined whether PC Kimens's opinion evidence was relevant and, if so, whether its probative value was outweighed "by such policy considerations as [the] danger of confusing the issues or misleading the jury". This would include an assessment of whether the probative value of that evidence was outweighed by the prejudicial effect of its admission.

105 Had the trial judge performed such an assessment, because of the highly subjective nature of the evidence, he might well have exercised his discretion to exclude it on the basis that the prejudicial effect of the evidence outweighed its probative value.

106 That said, in my view, the admission and use of the impugned evidence in this case did not impair a fair trial. I say this for two reasons.

107 First, the impugned evidence was very limited. . . .

108 Second, I see no basis for believing that the jury would have attached undue weight to the impugned evidence. The defence's effective and thorough cross-examination of PC Kimens served to diminish its weight and any prejudice that the opinion evidence might have occasioned. Through that cross-examination, it was clearly demonstrated that PC Kimens had no special training in psychology, human emotions or facial expressions, and he readily admitted that people react to shocking news in different ways. It also exposed the limits of PC Kimens's experience and education in forming his opinion, which served to address the policy consideration identified in *Graat*, namely, that the evidence might mislead the jury.

109 For these reasons, I would not give effect to the appellant's . . . argument.

Appeal dismissed

2. EXPERT EVIDENCE

Toward the end of the eighteenth century what appears to be an exception to the general rule forbidding testimony by witnesses who had no personal knowledge of the facts at issue was established. Expert assistance had been furnished to the court from very ancient times but not in the form normally used today.[299] Special juries of experts were commonly used in the fourteenth century to resolve trade disputes,[300] and as early as 1353 we find the court summoning surgeons to give an opinion on whether a wound amounted to mayhem.[301] The court summoned the expert, and on considering his advice, then directed the jury respecting the major premise that could be used by them in determining the particular fact situation. We find, toward the end of the eighteenth century, experts being called by the

---

[299]   See generally Hand, "Historical and Practical Considerations Regarding Expert Testimony" (1901) 15 Harv. L. Rev. 40; see also Thayer, *Cases on Evidence*, 2nd ed. (1900) at 672-673 and Rosenthal, "The Development of the Use of Expert Testimony" (1935) 2 L. & Contemp. Prob. 403.

[300]   See Hand, *ibid.* at 41, 42.

[301]   *Anonymous*, Lib. Ass. 28, pl. 5 (28 Edw. III); see also *Buller v. Crips* (1705), 87 E.R. 793.

parties, testifying as witnesses, and so furnishing their assistance directly to the jury.[302] To justify this apparent exception to the long-standing rule that witnesses have personal knowledge, the courts reasoned that to receive the same was *necessary*.[303] The expert then could give his opinion on matters of science, though he had no personal knowledge of the event being litigated, where to do so would be *helpful* to the jury's decision-making; where the major premise or premises against which the particular instance under review need(s) to be tested is/are lacking from the fund of knowledge possessed by the layman.

The expert's testimonial qualifications, just as those of lay witnesses, must be established before the trier of fact. It is for the trial judge in his discretion to rule whether the experiential qualifications of the witness have been made out,[304] and it is for the trial judge to rule whether the evidence will be helpful. As the state of the art varies with time so will the criterion of helpfulness. Professor McGuire wrote:

> The field of expertness is bounded on one side by the great area of the commonplace, supposedly within the ken of every person of moderate intelligence, and on the other by the even greater area of the speculative and uncertain. Of course both these boundaries constantly shift, as the former area enlarges and the latter diminishes. Only a few years ago it would have been necessary to take expert evidence on issues with respect to the operation of motor cars, airplanes, or radios which are now so completely inside the domain of popular understanding that such evidence would be rejected as superfluous. A century ago purportedly expert evidence on these topics would have been rejected as visionary.[305]

As the "speculative and uncertain" area changes, how should the court rule?

(a) Tests

In the United States[306] a special evidentiary rule was set out in a federal appellate opinion in 1923 and despite criticism over the years it lasted until its repudiation by the United States Supreme Court in 1993.[307] That rule, which became known as the *Frye* test, demanded general acceptance in the scientific community before expertise could be admitted.[308] McCormick recommended:

> The traditional standards of relevancy and the need for expertise — and nothing more — should govern. This method for evaluating the admissibility of scientific

---

302   See e.g. *Folkes v. Chad* (1782), 99 E.R. 589; (1783), 99 E.R. 686.
303   See note to *Carter v. Boehm* in *Smith's Leading Cases*, 13th ed., vol. 1 at 560.
304   *Preeper v. R.* (1888), 15 S.C.R. 401.
305   *Evidence: Common Sense and Common Law* (1947) at 30.
306   *Frye v. United States*, 293 F. 1013 (D.C. Cir. 1923).
307   See *Daubert, infra* note 310.
308   For criticism in the U.S. see e.g. Gianelli, "The Admissibility of Novel Scientific Evidence" (1980) 80 Col. L. Rev. 1197 and McCormick, "Scientific Evidence" (1982) 67 Iowa L. Rev. 879. The amount of writing on this issue was likened to "an academic cottage industry"; see Vu & Tamor, "Of *Daubert,* Elvis and Precedential Relevance" (1993) 41 U.C.L.A. L. Rev. 487 at 491.

evidence is the most appealing. It avoids the difficult problems of defining when "scientific" evidence is subject to the general acceptance requirement and how general this acceptance must be, of discerning exactly what it is that must be accepted, and of determining the "particular field" to which the scientific evidence belongs and in which it must be accepted.[309]

In 1975 the Federal Rules of Evidence were enacted by Congress. The impetus for these rules had been the United States Supreme Court and indeed the preliminary drafts were written pursuant to that Court's rule-making authority. It was only later that Congress involved itself in legislating the Rules. Rule 702 of the F.R.E. provides:

> If scientific, technical, or other specialized knowledge will assist the trier of fact to understand the evidence or to determine a fact in issue, a witness qualified as an expert by knowledge, skill, experience, training, or education, may testify thereto in the form of an opinion or otherwise.

This enactment caused many courts to disregard the *Frye* test. Finally, after 20 years of the rule's operation, the United States Supreme Court rejected the *Frye* test, saying it had been superseded by the F.R.E. rule.

In *Daubert v. Merrell Dow Pharmaceuticals Inc.,*[310] parents sued on their own behalf and on behalf of their children for birth defects. The plaintiffs maintained that these were due to the ingestion of Bendectin by the mother during her pregnancy. Bendectin was advertised as helpful to deal with morning sickness. The plaintiffs were unsuccessful in the lower courts. The trial court applied the *Frye* doctrine. The trial court granted summary judgment on the basis of an affidavit of a well-credentialed expert who deposed that having reviewed the literature, more than 30 published studies involving 130,000 patients, no study had found Bendectin to be a substance causing malformations in human fetuses. The plaintiffs did not contest this characterization of the published record regarding Bendectin. They responded with eight experts of their own, each with impressive credentials. They had concluded that Bendectin could cause birth defects. Their conclusions were based on animal studies; pharmacological studies of the chemical structure of Bendectin and the reanalysis of previously published, epidemiological, human statistical, studies. The trial court decided that scientific evidence was admissible only if the principle upon which it is based is sufficiently established to have general acceptance in the field to which it belongs. The Court decided that the plaintiffs' evidence did not meet that standard. Given the vast body of epidemiological data concerning Bendectin, the Court decided that expert opinion which was not based on epidemiological evidence was not admissible to establish causation. The epidemiological analyses were not admissible because they had not been published or subjected to peer review. The Court of Appeals affirmed holding that expert opinion based on a scientific technique is inadmissible unless the technique was generally accepted as reliable in the relevant scientific community.

---

[309] *McCormick on Evidence*, 4th ed. (1992) at 874.
[310] 113 S.Ct. 2786 (1993).

The Supreme Court granted *certiorari* in light of sharp divisions among the courts regarding the proper standard. When *certiorari* was granted this was front page news in the United States and 22 amicus briefs were filed.[311] The Court decided that the *Frye* test was superseded by the Federal Rules and general acceptance in the scientific community was not a prerequisite to admission of scientific evidence. The rejection of the *Frye* test does not mean however that a trial judge is deprived of authority to exclude expert testimony. Justice Blackmun for the court wrote:

> Nor is the trial judge disabled from screening such evidence. To the contrary, under the rules the trial judge must ensure that any and all scientific testimony or evidence admitted is not only relevant, but reliable.[312]

The Court recognized that scientists typically distinguish between "validity" (does the principle support what it purports to show?) and "reliability" (does application of the principle produce consistent results?). The Court was, however, at pains to point out that when they spoke of the need for reliability they were speaking of evidentiary reliability, i.e., trustworthiness, and that reliability would be based upon scientific validity.

The Court recognized that it would be wrong to demand that the subject of scientific testimony be known to a certainty. To qualify as scientific knowledge however an inference or assertion must be derived by the scientific method. The trial judge is expected to assess whether the reasoning or methodology underlying the testimony is scientifically valid and whether that reasoning or methodology can properly be applied to the facts in issue. The Court offered some observations as to how a trial judge might go about his or her task:

> [W]hether a theory or technique is scientific knowledge that will assist the trier of fact will [depend on] whether it can be and has been tested [and] whether the theory or technique has been subjected to peer review and publication. . . . The fact of publication, or lack thereof, in a peer-reviewed journal will be a relevant, though not dispositive, consideration. . . . [T]he court should consider the known or potential rate of error and the existence and maintenance of standards controlling the technique's operation. . . . Finally, "general acceptance" can yet have a bearing.[313]

Counsel for Merrell Dow Pharmaceuticals Inc. argued that abandoning the general acceptance test would result in a "free-for-all" in which juries would be confounded by irrational pseudoscientific assertions. The Court decided that along with the screening by the trial judge, the adversary system with vigorous cross-examination and presentation of contrary evidence were appropriate safeguards.

---

[311]   See Imwinkelried, "*Frye* Is Dead", *Trial* (September 1993) 60.

[312]   *Daubert, supra* note 310 at 2795.

[313]   *Ibid.* at 2796-2797.

WHITE BURGESS LANGILLE INMAN v. ABBOTT AND HALIBURTON CO.

2015 CSC 23, 2015 SCC 23, [2015] 2 S.C.R. 182, 18 C.R. (7th) 308 (S.C.C.)

CROMWELL J. (MCLACHLIN C.J. and ABELLA, ROTHSTEIN, MOLDAVER, WAGNER and GASCON JJ. concurring):

4 The appeal arises out of a professional negligence action by the respondents (who I will call the shareholders) against the appellants, the former auditors of their company (I will refer to them as the auditors). The shareholders started the action after they had retained a different accounting firm, the Kentville office of Grant Thornton LLP, to perform various accounting tasks and which in their view revealed problems with the auditors' previous work. The central allegation in the action is that the auditors' failure to apply generally accepted auditing and accounting standards while carrying out their functions caused financial loss to the shareholders. The main question in the action boils down to whether the auditors were negligent in the performance of their professional duties.

5 The auditors brought a motion for summary judgment in August of 2010, seeking to have the shareholders' action dismissed. In response, the shareholders retained Susan MacMillan, a forensic accounting partner at the Halifax office of Grant Thornton, to review all the relevant materials, including the documents filed in the action and to prepare a report of her findings. Her affidavit set out her findings, including her opinion that the auditors had not complied with their professional obligations to the shareholders. The auditors applied to strike out Ms. MacMillan's affidavit on the grounds that she was not an impartial expert witness. They argued that the action comes down to a battle of opinion between two accounting firms—the auditors' and the expert witness's. Ms. MacMillan's firm could be exposed to liability if its approach was not accepted by the court and, as a partner, Ms. MacMillan could be personally liable. Her potential liability if her opinion were not accepted gives her a personal financial interest in the outcome of the litigations and this, in the auditors' submission, ought to disqualify her from testifying.

6 The proceedings since have been neither summary nor resulted in a judgment. Instead, the litigation has been focused on the expert evidence issue; the summary judgment application has not yet been heard on its merits.

. . .

III. Analysis

. . .

B. Expert Witness Independence and Impartiality

11 There have been long-standing concerns about whether expert witnesses hired by the parties are impartial in the sense that they are expressing their own

unbiased professional opinion and whether they are independent in the sense that their opinion is the product of their own, independent conclusions based on their own knowledge and judgment: see, e.g., G. R. Anderson, *Expert Evidence* (3rd ed. 2014), at p. 509; S. N. Lederman, A. W. Bryant and M. K. Fuerst, *The Law of Evidence in Canada* (4th ed. 2014), at p. 783. As Sir George Jessel, M.R., put it in the 1870s, "[u]ndoubtedly there is a natural bias to do something serviceable for those who employ you and adequately remunerate you. It is very natural, and it is so effectual, that we constantly see persons, instead of considering themselves witnesses, rather consider themselves as the paid agents of the person who employs them": *Lord Abinger v. Ashton* (1873), L.R. 17 Eq. 358, at p. 374.

12 Recent experience has only exacerbated these concerns; we are now all too aware that an expert's lack of independence and impartiality can result in egregious miscarriages of justice: *R. v. D.D.*, 2000 SCC 43, [2000] 2 S.C.R. 275, at para. 52. As observed by Beveridge J.A. in this case, *The Commission on Proceedings Involving Guy Paul Morin: Report* (1998) authored by the Honourable Fred Kaufman and the *Inquiry into Pediatric Forensic Pathology in Ontario: Report* (2008) conducted by the Honourable Stephen T. Goudge provide two striking examples where "[s]eemingly solid and impartial, but flawed, forensic scientific opinion has played a prominent role in miscarriages of justice": para. 105. Other reports outline the critical need for impartial and independent expert evidence in civil litigation: *ibid.*, at para. 106; see the Right Honourable Lord Woolf, *Access to Justice: Final Report* (1996); the Honourable Coulter A. Osborne, *Civil Justice Reform Project: Summary of Findings & Recommendations* (2007).

13 To decide how our law of evidence should best respond to these concerns, we must confront several questions: Should concerns about potentially biased expert opinion go to admissibility or only to weight?; If to admissibility, should these concerns be addressed by a threshold requirement for admissibility, by a judicial discretion to exclude, or both?; At what point do these concerns justify exclusion of the evidence?; And finally, how is our response to these concerns integrated into the existing legal framework governing the admissibility of expert opinion evidence? To answer these questions, we must first consider the existing legal framework governing admissibility, identify the duties that an expert witness has to the court and then turn to how those duties are best reflected in that legal framework.

C. The Legal Framework

. . .

(2) The Current Legal Framework for Expert Opinion Evidence

16 Since at least the mid-1990s, the Court has responded to a number of concerns about the impact on the litigation process of expert evidence of dubious value. The jurisprudence has clarified and tightened the threshold requirements for admissibility, added new requirements in order to assure

reliability, particularly of novel scientific evidence, and emphasized the important role that judges should play as "gatekeepers" to screen out proposed evidence whose value does not justify the risk of confusion, time and expense that may result from its admission.

17 We can take as the starting point for these developments the Court's decision in *R. v. Mohan*, [1994] 2 S.C.R. 9. That case described the potential dangers of expert evidence and established a four-part threshold test for admissibility. The dangers are well known. One is that the trier of fact will inappropriately defer to the expert's opinion rather than carefully evaluate it.

As Sopinka J. observed in Mohan:

> There is a danger that expert evidence will be misused and will distort the fact-finding process. Dressed up in scientific language which the jury does not easily understand and submitted through a witness of impressive antecedents, this evidence is apt to be accepted by the jury as being virtually infallible and as having more weight than it deserves. [p. 21]

(See also *D.D.*, at para. 53; *R. v. J.-L.J.*, 2000 SCC 51, [2000] 2 S.C.R. 600, at paras. 25-26; *R. v. Sekhon*, 2014 SCC 15, [2014] 1 S.C.R. 272, at para. 46.)

18 The point is to preserve trial by judge and jury, not devolve to trial by expert. There is a risk that the jury "will be unable to make an effective and critical assessment of the evidence": *R. v. Abbey*, 2009 ONCA 624, 97 O.R. (3d) 330, at para. 90, leave to appeal refused, [2010] 2 S.C.R. v. The trier of fact must be able to use its "informed judgment", not simply decide on the basis of an "act of faith" in the expert's opinion: *J.-L.J.*, at para. 56. The risk of "attornment to the opinion of the expert" is also exacerbated by the fact that expert evidence is resistant to effective cross-examination by counsel who are not experts in that field: *D.D.*, at para. 54. The cases address a number of other related concerns: the potential prejudice created by the expert's reliance on unproven material not subject to cross-examination (*D.D.*, at para. 55); the risk of admitting "junk science" (*J.-L.J.*, at para. 25); and the risk that a "contest of experts" distracts rather than assists the trier of fact (*Mohan*, at p. 24). Another well-known danger associated with the admissibility of expert evidence is that it may lead to an inordinate expenditure of time and money: *Mohan*, at p. 21; *D.D.*, at para. 56; *Masterpiece Inc. v. Alavida Lifestyles Inc.*, 2011 SCC 27, [2011] 2 S.C.R. 387, at para. 76.

19 To address these dangers, *Mohan* established a basic structure for the law relating to the admissibility of expert opinion evidence. That structure has two main components. First, there are four threshold requirements that the proponent of the evidence must establish in order for proposed expert opinion evidence to be admissible: (1) relevance; (2) necessity in assisting the trier of fact; (3) absence of an exclusionary rule; and (4) a properly qualified expert (*Mohan*, at pp. 20-25; see also *Sekhon*, at para. 43). *Mohan* also underlined the important role of trial judges in assessing whether otherwise admissible expert

evidence should be excluded because its probative value was overborne by its prejudicial effect — a residual discretion to exclude evidence based on a cost-benefit analysis: p. 21. This is the second component, which the subsequent jurisprudence has further emphasized: Lederman, Bryant and Fuerst, at pp. 789-90; J.-L.J., at para. 28.

20 *Mohan* and the jurisprudence since, however, have not explicitly addressed how this "cost-benefit" component fits into the overall analysis. The reasons in *Mohan* engaged in a cost-benefit analysis with respect to particular elements of the four threshold requirements, but they also noted that the cost-benefit analysis could be an aspect of exercising the overall discretion to exclude evidence whose probative value does not justify its admission in light of its potentially prejudicial effects: p. 21. The jurisprudence since *Mohan* has also focused on particular aspects of expert opinion evidence, but again without always being explicit about where additional concerns fit into the analysis. The unmistakable overall trend of the jurisprudence, however, has been to tighten the admissibility requirements and to enhance the judge's gatekeeping role.

21 So, for example, the necessity threshold criterion was emphasized in cases such as *D.D.*. The majority underlined that the necessity requirement exists "to ensure that the dangers associated with expert evidence are not lightly tolerated" and that "[m]ere relevance or 'helpfulness' is not enough": para. 46. Other cases have addressed the reliability of the science underlying an opinion and indeed technical evidence in general: *J.-L.J.*; *R. v. Trochym*, 2007 SCC 6, [2007] 1 S.C.R. 239. The question remains, however, as to where the cost-benefit analysis and concerns such as those about reliability fit into the overall analysis.

22 *Abbey* (ONCA) introduced helpful analytical clarity by dividing the inquiry into two steps. With minor adjustments, I would adopt that approach.

23 At the first step, the proponent of the evidence must establish the threshold requirements of admissibility. These are the four *Mohan* factors (relevance, necessity, absence of an exclusionary rule and a properly qualified expert) and in addition, in the case of an opinion based on novel or contested science or science used for a novel purpose, the reliability of the underlying science for that purpose: *J.-L.J.*, at paras. 33, 35-36 and 47; *Trochym*, at para. 27; Lederman, Bryant and Fuerst, at pp. 788-89 and 800-801. Relevance at this threshold stage refers to logical relevance: *Abbey* (ONCA), at para. 82; *J.-L.J.*, at para. 47. Evidence that does not meet these threshold requirements should be excluded. Note that I would retain necessity as a threshold requirement: *D.D.*, at para. 57; see D. M. Paciocco and L. Stuesser, *The Law of Evidence* (7th ed. 2015), at pp. 209-10; *R. v. Boswell*, 2011 ONCA 283, 85 C.R. (6th) 290, at para. 13; *R. v. C. (M.)*, 2014 ONCA 611, 13 C.R. (7th) 396, at para. 72.

24 At the second discretionary gatekeeping step, the judge balances the potential risks and benefits of admitting the evidence in order to decide

whether the potential benefits justify the risks. The required balancing exercise has been described in various ways. In *Mohan*, Sopinka J. spoke of the "reliability versus effect factor" (p. 21), while in *J.-L.J.*, Binnie J. spoke about "relevance, reliability and necessity" being "measured against the counterweights of consumption of time, prejudice and confusion": para 47. Doherty J.A. summed it up well in *Abbey*, stating that the "trial judge must decide whether expert evidence that meets the preconditions to admissibility is sufficiently beneficial to the trial process to warrant its admission despite the potential harm to the trial process that may flow from the admission of the expert evidence": para. 76.

25 With this delineation of the analytical framework, we can turn to the nature of an expert's duty to the court and where it fits into that framework.

D. The Expert's Duty to the Court or Tribunal

26 There is little controversy about the broad outlines of the expert witness's duty to the court. As Anderson writes, "[t]he duty to provide independent assistance to the Court by way of objective unbiased opinion has been stated many times by common law courts around the world": p. 227. I would add that a similar duty exists in the civil law of Quebec: J.-C. Royer and S. Lavallée, *La preuve civile* (4th ed. 2008), at para. 468; D. Béchard with the collaboration of J. Béchard, *L'expert* (2011) ch. 9; *An Act to establish the new Code of Civil Procedure*, S.Q. 2014, c. 1, art. 22 (not yet in force); L. Chamberland, *Le nouveau Code de procédure civile commenté* (2014), at pp. 14 and 121.

27 One influential statement of the elements of this duty are found in the English case *National Justice Compania Naviera S.A. v. Prudential Assurance Co.*, [1993] 2 Lloyd's Rep. 68 (Q.B.). Following an 87-day trial, Cresswell J. believed that a misunderstanding of the duties and responsibilities of expert witnesses contributed to the length of the trial. He listed in obiter dictum duties and responsibilities of experts, the first two of which have particularly influenced the development of Canadian law:

> 1.   Expert evidence presented to the Court should be, and should be seen to be, the independent product of the expert uninfluenced as to form or content by the exigencies of litigation ... .
>
> 2.   An expert witness should provide independent assistance to the Court by way of objective unbiased opinion in relation to matters within his [or her] expertise ... . An expert witness in the High Court should never assume the role of an advocate. [Emphasis added; citation omitted; p. 81.]

(These duties were endorsed on appeal: [1995] 1 Lloyd's Rep. 455 (C.A.), at p. 496.)

28 Many provinces and territories have provided explicit guidance related to the duty of expert witnesses. In Nova Scotia, for example, the *Civil Procedure Rules* require that an expert's report be signed by the expert who must make (among others) the following representations to the court: that the expert is

providing an objective opinion for the assistance of the court; that the expert is prepared to apply independent judgment when assisting the court; and that the report includes everything the expert regards as relevant to the expressed opinion and draws attention to anything that could reasonably lead to a different conclusion (r. 55.04(1)(a), (b) and (c)). While these requirements do not affect the rules of evidence by which expert opinion is determined to be admissible or inadmissible, they provide a convenient summary of a fairly broadly shared sense of the duties of an expert witness to the court.

29 There are similar descriptions of the expert's duty in the civil procedure rules in other Canadian jurisdictions: Anderson, at p. 227; *The Queen's Bench Rules* (Saskatchewan), r. 5-37; *Supreme Court Civil Rules*, B.C. Reg. 168/2009, r. 11-2(1); *Rules of Civil Procedure*, R.R.O. 1990, Reg. 194, r. 4.1.01(1); *Rules of Court*, Y.O.I.C. 2009/65, r. 34(23); *An Act to establish the new Code of Civil Procedure*, art. 22. Moreover, the rules in Saskatchewan, British Columbia, Ontario, Nova Scotia, Prince Edward Island, Quebec and the Federal Courts require experts to certify that they are aware of and will comply with their duty to the court: Anderson, at p. 228; Saskatchewan *Queen's Bench Rules*, r. 5-37(3); British Columbia *Supreme Court Civil Rules*, r. 11-2(2); Ontario *Rules of Civil Procedure*, r. 53.03(2.1); Nova Scotia *Civil Procedure Rules*, r. 55.04(1)(a); Prince Edward Island *Rules of Civil Procedure*, r. 53.03(3)(g); *An Act to establish the new Code of Civil Procedure*, art. 235 (not yet in force); *Federal Courts Rules*, SOR/98-106, r. 52.2(1)(c).

30 The formulation in the Ontario *Rules of Civil Procedure* is perhaps the most succinct and complete statement of the expert's duty to the court: to provide opinion evidence that is fair, objective and non-partisan: r. 4.1.01(1)(a). The Rules are also explicit that this duty to the court prevails over any obligation owed by the expert to a party: r. 4.1.01(2). Likewise, the newly adopted *Act to establish the new Code of Civil Procedure* of Quebec explicitly provides, as a guiding principle, that the expert's duty to the court overrides the parties' interests, and that the expert must fulfill his or her primary duty to the court "objectively, impartially and thoroughly": art. 22; Chamberland, at pp. 14 and 121.

31 Many of the relevant rules of court simply reflect the duty that an expert witness owes to the court at common law: Anderson, at p. 227. In my opinion, this is true of the Nova Scotia rules that apply in this case. Of course, it is always open to each jurisdiction to impose different rules of admissibility, but in the absence of a clear indication to that effect, the common law rules apply in common law cases. I note that in Nova Scotia, the *Civil Procedure Rules* explicitly provide that they do not change the rules of evidence by which the admissibility of expert opinion evidence is determined: r. 55.01(2).

32 Underlying the various formulations of the duty are three related concepts: impartiality, independence and absence of bias. The expert's opinion must be impartial in the sense that it reflects an objective assessment of the questions at

hand. It must be independent in the sense that it is the product of the expert's independent judgment, uninfluenced by who has retained him or her or the outcome of the litigation. It must be unbiased in the sense that it does not unfairly favour one party's position over another. The acid test is whether the expert's opinion would not change regardless of which party retained him or her: P. Michell and R. Mandhane, "The Uncertain Duty of the Expert Witness" (2005), 42 Alta. L. Rev. 635, at pp. 638-39. These concepts, of course, must be applied to the realities of adversary litigation. Experts are generally retained, instructed and paid by one of the adversaries. These facts alone do not undermine the expert's independence, impartiality and freedom from bias.

E. The Expert's Duties and Admissibility

33 As we have seen, there is a broad consensus about the nature of an expert's duty to the court. There is no such consensus, however, about how that duty relates to the admissibility of an expert's evidence. There are two main questions: Should the elements of this duty go to admissibility of the evidence rather than simply to its weight?; And, if so, is there a threshold admissibility requirement in relation to independence and impartiality?

34 In this section, I will explain my view that the answer to both questions is yes: a proposed expert's independence and impartiality goes to admissibility and not simply to weight and there is a threshold admissibility requirement in relation to this duty. Once that threshold is met, remaining concerns about the expert's compliance with his or her duty should be considered as part of the overall cost-benefit analysis which the judge conducts to carry out his or her gatekeeping role.

(1) Admissibility or Only Weight?

(a) The Canadian Law

35 The weight of authority strongly supports the conclusion that at a certain point, expert evidence should be ruled inadmissible due to the expert's lack of impartiality and/or independence.

. . .

37 I will refer to a number of other cases that support this view. I do so by way of illustration and without commenting on the outcome of particular cases. An expert's interest in the litigation or relationship to the parties has led to exclusion in a number of cases: see, e.g., *Fellowes, McNeil v. Kansa General International Insurance Co.* (1998), 40 O.R. (3d) 456 (Gen. Div.) (proposed expert was the defendant's lawyer in related matters and had investigated from the outset of his retainer the matter of a potential negligence claim against the plaintiff); *Royal Trust Corp. of Canada v. Fisherman* (2000), 49 O.R. (3d) 187 (S.C.J.) (expert was the party's lawyer in related U.S. proceedings); *R v. Docherty*, 2010 ONSC 3628 (expert was the defence counsel's father); *Ocean v.*

Economical Mutual Insurance Co., 2010 NSSC 315, 293 N.S.R. (2d) 394 (expert was also a party to the litigation); *Handley v. Punnett*, 2003 BCSC 294 (expert was also a party to the litigation); *Bank of Montreal v. Citak*, [2001] O.J. No. 1096 (QL) (S.C.J.) (expert was effectively a "co-venturer" in the case due in part to the fact that 40 percent of his remuneration was contingent upon success at trial: para. 7); *Dean Construction Co. v. M.J. Dixon Construction Ltd.*, 2011 ONSC 4629, 5 C.L.R. (4th) 240 (expert's retainer agreement was inappropriate); *Hutchingame v. Johnstone*, 2006 BCSC 271 (expert stood to incur liability depending on the result of the trial). In other cases, the expert's stance or behaviour as an advocate has justified exclusion: see, e.g., *Alfano v. Piersanti*, 2012 ONCA 297, 291 O.A.C. 62; *Kirby Lowbed Services Ltd. v. Bank of Nova Scotia*, 2003 BCSC 617; *Gould v. Western Coal Corp.*, 2012 ONSC 5184, 7 B.L.R. (5th) 19.

38 Many other cases have accepted, in principle, that lack of independence or impartiality can lead to exclusion, but have ruled that the expert evidence did not warrant rejection on the particular facts: see, e.g., *United City Properties Ltd. v. Tong*, 2010 BCSC 111; *R. v. INCO Ltd.* (2006), 80 O.R. (3d) 594 (S.C.J.). This was the position of the Court of Appeal in this case: para. 109; see also para. 121.

39 Some Canadian courts, however, have treated these matters as going exclusively to weight rather than to admissibility. The most often cited cases for this proposition are probably *R. v. Klassen*, 2003 MBQB 253, 179 Man. R. (2d) 115, and *Gallant v. Brake-Patten*, 2012 NLCA 23, 321 Nfld. & P.E.I.R. 77. *Klassen* holds as admissible any expert evidence meeting the criteria from *Mohan*, with bias only becoming a factor as to the weight to be given to the evidence: see also *R. v. Violette*, 2008 BCSC 920. Similarly, the court in *Gallant* determined that a challenge to expert evidence that is based on the expert having a connection to a party or an issue in the case or a possible predetermined position on the case cannot take place at the admissibility stage: para. 89.

. . .

(c) Conclusion

45 Following what I take to be the dominant view in the Canadian cases, I would hold that an expert's lack of independence and impartiality goes to the admissibility of the evidence in addition to being considered in relation to the weight to be given to the evidence if admitted. That approach seems to me to be more in line with the basic structure of our law relating to expert evidence and with the importance our jurisprudence has attached to the gatekeeping role of trial judges. Binnie J. summed up the Canadian approach well in *J.-L.J.*: "The admissibility of the expert evidence should be scrutinized at the time it is proffered, and not allowed too easy an entry on the basis that all of the frailties could go at the end of the day to weight rather than admissibility" (para. 28).

(2) The Appropriate Threshold

46 I have already described the duty owed by an expert witness to the court: the expert must be fair, objective and non-partisan. As I see it, the appropriate threshold for admissibility flows from this duty. I agree with Prof. (now Justice of the Ontario Court of Justice) Paciocco that "the common law has come to accept . . . that expert witnesses have a duty to assist the court that overrides their obligation to the party calling them. If a witness is unable or unwilling to fulfill that duty, they do not qualify to perform the role of an expert and should be excluded": "Taking a 'Goudge' out of Bluster and Blarney: an 'Evidence-Based Approach' to Expert Testimony" (2009), 13 Can. Crim. L. R. 135, at p. 152 (footnote omitted). The expert witnesses must, therefore, be aware of this primary duty to the court and able and willing to carry it out.

47 Imposing this additional threshold requirement is not intended to and should not result in trials becoming longer or more complex. As Prof. Paciocco aptly observed, "if inquiries about bias or partiality become routine during *Mohan voir dires*, trial testimony will become nothing more than an inefficient reprise of the admissibility hearing": "Unplugging Jukebox Testimony in an Adversarial System: Strategies for Changing the Tune on Partial Experts" (2009), 34 Queen's L.J. 565 ("Jukebox"), at p. 597. While I would not go so far as to hold that the expert's independence and impartiality should be presumed absent challenge, my view is that absent such challenge, the expert's attestation or testimony recognizing and accepting the duty will generally be sufficient to establish that this threshold is met.

48 Once the expert attests or testifies on oath to this effect, the burden is on the party opposing the admission of the evidence to show that there is a realistic concern that the expert's evidence should not be received because the expert is unable and/or unwilling to comply with that duty. If the opponent does so, the burden to establish on a balance of probabilities this aspect of the admissibility threshold remains on the party proposing to call the evidence. If this is not done, the evidence, or those parts of it that are tainted by a lack of independence or by impartiality, should be excluded. This approach conforms to the general rule under the *Mohan* framework, and elsewhere in the law of evidence, that the proponent of the evidence has the burden of establishing its admissibility.

49 This threshold requirement is not particularly onerous and it will likely be quite rare that a proposed expert's evidence would be ruled inadmissible for failing to meet it. The trial judge must determine, having regard to both the particular circumstances of the proposed expert and the substance of the proposed evidence, whether the expert is able and willing to carry out his or her primary duty to the court. For example, it is the nature and extent of the interest or connection with the litigation or a party thereto which matters, not the mere fact of the interest or connection; the existence of some interest or a relationship does not automatically render the evidence of the proposed expert

inadmissible. In most cases, a mere employment relationship with the party calling the evidence will be insufficient to do so. On the other hand, a direct financial interest in the outcome of the litigation will be of more concern. The same can be said in the case of a very close familial relationship with one of the parties or situations in which the proposed expert will probably incur professional liability if his or her opinion is not accepted by the court. Similarly, an expert who, in his or her proposed evidence or otherwise, assumes the role of an advocate for a party is clearly unwilling and/or unable to carry out the primary duty to the court. I emphasize that exclusion at the threshold stage of the analysis should occur only in very clear cases in which the proposed expert is unable or unwilling to provide the court with fair, objective and non-partisan evidence. Anything less than clear unwillingness or inability to do so should not lead to exclusion, but be taken into account in the overall weighing of costs and benefits of receiving the evidence.

50 As discussed in the English case law, the decision as to whether an expert should be permitted to give evidence despite having an interest or connection with the litigation is a matter of fact and degree. The concept of apparent bias is not relevant to the quest ion of whether or not an expert witness will be unable or unwilling to fulfill its primary duty to the court. When looking at an expert's interest or relationship with a party, the question is not whether a reasonable observer would think that the expert is not independent. The question is whether the relationship or interest results in the expert being unable or unwilling to carry out his or her primary duty to the court to provide fair, non-partisan and objective assistance.

51 Having established the analytical framework, described the expert's duty and determined that compliance with this duty goes to admissibility and not simply to weight, I turn now to where this duty fits into the analytical framework for admission of expert opinion evidence.

F. Situating the Analysis in the Mohan Framework

(1) The Threshold Inquiry

52 Courts have addressed independence and impartiality at various points of the admissibility test. Almost every branch of the *Mohan* framework has been adapted to incorporate bias concerns one way or another: the proper qualifications component (see, e.g., *Bank of Montreal*; *Dean Construction*; *Agribrands Purina Canada Inc. v. Kasamekas*, 2010 ONSC 166; *R. v. Demetrius*, 2009 CanLII 22797 (Ont. S.C.J.); the necessity component (see, e.g., *Docherty*; *Alfano*); and during the discretionary cost-benefit analysis (see, e.g., *United City Properties*; *Abbey* (ONCA)). On other occasions, courts have found it to be a stand-alone requirement: see, e.g., *Docherty*; *International Hi-Tech Industries Inc. v. FANUC Robotics Canada Ltd.*, 2006 BCSC 2011; *Casurina Ltd. Partnership v. Rio Algom Ltd.* (2002), 28 B.L.R. (3d) 44 (Ont. S.C.J.);

Prairie Well Servicing Ltd. v. Tundra Oil and Gas Ltd., 2000 MBQB 52, 146 Man. R. (2d) 284. Some clarification of this point will therefore be useful.

53 In my opinion, concerns related to the expert's duty to the court and his or her willingness and capacity to comply with it are best addressed initially in the "qualified expert" element of the *Mohan* framework: S. C. Hill, D. M. Tanovich and L. P. Strezos, *McWilliams' Canadian Criminal Evidence* (5th ed. (loose-leaf)), vol. 2, at s. 12:30.20.50; see also *Deemar v. College of Veterinarians of Ontario*, 2008 ONCA 600, 92 O.R. (3d) 97, at para. 21; Lederman, Bryant and Fuerst, at pp. 826-27; *Halsbury's Laws of Canada: Evidence*, at para. HEV-152 "Partiality"; *The Canadian Encyclopedic Digest* (Ont. 4th ed. (loose-leaf)), vol. 24, Title 62—Evidence, at §469. A proposed expert witness who is unable or unwilling to fulfill this duty to the court is not properly qualified to perform the role of an expert. Situating this concern in the "properly qualified expert" ensures that the courts will focus expressly on the important risks associated with biased experts: Hill, Tanovich and Strezos, at s. 12:30.20.50; Paciocco, "Jukebox", at p. 595.

(2) The Gatekeeping Exclusionary Discretion

54 Finding that expert evidence meets the basic threshold does not end the inquiry. Consistent with the structure of the analysis developed following *Mohan* which I have discussed earlier, the judge must still take concerns about the expert's independence and impartiality into account in weighing the evidence at the gatekeeping stage. At this point, relevance, necessity, reliability and absence of bias can helpfully be seen as part of a sliding scale where a basic level must first be achieved in order to meet the admissibility threshold and thereafter continue to play a role in weighing the overall competing considerations in admitting the evidence. At the end of the day, the judge must be satisfied that the potential helpfulness of the evidence is not outweighed by the risk of the dangers materializing that are associated with expert evidence.

. . .

H. Application

56 I turn to the application of these principles to the facts of the case. In my respectful view, the record amply sustains the result reached by the majority of the Court of Appeal that Ms. MacMillan's evidence was admissible on the summary judgment application. Of course, the framework which I have set out in these reasons was not available to either the motions judge or to the Court of Appeal.

57 There was no finding by the motions judge that Ms. MacMillan was in fact biased or not impartial or that she was acting as an advocate for the shareholders: C.A. reasons, at para. 122. On the contrary, she specifically recognized that she was aware of the standards and requirements that experts be independent. She was aware of the precise guidelines in the accounting

industry concerning accountants acting as expert witnesses. She testified that she owed an ultimate duty to the court in testifying as an expert witness: A.R., vol. III, at pp. 75-76; C.A. reasons, at para. 134. To the extent that the motions judge was concerned about the "appearance" of impartiality, this factor plays no part in the test for admissibility, as I have explained earlier.

58 The auditors' claim that Ms. MacMillan lacks objectivity rests on two main points which I will address in turn.

59 First, the auditors say that the earlier work done for the shareholders by the Kentville office of Grant Thornton "served as a catalyst and foundation for the claim of negligence" against the auditors and that this "precluded [Grant Thornton] from acting as 'independent' experts in this case": A.F., at paras. 17 and 19. Ms. MacMilllan, the auditors submit, was in an "irreconcilable conflict of interest, in that she would inevitably have to opine on, and choose between, the actions taken and standard of care exercised by her own partners at Grant Thornton" and those of the auditors: A.F., at para. 21. This first submission, however, must be rejected.

60 The fact that one professional firm discovers what it thinks is or may be professional negligence does not, on its own, disqualify it from offering that opinion as an expert witness. Provided that the initial work is done independently and impartially and the person put forward as an expert understands and is able to comply with the duty to provide fair, objective and non-partisan assistance to the court, the expert meets the threshold qualification in that regard. There is no suggestion here that Grant Thornton was hired to take a position dictated to it by the shareholders or that there was anything more than a speculative possibility of Grant Thornton incurring liability to them if the firm's opinion was not ultimately accepted by the court. There was no finding that Ms. MacMillan was, in fact, biased or not impartial, or that she was acting as an advocate for the shareholders. The auditors' submission that she somehow "admitted" on her cross-examination that she was in an "irreconcilable conflict" is not borne out by a fair reading of her evidence in context: A.R., vol. III, at pp. 139-45. On the contrary, her evidence was clear that she understood her role as an expert and her duty to the court: *ibid.*, at pp. 75-76.

61 The auditors' second main point was that Ms. MacMillan was not independent because she had "incorporated" some of the work done by the Kentville office of her firm. This contention is also ill founded. To begin, I do not accept that an expert lacks the threshold qualification in relation to the duty to give fair, objective and non-partisan evidence simply because the expert relies on the work of other professionals in reaching his or her own opinion. Moreover, as Beveridge J.A. concluded, what was "incorporated" was essentially an exercise in arithmetic that had nothing to do with any accounting opinion expressed by the Kentville office: C.A. reasons, at paras. 146-49.

62 There was no basis disclosed in this record to find that Ms. MacMillan's evidence should be excluded because she was not able and willing to provide the court with fair, objective and non-partisan evidence. I agree with the majority of the Court of Appeal who concluded that the motions judge committed a palpable and overriding error in determining that Ms. MacMillan was in a conflict of interest that prevented her from giving impartial and objective evidence: paras. 136-50.

IV. Disposition

63 I would dismiss the appeal with costs.

Appeal dismissed with costs.

The issues of expert bias discussed in *White Burgess Langille Inman* have been a long-standing concern. Some commentators, including Professor (now Justice) David Paciocco,[314] have recommended the adoption of codes of conduct recognizing that experts owe a special duty of impartial advice to the courts. As Cromwell J. notes in *White Burgess Langille Inman* at paragraph 29, several provinces require expert witnesses in civil cases to certify an acknowledgement of their duties to the court. **Should a similar practice be adopted in criminal cases?**

In *R. v. France*,[315] part of the evidence of Dr. Michael Pollanen, Ontario's Chief Forensic Pathologist, was excluded on bias grounds. France was charged with murder in the death of a two-year-old boy who died from blunt force trauma to the abdomen. Dr. Pollanen had performed the post-mortem examination. At the preliminary hearing, he testified that the child's abdominal injury could not have been caused accidentally by a short fall onto an object, and stated that he was not aware of any studies dealing with abdominal injuries caused by short falls. Subsequently, Dr. Pollanen prepared a supplementary report surveying the medical literature on pediatric abdominal trauma to address the hypothesis that an accidental short fall could have caused the victim's fatal injury. That report concluded that it was possible but improbable that the injury was caused by an unprecedented accident, and referred to three documented cases out of hundreds studied where intestinal injuries were caused by a short fall onto a projected surface. Dr. Pollanen testified accordingly in chief on the *voir dire*.

In cross-examination, defence counsel presented Dr. Pollanen with 26 scholarly published articles on abdominal trauma causing injuries to the bowels. Three of these articles had been included in Dr. Pollanen's review of the literature, but he had not seen the other 23. Dr. Pollanen acknowledged in cross-examination that these articles showed many examples of children sustaining perforations of the intestines from short falls. He acknowledged on re-examination that, looking at the bowel injury alone, an accident was a

---

[314]   "Unplugging Jukebox Testimony in an Adversarial System: Strategies for Changing the Tune on Partial Experts" (2009) 34 Queen's L.J. 565.

[315]   2017 ONSC 2040, 36 C.R. (7th) 293 (Ont. S.C.J.).

possible explanation for the victim's injury. However, he maintained that an accidental mechanism of injury was statistically improbable and inconsistent with a holistic view of the case that would take the child's other injuries into account.

Justice Molloy ruled that Dr. Pollanen was permitted to provide expert opinion evidence in the field of forensic pathology and on the cause and mechanism of the victim's death and the nature of his other injuries. However, Dr. Pollanen was not permitted to testify to whether the victim's abdominal injury was more likely to have been deliberately inflicted or accidentally caused, to the probabilities of these causes, or to whether the child's other injuries made it more likely that the abdominal injury was caused by an assault.

Justice Molloy concluded that Dr. Pollanen showed bias in several respects. He exhibited unconscious bias when he prepared for the post-mortem examination by reading about abdominal trauma but limiting his research to assaults causing abdominal trauma. He was predisposed to see this case as an assault and failed to keep an open mind to other possible explanations for the abdominal injury. Dr. Pollanen's testimony at the preliminary hearing that a short fall could not cause this type of injury was dogmatic and incorrect. He acknowledged this error on the *voir dire*, but it was concerning that he was initially willing to take an extreme and rigid position without doing any research to support it. And while Dr. Pollanen acknowledged on the *voir dire* that an accidental mechanism of injury could not be completely ruled out, he stood by his characterization of this possibility as an unprecedented accident that was improbable. His position on this point illustrated professional credibility bias: having taken a position at the preliminary hearing, he looked for ways to support that opinion rather than looking objectively at the research and autopsy findings.

The trier of fact would be required to determine whether the injury was caused by a deliberate assault, and there was a wealth of case-specific evidence to draw upon in reaching that conclusion. It was not Dr. Pollanen's role to look at the other injuries on the victim's body and draw an inference that since they could not all be accidental, the blow to the abdomen was also an assault. Such an opinion would overstep the role of a forensic pathologist and usurp the role of the jury. The jury would have the evidence of the other injuries along with considerable other evidence in deciding whether the blow was an assault. They did not need Dr. Pollanen's opinion on the inferences he would draw based on part of the evidence, but there was a risk that they would rely unduly on the supposed scientific nature of his conclusion.

For another recent analysis of expert bias, see *R. v. McManus*,[316] where the Ontario Court of Appeal ruled expert evidence from a police officer in a narcotics prosecution inadmissible because it was in the circumstances neither independent nor impartial. The officer had known the accused longer than four years and had been involved in past investigations leading to drug charges.

---

[316]   2017 ONCA 188, 353 C.C.C. (3d) 493, 36 C.R. (7th) 261 (Ont. C.A.).

R. v. ABBEY
2017 ONCA 640, 350 C.C.C. (3d) 102, 39 C.R. (7th) 303 (Ont. C.A.)

LASKIN J.A. (DOHERTY and ROBERTS JJ.A. concurring):

A. INTRODUCTION

1 Warren Abbey has been tried twice before a judge and jury for the first degree murder of a young man named Simeon Peter. At his first trial Abbey was acquitted. At the second trial — after the Crown successfully appealed his acquittal and obtained an order for a new trial — Abbey was convicted. He appeals his conviction.

2 The main issue at both trials was the identity of the murderer: who killed Peter? And the Crown's theory at both trials was identical: Abbey, who was an associate of a street gang, shot and killed Peter because he believed — though mistakenly — that Peter was a member of a rival street gang.

3 However, the Crown's evidence against Abbey at the two trials differed in one important way. At Abbey's first trial the trial judge ruled that the Crown's expert on gang culture, Mark Totten, could not give an opinion on the meaning of a teardrop tattoo, which Abbey had obtained under his right eye some four months after the murder. At Abbey's second trial — after this court overturned the trial judge's ruling — Totten gave evidence about the meaning of a teardrop tattoo on the face of a young male gang member.

4 Totten testified that a teardrop tattoo meant one of three things: the wearer of the tattoo had lost a loved one or a fellow gang member; the wearer had spent "hard" time in prison; or the wearer had murdered a rival gang member. Then, Totten buttressed his opinion with a powerful set of statistics, which were drawn from six studies he authored between 1995 and 2005, and which the Crown relied on to argue Abbey had obtained a teardrop tattoo to signify he had killed a rival gang member.

5 On this appeal Abbey seeks to introduce fresh evidence to impeach the credibility and reliability of Totten's statistical evidence. The fresh evidence has three components: the evidence of Totten elicited by the Crown in an unrelated murder trial, *R. v. Gager*,[317] which took place after Abbey's second trial; eight research studies on street gangs conducted by Totten, of which six predated Abbey's two trials and formed the basis for Totten's statistical evidence on teardrop tattoos; and data from Statistics Canada on the number of homicides in Ontario.

. . .

---

[317]   See 2012 ONSC 1472 (Ont. S.C.J.), in which Clark J. provides his reasons for permitting Totten to testify on certain issues.

B. BACKGROUND

. . .

(d) The *voir dire* in *R. v. Gager*

37 Gager, too, was charged with murder. The Crown alleged that Gager was a member of a Toronto street gang and that the motive for the murder was a rivalry between his gang and another street gang. At this trial, however, the defence, not the Crown, proposed to call Totten as an expert on street gangs. The defence wanted to show, through Totten's opinion evidence, that Gager did not have the characteristics of a gang member.

38 The Crown did not concede that Totten was qualified to give expert evidence. Instead, at the beginning of the trial in February 2012, it challenged Totten's qualifications on a *voir dire* into the admissibility of his evidence. And the Crown's cross-examination revealed weaknesses and discrepancies in Totten's opinions . . .

39 Despite his reservations, the trial judge in *Gager*, Clark J., did qualify Totten to give expert evidence in several areas. In doing so he said that a court should be reluctant to disqualify an expert called by the defence. But in his lengthy ruling Clark J. was quite scathing of Totten and his proposed opinion evidence. For example, he regarded Totten's claim that he is a "Canadian expert on gangs" to signify the "sort of puffery" that suggests "a degree of immodesty on the witness' part that is not in keeping with the detachment and objectivity properly to be expected of an expert witness". He also found Totten's answers to questions about the sample size in his studies "both evasive and troubling". And he found Totten's answers to questions on his methodology also "evasive".

40 Although Clark J. did qualify Totten to give opinion evidence, the defence, no doubt concerned by the Crown's cross-examination on the *voir dire*, elected not to call him.

(e) Summary of the relevant chronology

41 The following is a bullet point summary of the relevant chronology and Totten's role:

- 1995-2005: Totten authors six studies, which he relies on for his opinion on the meaning of a teardrop tattoo.
- January 2004: Simeon Peter is murdered.
- 2007: The first Abbey trial is held. The Crown proposes to call Totten to give expert evidence on the meaning of a teardrop tattoo, but the trial judge rules he is not qualified to give that evidence because it is too unreliable. Abbey is acquitted.

- 2009: This court allows the Crown's appeal, sets aside Abbey's acquittal and orders a new trial. The court holds that Totten is qualified to give opinion evidence on the meaning of a teardrop tattoo.

- Winter 2011: The second Abbey trial is held. The Crown calls Totten as its expert witness on the meaning of a teardrop tattoo. Abbey is convicted of first degree murder.

- February 2012: In *R. v. Gager*, an unrelated murder trial, the defence proposes to call Totten as an expert witness on street gangs. The Crown objects to the admissibility of his evidence and cross-examines him on a *voir dire*. The defence then decides not to call Totten.

- February 2017: Abbey's appeal from his conviction is argued.

C. THE LEGAL FRAMEWORK

. . .

(b) The test for the admissibility of expert evidence

46 The modern Canadian law on the admissibility of expert evidence began with the judgment of Sopinka J. in *R. v. Mohan*, [1994] 2 S.C.R. 9. But in the last two decades since *Mohan* was decided the law on expert evidence has changed significantly. In *Abbey #1* itself — on the Crown's appeal from the acquittal at the first trial — my colleague Doherty J.A. reformulated the Mohan test for admissibility to make it easier to apply. And recently in *White Burgess Langille Inman v. Abbott and Haliburton Co.*, 2015 SCC 23, [2015] 2 S.C.R. 182, Cromwell J. adopted with "minor adjustments" Doherty J.A.'s reformulation of *Mohan*.[318]

47 The test in *White Burgess* is now the governing test for the admissibility of expert evidence. It adopts a two-stage approach, first suggested in *Abbey #1*: the first stage focuses on threshold requirements of admissibility; the second stage focuses on the trial judge's discretionary gatekeeper role. Each stage has a specific set of criteria.

48 The test may be summarized as follows:[319]

Expert evidence is admissible when:

   (1) It meets the threshold requirements of admissibility, which are:
       a. The evidence must be logically relevant;
       b. The evidence must be necessary to assist the trier of fact;
       c. The evidence must not be subject to any other exclusionary rule;

---

[318] For an excellent summary of the development of the law from *Mohan* to *Abbey #1* to *White Burgess* see Lisa Dufraimont, "Update on Admissibility of Expert Evidence" (paper presented to the Law Society of Upper Canada, Six Minute Criminal Lawyer 2016, April 9, 2016).

[319] In setting out this test I have largely adopted Lisa Dufraimont's useful summary at (2015), 18 C.R. (7th) 312-313.

d. The expert must be properly qualified, which includes the requirement that the expert be willing and able to fulfil the expert's duty to the court to provide evidence that is:
i. Impartial,
ii. Independent, and
iii. Unbiased.
e. For opinions based on novel or contested science or science used for a novel purpose, the underlying science must be reliable for that purpose,

and

(2) The trial judge, in a gatekeeper role, determines that the benefits of admitting the evidence outweigh its potential risks, considering such factors as:
a. Legal relevance,[320]
b. Necessity,
c. Reliability, and
b. Necessity,
d. Absence of bias.[321]

49 In short, if the proposed expert evidence does not meet the threshold requirements for admissibility it is excluded. If it does meet the threshold requirements, the trial judge then has a gatekeeper function. The trial judge must be satisfied that the benefits of admitting the evidence outweigh the costs of its admission. If the trial judge is so satisfied then the expert evidence may be admitted; if the trial judge is not so satisfied the evidence will be excluded even though it has met the threshold requirements.

50 On this appeal, of the threshold requirements for admissibility, only the fourth criterion — whether Totten is a properly qualified expert — is in issue. . .

---

[320] In *Abbey #1*, Doherty J.A. distinguished between the "logical relevance" of the evidence, which is a threshold requirement for admissibility, and "legal relevance", which trial judges must consider in their gatekeeper role. By legally relevant evidence Doherty J.A. means evidence that is sufficiently probative to justify its admission. In *White Burgess*, Cromwell J. referred expressly to logical relevance as a threshold requirement, but only relevance, not legal relevance, at the gatekeeper stage. Nonetheless, as confining relevance to logical relevance at the gatekeeper stage would be redundant, and as Cromwell J. said at para. 22 he would adopt the approach in *Abbey #1* with only "minor adjustments", I conclude that at the gatekeeper stage he meant legal relevance. I acknowledge that my conclusion introduces a small measure of duplication because the reliability of the evidence is a key component of legal relevance and Cromwell J. lists reliability as a separate factor.

[321] At para. 54, Cromwell J. lists these four factors but suggests they are not exhaustive.

D. THE ISSUES

. . .

(c) Totten's evidence at the second trial

63 In the light of this court's 2009 judgment, the trial judge qualified Totten, without objection from the defence, to give expert opinion evidence for the Crown "in relation to street gang culture and symbology ... in particular with respect to the interpretation of tattoos and more particularly the teardrop tattoo." In giving his opinion Totten said he relied on his clinical experience over two decades, his research projects, and his review of the academic literature.

64 His opinion on the meaning of a teardrop tattoo had two branches: a qualitative branch and a quantitative branch. The fresh evidence challenges the quantitative branch, not the qualitative branch. But the two branches are intertwined.

65 First, the qualitative branch. Totten testified that a teardrop tattoo on the face of a young member of a street gang means one of three things:

- The death of a family member of the wearer of the tattoo or of a fellow gang member;
- The wearer of the tattoo had served time in a correctional facility, usually ten years or more; or
- The wearer of the tattoo had murdered a rival gang member. Totten also said if this was the reason for the tattoo, typically the wearer would obtain it within six months of the homicide.

66 Second, the quantitative branch of Totten's opinion. Totten's evidence was that between 1995 and 2005 he conducted six studies on young gang members. The six studies yielded the following dramatic statistics:

- Totten studied a total of 290 young gang members;
- Of the 290, 97 gang members had been convicted of a homicide, either murder or manslaughter;
- Of the 97, 71 male gang members had teardrop tattoos; and
- Each of the 71 told Totten he had obtained a teardrop tattoo to signify he had killed a rival gang member.

In his evidence at trial Totten gave no breakdown of the number of homicides or teardrop tattoos attributable to each study.

67 That Totten's statistics are based on his six studies is critical to my assessment of the cogency of the fresh evidence. The six studies in chronological order are the following:

- Youth Services Bureau ("YSB") Survey (May 1999): a one-month study to get a snapshot of the youth who were living on the street in Ottawa;
- Youth Services Bureau ("YSB") Survey (May 1999): a one-month study to get a snapshot of the youth who were living on the street in Ottawa;
- Understanding Serious Youth Violence (2001): a three-month study to investigate various forms of extreme violence;
- When Children Kill (2002): a study into the lives of 19 young persons convicted of murder or manslaughter;
- Youth Literacy and Violence Prevention Research Project (2003): a study of the literacy level of young people engaging in violence; and
- The Gays in the Gang (2005): a report on the experiences of young gay, bisexual and transgender gang members who engaged in serious street violence.

68 The ages of the subjects studied ranged between 12 and 20. Most were male, but in a couple of the studies some of the subjects were female. None of the studies was geared toward the study of tattoos.

(d) The fresh evidence

(i) Introduction

69 Abbey has filed as fresh evidence relevant portions of the Crown's cross-examination of Totten in *Gager*, Totten's research studies and a small amount of Statistics Canada data. The purpose of the fresh evidence is to impeach the credibility and reliability of Totten's statistical evidence, which was a critical component of his opinion on the meaning of a teardrop tattoo. The fresh evidence seeks to demonstrate that Totten's opinion is replete with weaknesses, misrepresentations and even falsehoods.

70 Specifically, the fresh evidence mainly seeks to undermine the four key numbers that Totten said came from his six research studies and which he relied on for his opinion: 290 gang members; 97 convicted of a homicide; 71 wore a teardrop tattoo; all 71 obtained a teardrop tattoo to signify the killing of a rival gang member. In addition, the fresh evidence seeks to show duplication in Totten's studies, contrary to his sworn evidence in *Gager*, and misrepresentations in how he conducted his interviews.

71 The Crown has not disputed any of Abbey's fresh evidence, other than to contend that the Statistic Canada data are inadmissible because they are hearsay. The Crown has not filed any reply material. And neither side sought leave to call Totten to give evidence on the fresh evidence application. Thus for the purpose of this appeal I treat as unchallenged any problems with the reliability of Totten's opinion revealed by the fresh evidence.

(ii) 290 gang members

72 Totten testified that the total number of gang members in his six research studies was 290, broken down as follows:

- YSB Survey: 51
- Guys, Gangs and Girlfriend Abuse: 90
- Understanding Serious Youth Violence: 31
- When Children Kill: 9
- Youth Literacy and Violence Prevention Research Project: 84
- The Gays in the Gang: 25

73 Abbey challenges the figure of 90 gang members said to be between 13 and 17 years of age in what was Totten's biggest study up to the time of trial and also his doctoral dissertation: Guys, Gangs and Girlfriend Abuse. Abbey submits that 90 is a misrepresentation and that a review of the study shows that the accurate figure is 22, thus reducing Totten's sample size from 290 to 222. I agree with Abbey's submission.

. . .

81 Sample size is obviously important to Totten. In his second report for the first trial he claimed that his sample size of 290 street gang members was "considerably larger" than the sample size in any existing gang study,[322] and was large enough that his results could be "generalized" to other parts of Canada. In his report for *Gager* he claimed that his sample size of 519 was "many times larger" than the sample size used in previous Canadian studies. And, sample size is indeed important. The larger the sample the more significant the results derived from the data and the more confidence we can have in the inferences sought to be drawn from those results.

82 But inflating his sample size as Totten has done by misrepresenting the number of gang members casts a dark cloud over the reliability of his statistical evidence. The number of gang members in his study of Guys, Gangs and Girlfriend Abuse is 22 not 90, and his accurate total sample size is 222, not 290. The reduction in Totten's sample size likely affects, to an extent unknown, the numbers derived from it — 97 who committed a homicide, 71 of which had a teardrop tattoo.

(iii) 97 gang members were convicted of a homicide[323]

83 Totten claimed that of his sample size of 290 gang members, 97, fully one third, were convicted of homicide, either murder or manslaughter. Leaving aside that the sample size should be 222 not 290, I find it impossible to discern

---

[322]   The report states that the sample size was 300 gang members. In his testimony in *Gager*, Totten clarified that 300 was a typographical error and the correct number is 290.

[323]   Totten was not clear whether all 97 were male or whether some were female.

how Totten arrived at the figure of 97 or any number close to it from his six studies. The number may be correct but it cannot be found in the six studies.

84 The only study that expressly addresses homicides is When Children Kill, a small study of 19 children. All 19 killed another person but at most nine out of the 19 were gang members and none of the nine killed a rival gang member. At best one can assume nine gang members could have contributed to the 97 who committed a homicide. But none of the nine could have contributed to the 71 who obtained a teardrop tattoo to signify the killing of a rival gang member.

85 Very few individuals interviewed in Totten's five other studies were convicted of homicide. . .

86 In summary, only in the two studies When Children Kill and The Gays in the Gang did Totten specify that some of the gang members had committed a homicide. But the number who did was relatively small, less than ten in each study. The total of less than twenty falls far short of the 97 Totten claimed in his evidence.

. . .

89 Even without the Statistics Canada data the number of 97 is not supported by the written studies Totten authored. Neither that number nor any number close to it is disclosed by the six studies he claimed to have relied on. For that reason whether 97 young gang members in his studies were convicted of a homicide cannot be assessed or verified.

(iv) 71 males of the 97 gang members convicted of a homicide had a teardrop tattoo

90 Totten claimed that, of the 97 gang members in his studies who were convicted of murder or manslaughter, 71 males obtained a teardrop tattoo. This claim is even more troubling, even assuming the accuracy of the figure of 97. Not a single study lists the number of gang members who had a teardrop tattoo. Indeed, the texts of the six studies contain only a few references to tattoos and no reference at all to teardrop tattoos.

91 Nonetheless, Totten testified at the *Gager voir dire* that all six studies asked questions about tattoos. But the studies say otherwise . . .

92 In summary, in two of the six studies questions about tattoos were listed; in two they were not; and two were silent about the questions asked. And no study contained any discussion of or reference to teardrop tattoos, or a list of how many participants had them. Totten said it was not unusual that his studies failed to include questions on tattoos. But again his evidence cannot be verified by a review of the studies.

93 In his 2009 judgment in *Abbey #1*, at para. 119, Doherty J.A. suggested that in assessing the reliability of an expert's opinion that relies on data collected through various means such as interviews — as Totten's opinion does — one important question to ask is whether the data are accurately recorded, stored and available. In *Gager* the Crown asked Totten essentially this very question.

94 The Crown asked Totten for a breakdown of the number of tattoos, including teardrop tattoos, in each study, for a list of the 71 male gang members who had a teardrop tattoo and for the raw data supporting her request. Totten said he did not have the data with him. However, Totten told the Crown he had "masses of data" at home, and had collected and maintained his data on teardrop tattoos. He testified: "I can give you the numbers with teardrops, with the teardrop tattoo out of those six studies". He promised to get the data and bring them to court.

95 Surprisingly, after the luncheon recess, Totten did an about-face. He told the Crown and the trial judge he had no data on teardrop tattoos as he had destroyed all of his data in accordance with the guidelines of the "tri-council ethics committee". Totten said that under these guidelines he was bound to keep his raw data for 10 years, and then destroy them. Totten was not asked and did not say when he destroyed his data, and he did not produce a copy of the committee's guidelines.

. . .

97 . . . Totten's evidence raises serious concerns about his credibility and the reliability of his assertion that 71 of the 97 gang members had teardrop tattoos. The concerns are twofold. First, Totten's over-lunch about-face regarding whether he had his data is, at least, suspicious. Second, without access to the underlying data a court cannot test the reliability of Totten's claim that in his sample drawn from his six studies, 71 young male gang members who had been convicted of a homicide had a teardrop tattoo.

(v) Each of the 71 told Totten he had obtained a teardrop tattoo to signify the killing of a rival gang member

98 At trial the Crown asked Totten the following question:

> I just want to be certain I understand. So the 71 who had been convicted of murder or manslaughter that had a teardrop tattoo all indicated, told you, when you asked, that the teardrop signified killing of a rival gang member; is that right?

99 Totten answered: "That's right". His answer undoubtedly was one of the most powerful pieces of evidence, if not the most powerful piece of evidence, supporting the Crown's allegation that Abbey had murdered Peter. Yet on its face the answer seems implausible. Totten had testified that a young gang member would get a teardrop tattoo for one of three reasons. But according to his evidence not a single gang member among the 71 obtained a teardrop tattoo to signify the loss of a family member or fellow gang member, or to signify having been in a correctional facility. The implausibility of Totten's answer raises a concern about whether he had become a partisan advocate for the Crown, instead of an objective and impartial expert witness.

100 Even more significant, Totten's assertion that all 71 obtained a teardrop tattoo to signify the killing of a rival gang member cannot be tested or verified. All six of his studies are silent — none contains even a single reference to a teardrop tattoo, let alone the number of gang members who had one. In at least two of his studies the listed interview questions do not include a question on tattoos. Moreover, the figure from which the 71 is drawn, 97 who were convicted of a homicide, is itself suspect. And Totten claims to no longer have the raw data that could support his assertion.

(vi) Duplication

101 In *Gager*, Totten was asked: "Is there any duplication between the participants in any of these studies? Did you ever use gang members more than once in different studies?" He replied: "Never". His reply was false.

102 At least three participants were used in both Guys, Gangs and Girlfriend Abuse (2000) and The Gays in the Gang (2005). Their names are Bob, Phil and Brian. Identical quotes from these three participants are found in the interview summaries in both studies.

103 Other aspects of this duplication are even more concerning. Totten said that the primary research for Guys, Gangs and Girlfriend Abuse was done in 1993-4, and the interviews for The Gays in the Gang was done ten years later in 2004. Despite the ten-year gap the verbatim quotes attributed to Bob, Phil and Brian are identical in the two studies, as is the age of each one. In the first study, Guys, Gangs and Girlfriend Abuse, none of the three are overtly said to be gay (although there are suggestions that Bob and Phil are questioning their sexuality); in the second study The Gays in the Gang, all three are said to be gay.

104 The amount of duplication uncovered by the fresh evidence is small. But that it exists at all, contrary to Totten's sworn testimony, raises further concerns about the credibility and reliability of his opinion evidence. Indeed, the duplication raises a legitimate concern that Totten's interview summaries are fabrications.

(vii) Interview discrepancies

105 Totten's YSB May 1999 Youth Survey, a one-month study of the living circumstances and behaviour of Ottawa youth who were clients of the Youth Services Bureau, included interviews of 309 participants. The survey itself says that over one half of the interview questionnaire was completed by the young person "alone" and the remainder by the young person together with one of Totten's staff.

106 In his evidence at trial, however, Totten claimed that he was present for all the interviews and that each interview was at least one hour long. By the time he testified at the *Gager voir dire* each interview had become one to three hours long. He backtracked somewhat in his re-examination in *Gager*, and admitted some of the interviews were done by the staff and some were short. But he maintained that he was present at every interview. As Clark J. aptly commented at para. 54 of his ruling:

> Allowing time for sleep and other necessary daily activities, inasmuch as there are only 744 hours in the month of May, even using the lower figure of one hour for each interview simple arithmetic makes it difficult to accept that he could have performed that number of interviews in that time frame.

(e) Positions of the parties and analysis

. . .

121 The fresh evidence, in my view, shows that Totten's evidence is too unreliable to go to a jury. Because of its unreliability, its probative value and its benefit to the trial process would be minimal at best, and the prejudice and harm from admitting it would be great both because it would consume too much valuable court time and because the jury would likely be unable to effectively and critically assess the evidence. In short, the fresh evidence is so cogent that if known by the trial judge at the gatekeeper stage he would have ruled Totten's evidence on the meaning of a teardrop tattoo inadmissible.

. . .

E. CONCLUSION

155 I would admit the fresh evidence, allow the appeal, set aside Abbey's conviction for first degree murder and order a new trial.

While *White Burgess Langille Inman* is clearly now the leading decision on expert testimony, earlier Supreme Court rulings are still significant. In *R. v. J. (J.-L.)* the Supreme Court expressly adopted the U.S. Federal Rules of Evidence approach to novel scientific evidence.

R. v. J. (J.-L.)
[2000] 2 S.C.R. 600, 37 C.R. (5th) 203, 148 C.C.C. (3d) 487

The accused was charged with sexual offences in relation to two boys who were between three and five years old. The Crown called evidence of statements made by one of the children to a foster mother, the foster mother's sister and a police officer. The statements suggested that the accused had engaged in anal intercourse with the child. The Crown also called medical evidence to support this allegation. The defence sought to call expert evidence from a psychiatrist to establish that in all probability a serious sexual deviant had inflicted anal intercourse on two children of that age, and that no such deviant personality traits were disclosed in the psychiatrist's testing of the accused. In evidence given on a *voir dire*, the expert testified that it was not possible to establish a standard profile of individuals with a predisposition to sodomize young children, but that such individuals frequently exhibit certain distinctive identifiable characteristics. The accused had been tested for these characteristics and excluded. In reaching this conclusion, the psychiatrist had evaluated the results of a series of general personality tests, and a plethysmograph test, which was directed to the accused's sexual preferences by exposing him to images and sounds of sexual activity, both normal and deviant, and measuring his physiological reaction through a gauge attached to his penis. The expert testified that if the subject had previously derived pleasure from a specific form of sexual activity, the pleasure was imprinted on the brain and may be re-stimulated on further exposure to pictures or sounds of similar activity. The accused was never confronted with specific images designed to replicate the offences alleged against him. The expert concluded that the accused had a normal profile with a preference for adult women and a slight attraction to adolescents, but exhibited no deviation with respect to boys in general or prepubescent boys.

The trial judge held that the expert's evidence was inadmissible. He acquitted the accused on charges relating to one boy but convicted the accused of having invited, counselled or incited the other child to touch the accused for a sexual purpose, and having engaged in an act of anal intercourse.

The Quebec Court of Appeal allowed the accused's appeal from his convictions and ordered a new trial. The majority held that the trial judge erred in excluding the psychiatrist's evidence.

BINNIE J. (L'HEUREUX-DUBÉ, MCLACHLIN, IACOBUCCI, MAJOR, BASTARACHE and ARBOUR JJ. concurring):

. . .

In this appeal we are required to consider aspects of the "gatekeeper function" performed by trial judges in the reception of novel scientific evidence.

. . .

Expert witnesses have an essential role to play in the criminal courts. However, the dramatic growth in the frequency with which they have been called upon in recent years has led to ongoing debate about suitable controls on their participation, precautions to exclude "junk science", and the need to preserve and protect the role of the trier of fact—the judge or the jury. The law in this regard was significantly advanced by Mohan. . . . the course of Mohan and other judgments, the Court has emphasized that the trial judge should take seriously the role of "gatekeeper". The admissibility of the expert evidence should be scrutinized at the time it is proffered, and not allowed too easy an entry on the basis that all of the frailties could go at the end of the day to weight rather than admissibility.

. . .

Mohan kept the door open to novel science, rejecting the "general acceptance" test formulated in the United States in *Frye v. United States*, 293 F. 1013 (D.C. Cir. 1923), and moving in parallel with its replacement, the "reliable foundation" test more recently laid down by the US Supreme Court in *Daubert v. Merrell Dow Pharmaceuticals, Inc.* 509 U.S. 579 (1993). While Daubert must be read in light of the specific text of the Federal Rules of Evidence, which differs from our own procedures, the U.S. Supreme Court did list a number of factors that could be helpful in evaluating the soundness of novel science:

(1) whether the theory or technique can be and has been tested:

> Scientific methodology today is based on generating hypotheses and testing them to see if they can be falsified; indeed, this methodology is what distinguishes science from other fields of human inquiry.

(2) whether the theory or technique has been subjected to peer review and publication:

> [S]ubmission to the scrutiny of the scientific community is a component of "good science", in part because it increases the likelihood that substantive flaws in methodology will be detected.

(3) the known or potential rate of error or the existence of standards; and,

(4) whether the theory or technique used has been generally accepted:

> A "reliability assessment does not require, although it does permit, explicit identification of a relevant scientific community and an express determination of a particular degree of acceptance within that community."

> Widespread acceptance can be an important factor in ruling particular evidence admissible, and "a known technique which has been able to attract only minimal support within the community," . . . may properly be viewed with skepticism.

Thus, in the United States, as here, "general acceptance" is only one of several factors to be considered. A penile plethysmograph may not yet be generally accepted as a forensic tool, but it may become so. A case-by-case evaluation of novel science is necessary in light of the changing nature of our scientific knowledge: it was once accepted by the highest authorities of the western world that the earth was flat.

The Supreme Court allowed the appeal and restored the convictions. The Court believed the trial judge had not erred in excluding the expert's evidence.

R. v. TROCHYM
[2007] S.C.J. No. 6, 43 C.R. (6th) 217 (S.C.C.)

The Supreme Court considered the admissibility of evidence from a Crown witness who had recovered part of her memory of events after undergoing hypnosis. The majority applied the *J. (J.L.)* factors to determine the admissibility of post-hypnotic evidence. Writing for the five-member majority, Deschamps J. wrote:

31 Not all scientific evidence, or evidence that results from the use of a scientific technique, must be screened before being introduced into evidence. In some cases, the science in question is so well established that judges can rely on the fact that the admissibility of evidence based on it has been clearly recognized by the courts in the past. Other cases may not be so clear. Like the legal community, the scientific community continues to challenge and improve upon its existing base of knowledge. As a result, the admissibility of scientific evidence is not frozen in time.

32 While some forms of scientific evidence become more reliable over time, others may become less so as further studies reveal concerns. Thus, a technique that was once admissible may subsequently be found to be inadmissible. An example of the first situation, where, upon further refinement and study, a scientific technique becomes sufficiently reliable to be used in criminal trials, is DNA matching evidence, which this Court recognized in *R. v. Terceira*, [1999] 3 S.C.R. 866. An example of the second situation, where a technique that has been employed for some time comes to be questioned, is so-called "dock", or in-court, identification evidence. In *R. v. Hibbert*, [2002] 2 S.C.R. 445, 2002 SCC 39, at para. 50, Arbour J., writing for the majority, stated that despite its long-standing use, dock identification is almost totally unreliable. Therefore, even if it has received judicial recognition in the past, a technique or science whose underlying assumptions are challenged should not be admitted in evidence without first confirming the validity of those assumptions.

In determining that post-hypnotic evidence was inadmissible, Deschamps J. wrote:

55 When the factors set out in *J.-L.J.* are applied to hypnosis, it becomes evident that this technique and its impact on human memory are not understood well enough for post-hypnosis testimony to be sufficiently reliable to be used in a court of law. Although hypnosis has been the subject of numerous studies, these studies are either inconclusive or draw attention to the fact that hypnosis can, in certain circumstances, result in the distortion of memory. Perhaps most troubling is the potential rate of error in the additional information obtained through hypnosis when it is used for forensic purposes. At the present time, there is no way of knowing whether such information will be accurate or inaccurate. . .

. . .

61 In sum, it is evident, based on the scientific evidence on record, that post-hypnosis testimony does not satisfy the test for admissibility set out in *J.-L.J.* While hypnosis has been the subject of extensive study and peer review, much of the literature is inconclusive or highly contradictory regarding the reliability of the science in the judicial context. Unless a litigant reverses the presumption on the basis of the factors set out in *J.-L.J.*, post-hypnosis testimony should not be admitted in evidence.

Justice Bastarache dissented on behalf of three members of the Court. He argued that the *J. (J.L.)* factors should not be applied to hypnosis because it was not novel science:

131 Characterizing hypnosis as "novel science" by applying *R. v. J.-L.J.*, [2000] 2 S.C.R. 600, 2000 SCC 51, my colleague finds that hypnotically refreshed memories are, at least for now, presumptively inadmissible (para. 61).

132 This ignores the fact that the technique has been used in Canada for almost 30 years, and has been employed in Canadian criminal investigations to assist in memory retrieval of both Crown and defence witnesses for a similar amount of time. The earliest Canadian cases where this technique is reported are *R. v. Pitt*, [1968] 3 C.C.C. 342 (B.C.S.C.), and *R. v. K.*, [1979] 5 W.W.R. 105 (Man. Prov. Ct.). Many more cases emerged in the 1980s and 1990s. As well, as early as 1979, this Court specifically acknowledged the use of forensic hypnosis by police forces and by defence counsel: see *Horvath v. The Queen*, [1979] 2 S.C.R. 376, at pp. 433-34 (*per* Beetz J.). These cases stand for the proposition that hypnosis is in no way a novel science.

. . .

139 The point of both *Mohan* and *J.-L.J.* was to emphasize the need for courts to give special scrutiny to novel science or the new application of a recognized science, through a case-by-case evaluation, in light of the changing nature of our scientific knowledge (see *J.-L.J.*, at para. 34) . . . . *J.-L.J.* was not intended, as my colleague appears to suggest, to set down a rigid formula where the results must be proved beyond a reasonable doubt before scientific evidence can be admitted. The factors from *Daubert v. Merrell Dow Pharmaceuticals Inc.*, 509 U.S. 579(1993), adopted in *J.-L.J.* were designed to be flexible and non-exclusive. As noted above, similar factors to assist courts in assessing the reliability of scientific evidence have existed at common law long before *J.-L.J.* was decided. Well-established scientific methods accepted by our courts do not need to be systematically reassessed under *J.-L.J.* While my colleague suggests that not all previously accepted scientific techniques will have to be reassessed under *J.-L.J.*, her guidance that science which is "so well established" (at para. 31) need not be reassessed is so vague that it opens the door to most if not all previously accepted techniques being subject to challenge under *J.-L.J.*, without establishing a serious basis for the inquiry.

Justice Bastarache also questioned whether the evidentiary record was sufficient to ground the majority's conclusion that post-hypnotic evidence should be inadmissible:

141 Finally, I add that in order to come to the conclusion that hypnosis evidence does not meet the criteria of general acceptance, my colleague relies almost exclusively on the position of experts discussed in American cases. This is not a sufficient evidentiary foundation upon which to arrive at such a conclusion. However, this was the sole evidence the appellant advanced before this Court in support of his argument that it should adopt a general exclusionary rule towards hypnosis evidence . . .

. . .

147 . . . It is only before this Court and the Court of Appeal that Mr. Trochym sought to challenge the long-standing admissibility rule. In order to properly challenge such a rule, however, he was required to present direct expert evidence on why the rule should no longer be accepted, not just some academic commentary supporting this position. No such evidence was presented. I have serious reservations about courts conducting personal research — and forming conclusions on the basis of such research — in areas that require expertise, like the sciences.

The reliability factors developed in *Daubert* and adopted in *J. (J.-L.)* were framed with evidence from the "hard" sciences in mind. Other branches of knowledge, such as social sciences, may not rely on hypothesis testing and measurement of error rates in the same way. Determining how to gauge the reliability of expert evidence in the "soft" sciences has been a longstanding concern, one that was addressed at length in the judgment of Doherty J.A. in *Abbey #1*.[324] He wrote:

> [109] Scientific validity is not a condition precedent to the admissibility of expert opinion evidence. Most expert evidence routinely heard and acted upon in the courts cannot be scientifically validated. For example, psychiatrists testify to the existence of various mental states, doctors testify as to the cause of an injury or death, accident reconstructionists testify to the location or cause of an accident, economists or rehabilitation specialists testify to future employment prospects and future care costs, fire marshals testify about the cause of a fire, professionals from a wide variety of fields testify as to the operative standard of care in their profession or the cause of a particular event. Like Dr. Totten, these experts do not support their opinions by reference to error rates, random samplings or the replication of test results. Rather, they refer to specialized knowledge gained through experience and specialized training in the relevant field. To test the reliability of the opinion of these experts and Dr. Totten using reliability factors referable to scientific validity is to attempt to place the proverbial square peg into the round hole.[325]

> [110] Tested exclusively against the *Daubert* factors, much of the expert evidence routinely accepted and acted upon in courts would be excluded despite its obvious reliability and value to the trial process. However, *Daubert* does not

---

[324]   *R. v. Abbey*, 2009 ONCA 624, 246 C.C.C. (3d) 301, 68 C.R. (6th) 201 (Ont. C.A.).

[325]   Indeed, the evidence of professional experts as to the appropriate standard of care in negligence actions is not unlike Dr. Totten's evidence in that professional experts speak essentially to the culture of the profession by reference to the conduct expected of a reasonably competent member of the profession in a given fact situation.

suggest that the factors it proposes are essential to the reliability inquiry. Instead, *Daubert*, at p. 594 U.S., describes that inquiry as "a flexible one". This flexibility was subsequently emphasized in *Kumho Tire Co. v. Carmichael*, 526 U.S. 137, 119 S. Ct. 1167 (1999). Unlike *Daubert, Kumho Tire Co.* did not involve an opinion, the validity of which relied upon the scientific method. The expert's opinion in *Kumho Tire Co.* depended in part on scientific principles but also upon the knowledge of the witness gained through his experience and training.

. . .

[117] The proper question to be answered when addressing the reliability of Dr. Totten's opinion was not whether it was scientifically valid, but whether his research and experiences had permitted him to develop a specialized knowledge about gang culture, and specifically gang symbology, that was sufficiently reliable to justify placing his opinion as to the potential meanings of the teardrop tattoo within that culture before the jury: see David P. Leonard, Edward J. Imwinkelried, David H. Kaye, David E. Bernstein and Jennifer L. Mnookin, *The New Wigmore: A Treatise on Evidence* (New York: Aspen Publishers, 2004), at para. 9.3.4. . . .

[118] In holding that the trial judge improperly attempted to use the specific Daubert factors in assessing the reliability of Dr. Totten's evidence, I do not suggest that the Crown was not required to demonstrate threshold reliability. That reliability had to be determined, however, using tools appropriate to the nature of the opinion advanced by Dr. Totten.

[119] As with scientifically based opinion evidence, there is no closed list of the factors relevant to the reliability of an opinion like that offered by Dr. Totten. I would suggest, however, that the following are some questions that may be relevant to the reliability inquiry where an opinion like that offered by Dr. Totten is put forward:

- To what extent is the field in which the opinion is offered a recognized discipline, profession or area of specialized training?

- To what extent is the work within that field subject to quality assurance measures and appropriate independent review by others in the field?

- What are the particular expert's qualifications within that discipline, profession or area of specialized training?

- To the extent that the opinion rests on data accumulated through various means such as interviews, is the data accurately recorded, stored and available?

- To what extent are the reasoning processes underlying the opinion and the methods used to gather the relevant information clearly explained by the witness and susceptible to critical examination by a jury?

- To what extent has the expert arrived at his or her opinion using methodologies accepted by those working in the particular field in which the opinion is advanced?

- To what extent do the accepted methodologies promote and enhance the reliability of the information gathered and relied on by the expert?

- To what extent has the witness, in advancing the opinion, honoured the boundaries and limits of the discipline from which his or her expertise arises?

- To what extent is the proffered opinion based on data and other information gathered independently of the specific case or, more broadly, the litigation process?

R. v. SEKHON
2014 SCC 15, [2014] 1 S.C.R. 272, 307 C.C.C. (3d) 464,
8 C.R. (7th) 223 (S.C.C.)

In 2005 S was charged with importing cocaine and possession for the purposes of trafficking of 50 kg of cocaine. The pickup truck he was driving was stopped by border officers as he attempted to enter Canada from the United States. He was arrested when officers found the cocaine in a concealed compartment of his truck. The sole issue at trial was whether the Crown could prove beyond reasonable doubt that he knew of the cocaine. S claimed that an acquaintance had asked him to drive the truck to Canada and that he had no knowledge of the cocaine. The trial judge rejected S's testimony finding 12 problems which made his evidence illogical and completely unbelievable. The judge convicted. He found three pieces of circumstantial evidence very significant: the value of the cocaine would require a reliable driver with knowledge of the shipment, the evidence of a police officer qualified to give expert testimony regarding the customs and practices of the drug trade that in a thousand or more cocaine importing investigations he had never encountered a blind courier who did not know what he was moving, and evidence that S had detached the fob that controlled access to the secret compartment from his key chain before handing the keys to the border officer. On appeal, S argued that the trial judge should not have admitted or relied on the expert evidence of the police officer and, in particular, that portion of his evidence relating to his own experience with blind couriers. A majority of the B.C. Court of Appeal dismissed the appeal. The accused appealed.

MOLDAVER J. (ABELLA, ROTHSTEIN, KARAKATSANIS and WAGNER JJ. concurring):

46 Given the concerns about the impact expert evidence can have on a trial - including the possibility that experts may usurp the role of the trier of fact - trial judges must be vigilant in monitoring and enforcing the proper scope of expert evidence. While these concerns are perhaps more pronounced in jury trials, all trial judges — including those in judge-alone trials — have an ongoing duty to ensure that expert evidence remains within its proper scope. It is not enough to simply consider the *Mohan* criteria at the outset of the expert's testimony and make an initial ruling as to the admissibility of the evidence. The trial judge must do his or her best to ensure that, throughout the expert's testimony, the testimony remains within the proper boundaries of expert evidence. As noted by Doherty J.A. in *R. v. Abbey*, 2009 ONCA 624, 97 O.R. (3d) 330, at para. 62:

> The admissibility inquiry is not conducted in a vacuum. Before deciding admissibility, a trial judge must determine the nature and scope of the proposed expert evidence. In doing so, the trial judge sets not only the boundaries of the proposed expert evidence but also, if necessary, the language in which the expert's opinion may be proffered so as to minimize any potential harm to the trial process. A cautious delineation of the scope of the proposed expert evidence and strict adherence to those boundaries, if the evidence is admitted, are essential. The case law demonstrates that overreaching by expert witnesses is probably the most common fault leading to reversals on appeal . . . . [Emphasis added; citations omitted.]

47 The trial judge must both ensure that an expert stays within the proper bounds of his or her expertise and that the content of the evidence itself is properly the subject of expert evidence.

48 It is foreseeable that mistakes will be made and that, as happened in the instant case, testimony that strays beyond the proper scope of the expert evidence will be given. It is also foreseeable that defence counsel may fail to object to the testimony at the time the problematic statements are made. In a jury trial, once the statements have been made, it may be somewhat more difficult to address the problem — but a remedial instruction advising the jury to disabuse their minds of the inadmissible evidence will generally suffice. Judges, on the other hand, are accustomed to disabusing their minds of inadmissible evidence. It goes without saying that where the expert evidence strays beyond its proper scope, it is imperative that the trial judge not assign any weight to the inadmissible parts.

B. *Application to This Case*

49 In my view, the trial judge erred in relying upon the Impugned Testimony. The fact that Sgt. Arsenault did not personally encounter a blind courier over the course of his investigations is neither relevant nor necessary, within the meaning ascribed to those terms by this Court in *Mohan*, to the issue facing the trial judge — namely, whether Mr. Sekhon himself had knowledge of the drugs. The Impugned Testimony, though perhaps logically relevant, was not legally relevant because the guilt or innocence of accused persons that Sgt. Arsenault had encountered in the past is legally irrelevant to the guilt or innocence of Mr. Sekhon (see *Mohan*, at pp. 20-21). In other words, the Impugned Testimony was of no probative value in determining whether *Mr. Sekhon* knew about the cocaine in the hidden compartment. It is trite to say that a fundamental tenet of our criminal justice system is that the guilt of an accused cannot be determined by reference to the guilt of other, unrelated accused persons. Moreover, the Impugned Testimony was not necessary because determining whether Mr. Sekhon knew about the drugs is not beyond the knowledge and experience of the judge, and it is certainly not a matter that is technical or scientific in nature.

50 The lack of relevance or probative value is, in my view, sufficient to justify the exclusion of the Impugned Testimony. However, it is worth noting the prejudicial effect that such evidence may have on a trial. I agree with Newbury J.A. to the extent that she found little to no difference between the Impugned Testimony in this case and a homicide investigator being permitted to testify that in all of the cases she or he has worked on, the accused intended the death of his or her victim. Nor do I see a difference between the Impugned Testimony and a stolen goods investigator testifying that he or she has never seen a case of innocent possession of stolen property, or an experienced fraud investigator testifying that he or she has never seen a case where a senior manager was not aware of fraudulent conduct occurring within the company (A.F., at para. 60). The inherent danger of admitting such evidence is obvious — as Newbury J.A. pointed out:

> Anecdotal evidence of this kind is just that - anecdotal. It does not speak to the particular facts before the Court, but has the superficial attractiveness of seeming to show that the probabilities are very much in the Crown's favour, and of coming from the mouth of an "expert". If it can be said to be relevant to the case of a particular accused, it is also highly prejudicial. [para. 27]

This type of anecdotal evidence would appear to require the accused to somehow prove that, regardless of a particular expert's past experience, the accused's situation is different. Such a result is contrary to another fundamental tenet of our criminal justice system — that it is *the Crown* that bears the burden of proving the *mens rea* of an offence beyond a reasonable doubt. As the appellant points out, "such evidence would logically trigger a defence need to call evidence to refute such opinions, such as a retired investigator who did experience an innocent person in similar circumstances, or a witness who could testify that he or she was in the same circumstances of the accused and was innocent" (A.F., at para. 61). At that point, the trial would become a battle of experts — and a completely irrelevant battle at that.

51 For these reasons, I conclude that the Impugned Testimony was inadmissible.

The majority decided to apply the curative proviso under s. 686(1)(d)((iii) to avoid a new trial as the evidence of guilt was overwhelming. This resulted in a strongly worded dissent by LeBel J, (McLachlin C.J. concurring). In the view of the dissenters the curative proviso ought not to be used to override an accused's right to a fair trial based solely on admissible evidence.[326]

---

[326] For another recent case emphasizing the importance of delineating the proper scope of expert testimony, see *R. v. Singh*, 2014 ONCA 791, 16 C.R. (7th) 95 (Ont. C.A.).

R. v. BINGLEY

2017 SCC 12, [2017] 1 S.C.R. 170, 345 C.C.C. (3d) 306, 35 C.R. (7th) 1 (S.C.C.)

McLachlin C.J. (Abella, Moldaver, Côté and Brown JJ. concurring):

1 The issue on this appeal is narrow: Can a drug recognition expert ("DRE") testify about his or her determination under s. 254(3.1) of the *Criminal Code*, R.S.C. 1985, c. C-46, without a *voir dire* to determine the DRE's expertise? I conclude that in this case a *voir dire* was not required. I would therefore dismiss the appeal and confirm the order of the Ontario Court of Appeal for a new trial.

I. Facts

2 The appellant, Carson Bingley, was observed driving erratically, pulling into a parking lot, and striking a car. The police were called. Constable Jennifer Tennant arrived and interviewed Mr. Bingley. She testified that his eyes were "glossy" and bloodshot, and that he stumbled and slurred his words. She conducted a roadside screening device test, which Mr. Bingley passed. Constable Tennant then called for a field sobriety test. Constable Tommy Jellinek, a certified DRE under the *Criminal Code*, conducted the standard field sobriety test. Mr. Bingley failed the test, and was arrested for driving while impaired by a drug. Constable Jellinek took Mr. Bingley to a police station and conducted a drug recognition evaluation. During the evaluation, Mr. Bingley admitted he had smoked marijuana (cannabis) and taken two Xanax (alprazolam) in the previous 12 hours. Constable Jellinek concluded that Mr. Bingley was impaired by a drug. Based on his conclusion that Mr. Bingley was impaired, Constable Jellinek ordered a urinalysis under s. 254(3.4), which revealed the presence of cannabis, cocaine and alprazolam.

3 At trial, the Crown called Constable Jellinek to explain the results of his drug recognition evaluation as evidence of Mr. Bingley's impairment. The Crown relied on s. 254(3.1) of the *Criminal Code* as establishing the admissibility of Constable Jellinek's testimony, and argued that no *voir dire* was required.

II. Relevant Statutory Provisions

4 The relevant subsections of s. 254 of the *Criminal Code* are as follows:

Evaluation

(3.1) If a peace officer has reasonable grounds to believe that a person is committing, or at any time within the preceding three hours has committed, an offence under paragraph 253(1)(a) as a result of the consumption of a drug or of a combination of alcohol and a drug, the peace officer may, by demand made as soon as practicable, require the person to submit, as soon as practicable, to an evaluation conducted by an evaluating officer to determine whether the person's ability to operate a motor vehicle, a vessel, an aircraft or railway equipment is impaired by a drug or by a combination of alcohol and a drug, and to accompany the peace officer for that purpose.

. . .

Samples of bodily substances

(3.4) If, on completion of the evaluation, the evaluating officer has reasonable grounds to believe, based on the evaluation, that the person's ability to operate a motor vehicle, a vessel, an aircraft or railway equipment is impaired by a drug or by a combination of alcohol and a drug, the evaluating officer may, by demand made as soon as practicable, require the person to provide, as soon as practicable,

> **(a)** a sample of either oral fluid or urine that, in the evaluating officer's opinion, will enable a proper analysis to be made to determine whether the person has a drug in their body; or
>
> **(b)** samples of blood that, in the opinion of the qualified medical practitioner or qualified technician taking the samples, will enable a proper analysis to be made to determine whether the person has a drug in their body.

. . .

V. Analysis

8 Driving while impaired by drugs is a dangerous and, sadly, common activity, prohibited by the *Criminal Code*. Parliament long ago established a regime to enforce the law against alcohol-impaired driving, with breathalyzer testing and analyst certification at its centre. Enforcing the offence of drug-impaired driving was more elusive.

9 To meet the need to enforce the law against drug-impaired driving, Parliament set up a regime to test for drug impairment in 2008. The centrepiece of the regime is a 12-part evaluation for drug impairment, established by the Regulations, to be administered by police officers called DREs.[footnote omitted] DREs receive special training and certification. Section 254(3.1) of the *Criminal Code* provides law enforcement, for the first time, with the power to compel a person to submit to a drug recognition evaluation when there are reasonable grounds to believe that a person has driven while impaired by drugs or by a combination of drugs and alcohol. If the 12-step evaluation administered by a DRE provides him or her with reasonable grounds to believe that the person is impaired by a drug, s. 254(3.4) allows the police to take tests of oral fluid, urine or blood, to determine whether the person in fact has drugs in his or her body.

10 The Crown argues that s. 254(3.1) has supplanted the common law and that a DRE's determination is admissible at trial against the accused as evidence of impairment by drug. Mr. Bingley contends that the determination is only admissible if the DRE is established as an expert on a *voir dire*, pursuant to *Mohan*. To put it succinctly, the central issue on this appeal is whether s. 254(3.1) makes the DRE's opinion evidence *automatically admissible* (the Crown's position) or whether a *special hearing is required to determine admissibility*, as required at common law under *Mohan* (Mr. Bingley's position). In the alternative, the Crown argues that Constable Jellinek's evidence should be admitted as lay opinion evidence.

A. *Have the Common Law Rules of Evidence Been Displaced?*

11 Clear and unambiguous language is required to displace common law rules, including rules of evidence : see *Slaight Communications Inc. v. Davidson*, [1989] 1 S.C.R. 1038, at p. 1077; *Parry Sound (District) Social Services Administration Board v. O.P.S.E.U., Local 324*, 2003 SCC 42, [2003] 2 S.C.R. 157, at para. 39; *Heritage Capital Corp. v. Equitable Trust Co.*, 2016 SCC 19, [2016] 1 S.C.R. 306, at paras. 29-30. The Crown argues that the words "to determine" in s. 254(3.1) are clear enough to do this. I do not agree. Section 254(3.1) calls on the DRE to form an opinion about whether a person is impaired by drug. It does not follow that the opinion will be automatically admissible at trial.

12 The purpose of s. 254(3.1) confirms that a DRE's opinion is not automatically admissible at trial. Section 254(3.1) gives the police investigative tools to enforce laws against drug-impaired driving. It does not dictate whether evidence obtained through the use of those investigative tools will be admissible at trial. When Parliament intends to make evidence automatically admissible, it says so expressly: see, e.g., *Criminal Code*, ss. 723(5) (hearsay evidence) and 729(1) (analyst certificate on conditional sentence breaches). As section 254(3.1) does not speak to admissibility, the common law rules of evidence apply.

B. *Is the Evidence Admissible Expert Opinion?*

13 The modern legal framework for the admissibility of expert opinion evidence was set out in *Mohan* and clarified in *White Burgess Langille Inman v. Abbott and Haliburton Co.*, 2015 SCC 23, [2015] 2 S.C.R. 182 . . .

. . .

18 The only issue in this case is whether Constable Jellinek has special expertise as required by the fourth *Mohan* factor. Mr. Bingley concedes that the proposed evidence is logically relevant, necessary, and not subject to any other exclusionary rule. Nor does Mr. Bingley argue that the evidence should be excluded because its prejudicial effect outweighs its probative value. On the facts of this case, these were appropriate concessions.

19 The basic requirement of expertise for an expert witness is that the witness has expertise outside the experience and knowledge of the trier of fact. The question is whether Constable Jellinek, the DRE in this case, met this requirement. In my view, he did.

20 The DRE, literally, is a "drug recognition expert", certified as such for the purposes of the scheme. It is undisputed that the DRE receives special training in how to administer the 12-step drug recognition evaluation and in what inferences may be drawn from the factual data he or she notes. It is for this limited purpose that a DRE can assist the court by offering expert opinion evidence.

21 While a DRE's evaluation certainly has an investigative purpose, their application of the 12-step drug recognition evaluation and determination of impairment is relevant evidence and can assist the trier of fact. The DRE's opinion is based on his or her specialized training and experience in conducting the evaluation. By reason of this training and experience, all DREs undoubtedly possess expertise on determining drug impairment that is outside the experience and knowledge of the trier of fact.

22 This conclusion is not negated by the fact that a DRE is not trained in the science underlying the development of the 12-step evaluation. The test for expertise is merely knowledge outside the experience and knowledge of the trier of fact. Knowledge of the underlying science is not a precondition to the admissibility of a DRE's opinion. The scope of a DRE's expertise is in the application of the prescribed 12-step evaluation, not in its scientific foundation. Expert witnesses are not barred from assisting the court with their special knowledge simply because they are not trained in the underlying science of the field. Such knowledge is required only where the science is novel.

23 In his analysis, the trial judge focused on the reliability of the underlying science and determined that, as novel science, the DRE opinion evidence could not be admitted without a witness being able to explain the scientific validity of the evaluation. The purpose of the special rule for novel scientific evidence is to ensure that the reliability of the underlying technique or procedure used in forming the opinion has to be established by precedent, evidence, or statute.

24 In this case, the reliability of the 12-step evaluation comes from the statutory framework itself. Parliament has determined that the 12-step evaluation performed by a trained DRE constitutes evidence of drug impairment. It may not be conclusive, but it is evidence beyond the experience and knowledge of the trier of fact.

25 My colleague concludes that as s. 254(3.1) and the Regulations do not "clearly designat[e]" DRE opinion evidence admissible in evidence, reliability must be otherwise established. I cannot agree. It is true that s. 254(3.1) and the Regulations do not provide for the automatic admissibility of DRE opinion evidence. But that does not end the inquiry. The Regulations set out a uniform evaluative framework that a DRE must follow in order to reach a conclusion regarding drug impairment for the purposes of s. 254(3.1). Parliament is entitled to establish such a framework, and in doing so, establish that the 12-step drug evaluation is sufficiently reliable for the purposes of determining impairment. No further evaluation of the reliability of the steps mandated by the Regulations is required. Any challenge to the underlying effectiveness of the evaluation would require a challenge to the legislative framework itself.

26 Allowing a DRE to give relevant opinion evidence outside the experience and knowledge of the trier of fact is not "an unqualified endorsement of the underlying science" of the 12-step drug evaluations, as my colleague suggests (para. 46). Reliability is not assessed in a vacuum. Parliament has established, through the adoption of the Regulations, that the 12-step drug evaluation is sufficiently reliable for the purpose of a DRE's determination of impairment under s. 254(3.1). The scope of a DRE's expertise is limited to that determination, and it is only for the purpose of making that determination that Parliament has established the 12-step drug evaluation's reliability.

27 Mr. Bingley conceded that all the *Mohan* requirements other than special expertise were met and does not argue that the evidence should be excluded under the second stage of the admissibility analysis. Parliament has established the required expertise. It follows that the DRE's evidence is admissible in this case. To put it another way, the only purpose of a *voir dire* in this case would be to determine whether Constable Jellinek has expertise over and above an ordinary person. Normally, the judge determines this on evidence adduced at the *voir dire*. But s. 254(3.1) and the legislative and regulatory scheme that accompanies it conclusively answer the question of expertise. The DRE is established by Parliament to possess special expertise outside the experience and knowledge of the trier of fact. He is thus an expert for the purpose of applying the 12-step evaluation and determining whether that evaluation indicates drug impairment for the purposes of s. 254(3.1). His expertise has been conclusively and irrebuttably established by Parliament.

28 This compels the following conclusion. In the case at bar all the threshold requirements for admissibility of *Mohan* are established. Where it is clear that all the requirements of a common law rule of admissibility are established (the four *Mohan* threshold requirements for admissibility are met and there is no question that the probative value of the evidence outweighs its prejudicial effect), the trial judge is not obliged to hold a *voir dire* to determine the admissibility of the evidence. To so require would be otiose, if not absurd, not to mention a waste of judicial resources.

29 It is important to reiterate that a DRE's s. 254(3.1) determination is a result of administering the prescribed evaluation. That is the only expertise conferred on a DRE. The trial judge has an "ongoing duty to ensure that expert evidence remains within its proper scope": *Sekhon*, at para. 46. If opinions beyond the expertise of a DRE are solicited, a *Mohan voir dire* to establish further expertise may be required.

30 The statutory framework does not undermine a trial judge's important role as gatekeeper to safeguard the trial process and ensure that it is not distorted by improper expert opinion evidence. The trial judge always maintains residual discretion to exclude evidence if its probative value is outweighed by its prejudicial effect. Limitations, such as the absence of a standardized approach to weighing the various tests in reaching a determination, may affect the probative value of a DRE's opinion evidence. A DRE may be unable to explain how he or she made the determination based on the application of the 12-step evaluation. If the probative value of an individual DRE's evidence is so diminished that the benefits in admitting the evidence are outweighed by the potential harm to the trial process, a trial judge retains the discretion to exclude that evidence. I reiterate here that the focus of the analysis must be on the DRE's administration of the evaluation, not on the reliability of the steps underlying the evaluation, which have been prescribed by Parliament.

31 It is also important to note that the determination of the DRE is not conclusive of the ultimate question of whether the accused was driving while impaired by a drug. The DRE's task is to determine whether the evaluation indicates drug impairment. The DRE's evidence does not presume the ultimate issue of guilt; it is merely one piece of the picture for the judge or jury to consider.

32 That Parliament has established the reliability of the 12-step drug evaluation by statute does not hinder the trier of fact's ability to critically assess a DRE's conclusion of impairment or an accused person's right to test that evidence. Cross-examination of the DRE may undermine his or her conclusion. Evidence of bias may raise doubt about the officer's conclusion. The officer may fail to conduct the drug recognition evaluation in accordance with his or her training. A DRE may draw questionable inferences from his or her observations. Bodily sample evidence obtained under s. 254(3.4) may refute the DRE's assessment, as may evidence of bystanders or other experts. It will always be for the trier of fact to determine what weight to give a DRE's opinion. Any weight given to a DRE's evidence will necessarily respect the scope of the DRE's expertise and the fact that it is not conclusive of impairment.

33 The trial judge correctly found that the DRE in this case was an expert for purposes of administering the 12-step evaluation and determining whether Mr. Bingley was driving while impaired for the purpose of requiring further testing. He erred, however, in concluding that because the officer was not an expert in the scientific foundation of the various elements of the test, none of his opinion evidence was admissible. The DRE's expertise is not in the scientific foundation of the test but in the administration of the test itself. As the other criteria for admissibility are not in issue, Constable Jellinek's opinion evidence should have been admitted.

. . .

VI. Conclusion

35 I would dismiss the appeal and confirm the order for a new trial.

KARAKATSANIS (GASCON JJ. concurring) (dissenting):

. . .

38 I cannot agree . . . that Parliament has determined that the 12-step evaluation, when properly administered, is sufficiently reliable to be admitted as evidence of drug impairment at trial. In my view, it was open to the trial judge to refuse to admit the proposed opinion in the absence of evidence on the reliability and validity of the science underlying the 12-step evaluation.

39 As the Crown submits, evaluations performed by DREs pursuant to s. 254(3.1) of the *Criminal Code* rely on a science-based regime. As the DRE in this case acknowledged in cross-examination, the reliability of his opinion depends on the validity of the various tests and the reliability of the inferences he has been taught to draw from the results. Many of the "clues" and "cues" DREs rely on when making their overall determination would not obviously indicate impairment to a lay person. Tests such as the horizontal gaze nystagmus test or the lack-of-convergence test, which involve looking for irregularities in eye movements, are only reliable indicators of drug impairment if the science on which they are based is valid.

40 Parliament has endorsed the reliability of the 12-step evaluation as an investigative tool, not for the purpose of an evidentiary shortcut at trial. Without the ability to test the reliability of the scientific foundation of the evaluation, the trial judge — acting as gatekeeper — will be unable to assess the probative value of such evidence, and the trier of fact will be unable to assess the weight of such evidence. In my view, courts retain discretion to require — through evidence or precedent — confirmation that the science behind DRE evaluations meets the necessary level of reliability before admitting the evidence at trial. . . .

. . .

49 . . . [A]bsent statutory language that clearly designates DRE evaluations as admissible evidence, a basic threshold of reliability of the tests must be established through precedent or evidence on a *voir dire*.

. . .

51 The probative value of the evidence necessarily involves an assessment of the reliability of the underlying science : *Trochym,* at para. 28. Without evidence relating to the science, or the ability to cross-examine the expert about the science, how does the gatekeeper critically assess the probative value against the potential prejudice of the evidence, to ensure that it enhances, rather than distorts, the fact-finding process? (See *White Burgess*, at paras. 17-18.)

52 And without the ability to test its scientific foundation, how will the trier of fact ultimately assess the weight of the evaluation? The evidence has the potential to be highly prejudicial. In the context of a jury trial for impaired driving causing death, for example, there is a real danger that an opinion, coming from a police officer certified as a "Drug Recognition Expert", about whether the accused was impaired by a drug, would be given undue weight.

53 Nor can cross-examination of DREs effectively assist in understanding the probative value of the evidence and the strength of the inference that should be drawn from the opinion. Because a DRE's area of expertise is limited to administration of the prescribed evaluation rather than the scientific knowledge necessary to explain its effectiveness, cross-examination is unlikely to leave triers of fact with a real understanding of the weight that should be attached to the evidence.

54 Accused persons have a right to test the strength of the evidence against them. For those charged with alcohol-impaired driving, s. 258(1)(c) of the *Criminal Code* clearly designates breath sample results as "conclusive proof" of an accused's blood alcohol level (provided certain preconditions are met). Since there is no equivalent provision for DRE determinations, accused persons should not have to bring a constitutional challenge in order to question the strength of the 12-step evaluation.

55 The Chief Justice recognizes that Parliament has not displaced the common law rule requiring a *voir dire* on the admissibility of expert evidence. One important reason for this rule is to ensure that any novel science underpinning the expert's opinion is reliable. And yet, my colleague's reasons dispense with any inquiry into the reliability and validity of the 12-step evaluation. This displaces an important safeguard in our common law rule, without clear language to this effect. It effectively leads to the automatic admissibility of the evaluation upon proof it was properly administered. In my view, there is no clear indication that this was Parliament's intent.

· · ·

III. Conclusion

60 Accordingly, I would allow the appeal and reinstate the acquittal.

Do you agree with the majority or the dissenting view?

MOORE v. GETAHUN

2015 ONCA 55 (Ont. C.A.), additional reasons 2015 ONCA 443 (Ont. C.A.)

SHARPE J.A.:

[1] This appeal raises significant issues in relation to the preparation and use of expert reports in the context of a medical malpractice action.

[2] Following a motorcycle accident, the respondent (plaintiff) was treated by the appellant (defendant), a recently qualified orthopedic surgeon, for a fracture to his right wrist. The appellant applied a full circumferential cast to the respondent's wrist and forearm. The respondent suffered permanent damage to the muscles in his arm due to compartment syndrome that he alleged was caused by the appellant's negligence in the application of a full cast.

[3] The trial judge preferred the evidence of the respondent's expert witness over that of the appellant's expert witnesses and found that the application of the full circumferential cast was a breach of the standard of care and had caused the compartment syndrome to develop.

[4] The first and most significant legal issue raised on appeal involves the preparation of the written report of one of the appellant's expert witnesses. The trial judge held that it was improper for counsel to assist an expert witness in the preparation of the expert's report. That proposition is strongly challenged by the appellant and by all of the interveners. The respondent concedes that the view expressed by the trial judge is erroneous, but argues that her error had no impact on the outcome of the trial.

. . .

[7] For the following reasons, I conclude that the trial judge erred in holding that it was unacceptable for counsel to review and discuss the draft expert reports. She further erred in using the written expert reports that were neither entered into evidence, nor the subject of cross-examination, to contradict and discredit aspects of the *viva voce* evidence of the appellant's expert witnesses. I conclude, however, that these errors did not affect the outcome. As no substantial wrong or miscarriage of justice flowed from the errors, this court would not be justified in ordering a new trial.

ANALYSIS

1. (a) Did the trial judge err by criticizing the appellant's counsel for discussing with their expert witness the content of his draft report?

(i) Expert evidence

[33] Expert evidence is a significant and controversial feature of modern civil litigation. It constitutes an exception to the rule that witnesses may only testify

as to facts, not opinions, and that it is the exclusive prerogative of the trier of fact to draw inferences from proven facts. The expert evidence exception operates where specialized knowledge is required to determine the implications of the bare facts and where the trier of fact is not competent to draw the necessary inferences unaided: *R. v. Mohan*, [1994] 2 S.C.R. 9, at p. 23; *R. v. Abbey*, 2009 ONCA 624, 246 C.C.C. (3d) 301, at para. 94.

[34] Expert evidence has become more significant with the explosion of scientific knowledge and technical innovation. Many cases have been described as a "battle of experts". Medical negligence cases are a prime example. The trier of fact requires the assistance of expert witnesses to decide issues pertaining to the standard of care, causation and prognosis.

[35] The use of expert evidence poses difficult issues that have been the focus of consideration in civil justice reform. How do we control the added costs associated with the explosion of expert witnesses? How do we ensure that a party has a fair opportunity to challenge an adverse expert witness? How do we ensure that expert witnesses offer an unbiased scientific or technical opinion based upon their training and expertise, rather than act as "hired guns" who present unbalanced opinions unduly favouring the party that retains them?

(ii) 2010 amendments to rule 53.03

[36] Rule 53.03 establishes the framework that parties must follow when they intend to call an expert witness at trial. The rule requires a party to provide a signed report from the expert witness not less than 90 days before the pre-trial conference or, in the case of a responding report, not less than 60 days before the pre-trial conference (rules 53.03(1), (2)). Rule 53.03(3) provides that an expert witness may not testify with respect to an issue, except with leave of the trial judge, unless the substance of his or her testimony is set out in writing in compliance with the other provisions of the rule.

[37] In 2010, significant changes were made to the *Rules of Civil Procedure* relating to expert witnesses, following the recommendations of the Honourable Coulter Osborne contained in his review of the civil justice system, *Civil Justice Reform Project: Summary of Findings & Recommendations* (Toronto: Ontario Ministry of the Attorney General, 2007). His report highlighted, at p. 71, the common complaint that "too many experts are no more than hired guns who tailor their reports and evidence to suit the client's needs." Two significant recommendations of the Osborne Report, designed to foster unbiased expert evidence, were subsequently adopted.

[38] First, rule 4.1.01(1) specifically addresses the duty of an expert witness:

> It is the duty of every expert engaged by or on behalf of a party to provide evidence in relation to a proceeding under these rules,
> (a) to provide opinion evidence that is fair, objective and non-partisan;

    (b) to provide opinion evidence that is related only to matters that are within the expert's area of expertise; and

    (c) to provide such additional assistance as the court may reasonably require to determine a matter in issue.

[39] Second, rule 53.03(2.1) provides that an expert report must contain the following information:

1.   The expert's name, address and area of expertise.

2.   The expert's qualifications and employment and educational experiences in his or her area of expertise.

3.   The instructions provided to the expert in relation to the proceeding.

4.   The nature of the opinion being sought and each issue in the proceeding to which the opinion relates.

5.   The expert's opinion respecting each issue and, where there is a range of opinions given, a summary of the range and the reasons for the expert's own opinion within that range.

6.   The expert's reasons for his or her opinion, including,

      i.   a description of the factual assumptions on which the opinion is based,

      ii. a description of any research conducted by the expert that led him or her to form the opinion, and

      iii. a list of every document, if any, relied on by the expert in forming the opinion.

7.   An acknowledgement of expert's duty (Form 53) signed by the expert.

[40] The certificate mandated by rule 53.03(2.1) reads as follows:

ACKNOWLEDGMENT OF EXPERT'S DUTY

1. My name is . . . . *(name)*. I live at . . . . *(city)*, in the . . . . *(province/state)* of . . . . *(name of province/state)*.

2. I have been engaged by or on behalf of . . . . *(name of party/parties)* to provide evidence in relation to the above-noted court proceeding.

3. I acknowledge that it is my duty to provide evidence in relation to this proceeding as follows:

    (a) to provide opinion evidence that is fair, objective and non-partisan;

    (b) to provide opinion evidence that is related only to matters that are within my area of expertise; and

    (c) to provide such additional assistance as the court may reasonably require, to determine a matter in issue.

4. I acknowledge that the duty referred to above prevails over any obligation which I may owe to any party by whom or on whose behalf I am engaged.

Date . . . .

Signature

. . .

(v) Is it appropriate for counsel to review draft expert reports?

[50] I begin by considering the changes made to Dr. Taylor's report following discussion with counsel. Nowhere in her reasons does the trial judge explain which changes were significant. My review of the draft reports, the notes, the changes and Dr. Taylor's explanation indicates that the changes could be described as relatively minor editorial and stylistic modifications intended to improve the clarity of the reports. I can see no evidence of any significant change in substance, nor did counsel for the respondent on this appeal point to any such change. In my view, there is nothing in the record to indicate that either counsel or Dr. Taylor did anything improper or that Dr. Taylor's report reflected anything other than his own genuine and unbiased opinion.

[51] I now turn to the law. I disagree with the trial judge's statement that the 2010 amendments to rule 53.03 introduced a "change in the role of expert witnesses".

[52] As I read the amendments and the Osborne Report recommendations, the changes were intended to clarify and emphasize the existing duties of expert witnesses. I agree with Lederman J.'s statement in *Henderson v. Risi*, 2012 ONSC 3459, 111 O.R. (3d) 554 (S.C.), at para. 19, that these changes represent a restatement of the basic common law principle that it is the duty of an expert witness "to provide opinion evidence that is fair, objective and non-partisan." Those common law duties were summarized in an often cited passage from *National Justice Compania Naviera S.A. v. Prudential Assurance Co. Ltd.* (*"The Ikarian Reefer"*), [1993] 2 Lloyd's Rep. 68, at p. 81 (Eng. Q.B. Comm.), rev'd on other grounds but endorsed on this point, [1995] 1 Lloyd's Rep 455 (Eng. C.A. Civ.), at p. 496:

> 1. Expert evidence presented to the Court should be, and should be seen to be, the independent product of the expert uninfluenced as to form or content by the exigencies of litigation [citation omitted].

> 2. An expert witness should provide independent assistance to the Court by way of objective unbiased opinion in relation to matters within his expertise [citation omitted]. An expert witness. . . should never assume the role of an advocate.

The 2010 amendments to rule 53.03 did not create new duties but rather codified and reinforced these basic common law principles.

[53] The changes suggested by the trial judge find no support in the various reviews and studies on civil justice reform to which we have been referred. The Honourable Coulter Osborne certainly shared the trial judge's aspiration for a regime that fosters unbiased expert evidence, yet there is no suggestion in his report that the solution could be found by altering the long-standing practice of counsel reviewing draft reports.

[54] The *Inquiry into Pediatric Forensic Pathology in Ontario* (Toronto: Ontario Ministry of the Attorney General, 2008), conducted by Justice Stephen Goudge, looked into the shocking miscarriages of justice brought about by biased expert evidence. At p. 48 of his report, Justice Goudge stressed the importance of "[p]roperly prepared expert reports, along with a certification that the expert understands the duty to provide impartial advice to the court" in order to help ensure the reliability of expert evidence. Justice Goudge concluded, at p. 47, that proper communication with and preparation of expert witnesses was vital to enable them to communicate their opinions effectively to the court: "[C]ounsel, whether Crown or defence, should properly prepare forensic pathologists they intend to call to give evidence."

[55] While some judges have expressed concern that the impartiality of expert evidence may be tainted by discussions with counsel (see the cases cited below, at para. 72), banning undocumented discussions between counsel and expert witnesses or mandating disclosure of all written communications is unsupported by and contrary to existing authority: see *Maras v. Seemore Entertainment Ltd.,* 2014 BCSC 1109, [2014] B.C.W.L.D. 4470, at para. 90 ("[c]ounsel have a role in assisting experts to provide a report that satisfies the criteria of admissibility"); *Surrey Credit Union v. Willson* (1990), 45 B.C.L.R. (2d) 310 (S.C.), at para. 25 ("[t]here can be no criticism of counsel assisting an expert witness in the preparation of giving evidence"). In *Medimmune Ltd. v. Novartis Pharmaceuticals UK Ltd. & Anor*, [2011] EWHC 1669 (Pat.), the court pointed out, at para. 110, that in some highly technical areas such as patent law, expert witnesses "require a high level of instruction by the lawyers" which may necessitate "a high degree of consultation" involving "an iterative process through a number of drafts."

[56] As the court in *Medimmune* noted, at para. 111, "this process entails a risk of loss of objectivity on the part of the expert". However, the independence and objectivity of expert witnesses is fostered under existing law and practice in a number of ways.

[57] First, the ethical and professional standards of the legal profession forbid counsel from engaging in practices likely to interfere with the independence and objectivity of expert witnesses. I attach as an Appendix to these reasons The Advocates' Society's *Principles Governing Communications with Testifying Experts*, which provides a thorough and thoughtful statement of the professional standards pertaining to the preparation of expert witnesses. Principle 3 states:

> In fulfilling the advocate's duty to present clear, comprehensible and relevant expert evidence, the advocate should not communicate with an expert witness in any manner likely to interfere with the expert's duties of independence and objectivity.

[58] To the same effect, The Holland Group's position paper includes, at p. 4, its opinion "that it is inappropriate for counsel to persuade or attempt to

persuade experts to articulate opinions that they do not genuinely hold, and that it is of paramount importance that the expert genuinely believes the opinion that he or she articulates both in the expert report and in the witness box."

[59] In *Medimmune*, at para. 111, the court emphasized that it is "crucial that the lawyers involved should keep the expert's need to remain objective at the forefront of their minds at all times."

[60] Second, the ethical standards of other professional bodies place an obligation upon their members to be independent and impartial when giving expert evidence: see *Guideline: The Professional Engineer as an Expert Witness* (Toronto: Association of Professional Engineers of Ontario, September 2011); the Actuarial Standards Board's *Standards of Practice* (Ottawa: Canadian Institute of Actuaries, October 2014); the Canadian Institute of Chartered Business Valuators' *Code of Ethics* (Toronto: Canadian Institute of Chartered Business Valuators, 2012), *Standard No. 110: Valuation Reports* (Toronto: Canadian Institute of Chartered Business Valuators, 2009) and *Standard No. 310: Expert Reports* (Toronto: Canadian Institute of Chartered Business Valuators, 2010). Further, pursuant to the *Rules of Civil Procedure*, every expert witness is reminded of the duty imposed by rule 4.1.01 to be objective and impartial when signing the acknowledgment of expert's duty mandated by rule 53.03(2.1).

[61] Third, the adversarial process, particularly through cross-examination, provides an effective tool to deal with cases where there is an air of reality to the suggestion that counsel improperly influenced an expert witness. Judges have not shied away from rejecting or limiting the weight to be given to the evidence of an expert witness where there is evidence of a lack of independence or impartiality. In *Medimmune*, at para. 111, the court noted that "partisan expert evidence is almost always exposed as such in cross-examination, which is likely to reduce, if not eliminate, the value of the evidence to the client's case"; see also *Alfano v. Piersanti*, 2012 ONCA 297, 291 O.A.C. 62, at paras. 106-120.

[62] I agree with the submissions of the appellant and the interveners that it would be bad policy to disturb the well-established practice of counsel meeting with expert witnesses to review draft reports. Just as lawyers and judges need the input of experts, so too do expert witnesses need the assistance of lawyers in framing their reports in a way that is comprehensible and responsive to the pertinent legal issues in a case.

[63] Consultation and collaboration between counsel and expert witnesses is essential to ensure that the expert witness understands the duties reflected by rule 4.1.01 and contained in the Form 53 acknowledgment of expert's duty. Reviewing a draft report enables counsel to ensure that the report (i) complies with the *Rules of Civil Procedure* and the rules of evidence, (ii) addresses and is restricted to the relevant issues and (iii) is written in a manner and style that is

accessible and comprehensible. Counsel need to ensure that the expert witness understands matters such as the difference between the legal burden of proof and scientific certainty, the need to clarify the facts and assumptions underlying the expert's opinion, the need to confine the report to matters within the expert witness's area of expertise and the need to avoid usurping the court's function as the ultimate arbiter of the issues.

[64] Counsel play a crucial mediating role by explaining the legal issues to the expert witness and then by presenting complex expert evidence to the court. It is difficult to see how counsel could perform this role without engaging in communication with the expert as the report is being prepared.

[65] Leaving the expert witness entirely to his or her own devices, or requiring all changes to be documented in a formalized written exchange, would result in increased delay and cost in a regime already struggling to deliver justice in a timely and efficient manner. Such a rule would encourage the hiring of "shadow experts" to advise counsel. There would be an incentive to jettison rather than edit and improve badly drafted reports, causing added cost and delay. Precluding consultation would also encourage the use of those expert witnesses who make a career of testifying in court and who are often perceived to be hired guns likely to offer partisan opinions, as these expert witnesses may require less guidance and preparation. In my respectful view, the changes suggested by the trial judge would not be in the interests of justice and would frustrate the timely and cost-effective adjudication of civil disputes.

[66] For these reasons, I reject the trial judge's proclamation that the practice of consultation between counsel and expert witnesses to review draft reports must end. However, as I will discuss below, the trial judge's unwarranted criticism of the appellant's counsel on this basis did not, in my view, affect the outcome of the trial.

(b) Examples

Do you agree with the following applications of *Mohan* and *J. (J.-L.)*? Do you think that applying *White Burgess Langille Inman, Trochym* or *Abbey* would lead to a different result?

R. v. TERCEIRA
(1998), 15 C.R. (5th) 359, 123 C.C.C. (3d) 1 (Ont. C.A.)

The accused was convicted of murder. Hair, fibre, blood and DNA evidence which matched the accused was left on the floor at the attack site and on the victim's clothing. One of the main arguments on the appeal related to the admissibility of the DNA evidence and the instruction to the jury respecting it. The Supreme Court in an endorsement agreed with the courts below.

Finlayson J.A. (Brooke and Mckinlay JJ.A., concurring):—

. . .

DNA profiling is a comparatively new method of providing identification evidence for use in criminal cases. DNA evidence is used essentially for two purposes. The first use of DNA evidence is as evidence that the suspect's DNA "matches" the DNA found in blood, semen or tissue recovered at a crime scene. In this way, the DNA evidence serves an exclusionary purpose. In the absence of further qualifications, a "match" is no more than a failure to exclude a suspect's DNA from the crime scene. The debate at trial with respect to the determination of a match, as was the case during the trial of this matter, will often focus on the methodology used to determine a match. The second branch of the analysis of DNA evidence involves the application of population genetics. Probability statistics are introduced in an attempt to bolster the significance of a "match". The scientist determines, according to an established database of known DNA samples, the statistical likelihood that another individual person would have the same DNA pattern as that of the suspect. Simply stated, this second branch considers the statistical likelihood of a random DNA match. Cross-examination of the expert tendering DNA evidence serving this second purpose will usually focus on the methodology used to calculate the numbers reflecting the frequency of the DNA pattern. The DNA evidence in the present case was used by the Crown for the above two purposes.

. . .

Both Crown and defence counsel on the DNA *voir dire* devoted a considerable portion of their submissions to a discussion of the standard to be applied in relation to the admission of novel scientific evidence. Crown counsel discussed the standard of "relevancy and helpfulness" as well as "relevancy and reliability". Defence counsel made submissions in favour of the adoption of the more restrictive "*Frye*" test articulated by the United States Supreme Court in *Frye v. United States*, 293 F.1013. Both counsel explicitly referred the trial judge to the decision in *R. v. Johnston* (1992), 69 C.C.C. (3d) 395, 12 C.R. (4th) 99 (Ont. Gen. Div.), wherein Langdon J. adopted a "reliability" standard. The trial judge characterized the defence position on the *voir dire* as urging "that the Crown has not produced sufficient evidence on the *voir dire* to support the reliability and admissibility of Pamella Newall's techniques in analysis". The foregoing demonstrates that the trial judge was aware that initial determinations of reliability would be required before the proposed DNA evidence could be proffered at trial. Moreover, the appellant concedes that the trial judge recognized that reliability was a preliminary finding of fact that would need to be made before the proposed DNA evidence was admissible.

. . .

Relying upon the judgment of the Supreme Court of Canada in *R. v. Mohan*, counsel for the appellant submits that before the jury can be permitted to hear the evidence of DNA testing, the trial judge is required as a matter of law to conduct what he calls a "*Mohan* type hearing" in order to satisfy himself beyond a reasonable doubt as to the reliability of the evidence adduced by the experts for the Crown. By this counsel for the appellant suggests that the trial judge must satisfy himself as to the acceptance of the technology in the scientific community, the expertise of the Crown witnesses in that field, and the accuracy of the tests carried out pursuant to that technology, among other factors. All this to the criminal standard of proof. Then, and only then, can the same evidence be recalled for the consideration of the jury.

I have some considerable difficulty with this submission which, with respect, reflects a misreading of *Mohan*. In my opinion, the rules laid down by Sopinka J. in *R. v. Mohan* do not signify a departure from the common law rules relating to the admission of opinion evidence in a criminal trial, nor do they purport to do so. The four criteria for the admissibility of expert testimony are derived from case-law. . . . Prior to *Mohan*, when relevant expert opinion evidence has been proffered, Canadian courts focused on two factors in determining its admissibility: the special knowledge criterion and the expertise criterion. In *R. v. Abbey*, [1982] 2 S.C.R. 24 at p. 42, Dickson J. provided the following formulation of the "special knowledge" requirement for the admissibility of expert evidence:

> With respect to matters calling for special knowledge, an expert in the field may draw inferences and state his opinion. An expert's function is precisely this: to provide the judge and jury with a ready-made inference which the judge and jury, due to the technical nature of the facts, are unable to formulate. "An expert's opinion is admissible to furnish the Court with scientific information which is likely to be outside the experience and knowledge of a judge or jury. If on the proven facts a judge or jury can form their own conclusions without help, then the opinion of the expert is unnecessary (*R. v. Turner* (1974), 60 Cr. App. R. 80, at p. 83, per Lawton L.J.).

· · ·

It is to be observed that the word "reliable" is not listed among Sopinka J.'s four criteria. It is, however, discussed under "relevance" under his "cost-benefit analysis" as to whether expert evidence that is otherwise logically relevant may be excluded on the basis that its probative value is overborne by its prejudicial effect.

· · ·

In the appeal before this court the tension is between the probative value of the opinion evidence versus its prejudicial effect in the sense that its effect on the jury may be out of proportion to its reliability. *Mohan* stands as authority for the proposition that expert evidence which may be logically probative of an issue at trial may be nonetheless excluded in certain circumstances. Additionally, in light of the judicial reasoning from *Mohan*, since we are confronted with what was at the time of trial perceived to be a novel scientific theory or technique, we are concerned with the threshold issue of reliability, i.e., is the science itself valid. As I understand *Mohan*, with reference to the case in appeal, the requirement of a basic threshold of reliability as a pre-condition to admissibility is met where the trial judge is satisfied as to the reliability of DNA profiling as a novel scientific technique. Where the Crown and defence part company is with respect to the extent of the inquiry necessary to establish this pre-condition.

Our task is considerably narrowed by the concession of appellant's counsel that he is not suggesting that DNA profiling has not been found reliable in other jurisdictions. The appellant does not take issue with the microbiological aspects of DNA profiling. No general concern was raised at trial about the ability of the Centre of Forensic Science ("CFS") to extract DNA from biological substances and to isolate and remove regions on human chromosomes which are suitable for testing nor to determine whether any two samples were a "match" one to the other. Nor is counsel for the appellant suggesting that the process used by the CFS in this case, involving RFLP or "restriction fragment length polymorphism" analysis, is not an accepted methodology for DNA profiling. Rather, the complaint was that the DNA laboratory was only established by the CFS a few months prior to the testing in this case and there was no general acceptance of its specific methodology used to determine the statistical likelihood of a random match. The attack was not upon the technology of DNA profiling per se but upon the ability of the CFS, notably its principal expert Pamella Newall, to reliably utilize it. In addition, the appellant challenged the introduction of the probability figures as their prejudicial effect would exceed the probative value of presenting quantitative statements of random match probability as opposed to qualitative measures.

. . .

The jury was given frequency numbers that ranged from one in 1,500 to one in 1.8 million. The appellant concedes the admissibility of qualitative expressions of match significance (such as "rare" or "common") without the specifics afforded by statistics where DNA evidence is admitted showing a match between the DNA found on the crime scene and the DNA of a suspect, counsel for the appellant objects simply to the admission of the numbers themselves. In this case, it would be difficult to translate the figures the experts were prepared to use into neutral language, but all that aside, why would the defence want to do so? The fact that there are competing figures which differ so radically should be before the jury for its assessment. The range of numeric frequency determined by the various experts was fertile ground for cross-examination. This is a classic case for the application of the language of Dickson C.J.C. in *R. v. Corbett*, [1988] 1 S.C.R. 670 at p. 692:

> The very strength of the jury is that the ultimate issue of guilt or innocence is determined by a group of ordinary citizens who are not legal specialists and who bring to the legal process a healthy measure of common sense. The jury is, of course, bound to follow the law as it is explained by the trial judge. Jury directions are often long and difficult, but the experience of trial judges is that juries do perform their duty according to the law. We should regard with grave suspicion arguments which assert that depriving the jury of all relevant information is preferable to giving them everything, with a careful explanation as to any limitations on the use to which they may put that information.

I do not believe that there should be an absolute prohibition against the introduction of specific match figures. The appellant correctly notes that the case-law reflects conflicting conclusions as to the admissibility of DNA probability statistics in this case, and it might be in others. I would leave the matter to the discretion of the trial judge in the particular case.[327]

R. v. McINTOSH
(1997), 117 C.C.C. (3d) 385 (Ont. C.A.)

The accused were convicted of various offences as a result of a robbery. The case for the Crown consisted primarily of three eyewitnesses. The trial judge refused to admit expert opinion evidence from a defence psychologist tendered on the issue of eyewitness identification. The psychologist had written extensively on the psychology of witness testimony and claimed that it was a specialty which he had pursued over the years. His evidence related to the frailties of eyewitness identification, including factors present at the time of the offence that would impair the witness' ability to make an accurate identification, the problem of cross-racial identification, the quality of memory recall for perceived events over different time spans, and the influence of "post-event information" on memory.

FINLAYSON J.A. (LABROSSE and AUSTIN JJ.A. concurring):—

. . .

The general tenor of [the expert's] evidence is summed up in his own words:

> Well, the understanding of jurors, and how they perceive is what psychologists spend their lives doing. We hope to be able to assist the judge or the jury on the various levels and factors of what would lead to a good or a poor identification. It is not my job to decide whether or not that is the answer. All I can do is assist the trier in understanding, 'Here are the reasons why it could be a good identification or a poor one'.

I am astonished at the passivity of the Crown at trial and on appeal with respect to this type of evidence. At trial, Crown counsel contented himself with the early observation that the witness had said nothing that would convince him that a psychologist would know what information would be "probative" to the trial. However, he did not cross-examine Dr. Yarmey on his qualifications, or at all, and seemed to accept that the substance of his testimony was properly the subject-matter of expert evidence. On appeal, Crown counsel limited his argument to the submission that we should defer to the trial judge who rejected the evidence in the exercise of her discretion. He was careful, however, to state that there could be cases in which this evidence could be admitted.

This posture is not surprising given the reliance by the Crown on the "soft sciences" in other cases. In *R. v. Norman* (1993), 87 C.C.C. (3d) 153 (C.A.) the Crown introduced psychiatric evidence of child abuse accommodation syndrome which was misused by the trial judge and resulted in this court

---

[327]   *Terceira* was affirmed (1999), 142 C.C.C. (3d) 95 (S.C.C.) and applied in *R. v. Fisher* (2003), 18 C.R. (6th) 377, 179 C.C.C. (3d) 138 (Sask. C.A.).

setting aside the conviction of the accused. In *R. v. Edwards* (1996), 105 C.C.C. (3d) 21 (C.A.) (leave to appeal to S.C.C. refused August 29, 1996) the Crown attempted unsuccessfully to introduce expert testimony in the form of affidavits to support two Crown appeals against sentences imposed upon the respondents following their pleas of guilty to charges of attempted spousal homicide. The affidavits were sworn by three persons with differing professional backgrounds. All three deponents, however, had written extensively on issues relating to spousal abuse. They advocated the need for greater public awareness and participation in dealing with this pressing social problem. This court dismissed the motion for fresh evidence, holding that it was of marginal relevance to the sentencing issue and smacked of special pleading.

In the light of the limited argument before this court on the matter, it is evident that this is not the case to engage in a full-scale analysis as to whether the type of evidence proffered by Dr. Yarmey is admissible in any circumstance. However, I do not intend to leave the subject without raising some warning flags. In my respectful opinion, the courts are overly eager to abdicate their fact-finding responsibilities to "experts" in the field of the behavioural sciences. We are too quick to say that a particular witness possesses special knowledge and experience going beyond that of the trier of fact without engaging in an analysis of the subject-matter of that expertise. I do not want to be taken as denigrating the integrity of Dr. Yarmey's research or of his expertise in the field of psychology, clearly one of the learned sciences, but simply because a person has lectured and written extensively on a subject that is of interest to him or her does not constitute him or her an expert for the purposes of testifying in a court of law on the subject of that specialty. It seems to me that before we even get to the point of examining the witness's expertise, we must ask ourselves if the subject-matter of his testimony admits of expert testimony. Where is the evidence in this case that there is a recognized body of scientific knowledge that defines rules of human behaviour affecting memory patterns such that any expert in that field can evaluate the reliability of the identification made by a particular witness in a given case? Paraphrasing freely from the definition of "science" in *The Shorter Oxford English Dictionary on Historical Principles*, it seems to me that before a witness can be permitted to testify as an expert, the court must be satisfied that the subject-matter of his or her expertise is a branch of study in psychology concerned with a connected body of demonstrated truths or with observed facts systematically classified and more or less connected together by a common hypothesis operating under general laws. The branch should include trustworthy methods for the discovery of new truths within its own domain. I should add that it would be helpful if there was evidence that the existence of such a branch was generally accepted within the science of psychology.

The definitive judgment on the admissibility of expert evidence in criminal cases is *R. v. Mohan* which was relied upon by both parties to this appeal. . . . I would caution courts to scrutinize the nature of the subject-matter of the expert testimony. Any natural or unnatural phenomenon may become the subject of an investigation conducted according to the scientific method. The scientific method requires the formation of a hypothesis, the testing of the hypothesis using reliable methodology, the examination of the results (usually with statistical analysis) and the formation of a conclusion. However, the fact that the testimony recites the application of the scientific method does not necessarily render the original object of study a matter requiring opinion evidence at trial.

As is implicit in what I have written above, I have some serious reservations as to whether the "Psychology of Witness Testimony" is an appropriate area for opinion evidence at all. I acknowledge that the subject is interesting and Dr. Yarmey's presentation is informative. I also applaud his evidence that he lectures on the subject to police officers. We should all be reminded of the frailties of identification evidence. However, I would have to be persuaded that the subject is a recognized branch of psychology. Even if it is, I do not think that it meets the tests for relevance and necessity set out in *Mohan*.

In the case in appeal, I think that I can deal with relevance and necessity together because they appear to overlap. This opinion evidence is noteworthy in that, unlike most expert psychological or psychiatric testimony, it is not directed to making the testimony of a particular witness more understandable to the trier of fact and therefore more believable (e.g., an explanation of repressed memory syndrome or battered spouse syndrome). This opinion evidence is directed to instructing the jury that all witnesses have problems in perception and recall with respect to what occurred during any given circumstance that is brief and stressful. Accordingly, Dr. Yarmey is not testifying to matters that are outside the normal experience of the trier of fact: he is reminding the jury of the normal experience.

Perhaps I can develop this point through illustration. I suggest that it would be a different situation if a Crown witness had demonstrated remarkable memory feats which would strike the normal juror as startling and therefore less capable of belief. In this hypothetical situation, expert evidence might be admissible to show that the witness is an autistic savant and that such exceptional memory feats are often associated with this syndrome. Or to deal with an example closer to the case at hand, Dr. Yarmey was prepared to testify as to the problems of "cross-racial identification": the perception that members of one race tend to think that members of another race "all look alike". Dr. Yarmey's research supports this popular perception and his opinion on the subject is hardly surprising. But before this opinion evidence could be outside the normal experience of the jurors, would he not have had to conclude that the perception was false and that a cross-racial identification problem did not exist?

This is not to say that a reminder as to cross-racial identification is not appropriate in a case where it is an issue. However, the argument that impresses me is that such a reminder from the trial judge is more than adequate, especially when it is incorporated into the well-established warnings in the standard jury charge on the frailties of identification evidence. Writings, such as those of Dr. Yarmey, are helpful in stimulating an ongoing evaluation of the problem of witness identification, but they should be used to update the judge's charge, not instruct the jury. I think that there is a very real danger that such evidence would "distort the fact-finding process".

More than that I am concerned that much of what Dr. Yarmey and those who support him are saying is that our jury system is not adequate to the task of determining the guilt of an accused person beyond a reasonable doubt where identification evidence is pivotal to the case for the Crown. Much of Dr. Yarmey's evidence might well give us pause to consider whether our present jury instruction is adequate to the task, but to admit such evidence in the particular case may foster apprehension in the timorous juror and give him or her an excuse for not discharging that juror's duty to the community that he or she has sworn to serve.

An additional problem is that this evidence introduces yet another potentially contentious issue into the trial. If the defence is entitled to call this opinion evidence, the Crown is entitled to rebut it. This means that the jury has to be instructed as how conflicts in the opinions of experts are to be resolved, and when resolved, as to the limited use of the evidence. The jury must also be told that to the extent that the opinion evidence contradicts anything said by the trial judge in his or her charge, the jury must reject the evidence and accept what is said by the judge. Would it not be simpler to have the trial judge give the instruction in the first place?

In the case in appeal, the trial judge had the benefit of hearing all of Dr. Yarmey's evidence and of listening to full argument as to its merits and admissibility. In the end, she appears to have had the same reservations as I do with respect to its quality. While she premised her ultimate refusal to admit the evidence upon the failure to meet the necessity test in *Mohan*, in the course of delivering her reasons she stated:

> I do not agree, based on the evidence I've heard from Dr. Yarmey, that the science has advanced that far away from the common experience of jurors.

To address the specific ground of appeal in this case, I am of the opinion that the manner in which the issue of identification was handled by the court (and by "court" I mean the trial judge and counsel for the Crown and the defence) was a model of fairness. The trial judge was correct in rejecting the proffered expert evidence. Her charge to the jury, following the very full closing arguments of all counsel, was exemplary. She impressed upon the jury the frailties of witness identification evidence generally and then, in considerable detail, she set out the identification problems as they applied to the particular facts of the case.

. . .

We were referred to a number of cases from courts in the United States where expert evidence on identification has been accepted. We were also referred to *William Daubert v. Merrell Dow Pharmaceuticals Inc.*, 113 S.Ct. Rep. 2786 (1993), a decision of the United States Supreme Court which considered the admissibility of expert testimony generally under the Federal Rules of Evidence, Rule 702, 28 U.S.C.A. These cases must be approached with caution because the rules of court under consideration are dissimilar to ours. Moreover, juries in this jurisdiction receive significantly more assistance from the trial judge in their instruction than do juries in the United States. For this reason alone, expert testimony on matters which are covered by the jury instruction has less appeal. Our judges are not only encouraged to comment on the evidence, there are some cases in which they are obliged to do so.

This was such a case and the trial judge took full advantage of it. She was in a far better position than any witness or counsel to point out the frailties of the identification evidence, and her opinions, which she expressed, would have a very positive effect on the jury. She was also in a position to place these frailties in the context of the case for the Crown as a whole and she did that as well. This was not a "straight" identification case as counsel for the appellants submitted. After reading the complete charge of the trial judge on all of the evidence, I am left with no concern about the soundness of the verdict in this case. I would reject this ground of appeal.[328]

Given the findings of many inquiries and studies in Canada, the United States and England that identification evidence is a major cause of wrongful convictions[329] is it time to over-rule *McIntosh?*[330]

R. v. MARQUARD
[1993] 4 S.C.R. 223, 25 C.R. (4th) 1, 85 C.C.C. (3d) 193

The accused was charged with aggravated assault on her 3 1/2-year-old granddaughter. The allegation was that she put the complainant's face against a hot stove door as a way of disciplining her. In her unsworn testimony, the complainant testified that her "nana" had put her on the stove. The accused and her husband testified that they heard the complainant screaming and when they arrived saw that she had burned herself trying to light a cigarette with a butane lighter. The defence called Dr. Mian to testify that the complainant had told hospital staff that she had been burned with a lighter. The Crown cross-examined Dr. Mian and elicited evidence about whether in her opinion the complainant was telling the truth. The admissibility of this evidence was one of the issues before the Supreme Court.

MCLACHLIN J. (speaking for the Court on this point):

---

[328]   On the issue of the helpfulness of expert testimony on eyewitness identification, see Loftus & Doyle, *Eyewitness Testimony, Civil and Criminal*, 3rd ed. (Lexis Law Publishing, 1997).

[329]   See e.g. P. Cory, The Inquiry Regarding Thomas Sophonow, "Recommendations" at <http://www.gov.mb.ca/justice/sophonow/recommendations/english.html>. See also the discussion of the admissibility of expert evidence in this context in D. Schermbrucker, "Eyewitness Evidence: The Role of Experts in the Criminal Courts" ADGN/RP-186 and S. Woller, "Rethinking The Role of Expert Testimony Regarding the Reliability of Eyewitness Identifications in New York" (2004) 79 New York Law School Law Review 323.

[330]   *McIntosh* was followed in *R. v. Woodard* (2009), 245 C.C.C. (3d) 522, 67 C.R. (6th) 152 (Man. C.A.), holding that the eyewitness expert had been rightly rejected as superfluous. A week earlier, a trial judge, Sinclair J., in *R. v. Henderson* (2009), 67 C.R. (6th) 132 (Man. Q.B.) admitted the evidence of such an expert. In his view, eyewitness evidence should be excluded where it only reminds jurors of what they already know but admitted where it lies outside common experience, overcomes myths or provides scientifically sound counterintuitive information. In her C.R. annotation, Lisa Dufraimont applauds this test for deciding whether evidence of eyewitness experts should exceptionally be admitted.

5. Expert Comment on the Credibility of the Child

47 The defence called Dr. Mian to prove that the child, upon arriving at Sick Children's Hospital, told the staff that she had burned herself with a lighter. The Crown, in cross-examination, elicited from Dr. Mian the opinion that the child was lying when she told her that she had burned herself with a cigarette lighter. She testified that it is quite common that children "will initially. . . give the accidental explanation and later on will give us a story that is more consistent with her injury which is then put in a more convincing [manner] which we believe is the first disclosure of what actually happened." She also testified that even if the child's burn had looked like a lighter burn, she would have been suspicious of the child's story "because of the way the child said it. . ."

48 Dr. Mian went on to buttress her view that the child's actual explanation was a lie by reference to the behaviour of abused children:

> There's another reason [why children initially lie] which is that children who have been abused often feel that they are responsible for the behaviour that was done to them, for the injury that was inflicted on them.... Therefore if the care taker then takes them to the hospital and they're feeling that they did something wrong to elicit this punishment, they're certainly not going to want to tell the hospital staff that they did something wrong because they feel if my mom or whoever did this to me because of what I did, I wonder what these people who are strangers are going to do to me because of what I did.

The purport of this evidence was clear. Dr. Mian was of the view that the child was lying when she told the hospital staff that she had burned herself with a lighter, and that the child's second story—the one she told at trial—was the truth.

49 It is a fundamental axiom of our trial process that the ultimate conclusion as to the credibility or truthfulness of a particular witness is for the trier of fact, and is not the proper subject of expert opinion. This Court affirmed that proposition in *R. v. Béland, supra*, at p. 408, in rejecting the use of polygraph examinations as a tool to determine the credibility of witnesses:

> From the foregoing comments, it will be seen that the rule against oath-helping, that is, adducing evidence solely for the purpose of bolstering a witness's credibility, is well grounded in authority.

A judge or jury who simply accepts an expert's opinion on the credibility of a witness would be abandoning its duty to itself determine the credibility of the witness. Credibility must always be the product of the judge or jury's view of the diverse ingredients it has perceived at trial, combined with experience, logic and an intuitive sense of the matter: see *R. v. B. (G.)* (1988), 65 Sask. R. 134 (C.A.), at p. 149, per Wakeling J.A., affirmed [1990] 2 S.C.R. 3. Credibility is a matter within the competence of lay people. Ordinary people draw conclusions about whether someone is lying or telling the truth on a daily basis. The expert who testifies on credibility is not sworn to the heavy duty of a judge or juror. Moreover, the expert's opinion may be founded on factors which are not in the evidence upon which the judge and juror are duty-bound to render a true verdict. Finally, credibility is a notoriously difficult problem, and the expert's opinion may be all too readily accepted by a frustrated jury as a convenient basis upon which to resolve its difficulties. All these considerations have contributed to the wise policy of the law in rejecting expert evidence on the truthfulness of witnesses.

50 On the other hand, there may be features of a witness's evidence which go beyond the ability of a lay person to understand, and hence which may justify expert evidence. This is particularly the case in the evidence of children. For example, the ordinary inference from failure to complain promptly about a sexual assault might be that the story is a fabricated afterthought, born of malice or some other calculated stratagem. Expert evidence has been properly led to explain the reasons why young victims of sexual abuse often do not complain immediately. Such evidence is helpful; indeed it may be essential to a just verdict.

51 For this reason, there is a growing consensus that while expert evidence on the ultimate credibility of a witness is not admissible, expert evidence on human conduct and the psychological and physical factors which may lead to certain behaviour relevant to credibility, is admissible, provided the testimony goes beyond the ordinary experience of the trier of fact. Professor A. Mewett describes the permissible use of this sort of evidence as "putting the witness's testimony in its proper context." He states in the editorial "Credibility and Consistency" (1991), 33 *Crim. L.Q.* 385, at p. 386:

> The relevance of his testimony is to assist — no more — the jury in determining whether there is an explanation for what might otherwise be regarded as conduct that is inconsistent with that of a truthful witness. It does, of course, bolster the credibility of that witness, but it is evidence of how certain people react to certain experiences. Its relevance lies not in testimony that the prior witness is telling the truth but in testimony as to human behaviour. . . .
>
> There are concerns. As the court stated in *R. v. J. (F.E.)*, [(1990), 53 C.C.C. (3d) 94, 74 C.R. (3d) 269, 36 O.A.C. 348 (C.A.)], and *R. v. C. (R.A.)* (1990), 57 C.C.C. (3d) 522, 78 C.R. (3d) 390, the court must require that the witness be an expert in the particular area of human conduct in question; the evidence must be of the sort that the jury needs because the problem is beyond their ordinary experience; and the jury must be carefully instructed as to its function and duty in making the final decision without being unduly influenced by the expert nature of the evidence.

52 The conditions set out by Professor Mewett, reflecting the observations of various appellate courts which have considered the matter, recommend themselves as sound. To accept this approach is not to open the floodgates to expert testimony on whether witnesses are lying or telling the truth. It is rather to recognize that certain aspects of human behaviour which are important to the judge or jury's assessment of credibility may not be understood by the lay person and hence require elucidation by experts in human behaviour.

53 Had Dr. Mian confined her comments to expert evidence explaining why children may lie to hospital staff about the cause of their injuries, there could have been no objection to her evidence. She was an expert in child behaviour, and the evidence would arguably have been evidence needed by a lay jury to understand fully the implications of the witness's change in story. However, Dr. Mian went further. She clearly indicated that she personally did not believe the first story of the child, preferring the second version which the child told at trial. In so doing, she crossed the line between expert testimony on human behaviour and assessment of credibility of the witness herself. Moreover, the trial judge failed to instruct the jury that it was their duty to decide on the child's credibility without being unduly influenced by the expert evidence. In fact, the trial judge's statement that Dr. Mian gave "evidence as an expert in child abuse and relating to the truthfulness of the testimony of small children" actually reinforced the effect of the inadmissible evidence.

54 In my view, this error, considered with the others, requires that a new trial be directed.

R. v. D. (D.)
[2000] 2 S.C.R. 275, 36 C.R. (5th) 261, 148 C.C.C. (3d) 41

The accused was charged with sexual assault. The complainant alleged that the accused had sexually assaulted her when she was 5 to 6 years old. The complainant told no one about these events for 2 1/2 years. At trial, defence counsel cross-examined the complainant, who was 10 years old at the time, on the lengthy delay in reporting the incidents and suggested that she had fabricated the story. The Crown called a child psychologist to testify that a child's delay in alleging sexual abuse does not support an inference of falsehood. During a *voir dire*, the psychologist gave a general explanation applicable to all children that delayed disclosure could occur for a variety of reasons and did not indicate the lack of truth of an allegation. The trial judge admitted the expert evidence and the jury found the accused guilty of sexual assault and invitation to sexual touching. The Court of Appeal held that the expert evidence should not have been admitted because it was neither relevant nor necessary. The guilty verdict was set aside for this and other reasons, and a new trial was ordered. The Crown appealed from the finding that the expert evidence was inadmissible but agreed that the order for a new trial was warranted based on the Court of Appeal's other reasons for setting aside the verdict.

McLACHLIN C.J. (L'HEUREUX-DUBÉ and GONTHIER JJ. concurring), dissenting:—

. . .

During the *voir dire*, Dr. Marshall discussed delayed disclosure of child sexual abuse, based on his knowledge of the scientific literature in the area. He testified that there are many factors which can affect the timing of a complaint, including the relationship between the child and the abuser and the nature of the abuse. Some factors might discourage children from reporting abuse, such as embarrassment; fear of getting themselves or others into trouble; bribery or threats by the perpetrator; fear of being punished or sent away; disruption of the family; or fear that they would not be believed. Young children might also not fully comprehend what happened or not see anything wrong with the abuse.

Dr. Marshall also discussed the timing of allegations of abuse and its relevance to determining whether the abuse actually occurred. In his opinion, most sexual abuse is never disclosed, so one cannot assume that disclosure normally happens immediately. He testified that children disclose at various lengths of time after the event, so there is a continuum from immediate disclosure to delayed disclosure to no disclosure. When cross-examined by defence counsel as to whether the profile of a victim of abuse could be developed by reference to the timing of the complaint, Dr. Marshall stated "the fact of the delay . . . doesn't even enter into my thinking as to whether or not it happened. . . . [T]he research says that the length of time before a child reveals something is not diagnostic". The trial judge asked him to clarify what it means when delay is "not diagnostic", to which Dr. Marshall responded "[i]t proves nothing either way".

. . .

The test for the admissibility of expert evidence was consolidated in *Mohan*. Four criteria must be met by a party which seeks to introduce expert evidence: relevance, necessity, the lack of any other exclusionary rule, and a properly qualified expert. Even where these requirements are met, the evidence may be rejected if its prejudicial effect on the conduct of the trial outweighs its probative value.

The application of the four *Mohan* criteria is case-specific. Determinations of relevance and necessity, as well as the assessment of whether the prejudicial effect of the evidence outweighs its probative value, must be made within the factual context of the trial. . . . The case-specific nature of the inquiry means that an appellate court cannot lay down in advance broad rules that particular categories of expert evidence are always inadmissible. Such a categorical approach would undermine *Mohan*'s requirement of a case-by-case analysis of the four applicable criteria.

It follows that we cannot say as a general rule that expert evidence on a child's delay in reporting sexual assault is always admissible. Nor can we say it is never admissible. We can only say that it may be admissible if the four *Mohan* criteria are satisfied and if the prejudicial impact of the evidence does not outweigh its probative value. The trial judge erred if he took the comments in *Marquard* as indicating as a matter of stare decisis that expert evidence on delayed disclosure always meets the necessity test. By the same token, it would be erroneous to say that such evidence can never be admitted, as the Crown submits the Court of Appeal suggested. Admissibility of expert evidence must be determined on a case-by-case basis in the factual context of the case as it develops.

Against this background, I turn to the issue of whether the *Mohan* criteria for admissibility were met in this case.

A. Relevance

The trial judge found Dr. Marshall's evidence relevant to a fact in issue — the significance of the child's delay in reporting. The Court of Appeal, by contrast, held that the evidence was not relevant to a fact in issue, but only to the complainant's credibility.

In my view, the trial judge was correct in finding that Dr. Marshall's evidence was relevant to a fact in issue at the trial. The trial turned on the credibility of the complainant. If her testimony was believed, the offence was proved as charged. If there was a reasonable doubt about her credibility, the case was not made out. The issue of delay was subsidiary to the complainant's credibility. The "fact in issue" was whether a child's delay in reporting sexual abuse suggests that the alleged abuse did not occur. The defence put that fact in issue by indicating that it would ask the jury to infer from the delay in reporting that the alleged events were not real occurrences but fabrications. According to the defence, the complainant "was not credible because she waited too long". That was the fact in issue. Dr. Marshall's evidence was relevant to that issue because he discussed reasons other than fabrication, such as fear of not being believed, that might explain why a child would delay reporting sexual abuse.

. . .

The Court of Appeal reasoned that Dr. Marshall's evidence should be excluded because it represented "a blatant attempt to bolster the credibility of the only witness the Crown had to the alleged assault". Finlayson J.A. noted the principle, with which I agree, that the actual credibility of a particular witness is not generally the proper subject of opinion evidence: see *R. v. Béland*, [1987] 2 S.C.R. 398; *Marquard*, supra; *R. v. B. (F.F.)*, [1993] 1 S.C.R 697; *Mohan*, supra; *R. v. Burns*, [1994] 1 S.C.R. 656. This is known as the rule against oath-helping. In my view, Dr. Marshall's evidence did not violate that principle. In *Marquard*, supra, at p. 249, I noted that

> there is a growing consensus that while expert evidence on the ultimate credibility of a witness is not admissible, expert evidence on human conduct and the psychological and physical factors which may lead to certain behaviour relevant to credibility, is admissible, provided the testimony goes beyond the ordinary experience of the trier of fact.

. . .

B. Necessity

When it comes to necessity, the question is whether the expert will provide information which is likely to be outside the ordinary experience and knowledge of the trier of fact: *Burns*, supra; *Mohan*, supra; *R. v. Lavallee*, [1990] 1 S.C.R. 852; *R. v. Abbey*, [1982] 2 S.C.R. 24; *Kelliher (Village of) v. Smith*, [1931] S.C.R. 672. "Necessity" means that the evidence must be more than merely "helpful", but necessity need not be judged "by too strict a standard": *Mohan*, supra, at p. 23. Absolute necessity is not required.

. . .

The issue again may be put in simple terms: was there a sufficient basis for the trial judge to conclude that the issue of the child's delay in disclosure might involve matters beyond the ordinary knowledge and expertise of the jury? Was the evidence necessary to enable the trier of fact to properly dispose of the credibility issue? In answering this question, we must bear in mind that the trial judge is in the best position of determining the level of the jurors' understanding and what may assist them. In my view, there was an ample foundation for the trial judge's conclusion that Dr. Marshall's evidence went beyond the ordinary knowledge and expertise of the jury.

. . .

Given the additional assistance that Dr. Marshall's testimony may have provided to the jury, I cannot conclude that the trial judge erred by failing to find that it was unnecessary because he could have given a jury warning. This is particularly so in view of the fact that the defence never raised this argument at trial. That said, the trial judge on the new trial should consider whether the expert's testimony is necessary to that trial in light of all the relevant circumstances, including the arguments of counsel and the possibility of a judicial instruction.

C. No Other Exclusionary Rule

The third criterion for admitting expert evidence is that it must not be excluded by the operation of any other rule. The only exclusionary rule raised here is the principle that an expert may not testify on the ultimate issue of credibility. As discussed earlier, this rule was not violated because Dr. Marshall testified on an issue that was subsidiary to the complainant's credibility. He did not express an opinion on whether her allegations were true or false. It was left for the jury to determine whether they accepted all, some or none of the evidence of the complainant.

D. Properly Qualified Expert

The final requirement for admissibility is that the expert be properly qualified. Neither the accused nor the Court of Appeal suggested that Dr. Marshall was not properly qualified to testify on the subject of delayed disclosure.

E. Probative Value Versus Prejudicial Effects

As with the other elements of the *Mohan* test, probative value and prejudicial effects are case-specific. The determinations made by the trial judge deserve appellate deference. In this case, Dr. Marshall's evidence brought relevant facts and opinions to the case that were not within the jury's knowledge and would not otherwise have been available to assist them. Dr. Marshall's qualifications were not questioned. His testimony was understandable and convincing. Taken together, these factors suggest that the expert evidence possessed considerable probative value.

The accused argues that the probative value of the evidence was outweighed by two important prejudicial effects: (1) that Dr. Marshall's evidence would neutralize a legitimate line of argument and interfere with his right of self-defence; and (2) that Dr. Marshall's evidence would distort the trial process through the undue weight the jury may place on expert evidence. The first alleged prejudicial effect does not withstand scrutiny. As the trial judge noted in his decision on the *voir dire*, admitting Dr. Marshall's evidence would not prohibit defence counsel from making its "common sense" argument that delay casts doubt on whether the alleged assaults occurred. The Crown's expert evidence merely countered that argument by providing evidence that it was contrary to the current consensus in the scientific community. Conflicting evidence and inferences are the natural product of the adversarial nature of the trial process. Each side seeks to bring evidence to support its arguments. Expert witnesses are subject to cross-examination to probe the validity of their evidence and the weight to be assigned to it. At the end of the day, the jury decides what they accept and what they reject. Evidence is neither inadmissible nor unfair simply because it contradicts an argument put by the other side.

The second prejudicial effect merits closer consideration. Low value expert testimony can distort the fact-finding process by taking a relatively simple issue, dressing it up in scientific language and presenting the trier of fact with a ready-made decision. The jury may be tempted to avoid engaging in serious consideration of the actual facts and instead rely on the apparent expertise of the scientist. In effect, the expert may usurp the domain of the jury. Trial judges must take this possibility into account in determining whether the prejudicial effect of expert evidence outweighs its probative value.

Part of this concern is addressed at the necessity stage: a party seeking to call expert evidence must show that the subject matter of the expert's opinion falls outside the likely range of knowledge and experience of the trier of fact. Nonetheless, that may not suffice. Even if expert evidence may assist the judge or jury, that benefit must be balanced against its costs. Can the expert address the issue in understandable terms? Is the judge or jury likely to take the expert's word as unchallengeable truth, or will the trier of fact be able to examine it critically? At the same time, the judge must not underestimate the ability of jurors to assess evidence; they may be quite capable of discerning whether scientific information is legitimate or not, as long as it is presented in accessible language.

The concern that the jury may be misled was not made out in this case. Dr. Marshall testified in a clear and straightforward manner. He avoided scientific terms which might obfuscate the issue and confuse the jury. His evidence was easy to understand and well within the ability of the jury to evaluate. Unlike some expert witnesses, Dr. Marshall did not rely on his credentials or "the mystique of science" to bolster his testimony: see *Béland*, supra, at p. 434. Nor did his testimony verge on advocacy. He neither explicitly nor implicitly commented on the complainant's credibility or the ultimate issue of the guilt or innocence of the accused. Defence counsel engaged Dr. Marshall in cross-examination and did not seem hindered by the scientific nature of the evidence. On the circumstances that prevailed in the trial below, I cannot conclude that the trial judge erred in holding that the probative value of Dr. Marshall's evidence outweighed its prejudicial effects.

MAJOR J. (IACOBUCCI, BINNIE and ARBOUR JJ. concurring):—

. . .

I. General Approach to the Necessity Requirement

A. Standard of Necessity

The second requirement of the *Mohan* analysis exists to ensure that the dangers associated with expert evidence are not lightly tolerated. Mere relevance or "helpfulness" is not enough. The evidence must also be necessary.

I agree with the Chief Justice that some degree of deference is owed to the trial judge's discretionary determination of whether the *Mohan* requirements have been met on the facts of a particular case, but that discretion cannot be used erroneously to dilute the requirement of necessity. *Mohan* expressly states that mere helpfulness is too low a standard to warrant accepting the dangers inherent in the admission of expert evidence. A fortiori, a finding that some aspects of the evidence "might reasonably have assisted the jury" is not enough.

B. Dangers of Expert Evidence

In *Mohan*, Sopinka J. stated that the need for expert evidence must be assessed in light of its potential to distort the fact-finding process. A brief examination of the dangers associated with the admission of expert evidence is helpful to the analysis of this appeal.

A basic tenet of our law is that the usual witness may not give opinion evidence, but testify only to facts within his knowledge, observation and experience. This is a commendable principle since it is the task of the fact finder, whether a jury or judge alone, to decide what secondary inferences are to be drawn from the facts proved.

However, common law courts have since the 14th century recognized that certain exceptional issues require the application of special knowledge lying outside the experience of the usual trier of fact. Expert opinion evidence became admissible as an exception to the rule against opinion evidence in those cases where it was necessary to provide "a ready-made inference which the judge and jury, due to the technical nature of the facts, are unable to formulate" (*R. v. Abbey*, [1982] 2 S.C.R. 24, at p. 42).

Despite the emergence of the exception, it has been repeatedly recognized that the admissibility requirements of expert evidence do not eliminate the dangers traditionally associated with it. Nevertheless, they are tolerated in those exceptional cases where the jury would be unable to reach their own conclusions in the absence of assistance from experts with special knowledge.

Historically, there existed two modes of utilizing such expert knowledge as was available: first, to select jurors who by experience were best suited to deal with the facts before them, and second, to call experts as friends of the court rather than as witnesses for one side or the other. (See Learned Hand,

"Historical and Practical Considerations Regarding Expert Testimony" (1901), 15 Harv. L. Rev. 40.) In this manner, the neutrality of the experts was assured. This notion has long disappeared and now the "professional expert witness" has emerged. Although not biased in a dishonest sense, these witnesses frequently move from the impartiality generally associated with professionals to advocates in the case. In some notable instances, it has been recognized that this lack of independence and impartiality can contribute to miscarriages of justice. (See, e.g., *The Commission on Proceedings Involving Guy Paul Morin* (Kaufman Report) (1998), at p. 172.)

The primary danger arising from the admission of any opinion evidence is that the province of the jury might be usurped by that of the witness. This danger is especially prevalent in cases of expert opinion evidence. Faced with an expert's impressive credentials and mastery of scientific jargon, jurors are more likely to abdicate their role as fact-finders and simply attorn to the opinion of the expert in their desire to reach a just result. The danger of attornment to the opinion of the expert is further increased by the fact that expert evidence is highly resistant to effective cross-examination by counsel who are not experts in that field. In cases where there is no competing expert evidence, this will have the effect of depriving the jury of an effective framework within which to evaluate the merit of the evidence.

Additional dangers are created by the fact that expert opinions are usually derived from academic literature and out-of-court interviews, which material is unsworn and not available for cross-examination. Though not properly admissible as evidence for the proof of its contents, this material generally finds its way into the proceedings because "if an expert is permitted to give his opinion, he ought to be permitted to give the circumstances upon which that opinion is based" (*R. v. Dietrich* (1970), 1 C.C.C. (2d) 49 (Ont. C.A.), at p. 65). In many cases, this material carries with it prejudicial effects which require special instructions to the jury (*Abbey*, supra, at p. 45).

Finally, expert evidence is time-consuming and expensive. Modern litigation has introduced a proliferation of expert opinions of questionable value. The significance of the costs to the parties and the resulting strain upon judicial resources cannot be overstated. When the door to the admission of expert evidence is opened too widely, a trial has the tendency to degenerate into "a contest of experts with the trier of fact acting as referee in deciding which expert to accept" (*Mohan*, supra, at p. 24).

. . .

In my view, the content of the expert evidence admitted in this case was not unique or scientifically puzzling but was rather the proper subject for a simple jury instruction. This being the case, its admission was not necessary.

Distilling the probative elements of Dr. Marshall's testimony from its superfluous and prejudicial elements, one bald statement of principle emerges. In diagnosing cases of child sexual abuse, the timing of the disclosure, standing alone, signifies nothing. Not all victims of child sexual abuse will disclose the abuse immediately. It depends upon the circumstances of the particular victim. I find surprising the suggestion that a Canadian jury or judge alone would be incapable of understanding this simple fact. I cannot identify any technical quality to this evidence that necessitates expert opinion.

. . .

A trial judge should recognize and so instruct a jury that there is no inviolable rule on how people who are the victims of trauma like a sexual assault will behave. Some will make an immediate complaint, some will delay in disclosing the abuse, while some will never disclose the abuse. Reasons for delay are many and at least include embarrassment, fear, guilt, or a lack of understanding and knowledge. In assessing the credibility of a complainant, the timing of the complaint is simply one circumstance to consider in the factual mosaic of a particular case. A delay in disclosure, standing alone, will never give rise to an adverse inference against the credibility of the complainant.

It was submitted that it is preferable to introduce the concept contained in Dr. Marshall's evidence to the jury by way of expert testimony rather than by judicial instruction. In my view, this argument is flawed. There is nothing to be gained from a cross-examination of the simple and irrefutable proposition advanced in this case by the expert. As well, there is no benefit to be derived from the added flexibility of expert evidence since the undeniable nature of the proposition does not lend itself to future advancements in knowledge and understanding.

A jury instruction, in preference to expert opinion, where practicable, has advantages. It saves time and expense. But of greater importance, it is given by an impartial judicial officer, and any risk of superfluous or prejudicial content is eliminated. In this appeal, the evidence presented by the expert was precisely what the jury would have been instructed by a proper charge. There is no difference of substance between the two.

See Nick Bala, "*R. v. D. (D.D.)*: The Supreme Court and Filtering of Social Science Knowledge About Children"[331] and Nick Bala and Annelise Saunders, "Understanding the Family Context: Why the Law of Expert Evidence is Different in Family Law"[332] where it is suggested that the *Mohan* test needs to be applied less rigorously in family court. **Do you agree?**

R. v. TALBOT
(2002), 1 C.R. (6th) 396, 161 C.C.C. (3d) 256 (Ont. C.A.)

The accused was charged with three counts of sexual assault, three counts of anal intercourse, and 11 other sexual and non-sexual offences relating to three young boys. The evidence of the complainants was delayed, inconsistent, and marked by recantations. The Crown called a psychiatrist who testified that delayed or inconsistent disclosure and recantation were not unusual for child victims of sexual abuse, but that the nature of the disclosure by itself did not "tell us anything about the factual veracity of the disclosures

---

[331] (2001), 36 C.R. (5th) 283.
[332] (2003) 20 C.F.L.Q. 277.

that are ultimately made", and that it should not be seen as a certain indicator that a child has been sexually abused.

Per LASKIN J.A. (GOUDGE and SIMMONS JJ.A. concurring): —

. . .

The expert evidence

The Crown called two medical experts, Dr. Dirk Huyer, an expert in the medical aspects of child abuse. Dr. Huyer testified that anal penetration of a child is easier if the child has taken a muscle relaxant like Valium and Dr. Clive Chamberlain, a psychiatrist, who was qualified as an expert on the sexual abuse of children. On appeal the appellant challenges only the evidence of Dr. Chamberlain.

. . .

The three complainants did not disclose the accused's sexual abuse immediately after it occurred. Instead, disclosure was delayed, at times inconsistent, and marked by recantations. The defence relied on the way the complainants disclosed the abuse to argue that their allegations were fabricated. Dr. Chamberlain was called by the Crown to explain to the jury that delayed or inconsistent disclosure and even recantation of claims of sexual abuse by child victims is not unusual. He testified that it is "a very commonly observed pattern of behaviour of kids who have been involved in sexual situations with adults" and he discussed the reasons for it. But he also cautioned that "this kind of disclosure on and off and recantation, I don't think that it, by itself, should tell us anything about the factual veracity of the disclosures that are ultimately made . . . it ought not to be seen as a certain indicator that a child has been sexually abused".

At trial, defence counsel did not object to the admissibility of Dr. Chamberlain's opinion evidence. On appeal, however, relying on the recent Supreme Court of Canada decision in *R. v. D. (D.)* (2000), 148 C.C.C. (3d) 41, the appellant submits that Dr. Chamberlain should not have been allowed to testify because his testimony did not meet the necessity criterion for the admissibility of expert evidence. The appellant also submits that, once admitted, the trial judge failed to properly instruct the jury on how they could use Dr. Chamberlain's evidence.

. . .

Despite the holding in *D. (D.)* I would not give effect to the appellant's submission for two reasons. First, the expert evidence in *D. (D.)* differed materially from Dr. Chamberlain's evidence in this case. The expert evidence in *D. (D.)* related only to the significance of delay in disclosing sexual abuse allegations. As summarized by Major J., that expert testified that "the timing of the disclosure, standing alone, signifies nothing", at p. 64 [para. 59]. And the reason that delayed disclosure means nothing in and of itself is that, as a matter of law, no adverse inference can be drawn from a complainant's delay in disclosing the allegations. Major J. put it this way, at p. 66 [para. 63]: The significance of the complainant's failure to make a timely complaint must not be the subject of any presumptive adverse inference based upon now rejected stereotypical assumptions of how persons (particularly children) react to acts of sexual abuse: *R. v. M. (P.S.)* (1992), 77 C.C.C. (3d) 402 (Ont. C.A.) at pp. 408-9; *R. v. M. (T.E.)* (1996), 187 A.R. 273 (C.A.).

And further, at pp. 66-67:

A delay in disclosure, standing alone, will never give rise to an adverse inference against the credibility of the complainant.

Because this principle forms a recognized part of Canadian law, one can easily understand why the Supreme Court found that the information offered by the expert in D. (D.) should have gone to the jury in the form of an instruction from the trial judge. No expert evidence was needed to establish that the delay in the complainant's disclosure did not by itself impair her credibility. The jury was not permitted to draw an adverse inference from this delay as a matter of law and the trial judge should have instructed them accordingly.

The present case is very different. Instead of dealing with the relevance of delayed disclosure "standing alone", Dr. Chamberlain testified to patterns of disclosure among sexual abuse victims, patterns that include not only delays in disclosure but also inconsistencies in disclosure and recantations. Although no adverse inference can be drawn from the mere fact that disclosure is delayed, the same cannot be said for inconsistent disclosures or recantations. Indeed, prior inconsistent statements are typically highly damaging to a complainant's credibility.

Thus, there is, quite rightly, no existing principle of law that would prevent a jury from drawing an adverse inference from inconsistent disclosures or recantations by a complainant. But the jury should be allowed to put these inconsistent disclosures and recantations in context. If, as Dr. Chamberlain testified, child victims of sexual abuse often make disclosures marked by delay, inconsistencies, and recantations, then expert evidence may be required to help the jury make an appropriate and informed determination of the complainant's credibility. Patterns of disclosure among sexual abuse victims do not form a part of the ordinary experience and knowledge of jurors. Expert evidence may well be necessary to help jurors draw the proper inferences, and I conclude that it was necessary in this case.

In the light of *D. (D.)*, it might have seemed preferable for the trial judge to have dealt with the relevance of delay in a jury instruction, and for the Crown to have limited Dr. Chamberlain's testimony to the patterns of disclosure involving inconsistencies and recantations. Accepting, however, that Dr. Chamberlain's evidence was necessary to help the jury understand the significance of the complainants' inconsistent disclosures and recantations, to restrict him from offering an opinion on the relevance of delayed disclosure would be unworkable. Dr. Chamberlain's evidence dealt with patterns of disclosure among sexual abuse victims; delays in disclosure form an integral part of those patterns. Dr. Chamberlain's testimony was properly admitted.

Second, even if Dr. Chamberlain's evidence should not have been admitted, its admission caused no substantial wrong. If necessary, I would therefore apply the proviso in s. 686(1)(b)(iii) of the Code. Although the

Supreme Court of Canada did not address the proviso in D. (D.) because it had already decided to allow the appeal on another ground, the majority reasons affirm that the jury is entitled to the information on delayed disclosure. The majority said simply that the information should come from the trial judge, not from an expert witness. Major J. stressed, at p. 67 [para.67], that an important advantage of a jury instruction over expert evidence is that the information "is given by an impartial judicial officer, and any risk of superfluous or prejudicial content is eliminated".

Here, though the information on disclosure patterns was given by an expert, Dr. Chamberlain's evidence was short, balanced and avoided any superfluous or prejudicial content. In both his examination-in-chief and his cross-examination he emphasized that neither late or inconsistent disclosure nor recantation proves that sexual abuse has occurred. If the admission of his evidence amounted to an error of law, the error did not cause a miscarriage of justice.

The appellant also contends that the trial judge did not properly instruct the jury on how they could use Dr. Chamberlain's evidence. I do not agree with this contention. The trial judge quite properly told the jury that if they accepted Dr. Chamberlain's evidence they could take it into account in assessing the credibility of the complainants, that is in determining whether the complainants fabricated their evidence. But the trial judge cautioned the jury at least three times that they could not use Dr. Chamberlain's evidence to conclude that sexual abuse had occurred. For example, in discussing Dr. Chamberlain's evidence, the trial judge told the jury: However, it is very important that you understand and accept that this evidence cannot be used as confirming that the complaints by young persons of sexual acts performed upon them by Mr. Talbot are in fact true, or are more likely to be true because their conduct fits the so-called pattern described by Dr. Chamberlain. Dr. Chamberlain said himself that the pattern of secrecy, helplessness, denial, disclosure and further denial should not tell you anything about the truth of the matters disclosed.

And later, in comparing Dr. Chamberlain's evidence with similar fact evidence, he repeated this caution: This evidence of Dr. Chamberlain's was admitted since it may help you, if you accept it, in understanding how one or more young persons might not complain about sexual abuse or might deny sexual abuse. To that extent, Dr. Chamberlain's evidence may help you to determine the credibility of young persons who now allege various sexual acts performed on them by Mr. Talbot after not complaining or, alternatively, after denying such sexual acts. Such evidence, expert evidence, may explain away a problem with credibility, depending on how you view that evidence. However, that expert evidence cannot be used to bolster or add to the credibility of a complainant, because it cannot be used to say that sexual abuse did, in fact, occur. It is thus distinct from similar fact evidence.

I would not give effect to this ground of appeal.

R. v. G. (P.)
(2009), 242 C.C.C. (3d) 558, 63 C.R. (6th) 301 (Ont. C.A.)

The accused was charged with several sexual offences against his four-year-old daughter. The complainant initially disclosed the abuse to her foster parents, and she later provided two videotaped statements to police. These out-of-court statements by the complainant were admitted for the truth of their contents. She did not testify at trial. An expert on child sexual abuse offered his opinion at trial that the complainant had been sexually abused but did not identify the accused as the abuser. The jury found the accused guilty and the accused appealed.

JURIANSZ J.A. (SHARJE and ROULEAU JJ.A. concurring):

Analysis

[14] The most helpful case regarding the admissibility and ambit of an expert's opinion as to whether a child has suffered sexual abuse is *Khan v. College of Physicians and Surgeons of Ontario* (1992), 9 O.R. (3d) 641 (O.C.A.). This case presents the opportunity to repeat and expand upon the principles stated in that case.

[15] *Khan v. College of Physicians and Surgeons of Ontario* arose out of disciplinary proceedings against Dr. Khan before the College of Physicians and Surgeons of Ontario for the sexual assault of a patient, then 3 1/2 years old. One of the issues on the appeal was whether the two expert witnesses who had testified at Dr. Khan's hearing had gone beyond the scope of what was permissible by giving their opinions on the ultimate issue to be decided by the tribunal. Doherty J.A. reviewed the law and stated the following general principles.

[16] First, expert evidence is not rendered inadmissible simply because it may bear on the very factual issue to be decided by the trier of fact. Second, an expert witness may not offer an opinion as to the veracity of any witness, except in very exceptional cases. Third, expert opinion as to what factual inferences or conclusions should be drawn from the evidence concerning the "behaviour and symptomatology" of a child is admissible even though it indirectly enhances the credibility of the child's evidence. Fourth, the trial judge may control the format in which the expert evidence is given by excluding an expert's conclusory statements where the expert is able to express the opinion in less conclusory terms without detracting from its accuracy.

[17] These principles, taken together, allow the Crown to present expert evidence that will assist the trier of fact while protecting the accused from the trier of fact placing undue weight on the expert's opinion. There exists, however, potential tension between the second and third principles. The second principle is that the expert is not permitted to express an opinion about the veracity of any witness. Despite this, the third principle states that the expert is permitted to offer an opinion (based on the child's "behaviour and

symptomatology") that the child has been sexually abused even though it "indirectly enhances the credibility of the child's evidence."

[18] The third principle qualifies but does not annul the second principle. While the scope permitted an expert witness by the third principle is broad, the court should be vigilant in ensuring that the expert in expressing his or her opinions does not violate the second. As Doherty J.A. noted in *Khan v. College of Physicians and Surgeons of Ontario*, though there is strong value and need for evidence in cases of child sexual abuse, a trier of fact "[f]aced with the often intractable problem of trying to decide who is telling the truth in cases of alleged child abuse . . . may seek refuge in the apparent security and objectivity of the expert's opinion evidence." Major J. made much the same observation in *R. v. D. (D)*, [2000] 2 S.C.R. 275 at para. 53, that there is a danger that "faced with an expert's impressive credentials and mastery of scientific jargon, jurors are more likely to abdicate their role as fact-finders and simply attorn to the opinion of the expert in their desire to reach a just result."

[19] Turning back to this case, I do not accept that the subject matter which Dr. Wehrspann addressed strayed outside the broad range permitted by the third principle. The scope of the child's "behaviour and symptomatology" is not narrowly limited to the psychological, social and physical traits. It includes the child's verbal behaviour. Verbal behaviour may include the fact that the child makes reports of being involved in sexual activity or that the child makes such reports without prompting. It may also include the particular vocabulary the child uses in making those reports.

[20] Dr. Wehrspann noted that the complainant was observed at the daycare [acting in a sexually inappropriate manner], and that she was indiscriminate in her attachments in that she would go up to anybody and make physical contact with them. In addition, Dr. Wehrspann's opinion was also based on his view of the complainant's verbal behaviour. It was important to his analysis that the complainant did report sexual activity, she made these reports without prompting, and that she described the sexual activity in age appropriate language. These are all matters of the complainant's "behaviour and symptomatology".

[21] Properly elicited expert opinion based on such matters is admissible even though it may indirectly enhance the credibility of the child witness or of the witnesses who testify about the child's disclosure. The problem here is that Dr. Wehrspann's opinions were not properly elicited and the effect of his evidence was to indicate his views of the veracity of the complainant and the foster parents.

[22] As noted, Dr. Wehrspann's opinion was primarily on his review of the Children's Aid Society's file that contained the reports of her foster parents to the Society. The only matters he could address directly were his observation that when he tried to talk to the complainant about her father she became

fearful immediately and that she was too open and indiscriminate in her attachments to adults she did not know. His analysis, however, was based primarily on the material in the Children's Aid Society file, which included, notably, the reports from the complainant's foster parents, the veracity of which were disputed by the defence.

[27] Dr. Wehrspann's testimony clearly went beyond expressing an opinion based on the complainant's behaviour and symptomatology. His testimony would have left no doubt in the jury's mind that he believed the Crown's witnesses and disbelieved the appellant in arriving at his opinion that the complainant suffered sexual abuse. His testimony, in effect, directly addressed the credibility and reliability of other witnesses. As such it violated the second principle stated in *Khan v. College of Physicians and Surgeons of Ontario*. I would hold the trial judge erred in admitting it and that a new trial is necessary.

[28] This result could have been avoided had trial judge required that Dr. Wehrspann's testimony be elicited by hypothetical questions that incorporated all of the factual premises upon which his opinion was based. Properly framed hypothetical questions would have permitted Dr. Wehrspann to draw upon the foster parents' reports of the circumstances, manner and content of complainant's disclosure while leaving to the jury the task of deciding whether or not to believe them. This was especially important in this case as the defence attempted to implicate the foster father in the abuse and suggest that both foster parents helped concoct the allegations against him.

New trial ordered.

R. v. DIMITROV
(2003), 18 C.R. (6th) 36, 181 C.C.C. (3d) 554 (Ont. C.A.)

H V was murdered in the garage attached to his home. The accused, a boarder in the house at the time, was convicted by a jury of second degree murder. The central issue at the accused's trial was the identity of the killer. Four people lived at the house at the time of the murder: the victim, his wife, F V, and two tenants, Tzenev and the accused. The position of the Crown at trial was that the deceased was killed by one of the persons living in the house and that that person was the appellant.

WEILER and GILLESE JJ.A. (ARMSTRONG J.A. concurring): —

. . .

Did the trial judge err in admitting expert evidence of the barefoot impression in the Eagle Rock boots?

. . .

Barefoot impression evidence must be carefully evaluated on a case-by-case basis to determine its admissibility. Based on the current state of the jurisprudence, such evidence may be admissible where there are distinctive features of the barefoot impression that can connect the footwear to the accused's feet, as in Légère. It may also be admissible to show that an accused person has not worn a particular pair of shoes or to eliminate persons as regular wearers of shoes. The fact, however, that an accused person's footprint is "similar to" the barefoot impression in a boot or shoe ought not to be admissible as positive identification. As Sergeant Kennedy himself acknowledges, his research has not reached the stage where he can make a categorical identification from barefoot impressions.

. . .

We would allow the appeal, set aside the verdict of guilt and order a new trial.

R. v. KLYMCHUK
(2005), 203 C.C.C. (3d) 341 (Ont. C.A.)

The accused was convicted of first degree murder of his wife. The accused was home when she was killed. He called 911 and reported that he had found his wife dead in their shed. In addition to relying on evidence of the accused's extramarital affair as motive evidence, the Crown called an FBI expert to testify that the crime scene had been staged to look like a robbery. On appeal, the accused challenged the admissibility of this evidence.

DOHERTY J.A. (MOLDAVER and ARMSTRONG JJ.A. concurring): —

The admissibility of the expert evidence of "staging."

. . .

This court has considered the admissibility of expert evidence that a crime scene was "staged" in *R. v. Ranger* (2003), 178 C.C.C. (3d) 375 (Ont. C.A.) and *R. v. Clark* (2004), 182 C.C.C. (3d) 1 (Ont. C.A.). In the present context, staging refers to a deliberate alteration of the crime scene by the perpetrator of the crime to mislead the police as to the identity of the perpetrator. The decisions in *Ranger* and *Clark* go a long way to resolving the admissibility of the expert evidence tendered in this case. The trial judge, whose reasons reflect a careful consideration of the issues before her, did not have the benefit of this court's reasons in either *Ranger* or *Clark*.

In *Ranger*, Charron J.A. distinguished between expert evidence of crime scene analysis offered to assist the jury in deciding what had happened at the crime scene (the WHAT question) and expert evidence based on crime scene analysis offered to assist the jury in deciding why a crime was committed (the WHY question), or who committed the crime (the WHO question). She observed at paras. 71 and 72:

> Crime scene analysis (which I find useful to label as the "WHAT" referred to earlier) results in many forms of expert opinion evidence that regularly meets the legal requirements for admissibility. A few examples readily come to mind: an expert's opinion in an arson case that a fire was not accidental but, rather, deliberately set; opinion evidence explaining the significance of blood splatters; a pathologist's opinion about the likely cause of death or of injuries observed on a deceased victim; an expert's opinion on how a motor vehicle accident happened.

There are many more examples. *This kind of evidence assists the trier of fact in understanding WHAT the crime scene shows. The admissibility of that kind of evidence will usually turn on questions of relevance or the witness's particular expertise. Of course, issues may also arise under any other aspect of the Mohan test. However, the scientific basis for this kind of evidence is usually not contentious.*

By contrast, attempts to adduce expert opinion evidence about WHY an offence was committed in a particular manner and, more particularly, about WHO is more likely to have committed the offence, that is, the kinds of evidence that I have labelled more particularly as criminal profiling, have generally not met with success, either in this jurisdiction or elsewhere. I will refer to some American and English jurisprudence later in this judgment. However, in so far as Canadian jurisprudence is concerned, the best example is *Mohan* itself [emphasis added].

In *Clark* at paras. 83 and 84, Moldaver J.A. applied the distinction drawn in *Ranger*. He characterized expert evidence addressed to the WHAT question as "crime scene reconstruction evidence". That evidence was potentially admissible if relevant and offered through a properly qualified witness. He characterized expert evidence aimed at answering the WHO or the WHY questions as "impermissible criminal profiling evidence".

The distinction drawn in *Ranger* and *Clark* between expert evidence based on crime scene observations and reconstructions on the one hand, and expert evidence based on assessments of the type or category of person who committed a particular offence on the other, is rooted in the established reliability of the former and the unproven nature of the latter. Expert evidence describing the type of person who would or would not engage in a particular criminal activity is admitted only in that narrow class of cases where psychiatric knowledge has advanced sufficiently to allow a qualified expert to testify that the crime in question would in all likelihood have been committed by a person with a particular mental makeup, or alternatively that a person with the accused's mental makeup would in all likelihood not have committed the offence. Psychiatric profiling evidence is admissible only if the profile relied on by the expert is sufficiently precise and detailed to provide a meaningful distinction between the group said to fit the profile and the rest of the population. The evidence must also demonstrate that the profile has been developed and confirmed through an application of proper scientific methodology: *R. v. Mohan* (1994), 89 C.C.C. (3d) 402 at 423 (S.C.C.); *R. v. J. (J.L.)* (2000), 148 C.C.C. (3d) 487 at 500-507 (S.C.C.).

. . .

Agent Brantley's opinions as to the killer's motive and prior relationship with the victim were not founded on any scientific process of inquiry, but on his own experience as augmented by his review of similar case files and interviews with incarcerated felons. Agent Brantley's experience and review of the other sources led him to conclude that those who staged break-ins as part of a homicide probably had a personal motive for the homicide and probably had a prior association with the victim. Even if those opinions accurately reflect the statistical probabilities that a killer who stages a break-in as part of a homicide has a personal motive for the homicide and a prior relationship with the victim, conclusions based on statistical probabilities can offer no insight as to what happened in a specific case. For example, evidence from a homicide investigator that in his experience, his review of similar cases, and his interviews of killers, 85 percent of spousal homicides (a hypothetical figure) not involving a sexual assault or theft from the victim were committed by the surviving partner, could not be offered as evidence (expert or otherwise) that a specific spousal homicide was committed by the surviving partner. To borrow the words of Charron J.A. in Ranger, Agent Brantley's opinion as to the killer's motive and prior relationship with the deceased were "educated guesses" and not scientifically based opinions. As Charron J.A. indicated, those "educated guesses" can play a valuable role in the investigation of crime by directing the police to fruitful areas of investigation. They cannot, however, be admitted as evidence under the guise of expert opinion.

. . .

. . . As I explained earlier, statistical evidence of probabilities based on prior similar events, while useful in many disciplines, offers no admissible evidence as to what happened on a specific occasion in a criminal trial.

The Court ordered a new trial as the expert had gone beyond an assessment of the crime scene and testified about possible motives for the murder and the relationship between the victim and her killer. For example, he testified that the killer knew the victim and had a motive for killing her, a profile that fit the accused.

R. v. PERLETT
(2006), 212 C.C.C. (3d) 11 (Ont. C.A.)

The accused was charged with two counts of first degree murder in the shooting deaths of his parents while they were asleep. The accused testified that he had interrupted a masked intruder who had fired the fatal shots. The jury found him guilty of second degree murder. One of the issues on appeal was whether the trial judge had erred in excluding the evidence of an expert on the issue of memory.

LASKIN J.A. (GILLESE and MACFARLAND JJ.A.):

5. The trial judge erred in excluding the evidence of Dr. Loftus, or in failing to instruct the jury on the frailties of memories formed in traumatic situations

[94] Dr. Elizabeth Loftus is a renowned American psychologist. She has studied and written about human memory for many years. She is a recognized expert in the field.

[95] The defence sought to call Dr. Loftus as an expert witness for two purposes: to establish that a significant minority of the population mistakenly believe people are better able to remember details of traumatic events; and to establish that a witness to a traumatic event may have false memories of that event. By tendering Dr. Loftus' opinion evidence, the defence sought to counter the Crown's argument that the appellant's false statements and

inconsistent accounts of what occurred showed he had fabricated his intruder story.

[96] The trial judge, however, refused to permit the defence to call Dr. Loftus. The appellant submits that he erred in law in doing so because he incorrectly applied the test in *R. v. Mohan* (1994), 89 C.C.C. (3d) 402 (S.C.C.) for the admission of expert evidence, and he mischaracterized the nature of Dr. Loftus' evidence. Alternatively the appellant submits that the trial judge erred by failing to include the essence of Dr. Loftus' evidence in his jury charge, as he had said he would.

[97] The trial judge heard Dr. Loftus' proposed testimony on a voir dire. In his ruling he summarized the essence of her testimony concerning people's misconceptions about the memories of those who have had traumatic experiences:

> She testified that studies have shown that a significant minority — sometimes as great as fifty percent — of the general population have misconceptions about various aspects of human memory. In particular she testified that studies have shown that it is common for lay people to believe that traumatic experiences will leave participants with an imprinted memory of that event. However, she said that scientific evidence in fact contradicts this belief. She testified that memory of violent events is in fact weaker than that of non-violent events. Moreover, she said that witnesses to traumatic events often have false or illusory memories of these events.

[98] The trial judge then applied the Mohan test for the admission of expert evidence and decided to exclude Dr. Loftus' testimony. The Mohan test turns on four criteria: a properly qualified expert; relevance; necessity; and the absence of any exclusionary rule.

[99] Although not ruling definitively on the first criterion, the trial judge seemed willing to accept that "Dr. Loftus' area of research was an established and recognized area of scientific research."

[100] The trial judge also seemed to accept, albeit reluctantly, that the defence had established the second criterion, relevance. Initially, the trial judge held that as the defence tendered Dr. Loftus' testimony to explain inconsistencies in the appellant's account, the defence was simply seeking to bolster the appellant's credibility. Ordinarily evidence used solely to bolster credibility is inadmissible. However, the trial judge quoted McLachlin J.'s reasons in *R. v. Marquard* (1993), 85 C.C.C. (3d) 193 (S.C.C.) at 228-9, in which she said that "expert evidence of human conduct and the psychological and physical factors which may lead to certain behaviour relevant to credibility is admissible provided the testimony goes beyond the ordinary experience of the trier of fact." This type of expert evidence puts the witness' testimony in its proper context.

[101] The trial judge therefore accepted that although "Dr. Loftus's proposed testimony does indirectly go toward bolstering Mr. Perlett's credibility, it might be admissible if that testimony is needed because the problem is beyond their [the jury's] ordinary experience."

[102] The trial judge's decision to exclude Dr. Loftus' evidence was based on his application of the third criterion of the Mohan test, necessity. He ruled that her evidence was not "necessary." He correctly stated the test for necessity: for expert evidence to be admissible "the subject matter of the inquiry must be such that ordinary people are unlikely to form a correct judgment about it, if unassisted by persons with special knowledge." He held that Dr. Loftus' proposed evidence did not meet this test.

[103] The trial judge noted that Dr. Loftus could not say how large a segment of the population shared a misconception about memory of traumatic experiences. The most she could say was a significant minority, perhaps as high as fifty percent. The defence argued that her evidence suggested that at least some members of the jury were likely to have this opinion. The trial judge, however, was not convinced "that it is necessary to have expert opinion evidence every time it is statistically likely that a juror will have a relevant misconception about human behaviour". He referred to this Court's decision in *R. v. McIntosh* (1997), 117 C.C.C. (3d) 385 at 394-5 where Finlayson J.A. wrote that most people were aware that memories of brief and stressful incidents may be faulty. Thus the trial judge concluded that all that was needed was to caution the jury not to "draw too hasty a conclusion from any inconsistencies they may perceive in Mr. Perlett's statements."

[104] The trial judge also dealt with the fourth Mohan criterion and concluded that it provided an alternative basis to exclude Dr. Loftus' testimony. In his view the cost of admitting the testimony, including its potential to overwhelm the jury, substantially outweighed its "marginal probative value."

[105] The appellant makes two complaints about the trial judge's ruling on the admissibility of Dr. Loftus' testimony. His first complaint is that the trial judge wrongly characterized her testimony as being relevant only to bolster his credibility. I do not agree. As my summary of the trial judge's reasons endeavoured to show, the trial judge did acknowledge that although Dr. Loftus' evidence was relevant to the appellant's credibility, it might still be admissible to put the appellant's evidence in a proper context.

[106] The appellant's second and main complaint is that the trial judge misapplied the test for necessity. The appellant argues that to be admissible, Dr. Loftus' evidence does not have to go as far as to demonstrate that every juror would likely have this misconception. Instead necessity will be met if the risk of misconception among the jurors is material. Here, the appellant argues, the risk is material because Dr. Loftus' scientific findings show that a significant portion of the population, albeit less than fifty percent, perceive that

human memories of traumatic experiences will be keen and clear. And, critically, the perception is a misconception because it does not accord with the scientific evidence, but runs counter to it.

[107] This is a cogent and attractive argument. I found it a difficult argument to resolve. However, two things support the trial judge's ruling that Dr. Loftus' evidence does not meet the necessity criterion. First, Dr. Loftus' evidence about the extent of the population harbouring this misconception was not terribly precise; indeed it was quite vague.

[108] Second, the trial judge's ruling was consistent with this Court's judgments in McIntosh and *R v. M. (B.)* (1998), 130 C.C.C. (3d) 353. Admittedly, Dr. Loftus' evidence did not suffer from some of the frailties of the proposed experts in those two cases. Those frailties, however, related to the first Mohan criterion, a properly qualified expert. On the necessity criterion, both Finlayson J.A. in McIntosh and Rosenberg J.A. in *M. (B.)* accept that jurors are likely to understand that people have faulty perceptions and memories of brief and stressful events. Contrary to Dr. Loftus' opinion, these cases hold that it is within jurors' normal experience, not outside their experience, and thus expert assistance is not necessary. In the light of these cases and the vagueness of Dr. Loftus' evidence I am not persuaded that the trial judge erred in exercising his discretion to exclude her testimony.

R. v. OSMAR
(2007), 44 C.R. (6th) 276 (Ont. C.A.)

ROSENBERG J.A. (GOUDGE and LAFORME JJ.A. concurring): —

The defence sought to call Dr. Richard Ofshe to testify before the jury about false confessions. I will briefly summarize his evidence as it was disclosed during a *voir dire*. Dr. Ofshe is a social psychologist who has spent many years studying police interrogation. He has consulted widely with law enforcement agencies and testified in courts in the United States. He has authored many books and articles, including articles in peer-reviewed journals. The works of he and his associate, Richard Leo, were cited with approval in the leading recent decision on the common law confessions rule, *R. v. Oickle* . . . He testified that it is generally accepted that false confessions can be caused by interrogation tactics using psychological techniques. There is no credible empirical research that has attempted to quantify the rate of false confessions. His own view is that it is a relatively rare but regularly occurring phenomenon. Dr. Ofshe has done no study of the Mr. Big strategy. It is not a strategy used in the United States or Great Britain.

The defence proposed to call Dr. Ofshe to testify principally about three matters. First, that there is a bias among lay people against the idea that someone who is indeed innocent might falsely confess. Second, he would testify about what motivates a person, including an innocent person, to confess to a person in authority. Third, he would testify about the way to evaluate whether or not a confession is false. I will briefly expand on these themes.

. . .

I agree with the trial judge's conclusion that Dr. Ofshe's evidence was not admissible in the circumstances of this case. What I say here should not be taken as a finding that this kind of evidence could never be admitted in other circumstances. I also intend to limit my analysis to whether the evidence meets the necessity requirement for admission of expert evidence. I tend to agree with the appellant that the trial judge may have taken too narrow a view of the possible relevancy of the evidence by focusing solely on its value in determining the appellant's credibility. Dr. Ofshe's evidence was broader than that and went to the question of the reliability of the appellant's statements to the undercover officers in the context of the Mr. Big strategy. This would have been an issue in the case, even if the appellant did not testify.

As is well known, in *Mohan*, Sopinka J., speaking for the court, held that the admission of expert evidence depends on relevance, necessity in assisting the trier of fact, the absence of any exclusionary rule and a properly qualified expert (p. 411). He described necessity in these terms at p. 413:

> What is required is that the opinion be necessary in the sense that it provide information "which is likely to be outside the experience and knowledge of a judge or jury": as quoted by Dickson J. in *R. v. Abbey, supra*. As stated by Dickson J., the evidence must be necessary to enable the trier of fact to appreciate the matters in issue due to their technical nature. In *Kelliher v. Smith*, [1931] 4 D.L.R. 102, at p. 116, [1931] S.C.R. 672 (S.C.C.), this court, quoting from *Beven on Negligence*, 4th ed. (1928), p. 141, stated that in order for expert evidence to be admissible, "[t]he subject-matter of the inquiry must be such that ordinary people are unlikely to form a correct judgment about it, if unassisted by persons with special knowledge".

In my view, the three areas about which Dr. Ofshe proposed to testify did not meet this test. In particular, given the particular circumstances, his evidence was not about matters on which ordinary people are unlikely to form a correct judgment.

I start with his evidence about the bias among lay people against the idea that someone who is indeed innocent might falsely confess. As I have said, unfortunately Dr. Ofshe did not explain the reason for this phenomenon. I suspect that it comes from the difficulty that lay people have in applying their own experience to the circumstances of police interrogation. While most people would understand how a person could come to admit to almost anything, true or false, under torture or physical coercion, they would find it hard to understand why someone would admit to a crime they did not commit and thus place themselves in greater legal jeopardy than they would encounter from simply tolerating the psychological coercion of interrogation. If that is the explanation, Dr. Ofshe's evidence would not be helpful to the jury since it was anchored in formal police interrogation. If there is some other explanation for this bias, it was not forthcoming from Dr. Ofshe.

Similar considerations apply to Dr. Ofshe's evidence concerning the manner in which interrogations are conducted and the motivators for false confessions. I repeat a portion of Dr. Ofshe's evidence quoted above: "The significant question would be what's the motivator that is being offered to elicit the compliance. If the motivator is strong, if there is a powerful inducement, then depending on the power of that inducement, the risk of possibly eliciting a false confession goes up." In this case, the motive for a possible false confession was obvious, as was the fact that there was no downside to confessing to men the appellant believed were criminals. There were no myths to be dispelled; Dr. Ofshe would simply be describing what was obvious from the testimony of the police officers and, indeed, from the appellant's own evidence. The jury did not require Dr. Ofshe's evidence to arrive at a correct conclusion on this issue. He did not purport to offer an opinion as to how powerful the inducement was in this case nor whether it could have led to a false confession.

The final theme of Dr. Ofshe's evidence was that the way to determine whether the confession was true or false was to compare it to the known facts about the killing. He would also testify about the risk from contamination. Dr. Ofshe's evidence would have been helpful on this issue, but, as the trial judge observed, helpfulness is not enough. The entire defence was focused on this very issue. The defence theory was that the details in the confession came from the police. The defence also pointed out that some details that the killer would have known about were not contained in the confession. The jury did not need help understanding this point. As Dr. Ofshe testified, this is a straight-forward element of police investigation.[333]

On August 2, 2006, following an investigation and review into the 1972 murder conviction of Romeo Phillion, the Minister of Justice ordered a reference to the Ontario Court of Appeal. The reference raised questions as to the admissibility as fresh evidence of non-disclosure of alibi and other evidence, and expert opinion on the reliability of the confession.

A majority of the Court (per Moldaver J.A. (Laskin J.A. concurring), Macpherson J.A. dissenting) quashed the conviction mainly on the basis of the non-disclosed alibi evidence.[334]

The Court of Appeal were asked to consider the admissibility of reports presented to the Minister prepared by a psychologist and by Dr. Gisli Gudjonsson. Dr. Gudjonsson, who examined Phillion in 2003, is a leading British expert on the psychology of false confessions. He has testified in over 700 cases worldwide. In the result the Court largely avoids the question because this expert evidence was held not to meet the test for fresh evidence, as psychological evidence as to the reliability of the confession had in fact been lead at Phillion's original trial. However Justice Moldaver made a pointed comment as to the admissibility of such evidence:

> [The] admissibility of expert evidence on false confessions is anything but obvious and should be approached with considerable caution. Of particular

---

[333] See similarly *R. v. Warren* (1995), 35 C.R. (4th) 347 (N.W. T. S.C.) and *R. v. Bonisteel* (2008), 236 C.C.C. (3d) 170, 61 C.R. (6th) 64 (B.C. C.A.). In England expert evidence on false confessions is admissible: see *R. v. Fell* (2001), [2001] E.W.J. No. 1324 (C.A.). For an argument that *Osmar* does not absolutely preclude the admission of expert evidence as to the fallibility of a confession see Lisa Dufraimont, Annotation to *Osmar* (2007), 44 C.R (6th) 278.

[334] See *R. v. Phillion* (2009), 241 C.C.C. (3d) 193, 65 C.R. (6th) 255 (Ont. C.A.).

concern is whether the proposed evidence reaches the level of scientific reliability required by Mohan to warrant its reception. That said, I want to be clear that, in cases such as this where the reliability of a confession is in issue, expert evidence regarding an accused's personality traits that is relevant to and probative of the issue will be admissible. [paras. 217-218]

Justice Moldaver had earlier noted that Dr. Gudjonsson had been cross-examined on his report before Justice Sharpe of the Ontario Court of Appeal in May, 2008, and had admitted that his opinion that Phillion's confession was probably false had gone beyond the limits of scientific evaluation [para. 208].

The Ontario Court of Appeal has therefore once again, as previously in *Osmar,* left the door open to such evidence. The Court seems reluctant to follow the path of other countries and actually admit such expertise. For an argument that such expert evidence meets Canadian tests for reliability, see Timothy Moore and Cindy Wasser, "Social Science and Witness Reliability: Reliable Science Begets Reliable Evidence";[335] and see more generally Lisa Dufraimont, "Regulating Unreliable Evidence: Can Evidence Rules Guide Juries and Prevent Wrongful Convictions?"[336]

It is ironic that in 1972, the trial judge did admit expert evidence as to the reliability of Phillion's confession, with one of the experts even placing reliance on a polygraph test. On the appeal to the Supreme Court,[337] the Court held that evidence of the polygraph tendered by the defence had been properly excluded especially as the accused had chosen not to testify. This ruling was confirmed by a 5-2 majority in *R. v. Béland.*[338] Wilson and Lamer JJ. in dissent sought to distinguish *Phillion* on the basis that Béland had testified. They rejected oath-helping and other concerns advanced by the majority.

R. v. PEARCE
2014 MBCA 70, 318 C.C.C. (3d) 372, 13 C.R. (7th) 270 (Man. C.A.)

The accused was charged with manslaughter. The Crown alleged that the accused brutally killed his partner with blows using golf clubs. The theory was that the accused became enraged after having sex with a condom when the victim told him he was HIV-positive. Five months after the killing the accused went to the police to say he might be the male who had told a gas station employee intimate details about the killing. After a police interview he agreed to take a polygraph test. After the test the polygraph examiner told the accused and the detectives that in his opinion the accused had nothing to do with the death. The accused seemed to be upset by the news. Five days later the accused insisted on meeting again with the police. His initial statements led to his arrest. Two hours later he gave a videotaped statement to police in which he admitted to details of the killing that had not been made public.

---

[335]   (2006), 33 C.R. (6th) 316.
[336]   (2008) 33 Queen's L.J. 261.
[337]   *Phillion v. R.,* [1978] 1 S.C.R. 18.
[338]   (1987), 60 C.R. (3d) 1 (S.C.C.).

At trial, the accused testified that he did not kill the deceased. He testified that his confession was false because he was emotionally unstable at the time of the confession, confused because he had taken Tylenol 3 medication and that two officers had manipulated him into admitting something he did not do. He had learned the details of the killing from the media and the polygraph examination. The trial judge refused to admit evidence as to the risk of false confessions from two defence experts. He was convicted by a jury.

MAINELLA J.A. (HAMILTON AND MONNIN JJ.A. CONCURRING):

91 I. . . see no reason to interfere with the judge's decision to not admit Dr. Moore's evidence because it failed to meet the necessity criterion in *Mohan*.

92 The thesis of Dr. Moore is that while the Reid Technique is quite successful in getting true confessions from genuinely guilty people, it can also result in false confessions from innocent people. He conceded at the *voir dire* that the error rate of the Reid Technique is unknown and there is no interrogation procedure he knows of "that will elicit genuine valid confessions from the guilty but not from the innocent."

93 The methodology Dr. Moore uses to prepare an opinion about a confession's reliability is to review the context of the confession to identify what he believes are reliability risks. He explained his methodology during the *voir dire* as follows:

> . . . So when I look at the disclosures that I get, I mean I also look at the context, I mean where did this come from, I mean what was the crime, what other evidence, if there is any other evidence, is accompanying the so-called confession, how was the interrogation conducted, over what period of time, what do we know about the suspect, do they have any idiosyncratic susceptibilities. ....

94 Expert evidence directed solely to the question of credibility is not admissible because it usurps the function of the jury (*Marquard* at p. 248). I fail to see how Dr. Moore's opinion evidence is necessary for the jury. There is nothing unique or scientific to his methodology. He does exactly what the jury is asked to do, consider all the evidence in assessing the weight to give to a confession. If Dr. Moore's methodology can be described as a field of expertise, it would have to be treated as novel science requiring greater threshold reliability before being admissible. Sopinka J. explained in *Mohan* (at p. 25):

> In summary, therefore, it appears from the foregoing that expert evidence which advances a novel scientific theory or technique is subjected to special scrutiny to determine whether it meets a basic threshold of reliability and whether it is essential in the sense that the trier of fact will be unable to come to a satisfactory conclusion without the assistance of the expert. The closer the evidence approaches an opinion on an ultimate issue, the stricter the application of this principle.

95 Dr. Moore conceded in his evidence that his methodology is not "an exact science," nor does he claim that it is. The subject matter of his evidence is not outside the experience and knowledge of a jury; a jury is quite capable of determining the reliability of a confession looking at the overall context without the help of an expert (*Mohan* at p. 23-24). There is also a danger to the fact-finding process in allowing such expert evidence. Such evidence usurps the jury's province and the jury may simply attorn to the expert's opinion (*D.D.* at para. 53).

The Court, however, ordered a new trial. It decided that in the unusual circumstances of the case, the trial judge should have cautioned the jury regarding the phenomenon of false confessions.[339]

R. v. MELARAGNI
(1992), 76 C.C.C. (3d) 78 (Ont. Gen. Div.)

Two police officers were charged following an incident in which Wade Lawson, an unarmed young African Canadian, was shot in the back of the head as he fled the scene in his car.

MOLDAVER J.:—

. . .

The defence seeks to call expert evidence designed to rebut inferences which the jury might understandably choose to apply based upon their common everyday experience in life. The defence submits that there is a real risk that this jury will assume, absent the proposed evidence, that police officers are trained to react and do react in a cool, calm and deliberate fashion at all times, including situations of great stress, especially since stress is a regular component in the daily makeup of a police officer's existence. The defence submits that the jury would certainly be forgiven for asking questions such as, "How could a trained police officer miss his target by several feet at close range? How could a police officer think he had fired only two bullets when, in fact, he had fired four? How could a police officer possibly miss seeing his partner on the other side of a four and a half foot high motor vehicle if his partner was standing erect?"

The proposed evidence is sought to be tendered to dispell certain misperceptions that might exist in the minds of the jurors regarding these and other matters. While I have not received any evidence which would tend to confirm the existence of such misperceptions in the minds of the public, I cannot help but believe that the concerns expressed are real. As a society, we are generally unfamiliar through our common everyday experience as to just how police officers do react in situations of extreme stress and peril. What knowledge we do have is generally derived from Hollywood where police officers are for the most part portrayed as super human beings possessed of remarkable marksmanship skills with ice-water flowing through their veins. This perception, which I would describe as a myth, is one which the defence

---

[339] In a first degree murder trial in *R. v. Jeanvenne* (2011), 286 C.C.C. (3d) 65 (Ont. S.C.J.), Dr. Moore was also not allowed to testify as to the unreliability of confessions where the Mr. Big strategy had been employed. Ironically, his research was later relied on by the Supreme Court in *R. v. Hart* to ground the need for reliability inquiries respecting such police methods.

ought to be entitled to dispel. I am of the view that the proposed evidence is, therefore, not only relevant, but may well be helpful to the jury in dispelling the myth which I have described and in arriving at their ultimate decision in this case. Therefore, the evidence proposed by the defence is admissible.

The officers were acquitted. The verdict was one of the precipitating events that led to the decision by then-Premier Bob Rae to set up an inquiry into systemic racism in the criminal justice system in Ontario.

NASSIAH v. PEEL REGIONAL POLICE SERVICES BOARD
[2006] O.R.T.D. No. 18 (Ont. Human Rights Trib.)

The complainant alleged that she was the victim of racial discrimination during a police investigation of a purported theft from a Sears store. The Commission sought an interim ruling on the admissibility of expert evidence on racial profiling.

JOACHIM (MEMBER): —

Professor Norman Scot Wortley was called by the Commission as an expert witness on racial profiling in Canada to give opinion evidence of the nature of racial profiling in police investigations in general, and in this case, in particular. The Respondent objected both to Professor Wortley's expertise and to the necessity and relevance of his opinion evidence.

Professor Wortley gave evidence with respect to his qualifications before I made my order.

Professor Wortley has been an Associate Professor at the Centre for Criminology at the University of Toronto for five years; prior to that he was an Assistant Professor for five years. He holds a B.A., an M.A. and a Ph.D in Sociology. He has been personally involved in two large sociological studies into racial profiling in Canada and is currently completing work on a third. He was commissioned by the Kingston police for his current research to review information relating to race, age, etc. gathered during police stops over a period of one year.

. . .

I am persuaded that Professor Wortley's credentials, detailed above, qualify him as an expert in racial profiling in the criminal justice system and in police investigation in Canada.

The Respondents argued that the evidence proposed to be given by Professor Wortley could be highly prejudicial as it is akin to propensity evidence or similar fact evidence. That is, evidence that racial profiling exists could be highly prejudicial. They relied on the case of *R. v. Handy* (2000) 48 O.R. (3d) 257, [2000] O.J. No. 1373. I am not persuaded that the case of *R. v. Handy*, supra which is a criminal law case dealing with the test for admission of similar fact evidence, is useful to my determination on whether to hear expert evidence.

In the criminal context, the Courts have stated (*R. v. Mohan*, supra [1994] 2 S.C.R. 9) that they will only admit expert evidence that meets the following criteria:

> 1. relevance 2. necessity in assisting the trier of fact 3. the absence of any exclusionary rule 4. the proper qualification of the proposed witness.

The Respondents argued that the expert evidence was not relevant or necessary in this case.

Since I am not bound by the formal rules of evidence applied in the criminal law context, I have also taken note of principles developed in human rights proceedings in particular. The Respondents relied on *Omoruyi-Odin v. Toronto District School Board*, [[2002] O.H.R.B.I.D. No. 21], where the Tribunal declined to qualify certain witnesses as experts and refused to permit them to offer opinion evidence, in large part because the Tribunal determined that the proposed evidence was not relevant or necessary:

> [55] It was also proposed that Bernard proffer opinion evidence on the following topics: anti-Black racism in Canada and its manifestations in the workplace; the development and perpetuation of stereotypes and systemic barriers; and stereo-types directed against African Canadian men. None of these appear to be areas in which it is necessary that opinion evidence be adduced before the BOI, which is, after all, statutorily charged with and presumed to have the expertise to determine whether discrimination, including systemic discrimination, exists. Furthermore, it appears that this proposed evidence is all of a general or contextual nature in the sense that Bernard's views on these topics do not arise out of any examination of the circumstances obtaining in the Scarborough Board during the time covered by this Complaint.

The Respondents noted that in *Smith v. Canada Customs and Revenue Agency*, [2004] O.J. No. 3410 the Court did not permit Professor Wortley to testify on whether the Canada customs agent's actions amounted to racial profiling because he was not an expert on Canada customs enforcement practices. The Respondents argued that this is the same situation. Professor Wortley's evidence is not necessary. Nor is it relevant in that it is a general nature and not specific to the type of investigation at issue in this hearing. I note that in *Smith*, supra, Professor Wortley was qualified as an expert in racial profiling and permitted to testify about profiling in general.

Professor Wortley has not conducted any studies about the Peel police or the Greater Toronto police in particular. Also, Professor Wortley's research focuses primarily on police stops, which is not the situation in this complaint. However, Professor Wortley's research also focuses on the investigation by police after the initial stop, which may be analogous to the complaint before me.

The Respondents pointed out that in the case of *R. v. Brown*, [2003] 64 O.R. (3d) 161, a case involving racial profiling by the police, no expert evidence was needed. However, in that case the Crown conceded the existence of racial profiling, so the only issue was whether it had occurred in that case. I did not understand the Respondents to be conceding the existence of racial profiling in police investigations in Canada. At most, they agreed to a definition of racial profiling, not its existence.

I prefer the approach taken by the Nova Scotia Board in the case of *Johnson v. Halifax (Regional Municipality) Police Service*, [2003] N.S.H.R.B.I.D. No. 2 at paras. 92 and 93:

> . . . With all due respect to the board, expertise in racism and expertise in discrimination are two different things. Racism is a social phenomenon, discrimination a legally prohibited act. Boards are presumed to possess a certain expertise in the law of discrimination and human rights, but do not necessarily possess expert knowledge in the practices and impact of racism beyond a basic understanding of their dynamics (though obviously a range of knowledge on these topics exists on the part of boards of inquiry). Racism takes many guises, exists in many different environments and it is studied by a great variety of social scientists using various methodologies. A given board of inquiry is unlikely to be up to date on all this literature, and I would not wish to see *Omoruyi-Odin* cited as a way of cutting off recourse to expert evidence in discrimination cases. One method of providing this evidence to a board is of course simply to submit published works on the relevant matters, but works cannot be cross-examined.

> . . . In my view, the actual context of the *Mohan* decision must be kept in mind in understanding where to draw the line between "helpful" and "necessary" evidence. *Mohan* was a criminal case where the rules of evidence are highly structured, partly because of a historic concern to ensure that unduly prejudicial evidence does not go before a jury. I note that with only one exception all the case authorities cited in *Mohan* are criminal cases, suggesting that the concerns relating to criminal trials were uppermost in the Court's mind. In any case, immediately after noting that the descriptor "helpful" sets too low a standard, Justice Sopinka went on to say at 429, "I would not judge necessity by too strict a standard. What is required is that the opinion be necessary in the sense that it provide information 'which is likely to be outside the experience and knowledge of a judge or jury.'" I have found that it satisfies this test for the reasons stated above. Expert evidence in discrimination cases can be statistically based, with an air of scientific validity, but often it is highly qualitative and uses the "softer" methodologies of the social sciences. This is clearly appropriate when we are dealing with the elusive but nonetheless powerful concept of human dignity that underlies human rights law. The often subtle nature of discrimination puts a high burden on complainants, and I would urge future boards not to be too quick to characterize proffered expert evidence as merely "helpful" and thus excluded.

> . . .

In my view, while the standard remains "necessity," the assessment of "necessity" is somewhat lower in the context of a human rights hearing than in the context of a criminal proceeding. The "necessity" requirement must take into account the nature of human rights hearings and the often subtle nature of discrimination.

Regardless of the extent to which racial profiling has been raised in other cases, the Commission asserts that this is the first complaint before the Human Rights Tribunal in Ontario alleging racial profiling in a police investigation. I find that the proposed evidence would provide useful context about the meaning and existence of racial profiling (if any) in police investigations in

Canada against which I can better understand the circumstances in which it may occur and the factors indicative of it. In that sense I find the proposed evidence to be relevant and "necessary" using the less strict standard appropriate for a human rights process.

The Respondents also relied on the human rights case of case of *Orughu v. Canada Border Services Agency*, 2004 CHRT 35 where Professor Wortley, although accepted as an expert, was not permitted to tender parts of his report because they were not necessary and Professor Wortley would be opining on the very issue before the Tribunal. Similarly, in *Smith v. Canada Customs, supra*, the Court did not permit Professor Wortley to testify on whether the custom agent's action amounted to racial profiling, because that was the very issue before the Court.

On that point, I find the comments of Justice Lane in the civil case of *Peart v. Peel (Regional Municipality) Police Services Board*, [2003] O.J. No. 2669 on the use of opinion evidence on racial profiling very useful:

> [23] If I find that the underlying 'facts' upon which Dr. Agard's opinion is based actually existed on December 1, 1997, then his evidence provides me with a basis for an inference that racial profiling was being practiced that day by one or both officers. That is the classic role of the expert: to provide the court with a ready-made inference based on scientific, medical, psychiatric, engineering or similar learning, which the court can draw if certain identified underlying facts are demonstrated to exist. . . . But the inference is one that the court draws. Dr. Agard's opinion is not a substitute for the court's own analysis of the evidence, taking account in so doing of the societal background and the description of the indicia of racial profiling which he has provided, to determine what the facts actually were on that day. Nor is the inference a mandatory one; it is available for the court to draw if the court is persuaded on the balance of probabilities that it is the more probable explanation for the events in question . . .

Regardless of Professor Wortley's opinion on whether factors in this case point to racial profiling, that is my decision to make, and I will not be unduly influenced by his opinion on that issue. Accordingly, I concluded that Professor Wortley was properly qualified, and that the evidence he proposed to give was relevant, necessary and not excluded by any other exclusionary rule.

The Human Rights Tribunal concluded that Ms. Nassiah had been the victim of racial profiling. She was awarded $20,000 and a number of systemic remedies were ordered. See *Nassiah v. Regional Municipality of Peel Services Board.*[340]

---

340   2007 HRTO 14 (CanLII).

PROBLEM[341]

Gerald Stanley, 56, is charged with second degree murder in the death of Colten Boushie, 22, who died after being shot in the head on Stanley's farm. Stanley testified that he didn't mean to kill or even hurt anyone. The farmer said he fired two warning shots into the air, then pulled the trigger a few more times to clear the gun without shots going off. He approached the SUV, reaching in for the keys with one hand and holding the handgun in the other. Stanley testified that his finger was not on the trigger. Then the gun went off. The defence claims the shot was a rare "hang-fire" malfunction, a delay between pulling the trigger and the shot.

You are the trial judge. **Decide whether to admit evidence of three witnesses:** (1) a Crown RCMP firearms expert who tested Stanley's gun and ammunition in a lab; (2) a private sector defence firearms expert who is knowledgeable about Tokarev TT33 semi-automatic pistols and ammo but who never tested the Tokarev TT33 that killed Boushie; (3) a concerned citizen who approached Stanley's defence team after reading about the trial in the news with an account from 40 years ago in which he experienced a hang-fire of 10 to 12 seconds while gopher hunting.

3. EXPERT OPINION BASED ON HEARSAY

It is commonly said that an expert is confined to expressions of opinion based on facts proved at the trial, proved by the expert when he or she has had the advantage of personal observation of the facts at issue, or proved through the testimony of other witnesses, with the opinion elicited based on an assumption of their truthfulness using the device of hypothetical questions.[342] To this general proposition there has developed in Canada a seeming exception that, at least with respect to certain experts, an opinion may be expressed though based on facts not otherwise proved; i.e., where the basis for the expert's opinion consists partly of statements made to him or her prior to trial, and partly of where there are grounds of necessity in so proceeding or circumstances guaranteeing the trustworthiness of such statements.

R. v. JORDAN

(1983), 33 C.R. (3d) 394 (B.C. Co. Ct.)

WETMORE CO. CT. J.:—

The accused on arriving on a flight from Tokyo was searched at customs at the Vancouver airport. He was found in possession of narcotics. His statements to the customs officer confirm both the accused's knowledge of this

---

[341]   We thank Professor Noah Weisbord, Faculty of Law, Queen's University, for permission to include this problem he set as an exam question following the controversial jury acquittal of Gerald Stanley in 2018.
[342]   See e.g. Cross, *Evidence*, 5th ed. at 446 and Phipson, *Evidence*, 11th ed. at 507.

substance in his luggage and that it was a narcotic. It appears that there was never specific mention of the word "heroin" in the conversation.

The indictment charges importing heroin in count 1 and possession of heroin for the purposes of trafficking in count 2.

The Crown first produced certificates showing the substance to be heroin. The Crown then produced the analyst for cross-examination. It is on the basis of this evidence that the defence says there is no reliable evidence that the substance is heroin.

Mr. Clark, a duly appointed analyst, explained the process of analysis used. In the final analysis the questioned substance in a gaseous state is subjected to a spectrometric comparison with a known standard of heroin. The spectrometric comparisons being identical, heroin is concluded as being the questioned substance. There is a further comparative study made of a standard graph prepared from scientific literature and the spectrophotomatic characteristics of the questioned substance. Again the points of comparison unite.

Mr. Clark testifies that he would not certify the questioned substance as heroin without a positive identity existing in *both* comparative studies.

In operating his apparatus the "known heroin" comes from the crime detection laboratory in Ottawa to the Vancouver laboratory. There, this "known standard" is again analyzed by the same process before use. This is done not by Mr. Clark necessarily but by other analysts in the Vancouver laboratory. He cannot say who did the actual analysis of the known standard prior to its use as the standard in making the comparisons with the exhibits in this case.

Defence counsel therefore argues that the opinion evidence of Mr. Clark is based upon hearsay evidence, which is not admissible, thus destroying the value of his opinion.

The argument is developed from the judgment of Dickson J. in *R. v. Abbey*, 29 C.R. (3d) 193 (S.C.C.). In that case the accused related several bizarre incidents to the psychiatrist, which the doctor apparently accepted as truthful. The learned judge then dealt with the medical opinion as if those statements had been established as a fact. From pp. 208-14, Dickson J. discusses the problems of hearsay evidence and opinion evidence. He concludes [p. 214], "Before any weight can be given to an expert's opinion, the facts upon which the opinion is based must be found to exist."

It must be remembered that Dickson J. was dealing with a psychiatric opinion based upon facts which are unique to the particular inquiry. He was not commenting upon other types of information. For example, the psychiatrist's opinion in the final analysis is usually derived from three sources, the patient's comments, his own observations and experience, and the medical literature. Both the experience and medical literature elements involve a great deal of hearsay, but surely all knowledge need not be proved by primary research and observation. Indeed, if that were so, no scientific opinion beyond the most elementary could ever be forthcoming. There comes a time, after testing and observation, that some pragmatic conclusions legitimately arise which need no further verification from original sources.

With respect, I think that is the situation in the case at bar. If it had been established that either the spectrometric comparisons with the supplied "known source" or the published scientific journal graph had not all been consistent, a query may well arise which had not been settled by anything more reliable than hearsay evidence. That did not occur.

I can accept hearsay evidence as original evidence insofar as it relates to my evaluation of the expert's opinion. What I cannot do is accept, as proven for itself, the facts in that hearsay statement. What Mr. Clark really says is that in his opinion the fact that he compared the characteristics of this substance with two substances which he, for good reason, believed to be heroin standards satisfied him that the substance he was analyzing was heroin.

What I am then called upon to measure is my own judgment of his decision, that the conclusion was justified.

The standard is prepared in the crime detection laboratory for this specific purpose. It is then further checked for accuracy by analysts in the Vancouver lab. The standard graph from the scientific literature is likewise designed for this specific purpose. Using these techniques, Mr. Clark testifies to having done hundreds of tests of the same nature. Nothing in cross-examination suggests that observations of a suspicious nature relating to accuracy have ever occurred.

I conclude therefore that there is no reason to doubt the opinion of Mr. Clark that the substance involved in this case is heroin.

With respect to defence counsel, I think this sort of evidence is more analogous to such things as marine charts. Nobody suggests that those documents are inadmissible in proving depths of the ocean without calling the actual measurer and cartographer.

In dismissing the accused's appeal in *Jordan*, Anderson J.A. commented:

> . . . In the case on appeal the analyst testified that the substance received from Ottawa and labelled "heroin" was tested by an analyst in his office. Such a course is perfectly proper. To call the analyst who made the test of the "known" sample is unnecessary. If such an analyst was called, it would, according to the argument of the appellant, be necessary for him to prove that the substance that he used for comparison purposes was heroin, and so on down the line. Such an argument, while logical, cannot be accepted because it would make scientific proof so ponderous and expensive that in reality the evidence of experts could never be used. In my view, the argument that the judgment in *R. v. Abbey*, [1982] 2 S.C.R. 24, applies to scientific tests of the kind under consideration here is unacceptable.[343]

In *Worrall*, a manslaughter case, a very experienced trial judge, Watt J., provided a clear summary of the current law.

---

[343]   (1984), 39 C.R. (3d) 50 (B.C. C.A.) at 57.

R. v. WORRALL
(2004), 19 C.R. (6th) 213 (Ont. S.C.J.)

The accused was charged with unlawful act manslaughter in the death of his half-brother. It was alleged that he had injected a lethal dose of heroin or had given him a lethal dose to self-inject. The evidentiary issue was whether it was necessary to call technicians who had conducted tests as to whether the deceased had heroin in his blood.

WATT J.: —

It is well-established that, as a general rule, an expert may base his or her opinion on second-hand information. But when an opinion based on second-hand information is admitted,and the second-hand information is not otherwise established before the trier of fact, the weight of the opinion may recede accordingly. See, for example, *R. v. Lavallee*, [1990] 1 S.C.R. 852, 55 C.C.C. (3d) 97, 129-30 per Wilson J.

The nature of the second-hand information on which an expert may rely varies significantly. For example, a psychiatrist whose opinion is sought on an issue of criminal responsibility, or a toxicologist summoned to offer an opinion about a blood alcohol concentration will often rely on information provided on interview with an accused. On the other hand, experts in the physical sciences may rely on a variety of test results compiled by others in accordance with generally-accepted scientific principles.

In *R. v. Lavallee*, above, Sopinka J. drew a distinction between:

(i) evidence that an expert obtains and acts upon within the scope of his or her expertise; and

(ii) evidence that an expert obtains from a party to litigation about a matter directly in issue.

Where situation i, above, applies, the expert arrives at his or her opinion on the basis of forms of enquiry and practice that are accepted means of decision within that expertise.

Where the information on which the opinion is formed comes from the mouth of a party, or from any other source that is inherently suspect, we require independent proof of the information relied upon. See, *R. v. Lavallee*, above, at pp. 132-3 per Sopinka J.

And see, *City of Saint John v. Tans Oil Co. Ltd.*, [1966] S.C.R. 581; and *R. v. Abbey* (1982), 68 C.C.C. (2d) 97, 132 per Teeniest J.

. . .

The distinction drawn by Sopinka J. in his concurring judgment in R. v. Lavallee, above, has been recently re-affirmed in connection with data compiled by others and used by experts in offering opinions on the results tense analysis. . . .

This case involves the testimony of experts, forensic toxicologists and pathologists, who reached their stated opinions, to a greater or lesser extent, on the basis of scientific tests and analyses carried out by others as directed by those skilled in the field. There is no suggestion that the tests were scientifically unsound or unwarranted. The principal complaint is that further tests could have been done or findings better quantified.

This is not a case where an expert obtained information from a party about a matter directly in issue, then expressed an opinion before the trier of fact based on that information, which was not otherwise and properly established.

In my respectful view it is consistent with established and binding precedent to conclude, as I do, that there was no necessity to call the technicians as witnesses to prove the test results on which all experts relied.

Accused convicted.

MIZZI v. DEBARTOK
(1992), 9 O.R. (3d) 383 (Ont. Gen. Div.)

THE COURT [DUNNET, J.]:— The plaintiff wishes to call William Franks as his first witness. This is a personal injury action involving closed-head injury, and the plaintiff indicates that he wishes to present the medical evidence of the doctors who assessed the plaintiff at the outset. The defence objects, and says that if the plaintiff is not called first, it would be difficult to cross-examine the doctors on hearsay evidence and without the evidence of the plaintiff to lay the proper foundation for opinion evidence put to the doctors.

The plaintiff contends that the court will be in a better position to understand the nature of the injury to the plaintiff if the expert evidence of the treating doctors is called first, as well as the evidence as to the functioning of the brain, the physical damage that occurred and the psychological consequences.

In my view the plaintiff is a key witness. He is claiming damages and should have the opportunity to tell his story however best he can at the outset of the trial. As well, I find it is necessary for the court for the medical evidence to follow, and the plaintiff, if he is to be called, to be called at the outset of the trial.

Order accordingly.

4. EXAMINING EXPERT

(a) Hypothetical Questions

The reason for requiring the expert to provide the trier of fact with the basis for his or her opinion "is not a deduction from the opinion rule, but rests on the principle of testimonial qualifications that a witness' grounds of knowledge must be made to appear".[344] In a civil suit for negligence arising out of a motor vehicle accident, a witness is examined first respecting his past ability to observe the incident and his present ability to recollect and to communicate a description of the event. Without a demonstrated ability to observe and communicate, the witness' testimony is worthless. So, too, an

---

[344]   7 Wigmore, *Evidence* (Chad. Rev.), s. 1927.

expert's opinion, which rests always on certain premises of fact, must be directly coupled to those premises and both supplied to the jury.

The premises may be communicated by the same witness who expresses the opinion when the expert has had the opportunity of personal observation and so is able to recount, on request, the details observed forming the foundation of his or her opinion. It may be, however, that the factual premises are related by one witness and the opinion by another. Since it is the essential nature of an opinion that it is dependent on its premises, and since the premises can always be rejected by the jury whether testified to by the person giving the opinion or by another, it follows that all opinions in a sense are hypothetical. Is it necessary, therefore, that an expert testifying to an opinion based on personal observation must first state not only that he or she had an opportunity to observe, but also recount all the details of his or her observation, as premises, before being permitted to express his or her opinion?

To this Professor Wigmore answers:

> In academic nicety, yes; practically, no; and for the simple reason that either on direct examination or on cross-examination each and every detail of the appearance he observed can be brought out and thus associated with his general conclusion as the grounds for it, and the tribunal will understand that the rejection of these data will destroy the validity of his opinion.[345]

Where the expert is unable to supply from his or her own knowledge the details constituting his or her premises, then his or her opinion must be brought out by hypothetical presentation so that the jury will later be able to decide whether or not his or her opinion deserves acceptance after considering other testimony to its premises. As Professor Wigmore notes in describing "the orthodox and accepted theory of the hypothetical question":

> The key to the situation, in short is that there may be two distinct subjects of testimony, — premises, and inferences or conclusions; that the latter involves necessarily a consideration of the former; and that the tribunal must be furnished with the means of rejecting the latter if upon consultation they determine to reject the former, i.e. of distinguishing conclusions properly founded from conclusions improperly founded.[346]

Phipson describes the English attitude in a similar way when he notes:

> Where the issue is substantially one of science or skill merely, the expert may, if he has *himself* observed the facts, be asked the very question which the jury have to decide. If, however, his opinion is based merely upon facts proved by *others,* such a question is improper, for it practically asks him to determine the truth of their testimony, as well as to give an opinion upon it; the correct course is

---

[345] 2 Wigmore, *Evidence* (Chad. Rev.), s. 675. See also Chadbourn, *Study Relating to the Uniform Rules of Evidence,* commissioned by the California Law Revision Commission, 1964 at 937-939. But see *R. v. Turner* (1975), 60 Cr. App. R. 80 at 82.

[346] 2 Wigmore, *Evidence* (Chad. Rev.), s. 672; text quoted with approval by Ritchie J. in *Bleta v. R.,* [1965] 48 D.L.R. (2d) 139 (S.C.C.) at 143. See also Maule J. in *M'Naghten's Case* (1843), 10 Cl. & F. 200 at 207, 8 E.R. 718 at 721.

to put such facts to him *hypothetically,* but not *en bloc,* asking him to assume one or more of them to be true, and to state his opinion thereon; where, however, the facts are not in dispute, it has been said that the former question may be put as a matter of convenience, though not as of right.[347]

Where the expert is not speaking with personal knowledge, but basing his or her opinion on facts proved at the trial by other witnesses, then an expert cannot, where there has been conflict between the witnesses, be simply asked, "Having heard all the evidence led in this case, what is your opinion with respect to X?" As described by Ritchie J. in *Bleta v. R.:*[348]

> . . . it is obviously unsatisfactory to ask him to express an opinion based upon the evidence which he has heard because the answer to such a question involves the expert in having to resolve the conflict in accordance with his own view of the credibility of the witnesses and the jury has no way of knowing upon what evidence he based his opinion.

On the other hand, the Supreme Court of Canada did recognize in *Bleta* the same relaxation of attitude to hypothetical questions noted by Phipson when the evidence led by the "fact-witness" is all one way; i.e., depending on the particular case the hypothesis on which the expert is proceeding may be so readily apparent to the jury as to permit the trial judge "in the exercise of his discretion in the conduct of the trial"[349] to dispense with the necessity of abiding the formal hypothetical question technique usually demanded.

(b) Use of Textbooks

R. v. MARQUARD
25 C.R. (4th) 1, [1993] 4 S.C.R. 223, 85 C.C.C. (3d) 193

The accused was charged with aggravated assault of her granddaughter as a result of the child having received a severe facial burn. The theory of the defence was that the burn had been caused accidentally by the child playing with a lighter. At the trial the child was permitted to give unsworn testimony after the trial judge conducted an inquiry into the child's ability to tell the truth. At trial, the Crown called a physician who had treated the child at the hospital and a physician who was an expert on burns. The defence called another physician from the same hospital who was an expert on child abuse and had been consulted by the admitting physician. The child-abuse expert was called by the defence to testify concerning a statement made by the child when she was initially admitted, and which statement was consistent with the theory of accident. This witness in cross-examination testified that the fact that the child acted maturely in dealing with her injuries suggested that she had been the victim of long-term abuse. In addition, the expert testified that children will initially give an accidental explanation and only later give a story that is more consistent with the injury, in a more convincing manner. The

---

[347] Phipson, *Evidence,* 11th ed. at 518.
[348] *Bleta, supra* note 346 at 141; see also *R. v. Holmes,* [1953] 1 W.L.R. 686 (C.C.A.).
[349] *Bleta, ibid.* at 143. And see more recently *R. v. Swietlinski* (1978), 5 C.R. (3d) 324 (Ont. C.A.).

accused was convicted and her appeal to the Ontario Court of Appeal was dismissed.

Held: Appeal allowed and a new trial ordered.

[This case has been examined above under Competence and also under Evidence in Support of Credibility. In the course of the judgment comments were made regarding the use of Learned Treatises.]

Per McLACHLIN J. (SOPINKA J., GONTHIER J. and CORY JJ. concurring):—

Cross-examination of Dr. Tenace

Dr. Tenace was a psychiatrist called by the defence. In the course of cross-examination, the Crown put a series of reports and case studies to him and read extensively from them. Dr. Tenace testified that he was unaware of many of these studies and, for the most part, did not accept their conclusions. None of the experts specifically adopted as authoritative the studies of which Dr. Tenace was unaware and with which he did not agree. Some of the material was very prejudicial. For example, by one "question", some three and one-half pages in length, the Crown introduced opinions regarding the memory of a child who had been put through an extended traumatic and abusive experience, which was described in detail. Moreover, the impression may have been left that Dr. Tenace's unfamiliarity with these unproven studies reflected a lack of expertise.

The proper procedure to be followed in examining an expert witness on other expert opinions found in papers or books is to ask the witness if she knows the work. If the answer is "no", or if the witness denies the work's authority, that is the end of the matter. Counsel cannot read from the work, since that would be to introduce it as evidence. If the answer is "yes", and the witness acknowledges the work's authority, then the witness has confirmed it by the witness' own testimony. Parts of it may be read to the witness, and to the extent they are confirmed, they become evidence in the case. This procedure was laid out in *R. v. Anderson* (1914), 22 C.C.C. 455, 16 D.L.R. 203, [1914] 5 W.W.R. 1052 (Alta. S.C.), and has been followed by Canadian courts: *Holland v. P.E.I. School Board Regional Administrative Unit #4* (1986), 59 Teeniest. & P.E.I.R. 6 at pp. 21-2 (P.E.I. S.C.); *Tans Limited v. Reed Tenus Limited* (1986), 70 B.C.L.R. 189 at p. 193 (B.C. S.C.). The Crown urged us to adopt the American approach to putting scholarly works to an expert witness. The American approach varies from jurisdiction to jurisdiction. Some jurisdictions require that the witness have acknowledged the authority of the work before it can be read into the record on cross-examination. Others, however, appear to allow the works to be put into the record on cross-examination where there is some proof of, or where the judge is prepared to take judicial notice of, the general authority of the work. Even this more liberal standard was not met in the case of the material put to Dr. Tenace. I am satisfied that expert evidence, introduced in the guise of cross-examination of Dr. Tenace without any proof that it constituted reputable authority, was inadmissible. It was also, as noted, prejudicial. This is yet another ground which suggests that a new trial must be ordered.

L'HEUREUX-DUBÉ J. (dissenting): —

. . .

The law with respect to the admission of learned treatises into evidence has not been greatly altered since *R. v. Anderson* (1914), 22 C.C.C. 455, 16 D.L.R. 203, [1914] 5 W.W.R. 1052 (Alta. S.C.). Anderson requires that, in order for a learned treatise to be read into the body of evidence which the jury considers, it must first be adopted by the expert as authoritative. In this case, Dr. Tenace was unaware of the studies cited by the Crown, and of course, could not adopt them as authoritative.

There are a number of different views regarding the rules which should govern the admission of learned treatises. *Anderson* embodies a particularly strict approach: if a witness is asked about a text and expresses ignorance of it or denies its authority, no further use can be made of it by reading extracts of it into evidence. However, if the witness admits its authority, then he may be asked to explain any apparent differences between its opinion and his own: see Sopinka, Tannase and Tans, The Law of Evidence in Canada, *ibid.*, at p. 562.

By contrast, in many American jurisdictions, learned treatises may be put to considerably broader use. This explains the rationale behind the rule as follows: much expert testimony consists of information obtained from such sources and there are sufficient guarantees of trustworthiness to justify equating a learned treatise with the live testimony of an expert witness: Thins on Evidence (Thins rev. 1976), vol. 6, 1690-2. The hearsay exception to learned treatises under Rule 803(18) of the U.S. Federal Rules of Evidence, accordingly, permits such material to be read into evidence as long as it is called to the attention of the expert on cross-examination and its authoritativeness is reliably established. This may be done by the admission of the witness himself, by other experts who testify during the trial, or by judicial notice: J. W. Strong, ed., McCormick on Evidence, 4th ed. (1992), vol. 2, para. 321, at p. 351; see also, C. Tenace, "The Use of Learned Treatises in Canadian and United States Litigation", 24 U.T.L.J. 423 (1974).

I would be inclined to favour the American approach over Anderson, as it has the benefit of preventing the witness from foreclosing an inquiry into the depth or breadth of his or her knowledge by simply refusing to acknowledge a study. However, even if the law regarding the admission of learned treatises were not to be expanded in this way, while the examination in this case did not fall within the strict parameters of the rule in Anderson, no prejudice to the appellant arose from the cross-examination of Dr. Tenace considering the examination as a whole.

5. EXCHANGE OF EXPERTS' REPORTS

The *Criminal Code* now provides for an exchange of expert reports.

657.3 (1) In any proceedings, the evidence of a person as an expert may be given by means of a report accompanied by the affidavit or solemn declaration of the person, setting out, in particular, the qualifications of the person as an expert if

(a) the court recognizes that person as an expert; and

(b) the party intending to produce the report in evidence has, before the proceeding, given to the other party a copy of the affidavit or solemn declaration and the report and reasonable notice of the intention to produce it in evidence.

Attendance for examination

(2) Notwithstanding subsection (1), the court may require the person who appears to have signed an affidavit or solemn declaration referred to in that subsection to appear before it for examination or cross-examination in respect of the issue of proof of any of the statements contained in the affidavit or solemn declaration or report.

Notice for expert testimony

(3) For the purpose of promoting the fair, orderly and efficient presentation of the testimony of witnesses,

(a) a party who intends to call a person as an expert witness shall, at least thirty days before the commencement of the trial or within any other period fixed by the justice or judge, give notice to the other party or parties of his or her intention to do so, accompanied by

(i) the name of the proposed witness,

(ii) a description of the area of expertise of the proposed witness that is sufficient to permit the other parties to inform themselves about that area of expertise, and

(iii) a statement of the qualifications of the proposed witness as an expert;

(b) in addition to complying with paragraph (a), a prosecutor who intends to call a person as an expert witness shall, within a reasonable period before trial, provide to the other party or parties

(i) a copy of the report, if any, prepared by the proposed witness for the case, and

(ii) if no report is prepared, a summary of the opinion anticipated to be given by the proposed witness and the grounds on which it is based; and

(c) in addition to complying with paragraph (a), an accused, or his or her counsel, who intends to call a person as an expert witness shall, not later than the close of the case for the prosecution, provide to the other party or parties the material referred to in paragraph (b).

If notices not given

(4) If a party calls a person as an expert witness without complying with subsection (3), the court shall, at the request of any other party,

    (a) grant an adjournment of the proceedings to the party who requests it to allow him or her to prepare for cross-examination of the expert witness;

    (b) order the party who called the expert witness to provide that other party and any other party with the material referred to in paragraph (3)(b); and

    (c) order the calling or recalling of any witness for the purpose of giving testimony on matters related to those raised in the expert witness' testimony, unless the court considers it inappropriate to do so.

Additional court orders

(5) If, in the opinion of the court, a party who has received the notice and material referred to in subsection (3) has not been able to prepare for the evidence of the proposed witness, the court may do one or more of the following:

    (a) adjourn the proceedings;

    (b) order that further particulars be given of the evidence of the proposed witness; and

    (c) order the calling or recalling of any witness for the purpose of giving testimony on matters related to those raised in the expert witness' testimony.

Use of material by prosecution

(6) If the proposed witness does not testify, the prosecutor may not produce material provided to him or her under paragraph (3)(c) in evidence without the consent of the accused.

No further disclosure

(7) Unless otherwise ordered by a court, information disclosed under this section in relation to a proceeding may only be used for the purpose of that proceeding.

Note that there are statutory limits to the number of experts that can be called: 5 in the case of the *Canada Evidence Act*, s.7, subject to leave of the court, and 3 in the case of Provincial Evidence Acts.

WESTERHOF v. GEE ESTATE

2015 ONCA 206 (Ont. C.A.), additional reasons 2015 ONCA 456 (Ont. C.A.)

J.M. SIMMONS J.A.:—

A. INTRODUCTION

1 Rule 53.03 of the Rules of Civil Procedure, R.R.O. 1990, Reg. 194, sets out the requirements for introducing the evidence of expert witnesses at trial. These appeals, which were heard together, raise related issues about to whom 53.03 applies.

2 Both cases were tried following the 2010 amendments to the Rules, which were aimed at ensuring the neutrality and expertise of expert witnesses, as well as adequate disclosure of the basis for an expert's opinion.

3 Those amendments set out the overriding duty of an expert "engaged by or on behalf of a party" to provide opinion evidence "in relation to a proceeding" that is fair, neutral and non-partisan and within the expert's area of expertise: rule 4.1.01.

4 The 2010 amendments also specified certain information relating to an expert's opinion and expertise that must be included in an expert's report and required that the expert sign an acknowledgement of his or her duty, which identifies the party by or on behalf of whom the expert was engaged: rule 53.03(2.1), Form 53.

5 Both appeals arise from claims for damages for injuries suffered in car accidents. Both cases were tried before a judge and jury. In each case, the defendant admitted liability for causing the accident, and the issues at trial related to whether the accidents caused the plaintiffs' injuries and the quantum of damages.

6 The Westerhof appeal raises the question of whether rule 53.03 applies only to experts described in rule 4.1.01 and Form 53 - experts "engaged by or on behalf of a party to provide [opinion] evidence in relation to a proceeding" (referred to in these reasons as "litigation experts") - or whether it applies more broadly to all witnesses with special expertise who give opinion evidence. This broader group of witnesses would include, for example, treating physicians, who form opinions based on their participation in the underlying events (referred to in these reasons as "participant experts") rather than because they were engaged by a party to the litigation to form an opinion. It would also include experts retained by a non-party to the litigation (for example, statutory accident benefits ("SABS") insurers), who form opinions based on personal observations or examinations relating to the subject matter of the litigation for a purpose other than the litigation (referred to in these reasons as "non-party experts").

7 At the Westerhof trial, the trial judge ruled inadmissible opinion evidence concerning history, diagnosis and prognosis from various medical practitioners who were either participant experts or non-party experts. The trial judge found that these witnesses were required to comply with rule 53.03 and had not done so.

. . .

14 In my opinion, participant experts and non-party experts may give opinion evidence without complying with rule 53.03. Accordingly, I conclude that the trial judge in Westerhof erred in excluding the evidence of several witnesses. For that reason, I would order a new trial.

. . .

(3) Analysis: To Whom Does Rule 53.03 Apply?

(a) General principles

59 As I have said, I do not agree with the Divisional Court's conclusion that the type of evidence - whether fact or opinion - is the key factor in determining to whom rule 53.03 applies.

60 Instead, I conclude that a witness with special skill, knowledge, training, or experience who has not been engaged by or on behalf of a party to the litigation may give opinion evidence for the truth of its contents without complying with rule 53.03 where:

* the opinion to be given is based on the witness's observation of or participation in the events at issue; and
* the witness formed the opinion to be given as part of the ordinary exercise of his or her skill, knowledge, training and experience while observing or participating in such events.

61 Such witnesses have sometimes been referred to as "fact witnesses" because their evidence is derived from their observations of or involvement in the underlying facts. Yet, describing such witnesses as "fact witness" risks confusion because the term "fact witness" does not make clear whether the witness's evidence must relate solely to their observations of the underlying facts or whether they may give opinion evidence admissible for its truth. I have therefore referred to such witnesses as "participant experts".

62 Similarly, I conclude that rule 53.03 does not apply to the opinion evidence of a non-party expert where the non-party expert has formed a relevant opinion based on personal observations or examinations relating to the subject matter of the litigation for a purpose other than the litigation.

63 If participant experts or non-party experts also proffer opinion evidence extending beyond the limits I have described, they must comply with rule 53.03 with respect to the portion of their opinions extending beyond those limits.

64 As with all evidence, and especially all opinion evidence, the court retains its gatekeeper function in relation to opinion evidence from participant experts and non-party experts. In exercising that function, a court could, if the evidence did not meet the test for admissibility, exclude all or part of the opinion evidence of a participant expert or non-party expert or rule that all or part of such evidence is not admissible for the truth of its contents. The court could also require that the participant expert or non-party expert comply with rule 53.03 if the participant or non-party expert's opinion went beyond the scope of an opinion formed in the course of treatment or observation for purposes other than the litigation.

E. PRIVILEGE

1. PRIVILEGED COMMUNICATIONS

(a) Introduction

Evidentiary rules respecting privilege differ from the rules we have so far examined in that the earlier rules were, largely, designed to promote an approximation to truth; the rules we are about to examine clearly operate to restrict the search for truth and must, therefore, be justified by some other value. Rand, J. in *R. v. Snider*[350] wrote of privilege:

> It requires as its essential condition that there be a public interest recognized as overriding the general principle that in a Court of justice every person and every fact must be available to the execution of its supreme functions.

R. v. GRUENKE
[1991] 3 S.C.R. 263, 67 C.C.C. (3d) 289, 8 C.R. (4th) 368

The accused was convicted of first degree murder. The Crown's theory was that the accused had enlisted the aid of her boyfriend in the planning and commission of the murder, which she committed, to stop the victim's sexual harassment of her and to benefit from the provisions of his will. The evidence of the accused's pastor and the lay counsellor, which directly supported the Crown's theory, was ruled admissible at trial. The communications between the accused, the pastor and the lay counsellor took place when the lay counsellor, on hearing of the victim's death two days earlier, visited the accused. When the accused began speaking of her involvement in the murder, the pastor was called and the conversation continued. The accused unsuccessfully appealed her conviction.

LAMER C.J. (LA FOREST, SOPINKA, CORY, MCLACHLIN, STEVENSON and IACOBUCCI JJ. concurring):—

. . .

This case requires the Court to consider whether a common law prima facie privilege for religious communications should be recognized or whether claims of privilege for such communications should be dealt with on a case-by-case basis.

. . .

Given that the Wigmorean criteria (for privilege) play a central role in this case, I will set out the "test" below for ease of reference (Wigmore, *Evidence in Trials at Common Law*, vol. 8, McNaughton Revision, para. 2285):

(1) The communications must originate in a confidence that they will not be disclosed.

(2) This element of confidentiality must be essential to the full and satisfactory maintenance of the relation between the parties.

---

[350]   [1954] 4 D.L.R. 483 (S.C.C.) at 486.

(3) The relation must be one which in the opinion of the community ought to be sedulously fostered.

(4) The injury that would inure to the relation by the disclosure of the communications must be greater than the benefit thereby gained for the correct disposal of litigation.

Analysis

Before delving into an analysis of the issues raised by this appeal, I think it is important to clarify the terminology being used in this case. The parties have tended to distinguish between two categories: a "blanket", prima facie, common law, or "class" privilege on the one hand, and a "case-by-case" privilege on the other. The first four terms are used to refer to a privilege which was recognized at common law and one for which there is a prima facie presumption of inadmissibility (once it has been established that the relationship fits within the class) unless the party urging admission can show why the communications should not be privileged (i.e., why they should be admitted into evidence as an exception to the general rule). Such communications are excluded not because the evidence is not relevant, but rather, because there are overriding policy reasons to exclude this relevant evidence. Solicitor-client communications appear to fall within this first category. The term "case-by-case" privilege is used to refer to communications for which there is a prima facie assumption that they are not privileged, i.e., are admissible. The case-by-case analysis has generally involved an application of the "Wigmore test", which is a set of criteria for determining whether communications should be privileged (and therefore not admitted) in particular cases. In other words, the case-by-case analysis requires that the policy reasons for excluding otherwise relevant evidence be weighed in each particular case.

Throughout these reasons, I will be using the terms "class privilege" and prima facie privilege to refer to the first category of communications and will generally use the term "case-by-case privilege" to refer to the second category of communications. I should note that some writers tend to use the term "privileged communications" or "privilege" only in relation to communications which are class-based or prima facie inadmissible. I will be using the term "privilege" in relation to both types of communications.

. . .

Common Law, prima facie Privilege

A prima facie privilege for religious communications would constitute an exception to the general principle that all relevant evidence is admissible. Unless it can be said that the policy reasons to support a class privilege for religious communications are as compelling as the policy reasons which underlay the class privilege for solicitor-client communications, there is no basis for departing from the fundamental "first principle" that all relevant evidence is admissible until proven otherwise.

In my view, the policy reasons which underlay the treatment of solicitor-client communications as a separate class from most other confidential communications, are not equally applicable to religious communications. The prima facie protection for solicitor-client communications is based on the fact that the relationship and the communications between solicitor and client are essential to the effective operation of the legal system. Such communications are inextricably linked with the very system which desires the disclosure of the communication. In my view, religious communications, notwithstanding their social importance, are not inextricably linked with the justice system in the way that solicitor-client communications surely are.

. . .

Having found no common law, prima facie privilege for religious communications, I will consider whether such communications can be excluded in particular cases by applying the Wigmore criteria on a case-by-case basis.

2. Case-by-Case Privilege

In *Re Church of Scientology and The Queen (No. 6)* the Ontario Court of Appeal recognized the existence of a "priest and penitent" privilege determined on a case-by-case basis, having regard to the Wigmore criteria. This approach is consistent with the approach taken by this Court in *Slavutych v. Baker*, and is, in my view, consistent with a principled approach to the question which properly takes into account the particular circumstances of each case. This is not to say that the Wigmore criteria are now "carved in stone", but rather that these considerations provide a general framework within which policy considerations and the requirements of fact-finding can be weighed and balanced on the basis of their relative importance in the particular case before the court. Nor does this preclude the identification of a new class on a principled basis. Furthermore, a case-by-case analysis will allow courts to determine whether, in the particular circumstances, the individual's freedom of religion will be imperilled by the admission of the evidence.

. . .

Having found that religious communications can be excluded in particular cases where the Wigmore criteria are satisfied, I turn now to the question of whether the communications involved in this case satisfy the Wigmore criteria.

Application of the Wigmore Criteria

In my opinion, a consideration of the Wigmore criteria and the facts of this case reveals that the communications between the appellant, Pastor Thiessen and Janine Frovich were properly admitted at trial. In my view, these communications do not even satisfy the first requirement; namely, that they originate in a confidence that they will not be disclosed. Leaving aside the other components of the Wigmore test, it is absolutely crucial that the communications originate with an expectation of confidentiality (in order for those communications to be qualify as "privileged" and to thereby be excluded from evidence). Without this expectation of confidentiality, the raison d'être of the privilege is missing.

In the case at bar, there is evidence that Ms. Gruenke's communications to Pastor Thiessen and Ms. Frovich did not originate in a confidence that they would not be disclosed. The testimony of Pastor Thiessen and Janine Frovich indicates that they were unclear as to whether they were expected to keep confidential what Ms. Gruenke had told them about her involvement in the murder. As was stated by Twaddle J.A. in the Court of Appeal judgment at p. 300, "there was no evidence that the accused Gruenke made her admissions to them in the confident belief that they would be disclosed to no one". Ms. Gruenke did not approach Ms. Frovich and the Pastor on the basis that the communications were to be confidential. In fact, Ms. Frovich initiated the meeting and Ms. Gruenke testified that she saw no harm in speaking to Janine Frovich because she had already made up her mind to turn herself in to the police and "take the blame". In my view, the Court of Appeal accurately described these communications as being made more to relieve Ms. Gruenke's emotional stress than for a religious or spiritual purpose. I note that my view is based on the parties' statements and behaviour in relation to the communication and not on the lack of a formal practice of "confession" in the Victorious Faith Centre Church. While the existence of a formal practice of "confession" may well be a strong indication that the parties expected the communication to be confidential, the lack of such a formal practice is not, in and of itself, determinative.

The communications in question do not satisfy the first Wigmore criterion and their admission into evidence does not infringe Ms. Gruenke's freedom of religion. As I have stated above, whether an individual's freedom of religion will be infringed by the admission of religious communications will depend on the particular facts of each case. In the case at bar, there is no such infringement.I would dismiss the appeal.

L'Heureux-Dubé J., Gonthier J. concurring, agreed with the majority that the appeal should be dismissed, substantially for the reasons given. However, they would prefer, for utilitarian reasons, to recognize a class privilege for pastor-penitent communications. They concluded:

In my view, it is more in line with the rationales identified earlier, the spirit of the Charter and the goal of assuring the certainty of the law, to recognize a pastor-penitent category of privilege in this country. If our society truly wishes to encourage the creation and development of spiritual relationships, individuals must have a certain amount of confidence that their religious confessions, given in confidence and for spiritual relief, will not be disclosed. Not knowing in advance whether his or her confession will be afforded any protection, a penitent may not confess, or may not confess as freely as he or she otherwise would. Both the number of confessions and their quality will be affected. The special relationship between clergy and parishioners may not develop, resulting in a chilling effect on the spiritual relationship within our society. In that case, the very rationale for the pastor-penitent privilege may be defeated.

However, L'Heureux-Dubé J. and Gonthier J. decided that in the circumstances of this particular case the communications did not originate in the confidence that they would not be disclosed and therefore the communications were not covered by such a privilege.[351]

Both Quebec and Newfoundland have legislated a class privilege for religious communications.[352]

Six years after the Supreme Court dismissed Gruenke's appeal, the Self Defence Review Committee which had been established to review cases of battered women convicted before *Lavallee* recommended that the Minister of Justice refer her case to the Manitoba Court of Appeal pursuant to s. 690 of the *Criminal Code*. The issue was whether evidence surrounding her relationship with the deceased was admissible as fresh evidence on the issue of planning and deliberation. The Manitoba Court of Appeal concluded that the evidence was not admissible as fresh evidence.[353] The Supreme Court of Canada dismissed a further appeal.[354]

We will later further consider Wigmore's case-by-case approach and also the impact of the *Charter*. We first examine existing class privileges.

(b) Solicitor-Client Privilege

(i) *Generally*

> . . . the first duty of an attorney is to keep the secrets of his client.[355]

The privilege belongs to the client, not the attorney, and protects the client from the disclosure of any confidential communications made by him or her, or his or her agent, to his or her solicitor, or communications by the solicitor in response, while the client was engaged in seeking legal advice.

Consider the following views favouring and opposing the privilege. J.C. McRuer, in his Royal Commission Inquiry into Civil Rights,[356] justified the privilege:

> Without the solicitor and client privilege the whole structure of our adversary system of administering justice would collapse, for the object of that system is that the rights of all persons shall be submitted with equal force to the courts. The only way that the imbalance between the learned and the unlearned, the wise and the foolish, can be redressed is that every man's case be brought before the courts with as nearly equal ability as possible. If a lawyer is to give useful service to his client, he must be free to learn the whole of his client's case. The basis of the privilege between solicitor and client is not, therefore, that the relationship is confidential but that confidentiality is necessary to insure that the public, with safety, may substitute legal advisers in their place instead of having to conduct their own cases and advise themselves.

But Jeremy Bentham argued against the privilege:

351 For an application of *Gruenke*, see *R. v. Welsh* (2007), 51 C.R. (6th) 33 (Ont. S.C.J.).
352 See Newfoundland *Evidence Act*, R.S.N. 1990, c. E-16, s. 8; Quebec *Charter of Rights and Freedoms*, R.S.Q. 1977, c. C-12, s. 9. See generally H.R.S. Ryan, "Obligation of the Clergy Not to Reveal Confidential Information" (1990), 73 C.R. (3d) 217.
353 *R. v. Fosty* (1998), (*Reference re Gruenke*) 131 C.C.C. (3d) 72 (Man. C.A.).
354 *R. v. Fosty* [2000] 1 S.C.R. 836.
355 Per Gaselee, J. in *Taylor v. Blacklow* (1836), 132 E.R. 401 at 406.
356 Province of Ontario, Vol. 2, Report No. I (1968) at 819.

A counsel, solicitor, or attorney, cannot conduct the cause of his client" (it has been observed) "if he is not fully instructed in the circumstances attending it: but the client" (it is added) "could not give the instructions *with safety*, if the facts confided to his advocate were to be disclosed." Not with safety? So much the better. To what object is the whole system of penal law directed, if it be not that no man shall have it in his power to flatter himself with the hope of safety, in the event of his engaging in the commission of an act which the law, on account of its supposed mischievousness, has thought fit to prohibit? The argument employed as a reason against the compelling such disclosure, is the very argument that pleads in favour of it.[357]

DESCÔTEAUX v. MIERZWINSKI
[1982] 1 S.C.R. 860, 28 C.R. (3d) 289, 70 C.C.C. (2d) 385

The judgment of the court was delivered by

LAMER J.:—

A citizen who lies about his financial means in order to obtain legal aid is committing a crime. This appeal concerns the right of the police to be authorized by a search warrant to search a legal aid bureau and seize the form filled out by the citizen at his interview, for purposes of proving that this crime was committed. This issue raises several others, including, in particular, the scope of and procedures for exercising the authority to search lawyers' offices, in view of the confidential nature of their clients' files. This appeal will also give everyone an opportunity to note the deficiencies in the law in this area and the limited ability of the courts to compensate for them since their role is not primarily legislative.

. . .

In the Superior Court

After the documents had been seized and sealed, Mr. Descôteaux and the legal aid bureau (Le Centre communautaire juridique de Montréal) presented to a judge of the Superior Court, District of Montreal, a motion for the issuance of a writ of *certiorari* requesting that the seizure be quashed on the grounds of nullity and requesting the Superior Court Judge to order the justice of the peace to return the sealed envelope and its contents to them.

The motion was dismissed, but the judge amended the wording of the warrant, stating that [translation] "the words 'other documents concerning this case' should be struck out and no longer regarded as forming part of the said search warrant".

The Superior Court Judge stated that he was of the view that solicitor-client privilege could be invoked as soon as confidentiality was threatened, "without waiting until the person or persons disregarding the privilege attempted to tender the information thus obtained as evidence". He found, however, that the documents seized were not privileged since they had been prepared before the solicitor-client relationship came into existence.

---

[357] "Rationale of Judicial Evidence" (1827), 7 The Works of Jeremy Bentham, 475 (Bowring ed., 1842) quoted in 8 Wigmore, *Evidence* (McNaughton Rev.), s. 2291 at 550.

. . .

In the Court of Appeal

The Court of Appeal adopted the conclusions of the Superior Court Judge, together with his reasons [16 C.R. (3d) 188]. To these Bélanger J.A. added on behalf of the court that in any event solicitor-client privilege could not have operated to protect the communication, since the latter was precisely what had been resorted to in order to mislead a representative of the legal aid bureau. On that matter, he stated the following (translation) [at p. 192]:

> In the case at bar the communications or documents that are alleged to be confidential are those referred to in the charge as having been used in the commission of the offence in question. Apart from common law principles, they are no more privileged than if the same information and documents had been used to mislead the lawyer himself in order to fraudulently obtain his services on special terms. In either case I do not think that false communications made to the eventual victim who will have to bear the cost of the services are confidential in any way. In short, a communication made to a representative of the Commission des services juridiques [Legal Services Commission] is in no way confidential if it is an element of an offence committed to the latter's prejudice, since in such circumstances there is no confidentiality between solicitor and client.

I think that at this point I should state my findings in the case at bar; I shall give reasons for them later.

In my view, it was correctly decided that it is not necessary to wait for the trial or preliminary inquiry at which the communication is to be adduced or sought in evidence before raising its confidentiality.

. . .

The right to confidentiality

It is not necessary to demonstrate the existence of a person's right to have communications with his lawyer kept confidential. Its existence has been affirmed numerous times and was recently reconfirmed by this court in *Solosky v. The Queen*, [1980] 1 S.C.R. 821 at p. 839, where Dickson J. stated:

> One may depart from the current concept of privilege and approach the case on the broader basis that (i) *the right to communicate in confidence with one's legal adviser is a fundamental civil and legal right, founded upon the unique relationship of solicitor and client*, and (ii) a person confined to prison retains all of his civil rights, other than those expressly or impliedly taken from him by law.

(Emphasis added.) There is no denying that a person has a right to communicate with a legal adviser in all confidence, a right that is "founded upon the unique relationship of solicitor and client" (*Solosky, supra*). It is a personal and extra-patrimonial right which follows a citizen throughout his dealings with others. Like other personal, extra-patrimonial rights, it gives rise to preventive or curative remedies provided for by law, depending on the nature of the aggression threatening it or of which it was the object. Thus a lawyer who communicates a confidential communication to others without his client's authorization could be sued by his client for damages; or a third party who had accidentally seen the contents of a lawyer's file could be prohibited by injunction from disclosing them. (I am dealing here generally with the effects of the right to confidentiality. In its present state, the rule of evidence, which I shall discuss later, would not prohibit a third party from making such a disclosure: see 8 Wigmore, *Evidence*, §2326, pp. 633-4 (McNaughton Rev. 1961.)

. . .

There is no doubt that this right belonging to a person in his dealings with others, including the State, is part of our Quebec public law as well as of the common law.

Although we recognize numerous applications of it today, the right to confidentiality did not first appear until the 16th century, and then did so as a rule of evidence: see, *inter alia, Berd v. Lovelace* (1577), Cary 62, 21 E.R. 33; *Dennis v. Codrington* (1580), Cary 100, 21 E.R. 53.

The rule of evidence is well known; it has often been stated. This court referred to it again recently in *Solosky, supra*. That decision sets out the conditions precedent to the existence of the privilege, as well as its limits and exceptions. It should be pointed out that the substantive conditions precedent to the existence of the privilege, which the judges have gradually established and defined, are in fact the substantive conditions precedent to the existence of the right to confidentiality, the former being merely the earliest manifestation of the latter. There is no need to list those conditions exhaustively here or to review all the nuances that have been developed by the courts over the years. It will be sufficient to review them in broad outline and to emphasize certain aspects of particular relevance to this appeal.

The following statement by Wigmore (8 Wigmore, *Evidence*, §2292, p. 554 (McNaughton Rev. 1961)), of the rule of evidence is a good summary, in my view, of the substantive conditions precedent to the existence of the right of the lawyer's client to confidentiality:

> Where legal advice of any kind is sought from a professional legal adviser in his capacity as such, the communications relating to that purpose, made in confidence by the client, are at his instance permanently protected from disclosure by himself or by the legal adviser, except the protection be waived.

Seeking advice from a legal adviser includes consulting those who assist him professionally (for example, his secretary or articling student) and who have as such had access to the communications made by the client for the purpose of obtaining legal advice.

There are exceptions. It is not sufficient to speak to a lawyer or one of his associates for everything to become confidential from that point on. The communication must be made to the lawyer or his assistants in their professional capacity; the relationship must be a professional one at the exact moment of the communication. Communications made in order to facilitate the commission of a crime or fraud will not be confidential either, regardless of whether or not the lawyer is acting in good faith.

The substantive rule

Although the right to confidentiality first took the form of a rule of evidence, it is now recognized as having a much broader scope, as can be seen from the manner in which this court dealt with the issues raised in *Solosky, supra.*

. . .

It is quite apparent that the court in that case applied a standard that has nothing to do with the rule of evidence, the privilege, since there was never any question of testimony before a tribunal or court. The court in fact, in my view, applied a substantive rule, without actually formulating it, and, consequently, recognized implicitly that the right to confidentiality, which had long ago given rise to a rule of evidence, had also since given rise to a substantive rule.

It would, I think, be useful for us to formulate this substantive rule, as the judges formerly did with the rule of evidence; it could, in my view, be stated as follows:

1. The confidentiality of communications between solicitor and client may be raised in any circumstances where such communications are likely to be disclosed without the client's consent.

2. Unless the law provides otherwise, when and to the extent that the legitimate exercise of a right would interfere with another person's right to have his communications with his lawyer kept confidential, the resulting conflict should be resolved in favour of protecting the confidentiality.

3. When the law gives someone the authority to do something which, in the circumstances of the case, might interfere with that confidentiality, the decision to do so and the choice of means of exercising that authority should be determined with a view to not interfering with it except to the extent absolutely necessary in order to achieve the ends sought by the enabling legislation.

4. Acts providing otherwise in situations under para. 2 and enabling legislation referred to in para. 3 must be interpreted restrictively.

The rule of evidence

The rule of evidence is formulated by Cross (*Cross on Evidence*, 5th ed. (1979), p. 282), as follows:

> In civil and criminal cases, confidential communications passing between a client and his legal adviser need not be given in evidence by the client and, without the client's consent, may not be given in evidence by the legal adviser in a judicial proceeding. . .

The rule of evidence does not in any way prevent a third party witness (I am referring here to someone other than an agent of the client or the lawyer) from introducing in evidence confidential communications made by a client to his lawyer. It is important to note, however, that before allowing such evidence to be introduced and in determining to what extent to allow it, the judge must satisfy himself, through the application of the substantive rule (No. 3), that what is being sought to be proved by the communications is important to the outcome of the case and that there is no reasonable alternative form of evidence that could be used for that purpose.

Confidentiality in the case at bar

In the case at bar the principal issue is to determine when the solicitor-client relationship, which confers the confidentiality protected by the substantive rule and the rule of evidence, arises.

The Superior Court Judge, as we have seen, was of the view that this relationship, and consequently the right to confidentiality, did not arise until the legal aid applicant had been accepted, that is, until the retainer was established.

When dealing with the right to confidentiality it is necessary, in my view, to distinguish between the moment when the retainer is established and the moment when the solicitor-client relationship arises. The latter arises as soon as the potential client has his first dealings with the lawyer's office in order to obtain legal advice.

The items of information that a lawyer requires from a person in order to decide if he will agree to advise or represent him are just as much communications made in order to obtain legal advice as any information communicated to him subsequently. It has long been recognized that even if the lawyer does not agree to advise the person seeking his services, communications made by the person to the lawyer or his staff for that purpose are none the less privileged: *Minter v. Priest*, [1930] A.C. 558; *Phipson on Evidence*, 12th ed. (1976), p. 244, para. 590; 8 Wigmore, *Evidence* §2304, pp. 586-7 (McNaughton Rev. 1961).

. . .

Conclusion

In summary, a lawyer's client is entitled to have all communications made with a view to obtaining legal advice kept confidential. Whether communications are made to the lawyer himself or to employees, and whether they deal with matters of an administrative nature such as financial means or with the actual nature of the legal problem, all information which a person must provide in order to obtain legal advice and which is given in confidence for that purpose enjoys the privileges attached to confidentiality. This confidentiality attaches to all communications made within the framework of the solicitor-client relationship, which arises as soon as the potential client takes the first steps, and consequently even before the formal retainer is established.

There are certain exceptions to the principle of the confidentiality of solicitor-client communications, however. Thus communications that are in themselves criminal or that are made with a view to obtaining legal advice to facilitate the commission of a crime will not be privileged, *inter alia*.

The fundamental right to communicate with one's legal adviser in confidence has given rise to a rule of evidence and a substantive rule. Whether through the rule of evidence or the substantive rule, the client's right to have his communications to his lawyer kept confidential will have an effect when the search warrant provided for in s. 443 of the *Criminal Code* is being issued and executed.

Thus the justice of the peace has no jurisdiction to order the seizure of documents that would not be admissible in evidence in court on the ground that they are privileged (the rule of evidence).

Before authorizing a search of a lawyer's officer for evidence of a crime, the justice of the peace should refuse to issue the warrant unless he is satisfied that there is no reasonable alternative to the search, or he will be exceeding his jurisdiction (the substantive rule). When issuing the warrant, to search for evidence or other things, he must in any event attach terms of execution to the warrant designed to protect the right to confidentiality of the lawyer's clients as much as possible.

Applying these principles to the case at bar, I have arrived at the following conclusions.

First, all information contained in the form that applicants for legal aid must fill out is provided for the purpose of obtaining legal advice, is given in confidence for that purpose and, consequently, is subject to the applicant's fundamental right to have such communications kept confidential and, as such, is protected by the rule of evidence and the substantive rule.

It is alleged in the information laid that the communications made by Ledoux with respect to his financial means are criminal in themselves since they constitute the material element of the crime charged. This is an exception to the principle of confidentiality and these communications are accordingly not protected (this does not mean that we are expressing an opinion as to the validity of the allegations in the information). However, since the allegation concerns only the information dealing with the applicant's financial means, all other information on the form remains confidential.

Since the part of the form dealing with Ledoux's financial situation was as an exception admissible in evidence, the justice of the peace had jurisdiction to order its seizure.

For these reasons I would dismiss this appeal and refer the matter back to the justice of the peace, ordering him to deal with the envelope and its contents as stated above.

In response to *Descôteaux*, Parliament enacted s. 488.1 of the *Criminal Code* which set out a detailed code of procedure to deal with search warrants issued to search lawyer's offices, striving to arrive at a procedure to protect against undue invasions of solicitor-client privilege. A series of Court of Appeal decisions and then finally the Supreme Court of Canada in *R. v. Lavallee, Rackel & Heintz*[358] decided that s. 488.1 was insufficiently

---

[358] (2002), 167 C.C.C. (3d) 1 (S.C.C.). In *Federation of Law Societies of Canada v. Canada (Attorney General)*, 2015 CSC 7, 2015 SCC 7, [2015] 1 S.C.R. 401, 322 C.C.C. (3d) 1, 17 C.R. (7th) 57 (S.C.C.) a 5-2 majority declared that another central dimension of the solicitor-client relationship and a principle of fundamental justice was the lawyer's duty of commitment to the

protective of solicitor-client privilege and therefore an unconstitutional violation of the *Charter* right to make full answer and defence.[359] The Supreme Court emphasized in *Maranda v. Richer*[360] that even where there is authorization to search a lawyer's office the impairment of solicitor-client privilege must be as little as possible.

The rules of privilege prevent a client from being <u>compelled</u> by the State or a third party to reveal a confidential solicitor-client communication. It is important to recognize that a lawyer's duty of confidentiality is broader than the privilege. It requires a lawyer, subject to a number of exceptions, to not <u>disclose</u> any information about the client obtained during the course of the relationship. This duty of confidentiality is enforced through the rules of professional conduct enacted by each provincial law society.

CANADA (PRIVACY COMMISSIONER) v. BLOOD TRIBE DEPARTMENT OF HEALTH
[2008] 2 S.C.R. 574

An employee with the Blood Tribe Department of Health was dismissed. At the time of her dismissal, her employer sought legal advice. Following her dismissal, the employee sought access to her file. She suspected that her employer may have collected inaccurate information. Her employer refused. She then brought an application under the relevant provisions of the *Personal Information Protection and Electronic Documents Act (PIPEDA)* to the Privacy Commissioner. The issue before the Supreme Court was whether the Commissioner could order production of documents protected by solicitor-client privilege. Writing for the Court, Justice Binnie held that the Privacy Commissioner, while an officer of Parliament and administrative adjudicator, has no jurisdiction to order disclosure as the position lacks the independence and authority of a court. In so holding, the Court provided a concise summary of the solicitor-client privilege.

BINNIE J. (for the Court):

. . .

IV. Analysis

9 Solicitor-client privilege is fundamental to the proper functioning of our legal system. The complex of rules and procedures is such that, realistically speaking, it cannot be navigated without a lawyer's expert advice. It is said that anyone who represents himself or herself has a fool for a client, yet a lawyer's

---

client's cause. In *R. v. Lavallee, Rackel & Heintz* the Supreme Court of Canada took issue with Parliament's attempt to set out a legal regime in the *Criminal Code* (s. 488.1) for searches and seizures conducted at law offices. The Court recognized that solicitor-client privilege was a principle of fundamental justice under s. 7 of the *Charter*. The Court declared s. 488.1 inoperative and set out a number of standards to be followed in such searches.

[359]   For comment see M.C. Plaxton, "*R. v. Lavallee, Rackel & Heintz*: Jiminy Cricket Has Left The Building" (2002), 3 C.R. (6th) 253. See further *Festing v. Canada (Attorney General)* (2003), 172 C.C.C. (3d) 321 (B.C. C.A.) and *Maranda v. Richer, infra* note 360. The Court has declared procedures to be applied in such cases pending any new legislation.

[360]   (2003), 15 C.R. (6th) 1 (S.C.C.).

advice is only as good as the factual information the client provides. Experience shows that people who have a legal problem will often not make a clean breast of the facts to a lawyer without an assurance of confidentiality "as close to absolute as possible":

> [S]olicitor-client privilege must be as close to absolute as possible to ensure public confidence and retain relevance. As such, it will only yield in certain clearly defined circumstances, and does not involve a balancing of interests on a case-by-case basis.
>
> (*R. v. McClure*, [2001] 1 S.C.R. 445, 2001 SCC 14, at para. 35, quoted with approval in *Lavallee, Rackel & Heintz v. Canada (Attorney General)*, [2002] 3 S.C.R. 209, 2002 SCC 61, at para. 36.)

It is in the public interest that this free flow of legal advice be encouraged. Without it, access to justice and the quality of justice in this country would be severely compromised. The privilege belongs to the client not the lawyer. In *Andrews v. Law Society of British Columbia*, [1989] 1 S.C.R. 143, at p. 188, McIntyre J. affirmed yet again that the Court will not permit a solicitor to disclose a client's confidence.

10 At the time the employer in this case consulted its lawyer, litigation may or may not have been in contemplation. It does not matter. While the solicitor-client privilege may have started life as a rule of evidence, it is now unquestionably a rule of substance applicable to all interactions between a client and his or her lawyer when the lawyer is engaged in providing legal advice or otherwise acting as a lawyer rather than as a business counsellor or in some other non-legal capacity: *Solosky v. The Queen*, [1980] 1 S.C.R. 821, at p. 837; *Descôteaux v. Mierzwinski*, [1982] 1 S.C.R. 860, at pp. 885-87; *R. v. Gruenke*, [1991] 3 S.C.R. 263; *Smith v. Jones*, [1999] 1 S.C.R. 455; *Foster Wheeler Power Co. v. Société intermunicipale de gestion et d'élimination des déchets (SIGED) inc.*, [2004] 1 S.C.R. 456, 2004 SCC 18, at paras. 40-47; *McClure*, at paras. 23-27; *Blank v. Canada (Minister of Justice)*, [2006] 2 S.C.R. 319, 2006 SCC 39, at para. 26; *Goodis v. Ontario (Ministry of Correctional Services)*, [2006] 2 S.C.R. 32, 2006 SCC 31; *Celanese Canada Inc. v. Murray Demolition Corp.*, [2006] 2 S.C.R. 189, 2006 SCC 36; *Juman v. Doucette*, [2008] 1 S.C.R. 157, 2008 SCC 8. A rare exception, which has no application here, is that no privilege attaches to communications criminal in themselves or intended to further criminal purposes: *Descôteaux*, at p. 881; *R. v. Campbell*, [1999] 1 S.C.R. 565. The extremely limited nature of the exception emphasizes, rather than dilutes, the paramountcy of the general rule whereby solicitor-client privilege is created and maintained "as close to absolute as possible to ensure public confidence and retain relevance" (*McClure*, at para. 35).

11 To give effect to this fundamental policy of the law, our Court has held that legislative language that may (if broadly construed) allow incursions on solicitor-client privilege must be interpreted restrictively. The privilege cannot be abrogated by inference. Open-textured language governing production of

documents will be read not to include solicitor-client documents: *Lavallee*, at para. 18; *Pritchard*, at para. 33. This case falls squarely within that principle.

As we will see in the next section (*(ii) Exceptions*), the privilege is not absolute, although *Blood Tribe* reveals how jealously guarded it is as a substantive organizing principle of our legal system and the rule of law. In the following case, the Supreme Court, applying its earlier decision in *Descôteaux*, set out a general "absolute necessity" test for when the privilege will be pierced. The issue was whether a judge could order disclosure of privileged records to a lawyer representing a client who sought production under the *Freedom of Information and Protection of Privacy Act* to enable the lawyer to make submissions on whether the records should be disclosed. The lawyer provided a non-disclosure undertaking.

GOODIS v. ONTARIO (MINISTRY OF CORRECTIONAL SERVICES)
[2006] 2 S.C.R. 32

ROTHSTEIN J. (for the Court):

. . .

15 The substantive rule laid down in *Descôteaux* is that a judge must not interfere with the confidentiality of communications between solicitor and client "except to the extent absolutely necessary in order to achieve the ends sought by the enabling legislation". In *Lavallee, Rackel & Heintz v. Canada (Attorney General)*, [2002] 3 S.C.R. 209, 2002 SCC 61, it was found that a provision of the *Criminal Code*, R.S.C. 1985, c. C-46, that authorized the seizure of documents from a law office was unreasonable within the meaning of s. 8 of the *Canadian Charter of Rights and Freedoms* because it permitted the automatic loss of solicitor-client privilege. That decision further emphasized the fundamental nature of the substantive rule. It is, therefore, incumbent on a judge to apply the "absolutely necessary" test when deciding an application for disclosure of such records.

. . .

17 Of particular significance is that the question of disclosure of solicitor-client privileged communications does not involve a balancing of interests on a case-by-case basis.

. . .

(3) Meaning of Absolute Necessity

20 Absolute necessity is as restrictive a test as may be formulated short of an absolute prohibition in every case. The circumstances in which the test has been met exemplify its restrictive nature. In *Solosky v. The Queen*, [1980] 1 S.C.R. 821, at p. 841, for example, it was found that subject to strict safeguards, mail received by an inmate at a penitentiary could be inspected to maintain the safety and security of the penitentiary. Similarly, in *McClure* [discussed in the next section], it was found that documents subject to privilege

could be disclosed where there was a genuine danger of wrongful conviction because the information was not available from other sources and the accused could not otherwise raise a reasonable doubt as to his guilt.

21 While I cannot rule out the possibility, it is difficult to envisage circumstances where the absolute necessity test could be met if the sole purpose of disclosure is to facilitate argument by the requester's counsel on the question of whether privilege is properly claimed. Hearing from both sides of an issue is a principle to be departed from only in exceptional circumstances. However, privilege is a subject with which judges are acquainted. They are well equipped in the ordinary case to determine whether a record is subject to privilege. There is no evidence in this case that disclosure of records to counsel for the purpose of arguing whether or not they are privileged is absolutely necessary.

(4) Judicial Workload

22 It is suggested that the need to examine many records could place an undue burden on the reviewing judge. It is not obvious that disclosure to the requester's counsel will necessarily reduce that workload. In any event, there are techniques available to help reduce the volume of information that must be reviewed. At a minimum, for example, the 459 pages could be organized in categories that exhibit common characteristics relevant to the solicitor-client privilege. Nor do I see how an increase in judicial workload or other administrative considerations make absolutely necessary disclosure to the requester's counsel for the purpose of arguing the judicial review application. Convenience is not a reason to release information subject to a claim of solicitor-client privilege.

(5) Conclusion on Solicitor-Client Privilege

23 In sum, I agree with the Ministry that there is no justification for establishing a new or different test for disclosure of records subject to a claim for solicitor-client privilege in an access to information case.

24 I am of the respectful opinion that the Ontario courts were in error in permitting disclosure of all the documents in this case. The appropriate test for any document claimed to be subject to solicitor-client privilege is "absolute necessity". That test was not applied. Had it been, disclosure of all the records would not have been ordered.

25 I am mindful that openness of the court's process is a recognized principle. However, as with all general principles, there are exceptions. Records that are subject to a claim of solicitor-client privilege in an access to information case are such an exception. Absent absolute necessity in order to achieve the end sought by the enabling legislation, such records may not be disclosed. As stated, the evidence disclosed no such absolute necessity in this case.

What if the client believes he or she is communicating with a lawyer but, in fact, the person is not licensed?

MINISTER OF NATIONAL REVENUE v. NEWPORT PACIFIC FINANCIAL GROUP SA
2010 ABQB 568, 34 Alta. L.R. (5th) 285 (Alta. Q.B.)

GRAESSER, J.:

. . .

31 Can solicitor and client privilege be extended to communications between a client and a lawyer who is not authorized to practice law in the jurisdiction?

32 *The Legal Profession Act*, RSA 2000, c. L-8, provides in para. 106(1):

> 106.
>
> (1) No person shall, unless the person is an active member of the Society,
>
> (a) practise as a barrister or as a solicitor

. . .

39 Mr. Ziv, on behalf of Mr. O'Byrne and Sunny Shores Ltd., has not provided any authority suggesting that communications with a non-lawyer are privileged. Solicitor client privilege must be a communication between a lawyer and his or her client, or part of the lawyer's work product in the giving of legal advice.

40 There may be some debate as to what a "lawyer" is. It may well be that someone who has a law degree can legitimately claim to be a "lawyer". In Alberta, a "lawyer" has no particular status. Legal services are provided by barristers and solicitors who are members of the Law Society.

41 There are many people with law degrees who are not "barristers and solicitors". Non-practising members of the Law Society are in that category, yet they are still lawyers. Disbarred members of the Law Society may still be "lawyers" even though they have no ability to practice law lawfully in Alberta. There are others: law school graduates who have chosen not to be admitted to the bar; lawyers from other jurisdictions who have not sought to be admitted to the bar here; and former members of the Law Society who have ceased to have any relationship with the Law Society.

42 Solicitor client privilege is a significant protection given to clients of barristers and solicitors, so that they can be frank with their barrister and solicitor to obtain appropriate legal advice. Solicitor client privilege enjoys a higher status in law than any other form of confidential communications, including those between priest and penitent, doctor and patient, or journalist and source.

43 In my view, the essence of solicitor client privilege is that it must involve a lawyer who is regulated as part of the legal profession. People can seek advice from anyone they choose. But if they want legal advice, and the protection of solicitor client privilege with respect to their communications for the purpose of obtaining legal advice, the person they communicate with must be part of the recognized legal profession in the jurisdiction where they seek the advice.

44 There is no public interest served in protecting communications between someone and a disbarred lawyer, or someone who has never passed the bar exams, or someone who is not subject to regulatory oversight by the body charged with regulating the provision of legal services in the jurisdiction.

45 In Alberta, that is the Law Society. If someone is not an active member of the Law Society of Alberta, he or she cannot practice law in Alberta. He or she cannot give legal advice. Thus there can be no communications with that person for the purposes of obtaining legal advice.

. . .

52 Mr. O'Byrne complains that he was misled by representations and advertising from NPC as to the nature of their services and the presence of lawyers there. Those concerns might be the subject of litigation between Mr. O' Byrne and those who made those representations or placed such advertising, but solicitor client privilege is a function of a relationship between a person and his or her barrister and solicitor. Privilege does not exist between a person and someone he or she believes to be a barrister and solicitor.

53 Otherwise, communications with a disbarred lawyer, or with someone who has never been admitted to the bar, or with someone falsely holding him or herself out to be a lawyer entitled to practice, might be privileged. That cannot be correct.

. . .

55 If a member of the public believes someone to be a barrister and solicitor, entitled to practice law in Alberta, and does not verify that with the Law Society, he or she proceeds at his or her peril. If the advisor turns out to not be a member in good standing with the Law Society, the person has not been dealing with a barrister or solicitor and any communications cannot be protected by solicitor client privilege.

But see *R. v. Choney* (1908), 17 Man. R. 467 (C.A.), in which the accused's confession was protected by solicitor-client privilege when he reasonably but mistakenly believed he was speaking to his lawyer's representative.

Does the privilege apply to licensed paralegals?

Is there a litigation or work-product privilege in Canada? Is it accorded the same status as solicitor-client privilege? The following case is the first time the Supreme Court of Canada had occasion to answer these questions.

BLANK v. CANADA (MINISTER OF JUSTICE)
40 C.R. (6th) 1, [2006] 2 S.C.R. 319

Blank and a company were twice charged with regulatory offences. All of the charges were eventually quashed or stayed by the Crown. Blank and the company eventually sued the federal government for fraud, conspiracy, perjury and abuse of process. Blank sought all of the records pertaining to his prosecution. When his request was refused, he brought an application under the *Access Act*. The Minister of Justice claimed that the documents prepared for the dominant purpose of a criminal investigation were covered by litigation privilege. The Supreme Court was asked to determine whether some of the documents that fell within litigation privilege should be released if the original litigation that led to their creation had ended.

FISH J. (for the majority):

. . .

1 This appeal requires the Court, for the first time, to distinguish between two related but conceptually distinct exemptions from compelled disclosure: the solicitor-client privilege and the litigation privilege. They often co-exist and one is sometimes mistakenly called by the other's name, but they are not coterminous in space, time or meaning.

2 More particularly, we are concerned in this case with the litigation privilege, with how it is born and when it must be laid to rest.

. . .

5 In short, we are not asked in this case to decide whether the government can invoke litigation privilege. Quite properly, the parties agree that it can. Our task, rather, is to examine the defining characteristics of that privilege and, more particularly, to determine its lifespan.

6 The Minister contends that the solicitor-client privilege has two "branches", one concerned with confidential communications between lawyers and their clients, the other relating to information and materials gathered or created in the litigation context. The first of these branches, as already indicated, is generally characterized as the "legal advice privilege"; the second, as the "litigation privilege".

7 Bearing in mind their different scope, purpose and rationale, it would be preferable, in my view, to recognize that we are dealing here with distinct conceptual animals and not with two branches of the same tree. Accordingly, I shall refer in these reasons to the solicitor-client privilege as if it includes only the legal advice privilege, and shall indeed use the two phrases—solicitor-client privilege and legal advice privilege—synonymously and interchangeably, except where otherwise indicated.

8 As a matter of substance and not mere terminology, the distinction between litigation privilege and the solicitor-client privilege is decisive in this case. The former, unlike the latter, is of temporary duration. It expires with the litigation

of which it was born. Characterizing litigation privilege as a "branch" of the solicitor-client privilege, as the Minister would, does not envelop it in a shared cloak of permanency.

9 The Minister's claim of litigation privilege fails in this case because the privilege claimed, by whatever name, has expired: The files to which the respondent seeks access relate to penal proceedings that have long terminated. By seeking civil redress for the manner in which those proceedings were conducted, the respondent has given them neither fresh life nor a posthumous and parallel existence.

. . .

26 . . . The solicitor-client privilege has been firmly entrenched for centuries. It recognizes that the justice system depends for its vitality on full, free and frank communication between those who need legal advice and those who are best able to provide it. Society has entrusted to lawyers the task of advancing their clients' cases with the skill and expertise available only to those who are trained in the law. They alone can discharge these duties effectively, but only if those who depend on them for counsel may consult with them in confidence. The resulting confidential relationship between solicitor and client is a necessary and essential condition of the effective administration of justice.

27 Litigation privilege, on the other hand, is not directed at, still less, restricted to, communications between solicitor and client. It contemplates, as well, communications between a solicitor and third parties or, in the case of an unrepresented litigant, between the litigant and third parties. Its object is to ensure the efficacy of the adversarial process and not to promote the solicitor-client relationship. And to achieve this purpose, parties to litigation, represented or not, must be left to prepare their contending positions in private, without adversarial interference and without fear of premature disclosure.

28 R. J. Sharpe (now Sharpe J.A.) has explained particularly well the differences between litigation privilege and solicitor-client privilege:

> It is crucially important to distinguish litigation privilege from solicitor-client privilege. There are, I suggest, at least three important differences between the two. First, solicitor-client privilege applies only to confidential communications between the client and his solicitor. Litigation privilege, on the other hand, applies to communications of a non-confidential nature between the solicitor and third parties and even includes material of a non-communicative nature. Secondly, solicitor-client privilege exists any time a client seeks legal advice from his solicitor whether or not litigation is involved. Litigation privilege, on the other hand, applies only in the context of litigation itself. Thirdly, and most important, the rationale for solicitor-client privilege is very different from that which underlies litigation privilege. This difference merits close attention. The interest which underlies the protection accorded communications between a client and a solicitor from disclosure is the interest of all citizens to have full and ready access to legal

advice. If an individual cannot confide in a solicitor knowing that what is said will not be revealed, it will be difficult, if not impossible, for that individual to obtain proper candid legal advice.

Litigation privilege, on the other hand, is geared directly to the process of litigation. Its purpose is not explained adequately by the protection afforded lawyer-client communications deemed necessary to allow clients to obtain legal advice, the interest protected by solicitor-client privilege. Its purpose is more particularly related to the needs of the adversarial trial process. Litigation privilege is based upon the need for a protected area to facilitate investigation and preparation of a case for trial by the adversarial advocate. In other words, litigation privilege aims to facilitate a process (namely, the adversary process), while solicitor-client privilege aims to protect a relationship (namely, the confidential relationship between a lawyer and a client).

("Claiming Privilege in the Discovery Process", in *Special Lectures of the Law Society of Upper Canada* (1984), 163, at pp. 164-65)

29 With the exception of *Hodgkinson v. Simms* (1988), 33 B.C.L.R. (2d) 129, a decision of the British Columbia Court of Appeal, the decisions of appellate courts in this country have consistently found that litigation privilege is based on a different rationale than solicitor-client privilege . . .

30 American and English authorities are to the same effect . . . . In the United States communications with third parties and other materials prepared in anticipation of litigation are covered by the similar "attorney work product" doctrine. This "distinct rationale" theory is also supported by the majority of academics . . . .

31 Though conceptually distinct, litigation privilege and legal advice privilege serve a common cause: The secure and effective administration of justice according to law. And they are complementary and not competing in their operation. But treating litigation privilege and legal advice privilege as two branches of the same tree tends to obscure the true nature of both.

32 Unlike the solicitor-client privilege, the litigation privilege arises and operates even in the absence of a solicitor-client relationship, and it applies indiscriminately to all litigants, whether or not they are represented by counsel: see *Alberta (Treasury Branches) v. Ghermezian* (1999), 242 A.R. 326, 1999 ABQB 407. A self-represented litigant is no less in need of, and therefore entitled to, a "zone" or [page333] "chamber" of privacy. Another important distinction leads to the same conclusion. Confidentiality, the sine qua non of the solicitor-client privilege, is not an essential component of the litigation privilege. In preparing for trial, lawyers as a matter of course obtain information from third parties who have no need nor any expectation of confidentiality; yet the litigation privilege attaches nonetheless.

33 In short, the litigation privilege and the solicitor-client privilege are driven by different policy considerations and generate different legal consequences.

34 The purpose of the litigation privilege, I repeat, is to create a "zone of privacy" in relation to pending or apprehended litigation. Once the litigation has ended, the privilege to which it gave rise has lost its specific and concrete purpose—and therefore its justification. But to borrow a phrase, the litigation is not over until it is over: It cannot be said to have "terminated", in any meaningful sense of that term, where litigants or related parties remain locked in what is essentially the same legal combat.

35 Except where such related litigation persists, there is no need and no reason to protect from discovery anything that would have been subject to compellable disclosure but for the pending or apprehended proceedings which provided its shield. Where the litigation has indeed ended, there is little room for concern lest opposing counsel or their clients argue their case "on wits borrowed from the adversary", to use the language of the U.S. Supreme Court in *Hickman*, at p. 516.

36 I therefore agree with the majority in the Federal Court of Appeal and others who share their view that the common law litigation privilege comes to an end, absent closely related proceedings, upon the termination of the litigation that gave rise to the privilege. . .

37 Thus, the principle "once privileged, always privileged", so vital to the solicitor-client privilege, is foreign to the litigation privilege. The litigation privilege, unlike the solicitor-client privilege, is neither absolute in scope nor permanent in duration.

38 As mentioned earlier, however, the privilege may retain its purpose—and, therefore, its effect—where the litigation that gave rise to the privilege has ended, but related litigation remains pending or may reasonably be apprehended. In this regard, I agree with Pelletier J.A. regarding "the possibility of defining ... litigation more broadly than the particular proceeding which gave rise to the claim" (para. 89); see *Ed Miller Sales & Rentals Ltd. v. Caterpillar Tractor Co.* (1988), 90 A.R. 323 (C.A.).

39 At a minimum, it seems to me, this enlarged definition of "litigation" includes separate proceedings that involve the same or related parties and arise from the same or a related cause of action (or "juridical source"). Proceedings that raise issues common to the initial action and share its essential purpose would in my view qualify as well.

40 As a matter of principle, the boundaries of this extended meaning of "litigation" are limited by the purpose for which litigation privilege is granted, namely, as mentioned, "the need for a protected area to facilitate investigation and preparation of a case for trial by the adversarial advocate" (Sharpe, at p. 165).

. . .

42 In this case, the respondent claims damages from the federal government for fraud, conspiracy, perjury and abuse of prosecutorial powers. Pursuant to the *Access Act*, he demands the disclosure to him of all documents relating to the Crown's conduct of its proceedings against him. The source of those proceedings is the alleged pollution and breach of reporting requirements by the respondent and his company.

43 The Minister's claim of privilege thus concerns documents that were prepared for the dominant purpose of a criminal prosecution relating to environmental matters and reporting requirements. The respondent's action, on the other hand, seeks civil redress for the manner in which the government conducted that prosecution. It springs from a different juridical source and is in that sense unrelated to the litigation of which the privilege claimed was born.

44 The litigation privilege would not in any event protect from disclosure evidence of the claimant party's abuse of process or similar blameworthy conduct. It is not a black hole from which evidence of one's own misconduct can never be exposed to the light of day.

45 Even where the materials sought would otherwise be subject to litigation privilege, the party seeking their disclosure may be granted access to them upon a prima facie showing of actionable misconduct by the other party in relation to the proceedings with respect to which litigation privilege is claimed. Whether privilege is claimed in the originating or in related litigation, the court may review the materials to determine whether their disclosure should be ordered on this ground.

46 Finally, in the Court of Appeal, Létourneau J.A., dissenting on the cross-appeal, found that the government's status as a "recurring litigant" could justify a litigation privilege that outlives its common law equivalent. In his view, the "[a]utomatic and uncontrolled access to the government lawyer's brief, once the first litigation is over, may impede the possibility of effectively adopting and implementing [general policies and strategies]" (para. 42).

47 I hesitate to characterize as "[a]utomatic and uncontrolled" access to the government lawyer's brief once the subject proceedings have ended. In my respectful view, access will in fact be neither automatic nor uncontrolled.

48 First, as mentioned earlier, it will not be automatic because all subsequent litigation will remain subject to a claim of privilege if it involves the same or related parties and the same or related source. It will fall within the protective orbit of the same litigation defined broadly.

49 Second, access will not be uncontrolled because many of the documents in the lawyer's brief will, in any event, remain exempt from disclosure by virtue of the legal advice privilege. In practice, a lawyer's brief normally includes materials covered by the solicitor-client privilege because of their evident connection to legal advice sought or given in the course of, or in relation to, the

originating proceedings. The distinction between the solicitor-client privilege and the litigation privilege does not preclude their potential overlap in a litigation context.

50 Commensurate with its importance, the solicitor-client privilege has over the years been broadly interpreted by this Court. In that light, anything in a litigation file that falls within the solicitor-client privilege will remain clearly and forever privileged.

. . .

55 Finally, we should not disregard the origins of this dispute between the respondent and the Minister. It arose in the context of a criminal prosecution by the Crown against the respondent. In criminal proceedings, the accused's right to discovery is constitutionally guaranteed. The prosecution is obliged under *Stinchcombe* to make available to the accused all relevant information if there is a "reasonable possibility that the withholding of information will impair the right of the accused to make full answer and defence" (p. 340). This added burden of disclosure is placed on the Crown in light of its overwhelming advantage in resources and the corresponding risk that the accused might otherwise be unfairly disadvantaged.

56 I am not unmindful of the fact that *Stinchcombe* does not require the prosecution to disclose everything in its file, privileged or not. Materials that might in civil proceedings be covered by one privilege or another will nonetheless be subject, in the criminal context, to the "innocence at stake" exception—at the very least: see *McClure*. In criminal proceedings, as the Court noted in *Stinchcombe*:

> The trial judge might also, in certain circumstances, conclude that the recognition of an existing privilege does not constitute a reasonable limit on the constitutional right to make full answer and defence and thus require disclosure in spite of the law of privilege. [p. 340]

57 On any view of the matter, I would think it incongruous if the litigation privilege were found in civil proceedings to insulate the Crown from the disclosure it was bound but failed to provide in criminal proceedings that have ended.

58 The result in this case is dictated by a finding that the litigation privilege expires when the litigation ends. I wish nonetheless to add a few words regarding its birth.

59 The question has arisen whether the litigation privilege should attach to documents created for the substantial purpose of litigation, the dominant purpose of litigation or the sole purpose of litigation. . . .

60 I see no reason to depart from the dominant purpose test. Though it provides narrower protection than would a substantial purpose test, the dominant purpose standard appears to me consistent with the notion that the

litigation privilege should be viewed as a limited exception to the principle of full disclosure and not as an equal partner of the broadly interpreted solicitor-client privilege. . . .

. . .

62 A related issue is whether the litigation privilege attaches to documents gathered or copied—but not created—for the purpose of litigation. This issue arose in *Hodgkinson*, where a majority of the British Columbia Court of Appeal, relying on *Lyell v. Kennedy* (1884), 27 Ch. D. 1 (C.A.), concluded that copies of public documents gathered by a solicitor were privileged. McEachern C.J.B.C. stated:

> It is my conclusion that the law has always been, and, in my view, should continue to be, that in circumstances such as these, where a lawyer exercising legal knowledge, skill, judgment and industry has assembled a collection of relevant copy documents for his brief for the purpose of advising on or conducting anticipated or pending litigation he is entitled, indeed required, unless the client consents, to claim privilege for such collection and to refuse production. [p. 142]

63 This approach was rejected by the majority of the Ontario Court of Appeal in *Chrusz*.

64 The conflict of appellate opinion on this issue should be left to be resolved in a case where it is explicitly raised and fully argued. Extending the privilege to the gathering of documents resulting from research or the exercise of skill and knowledge does appear to be more consistent with the rationale and purpose of the litigation privilege. That being said, I take care to mention that assigning such a broad scope to the litigation privilege is not intended to automatically exempt from disclosure anything that would have been subject to discovery if it had not been remitted to counsel or placed in one's own litigation files. Nor should it have that effect.

For a recent discussion of *Blank* and the issue of litigation privilege in the context of related criminal investigations, see *R. v. Basi* (2009), 244 C.C.C. (3d) 537 (B.C. S.C.).

(ii) *Exceptions*

Inadvertent Disclosure

AIRST v. AIRST
(1998), 37 O.R. (3d) 654 (Ont. Gen. Div.)

During pre-trial proceedings in a matrimonial case, it was ordered that a joint evaluation report be prepared in relation to certain assets. The husband was required to send a number of documents to the valuators. Included in the documents he sent were two letters from his lawyer that were privileged. The wife now claimed that privilege was lost and the letters should be admissible in evidence. It was agreed that the letters were inadvertently sent.

WEIN J.:

. . .

Case-law Relating to Waiver of the Privilege Upon Inadvertent Disclosure

The traditional common law approach, as set out in the English Court of Appeal in *Calcraft v. Guest*, [1898] 1 Q.B. 759, [1895-9] All E.R. Rep. 346 (C.A.), has been that the privilege is lost whether the disclosure is by accident or by design. This traditional approach has been adopted by the Supreme Court of Canada in *Descôteaux v. Mierzwinski*, [1982] 1 S.C.R. 860, 141 D.L.R. (3d) 592.

However, in the civil context, in cases where the disclosure is found to be inadvertent, more recent authority in this court and other courts has held that, Descôteaux notwithstanding, there is a discretion that may be properly exercised in favour of non-disclosure where the release of the documents or information has been found to be inadvertent: see *Unit Park Management Co. v. Nissan Canada Inc.*, [1997] O.J. No. 3265 (Gen. Div.), per Gans J.; ..[further citations omitted.]

The competing policy interests are obvious. The basic rationale behind the solicitor-client privilege is to permit people to speak frankly and openly with their solicitors. Inadvertent disclosure should not logically override the privilege in all cases, though there may be some level of obligation upon the solicitor and the client to take steps to ensure that their communications remain confidential.

Yet another important policy interest dictates that all relevant facts be disclosed, such that in a case where information has come to the knowledge of a third party, it may be contrary to public policy to allow the privilege to stand. For example, if a third party is in possession of information which contradicts evidence that may have been given in pre-trial disclosure or during a trial, it might be said to be improper to require the court to rule on that evidence without the benefit of weighing the contradictory material.

Certainly where the evidence is unlawfully or improperly obtained, the principle has emerged that a party may be restrained from introducing such evidence, at least in civil proceedings: see *Ashburton (Lord) v. Pape*, [1913] 2 Ch. 469, [1911-13] All E.R. Rep. 708 (C.A.). Under this line of authority, injunctive relief will be granted to restrain the use of confidential material obtained in such a manner. However, *Calcraft v. Guest*, supra, suggests that the material, if not so restrained, may be introduced in court. This conflict relating to resultant use appears dichotomous: see J. Sopinka, S.N. Lederman and A. Bryant, The Law of Evidence in Canada (Toronto: Butterworths, 1992) at pp. 672-77.

The more recent trend in the authorities is to permit the courts to enquire into the circumstances by which the privileged information has come to the attention of the third party. Where a third party has obtained the information by improper means, courts have held that the privileged information ought not to be disclosed. On the other hand, Charter principles, applicable in criminal cases, may override traditional approaches to the law of privilege.

In the criminal law context where Charter principles have overlaid a rights-based matrix onto the development of law, it has been fully recognized that interpretations of privilege and the scope of a waiver may be affected by Charter-based rights. So for example in *R. v. O'Connor*, [1995] 4 S.C.R. 411 at p. 431, 103 C.C.C. (3d) 1 at p. 15, it was noted that: "it must be recognized that any form of privilege may be forced to yield where such a privilege would preclude the accused's right to make full answer and defence" (per Lamer C.J.C and Sopinka J. dissenting on another point).

This principled approach to the law of evidence must clearly be given application in the civil law context: it has been acknowledged that the common law should develop in accordance with Charter principles and values, even though the Charter may not have direct application to the case: "ensuring that the common law of privilege develops in accordance with 'Charter values' requires that the existing rules be scrutinized to ensure that they reflect the values the Charter enshrines": see *M. (A.) v. Ryan*, [1997] 1 S.C.R. 157 at pp. 170-72, 143 D.L.R. (4th) 1, per McLachlin J.; see also *Hill v. Church of Scientology of Toronto*, [1995] 2 S.C.R. 1130 at paras. 93, 95, 121, 126 D.L.R. (4th) 129.

In this context, that principle dictates that the rigid approach embodied in *Calcraft v. Guest, supra*, must be modified to reflect the fairness approach developed in more recent cases.

General Conclusions

In balancing the competing interests in a case involving inadvertent disclosure, the court must exercise a discretion and determine the issue based on the particular circumstances. Factors relevant to the court's consideration will include the way in which the documents came to be released, whether there was a prompt attempt to retrieve the documents after the disclosure was discovered, the timing of the discovery of the disclosure and, sometimes, the timing of the application, the number and nature of the third parties who have become aware of the documents, whether maintenance of the privilege will create an actual or perceived unfairness to the opposing party, and the impact on the fairness, both actual and perceived, of the processes of the court.

In some cases of inadvertent disclosure there may be a limited risk that the information has become or will become widely known beyond the party to whom the disclosure was made. The information may not even have been fully released, as in cases where documents are released but not opened or read. In other circumstances, the balance may favour admission of the evidence, such as where the documents have come into the hands of the opposing party through the carelessness of the party claiming privilege, but not through any wrongdoing of the opposing party. In some such situations the failure to permit the introduction of the evidence could leave the party with a sense that the court was denying itself the opportunity to assess conflicting information on a material point, and consequently could negatively reflect on the public perception of the administration of justice. In other cases the information might have been so widely distributed that it would be futile as a practical matter to attempt to prevent its admission. In every case there must be a balancing of the relevant factors in the individual circumstances of the case, thus no hard rule can be laid down.

Findings in this Case

In this case, there is no issue that the disclosure was inadvertent. A review of the documents confirms that solicitor-client privilege would apply to all of the content of the documents. Notwithstanding that the content may in some way be relevant to the issues before the court, in my view the equities favour the holding that the privilege has not been lost in this case. The release of the documents was entirely inadvertent, apparently through the carelessness of a party of advanced years required to find documents relating to many years of transactions. The disclosure was limited in scope and restricted to one individual retained in a capacity that may be broadly construed as confidential. There has been no "public" disclosure of the documents. The content of the documents does not bear in any direct way on the third party's assessment of the material he was retained to review. The court's ability to assess the facts underlying the issues in the case will not be impaired by lack of disclosure. To the contrary, release of the solicitor-client instructions might well be seen, in this case, as giving the opposing party an unfair "windfall" advantage of revealing tactical approaches taken at one point in time by the other side. Given the timing of the discovery of the issue, well after both parties had testified, disclosure at this time is additionally problematic. All of these factors are relevant to my consideration.

Accordingly, in this case the letters will not be released to counsel for the wife. The court copies of the letters will remain sealed and are not to be opened without further court order.[361]

Public Safety — Future Harm Exception

SMITH v. JONES
[1999] 1 S.C.R. 455, 22 C.R. (5th) 203, 132 C.C.C. (3d) 225

The accused was charged with aggravated sexual assault on a prostitute. His counsel referred him to a psychiatrist hoping that it would be of assistance in the preparation of the defence or with submissions on sentencing in the event of a guilty plea. Counsel informed the accused that the consultation was privileged in the same way as a consultation with him would be. During his interview with the psychiatrist, the accused described in considerable detail his plan to kidnap, rape and kill prostitutes. The psychiatrist informed defence counsel that in his opinion the accused was a dangerous individual who would, more likely than not, commit future offences unless he received sufficient treatment. The accused later pled guilty to the included offence of aggravated assault. The psychiatrist phoned defence counsel to inquire about the status of the proceedings and learned

---

[361]   On the issue of inadvertent disclosure see further *Canada v. Chapelstone Developments Inc.* (2004), 191 C.C.C. (3d) 152 (N.B. C.A.).

that his concerns about the accused would not be addressed in the sentencing hearing. The psychiatrist commenced this action for a declaration that he was entitled to disclose the information he had in his possession in the interests of public safety. He filed an affidavit describing his interview with the accused and his opinion based upon the interview. The trial judge ruled that the public safety exception to the solicitor-client privilege and doctor-patient confidentiality released the psychiatrist from his duties of confidentiality and concluded that he was under a duty to disclose to the police and the Crown both the statements made by the accused and his opinion based upon them. The Court of Appeal allowed the accused's appeal but only to the extent that the mandatory order was changed to one permitting the psychiatrist to disclose the information to the Crown and police.

CORY J. (L'HEUREUX-DUBÉ, GONTHIER, MCLACHLIN, IACOBUCCI and BASTARACHE JJ. concurring):—

. . .

Dr. Smith reported that Mr. Jones described in considerable detail his plan for the crime to which he subsequently pled guilty. It involved deliberately choosing as a victim a small prostitute who could be readily overwhelmed. He planned to have sex with her and then to kidnap her. He took duct tape and rope with him, as well as a small blue ball that he tried to force into the woman's mouth. Because he planned to kill her after the sexual assault he made no attempt to hide his identity. Mr. Jones planned to strangle the victim and to dispose of her body in the bush area near Hope, British Columbia. He was going to shoot the woman in the face before burying her to impede identification. He had arranged time off from his work and had carefully prepared his basement apartment to facilitate his planned sexual assault and murder. He had told people he would be going away on vacation so that no one would visit him and he had fixed dead bolts on all the doors so that a key alone would not open them. Mr. Jones told Dr. Smith that his first victim would be a "trial run" to see if he could "live with" what he had done. If he could, he planned to seek out similar victims. He stated that, by the time he had kidnapped his first victim, he expected that he would be "in so deep" that he would have no choice but to carry out his plans.

. . .

Just as no right is absolute so too the privilege, even that between solicitor and client, is subject to clearly defined exceptions. The decision to exclude evidence that would be both relevant and of substantial probative value because it is protected by the solicitor-client privilege represents a policy decision. It is based upon the importance to our legal system in general of the solicitor-client privilege. In certain circumstances, however, other societal values must prevail.

. . .

Quite simply society recognizes that the safety of the public is of such importance that in appropriate circumstances it will warrant setting aside solicitor-client privilege. What factors should be taken into consideration in determining whether that privilege should be displaced?

There are three factors to be considered: First, is there a clear risk to an identifiable person or group of persons? Second, is there a risk of serious bodily harm or death? Third, is the danger imminent? Clearly if the risk is imminent, the danger is serious.

These factors will often overlap and vary in their importance and significance. The weight to be attached to each will vary with the circumstances presented by each case, but they all must be considered. As well, each factor is composed of various aspects, and, like the factors themselves, these aspects may overlap and the weight to be given to them will vary depending on the circumstances of each case. Yet as a general rule, if the privilege is to be set aside the court must find that there is an imminent risk of serious bodily harm or death to an identifiable person or group.

(a) Clarity

What should be considered in determining if there is a clear risk to an identifiable group or person? It will be appropriate and relevant to consider the answers a particular case may provide to the following questions: Is there evidence of long range planning? Has a method for effecting the specific attack been suggested? Is there a prior history of violence or threats of violence? Are the prior assaults or threats of violence similar to that which was planned? If there is a history of violence, has the violence increased in severity? Is the violence directed to an identifiable person or group of persons? This is not an all-encompassing list. It is important to note, however, that as a general rule a group or person must be ascertainable. The requisite specificity of that identification will vary depending on the other factors discussed here.

The specific questions to be considered under this heading will vary with the particular circumstances of each case. Great significance might, in some situations, be given to the particularly clear identification of a particular individual or group of intended victims. Even if the group of intended victims is large considerable significance can be given to the threat if the identification of the group is clear and forceful. For example, a threat, put forward with chilling detail, to kill or seriously injure children five years of age and under would have to be given very careful consideration. In certain circumstances it might be that a threat of death directed toward single women living in apartment buildings could in combination with other factors be sufficient in the particular circumstances to justify setting aside the privilege. At the same time, a general threat of death or violence directed to everyone in a city or community, or anyone with whom the person may come into contact, may be too vague to warrant setting aside the privilege. However, if the threatened harm to the members of the public was particularly compelling, extremely serious and imminent, it might well be appropriate to lift the privilege. All the surrounding circumstances will have to be taken into consideration in every case.

In sum, the threatened group may be large but if it is clearly identifiable then it is a factor — indeed an essential factor — that must be considered together with others in determining whether the solicitor-client privilege should be set aside. A test that requires that the class of victim be ascertainable allows the trial judge sufficient flexibility to determine whether the public safety exception has been made out.

(b) Seriousness

The "seriousness" factor requires that the threat be such that the intended victim is in danger of being killed or of suffering serious bodily harm. Many persons involved in criminal justice proceedings will have committed prior crimes or may be planning to commit crimes in the future. The disclosure of planned future crimes without an element of violence would be an insufficient reason to set aside solicitor-client privilege because of fears for public safety. For the public safety interest to be of sufficient importance to displace solicitor-client privilege, the threat must be to occasion serious bodily harm or death.

It should be observed that serious psychological harm may constitute serious bodily harm.

(c) Imminence

The risk of serious bodily harm or death must be imminent if solicitor-client communications are to be disclosed. That is, the risk itself must be serious: a serious risk of serious bodily harm. The nature of the threat must be such that it creates a sense of urgency. This sense of urgency may be applicable to some time in the future. Depending on the seriousness and clarity of the threat, it will not always be necessary to impose a particular time limit on the risk. It is sufficient if there is a clear and imminent threat of serious bodily harm to an identifiable group, and if this threat is made in such a manner that a sense of urgency is created. A statement made in a fleeting fit of anger will usually be insufficient to disturb the solicitor-client privilege. On the other hand, imminence as a factor may be satisfied if a person makes a clear threat to kill someone that he vows to carry out three years hence when he is released from prison. If that threat is made with such chilling intensity and graphic detail that a reasonable bystander would be convinced that the killing would be carried out the threat could be considered to be imminent. Imminence, like the other two criteria, must be defined in the context of each situation.

In summary, solicitor-client privilege should only be set aside in situations where the facts raise real concerns that an identifiable individual or group is in imminent danger of death or serious bodily harm. The facts must be carefully considered to determine whether the three factors of seriousness, clarity, and imminence indicate that the privilege cannot be maintained. Different weights will be given to each factor in any particular case. If after considering all appropriate factors it is determined that the threat to public safety outweighs the need to preserve solicitor-client privilege, then the privilege must be set aside. When it is, the disclosure should be limited so that it includes only the information necessary to protect public safety.

The disclosure of the privileged communication should generally be limited as much as possible. The judge setting aside the solicitor-client privilege should strive to strictly limit disclosure to those aspects of the report or document which indicate that there is an imminent risk of serious bodily harm or death to an identifiable person or group. In undertaking this task consideration should be given to those portions of the report which refer to the risk of serious harm to an identifiable group; that the risk is serious in that it involves a danger of death or serious bodily harm; and that the serious risk is imminent in the sense given to that word above. The requirement that the disclosure be limited must be emphasized. For example, if a report contained references to criminal behaviour that did not have an imminent risk of serious bodily harm but disclosed, for example, the commission of crimes of fraud, counterfeiting or the sale of stolen goods, those references would necessarily be deleted.

[In applying the criteria set out the majority found sufficient clarity, seriousness and imminence to satisfy the Public Safety Exception to Solicitor-Client Privilege.]

. . .

Dr. Smith chose to bring a legal action for a declaration that he was entitled to disclose the information he had in his possession in the interests of public safety. However, this is not the only manner in which experts may proceed. Although it is true that this procedure may protect the expert from legal consequences, there may not always be time for such an action. In whatever action is taken by the expert, care should be exercised that only that information which is necessary to alleviate the threat to public safety is revealed.

It is not appropriate in these reasons to consider the precise steps an expert might take to prevent the harm to the public. It is sufficient to observe that it might be appropriate to notify the potential victim or the police or a Crown prosecutor, depending on the specific circumstances.

. . .

The order of the British Columbia Court of Appeal is affirmed. . . . Dr. Smith seeks to recover his costs. He should not have them. This case raised the issue of when solicitor-client privilege can be set aside. It has been found that, because of the danger posed by Mr. Jones to the public, solicitor-client privilege, which Mr. Jones had every right to believe attached to Dr. Smith's report, was set aside. This case arises in the context of criminal proceedings and the result may well affect the sentence imposed on Mr. Jones. It would be unfair and unjust in the circumstances to impose the burden of costs on Mr. Jones and I would not do so.

MAJOR J. (LAMER, C.J. and BINNIE J. concurring) (dissenting):—

. . .

In my opinion a limited exception which does not include conscriptive evidence against the accused would address the immediate concern for public safety in this appeal while respecting the importance of the privilege. I do not read Cory J.'s reasons as imposing that limitation. This approach will in my view foster a climate in which dangerous individuals are more likely to disclose their disorders, seek treatment and pose less danger to the public.

. . .

I agree with Cory J. that the standard of a "clear, serious and imminent" danger is the appropriate test for disclosure of privileged communications. There are compelling public policy reasons for limiting disclosure to cases of clear and imminent danger. The record confirms that Mr. Jones only disclosed his secret plans because his lawyer had properly advised him that anything he said to Dr. Smith would be confidential. If Cory J. is correct in holding that, in cases where the necessity test is met, the privilege is overridden to the extent of allowing disclosure of self-incriminating evidence, the result might endanger the public more than the public safety exception would protect them.

If defence counsel cannot freely refer clients, particularly dangerous ones, to medical or other experts without running a serious risk of the privilege being set aside, their response will be not to refer clients until after trial, if at all. This could result in dangerous people remaining free on bail for long periods of time, undiagnosed and untreated, presenting a danger to society.

The chilling effect of completely breaching the privilege would have the undesired effect of discouraging those individuals in need of treatment for serious and dangerous conditions from consulting professional help. In this case the interests of the appellant and more importantly the interests of society would be better served by his obtaining treatment. This Court has recognized that mental health, including those suffering from potentially dangerous illnesses, is an important public good: see *M. (A.) v. Ryan*, [1997] 1 S.C.R. 157, at para. 27.

Although the appellant did not go to Dr. Smith to seek treatment, it is obvious that he is more likely to get treatment when his condition is diagnosed than someone who keeps the secret of their illness to themselves. It seems apparent that society will suffer by imposing a disincentive for patients and criminally accused persons to speak frankly with counsel and medical experts retained on their behalf.

As appealing as it may be to ensure that Mr. Jones does not slip back into the community without treatment for his condition, completely lifting the privilege and allowing his confidential communications to his legal advisor to be used against him in the most detrimental ways will not promote public safety, only silence. For this doubtful gain, the Court will have imposed a veil of secrecy between criminal accused and their counsel which the solicitor-client privilege was developed to prevent. Sanctioning a breach of privilege too hastily erodes the workings of the system of law in exchange for an illusory gain in public safety.

While I agree with Cory J. that the danger in this case is sufficiently clear, serious and imminent to justify some warning to the relevant authorities, I find that the balance between the public interests in safety and the proper administration of justice is best struck by a more limited disclosure than the broader abrogation of privilege he proposes. In particular, Cory J. endorses the trial judge's limitation of Dr. Smith's affidavit to those portions which indicate an imminent risk of serious harm or death. In the result, conscriptive evidence such as the accused's confession can be disclosed. In my opinion, the danger posed by the accused can be adequately addressed by the expression of that opinion by Dr. Smith without disclosing the confession.

. . .

Courts are obligated to craft the narrowest possible exception to privilege which accomplishes this purpose. Accordingly, Dr. Smith should be permitted to warn the relevant authorities (i.e., the Attorney General and sentencing judge) that Mr. Jones poses a threat to prostitutes in the Vancouver area. However, Dr. Smith should only disclose his opinion and the fact that it is based on a consultation with Mr. Jones. Specifically, he should not disclose any communication from the accused relating to the circumstances of the offence, nor should he be permitted to reveal any of the personal information which the trial judge excluded from his original order for disclosure.

I agree with Cory J. that in rare cases where an individual poses an instant risk such that even an ex parte application to the court is not possible, the person reviewing the otherwise privileged information may issue a timely warning to the police. Otherwise, the scope and timing of disclosures should be dealt with by the courts on a case-by-case basis.

. . .

I would allow the appeal without costs, confirm the entirety of Mr. Jones's communications to Dr. Smith to be privileged, but permit Dr. Smith to give his opinion and diagnosis of the danger posed by Mr. Jones.

Smith and Jones were aliases to keep matters confidential until the Supreme Court had ruled. Jones was in fact a man named Leopold and Dr. Smith was Dr. O'Shaughnessy, chairman of forensic psychiatry at the University of British Columbia. Leopold's sentence hearing proceeded after the Supreme Court's ruling. Dr. O'Shaughnessy now testified for the Crown. There had been plea negotiations for a reformatory sentence but now the Crown brought a dangerous offender application. The trial judge rejected that motion but imposed an 11-year sentence. On a further appeal the B.C. Court of Appeal held that Leopold should be declared to be a dangerous offender: *R. v. Leopold.*[362]

The future harm exception carved out by the Supreme Court is not limited to future crimes and includes serious psychological harm. **What is the significance of this broader approach to harm? Could a lawyer rely on *Smith v. Jones* to disclose that his or her client confessed to a crime for which another individual was convicted?**

---

[362] (2001), 155 C.C.C. (3d) 251 (B.C. C.A.). For further discussion of *Smith v. Jones* and many of these issues see D. Layton, "The Public Safety Exception: Confusing Confidentiality, Privilege and Ethics" (2001) 6 Can. Crim. L. Rev. 217; "*R. v. Leopold*: The Public Safety Exception and Defence Counsel as Confidential Informant" (2001), 43 C.R. (5th) 319; and A. Dodek, "The Public Safety Exception to Solicitor-Client Privilege: *Smith v. Jones*" (2000) 34 U.B.C. L. Rev. 292.

Innocence at Stake Exception

R. v. McCLURE
[2001] 1 S.C.R. 445, 40 C.R. (5th) 1, 151 C.C.C. (3d) 321

The accused was a librarian and teacher at the school attended by J.C. in the mid-1970s. In 1997, the accused was charged with sexual offences against 11 former students. After reading about the accused's arrest, J.C. gave a statement to the police alleging incidents of sexual touching by the accused. His allegations were later added to the indictment. J.C. also brought a civil action against the accused. The accused sought production of J.C.'s civil litigation file to determine the nature of the allegations and to assess his motive to fabricate or exaggerate incidents of abuse. In his first ruling, the trial judge ordered the production of J.C.'s civil litigation file for his review. In a second ruling, he granted the accused access to the file but ordered all references to quantum of settlement and fees deleted from the produced file. The trial judge ruled that certain matters of sequence were significant, and not available to the defence without access to J.C.'s file. The order granting access was stayed pending appeal. J.C., who was not a party in the criminal trial, was granted leave to appeal the order to the Supreme Court pursuant to s. 40 of the *Supreme Court Act.*

MAJOR J. (McLACHLIN, C.J. and L'HEUREUX-DUBÉ, GONTHIER, IACOBUCCI, BASTARACHE, BINNIE, ARBOUR and LEBEL JJ. concurring):—

. . .

There are two useful tests which help to identify when the right to make full answer and defence will prevail over the need for confidentiality. While useful, neither test sufficiently addresses the unique concerns evoked by solicitor-client privilege and, as explained later, more is needed.

The first test originated in *O'Connor*, relative to procedures to govern production of medical or therapeutic records that are in the hands of third parties. Subsequently, Parliament codified the procedure in ss. 278.1 to 278.9 of the Criminal Code and its constitutionality was upheld in *R. v. Mills*, [1999] 3 S.C.R. 668. The *O'Connor* test and ss. 278.1 to 278.9 of the Criminal Code were created with the sensitivity and unique character of third party therapeutic records in mind. They focus on an individual's privacy interest and not the broader policy objectives underlying the administration of justice.

The other test is the innocence at stake test for informer privilege, see *Leipert*. This test details the circumstances under which the identity of an informer might have to be revealed. The value of reliable informers to the administration of justice has been recognized for a long time, so much so that it too is a class privilege. This explains why the high standard of showing that the innocence of the accused is at stake before permitting invasion of the privilege is necessary. Should the privilege be invaded, the state then generally provides for the protection of the informer through various safety programs, again illustrating the public importance of that privilege. The threshold created by the innocence at stake test comes the closest to addressing the concerns raised in this appeal as it is appropriately high. Both informer privilege and solicitor-client privilege are ancient and hallowed protections.

The Innocence at Stake Test for Solicitor-Client Privilege

In granting the respondent McClure access to the complainant's civil litigation file, the trial judge applied the *O'Connor* test for disclosure of confidential therapeutic records. With respect, this was an error. The appropriate test by which to determine whether to set aside solicitor-client privilege is the innocence at stake test, set out below. Solicitor-client privilege should be set aside only in the most unusual cases. Unless individuals can be certain that their communications with their solicitors will remain entirely confidential, their ability to speak freely will be undermined.

In recognition of the central place of solicitor-client privilege within the administration of justice, the innocence at stake test should be stringent. The privilege should be infringed only where core issues going to the guilt of the accused are involved and there is a genuine risk of a wrongful conviction.

Before the test is even considered, the accused must establish that the information he is seeking in the solicitor-client file is not available from any other source and he is otherwise unable to raise a reasonable doubt as to his guilt in any other way.

By way of illustration, if the accused could raise a reasonable doubt at his trial on the question of mens rea by access to the solicitor-client file but could also raise a reasonable doubt with the defence of alibi and/or identification, then it would be unnecessary to use the solicitor-client file. The innocence of the accused would not be at stake but instead it is his wish to mount a more complete defence that would be affected. On the surface it may appear harsh to deny access as the particular privileged evidence might raise a reasonable doubt, nonetheless, the policy reasons favouring the protection of the confidentiality of solicitor-client communications must prevail unless there is a genuine danger of wrongful conviction.

The innocence at stake test is applied in two stages in order to reflect the dual nature of the judge's inquiry. At the first stage, the accused seeking production of a solicitor-client communication must provide some evidentiary basis upon which to conclude that there exists a communication that could raise a reasonable doubt as to his guilt. At this stage, the judge has to decide whether she will review the evidence.

If the trial judge is satisfied that such an evidentiary basis exists, then she should proceed to stage two. At that stage, the trial judge must examine the solicitor-client file to determine whether, in fact, there is a communication that is likely to raise a reasonable doubt as to the guilt of the accused. It is evident that the test in the first stage (could raise a reasonable doubt) is different than that of the second stage (likely to raise a reasonable doubt). If the second stage of the test is met, then the trial judge should order the production but only of that portion of the solicitor-client file that is necessary to raise the defence claimed.

(1) Stage #1

The first stage of the innocence at stake test for invading the solicitor-client privilege requires production of the material to the trial judge for review. There has to be some evidentiary basis for the request. This is a threshold requirement designed to prevent "fishing expeditions". Without it, it would be too easy for the accused to demand examination of solicitor-client privileged communications by the trial judge. As this request constitutes a significant invasion of solicitor-client privilege, it should not be entered into lightly. On the other hand, the bar cannot be set so high that it can never be met. The trial judge must ask: "Is there some evidentiary basis for the claim that a solicitor-client communication exists that could raise a reasonable doubt about the guilt of the accused?"

It falls to the accused to demonstrate some evidentiary basis for his claim that there exists a solicitor-client communication relevant to the defence he raises. Mere speculation as to what a file might contain is insufficient.

That is then followed by a requirement that the communication sought by the accused could raise a reasonable doubt as to his guilt. This must be considered in light of what the accused knows. It is likely that the accused who, it must be remembered, has had no access to the file sought, may only provide a description of a possible communication. It would be difficult to produce and unfair to demand anything more precise. It is only at stage two that a court determines conclusively that such a communication actually exists.

The evidence sought should be considered in conjunction with other available evidence in order to determine its importance. It is the totality of the evidence that governs. However, when the accused is either challenging credibility or raising collateral matters, it will be difficult to meet the standards required of stage one.

Where an accused fails to show that the information sought could raise a reasonable doubt as to guilt, the solicitor-client privilege prevails.

(2) Stage #2

Once the first stage of the innocence at stake test for setting aside the solicitor-client privilege has been met, the trial judge must examine that record to determine whether, in fact, there exists a communication that is likely to raise a reasonable doubt as to the accused's guilt. The trial judge must ask herself the following question: "Is there something in the solicitor-client communication that is likely to raise a reasonable doubt about the accused's guilt?"

After a review of the evidence of the solicitor-client communication in question, the judge must decide whether the communication is likely to raise a reasonable doubt as to the guilt of the accused. In most cases, this means that, unless the solicitor-client communication goes directly to one of the elements of the offence, it will not be sufficient to meet this requirement. Simply providing evidence that advances ancillary attacks on the Crown's case (e.g., by impugning the credibility of a Crown witness, or by providing evidence that suggest that some Crown evidence was obtained unconstitutionally) will very seldom be sufficient to meet this requirement.

The trial judge does not have to conclude that the information definitely will raise a reasonable doubt. If this were the case, the trial would effectively be over as soon as the trial judge ordered the solicitor-client file to be produced. There would be nothing left to decide. Instead, the information must likely raise a reasonable doubt as to the accused's guilt. Also, upon reviewing the evidence, if the trial judge finds material that will likely raise a reasonable doubt, stage two of the test is satisfied and the information should be produced to the defence even if this information was not argued as a basis for production by the defence at stage one.

In determining whether or not the solicitor-client communication in question is likely to raise a reasonable doubt as to the guilt of the accused, the trial judge should consider that the communication in the solicitor-client file cannot be marginal but must be sufficient to establish the basis for its admission. It is the totality of the evidence then available that the trial judge considers in determining whether it is likely that the evidence can raise a reasonable doubt.

The difficulties described in successfully overcoming solicitor-client privilege illustrate the importance and solemnity attached to it. As described earlier, it is a cornerstone of our judicial system and any impediment to open candid and confidential discussion between lawyers and their clients will be rare and reluctantly imposed.

Application to the Case at Bar

In this case, the litigation file should not have been produced to the defence. With respect, the trial judge erred in using the earlier *O'Connor* test for the production of third party confidential therapeutic records to govern whether the litigation file should have been produced to the defence.

The first stage of the innocence at stake test for solicitor-client privilege was not met. There was no evidence that the information sought by the respondent McClure could raise a reasonable doubt as to his guilt. Even if the chronology of events in this case — i.e. lawyer, police, therapist, civil suit — was unusual, it does not justify overriding solicitor-client privilege. This "unusual" chronology does not rise to a level that demonstrates that the litigation file could raise a reasonable doubt as to guilt and so fails at the first stage.

In addition, the accused would be able to raise the issue of the complainant's motive to fabricate events for the sake of a civil action at trial from another source, simply by pointing out the sequence of events and the fact that a civil action was initiated.

The third party appellant, J.C., could not appeal the interlocutory order for production of his litigation file because he was not a party in the criminal trial. Instead, he applied directly to this Court pursuant to s. 40(1) of the Supreme Court Act for leave to appeal the final order ordering production of his litigation file. This avenue of appeal is unsatisfactory. The usual avenue for appeal should be to the court of appeal of the province. That court has broad powers of review and is the desirable forum for appeals of first instance. This appeal is not the first demonstration of the anomaly of a direct appeal of an interlocutory order to the Supreme Court of Canada. The only apparent method of resolving this problem is by legislative amendment.

The appeal is allowed and the order for production by Hawkins J. is set aside.[363]

One important refinement of *McClure* by the Supreme Court in *Brown* was the granting of use and derivative use immunity to the privilege holder. As Justice Major held:

> The invasion of solicitor-client privilege exposes the privilege holder to potential future liability, particularly in cases, such as the present one, that may involve a confession to a serious crime. . . .
>
> As described, solicitor-client privilege is a fundamental tenet of our legal system. Clients must be comfortable in making free and candid disclosure to their solicitors without fear that their communications will be later used against them. This principle should in no way be diminished by the limited disclosure allowed in *McClure*. The test established in that case provides for disclosure in the exceptional circumstance that it is necessary to prevent a wrongful conviction. . . . It should not be used to incriminate the privilege holder, who would have been protected but for the operation of *McClure*. . . .
>
> This means that the privilege holder's communications and any evidence derived therefrom cannot be used in a subsequent case against the privilege holder. . . . Use and derivative use immunity should prohibit the Crown both from using the communications as direct evidence against the privilege holder and from using the communications to impeach the privilege holder if and when he is himself an accused.

In the next two cases which deal with the future crime/fraud and common interest exceptions, we will see the Supreme Court recognizing solicitor-client privilege in the context of Crown/police relationships and those between in-house counsel and their clients, including government agencies.

Legal Advice About Police Legality

R. v. SHIROSE AND CAMPBELL
[1999] 1 S.C.R. 565, 24 C.R. (5th) 365, 133 C.C.C. (3d) 257

As part of an undercover drug operation in Quebec, a number of police officers posing as large-scale hashish vendors contacted two potential groups of purchasers. Negotiations included showing the hashish to them. The operation was discussed with a Department of Justice lawyer and approved by two senior RCMP officers. Following their conviction, the

---

[363] For comments on *McClure* see Manson, "Annotation: *R. v. McClure*" (2001), 40 C.R. (5th) 1 and Layton, "*R. v. McClure*: The Privilege on the Pea" (2001), 40 C.R. (5th) 19. The Supreme Court considered further procedural issues on *McLure* applications in *R. v. Brown* (2002), 50 C.R. (5th) 1 (S.C.C.). See comment by David Layton, "*R. v. Brown*: Protecting Legal-Professional Privilege" (2002), 50 C.R. (5th) 37.

accused brought a stay application alleging that the reverse-sting used by the police was unlawful and an abuse of process. The position of the RCMP was that they were acting in good faith based on the advice they had received. In support of their application, the accused sought to subpoena the Justice lawyer in relation to the communications with the police as to the legality of the reverse sting. The trial judge quashed the subpoena on the grounds that the communications were protected by solicitor-client privilege. The Court of Appeal dismissed the accused's appeal. On further appeal, the Supreme Court ordered a new trial and held that the legal advice should have been disclosed.

BINNIE J., speaking for the Court, held: —

. . .

Existence of a Solicitor-Client Relationship between the RCMP Officers and Lawyers in the Department of Justice

The solicitor-client privilege is based on the functional needs of the administration of justice. The legal system, complicated as it is, calls for professional expertise. Access to justice is compromised where legal advice is unavailable. It is of great importance, therefore, that the RCMP be able to obtain professional legal advice in connection with criminal investigations without the chilling effect of potential disclosure of their confidences in subsequent proceedings. As Lamer C.J. stated in *R. v. Gruenke*, [1991] 3 S.C.R. 263, at p. 289:

> The prima facie protection for solicitor-client communications is based on the fact that the relationship and the communications between solicitor and client are essential to the effective operation of the legal system. Such communications are inextricably linked with the very system which desires the disclosure of the communication. . . .

See also *Smith v. Jones*, [1999] 1 S.C.R. 455, per Cory J., at para. 46, and per Major J., at para. 5. This Court had previously, in *Descôteaux v. Mierzwinski*, [1982] 1 S.C.R. 860, at p. 872, adopted Wigmore's formulation of the substantive conditions precedent to the existence of the right of the lawyer's client to confidentiality (Wigmore on Evidence, vol. 8 (McNaughton rev. 1961), sec. 2292, at p. 554):

> Where legal advice of any kind is sought from a professional legal adviser in his capacity as such, the communications relating to that purpose, made in confidence by the client, are at his instance permanently protected from disclosure by himself or by the legal adviser, except the protection be waived. [Emphasis and numerotation deleted.]

Cpl. Reynolds' consultation with Mr. Leising of the Department of Justice falls squarely within this functional definition, and the fact that Mr. Leising works for an "in-house" government legal service does not affect the creation or character of the privilege.

It is, of course, not everything done by a government (or other) lawyer that attracts solicitor-client privilege. While some of what government lawyers do is indistinguishable from the work of private practitioners, they may and frequently do have multiple responsibilities including, for example, participation in various operating committees of their respective departments. Government lawyers who have spent years with a particular client department may be called upon to offer policy advice that has nothing to do with their legal training or expertise, but draws on departmental know-how. Advice given by lawyers on matters outside the solicitor-client relationship is not protected. A comparable range of functions is exhibited by salaried corporate counsel employed by business organizations. Solicitor-client communications by corporate employees with in-house counsel enjoy the privilege, although (as in government) the corporate context creates special problems: see, for example, the in-house inquiry into "questionable payments" to foreign governments at issue in *Upjohn Co. v. United States*, 449 U.S. 383 (1981), per Rehnquist J. (as he then was), at pp. 394-95. In private practice some lawyers are valued as much (or more) for raw business sense as for legal acumen. No solicitor-client privilege attaches to advice on purely business matters even where it is provided by a lawyer. As Lord Hanworth, M.R., stated in *Minter v. Priest*, [1929] 1 K.B. 655 (C.A.), at pp. 668-69:

> [I]t is not sufficient for the witness to say, "I went to a solicitor's office." . . . Questions are admissible to reveal and determine for what purpose and under what circumstances the intending client went to the office.

Whether or not solicitor-client privilege attaches in any of these situations depends on the nature of the relationship, the subject matter of the advice and the circumstances in which it is sought and rendered. One thing is clear: the fact that Mr. Leising is a salaried employee did not prevent the formation of a solicitor-client relationship and the attendant duties, responsibilities and privileges. . . .

Subject to what is said below, when Mr. Leising of the Department of Justice initially advised Cpl. Reynolds about the legality of a reverse sting operation, these communications were protected by solicitor-client privilege.

The "Future Crimes and Fraud" Exception

It is well established, as the appellants argue, that there is an exception to the principle of confidentiality of solicitor-client communications where those communications are criminal or else made with a view to obtaining legal advice to facilitate the commission of a crime. . . .

In this case, however, I think the RCMP did waive the privilege, as discussed below. The relevant solicitor-client communications that came within the scope of the waiver ought therefore to be turned over directly to the appellants without the need in the first instance of a two-stage procedure involving the trial judge.

. . .

Waiver of Solicitor-Client Privilege

The record is clear that the RCMP put in issue Cpl. Reynolds' good faith belief in the legality of the reverse sting, and asserted its reliance upon his consultations with the Department of Justice to buttress that position. The

RCMP factum in the Ontario Court of Appeal has already been quoted in para. 46. In my view, the RCMP waived the right to shelter behind solicitor-client privilege the contents of the advice thus exposed and relied upon. . . .

The scope of Crown-police privilege and in particular whether entrapment falls within the "innocence at stake" *McClure* exception to this privilege has been considered in a number of recent cases.[364]

Claims of Crown privilege including those of work product have succeeded in the face of disclosure requests in recent gangsterism trials.[365]

The Common Interest Exception

PRITCHARD v. ONTARIO (HUMAN RIGHTS COMMISSION)
19 C.R. (6th) 203, [2004] 1 S.C.R. 809

The appellant filed a human rights complaint against her employer, Sears Canada, alleging gender discrimination, sexual harassment and reprisal. The Ontario Human Rights Commission decided not to proceed with her complaint. She sought judicial review and brought a motion for production of all documents. One of those documents was a legal opinion provided to the Commission by in-house counsel.

MAJOR J. (for the Court):

. . .

Solicitor-client privilege has been held to arise when in-house government lawyers provide legal advice to their client, a government agency: see *R. v. Campbell*, [1999] 1 S.C.R. 565, at para. 49. In *Campbell*, the appellant police officers sought access to the legal advice provided to the RCMP by the Department of Justice and on which the RCMP claimed to have placed good faith reliance. In identifying solicitor-client privilege as it applies to government lawyers, Binnie J. compared the function of public lawyers in government agencies with corporate in-house counsel. He explained that where government lawyers give legal advice to a "client department" that traditionally would engage solicitor-client privilege, and the privilege would apply. However, like corporate lawyers who also may give advice in an executive or non-legal capacity, where government lawyers give policy advice outside the realm of their legal responsibilities, such advice is not protected by the privilege.

Owing to the nature of the work of in-house counsel, often having both legal and non-legal responsibilities, each situation must be assessed on a case-by-case basis to determine if the circumstances were such that the privilege

---

[364] See *R. v. Schacher* (2003), 179 C.C.C. (3d) 561 (Alta. C.A.) and *R. v. Castro* (2001), 157 C.C.C. (3d) 255 (B.C. C.A.); *R. v. Trang* (2002), 168 C.C.C. (3d) 145 (Alta. Q.B.) and *R. v. Chan* (2002), 168 C.C.C. (3d) 396 (Alta. Q.B.).

[365] See Ian Carter, "Chipping Away at *Stinchcombe*: the Expanding Privilege Exception to Disclosure" (2002), 50 C.R. (5th) 332.

arose. Whether or not the privilege will attach depends on the nature of the relationship, the subject matter of the advice, and the circumstances in which it is sought and rendered: *Campbell, supra*, at para. 50.

Where solicitor-client privilege is found, it applies to a broad range of communications between lawyer and client as outlined above. It will apply with equal force in the context of advice given to an administrative board by in-house counsel as it does to advice given in the realm of private law. If an in-house lawyer is conveying advice that would be characterized as privileged, the fact that he or she is "in-house" does not remove the privilege, or change its nature.

B. *The Common Interest Exception*

The appellant submitted that solicitor-client privilege does not attach to communications between a solicitor and client as against persons having a "joint interest" with the client in the subject-matter of the communication. This "common interest", or "joint interest" exception does not apply to the Commission because it does not share an interest with the parties before it. The Commission is a disinterested gatekeeper for human rights complaints and, by definition, does not have a stake in the outcome of any claim.

The common interest exception to solicitor-client privilege arose in the context of two parties jointly consulting one solicitor. See *R. v. Dunbar and Logan* (1982), 138 D.L.R. (3d) 221, *per* Martin J.A. at p. 245:

> The authorities are clear that where two or more persons, each having an interest in some matter, jointly consult a solicitor, their confidential communications with the solicitor, although known to each other, are privileged against the outside world. However, as between themselves, each party is expected to share in and be privy to all communications passing between each of them and their solicitor. Consequently, should any controversy or dispute arise between them, the privilege is inapplicable, and either party may demand disclosure of the communication. . . .

The common interest exception originated in the context of parties sharing a common goal or seeking a common outcome, a "selfsame interest" as Lord Denning, M.R., described it in *Buttes Gas & Oil Co. v. Hammer (No. 3)*, [1980] 3 All E.R. 475 (C.A.), at p. 483. It has since been narrowly expanded to cover those situations in which a fiduciary or like duty has been found to exist between the parties so as to create common interest. These include trustee-beneficiary relations, fiduciary aspects of Crown-aboriginal relations and certain types of contractual or agency relations, none of which are at issue here.

The Commission neither has a trust relationship with, nor owes a fiduciary duty to, the parties appearing before it. The Commission is a statutory decision-maker. The cases relied on by the appellant related to trusts, fiduciary duty, and contractual obligations. These cases are readily distinguishable and do not support the position advanced by the appellant. The common interest exception does not apply to an administrative board with respect to the parties before it.

The appellant relied heavily on the decision of the New Brunswick Court of Appeal in *Melanson v. New Brunswick (Workers' Compensation Board)*

(1994), 146 N.B.R. (2d) 294. In that case, the court ordered a new hearing based on a failure by the Workers' Compensation Board to observe procedural fairness in the processing of the appellant's claim. The court held that several significant errors were made at the review committee level, negating the review committee's duty to act fairly. Among these errors were the failure to provide the appellant with its first decision, the decision to turn the appellant's claim into a test case without her knowledge and partly at her expense, and the introduction of new evidence not disclosed to the appellant. For these reasons the court, in its *ratio*, concluded that "the taint at the intermediate level of the Review Committee has irrevocably blemished the proceedings" (para. 31). Other comments made by the Court of Appeal, pertaining to the production of legal opinions, were *obiter dicta*. The proper approach to legal opinions is to determine if they are of such a kind as would fall into the privileged class. If so, they are privileged. To the extent that *Melanson* is otherwise relied on is error.

C. *Application to the Case At Bar*

As stated, the communication between the Commission and its in-house counsel was protected by solicitor-client privilege.

The opinion provided to the Commission by staff counsel was a *legal opinion*. It was provided to the Commission by in-house or "staff" counsel to be considered or not considered at their discretion. It is a communication that falls within the class of communications protected by solicitor-client privilege. The fact that it was provided by in-house counsel does not alter the nature of the communication or the privilege.

There is no applicable exception that can remove the communication from the privileged class. There is no common interest between this Commission and the parties before it that could justify disclosure; nor is this Court prepared to create a new common law exception on these facts.

(c) Marital Communications

We will see later in Chapter 5 that Parliament finally abolished the spousal incompetence rule with Bill C-32 (*Victims Bill of Rights Act*), which received Royal Assent on April 23, 2015. Section 4(2) of the *Canada Evidence Act* now reads:

Spouse of accused

(2) No person is incompetent, or uncompellable, to testify for the prosecution by reason only that they are married to the accused.

However, Parliament retained the spousal privilege rule in s. 4(3):

No husband is compellable to disclose any communication made to him by his wife during their marriage, and no wife is compellable to disclose any communication made by her husband during their marriage.

Similarly, the *Ontario Evidence Act* abolished rules against spousal competence and compellability but retained a spousal privilege. Section 11 of that Act was amended in 2005 to ensure that all married spouses, including same-sex spouses, get the benefit of the marital privilege. It now reads:

Communications made during marriage

11. A person is not compellable to disclose any communication made to the person by his or her spouse during the marriage,

Can you justify abolishing rules against spousal competence and compellability but retaining the traditional marital privilege?

Notice, at the outset, that the privilege provided, unlike the case of solicitor-client communications, belongs to the recipient of the communication rather than to the communicant; "it is a mystery to me why it was decided to give this privilege to the spouse who is a witness".[366]

At face value these privilege provisions do not protect common-law relationships. This could lead to s. 15 challenges. In *R. v. Nguyen*,[367] the Ontario Court of Appeal found the now-repealed spousal incompetency rules law discriminatory against common-law partners under s. 15 of the *Charter* but upheld the limitation to married spouses under s. 1 of the *Charter*.[368]

R. v. NERO
2016 ONCA 160, 334 C.C.C. (3d) 148 (Ont. C.A.)

WATT J.A.:

[1] Spring 2011 and Nicola Nero was on parole. Finishing up a penitentiary sentence of almost nine years in a halfway house down Niagara way. Allowed out on weekdays. Required to return on weeknights. Weekends, out and about.

[2] Parole includes restrictions. Where you can go. What you can do. Who you can talk to and hang around with. No association with others convicted of crime. And for Nicola Nero, no cellphones.

[3] But old habits are hard to break. Especially lucrative old habits. Like trafficking in cocaine. And keeping in touch with those like-minded. By cellphone and text message.

[4] Police suspected Nicola Nero had returned to the life. They began an investigation. In Niagara Region. But soon, elsewhere, including York Region.

---

[366] Echoing the words of Lord Reid in *Rumping v. D.P.P.* (1962), 46 Cr. App. R. 398 (H.L.) at 409.
[367] 2015 ONCA 278, 323 C.C.C. (3d) 240, 20 C.R. (7th) 287 (Ont. C.A.).
[368] Justice Gillese explained at para. 8 that by giving common-law spouses the freedom to choose to testify, "the limit to the spousal incompetency rule has the effect of affirming the dignity and self-worth of witness spouses, except where those individuals have chosen to marry and thereby accept the state-imposed responsibilities and protections flowing from that status".

[5] About a year later, the police investigation ended. Nero; his girlfriend or common-law spouse, Tawnya Fletcher; Martino Caputo; and some others were charged with several offences relating to unlawful traffic in cocaine.

. . .

Ground #6: Spousal Communication Privilege

[166] The final ground of appeal invokes spousal communication privilege and its implications for certain interceptions made under the Part VI authorizations and the use of information obtained by interception to assist in establishing the conditions precedent for issuance of the search warrant on May 22, 2012.

The Background

The Nero/Fletcher Relationship

[167] Before the motion judge, Nero took the position that at the relevant time, he and Fletcher were common-law spouses. Each filed an affidavit describing the nature of their relationship.

[168] Nero explained that his parole conditions required him to spend Monday to Thursday evenings of each week at the halfway house in which he resided. He and Fletcher lived together on weekends in various hotels and spent weekday evenings together before he was required to return to the halfway house.

[169] Each considered the other their common-law spouse beginning in early spring 2011. Each claimed to have begun residing with the other in August 2011. In fall 2011, they became engaged and purchased property together.

[170] The trial Crown advised the motion judge that he wished to cross-examine Nero and Fletcher on their affidavits. The cross-examination did not take place, however, because the motion judge decided not to hear any submissions by the Crown on the spousal communication privilege issue.

[171] In response to the spousal privilege claim, the trial Crown filed an affidavit from Nero's parole officer. In his application for parole, Nero provided information that he was involved in a common-law relationship with another woman. He was given weekend passes to be out of custody, provided he was with this common-law spouse or at his mother's home. The parole officer was not told that this relationship had ended until July 2011.

[172] In official documents, such as driver's licences and tax returns, Fletcher described herself as single and her place of residence as some place other than with Nero at the home on River Beach Drive. Nero's documents described him as separated and living with his mother.

The Ruling of the Motion Judge

[173] The motion judge found as a fact that Nero and Fletcher were not common-law spouses at any time material to their claim of spousal communication privilege. He further found that the exclusion of common-law spouses from the spousal communication privilege described in s. 4(3) of the *Canada Evidence Act, R.S.C., 1985, c. C-5 ("CEA")*, offended s. 15 of the Charter, but was saved by s. 1. It followed that s. 4(3) barred neither the interception of private communications between Nero and Fletcher or use of those communications in the ITO filed to obtain the search warrant executed at the Nero/Fletcher residence.

The Arguments on Appeal

[174] Nero submits that the motion judge erred in finding that he and Fletcher were not common-law spouses. They were in a committed relationship, had purchased property and lived together and were engaged to be married. Their relationship was of sufficient permanency and duration to make them common-law spouses.

[175] Nero says that as common-law spouses, the spousal communication privilege applies because s. 4(3) of the CEA violates s. 15 of the Charter and is not saved by s. 1. The remedy for this unconstitutionality is to extend the privilege to common-law spouses. This would render interception of their private communications a breach of s. 189(6) of the Criminal Code. It would follow, Nero continues, that the intercepted private communications would be inadmissible as evidence and could not be relied upon as part of the ITO in connection with the search warrant.

[176] The respondent contends that Nero's claim of spousal communication privilege fails both factually and legally.

[177] The respondent begins with the submission that Nero and Fletcher were not common-law spouses when the interceptions were made. They began to cohabit only seven months before interception of their private communications began. While there is admittedly no universal definition of the period of cohabitation required to establish a common-law relationship, even the most generous definition would require a significantly longer period than seven months to qualify. Further, the relationship was shrouded in secrecy, belied by public documents and Nero's own representations to parole authorities, and lacked the essential public acknowledgement and recognition required to constitute a common-law relationship.

[178] The respondent adds that the claim also fails as a matter of law. Nero and Fletcher were not "husband" and "wife" for the purpose of the then provisions of s. 4 of the CEA. The spousal communication privilege of s. 4(3) does not apply to common-law spouses. Binding authority establishes that the failure of s. 4(3) to reach so far as common-law spouses is constitutionally valid. Besides,

spousal communication privilege is testimonial only. Neither interception of these communications nor their use in the ITO was barred by the privilege.

The Governing Principles

[179] Section 4(3) of the CEA is a statutory enactment of a common law class privilege. The subsection provides that no "husband" is compellable to disclose any communications made to him by his "wife" during their marriage, and no "wife" is compellable to disclose any communication made to her by her "husband" during their marriage.

[180] Section 4(3) CEA consists of three elements:

    i. status ("husband" and "wife");

    ii. subject-matter ("a communication"); and

    iii. timing ("during their marriage").

[181] Section 4 does not define "husband" or "wife" for the purposes of the section or more generally. As a general rule, however, courts have held that the former rules of spousal competency and the preservation of spousal communication privilege do not apply to common-law spouses: see e.g. *R. v. Martin*, 2009 SKCA 37 (CanLII), 244 C.C.C. (3d) 206, at paras. 15-25.

[182] In *R. v. Nguyen*, 2015 ONCA 278 (CanLII), 125 O.R. (3d) 321, leave to appeal ref'd, 2016 CarswellOnt 473 (S.C.C.), this court considered, whether the then spousal incompetency rule extended to common-law spouses. At trial, the Crown had called the common-law spouses of two accused as witnesses for the prosecution. The evidence adduced also included what one accused told his common-law spouse in a conversation after the offence has been committed. The admissibility of this evidence was challenged as barred by spousal communication privilege.

[183] Three points of significance to this case emerge from the decision in *Nguyen*.

[184] First, the spousal incompetency rule, as it then existed, did not extend to common-law relationships. As a result, an accused's common-law spouse was a competent and compellable witness for the Crown at the accused's trial: *Nguyen*, at paras. 7, 158.

[185] Second, the spousal communication privilege in s. 4(3) of the CEA does not extend to common-law spouses. As a result, a recipient spouse who testifies at trial cannot invoke the privilege to refuse to answer questions about communications passing between spouses during their common-law marriage: *Nguyen*, at paras. 16-18.

[186] Third, the spousal communication privilege is testimonial in nature. Properly invoked by the recipient spouse, it precludes the reception of

communications during marriage as evidence in the proceedings. The information conveyed, however, is not itself privileged: *Nguyen*, at paras. 134-136; *R. v. Couture*, 2007 SCC 28 (CanLII), [2007] 2 S.C.R. 517, at para. 41; *R. v. Siniscalchi*, 2010 BCCA 354 (CanLII), 257 C.C.C. (3d) 329, at paras. 31-32.

[187] Section 189(6) of the Criminal Code is in these terms:

> Any information obtained by an interception that, but for the interception, would have been privileged remains privileged and inadmissible as evidence without the consent of the person enjoying the privilege.

[188] Section 189(6) does not create a privilege, but rather preserves any existing privilege that attaches to information despite its interception. It logically follows that if the information obtained by interception is *not* privileged, s. 189(6) is not engaged and the information, if otherwise relevant, material and not barred by some other evidentiary rule, would be received for consideration by the trier of fact.

[189] For the purposes of the spousal communication privilege, and despite pronouncements that the information itself is not privileged, s. 189(6) excludes as privileged any information the recipient "husband" or "wife" had a right not to disclose: *R. v. Jean* (1979), 1979 ALTASCAD 89 (CanLII), 46 C.C.C. (2d) 176 (Alta. S.C., AD), at p. 187, aff'd 1980 CanLII 163 (SCC), [1980] 1 S.C.R. 400; *Lloyd et al. v. The Queen*, 1981 CanLII 219 (SCC), [1981] 2 S.C.R. 645, at pp. 650-51.

The Principles Applied

[190] I would not give effect to this ground of appeal. My reasons are two-fold and brief.

[191] First, it is at least open to serious question on the evidence before the motion judge whether during the period of authorized interceptions Nero and Fletcher were in a *bona fide* common-law spousal relationship. Any period of cohabitation was brief. The assertion of such a relationship lacked public acknowledgement and was contradicted by official documents the "spouses" created themselves.

[192] Second, and more importantly, neither the spousal competency rule as it then existed, nor the spousal communication privilege, extends to common-law spouses. It follows that Fletcher could not have asserted privilege if called as a witness, nor could s. 189(6) of the Criminal Code have barred the reception of the intercepted private communications if tendered as evidence by the Crown.

In *R. v. Zylstra*,[369] the Ontario Court of Appeal held that marital privilege does not prevent counsel from asking questions about marital

---

[369]   (1995), 99 C.C.C. (3d) 477, 41 C.R. (4th) 130 (Ont. C.A.).

communications. The witness spouse who holds the privilege may choose whether or not to answer when asked. In a jury case, this means a witness who asserts the privilege must do so in front of the jury. The judge should then instruct the jury that the marital communications privilege is a statutory privilege that all legally married witnesses are entitled to assert.

In contrast there is no class privilege for communications between parent and child: *R. v. E. (T.K.).*[370]

(d) Privilege for Without Prejudice Communications

MIDDELKAMP v. FRASER VALLEY REAL ESTATE BOARD
(1992), 71 B.C.L.R. (2d) 276 (B.C. C.A.)

The plaintiffs complained to the Director of the Competition Act about the defendant real estate board's conduct. The Director referred the matter to the Attorney General of Canada who proceeded against the board by way of information. There were lengthy negotiations. In the result there was a consent prohibition order in Federal Court. During the negotiations the board and the federal authorities exchanged numerous documents. In the plaintiffs' civil action against the board, the defendant board claimed privilege with respect to these documents on the ground that they were exchanged on a without prejudice basis. An order to produce the documents was made. The defendant successfully appealed.

McEACHERN C.J.B.C. (PROUDFOOT, GIBBS and HOLLINRAKE JJ.A. concurring):— Mr. Justice Locke has fully stated the facts of this case which I need not repeat. He bases his judgment upon an immunity equivalent to privilege arising out of the interest the public has in the settlement of disputes. While reaching the same conclusion I prefer, with respect, to base my judgment on slightly different grounds. . . .

I have no doubt that it is in the public interest, that parties to disputes should be free to negotiate *Competition Act* matters and other disputes freely, and without fear of later prejudice arising out of the steps taken during efforts to arrange settlements.

I am, however, hesitant to establish an immunity other than privilege because parties to negotiations, such as the appellant in this case, have no control over without prejudice communications once they are sent off to the other side, and documents of the kind in question in this case can easily find their way into the hands of strangers to the dispute being settled. There is no effective protection against the prejudice caused by such communications unless they are characterized as privileged.

. . .

Considering the enormous scope of production which is required by our almost slavish adherence to the *Peruvian Guano* principle, the questionable relevance and value of documents prepared for the settlement of disputes, and

---

[370]   (2005), 194 C.C.C. (3d) 496, 28 C.R. (6th) 366 (N.B. C.A.).

the public interest, I find myself in agreement with the House of Lords that the public interest in the settlement of disputes generally requires "without prejudice" documents or communications created for, or communicated in the course of, settlement negotiations to be privileged. I would classify this as a " 'blanket', *prima facie*, common law, or 'class' " privilege because it arises from settlement negotiations and protects the class of communications exchanged in the course of that worthwhile endeavour.

In my judgment this privilege protects documents and communications created for such purposes both from production to other parties to the negotiations and to strangers, and extends as well to admissibility, and whether or not a settlement is reached. This is because, as I have said, a party communicating a proposal related to settlement, or responding to one, usually has no control over what the other side may do with such documents. Without such protection, the public interest in encouraging settlements will not be served.

. . .

I would allow the appeal accordingly.

LOCKE J.A.:— This appeal deals with a litigant's obligation to produce certain documents for inspection prior to a civil trial when those documents were generated in negotiating the resolution of potential criminal charges against him.

. . .

The trial judge examined the existing law at some length. He decided he was bound by previous authority in this court. He identified two competing issues: the promotion of negotiations leading to compromise, and the desirability of full discovery. He followed the case of *Derco Industries Ltd. v. A.R. Grimwood Ltd.* (1984), 57 B.C.L.R. 395, and ordered production.

. . .

[There then follows a very thorough review of the jurisprudence in this area in other provinces and in England.]

This claim for protection from production of documents "without prejudice" is often considered to be one that the documents are "privileged" and the cases and writers on occasion classify it as a branch of this doctrine. This is no doubt satisfactory provided it is understood that the claim rests on a very different theoretical base than those other forms which arise because of the relationship between two parties which prohibits admission of their evidence at trial without the consent of the other: legal professional privilege, marital privilege, and concerning landlord and tenant as against disclosure of title deeds, by way of example. Those arise because society deems the relationships to be of such importance that it will not permit their sanctity to be undermined. The "privilege" with which we are concerned here deals not with a relationship but with competing legal interests, both of which are intrinsically meritorious. But as the doctrine we discuss is not a true "privilege" but really a rule of public policy, in my opinion papers leading up to a settlement, no matter how obtained, could not be produced in evidence at all.

Some of the difficulties of dealing with it as a "privilege" are dealt with in an article entitled " 'Without Prejudice' Communications — Their Admissibility and Effect" (1974), 9 U.B.C. Law Review 85, where the author D. Vaver has this to say at p. 107 of his dissertation:

> The undesirability of calling the "without prejudice" rule a "privilege" may also be pointed out in those cases where inadmissibility depends on irrelevancy and where the assertion of a privilege is an impossibility. Suppose that a motor accident arises involving A, B and C. A alleges that B is at fault and B alleges that C is at fault. C compromises with B, but A sues B alone, claiming the accident was solely B's fault. B calls C to testify as to the fact of the offer of compromise. A is unable to object to the evidence on the grounds of privilege, for B and C alone can claim privilege. However, the evidence ought to be excluded on the grounds of irrelevancy, for a compromise *per se* is not evidence of an admission but merely implies a desire to buy peace. If the offer of compromise did contain an admission of liability by C and was thus admissible, "privilege" being waived by B and C, A could not prevent inclusion of the evidence. He could not claim privilege, since privilege is personal to the parties, and the evidence was clearly relevant. It may therefore be seen that there are good reasons for eschewing the use of the description "privilege" in the context of the "without prejudice" rule and for not considering the basis of the rule as one of "privilege".

. . .

And so it is seen that the overwhelming current of authority is in favour of endorsing the protection from production with the aim of curtailing or shortening litigation. This has been the underlying object. I have laboriously canvassed all these cases to show that the principle has always been accepted from the earliest times. There has been much litigation, but it has all been to define the scope of the doctrine: Does it apply to arbitrations? Does it apply to opinion evidence? Does it apply to lawyers as well as clients? Does it apply when there has been a concluded settlement? And so on. Never has the principle, which is really one example of applying the principle of economy of means, been doubted.

In later times much intellectual powder has been expended in attempting to state the true theoretical basis for the doctrine. *Hoghton v. Hoghton* in 1852, *Underwood v. Cox* in 1912, one judge in *Schetky v. Cochrane* in 1918, *Scott Paper* in 1927, *Waxman* in 1968 and *Rush v. Tomkins* in 1988 have all placed it in the ground of public interest.

I agree with this. It has to my mind the immense advantage of enabling one to balance competing interests not on forms of words but on intrinsic strengths. One is enabled to apply principle to the kaleidoscope of circumstance.

The present case

. . .

With all respect I cannot in law see one reason why this province, alone in the Commonwealth, should not recognize the overriding importance of this protection from the eyes of a third party. To refuse it is to inhibit and penalize one who wishes to settle. It is easy to envisage a building owner loath to compromise the minor claim of a small subcontractor, because of concern an admission of fact would be held against him in another major subcontractor's proceeding.

All the cases emphasize that no bars should be placed in the way of one who wishes to compromise, and to allow the production is by definition to inhibit. Such barriers to settlement should only be permitted if the other competing interest absolutely demands it.

. . .

In my view, the guiding principle and one promising the greatest good for the greatest number of disputants is to shield these documents from production.[371]

In *British Columbia Children's Hospital v. Air Products Canada Ltd./ Prodair Canada Ltée*,[372] a majority of the Court of Appeal took *Middelkamp* one step further and concluded that settlement privilege protected not only "without prejudice" communications made in furtherance of settlement but also the settlement agreements themselves. Justice Huddart dissented. In her view, a case-by-case determination of privilege should be applied.

In *R. v. Delchev*,[373] the Court held that a plea-bargaining discussion is subject to settlement privilege. However the Court recognized an exception that evidence of such a discussion was admissible for the purpose of an abuse of process application against the Crown.

2. PUBLIC INTEREST IMMUNITY

(a) Statutory Provisions

Sections 37 to 39 of the *Canada Evidence Act* govern claims of public interest immunity. Section 37 applies where a "specified public interest" is asserted such as the identity of an informer privilege[374] or law enforcement investigative technique.[375] Section 38 applies where the immunity from production is sought to protect international relations, national defence or national security. Finally, s. 39 applies to confidences of the Privy Council or Cabinet.

Following the attacks of September 11, 2001, Canada moved quickly and passed its *Anti-terrorism Act* (Bill C-36) in December, 2001.[376] Bill C-36 amended ss. 37 and 38 of the *Canada Evidence Act*. Generally speaking, Bill C-36 did not substantially alter the parameters of the balancing required to determine whether disclosure should be permitted. Under both ss. 37(5) and 38.06(2), a judge is to determine whether the public interest in disclosure (usually the fair trial rights of the individual) outweighs the harm to a specified public interest or to international relations, national defence or security.

---

[371] See further *Gay (Guardian ad litem of) v. UNUM Life Insurance Co. of America* (2003), 219 N.S.R. (2d) 175, 42 C.P.C. (5th) 151 (N.S. S.C. [In Chambers]).
[372] (2003), 224 D.L.R. (4th) 23 (B.C. C.A.), leave to appeal allowed (2004), 233 D.L.R. (4th) vi (S.C.C.).
[373] 2015 ONCA 381, 325 C.C.C. (3d) 447 (Ont. C.A.).
[374] See *R. v. Pilotte* (2002), 163 C.C.C. (3d) 225 (Ont. C.A.).
[375] See *R. v. Richards* (1997), 115 C.C.C. (3d) 377 (Ont. C.A.).
[376] S.C. 2001, c. 41 (Bill C-36). Section 43 of Bill C-46 amends the *Canada Evidence Act*.

However, there are some significant additions to the national defence and security section (i.e., s. 38).[377] These include:

- an expansion of the kind of information that triggers scrutiny. Objections under the old s. 38, for example, could only be made where it was alleged that disclosure *would* injure international relations or national defence or security. Under the new regime, objection can be made in relation to "potentially injurious information" which is defined as *could* rather than would injure . . . and "sensitive information" defined as "information relating to international relations or national defence or national security that is in the possession of the Government of Canada, whether originating from inside or outside of Canada, and is of the type that the Government of Canada is taking measures to safeguard";[378]

- an obligation on both parties (including the defence)[379] to notify the federal Attorney General of the possibility that he or she or anyone else may disclose sensitive or potentially injurious information;[380]

- a power vested in the federal Attorney General to issue a certificate that prohibits disclosure of information in connection with a proceeding for the purpose of protecting information obtained in confidence from, or in relation to, a foreign entity or for the purpose of protecting national defence or national security.[381]

Most of the provinces in Canada have enacted legislation providing for immunity claims in proceedings where the Crown is a party. For example, the *Proceedings Against the Crown Act* in Alberta provides:

> 11. In proceedings against the Crown, the rules of court as to discovery and inspection of documents and examination for discovery apply in the same manner as if the Crown were a corporation, except that the Crown may refuse to produce a document or to make answer to a

---

[377] See J. Kalajdzic, "Litigating State Secrets: A Comparative Study of National Security Privilege in Canadian, U.S. and British Civil Cases" (2010) 41:2 Ottawa L. Rev. 289; Cohen, *Privacy, Crime and Terror— Legal Rights and Security in a Time of Peril* (Toronto: Butterworths, 2005); H. Stewart, "Public Interest Immunity After Bill C-36" (2003) 47 Crim. L.Q. 249; and P. Rosenthal, "Disclosure To The Defence After September 11: Sections 37 and 38 Of The *Canada Evidence Act*" (2003) 48 Crim. L.Q. 186.

[378] Section 38. In *O'Neill v. Canada (Attorney General)* (2006), 42 C.R. (6th) 63, 213 C.C.C. (3d) 389 (Ont. S.C.J.), Ratushny J. of the Ontario Superior Court struck down portions of the *Security of Information Act* concerning unauthorized release of secret information as vague, overbroad and not requiring fault. See "Annotation" by Steve Coughlan, C.R. *ibid.* The Federal Minister of Justice announced that an appeal of *O'Neill* was not in the public interest. For an application of s. 38.04 in the context of a terrorism trial, see *Canada (Attorney General) v. Khawaja* (2007), 52 C.R. (6th) 107 (F.C.A.). The Supreme Court decided that such a review of public interest immunity concerns was required by s. 7 of the *Charter* respecting an applicant captured by the United States forces, detained and charged with offences before military tribunals: *Khadr v. Canada (Minister of Justice)*, [2008] 2 S.C.R. 125, 232 C.C.C. (3d) 101, 56 C.R. (6th) 255 (S.C.C.). See Benjamin Berger, "The Reach of Rights in the Security State: Reflections on *Khadr v. Canada (Minister of Justice)*", C.R. *ibid.* 268.

[379] See *Canada (Attorney General) v. Ribic* (2003), 185 C.C.C. (3d) 129 (Fed. C.A.).

[380] Section 38.02.

[381] Section 38.13.

question on discovery on the ground that the production of it or the answer would be injurious to the public interest.[382]

In addition, some provinces have enacted legislation regarding the procedure for immunity claims in suits between parties. For example, the *Ontario Evidence Act* provides:

> 30. Where a document is in the official possession, custody or power of a member of the Executive Council, or of the head of a ministry of the public service of Ontario, if the deputy head or other officer of the ministry has the document in his or her personal possession, and is called as a witness, he or she is entitled, acting herein by the direction and on behalf of such member of the Executive Council or head of the ministry, to object to producing the document on the ground that it is privileged, and such objection may be taken by him or her in the same manner, and has the same effect, as if such member of the Executive Council or head of the ministry were personally present and made the objection.[383]

Where there is no specific statutory provision that is comparable to ss. 37 to 39 of the *Canada Evidence Act*, then the common law will apply to claims of immunity by the provinces. The leading case setting out the common law procedure is *Carey v. Ontario*[384] which dealt with Cabinet documents of the Ontario Legislature.

(b) Identity of Informers

R. v. DURHAM REGIONAL CRIME STOPPERS INC.
2017 CSC 45, 2017 SCC 45, [2017] 2 S.C.R. 157, 355 C.C.C. (3d) 324,
41 C.R. (7th) 1 (S.C.C.)

A week after a fatal shooting, Crime Stoppers received an anonymous tip from a caller. The caller reported that on the day of the shooting he observed four men in the backyard of a house neighbouring on the crime scene and that he then saw the men drive to a lake where they threw things into the water. The accused was charged with second degree murder for the shooting. The Crown disclosed to the defence the anonymous tip and all relevant evidence in its possession and brought a pre trial application to introduce the evidence of the tip. The Crown maintained that the call was made by the accused to divert attention away from himself during the police investigation. The accused denied making the call. In addition, he and Crime Stoppers submitted that the call was covered by informer privilege. The application judge, at an *in camera* hearing, found that informer privilege did not apply. His ruling was appealed to the Supreme Court pursuant to s. 40(1) of the *Supreme Court Act*.

The Supreme Court was unanimous in dismissing the appeal.

---

[382]   R.S.A. 2000, c. P-25.
[383]   R.S.O. 1990, c. E.23.
[384]   [1986] 2 S.C.R. 637.

MOLDAVER J.:

I. Overview

[1] The informer privilege rule is a common law rule of long standing — and it is fundamentally important to the criminal justice system. Informers play a critical role in law enforcement by providing police with information that is otherwise difficult or impossible to obtain. By protecting the identity of individuals who supply information to the police — and encouraging others to do the same — informer privilege greatly assists the police in the investigation of crime and the protection of the public. Subject to the innocence at stake exception, the privilege acts as a complete bar on the disclosure of the informer's identity, and the police, the Crown and the courts are bound to uphold it.

. . .

A. *Does Informer Privilege Apply to the Anonymous Tip Made to Crime Stoppers in This Case?*

(1) The Underlying Rationales of the Informer Privilege Rule

[11] Informer privilege is a common law rule that prohibits the disclosure of an informer's identity in public or in court. As a class privilege, informer privilege is not determined on a case-by-case basis. It exists where a police officer, in the course of an investigation, guarantees confidentiality to a prospective informer in exchange for information: *R. v. Basi*, 2009 SCC 52, [2009] 3 S.C.R. 389, at para. 36; *Bisaillon v. Keable*, [1983] 2 S.C.R. 60, at p. 105. The privilege acts as "a complete and total bar" on any disclosure of the informer's identity, subject only to the innocence at stake exception: *Named Person v. Vancouver Sun*, 2007 SCC 43, [2007] 3 S.C.R. 253, at para. 30. All information which might tend to identify the informer is protected by the privilege: *ibid.* The privilege belongs both to the Crown and to the informer and neither can waive it without the consent of the other: *ibid.*, at para. 25.

[12] As with all privileges, informer privilege is granted in the public interest. Informers pass on useful information to the police which may otherwise be difficult or even impossible to obtain. They thus play a critical role in the investigation of crime and the apprehension of criminals. The police and the criminal justice system rely on informers — and society as a whole benefits from their assistance: see *R. v. Leipert*, [1997] 1 S.C.R. 281, at para. 9; *R. v. Barros*, 2011 SCC 51, [2011] 3 S.C.R. 368, at para. 30. In fulfilling this important role, informers often face the risk of retribution from those involved in criminal activity: *Leipert*, at para. 9. Accordingly, informer privilege was developed to protect the identity of citizens who provide information to law enforcement: *ibid.* By protecting those who assist the police in this manner — and encouraging others to do the same — the privilege furthers the interests of justice and the maintenance of public order: see *R. v. Hiscock* (1992), 72 C.C.C. (3d) 303 (Que. C.A.), at p. 328, leave to appeal refused, [1993] 1 S.C.R. vi. As this Court noted in *Bisaillon*:

> The public interest which requires secrecy regarding police informers' identity is the maintenance of an efficient police force and an effective implementation of the criminal law. [p. 97]

Likewise, in *Named Person*, LeBel J., writing in dissent, but not on this point, stated that:

> the social justification for this privilege was found in the need to ensure performance of the policing function and maintenance of law and order. [para. 111]

[13] Informer privilege is particularly important in the context of anonymous informers. In *Leipert*, this Court noted that preserving the anonymity of callers to Crime Stoppers and other public service organizations working to combat crime is critical to the effectiveness of law enforcement:

> It is the promise of anonymity which allays the fear of criminal retaliation which otherwise discourages citizen involvement in reporting crime. In turn, by guaranteeing anonymity, Crimestoppers provides law enforcement with information it might never otherwise obtain.

> (para. 11, quoting *People v. Callen*, 194 Cal.App. 3d 558 (1987), at p. 563.)

In *Leipert*, the Court recognized that informer privilege may apply where an anonymous tip is made to Crime Stoppers.

[14] Informer privilege is of such fundamental importance to the criminal justice system and to society at large that it is "near absolute" and is subject to only the innocence at stake exception: *Basi*, at para. 37; *Barros*, at para. 1. This exception provides that where disclosure of the informer's identity is necessary to show the innocence of an accused, the informer's identity can be disclosed for that limited purpose: *Leipert*, at para. 20. Our abhorrence of wrongful convictions requires no less. As such, the right of an accused to establish his or her innocence by raising a reasonable doubt takes precedence over protecting an informer's identity: *R. v. Scott*, [1990] 3 S.C.R. 979, at pp. 995-96.

[15] Apart from the innocence at stake exception, the informer privilege rule is absolute. Courts must give effect to it and are not entitled to balance the benefit of the privilege against countervailing considerations: *Leipert*, at paras. 12-13. Through informer privilege, the law recognizes that the public interest in protecting the identity of informants prevails over other policy concerns: see D. M. Paciocco and L. Stuesser, *The Law of Evidence* (7th ed. 2015), at p. 302. The police, the Crown and courts are bound by the rule and are under a duty to protect the informer's identity: *Barros*, at para. 37.

(2) The Scope of Informer Privilege

(a) *The Scope of Informer Privilege is Limited by its Underlying Rationales*

[16] Keenan Corner and Crime Stoppers submit that all persons who call Crime Stoppers are confidential informers and are entitled to informer privilege. They assert that the "privilege attaches automatically: literally, as

soon as the phone rings" (A.F. (Crime Stoppers), at para. 54). I would not give effect to this submission. As I will explain, informer privilege does not apply where a person has made a communication to Crime Stoppers with the intention of furthering criminal activity or interfering with the administration of justice. In such circumstances, unlike a claim of innocence at stake which is treated as an exception to a communication that otherwise comes within the scope of informer privilege, a communication in furtherance of criminality is excluded from the scope of informer privilege.

[17] The scope of informer privilege is limited by its underlying rationales. As Binnie J. noted in Barros, "it is important not to extend [the privilege's] scope beyond what is necessary to achieve its purpose of protecting informers and encouraging individuals with knowledge of criminal activities to come forward to speak to the authorities": para. 28.

. . .

(c) *The Policy Concern About Chilling Effects*

[27] Crime Stoppers and Keenan Corner submit that if privilege does not automatically apply to anonymous tips made to Crime Stoppers, this will have a chilling effect on citizens who provide information to Crime Stoppers: A.F. (Crime Stoppers), at para. 78. The privilege must apply "as soon as the phone rings" at Crime Stoppers, otherwise callers who are misinformed about the details of suspects or events, or those who deliberately distort or disguise certain details to protect themselves, may be investigated by the police or exposed to the risk of criminal sanction: *ibid.*, at paras. 74 and 78. This, they say, will dissuade citizens from providing information to Crime Stoppers.

[28] With respect, I do not share their concern. In the case of anonymous tips made to Crime Stoppers, informer privilege will apply except in those cases where it can be shown that the person called with the intention of furthering criminal activity or interfering with the administration of justice. This is a high bar to meet. It requires a heightened mental element and involves a high degree of moral blameworthiness. Callers who are *bona fide* informers have no cause to be concerned about being excluded from the protection of the privilege. In the vast majority of cases, informer privilege will apply to a tip made to Crime Stoppers. Only those who possess the requisite intent need be concerned.

[29] Furthermore, informer privilege is not an absolute rule. As indicated, it is subject to one exception: where an accused's innocence is at stake. Callers cannot know whether their identities will be disclosed through the innocence at stake exception, yet this has not been shown to deter people from providing information to Crime Stoppers. By contrast, where a person calls with an intention of furthering criminal activity or interfering with the administration of justice, informer privilege will not apply for precisely that reason — something entirely within the person's control. Given that the innocence at stake exception has not been shown to deter callers, I fail to see how such an exclusion could have a deterrent effect on *bona fide* informers.

. . .

(e) *Application to This Case*

[32] The application judge did not err in concluding that privilege did not apply to the Crime Stoppers tip. It was reasonable for the application judge to find, on a balance of probabilities, that Keenan Corner made the tip and that he did so to divert attention away from himself in a police investigation. This finding was well-supported by the following evidence, upon which the application judge relied:

1. The caller's report that the four men waited near the crime scene for five to ten minutes after the fatal shooting of Mr. Niazi was unlikely to be true;

2. Police examination of the area around the crime scene was inconsistent with the caller's report that he saw four male persons there;

3. Keenan Corner was observed by the police ending a call on a public pay phone around the same time the call to Crime Stoppers was terminated; and

4. There were significant similarities between Keenan Corner's statements to the police about three male persons at the crime scene — which he later admitted were false — and the descriptions of the four male persons given by the anonymous caller.

[33] In light of this evidence, I see no basis for interfering with the application judge's finding that Keenan Corner was the caller and that he made the call with the intention of interfering with the administration of justice. I would therefore uphold the application judge's decision that informer privilege does not apply to the tip.

Should individuals who allow the police to use their homes as location posts for surveillance be entitled to the same protection as police informers?[385]

In *R. v. Barros*[386] the Court held that the accused has a right to conduct lawful investigations to discover the identity of a confidential source. However, intimidating investigations by a former police officer on behalf of the accused could, the Court held, amount to obstruction and extortion.[387]

The Supreme Court held in *R. v. B.*[388] that not everyone who provides information to the police becomes a confidential informant but the promise of protection and confidentiality may be inferred from the circumstances.

---

[385]   Compare *R. v. Lam* (2000), 148 C.C.C. (3d) 379 (B.C. C.A.) with *R. v. Thomas* (1998), 124 C.C.C. (3d) 178 (Ont. Gen. Div.). See also *R. v. Richards* (1997), 115 C.C.C. (3d) 377 (Ont. C.A.); *R. v. Meuckon* (1990), 57 C.C.C. (3d) 193 (B.C. C.A.) and R.W. Hubbard et al., "Informer and Police Investigatory Privilege At The Preliminary Inquiry" (1999) 41 Crim. L.Q. 68 on the issue of privilege and police investigatory techniques.

[386]   [2011] 3 S.C.R. 368, 88 C.R. (6th) 33, 273 C.C.C. (3d) 129 (S.C.C.).

[387]   See discussion by Philip Wright, "*Barros:* Legal Limits on Active Defence Investigations into the Identity of an Informant and the Need to Confront Ethical Issues" (2011), 88 C.R. (6th) 77.

[388]   [2013] 1 S.C.R. 405 (S.C.C.).

In *Harkat, Re*[389] the Supreme Court held that the police informer privilege was not to be extended to Canadian Security Intelligence Service human sources.

3. CASE-BY-CASE PRIVILEGE

Wigmore recognized that to suppress relevant evidence and so inhibit the search for truth required a public interest weightier than the public's general right to everyman's evidence. He suggested then four conditions as necessary to the establishment of a privilege for confidential communications:

(1) The communications must originate in a *confidence* that they will not be disclosed.

(2) This element of *confidentiality must be essential* to the full and satisfactory maintenance of the relation between the parties.

(3) The *relation* must be one which in the opinion of the community ought to be sedulously *fostered.*

(4) The *injury* that would inure to the relation by the disclosure of the communications must be *greater than the benefit* thereby gained for the correct disposal of litigation.

Only if these four conditions are present should a privilege be recognized.[390]

In *Slavutych v. Baker*[391] the appellant appealed against his dismissal as a university professor. Slavutych had been asked for a confidential report on a colleague's suitability for tenure and this report was used against Slavutych to justify his dismissal; the actual charge against Slavutych was that he had in his report, made a "very serious charge on the flimsiest basis". A board of arbitration upheld the dismissal. The Supreme Court of Canada quashed the award of the arbitration board on the substantive law basis that a party who obtains information in confidence shall not be allowed to use it as a springboard for an action against the person who made the confidential communication. It was not necessary then for the Court to consider the admissibility of the document as an evidentiary matter but, speaking for a unanimous Court, Spence, J. measured the communication against Wigmore's criteria and concluded:

> . . . considering this matter only an evidentiary one and under the doctrine of privilege as so ably considered in Wigmore the confidential document should have been ruled inadmissible.[392]

The Court's lead, adopting Wigmore's criteria as a guide for the recognition of future privileged communications, has since been followed in a number of cases[393] as the courts seemingly agree with the observation of Laskin, C.J.C.:

---

[389] [2014] 2 S.C.R. 33 (S.C.C.). See C.R. comment by Tim Quigley.

[390] 8 Wigmore, *Evidence* (McNaughton Rev.), s. 2285.

[391] (1975), 55 D.L.R. (3d) 224 (S.C.C.).

[392] *Ibid.* at 229.

[393] See e.g. *Jones v. Crompton*, [1977] 4 W.W.R. 440 (B.C. S.C.), diary not prepared in a confidence not privileged.

What *Slavutych v. Baker* established is that the categories of privilege are not closed.[394]

For a consideration of the *Slavutych* criteria see *R. v. Delong*.[395] The accused was charged with assaulting police. The question was whether the trial judge should have ordered production of statements given to police complaints investigators for use in the defence of the accused. The statements were those previously given by Crown witnesses to investigators on a complaint made by the accused to the Complaint Investigation Bureau of the Peel Regional Police, arising out of the same circumstances. The Court decided that it was doubtful whether there was true confidentiality established by the informal understanding with the police association. Nor was the relationship one which needed to be "sedulously fostered". Finally, the Court decided that it was not satisfied that, under condition 4, the "injury" that would result to the relationship between the police officers and the Complaint Bureau had a social value that would outweigh the public interest in favour of the accused facing a serious criminal charge having the right to disclosure to enable him to make full answer and defence. The Court decided that the statements should have been produced and allowed the accused's appeal.

In *R. v. National Post*[396] the Supreme Court decided that there was no class privilege for journalistic sources. Confidentiality was to be determined on the case-by-case Wigmore criteria. Privacy interests of the press are to be balanced against law enforcement interests of the State. Access to documents suspected to be forged was ordered.[397]

4. BALANCING CHARTER VALUES

The constitutional right to full disclosure has proved particularly controversial where relied upon by defence counsel to gain access to medical records of sexual assault complainants. The matter reached the Supreme Court in *R. v. O'Connor*[398] and *A. (L.L.) v. B. (A.).*[399] The Court in *O'Connor* announced a special procedure respecting discovery of medical records in the possession of third parties. The decision represents a fundamental broadening of the *Stinchcombe* right to disclosure of material in the Crown's possession or control to a right to discovery.

Through the judgment of Madam Justice L'Heureux-Dubé in *A. (L.L.) v. B. (A.)*, the Court unanimously decided that production should not be determined by class or case-by-case privilege. According to L'Heureux-Dubé J., the creation of a class privilege in favour of private records in criminal law raised concerns relating to

---

[394]   *Sol. Gen. Can. v. Royal Commn. Re Health Records* (1982) 62 C.C.C. (2d) 173 (S.C.C.) at 207.
[395]   (1989), 69 C.R. (3d) 147 (Ont. C.A.).
[396]   [2010] 1 S.C.R. 477, 254 C.C.C. (3d) 469, 74 C.R. (6th) 1 (S.C.C.).
[397]   See C.R. annotation by Janine Benedet.
[398]   (1996), 44 C.R. (4th) 1.
[399]   (1996), 44 C.R. (4th) 91.

(1) the truth-finding process of our adversarial trial procedure;

(2) the possible relevance of some private records;

(3) the accused's right to make full answer and defence;

(4) the categories of actors included in a class privilege; and

(5) the experience of other countries.

Carefully examining case law dealing with privilege and confidential information, including that relating to police informants, solicitor-client privilege and public interest immunity, she points out that the courts have consistently ordered production where necessary to establish innocence. While there was ground to recognize a case-by-case privilege along Wigmore lines for private records in some instances, such exceptions to the general evidentiary rule of admissibility and disclosure "should not be encouraged". The better approach was one of balancing competing *Charter* rights. L'Heureux-Dubé J. with La Forest, Gonthier and McLachlin JJ. concurring, saw the need to balance the accused's right to a fair trial and full answer and defence with the complainant's rights to privacy and to equality without discrimination. The majority through a joint judgment by Lamer C.J. and Sopinka J. with Cory, Iacobucci and Major JJ. concurring, determined that the accused's right to full answer and defence should be balanced against the complainant's rights to privacy under ss. 7 and 8. However the majority, in not referring to a s. 15 equality right for complainants although it was fully argued, implicitly reject it.

The Court agreed that there should be a two-stage procedure but divided 5-4 as to the precise tests. For the majority Lamer C.J. and Sopinka J. decided that when the defence seeks information in the hands of a third party the onus should be on the accused to satisfy a judge that the information is likely to be relevant. In the context of disclosure, the meaning of relevance was whether the information might be useful to the defence. In the context of production, the test of relevance should be higher: the presiding judge must be satisfied that there is a reasonable possibility that the information is logically probative to an issue at trial or the competence of a witness to testify. While likely relevance was the appropriate threshold for the first stage of the two-step procedure, the majority determined that it should not be interpreted as an onerous burden upon the accused. A relevance threshold, at this stage, was simply a requirement to prevent the defence from engaging in speculative, fanciful, disruptive, unmeritorious, obstructive and time-consuming requests for production. The crux of the *O'Connor* regime is the determination by the majority that the first stage of establishing likely relevance had to be a low threshold as the accused might often be in a catch-22 situation where he or she was disadvantaged by arguing relevance of a document he or she had not seen. The majority in *O'Connor* disagreed with L'Heureux-Dubé J.'s position that such records would only be relevant in rare cases. They gave as examples of possible relevance records which may contain information about the unfolding of the complaint about the use of therapy to influence memory, and bearing on credibility. L'Heureux-Dubé J. thought the *Charter* mandated less, but she did not carry the day. Upon their production to the court, the judge should examine the records to determine whether, and to what extent, they should be produced to the accused. In making that determination, the judge must examine and weigh the salutary and deleterious effects of a production order and determine whether a non-production order would constitute a reasonable limit on the ability of the accused to make full answer and defence.

For the minority, L'Heureux-Dubé J. saw the first-stage burden on an accused to demonstrate likely relevance as significant and, if it could not be met, the application for production should be dismissed as amounting to no more than a fishing expedition. The mere fact that the complainant had received treatment or counselling could not be presumed to be relevant to the trial as therapy generally focuses on emotional and psychological responses rather than being oriented to ascertaining historical truth.

There was a further difference of opinion as to the criteria at the production stage. Lamer C.J. and Sopinka J., for the majority, agreed with L'Heureux-Dubé J. that the following factors should be considered:

(1) the extent to which the record is necessary for the accused to make full answer and defence;
(2) the probative value of the record in question;
(3) the nature and extent of the reasonable expectation of privacy vested in that record;
(4) whether production of the record would be premised upon any discriminatory belief or bias; and
(5) the potential prejudice to the complainant's dignity, privacy or security of the person that would be occasioned by production of the record in question.

However, the majority departed from L'Heureux-Dubé J.'s further view that it was also necessary to balance two other factors:

(1) the extent to which production of records of this nature would frustrate society's interest in encouraging the reporting of sexual offences, and
(2) the acquisition of treatment by victims [and] the effect on the integrity of the trial process of producing, or failing to produce, the record, having in mind the need to maintain consideration in the outcome.

According to the majority the second factor was more appropriately dealt with at the admissibility stage and not in deciding whether the information should be produced. As for society's interest in the reporting of sexual crimes, the majority pointed to other avenues available to the judge to ensure that production does not frustrate the societal interests, such as publication bans and barring spectators.

The majority decided that quite different considerations should apply where records were in the possession of the Crown. In such cases the complainant's privacy interests in medical records would not have to be balanced. The Crown's disclosure obligations established in *Stinchcombe* were not to be affected. Concerns relating to privacy or privilege disappeared when the documents were in the Crown' s possession. If the records were in the possession of the Crown their relevance was to be presumed. It was unfair in the adversarial process for the Crown to have knowledge that was not shared with the accused. When the records had been shared with the

Crown, an agent of the State, the records had become the property of the public to be used to ensure that justice was done. In deciding whether the complainant had waived any potential claim of privilege the waiver would have to be informed. There was to be an onus on the Crown to inform the complainant of the potential for disclosure. Any form of privilege would in any event have to yield where such a privilege precluded the accused's right to full answer and defence.

The majority opinion that privacy issues disappear where the medical records are in the possession of the Crown is utterly unconvincing and has been strongly criticized. Heather Holmes puts the problem well:

> This reasoning appears to assume a formal investigative dialogue by which relevant information is requested by the police or Crown and either provided or refused by the witness, with full opportunity for discussion of legal consequences. It cannot have been intended to apply to the hurly-burly of ordinary existence. A wide variety of material will make its way into the police or Crown files by accident, inadvertence, or because of an investigator' s less than perfect appreciation of relevance.

> Complainants who muster the considerable courage required for the bringing of criminal charges usually do so without counsel. The Crown prosecutor, as the lawyer tasked with presenting the complainant's report to the court, may appear to the complainant to be "her" lawyer. It is not unusual or unreasonable for a complainant to tacitly consider her relationship with the prosecutor to have a special, albeit undefined, legal status, that at the very least provides some basic protection of confidentiality. Waiver is a strained concept in this situation. See Holmes, "An Analysis of Bill C-46, Production of Records . . ." (1997), 2 Can. Crim. L.R. 71.

Even under *Stinchcombe* there is no absolute duty for the Crown to disclose. Disclosure is subject to determinations of relevance and privilege, both issues here predetermined against the Crown. The notion that the complainant no longer has a privacy issue in the records simply because they are in the possession of the Crown is extraordinary. What if they were stolen, given to the Crown by a therapist without the knowledge of the complainant or handed over to the police by the complainant on the basis that there would otherwise be no prosecution. The minority, through L'Heureux-Dubé J., point out that the majority opinion is *obiter* as the appeal did not concern the extent of the Crown's obligation to disclose private records in its possession.

Following *O'Connor* the Parliament of Canada passed the comprehensive Bill C-46 to restrict the production of records in sexual offence proceedings.

In essence the legislation now contained in ss. 278.1 to 278.9 of the *Criminal Code* in large measure reflects word for word the minority position of L'Heureux-Dubé J. in *O'Connor*. In particular:

1. The preamble asserts a s. 15 equality right for women and children who are complainants in sexual cases.

2. Although the *O'Connor* likely relevance test is maintained, s. 278.3(4) specifies ten assertions which are declared not sufficient

on their own to establish that a record is likely relevant to an issue at trial or to the competence of a witness to testify.

3. Under s. 278.5 a trial judge has to balance privacy and the interests of justice before deciding whether to order the production of a record for review by the court.

4. Under s. 278.7 the trial judge may only order production to the accused on consideration of all seven factors listed by L'Heureux-Dubé, J. rather than the five adopted by the *O'Connor* majority.

5. Under s. 278.2 the two-stage balancing process must be applied to records in the possession of the Crown.

In *Mills* a joint judgment by Justices McLachlin and Iacobucci holds constitutional the more comprehensive Parliamentary scheme for access to complainants' records in sexual assault cases, which had enacted the minority approach in *O'Connor*. Of the *O'Connor* majority, only Lamer, C.J. dissented in *Mills* and only on the issue of applying the balancing of complainants' rights approach to records in the possession of the Crown. Justice Cory chose not to participate before his retirement and Justices Iacobucci and Major no longer supported their earlier positions.

R. v. MILLS
[1999] 3 S.C.R. 668, 28 C.R. (5th) 207, 139 C.C.C. (3d) 321

McLachlin and Iacobucci JJ. (L'Heureux-Dubé, Gonthier, Major, Bastarache and Binnie JJ. concurring):—

. . .

The law develops through dialogue between courts and legislatures: see *Vriend v. Alberta*, [1998] 1 S.C.R. 493. Against the backdrop of *O'Connor*, Parliament was free to craft its own solution to the problem consistent with the Charter. Turning to the legislation at issue in this appeal, we find it constitutional. It is undisputed that there are several important respects in which Bill C-46 differs from the regime set out in *O'Connor*, supra. However, these differences are not fatal because Bill C-46 provides sufficient protection for all relevant Charter rights. There are, admittedly, several provisions in the Bill that are subject to differing interpretations. However, in such situations we will interpret the legislation in a constitutional manner where possible: see *Slaight Communications Inc. v. Davidson*, [1989] 1 S.C.R. 1038, at p. 1078. By so doing, we conclude that Bill C-46 is a constitutional response to the problem of production of records of complainants or witnesses in sexual assault proceedings.

. . .

Like *O'Connor*, Parliament has set up a two-stage process: (1) disclosure to the judge; and (2) production to the accused. At the first stage, the accused must establish that the record sought is "likely relevant to an issue at trial or to the competence of a witness to testify" and that "the production of the record is necessary in the interests of justice" (s. 278.5(1)). Bill C-46 diverges from

O'Connor by directing the trial judge to consider the salutary and deleterious effects of production to the court on the accused's right to full answer and defence and the complainant or witness's right to privacy and equality. A series of factors is listed that the trial judge is directed to take into account in deciding whether the document should be produced to the court (s. 278.5(2)). If the requirements of this first stage are met, the record will be ordered produced to the trial judge. At the second stage, the judge looks at the record in the absence of the parties (s. 278.6(1)), holds a hearing if necessary (s. 278.6(2)), and determines whether the record should be produced on the basis that it is "likely relevant to an issue at trial or to the competence of a witness to testify" and that its production is "necessary in the interests of justice" (s. 278.7). Again at this stage, the judge must consider the salutary and deleterious effects on the accused's right to make full answer and defence and on the right to privacy and equality of the complainant or witness, and is directed to "take into account" the factors set out at s. 278.5(2): s. 278.7(2). When ordering production, the judge may impose conditions on production: s. 278.7(3).

The respondent and several supporting interveners argue that Bill C-46 is unconstitutional to the extent that it establishes a regime for production that differs from or is inconsistent with that established by the majority in *O'Connor*. However, it does not follow from the fact that a law passed by Parliament differs from a regime envisaged by the Court in the absence of a statutory scheme, that Parliament's law is unconstitutional. Parliament may build on the Court's decision, and develop a different scheme as long as it remains constitutional. Just as Parliament must respect the Court's rulings, so the Court must respect Parliament's determination that the judicial scheme can be improved. To insist on slavish conformity would belie the mutual respect that underpins the relationship between the courts and legislature that is so essential to our constitutional democracy: *Vriend*, supra. . . .

Relationship Between the Courts and the Legislature Generally

A posture of respect towards Parliament was endorsed by this Court in *Slaight Communications*, supra, at p. 1078, where we held that if legislation is amenable to two interpretations, a court should choose that interpretation that upholds the legislation as constitutional. Thus courts must presume that Parliament intended to enact constitutional legislation and strive, where possible, to give effect to this intention. This Court has also discussed the relationship between the courts and the legislature in terms of a dialogue, and emphasized its importance to the democratic process. In *Vriend*, supra, at para. 139, Iacobucci J. stated:

> To my mind, a great value of judicial review and this dialogue among the branches is that each of the branches is made somewhat accountable to the other. The work of the legislature is reviewed by the courts and the work of the court in its decisions can be reacted to by the legislature in the passing of new legislation (or even overarching laws under s. 33 of the Charter). This dialogue between and accountability of each of the branches have the effect of enhancing the democratic process, not denying it.

See also Peter W. Hogg and Allison A. Bushell, "The Charter Dialogue Between Courts and Legislatures" (1997), 35 Osgoode Hall L.J. 75. If the common law were to be taken as establishing the only possible constitutional regime, then we could not speak of a dialogue with the legislature. Such a situation could only undermine rather than enhance democracy. Legislative change and the development of the common law are different.

. . .

Courts do not hold a monopoly on the protection and promotion of rights and freedoms; Parliament also plays a role in this regard and is often able to act as a significant ally for vulnerable groups. This is especially important to recognize in the context of sexual violence. The history of the treatment of sexual assault complainants by our society and our legal system is an unfortunate one. Important change has occurred through legislation aimed at both recognizing the rights and interests of complainants in criminal proceedings, and debunking the stereotypes that have been so damaging to women and children, but the treatment of sexual assault complainants remains an ongoing problem. If constitutional democracy is meant to ensure that due regard is given to the voices of those vulnerable to being overlooked by the majority, then this court has an obligation to consider respectfully Parliament's attempt to respond to such voices.

Parliament has enacted this legislation after a long consultation process that included a consideration of the constitutional standards outlined by this Court in *O'Connor*. While it is the role of the courts to specify such standards, there may be a range of permissible regimes that can meet these standards. It goes without saying that this range is not confined to the specific rule adopted by the Court pursuant to its competence in the common law. In the present case, Parliament decided that legislation was necessary in order to address the issue of third-party records more comprehensively. As is evident from the language of the preamble to Bill C-46, Parliament also sought to recognize the prevalence of sexual violence against women and children and its disadvantageous impact on their rights, to encourage the reporting of incidents of sexual violence, to recognize the impact of the production of personal information on the efficacy of treatment, and to reconcile fairness to complainants with the rights of the accused. Many of these concerns involve policy decisions regarding criminal procedure and its relationship to the community at large. Parliament may also be understood to be recognizing "horizontal" equality concerns, where women's inequality results from the acts of other individuals and groups rather than the state, but which nonetheless may have many consequences for the criminal justice system. It is perfectly reasonable that these many concerns may lead to a procedure that is different from the common law position but that nonetheless meets the required constitutional standards.

We cannot presume that the legislation is unconstitutional simply because it is different from the common law position. The question before us is not whether Parliament can amend the common law; it clearly can. The question before us is whether in doing so Parliament has nonetheless outlined a constitutionally acceptable procedure for the production of private records of complainants in sexual assault trials.

. . .

Tensions Among Full Answer and Defence, Privacy, and Equality

(a) Balancing Interests and Defining Rights

At play in this appeal are three principles, which find their support in specific provisions of the Charter. These are full answer and defence, privacy, and equality. No single principle is absolute and capable of trumping the others; all must be defined in light of competing claims. As Lamer C.J. stated in *Dagenais*, supra, at p. 877:

> When the protected rights of two individuals come into conflict . . . Charter principles require a balance to be achieved that fully respects the importance of both sets of rights.

. . .

Whether or not all the rights involved are "principles of fundamental justice", Charter rights must always be defined contextually.

. . .

(b) Nature of the Charter Principles

(i) Full Answer and Defence

It is well established that the ability of the accused to make full answer and defence is a principle of fundamental justice protected by s. 7. . . . Many of these principles of fundamental justice are informed by the legal rights outlined in ss. 8 to 14 of the Charter. . . . Our jurisprudence has recognized on several occasions "the danger of placing the accused in a 'Catch-22' situation as a condition of making full answer and defence". This is an important consideration in the context of records production as often the accused may be in the difficult position of making submissions regarding the importance to full answer and defence of records that he or she has not seen. Where the records are part of the case to meet, this concern is particularly acute as such a situation very directly implicates the accused's ability to raise a doubt concerning his or her innocence. As the Court stated in *R. v. Leipert*, [1997] 1 S.C.R. 281, at para. 24, "[t]his Court has consistently affirmed that it is a fundamental principle of justice, protected by the Charter, that the innocent must not be convicted". Where the records to which the accused seeks access are not part of the case to meet, however, privacy and equality considerations may require that it be more difficult for accused persons to gain access to therapeutic or other records.

That said, the principles of fundamental justice do not entitle the accused to "the most favourable procedures that could possibly be imagined": *R. v. Lyons*, [1987] 2 S.C.R. 309, per La Forest J., at p. 362. This is because fundamental justice embraces more than the rights of the accused. For example, this Court has held that an assessment of the fairness of the trial process must be made "from the point of view of fairness in the eyes of the community and the complainant" and not just the accused: *R. v. E. (A.W.)*, [1993] 3 S.C.R. 155, per Cory J., at p. 198. . . . This spectrum of interests reflected in the principles of fundamental justice highlights the need to avoid viewing any particular principle in isolation from the others.

. . .

Several principles regarding the right to make full answer and defence emerge from the preceding discussion. First, the right to make full answer and defence is crucial to ensuring that the innocent are not convicted. To that end, courts must consider the danger of placing the accused in a Catch-22 situation as a condition of making full answer and defence, and will even override competing considerations in order to protect the right to make full answer and defence in certain circumstances, such as the "innocence at stake" exception to informer privilege. Second, the accused's right must be defined in a context that includes other principles of fundamental justice and Charter provisions. Third, full answer and defence does not include the right to evidence that would distort the search for truth inherent in the trial process.

(ii) Privacy

Since *Hunter v. Southam Inc.*, [1984] 2 S.C.R. 145, this Court has recognized that s. 8 of the Charter protects a person's reasonable expectation of privacy. This right is relevant to the present appeal, as an order for the production of documents is a seizure within the meaning of s. 8 of the Charter [citations omitted]. Therefore an order for the production of records made pursuant to ss. 278.1 to 278.91 of the Criminal Code, falls within the ambit of s. 8.

. . .

This Court has most often characterized the values engaged by privacy in terms of liberty, or the right to be left alone by the state. . . . This interest in being left alone by the state includes the ability to control the dissemination of confidential information. These privacy concerns are at their strongest where aspects of one's individual identity are at stake, such as in the context of information "about one's lifestyle, intimate relations or political or religious opinions".

. . .

In fostering the underlying values of dignity, integrity and autonomy, it is fitting that s. 8 of the Charter should seek to protect a biographical core of personal information which individuals in a free and democratic society would wish to maintain and control from dissemination to the state. This would include information which tends to reveal intimate details of the lifestyle and personal choices of the individual. That privacy is essential to maintaining relationships of trust was stressed to this Court by the eloquent submissions of many interveners in this case regarding counselling records. The therapeutic relationship is one that is characterized by trust, an element of which is confidentiality. Therefore the protection of the complainant's reasonable expectation of privacy in her therapeutic records protects the therapeutic relationship.

. . .

Given that s. 8 protects a person's privacy by prohibiting unreasonable searches or seizures, and given that s. 8 addresses a particular application of the principles of fundamental justice, we can infer that a reasonable search or seizure is consistent with the principles of fundamental justice. Moreover, as we have already discussed, the principles of fundamental justice include the right to make full answer and defence. Therefore a reasonable search and seizure will be one that accommodates both the accused's ability to make full answer and defence and the complainant's privacy right.

From our preceding discussion of the right to make full answer and defence, it is clear that the accused will have no right to the records in question insofar as they contain information that is either irrelevant or would serve to distort the search for truth, as access to such information is not included within the ambit of the accused's right. . . . The values protected by privacy rights will be most directly at stake where the confidential information contained in a record concerns aspects of one's individual identity or where the maintenance of confidentiality is crucial to a therapeutic, or other trust-like, relationship.

(iii) Equality

Equality concerns must also inform the contextual circumstances in which the rights of full answer and defence and privacy will come into play. In this respect, an appreciation of myths and stereotypes in the context of sexual violence is essential to delineate properly the boundaries of full answer and defence. As we have already discussed, the right to make full answer and defence does not include the right to information that would only distort the truth-seeking goal of the trial process. In *R. v. Osolin*, [1993] 4 S.C.R. 595, Cory J., for the majority on this issue, stated, at pp. 669 and 670:

> The provisions of ss. 15 and 28 of the Charter guaranteeing equality to men and women, although not determinative should be taken into account in determining the reasonable limitations that should be placed upon the cross-examination of a complainant. . . . A complainant should not be unduly harassed and pilloried to the extent of becoming a victim of an insensitive judicial system.

The reasons in *Seaboyer* make it clear that eliciting evidence from a complainant for the purpose of encouraging inferences pertaining to consent or the credibility of rape victims which are based on groundless myths and fantasized stereotypes is improper. The accused is not permitted to "whack the complainant" through the use of stereotypes regarding victims of sexual assault.

. . .

When the boundary between privacy and full answer and defence is not properly delineated, the equality of individuals whose lives are heavily documented is also affected, as these individuals have more records that will be subject to wrongful scrutiny. Karen Busby cautions that the use of records to challenge credibility at large will subject those whose lives already have been subject to extensive documentation to extraordinarily invasive review. This would include women whose lives have been documented under conditions of multiple inequalities and institutionalization such as Aboriginal women, women with disabilities, or women who have been imprisoned or involved with child welfare agencies ("Discriminatory Uses of Personal Records in Sexual Violence Cases" (1997), 9 C.J.W.L. 148, at pp. 161-62).

These concerns highlight the need for an acute sensitivity to context when determining the content of the accused's right to make full answer and defence, and its relationship to the complainant's privacy right.

Summary

In summary, the following broad considerations apply to the definition of the rights at stake in this appeal. The right of the accused to make full answer and defence is a core principle of fundamental justice, but it does not automatically entitle the accused to gain access to information contained in the private records of complainants and witnesses. Rather, the scope of the right to make full answer and defence must be determined in light of privacy and equality rights of complainants and witnesses. It is clear that the right to full answer and defence is not engaged where the accused seeks information that will only serve to distort the truth-seeking purpose of a trial, and in such a situation, privacy and equality rights are paramount. On the other hand, where the information contained in a record directly bears on the right to make full answer and defence, privacy rights must yield to the need to avoid convicting the innocent. Most cases, however, will not be so clear, and in assessing applications for production courts must determine the weight to be granted to the interests protected by privacy and full answer and defence in the particular circumstances of each case. Full answer and defence will be more centrally implicated where the information contained in a record is part of the case to meet or where its potential probative value is high. A complainant's privacy interest is very high where the confidential information contained in a record concerns the complainant's personal identity or where the confidentiality of the record is vital to protect a therapeutic relationship.

With this background in mind, we now proceed to discuss the statutory provisions under attack.

. . .

The Statutory Provisions

Section 278.3(4) lists a series of "assertions" that cannot "on their own" establish that a record is likely relevant. The respondent submits that on a plain reading, this provision prevents the accused from relying on the listed factors when attempting to establish the likely relevance of the records. This, he argues, interferes with the right to make full answer and defence by restricting what the judge can consider in determining whether the records must be produced to the defence. The legislation raises the bar for production, he asserts, making it difficult if not impossible for the accused to meet the likely relevance test of ss. 278.5 and 278.7. The respondent contends that it is unconstitutional to exclude the assertions listed in s. 278.3(4) as irrelevant.

This submission forgets that when legislation is susceptible to more than one interpretation, we must always choose the constitutional reading. See *Slaight*, supra, at p. 1078. This mistake leads the respondent to overstate the purpose and effect of s. 278.3(4). As has frequently been held, its purpose is to prevent speculative and unmeritorious requests for production [citations omitted]. It does not entirely prevent an accused from relying on the factors listed, but simply prevents reliance on bare "assertions" of the listed matters, where there is no other evidence and they stand "on their own".

The purpose and wording of s. 278.3 does not prevent an accused from relying on the assertions set out in subsection 278.3(4) where there is an evidentiary or informational foundation to suggest that they may be related to likely relevance. . . . The section requires only that the accused be able to point to case specific evidence or information to show that the record in issue is likely relevant to an issue at trial or the competence of a witness to testify, see *Leipert*, supra, at para. 21. Conversely, where an accused does provide evidence or information to support an assertion listed in s. 278.3(4), this does not mean that likely relevance is made out. Section 278.3(4) does not supplant the ultimate discretion of the trial judge. Where any one of the listed assertions is made and supported by the required evidentiary and informational foundation, the trial judge is the ultimate arbiter in deciding whether the likely relevance threshold set out in s. 278.5 and 278.7 is met. We conclude that s. 278.3(4) does not violate ss. 7 or 11(d) of the Charter.

. . .

Both the majority and minority of this Court in *O'Connor*, supra, held that records must be produced to the judge for inspection if the accused can demonstrate that the information is "likely to be relevant": *O'Connor*, supra, at para. 19, per Lamer C.J. and Sopinka J., and at para. 138, per L'Heureux-Dubé J. The Court defined the standard of likely relevance as "a reasonable possibility that the information is logically probative to an issue at trial or the competence of a witness to testify". Although the majority recognized that complainants have a constitutional right to privacy it held that no balancing of rights should be undertaken at the first stage. This conclusion was premised on the finding that: (1) to require the accused to meet more than the likely relevance stage would be to "put the accused in the difficult situation of having to make submissions to the judge without precisely knowing what is contained in the records"; and (2) there is not enough information before a trial judge at this initial stage of production for an informed balancing procedure to take place. To this end, the majority held that the analysis should be confined to determining "likely relevance" and "whether the right to make full answer and defence is implicated by information contained in the records". In contrast, the minority held that once the accused meets the "likely relevance" threshold, he must then satisfy the judge that the salutary effects of ordering the documents produced to the court for inspection outweigh the deleterious effects of such production, having regard to the accused's right to make full answer and defence, and the effect of such production on the privacy and equality rights of the subject of the records. L'Heureux-Dubé J. found that a sufficient evidentiary basis could be established at this stage through Crown disclosure, defence witnesses, the cross-examination of Crown witnesses at both the preliminary inquiry and the trial and, on some occasions, expert evidence. Parliament, after studying the issue, concluded that the rights of both the complainant and the accused should be considered when deciding whether to order production to the judge. In coming to this conclusion, Parliament must be taken to have determined, as a result of lengthy consultations, and years of Parliamentary study and debate, that trial judges have sufficient evidence to engage in an informed balancing process at this stage. . . . As a result of the consultation process, Parliament decided to supplement the "likely relevant" standard for production to the judge proposed in *O'Connor* with the further requirement that production be "necessary in the interests of justice". The result was s. 278.5. This process is a notable example of the dialogue between the judicial and legislative branches discussed above. This Court acted in *O'Connor*, and the legislature responded with Bill C-46. As already mentioned, the mere fact that Bill C-46 does not mirror *O'Connor* does not render it unconstitutional.

The question comes down to this: once likely relevance is established, is it necessarily unconstitutional that a consideration of the rights and interests of those affected by production to the court might result in production not being ordered? The answer to this question depends on whether a consideration of the range of rights and interests affected, in addition to a finding of likely relevance, will ultimately prevent the accused from seeing documents that are necessary to enable him to defend himself — to raise all the defences that might be open to him at trial. The non-disclosure of third party records with a high privacy interest that may contain relevant evidence will not compromise trial fairness where such non-disclosure would not prejudice the accused's right to full answer and defence.

Section 278.5(1) is a very wide and flexible section. It accords the trial judge great latitude. Parliament must be taken to have intended that judges, within the broad scope of the powers conferred, would apply it in a constitutional manner — a way that would ultimately permit the accused access to all documents that may be constitutionally required. Indeed, a production regime that denied this would not be production "necessary in the interests of justice".

. . .

While this Court may have considered it preferable not to consider privacy rights at the production stage, that does not preclude Parliament from coming to a different conclusion, so long as its conclusion is consistent with the Charter in its own right. As we have explained, the Bill's directive to consider what is "necessary in the interests of justice", read correctly, does include appropriate respect for the right to full answer and defence.

This leaves the argument that the judge cannot consider the factors listed in s. 278.5(2) without looking at the documents. However, s. 278.5(2) does not require that the judge engage in a conclusive and in-depth evaluation of each of the factors. It rather requires the judge to "take them into account" — to the extent possible at this early stage of proceedings — in deciding whether to order a particular record produced to himself or herself for inspection. Section 278.5(2) serves as a check-list of the various factors that may come into play in making the decision regarding production to the judge. Therefore, while the s. 278.5(2) factors are relevant, in the final analysis the judge is free to make whatever order is "necessary in the interests of justice" — a mandate that includes all of the applicable "principles of fundamental justice" at stake.

Furthermore, contrary to the respondent's submissions, there is a sufficient evidentiary basis to support such an analysis at this early stage. This basis can be established through Crown disclosure, defence witnesses, the cross-examination of Crown witnesses at both the preliminary inquiry and the trial, and expert evidence, see: *O'Connor*, supra, at para. 146, per L'Heureux-Dubé J. As noted by Taylor J. for the British Columbia Supreme Court, "the criminal process provides a reasonable process for the acquisition of the evidentiary basis", *Hurrie*, supra, at para. 39. To this end, as the Attorney of British Columbia submitted: "Laying the groundwork prior to trial, or comprehensive examination of witnesses at trial, will go a long way to establishing a meritorious application under this legislation".

The nature of the records in question will also often provide the trial judge with an important informational foundation. For example, with respect to the privacy interest in records, the expectation of privacy in adoption or counselling records may be very different from that in school attendance records, see for example, *R. v. J.S.P.*, B.C. S.C., Vancouver Registry Nos. CC970130 & CC960237, May 15, 1997. Similarly, a consideration of the probative value of records can often be informed by the nature and purposes of a record, as well as the record-taking practices used to create it. As noted above, many submissions were made regarding the different levels of reliability of certain records. Counselling or therapeutic records, for example, can be highly subjective documents which attempt merely to record an individual's emotions and psychological state. Often such records have not been checked for accuracy by the subject of the records, nor have they been recorded verbatim. All of these factors may help a trial judge when considering the probative value of a record being sought by an accused.

As discussed above in the context of defining the right to full answer and defence, courts must as a general matter ensure that the accused can obtain all pertinent evidence required to make full answer and defence, and must be wary of the danger of putting the accused in a Catch-22 situation in seeking to obtain such evidence. Where there is a danger that the accused's right to make full answer and defence will be violated, the trial judge should err on the side of production to the court. We conclude that s. 278.5 is constitutional.

Once the first hurdle is passed and the records are produced to the judge, the judge must determine whether it is in the interests of justice that they be produced to the defence. Again the judge must be satisfied that the records are "likely relevant" and that production, this time to the accused, is necessary in the interests of justice. In making this decision, the judge must once again consider the factors set out in s. 278.5(2).

The respondent accepts that weighing competing interests is appropriate at this second stage of the analysis. However, the respondent contends that the requirement under s. 278.7(2), that the trial judge take the factors specified in paragraphs s. 278.5(2)(a) to (h) into account, inappropriately alters the constitutional balance established in *O'Connor*. Specifically, the respondent contends that ss. 278.5(2)(f) and (g) elevate the societal interest in encouraging the reporting of sexual offences and encouraging of treatment of complainants of sexual offences, to a status equal to the accused's right to make full answer and defence. This, he suggests, alters the constitutional balance established in *O'Connor*, where the majority specifically determined these factors to be of secondary importance to defence interests in any balancing of competing interests and better taken into account through other avenues. The respondent also contends that s. 278.5(2)(h) unfairly requires trial judges to consider the effect of disclosure on the integrity of the trial process. The respondent submits that this is a question going to admissibility.

These concerns are largely answered by the analysis advanced under s. 278.5(2), discussed at greater length above. Trial judges are not required to rule conclusively on each of the factors nor are they required to determine whether factors relating to the privacy and equality of the complainant or witness "outweigh" factors relating to the accused's right to full answer and defence. To repeat, trial judges are only asked to "take into account" the factors listed in s. 278.5(2) when determining whether production of part or all of the impugned record to the accused is necessary in the interest of justice, s. 278.7(1).

The respondent argues that the inclusion of the societal interest factors in ss. 278.5(2)(f) and (g) alters the constitutional balance established by the *O'Connor* majority. With respect, this argument is unsound. . . . As noted above, when preparing Bill C-46 Parliament had the advantage of being able to assess how the *O'Connor* regime was operating. From the information available to Parliament and the submissions it received during the consultation process, Parliament concluded that the effect of production on the integrity of the trial was a factor that should be included in the list of factors for trial judges to "take into account" at both stages of an application for production. Several interveners have interpreted this factor as requiring courts to consider, along with the other enumerated factors, whether the search for truth would be advanced by the production of the records in question; that is, the question is whether the material in question would introduce discriminatory biases and beliefs into the fact-finding process. We agree with this interpretation of the inquiry required by s. 278.5(2)(h) and believe it to be in keeping with the purposes set out in the preamble of the legislation.

By giving judges wide discretion to consider a variety of factors and requiring them to make whatever order is necessary in the interest of justice at both stages of an application for production, Parliament has created a scheme that permits judges not only to preserve the complainant's privacy and equality rights to the maximum extent possible, but also to ensure that the accused has access to the documents required to make full answer and defence.

LAMER C.J.:—

. . .

While I agree with McLachlin and Iacobucci JJ.'s finding that Bill C-46 complies with ss. 7 and 11(d) of the Canadian Charter of Rights and Freedoms as it applies to the production of records in the possession of third parties, I take a different view of the legislative regime's approach to records in the hands of the Crown. In my opinion, Bill C-46's treatment of records that form part of the case to meet tips the balance too heavily in favour of privacy to the detriment of the accused's right to make full answer and defence.

The implications of an enforceable s. 15 claim for complainants in sexual assault cases is left unexplored. The policy issues are far wider than establishing privacy rights for therapeutic and other records of complainants. Can complainants now seek status to be represented throughout a sexual assault trial? How about rights to cross-examine the accused, to challenge the similar fact evidence rule or to reverse the presumption of innocence?

For an analysis that *O'Connor* applications were used almost always against female complainants see Karen Busby, "Third Party Records Cases Since *R. v. O'Connor*".[400]

Professor Stephen Coughlan, "Complainants' Records After *Mills*: Same as it Ever Was",[401] has suggested that a close reading of *Mills* is that, although the language is deference to Parliament, the Court has read in discretion at every point such that its regime still conforms to its earlier majority judgment in *O'Connor*. Accepting that there is reading down in *Mills*, this appears to place far too little emphasis on the raising of the bar at the first stage of production to the judge. Several courts have already decided that *Mills* has indeed raised that threshold test.[402]

The Court in *Mills* certainly reads down the "insufficient grounds" s. 278.3(4) which declares the long list of assertions which would not meet the likely relevant test. Pointing to words "on their own" the Court holds this merely requires an evidentiary foundation. The Court sees the purpose of the provision to be the prevention of speculative myths, stereotypes, and generalized assumptions about sexual assault victims and classes of records from forming the entire basis of an otherwise unsubstantiated order for production of private records. The problem, as Kent Roach points out in "Editorial on *Mills*"[403] is that only some of the prohibited assertions involve sexist rape myths. Those relating to credibility do not. The section requires only, holds the Court in reading the section down, that the accused be able to point to case-specific evidence or information to show that the record in issue

---

[400] (2000) 27 Man. L.J. 355. For critical comments on *Mills* see Stuart, "*Mills*: Dialogue with Parliament and Equality by Assertion at What Cost?" (2000), 28 C.R. (5th) 275 and Peter Sankoff, "Crown Disclosure After *Mills*: Have the Ground Rules Suddenly Changed?" (2000), 28 C.R. (5th) 285.

[401] (2000), 33 C.R. (5th) 300.

[402] See *R. v. Batte* (2000), 34 C.R. (5th) 197 (Ont. C.A.) (criticized by Joseph Wilkinson, "*Batte*: Raising the Defence Hurdle for Access to Third Party Records" (2000), 34 C.R. (5th) 257) and *R. v. M. (D.)* (2000), 37 C.R. (5th) 80 (Ont. S.C.J.) (denying access to a diary and counselling records because the evidentiary foundation was not laid at the preliminary inquiry).

[403] (2000) 43 Crim. L.Q. 145.

is likely relevant to an issue at trial or the competence of a witness to testify. The Court indicates one source of such an evidentiary base to be the preliminary inquiry. The difficulty here is that many sexual assault trials across Canada are now proceeded with, through Crown election, by way of summary proceedings where there is no preliminary (and no jury trial).

In such cases is it a good idea to encourage free-ranging and intrusive inquiries into the existence and type of records presumably necessitating adjournments where production is ordered?

The various other rulings in *Mills* on the records issues are supportable. This includes the acceptance by the majority of Parliament's view that the balancing of rights of complainants must also occur, in the absence of express waiver, where the records are in the possession of the Crown. We have seen that the majority ruling to the contrary in *O'Connor* was *obiter* and not persuasive in holding that privacy had necessarily been waived by complainants in such cases.

Subsequently the majority of the Supreme Court appears to have changed the balance again in favour of rights of accused. The context was a cross-examination of a diary in the possession of the accused as to why the complainant had not mentioned abuse by the accused.

R. v. SHEARING
[2002] 3 S.C.R. 33, 2 C.R. (6th) 213, 165 C.C.C. (3d) 225

The accused was charged with 20 counts of sexual offences alleged to have occurred between 1965 and 1989. The accused was the leader of a cult. He preached that sexual experience was a way to progress to higher levels of consciousness and that he, as a cult leader, could be instrumental in enabling young girls to reach these higher levels. Two of the complainants were sisters who lived in a group home. One kept a daily diary for eight months in 1970. The day-to-day entries covered part of the 10-year period when she alleged sexual abuse by the accused. When the complainant left the group home her mother put some of her belongings in a cardboard box in the storage area shared with other residents. About 18 months later, after the accused had been indicted, another resident of the house opened the cardboard box, found the complainant's diary and gave it to the defence.

At trial, the defence sought to use the diary to contradict the complainant on the basis of entries arguably inconsistent with her evidence in chief, and by showing the absence of any entry chronicling physical or sexual abuse. The complainant objected and, at the *voir dire* into the admissibility of the diary, asserted a privacy interest. The trial judge permitted the accused to use the diary to cross-examine the complainant on entries the defence considered probative but did not permit cross-examination on the absence of any entries recording physical abuse by the complainant's mother or sexual abuse by the accused. The trial judge refused to allow cross-examination of the complainant's diary as to the fact there was no mention of the alleged abuse. The trial judge applied the *O'Connor* principles respecting production of therapeutic and other records of complainants. Justice Donald for the B.C. Court of Appeal approved the trial judge's decision and approach with these words:

> Mills has shifted the balance away from the primary emphasis on the rights of the accused. The decision requires a reconsideration of the position of the complainant, and in particular the equality rights of the complainant, so as to effectively guard against procedures which deny complainants equal access to and benefit of the law.

When the matter reached the Supreme Court, the Court divided 7-2 on this issue. The majority held that the trial judge ought to have allowed the cross-examination and ordered a new trial on the count for which the accused had been convicted.

Per BINNIE J. (MCLACHLIN C.J. and IACOBUCCI, MAJOR, BASTARACHE, ARBOUR and LEBEL JJ. concurring): —

. . .

Limiting the Scope of Cross-examination

The critical importance of cross-examination is not doubted. The appellant stood before the court accused of crimes by numerous complainants but he was presumed to be innocent of each and every count. All of the alleged sexual misconduct, by its very nature, was in private. At trial, it was his word against the credibility of his accusers, individually and (by virtue of the similar fact evidence) collectively. If the complainants were untruthful about what happened in the privacy of their encounters, the most effective tool he possessed to get at the truth was a full and pointed cross-examination. The general principle was stated in *Seaboyer, supra*, per McLachlin J. at p. 611:

> Canadian courts, like courts in most common law jurisdictions, have been extremely cautious in restricting the power of the accused to call evidence in his or her defence, a reluctance founded in the fundamental tenet of our judicial system that an innocent person must not be convicted. It follows from this that the prejudice must substantially outweigh the value of the evidence before a judge can exclude evidence relevant to a defence allowed by law.

It has been increasingly recognized in recent years, however, that cross-examination techniques in sexual assault cases that seek to put the complainant on trial rather than the accused are abusive and distort rather than enhance the search for truth. Various limitations have been imposed. One of these limits is the privacy interest of the complainant, which is not to be needlessly sacrificed. This was explored by Cory J. writing for the majority in *Osolin, supra*, at pp. 669 and 671, as follows:

> A complainant should not be unduly harassed and pilloried to the extent of becoming a victim of an insensitive judicial system. Yet a fair balance must be achieved so that the limitations on the cross-examination of complainants in sexual assault cases do not interfere with the right of the accused to a fair trial.

. . .

In each case the trial judge must carefully balance the fundamentally important right of the accused to a fair trial against the need for reasonable protection of a complainant, particularly where the purpose of the cross-examination may be directed to the "rape myths".

I underline the reference to "rape myths" because in my view it is a concern about a potential revival of the shibboleth of "recent complaint" in sexual assault cases rather than a privacy concern as such, that lies at the heart of the trial judge's ruling.

In *Seaboyer*, the accused sought to cross-examine the complainant on her sexual conduct on other occasions to explain the "bruises and other aspects of the complainant's condition which the Crown had put in evidence". In *Osolin*, the accused sought to cross-examine a notation in the complainant's medical record of a concern she had expressed to her therapist that her attitude and behaviour may have influenced the accused to some extent. This case is different. The focus is not private information as such because, as stated, the trial judge allowed cross-examination by the defence on each of the specific diary entries the defence sought to utilize. The defence objection is to the restriction on its ability to cross-examine on the significance (if any) of what was not recorded. It is common ground that KWG's diary contains no references to beatings by the mother or to sexual abuse by the appellant.

The cogency of this line of questioning rested on the premise that if these assaults had happened, they would have been recorded, and because the events were not recorded,they did not happen. That, in the Crown's view, is where one of the "rape myths" surfaces. The trial judge agreed:

> In essence, [the appellant] wants to go to the jury and argue that the witness has made no "complaint", if I may use that word, to her private, confidential diary about the sexual assaults that she now testifies to.
>
> . . .
>
> [Counsel for KWG] argues strongly that there is no probative value in a lack of complaint in these circumstances, and that to allow cross-examination and argument on the issue is premised upon a discriminatory belief or bias.

The trial judge's trade-off of permitting questions on actual entries but disallowing questions on the absence of entries was criticized in about equal measure by the appellant and the Criminal Lawyers' Association on the one hand, who thought it too restrictive on the defence, and on the other hand by the Crown and Women's Legal Education and Action Fund ("LEAF"), who thought it went too far against the complainant.

The Crown and LEAF took the position that KWG's diary was and remained her property, and that the appellant came into possession of it without colour of right. That being the case, the trial judge ought to have ignored the reality of the appellant's possession (a sort of constructive dispossession) and required the appellant to make anapplication for compelled production of documents under ss. 278.1 to 278.9, just as if KWG rather than the appellant had possession of it.

I will deal with these points in turn.

(1) Surprise Disclosure of the Diary

In her evidence-in-chief and in the initial cross-examination KWG committed herself to having experienced a profoundly unhappy childhood (a "chamber of horrors" is how the defence put it, somewhat sarcastically), lack of friends at school, prohibition on participation in extracurricular school activities, and not being allowed to wear ordinary teenager clothing. All of this was the background to alleged constant physical abuse by the mother and alleged sexual abuse by the appellant, the latter occurring mainly in the appellant's den at the Centre.

She was asked by the defence about the possible existence of a diary and she said she thought she had received one as a present at Christmas in her early teens, but had only made entries for two weeks or so.

At this point in the trial, counsel for the defence flourished KWG's original diary which she had not seen for 22 years, and announced that it contained day-by-day entries for a period of eight months (not the two weeks she had recalled) commencing January 1970, in the midst of the period of alleged abuse. It recorded what KWG herself described as "mundane" entries about schoolmates, participation in school functions, family outings to see films, Easter presents and some positive references to the appellant (e.g., "Stayed home from school today and had a nice talk with Ivon. He makes you want to work harder"). The defence wished to raise a doubt about the reliability and completeness of KWG's memory by contradicting her testimonywith what the defence viewed as inconsistent entries written under her own hand in the diary, and the omission of any entry chronicling physical or sexual abuse.

KWG's response to the surprise disclosure of her 1970 diary was to obtain a short adjournment, and to retain her own Counsel who argued that (1) the diary was the property of KWG and should be returned forthwith and (2) thereafter dealt with under the documentary production provisions of ss. 278.1 to 278.9 of the Criminal Code.

(2) Wrongful Possession of the Diary

KWG testified on the *voir dire* that she did "not at all" intend to give up her privacy rights. She was "appalled" and wanted the diary and all the copies returned to her as the defence had no right to "the little bit of privacy that [she] had". On cross-examination, KWG described the diary entries as "very mundane", "[b]ut it's still mine. . . . I don't understand what that has to do with anything. This is still mine. Whether it's mundane or exciting or boring, it's still mine". The trial judge found that KWG had never waived or abandoned her privacy interest in the diary and I agree with him.

The *voir dire* included a lengthy legal debate about whether KWG had or had not abandoned her property interest in her diary, and whether the appellant's possession of it amounted to conversion. I do not think KWG was illegally deprived of possession of the diary (unlike the Chinese restaurateurs whose safe containing private documents was stolen by thieves in *R. v. Law*, 2002 SCC 10). She simply left it behind in a common storage room with other possessions no longer required for day-to-day living. When her mother forwarded her possessions to her in 1995, the diary was not among them. When the diary fell into the appellant's possession 22 years after KWG left home, it was not a "wrongful" taking in any legal sense, although I agree with KWG that it underlined the extent of his unwelcome access to KWG's private life as a by-product of her mother's adherence to the cult.

I do not propose to pursue the property ownership debate. The issue for present purposes is not the "ownership of the diary" (which could be the subject of a civil cause of action) but the status of information contained within the diary. Return of the diary, as proposed by my colleague L'Heureux-Dubé J. at para. 161, would seem to me to shut the barn door after the horse had escaped. . . .

Our concern here is with the privacy interest not the property interest.

(3) Applicability of Sections 278.1 to 278.9 of the Criminal Code

Sections 278.1 to 278.9 on their face address the production not the use or admissibility of personal information, as stated by Parliament itself in the Preamble (S.C. 1997, c. 30):

> WHEREAS the Parliament of Canada recognizes that the *compelled production* of personal information may deter complainants of sexual offences from reporting the offence to the police and may deter complainants from seeking necessary treatment, counselling or advice;
>
> WHEREAS the Parliament of Canada recognizes that the work of those who provide services and assistance to complainants of sexual offences is detrimentally affected by the *compelled production* of records and by the process to compel that production;
>
> AND WHEREAS the Parliament of Canada recognizes that, while *production* to the court and to the accused of personal information regarding any person may be necessary in order for an accused to make a full answer and defence, *that production* may breach the person's right to privacy and equality and *therefore the determination as to whether to order production should be subject to careful scrutiny.* . . . [Emphasis added.]

The text of ss. 278.1 to 278.9 that follows is consistent with such a purpose. Counsel for KWG at trial and LEAF before this Court, argued that the machinery of ss. 278.1 to 278.9 can be put into reverse, i.e., it contemplates taking documents already in the hands of the defence and restoring these to the complainant, thus requiring the defence to make a fresh application for the document just removed from its possession. In my view, this interpretation is unduly contrived and does violence to the statutory language.

(4) The Issue Here is Admissibility of Evidence, Not Production and Disclosure

The confusion between production (O'Connor) and admissibility (Osolin) took hold at an early stage of the *voir dire* in this case. Having rightly rejected the applicability of ss. 278.1 to 278.9 on the ground that there was no issue here of production or disclosure, the trial judge prefaced the opening of submissions on admissibility as "what I'll call an *O'Connor* application at this stage".

Although well aware of *Seaboyer* (1991) and *Osolin* (1993), the trial judge (and eventually the Court of Appeal) seems to have concluded that these earlier authorities had been overtaken by this Court's subsequent pronouncements in *O'Connor* (1995). I do not agree that *O'Connor* can substitute for *Osolin* or indeed that the two tests are equivalent or interchangeable.

The trial judge heard several days of argument from counsel for KWG as well as counsel for the prosecution and the defence on the use that would be made of KWG's diary in cross-examination before the jury. Much of this argument was directed explicitly to various dicta in *O'Connor, supra*. In his ruling on the permissible scope of the cross-examination, the trial judge "applied" the *O'Connor* principles. . . .

In my view, the trial judge erred in extrapolating the *O'Connor* test from the issue of production of information not previously disclosed to the defence and applying it to the admissibility (or use in cross-examination) before the jury of evidence already in the possession of the defence.

A simple "balancing of interests" test (*O'Connor, supra*, at paras. 129 and 150) cannot be equated to "substantially outweighs" (*Seaboyer, Osolin*). Under *O'Connor*, the default position is that the third party information is not produced to the defence. Under *Seaboyer* and *Osolin*, the default position is that the defence is allowed to proceed with its cross-examination. . . .

(5) The Proper Limits of Cross-examination

In *Seaboyer*, McLachlin J. noted that "our courts have traditionally been reluctant to exclude even tenuous defence evidence" (p. 607) and affirmed that the defence has a right to use evidence in its possession unless its prejudicial effect "substantially outweighs" (p. 611) its probative value. The reason for the different orientation is apparent. In the *O'Connor* situation, the accused is not entitled to disclosure, and seeks the intervention of the state to put aside theprivacy of a third party complainant. In the *Seaboyer* situation, the state is asked by the complainant to intervene against the accused to deny him the use of information already in his possession. It is true that some of the same values must be weighed (e.g., full answer and defence, privacy, equality rights, etc.) but both the purpose and the context are quite different.

The issue for the trial judge here, therefore, was whether cross-examination on the diary would create prejudice to the complainant that "substantially outweighed" its potential probative value to the appellant, and in that regard whether cross-examination on the absence of entries recording abuse relied upon "rape myths" or the equivalent.

(6) KWG's Privacy Concerns

The fact KWG conceded that the diary contained "mundane" sorts of information is not, in my view, fatal to her wish to keep private the entries she did choose to record in her private diary, but the fact KWG freely acknowledged that her teenage diary was not written in any kind of confessional spirit does go to the weight of the privacy interest.

On this point, however, it is KWG not the appellant who might be expected to complain of the trial judge's ruling. He allowed the defence to put to KWG whatever entries it wished where specific entries arguably contradicted KWG on some of the statements she had made in her evidence-in-chief.

All that was left to explore was what she did not write down. Cross-examination on that point would be a high-risk tactic for the defence capable of generating some devastating answers, to put it mildly. However, the appellant considered pursuit of that point to be crucial to his defence.

(7)   Omission of Entries Recording Abuse

We arrive then at the appellant's real grievance. He was not allowed to challenge the credibility of KWG based on the absence of any entries dealing with physical or sexual abuse in an important and relevant 8-month period in 1970.

In fact, the jury was never told the omissions existed.

The Crown contends that the effect of this restriction was marginal at best:

> The Respondent submits that the non-recording of an event is generally of much lower probative value than the recording of an event. If an event is recorded which a witness denies, that contradiction cries out for an explanation. Where an event is not recorded, however, that fact is not in itself logically inconsistent with the event having occurred.

The Crown's argument assumes the point in issue, of course. If we assume KWG intended a type of diary that would not be expected to contain entries recording abuse, the omissions would be irrelevant. It is that assumption, however, which the defence sought to explore in cross-examination.

The courts have recognized, no doubt belatedly, that certain techniques of cross-examination traditionally employed in sexual assault cases have distorted rather than advanced the search for truth. This case illustrates one of the problem areas. The omission to record some piece of information is only probative if there is a reasonable expectation that such a record would be made (*R. v. R.M.* (1997), 93 B.C.A.C. 81, at paras. 45-49; Wigmore on Evidence, Vol. IIIA (Chadbourn rev. 1970), at para. 1042). A pilot's log will record relevant flight information, because that is its purpose, but not what he or she had to eat for breakfast over the Atlantic Ocean. Hospital records will include medical observations but not what television station the patient happened to be watching that evening. What was objectionable about the defence approach here was that it overlooked (or perhaps resolutely resisted) the need to lay before the jury a rational basis for the inference it ultimately wished to draw, namely that the non-recording of a certain type of information was circumstantial evidence that the alleged abuse never happened.

The problem lies in the unspoken and unproven premise. KWG was obviously under no legal or other duty to record such observations. She clearly did not follow a regular practice of making such entries because no entries of any kind of abuse were made. All sides agree that the diary entries were "mundane". Why assume that a diary devoted to "mundane" entries would necessarily report on episodes of physical and sexual abuse? On what logical basis would such a non-record give rise to an inference of testimonial deficiency or fabrication? In the absence of some evidentiary basis for the premise that abuse ought to have been recorded, the result of allowing the cross-examination to proceed as proposed by the defence ("the entire contents are fair game") would be to allow the defence to go to the jury at the end of the trial and to point to the absence of entries in an effort to suggest—nod nod wink wink—that women and children who are sexually and physically abused do not suffer in silence, but must and do confide their inner hurt even if only to their private diaries.

(8)   Legitimate Scope for Cross-examination

This does not turn persons accused of sexual abuse into second class litigants. It simply means that the defence has to work with facts rather than rely on innuendoes and wishful assumptions. This means, in turn, that the defence should not be prevented from getting at the facts. As L'Heureux-Dubé J. wrote in *O'Connor, supra*, at para. 124:

> Although the defence must be free to demonstrate, without resort to stereotypical lines of reasoning, that such information is actually relevant to a live issue at trial, it would mark the triumph of stereotype over logic if courts and lawyers were simply to assume such relevance to exist, without requiring any evidence to this effect whatsoever. [Emphasis in original]

At the time of the trial, KWG was a mature and well-spoken 42-year-old adult. She was (or had been) an airline stewardess. She was not a child in need of any special protection from the court. There were arguably some contradictions between her testimony as an adult and what she had written as a teenager 27 years before, as the trial judge recognized. These arguable contradictions nourished the defence argument that the diary (including omissions) provided a more accurate picture of events in 1970 than KWG's unaided recollection. I therefore do not, with respect, agree with my colleague L'Heureux-Dubé J. at para. 176 that cross-examination on such issues would serve "no legitimate purpose".

A witness's powers of recall and the reliability of his or her memory are important issues in a trial of events that took place 27 years previously.

(9)   The Trial Judge's Ruling with Respect to the Absence of Entries

The trial judge's ruling was certainly understood by Donald J.A. in the British Columbia Court of Appeal, as based on *O'Connor*. He concluded that *Mills, supra*, following on *O'Connor, supra*, "casts a new light on the question of the complainant's privacy and supports the impugned ruling" (para. 83). Further, "Mills . . . shifted the balance away from the primary emphasis on the rights of the accused" (para. 93), and again, "[t]he majority in Mills emphasized the need to concentrate on the context in which the competing rights arise in order to strike the right balance in each case" (para. 94).

Mills, of course, dealt with the constitutional validity of the procedure set out in ss. 278.1 to 278.9 of the Criminal Code for the production of third party records. It did not purport to deal with the proper limits of cross-examination using evidence already in the possession of the defence. Moreover, even in terms of production of third party documents, I do not, with respect, agree that "*Mills* has shifted the balance away from the primary emphasis on the rights of the accused" (para. 93 (emphasis added)) because *Mills* itself affirms the primacy — in the last resort of the requirement of a fair trial to avoid the wrongful conviction of the innocent. *Mills* states in para. 94 that:

> where the information contained in a record directly bears on the right to make full answer and defence, privacy rights must yield to the need to avoid convicting the innocent.

I agree with Donald J.A. that the trial judge applied *O'Connor* to limit the defence cross-examination of the complainant but I do not agree, with respect, that this Court in *O'Connor* or *Mills* either intended to or did substitute a test intended for the production of third party documents to the quite different problem of imposing limits on cross-examination as laid down in *Seaboyer* and *Osolin*.

. . .

The appeal is therefore allowed with respect to the counts pertaining to KWG but is dismissed with respect to the other convictions of the appellant, the validity of which is affirmed.

L'HEUREUX-DUBÉ J. (Gonthier J. concurring, dissenting):— . . . I respectfully disagree that the defence should have been permitted to question KWG on the absence of reference to abuse in her diary. The reasons for my disagreement are twofold. First, the trial judge should have ordered the diary returned to KWG, its rightful owner, and required the appellant to seek production of it through the appropriate statutory channels. Second, even if the appellant had acquired the diary through the proper channels in the first place, the prejudicial effect of the proposed line of questions on the absence of entries substantially outweighs its probative value.

Like my colleague, however, I do not think it is necessary to dwell on the property ownership debate. Even if we assume, in the appellant's favour, that the diary came into his hands in a manner consistent with the statutory scheme, I believe both the trial judge and the Court of Appeal were nonetheless correct to prohibit the proposed line of cross-examination on the diary. . . .

The test for admissibility of defence evidence is whether the prejudicial effect of that evidence substantially outweighs its probative value: *R. v. Seaboyer*. . . . In weighing prejudicial and probative value, the trial judge must consider not only the accused's right to full answer and defence, but also the importance of the complainant's and other witnesses' privacy and equality rights, as outlined in *R. v. O'Connor* . . . and *R. v. Mills*. . . . The majority decision in *Osolin*, *supra*, clearly held that, similar to *O'Connor*, *supra*, and *Mills*, *supra*, the privacy and equality rights of the complainant as protected by the Charter should inform the trial judge's decision on whether to restrict the defence's cross-examination.

On this point, I disagree with my colleague that "the nature and scope of KWG's diary did not raise privacy or other concerns of such importance as to 'substantially outweigh' the appellant's fair trial right to cross-examine on the [absence of entries in the diary] . . . to test the accuracy and completeness of KWG's recollection of events 27 years previously" (para. 150). Instead, I believe that such cross-examination would introduce a high potential of prejudice. That possibility substantially outweighs the minimal probative value of questions concerning the absence of entries in the complainant's diary. . . .

Proper consideration of the complainant's equality rights also requires an appreciation of myths and stereotypes in the context of sexual violence: see *Mills, supra; O'Connor, supra; Osolin, supra; Seaboyer, supra*. Allowing questioning on the absence of the mention of sexual assault in the diary would be to endorse the same discriminatory beliefs that underlie the "recent complaint" myth. As I explained in *Osolin, supra*, at p. 625, the recent complaint myth "suggest[s] that the presence of certain emotional reactions and immediate reporting of the assault, despite all of the barriers that might discourage such reports, lend credibility to the assault report, whereas the opposite reactions lead to the conclusion that the complainant must be fabricating the event". Similarly, questioning the complainant as to why certain reactions are not present in her diary or why she did not "report" the incident by recording it in her diary, implies that the absence of such writings is support for the conclusion that she fabricated the events.

The rape myth of "recent complaint" has long been dismissed by this Court and, if used to draw a negative inference about the complainant's credibility, constitutes a reversible error: see *R. v. D.D.*, [2000] 2 S.C.R. 275, at para. 63. As this Court firmly explained in *Mills, supra*, at para. 90: "The accused is not permitted to 'whack the complainant' through the use of [such] stereotypes regarding victims of sexual assault." Oftentimes, merely posing a question that may be directed to myths and stereotypes in the sexual assault context is enough to distort the truth-seeking goal of the trial process because the prejudice derives from the innuendo imbedded in the question.

In summary, an application of the *Seaboyer/Osolin, supra*, test that cross-examination should be restricted if the prejudicial impact substantially outweighs the probative value, reveals that the trial judge and Court of Appeal in this case were correct to prohibit the particular line of questioning proposed by the defence. In applying this test, we must consider the accused's right to full answer and defence and the complainant's privacy and equality rights. In the case at bar, the prejudicial effect is very high, while the probative value is, at best, minimal. The diary is an intimate record of the complainant's life during that period of time and the proposed line of cross-examination would necessarily open up much of the diary's contents to scrutiny.

Besides constituting a wide-ranging violation of the complainant's privacy rights, the proposed cross-examination also has potential equality implications, as victims would naturally be loath to report sexual assaults if they feared that their entire private lives would be intensely scrutinized at trial. Given that a diary is an individualistic exercise, questioning a complainant on the failure to record a sexual assault is akin to questioning a complainant as to why she failed to raise a "hue and cry" immediately after the assault. As the proposed line of questioning is animated by a discriminatory belief, the prejudice is high and the potential probative value is very low, if anything. In addition, the defence has the benefit of getting evidence by directly cross-examining the complainant on her version of events, and thus does not require the additional evidence that would result from questioning the complainant on why she did not write about the assaults. Therefore, the evidence is neither relevant nor necessary for the accused to exercise his right to full answer and defence. A review of all of these factors strongly indicates that the trial judge and Court of Appeal were correct to prohibit the proposed line of cross-examination on the diary, as the potential prejudice substantially outweighs the probative value of such an exercise.

Has the majority in *Shearing* changed the balance between rights of accused and those of complainants in sexual assault cases the Court recognized in *Mills*? Is there now a hierarchy of rights where the right of an accused to full answer and defence trumps rights of complainants? Is L'Heureux-Dubé J. correct in suggesting that the majority ruling allowing cross-examination on the lack of mention of abuse in the diary wrongly revives recent complaint myths and stereotypes?[404]

The *Code* provisions for production of third-party records as interpreted in *Mills* apply only to sexual offences.

In *R. v. McNeil*[405] Charron J., speaking for a unanimous Court, made it clear that the common law regime set out in *O'Connor* is applicable to applications for the production of third-party records for offences other than sexual offences *whether or not there is a privacy interest in the record*. The Court also provided welcome clarification of the distinction between an *O'Connor* application and an application under the statutory regime for sexual offences. The Court made clear that *O'Connor* applications are different from those under the statutory regime. First, the likely relevance standard serves a different purpose. Where a sexual offence is involved, the standard is intended to counter myths and stereotypes regarding sexual assault victims; in the case of *O'Connor* applications, it is intended only to screen out unmeritorious applications so as to avoid wasting valuable court time and resources. It reaffirmed that the likely relevance burden to be met to get courts to inspect third-party records had to be realistic. The accused could not be expected to identify the precise use to which the record would be put if counsel hadn't seen the record. Second, under the *O'Connor* regime, much more balancing of the interests of the accused and that of the

---

[404]   For comments see Stuart, "*Shearing*: Admitting Similar Fact Evidence and Re-asserting The Priority of Rights of Accused in Sexual Assault in Sexual Assault Trials" (2002), 2 C.R. (6th) 222 and "Zigzags on Rights of Accused: Brittle Majorities Manipulate Weasel Words of Dialogue, Deference and *Charter* Values" (2003) (20) Supreme Court L. Rev. 267-296.

[405]   [2009] 1 S.C.R. 66, 238 C.C.C. (3d) 353, 62 C.R. (6th) 1 (S.C.C.).

third party occurs at the second stage of determining whether production to the defence should occur, rather than at the likely relevance stage under the statutory regime. Justice Charron finally streamlined the two-part inquiry for *O'Connor* applications with the remarks that the relevancy assessment will usually be largely determinative of the production issue (para. 30) and if the claim of likely relevance is borne out on inspection, the accused's right to full answer and defence will, with few exceptions, tip the balance in favour of allowing the application for production (para. 41).

Indeed, the Court further offered a simple test at the second stage: If the third-party record happened to be in the Crown's file, would there be any basis for refusing to disclose it under *Stinchcombe* disclosure obligations? If not, the record should be produced to the defence.

Bill C-51, *An Act to amend the Criminal Code and the Department of Justice Act and to make consequential amendments to another Act*, was introduced in Parliament on June 6, 2017. The Act would amend the *Criminal Code* by introducing a new process requiring the defence to bring an application to admit evidence of any records relating to a sexual assault complainant in which there is a reasonable expectation of privacy. Section 278.92(1) applies to sexual offence proceedings and provides:

> 278.92(1) Except in accordance with this section, no record relating to a complainant that is in the possession or control of the accused — and which the accused intends to adduce — shall be admitted. . .

The proposed legislation would strictly limit the admissibility of private records relating to the complainant by adding the following provision to the *Code*:

> 278.92(2)(b) The evidence is inadmissible unless the judge, provincial court judge or justice determines . . . that the evidence is relevant to an issue at trial and has significant probative value that is not substantially outweighed by the danger of prejudice to the proper administration of justice.

This new process would apply to records relating to the complainant that are legitimately in the hands of the accused. Indeed, on its face, the new process would seem to apply even to records that have been produced to the accused as a result of a successful third-party records application under s. 278 of the *Code*.

The records covered by the new proposed regime are defined in s. 278.1 of the *Code* as "any form of record that contains personal information for which there is a reasonable expectation of privacy and includes medical, psychiatric, therapeutic, counselling, education, employment, child welfare, adoption and social services records, personal journals and diaries . . .". This definition would certainly have covered the complainant's diary in *Shearing*. This broad definition might also be read to include electronic and social media messages from the complainant, even if those messages were addressed to the accused. **Is there a reasonable expectation of privacy in messages sent by the complainant to the accused?**

M. (A.) v. RYAN
[1997] 1 S.C.R. 157, 4 C.R. (5th) 220

McLACHLIN J. (LA FOREST, SOPINKA, CORY, IACOBUCCI and MAJOR JJ. concurring):—

After having been sexually assaulted by the respondent Dr. Ryan, the appellant sought counselling from a psychiatrist. The question on this appeal is whether the psychiatrist's notes and records containing statements the appellant made in the course of treatment are protected from disclosure in a civil suit brought by the appellant against Dr. Ryan. Put in terms of principle, should a defendant's right to relevant material to the end of testing the plaintiff's case outweigh the plaintiff's expectation that communications between her and her psychiatrist will be kept in confidence?

. . .

IV.   General Principles

The common law principles underlying the recognition of privilege from disclosure are simply stated. They proceed from the fundamental proposition that everyone owes a general duty to give evidence relevant to the matter before the court, so that the truth may be ascertained. To this fundamental duty, the law permits certain exceptions, known as privileges, where it can be shown that they are required by a "public good transcending the normally predominant principle of utilizing all rational means for ascertaining truth": *Trammel v. United States*, 445 U.S. 40 (1980), at p. 50.

While the circumstances giving rise to a privilege were once thought to be fixed by categories defined in previous centuries — categories that do not include communications between a psychiatrist and her patient — it is now accepted that the common law permits privilege in new situations where reason, experience and application of the principles that underlie the traditional privileges so dictate: *Slavutych v. Baker*, [1976] 1 S.C.R. 254; *R. v. Gruenke*, [1991] 3 S.C.R. 263, at p. 286. The applicable principles are derived from those set forth in *Wigmore on Evidence*, vol. 8 (McNaughton rev. 1961), sec. 2285. First, the communication must originate in a confidence. Second, the confidence must be essential to the relationship in which the communication arises. Third, the relationship must be one which should be "sedulously fostered" in the public good. Finally, if all these requirements are met, the court must consider whether the interests served by protecting the communications from disclosure outweigh the interest in getting at the truth and disposing correctly of the litigation.

It follows that the law of privilege may evolve to reflect the social and legal realities of our time. One such reality is the law's increasing concern with the wrongs perpetrated by sexual abuse and the serious effect such abuse has on the health and productivity of the many members of our society it victimizes. Another modern reality is the extension of medical assistance from treatment of its physical effects to treatment of its mental and emotional aftermath through techniques such as psychiatric counselling. Yet another development of recent vintage which may be considered in connection with new claims for privilege is the Canadian Charter of Rights and Freedoms, adopted in 1982.

. . .

The first requirement for privilege is that the communications at issue have originated in a confidence that they will not be disclosed. The Master held that this condition was not met because both the appellant and Dr. Parfitt had concerns that notwithstanding their desire for confidentiality, the records might someday be ordered disclosed in the course of litigation. With respect, I do not agree. The communications were made in confidence. The appellant stipulated that they should remain confidential and Dr. Parfitt agreed that she would do everything possible to keep them confidential. The possibility that a court might order them disclosed at some future date over their objections does not change the fact that the communications were made in confidence. With the possible exception of communications falling in the traditional categories, there can never be an absolute guarantee of confidentiality; there is always the possibility that a court may order disclosure. Even for documents within the traditional categories, inadvertent disclosure is always a possibility. If the apprehended possibility of disclosure negated privilege, privilege would seldom if ever be found.

The second requirement — that the element of confidentiality be essential to the full and satisfactory maintenance of the relation between the parties to the communication — is clearly satisfied in the case at bar. It is not disputed that Dr. Parfitt's practice in general and her ability to help the appellant in particular required that she hold her discussions with the appellant in confidence. Dr. Parfitt's evidence establishes that confidentiality is essential to the continued existence and effectiveness of the therapeutic relations between a psychiatrist and a patient seeking treatment for the psychiatric harm resulting from sexual abuse. Once psychiatrist-patient confidentiality is broken and the psychiatrist becomes involved in the patient's external world, the "frame" of the therapy is broken. At that point, it is Dr. Parfitt's practice to discontinue psychotherapy with the patient. The result is both confusing and damaging to the patient. At a time when she would normally find support in the therapeutic relationship, as during the trial, she finds herself without support. In the result, the patient's treatment may cease, her distrustfulness be exacerbated, and her personal and work relations be adversely affected.

The appellant too sees confidentiality as essential to her relationship with Dr. Parfitt. She insisted from the first that her communications to Dr. Parfitt be held in confidence, suggesting that this was a condition of her entering and continuing treatment. The fact that she and Dr. Parfitt feared the possibility of court-ordered disclosure at some future date does not negate the fact that confidentiality was essential "to the full and satisfactory maintenance" of their relationship.

The third requirement — that the relation must be one which in the opinion of the community ought to be sedulously fostered — is equally satisfied. Victims of sexual abuse often suffer serious trauma, which, left untreated, may mar their entire lives. It is widely accepted that it is in the interests of the victim and society that such help be obtained. The mental health of the citizenry, no less than its physical health, is a public good of great importance. Just as it is in the interest of the sexual abuse victim to be restored to full and healthy functioning, so is it in the interest of the public that she take her place as a healthy and productive member of society.

It may thus be concluded that the first three conditions for privilege for communications between a psychiatrist and the victim of a sexual assault are met in the case at bar. The communications were confidential. Their confidence is essential to the psychiatrist-patient relationship. The relationship itself and the treatment it makes possible are of transcendent public importance.

The fourth requirement is that the interests served by protecting the communications from disclosure outweigh the interest of pursuing the truth and disposing correctly of the litigation. This requires first an assessment of the interests served by protecting the communications from disclosure. These include injury to the appellant's ongoing relationship with Dr. Parfitt and her future treatment. They also include the effect that a finding of no privilege would have on the ability of other persons suffering from similar trauma to obtain needed treatment and of psychiatrists to provide it. The interests served by non-disclosure must extend to any effect on society of the failure of individuals to obtain treatment restoring them to healthy and contributing members of society. Finally, the interests served by protection from disclosure must include the privacy interest of the person claiming privilege and inequalities which may be perpetuated by the absence of protection.

As noted, the common law must develop in a way that reflects emerging Charter values. It follows that the factors balanced under the fourth part of the test for privilege should be updated to reflect relevant Charter values. One such value is the interest affirmed by s. 8 of the Charter of each person in privacy. Another is the right of every person embodied in s. 15 of the Charter to equal treatment and benefit of the law. A rule of privilege which fails to protect confidential doctor/patient communications in the context of an action arising out of sexual assault perpetuates the disadvantage felt by victims of sexual assault, often women. The intimate nature of sexual assault heightens the privacy concerns of the victim and may increase, if automatic disclosure is the rule, the difficulty of obtaining redress for the wrong. The victim of a sexual assault is thus placed in a disadvantaged position as compared with the victim of a different wrong. The result may be that the victim of sexual assault does not obtain the equal benefit of the law to which s. 15 of the Charter entitles her. She is doubly victimized, initially by the sexual assault and later by the price she must pay to claim redress — redress which in some cases may be part of her program of therapy. These are factors which may properly be considered in determining the interests served by an order for protection from disclosure of confidential patient-psychiatrist communications in sexual assault cases.

These criteria, applied to the case at bar, demonstrate a compelling interest in protecting the communications at issue from disclosure. More, however, is required to establish privilege. For privilege to exist, it must be shown that the benefit that inures from privilege, however great it may seem, in fact outweighs the interest in the correct disposal of the litigation.

At this stage, the court considering an application for privilege must balance one alternative against the other. The exercise is essentially one of common sense and good judgment. This said, it is important to establish the outer limits of acceptability. I for one cannot accept the proposition that "occasional injustice" should be accepted as the price of the privilege. It is true that the traditional categories of privilege, cast as they are in absolute all-or-nothing terms, necessarily run the risk of occasional injustice. But that does not mean that courts, in invoking new privileges, should lightly condone its extension. In the words of Scalia J. (dissenting) in *Jaffee v. Redmond*, 116 S. Ct. 1923 (1996), at p. 1941:

> It is no small matter to say that, in some cases, our federal courts will be the tools of injustice rather than unearth the truth where it is available to be found. The common law has identified a few instances where that is tolerable. Perhaps Congress may conclude that it is also tolerable. . . . But that conclusion assuredly does not burst upon the mind with such clarity that a judgment in favor of suppressing the truth ought to be pronounced by this honorable Court.

It follows that if the court considering a claim for privilege determines that a particular document or class of documents must be produced to get at the truth and prevent an unjust verdict, it must permit production to the extent required to avoid that result. On the other hand, the need to get at the truth and avoid injustice does not automatically negate the possibility of protection from full disclosure. In some cases, the court may well decide that the truth permits of nothing less than full production. This said, I would venture to say that an order for partial privilege will more often be appropriate in civil cases where, as here, the privacy interest is compelling. Disclosure of a limited number of documents, editing by the court to remove non-essential material, and the imposition of conditions on who may see and copy the documents are techniques which may be used to ensure the highest degree of confidentiality and the least damage to the protected relationship, while guarding against the injustice of cloaking the truth.

It must be conceded that a test for privilege which permits the court to occasionally reject an otherwise well-founded claim for privilege in the interests of getting at the truth may not offer patients a guarantee that communications with their psychiatrists will never be disclosed. On the other hand, the assurance that disclosure will be ordered only where clearly necessary and then only to the extent necessary is likely to permit many to avail themselves of psychiatric counselling when certain disclosure might make them hesitate or decline. The facts in this case demonstrate as much. I am reinforced in this view by the fact, as Scalia J. points out in his dissenting reasons in *Jaffee v. Redmond*, that of the 50 states and the District of Columbia which have enacted some form of psychotherapist privilege, none have adopted it in absolute form. All have found it necessary to specify circumstances in which it will not apply, usually related to the need to get at the truth in vital situations. Partial privilege, in the views of these legislators, can be effective.

The view that privilege may exist where the interest in protecting the privacy of the records is compelling and the threat to proper disposition of the litigation either is not apparent or can be offset by partial or conditional discovery is consistent with this Court's view in *R. v. O'Connor*, [1995] 4 S.C.R. 411. The majority there did not deny that privilege in psychotherapeutic records may exist in appropriate circumstances. Without referring directly to privilege, it developed a test for production of third party therapeutic and other records which balances the competing interests by reference to a number of factors including the right of the accused to full answer and defence and the right of the complainant to privacy. Just as justice requires that the accused in a criminal case be permitted to answer the Crown's case, so justice requires that a defendant in a civil suit be permitted to answer the plaintiff's case. In deciding whether he or she is entitled to production of confidential documents, this requirement must be balanced against the privacy interest of the complainant. This said, the interest in disclosure of a defendant in a civil suit may be less compelling than the parallel interest of an accused charged with a crime. The defendant in a civil suit stands to lose money and repute; the accused in a criminal proceeding stands to lose his or her very liberty. As a consequence, the balance between the interest in disclosure and the complainant's interest in privacy may be struck at a different level in the civil and criminal case; documents produced in a criminal case may not always be producible in a civil case, where the privacy interest of the complainant may more easily outweigh the defendant's interest in production.

My conclusion is that it is open to a judge to conclude that psychiatrist-patient records are privileged in appropriate circumstances. Once the first three requirements are met and a compelling prima facie case for protection is established, the focus will be on the balancing under the fourth head. A document relevant to a defence or claim may be required to be disclosed, notwithstanding the high interest of the plaintiff in keeping it confidential. On the other hand, documents of questionable relevance or which contain information available from other sources may be declared privileged. The result depends on the balance of the competing interests of disclosure and privacy in each case. It must be borne in mind that in most cases, the majority of the communications between a psychiatrist and her patient will have little or no bearing on the case at bar and can safely be excluded from production. Fishing expeditions are not appropriate where there is a compelling privacy interest at stake, even at the discovery stage. Finally, where justice requires that communications be disclosed, the court should consider qualifying the disclosure by imposing limits aimed at permitting the opponent to have the access justice requires while preserving the confidential nature of the documents to the greatest degree possible.

It remains to consider the argument that by commencing the proceedings against the respondent Dr. Ryan, the appellant has forfeited her right to confidentiality. I accept that a litigant must accept such intrusions upon her privacy as are necessary to enable the judge or jury to get to the truth and render a just verdict. But I do not accept that by claiming such damages as the law allows, a litigant grants her opponent a licence to delve into private aspects of her life which need not be probed for the proper disposition of the litigation.

VI. Procedure for Ascertaining Privilege

In order to determine whether privilege should be accorded to a particular document or class of documents and, if so, what conditions should attach, the judge must consider the circumstances of the privilege alleged, the documents, and the case. While it is not essential in a civil case such as this that the judge examine every document, the court may do so if necessary to the inquiry. On the other hand, a judge does not necessarily err by proceeding on affidavit material indicating the nature of the information and its expected relevance without inspecting each document individually. The requirement that the court minutely examine numerous or lengthy documents may prove time-consuming, expensive and delay the resolution of the litigation. Where necessary to the proper determination of the claim for privilege, it must be undertaken. But I would not lay down an absolute rule that as a matter of law, the judge must personally inspect every document at issue in every case. Where the judge is satisfied on reasonable grounds that the interests at stake can properly be balanced without individual examination of each document, failure to do so does not constitute error of law.

VII. Application to This Case

The Court of Appeal declined to order production of Dr. Parfitt's notes to herself on the ground that they were unnecessary given that she would not be called to testify. It ordered the production of notes and records of consultations with the appellant, but under stringent conditions. While the Court of Appeal did not proceed on the basis of privilege, its orders are supported by the principles relating to privilege that I have attempted to set forth.

The interest in preserving the confidentiality of the communications here at issue was, as discussed, compelling. On the other hand, the communications might be expected to bear on the critical issue of the extent to which the respondent Dr. Ryan's conduct caused the difficulties the appellant was experiencing. A court, in a case such as this, might well consider it best to inspect the records individually to the end of weeding out those which were irrelevant to this defence. However, the alternative chosen by the Court of Appeal in this case of refusing to order production of one group of documents and imposing stringent conditions on who could see the others and what use could be made of them cannot be said to be in error. In the end, the only persons to see the documents in question will be the lawyers for the respondent Dr. Ryan and his expert witnesses. Copies will not be made, and disclosure of the contents to other people will not be permitted. In short, the plaintiff's private disclosures to her psychiatrist will be disclosed only to a small group of trustworthy professionals, much in the fashion that confidential medical records may be disclosed in a hospital setting. I am not persuaded that the order of the Court of Appeal should be disturbed.

VIII. Conclusion

I would dismiss the appeal with costs.

[L'HEUREUX-DUBÉ J. would have allowed the appeal and set aside the decision of the Court of Appeal. In conclusion she reasoned as follows.]

L'HEUREUX-DUBÉ J.:—

. . .

The Court of Appeal in the present case allowed the appeal in part. It did so after attempting some balancing of the privacy interests of the plaintiff and the interests in a fair trial. Consequently, it withheld the notes made for diagnostic purposes and restricted the dissemination and reproduction of the records once produced. Nonetheless, it did not review the documents before ordering their production. In my view, such a process does not give due consideration to the appropriate balance of the Charter values engaged by the discovery procedures.

Indeed, in these particular circumstances, and given the nature of the damages claimed and the information sought by the defence, very little meaningful protection has been accorded to these private records. If plaintiffs in such cases know that the entire contents of their discussion with their therapists or any other private records may be revealed to the lawyers and expert witnesses of the defendant, they may very well be deterred from seeking civil remedies. Without anyone reviewing the documents to remove information which is private, irrelevant or of very limited probative value, an order of production constitutes a serious breach of privacy while affording potentially limited benefit to the defence. A hierarchy of Charter values has been created, one where the defence is greatly advantaged while the effect on the plaintiff may be highly detrimental. In striking an appropriate balance of Charter values, such a hierarchy is impermissible. The Court of Appeal's decision must, therefore, be revisited. While the Court of Appeal's general approach was correct and while it did not have the benefit of our judgments in *O'Connor* and *L.L.A.*, at the time its decision was rendered, the process it adopted is infirm.

As regards the first issue, that relating to the privileged nature of the communications between the appellant and Dr. Parfitt, I agree with McLachlin J. that a successful claim of privilege has clearly been established for the records which were exempt from disclosure. I also affirm the Court of Appeal's general conclusion that it had a broader discretion to control the process of discovery for the remaining documents to ensure that it not affect one of the parties unjustly.

The exercise of discretion upon which the order was based did not effect an appropriate balance of the Charter values of privacy, equality, and fair trial. By failing to screen private records in such cases, the court creates a hierarchy of Charter values, where interests in privacy and equality may be seriously affected for records or parts thereof which may provide very little if any benefit to the defence or be unnecessary to ensure the fairness of the proceedings. Procedures adapted to the context of discovery in civil proceedings from the principles developed by this Court in *O'Connor* are in order.

I would allow the appeal with costs. The decision of the Court of Appeal should be set aside, except as regards the notes which were not disclosed, and the matter remitted back to the Master for determination in a manner consistent with the foregoing reasons.

Chapter 5

Mechanics of Proof

A. MATTERS NOT REQUIRING PROOF

1. FORMAL ADMISSIONS OF FACT

In civil cases pleadings are designed to narrow issues and determine facts not in dispute. Failure to admit facts can result in an award of costs. Admissions of fact, law or mixed law and facts can occur in a number of ways including pleadings, a failure to respond, an agreed statement in a signed letter, or orally at trial.

In criminal trials s. 655 of the *Criminal Code* allows the accused or his or her counsel to admit any fact alleged against him or her thereby dispensing with the need for proof.

R. v. FALCONER
2016 NSCA 22, 372 N.S.R. (2d) 186 (N.S. C.A.)

BEVERIDGE JA (MACDONALD CJNS and BOURGEOIS JA concurring)

THE GOVERNING PRINCIPLES OF ADMISSIONS

[39] The common law did not permit an accused charged with a felony to make admissions at or during his or her trial (other than a plea of guilty). Since its inception, the *Criminal Code* cured this inconvenience . . . .

[40] This provision now exists as s. 655, with no substantive change in the wording:

> 655. Where an accused is on trial for an indictable offence, he or his counsel may admit any fact alleged against him for the purpose of dispensing with proof thereof.

[41] The common law and the import of the *Criminal Code* provision was considered by the Supreme Court of Canada in *R. v. Castellani*, 1969 CanLII 57 (SCC), [1970] S.C.R. 310. At the accused's trial for the murder of his wife, his counsel produced an eight paragraph document purporting to admit to certain facts pursuant to the predecessor section to s. 655. The Crown objected to the eighth paragraph. The Admissions were amended to delete that paragraph and were tendered at trial.

[42] The accused was convicted. The British Columbia Court of Appeal concluded that the trial judge should have permitted all of the admissions, but

dismissed the appeal from conviction on the basis that the error by the trial judge had caused no prejudice. The accused's further appeal to the Supreme Court was unsuccessful.

[43] Cartwright C.J., writing for the full Court, concluded that the trial judge had not erred. He explained it is for the Crown to propose admissions, and the accused to admit or decline:

> In a criminal case, there being no pleadings, there are no precisely worded allegations of fact which are susceptible of categorical admission. An accused cannot admit a fact alleged against him until the allegation has been made. When recourse is proposed to be had to s. 562 it is for the Crown, not for the defence, to state the fact or facts which it alleges against the accused and of which it seeks admission. The accused, of course, is under no obligation to admit the fact so alleged but his choice is to admit it or to decline to do so. He cannot frame the wording of the allegation to suit his own purposes and then insist on admitting it. To permit such a course could only lead to confusion. The idea of the admission of an allegation involves action by two persons, one who makes the allegation and another who admits it.

[44] Chief Justice Cartwright explained that his conclusion was directed by the wording of the *Criminal Code*, and by what is necessarily involved in the idea of an accused admitting an allegation of fact in a criminal case. He viewed his conclusion as being strengthened by the purpose of the statutory provision. After referring to the common law, he explained the purpose of the section:

> In my opinion the purpose of enacting s. 562 and its predecessors was to alter the common law rule by eliminating the necessity, on the trial of an indictable offence, of proof by the Crown of any fact which it desires to prove and which the accused is prepared to admit at his trial.

[45] Once tendered, formal admissions under s. 655 of the *Criminal Code* are conclusive for the trier of fact. Subject to relief being granted from the consequence of the admission, the fact admitted is conclusively established. It is not open to challenge.

[46] In *R. v. Baksh*, 2005 CanLII 24918 (ON SC), [2005] O.J. No. 2971, the Crown wanted to tender s. 655 admissions previously made in a trial (that had resulted in a mistrial) in a subsequent trial. Justice Hill explained the import of s. 655 admissions:

> [84] An admission validly made in the context of s. 655 of the *Code* is an acknowledgement that some fact alleged by the prosecution is true. Such an admission dispenses with proof of that fact by testimony or ordinary exhibit and the accused is not entitled to set up competing contradictory evidence in an attempt to disprove the judicial or formal admission. In other words, the formal admission is conclusive of the admitted fact . . .

[47] After a thorough review of the governing case law, Hill J. concluded that the agreed statement of facts was admissible as evidence at the subsequent trial,

but as rebuttable, not binding, admissions. He set out his conclusion as follows:

[118] In summary, in the January 5, 2004 trial, the Agreed Statement amounted to judicial or formal admissions. Voluntarily made, with the benefit of legal advice, the unqualified admissions were, in the former trial, conclusive proof against both parties of the matters asserted. The mistrial, in my view, was precipitated by Mr. Baksh's desire to no longer be bound by the entirety of the Agreed Statement as formal admissions. Having already benefitted from the withdrawal of charges and certain advantages associated with the delay of the trial's completion, the mistrial order then freed the accused from the conclusive nature of those admissions although the accused had raised no demonstrable case of mistake or ineffective assistance of counsel justifying repudiation of para. 15 of the Agreed Statement. In these circumstances, the admissions in the first trial survive as ordinary admissions . . .

[48] Parties pursuing the laudable goal of shortening and streamlining trials frequently enter into informal agreements about admissibility of evidence or other matters that fall outside the parameters of s. 655. Care is required by the parties and the trial judge to understand the difference and understand the consequences that flow from such agreements. *McWilliams' Canadian Criminal Evidence* explains the distinction:

The distinction between the solemn or formal admission and an evidentiary or informal admission is "a radical one" as the former "more stringent" form of admission admits of no contradiction while the latter genre of admission, for example, agreeing what a witness if present would testify to without any agreement "that the tenor of the desired testimony is true", leaves it open to impeach or contradict the credibility of the absent witness by other evidence.

[49] There are a number of cases where the parties appear to have misunderstood this difference. *R. v. Korski*, 2009 MBCA 37 (CanLII) illustrates. There were several agreed statements of fact. The ones that turned out to be contentious dealt with the introduction of evidence by tendering witness statements. The judge told the jury that they could weigh the "agreed statements of fact" along with the *viva voce* evidence. The appellant claimed this was wrong — the agreed statements of facts were formal agreements and hence amounted to proven facts. Steel J.A., for the Court, quoted with approval the discussion from *McWilliams* about the difference between formal and informal admissions. She then explained the role that the latter played in general and in the trial of Mr. Korski:

[125] In the case at bar, counsel may have labelled all the exhibits agreed statements of facts, but that does not make them so. Instead, what in fact happened was that some of the seven exhibits were formal admissions and some were informal admissions and they should have not been lumped together. There is a distinction between agreed facts and a statement that a certain witness will say a certain thing. The various "Agreed Statement of Fact re: Evidence of [a witness]" were merely agreements as to what the witnesses would have said, not that what they say is necessarily true. The trial judge recognized the difference and brought it

to the attention of defence counsel in the excerpt from the transcripts referred to previously, and to the attention of Crown counsel . . .

[50] The last type of admission has to do with the admissibility of evidence. Ordinarily, if a party objects to evidence being proferred during a trial, an objection is made. The objection can be disposed of after argument in the presence or absence of the jury without the hearing of the contentious evidence in a separate proceeding (a *voir dire*).

[51] But there are some types of evidence that should not be heard by the trier of fact without the trial judge first being satisfied as to certain requirements. Statements allegedly made by an accused to persons whom he believes to be in authority and expert opinion evidence are two of them. Both were adduced at the appellant's trial, and their admissibility were conceded in Ex. #2.

[52] The requirements for admissibility for these two types of evidence and the burden of proof the proponent must meet to gain admission are different.

[53] A trier of fact should not hear evidence describing statements made by an accused to persons in authority (usually police officers) unless the Crown first establishes, in a separate proceeding (a *voir dire*), that the statements were made "voluntarily".

[54] Neither should a trier of fact hear expert opinion evidence without being satisfied that it meets the criteria for admission set out in *R. v. Mohan*, 1994 CanLII 80 (SCC), [1994] 2 S.C.R. 9, and recently refined by the Supreme Court in *White Burgess Langille Inman v. Abbott and Haliburton Co.*, 2015 SCC 23 (CanLII).

[55] Yet, for both types of evidence, the Crown and the accused routinely agree that the intended evidence is admissible without the necessity of a formal or even informal *voir dire*.

[56] The rules are strict with respect to statements by an accused to a person in authority. To gain admission, the Crown must establish beyond a reasonable doubt that the statement was voluntary, in the sense that it was not obtained by either fear of prejudice, or hope of advantage exercised or held out by a person in authority, or other oppressive conduct. (See, for example, *R. v. Erven*, 1978 CanLII 19 (SCC), [1979] 1 S.C.R. 926; *R. v. Oickle*, 2000 SCC 38 (CanLII).)

[57] The rule applies whether the statement is inculpatory or exculpatory and whether the trial is by judge and jury or by judge alone. (See: *R. v. Piché*, 1970 CanLII 182 (SCC), [1971] S.C.R. 23; *R. v. Gauthier*, 1975 CanLII 193 (SCC), [1977] 1 S.C.R. 441; *R. v. Powell*, 1976 CanLII 155 (SCC), [1977] 1 S.C.R. 362.) A *voir dire* is required to be held whether the accused was even a suspect at the time or that the circumstances appear to make it plain that the statement in question was voluntary (*R. v. Erven, supra*.)

[58] The sole exception is where an accused waives the requirement for a *voir dire*. In other words, an admission by the accused that the statements in question are "voluntary". The juridicial basis to permit such an admission was debated for many years. It is not necessary to delve too deeply into the controversy, other than to say that the ability to make the admission exists either as a formal admission under s. 655 or independently of it (see *R. v. Park*, 1981 CanLII 56 (SCC), [1981] 2 S.C.R. 64).

The issue of formal admissions and the ethical obligations of counsel to use them to shorten the length of criminal trials was the subject of comment by two experienced criminal law participants who issued the following two recommendations in their report *"Report of the Review of Large and Complex Criminal Cases Procedures".*[1]

Recommendation 18:

Counsel for the Crown and for the defence are both under ethical duties to make reasonable admissions of facts that are not legitimately in dispute. The court should encourage and mediate efforts to frame reasonable admissions. When the defence fully admits facts alleged by the Crown, the court has the power to require the Crown to accept a properly framed admission and to exclude evidence on that issue.

Recommendation 19:

Federal, Provincial and Territorial Justice Ministers ought to instruct their officials to consider expanding s. 657.1 of the *Criminal Code* to include other routine factual issues that can properly be proved by way of affidavit, subject to a right to cross-examine the affiant where some live issue exists.

Another type of formal admission of fact is a plea of guilt. Section 606 of the *Criminal Code* provides:

Pleas permitted

(1) An accused who is called on to plead may plead guilty or not guilty, or the special pleas authorized by this Part and no others.

Conditions for accepting guilty plea

(1.1) A court may accept a plea of guilty only if it is satisfied that the accused

(a) is making the plea voluntarily; and

(b) understands

(i)   that the plea is an admission of the essential elements of the offence,

(ii) the nature and consequences of the plea, and

(iii) that the court is not bound by any agreement made between the accused and the prosecutor.

---

[1]   The Honourable Patrick Lesage and Professor Michael Code (November, 2008) (Ministry of the Attorney General of Ontario).

Validity of plea

(1.2) The failure of the court to fully inquire whether the conditions set out in subsection (1.1) are met does not affect the validity of the plea.

What is the purpose of s. 606(1.2)? Is it not preferable for a trial judge to inquire to ensure that an innocent person does not plead guilty to an offence he or she did not commit?

R. v. G. (D.M.)
(2011), 84 C.R. (6th) 420, 275 C.C.C. (3d) 295 (Ont. C.A.)

WATT J.A.:

39 The Criminal Code describes the pleas available to an accused. A plea represents an accused's formal response to the allegations contained in an indictment or information. The only pleas available to an accused are the general or special pleas authorized in Part XX of the Criminal Code. No other pleas are permitted: Criminal Code, s. 606(1).

40 A general plea of not guilty is or represents an accused's formal, in-court denial of having committed the offence to which the plea has been entered. A plea of not guilty provides notice to the prosecutor and to the trier of fact that the person charged requires the prosecutor to prove each essential element of the offence charged by evidence that is relevant, material and admissible at trial. A general plea of not guilty does not involve any admission about any essential element of any offence charged or its proof.

41 On the other hand, a plea of guilty is a formal, in-court admission by an accused that she or he committed the offence to which the plea has been entered. An accused who pleads guilty consents to entry of a finding of guilt, or conviction without a trial and relieves the prosecutor of the burden of proving guilt, by relevant, material and admissible evidence, beyond a reasonable doubt. An accused who pleads guilty abandons his or her non-compellability as a witness, as well the right to remain silent, and surrenders his or her right to offer full answer and defence to the charge: Adgey v. The Queen, [1975] 2 S.C.R. 426, at p. 440, per Laskin J., in dissent on other grounds.

42 The nature and effect of a plea of guilty makes it essential that the plea be unequivocal, voluntary and informed. To ensure that pleas of guilty meet these requirements, s. 606(1.1) imposes an obligation on the presiding judge to satisfy him or herself of the voluntary and informed nature of the plea. For the plea to be informed, the accused must understand that the plea is an admission of the essential elements of the offence and that the presiding judge is not bound by any agreement made by the accused and the prosecutor. The accused must also understand the nature and consequences of a guilty plea. Under s. 606(1.2) the failure of the trial judge to fully inquire about the voluntary and informed nature of the accused's plea does not affect the validity of that plea. But an inquiry is mandatory nonetheless.

. . .

The Relationship Between the General Pleas and Admissions

47 In criminal proceedings, we recognize two kinds of formal admissions:

    i.   a plea of guilty, other than an unaccepted plea of guilty under s. 606(4); and

    ii.   an admission of specific facts under s. 655 of the Criminal Code.

48 After a plea of guilty has been entered, and where necessary accepted by the prosecutor, the usual practice in this province is that the prosecutor reads into the record the allegations relied upon to establish the essential elements of the offence the accused is alleged to have committed. Defence counsel is asked whether the allegations read are correct or substantially correct. Provided there is no dispute about the essential elements of the offence, and the judge is satisfied after inquiry of the accused that the plea of guilty is unequivocal, informed and voluntary, the trial judge enters a finding of guilt and records a conviction of the offence to which the plea of guilty was entered. Apart from the requirement of a plea inquiry, the Criminal Code says nothing about the procedure to be followed after entry of a plea of guilty.

49 Where an accused pleads not guilty, the prosecutor bears the onus of proof. The manner in which the prosecutor chooses to prove the allegations contained in an information or indictment is up to the prosecutor, but subject to the supervision of the trial judge who must ensure that any evidence adduced is relevant, material and admissible. The prosecutor's case may include or consist entirely of admissions of fact under s. 655 of the Criminal Code.

The Principles Applied

50 In my view, for reasons that I will develop, the proceedings that followed the appellant's plea of not guilty were sufficiently flawed that the conviction entered by the trial judge must be set aside and a new trial ordered.

. . .

55 This case proceeded on the basis of a plea of not guilty, a plea by which the appellant denied having committed the offence charged and required the prosecutor to prove the essential elements of that offence by relevant, material and admissible evidence beyond a reasonable doubt.

56 After the plea of not guilty, the prosecutor adduced no evidence. No viva voce testimony. No real evidence. As a surrogate for evidence, the prosecutor read the allegations made against the appellant. It is fundamental that prosecutorial allegations are not evidence. Nor did they become admissions under s. 655 of the Criminal Code by the failure of the appellant's trial counsel to make submissions.

57 To some it may seem a mere quibble, a swap of form for substance, to conclude that what occurred here was not at least a reasonable facsimile of a

formal admission under s. 655. I do not agree. To admit something is to accept it as valid or as true. By an admission under s. 655 an accused admits a fact or the facts alleged as true.

58 The allegation of ineffective assistance of counsel has provided us with information not available to the trial judge. That information makes it plain and obvious that the appellant consistently denied that the complainant's allegations ever occurred, a position inconsistent with their formal admission before the trial judge. The appellant was never asked, nor did his counsel ever expressly admit on his behalf the prosecutor's allegations. What occurred here did not amount to an admission of fact under s. 655.

. . .

67 After anxious consideration, I am satisfied that the procedure followed in the proceedings of February 21, 2008, caused a miscarriage of justice through procedural unfairness. The appellant's unwavering denial of guilt was sideswiped by a procedure that resulted in a de facto admission of guilt without any inquiry into voluntariness or the appellant's understanding of the nature and effect of this procedure.

. . .

69 Persons who admit their guilt should plead guilty. The plea inquiry that s. 606(1.1) requires ensures that the plea is unequivocal, voluntary and informed.

70 Persons who deny guilt should plead not guilty and have a trial at which proper proof may be offered and its sufficiency or inadequacy assessed by the trier of fact. The cannibalized procedure followed here blurs the distinction between admissions and denials of guilt, is unauthorized and, as this case demonstrates, is capable of great mischief.

2. JUDICIAL NOTICE

(a) Introduction

. . . [T]o require that a judge should affect a cloistered aloofness from facts that every other man in Court is fully aware of, and should insist on having proof on oath of what, as a man of the world, he knows already better than any witness can tell him, is a rule that may easily become pedantic and futile. . . Judicial notice . . . involves that, at the stage when evidence of material facts can be properly received, certain facts may be deemed to be established, although not proved by sworn testimony, or by the production, out of the proper custody, of documents, which speak for themselves. Judicial notice refers to facts, which a judge can be called upon to receive and to act upon, either from his general knowledge of them, or from inquiries to be made by himself for his own information from sources to which it is proper for him to refer. . .[2]

---

[2]   *Commonwealth Shipping Representative v. P. & O. Branch Service*, [1923] A.C. 191 (H.L.) at 211-212 per Lord Sumner.

The judicial process cannot construct every case from scratch, like Descartes creating a world based on the postulate Cogito, ergo sum.[3]

We do not prove by evidence, indeed we cannot prove by evidence, all the facts that are necessary to a judicial decision. Certain matters are so well-known in the community or so easily determinable as to be indisputable.

Consider a civil suit for damages for injuries sustained in an automobile accident. The defendant describes his speed and handling of the car. He maintains that the accident was unavoidable as he was unable to bring his vehicle to a stop. The plaintiff maintains that the defendant was negligent in that he was driving too fast for the conditions of the road at the time of the accident. The evidence indicates that it was raining at the time of the accident. To resolve the issue of liability, do we need evidence to be led to establish that rain makes road surfaces wet, that the coefficient of friction between tires and asphalt is thereby reduced, that such a fact is known to most drivers, and that careful drivers lower their speed in such conditions? Such matters are so well-known in the community as to be indisputable. This material need not be proved according to the normal rules of evidence. This knowledge is assumed to be already possessed by the judge and the party who has the burden on the issue may simply call on the judge to judicially notice those facts which are necessary to the determination of the question. The judge, at times, may not himself or herself have the knowledge and may need to be informed, but when the judge is informed about such matters it is not through material filtered through the various rules of evidence. Dictionaries, atlases and the like are ready at hand and may freely be consulted by him or her.

(b) Disputed Boundaries of Judicial Notice

Illustrations from reported cases give us a notion of what is traditionally described as judicial notice. For example, we see court rulings that evidence is not necessary to establish that Victoria is in British Columbia,[4] that Toronto is in Canada,[5] that LSD can be a mind destroying drug,[6] that Colonel By Drive in Ottawa is National Commission property,[7] that big horn sheep are mountain sheep,[8] that a pizza costs less than $200,[9] that "OD'd" means overdosed on a drug,[10] or that the incidence of a particular crime has reached such a high level that deterrence is mandated.[11] All these things can

---

[3]   Advisory Committee's Note to Rule 201 of the U.S. Federal Rules of Evidence.
[4]   R. v. Kuhn (1970), 1 C.C.C. (2d) 132 (B.C. Co. Ct.).
[5]   R. v. Cerniuk (1948), 91 C.C.C. 56 (B.C. C.A.).
[6]   R. v. Shaw (1977), 36 C.R.N.S. 358 (Ont. C.A.).
[7]   R. v. Potts (1982), 134 D.L.R. (3d) 227 (Ont. C.A.).
[8]   R. v. Quinn (1975), 27 C.C.C. (2d) 543 (Alta. S.C.). See also Sigeareak v. R., [1966] S.C.R. 645.
[9]   Re Livingstone and R. (1975), 29 C.C.C. (2d) 557 (B.C. S.C.).
[10]   R. v. MacAulay (1975), 25 C.C.C. (2d) 1 (N.B. C.A.).
[11]   See e.g. R. v. McNicol, [1969] 3 C.C.C. 56 (Man. C.A.) and R. v. Adelman, [1968] 3 C.C.C. 311 (B.C. C.A.). But see R. v. Priest (1996), 1 C.R. (5th) 275 (Ont. C.A.) where the trial judge was criticized by Rosenberg J.A. for relying too heavily on general deterrence for a youthful first offender based on the prevalence of break and enter cases. It was noted that the judge had no

be judicially noticed. The judge does not need to be informed about these matters by evidence.

Judicially noticing geographic locations and the meaning of words presents few real problems. When the facts are indisputable, no one has a basis to object. But suppose a judge notices or assumes something about which there are different opinions. Is this also judicial notice? Is it permissible?

There are different schools of thought concerning the boundaries of judicial notice. Professor Thayer regarded judicial notice not as belonging peculiarly to the law of evidence, but rather

> to the general topic of legal or judicial reasoning. It is, indeed, woven into the very texture of the judicial function. In conducting a process of judicial reasoning, as of other reasoning, not a step can be taken without assuming something which has not been proved; and the capacity to do this, with competent judgment and efficiency, is imputed to judges and juries as part of their necessary mental outfit . . . What are the things of which judicial tribunals may take notice, and should take notice, without proof? It is possible to indicate with exactness only a part of these matters. Some things are thus dealt with by virtue of express statutory law; some in a manner that is referable merely to precedent — to the actual decision, which have selected some things and omitted others in a way that is not always explicable upon any general principle; others upon a general maxim of reason and good sense, the application of which must rest mainly with the discretion of the tribunal, and, in any general discussion, must rather be illustrated than defined.[12]

Cross on Evidence similarly concludes:

> The tacit applications of the doctrine of judicial notice are more numerous and more important that the express ones. A great deal is taken for granted when any question of relevance is considered or assumed. For example, evidence is constantly given that persons accused of burglary were found in possession of jemmies or skeleton keys, that the accused became confused when charged; these are relevant only provided there is a common practice to use such things in the commission of crime, or provided that guilty people tend more to become confused when charged, but no one ever thinks of calling evidence on such a subject.[13]

Professor Morgan, on the other hand, in his classic article on the subject, so viewed the purpose of judicial notice that he limited its application to those facts which were indisputable:

> Just as the court cannot function unless the judge knows the law and unless the judge and jury have the fund of information common to all intelligent men in the community as well as the capacity to use the ordinary processes of reasoning, so it cannot adjust legal relations among members of society and thus fulfil the sole

---

statistics before him; and see similarly *R. v. Mallory*, (2004) 25 C.R. (6th) 182 (B.C. C.A.). See now *R. c. Lacasse*, 2015 CSC 64, 2015 SCC 64, [2015] 3 S.C.R. 1089, 333 C.C.C. (3d) 450, 24 C.R. (7th) 225 (S.C.C.). However in dissent Gascon J. was of the view that the trial judge should not have taken judicial notice that impaired driving had been trivialized in his region.

[12]   Thayer, *A Preliminary Treatise on Evidence at the Common Law* (1898) at 279, 299.

[13]   *Cross and Tapper on Evidence*, 8th ed. at 79.

purpose of its creation if it permits the parties to take issue on, and thus secure results contrary to, what is so notoriously true as not to be the subject of reasonable dispute, or what is capable of immediate and accurate demonstration by resort to sources of indisputable accuracy easily accessible to men in the situation of members of the court. This, it is submitted, is the rock of reason and policy upon which judicial notice of facts is built. . . To warrant judicial notice the probability must be so great as to make the truth of the proposition notoriously indisputable among reasonable men.[14]

It has been noted that the Morgan thesis thrived in an era dominated by a mood of judicial restraint.[15] How the particular judge views his role will probably dictate how much he or she will rely on materials not introduced by the parties. It depends on "whether he will play an affirmative or quiescent role in the performance of his duties".[16]

In contrast to Morgan's view, Professor Thayer believed that there were instances when a court, in its discretion, might judicially notice facts which could not be demonstrated as being indisputable. While Professor Morgan saw the purpose of judicial notice as ensuring that courts did not make decisions contrary to nature, and therefore would confine it to instances where the facts were notoriously indisputable, Professor Thayer saw another purpose for the doctrine: efficiency. Professor Thayer wrote:

> Taking judicial notice does not import that the matter is indisputable. It is not necessarily anything more than a *prima facie* recognition, leaving the matter still open to controversy. . . Courts may judicially notice much which they cannot be required to notice. That is well worth emphasizing, for it points to a great possible usefulness in this doctrine, in helping to shorten and simplify trials; it is an instrument of great capacity in the hands of a competent judge; and is not nearly as much used, in the region of practice and evidence, as it should be.[17]

Professor Kenneth Culp Davis, also disagreeing with Morgan's thesis, wrote:

> The plain fact is, however, that judges and administrative officers necessarily use extra-record facts which are neither indisputable nor found in sources of indisputable accuracy. A human being is probably unable to consider a problem — whether of fact, law, policy, judgment or discretion — without using his past experience, much of which may be factual and much highly disputable. Judges and administrators are at their best when they are well informed; their understanding and information must be used to the full if their decisions are to be wise and sound. Fact finding, law making, and policy formulation should be guided by experience and understanding, not limited to wooden judgments predicated upon the literal words of witnesses.[18]

---

14 Morgan, "Judicial Notice" (1944) 57 Harv. L. Rev. 269 at 273-274.
15 Roberts, "Preliminary Notes Toward a Study of Judicial Notice" (1966-67) 52 Cornell Law Q. 210 at 230.
16 Weinstein's *Evidence* at 200-204. The authors note that this phrase was termed "the most important decision the judge makes for himself" by Judge Breitel, "Ethical Problems in the Performance of the Judicial Function" (Chicago University Conference of Judicial Ethics) at 65.
17 *Supra* note 12 at 308-309.
18 Davis, "Judicial Notice" (1955) 55 Col. L. Rev. 945 at 948-49. In Davis, *A System of Judicial Notice Based on Fairness and Convenience, Perspectives of Law* (1964) at 69, 74, Davis explained that the boundaries of judicial notice coincide with those of judicial reasoning: When

In his textbook, Davis later emphasized that judicial notice was *not* based simply on ensuring that courts were protected from making findings which did not accord with reality, but that

> the basic principle is that extra-record facts should be assumed whenever it is convenient to assume them, except that convenience should always yield to the requirement of procedural fairness that parties should have an opportunity to meet in the appropriate fashion all facts that influence the disposition of the case.[19]

Professor Roberts commented:

> The Davis theory of judicial notice is just as much a product of the times as was the Morgan theory. Courts seen as super-legislatures must be allowed to roam far and wide and must at all costs not be inhibited by any requirement that the facts with which they deal must be either found in the record or attributable to common knowledge or sources of indisputable accuracy. The law, in short, must be seen as a creative process and the rules of judicial notice recast to expedite this creativity.[20]

In *R. v. Zundel*, Zundel was charged with the *Criminal Code* offence of spreading false news in his denial of the Holocaust. One of his publications was entitled "Did Six Million Jews Really Die?" He was convicted. On his appeal an issue was whether the trial judge had erred in not taking judicial notice of the Holocaust. The Court of Appeal responded as follows:[21]

> It is well established that the court may take judicial notice of an historical fact. The court may, on its own initiative, consult historical works or documents, or the court may be referred to them: see *Read v. Lincoln (Bishop)*, [1892] A.C. 644 (P.C.); *R. v. Bartleman*, 55 B.C.L.R. 78, [1984] 3 C.N.L.R. 114, 13 C.C.C. (3d) 488 at 491-92, 12 D.L.R. (4th) 73 (C.A.). The court may even hear sworn testimony before judicial notice is taken: see *McQuaker v. Goddard*, [1940] 1 K.B. 687, [1940] 1 All E.R. 471 (C.A.).
>
> As Professor Cross points out, the distinction between the process of taking judicial notice and the reception of evidence begins to fade when the judge makes inquiries before deciding to take judicial notice of a matter. He points out

---

the judge reads a pleading or listens to a witness testify, he cannot know the meaning of the words used except through extra-record information, and apart from the meaning of words, he cannot understand the significance of the ideas expressed unless he uses his general background of knowledge — knowledge that cannot conceivably be captured and penned up within the pages of a formal record. As judges go about their workaday tasks, they assume facts all along the line without either thinking or speaking in terms of judicial notice. They assume facts without mentioning that they do so, and when they mention that they do so, they are more likely to say that they "assume" the facts than that they "take judicial notice" of them. Nothing hinges — and nothing should hinge — on the form of words that happen to be used. Compare Carter, "Do Courts Decide According to the Evidence?" (1988) 22 U.B.C. L. Rev. 51 at 363: When assessing any evidence given in court, the trier of fact must obviously draw upon a vast mass of previously acquired factual information, knowledge and experience. The use of the terminology of judicial notice to describe this may be confusing. This is not a question of judicial notice, but of the tribunal relying on its own experience as to the ordinary course of human affairs.

[19] Davis, *Administrative Law*, 3rd ed. (1972) at 314.
[20] Roberts, *supra* note 15 at 233.
[21] (1987), 56 C.R. (3d) 1 at 56.

that if learned treatises are consulted it is not easy to say whether evidence is being received under an exception to the hearsay rule or whether the judge is equipping himself to take judicial notice. The resemblance of taking judicial notice to the reception of evidence is even more marked when sworn testimony is heard before judicial notice is taken. He concludes, however, that, even where the processes of taking judicial notice and receiving evidence approximate most closely, they are essentially different: see Cross on Evidence, pp. 67-68. The essential difference is that, when the judge is equipping himself to take judicial notice, the hearsay rule does not apply.

The Court recognized that it was fitting and proper to judicially notice historical facts. The Court in *Zundel* recognized that the fact of the Holocaust was generally known and accepted and that the trial judge would be entitled, therefore, to judicially notice it. The Court decided, however, that judicial notice was a discretionary matter and that the trial judge was right to refuse the Crown's application for judicial notice and to insist that the Crown prove it. The Court exhibited concern that judicially noticing that the Holocaust occurred would be "gravely prejudicial" to the accused's defence. Ask yourself whether it is proper to refuse to judicially notice that which is generally known and accepted. **Should the accused be provided an opportunity to try to prove, in a courtroom, the opposite of what everyone knows, and accepts as true?** Professor Thayer had written: "Courts may judicially notice much which they cannot be required to notice." The Court relied on this sentence for saying that a judge had a discretion whether or not to judicially notice. But Thayer was saying that besides noticing things that they were required to notice, things which were indisputable, judges could also judicially notice other things. He never said that a judge could refuse to notice things that were indisputable! The Court repeated this "error" when sitting on appeal from the second *Zundel* trial: *R. v. Zundel* (1990), 53 C.C.C. (3d) 161 (Ont. C.A.).

Professor Davis drew a distinction between judicially noticing adjudicative facts and legislative facts. He wrote:

> When a court or an agency finds facts concerning the immediate parties — who did what, where, when, how, and with what motive or intent — the court or agency is performing an adjudicative function, and the facts so determined are conveniently called adjudicative facts. When a court or an agency develops law or policy, it is acting legislatively; the courts have created the common law through judicial legislation, and the facts which inform the tribunal's legislative judgment are called legislative facts.[22]

These legislative facts, by their nature, are generally known or discovered by the judge from sources outside the formal proof offered by the parties. Unlike adjudicative facts they can seldom be indisputable and knowledge of them is more properly labelled belief:

---

[22] Davis, "Judicial Notice", *supra* note 18. The distinction was coined in an earlier article: Davis, "An Approach to Problems of Evidence in the Administrative Process" (1942) 55 Harv. L. Rev. 364.

> The bulk of social science probably cannot be called "clearly indisputable". Even though anyone would prefer to found lawmaking upon clearly indisputable facts, the practical choice is often between proceeding in ignorance and following the uncertain, tentative, and far from indisputable searchings of social science such as they are, for the simple reason that clearly indisputable facts are unavailable.[23]

These legislative facts are necessary, however, to an informed policy choice between competing rules or interpretations and also decisions on constitutional validity. Judge Weinstein explains why consultation with the parties concerning notice of legislative fact is appropriate:

> In taking judicial notice of legislative facts, courts frequently take cognizance of matter which is neither indisputable nor easily verifiable. . . Is such power compatible with our adversary system, which presupposes that disputed facts must be brought into the open, subject to cross-examination? . . . Legislative facts . . . relate to substantive law, and if the judge is to exercise the function of shaping the law he must have discretion to consider those factors essential to the process. Limitations in the form of indisputability or rigid and formal requirements of notice are inappropriate. . . Once the court decides to advise itself in order to make new law, it ought not to add to the risk of a poor decision by denying itself whatever help on the facts it can with propriety obtain. Informal consultation with the parties enables the court to enlist their aid in obtaining further information, guarantees that differing points of view will be consulted, and is especially appropriate in those cases where the facts the judge is noticing may have adjudicative as well as legislative implications.[24]

With the advent of the *Charter of Rights* and the new task of determining the constitutional validity of legislation, the courts are, of necessity, called on to judicially notice legislative facts. For example, in *R. v. Oakes*[25] the government had the task of justifying a violation of a constitutional right under s. 1: to establish that the violation of the accused's right to be presumed innocent was justified as a reasonable limit in a free and democratic society. In that case, the Court noted:

> Where evidence is required in order to prove the constituent elements of a s. 1 inquiry, *and this will generally be the case*, it should be cogent and persuasive and make clear to the court the consequences of imposing or not imposing the limit. [Emphasis added.][26]

Nevertheless, the Court, in deciding that the legislative objective was of sufficient importance to warrant overriding a constitutionally protected right, relied on all manner of material to inform itself regarding the legislative facts. The Court noted:

---

[23]   Davis, *A System of Judicial Notice Based on Fairness and Convenience, supra* note 18 at 69, 87, quoted in Weinstein's *Evidence* at 200-216.
[24]   Weinstein's *Evidence* at 200-217.
[25]   (1986), 50 C.R. (3d) 1 (S.C.C.).
[26]   *Ibid.* at 29-30.

In my opinion, Parliament's concern that drug trafficking be decreased can be characterized as substantial and pressing. The problem of drug trafficking has been increasing since the 1950s, at which time there was already considerable concern: see Report of the Special Committee on Traffic in Narcotic Drugs, Appendix to Debates of the Senate of Canada, session of 1955, pp. 690-700; see also Final Report, Commission of Inquiry into the Non-Medical Use of Drugs (Ottawa, 1973). Throughout this period, numerous measures were adopted by free and democratic societies, at both the international and national levels.

At the international level, on 23rd June 1953, the Protocol for Limiting and Regulating the Cultivation of the Poppy Plant, the Production of, International and Wholesale Trade in, and Use of Opium, to which Canada is a signatory, was adopted by the United Nations Opium Conference held in New York. The Single Convention on Narcotic Drugs (1961), was acceded to in New York on 30th March 1961. This treaty was signed by Canada on 30th March 1961. It entered into force on 13th December 1964. As stated in the preamble, "addiction to narcotic drugs constitutes a serious evil for the individual and is fraught with social and economic danger to mankind".

At the national level, statutory provisions have been enacted by numerous countries which, inter alia, attempt to deter drug trafficking by imposing criminal sanctions: see, for example, Misuse of Drugs Act, 1975 (New Zealand), no. 116; Misuse of Drugs Act, 1971 (Eng.), c. 38.

The objective of protecting our society from the grave ills associated with drug trafficking is, in my view, one of sufficient importance to warrant overriding a constitutionally-protected right or freedom in certain cases. Moreover, the degree of seriousness of drug trafficking makes its acknowledgement as a sufficiently important objective for the purposes of s. 1 to a large extent self-evident. The first criterion of a s. 1 inquiry, therefore, has been satisfied by the Crown.[27]

Judicial notice of social facts or social context evidence has also arisen in cases attempting to address inequality or gender bias.

R. v. LAVALLEE
[1990] 1 S.C.R. 852, 76 C.R. (3d) 329, 55 C.C.C. (3d) 97

The accused, a battered woman in a volatile common-law relationship, killed her partner, Rust, late one night by shooting him in the back of the head as he left her room. The shooting occurred after an argument where the accused had been physically abused. She was fearful for her life after being taunted with the threat that either she kill him or he would get her. She had frequently been a victim of his physical abuse and had concocted excuses to explain her injuries to medical staff on those occasions. A psychiatrist with extensive professional experience in the treatment of battered wives prepared a psychiatric assessment of the appellant which was used in support of her defence of self-defence. The jury acquitted the accused but its

---

[27] *Ibid.* at 31-32. See also *R. v. Clayton*, [2007] 2 S.C.R. 725; *R. v. Edwards Books & Art Ltd.*, [1986] 2 S.C.R. 713; *R. v. Thomsen* (1988), 63 C.R. (3d) 1 (S.C.C.); and *R. v. Hufsky* (1988), 63 C.R. (3d) 14 (S.C.C.). And see generally Maybank, "Proof of Facts Under S. 1 of the *Charter*" (1990), 77 C.R. (3d) 260; and Morgan, "Proof of Facts in *Charter* Litigation" in Sharpe, ed., *Charter Litigation* (1987). See also McEachern, "*Viva Voce* Evidence in *Charter* Cases" (1989) 23 U.B.C. L. Rev. 591.

verdict was overturned by a majority of the Manitoba Court of Appeal. The Supreme Court allowed the accused's appeal deciding that the expert's opinion was admissible as relevant to her claim of self-defence.

Notice the Court's reasoning. Notice how it judicially notices legislative facts; how it decides; how it reforms the law to fit society's attitude. Notice the literature relied on which was not proved in evidence.

WILSON J. (DICKSON C.J.C and LAMER, L'HEUREUX-DUBÉ, GONTHIER and CORY JJ. concurring):—

. . .

The gravity, indeed, the tragedy of domestic violence can hardly be overstated. Greater media attention to this phenomenon in recent years has revealed both its prevalence and its horrific impact on women from all walks of life. Far from protecting women from it, the law historically sanctioned the abuse of women within marriage as an aspect of the husband's ownership of his wife and his "right" to chastise her. One need only recall the centuries old law that a man is entitled to beat his wife with a stick "no thicker than his thumb".

Laws do not spring out of a social vacuum. The notion that a man has a right to "discipline" his wife is deeply rooted in the history of our society. The woman's duty was to serve her husband and to stay in the marriage at all costs "till death do us part" and to accept as her due any "punishment" that was meted out for failing to please her husband. One consequence of this attitude was that "wife battering" was rarely spoken of, rarely reported, rarely prosecuted, and even more rarely punished. Long after society abandoned its formal approval of spousal abuse, tolerance of it continued and continues in some circles to this day.

Fortunately, there has been a growing awareness in recent years that no man has a right to abuse any woman under any circumstances. Legislative initiatives designed to educate police, judicial officers and the public, as well as more aggressive investigation and charging policies all signal a concerted effort by the criminal justice system to take spousal abuse seriously. However, a woman who comes before a judge or jury with the claim that she has been battered and suggests that this may be a relevant factor in evaluating her subsequent actions still faces the prospect of being condemned by popular mythology about domestic violence. Either she was not as badly beaten as she claims or she would have left the man long ago. Or, if she was battered that severely, she must have stayed out of some masochistic enjoyment of it.

. . .

. . . Was the appellant "under reasonable apprehension of death or grievous bodily harm" from Rust as he was walking out of the room? The second is the assessment in s. 34(2)(b) of the magnitude of the force used by the accused. Was the accused's belief that she could not "otherwise preserve herself from death or grievous bodily harm" except by shooting the deceased based "on reasonable grounds"?

. . .

If it strains credulity to imagine what the "ordinary man" would do in the position of a battered spouse, it is probably because men do not typically find themselves in that situation. Some women do, however. The definition of what is reasonable must be adapted to circumstances which are, by and large, foreign to the world inhabited by the hypothetical "reasonable man".

. . .

The cycle described by Dr. Shane conforms to the Walker Cycle Theory of Violence named for clinical psychologist Dr. Lenore Walker, the pioneer researcher in the field of the battered wife syndrome. Dr. Shane acknowledged his debt to Dr. Walker in the course of establishing his credentials as an expert at trial. Dr. Walker first describes the cycle in the book The Battered Woman, (1979). In her 1984 book, The Battered Woman Syndrome, Dr. Walker reports the results of a study involving 400 battered women. Her research was designed to test empirically the theories expounded in her earlier book. At pp. 95-96 of The Battered Woman Syndrome she summarizes the Cycle Theory as follows:

[There follows a lengthy extract from the book.]

Dr. Walker defines a battered woman as a woman who has gone through the battering cycle at least twice. As she explains in her introduction to The Battered Woman, at p. xv, "Any woman may find herself in an abusive relationship with a man once. If it occurs a second time, and she remains in the situation, she is defined as a battered woman."

. . .

Another aspect of the cyclical nature of the abuse is that it begets a degree of predictability to the violence that is absent in an isolated violent enounter between two strangers. This also means that it may in fact be possible for a battered spouse to accurately predict the onset of violence before the first blow is struck, even if an outsider to the relationship cannot. Indeed, it has been suggested that a battered woman's knowledge of her partner's violence is so heightened that she is able to anticipate the nature and extent (though not the onset) of the violence by his conduct beforehand. In her article "Potential Uses for Expert Testimony: Ideas Toward the Representation of Battered Women Who Kill" (1986), 9 Women's Rights Law Reporter 227, psychologist Julie Blackman describes this characteristic, at p. 229:

[Another lengthy quote.]

. . . The requirement imposed in *Whynot* that a battered woman wait until the physical assault is "underway" before her apprehensions can be validated in law would, in the words of an American court, be tantamount to sentencing her to "murder by instalment": *State v. Gallegos*, 719 P.2d 1268 (N.M. 1986), at p. 1271. I share the view expressed by Willoughby in "Rendering Each Woman Her Due: Can a Battered Woman Claim Self-Defense When She Kills Her Sleeping Batterer" (1989), 38 Kan. L. Rev. 169, at p. 184, that "society gains nothing, except perhaps the additional risk that the battered woman will herself be killed, because she must wait until her abusive husband instigates another battering episode before she can justifiably act".

. . .

R. v. MALOTT
[1998] 1 S.C.R. 123, 12 C.R. (5th) 207, 121 C.C.C. (3d) 456

The accused was charged with murder. The accused and the deceased had lived as common-law spouses for almost 20 years. The deceased abused the accused physically, sexually, psychologically and emotionally. The jury found the accused guilty of second degree murder in the death of the deceased and of the attempted murder of his girlfriend. A majority of the Court of Appeal affirmed the convictions. The accused appealed, complaining about the adequacy of the trial judge's charge to the jury on the murder charge with regard to the issue of battered woman syndrome as a defence. The appeal was dismissed. Concurring in the result, Justice L'Heureux-Dubé, McLachlin J. concurring, noted that concerns had been expressed that the treatment of expert evidence on battered woman syndrome, admissible in order to combat the myths and stereotypes which society has about battered women, had led to a new stereotype of the battered woman.

L'HEUREUX-DUBÉ J. (MCLACHLIN J. concurring):— I have read the reasons of my colleague Justice Major, and I concur with the result that he reaches. However, given that this Court has not had the opportunity to discuss the value of evidence of "battered woman syndrome" since *R. v. Lavallee*, [1990] 1 S.C.R. 852, and given the evolving discourse on "battered woman syndrome" in the legal community, I will make a few comments on the importance of this kind of evidence to the just adjudication of charges involving battered women.

. . .

. . . Concerns have been expressed that the treatment of expert evidence on battered women syndrome, which is itself admissible in order to combat the myths and stereotypes which society has about battered women, has led to a new stereotype of the "battered woman": see, e.g., Martha Shaffer, "The battered woman syndrome revisited: Some complicating thoughts five years after *R. v. Lavallee*" (1997), 47 *U.T.L.J.* 1, at p. 9; Sheila Noonan, "Strategies of Survival: Moving Beyond the Battered Woman Syndrome", in Ellen Adelberg and Claudia Currie, eds., *In Conflict with the Law: Women and the Canadian Justice System* (1993), 247, at p. 254; Isabel Grant, "The 'syndromization' of women's experience", in Donna Martinson et al., "A Forum on *Lavallee v. R.*: Women and Self-Defence" (1991), 25 *U.B.C. L. Rev.* 23, 51, at pp. 53-54; and Martha R. Mahoney, "Legal Images of Battered Women: Redefining the Issue of Separation" (1991), 90 *Mich. L. Rev.* 1, at p. 42.

It is possible that those women who are unable to fit themselves within the stereotype of a victimized, passive, helpless, dependent, battered woman will not have their claims to self-defence fairly decided. For instance, women who have demonstrated too much strength or initiative, women of colour, women who are professionals, or women who might have fought back against their abusers on previous occasions, should not be penalized for failing to accord with the stereotypical image of the archetypal battered woman. See, e.g., Julie Stubbs and Julia Tolmie, "Race, Gender, and the Battered Woman Syndrome: An Australia Case Study" (1995), 8 *C.J.W.L.* 122. Needless to say, women with these characteristics are still entitled to have their claims of self-defence fairly adjudicated, and they are also still entitled to have their experiences as battered women inform the analysis. Professor Grant, *supra*, at p. 52, warns against allowing the law to develop such that a woman accused of killing her abuser must either have been "reasonable 'like a man' or reasonable 'like a battered woman'". I agree that this must be avoided. The "reasonable woman" must not be forgotten in the analysis, and deserves to be as much a part of the objective standard of the reasonable person as does the "reasonable man".

How should the courts combat the "syndromization", as Professor Grant refers to it, of battered women who act in self-defence? The legal inquiry into the moral culpability of a woman who is, for instance, claiming self-defence must focus on the *reasonableness* of her actions in the context of her personal experiences, and her experiences as a woman, not on her status as a battered woman and her entitlement to claim that she is suffering from "battered woman syndrome". This point has been made convincingly by many academics reviewing the relevant cases: see, e.g., Wendy Chan, "A Feminist Critique of Self-Defense and Provocation in Battered Women's Cases in England and Wales" (1994), 6 *Women & Crim. Just.* 39, at pp. 56-57; Elizabeth M. Schneider, "Describing and Changing: Women's Self-Defense Work and the Problem of Expert Testimony on Battering" (1992), 14 *Women's Rts. L. Rep.* 213, at pp. 216-17; and Marilyn MacCrimmon, "The social construction of reality and the rules of evidence", in Donna Martinson et al., *supra,* 36, at pp. 48-49. By emphasizing a woman's "learned helplessness", her dependence, her victimization, and her low self-esteem, in order to establish that she suffers from "battered woman syndrome", the legal debate shifts from the objective rationality of her actions to preserve her own life to those personal inadequacies which apparently explain her failure to flee from her abuser. Such an emphasis comports too well with society's stereotypes about women. Therefore, it should be scrupulously avoided because it only serves to undermine the important advancements achieved by the decision in Lavallee.

. . .

My focus on women as the victims of battering and as the subjects of "battered woman syndrome" is not intended to exclude from consideration those men who find themselves in abusive relationships. However, the reality of our society is that typically, it is women who are the victims of domestic violence, at the hands of their male intimate partners. To assume that men who are victims of spousal abuse are affected by the abuse in the same way, without benefit of the research and expert opinion evidence which has informed the courts of the existence and details of "battered woman syndrome", would be imprudent.

Alan Gold, in response to *Malott*,[28] highlights an article by Faigman and Wright, "The Battered Woman Syndrome in the Age of Science".[29] The article begins with a scathing denunciation of Lenore Walker's book, *The Battered Woman* (New York: Harper Collins, 1980), which figured so prominently in Justice Wilson's judgment in *R. v. Lavallee:*

> The battered woman syndrome illustrates all that is wrong with the law's use of science. The working hypothesis of the battered woman syndrome was first introduced in Lenore Walker's 1979 book, *The Battered Woman*. When it made its debut, this hypothesis had little more to support it beyond the clinical impressions of a single researcher. Five years later, Walker published a second book that promised a more thorough investigation of the hypothesis. However, this book contains little more than a patchwork of pseudo-scientific methods employed to confirm a hypothesis that its author and participating researchers never seriously doubted. Indeed, the 1984 book would provide an excellent case study for psychology graduate students on how not to conduct empirical research. Yet, largely based upon the same political ideology driving the researchers, judges have welcomed the battered woman syndrome into their courts. Because the law is driven by precedent, it quickly petrified around the original conception of the defense. Increasingly, observers are realizing that the evidence purportedly supporting the battered woman syndrome is without empirical foundation, and, perhaps more troubling, that the syndrome itself is inimical to the political ideology originally supporting it. In short, in the law's hasty effort to use science to further good policy, it is now obvious that the battered woman syndrome is not good science nor does it generate good policy.

In *Lavallee*, the Court announced a major change in the law. It was informed partly by the expert opinion given at the trial, but also by books and articles which the Court read for itself. The Court judicially noticed legislative facts outlined in Lenore Walker's books, and formed the law to fit the Court's view of society's present attitude. But the literature, before and after *Lavallee*, is replete with research disagreeing with Walker's description of battered woman syndrome, which description was adopted in *Lavallee*. Some are mentioned in Justice L'Heureux-Dubé's opinion in *Malott*. For citations to literature disagreeing with the Court's description of battered woman syndrome, see Fischer, Vidmar & Ellis, "The Culture of Battering and the Role of Mediation in Domestic Violence Cases".[30]

It is a welcome advance that the Court in *Malott*, or at least two members of the Court, were prepared to admit that the Court's reliance on the battered woman syndrome was in error and too restrictive for developing appropriate sensitivity to the situation of the abused partner. Justice L'Heureux-Dubé in *Malott* speaks of courts having been informed by expert opinion evidence. In truth the Supreme Court frequently informs itself through its own research, judicially noticing facts found in the literature, and not by expert witnesses. Using expert witnesses has the advantage that their opinions can be challenged by cross-examination and by competing experts and a truer

---

[28]   ADGN/98-075 (QUICKLAW database Gold).
[29]   (1997) 39 Ariz. L. Rev. 67.
[30]   (1993) 46 S.M.U. L. Rev. 2117.

picture will then emerge. Also it would be fairer to the parties. To use *Lavallee* as but one example, the Court would have been better off, before issuing its opinion, had it advised counsel that it was about to rely on this book by Lenore Walker so that the parties might have had the opportunity to inform the Court of other sources. When the courts decide to use science to inform the law they will be better informed if the parties are engaged. The joint endeavour will improve the court's ability to recognize junk science when it comes across it.

MOGE v. MOGE
[1992] 3 S.C.R. 813

The parties were married in the mid-1950s in Poland and moved to Canada in 1960. They separated in 1973 and divorced in 1980. The wife had a grade seven education and no special skills or training. During the marriage, she cared for the house and their three children and, except for a brief period, also worked six hours per day in the evenings cleaning offices. After the separation, she was awarded custody of the children and received $150 per month spousal and child support and continued to work cleaning offices. The husband remarried in 1984 and continued to pay support to his former wife. She was laid off in 1987 and, as a result of an application to vary, her spousal and child support was increased to $400. She was later able to secure part-time and intermittent cleaning work. In 1989, the husband was granted an order terminating support. The trial judge found that the former wife had had time to become financially independent and that her husband had supported her as long as he could be required to do. The Court of Appeal set aside the judgment and ordered spousal support in the amount of $150 per month for an indefinite period. The appeal to the Supreme Court of Canada was then to determine whether the wife was entitled to ongoing support for an indefinite period of time or whether spousal support should be terminated. The Court decided to reverse a series of cases that had been based on a self-suffiency model of spousal support. Justice L'Heureux-Dubé noted the heavy costs that would be involved if expert evidence was necessary and decided the answer lay in judicial notice. She was influenced by a number of writings.

L'HEUREUX-DUBÉ J. (LA FOREST, GONTHIER, CORY and IACOBUCCI JJ. concurring):—

. . .

In Canada, the feminization of poverty is an entrenched social phenomenon. Between 1971 and 1986 the percentage of poor women found among all women in this country more than doubled. During the same period the percentage of poor among all men climbed by 24 percent. The results were such that by 1986, 16 percent of all women in this country were considered poor: M. Gunderson, L. Muszynski and J. Keck, *Women and Labour Market Poverty* (1990), at p. 8.

Given the multiplicity of economic barriers women face in society, decline into poverty cannot be attributed entirely to the financial burdens arising from the dissolution of marriage: J.D. Payne, "The Dichotomy between Family Law and Family Crises on Marriage Breakdown" (1989), 20 *R.G.D.* 109, at pp. 116-17. However, there is no doubt that divorce and its economic effects are playing a role. Several years ago, L.J. Weitzman released her landmark study on divorce, The Divorce Revolution: The Unexpected Social and Economic Consequences for Women and Children in America (1985), and concluded at p. 323:

> On a societal level, divorce increases female and child poverty and creates an ever-widening gap between the economic well-being of divorced men, on the one hand, and their children and former wives on the other.
>
> . . .

One proposal put forth by Professor Rogerson would be for Parliament to consider enacting a set of legislative guidelines. . .

One possible disadvantage of such a solution lies in the risk that it may impose a strait-jacket which precludes the accommodation of the many economic variables susceptible to be encountered in spousal support litigation.

Another alternative might lie in the doctrine of judicial notice. The doctrine itself grew from a need to promote efficiency in the litigation process and may very well be applicable to spousal support. One classic statement of the content and purpose of the doctrine is outlined in *Varcoe v. Lee*, 181 P. 223 (Cal. 1919), at p. 226:

> The three requirements . . . — that the matter be one of common and general knowledge, that it be well established and authoritatively settled, be practically indisputable, and that this common, general, and certain knowledge exist in the particular jurisdiction — all are requirements dictated by the reason and purpose of the rule, which is to obviate the formal necessity for proof when the matter does not require proof.

As E.M. Morgan noted in "Judicial Notice" (1944), 57 Harv. L. Rev. 269, at p. 272:

> . . . the judge . . . must be assumed to have a fund of general information, consisting of both generalized capacity to relate it to what he has perceived during the proceeding, as well as the ability to draw reasonable deductions from the combination by using the ordinary processes of thought. That fund of general information must be at least as great as that of all reasonably well-informed persons in the community. He cannot be assumed to be ignorant of what is so generally accepted as to be incapable of dispute among reasonable men.
>
> . . .

Based upon the studies which I have cited earlier in these reasons, the general economic impact of divorce on women is a phenomenon the existence of which cannot reasonably be questioned and should be amenable to judicial notice. More extensive social science data are also appearing. Such studies are beginning to provide reasonable assessments of some of the disadvantages incurred and advantages conferred post-divorce. . . While quantification will remain difficult and fact related in each particular case, judicial notice should be taken of such studies, subject to other expert evidence which may bear on them, as background information at the very least. . .

In all events, whether judicial notice of the circumstances generally encountered by spouses at the dissolution of a marriage is to be a formal part of the trial process or whether such circumstances merely provide the necessary background information, it is important that judges be aware of the social reality in which support decisions are experienced when engaging in the examination of the objectives of the Act.

In an article written by L'Heureux-Dubé which had justified her decision in *Moge v. Moge,* Justice L'Heureux-Dubé discussed the propriety of bringing social reality into the courtroom by way of judicial notice and concluded:

> Judicial notice of evidence of a general character has the potential to simplify the judges' task of assessing the true consequences flowing from the relationship and its breakup and of formulating a more accurate picture of the realistic needs of the parties, particularly when self-sufficiency, market conditions and real estate situations are at issue. It promotes judicial awareness of the context in which support awards are experienced, rather than merely contemplated.

> Though judicial notice as a proper device in family law is not new, its use appears to have escalated since it received the Court's blessing in *Moge.* It has been taken of many different facts in Canadian matrimonial cases. A recent article itemizes fifty- nine cases where judicial notice was taken in Canadian family law cases on subjects such as the following: the employment market for women; the impairment of the economic ability of a woman at the end of a relationship; the increase in the cost of raising children as they grow older; the effects of inflation on the parties; the tax implications to the parties; changes in the value of property, including changes in the real estate market; and the costs of disposition of property. *Moge* has acknowledged that as much as laws are not enacted in a Judicial vacuum, judicial decisions should not be made in isolation, particularly of the socio-economic research and data of the time. It is now up to courts in support and custody disputes to take the baton and run with it.

> Judicial notice of the general economic impact of divorce on women and children and of studies providing social science data on related matters also serves important ends of judicial efficiency. Specifically, it helps to moderate the high cost of family law litigation by reducing the need for experts, and frees for more important matters court time that would otherwise be required in order to deal with evidence on socio-economic context. Moreover, it reduces the burden on many spouses (most often women) who do not have the resources necessary to bring to the court's attention the studies and expert evidence which might demonstrate such context. In other cases, the small sums involved simply would not justify the expenditure of such resources. Finally, requiring that such facts be proven in each individual case would undoubtedly spawn needless duplication. The value of judicial notice, responsibly exercised, as a practical and economic measure to increase judicial consciousness on the social realities of support should therefore not be underestimated.

> In parting, it should be evident that I do not mean to suggest that judicial notice can take the place of effective counsel and situation-specific evidence. It cannot. Moreover, whenever possible, I think that, participation of counsel in determinations of what is to be noticed judicially should be encouraged. I do think it

important to emphasize, however, that courts should be willing to join hands with the legislature in promoting family law legislation that truly and effectively addresses the needs and concerns of those individuals falling within its ambit. By recognizing that exclusive reliance on the adversarial framework, and all of its accompanying legal baggage, may not be the best means by which to address family law concerns, we open the door for more innovative and co-operative solutions that should ultimately improve both the interpretation and application of family law in Canada.[31]

But not all agree! *Willick v. Willick*[32] was concerned with an application to vary the amount of child support which had been set in a separation agreement later incorporated into a divorce judgment. The Court was unanimous that the conditions necessary for a variation had been satisfied. There was a difference of opinion regarding the propriety of judicial notice. Justice Sopinka, La Forest, Cory and Iacobucci JJ. concurring, decided that he was able to arrive at the same result as Justice L'Heureux-Dubé on the basis of the rules of statutory construction as to the proper statutory interpretation of s. 17(4) of the *Divorce Act*, without resort to extensive extrinsic materials. He wrote:

A contextual approach to the interpretation of the statutory provisions is appropriate but does not require an examination of the broad policy grounds to which my colleague refers. Following that course would require us to resolve the thorny question of the use of extraneous materials such as studies, opinions and reports and whether it is appropriate to take judicial notice of them and what notice to counsel, if any, is required. We would also have to consider the extent to which our approach is different in a case such as this from a constitutional case in which wider latitude is allowed.

Justice L'Heureux-Dubé, Gonthier and McLachlin JJ. concurring, wrote:

Social science research and socio-economic data are longstanding judicial tools in both Canada and the United States. The judiciary's long-recognized function as a policy finder sometimes compels it to consider social authority even when the parties do not, themselves, present relevant evidence on relevant questions of public policy. In the course of Charter interpretations, this Court has often taken judicial notice of reliable social research and socio-economic data in order to assist its contextual s. 1 analysis of a rights violation. Social authority can be an indispensable element to this approach and this Court has accepted its value in non-constitutional contexts which nonetheless raise broad questions of public policy. See *R. v. Lavallee.*

Justice L'Heureux-Dubé then went on to consider a variety of studies.

A trial judge, Judge Williams, was critical of Justice L'Heureux-Dubé's willingness to use judicial notice without informing the parties and seeking their involvement.[33] Justice L'Heureux-Dubé responded and maintained her position:

---

[31] L'Heureux-Dubé, "Re-examining the Doctrine of Judicial Notice in the Family Law Context" (1994) 26 Ottawa L. Rev. 551.
[32] [1994] 3 S.C.R. 670.
[33] Williams, "Grasping a Thorny Baton" (1996) 14 C.F.L.Q. 179.

In his view, judicial notice of social framework evidence should not be undertaken without providing the parties with the opportunity to make submissions at trial on this evidence or other evidence which refutes it. I, on the other hand, believe that, while desirable in certain cases, strict procedural requirements applied uniformly to all cases may too readily ignore the very reasons for which judicial notice is both needed and appropriate in the family law context. I have already underlined the significance of cost and the unfairly onerous burden a lengthy trial may place on the spouse with more limited resources. I have also demonstrated the need for tempering the adversarial process in family law matters.[34]

On this view, tempering the adversarial process with liberal use of judicial notice can advance access to justice. Similar arguments were considered in the following influential American case.

ROWE v. GIBSON
798 F.3d 622 (U.S. C.A. 7th Cir., 2015)

The plaintiff Rowe, an Indiana prison inmate, claimed that the prison administrators and medical staff had violated his civil rights by acting with deliberate indifference to his serious medical needs. Such indifference can amount to cruel and unusual punishment under the United States Constitution. The district judge granted summary judgment in favour of the defendants and dismissed Rowe's suit. The plaintiff appealed and the Seventh Circuit Court of Appeals reversed the district court's ruling.

POSNER, *Circuit Judge* (for the majority):

In 2009, already an inmate at Pendleton, Rowe was diagnosed with reflux esophagitis, also known as gastroesophageal reflux disease (GERD). See National Institutes of Health, "Gastroesophageal reflux disease," www.nlm.nih.gov/medlineplus/ency/article/000265.htm (visited August 17, 2015, as were the other websites cited in this opinion). The Mayo Clinic explains that "a valve-like structure called the lower esophageal sphincter usually keeps the acidic contents of the stomach out of the esophagus. If this valve opens when it shouldn't or doesn't close properly, the contents of the stomach may back up into the esophagus (gastroesophageal reflux).... [GERD] is a condition in which this backflow of acid is a frequent or ongoing problem. A complication of GERD is chronic inflammation and tissue damage in the esophagus." *Mayo Clinic*, "Diseases and Conditions, Esophagitis: Reflux Esophagitis," www.mayoclinic.org/diseasesconditions/esophagitis/basics/causes/con-20034313.... Rowe complains of pain based on neglect of his need for symptomatic relief; continued neglect will endanger him more profoundly.

The prison physician who diagnosed Rowe with GERD told him to take a 150-milligram Zantac pill twice a day. . . .

---

[34]   L'Heureux-Dubé, "Making Equality Work in Family Law" (1997) 14 Can. J. Fam. Law 103 at 119.

After the diagnosis Rowe was given Zantac pills and was permitted to keep them in his cell and take them when he felt the need to. This regimen continued for more than a year. But in January 2011 his pills were confiscated and he was told that he would be allowed to take a Zantac pill only when a prison nurse gave it to him, and that would be at 9:30 a.m. and then at 9:30 p.m. He complained that he needed to take Zantac with his meals, which were, oddly enough, scheduled by the prison for 4 a.m. and 4 p.m. (why these times, we are not told). The prison had decided that inmates such as Rowe who take psychiatric medications should not be allowed to keep any pills in their cells — yet the head of health care at the prison told Rowe that he could keep in his cell (and thus take whenever he wanted) any Zantac pills that he bought at the prison commissary — which, however, as we're about to see, he couldn't afford. No reason has been articulated for forbidding him to keep Zantac given him by prison staff while permitting him to keep Zantac that he bought at the commissary and take it whenever he needs to in order to prevent or alleviate pain. There is no suggestion that Zantac is a narcotic or otherwise consumed for nonmedical as well as medical reasons.

. . .

To continue the narrative of what seems a senseless series of decisions by the prison's medical staff, as well as heartless given what the staff knew about the disease and Rowe's continuous claims of severe pain: at the beginning of July 2011, a month after he filed suit, he ceased receiving Zantac because his "prescription" (that is, his authorization to receive over-the-counter Zantac free of charge on a continuing basis) had lapsed. He made a series of requests for the drug beginning on July 3, but the nurse defendants denied all of them because he had no prescription. When he complained he was told by the administrative director of the medical staff: "Your chronic care condition does not warrant the continued use of Zantac. The continual use of over-the-counter medications can create further health problems in many instances. You will have to purchase this off of commissary if you wish to continue taking it.". . .

On July 13, 2011, in response to Rowe's continued requests for a renewed prescription for Zantac, a physician who works at the prison . . . named William H. Wolfe, whose professional specialty is preventive medicine . . ., and who is a frequent defendant in prisoner civil rights suits, reviewed Rowe's medical records and opined that his condition didn't require Zantac at all — this despite the fact that Rowe had been continuously prescribed Zantac for almost two years and that Wolfe himself had been the prescribing doctor for a quarter of that period. But though initially refusing to provide a new prescription for Zantac, Wolfe later relented and on August 2 prescribed it though he later stated in an affidavit that he had done so as a "courtesy" to Rowe and not out of medical necessity. (Prescribing drugs for prison inmates as a "courtesy" seems very odd; it is not explained.) The upshot was that Rowe had no access to Zantac for more than a month (between July 1 and August 3) — a significant deprivation. Even after Zantac was restored to him, he continued to be allowed to take it only at 9:30 a.m. and 9:30 p.m., both times being many hours distant from his meals.

In another affidavit Wolfe stated that "it does not matter what time of day Mr. Rowe receives his Zantac prescription. Each Zantac pill is fully effective for twelve hour increments. Zantac does not have to be taken before or with a meal to be effective." However, according to Boehringer Ingelheim, the manufacturer of over-the-counter Zantac, while Zantac can be taken at any time "to relieve symptoms," in order "to prevent symptoms" it should be taken "30 to 60 minutes before eating food or drinking beverages that cause heartburn." *Zantac*, "Maximum Strength Zantac 150," www.zantacotc.com/zantac-maximumstrength.html# faqs, and this advice is repeated on the labels of the boxes in which over-the-counter Zantac is sold. Were Zantac equipotent whenever taken, the manufacturer would not tell consumers to take it 30 to 60 minutes before eating, for having to remember when to take a pill adds a complication that the consumer would rather do without. There is thus no reason for the manufacturer to be lying, and it would be absurd to think that Dr. Wolfe, a defendant who is not a gastroenterologist, knows more about treatment of esophagitis with Zantac than the manufacturer does.

. . .

The evidence that Rowe was in pain for five and a half hours after eating is his repeated attestation — in his verified federal complaint and his declarations — that he experienced pain for that length of time when he was not allowed to take Zantac with or shortly before his meals. For purposes of summary judgment his attestations of extreme pain must be credited. See 28 U.S.C. § 1746; Fed.R.Civ.P. 56(c). There was no plausible contrary evidence. The affidavits of the only expert witness on the proper times at which to take Zantac, defendants' witness Wolfe, were highly vulnerable. Wolfe is not a gastroenterologist. He says that Rowe didn't need Zantac yet prescribed Zantac for him. He opined with confidence about what Rowe needed or didn't need — yet never examined him — and offered no basis for his off-the-cuff medical opinion . . . .

In citing even highly reputable medical websites in support of our conclusion that summary judgment was premature we may be thought to be "going outside the record" in an improper sense. It may be said that judges should confine their role to choosing between the evidentiary presentations of the opposing parties, much like referees of athletic events. . . .

Rule 201 of the Federal Rules of Evidence makes facts of which judicial notice is properly taken conclusive, and therefore requires that their accuracy be indisputable for judicial notice to be taken of them. We are not deeming the Internet evidence cited in this opinion conclusive or even certifying it as being probably correct, though it may well be correct since it is drawn from reputable medical websites. We use it only to underscore the existence of a genuine dispute of material fact created in the district court proceedings by entirely conventional evidence, namely Rowe's reported pain.

There is a high standard for taking judicial notice of a fact, and a low standard for allowing evidence to be presented in the conventional way, by testimony subject to cross-examination, but is there no room for anything in between? Must judges abjure visits to Internet web sites of premier hospitals and drug companies, not in order to take judicial notice but to assure the existence of a genuine issue of material fact that precludes summary judgment?... Shall the unreliability of the unalloyed adversary process in a case of such dramatic inequality of resources and capabilities of the parties as this case be an unalterable bar to justice? Must our system of justice allow the muddled affidavit of a defendant who may well be unqualified to be an expert witness in this case to carry the day against a pro se plaintiff helpless to contest the affidavit?

This is not the case in which to fetishize adversary procedure in a pure eighteenth-century form, given the inadequacy of the key defense witness, Dr. Wolfe. Let's review: Wolfe refused to continue Rowe's Zantac prescription in July 2011 while Rowe was being kept waiting for three weeks before being seen by a doctor. Wolfe knew Rowe had esophagitis: he reviewed Rowe's medical records, which contained the 2009 diagnosis and revealed nearly two years of physicians' having prescribed Zantac for him continuously. Wolfe had *personally* prescribed Zantac for Rowe for six months of those two years and must have known that the Department of Correction authorizes such treatment only for a *serious* health condition. Rowe was complaining of continuing reflux pain; and while Wolfe denied a prescription renewal on July 13, he demonstrated his awareness that Rowe might need treatment by scheduling him for a later appointment (the August 2 appointment) to evaluate his request to resume taking Zantac.

Against this background, to credit Wolfe's evidence that it doesn't matter when you take Zantac for relief of GERD symptoms (evidence that may well have failed to satisfy the criteria for the admissibility of expert evidence that are set forth in Fed.R.Evid. 702) just because Rowe didn't present his own expert witness would make no sense — for how could Rowe find such an expert and persuade him to testify? He could not afford to pay an expert witness. He had no lawyer in the district court and has no lawyer in this court; and so throughout this litigation (now in its fourth year) he has been at a decided litigating disadvantage. He requested the appointment of counsel and of an expert witness to assist him in the litigation, pointing out sensibly that he needed "verifying medical evidence" to support his claim. The district judge denied both requests, leaving Rowe unable to offer evidence beyond his own testimony that he was in extreme pain when forbidden to take his medication with his meals.

The web sites give credence to Rowe's assertion that he was in pain. But the information gleaned from them did not *create* a dispute of fact that was not already in the record. Rowe presented enough evidence to call Dr. Wolfe's assessment into question — Rowe claims that after his medication was switched to the 12-hour schedule he was in extreme pain and Dr. Wolfe, without examining Rowe or disclosing the basis for his opinion (as we require experts to do), stated cursorily that the medicine would be effective for 12 hours. It will be up to the factfinder to decide, on a better developed record, who is right.

. . .

It is heartless to make a fetish of adversary procedure if by doing so feeble evidence is credited because the opponent has no practical access to offsetting evidence. To say for example that however implausible Dr. Wolfe's evidence is, it must be accepted because not contested, is to doom the plaintiff's case regardless of the merits simply because the plaintiff lacks the wherewithal to obtain and present conflicting evidence. Rowe did not move to exclude Wolfe as an expert witness on the ground that Wolfe neither qualified to give expert evidence in this case (because he is not a gastroenterologist) nor, as a defendant, was likely to be even minimally impartial. But Rowe does not have the legal knowledge that would enable him to file such a motion.

We have decided to reverse the judgment. We base this decision on Rowe's declarations, the timeline of his inability to obtain Zantac, the manifold contradictions in Dr. Wolfe's affidavits, and, last, the cautious, limited Internet research that we have conducted in default of the parties' having done so. . . .

Judge Hamilton dissented in part on the basis that the majority improperly relied on "evidence" found by the appellate court on the Internet.[35] Canadian courts have cautioned against judges doing Internet searches, citing the "basic principle that judges and jurors must make their judicial decisions based only on the evidence presented in court on the record. Jurors are specifically told not to conduct any Internet searches about anything in the case."[36]

CRONK v. CANADIAN GENERAL INSURANCE CO.
(1995), 25 O.R. (3d) 505 (Ont. C.A.)

The plaintiff was employed as a clerk-stenographer. In 1993, as a result of internal reorganization by the defendant, the plaintiff's employment was terminated. She brought an action for damages for wrongful dismissal and moved for summary judgment, seeking damages based on a notice period of 20 months. The plaintiff was awarded damages of 20 months' salary and the defendant appealed.

---

[35] For commentary, see e.g. M.C. Martin, "'Googling' Your Way to Justice: How Judge Posner Was (Almost) Correct in His Use of Internet Research in *Rowe v. Gibson*" (2015) 11 Seventh Circuit Rev. 1.

[36] *R. v. H. (C.D.)*, 2015 ONCA 102, 322 C.C.C. (3d) 468, 19 C.R. (7th) 375 (Ont. C.A.). See also *R. v. Bahamonde*, 2016 BCCA 505, 343 C.C.C. (3d) 1 (B.C. C.A.).

LACOURCIÈRE J.A.:—

. . .

In granting judgment in her favour, MacPherson J. noted that "the factors to be considered in determining reasonable notice have remained more or less constant for over 30 years", having been enunciated by McRuer C.J.H.C. in *Bardal v. Globe & Mail Ltd.*, [1960] O.W.N. 253 (H.C.J.) at p. 255:

> There could be no catalogue laid down as to what was reasonable notice in particular classes of cases. The reasonableness of the notice must be decided with reference to each particular case, having regard to the character of the employ-ment, the length of service of the servant, the age of the servant and the availability of similar employment, having regard to the experience, training and qualifications of the servant.

. . .

Addressing the role played by the character of employment in determining the requisite notice period, MacPherson J. observed that the length of notice requested by the respondent had traditionally been reserved for persons with positions more senior to hers. Having said that, he could find no principled reason why this should be so. He rejected the proposition that senior employees are more stigmatized by the loss of employment than are their underlings. Likewise, he could find no support for the notion, frequently articulated in the case-law, that senior, specialized employees have greater difficulty in securing new employment. Apart from the fact that the appellant had not provided any evidence to that effect, and the fact that the respondent was still out of work eight months after her dismissal, MacPherson J. found another basis on which to dismiss the proposition (at p. 25):

> Third, the reality is — as we are all told by our parents at a young age — that education and training *are* directly related to employment. The senior manager and the professional person are better, not worse, positioned to obtain employ-ment, both initially and later in a post-dismissal context. Higher education and specialized training correlate directly with *increased* access to employment.

In support of this assertion, the learned motions court judge cited two studies published by the Council of Ontario Universities, as well as a May 21, 1994 article in the *Economist* magazine. He discovered these materials through his own research. For those reasons, he refused to accept the defendant's argument based on a managerial-clerical distinction.

. . .

In my opinion, the learned motion court judge's reasons do not justify departing from the widely accepted principle. He erred in doing so on the basis of his own sociological research without providing counsel an opportunity to challenge or respond to the results of the two studies relied upon. I agree with the appellant that the factual conclusions which he drew from these studies are beyond the scope of proper judicial notice.

. . .

The conclusion of the motions court judge based on the studies prepared by the Council of Ontario Universities are obviously not so generally known or accepted as to challenge the validity of an established principle which has found judicial acceptance for over three decades. It is not, as the respondent contended, an undisputed "social reality" as was the background information concerning the circumstances encountered by spouses at the dissolution of a marriage, in *Moge v. Moge*, [1992] 3 S.C.R. 813 at p. 874.

Before taking new matters into account based on statistics which have not been considered in the judgment under appeal, the adversarial process requires that the court ensure that the parties are given an opportunity to deal with the new information by making further submissions, oral or written, and allowing, if requested, fresh material in response.

The result arrived at has the potential of disrupting the practices of the commercial and industrial world, wherein employers have to predict with reasonable certainty the cost of downsizing or increasing their operations, particularly in difficult economic times. As well, legal practitioners specializing in employment law and the legal profession generally have to give advice to employers and employees in respect of termination of employment with reasonable certainty. Adherence to the doctrine of *stare decisis* plays an important role in that respect: *Cassell & Co. v. Broome*, [1972] 1 All E.R. 801 at p. 809, [1972] A.C. 1027 (H.L.).

. . .

In my opinion, the character of the employment of the respondent does not entitle her to a lengthy period of notice.

. . .

For these reasons, I would vary the judgment of MacPherson J. so that the plaintiff respondent will recover damages based on a salary calculation covering 12 months from September 9, 1993.

WEILER J.A. (dissenting in part):—

. . .

The justification for placing less weight on the factor of character of employment in the case of a clerical employee is based on several factual propositions or assumptions put forward by the appellant. Lacourcière J.A. does not find it necessary to deal with the validity of these propositions because they were not challenged in argument before MacPherson J. MacPherson J. did, however, question the validity of these factual propositions. In my opinion he was not prevented from doing so although he erred in not giving the parties an opportunity to lead evidence and to make submissions respecting his rejection of these factual propositions.

. . .

A trial is a search for the truth. When a trial judge reviews jurisprudence and finds it rests on a factual assumption, that may no longer be true or which may not apply in all cases, the judge is not obliged to continue to accept this assumption as a fact. Naturally, the judge wishes to avoid the expense and delay of requiring counsel to re-attend for further argument concerning the material he has discovered and upon which he seeks to rely. However, where a judicial approach rests on a factual proposition with which the judge disagrees, and counsel are unaware that the judge is considering a break with the past, I can see no alternative but for the judge to allow counsel an opportunity to call evidence and to make submissions. The reason for this is two-fold. The general studies or material that the judge sees as rebutting the factual proposition may, as a result of expert evidence, be susceptible to other interpretation. In addition, the parties have a right to expect that if a judge disagrees with a factual assumption, which has found its way into the jurisprudence and which has gone unchallenged, the judge will give the parties an opportunity to make submissions concerning the studies he sees as rebutting this assumption. MacPherson J. erred in not doing so. The parties should have been recalled.

. . .

I would allow the appeal, set aside the judgment of MacPherson J. respecting reasonable notice, and in its place, substitute an order pursuant to rule 20.04(3) directing the trial of an issue as to the amount that Ms. Cronk is entitled to be paid in lieu of notice.

MORDEN A.C.J.O.:— I have had the benefit of reading the reasons of Lacourcière J.A. and Weiler J.A. I agree with Lacourcière J.A.'s propspace = "t"osed disposition of this appeal and agree, generally, with his reasons. I shall state my particular reasons briefly.

. . .

The parties were content to have MacPherson J. and this court dispose of Ms. Cronk's motion for summary judgment on the basis of the materials which they had filed with the court. They were satisfied that the court could come to a just conclusion on what was a reasonable notice period on these materials. Although this would involve the court's consideration of the parties' competing contentions on the application of the reasonable notice standard to differing views of the facts, a trial was not required for this purpose. There was no genuine issue requiring a trial: see *Ron Miller Realty v. Honeywell, Wotherspoon* (1991), 4 O.R. (3d) 492 (Gen. Div.). I think that the parties are to be commended for adopting this approach. In the light of this and, also, the consideration that character of employment is not commensurate with availability of other employment, and, even if it were, my doubt that this would necessarily result in the upward adjustment of notice periods for clerical employees (rather than the downward adjustment of those for senior employees), I do not think, with respect, that a trial should be directed.

Do you see why it was undisputed social reality in *Moge v. Moge* and therefore amenable to judicial notice, but not in *Cronk*?

(c) *Spence*: Revised Standards

R. v. SPENCE
33 C.R. (6th) 1, [2005] 3 S.C.R. 458, 202 C.C.C. (3d) 1

A Black accused was charged with robbery of a South Asian pizza deliveryman in the hallway of an apartment block. The trial judge permitted the defence to challenge potential jurors for cause on the basis of potential bias against a Black accused, but refused to allow a question addressing the interracial nature of the crimes. He held that the "interracial" element was irrelevant on the facts of this case. The accused was convicted.

On appeal, the accused argued that he was deprived of his right to an impartial jury and therefore to a fair trial. The majority of the Ontario Court of Appeal set aside the conviction. The trial judge had misinterpreted the ruling in *R. v. Parks*[37] entitling Black accused to challenge prospective jurors for cause on the basis of race. The majority held that where an accused entitled to challenge the jury for cause on the basis of race wishes to include the interracial nature of the crime in the question for potential jurors, he or she is entitled to have the question posed in that way.

On further appeal, the Supreme Court allowed the appeal and restored the conviction. Justice Binnie wrote the unanimous judgment of the Court. He held it was up to the defence to show an "air of reality" to the assertion that the complainant's South Asian origin had the realistic potential of aggravating jurors' prejudice against the Black accused because of natural sympathy for the victim by jurors who might be South Asian. This burden was not met. While it was open to the trial judge to include the "interracial" aspect of the crime in the challenge for cause, neither the case law, nor the studies on which case law was based, supported the need for a broad entitlement in every case to challenge for cause based on racial sympathy as distinguished from potential racial hostility. The majority in the court below had pushed judicial notice beyond its proper limits. It was within the trial judge's discretion to allow the interracial question but it was not an error of law for the trial judge to draw the line where he did. This had not resulted in an unfair trial. In the course of the judgment the Court revised its approach to judicial notice.

BINNIE J. (MAJOR, LEBEL, DESCHAMPS, FISH, ABELLA and CHARRON JJ. concurring): —

It is not to be doubted that evidence of *how* and *to what extent* racial discrimination affects the behaviour of jurors is difficult to come by, as noted by Finlayson J.A. in *Koh* (paras. 28 and 41). The intervener, African Canadian Legal Clinic, in a useful submission that went beyond the more case law oriented argument of the respondent, urged the Court to fill the evidentiary gap with the taking of judicial notice that where the complainant is also a member of a visible minority:

---

[37]   (1993) 24 C.R. (4th) 81 (Ont. C.A.), later adopted in *R. v. Williams*, [1998] 1 S.C.R. 1128.

[r]acial bias can affect the fairness of the trial process ... for example affecting juror assessment of credibility and weight of the evidence, shaping information received during the trial, consideration of the accused's propensity for criminality, and favouring of the Crown or witnesses. During the trial process stereotypes relating to both the complainant and the accused may interact and affect a potential juror. The operation of biases in this context is potentially harmful, unpredictable, and can skew the outcome in innumerable ways.

Juror impartiality may arise from a favouring of the victim over the accused because the victim is from the same racialized group as the juror. [paras. 34-35]

In taking this broad approach to judicial notice, the intervener was perhaps invoking the work of the great American expert on the law of evidence, Professor James Thayer, who wrote in 1890 that "courts may and should notice without proof, and assume as known by others, whatever, as the phrase is, everybody knows" (emphasis added) (J.B. Thayer, "Judicial Notice and the Law of Evidence" (1889-90), 3 *Harv. L. Rev.* 285, at p. 305.) In taking this view, he is largely supported by Dean Wigmore. (See J.H. Wigmore, *Evidence in Trials at Common Law* (Chadbourn rev. 1981), vol. 9, at p. 732.) From time to time, similarly broad statements have issued from this Court. No less strict a judge than Duff C.J.C. was prepared in 1938 to take judicial notice of "facts which are known to intelligent persons generally": *Reference re Alberta Statutes*, [1938] S.C.R. 100 at p. 128, [1938] 2 D.L.R. 81 *sub nom. Reference re Alberta Legislation.* More recently Beetz J. in *Montréal (City of) v. Arcade Amusements Inc.*, [1985] 1 S.C.R. 368, 18 D.L.R. (4th) 161, took judicial notice of a number of "facts" dealing with the habits and lifestyles of children and adolescents on the basis that judges "cannot disregard" such obvious things that are part of our everyday experience:

The courts cannot be unaware that children and adolescents generally have limited financial resources. . .The courts cannot disregard the attraction which amusement machines and amusement halls are likely to exert on children and adolescents,... both while they have money and when they run out of it. [pp. 382-83]

Professor Thayer's view was that "[i]n conducting a process of judicial reasoning, as of other reasoning, not a step can be taken without assuming something which has not been proved" (pp. 287-88). I would add the comment of Scrutton L.J.:

It is difficult to know what judges are allowed to know, though they are ridiculed if they pretend not to know. (*Tolley v. Fry*, [1930] 1 K.B. 467 (Eng. C.A.) at p. 475)

This is true, so far as it goes. The Court's judgment in *Whirlpool Corp. v. Camco Inc.*, [2000] 2 S.C.R. 1067, 2000 SCC 67, 194 D.L.R. (4th) 193, for instance, talked at length about the functioning of clothes washing machines, even though no washing machine had been filed as a trial exhibit, and no special instruction about their general operations was offered through the expert witnesses. It was just that "everyone" knew.

Thayer's approach to judicial notice has its role but I do not think it helps us to solve the issue posed by the African Canadian Legal Clinic. There are at least three difficulties standing in its way. Firstly what "everybody knows" may be wrong. Until *Parks*, "everybody" knew the solemnity of a criminal trial and careful jury instructions from the judge meant there was little possibility that potential jurors in Toronto would be influenced by racial prejudice (Doherty J.A., at p. 360 of *Parks*, cites a number of trial decisions where race-based challenges for cause were rejected for that reason). Common law judges in early Tudor England would presumably have taken judicial notice of the "fact" that the sun revolves around the earth. Secondly, there is the problem of trial fairness. Where do these facts come from and how are the parties going to address them? How can parties who are prejudiced by the taking of judicial notice rebut what "everybody" knows unless a plausible source is put to them for their comment and potential disagreement? (See *R. v. Parnell* (1995), 98 C.C.C. (3d) 83 (Ont. C.A.) at p. 94.) A third problem is that judges occasionally contradict each other about some "fact" that "everybody" knows, even on the same court in the same case. Thus, in *Campbell v. Royal Bank of Canada*, [1964] S.C.R. 85, 43 D.L.R. (2d) 341, Martland and Ritchie JJ., dissenting, pointed out, at p. 91, that the majority and dissenting judges in the court below had taken judicial notice of flatly contradictory facts, namely whether it was usual or unusual to find water in substantial quantities on the floor of a Manitoba bank in wintertime. More dramatically, in *Clinton v. Jones*, 520 U.S. 681 (1997), where the issue before the Supreme Court of the United States was whether a sitting President is entitled to automatic immunity during his term of office with respect to private conduct prior to his election to the presidency, the court stated with confidence with respect to the Paula Jones affair that "it appears to us highly unlikely to occupy any substantial amount of petitioner's time" (p. 702).

While courts have accepted the widespread existence of racism, and the likelihood that anti-black racism is aggravated when the alleged victim is white, there is no similar consensus that "everybody knows" a juror of a particular race is likely to favour a complainant or witness of the same race, despite the trial safeguards and the trial judge's instruction to the contrary.

Still less can it be said that such favouritism satisfies the more stringent test of judicial notice adopted by this Court in *Find*, at para. 48, per McLachlin C.J.C.:

> Judicial notice dispenses with the need for proof of facts that are clearly uncontroversial or beyond reasonable dispute. Facts judicially noticed are not proved by evidence under oath. Nor are they tested by cross-examination. Therefore, the threshold for judicial notice is strict: a court may properly take judicial notice of facts that are either: (1) so notorious or generally accepted as not to be the subject of debate among reasonable persons; or (2) capable of immediate and accurate demonstration by resort to readily accessible sources of indisputable accuracy.

This stricter formulation adopted in *Find* was originally put forward by Professor E.M. Morgan in "Judicial Notice" (1943-1944), 57 *Harv. L. Rev.* 269. Morgan, in common with other critics, took the view that the Thayer formulation of judicial notice was too broad. It allowed the courts to make too much use of out-of-court information, and did not sufficiently recognize the limitations on a judge imposed by the adversarial process and fair trial considerations. The narrower Morgan view is found in J. Sopinka, S.N.

Lederman and A.W. Bryant, *The Law of Evidence* (2nd ed. 1999), p. 1055, and D.M. Paciocco and L. Stuesser, *The Law of Evidence* (2nd ed. 1999), at p. 285. I do not think the African Canadian Legal Clinic's view of race-based sympathy for victims (or partiality in favour of certain witnesses) is so notoriously correct as "not to be the subject of debate among reasonable persons". Nor is it capable of immediate demonstration by resort to "readily accessible sources of indisputable accuracy" (*Find*, at para. 48).

Unlike Professor Thayer, for whom judicial notice created a rebuttable presumption of accuracy, Professor Morgan (p. 273) necessarily concluded that if certain facts were properly made subject to judicial notice, they were, by definition, not open to rebuttal. In this, he was supported by Professor C.T. McCormick, who wrote that "a ruling that a fact will be judicially noticed precludes contradictory evidence"; see "Judicial Notice" (1951-1952), 5 Vand. L. Rev. 296, at p. 322. In *R. v. Zundel* (1987), 31 C.C.C. (3d) 97, 35 D.L.R. (4th) 338 (Ont. C.A.), the court said that "[t]he generally accepted modern view . . . is that where the court takes judicial notice of a matter, the judicial notice is final" (p. 150). On this view, acceptance through judicial notice of the broad race-based thesis of the intervener African Canadian Legal Clinic would not only stretch the elasticity of judicial notice, it would create a set of irrebuttable presumptions about how individuals called to jury duty can be expected to think. If there is one thing most of the social science studies agree upon, it is that much work remains to be done in Canada within the limits imposed by s. 649 of the *Criminal Code* to clarify our working assumptions about jury behaviour.

It could be argued that the requirements of judicial notice accepted in Find should be relaxed in relation to such matters as laying a factual basis for the exercise of a discretion to permit challenges for cause. These are matters difficult to prove, and they do not strictly relate to the adjudication of guilt or innocence, but rather to the framework within which that adjudication is to take place. Such non-adjudicative facts are now generally called "social facts" when they relate to the fact-finding process and "legislative facts" in relation to legislation or judicial policy. Juror partiality is a question of fact, and what the African Canadian Legal Clinic invites us to do is to take judicial notice of the "social facts" of different aspects of racism.

"Social fact" evidence has been defined as social science research that is used to construct a frame of reference or background context for deciding factual issues crucial to the resolution of a particular case: see, e.g., C. L'Heureux-Dubé "Re-examining the Doctrine of Judicial Notice in the Family Law Context" (1994), 26 *Ottawa L. Rev.* 551, at p. 556. As with their better known "legislative fact" cousins, "social facts" are general. They are not specific to the circumstances of a particular case, but if properly linked to the adjudicative facts, they help to explain aspects of the evidence. Examples are the Court's acceptance of the "battered wife syndrome" to explain the wife's conduct in *R. v. Lavallée*, [1990] 1 S.C.R. 852, 55 C.C.C. (3d) 97, or the effect of the "feminization of poverty" judicially noticed in *Moge v. Moge*, [1992] 3 S.C.R. 813 at p. 853, 99 D.L.R. (4th) 456, and of the systemic or background factors that have contributed to the difficulties faced by aboriginal people in both the criminal justice system and throughout society at large in *R. v. Wells*, [2000] 1 S.C.R. 207, 2000 SCC 10, 141 C.C.C. (3d) 368, 182 D.L.R. (4th) 257, at para. 53, and in *R. v. Gladue*, [1999] 1 S.C.R. 688, 133 C.C.C. (3d) 385, 171 D.L.R. (4th) 385, at para. 83.

No doubt there is a useful distinction between adjudicative facts (the where, when and why of what the accused is alleged to have done) and "social facts" and "legislative facts" which have relevance to the reasoning process and may involve broad considerations of policy: Paciocco and Stuesser, at p. 286. However, simply categorizing an issue as "social fact" or "legislative fact" does not license the court to put aside the need to examine the trustworthiness of the "facts" sought to be judicially noticed. Nor are counsel encouraged to bootleg "evidence in the guise of authorities": *Public School Boards' Assn. of Alberta v. Alberta (Attorney General)*, [1999] 3 S.C.R. 845, 180 D.L.R. (4th) 670, at para. 3.

The distinction between legislative and adjudicative facts was formulated by the astute administrative law expert, Kenneth Culp Davis, who thought it important to distinguish for purposes of judicial notice between "adjudicative" fact (where he thought the Morgan criteria should apply) and "legislative" fact (where he tended to side with Thayer): K.C. Davis, *Administrative Law Treatise* (2nd ed. 1980), vol. 3, at p. 139. The proof of facts about widespread racism in the community, and whether or not it is so strong as to create a "realistic possibility" of overcoming a juror's presumed impartiality, has to do with juries in general and judicial policy towards their composition. Such matters, according to Sopinka J., "are subject to less stringent admissibility requirements": (*Danson v. Ontario (Attorney General)*, [1990] 2 S.C.R. 1086 at p. 1099, 73 D.L.R. (4th) 686. The "less stringent" standard was not defined.

Professor Davis' useful distinction between adjudicative facts and legislative facts is part of his larger insight, highly relevant for present purposes, that *the permissible scope of judicial notice should vary according to the nature of the issue under consideration*. For example, more stringent proof may be called for of facts that are close to the center of the controversy between the parties (whether social, legislative or adjudicative) as distinguished from background facts at or near the periphery.

To put it another way, the closer the fact approaches the dispositive issue, the more the court ought to insist on compliance with the stricter Morgan criteria. Thus in *Find*, the Court's consideration of alleged juror bias arising out of the repellant nature of the offences against the accused did not relate to the issue of guilt or innocence, and was not "adjudicative" fact in that sense, but nevertheless the Court insisted on compliance with the Morgan criteria because of the centrality of the issue, which was hotly disputed, to the disposition of the appeal. While some learned commentators seek to limit the Morgan criteria to adjudicative fact (see, e.g., Paciocco and Stuesser, at p. 286; McCormick, at p. 316), I believe the Court's decision in Find takes a firmer line. I believe a review of our jurisprudence suggests that the Court will start with the Morgan criteria, whatever may be the type of "fact" that is sought to be judicially noticed. The Morgan criteria represent the gold standard and, if satisfied, the "fact" will be judicially noticed, and that is the end of the matter.

If the Morgan criteria are not satisfied, and the fact is "adjudicative" in nature, the fact will not be judicially recognized, and that too is the end of the matter.

It is when dealing with social facts and legislative facts that the Morgan criteria, while relevant, are not necessarily conclusive. There are levels of notoriety and indisputability. Some legislative "facts" are necessarily laced with supposition, prediction, presumption, perception and wishful thinking. Outside the realm of adjudicative fact, the limits of judicial notice are inevitably somewhat elastic. Still, the Morgan criteria will have great weight when the legislative fact or social fact approaches the dispositive issue. For example, in *R. v. Advance Cutting & Coring Ltd.*, [2001] 3 S.C.R. 209, 2001 SCC 70, 205 D.L.R. (4th) 385, LeBel J. observed:

> The fact that unions intervene in political social debate is well known and well documented and might be the object of judicial notice. ... Taking judicial notice of the fact that Quebec unions have a constant ideology, act in constant support of a particular cause or policy, and seek to impose that ideology on their members seems far more controversial. It would require a leap of faith and logic, absent a proper factual record on the question. [paras. 226-27]

See also *Gladue*, at para. 83.

The reality is that in many *Charter* cases (for example), the adjudicative facts are admitted. It is the legislative facts or social facts that are likely to prove dispositive (e.g., *R. v. Sharpe*, [2001] 1 S.C.R. 45, 2001 SCC 2, 150 C.C.C. (3d) 321, 194 D.L.R. (4th) 1; *R. v. Butler*, [1992] 1 S.C.R. 452, 70 C.C.C. (3d) 129, 89 D.L.R. (4th) 449; *Little Sisters Book and Art Emporium v. Canada (Minister of Justice)*, [2000] 2 S.C.R. 1120, 2000 SCC 69, 150 C.C.C. (3d) 1, 193 D.L.R. (4th) 193). The Court in those cases was rightly careful to keep judicial notice on a relatively short leash, while at the same time acknowledging that facts cannot be demonstrated with greater precision than the subject matter permits.

When asked to take judicial notice of matters falling between the high end already discussed where the Morgan criteria will be insisted upon, and the low end of background facts where the court will likely proceed (consciously or unconsciously) on the basis that the matter is beyond serious controversy, I believe a court ought to ask itself whether such "fact" would be accepted by reasonable people who have taken the trouble to inform themselves on the topic as not being the subject of reasonable dispute for the particular purpose for which it is to be used, keeping in mind that the need for reliability and trustworthiness increases directly with the centrality of the "fact" to the disposition of the controversy. Thus, for example, journalists claim that "everybody knows" some important news sources will dry up unless their identity can be kept secret. On that basis, some courts have been prepared to refuse (or delay) compelling journalists to disclose confidential sources for the purpose of defamation proceedings, e.g., *Hays v. Weiland* (1918), 43 D.L.R. 137 (Ont. C.A.); *Reid v. Telegram Publishing Co.*, [1961] O.R. 418, 28 D.L.R. (2d) 6 (H.C.); *Drabinsky v. Maclean-Hunter Ltd.* (1980), 28 O.R. (2d) 23, 108 D.L.R. (3d) 390 (H.C.J.); *McInnis v. University Students' Council of University of Western Ontario* (1984), 14 D.L.R. (4th) 126n (Ont. H.C.), leave to appeal to Divisional Court refused, at p. 127. However, when the issue of compelled disclosure of confidential sources became dispositive in *Moysa v. Alberta (Labour Relations Board)*, [1989] 1 S.C.R. 1572, 60 D.L.R. (4th) 1, the Court declined to recognize any Charter entitlement for journalists to refuse to disclose "secret" sources before an administrative tribunal, at p. 1581, per Sopinka J.:

> While judicial notice may be taken of self-evident facts, I am not convinced that it is indisputable that there is a direct relationship between testimonial compulsion and a "drying-up" of news sources as alleged by the appellant. The burden of proof that there has been a violation of s. 2(b) rests on the appellant. Absent any evidence that there is a tie between the impairment of the alleged right to gather information and the requirement that journalists testify before the Labour Relations Board, I cannot find that there has been a breach of s. 2(b) in this case.

Both of these examples dealt with the "legislative facts" underlying a claimed rule giving effect to journalistic privilege. For the purposes of regulating procedures in defamation proceedings, the courts were prepared to accept as a reasonable generalization that failure to respect confidential sources would "chill" the gathering of news, which would not be in the public interest. In *Moysa*, however, for the very different purpose of considering whether the underlying "legislative fact" was sufficiently beyond controversy to support a claim to entrenchment as a *Charter* privilege, the generalization was subjected to closer scrutiny.

Here, the respondent and the African Canadian Legal Clinic are asking the Court to make some fundamental shifts in the law's understanding of how juries function and how the selection of their members should be approached. Their submissions carry us well beyond the specific context in which *Williams* and *Parks* were decided. The facts of which they ask us to take judicial notice would be dispositive of the appeal; yet they are neither notorious nor easily verified by reference to works of "indisputable accuracy". We are urged to pile inference onto inference. To take judicial notice of such matters for this purpose would, in my opinion, be to take even a generous view of judicial notice a leap too far. We do not know whether a favourable predisposition based on race—to the extent it exists—is any more prevalent than it is for people who share the same religion, or language, or national origin, or old school. On the present state of our knowledge, I think we should decline, at least for now, to proceed by way of judicial notice down the road the African Canadian Legal Clinic has laid out for us.

I would add this comment: in *R. v. Malmo-Levine*, [2003] 3 S.C.R. 571, 2003 SCC 74, 179 C.C.C. (3d) 417, 233 D.L.R. (4th) 415, a majority of our Court expressed a preference for social science evidence to be presented through an expert witness who could be cross-examined as to the value and weight to be given to such studies and reports. This is the approach that had been taken by the litigants in *Sharpe, Little Sisters, Malmo-Levine* itself and subsequently in *Canadian Foundation for Children, Youth and the Law v. Canada (Attorney General)*, [2004] 1 S.C.R. 76, 2004 SCC 4, 180 C.C.C. (3d) 353, 234 D.L.R. (4th) 257. We said in *Malmo-Levine* that

> . . . courts should nevertheless proceed cautiously to take judicial notice even as "legislative facts" of matters . . . are reasonably open to dispute, particularly where they relate to an issue that could be dispositive. [para. 28]

The suggestion that even legislative fact and social "facts" should be established by expert testimony rather than reliance on judicial notice was also made in cases as different from one another as *Find*, *Moysa*, *Danson*, at p. 1101, *Symes v. Canada*, [1993] 4 S.C.R. 695, 110 D.L.R. (4th) 470, *Waldick v. Malcolm*, [1991] 2 S.C.R. 456 at pp. 472-73, 83 D.L.R. (4th) 114, *Stoffman v. Vancouver General Hospital*, [1990] 3 S.C.R. 483 at pp. 549-50, 76 D.L.R. (4th) 700, *R. v. Penno*, [1990] 2 S.C.R. 865 at pp. 881-82, 59 C.C.C. (3d) 344, and *MacKay v. Manitoba*, [1989] 2 S.C.R. 357, 61 D.L.R. (4th) 385. Litigants who disregard the suggestion proceed at some risk.

Spence is now the controlling authority on judicial notice. Justice Binnie is clearly at pains to establish principles upon which all issues of judicial notice are to be based. On the one hand, the Court is cautious. The closer any issue is to the dispositive issue, the less scope there is for judicial notice. If the matter relates to adjudicative issues, the strict Morgan criteria of notorious or indisputable govern. When it comes to social or legislative facts, the Court opens the door a little wider. However a judge must still ask whether the alleged fact would be accepted by a properly informed reasonable person as not subject to reasonable dispute. This latter test is new. Binnie J. clearly prefers notice to counsel before judicial notice is taken and prefers that social science evidence be presented through experts who can be cross-examined.

These views appear to diverge considerably from those of L'Heureux-Dubé J. we examined earlier. She championed the need for a wide approach to judicial notice to bring social context into the courtroom, saw no distinction between the role of trial or appeal judges, did not stress the distinction between adjudicative and other facts and indicated that it is not necessary to alert counsel as to when judicial notice may be taken. She also wrote that family law matters require an especially generous approach to judicial notice. **Which view do you prefer and why?**

It will be interesting to see whether the Supreme Court extends its new approach to judicial notice to contexts other than criminal matters and whether it will be able to satisfactorily distinguish between adjudicative facts where there is to be a strict standard for judicial notice, and social and legal facts where there is now a slightly relaxed standard.

In the meantime, trial judges in particular would be well-advised to alert counsel as to matters seen to be subject to judicial notice. Alerting counsel requires a delicate balance that must avoid taking on the role of a research director.[38]

------

[38]   See Doherty J.A. in *R. v. Hamilton* (2004), 186 C.C.C. (3d) 129, 22 C.R. (6th) 1 (Ont. C.A.).

CTV TELEVISION v. THE QUEEN [R. v. Hogg]
(2006), 214 C.C.C. (3d) 70 (C.A.)

The accused pleaded guilty to a vicious and unprovoked aggravated assault that garnered public and media attention. He was sentenced to a conditional sentence. On appeal, the sentenced was varied to three years imprisonment. Given the public and political debate surrounding conditional sentences, W-Five intended to use the case in an upcoming episode. It attempted to obtain a copy of the videotaped statement. Its application was denied. CTV successfully appealed.

MONNIN J.A. (SCOTT C.J.M. and STEEL J.A. concurring): —

The judge's conclusion that the releasing of the videotape would hamper the process of obtaining videotaped statements generally, and therefore hinder the administration of justice, is based, as he himself states, on common sense and logic or judicial experience. He bases his authority for doing so on the decisions of *Harper v. Canada (Attorney General)*, 2004 SCC 33, [2004] 1 S.C.R. 827, and *RJR-MacDonald Inc. v. Canada (Attorney General)*, [1995] 3 S.C.R. 199, 100 C.C.C. (3d) 449.

With respect, I am of the view that in the circumstances of this case, the judge erred when he based his conclusion on common sense and logic alone, without the benefit of real and substantial evidence.

I distinguish the cases that the judge relied on because they only place reliance on common sense and logic after considering some social science evidence. That type of evidence was lacking in the present case. In fact, in this case, the judge had no evidence, let alone social science evidence on which to apply logic and common sense.

Furthermore, the cases on which the judge relied are cases dealing with legislative enactments as opposed to common law rights, and in each case there existed bodies of work or commission reports that the Legislature relied upon prior to enacting the legislation being challenged.

A court in and of its own, without anything further, should not be relying on simple common sense and logic when the effect of a decision is to limit a *Charter* right. The analysis that the judge conducted with respect to the difficulty in having videotaped statements presented in court cannot be the justification for the conclusion that the judge arrives at absent some evidence. That requires a speculative leap of faith that cannot be countenanced.

To a certain degree, the judge could be said to have taken judicial notice of facts he found central to the resolution of the controversy, and in doing so, he erred. This is even more so since the decision of the Supreme Court of Canada in *R. v. Spence*, 2005 SCC 71, [2005] 3 S.C.R. 458, 202 C.C.C. (3d) 1, a case dealing with the racial makeup of juries.

In *Spence*, Binnie J. proceeds to an all-encompassing review of the application of the concept of judicial notice. In his analysis he goes back to the work of Professor James Thayer, who in 1890 laid down a broad approach to judicial notice ("Judicial Notice and the Law of Evidence" (1889-1890), 3 *Harv. L. Rev.* 285). The analysis encompasses the 2001 Supreme Court decision in *R. v. Find*, 2001 SCC 32, [2001] 1 S.C.R. 863, 154 C.C.C. (3d) 97, which adopted a stricter approach to the reliance on judicial notice. This approach, according to Binnie J. is based on the writings of Professor Edmund M. Morgan, "Judicial Notice" (1943-44), 57 *Harv. L. Rev.* 269.

. . .

In an annotation by Professor Don Stuart published along with *Spence* the decision is summarized in these words (2005 CarswellOnt 6824):

> *Spence* is now the controlling authority on judicial notice. Justice Binnie is clearly at pains to establish principles upon which all issues of judicial notice are to be based. On the one hand the Court is cautious. The closer any matter is to the dispositive issue, the less scope there is for judicial notice. If the matter relates to adjudicative issues, the strict Morgan criteria of notorious or indisputable fact govern. When it comes to social or legislative facts, the Court opens the door a little wider. However, a judge must still ask whether the alleged fact would be accepted by a properly informed reasonable person as not subject to reasonable dispute. This latter test is new.

[The Court quotes from *Spence* where Justice Binnie expresses the Court's preference for social science evidence to be presented even for legislative and "social" facts.]

In the present case, when the judge speaks of "compelling common sense and logic" and "judicial experience" he can only be referring to judicial notice under another name. His reasoning, therefore, must be subject to the restrictions that the Supreme Court has expressed in *Spence*, as well as the evidentiary requirements referred to therein. In this case, there was no evidence that could permit him to link the difficulty courts have had in convincing police services to videotape statements of accused persons with the release of the respondent's videotaped statement, sufficient to displace the presumption of openness of the courts.

The simple fact of this appeal and the Crown's argument in support of the appellant's position demonstrate that reasonable people are debating the accuracy of what the judge concluded as being a fact. As such, that fact cannot be taken judicial notice of, based on the first prong of the Morgan criteria.

Furthermore, if readily accessible sources were available, they were not advanced before the judge. Satisfaction of this criterion would have required the judge to take judicial notice of the existence of such sources, and then make a further inference that these sources confirmed that releasing the videotape would create reluctance to consenting to future videotaping. Simply piling inference upon inference does not satisfy the second prong of the Morgan criteria.

When the judge took judicial notice of the fact that the releasing of the videotape would hinder the producing of videotaped statements before the courts, that conclusion became determinative of the application. Being so central to the issue at hand, the dicta of *Spence* should have been applied and the Morgan criteria should have been adhered to strictly. Neither prong of the Morgan criteria being satisfied, the social fact that releasing the respondent's videotaped statement would deter the producing of videotaped statements before the courts should not have been a fact accepted without proof.

I conclude, therefore, that in the case before us, the judge simply did not have the proper factual foundation or evidence that would have permitted him to come to the conclusion that he did. He was in error when he denied the appellant access to the videotape.

PROBLEMS

Problem 1

How would the *Zundel* case, discussed earlier at note 21, be decided under *Spence*?

Problem 2

In May of 1997, a trial judge listens to a lecture by a psychologist to Family Court judges respecting a "compelling cultural disinclination" for Aboriginals to "relive past events of an unpleasant nature". Presiding at a sexual assault trial, he notes that the Aboriginal complainant has difficulty in responding to questions. In the course of convicting, he puts the complainant's difficulty down to "cultural disinclination". The accused appeals on the basis that there was no evidence of this put before the Court and the judge was relying on personal knowledge he did not share. **Applying *Spence*, should the accused receive a new trial?** Compare *R. v. S. (W.)* (1991), 6 C.R. (4th) 373 (Ont. C.A.).

Problem 3

The accused is charged with the wilful promotion of hatred arising from his participation in a demonstration to protest against the entry of Roma refugee claimants into Canada. At the end of the Crown's case, the defence called no evidence and argued that the Crown had failed to prove that there was hatred promoted against "Roma". Counsel argued that the evidence only showed that the actions of the demonstrators were directed toward "gypsies" and that there was no evidence that Roma is the same as "gypsies". The Crown presented the trial judge with five dictionaries that linked "Roma" and "gypsy". The trial judge refused to take judicial notice and acquitted the accused. **Is there a ground of appeal?** See *R. v. Krymowski*, [2005] 1 S.C.R. 101, 26 C.R. (6th) 207, 193 C.C.C. (3d) 129.

Problem 4

In a sexual assault trial, the only issue was whether the accused was wearing a condom. It was common ground that the accused was not wearing a condom when he ejaculated and that the complainant would never have consented to unprotected sex. The accused maintained that he was wearing a condom but that it had slipped off as he had lost his erection shortly before ejaculating. The trial judge convicted, in part, on the basis that "[a] virile young man with a full erection bound on having a climax would not lose his erection". **Is this a matter of the judge taking judicial notice? If so, did the judge comply with *Spence*?** Compare *R. v. Perkins* (2007), 51 C.R. (6th) 116 (Ont. C.A.).

Problem 5

The accused was charged with aggravated assault arising from a collision at a recreational no-contact hockey game. The defence was that this was an unavoidable accident. The Crown argued that the contact resulted from a deliberate blindside hit. The complainant suffered a concussion and significant facial injuries. The trial judge found that most of the witnesses showed a bias depending on which team they were on. She rejected the evidence of some defence witnesses on her view that three defencemen would not have been on the ice with the accused's team down by two goals with time running out. She rejected the accused's account in part because if he truly had been trying to get hold of the puck he would not have been skating at full speed. She convicted and the accused appealed. **Did the trial judge exceed the bounds of judicial notice?**

See *R. v. MacIsaac*, 2015 ONCA 587, 23 C.R. (7th) 313 (Ont. C.A.).

Problem 6

The accused was charged with assault causing bodily harm. The Crown alleged that he had punched a woman outside a nightclub at about 3 a.m. and that he cut his hand on her teeth. She suffered a broken tooth and other injuries. The accused testified that he had not assaulted the victim and that he had cut his knuckle on a fence in a fight with another man. A later witness testified he had seen the two men fighting near a fence. The trial judge then downloaded the image of the fence from Google Street View from his computer. The image showed the fence at the nightclub. The trial judge used the image to make an adverse finding against the accused, holding that he was unlikely to have cut his hand on the fence the way he had described it as the fence was tubular. The accused was never asked to comment on the image. The trial judge convicted. The accused appealed. **Should a new trial be ordered?**

See *R. v. Ghaleenovee*, 2015 ONSC 1707, 19 C.R. (7th) 154 (Ont. S.C.J.) and *R. v. Synkiw* (2012), 292 C.C.C. (3d) 53 (Sask. Q.B.).

B. REAL EVIDENCE

1. AUTHENTICATION

Wigmore distinguished the three modes by which a trier may acquire knowledge: testimonial evidence, circumstantial evidence, and real evidence:

> If, for example, it is desired to ascertain whether the accused has lost his right hand and wears an iron hook in place of it, one source of belief on the subject would be the testimony of a witness who had seen the arm; in believing this testimonial evidence, there is an inference from the human assertion to the fact

asserted. A second source of belief would be the mark left on some substance grasped or carried by the accused; in believing this circumstantial evidence, there is an inference from the circumstance to the thing producing it. A third source of belief remains, namely, the *inspection by the tribunal* of the accused's arm. This source differs from the other two in omitting any step of conscious inference or reasoning, and in proceeding by direct self-perception, or autopsy . . . From the point of view of the litigant party furnishing the source of belief, it may be termed *autoptic proference.*[39]

His term "autoptic proference" has not gained much acceptance and the third source of belief is commonly referred to in England and Canada as real evidence.[40] The types or kinds of real evidence are infinitely variable and may affect any of the senses. Here we are content to explore some general principles applicable to all.

To be receivable, real evidence must of course be relevant and it will only be relevant to the matters in issue if the item proffered is identified as genuine (i.e., if the item tendered as an exhibit is authenticated to be what it is represented to be by its proponent). In a prosecution for assault causing bodily harm, a blood-stained shirt is not relevant evidence unless it is identified as having been worn by the victim on the evening of the altercation. There are functions here for both the judge and the jury. The judge must be satisfied that there is sufficient evidence introduced to permit a rational finding by the jury that the item is as claimed; the jury then weighs the evidence and determines whether the item is authentic.[41]

In the absence of agreement of counsel, real evidence, whether this be the gun, the drugs, a photograph or a letter, must be tendered through witnesses and be authenticated. There is no set procedure and there are no questions that must be asked. The usual steps for counsel seeking to tender a piece of real evidence are:

1. call a witness with personal knowledge of the object,
2. ask the witness to describe the object before showing it to the witness,
3. allow the witness to examine and identify it as genuine, and
4. ask that the object be entered as an exhibit, with an appropriate stamp applied by the clerk.

Sometimes the witness will not be able to identify the object as that previously seen. In such cases the accepted practice is to have it marked as an "exhibit for identification". Hopefully there will be a later witness to call who can properly authenticate it so that it can then be marked as an exhibit as a piece of evidence in the case. If entered as an exhibit in jury trials the jury is usually allowed to take the exhibit into the jury room during their deliberations.[42] In *R. v. Patterson,*[43] Gillese J.A. held that it is within the trial judge's discretion as to whether exhibits go to the jury:

39   4 Wigmore, *Evidence* (Chad. Rev.), s. 1150 at 322.
40   See generally Nokes, "Real Evidence" (1949) 65 L.Q.R. 57. McCormick, *Evidence*, 2nd ed. (1972) at 524 notes that "it will be seen variously referred to as real, autoptic, demonstrative, tangible, and objective".
41   See *R. v. Parsons* (1977), 37 C.C.C. (2d) 497 (Ont. C.A.).
42   See further Lee Stuesser, *An Advocacy Primer*, 3rd ed. (2005) at 227-232.

It was open to the trial judge to permit the videotape to go to the jury room during deliberations. This was a matter within his discretion and there is no basis to suggest he erred in law. The trial judge was not required to depart from the general practice of giving the jury all exhibits whenever feasible. He heard submissions on the issue and declined to adopt the suggestion that the video go to the jury only if they requested it. He was entitled to reach this decision. The trial judge was correct in his assessment that any concern about potential misuse of the video could be avoided by clear cautionary instructions and he gave those instructions. *R. v. Pleich* (1980), 55 C.C.C. (2d) 13 at 32-33 (Ont. C.A.).

An important part of authentication, particularly in drug cases, is the issue of continuity. **Is this an issue of weight or admissibility?** The current law respecting proof of continuity was reviewed by Owen-Flood J. in *R. v. MacPherson:*[44]

> There were a number of problems relating to the continuity of the evidence in this case. Unfortunately, Cst. Banky, the exhibits officer assigned to this case, died unexpectedly in October 2003. Because Cst. Banky could not testify at trial, there is a break in the continuity of the evidence. No alternate evidence as to the chain of custody of the real evidence was proferred by the Crown.

> The extent to which the Crown proves the continuity of real evidence in a narcotics case, and whether or not breaks in continuity makes evidence inadmissible are questions of fact for the trier of fact to decide. Breaks in the chain of continuity reduce the weight which can be given to the proferred evidence: *R. v. Andrade* (1985), 18 C.C.C. (3d) 41 (Ont. C.A.). In *R. v. Larsen*, [2001] B.C.J. No. 824, 2001 BCSC 597, aff'd on other grounds, [2003] B.C.J. No. 45, 2003 BCCA 18, Romilly J. held as follows:

>> It is important to appreciate what the Crown must prove in a narcotics-related case. In essence, the Crown must show beyond a reasonable doubt that the material seized from an accused was a prohibited substance. To that end, the Crown must prove that the substance dealt with by, or in the possession of, the accused is the same substance that is alleged in the information or indictment (and prohibited by law). Undoubtedly, then, continuity of possession of the substance from the accused to the law enforcement officer to the analyst is crucial. However, Canadian case law makes it clear that proof of continuity is not a legal requirement and that gaps in continuity are not fatal to the Crown's case unless they raise a reasonable doubt about the exhibit's integrity. See *R. v. Dawdy and Lamoureaux* (1971), 4 C.C.C. (2d) 122 (Ont. C.A.); *R. v. Oracheski* (1979), 48 C.C.C. (2d) 217 (Alta. C.A.), *R. v. DeGraaf* (1981), 60 C.C.C. (2d) 315 (B.C. C.A.); and *R. v. Taylor* (1988), 93 N.B.R. (2d) 246 (N.B. Q.B.). These cases establish there is no duty upon the Crown to show detailed continuity of the location and handling of the exhibits from the time of their seizure by law enforcement officers to their deposit with analysts.[45]

Authentication presents special problems with evidence in the form of photographs and video recordings.

---

[43]   (2003), 174 C.C.C. (3d) 193 (Ont. C.A.).
[44]   2005 BCSC 381 (B.C. S.C.).
[45]   See also *R. v. Wilder*, 2002 BCSC 1333.

R. v. NIKOLOVSKI

[1996] 3 S.C.R. 1197, 3 C.R. (5th) 362, 111 C.C.C. (3d) 403

The accused was convicted of robbing a convenience store. The sole witness, the store clerk, could not identify the accused with any certainty and, when shown a videotape of the robbery during his testimony, did not identify the person in the videotape as the accused. The Crown called no other identification evidence. The trial judge relied on her own comparison between the accused and the robber in the videotape to conclude that the accused was the robber.

CORY J. (LAMER C.J. and LA FOREST, L'HEUREUX-DUBÉ, GONTHIER, MCLACHLIN and IACOBUCCI JJ. concurring):—

Can a videotape alone provide the necessary evidence to enable the trier of fact to identify the accused as the perpetrator of the crime? That is the question that must be resolved on this appeal.

. . .

In 1991, during the early morning hours of May 13, Mahmood Wahabzada was the sole employee in a Mac's Milk store. At about 2:00 a.m., a man armed with a knife entered the store and ordered him to open the cash register. Mr. Wahabzada complied. The robber took some $230 from the register and fled. The store clerk described the robber to the police as hefty with a strong build, blond hair, a mustache and taller than his own height of 175 centimetres. He could not recall the clothes worn by the robber. As he explained at the trial "You know that time is a very panic time. One cannot remember everything". Two days after the robbery, the store clerk was shown photos of 12 men. He suspected three of the men shown, one of whom was the respondent (accused). At the trial, he testified that he thought that the man shown in photograph number 8, who was not the respondent, could be the robber but he was only 25 to 30 percent sure. He said that when he was first shown the photos he could be no more definite than to say that he "mostly" suspected photograph number 8.

The police officers gave evidence that when he was shown the photos the store clerk exclaimed "that's him" when looking at photo number 6 (which was of the respondent) or "He looks just like him" referring to the same photo, but added "He looks a bit like him also" when referring to photo number 8.

The Crown introduced as evidence the videotape of the robbery, recorded by the store security camera. The store clerk testified that it showed all of the robbery. At the conclusion of the review of the videotape, the clerk was asked if the man who robbed him was in court, to which he replied that he did not think so.

A detective who had known the respondent for some years was present at the time of his arrest. He testified that the respondent then had a sparse mustache covering the upper part of his lip, which was not present on the day of the trial. In cross-examination, the officer acknowledged that the respondent had denied committing the robbery and said that he'd been home with his mother and brother. The defence did not present any evidence.

. . .

. . . Counsel for the respondent cautioned the trial judge of the frailties of eyewitness identification. In response and as part of her reasons, the trial judge stated:

> I have directed my mind, but what about that video tape? I mean the video tape does away with a lot of the frailty of identification by a witness who said to me he was frightened, he was nervous, he couldn't recall some of it. And look at the tape. The tape doesn't lie.
>
> . . . a movie showing the robbery being committed is surely one of the best forms of evidence you've got. And not only was the movie—the man's face was practically in front of the screen. . .
>
> I looked at that video, and I looked at it very carefully, and I can honestly tell you there is no doubt in my mind that the man who committed that robbery on that video was your client. . .
>
> As I said earlier, I've directed myself to all the frailties of the I.D. cases. And over my years as counsel, I know I was involved in a number where it was a serious issue, and I'm well aware of all of it, and the reason behind the case law.
>
> And a lot of the reasons for those frailties are the very things that exist in this case. An act of violence, which happens quickly and unexpectedly to a victim who is terrified.
>
> At best he could say that Photograph 6 looked like, and he also pointed to 8 and to 11. He said quite bluntly: I was afraid. I can't remember all. He also doesn't have English as a first language.
>
> Now, I've seen video tapes in the past that have been grainy, where the lighting hasn't been good, where there's no clear view over a period of time of the robbery and of the perpetrator.
>
> This particular video tape is very clear. The lighting is very good. The man is in the camera for long enough to make a careful observation. And the issue of beyond a reasonable doubt is when I'm obliged to make a decision, and I cannot ignore what my eyes tell me, and my eyes tell me, and there's no dispute this isn't a video tape of the robbery, that the person who committed that robbery is Mr. Nikolovski, and I can't ignore that. . .
>
> It would be mere speculation for me to say, there's one chance in a million he's got an absolute twin running around, who happened to rob that store, that's getting into the realm of speculation at that point.

The trial judge concluded, without calling upon the Crown:

> . . . I think we've beaten this to death. . . I'm satisfied that the robbery was committed by your client. I'm satisfied on looking at that tape that that's him and he's convicted.

. . .

The courts have long recognized the frailties of identification evidence given by independent, honest and well-meaning eyewitnesses. This recognized frailty served to emphasize the essential need to cross-examine eyewitnesses. So many factors come into play with the human identification witness. As a minimum it must be determined whether the witness was physically in a position to see the accused and, if so, whether that witness had sound vision, good hearing, intelligence and the ability to communicate what was seen and heard. Did the witness have the ability to understand and recount what had been perceived? Did the witness have a sound memory? What was the effect of fear or excitement on the ability of the witness to perceive clearly and to later recount the events accurately? Did the witness have a bias or at least a biased perception of the event or the parties involved? This foreshortened list of the frailties of eyewitness identification may serve as a basis for considering the comparative strengths of videotape evidence.

It cannot be forgotten that a robbery can be a terrifyingly traumatic event for the victim and witnesses. Not every witness can have the fictional James Bond's cool and unflinching ability to act and observe in the face of flying bullets and flashing knives. Even Bond might have difficulty accurately describing his would be assassin. He certainly might earnestly desire his attacker's conviction and be biased in that direction.

The video camera on the other hand is never subject to stress. Through tumultuous events it continues to record accurately and dispassionately all that comes before it. Although silent, it remains a constant, unbiased witness with instant and total recall of all that it observed. The trier of fact may review the evidence of this silent witness as often as desired. The tape may be stopped and studied at a critical juncture.

So long as the videotape is of good quality and gives a clear picture of events and the perpetrator, it may provide the best evidence of the identity of the perpetrator. It is relevant and admissible evidence that can by itself be cogent and convincing evidence on the issue of identity. Indeed, it may be the only evidence available. For example, in the course of a robbery, every eyewitness may be killed yet the video camera will steadfastly continue to impassively record the robbery and the actions of the robbers. Should a trier of fact be denied the use of the videotape because there is no intermediary in the form of a human witness to make some identification of the accused? Such a conclusion would be contrary to common sense and a totally unacceptable result. It would deny the trier of fact the use of clear, accurate and convincing evidence readily available by modern technology. The powerful and probative record provided by the videotape should not be excluded when it can provide such valuable assistance in the search for truth. In the course of their deliberations, triers of fact will make their assessment of the weight that should be accorded the evidence of the videotape just as they assess the weight of the evidence given by viva voce testimony.

It is precisely because videotape evidence can present such very clear and convincing evidence of identification that triers of fact can use it as the sole basis for the identification of the accused before them as the perpetrator of the crime. It is clear that a trier of fact may, despite all the potential frailties, find an accused guilty beyond a reasonable doubt on the basis of the testimony of a single eyewitness. It follows that the same result may be reached with even greater certainty upon the basis of good quality video evidence. Surely, if a jury had only the videotape and the accused before them, they would be at liberty to find that the accused they see in the box was the person shown in the videotape at the scene of the crime committing the offence. If an appellate court, upon a review of the tape, is satisfied that it is of sufficient clarity and quality that it would be reasonable for the trier of fact to identify the accused as the person in the tape beyond any reasonable doubt then that decision should not be disturbed. Similarly, a judge sitting alone can identify the accused as the person depicted in the videotape.

. . .

Once it is established that a videotape has not been altered or changed, and that it depicts the scene of a crime, then it becomes admissible and relevant evidence. Not only is the tape (or photograph) real evidence in the sense that that term has been used in earlier cases, but it is to a certain extent, testimonial evidence as well. It can and should be used by a trier of fact in determining whether a crime has been committed and whether the accused before the court committed the crime. It may indeed be a silent, trustworthy, unemotional, unbiased and accurate witness who has complete and instant recall of events. It may provide such strong and convincing evidence that of itself it will demonstrate clearly either the innocence or guilt of the accused.

The weight to be accorded that evidence can be assessed from a viewing of the videotape. The degree of clarity and quality of the tape, and to a lesser extent the length of time during which the accused appears on the videotape, will all go towards establishing the weight which a trier of fact may properly place upon the evidence. The time of depiction may not be significant for even if there are but a few frames which clearly show the perpetrator that may be sufficient to identify the accused. Particularly will this be true if the trier of fact has reviewed the tape on several occasions and stopped it to study the pertinent frames.

Although triers of fact are entitled to reach a conclusion as to identification based solely on videotape evidence, they must exercise care in doing so. For example, when a jury is asked to identify an accused in this manner, it is essential that clear directions be given to them as to how they are to approach this task. They should be instructed to consider carefully whether the video is of sufficient clarity and quality and shows the accused for a sufficient time to enable them to conclude that identification has been proven beyond a reasonable doubt. If it is the only evidence adduced as to identity, the jury should be reminded of this. Further, they should be told once again of the importance that, in order to convict on the basis of the videotape alone, they must be satisfied beyond a reasonable doubt that it identifies the accused.

The jury or trial judge sitting alone must be able to review the videotape during their deliberations. However, the viewing equipment used at that time should be the same or similar to that used during the trial. I would think that very often triers of fact will want to review the tape on more than one occasion.

A trial judge sitting alone must be subject to the same cautions and directions as a jury in considering videotape evidence of identification. It would be helpful if, after reviewing the tape, the trial judge indicated that he or she was impressed with its clarity and quality to the extent that a finding of identity could be based upon it. This courtesy would permit Crown or particularly defence counsel to call, for example, expert evidence as to the quality of the tape or evidence as to any changes in appearance of the accused between the taking of the videotape and the trial and to prepare submissions pertaining to identification based on the tape.

I viewed the tape and it is indeed of excellent quality and great clarity. The accused is depicted for a significant period of time. At one point, it is almost as though there was a close-up of the accused taken specifically for identification purposes. There is certainly more than adequate evidence on the tape itself from which the trial judge could determine whether or not the person before her was the one who committed the robbery. The fact that the store clerk could not identify the accused is not of great significance. When the tape is viewed, it is easy to appreciate that the clerk might not have been able to properly focus upon the identity of the robber. The violent and savagely menacing jab made by the robber with a large knife directed towards the clerk suggests that self-preservation, not identification, may very reasonably have been the clerk's prime concern at the time of the robbery. Yet, the tape remained cool, collected, unbiased and accurate. It provides as clear a picture of the robbery today as it did when the traumatic events took place. The evidence of the tape is of such clarity and strength that it was certainly open to the trial judge to conclude that the accused before her was the person depicted on the tape. The trial judge was aware of the difficulties and frailties of identification evidence and acknowledged them in her reasons. Nonetheless, she was entitled on the evidence before her to conclude beyond a reasonable doubt that the accused was guilty. There was no need for corroboration of this tape.

SOPINKA J. and MAJOR J. dissenting:—

. . .

It is significant that the judge's observations are entirely untested by cross-examination. Cross-examination in identification is of special importance. Here, not only was there no opportunity to cross-examine, but the substance of the judge's observations was unknown until the case for both the Crown and defence was closed. Not only are the judge's subjective observations not tested by cross-examination but they cannot be tested on appeal. In order to evaluate the reasonableness of the evidence upon which a trier of fact relies, the Court of Appeal must be able to examine all the evidence. All we can do is see one side of a coin that has two sides. All the assurances about the clarity of the video are of no avail if we cannot see the person with whom the comparison is being made.

In summary, this conviction was based on evidence that amounted to no more than the untested opinion of the trial judge which was contradicted by other evidence that the trial judge did not reject. This included evidence that the victim, a few days after the robbery, identified a person other than the accused as the more likely perpetrator of the crime. The trial judge simply relied on her own observations, the accuracy of which we are not in a position to assess. Having regard for the inherent frailties in identification evidence, I conclude that the conviction rests on a shaky foundation and is unsafe and unsatisfactory. I am satisfied that the verdict is unreasonable and cannot be supported by the evidence.[46]

Which opinion do you find more compelling?

R. v. ANDALIB-GOORTANI
2014 ONSC 4690, 13 C.R. (7th) 128 (Ont. S.C.J.)

TROTTER J.:

INTRODUCTION

1 A photograph can be a powerful piece of evidence, especially when it purports to show a crime in progress. Photographs are introduced into evidence on a daily basis in our courts. Most of the time, no objection is taken to the admission of this type of evidence.

2 This case is different. Babak Andalib-Goortani is a Toronto Police Service (TPS) officer who is charged with assault with a weapon. The Crown seeks to rely upon a photograph that purports to record the alleged assault. The problem is that no one knows who took the photo because it was posted anonymously to a website.

3 The defence opposes the admission of the photo, arguing that the Crown is unable to establish its authenticity. The Crown contends that it has authenticated the image and that the issue is one of weight for the trier of fact.

THE FACTS

(a)   Photographs at the Scene

4 The alleged assault occurred on June 26, 2010 during the G20 Summit in Toronto. I need not say much about the G20 Summit, except to mention that it was marked with violent protests and clashes between protesters and the police. It is alleged that, during a protest at the Ontario Legislature at Queen's Park, P.C. Andalib-Goortani struck Ms. Wyndham Bettencourt-McCarthy (the complainant) with a baton, causing a nasty bruise to her hip.

5 Many photographs were taken at the protest. Mr. Vincenzo D'Alto, an accredited photojournalist from Quebec, took photos that day. He testified at the preliminary inquiry and authenticated many images. Mr. D'Alto did not take the photo in question, which depicts a police officer winding up and about to hit a female with a baton. There is no doubt that the female image in the photo is that of the complainant. The question is whether P.C. Andalib-

---

[46]   In *R. v. K. (T.A.)* (2006), 207 C.C.C. (3d) 547 (C.A.), a new trial was ordered because of the failure of the trial judge to permit defence counsel an opportunity to make submissions about the quality and content of the videotape.

Goortani is the police officer and whether the image accurately reflects what occurred that day.

6 At the preliminary inquiry, the complainant said that she saw the photograph in question several days after the event. She testified that her friend told her he found it on a site called www.g20justice.com. There is no evidence as to who uploaded the photograph to the site. The complainant was shown the photograph at the preliminary inquiry and said:

> Ah, this is a photograph of the officer who struck me, and this is a photograph of him with his arm raised and his baton out. Ah, about the moment, the moment before he struck me and in the background, there are a group of officers who are engaged in...forcibly detaining...the man who is, who is lying on the ground.

Asked what she remembered about the officer, the complainant said:

> . . . I was not able to see his face...very clearly as, as you can see in the photo, um, he has a helmet and a face shield that is...partially concealing his face. Um, but I remember seeing him come towards me and, ah, seeing a man who was...a bit shorter than me and somewhat stalky and who had facial hair, goatee style of facial hair.

The complainant is unable to identify the person who struck her.

7 The Crown intends to rely on other photographs of P.C. Andalib-Goortani at the scene, as well as other photos of him, out of uniform, on a different day. These photos are included as part of this application because the Crown intends to call another TPS officer, Sgt. Angelo Costa, to identify the face of P.C. Andalib-Goortani in some of those photographs as a step towards identifying him in the photograph in question.

• • •

(b) Expert Evidence

9 Both parties adduced expert evidence concerning the photograph. The Crown called Tracy D. Peloquin, a civilian member of the Ontario Provincial Police. Among other things, she is a Certified Forensic Video Analyst and a Forensic Identification Analyst. Her extensive *curriculum vitae* demonstrated that she is well qualified to provide an opinion on the authenticity of the photograph. She has attended many courses in her area of expertise.

• • •

12 After reviewing her findings dealing with a comparative analysis (*i.e.*, a comparison of the photograph in question with other known images of P.C. Andalib-Goortani), which is not relevant to this application, Ms. Peloquin concluded:

> It is the writer's opinion that there are no clear indications of manipulation in the suspect image...around the persons of interest or otherwise. The images show no artifacts that can be a result of being added or manipulated with an image-editing

<u>program.</u> Depth of field, lighting, shadowing and digital compression remain consistent throughout the image. <u>No visual evidence of image alteration and/or changes to the image structure was found.</u> [Emphasis added.]

13 Ms. Peloquin confirmed her opinion during her testimony before me. Upon a visual examination of the image, Ms. Peloquin did not notice anything that would raise alarms that it had been tampered with. She noticed no problems with shadowing, nor did she observe any sharp edges that might be indicative of an image being superimposed onto another image. Ms. Peloquin could only find evidence that the size of the image had been altered.

14 Towards the end of her examination-in-chief, Ms. Peloquin said that, if someone did alter the image, they would have to be possessed of strong knowledge of the relevant software to do so without being detected. Mr. Black picked up on this cross-examination. Ms. Peloquin agreed that she was unable to say that the image had *not* been altered; all she could say was that there was no evidence it *had been* altered. For example, she could not say that the face of the police officer in the photo had not been changed or that the distance between the officer and the complainant had not been adjusted. Ms. Peloquin agreed that it is impossible to determine whether the image originated from a digital or analog device, or whether it is a still shot taken from a video. Moreover, Ms. Peloquin testified that there is no way to determine how many computers or websites the image has been uploaded to and downloaded from. She was able to locate the image on ten different websites.

• • •

17 As in Ms. Peloquin's report, Mr. Musters' report discussed the easy availability of Photoshop, a program used to edit photos. Mr. Musters noted that, if a photo has been modified with Photoshop, and then uploaded to a website, evidence of the alteration would be removed when the image is stripped of its metadata.

18 Mr. Musters testified that the dpi (dots per inch) of the photo is 300. At the time of the G20 Summit in 2010, a typical camera would take a photo at a value of 72 dpi. Based on this observation, and running the image through a forensic program called FOURMatch (a program developed by a company in the field of image validation), Mr. Musters concluded:

> In our opinion the absence of metadata is indicative that the photograph was uploaded to Facebook at some point in its life cycle. The fact that the dpi of [the image] is 300 on the www.G20justice.com site points to it being altered manually with a photo editing software before it was posted to that website.

> Based on our analysis, we can conclude that this image... was processed/edited with a software program, likely one of the ones listed by FOURMatch.

> We support the "Verdict" of FOURMatch which states "that the file has been changed, though the amount of change is unknown.

19 Mr. Musters elaborated on his opinion during his testimony. In addition to noting the unusual dpi feature of the image, he said that the image taken from the website was 61.2 kb in size. Mr. Musters testified that, in the unlikely event that the photo was taken with a camera set to 300 dpi, the size of the photo would have been far larger than 61.2 kb. This led him to conclude that the image taken from the website is not the original photo from the camera. Furthermore, Mr. Musters testified that it is possible to alter facial hair on an image and not see any forensic abnormalities. In short, Mr. Musters said that one could make changes to facial hair with Photoshop and not leave any evidence of having done so because Photoshop does a "really good job" of editing without detection because it blends colours to make it look as if no alternations have been made.

. . .

ANALYSIS

(a) Framing the Issue

23 As part of its application, the Crown seeks a ruling on the admissibility of the photograph. . .

(b) Onus and Threshold

24 The Crown argues that, because photographic evidence is not presumptively inadmissible, it bears no burden in establishing the admissibility of the image in question. The Crown submits that the onus is on the defence to bring a motion to exclude the evidence. This is incorrect.

25 Some types of evidence are considered presumptively inadmissible, such as similar fact evidence (*R. v. Handy* (2002), 164 C.C.C. (3d) 481 (S.C.C.)), hearsay (*R. v. Baldree* (2013), 298 C.C.C. (3d) 425 (S.C.C.)), prior consistent statements (*R. v. Ellard* (2009), 245 C.C.C. (3d) 183 (S.C.C.)) and statements of an accused made during a "Mr. Big" operation (*R. v. Hart*, 2014 SCC 52). Photographic evidence has not been so categorized. However, this does not mean that it is *automatically* admissible; instead, photographs are *conditionally* admissible. Certain pre-conditions must be "established" on the basis of "some evidence" before a photograph is admissible and made available to a witness and the trier of fact: see S.C. Hill, D.M. Tanovich and L.P. Strezos, *McWilliams' Canadian Criminal Evidence*, 5th ed. (Toronto: Canada Law Book, 2013) (looseleaf), at pp. 23-5 to 23-9.

26 This proposition is demonstrated in *R. v. Nikolovski* (1996), 111 C.C.C. (3d) 403 (S.C.C.), in which the Court considered the admissibility of videotape evidence. Writing many years ago, Cory J. said the following at p. 416:

> Once it is established that a videotape has not been altered or changed, and it depicts the scene of a crime, then it becomes admissible and relevant evidence. Not only is the tape (or photograph) real evidence in the sense that that term has been

used in earlier cases, but is to a certain extent, testimonial evidence as well. [Emphasis added.]

See also *R. v. Penney* (2002), 163 C.C.C. (3d) 329 (Nfld. & Lab. C.A.), at pp. 335 and 342.

27 In a criminal trial, it would be improper for counsel to wave a photograph around in front of the jury, or thrust it under the nose of a witness, without first addressing the issue of authenticity. The potential for unfairness is obvious. In this case it is very real. The party wishing to make use of a photograph bears the burden of authentication, not the other way around.

(c)   Authentication

28 The leading Canadian case on authenticating images is *R. v. Creemer and Cormier*, [1968] 1 C.C.C. 14 (N.S.S.C. App. Div.). McKinnon J.A. noted the following requirements for authentication at p. 22:

> All the cases dealing with the admissibility of photographs go to show that such admissibility depends upon (1) their accuracy in truly representing the facts; (2) their fairness and absence of any intention to mislead; and (3) their verification on oath by a person capable of doing so.

This formulation has been widely accepted in many subsequent decisions and by numerous commentators: see, for example, *R. v. Maloney (No. 2)* (1976), 29 C.C.C. (2d) 431 (Ont. Co. Ct.), *R. v. Penney, supra*, *R. v. Schaffner* (1988), 44 C.C.C. (3d) 507 (N.S.C.A.), at pp. 509-511, *R. v. J.S.C.*, [2013] A.J. No. 455 (C.A.), *R. v. Adams* (2011), 274 C.C.C. (3d) 502 (N.S.C.A.), Sydney N. Lederman, Alan W. Bryant and Michelle K. Fuerst, *The Law of Evidence in Canada*, 4th edition (Toronto: LexisNexis, 2014), at pp. 44-45 and pp. 1294-1296, David Watt, *Watt's Manual of Criminal Evidence*, 2013 (Toronto: Thomson Reuters, 2014), at p. 88 and David Paciocco, *The Law of Evidence*, 6th ed. (Toronto: Irwin Law, 2011), at p. 462.

29 The Crown's attempt to authenticate the image in this case may be addressed by the application of the second criterion—fairness and absence of an intention to mislead. I conclude that the Crown has failed to establish that the image was not tampered with or altered before it came into its possession.

30 Both Ms. Peloquin and Mr. Musters agree that some properties of the image have been altered through the process of being uploaded. However, neither could say to which site it was initially uploaded. Neither is able to discern whether the image was automatically stripped of its metadata during this process, or whether it was intentionally removed (and by whom). Nor can the experts determine how many websites and/or computers this image has been uploaded to or downloaded from.

31 I appreciate that Ms. Peloquin has more formal training than Mr. Musters in this area. However, Mr. Musters' practical experience over the years equally qualifies him to provide an opinion on this matter. In his report and his testimony, Mr. Musters expressed more concern than Ms. Peloquin that the image had been tampered with or altered, and in more serious ways. He had the image analyzed by FOURMatch, which Ms. Peloquin did not. He refused to use so-called "freeware" (*i.e.*, free software available from the internet) because of his concerns about its reliability, whereas Ms. Peloquin relied on at least one of these free products ("JPEGsnoop"). In the end, I am not prepared to discount the weight of Mr. Musters' opinion in the manner that the Crown submits.

32 Some of the observed changes to the image may, at first blush, appear innocuous. However, given that the image has been changed in these ways (for reasons and by persons unknown), there is a lingering concern that it has been manipulated in other ways, ways that are intended to distort the true state of affairs that the image purports to capture. Neither expert could say that the image has not been altered in this manner. Ms. Peloquin said that it would take considerable skill for someone to alter an image and elude forensic testing. Mr. Musters suggested it would take less skill to pull off such a feat, especially with the widely available Photoshop software.

33 Materials taken from websites and offered as evidence in court must be approached with caution, especially in a case such as this where no one is prepared to step forward to say, "I took that photo and it has not been altered or changed in anyway." Several U.S. cases warn about the possibility of tampering in this context. In *People v. Beckley*, 110 Cal. Rptr. (3d) 362 (Ct. App. 2010), the Court expressed concern about the dangers of unauthenticated digital images at pp. 515-516:

> Recent experience shows that digital photographs can be changed to produce false images . . . Indeed, with the advent of computer software programs such as Adobe Photoshop "it does not always take skill, experience, or even cognizance to alter a digital photo." (Parry, Digital Manipulation and Photographic Evidence: Defrauding The Courts One Thousand Words At A Time" (2009), 2009 J.L. Tech. & Pol'y 175, 183).

Similar concerns were expressed in *St. Clair v. Johnny's Oyster & Shrimp, Inc.*, 76 F. Supp. (2d) 773 (Tex. Dist. Ct. 1999), *Griffin v. State*, 19 A. (3d) 415 (Ct. App. Md. 2010) and *People v. Lenihan*, 911 N.Y.S. (2d) 588 (Sup. Ct. N.Y. 2010). These common sense warnings take on special significance when eyewitness identification is critical, as it is in this case.

34 The Crown has failed to satisfy me that the image has not been tampered with or altered in some material way. For this reason alone, the image cannot be authenticated. In the circumstances, it is not necessary to addresses the other authentication criteria mentioned above.

CONCLUSION

35 The photograph has not been properly authenticated. It is not admissible at P.C. Andalib-Goortani's trial. The Crown's application is dismissed.

Do you think Justice Trotter came to the correct decision? David Tanovich argues:[47]

> In *Andalib-Goortani*, Justice Trotter properly recognizes that the burden rests with the proponent of the evidence to establish threshold reliability on a "some evidence" standard. Ultimately, he concluded that the G20 photograph was inadmissible because the Crown had failed to establish "that the image has not been tampered with or altered in some material way." The case leaves one wondering whether the bar has been set too high, making it almost impossible now to admit photos or other evidence uploaded to the internet. Justice Trotter was concerned that:
>
> > . . . there is a lingering concern that [the photo] has been manipulated in other ways, ways that are intended to distort the true state of affairs that the image purports to capture. Neither expert could say that the image has not been altered in this manner. Ms. Peloquin said that it would take considerable skill for someone to alter an image and elude forensic testing. Mr. Musters suggested that it would take less skill to pull off such a feat, especially with the widely available Photoshop software.
>
> Presumably, a party will always be able to find an expert to say that material downloaded to the internet "could be" manipulated without easy detection or that they cannot say for certain that it was not. Arguably, that is a question of weight and ultimate reliability.
>
> In this case, the Crown's expert offered the most definitive opinion on the issue when she concluded that "It is the writer's opinion that there are no clear indications of manipulation in the suspect image . . . around the persons of interest or otherwise. The images show no artifacts that can be as a result of being added or manipulated with an image-editing program." Moreover, the complainant did testify at the preliminary inquiry that the photograph was an accurate representation of her memory of the assault including her memory of the height and facial hair of the officer who struck her. Normally, this kind of evidence has been sufficient to authenticate a video or photograph.

In light of the authentication ruling, the officer was acquitted.[48] The same officer was previously convicted of assaulting Adam Nobody during those protests and sentenced to 45 days' imprisonment although that sentence was reduced on appeal to time served.[49]

---

[47]   *R. v. Andalib-Goortani: Authentication & the Internet*, C.R comment.

[48]   See Alysah Hasham, "Cop acquitted on second G20 assault charge", *Toronto Star* (24 September 2014).

[49]   See *R. v. Andalib-Goortani*, 2015 ONSC 1403 (Ont. S.C.J.), additional reasons 2015 ONSC 1445 (Ont. S.C.J.).

2. DOCUMENTS

Documents are the most common form of real evidence. Their authenticity may be established by calling the suggested writer, by calling one who saw him or her write the document or who has an awareness of his or her handwriting, by direct comparison of the handwriting in dispute with handwriting known to be that of the suggested writer, by the testimony of experts, or by admission of authenticity by the party against whom the document is tendered.

Section 8 of the *Canada Evidence Act* provides:

> Comparison of a disputed writing with any writing proved to the satisfaction of the court to be genuine shall be permitted to be made by witnesses, and such writings, and the evidence of witnesses respecting those writings, may be submitted to the court and jury as proof of the genuineness or otherwise of the writing in dispute.

In *R. v. Abdi*[50] it was held that s. 8 did not preclude a common law option of allowing a jury to compare writing samples without witness testimony. The Court relied on *Nikolovski* but also decided that the jury should be warned to be cautious in reaching a conclusion without expert or witness testimony as to the handwriting. In addition, there are some documents which so regularly have significance in legal proceedings that the common law has developed rules allowing the documents to authenticate themselves because of the circumstances in which they are generated or kept in custody.

Two examples of such rules allowing authentication by circumstantial evidence are those affecting ancient documents and reply letters. If a document is over 30 years old, there are no circumstances indicating fraud, and it is produced from a place where its custody is natural, the circumstances call for it to be presumed authentic; the courts were also moved by the fact that circumstantial evidence would often be necessary as the maker or witnesses might no longer be available.[51] If a letter is received purportedly signed by Smith, the law will presume the letter authentic if it was received in response to an earlier letter; the reply indicates knowledge in the signer which, relying on the habitual accuracy of the mails, could only have come from the earlier letter addressed to Smith.[52]

In addition to the rules developed at common law, the various Evidence Acts in Canada and the *Criminal Code* are filled with provisions to aid the authentication of official and government documents.[53]

It must be borne in mind that even where a statutory provision operates to authenticate a document, the effect is merely to establish that in fact the statement was made. If the statement is to be introduced to establish the truth

---

[50]   (1997), 116 C.C.C. (3d) 385, 11 C.R. (5th) 197 (Ont. C.A.).
[51]   See *Stevenson v. Dandy*, [1920] 2 W.W.R. 643 (Alta. C.A.) at 661.
[52]   See *Montgomery v. Graham* (1871), 31 U.C.Q.B. 57 (C.A.). Note that the document though authenticated as genuine may still be held inadmissible as violative of the hearsay rule. A hearsay exception for ancient writings deserves further consideration.
[53]   See e.g. *Canada Evidence Act*, R.S.C. 1985, c. C-5, ss. 19-23.

of the matter stated, its receivability will be conditioned by the hearsay rule which will be examined later.[54]

3. BEST EVIDENCE RULE

In contrast to the above rules which *facilitate* the proof of a document there is an ancient rule which *requires* that, when the terms of a document are material, proof of the terms of the document must be by production of the original. The documentary originals rule, sometimes called the best evidence rule, existed even before witnesses were called to testify before a jury,[55] but as the new system of inquiry took hold, the rule was retained, as it was seen to be beneficial; production of the original avoided possible errors in copying or in oral evidence regarding the contents. Some text-writers in the nineteenth century spoke of a wider best evidence rule applicable to *all* forms of evidence which *required* the best evidence that could be given and also *allowed* the best evidence that could be given. Thayer described this as "an old principle which had served a useful purpose for the century while rules of evidence had been forming and . . . was no longer fit to serve any purpose as a working rule of exclusion".[56] Restricting the rule's use to documents, perhaps jettisoning its use completely in favour of the name "documentary originals rule", would bring needed clarity. As opposed to a general rule of exclusion for the other forms of real evidence, we would have then simply the application of common sense that the failure to produce the best evidence available to the proponent might yield a distrust for the evidence that was produced. As Lord Denning put it:

> . . . the old rule that a party must produce the best evidence that the nature of the case will allow, and that any less good evidence is to be excluded. That old rule has gone by the board long ago. The only remaining instance of it that I know is that if an original document is available in one's hands, one must produce it. One cannot give secondary evidence by producing a copy. Nowadays we do not confine ourselves to the best evidence. We admit all relevant evidence. The goodness or badness of it goes only to weight, and not to admissibility.[57]

The documentary originals rule requires production of the original unless the proponent is unable to do so. Secondary evidence may be introduced if the proponent can satisfy the court that the original is lost or destroyed or is in the possession of another and cannot be obtained.[58]

In *R. v. Betterest Vinyl Manufacturing Ltd.*[59] Justice Taggart wrote for the B.C. Court of Appeal:

---

[54]   See Lester, "The Rules of Evidence Governing Cross-Examination Based on Documents: A Practical Guide" (1996) 18 Advocates' Quarterly 261.

[55]   Thayer, *A Preliminary Treatise on Evidence at the Common Law* (1898) at 503.

[56]   *Ibid.* at 495.

[57]   *Garton v. Hunter*, [1969] 1 All E.R. 451 (C.A.) at 453, followed in *Kajala v. Noble* (1982), 75 Cr. App. R. 149 (C.A.) at 152 per Arkner, L.J.: "In our judgment the old rule is limited and confined to written documents in the strict sense of the term, and has no relevance to tapes or films." See also *R. v. Donald* (1958), 121 C.C.C. 304, 306 (N.B. C.A.) and *R. v. Galarce* (1983), 35 C.R. (3d) 268 (Sask. Q.B.).

[58]   See e.g. *R. v. Wayte* (1983), 76 Cr. App. R. 110.

[59]   (1989) 52 C.C.C. (3d) 441.

As I read the textwriters and the authorities we are no longer bound to apply strictly the best evidence rule as it relates to copies of documents and especially photocopies of them. . . An over-technical and strained application of the best evidence rule served only to hamper the inquiry without at all advancing the cause of truth.[60]

In addition, various statutory provisions have been enacted to provide for the introduction of copies when to require the original would produce great inconvenience. For example, s. 29 of the *Canada Evidence Act*[61] provides for the receipt of copies of entries in bankers' books, s. 30(3) for copies of records made in the usual and ordinary course of business, and s. 31(2)(c) for copies of records belonging to or deposited with any government or corporation there defined.

R. v. COTRONI

(1977), 37 C.C.C. (2d) 409 (Ont. C.A.), affirmed (*sub nom. Papalia v. R.*) [1979] 2 S.C.R. 256, 45 C.C.C. (2d) 1, (*sub nom. R. v. Swartz*) 7 C.R. (3d) 185, 11 C.R. (3d) 150

The accused were charged with conspiracy to possess money obtained by extortion.

JESSUP J.A. (ARNUP and ZUBER JJ.A. concurring):—

. . .

The only evidence incriminating Violi and Cotroni, and essential evidence against Swartz and Papalia, consisted of the tape recordings of three conversations which took place in premises at Montreal. The recordings proffered in evidence were re-recordings. The explanation for this was that, after re-recording, the original recordings had been erased and the tapes of them reused. The reason was that at that time it was not the practice of the Montreal police to use tape recordings as evidence in Court. The further reason was that electronic surveillance of the premises in Montreal had extended over a protracted period and the storage of the many resultant tapes presented a problem. As a result, a record only of significant conversations was kept by re-recording such significant parts on fresh tapes which were preserved.

It was argued that the re-recordings proffered were inadmissible as not being the best evidence of the conversations they reproduced. However, counsel made the significant admission that no question was raised as to the authenticity of the re- recordings.

Of the "best evidence" rule Halsbury states in 17 Hals., 4th ed., pp. 8-9, para. 8:

That evidence should be the best that the nature of the case will allow is, besides being a matter of obvious prudence, a principle with a considerable pedigree. However, any strict interpretation of this principle has long been obsolete, and the rule is now only of importance in regard to the primary evidence of private documents. The logic of requiring the production of an original document where it

---

[60] *Ibid.* at 447-448.
[61] R.S.C. 1985, c. C-5.

is available rather than relying on possibly unsatisfactory copies, or the recollections of witnesses, is clear, although modern techniques make objections to the first alternative less strong.

The rule itself, in its relatively modern form, did not absolutely exclude evidence. It is stated by Lord Esher, M.R., in *Lucas v. Williams & Sons*, [1892] 2 Q.B. 113 at p. 116:

> "Primary" and "secondary" evidence mean this: primary evidence is evidence which the law requires to be given first; secondary evidence is evidence which may be given in the absence of the better evidence which the law requires to be given first, when a proper explanation is given of the absence of that better evidence.

Lord Denning would remove the question of secondary evidence entirely from the area of admissibility to that of weight. In *Garton v. Hunter*, [1969] 2 Q.B. 37 at p. 44 he said:

> It is plain that Scott L.J. had in mind the old rule that a party must produce the best evidence that the nature of the case will allow, and that any less good evidence is to be excluded. That old rule has gone by the board long ago. The only remaining instance of it that I know is that if an original document is available in your hands, you must produce it. You cannot give secondary evidence by producing a copy. Nowadays we do not confine ourselves to the best evidence. We admit all relevant evidence. The goodness or badness of it goes only to weight, and not to admissibility.

However, the counsel of prudence mentioned by Halsbury accords with the principle stated by *McCormick's Handbook of the Law of Evidence*, 2nd ed. (1972), p. 571:

> If the original document has been destroyed by the person who offers evidence of its contents, the evidence is not admissible unless, by showing that the destruction was accidental or was done in good faith, without intention to prevent its use as evidence, he rebuts to the satisfaction of the trial judge, any inference of fraud.

The same principle should apply to tape recordings.

. . .

. . . In my opinion, the learned trial Judge properly received in evidence in the present case the re-recordings proffered.

The notion of "best evidence" has arisen again with the admissibility regime in the *Canada Evidence Act* concerning electronic evidence.

R. v. HIRSCH
2017 SKCA 14, 353 C.C.C. (3d) 230, 36 C.R. (7th) 216 (Sask. C.A.)

CALDWELL J.A.

[1] Christopher Donald Hirsch appeals against his conviction and sentence . . . on the charge that he "did by facebook [*sic*] message, knowingly utter threats to cause bodily harm to [the complainant], by saying he was going to choke her

and end it with a shotgun shell, contrary to Section 264.1(1) of the Criminal Code." The charge followed from the posting, ostensibly on Mr. Hirsch's Facebook account, of a message stating intentions to choke the complainant, Mr. Hirsch's former girlfriend, and to shoot her. The message was accompanied by a nude photograph of the complainant.

. . .

[4] I would also dismiss the conviction appeal for the reasons that follow.

. . .

A. Authentication of documentary evidence

[14] The primary allegation of error in this appeal is that the trial judge admitted and relied on digital photographs—namely, the screen captures of what was, ostensibly, Mr. Hirsch's Facebook page—to convict Mr. Hirsch, without requiring the Crown to authenticate that evidence and despite his trial counsel's objections to admissibility and authenticity. The screen captures included images of a Facebook page showing a post of a nude photograph of the complainant as well as a post of the textual message complained of in this case.

[15] In his factum, Mr. Hirsch confined his argument to the authentication of the screen captures and, relatedly, authorship of the Facebook posts. In that regard, the Crown had adduced evidence through the complainant to the effect that she recognised the Facebook page shown in screen captures as that of Mr. Hirsch. In his factum, Mr. Hirsch takes issue with this because, as the complainant admitted, Mr. Hirsch had blocked her access to his Facebook page about two months before the offence and, therefore, she had had no recent, direct access to his page and was not in a position to authenticate it. Mr. Hirsch also says the Crown ought to have called the complainant's friend, who had taken the screen captures and given them to the complainant, for authentication purposes and to dispel any speculation about editing or tampering.

[16] In oral argument before this Court, Mr. Hirsch additionally alleged the Crown had failed to comply with the requirements of the Canada Evidence Act, RSC 1985, c C-5, as they relate to electronic documents. In particular, the Canada Evidence Act provides:

Authentication of electronic documents

31.1 Any person seeking to admit an electronic document as evidence has the burden of proving its authenticity by evidence capable of supporting a finding that the electronic document is that which it is purported to be.

Application of best evidence rule — electronic documents

31.2(1) The best evidence rule in respect of an electronic document is satisfied

(a) on proof of the integrity of the electronic documents system by or in which the electronic document was recorded or stored; . . .

Presumption of integrity

31.3 For the purposes of subsection 31.2(1), in the absence of evidence to the contrary, the integrity of an electronic documents system by or in which an electronic document is recorded or stored is proven

(a) by evidence capable of supporting a finding that at all material times the computer system or other similar device used by the electronic documents system was operating properly or, if it was not, the fact of its not operating properly did not affect the integrity of the electronic document and there are no other reasonable grounds to doubt the integrity of the electronic documents system;

(b) if it is established that the electronic document was recorded or stored by a party who is adverse in interest to the party seeking to introduce it; or

(c) if it is established that the electronic document was recorded or stored in the usual and ordinary course of business by a person who is not a party and who did not record or store it under the control of the party seeking to introduce it.

. . .

Application

31.7 Sections 31.1 to 31.4 do not affect any rule of law relating to the admissibility of evidence, except the rules relating to authentication and best evidence.

Definitions

31.8 The definitions in this section apply in sections 31.1 to 31.6.

computer system means a device that, or a group of interconnected or related devices one or more of which,

(a) contains computer programs or other data; and

(b) pursuant to computer programs, performs logic and control, and may perform any other function.

data means representations of information or of concepts, in any form.

electronic document means data that is recorded or stored on any medium in or by a computer system or other similar device and that can be read or perceived by a person or a computer system or other similar device. It includes a display, printout or other output of that data.

electronic documents system includes a computer system or other similar device by or in which data is recorded or stored and any procedures related to the recording or storage of electronic documents.

[17] On the basis of his factum and oral arguments, I would identify the issues raised by Mr. Hirsch in relation to this aspect of the appeal as being twofold:

(a) whether the Crown had authenticated an electronic document; and

(b) whether the Crown had proven the integrity of an electronic document.

1. Authentication of an electronic document

[18] I am not persuaded by Mr. Hirsch's arguments on authentication and the related issue of authorship. In my assessment, s. 31.1 of the Canada Evidence Act is a codification of the common law rule of evidence authentication. The provision merely requires the party seeking to adduce an electronic document into evidence to prove that the electronic document is what it purports to be. This may be done through direct or circumstantial evidence: The Honourable Justice David Watt, *Watt's Manual of Criminal Evidence, 2016* (Toronto: Thomson Reuters, 2016) at 104 [*Watt's Manual*]. Quite simply, to authenticate an electronic document, counsel could present it to a witness for identification and, presumably, the witness would articulate some basis for authenticating it as what it purported to be (see: *Pfizer Canada Inc. v Teva Canada Limited*, 2016 FCA 161 (CanLII) at para 93, 400 DLR (4th) 723). That is, while authentication is required, it is not an onerous requirement. In *Watt's Manual*, the author notes at 1115:

> The *burden* of proving authenticity of an electronic document is on the person who seeks its admission. The *standard* of proof required is the introduction of evidence capable of supporting a finding that the electronic document is as it claims to be. In essence, the threshold is met and admissibility achieved by the introduction of some evidence of authenticity.
>
> [Emphasis in original]

As this suggests, the integrity (or reliability) of the electronic document is not open to attack at the authentication stage of the inquiry. Those questions are to be resolved under s. 31.2 of the Canada Evidence Act—*i.e.*, the best evidence rule, as it relates to electronic documents. (See, as examples, the applications of ss. 31.1 and 31.2 in *R v Himes*, 2016 ONSC 249 (CanLII) at paras 45-48; *R v K.M.*, 2016 NWTSC 36 (CanLII); *R v Oland*, 2015 NBQB 245 (CanLII) at paras 52-91, 446 NBR (2d) 224; and *R v Moon*, 2016 ABPC 103 (CanLII), 36 Alta LR (6th) 386; but see *R v Moise*, 2016 MBCA 61 (CanLII), decided under the test in *R v Palmer*, 1979 CanLII 8 (SCC), [1980] 1 SCR 759, for admissibility of fresh evidence on appeal.)

[19] As to authentication in this case, as noted, the Crown put the screen captures to the complainant and she testified as to recognising them as depicting Mr. Hirsch's Facebook page. She gave reasons to support her identification of it and its author: a) she was familiar with Mr. Hirsch's

Facebook page; b) she recognised the Facebook page as being that of Mr. Hirsch; c) she recognised a nude photograph of herself that she had sent only to Mr. Hirsch; d) he was shown as the author of the posts; and e) the textual postings were consistent with the manner in which Mr. Hirsch communicated.

[20] In cross-examination, the complainant acknowledged she had no way of knowing whether her friend, who had sent her the screen captures, had edited or changed what they purported to show. However, when Mr. Hirsch's trial counsel asked her whether she recognised the words complained of as a quote from a Dave Chappelle comedy sketch, she agreed it was, or some of it was, namely, the choking part. But, she recognised the words "because he [Mr. Hirsch] used to always say that." She had no direct knowledge of the comedy sketch. She also testified under cross-examination that she recognised a small photograph of her cat on the Facebook page, located right beside Mr. Hirsch's name. She said she knew the screen captures had been taken 31 minutes after the nude photograph and threat had been posted to Facebook by reason of the timestamp on the postings shown in the screen captures, but acknowledged she had no idea when the postings themselves had occurred.

[21] From the transcript, it is clear the trial judge was alive to the issues of authentication and authorship, although perhaps not to the requirements of s. 31.1 of the Canada Evidence Act, which had not been raised at trial. Nevertheless, I am satisfied the evidence adduced in this respect was *capable* of authenticating the screen captures as a record of Mr. Hirsch's Facebook page. While it might have been preferable to have the complainant's friend testify as to authenticity, there was sufficient evidence of authentication before the trial judge for him to reach the conclusion that he did and, because of that, I find no compelling reason to interfere with his conclusion that the screen captures were admissible.

2. Proof of integrity

[22] At common law, the best evidence rule requires the proponent of a record to produce the original record or the next best available record: *Watt's Manual* at 106. However, the concept of an *original* is not readily applied to electronic documents. Further, due to the inherent nature of electronic documents, it is often impossible to provide direct evidence of the integrity of an electronic document sought to be adduced into evidence. For this reason, the Canada Evidence Act dispenses with the common law requirement of an *original* record and substitutes other means of satisfying the purpose that underpins the best evidence rule. See, for example, the application of these provisions in *R v Nde Soh*, 2014 NBQB 20 (CanLII), 416 NBR (2d) 328.

[23] The purpose of the best evidence rule is to assist the trier of fact with the verification of the integrity of documents because alterations are more readily detectible on original documents. Sections 31.2 to 31.6 of the Canada Evidence Act set out the means by which a party may prove the integrity of an electronic

document. In simple terms, under that *Act*, the integrity of an electronic document is proven by establishing the integrity or reliability of the electronic document system in which it is recorded or stored. That is, proof of electronic document *system integrity* is a substitute for proof of electronic *document integrity*.

[24] Of importance in this case, s. 31.3(b) provides for a *presumption of integrity* in the circumstances where a party has established that the electronic document the party seeks to adduce into evidence was recorded or stored by another party who is adverse in interest to the party seeking to introduce it. Although no reference was made to the Canada Evidence Act at trial, this was largely the circumstance before the trial judge. The Crown sought to introduce copies of Mr. Hirsch's Facebook page—an electronic document recorded and stored by Mr. Hirsch—through screen captures of that electronic document. It might be suggested that, in one sense, there were actually two electronic documents at issue: the screen captures themselves and the Facebook page itself. However, the more compelling conclusion is that the screen captures are the best evidence available to the Crown to adduce Mr. Hirsch's Facebook page itself into evidence. Indeed, given the fluidity and impermanence of postings on a Facebook page, a screen capture may be one of the few ways of establishing what was actually posted on a Facebook page at any point in time. On this basis, I am satisfied the presumption of integrity under s. 31.3(b) of the Canada Evidence Act applied in these circumstances and was not rebutted (Mr. Hirsch adduced no evidence).

[25] However, as the Canada Evidence Act had not been raised, the trial judge approached the matter differently. He addressed only the arguments raised at trial by Mr. Hirsh against admissibility and authentication. In that respect, Mr. Hirsch had argued the complainant's lack of direct access to his Facebook page meant there was no direct evidence that there were nude photographs of her on it or that threats had been conveyed through it. That is, Mr. Hirsch argued identity or authorship could not be proven beyond a reasonable doubt because the screen captures had not been authenticated by the person who had sent them to the complainant.

[26] The trial judge rejected these arguments because, in his assessment, the evidence considered as a whole proved the screen captures accurately depicted Mr. Hirsch's Facebook page. Critically, the trial judge found that Mr. Hirsch was the author of the text messages subsequently sent to the complainant and that those messages were capable of proving Mr. Hirsch had also posted the threatening message on his Facebook page. He marshalled the following evidence in support of his findings:

(a) the complainant was familiar with and recognized Mr. Hirsch's Facebook page;

(b) it was highly likely the Facebook post and the text messages sent to the complainant were authored by the same person given the similarity in the nature of the language used in both;

(c) the language of the threatening Facebook post was similar to how Mr. Hirsch normally spoke to the complainant;

(d) the author of the Facebook post and the text messages referred to the complainant by her first name;

(e) the author of the Facebook post and the text messages referred to the complainant by her first name;

(f) Mr. Hirsch was the only person who had nude photographs of the complainant;

(g) it would be highly speculative to find the complainant's friend had modified the screen captures; and

(h) it would be highly speculative to find that someone other than Mr. Hirsch had posted the threatening message on Mr. Hirsch's Facebook page.

[27] Moreover, when discussing the issue of whether time was an essential element of the charge, the trial judge made a finding on the basis of the text messages that I can only interpret as his conclusion that Mr. Hirsch had *admitted* responsibility for posting the threatening message and nude photograph to his Facebook page. In his oral reasons in this regard, the trial judge said:

> In fact, based on Mr. Hirsch's texts, subsequent to [the complainant] raising the issue, *it seems Mr. Hirsch was quite content to take responsibility for the Facebook post*. Again, I look to the upper screen shot on page 4 of Exhibit P-1 [*i.e.*, screen-captures of the text messages], and note that below the shot of the exposed breast, Mr. Hirsch writes: (as read)
>
> > Fuck, I wish I would have kept them ugly pics of you and Facebooked them. I got – only had a tit shot, but I decided disrespect will get you disrespect like I told you over and over.
>
> I note there is nothing in any of these emails that would suggest Mr. Hirsch felt he had been framed by somebody else. There is no doubt in my mind that Mr. Hirsch also authored the incoming text messages in Exhibit P-1. To find otherwise would be to engage in even greater speculation. . . .

[28] In addition, although not specifically referenced by the trial judge in his reasons, the evidence was that Mr. Hirsch had also sent the following text messages to the complainant:

> That just got sent to fb and every contact and email in my pphone . . . have a.goood day looper

and

Fucking delete it urself. cause i got more . . cunt. disrespect me and ull getvit worse in return . . . if ud have learned this wouldn't happen but ur to outta control to make it throughh a fucking day without disrespecting me . . . I WANT U DEAD

and

I'm goonna torment u till u fucking leave me alone.do u think i want u.i can't stand fucking u.its been boring and lame since i met u.

[29] Given the evidence and the presumption of integrity under the Canada Evidence Act, I find no reason to disturb the trial judge's decision to admit the screen captures into evidence as an authenticated electronic document depicting Facebook postings authored by Mr. Hirsch.[62]

4. DEMONSTRATIVE EVIDENCE

One needs to recognize a distinction between real evidence and demonstrative evidence. Demonstrative evidence, charts, models and the like are tools to assist the trier in understanding the evidence. Real evidence, the gun, the narcotics, the bloodstained shirt, tendered as an object within the courtroom is not a helpful aid but rather is evidence itself. Real evidence needs to be authenticated. With items of demonstrative evidence their worth depends on whether they are accurate representations of what happened. The judge needs to be satisfied that the demonstration will genuinely assist the trier of fact and not distort the fact-finding process. There is concern that the demonstration might overpower the trier. In the end we can do little more than trust the discretion of the trial judge.

R. v. MACDONALD
(2000), 35 C.R. (5th) 130, 146 C.C.C. (3d) 525 (Ont. C.A.)

The accused M was a fugitive from justice. He and his co-accused V were the targets of a police "takedown" which did not go smoothly. As a result, M was charged with two counts of aggravated assault and one count of dangerous driving, and V was charged with possession of a restricted weapon, possession of a weapon for a purpose dangerous to the public peace and assault with a weapon. Twenty months after the attempted takedown, the police made a video in which they attempted to reconstruct and re-enact the takedown. The finished product reflected the recollections of four police officers. Defence counsel objected to the admissibility of the video at trial on the ground that it was more prejudicial than probative. The trial judge ruled that the video was admissible. The Crown played the video twice during the examination-in-chief of one of the police officers.

---

[62]   See too *R. v. Avanes*, 2015 ONCJ 606, 25 C.R. (7th) 26 (Ont. C.J.) (Blackberries chipped off and saved to DVD); *R. v. Hamdan*, 2017 BCSC 676, 349 C.C.C. (3d) 338, 37 C.R. (7th) 384 (B.C. S.C.) (Facebook posts and profiles); *R. v. Hirsch*, 2017 SKCA 14, 353 C.C.C. (3d) 230, 36 C.R. (7th) 216 (Sask. C.A.). See more generally Brock Jones, "The Courts 'Liked' Your Post: Assessing Social Media Evidence in Criminal Proceedings" (2015) 62 Crim. L.Q. 372.

PER CURIAM:—

. . .

We will first describe how the video was made and its contents, then discuss the applicable principles governing its admissibility and, finally, apply the principles to this case.

The evidence on the *voir dire* explained how the video re-enactment was produced and what it showed. The police acquired a car similar to the car MacDonald was driving and another car to be positioned behind the "suspect car". During the takedown, the car behind had been a large sport-utility vehicle, a Ford Explorer; its replacement in the video was much smaller, a 1987 Toyota. The location chosen for the video, apparently a deserted sand quarry, differed from the location of the actual incident, a controlled intersection with a traffic light in the town of Markham. The video lasted 20 seconds. Officer Brown testified that it showed the cars moving "much slower" than they did during the actual incident and, therefore, the length of the video was also longer than the time of the incident.

The video re-enacts the police's version of what occurred during the attempted takedown. Four police officers — Brown, Wright, Rodgers and Giangrande — played themselves, recreating what each claimed to have done during the incident. The video shows the four officers getting out of the emergency response unit van, which is partly blocking the suspect car. Three officers take up positions several feet in front of the car with their guns aimed at the occupants. All three are shouting loudly: "Police, don't move." Four seconds elapse between the police first shouting and the suspect car backing up. The camera shows the police from behind facing the suspect car. The camera is then set inside the car to show the driver's perspective looking out at the officers through the windshield. The police are clearly visible to the driver of the suspect car.

After the suspect car backs up a considerable distance, the camera shows the car from the outside, advancing on the officers. Brown, the officer nearest the passenger side, shoots twice into the windshield on that side of the car. Rodgers, the officer at the driver's window, fires four shots in rapid succession at the windshield on the driver's side. Red lines were added to the video to show the trajectory of the bullets but the trial judge ruled they be deleted before the video was shown to the jury. As the car moves forward on the video it hits Brown, who rolls onto the hood in a fetal position. The video ends with the car driving away, Brown still on the hood.

The video re-enactment took two hours to make. The finished product reflected the recollections of the four officers. Although each officer tried to recreate his own actions, the four discussed the incident among themselves before making the video.

We turn now to the applicable legal principles. A serious concern with videotaped re-enactments, particularly those created without the participation of the accused, is their potential to unfairly influence the jury's decision-making. Because a video re-enactment has an immediate visual impact, jurors may be induced to give it more weight than it deserves and, correspondingly, to discount less compelling or less vivid evidence which is nonetheless more probative of the facts in dispute. Several commentators and courts have warned against this danger. Dean Wigmore adverted to it in his classic treatise on evidence, *Wigmore, Evidence in Trials at Common Law* (1970), at s. 798a:

> In so far as such a [motion] picture has any value beyond a still picture, this value depends on the correctness of the *artificial reconstruction* of a complex series of movements and erections, usually involving several actors, each of them the paid agent of the party and acting under his direction. Hence its reliability, as identical with the original scene, is decreased and may be minimized to the point of worthlessness.
>
> Where this possibility is serious, what should be done? Theoretically, of course, the motion picture can never be assumed to represent the actual occurrence: what is seen in it is merely what certain witnesses say was the thing that happened. And, moreover, the party's hired agents may so construct it as to go considerably further in his favor than the witnesses' testimony has gone. And yet, any motion picture is apt to cause forgetfulness of this and to impress the jury with the convincing impartiality of Nature herself...

So too did Professor McCormick in his evidence text, *McCormick on Evidence*, 4th ed. (1992), vol. 2, at pp. 3-4:

> It has already been noted that evidence from which the trier of fact may derive his own perceptions, rather than evidence consisting of the reported perceptions of others, possesses unusual force. Consequently, demonstrative evidence is frequently objected to as prejudicial, a term which is today generally defined as suggesting "decision on an improper basis, commonly, though not necessarily, an emotional one." A great deal of demonstrative evidence has the capacity to generate emotional responses such as pity, revulsion, or contempt, and where this capacity outweighs the value of the evidence on the issues in litigation, exclusion is appropriate. Again, even if no essentially emotional response is likely to result, demonstrative evidence may convey an impression of objective reality to the trier. Thus, the courts are frequently sensitive to the objection that the evidence is "misleading", and zealous to insure that there is no misleading differential between objective things offered at trial and the same or different objective things as they existed at the time of the events or occurrences in litigation.

This danger increases when the videotape depicts not just the undisputed positions of persons and things, but one side's version of disputed facts. McCormick makes this point in discussing the admissibility of photographs, at p. 17:

> A somewhat . . . troublesome problem is presented by posed or artificially reconstructed scenes, in which people, automobiles, and other objects are placed so as to conform to the descriptions of the original crime or collision given by the witnesses. When the posed photographs go no further than to portray the positions of persons and objects as reflected in the undisputed testimony, their admission has long been generally approved. Frequently, however, a posed photograph will portray only the version of the facts supported by the testimony of the proponent's witness. The dangers inherent in this situation, i.e., the tendency of the photographs unduly to emphasize certain testimony and the possibility that the jury may confuse one party's reconstruction with objective fact, have led many

courts to exclude photographs of this type . . . the current trend would appear to be to permit even photos of disputed reconstructions in some instances [e.g., if pressing necessity].

In a comprehensive article on the subject, "Manufacturing Evidence for Trial: The Prejudicial Implications of Videotaped Crime Scenery Re-enactments" (1994), 142 *U. Pa. L. R.* 2125, David B. Hennes examined the high sensory impact of video images and their tendency to stay at the front of the viewer's mind. He summarized why admitting videotaped re-enactments may be unfair at pp. 2179-80:

> The danger of unfair prejudice presented by the videotaped re-enactment is a function of both the manner of the presentation and the content of the presentation. That danger is only accentuated by its stark lack of probative value. The availability heuristic suggests that the re-enactment will be readily recalled and heavily relied upon during the decision-making process. Individuals learn more readily through sight, and a key component of the learning process comes through the use of the television, an everyday source of entertainment and information. A television videotape, much more than other forms of demonstrative visual evidence, leaves a lasting impression on jurors' mental processes, since its vividness dictates that it will be readily available for cognitive recall. The videotaped re-enactment, because of its mental impressionability, is exactly the type of vivid information to which the availability heuristic grants cognitive priority during decision-making.

Mr. Hennes approved of the majority opinion of the Texas Court of Appeals in *Lopez v. State*, 651 S.W. 2d 413 (1983) at p. 416, banning video re-enactments. Burdock J. wrote:

> . . . We find that any staged, re-enacted criminal acts or defensive issues involving human beings are impossible to duplicate in every minute detail and are therefore inherently dangerous, offer little in substance and the impact of re-enactments is too highly prejudicial to insure the State or the defendant a fair trial.

In addition to the concerns about video re-enactments discussed by courts and commentators, we cannot ignore the reality that usually only the Crown has the resources to produce a video and thus, in many cases, the re-enactment will be an "extra witness for the state".

Despite these concerns, however, we think it would be unwise to lay down rigid rules governing the admissibility of video re-enactments. In an era of rapidly changing technology we would take a step backward were we to prohibit the use of video re-enactments in the courtroom. Further, an outright prohibition would hinder the efforts of today's advocates to devise new and creative ways to promote their clients' causes.

In our view, the preferable approach recognizes the dangers of video re-enactments but adopts a case-by-case analysis. As with the admissibility of other kinds of evidence, the overriding principle should be whether the prejudicial effect of the video re-enactment outweighs its probative value. If it does, the video re-enactment should not be admitted. In balancing the prejudicial and probative value of a video re-enactment, trial judges should at least consider the video's relevance, its accuracy, its fairness, and whether what it portrays can be verified under oath: see *R. v. Creemer*, [1968] 1 C.C.C. 14 at p. 22 (N.S. C.A.). Other considerations may be material depending on the case. And as with rulings on the admissibility of other kinds of evidence, the trial judge's decision to admit or exclude a video re-enactment is entitled to deference on appeal.

The appellants contend that another consideration should be necessity, whether the video is needed in the light of the other evidence in the case. According to the appellants, if a taped re-enactment merely repeats what witnesses have already testified to, it adds nothing new and accordingly should not be admitted. This argument, however, applies equally to other kinds of demonstrative evidence — charts, graphs, diagrams and photographs — that courts routinely admit to help the trier of fact understand the testimony of witnesses. The question of necessity is, therefore, better dealt with as yet another aspect of evaluating the prejudicial effect and probative value of a video re-enactment in a given case.

With these principles in mind, we consider the use of the video by the Crown in this case. We accept that the video was relevant because it sought to portray the incident that gave rise to the charges against the appellants. We also accept that Officer Rodgers testified under oath about the video and explained it to the jury. In our view, however, the trial judge erred in admitting the video for two main reasons: first, he failed to appreciate that its many inaccuracies undermined its probative value; and, second, he was not sensitive enough to the prejudice caused by re-enacting one side's version of events.

A video's probative value rests on the accuracy of its re-enactment of undisputed facts. This video failed to meet this requirement. It did not accurately represent the undisputed facts and even ventured into the realm of disputed facts. Variation from the actual facts may be permissible but only if the variation can be fully explained to and properly understood by the trier of fact. No explanation was given to the jury in this case.

Accuracy imports many different factors. LeSage J. observed in *R. v. Maloney (No. 2)* (1976), 29 C.C.C. (2d) 431 (Ont. Co. Ct.) at p. 436 that accuracy means "consistent with facts, agreeing with reality . . . reality therefore includes not only material objects but also the immaterial such as light, sound, and the dimensions of space and *time*". Discrepancies in various factors may affect the accuracy of a videotaped re-enactment, including time of day, time of year, weather conditions, lighting or visibility, speed of action, distance, location, physical characteristics of the individuals portrayed, physical characteristics of the "props", and complexity of the events depicted. Many of these factors are inaccurately represented in this video re-enactment. The following table shows how the undisputed evidence at trial about the attempted takedown differed from the video re-enactment of it:

Facts	Actual Takedown	Video Re-enactment
Time of year	June 20	February
Time of day	4:00 p.m.	Morning
Location	Markham intersection at stop light	Deserted sand quarry
Speed	Actual	Slower
Distance (of suspect's car from Officer Rodgers)	3 — 4 feet	Inches
Type of car behind the suspect car	Ford Explorer	Toyota

These inaccuracies distorted the reality of the takedown. The jurors were given a powerful and misleading image of what occurred, which could only have undermined their ability to fairly determine the crucial fact in the case, whether MacDonald could see that those who surrounded his car were police officers. Moreover, the video re-enactment was superfluous. The jury heard ample evidence from the Crown and the defence about what happened during the takedown. They were also given maps and diagrams of the scene. Overall, in our view, the video re-enactment had little or no probative value.

In contrast, the video was highly prejudicial. The trial judge dismissed the claim of prejudice by stating that the video re-enactment "is not more prejudicial than oral testimony". This is surely wrong. All of the authorities say the opposite. The video permitted the prosecution to put before the jury its own version of what occurred, distilled into a neatly packaged, compressed, and easily assimilated sight and sound bite. The violent, visual, highly impressionistic imagery gave the Crown an unfair advantage in this trial. Courts must be sensitive to how a video re-enactment that depicts only the Crown's version of disputed facts may distort the jury's decision-making and thus prejudice an accused's right to a fair trial.

In this case, the Crown's video re-enactment contradicted in material ways not just MacDonald's testimony but even the evidence of the Crown's ballistics expert. For example, the video depicts the police van cutting off MacDonald's car; MacDonald testified that he did not see the van. In the video the police are yelling loudly; MacDonald testified that he did not hear the police announce their presence. In the video the police are plainly visible in front of the car; MacDonald said that he did not see the police at first and then mistook them. On the video MacDonald's car backs up; MacDonald testified that the unmarked police car bumped him from behind. The video showed two shots fired into the front windshield on the passenger's side and four shots into the windshield on the driver's side; MacDonald's evidence, supported by the Crown's ballistics expert, was that shots were fired through the window on the driver's door.

These examples demonstrate how one-sided the video re-enactment was. This one-sided depiction of what occurred, presented in vivid and forceful imagery, was highly prejudicial. The distortion of even undisputed facts only added to the prejudice.

. . .

[Appeals against conviction were allowed, the convictions were set aside and a new trial was ordered.]

McCUTCHEON v. CHRYSLER CANADA LTD.
(1998), 32 C.P.C. (4th) 61 (Ont. Gen. Div.)

PER SHAUGHNESSY J.: —

On the second day of this trial a Voir Dire has been conducted to determine the admissibility of a computer generated animated video detailing the premorbid and post accident gait of the Plaintiff, Dr. Larry McCutcheon. There appears to be some controversy as to the admissibility of such evidence. The obvious objection is that such evidence has the appearance of authenticity which may not exist.

Filed as exhibits on the voir dire are the computer video animation depicting the premorbid and post accident gait of the Plaintiff; a further VHS home video taken of the Plaintiff in or about the Spring of 1995 which was viewed but not used by the video animator; photographs of Larry McCutcheon pre and post accident which were viewed by the video animator and there was also filed as an exhibit the curriculum vitae of the video animator, as well as a further video made by the animator, Mr. Lenartowich, which details the Plaintiff walking to and fro, as well as on stairs and without his leg brace in a locked position, as well as in a locked position.

The computer generated video which the Plaintiff proposes to introduce details a computer humanoid figure which visually presents the gait of the Plaintiff before the accident, as well as after the accident. The scene changes at various times to show the bone structure of the legs and feet pre and post accident and also, at one point, shows an actual picture of the Plaintiff walking with his brace on. There are also on the screen split scene comparisons showing the humanoid in gaits pre and post accident.

The Plaintiff, Larry McCutcheon, and his wife, Marilyn, were called to give evidence on the voir dire. It was their evidence that the computer video was an accurate depiction of the Plaintiff's gait both before and after the accident. In particular the change of pace in his gait as well as a change in the positioning of his leg in order to enable the swing of his leg above the ground with the brace on is stated to be an accurate depiction on the video.

Mr. Brian Lenartowich gave evidence on the voir dire. His curriculum vitae was filed as Exhibit #5 and he was qualified to give expert opinion evidence as a professional animator. While he has no medical training, his assignment was to provide animation of a gait, premorbid and post accident. His evidence was that he met with the Plaintiff and Dr. Anthony Newall to establish how a computer generated animation would illustrate the differences in the gait before and after the accident. The technical detail concerning the hardware and software used the 3D models employed in the animation are detailed in his report dated November 6, 1998, which was also filed as an exhibit. If I understand the submissions of Defence counsel he has really no serious objection concerning the technical aspects of the evidence and he accepted that the equipment and software used was what is described as the high end of the state of art for computer generated animation.

. . .

The position of counsel for the Plaintiff is that while this technology is somewhat new, nevertheless this type of demonstrative evidence should be entered into evidence in accordance with the Rules of Evidence governing same. The Plaintiff refers to two fairly recent decisions. . . Essentially, the Plaintiff's argument is that the evidence would be helpful and relevant to the issues in this case. It is argued that the animator has provided evidence relating to the technical requirements of the hardware and software and the method of computer animation and that the animator employed reliable software and hardware to the application of the information provided to him. Finally, the Plaintiff argues that the animator, to a tolerable level, accurately produced a computer animation which reasonably represents what it is intended to illustrate.

The Defendant's position is that the animation is far too subjective a depiction in which the animator solely relied on information provided to him by the Plaintiff. Counsel for the Defendant argues that the animation depicts something that is not entirely accurate. His principal objection is that the video animation is extremely prejudicial to his client. He argues that the video presentation is not accurate in that it does not clearly delineate a premorbid leg shortage of three-quarters of an inch — relating to the Plaintiff's polio condition and it does not depict the hardware in the hip joint. Counsel for the Defendant further argues that the depiction is prejudicial because it can mislead the Jury and it is not an objective assessment of the Plaintiff's pace or his tiring at the end of the day. In fairness to counsel for the Defence, there are subjective components to the animation which I noted and it was clear that the Plaintiff had direct input in terms of the information provided to the animator. In particular, decisions were made by the Plaintiff's counsel to display only a post accident gait with the knee brace locked and as well, it was subjectively decided that the pace of the Plaintiff's gait was one-half of the pre-accident pace. The Defendants referred me to *Draper v. Jacklyn* (1970), 9 D.L.R. (3d) 264. At p. 270 there is cited the case of *Noor Mohamed v. The King*, [1949] A.C. 182 where it is stated:

> It is right to add, however, that in all such cases the judge ought to consider whether the evidence which it is proposed to adduce is sufficiently substantial, having regard to the purpose to which it is professedly directed, to make it desirable in the interest of justice that it should be admitted. If, so far as that purpose is concerned, it can in the circumstances of the case have only trifling weight, the judge will be right to exclude it. To say this is not to confuse weight with admissibility. The distinction is plain, but cases must occur in which it would be unjust to admit evidence of a character gravely prejudicial to the accused even

though there may be some tenuous ground for holding it technically admissible. The decision must then be left to the discretion and the sense of fairness of the judge."

Therefore Defence counsel argues that although the video may be technically admissible, nevertheless, its prejudicial value outweighs its probative value. I should indicate that counsel for the Defence stated on the Record that he was not challenging the introduction of the evidence based on Rule 53.04 of the Ontario Rules of Civil Procedure. Ultimately the matter has to be determined by the trial judge exercising his discretion judicially and the test applicable in terms of judicial discretion is whether the prejudicial effect of demonstrative evidence outweighs its probative value. The Supreme Court of Canada in *Draper v. Jacklyn, supra,* held that demonstrative evidence is admissible where it is relevant to the issues in dispute and where it would assist the jury to better understand the conditions alleged so long as its prejudicial value does not outweigh its probative value.

. . .

I find the following:

The computer generated video animation will assist the Jury and will provide some evidence by which to compare the premorbid and post traumatic gait of the Plaintiff. The only other home video of the Plaintiff is not adequate or sufficient in the circumstances for the reasons which I have outlined previously.

I further find the video animation is relevant to the issues in this proceeding. It is the Plaintiff's position in this proceeding that the change in the Plaintiff's gait has caused the thigh muscle to weaken and which has resulted in the onset of fatigue, reduced and deteriorating function, including the ability to walk. This accordingly has affected his enjoyment of life as well as requiring future care. I further find that the hardware and software methods employed by the animator have been verified by the witness Mr. Lenartowich. I have viewed the video and it does not contain any editorial comments, other than the usual headings one might expect, detailing premorbid, versus post traumatic viewings of the humanoid figure and there are some isolated measurements involving the foot.

I find that the evidence adduced before me establishes that the video animation accurately represents the Plaintiff's premorbid and post traumatic gaits. The objection raised by Defence counsel concerning the leg shortening and hip hardware are, in my opinion, not relevant in these proceedings as these conditions remained the same before and after the accident and have no real value or effect on the fairness of the video animation. However, it is not enough to end my consideration at this point. I have also considered whether the prejudicial value outweighs the probative value and as well, the considerations that Morin J. put forward, namely whether the evidence is relevant and necessary.

I have provided my findings concerning relevancy. As to the matter of whether the evidence is necessary, I have considered that it is difficult for a witness to describe a person's gait or limp. It is ever more difficult, as in the present case, to describe a change in the gait. The Plaintiff had a noticeable limp before this accident occurred. The gait has, to some degree, become more pronounced since the accident and it is the Plaintiff's case that his pace and manner of walking has changed as depicted on the animation with resultant serious consequences. I find the animations are helpful, not only in relationship to the medical evidence that will be forthcoming in this trial, but also in helping the jury to understand the evidence of other witnesses. I believe the Jury's understanding of the issues will be greatly assisted by the use of the computer animation. Therefore, I find that the computer animation is necessary.

Finally, even though I may have found that the evidence is relevant and necessary I still have directed my mind to a determination as to whether the prejudicial value outweighs the probative value. Again, as I stated, I have reviewed the video on the Voir Dire. It is presented in a very simple, straightforward manner. There is no sound. There were few headings and no editorializing. It lasts approximately ten minutes. In essence, it depicts a humanoid with a very clear limp premorbid and a gait that is different but still a limp, post accident. I do not find that it is inflammatory. Nor do I think that the presentation is much different than any member of this jury might see on any television commercial. I find that it will not inflame the Jury, nor will it negatively impact on the fairness of this trial. I do not find that the presentation is misleading, or unfair to the Defendant.

While there are perceived frailties in the evidence, in particular the subjective component in the information and involvement of the Plaintiff before the production of the video, nevertheless I find that these are all matters that counsel for the Defendant may adequately pursue on cross-examination and go to the weight of the evidence.

My Ruling is that the computer video animation shall not be excluded as evidence in this case and I expect that Mr. Oatley will follow the proper procedure in terms of introducing that evidence before the Jury.

R. v. COLLINS
(2001), 160 C.C.C. (3d) 85 (Ont. C.A.)

The accused was charged with criminal negligence causing death. The victim was a 7-year-old boy who was camping with his father, two siblings and the accused. The accused shot a number of rounds from a rifle into the lake, close to where the victim was sitting on a log, about 45 metres away. The victim was hit by one bullet and died from his injury. The Crown lead evidence of a police officer who was qualified as an expert in handling firearms. He testified to an experiment he conducted whereby he shot the accused's rifle 16 times aiming at the water at various distances from where the victim was positioned. All but one of the bullets struck a large target placed in the area where the victim was sitting. The trial judge ruled that the evidence was admissible to show what happened when a gun was fired in the way suggested by the witnesses. The accused was convicted. His appeal was dismissed.

CHARRON J.A. (SHARPE J.A. concurring): —

. . .

The Law on the Admissibility of Experiment Evidence

Despite the fact that experiment evidence is often, and at times routinely, admitted at trials, there is a paucity of Canadian jurisprudence relating to this kind of evidence. Perhaps this is explained by the fact that experiment evidence often goes unrecognized for what it is: in some cases, it consists of mere factual evidence, much like any other sworn testimony; in other cases, it is a combination of factual and opinion evidence. In either situation, its admissibility is governed by well-established rules of evidence.

. . .

A witness's testimony as to observed facts is, of course, subject to the general principles governing the admissibility of any evidence: relevance and materiality. Relevance is established at law if, as a matter of logic and experience, the evidence tends to prove the proposition for which it is advanced. The evidence is material if it is directed at a matter in issue in the case. Hence, evidence that is relevant to an issue in the case will generally be admitted. Indeed, it is a fundamental principle of our law of evidence that any information that has any tendency to prove a fact in issue should be admitted in evidence unless its exclusion is justified on some other grounds. [Citations omitted.]

. . .

These general principles apply to experiment evidence. A pre-trial experiment can be as simple as driving from one location to another to determine the time it takes to cover the distance in order to substantiate or disprove an alibi, or driving along a particular stretch of road to determine at what point a stop sign becomes visible. The evidence in such cases, provided that it is relevant to an issue in the case, will usually be admitted without argument. It is entirely factual, and its admissibility is only subject to the general principles of relevance, materiality and discretion as discussed earlier.

. . .

In a nutshell, experiment evidence, if it is relevant to an issue in the case, should generally be admitted, subject to the trial judge's residuary discretion to exclude the evidence where the prejudice that would flow from its admission clearly outweighs its value.

. . .

In most cases, the relevance of the experiment evidence will depend on the degree of similarity between the replication and the original event. Consider the example given earlier where the experiment consists of the driving along a particular stretch of road to determine at what point a stop sign becomes visible. If the distance at which the stop sign becomes visible is in issue at trial, the experiment evidence will be material, but will only be relevant if the replication bears some similarity to the original event. For example, if the original event occurred in the summer when vegetation partly obstructed the driver's view but the experiment was conducted in winter after all the leaves had fallen, the relevance of the evidence will be greatly diminished. Depending on all the circumstances, it may not be worth receiving.

. . .

In my view, the appellant has not shown any prejudice that would justify the exclusion of the evidence. I see no merit to the contention that the jury would not be able to properly interpret the results of the experiment without expert opinion evidence. The evidence was introduced simply to show how bullets can ricochet off water. It was entirely open to the jury to draw their own inferences on this issue from the results of the experiment.

Simmons, J.A. concurred in a separate opinion.

_____

Collins was applied as the "leading case" in *R. v. Nikitin*[63] to admit into evidence a videotaped re-enactment of a school bus crossing accident in which a 5-year-old child was killed. The accused was convicted of manslaughter.

In *Nikitin*, the re-enactment was made an exhibit and this was not discussed in the Court of Appeal judgment which upheld the decision of the trial judge to admit the videotape. **Are there dangers in making the demonstration an exhibit?**[64]

5. VIEWS

If it is physically impossible to bring the real evidence into the courtroom, the courtroom may have to go to the evidence and take a view. Statutory authority for taking a view in criminal cases is found in the *Criminal Code*:

652. (1) The judge may, where it appears to be in the interests of justice, at any time after the jury has been sworn and before it gives its verdict, direct the jury to have a view of any place, thing or person, and shall give directions respecting the manner in which, and the persons by whom, the place, thing or person shall be shown to the jury, and may for that purpose adjourn the trial.

(2) Where a view is ordered under subsection (1), the judge shall give any directions that he considers necessary for the purpose of preventing undue communication by any person with members of the jury, but

_____

[63]   (2003), 176 C.C.C. (3d) 225 (C.A.).

[64]   For a discussion of the recent developments in using computer animation to demonstrate a litigant's position see D'Angelo, "The Snoop Doggy Dogg Trial: A Look at How Computer Animation Will Impact Litigation in the Next Century" (1998) 32 Univ. of San. Fran. Law Rev. 561. See also B.S. Fiedler, "Are Your Eyes Deceiving You?: The Evidentiary Crisis Regarding The Admissibility Of Computer Generated Evidence" (2004) 79 New York Law School Law Review 295; E.E. Weinreb, "'Counselor Proceed With Caution': The Use Of Integrated Evidence Presentation Systems And Computer-Generated Evidence In The Courtroom" (2001) 23 Cardoza L. Rev. 393; N. Wiebe, "Regarding Digital Images: Determining Courtroom Admissibility Standards" (2000) 28 Manitoba L.J. 61; Legate, "The Admissibility of Demonstrative Evidence in Jury Trials: Applying the Principled Approach to the Law of Evidence" (2006) 31 Advocates' Quarterly 316.

failure to comply with any directions given under this subsection does not affect the validity of the proceedings.

(3) Where a view is ordered under subsection (1) the accused and the judge shall attend.

and in civil cases is located in the various rules of court. For example, the Ontario Rules[65] provide:

52.05 The judge or judge and jury by whom an action is being tried or the court before whom an appeal is being heard may, in the presence of the parties or their counsel, inspect any property concerning which any question arises in the action, or the place where the cause of action arose.

The decision as to whether a view will be taken is properly within the discretion of the judge, who will assess the importance of the evidence against the disruption of the trial necessitated by the adjournment.[66]

On the question of whether a view is evidence or is only a device for better understanding the evidence the courts have divided. In *Chambers v. Murphy*[67] the trial judge had taken a view of the motor vehicle accident scene. He rejected the defendant's evidence as to how the accident had taken place:

When the defendant Peter Murphy told me that he stopped, that his vision was obstructed, and that he started into Tashmoo Avenue so that he could see, he told me what was not so.[68]

A new trial was ordered as the Ontario Court of Appeal believed it was

... well settled and beyond all controversy that the purpose of a view by a Judge or jury of any place is "in order to understand better the evidence"...

I have no doubt that the learned Judge proceeded quite innocently in taking the course he did, and indeed counsel assented to that course and were present at the time of the making of the tests. Nevertheless the facts ascertained from those tests were evidence that might properly have been received from a witness at the trial, but was not so given. The learned Judge in reality supplied that evidence himself and erroneously acted upon it.[69]

The decision of the English Court of Appeal[70] relied on for this holding was, however, later regarded by that court, per Lord Denning, as

unduly restrict[ive of] the function of a view. Everyday practice in these courts shows that, where the matter for decision is one of ordinary common sense, the judge of fact is entitled to form his own judgment on the real evidence of a view, just as much as on the oral evidence of witnesses.[71]

---

65 *Rules of Civil Procedure*, R.R.O. 1990, Reg. 194.
66 See generally 4 Wigmore, *Evidence* (Chad. Rev.), s. 1164.
67 [1953] 2 D.L.R. 705 (Ont. C.A.).
68 *Ibid.* at 706.
69 *Ibid.* See criticism of this case by Milner (1953) 31 Can. Bar Rev. 305.
70 *London Gen. Omnibus Co. v. Lavell*, [1901] 1 Ch. 135 (C.A.).
71 *Buckingham v. Daily News Ltd.*, [1956] 2 All E.R. 904 (C.A.) at 914.

This approach to views was adopted by the Manitoba Court of Appeal in *Meyers v. Govt. of Man.*[72] It seems preferable to regard the view as evidence and allow all reasonable inferences to be drawn therefrom as

> it is unreasonable to assume that jurors, however they may be instructed, will apply the metaphysical distinction suggested and ignore the evidence of their own senses when it conflicts with the testimony of the witnesses.[73]

Nevertheless, in Canada some appeal courts continue to apply the *Chambers* approach.[74]

C. WITNESSES

1. COMPETENCE AND COMPELLABILITY

(a) Introduction

Competence deals with the ability of a witness to testify. Compellability deals with compelling a witness who is competent to testify when that witness does not wish to.

The testimonial qualifications of any witness are to be gauged according to that witness' ability, first, to observe, second, to accurately recall his or her observation, and, third, to communicate his or her recollection to the trier of fact. The witness' ability to communicate has two aspects: the *intellectual* ability to understand questions and to give intelligent answers, and the *moral responsibility* to speak the truth.[75]

Each of these qualifications provides fertile ground for the cross-examiner to explore, for the benefit of the trier of fact, the credibility of the testimony offered.

The early common law also erected rules which completely forbade testimony from those witnesses who were seen from the outset as incapable of exercising the necessary powers of observation, recollection and communication. These witnesses were regarded as incompetent, and their incompetency was determined not by the jury but by the trial judge. As the common law matured the blanket rules were refined.

(b) Oath

At common law, a person was obliged to take an oath in order to be a competent witness. In the earlier modes of trial, the oath was a direct appeal to the Almighty to witness the justness of the party's claim, and since it was

---

[72]   (1960), 26 D.L.R. (2d) 550 (Man. C.A.).
[73]   McCormick, *Evidence* (1972) at 539.
[74]   See *R.v. Welsh* (1997), 120 C.C.C. (3d) 68 (B.C. C.A.); *Triple A Invt. Ltd. v. Adams Bros. Ltd.* (1985), 56 Nfld. & P.E.I.R. 272 (Nfld. C.A.); and *Swadron v. North York* (1985), 8 O.A.C. 204 (Div. Ct.). See Peter Sankoff, "We Should Probably Take a Look at That: The Process of Taking a View in Criminal Proceedings" (2017) 65 Crim. L.Q. 140. He advocates that view procedure should be used more regularly given the utility of gaining first-hand experience of the scene where the crime is alleged to have taken place.
[75]   See 2 Wigmore, *Evidence* (Chad. Rev.), s. 506, approved in *R. v. Kendall* (1962), 132 C.C.C. 216 (S.C.C.) at 220.

then believed that a false appeal would be immediately visited with punishment, the claim would be upheld if the party survived the oath. As the mode of trial changed and witnesses informed the trier, the oath was given to the witnesses to guard against false evidence; the witnesses were advised that they were undertaking a solemn obligation, and it was hoped that bringing to their mind the threat of retribution from some Superior Being would cause the witnesses to be truthful:

> The object of the law in requiring an oath is to get at the truth by obtaining a hold on the conscience of the witness.[76]

Since this is the purpose of the oath it must be determined what form, if any, would act as an assurance of trustworthiness. Although in Canada a fear of divine retribution may no longer be necessary,[77] there must be some belief in the witness of something sacred called to witness his or her evidence. The form of the oath must then vary according to the witness. This was recognized in 1744 in *Omychund v. Barker*:[78]

> But oaths are as old as the creation. . .
>
> The nature of an oath is not at all altered by Christianity, but only made more solemn from the sanction of rewards and punishments being more openly declared.
>
> . . .
>
> The form of oaths varies in countries according to different laws and constitutions, but the substance is the same in all.
>
> . . .
>
> There can be no evidence admitted without oath, it would be absurd for him to swear according to the Christian oath, which he does not believe; and therefore, out of necessity, he must be allowed to swear according to his own notion of an oath.
>
> . . .
>
> I found my opinion upon the certificate, which says, the *Gentoos* believe in a God as the Creator of the universe, and that He is a rewarder of those who do well, and an avenger of those who do ill.

As emphasis that there is no "correct" form of oath, see the *Ontario Evidence Act* which provides:

> 16. Where an oath may be lawfully taken, it may be administered to a person while such person holds in his or her hand a copy of the Old or New Testament without requiring him or her to kiss the same, or, when the person objects to being sworn in this manner or declares that the oath so administered is not binding upon the person's conscience, then *in such*

---

[76]   Best, *Evidence* (1849), s. 161 as quoted in 6 Wigmore, *Evidence* (Chad. Rev.), s. 1816.

[77]   See (c) Age, below respecting child witnesses.

[78]   (1744), 26 E.R. 15 (C.A.) at 30, 31 per Willes, L.C.J. See *R. v. Lai Ping* (1904), 11 B.C.R. 102 (C.A.) (paper oath administered wherein witness writes his name on paper which is then burned); and *R. v. Lee Tuck* (1912), 4 Alta. L.R. 388 (S.C.). See also *R. v. Ah Wooey* (1902), 8 C.C.C. 25 (B.C. S.C.) (chicken oath administered). And see generally Silving, *Essays on Criminal Procedure* (1964) for a thorough description of many forms of oaths.

> *manner and form and with such ceremonies as he or she declares to be binding.* [Emphasis added.][79]

The *Canada Evidence Act* prescribes no particular form of oath. The traditional form of oath which developed in England, and which will be normally administered in Canada unless the witness requests otherwise, varies slightly between criminal and civil cases. In criminal cases the witness is addressed:

> You swear that the evidence to be given by you to the Court (and jury sworn between our Sovereign Lady the Queen and the prisoner at the Bar) shall be the truth, the whole truth, and nothing but the truth. So help you God.[80]

And in civil cases:

> You swear that the evidence to be given by you to the Court (and jury sworn) touching the matters in question, shall be the truth, the whole truth, and nothing but the truth. So help you God.

R. v. KALEVAR
(1991), 4 C.R. (4th) 114 (Ont. Gen. Div.)

The accused was charged with theft under $1,000. He represented himself at his trial. When he came forward to testify he objected to the Bible that was offered to him for taking the oath. The Court instructed that he be affirmed. The accused sought to give notice that he wished to raise a constitutional question. The Court admonished him that he was to give his evidence under oath or affirmation. In the result the accused gave no evidence. A conviction was entered and the accused appealed.

HALEY J.: —

. . .

. . . [T]he appellant gave no evidence and the matter was put over for submissions. On the subsequent hearing the Crown suggested to the Judge that the wording of the *Canada Evidence Act*, . . . dealing with oaths was such that an oath need not be taken on the Bible, and that some other religious oath could bind the appellant as a solemn oath so that he could give evidence in the proceedings. The Judge held that the appellant had refused to be affirmed, and there was no other course now open to him to permit him to give evidence except to give unsworn evidence as a "dock statement" from the body of the Court. The appellant refused and a conviction was entered.

On this appeal, the Crown took the position that the Judge had erred in not giving the appellant the right to a religious oath other than on the Bible and, accordingly, the appellant had not had the opportunity to make full answer and defence. In those circumstances the Crown agreed that the appeal should be allowed, the conviction set aside and an acquittal entered. This was

---

[79]   R.S.O. 1990, c. E-23.
[80]   See *R. v. Budin* (1981), 58 C.C.C. (2d) 352 (Ont. C.A.) at 354. See also 6 Wigmore, *Evidence* (Chad. Rev.), s. 1818 and Crankshaw's *Criminal Code of Canada*, 7th ed. (1959) at 622.

done as I was in agreement that a solemn oath was not limited to one taken on the Bible.

Section 13 of the *Canada Evidence Act* reads as follows:

Every court and judge, and every person having, by law or consent of parties, authority to hear and receive evidence, has power to administer an oath to every witness who is legally called to give evidence before that court, judge or person.

The *Shorter Oxford Dictionary* . . . defines oath as "a solemn appeal to God (or something sacred) in witness that a statement is true, or a promise binding."

The use of oaths other than those taken on the Bible are not unknown in this country. *R. v. Ah Wooey* (1902), 8 C.C.C. 25 (S.C.) was a case in the Supreme Court of British Columbia in which the following decision was taken [p. 25 C.C.C.]:

For taking the evidence of a Canton Chinaman not a believer in Christianity, the oath known as the 'chicken oath' should be administered instead of the less solemn 'paper oath', if the trial is for a capital offence.

In those circumstances an oath in writing to the King of Heaven was signed by the witness. "The oath was then read out loud by the witness, after which he wrapped it in Joss-paper as used in religious ceremonies, then laid the cock on the block and chopped its head off, and then set fire to the oath from the candles and held it until it was consumed" [pp. 26-27].

Clearly, Canada's emerging multi-cultural society requires an acknowledgement in the courts that the Judaic-Christian form of oath is not necessarily the only form of religious oath to be administered, and that persons of other religious persuasions should not automatically be given affirmation as the only alternative.

The appellant wishes to go further and have me decide his appeal on the ground that his right to freedom of conscience and religion under the *Canadian Charter of Rights and Freedoms* has been breached by the offering to him of an oath on the Bible. He argues strenuously that this freedom has been offended by the presence of the Bible in the courtroom to the exclusion of all other holy books, and that steps should be taken to remove any suggestion of paramountcy of the Bible in the court process.

It is perhaps disappointing from the appellant's point of view that this ground is not necessary to the success of his appeal. Throughout the transcripts it is plain that his main concern was the making of the constitutional argument. However, in the circumstances anything I might decide on the *Charter* issue would be only obiter dicta as unnecessary for the appeal, and the argument must wait until a new case with the proper factual basis can be found to place the argument before the Court for decision.

Rather than automatically proffering a Bible to every witness who comes forward, it might be better to ask each witness whether he or she wishes to be sworn and, if so, in what manner. A witness is normally frightened attending court and the court taking this initiative would avoid yet another burden on the witness of objecting to the oath. Or, counsel might best inquire of the witness what he or she prefers and make the announcement for the witness as he or she goes to the witness stand. Or, one might see the wisdom of the "oath ceremony" devised by His Honour Judge Peter Nasmith.[81] His Honour described the way in which witnesses in his court, over the age of 12, had been treated. His clerk addressed the witness as follows:

> Do you know that it is a criminal offence to intentionally give false evidence in a judicial proceeding?
>
> Do you solemnly promise to tell the truth in this proceeding?

His Honour noted that the answers were invariably "Yes" and the witness was then considered to be under oath.

Though the common law developed some flexibility in the form of the oath, there were people still excluded as witnesses though they were competent in all other respects: those who were children and had not yet formed any religious beliefs, those who had religious beliefs which forbade taking an oath (e.g., Quakers) and those who were atheists or agnostics. These groups were accommodated by legislation enacted during the nineteenth century. See now s. 14 of the *Canada Evidence Act*,[82] which provides:

> 14. (1) A person may, instead of taking an oath, make the following solemn affirmation:
>
> I solemnly affirm that the evidence to be given by me shall be the truth, the whole truth and nothing but the truth,
>
> (2) Where a person makes a solemn affirmation in accordance with subsection (1), his evidence shall be taken and have the same effect as if taken under oath.

Should the distinction between an oath and solemn affirmation be abolished?

R. v. J. (T.R.)
2013 BCCA 449, 6 C.R. (7th) 207 (B.C. C.A.)

1 J.E. HALL J.A. (orally):— In this case, the appellant was charged with sexual interference with his granddaughter then aged about four or five years. At the time of trial, she was aged about nine. Having no apparent memory of the alleged events at the time of trial, the substantial evidence emanating from the young child concerning the alleged assault consisted of a videotaped statement of the child taken near to the time of the alleged events about four years prior to trial. The appellant was tried by a judge sitting without a jury and was found guilty.

2 A number of grounds of appeal are advanced including issues about identification, burden of proof, and unreasonable verdict. As in my opinion, this case may be decided on one particular ground of appeal, it is only

---

[81] See "High Time for One Secular Oath" (1990) L. Soc. Gaz. 230.
[82] R.S.C. 1985, c. C-5 [am. S.C. 1994, c. 44, s. 87].

necessary to deal with that ground. This has to do with the matter concerning affirmation by the appellant prior to the giving of his evidence. The appellant identifies the error as, "The learned trial judge erred by considering the appellant's decision to affirm rather than swear to tell the truth in assessing his credibility".

3 Section 14 of the *Canada Evidence Act*, R.S.C. 1985, c. C-5, provides:

> (1) A person may, instead of taking an oath, make the following solemn affirmation: I solemnly affirm that the evidence to be given by me shall be the truth, the whole truth and nothing but the truth.

> (2) Where a person makes a solemn affirmation in accordance with subsection (1), his evidence shall be taken and have the same effect as if taken under oath.

> R.S., 1985, c. C-5, s. 14; 1994, c. 44, s. 87.

I specifically note the language "that solemn affirmation has the same force and effect as if that person had taken an oath."

4 While I consider there may be factual circumstances where it could be appropriate for a judge to permit some exploration of the issue of the degree to which an oath or affirmation may bind the conscience of a witness, I do not discern any basis for such an exploration in the circumstances of this case. I doubt that I would have permitted cross-examination on this issue as appears to have occurred at the trial in this case

5 The judge noted at para. 67 of his reasons:

> The Crown submits that for a religious individual to affirm instead of swearing on the Bible leads to an inference that he was not telling the truth. They refer to *R. v. K. (A.H.)*, 2011 ONSC 5510 and *R. v. Bell*, 2011 ONSC 1218.

6 This submission on the face of it, seems out of accord with the statutory provision above quoted. The judge quite properly exhibited some degree of skepticism about this submission. However he did go on to observe:

> [70] In my view there is a difference between a Muslim choosing to swear on the Bible and a Christian choosing to affirm. The former is a competing faith; the latter is not. The distinction from the situations in *K. (A.H.)* and *Bell* is important. As a result I do not view the accused's choice to affirm as raising a significant concern respecting his credibility as was the situation in the cases cited. However it is a factor to be considered in assessing his evidence.

7 I particularly note the observation of the judge in the final sentence of para. 70, that "it is a factor to be considered in assessing his evidence" the circumstance that the appellant affirmed. The reality of this case was that if the accused appellant was to successfully exculpate himself from the allegation of wrongful conduct he faced, his evidence would be crucial. Any factor that weighed in the mind of the trier of fact to the disadvantage of the appellant concerning his credibility was highly significant.

8 At para. 94 the judge observed:

> The evidence of the accused did not raise a reasonable doubt. I do not find his denials, in the context of the whole of the evidence to be credible. I am satisfied on the whole of the evidence that the conduct complained of occurred and was that of the accused, and therefore I am satisfied the Crown has proven its case beyond a reasonable doubt.

Thus, it can be seen that the trial judge found the evidence of the appellant not credible.

9 Ms. Ainslie, with her usual competence, has submitted that the analytical approach of the judge here, being substantially based on the reliability of the Crown evidence, did not result in any deficiency in a credibility analysis being of any great significance. She urges us to apply the curative provision to sustain this conviction. As I observed during the argument, there is usually going to be some interplay in the analysis of evidence between reliability and credibility. While cases can arise where an erroneous approach to an issue of credibility may be susceptible to application of the curative proviso, credibility cases in my respectful opinion form a class of cases in which such application may be often inappropriate and problematical. Because I view the issue of the credibility of this appellant to have been of centrality in this case, I would not accede to the suggestion that it would be appropriate to apply here the provisions of the *Criminal Code*, s. 686 (1)(b)(iii).

10 In my respectful view, the legal error in the approach of the judge to a credibility assessment of the appellant makes unsustainable the verdict of guilty rendered against the appellant at trial. I consider that the appropriate disposition of the appeal is to allow the appeal from conviction and to order a new trial.

Do you agree with the statement at paragraph 6 that there is a distinction between what happened in this case and a Muslim accused swearing an oath on the Bible? **Should we abolish the oath requirement?**[83]

(c) Age

The evidence of children (defined as persons under the age of 14) has traditionally been regarded with some circumspection. In *Horsburgh v. R.*,[84] Spence J. said:

> The view expressed by the learned trial Judge is not only that the evidence of children, once sworn, must be received, but it must be treated as that of a competent adult witness. In my opinion, this is a serious misdirection, as the witnesses, despite the fact that it was determined, in my opinion properly, that they were capable of being sworn, were nevertheless child witnesses and their

---

[83]   See Tanovich, "*J. (T.R.)*: Time to Remove Religion from the Oath" (2013), 6 CR (7th) 211.
[84]   [1968] 2 C.C.C. 288 (S.C.C.) at 320.

testimony bore all the frailties of testimony of children, such frailties as Judson, J., in this Court referred to in *R. v. Kendall* . . . The evidence of such children was, as Judson, J., pointed out, subject to the difficulties related to (1) capacity of observation, (2) capacity to recollect, (3) capacity to understand questions put and frame intelligent answers, and (4) the moral responsibility of the witness. It is this fourth difficulty which is very marked in the present case.

We should note, however, that the difficulties enumerated as particularly referable to the evidence of children are, on reflection, the difficulties inherent in the testimony of all witnesses, including adults!

Dr. Haka-Ikse explained:

> Children are not necessarily incompetent morally or cognitively to testify as implied by the present legal system. The assumptions about the testimonial limitations of children do not as an example take into consideration the significant differences between pre-school and adolescent children just under 14 years of age. Conversely, the law considers as competent witness any individual after his or her 14th birthday, which is a totally arbitrary division. Also, the law fails to consider the very wide range of verbal, cognitive and perceptual abilities between children of the same age. The assumption that every individual of older age has the necessary moral judgement, impartiality, objectivity and rationality to give competent testimony is at best questionable. Long pediatric experience in interviewing and coming to know sufficiently close large numbers of pre-latency and latency age children and their parents, indicate that children are able to talk about events that are important to them with simplicity, candor and without excursions to fantasy. The normal pre-schooler or young school age child may have fears about ghosts or the boogey man (and so do some adults by the way) but he or she does not mistake the parent, the babysitter or the teacher as the ghost or the monster. Many children have imaginary companions but they only play with or talk to them in the privacy of their room. The memory of children is often surprising. I have seen 4 and 5 year olds returning to the clinic for a visit after several months and remember where they had sat or where the toys were kept. Conversely the memory of some parents I interview is subjective, bound to interpretation rather than facts, indicating poor recall or understanding of events and often being colored by the parents' emotional status and wishful thinking. The competence of a person to present facts either in giving medical history or in testifying in court, depends on the particular individual's qualities and is not a function of age. I recall many situations when parents interviewed in the presence of their child turn to the child for assistance in answering some questions they ignore or cannot recall the answers. In other instances I recall children interrupting parents to correct or clarify what the parents are reporting. In terms of moral judgement although it is true that the younger the individual is the more he or she relies on authority figures to define or set moral standards rather than to absolute moral imperatives, and their actions are not perceived as "bad" as long as nobody knows about them. The same is true for a good number of adults. Discrimination against children by the law on such grounds is developmentally unfounded and unconstitutional.[85]

---

[85]   Haka-Ikse, "The Child as Witness in Sexual Abuse Cases: A Developmental Perspective", unreported paper delivered September 10, 1985, University of Toronto. See also Goodman, "The Child Witness" (1984) 40 J. of Social Issues 157; Wehrspann & Steinhauer, "Assessing the Credibility of Young Children's Allegations of Sexual Abuse" (1987) 32 Can. J. of Psychiatry 610 at 615.

To what extent have the rules governing the competency of children and the assessment of their evidence evolved to give effect to the concerns expressed by Dr. Haka-Ikse?

R. v. W. (R.)
[1992] 2 S.C.R. 122, 13 C.R. (4th) 257, 74 C.C.C. (3d) 134

The accused was charged with indecent assault, gross indecency and sexual assault against three young girls. The evidence of the oldest child, S.W., was internally consistent. The evidence of the two younger children, however, revealed a number of inconsistencies and was contradicted in some respects. The accused was convicted on all counts and appealed. The convictions were set aside on the basis that there was no confirmatory evidence and the evidence of the younger children was fraught with inaccuracy. The Crown appealed.

McLACHLIN J. (LA FOREST, L'HEUREUX-DUBÉ, GONTHIER, CORY, and IACOBUCCI JJ. concurring):—

. . .

The following is the text of the Court of Appeal's endorsement:

This case has caused us very great concern. The case has been carefully argued. We recognize the advantage of the trial judge, but also the responsibility of this court. . . Giving the matter our best consideration, we are all of the opinion that on this evidence these convictions cannot safely stand. There was really no confirmatory evidence, the evidence of the two younger children was fraught with inaccuracy and in the case of the older children [it was] perfectly clear that neither was aware or concerned that anything untoward occurred which is really the best test of the quality of the acts. The appeal is allowed, the conviction is set aside and an acquittal is entered.

. . .

. . . I pause to consider the general question of how courts should approach the evidence of young children. The law affecting the evidence of children has undergone two major changes in recent years. The first is removal of the notion, found at common law and codified in legislation, that the evidence of children was inherently unreliable and therefore to be treated with special caution. Thus, for example, the requirement that a child's evidence be corroborated has been removed. . . The repeal of provisions creating a legal requirement that children's evidence be corroborated does not prevent the judge or jury from treating a child's evidence with caution where such caution is merited in the circumstances of the case. But it does revoke the assumption formerly applied to all evidence of children, often unjustly, that children's evidence is always less reliable than the evidence of adults. So if a court proceeds to discount a child's evidence automatically, without regard to the circumstances of the particular case, it will have fallen into an error.

The second change in the attitude of the law toward the evidence of children in recent years is a new appreciation that it may be wrong to apply adult tests for credibility to the evidence of children. One finds emerging a new sensitivity to the peculiar perspectives of children. Since children may experience the world differently from adults, it is hardly surprising that details important to adults, like time and place, may be missing from their recollection. Wilson J. recognized this in *R. v. B. (G.)*, [1990] 2 S.C.R. 30, at pp. 54-55, when, in referring to submissions regarding the court of appeal judge's treatment of the evidence of the complainant, she said that:

> . . . it seems to me that he was simply suggesting that the judiciary should take a common sense approach when dealing with the testimony of young children and not impose the same exacting standard on them as it does on adults. However, this is not to say that the courts should not carefully assess the credibility of child witnesses and I do not read his reasons as suggesting that the standard of proof must be lowered when dealing with children as the appellants submit. Rather, he was expressing concern that a flaw, such as a contradiction, in a child's testimony should not be given the same effect as a similar flaw in the testimony of an adult. I think his concern is well founded and his comments entirely appropriate. While children may not be able to recount precise details and communicate the when and where of an event with exactitude, this does not mean that they have misconceived what happened to them and who did it. In recent years we have adopted a much more benign attitude to children's evidence, lessening the strict standards of oath taking and corroboration, and I believe that this is a desirable development. The credibility of every witness who testifies before the courts must, of course, be carefully assessed but the standard of the 'reasonable adult' is not necessarily appropriate in assessing the credibility of young children.

As Wilson J. emphasized in *B. (G.)*, these changes in the way the courts look at the evidence of children do not mean that the evidence of children should not be subject to the same standard of proof as the evidence of adult witnesses in criminal cases. Protecting the liberty of the accused and guarding against the injustice of the conviction of an innocent person require a solid foundation for a verdict of guilt, whether the complainant be an adult or a child. What the changes do mean is that we approach the evidence of children not from the perspective of rigid stereotypes, but on what Wilson J. called a "common sense" basis, taking into account the strengths and weaknesses which characterize the evidence offered in the particular case.

It is neither desirable nor possible to state hard and fast rules as to when a witness's evidence should be assessed by reference to "adult" or "child" standards — to do so would be to create anew stereotypes potentially as rigid and unjust as those which the recent developments in the law's approach to children's evidence have been designed to dispel. Every person giving testimony in court, of whatever age, is an individual, whose credibility and evidence must be assessed by reference to criteria appropriate to her mental development, understanding and ability to communicate. But I would add this. In general, where an adult is testifying as to events which occurred when she was a child, her credibility should be assessed according to criteria applicable to her as an adult witness. Yet with regard to her evidence pertaining to events which occurred in childhood, the presence of inconsistencies, particularly as to peripheral matters such as time and location, should be considered in the context of the age of the witness at the time of the events to which she is testifying.

Against this background, I turn to a more particular consideration of the Court of Appeal's treatment of the evidence in this case. First, the Court referred to the fact that "there was really no confirmatory evidence". This suggests that the Court may have been applying the old rule that the evidence of a child could not found a conviction unless it was confirmed or corroborated by independent evidence. It may be that in considering the whole of the evidence in accordance with the *Yebes* test, a court of appeal will take into account, along with other factors, the presence or absence of confirmatory evidence. So the reference to lack of confirmatory evidence is not in itself an error of law. But standing as it does as a bald proposition unrelated to a detailed examination of the evidence, it does support the submission that the Court of Appeal was treating the evidence of the children as being inherently less reliable than adult evidence might be.

. . .

The Court of Appeal next referred to the fact that the evidence of the younger children was fraught with inaccuracy. This is true, particularly with respect to B.W.'s evidence. Some of the inconsistencies are minor, for example an error on the distance from a van to a ball game many years ago. Others are more significant, relating to the sleeping arrangements of the three children, the location of bedrooms in the house and possibly the respondent's nighttime attire. While it was the proper task of the Court of Appeal to consider such inconsistencies, one finds no mention of the fact that the trial judge was alive to them and resolved them to his satisfaction in his reasons for judgment, nor of the fact that many of the inconsistencies may be explained by reference to the fact that a young child might not be paying particular attention to sleeping arrangements or clothing or that the children had lived in a variety of different arrangements, which might well have given rise to confusion on such details.

Finally, the Court of Appeal relied on the fact that neither of the older children was "aware or concerned that anything untoward occurred which is really the best test of the quality of the acts." This reference reveals reliance on the stereotypical but suspect view that the victims of sexual aggression are likely to report the acts, a stereotype which found expression in the now discounted doctrine of recent complaint. In fact, the literature suggests the converse may be true; victims of abuse often in fact do not disclose it, and if they do, it may not be until a substantial length of time has passed. . .

In summary, the Court of Appeal was right to be concerned about the quality of the evidence and correct in entering upon a re-examination and reweighing, to some extent, of the evidence. It went too far, however, in finding lacunae in the evidence which did not exist and in applying too critical an approach to the evidence, an approach which appears to have placed insufficient weight on the trial judge's findings of credibility, influenced as the Court of Appeal appears to have been by the old stereotypes relating to the inherent unreliability of children's evidence and the "normal" behaviour of victims of sexual abuse.

Placing myself, as I must, in the position of the Court of Appeal . . . I conclude that we are here concerned with verdicts which "a properly instructed jury [or judge], acting judicially, could reasonably have rendered", to repeat the words of *Yebes*. I would allow the appeal and restore the convictions.[86]

Both the *Ontario Evidence Act* and the *Canada Evidence Act* have been amended over the last 20 years to remove barriers to the evidence of children and to facilitiate their testimony. At the federal level, Bill C-2 (S.C. 2005, c. 32) came into effect at the start of 2006. It amended the competency provisions in the *Canada Evidence Act* and introduced a range of protective measures for young witnesses in the *Criminal Code*. Professor Nick Bala of Queen's University served as an expert consultant to the Department of Justice with respect to Bill C-2. The following is an article co-written by Nick Bala, Katherine Duvall-Antonacopoulos, R.C.L. Lindsay, Kang Lee and Victoria Talwar.

Bill C-2: A New Law for Canada's Child Witnesses
(2006), 32 C.R. (6th) 48

Bill C-2 . . . introduces significant procedural and substantive amendments that are intended to increase protections for children, women and vulnerable adults from various forms of exploitation . . . This article deals with the procedural and evidentiary reforms in Bill C-2, and considers their effect on Canada's criminal justice system . . . [T]he procedural and evidentiary provisions which amend the Criminal Code and Evidence Act apply to trials held after the law is in force, even if the offences occurred earlier.[87]

Overview and Context

Historically, the common law regarded children as inherently unreliable. In 1893, Canada enacted its first statutory provisions concerning child witnesses, permitting children to give unsworn evidence, provided a court found that the child "possessed sufficient intelligence" and understood "the duty to speak the truth".[88] A child's unsworn evidence was viewed with suspicion, and there was a statutory requirement for corroboration of a child's unsworn testimony. Further, no steps were taken to accommodate children when they testified in court, and children did not frequently testify. In the

---

[86]   For commentary on *W. (R.)* see Bala, "More Sensitivity to Child Witnesses" (1992), 13 C.R. (4th) 270 and Rauf, "Questioning the New Orthodoxy of the Proper Approach to Child Witnesses" (1993), 17 C.R. (4th) 305. Consider the Martensville cases involving several false charges of child abuse: see *R. v. S. (T.)* (1995), 40 C.R. (4th) 1 (Sask. C.A.). See also David Paciocco, "The Evidence of Children: Testing the Rule Against What We Know" (1996) 21 Queen's L.J. 345; and Nick Bala, "Developmentally Appropriate Questions for Child Witnesses" (1999) 25 Queen's L.J. 252 and "A Legal and Psychological Critique of the Present Approach to the Assessment of the Competence of Child Witnesses" (2001) 38 Osgoode Hall L.J.

[87]   See R. Sullivan, *Statutory Interpretation* (Toronto: Irwin Law, 1997) at 190.

[88]   For a discussion of the history and development of Canada's child witness laws, see Bala, "Child Witnesses in the Canadian Criminal Justice System: Recognizing Their Needs & Capacities" (1999) 5(2) Psychology, Public Policy and the Law 323.

1980s there was an increased awareness of the under-reporting of child abuse, and a growing body of research about child witnesses. There is a large body of psychological research which establishes that children as young as four years of age can provide important, reliable evidence about events that they have experienced or observed.[89]

In 1988, there were significant amendments to the procedural and evidentiary law governing child witnesses, allowing the use of such testimonial aids as videotaped statements, screens and closed circuit television.[90] The Canada Evidence Act was also amended to permit a child who was able to "communicate the evidence" to testify on a promise to tell the truth. In 1993, the Supreme Court of Canada upheld the constitutional validity of a number of these provisions, emphasizing that these reforms facilitated the truth-seeking function of the criminal justice process without compromising the rights of the accused to a fair trial.[91]

While prior reforms have been significant, there remained substantial concerns about the treatment of vulnerable persons in the justice system, and the difficulty in prosecuting cases in which they are witnesses. Even after the 1988 reforms, in some important respects the justice system failed to treat child witnesses fairly. The Preamble to Bill C-2 states that Parliament "wishes to facilitate the participation of children and other vulnerable witnesses" in the criminal justice system "while ensuring that the rights of accused persons are respected." The court system requires a fair and balanced approach to witnesses, one that recognizes that children have different needs and capacities than adults, and that, like adults, they can provide reliable evidence, as well as lie or make mistakes in their recollection of events.

Bill C-2 changes the approach for determining if child witnesses are competent to testify, allowing children to testify if they are able to understand and respond to questions. The new legislation will facilitate use of testimonial aids, including support persons, screens and closed circuit television, in cases involving children and vulnerable adults. It also facilitates the use in court of video recorded statements made by a child or disabled adult, if the witness adopts the content of the recording when he or she testifies. . .

The Competency Requirement: Section 16 of the *Canada Evidence Act*

The competency inquiry (or *voir dire*) has long been a critical, initial challenge for child witnesses. For young children these inquiries could be confusing and intimidating, and sometimes resulted in children who were capable of giving important evidence being prevented from testifying.

Under the 1988 version of s.16 of the *Canada Evidence Act*, before a child under the age of fourteen can testify, the court is required to conduct an

---

[89]   See e.g. Carole Peterson, "Children's long-term memory for autobiographical events" (2002) 22 Developmental Review 370 and S.J. Ceci & M.Bruck, *Jeopardy in the Courtroom: A Scientific Analysis of Children's Testimony* (Washington, DC: American Psychological Association, 1995).

[90]   R.S.C. 1985, c. 19 (3rd Supp.).

[91]   *R. v. L. (D.O.)*, [1993] 4 S.C.R. 419, 85 C.C.C. (3d) 289, 25 C.R. (4th) 285; *R. v. Levogiannis*, [1993] 4 S.C.R. 475, 85 C.C.C. (3d) 327, 25 C.R. (4th) 325. See also *R. v. F. (C.)*, [1997] 3 S.C.R. 1183, 120 C.C.C. (3d) 225, 11 C.R. (5th) 209.

inquiry to determine if the child understands "the nature of an oath" or solemn affirmation. Those without religious beliefs relating to an oath or who choose not to testify under oath may solemnly affirm, which has the same legal effect as testimony under oath. Interestingly, it seems that judges rarely ask children to affirm, and there are no reported Canadian cases in which children have been asked questions about their understanding of the solemn affirmation.

Historically, in order to demonstrate an understanding of the oath, children were required to state that they expected "divine sanctions" if they told a lie under oath. More recently, it has been accepted that the focus of the inquiry about the oath should be whether the child understands the moral significance of making a commitment to tell the truth, and appreciates the importance of telling the truth in court proceedings, and not on the spiritual significance of an oath.[92] However, many trial judges have continued to ask children intrusive questions about religious beliefs and observances as part of the inquiry about the oath.[93]

If the child cannot demonstrate an understanding of the nature of an oath, s. 16(3) permits a child to testify if the child is "able to communicate in court. . .on promising to tell the truth." While the 1988 legislation did *not* state that there should be an inquiry into a child's understanding of such concepts as "truth," "lie" or "promise," the courts have interpreted s. 16(3) to mean that a child could only give unsworn testimony if the court conducts an inquiry to satisfy itself that the child can *demonstrate* an understanding of the duty to speak the truth.[94] This involves inquiring into the child's understanding of the nature of a "promise," and into the child's understanding of the meaning of "truth" and "lie." [95]Adults are not asked these challenging questions before being asked to testify, and laboratory based psychological research has established (not surprisingly) that a child's ability to correctly answer questions about the meaning of various such abstract concepts as "truth" and "promise" is not related to whether a child will actually tell the truth.[96]

The final requirement for competency to testify under the 1988 *Canada Evidence Act* is that a child, giving either sworn or unsworn testimony, must be "able to communicate the evidence." In *R. v. Marquard,* McLachlin J. indicated a relatively brief inquiry could satisfy the "ability to communicate" test, stating that the judge should explore "in a general way whether the witness is capable of perceiving events, remembering events and communicating events

---

[92]   *R. v. Fletcher* (1982), 1 C.C.C. (3d) 370 (Ont. C.A.). In *R. v. F. (W.J.)*, [1999] 3 S.C.R. 569, 27 C.R. (5th) 169, 138 C.C.C. (3d) 1 (S.C.C.) at 591 [S.C.R.], McLachlin J. commented on the "absurdity of subjecting children to examination on whether they understood the religious consequences of the oath".

[93]   N. Bala, K. Lee, R.C.L. Lindsay & V. Talwar, "A Legal & Psychological Critique of the Present Approach to the Assessment of the Competence of Child Witnesses" (2000) 38(3) Osgoode Hall L.J. 409.

[94]   See *R. v. McGovern* (1993), 82 C.C.C. (3d) 301, 22 C.R. (4th) 359 (Man. C.A.) at 304-305 [C.C.C.] and *R. v. Ferguson* (1996), 112 C.C.C. (3d) 342 (B.C. C.A).

[95]   N. Bala, J. Lee & R.C.L. Lindsay, "*R. v. M. (M.A.)*: Failing to Appreciate the Testimonial Capacity of Children" (2001), 40 C.R. (4th) 93.

[96]   V. Talwar, K. Lee, N. Bala & R.C.L. Lindsay, "Children's Conceptual Knowledge of Lying and its Relation to their Actual Behaviors: Implications for the Court Competence Examination" (2002) 26 Law & Human Behavior 395.

to the court."[97] This is usually done by asking the child questions about a past event, like a previous birthday, that is not the subject of the proceedings.

The New Competency Standard: s. 16.1 of the *Evidence Act*

Bill C-2 leaves s.16 of the *Canada Evidence Act* essentially unchanged for proposed witnesses fourteen or older whose mental capacity is challenged. A new s. 16.1 establishes a completely new approach for qualifying children under the age of fourteen, and securing their commitment to telling the truth to the best of their ability.

Person under fourteen years of age

16.1 (1) A person under fourteen years of age is presumed to have the capacity to testify.

No oath or solemn affirmation

(2) A proposed witness under fourteen years of age shall not take an oath or make a solemn affirmation despite a provision of any Act that requires an oath or a solemn affirmation.

Evidence shall be received

(3) The evidence of a proposed witness under fourteen years of age shall be received if they are able to understand and respond to questions.

Burden as to capacity of witness

(4) A party who challenges the capacity of a proposed witness under fourteen years of age has the burden of satisfying the court that there is an issue as to the capacity of the proposed witness to understand and respond to questions.

Court inquiry

(5) If the court is satisfied that there is an issue as to the capacity of a proposed witness under fourteen years of age to understand and respond to questions, it shall, before permitting them to give evidence, conduct an inquiry to determine whether they are able to understand and respond to questions.

Promise to tell truth

(6) The court shall, before permitting a proposed witness under fourteen years of age to give evidence, require them to promise to tell the truth.

Understanding of promise

(7) No proposed witness under fourteen years of age shall be asked any questions regarding their understanding of the nature of the promise to tell the truth for the purpose of determining whether their evidence shall be received by the court.

Effect

(8) For greater certainty, if the evidence of a witness under fourteen years of age is received by the court, it shall have the same effect as if it were taken under oath.

---

[97]   *R. v. Marquard,* [1993] 4 S.C.R. 223, 25 C.R. (4th) 1, 85 C.C.C. (3d) 193 (S.C.C.) at paras. 236-237.

The new provision begins with the statement in s 16.1 (1) that children are "presumed to have the capacity to testify," while s. 16.1(4) places a burden on the "party who challenges the capacity" of a child to "satisfy the court that there is an issue as to the capacity" of the child "to understand and respond to questions." Subsection 16.1(4) might suggest that there is an onus on the party not calling the child as a witness (usually the accused) to raise the issue of competence. However, s. 16.1(5) provides that if the judge "is satisfied that there is an issue" as to a child's capacity to "understand and respond to questions," then before permitting the child to testify, the judge "shall conduct an inquiry" to determine whether the child is "able to understand and respond to questions." The words of s. 16.1(5) clearly suggest that the court itself or the party calling the child witness (usually the Crown), may also raise the issue of a child's competence, though the effect of ss. 16.1 (1) and (4) is that there will be a presumption of competence at the inquiry.

It is clearly preferable for the child for any issues about competency to be dealt with prior to the child giving evidence; further, there might be some risk of a mistrial if a child is called as a witness and begins to testify without an inquiry and then proves unable to answer most of the questions posed. The practice of taping of investigative interviews with the child by police or social workers and disclosure to defence counsel of the tapes should minimize these risks, as defence counsel should be in a position to have assessed whether the child is competent to answer questions prior to the child being called to the stand. It would also be a good practice for judges to ascertain at the time that a child is called to the stand whether the defence is challenging the competence of the witness, or accepts the child's competence.

The words of the new s. 16.1(5) are different from the words of the inquiry carried out under the 1988 provisions, which focused on whether the child "is able to communicate the evidence." The former competence inquiry concerned the capacity of the child to communicate about past events in general.[98] A child was required to be capable of giving more than "yes" or "no" responses to straightforward questions.[99] The courts also required that the child demonstrate an ability to distinguish between fact and fiction, and a capacity and a willingness to relate to the court the essence of what happened to her.[100]

Given the new test of "ability to understand and respond to questions," the issue under the new test is whether the child has basic cognitive and language abilities. The ability to observe and recollect now will be dealt with as matters of evidentiary weight. Whether a child witness is able to understand and respond to questions will be a matter for the judge to determine, and expert testimony will not normally be required.[101] In "exceptional circumstances," where the child would be so traumatized by the experience of appearing in court even for the limited purpose of establishing the inability to understand and respond to questions, an expert might be called to establish

[98]   *Marquard, supra* note 97.
[99]   *R. v. Caron* (1994), 94 C.C.C. (3d) 466 (Ont. C.A.).
[100] *Ibid.* at 471.
[101] *R. v. Parrott*, [2001] 1 S.C.R. 178, 39 C.R. (5th) 255, 150 C.C.C. (3d) 449.

that the child is *not* able to testify.[102] If the inability to testify is established to the satisfaction of the court, this may be a ground for establishing the "necessity" for the admission of hearsay evidence instead of having the child testify.

In theory, the new words suggest a somewhat less onerous inquiry, but in practice the application of the test is likely to be very similar to the part of the old inquiry that focused on the child's capacity to meaningfully communicate evidence in court. It is submitted that, as required by the Supreme Court in applying the test in the 1988 *Evidence Act* in *R. v. Marquard,*[103] there should be a relatively brief inquiry into whether the child has the capacity to remember events and answer questions about those events. The inquiry into the child's capacity should be conducted by having the judge or counsel ask the child questions about a non-contentious past event. The judge has a duty to ensure that the questions that are posed to the child during this inquiry, and later in the proceedings, are appropriate to the child's stage of development, with age appropriate vocabulary and sentence structure.[104]

Prior to the 1988 amendments, trial judges always took the lead in actually asking the child questions, and counsel would then be given the opportunity to ask further questions. As with the 1988 provisions, Bill C-2 specifies that "the court shall conduct" an inquiry, if necessary because the capacity of a child witness has been challenged. It has been held that under the 1988 provisions it is sufficient for the judge to control the process and make the determination of competency to testify, but it is not necessary for the judge to take the lead in asking the questions.[105]

Judges increasingly appreciate that the counsel who calls the child as a witness (almost always the prosecutor) is a more suitable person to take the lead in questioning the child. The prosecutor should have met the child before court and the child will be more familiar with that counsel, and more comfortable in answering questions from that person during the invariably stressful first minutes in the courtroom.[106] This approach continues to be appropriate under the new provisions in s.16.1.

Subsection 16.1(2) and (6) provide that a child under fourteen years of age shall not testify under oath or solemn affirmation, but rather shall give a "promise to tell the truth." These provisions remove the possibility that a judge or counsel might want to attempt to determine whether a child might be

---

[102]   *Ibid.*

[103]   *Marquard, supra* note 97.

[104]   See J. Schuman, N. Bala & K. Lee, "Developmentally Appropriate Questions for Child Witnesses" (1999) 25 Queen's L.J. 251. In *R. v. L. (D.O.),* [1993] 4 S.C.R. 419, 25 C.R. (4th) 285, 85 C.C.C. (3d) 289, L'Heureux-Dubé J., writing for the entire Supreme Court of Canada on this point, gave judges the authority to intervene whenever a child is asked inappropriate questions (at 471 [S.C.R.], emphasis added):

in . . . cases involving fragile witnesses such as children, *the trial judge has a responsibility to ensure that the child understands the question being asked and that the evidence given by the child is clear and unambiguous. To accomplish this end, the trial judge may be required to clarify and rephrase questions asked by counsel and to ask subsequent questions to the child to clarify the child's responses. In order to ensure the appropriate conduct of the trial, the judge should provide a suitable atmosphere to ease the tension so that the child is relaxed and calm.*

[105]   *R. v. F. (R.G.)* (1997), 6 W.W.R. 273, 50 Alta. L.R. (3d) 1 (Alta. C.A.) at paras. 24-26.

[106]   *R. v. Peterson* (1996), 106 C.C.C. (3d) 64, 27 O.R. (3d) 739, 47 C.R. (4th) 161 (C.A.).

permitted to testify under oath by requiring the child to answer questions about the nature of an oath, or intrusive questions about religious understandings or observance. This will ensure that all child witnesses receive the same treatment.

Subsection 16.1(6) specifically requires a child to make a "promise to tell the truth" before testifying. The process of a witness, whether a child or adult, making a commitment to tell the truth has symbolic importance for all of those involved in the justice process. Further, psychological research suggests that children who have promised to tell the truth may be more likely to tell the truth, even if they are not able to provide a *definition* of "promise" or "truth".[107] (Interestingly, there is no comparable research for the effect of an oath, solemn affirmation or promise on adults.)

However, in a very significant change from practice under the 1988 law, s.16.1(7) specifies that "[n]o proposed witness under fourteen years of age shall be asked any questions regarding their understanding of the nature of the promise to tell the truth for the purpose of determining whether their evidence shall be received by the court." This provision is clearly intended to preclude the judge or counsel from asking a child questions about the meaning of such abstract concepts as "promise", "truth" and "lie" as a condition of being permitted to testify. Under the new provision, it is clear that children are not expected to demonstrate that they understand the duty to speak the truth or can define abstract concepts. These changes to the competency inquiry reflect the psychological research which demonstrates that the previous cognitively based inquiry might exclude children who were in fact competent to give honest, reliable answers to questions.

A result of the changes to the competency test for children is that children and adults are now treated in a more similar manner. By requiring children to demonstrate that they understood the "nature of an oath or solemn affirmation," judges were requiring more of children than of adults. Adults are not asked to define abstract concepts like "oath" before they are permitted to testify, even though a significant portion of adult witnesses are not able to give a good definition of this abstract concept. Children (and often adults) often understand and correctly use words without being able to answer questions that require them to provide a definition. For both adults and children, the process of promising or swearing an oath may serve to impress on the witness and others in the court the solemnity of the occasion. While having a child promise to tell the truth provides no guarantee of the honesty of the witness, it does no harm, and may do some good.

---

[107] V. Talwar, K. Lee, N. Bala, & R.C.L. Lindsay, "Children's conceptual knowledge of lie-telling and its relation to their actual behaviors: Implications for court competence examination" (2002) 26 Law & Human Behavior 395; V. Talwar, K. Lee, N. Bala, & R.C.L. Lindsay, "Children's lie-telling to conceal a parent's transgression: Legal implications" (2004) 8 Law & Human Behavior 411.

Though Bill C-2 does not provide detailed directions about how a judge is to deal with a child who is called as a witness, the language used in the new s.16.1 suggests that when the child takes the stand, after initial introductions, the judge, or counsel who has called the child as a witness, should ask the child preliminary questions about name, and such matters as age, school, and residence, and then about one or two past events, such as a holiday, not related to the matters at issue.[108] This initial questioning is intended to allow the court to ascertain whether the child is "able to understand and respond to questions." This questioning about non-contentious matters may also help the court to understand the child's speech and vocabulary, and will help the child feel less uncomfortable in court and hence able to be a more effective witness.

While s. 16.1(7) makes clear that the answering of questions about the promise is not to be a condition of the child testifying, it is submitted that the judge may give the child simple instructions about the role of a witness in court.[109] This might include brief instructions about the importance of telling the truth.[110] The child could also be encouraged and instructed during this initial period about the need to give responses that are as detailed as possible. Children should also be reminded that if there are questions which they do not understand, that they should indicate this to the court, and if there are questions that they cannot answer, they should not guess at answers, but rather should respond "I don't know."[111]

Section 16.1 (8) makes clear that if a child testifies after giving a promise to tell the truth, this "shall have the same effect" as if the child testified under oath; that is, there is to be no discounting of the evidence of a child merely because the child has not given an oath. This new provision addresses a common judicial view that, under the 1988 *Act*, there was a distinction between the sworn and unsworn testimony of a child. It has not been uncommon, in the

---

[108]   For a discussion of the type of "pre-interview" questioning that should be carried out to allow for the best "interview", see J. Schuman, N. Bala & K. Lee, "Developmentally Appropriate Questions for Child Witnesses" (1999) 25 Queen's L.J. 251; and M.E. Lamb, K.K. Sternberg & P.W. Esplin, "Conducting Investigative Interviews of Alleged Sexual Abuse Victims" (1998) 22 Child Abuse and Neglect 813 at 818-819.

[109]   It is submitted that this is as an aspect of the inherent obligation and power of the presiding judge to control the court process. See *R. v. A. (A.)* (2003), 170 C.C.C. (3d) 449 (Ont. C.A.) on the inherent powers of a presiding judge, including a justice of the peace, to control the court process, and in the context of a youth court proceeding to ensure that a young person understands the significance of the charges that he or she faces, even if his or her counsel waives the reading of the charges.

[110]   *The Youth Criminal Justice Act*, S.C. 2002, c. 1, s. 151 provides that a youth justice court judge shall "instruct" a child witness under 12 "as to the duty to speak the truth and the consequences of failing to do so", and may give such instructions to a young person who testifies.

[111]   Young children often do not understand all that an adult questioner asks, but have been socially trained to "guess" at what is being asked and "respond". They will usually try to provide an answer to a question even if they did not understand it, or do not know how to answer it. It is appropriate for the judge to remind a child of the importance of saying that he or she did not understand a question, and to not guess at answers.

charge to the jury, for the judge to advert to the fact that a child did not testify under oath as a possible reason for discounting the child's testimony,[112] even though there is no legislative authority for this practice and no research to support it. This practice should no longer occur, since all children will testify on the basis of a promise to the truth. While a judge might caution a jury about inconsistencies or frailties in the testimony of any individual witness, including a child, there should not be a warning for classes of witnesses, such as children.

In the past, the intrusive inquiry required by s.16 was upsetting to children, a waste of court time and did nothing to promote the search for the truth. Some children who could give honest, reliable evidence were precluded from testifying, potentially resulting in miscarriages of justice. The changes created with the passage of Bill C-2 should address those concerns, by making it simpler for child witnesses to testify, through the introduction of a more logical competency test. Social science research establishes that the old practice of requiring children to "correctly" answer cognitive questions about the meaning of such abstract concepts as "oath", "truth", or "promise" did not increase the likelihood that a child would give honest or reliable testimony. Examining a child witness' ability to meaningfully understand and answer questions is a more realistic criterion to use to determine whether a child is competent to testify. If the child is found "able to understand and respond to questions" about past events, the child will invariably have sufficient basic understanding of the concepts involved to give the child some appreciation for the significance of "promising to tell the truth." Asking the child to promise to tell the truth, but not expecting the child to explain the significance of this undertaking is similar to how adults are treated.

Conclusion

While the justice system at one time operated on the basis of erroneous stereotypes about the inherent unreliability of children, psychological research conducted over the past two decades has led to a better understanding of children as witnesses. Research also has examined the experience of children as witnesses, and the changes enacted by the passage of Bill C-2 reflect the increased awareness of the capacities and needs of children and other vulnerable witnesses. Some of the changes, such as the new competency test in s. 16.1 of the *Canada Evidence Act,* will permit children to serve as witnesses who previously would have been prevented from testifying. Other changes in Bill C-2 will enable children and other vulnerable witnesses to testify in a more

---

[112]   See *R. v. Demerchant* (1991), 66 C.C.C. (3d) 49 (N.B. C.A.). In G.A. Ferguson & J.C. Bouck, *Canadian Criminal Jury Instructions*, 3rd ed. (Vancouver, Continuing Legal Education Society of British Columbia, 2002), vol. 1 at 4-65-2, it is suggested that a judge should charge the jury in the following way:

> Despite the fact that [the child witness] did not testify under oath. . .to tell the truth, you may still accept or reject (his/her) evidence in the same way you accept or reject the evidence of any other witness.

They go on to propose a further "discretionary instruction that may be given in appropriate circumstances" that would summarize the specific concerns about a particular child's testimony, and then conclude that "there is a dangerous risk of relying on (his/her) unsworn evidence standing alone without some other supporting or confirming evidence".

effective manner, while experiencing less trauma and anxiety. While children will continue to feel a great deal of stress, and in some cases suffer emotional trauma, from the testifying, the new provisions are a clear improvement. The changes in Bill C-2 should both enhance the truth-seeking function of the criminal justice system and reduce the stress on children and other vulnerable witnesses from their involvement in the legal process.

The constitutionality of s. 16.1 was upheld by the Supreme Court in *R. v. S. (J.)*.[113]

The *Ontario Evidence Act* has arguably not yet caught up to its federal counterpart. Section 18.1 reads:

Evidence of witness under 14

18.1 (1) When the competence of a proposed witness who is a person under the age of 14 is challenged, the court may admit the person's evidence if the person is able to communicate the evidence, understands the nature of an oath or solemn affirmation and testifies under oath or solemn affirmation.

Same

(2) The court may admit the person's evidence, if the person is able to communicate the evidence, even though the person does not understand the nature of an oath or solemn affirmation, if the person understands what it means to tell the truth and promises to tell the truth.

Further discretion

(3) If the court is of the opinion that the person's evidence is sufficiently reliable, the court has discretion to admit it, if the person is able to communicate the evidence, even if the person understands neither the nature of an oath or solemn affirmation nor what it means to tell the truth.

Bill C-2 also added to the procedures in the *Criminal Code* that were enacted in 1988 to accommodate the evidence of children. As a result of both amendments, witnesses under the age of 18 can testify with a support person (s. 486.1), and behind a screen or with the aid of a closed circuit television (s. 486.2). There is also a requirement that an accused must apply to the judge to personally cross-examine the complainant (s. 486.3).

The constitutionality of the 1988 amendments was upheld in the following case:

R. v. LEVOGIANNIS
[1993] 4 S.C.R. 475, 25 C.R. (4th) 325, 85 C.C.C. (3d) 327

The accused was charged with touching a child for a sexual purpose. The Crown requested that the 12-year-old complainant be allowed to testify behind a screen pursuant to s. 486(2.1) of the *Code*. The trial judge granted

---

[113]   [2010] 1 S.C.R. 3, 251 C.C.C. (3d) 1, 72 C.R. (6th) 42 (S.C.C.). The Court was content to adopt the judgment of the B.C. Court of Appeal: (2008), 238 C.C.C. (3d) 522, 61 C.R. (6th) 282 (B.C. C.A.) — see laudatory C.R. annotation to that ruling by Lisa Dufraimont.

the Crown's motion following the testimony of a clinical psychologist who indicated that the complainant was experiencing a great deal of fear about testifying. The accused challenged the constitutional validity of s. 486(2.1) on the grounds that it violated his right to a fair trial guaranteed by ss. 7 and 11(d) of the *Charter*. Both the trial judge and the Court of Appeal held that s. 486(2.1) of the *Code* did not infringe ss. 7 and 11(d). The Court of Appeal added that even if s. 486(2.1) infringed these sections, the infringement would be justified under s. 1 of the *Charter*.

L'HEUREUX-DUBÉ J.:—

. . .

The examination of whether an accused's rights are infringed encompasses multifaceted considerations, such as the rights of witnesses, in this case children, the rights of accused and courts' duties to ascertain the truth. The goal of the court process is truth seeking and, to that end, the evidence of all those involved in judicial proceedings must be given in a way that is most favourable to eliciting the truth. In ascertaining the constitutionality of s. 486(2.1) of the *Criminal Code*, one cannot ignore the fact that, in many instances, the court process is failing children, especially those who have been victims of abuse, who are then subjected to further trauma as participants in the judicial process.

. . .

The plight of children who testify and the role courts must play in ascertaining the truth must not be overlooked in the context of the constitutional analysis in the case at hand. As this Court has said, children may require different treatment than adults in the courtroom setting.

. . .

An order under s. 486(2.1) simply blocks the complainant's view of the accused and not vice versa. The wording of s. 486(2.1) merely provides that the screen "would allow the complainant not to see the accused". The screen does not obstruct the view of the complainant by the accused, his counsel, the Crown or the judge. All are present in court. The evidence is given and the trial is conducted in the usual manner, including cross-examination. As a result, the issue before this Court, is, simply put, whether a witness's obstructed view of an accused, infringes the rights of such accused under s. 7 or 11(*d*) of the *Charter*.

. . .

In my view, the main objective pursued by the legislative enactment presently challenged is to better "get at the truth", by recognizing that a young child abuse victim's evidence may, in certain circumstances, be facilitated if the child is able to focus his or her attention on giving testimony, rather than experiencing difficulties in facing the accused. Section 486(2.1) of the *Criminal Code* recognizes that a child may react negatively to a face-to-face confrontation and, as a result, special procedures may be required to alleviate these concerns.

. . .

The appellant submits that his right to "be presumed innocent until proven guilty according to law in a fair and public hearing by an independent and impartial tribunal" is violated, as the screen undermines the presumption of innocence, operates unfairly against the accused and hampers cross-examination. . .

According to the appellant, the use of a screen lends an air of credence to the witness' testimony and, since the courtroom has been altered for the protection of the young complainant, the accused may appear guilty. In the case at bar, the appellant was tried before a judge sitting alone and, as a result, the issue of appearance to the jury is not relevant. Had a jury been present, however, I suggest that, properly informed, they would not have been swayed by the use of the screen. As Dickson C.J. said in *R. v. Corbett*, [1988] 1 S.C.R. 670, at p. 692:

> In my view, it would be quite wrong to make too much of the risk that the jury might use the evidence for an improper purpose.

In a similar vein, I suggest that one should assume that a jury will follow judicial instruction and will not be biased by the use of such a device. In fact, in contrast to the perspective raised by the appellant, it has been remarked that Crown prosecutors are reluctant to request the use of screens because they are concerned that the young complainant may not come across as credible or the child's testimony may have less of an impact. . . The use of a screen could very well be held against a child complainant, who might be judged to be an unreliable witness, because she or he is unable to look the accused in the eye, rather than against the accused. If screens were used more regularly as part of the courtroom procedure, as recommended by the Family Court Clinic in London, these perceptions may well be totally eliminated. Finally, while it is true, as the appellant contends, that s. 486(2.1) of the *Criminal Code*, similar in this regard to most sections of the *Code*, does not contain prescribed jury instructions, such instructions are routinely given by judges and such a caution is no more a constitutional prerequisite with respect to this section than with respect to any other section of the *Criminal Code*. Such caution may not be necessary or, if it is, it will be a function of the circumstances of the case.

Similar provisions aimed at accommodating child witnesses have been adopted at the provincial level. For example, the *Ontario Evidence Act* provides:

> 18.4 (1) A witness under the age of 18 may testify behind a screen or similar device that allows the witness not to see an adverse party, if the court is of the opinion that this is likely to help the witness give complete and accurate testimony or that it is in the best interests of the witness, and if the condition set out in subsection (4) is satisfied.
>
> (2) The court may order that closed-circuit television be used instead of a screen or similar device if the court is of the opinion that,
>
>> (a) a screen or similar device is insufficient to allow the witness to give complete and accurate testimony; or

(b) the best interests of the witness require the use of closed-circuit television.

(3) If the court makes an order under subsection (2), the witness shall testify outside the courtroom and his or her testimony shall be shown in the courtroom by means of closed-circuit television.

(4) When a screen or similar device or closed-circuit television is used, the judge and jury and the parties to the proceeding and their lawyers shall be able to see and hear the witness testify.

18.5 (1) During the testimony of a witness under the age of 18, a support person chosen by the witness may accompany him or her.

(2) If the court determines that the support person chosen by the witness is not appropriate for any reason, the witness is entitled to choose another support person.

(3) The following are examples of reasons on the basis of which the court may determine that the support person chosen by a witness is not appropriate:

1. The court is of the opinion that the support person may attempt to influence the testimony of the witness.

2. The support person behaves in a disruptive manner.

3. The support person is also a witness in the proceeding.

18.6 (1) The court may prohibit personal cross-examination of a witness under the age of 18 by an adverse party if the court is of the opinion that such a cross-examination,

(a) would be likely to affect adversely the ability of the witness to give evidence; or

(b) would not be in the best interests of the witness.

(2) If the court prohibits personal cross-examination by the adverse party, the cross-examination may be conducted in some other appropriate way (for example, by means of questions written by the adverse party and read to the witness by court).

Another kind of accommodation for child witnesses is to allow their video-recorded statements to be admitted in evidence as an exception to the hearsay rule. The *Criminal Code* provides:

VIDEO-RECORDED EVIDENCE

Evidence of victim or witness under 18

715.1 (1) In any proceeding against an accused in which a victim or other witness was under the age of eighteen years at the time the offence is alleged to have been committed, a video recording made within a reasonable time after the alleged offence, in which the victim or witness describes the acts complained of, is admissible in evidence if the victim or witness, while testifying, adopts the contents of the video recording, unless the presiding judge or justice is of the opinion that admission of the video recording in evidence would interfere with the proper administration of justice.

R.S., 1985, c. 19 (3rd Supp.), s. 16; 1997, c. 16, s. 7; 2005, c. 32, s. 23.

Evidence of victim or witness who has a disability

715.2 (1) In any proceeding against an accused in which a victim or other witness is able to communicate evidence but may have difficulty doing so by reason of a mental or physical disability, a video recording made within a reasonable time after the alleged offence, in which the victim or witness describes the acts complained of, is admissible in evidence if the victim or witness, while testifying, adopts the contents of the video recording, unless the presiding judge or justice is of the opinion that admission of the video recording in evidence would interfere with the proper administration of justice.

1998, c. 9, s. 8; 2005, c. 32, s. 23.

R. v. L. (D.O.)
[1993] 4 S.C.R. 419, 25 C.R. (4th) 285, 85 C.C.C. (3d) 289

The accused was charged with sexual assault alleged to have taken place between September 1985 and March 1988. Following a medical examination of the complainant, a 9-year-old girl, the police began their investigation in May 1988 and a videotaped interview of the complainant took place in August 1988. At the preliminary inquiry, the complainant testified before the court. At trial, the Crown sought to introduce the videotaped interview of the complainant pursuant to s. 715.1 of the *Criminal Code*. The accused sought a declaration that s. 715.1 was unconstitutional but the trial judge upheld the section. Following a *voir dire*, the videotaped interview was admitted into evidence and the accused was convicted. The Court of Appeal allowed the accused's appeal and declared s. 715.1 unconstitutional.

LAMER C.J. (LA FOREST, SOPINKA, CORY, MCLACHLIN and IACOBUCCI JJ. concurring):—

I have read the reasons of Justice L'Heureux-Dubé and concur in her result. It is my view that s. 715.1 of the *Criminal Code* . . . is a response to the dominance and power which adults, by virtue of their age, have over children. Accordingly, s. 715.1 is designed to accommodate the needs and to safeguard the interests of young victims of various forms of sexual abuse, irrespective of their sex. By allowing for the videotaping of evidence under certain express conditions, s. 715.1 not only makes participation in the criminal justice system less stressful and traumatic for child and adolescent complainants, but also aids in the preservation of evidence and the discovery of truth.

. . . As s. 715.1 neither offends the principles of fundamental justice nor violates the right a fair trial, it cannot be said to limit the rights guaranteed under s. 7 or 11(*d*) of the *Canadian Charter of Rights and Freedoms*. The respondent has failed to establish that s. 715.1 offends the rules of evidence against the admission of hearsay evidence and prior consistent statements. In addition, as there is no constitutionally protected requirement that cross-examination be contemporaneous with the giving of evidence, the respondent has failed to show that his fundamental right to cross-examine has been violated. The admission of the videotaped evidence does not make the trial unfair or not public, nor does it in any way affect an accused's right to be presumed innocent.

[L'Heureux-Dubé J., in a lengthy judgment, Gonthier J. concurring, also found s. 715.1 to be not violative of the accused's *Charter rights*.]

R. v. F. (C.)
[1997] 3 S.C.R. 1183, 11 C.R. (5th) 209, 120 C.C.C. (3d) 225

The accused was charged with touching his 6-year-old daughter for a sexual purpose. The police investigated the complaint the evening it was made and videotaped the complainant's statement describing the incident. At trial, the complainant was shown the videotape following her examination-in-chief. She confirmed that she made the statements on the videotape and that they were true. The trial judge ruled that the complainant had adopted the videotaped statement and admitted it as evidence pursuant to s. 715.1 of the *Criminal Code*. On cross-examination the complainant made statements which contradicted in part the videotaped statements. The Ontario Court of Appeal overturned the conviction and directed a new trial. The Court of Appeal held that the videotaped evidence that was later disavowed could not be considered as having been adopted under s. 715.1.

The judgment of the Court was delivered by Cory J.:—

. . .

The appellate courts of Alberta and Ontario have given different meaning to the word "adopted". What constitutes the adoption of a videotape statement is the first and paramount issue that must be resolved in this appeal. The second is a consideration of what effect, if any, subsequent contradictory evidence of the complainant will have upon the admissibility of the videotape statement.

. . .

It will be self-evident to every observant parent and to all who have worked closely with young people that children, even more than adults, will have a better recollection of events shortly after they occurred than they will some weeks, months or years later. The younger the child, the more pronounced will this be. Indeed to state this simply expresses the observations of most Canadians. It is a common experience that anyone, and particularly children, will have a better recollection of events closer to their occurrence than he or she will later on. It follows that the videotape which is made within a reasonable time after the alleged offence and which describes the act will almost inevitably reflect a more accurate recollection of events than will testimony given later at trial. Thus the section enhances the ability of a court to find the truth by preserving a very recent recollection of the event in question. . . . The important subsidiary aim of the section is to prevent or reduce materially the likelihood of inflicting further injury upon a child as a result of participating in court proceedings. This will be accomplished by reducing the number of interviews that the child must undergo and thereby diminish the stress occasioned a child by repeated questioning on a painful incident. Further, the videotaping will take place in surroundings that are less overwhelming for a child than the courtroom.

. . .

Section 715.1 provides that a videotaped statement is admissible in evidence if the complainant "adopts the contents of the videotape" while testifying. What meaning should be attributed to that phrase?.... Black's Law Dictionary defines "adopt" as follows:

> To accept, appropriate, choose, or select. To make that one's own, property or act, which was not so originally.

Obviously the term "adoption" is capable of several meanings. However, in the context of s. 715.1 the proper interpretation should be one which accords with its aim and purpose. The Alberta and Ontario Courts of Appeal have taken different approaches to the adoption of videotaped evidence. In *R. v. Meddoui* (1990), 61 C.C.C. (3d) 345, the Alberta Court of Appeal found that a witness "adopted" her statement within the meaning of s. 715.1 when she recalled giving the statement and testified that she was then attempting to be honest and truthful. It was held that the complainant need not have a present recollection of the events discussed. The decision approved the use of the videotape as evidence of the events described, even if the complainant is unable to recall the events discussed in the tape which formed the basis for the charge . . . In *R. v. Toten* (1993), 83 C.C.C. (3d) 5, the Ontario Court of Appeal rejected the *Meddoui* interpretation of "adopts" in favour of a narrower one. It was held that in order to adopt the contents of a videotaped statement, the child complainant must be able, based on a present memory of the events referred to in the videotape, to verify the accuracy and contents of the statement. The child must not only acknowledge making the statement but also the truth of its contents. In light of the clear aim and purpose of s. 715.1, I cannot accept the Ontario Court of Appeal position. . . S. 715.1 has built-in guarantees of trustworthiness and reliability which eliminate the need for such a stringent requirement for adoption. Further, a lack of present memory or an inability to provide testimony at trial regarding the events referred to in the videotape as a result of the youthfulness and the emotional state of the complainant increases the need to consider the videotaped statement.

The test set out in *Toten* would prevent a child who has little, or no memory of the events from "adopting" the video and it would therefore be inadmissible under s. 715.1. However, it is precisely in this situation that the video is most needed. Children, particularly younger ones, are prone to forget details of an event with the passage of time. A videotape made shortly after the event is more likely to be accurate than the child's viva voce testimony, given months later, at trial. It is quite possible that a young child will have a recollection of going to the police station and making the statement and of her attempt to be truthful at the time yet have no memory of the unpleasant events. This is particularly true where the elapsed time between the initial complaint and the date of trial is lengthy. If effect is to be given to the aims of s. 715.1 of enhancing the truth-seeking role of the courts by preserving an early account of the incident and of preventing further injury to vulnerable children as a result of their involvement in the criminal process, then the videotape should generally be admitted.

. . .

I recognize that the *Meddoui* approach to "adoption" gives rise to another problem. Specifically, a witness who cannot remember the events cannot be effectively cross-examined on the contents of his or her statement, and therefore the reliability of his or her testimony cannot be tested in that way. However, it was recognized in *R. v. Khan*, [1990] 2 S.C.R. 531; *R. v. Smith*, [1992] 2 S.C.R. 915, and *R. v. B. (K.G.)*, [1993] 1 S.C.R. 740, that cross-examination is not the only guarantee of reliability. There are several factors present in s. 715.1 which provide the requisite reliability of the videotaped statement. They include: (a) the requirement that the statement be made within a reasonable time; (b) the trier of fact can watch the entire interview, which provides an opportunity to observe the demeanor, and assess the personality and intelligence of the child; (c) the requirement that the child attest that she was attempting to be truthful at the time that the statement was made. As well, the child can be cross-examined at trial as to whether he or she was actually being truthful when the statement was made. These indicia provide enough guarantees of reliability to compensate for the inability to cross-examine as to the forgotten events. Moreover, where the complainant has no independent memory of the events there is an obvious necessity for the videotaped evidence. In *Meddoui*, it was recommended that in such circumstances, the trier of fact should be given a special warning (similar to the one given in *Vetrovec v. The Queen*, [1982] 1 S.C.R. 811) of the dangers of convicting based on the videotape alone. In my view, this was sage advice that should be followed.

. . .

After the videotaped evidence has been admitted, any questions which arise concerning the circumstances in which the video was made, the veracity of the witness' statements, or the overall reliability of the evidence, will be matters for the trier of fact to consider in determining how much weight the videotaped statement should be given. If, in the course of cross-examination, defence counsel elicits evidence which contradicts any part of the video, this does not render those parts inadmissible. Obviously a contradicted videotape may well be given less weight in the final determination of the issues. However, the fact that the video is contradicted in cross-examination does not necessarily mean that the video is wrong or unreliable. The trial judge may still conclude, as in this case, that the inconsistencies are insignificant and find the video more reliable than the evidence elicited at trial. . . Although each witness' credibility must be assessed, the standard which would be applied to an adult's evidence is not always appropriate in assessing the credibility of young children. This approach to the evidence of children was reiterated in *R. v. W. (R.)*, [1992] 2 S.C.R. 122, at pp. 132-34. There McLachlin J. acknowledged that the peculiar perspectives of children can affect their recollection of events and that the presence of inconsistencies, especially those related to peripheral matters, should be assessed in context. A skilful cross-examination is almost certain to confuse a child, even if she is telling the truth. That confusion can lead to inconsistencies in her testimony. Although the trier of fact must be wary of any evidence which has been contradicted, this is a matter which goes to the weight which should be attached to the videotape and not to its admissibility.[114]

The *Ontario Evidence Act* was amended to provide:

18.3 (1) A videotape of the testimony of a witness under the age of 18 that satisfies the conditions set out in subsection (2) may be admitted in evidence, if the court is of the opinion that this is likely to help the witness give complete and accurate testimony or that it is in the best interests of the witness.

(2) The judge or other person who is to preside at the trial and the lawyers of the parties to the proceeding shall be present when the testimony is given, and the lawyers shall be given an opportunity to examine the witness in the same way as if he or she were testifying in the courtroom.

(3) Subsection 18.4(1) and section 18.5 apply with necessary modifications when testimony is being videotaped.

(4) If a videotape is admitted under subsection (1), the witness need not attend or testify and shall not be summoned to testify.

(5) However, in exceptional circumstances, the court may require the witness to attend and testify even though a videotape of his or her testimony has been admitted in evidence.

(6) With the leave of the court, a videotape of an interview with a person under the age of 18 may be admitted in evidence if the person, while testifying, adopts the contents of the videotape.

(7) Subsection (6) is in addition to any rule of law under which a videotape may be admitted in evidence.

(d) Mental Capacity

Section 16 of the *Canada Evidence Act* now reads:

Witness whose capacity is in question

16. (1) If a proposed witness is a person of fourteen years of age or older whose mental capacity is challenged, the court shall, before permitting the person to give evidence, conduct an inquiry to determine

   (a) whether the person understands the nature of an oath or a solemn affirmation; and

   (b) whether the person is able to communicate the evidence.

---

[114]   For critical commentary see Moore & Green, "Truth and the Reliability of Children's Evidence: Problems With S. 715 of the *Criminal Code*" (2000), 30 C.R. (5th) 148, who argue that overly generous court interpretations of reasonable time and adoption have raised significant threats to reliability.

Testimony under oath or solemn affirmation

(2) A person referred to in subsection (1) who understands the nature of an oath or a solemn affirmation and is able to communicate the evidence shall testify under oath or solemn affirmation.

Testimony on promise to tell truth

(3) A person referred to in subsection (1) who does not understand the nature of an oath or a solemn affirmation but is able to communicate the evidence may, notwithstanding any provision of any Act requiring an oath or a solemn affirmation, testify on promising to tell the truth.

No questions regarding understanding of promise

(3.1) A person referred to in subsection (3) shall not be asked any questions regarding their understanding of the nature of the promise to tell the truth for the purpose of determining whether their evidence shall be received by the court.

Inability to testify

(4) A person referred to in subsection (1) who neither understands the nature of an oath or a solemn affirmation nor is able to communicate the evidence shall not testify.

Burden as to capacity of witness

(5) A party who challenges the mental capacity of a proposed witness of fourteen years of age or more has the burden of satisfying the court that there is an issue as to the capacity of the proposed witness to testify under an oath or a solemn affirmation.

Subsection 16(3.1) was added to the *Canada Evidence Act* in Bill C-32, the *Victims Bill of Rights Act*, which received Royal Assent on April 23, 2015.

Before this amendment, the Act neither specifically required nor explicitly prohibited questioning adult witnesses whose mental competency was challenged on their understanding of the promise to tell the truth. In *R. v. I. (D.)*,[115] the Supreme Court was sharply divided on this question. The majority holding that such witnesses must not be questioned on their understanding of the promise to tell the truth was ultimately adopted in the legislation.

R. v. I. (D.)
[2012] 1 S.C.R. 149, 280 C.C.C. (3d) 127, 89 C.R. (6th) 221 (S.C.C.)

McLACHLIN C.J. (DESCHAMPS, ABELLA, CHARRON, ROTHSTEIN and CROMWELL JJ. concurring)—

3 At the heart of this case is a young woman, K.B., aged 26, with the mental age of a three- to six-year-old. The Crown alleges that she was repeatedly sexually assaulted by her mother's partner at the time, D.A.I. The prosecution sought to call the young woman to testify about the alleged assaults. It also

---

[115]   [2012] 1 S.C.R. 149, 280 C.C.C. (3d) 127, 89 C.R. (6th) 221 (S.C.C.).

sought to adduce evidence through her school teacher and a police officer of what she told them.

4 The trial judge excluded this evidence, on the ground that K.B. was not competent to testify in a court of law (A.R., vol. I, at p. 2). As a result, the case collapsed and D.A.I. was acquitted (2008 CanLII 21725 (Ont. S.C.J.)). The Ontario Court of Appeal affirmed the acquittal (2010 ONCA 133, 260 O.A.C. 96).

5 I respectfully disagree. In my view, the trial judge made a fundamental error of law in interpreting and applying the provisions of the *Canada Evidence Act* governing the testimonial competence of adult witnesses with mental disabilities. This error of law vitiates the trial judge's ruling that K.B. could not be allowed to testify. Subsequent evidence on other matters cannot overcome this fatal defect. I would therefore set aside the acquittal of D.A.I. and order a new trial.

. . .

34 . . . [Section] 16(3) should be read as requiring only two requirements for competence of an adult with mental disabilities: (1) ability to communicate the evidence; and (2) a promise to tell the truth. . .

35 [The defence argues] that unless an adult witness with mental disabilities is required to demonstrate that she understands the nature of the obligation to tell the truth, the promise is an "empty gesture". However, this submission's shortcoming is that it departs from the plain words of s. 16(3), on the basis of an assumption that is unsupported by any evidence and contrary to Parliament's intent. Imposing an additional qualitative condition for competence that is not provided in the text of s. 16(3) would demand compelling demonstration that a promise to tell the truth cannot amount to a meaningful procedure for adults with mental disabilities. No such demonstration has been made. On the contrary, common sense suggests that the act of promising to tell the truth may be useful, even in the absence of the witness's ability to explain what telling the truth means in abstract terms.

36 Promising is an act aimed at bringing home to the witness the seriousness of the situation and the importance of being careful and correct. The promise thus serves a practical, prophylactic purpose. A witness who is able to communicate the evidence, as required by s. 16(3), is necessarily able to relate events. This in turn implies an understanding of what really happened — i.e. the truth — as opposed to fantasy. When such a witness promises to tell the truth, this reinforces the seriousness of the occasion and the need to do so. In dealing with the evidence of children in s. 16.1, Parliament held that a promise to tell the truth was all that is required of a child capable of responding to questions. Parliament did not think a child's promise, without more, is an empty gesture. Why should it be otherwise for an adult with the mental ability of a child?

. . .

70 . . . Does allowing an adult witness with mental disabilities to testify when the witness can communicate the evidence and promises to tell the truth render a trial unfair? In my view, the answer to this question is no.

71 The common law, upon which our current rules of evidence are founded, recognized a variety of rules governing the capacity to testify in different circumstances. The golden thread uniting these varying and different rules is the principle that the evidence must meet a minimal threshold or reliability as a condition of being heard by a judge or jury. Generally speaking, this threshold of reliability is met by establishing that the witness has the capacity to understand and answer the questions put to her, and by bringing home to the witness the need to tell the truth by securing an oath, affirmation or promise. There is no guarantee that any witness — even those of normal intelligence who can take the oath or affirm — will in fact tell the truth, all the truth, or nothing but the truth. What the trial process seeks is merely a basic indication of reliability.

72 Many cases, including *Khan*, have warned against setting the threshold for the testimonial competence too high for adults with mental disabilities: *R. v. Caron* (1994), 72 O.A.C. 287; *Farley*; *Parrott*. This reflects the fact that such witnesses may be capable of giving useful, relevant and reliable evidence. It also reflects the fact that allowing the witness to testify is only the first step in the process. The witness's evidence will be tested by cross-examination. The trier of fact will observe the witness's demeanour and the way she answers the questions. The result may be that the trier of fact does not accept the witness's evidence, accepts only part of her evidence, or reduces the weight accorded to her evidence. This is a task that judges and juries perform routinely in a myriad of cases involving witnesses of unchallenged as well as challenged mental ability.

. . .

84 During the voir dire on K.B.'s testimonial capacity, the Crown posed a line of questions going to whether she could tell the difference between true and false factual statements in concrete circumstances. These were relevant to K.B.'s basic ability to communicate the evidence. . .:

MR. SEMENOFF:

Q. How old are you now, [K.B.]?

A. I'm 22, you know that.

Q. 22? When's your birthday?

A. [Birth date].

Q. [Birth date]. Are you going to school now or are you done with school?

A. I'm not done in school yet.

Q. What school do you go to, [K.B.]?

A. [Name of school].

Q. How long—do you know how long you've been going to [name of school]?

A. I don't know.

Q. Did you go to any school before you went to [name of school]?

A. From [name of previous school].

Q. From [name of previous school]. Okay. [page189] Did you have a teacher from that school, a Ms. [W.]?

A. Ms. [R.].

Q. Oh, [R.]. Okay. And I call her Ms. [W.], do you know what her name is, is it [R.] or is it Ms. [W.]?

A. [R.].

Q. Okay.

. . .

Q. [K.B.], if I were to tell you that the room that we're in that the walls in the room are black[,] would that be a truth or a lie, [K.B.]?

A. A lie.

Q. Why would it be a lie?

A. It's different colours in here.

Q. There are different colours in here. What colour are the walls?

A. Purple.

Q. Purple. Okay. If I were to tell you that the gown that I'm wearing that that is black, would that be a truth or a lie?

A. The truth.

Q. And why is that?

A. I don't know.

Q. You don't know. Is it a good thing or a bad thing to tell the truth?

A. Good thing.

Q. Is it a good thing or a bad thing to tell a lie?

A. Bad thing.

(A.R., vol. I, at pp. 111-13)

However, the trial judge went on to question K.B. on her understanding of the meaning of truth, religious concepts, and the consequences of lying.

[THE COURT:]

[Q.] Do you go to church, [K.B.]?

A. No.

Q. No. Have you ever been taught about God or anything like that?

A. No.

Q. No? All right. What happens if you steal something?

A. I don't know.

Q. You don't know. If you steal something and no one sees it, will anything happen to you? Nothing will happen. Why won't anything happen?

A. I don't know.

Q. You don't know. Tell me what you think about the truth.

A. I don't know.

Q. You don't know. All right. Is it important to tell the truth?

A. I don't know.

Q. You don't know. Tell me what a promise is when you make a —

A. I don't know.

Q.— promise. What's a promise?

A. I don't know.

Q. You don't know what a promise is. Okay. Have you ever been in court before?

A. Once.

Q. Once? And do you think it's an important thing to be in court?

A. I don't know.

Q. You don't know. All right. Do you know what an oath is, to take an oath?

A. I don't know.

Q. No. Do you have any idea what it means to tell the truth?

A. I don't know.

Q. You don't know. If you tell a lie does anything happen to you? Nothing happens.

A. No.

. . .

[THE COURT:]

[Q.] Do you know why you're here today?

A. I don't know. To talk about [D.A.I.].

Q. Yes, and do you think that's really important?

A. Maybe yeah.

Q. Maybe yeah? Remember earlier I was asking you about a promise?

A. No.

Q. Have you ever made a promise to anybody?

A. I don't know.

Q. That you promised you'll be good, did you ever say that? Have you ever heard that expression "I promise to be good, mommy"?

A. Okay.

Q. All right. So do you know what a promise is, that you're going to do something the right way? Do you understand that?

A. Okay.

Q. Can you tell me whether you understand that, [K.B.]?

A. I don't know.

Q. Does anything happen if you break a promise?

A. I don't know.

Q. You told me you don't go to church, right?

A. Right.

Q. And no one has ever told you about God; is that correct? No one has ever told you about God?

A. No.

Q. Has anyone ever told you that if you tell big lies you'll go to jail?

A. Right.

Q. If you tell big lies will you go to jail?

A. No.

(Ibid., at pp. 117-19 and 155-56)

85 As these passages demonstrate, the trial judge was not satisfied with the Crown's questions on K.B.'s ability to recount events and distinguish between telling the truth and lying in concrete, real-life situations. He went on to question her on the nature of truth, religious obligations and the consequences of failing to tell the truth. Because K.B. was unable to satisfactorily answer these more abstract questions, he ruled that she could not be allowed to promise to tell the truth and refused to allow her to testify.

86 This ruling was based on an erroneous interpretation of s. 16(3), which the trial judge read as requiring an understanding of the duty to speak the truth. Hence, K.B. was precluded from testifying on promising to tell the truth. . . .

90 I would allow the appeal, set aside the acquittal, and direct a new trial.

A strong dissent was delivered by Binnie J. (LeBel J. and Fish JJ., concurring).

Does the witness have to be called on the s. 16 competency hearing?

R. v. PARROTT

[2001] 1 S.C.R. 178, 39 C.R. (5th) 255, 150 C.C.C. (3d) 449

The accused was charged with offences in relation to a woman who suffered from Down's Syndrome. The complainant made statements to the police when she was found, and to the doctor who first examined her. The police also conducted a videotaped interview the following day. As we saw in Chapter 4 dealing with Hearsay, out-of-court statements may be received for their truth if there are grounds of necessity and the statements were made in circumstances that indicated they were reliable. This case deals with the requirement of necessity.

BINNIE J. (MAJOR, BASTARACHE and ARBOUR JJ. concurring): —

This appeal tests the limits of the principled hearsay exception that allows the Crown in exceptional circumstances to lead the out-of-court evidence of a complainant at a criminal trial without having him or her present in court and available for cross-examination by the defence.

In this case, the complainant in a kidnapping and sexual assault case was a mature woman who had suffered since birth from Down's Syndrome. She was considered mildly to moderately retarded and had been in institutional care for almost 20 years. Expert evidence was called to establish that her mental development was equivalent to that of a three- or four-year-old child and that her memory of events was poor. Her response to even the simplest questions was said to be not very coherent. The complainant herself was never called into the presence of the trial judge so that these attributes could be verified even though she was available and there was no suggestion that she would suffer any trauma or other adverse effect by appearing in court. Instead the court received evidence of out-of-court statements that she had earlier made to the police and to a doctor.

. . .

Analysis

While in this country an accused does not have an absolute right to confront his or her accuser in the course of a criminal trial, the right to full answer and defence generally produces this result. In this case, unusually, the Crown precipitated an inquiry under s. 16 of the Canada Evidence Act not for the purpose of establishing the testimonial competence of "a proposed witness", namely the complainant, but to lay an evidentiary basis to keep her out of the witness box. Having satisfied the trial judge entirely through expert evidence that the complainant neither understood the nature of an oath nor could communicate her evidence, the Crown used the *voir dire* as a springboard to establish the admissibility of hearsay evidence of her out-of-court statements under the principles established in *Khan*.

This procedure raises two distinct though related issues, firstly the admissibility of the expert evidence at the *voir dire*, and secondly the admissibility of the complainant's out-of-court statements at the trial. In my view, these issues ought to have been resolved in favour of the respondent, as held by the majority judgment of the Newfoundland Court of Appeal, for the following reasons:

1. The expert evidence was improperly admitted at the *voir dire*. Trial judges are eminently qualified to assess the testimonial competence of a witness. The trial judge, after all, was to be at the receiving end of the complainant's communication, and could have determined whether or not she was able to communicate her evidence to him. If she had been called and it became evident that the trial judge required expert assistance to draw appropriate inferences from what he had heard her say (or not say), or if either the defence or the Crown had wished to pursue the issue of requiring an oath or solemn affirmation, expert evidence might then have become admissible to assist the judge. At the time the expert testimony was called, it had not been shown that expert evidence as such was necessary, and the testimony of Drs. Gillespie, Morley and Parsons was therefore inadmissible: *R. v. Mohan*, [1994] 2 S.C.R. 9.

2. Consequently, the trial judge erred in ruling at the conclusion of the *voir dire* that the complainant's out-of-court statements would be admissible at trial. Having dispensed with hearing from the complainant, and the expert medical testimony having been improperly admitted, the trial judge had no admissible evidence on which to exercise a discretion to admit the complainant's out-of-court statements.

. . .

At the threshold stands the question of why expert evidence was admitted in the first place to establish the competency of a witness, a task which is specifically assigned by s. 16 of the Canada Evidence Act to the trial judge. In *R. v. Abbey*, [1982] 2 S.C.R. 24, the Court adopted as correct the statement that "[i]f on the proven facts a judge or jury can form their own conclusions without help, then the opinion of the expert is unnecessary".

The key and undisputed facts of this case are that the complainant was available to testify and there was no suggestion by anybody that she might be harmed thereby. She was not called simply because the Crown made the tactical decision to proceed without calling her. The medical experts were not called to assist the judge to interpret what he had seen or heard from the complainant in the witness box, but in substitution for any such opportunity of direct observation.

The special role of the expert witness is not to testify to the facts, but to provide an opinion based on the facts, to assist the trier of fact to draw the appropriate inferences from the facts as found "which the judge and jury, due to the technical nature of the facts, are unable to formulate" (*Abbey, supra.*)

. . .

Whether a complainant "is able to communicate the evidence" in this broad sense is a matter on which a trial judge can (and invariably does) form his or her own opinion. It is not a matter "outside the experience and knowledge of a judge or jury" (*Mohan, supra*, at p. 23). It is the very meat and potatoes of a trial court's existence.

LeBel J. (L'Heureux-Dubé and Gonthier JJ. concurring) dissenting: —

. . . The question at issue in this appeal is whether, on the *voir dire* to determine necessity, the Crown was *obliged* to put the complainant forward as a witness in order for the trial judge to evaluate her testimonial capacity. While I agree with my colleague, Binnie J., that it is generally a prudent practice to have the Crown do so, I would not elevate it to an absolute legal requirement in every case. In my view, the evidence before the trial judge in the present case amply supports his findings of necessity and reliability. . .

(e) Interest

When witnesses first began informing the jury in the fifteenth century, there was no bar against witnesses who were interested in the outcome. Indeed, witnesses who were disinterested were regarded as meddling and unless summoned by the court or the jury they might risk a maintenance prosecution.[116] Originally witnesses were interested in the outcome and as a result distinctly partisan. To this there was one major exception: the parties themselves. The party could plead or argue but could not be sworn since to do so would be to mix two kinds of proof; during the fifteenth century, and indeed continuing into the sixteenth, the party could elect trial by wager of law rather than by jury, and in that mode of proceeding he was entitled to the use of his own oath. Later, as trial by witnesses before a jury became the predominant mode of proceeding in civil cases, the disqualification of parties was extended, by analogy, to include other persons interested in the outcome and by 1650 the disqualification was firmly established. One particular group of readily identifiable interested persons were the spouses of the parties. Curiously, while the disqualification was extended to cover the spouse, the common law did not go further and extend it to children or other relatives; perhaps the extension to spouses was grounded on the then-current notion of identity or merger of the two spouses into a single person. In criminal trials the accused had been entitled, like a party in a civil case, to plead and argue orally, by himself, and later, through his counsel. The accused then presented his own "evidence" and was questioned though he was not sworn. By analogy to the civil cases his statements were not to be

---

[116] See Thayer, *Preliminary Treatise on Evidence at the Common Law* (1898) at 125-129. Quoting Paston, J. in 1442 (at 128): "If one who has no reason to meddle in the matter and is not learned in the law shows the jury, or the party himself, or his counsel, the truth of the matter and opens evidence of it as well and as fully as one who was learned in the law could, yet this is a maintenance in his person."

regarded as testimony since he was disqualified as a witness from his own interest in the outcome.[117]

As in civil cases, the spouse was incompetent in criminal trials:

. . . except in case of necessity, and that necessity is not a general necessity, as where no other witness can be had, but a particular necessity, as where, for instance, the wife would otherwise be exposed without remedy to personal injury.[118]

Inspired by Bentham, the reformers in the mid to late nineteenth century gradually discarded these disqualifications for interest, preferring that the proposed witness' interest be displayed to, and taken into account by, the trier of fact, who could then evaluate to what particular extent the interest may have impaired credibility. As Bentham noted:

Any interest, interest of any sort and quantity, sufficient to prove mendacity? As rational would be it to say, any horse, or dog, or flea, put to a wagon, is sufficient to move it . . .

. . . In the eyes of the English lawyer, one thing, and one thing only, has a value: that thing is money. On the will of man, if you believe the English lawyer, one thing, and one thing only, has influence: that thing is money. Such is his system of psychological dynamics. If you will believe the man of law, there is no such thing as the fear of God; no such thing as regard for reputation; no such thing as fear of legal punishment; no such thing as ambition; no such thing as the love of power; no such thing as filial, no such thing as parental, affection; no such thing as party attachment; no such thing as party enmity; no such thing as public spirit, patriotism, or general benevolence; no such thing as compassion; no such thing as gratitude; no such thing as revenge.[119]

The reforming legislation enacted in England was copied in Canada. The incremental nature of the change in England by individual statutes over a period of years is seen reflected in the provincial legislation, which in its present form consequently appears duplicative. For example, the *Ontario Evidence Act* provides:[120]

---

[117] The detailed history of the development here briefly described may be seen in 2 Wigmore, *Evidence* (Chad. Rev.), ss. 575, 601. See also *Coleman's Trial* (1678), 7 Howell's State Trials 1, 65: the prosecution witness maintained the prisoner's treasonous act was done about the 21st of August and the prisoner said to the court:

- Prisoner: I went out of town on the 10th of August, it was the latter end I came home.

- L.C.J.:   Have you any witness to prove that?

- Prisoner: I cannot say I have a witness.

- L.C.J.:   They say, she is so big with child she can't come.

- L.C.J.:   Then you say nothing. . . You say you went out of town the 10th and came home the last of August; you say it is impossible that he should say right, but yet you do not prove it.

[118] *Bentley v. Cooke* (1784), 99 E.R. 729, per Lord Mansfield.

[119] Bentham, *Rationale of Judicial Evidence* (1827), cited in 2 Wigmore, *Evidence* (Chad. Rev.), s. 576.

[120] R.S.O. 1990, c. E-23.

6. No person offered as a witness in an action shall be excluded from giving evidence by reason of any alleged incapacity from crime or interest.

7. Every person offered as a witness shall be admitted to give evidence notwithstanding that he has an interest in the matter in question or in the event of the action and notwithstanding that he has been previously convicted of a crime or offence.

8. (1) The parties to an action and the persons on whose behalf it is brought, instituted, opposed or defended are, except as hereinafter otherwise provided, competent and compellable to give evidence on behalf of themselves or of any of the parties, and the spouses of such parties and persons are, except as hereinafter otherwise provided, competent and compellable to give evidence on behalf of any of the parties. R.S.O. 1990, c. E.23, s. 8 (1); 2005, c. 5, s. 25 (2).

. . .

10. (1) The parties to a proceeding instituted in consequence of adultery and the spouses of such parties are competent to give evidence in such proceedings, but no witness in any such proceeding, whether a party to the suit or not, is liable to be asked or bound to answer any question tending to show that he or she is guilty of adultery, unless such witness has already given evidence in the same proceeding in disproof of his or her alleged adultery. R.S.O. 1990, c. E.23, s. 10; 2005, c. 5, s. 25 (4).

The Canada Evidence Act provides:[121]

3. A person is not incompetent to give evidence by reason of interest or crime.

(f) Spousal Competence and Compellability

After decades of recommendations and calls for reform by academics (see e.g. Ronda Bessner, "Spousal Competency and Compellability in Criminal Proceedings: Proposals for Reform" (2014) 18 Can. Crim. L. Rev. 7) and courts (see *R. v. Schell*),[122] Parliament finally abolished the spousal incompetence rule with Bill C-32 (*Victims Bill of Rights Act*) which received Royal Assent on April 23, 2015. Section 4(2) of the *Canada Evidence Act* now reads:

Spouse of accused

(2) No person is incompetent, or uncompellable, to testify for the prosecution by reason only that they are married to the accused.

Sections 4(4) and (5) have also been repealed. These amendments do not impact marital privilege recognized in s. 4(3) of the *Canada Evidence Act*. See discussion in Chapter 4 under Privilege. In civil cases, there is also no spousal incompetence rule. Section 8(1) of the *Ontario Evidence Act* (reproduced above) is representative of provincial legislation making the parties and their spouses competent and compellable witnesses for either side in civil cases.

---

[121]   R.S.C. 1985, c. C-5.
[122]   (2004), 188 C.C.C. (3d) 254, 20 C.R. (6th) 1 (Alta. C.A.).

(g) Compellability of Accused

(i) *History of Privilege Against Self-incrimination*[123]

Prior to the thirteenth century, criminal procedure was basically accusatorial. Both on the continent and in England, a private person accused another, provided details of the complaint, conducted the prosecution and led the proof. The resultant trial might be by compurgation, battle, or ordeal. By the thirteenth century, trials by battle and compurgation had fallen into disfavour as they were increasingly seen as irrational and untrustworthy. In 1215, the church forbade its clergy from participating in trials by ordeal and new methods of proceeding became necessary. England retained the accusatorial method and gave its grand jury of presentment the additional task of finding a verdict. In England the perceived lack of impartiality in the trier gradually gave birth to a separate, petit jury for the latter task. The ecclesiastical courts and the continental civilian courts on the other hand embraced the inquisitorial method as a replacement.

The inquisitorial method allowed the judge to fill all the roles; he was accuser, prosecutor and trier. The judge, and not a jury of presentment, decided whether there were sufficient grounds to call the individual to answer. The method also provided for a new oath to be taken by the accused at the beginning of the inquiry whereby he promised to answer all questions put to him though he be given no information regarding the charges against him nor the evidence, if any, which supported them. This type of oath became known as the oath *ex officio* as it was administered by the judge by virtue of his office.

The oath *ex officio* was introduced into the ecclesiastical courts in England in 1236, and was adopted by the judicial arm of the King's Council, the Court of Star Chamber, in 1487. In the common law courts at this time the accused was interrogated but he was not sworn. On taking the oath *ex officio* the accused was compelled to choose between offending his God and risking punishment for perjury or accusing himself of crime; failing to take the oath was regarded by the court as a confession of guilt. Placing an individual in such a dilemma was regarded by many as more cruel than physical torture. With no requirement of a charge in advance, much less a demonstrated basis for the same, the individual became his own accuser and his own means of destruction.

During the sixteenth and seventeenth centuries the *ex officio* oath was used in England by the Court of Star Chamber and the Court of the High Commission in Causes Ecclesiastical for the purposes of stamping out non-conforming political and religious views. Opposition to this method of inquiry,

---

[123] See Levy, *Origins of the Fifth Amendment* (1968, Oxford). But compare Langbein, "The Historical Origins of the Privilege" (1994) 92 Mich. L. Rev. 1047. And note the comment of Frankfurter, J.: "The privilege against self-incrimination is a specific provision of which it is peculiarly true that 'a page of history is worth a volume of logic'", in *Ullman v. U.S.*, 350 U.S. 422 (1956) at 438. See also Morgan, "The Privilege Against Self-Incrimination" (1949) 34 Minn. L. Rev. 1; and 8 Wigmore, *Evidence* (McNaughton Rev.), s. 2250.

wide-ranging and without benefit of accusation, steadily grew and reached its culmination in 1638 in the trial in the Court of Star Chamber of a young Puritan named John Lilburne. The offence was importing seditious books into England, and while it would appear that he knew the nature of the charge against him, no bill of complaint was proferred before he was requested to take the oath. Lilburne denied the charges against him but refused to take the oath. Rather than taking this as a confession of guilt, the court found him guilty of contempt and sentenced him to a fine, corporal punishment and imprisonment until he conformed by taking the oath. Lilburne's martyrdom, and his numerous pamphlets against the excesses of the High Commission and Star Chamber smuggled out of his prison, caused others to follow his example, public discontent to swell, and the way to be paved for radical reforms. In 1641 the High Commission and Star Chamber were abolished and the *ex officio* oath outlawed. The opposition had been to the far-ranging inquiry on oath without benefit of accusation or bill of complaint; but such was the depth of emotion over the excesses of those courts that anything akin to their procedures was regarded as odious. Gradually, in the common law courts, accused persons, even though properly charged, began to resist their questioning on the basis that no man is bound to incriminate himself. By 1700 it was firmly recognized that no person, in any court, whether he be accused or merely witness, could be compelled to answer if the answer would tend to incriminate. The common law privilege was born.

It should be noted, however, that accused persons continued being questioned by examining justices of the peace prior to trial, although that examination was not on oath. The normal criminal trial would begin with a reading of the accused's earlier compulsory examination.[124] The privilege against self-incrimination, at least in its formative years, was confined to foreclose only compulsory examination at trial. It was not until *Jervis's Act* of 1848[125] that we see the accused being advised that he need not make a statement to the examining justices prior to committal.

Until the end of the nineteenth century the accused was not able to give testimony on oath for two reasons. First, he was regarded as incompetent because of his obvious interest in the outcome of the proceedings. Second, it was regarded as a violation of his privilege against self-incrimination to place him on the horns of a dilemma: should he choose to testify falsely gaining temporal relief but everlasting damnation or testify truthfully and forfeit his liberty? Perhaps a trilemma in that should he choose not to testify, and it being known that he was able, he risked an inference of guilt being drawn from his silence.

(ii) *Canada Evidence Act*

By the end of the nineteenth century statutory reforms made the accused competent for the defence. The common law position of non-

---

[124] The compulsory examination was provided for by statute: (1554), 1 & 2 Phil. & Mar., c. 13, s. 4.
[125] 11 & 12 Vict., c. 42, s. 18, the predecessor to the present Canadian provision used in the preliminary hearing: see *Criminal Code*, R.S.C. 1985, c. C-46, ss. 540, 541.

compellability at the instance of the prosecution remained. Section 4 of the *Canada Evidence Act* provides:

> (1) Every person charged with an offence, and, except as otherwise provided in this section, the wife or husband, as the case may be, of the person so charged, is a competent witness for the defence, whether the person so charged is charged solely or jointly with any other person.

It is important to recognize that this privilege, in its origins and as later interpreted in Canada, operated to protect a person from being compelled to give evidence before a court or like tribunal. It was also restricted to testimonial evidence. Taking bodily samples, fingerprints or photographs were not seen as captured by the privilege.[126] In short, the privilege in Canada was seen to be reflected simply, and solely, in the accused's non-compellability at trial. The accused, pursuant to the legislation, was a competent witness for the defence. It was up to the accused to decide whether he or she would go into the box.

In Canada, the legislation also provided that no witness, including the accused who chose to become a witness, could refuse to answer a question on the grounds that the answer might tend to incriminate. Rather, the legislation provided that he or she was obliged to answer but the answer could not be used against him or her in later proceedings. For example, the *Canada Evidence Act* provides:

> 5. (1) No witness shall be excused from answering any question on the ground that the answer to the question may tend to criminate him, or may tend to establish his liability to a civil proceeding at the instance of the Crown or of any person.
>
> (2) Where with respect to any question a witness objects to answer on the ground that his answer may tend to criminate him, or may tend to establish his liability to a civil proceeding at the instance of the Crown or of any person, and if but for this Act, or the Act of any provincial legislature, the witness would therefore have been excused from answering the question, then although the witness is by reason of this Act or the provincial Act compelled to answer, the answer so given shall not be used or admissible in evidence against him in any criminal trial or other criminal proceeding against him thereafter taking place, other than a prosecution for perjury in the giving of that evidence or for the giving of contradictory evidence.

Similar provisions exist in provincial legislation.[127]

In *R. v. Mottola*[128] Morden J.A. explained the proper procedure to be followed:

> An accused person who is a witness and any other witness is not excused from answering incriminating questions. However, if the witness objects to

---

[126]   *Marcoux v. R.* (1975), 24 C.C.C. (2d) 1 (S.C.C.).

[127]   For similar provincial and territorial provisions. see: R.S.A. 1980, c. A-21, s. 6; R.S.B.C. 1979, c. 116, s. 4; R.S.M. 1987, c. E-150, s. 6; R.S.N.B. 1973, c. E-II, s. 6; R.S.N. 1970, c. 115, s. 3A; R.S.N.W.T. 1974, c. E-4, s. 8; R.S.N.S. 1989, c. 154, s. 59; R.S.O. 1990, c. E.23, s. 9; R.S.P.E.I. 1988, c. E-11, s. 6; R.S.S. 1978, c. S-16, s. 37; and R.S.Y.T. 1986, c. 57, s. 7.

[128]   (1959), 124 C.C.C. 288 (Ont. C.A.) at 295.

answering a question upon the ground that his answer may tend to incriminate him and he then answers it as he is bound by the Act to do, the answer shall not be used in evidence against him in any criminal proceedings against him thereafter taking place with the necessary exception for a perjury charge in the giving of such evidence. The objection must be taken by the witness to the question. In practice when a witness is being examined upon an incident or series of incidents and he thinks that all or any of his answers might tend to incriminate him, the Judge might of course permit a general objection to the series of such questions and not require a specific objection to each and every question. But the objection cannot be taken before the witness is sworn and before he is asked any questions. Any protection the witness has if he objects to the question, as provided by s. 5(2), is against the use of his answer in independent, contemporaneous or subsequent prosecutions. This protection is conferred by the Act and not by any ruling of the Judge when objection is taken to a question. The procedure followed in the case under appeal was unwarranted. The Magistrate had no authority to confer or withhold "the protection of the Court" upon the witness Boule or upon the appellant Vallee. Both these witnesses could at any time during their examination object to answer questions — they had no right to refuse to answer — but if they would have been excused at common law from answering such questions, their answers could not be used against them in other criminal proceedings. The accused has the same rights in this regard as any other witness at his trial.

(iii) *Sections 11(c) and 13 of Charter*

The *Charter of Rights* provides:

11. (c) Any person charged with an offence has the right. . . not to be compelled to be a witness in proceedings against that person in respect of the offence.

. . .

13. A witness who testifies in any proceedings has the right not to have any incriminating evidence so given used to incriminate that witness in any other proceedings, except in a prosecution for perjury or for the giving of contradictory evidence.

Section 11(c) confirms that the Crown or co-accused cannot compel an accused to testify. Section 13 entrenches a privilege against incrimination which results in use immunity. Note that s. 13 provides for blanket exclusion without the necessity of objection. **Is this a welcome advance?**

In *R. v. Dubois*[129] the Supreme Court held that "in any other proceeding" in s. 13 included a second trial. The Crown could not adduce into evidence statements made by the accused at his first trial for murder into the second trial. Otherwise this would allow the accused to indirectly compel the accused to testify contrary to s. 11(c). This was extended in *R. v. Mannion*[130] to prevent cross-examination by the Crown on the accused's testimony from the first trial, although this ruling was on the narrow footing that the purpose of the cross-examination was to incriminate Mannion. Then, in *R. v. Kuldip*[131] the

---

129   [1985] 2 S.C.R. 350.
130   (1986), 53 C.R. (3d) 193 (S.C.C.).
131   (1990), 1 C.R. (4th) 285 (S.C.C.).

Supreme Court held that cross-examination on the accused's previous voluntary testimony is permitted if the purpose is to impugn his her credibility, rather than to incriminate him or her. The policy behind *Kuldip* was laudable — to prevent an accused from advancing conflicting versions without being faced with the inconsistency — but the distinction between an incriminating purpose and impugning credibility was sometimes difficult to draw and to explain clearly to a jury. In *R. v. Noël*[132] the Supreme Court decided that under s. 13 of the *Charter*, when an accused testifies at trial he or she cannot be cross-examined on prior testimony from an earlier trial unless the trial judge is satisfied that there is no realistic danger that the prior testimony could be used to incriminate the accused.

With this background of complex rulings, the Supreme Court in *R. v. Henry*[133] attempted to simplify the Court's interpretation of s. 13. In *Henry*, the two accused had voluntarily testified at their first trial and then, after a new trial was ordered, provided quite different testimony at their second trial. The s. 13 issue arose because the Crown cross-examined them on their prior inconsistent testimony. On the previous jurisprudence, *Mannion* would have barred the cross-examination. However, the Supreme Court departed from its previous position and overruled *Mannion* and modified *Kuldip*. The focus has shifted to whether or not the accused voluntarily testified at the other proceeding. If so, the Crown may cross-examine on the prior testimony, regardless of whether the purpose is to impeach credibility or to incriminate. As Justice Binnie, for the Court, held:

> 60 The result of a purposeful interpretation of s. 13 is that an accused will lose the *Mannion* advantage in relation to prior *volunteered* testimony but his or her protection against the use of prior *compelled* testimony will be strengthened. The two different situations will be treated differently instead of homogenized, and the unpredictability inherent in sorting out attacks on credibility from attempts at incrimination will be avoided.
>
> 61 For the foregoing reasons, I conclude that the s. 13 *Charter* rights of the appellants (who were volunteers at both trials) were not violated by the Crown's cross- examination. Their appeals must therefore be dismissed.

Like the majority judges in the B.C. Court of Appeal, the Supreme Court could not see why s. 13 should protect an accused from cross-examination where he or she chose to testify one way at his or her first trial then differently on the re-trial.

Some had thought that the Court might have been prepared to reverse the *Dubois* ruling so that when a new trial is ordered the trial does not constitute "other proceedings" to trigger any s. 13 protection. Justice Binnie did not accept this view. The Court declined, however, to overrule *Dubois*, with the result that the Crown may not introduce the prior testimony as a part of its case in chief even if the accused voluntarily testified at the previous trial.

---

[132]   [2002] 3 S.C.R. 433.
[133]   [2005] 3 S.C.R. 609. For comments on *Henry*, see Stuart, "Annotation" (2005), 33 C.R. (6th) 215 and Hamish Stewart, "*Henry* in the Supreme Court of Canada: Reorienting the s. 13 Right against Self-incrimination" (2006), 34 C.R. (6th) 112, especially at 119.

On the other hand, where the accused has been compelled to testify in the previous proceeding, usually at the trial of another person, the Supreme Court now gives the accused greater s. 13 protection. The prior testimony may not be used by the Crown to incriminate or attack credibility. Thus, the decision leaves *Noël* intact as well. The courts will now be spared the task of trying to draw a distinction that the Supreme Court now says has been, in this context, too difficult to draw.

Henry is also significant because it confirms that s. 13 does not require an objection to be compelled as does s. 5(2), and that its use immunity extends to all other proceedings and not just criminal. As Justice Binnie observed:

> 22 The consistent theme in the s. 13 jurisprudence is that "the purpose of s. 13 . . . is to protect individuals from being indirectly compelled to incriminate themselves" (*Dubois*, at p. 358, and reiterated in *Kuldip*, at p. 629). That same purpose was flagged in *Noël*, the Court's most recent examination of s. 13, by Arbour J., at para. 21: Section 13 reflects a long-standing form of statutory protection against compulsory self-incrimination in Canadian law, and is best understood by reference to s. 5 of the *Canada Evidence Act*. Like the statutory protection, the constitutional one represents what Fish J.A. called a *quid pro quo*: when a witness who is compelled to give evidence in a court proceeding is exposed to the risk of self-incrimination, the state offers protection against the subsequent use of that evidence against the witness in exchange for his or her full and frank testimony. [Emphasis added.]
>
> 23 There is thus a consensus that s. 13 was intended to extend s. 5 of the *Canada Evidence Act* to give further and better effect to this purpose. As McIntyre J. pointed out in *Dubois*, in reasons that dissented in the result but not on this point, s. 13 "does not depend on any objection made by the witness giving the evidence. It is applicable and effective without invocation, and even where the witness in question is unaware of his rights" (p. 377). Further, s. 13 "is not limited to a question in respect of which a witness would have been entitled to refuse to answer at common law and its prohibition against the use of incriminating evidence is not limited to criminal proceedings. It confers a right against incrimination by the use of evidence given in one proceeding in any other proceedings" (p. 377).

However, *Henry* was partially reversed in the Supreme Court's complex divided ruling in *Nedelcu*. In essence, the full Court first confirms the basic ruling in *Henry* that use immunity under s. 13 of the *Charter* only applies where an accused gave incriminating evidence under compulsion at a prior proceeding. However, Justice Moldaver for a 6-3 majority held the trial judge had not erred in permitting the Crown to cross-examine the accused on civil discovery statements because the statements were not incriminating, as "incriminating evidence" only refers to evidence the Crown could (if permitted) use in subsequent proceedings to prove or assist in proving one or more essential elements of the offence charged.

This effectively reversed the clear bright line approach under *Henry* that previously compelled testimony is always inadmissible even if

tendered for credibility, a pragmatic decision widely applauded by judges and commentators.[134]

R. v. NEDELCU

[2012] 3 S.C.R. 311, 290 C.C.C. (3d) 153, 96 C.R. (6th) 391

The accused took a fellow employee P for a motorcycle ride on the company property. There was a crash. P was not wearing a helmet and suffered permanent brain damage. The accused suffered minor brain damage and was hospitalized overnight. The accused was charged with dangerous driving causing bodily harm. At trial the Crown sought to cross-examine the accused on his examination for discovery in a civil suit by P and his family. In his discovery answers on oath the accused indicated he had no memory of the accident until he woke up the next day in hospital. At the criminal trial 14 months later he gave a detailed account of how the accident occurred. The trial judge allowed the Crown to cross-examine on the statement as to credibility on the basis that s. 13 of the *Charter* did not apply to compelled discovery evidence in a civil case. The accused was not afforded the protection of s. 13 of the *Charter* because his situation did not meet the *quid pro quo* rationale of compulsion. The accused had given his discovery evidence to further his own private interest in a civil action against him. The accused was convicted and appealed.

The Ontario Court of Appeal, applying *Henry*, allowed the appeal, quashed the conviction and ordered a new trial. The Court held that under s. 13 of the *Charter* the accused's compelled testimony on civil discovery is inadmissible at the subsequent criminal trial for purposes of incrimination or for testing credibility. The protection was not only available where the prior testimony assists the Crown. The accused had been compelled to testify on the examination for discovery solely for the benefit of the plaintiffs. *Quid pro quo* had a wider meaning than that given by the trial judge. Any other proceeding in s. 13 includes royal commissions, statutory boards and tribunals, bankruptcy proceedings and other forms of judicial and quasi-judicial proceedings. The trial judge's distinction between criminal and non-criminal interrogatories was not relevant.

On further appeal a 6-3 majority allowed the Crown appeal and substituted a conviction.

MOLDAVER J. (MCLACHLIN C.J. and DESCHAMPS, ABELLA, ROTHSTEIN, and KARAKATSANIS JJ. concurring):

1   I have had the privilege of reading Justice LeBel's reasons for judgment and I agree with him on the issue of compulsion. In particular, I accept his conclusion, at para. 109, that Mr. Nedelcu "was statutorily compellable, and therefore 'compelled' ... for the purposes of s. 13 [of the Canadian

---

[134]   See comments of Stuart, *Charter Justice in Canadian Criminal Law*, 7th ed. (2018) at 598-603; Paul Calarco, "*R. v. Nedelcu:* Whatever Happened to a Large and Liberal Interpretation of the *Charter?*" (2013), 96 C.R. (6th) 438; and Lisa Dufraimont, "Section 13 Use Immunity After *R. v. Nedelcu*" (2013), 96 C.R. (6th) 431.

Charter of Rights and Freedoms]" to testify at his examination for discovery in the civil action.

2   Where I part company with my colleague is on the interpretation of s. 13 and in particular, its application to the facts of this case. In my respectful view, s. 13 was never meant to apply to a case such as this—and I am convinced it does not. This Court's decision in *R. v. Henry*, 2005 SCC 76, [2005] 3 S.C.R. 609, does not provide otherwise.

4   The difficulty I have with the present case is that there was no "quid" for there to be a "quo"—and hence, in my view, s. 13 was never engaged. I would accordingly allow the appeal.

6   As I read [section 13] , the "quid" that forms the critical first branch of the historical rationale, refers to "incriminating evidence" the witness has given at a prior proceeding in which the witness could not refuse to answer. The section does not refer to all manner of evidence the witness has given at the prior proceeding. It refers to "incriminating evidence" the witness has given under compulsion.

7   The "quo" refers to the state's side of the bargain. In return for having compelled the witness to testify, to the extent the witness has provided "incriminating evidence", the state undertakes that it will not use that evidence to incriminate the witness in any other proceeding, except in a prosecution for perjury or for the giving of contradictory evidence.

8   Thus, a party seeking to invoke s. 13 must first establish that he or she gave "incriminating evidence" under compulsion at the prior proceeding. If the party fails to meet these twin requirements, s. 13 is not engaged and that ends the matter.

9   What then is "incriminating evidence"? The answer, I believe, should be straightforward. In my view, it can only mean evidence given by the witness at the prior proceeding that the Crown could use at the subsequent proceeding, if it were permitted to do so, to prove guilt, i.e. to prove or assist in proving one or more of the essential elements of the offence for which the witness is being tried.

. . .

16   The law is clear and I accept it to be so, that the time for determining whether the evidence given at the prior proceeding may properly be characterized as "incriminating evidence" is the time when the Crown seeks to use it at the subsequent hearing. (See *Dubois v. The Queen*, [1985] 2 S.C.R. 350, at pp. 363-64). That however, does not detract from my contention that the evidence to which s. 13 is directed is not "any evidence" the witness may have been compelled to give at the prior proceeding, but evidence that the Crown could use at the subsequent proceeding, if permitted to do so, to prove the witness's guilt on the charge for which he or she is being tried.

17   In so concluding, I recognize that there will be instances where evidence given at the prior proceeding, though seemingly innocuous or exculpatory at the time, may become "incriminating evidence" at the subsequent proceeding, thereby triggering the application of s. 13.

18   Take for example, the witness who, at the trial of a third party for robbery, admits to having been present at the scene of the crime but denies any involvement in it. If the witness is subsequently charged with the same robbery and testifies that he was not present when the robbery occurred, his evidence from the prior proceeding, though innocuous at the time, will have taken on new meaning. For purposes of s. 13, it would now be treated as "incriminating evidence" because it is evidence that the Crown could use at the witness's robbery trial, if permitted to do so, to prove the essential element of identity. And that is where s. 13 comes in. It precludes the Crown from introducing it for any purpose, whether as part of its case to prove identity or as a means of impeaching the witness's testimony.

19   Manifestly, I take a different view where the evidence given by the witness at the prior proceeding could not be used by the Crown at the subsequent proceeding to prove the witness's guilt on the charge for which he or she is being tried. In such circumstances, because the prior evidence is not "incriminating evidence", there can be no "quid" for purposes of s. 13—and because there is no "quid", no "quo" is owed in return. The case at hand provides a classic example of this.

LEBEL J. (FISH and CROMWELL JJ. concurring) (dissenting):

44   The right against self-incrimination is a principle that lies at the heart of our justice system and is enshrined in the *Canadian Charter of Rights and Freedoms*. A specific form of protection against self-incrimination is the right against testimonial self-incrimination provided for in s. 13 of the *Charter*. Section 13 protects a witness who gives evidence in any proceeding from having that evidence used against him or her in a subsequent proceeding. This *Charter* guarantee has engendered many decisions of this Court, the latest significant pronouncement being *R. v. Henry*, 2005 SCC 76, [2005] 3 S.C.R. 609.

45   The Crown asks this Court to reconsider the s. 13 principles it unanimously espoused in *Henry*. For the reasons that follow, I would decline to do so. I would therefore dismiss the appeal.

D. Compelled Testimony

101   One of the Crown's main submissions is that the respondent was not "compelled" to testify at his examination for discovery in the civil action against him in the sense described in *Henry*. The Crown argues that the respondent was not subjectively compelled, because he freely decided to attend the discovery proceeding [FAP 36], and that he was not objectively compelled, because he chose to file a statement of defence

and to therefore put himself "within the grasp of procedural rules ... that would, only then, compel his evidence" (A.F., at para. 37).

102   Although Binnie J. did not fully canvass what constitutes "compelled" evidence in the *Henry* sense, he did note that an accused who chooses to testify freely at his or her first trial and then at a retrial is not "compelled" and so does not qualify for s. 13 protection (para. 43). He also stated parenthetically that "[f]or present purposes, evidence of compellable witnesses should be treated as compelled even if their attendance was not enforced by a subpoena" (para. 34; emphasis added).

103   Binnie J.'s observation that evidence from an accused who decides to testify is "voluntary" simply means that, because accused persons have a right not to be called to testify in their own defence under s. 11(c) of the *Charter*, any accused who chooses to testify waives his or her right not to be compellable. In contrast, a witness who voluntarily gives evidence at someone else's trial is not giving evidence "voluntarily" within the meaning of *Henry* even if the witness decides to testify on his or her own volition, for example, to assist the accused. The difference is this: An accused who testifies voluntarily is waiving a constitutional right by choosing to testify. Any other witness can otherwise be compelled, meaning the witness is statutorily compellable regardless of whether he or she "volunteers" to take the stand. This view is confirmed by Binnie J.'s observation that "evidence of compellable witnesses should be treated as compelled even if their attendance was not enforced by a subpoena".

104   Therefore, whether the respondent freely decided to attend the discovery proceeding is irrelevant. Whether a witness was compelled should not be determined on a subjective standard. It would be unprincipled to give a lesser degree of *Charter* protection to a witness who testifies willingly than to a witness who must be subpoenaed or otherwise forced to give evidence, if both could have been statutorily compelled to testify in any event. Therefore, to determine whether the quid pro quo is engaged in a particular case, the court should consider whether the witness was statutorily compellable and not whether the witness felt subjectively compelled to testify. The relevant question is this: Was the respondent statutorily compelled to give evidence in the proceeding?

105   The Crown's second argument on compulsion is that the respondent was not objectively compelled because he chose to file a statement of defence, and therefore that he voluntarily put himself within the grasp of the powers of civil discovery.

106   This argument must also fail. First, as noted by the intervener Advocates' Society, the integrity of the civil discovery process could be undermined if courts considered that those who defend civil actions are not "compelled" for the purposes of s. 13. Parties facing criminal proceedings might then find it advantageous not to co-operate in any civil action,

thereby forcing the other party to obtain a court order compelling their testimony on discovery.

E. Should the Court Revisit *Henry*?

110   *Henry* makes it quite clear that the distinction between using prior compelled testimony to impeach credibility and using it to incriminate the accused is unworkable. Even using so-called "innocent statements" to expose inconsistencies in the testimony of an accused will, as Martin J.A. said in *Kuldip*, "assist the Crown in its case and, in a broad sense, may help to prove guilt" (p. 23). Counsel for the respondent summarized this concern in oral argument before this Court: "... the distinction doesn't really exist between incriminating and impeaching. If you are impeaching, you are advancing the Crown's case. There may be an inference of consciousness of guilt" (transcript, at p. 52).

111   I agree that, in the context of s. 13, there can be no such distinction in practice. Any evidence that may assist the Crown in proving its case, including evidence impeaching the credibility of the accused, will have an incriminating effect and must therefore be subject to s. 13 protection.

112   It seems evident, therefore, that this distinction is not compatible with the underlying purpose of s. 13. One need only go back to the cases in which the distinction was maintained to see just how inconsistently—and at times arbitrarily—it was applied in practice. There were undoubtedly accused persons whose s. 13 *Charter* rights were unduly diminished under this approach. It is for this reason that the Court abolished this problematic distinction in *Henry*.

113   The concerns expressed in Henry with respect to the difference between using prior compelled testimony to impeach credibility and using it to incriminate still exist. Should this Court nevertheless revisit *Henry* on this point?

. . .

115   In my view, there are no substantial reasons to believe *Henry* was wrongly decided. Nor are there any compelling or principled reasons to reintroduce the distinction between impeachment and incrimination, thereby reducing the scope of s. 13 of the Charter. *Henry* is a fairly recent, unanimous decision of this Court, which has largely been welcomed by the profession for providing predictability and simplifying the law in this area . . .

116   Nothing has changed since *Henry*, and it should not be revisited.

128   . . ., my colleague's approach dilutes *Henry*. As I stated earlier in these reasons, *Henry* has been lauded as a decision that brought predictability and clarity to a previously murky area of law. This interpretation of *Henry* will again send the application of s. 13 into a state of confusion. It will cause uncertainty regarding the s. 13 rights of an accused.

129   I am not aware of any decision since *Henry* in which a court has inquired into whether the statements of an accused were "innocent" or "incriminating" in order to determine whether s. 13 applied. Courts will now have to conduct voir dires to make this determination, which will both encumber the trial process and render the scope of s. 13 dubious in theory and uncertain in practice. Such uncertainty undermines the objective of the quid pro quo, which is to encourage full and frank testimony. Without knowing in advance how their evidence might be used in future proceedings, witnesses will undoubtedly be less likely to display candour, a consequence that is completely at odds with what this Court sought to accomplish in *Henry*. This will also undoubtedly reduce the scope of the s. 13 protection that previously compelled witnesses have had since *Henry*.

130   In *Henry*, Binnie J. recognized the importance of ensuring predictability in the application of s. 13. He concluded his reasons by stating that the approach he proposed would avert the "unpredictability inherent in sorting out attacks on credibility from attempts at incrimination" (para. 60). In my view, my colleague's opinion reintroduces uncertainty by resurrecting the abandoned distinction, for s. 13 purposes, between "innocuous" and "incriminating" evidence. Witnesses will be less likely to testify truthfully if they do not know, when called to testify, whether and to what extent the evidence they give will be admissible against them in future proceedings.

With whom do you agree?

In *R. v. Schertzer*[135] the Ontario Court of Appeal held that the perjury exception under s. 13 included charges of attempting to obstruct justice laid. Drug squad officers had been properly convicted based on their false testimony given at a preliminary inquiry.

PROBLEMS

Problem 1

At his friend's trial, the accused agrees to testify. He admits that he committed the offence. His friend is acquitted. The accused is now charged with the very same offence based on evidence the police had prior to his testimony. At his trial, he testifies that he did not commit the offence. **Can the Crown confront him with his earlier admission?**

Problem 2

The accused is charged with a bank robbery in Windsor. At his trial, he testifies that he didn't commit the offence. His defence is alibi. He was in Kingston at the time of the robbery committing an armoured car robbery. The accused is acquitted. The Kingston police are unaware of the accused's testimony and are independently investigating the armoured car robbery.

---

[135]   2015 ONCA 259, 325 C.C.C. (3d) 202, 20 C.R. (7th) 187 (Ont. C.A.).

They discover the accused's fingerprints on the back of the vehicle and a videotape showing him in the vicinity of the robbery. The accused is now charged with the Kingston armoured car robbery. He testifies at his trial. **Can the Crown confront him with his earlier testimony? What if he testified at his bail hearing on the armoured car charge? Can the Crown cross-examine him at trial on this testimony?**

KNUTSON v. REGISTERED NURSES' ASSN. (SASKATCHEWAN)
(1990), 90 Sask. R. 120 (Sask. C.A.)

The issue was whether s. 13 of the *Charter of Rights and Freedoms* applied to discipline proceedings under the *Registered Nurses Act* so that evidence given in criminal proceedings by the respondent nurse could not be subsequently used against her in discipline proceedings. When the respondent gave evidence at the criminal trial she did not invoke the provisions of s. 5 of the *Canada Evidence Act* or the provincial counterpart to protect her against use of any of her evidence in subsequent proceedings.

SHERSTOBITOFF J.A. (VANCISE and WAKELING JJ.A. concurring):—

. . .

The right protected by s. 13 is the right against use of incriminating evidence given a person in one proceeding to incriminate that person in subsequent proceedings.

. . .

Accordingly, one can only incriminate oneself as defined by s. 13 in respect of matters which may be described as criminal, quasi-criminal, or proceedings with penal consequences.

. . .

The disciplinary proceedings under review in this case are neither criminal nor quasicriminal.

. . .

In this case, there is no liability to imprisonment or fine, and thus no possible element of punishment. There is no matter of public order or welfare in a public sphere of activity. The disqualification is an internal and private disciplinary matter imposed as part of a scheme for regulating an activity in order to protect the public. The respondent is entitled to apply for reinstatement at any time and has an appeal to the courts from an adverse decision, so that her expulsion is not permanent if she can show fitness to practice her profession. . . [T]he result must be the same as in the related police discipline cases: a finding that there were no penal consequences, and thus s. 13 did not apply. The impugned evidence was therefore admissible.[136]

---

[136]   See too *R. v. Jones*, 89 C.C.C. (3d) 353, 30 C.R. (4th) 1, [1994] 2 S.C.R. 229 (s. 13 not available at sentencing proceedings); *Martineau c. Ministre du Revenu national* (2004), 192 C.C.C. (3d) 129, 24 C.R. (6th) 207 (S.C.C.) (no s. 11(c) protection at *Customs Act* proceedings); and *R. v. D. (R.)* (2004), 182 C.C.C. (3d) 545 (Ont. S.C.J.) (s. 13 not available in perjury proceedings).

(iv) *Pre-trial Right to Silence: Charter section 7*

See earlier analysis of the lead decision in *R. v. Hebert*[137] in Chapter 4 under Confessions.

(v) *Principle Against Self-incrimination: Charter section 7*

In a series of complex and split Supreme Court decisions, a majority position has emerged through the judgments of Chief Justice Lamer that within principles of fundamental justice guaranteed by s. 7 there is a "principle against self-incrimination" wider than the pre-trial right to silence recognized in *R. v. Hebert*,[138] the protections against compellability in s. 11(c) and the privilege against self-incrimination in s. 13. The Chief Justice put it best for the majority of the Court in *R. v. P. (M.B.)*.[139]

> Perhaps the single most important organizing principle in criminal law is the right of an accused not to be forced into assisting in his or her own prosecution. . . This means, in effect, that an accused is under no obligation to respond until the state has succeeded in making out a *prima facie* case against him or her. In other words, until the Crown establishes that there is a "case to meet", an accused is not compellable in a general sense (as opposed to the narrow, testimonial sense) and need not answer the allegations against him or her.[140]

The Chief Justice saw the presumption of innocence and the power imbalance between the state and the individual as being at the root of the principle. In a later judgment, he describes the principle against self-incrimination in even broader terms:

> Any state action that coerces an individual to furnish evidence against him or herself in a proceeding in which the individual and the state are adversaries violates the principle against self-incrimination. Coercion means the denial of free and informed consent.[141]

This principle against self-incrimination or a "case to meet" is not merely an organizing principle of existing rules and principles but one that has the capacity to introduce new rules.[142] It is now seen to be the explanation of the recognition of a pre-trial right to silence in *Hebert*.

It also led the Court in *B.C. Securities Commission v. Branch*[143] to create a doctrine of derivative use immunity and also a discretion to prevent the

---

[137] [1990] 2 S.C.R. 151, 57 C.C.C. (3d) 1, 77 C.R. (3d) 145 (S.C.C.).
[138] *Ibid.*
[139] (1994), 29 C.R. (4th) 209 (S.C.C.). In *S. (R.J.)* (1995), 36 C.R. (4th) 1 (S.C.C.) Iacobucci J., speaking for four justices not including Lamer C.J., expressly adopted the principle of self-incrimination outlined by the Chief Justice in *P. (M.B.)*.
[140] *P. (M.B.), supra* note 139 at 226.
[141] *Jones, supra* note 136 at 41 [*C.R.*]. This statement was adopted by La Forest J. for a unanimous Court in *R. v. Fitzpatrick* (1995), 43 C.R (4th) 343 (S.C.C.), although distinguished on the facts.
[142] Iacobucci J. in *S. (R.J.), supra* note 139 at 49.
[143] (1995), 38 C.R. (4th) 133 (S.C.C.), where Sopinka J. and Iacobucci J. reached a consensus majority position not evident in the earlier 229-page inconclusively split decision in *S. (R.J.)* (1995), 36 C.R. (4th) 1 (S.C.C.). See further *R. v. Jobin* (1995), 38 C.R. (4th) 176 (S.C.C.) and *R. v. Primeau* (1995), 38 C.R. (4th) 189 (S.C.C.).

compellability of a witness who is (or may be) charged with an offence. Two officers of a company were served with summonses from the Securities Commission under the provincial *Securities Act* compelling their attendance for examination and requiring them to produce all records in their possession. When the officers failed to appear, the Commission sought an order from the court committing the officers for contempt. The officers applied for a declaration that the Act violated s. 7 of the *Charter*. The Supreme Court decided that the principle against self-incrimination required that persons compelled to testify be provided with subsequent derivative-use immunity in addition to the use immunity guaranteed by s. 13 of the *Charter*. The accused would have the evidentiary burden of showing a plausible connection between the compelled testimony and the evidence later sought to be adduced. Once this was done, in order to have the evidence admitted, the Crown would have to satisfy the court on a balance of probabilities that the authorities would have discovered the impugned derivative evidence absent the compelled testimony. The Court also decided that, in addition, courts can, in certain circumstances, grant exemptions from compulsion to testify. The crucial question was whether the predominant purpose for seeking the evidence was to obtain incriminating evidence against the person compelled to testify or rather for some other legitimate public purpose. That test was seen to strike the appropriate balance between the interests of the State in obtaining the evidence for a valid public purpose on the one hand, and the right to silence of the person compelled to testify on the other.[144]

Branch was distinguished by La Forest J. for the Court in *R. v. Fitzpatrick*,[145] in holding that s. 7 did not prevent the Crown from relying on statutorily required fishing logs on a charge of overfishing. The Court held that the principle against self-incrimination should not be applied as rigidly as it might in the context of a purely criminal offence. Fishing logs were required from all commercial fishers as conditions of their licence to assist in the routine administration of a regulated industry.

In *R. v. G. (S.G.)*,[146] the Supreme Court held 5-2[147] that the discretion to allow the Crown to reopen its case after the defence had begun to answer was extremely narrow and far less likely to be exercised, otherwise the s. 7 right of an accused not to be conscripted would be compromised. The minority pointed to the fact the late evidence had been unforeseen, had not arisen through fault of the Crown and should be left to a determination of whether there was prejudice to the defence case.[148]

In *R. v. White*,[149] Iacobucci J. held for a 6-1 majority[150] of the Supreme Court that the s. 7 principle against self-incrimination barred the admission of

---

[144]   This is further addressed by Cory J. (Iacobucci and Major JJ. concurring) in concurring reasons in *Phillips v. Nova Scotia (Commissioner, Public Inquiries Act)* (1995), 39 C.R. (4th) 141 (S.C.C.).

[145]   *Fitzpatrick, supra* note 141.

[146]   (1997), 8 C.R. (5th) 198 (S.C.C.).

[147]   Per Cory J. (Lamer C.J., Sopinka, Iacobucci and Major JJ. concurring). McLachlin J. (L'Heureux-Dubé J. concurring) dissented on this point.

[148]   See comment by Delisle, "Annotation" (1997), 8 C.R. (5th) 204 in favour of the majority position.

motor vehicle accident reports made under the compulsion of a provincial *Motor Vehicle Act* at a trial for failing to stop at the scene of an accident under s. 252(1)(a) of the *Criminal Code*. To obtain this use immunity, the person who made the statement would have to prove compulsion on a balance of probabilities. The test was whether the declarant held an honest and reasonable belief that he or she was required by law to report the accident to the person to whom the report was given.[151]

Iacobucci J. restated the residual principle against self-incrimination in the following broad terms:

> It is now well-established that there exists, in Canadian law, a principle against self- incrimination that is a principle of fundamental justice under s. 7 of the Charter. [The] principle has at least two key purposes, namely to protect against unreliable confessions, and to protect against abuses of power by the state. There is both an individual and a societal interest in achieving both of these protections. Both protections are linked to the value placed by Canadian society upon individual privacy, personal autonomy and dignity. . . A state which arbitrarily intrudes upon its citizens' personal sphere will inevitably cause more injustice than it cures.
>
> The jurisprudence of this Court is clear that [it] . . . is an overarching principle within our criminal justice system, from which a number of specific common law and Charter rules emanate, such as the confessions rule, and the right to silence, among many others.[152]

However he also added an important general caveat.[153] The fact that the principle against self-incrimination had the status of an overarching principle did not imply that it provided absolute protection for an accused against all uses of information compelled by statute or otherwise. The residual protections were specific, contextually sensitive and required a balancing process. In some contexts, the factors that favoured the importance of the search for truth would outweigh the factors that favour protecting the individual against undue compulsion by the State.

The principle against self-incrimination has not caught fire in lower courts, but there are some signs of life. The Ontario Court had no difficulty in holding that the principle did not bar the admission of a guilty plea at a subsequent criminal proceeding.[154]

So too the B.C. Court of Appeal determined that the principle against self-incrimination did not bar the admissibility of information provided to Revenue Canada in a fraud prosecution.[155] The principle has not availed in the context of compelled testimony under the *Mutual Legal Assistance in*

---

[149]   (1999), 24 C.R. (5th) 201 (S.C.C.). See criticism by Steven Penney, "The Continuing Evolution of the s. 7 Self-Incrimination Principle: *R. v. White*" (1999), 24 C.R. (5th) 247 and the reply by Michael Plaxton, "An Analysis and Defence of Free Choice Theory: A Response to Professor Penney" (1999), 27 C.R. (5th) 218.

[150]   L'Heureux-Dubé J. dissented.

[151]   *White, supra* note 149 at 230-232, applied in *R. v. Gibb* (1999), 30 C.R. (5th) 189 (Sask. Q.B.) (admitting statement made to parole officer after arrest).

[152]   *White, ibid.* at 219-220.

[153]   *Ibid.* at 220-221.

[154]   *R. v. Ford* (2000), 33 C.R. (5th) 178 (Ont. C.A.). See too *R. v. Thompson* (2001),151 C.C.C. (3d) 339 (Ont. C.A.) (upholding offence of failing to provide roadside test).

Criminal Matters Act given the evidentiary immunity provided.[156] On the other hand, the Quebec Court of Appeal excluded the evidence of an accused and his wife compelled at a fire commissioner's inquiry from the subsequent arson trial.[157]

In *R. v. B. (S.A.),*[158] the Supreme Court dismissed a number of *Charter* challenges to the DNA warrant powers. In the course of this ruling Justice Arbour, speaking for the full Court, asserted that the principle against self-incrimination developed under s. 7 of the *Charter* is of "limited application". Previously we saw that in *P. (M.B).* the Court had described the principle as the "single most important organizing principle in criminal law" and one capable of growth. Growth is clearly now stunted. This may well come as a relief to lower court judges who have often been resistant to wide applications. Arbour J. sees the application of the principle as depending on context (that unruly horse), and hinging on consideration of factors of reliability and State abuse of no concern in the DNA legislation.[159]

The Supreme Court later rejected a principle against self-incrimination challenge to investigative hearings under anti-terrorism provisions: see *Application under s. 83.28 of the Criminal Code.*[160] As a result of a vote in Parliament (159-124), the investigative hearing provision of the *Criminal Code* expired as of March 1, 2007.[161]

(vi) *No Adverse Inference from Pre-trial Silence*

Can guilt be inferred from pre-trial silence? Should it be? Can pre-trial silence impair credibility about a defence first raised at trial?

R. v. TURCOTTE
31 C.R. (6th) 197, 200 C.C.C. (3d) 289, [2005] 2 S.C.R. 519

The accused went to a police station and asked that a car be sent to the ranch where he lived and worked. According to the police evidence, he also told them to put him in "jail" although Turcotte denied making this statement but did admit that he could have said to "lock him up" to shift their focus from him to the investigation of the farm. Turcotte also told the police in response to a question that there was no danger to the officers or anyone else at the farm. Despite repeated questions from the police, he refused to explain why a car was necessary or what would be found there. He indicated there was a rifle in his truck. Officers found three victims at the ranch. All three died from

---

[155] *R. v. Wilder* (2000), 142 C.C.C. (3d) 418 (B.C. C.A.). See also *R. v. Graham* (1997), 121 C.C.C. (3d) 76 (B.C. S.C.).

[156] *États-Unis c. Ross* (1995), 41 C.R. (4th) 358, (*sub nom.* United States of America v. Ross) 100 C.C.C. (3d) 320 (Que. C.A.); *U.K. v. Hrynyk* (1996), 107 C.C.C. (3d) 104 (Ont. Gen. Div.).

[157] *R. v. Kabbabe* (1997), 6 C.R. (5th) 82 (Que. C.A.).

[158] (2003), 14 C.R. (6th) 205 (S.C.C.).

[159] See further David Stratas, "*R. v. B. (S.A.)* and the Right Against Self-Incrimination: A Confusing Change of Direction?" (2003), 14 C.R. (6th) 227.

[160] (2004), 21 C.R. (6th) 82 (S.C.C.).

[161] O'Neill & Mayeda, "Anti-Terrorism Measures Defeated", *Montreal Gazette* (28 February 2007) A12.

axe wounds to the head. The accused was charged with three counts of second degree murder. At trial, the evidence against the accused was entirely circumstantial, including his conduct at the police station, fingerprints on two items at the farm and small bloodstains from two of the victims found on his clothing. The accused admitted finding the victims, but denied killing them. With respect to the accused's refusal to respond to police questioning as to why they should go to the farm, the trial judge told the jury that they could not draw inferences of guilt or innocence from the accused's silence but that this silence could be considered as relevant to his state of mind. He later instructed the jury that it could be considered "post-offence conduct", and that it was the only substantial evidence proving guilt. The jury returned a verdict of guilty on each count.

The B.C. Court of Appeal set aside the convictions and ordered a new trial. It held that no adverse inference should have been drawn from the accused's silence. The Crown appealed.

ABELLA J. (MCLACHLIN C.J.C, MAJOR, BASTARACHE, BINNIE, LEBEL, DESCHAMPS, FISH and CHARRON JJ. concurring): —

. . .

The essence of the Crown's argument is that Mr. Turcotte's refusal to respond to some of the questions from the police can be relied on as post-offence conduct from which an inference of guilt can be drawn.

"Post-offence conduct" is a legal term of art. It is not meant to be a neutral term embracing all behaviour by an accused after a crime has been committed, but only that conduct which is probative of guilt. It is, by its nature, circumstantial evidence.

The more traditional designation of such conduct, "consciousness of guilt" evidence, was changed by this Court to "post-offence conduct" evidence in *R. v. White*, [1998] 2 S.C.R. 72, 125 C.C.C. (3d) 385, 161 D.L.R. (4th) 590. Major J. held, at para. 20, that use of the phrase "consciousness of guilt" should be discouraged because it might undermine the presumption of innocence or may mislead the jury. In *White*, at para. 19, Major J. provided a non-exhaustive list of conduct that is typically admitted as post-offence conduct evidence: flight from the scene of the crime or the jurisdiction in which the crime was committed; attempts to resist arrest; failure to appear at trial; and acts of concealment such as lying, assuming a false name, changing one's appearance, and hiding or disposing of evidence. In *White*, the post-offence conduct was the accused's running from the police to avoid arrest, the attempted disposal of one of the murder weapons, and fleeing the jurisdiction following the killing.

Although the terminology has been changed, the evidentiary concept has not. As with evidence of "consciousness of guilt", only evidence after a crime has been committed that is probative of guilt can be relied on as "post-offence conduct".

The first issue, therefore, is to determine whether the trial judge erred in designating Mr. Turcotte's refusal to answer some of the police questions as "post-offence conduct" capable of supporting an inference of guilt. This in turn requires a determination of whether Mr. Turcotte had the right to refuse to answer the police's questions. The Crown's dual argument is that no right to silence was engaged in this case, but that even if it was, Mr. Turcotte's conduct in going to the police station and answering some of the police's questions, showed that it was a right he chose to waive.

Under the traditional common law rules, absent statutory compulsion, everyone has the right to be silent in the face of police questioning. This right to refuse to provide information or answer inquiries finds cogent and defining expression in *Rothman v. The Queen*, [1981] 1 S.C.R. 640, 59 C.C.C. (2d) 30, 121 D.L.R. (3d) 578, per Lamer J.:

> In Canada the right of a suspect not to say anything to the police... is merely the exercise by him of the general right enjoyed in this country by anyone to do whatever one pleases, saying what one pleases or choosing not to say certain things, unless obliged to do otherwise by law. It is because no law says that a suspect, save in certain circumstances, must say anything to the police that we say that he has the right to remain silent, which is a positive way of explaining that there is on his part no legal obligation to do otherwise. [Footnotes omitted; p. 683]

Although its temporal limits have not yet been fully defined, the right to silence has also received *Charter* benediction. In *R. v. Hebert*, [1990] 2 S.C.R. 151, 57 C.C.C. (3d) 1, the first decision from this Court recognizing it as a s. 7 right, an accused, who had been arrested and advised of his rights, refused to provide a statement to the police after consulting counsel. He was then placed in a cell with an undercover officer posing as a suspect under arrest. During the course of their conversation, the accused incriminated himself. The question before the Court was whether the statement to the undercover officer was admissible. Writing for the majority, McLachlin J. held that it was not admissible because it violated the accused's right to silence found in s. 7 of the *Canadian Charter of Rights and Freedoms*.

In addition to emphasizing the importance of providing protection from the power of the state, McLachlin J. founded the s. 7 right to silence in two common law doctrines: the confessions rule and the privilege against self-incrimination, explaining that both emerge from the following unifying theme:

> [T]he idea that a person in the power of the state in the course of the criminal process has the right to choose whether to speak to the police or remain silent. [p. 164]

It would be an illusory right if the decision not to speak to the police could be used by the Crown as evidence of guilt. As Cory J. explained in *Chambers*, where the trial judge failed to instruct the jury that the accused's silence could not be used as evidence of guilt:

> It has as well been recognized that since there is a right to silence, it would be a snare and a delusion to caution the accused that he need not say anything in response to a police officer's question but nonetheless put in evidence that the accused clearly exercised his right and remained silent in the face of a question which suggested his guilt. [p. 1316]

Although *Chambers* dealt specifically with silence after the accused had been cautioned, it would equally be "a snare and a delusion" to allow evidence of any valid exercise of the right to be used as evidence of guilt.

Moreover, as Doherty and Rosenberg JJ.A. explained in *R. v. B. (S.C.)* (1997), 36 O.R. (3d) 516, 119 C.C.C. (3d) 530 (C.A.), since, in most circumstances, individuals are under no obligation to assist the police, their silence cannot, on its own, be probative of guilt:

> a refusal to assist is nothing more than the exercise of a recognized liberty and, standing alone, says nothing about that person's culpability. [p. 529]

Evidence of silence is, however, admissible in limited circumstances. As Cory J. held in *Chambers*, at p. 1318, if "the Crown can establish a real relevance and a proper basis", evidence of silence can be admitted with an appropriate warning to the jury.

There are circumstances where the right to silence must bend. In *R. v. Crawford*, [1995] 1 S.C.R. 858, 96 C.C.C. (3d) 481, for example, the Court was confronted with a conflict between the right to silence and the right to full answer and defence. Two men were charged with second degree murder after a man was beaten to death. At their joint trial, each blamed the other. Crawford, one of the accused, had not given the police a statement, but he chose to testify at trial in his own defence. His co-accused's counsel cross-examined him on his failure to make a statement to the police. This failure was negatively contrasted with the fact that his co-accused had given a full statement to the police at the earliest opportunity. Sopinka J., writing for the majority, held that a balance between the two competing rights can be achieved if the evidence of silence is admitted, but used only to assess credibility and not to infer guilt. Since the jury had been invited to infer guilt from Crawford's silence, the Court ordered a new trial.

Evidence of silence may also be admissible when the defence raises an issue that renders the accused's silence relevant. Examples include circumstances where the defence seeks to emphasize the accused's cooperation with the authorities (*R. v. Lavallee*, [1980] O.J. No. 540 (QL) (C.A.)); where the accused testified that he had denied the charges against him at the time he was arrested (*R. v. Ouellette* (1997), 200 A.R. 363, 119 C.C.C. (3d) 30 sub nom. *R. v. O. (G.A.)* (C.A.)); or where silence is relevant to the defence theory of mistaken identity and a flawed police investigation (*R. v. M.C.W.* (2002), 169 B.C.A.C. 128, 2002 BCCA 341, 165 C.C.C. (3d) 129).

Similarly, cases where the accused failed to disclose his or her alibi in a timely or adequate manner provide a well established exception to the prohibition on using pre-trial silence against an accused: *R. v. Cleghorn*, [1995] 3 S.C.R. 175, 100 C.C.C. (3d) 393.[162] Silence might also be admissible if it is inextricably bound up with the narrative or other evidence and cannot easily be extricated.

---

[162]   For a careful analysis of the traditional alibi exception see Doherty J.A. in *R. v. Wright* (2009), 247 C.C.C. (3d) 1 (Ont. C.A.).

The Crown argued that any right to silence is engaged only when the accused comes within "the power of the state" and that the right has no relevance when the state has done nothing to use that power against the individual. This, with respect, makes the right's borders too confining. In general, absent a statutory requirement to the contrary, individuals have the right to choose whether to speak to the police, even if they are not detained or arrested. The common law right to silence exists at all times against the state, whether or not the person asserting it is within its power or control. Like the confessions rule, an accused's right to silence applies any time he or she interacts with a person in authority, whether detained or not. It is a right premised on an individual's freedom to choose the extent of his or her cooperation with the police, and is animated by a recognition of the potentially coercive impact of the state's authority and a concern that individuals not be required to incriminate themselves. These policy considerations exist both before and after arrest or detention. There is, as a result, no principled basis for failing to extend the common law right to silence to both periods.

Nor do I share the Crown's view that by attending at the detachment and answering some of the police's questions, Mr. Turcotte waived any right he might otherwise have had. A willingness to impart some information to the police does not completely submerge an individual's right not to respond to police questioning. He or she need not be mute to reflect an intention to invoke it. An individual can provide some, none, or all of the information he or she has. A voluntary interaction with the police, even one initiated by an individual, does not constitute a waiver of the right to silence. The right to choose whether to speak is retained throughout the interaction.

At various points throughout the trial, the Crown, and the trial judge at the Crown's request, characterized Mr. Turcotte's silence in two ways: as post-offence conduct evidence (called "consciousness of guilt" evidence by the Crown), and as state of mind evidence rebutting his claim to be in shock and panic. Most troubling was the trial judge's final instructions on post-offence conduct. During this portion of his instructions, the trial judge told the jury that Mr. Turcotte's silence was post-offence conduct and zeroed in on his silence as the only relevant post-offence conduct. His invocation was: "[y]ou may decide that the only substantial evidence proving the guilt of Mr. Turcotte arises from his post-offence conduct".

Even before his detention at 10:06 a.m., Mr. Turcotte had no duty to speak to or cooperate with the police. He exercised this right by refusing to answer some of the questions put to him by the police, declining to explain why a car should be sent to the Erhorn Ranch and refusing to say what the police would find there. Although he answered some of the police's questions, when he did not answer others he was nonetheless exercising his right to silence.

This is significant in deciding whether evidence of his silence was admissible as post-offence conduct, that is, evidence that is probative of guilt. Conduct after a crime has been committed is only admissible as "post-offence conduct" when it provides circumstantial evidence of guilt. The necessary relevance is lost if there is no connection between the conduct and guilt. The law imposes no duty to speak to or cooperate with the police. This fact alone severs any link between silence and guilt. Silence in the face of police questioning will, therefore, rarely be admissible as post-offence conduct because it is rarely probative of guilt. Refusing to do what one has a right to refuse to do reveals nothing. An inference of guilt cannot logically or morally emerge from the exercise of a protected right. Using silence as evidence of guilt artificially creates a duty, despite a right to the contrary, to answer all police questions.

Since there was no duty on Mr. Turcotte's part to speak to the police, his failure to do so was irrelevant; because it was irrelevant, no rational conclusion about guilt or innocence can be drawn from it; and because it was not probative of guilt, it could not be characterized for the jury as "post-offence conduct".

Nor do I see how Mr. Turcotte's silence could be used as "state of mind" evidence from which guilt could be inferred. The Crown argued that Mr. Turcotte's silence negated his claim that his state of mind was one of shock and panic. It is clear from the Crown's closing argument that there was little difference between asking the jury to consider Mr. Turcotte's silence as evidence of his state of mind, and asking them to consider it as evidence of his guilty conscience. So, for example, during his closing argument the Crown argued:

> That may tell you something about the guilty mind of Mr. Turcotte at the time. But again, it doesn't show that he was in a state of shock or panic, but rather that he was thinking about what he said and chose to say what he wanted to say and didn't want to say.

In order to make this claim, it was necessary for the Crown to suggest that his silence was motivated by a different state of mind, namely his guilty conscience. Characterizing the silence as state of mind evidence was simply another way of arguing that the silence was post-offence conduct probative of Mr. Turcotte's guilt.

While not admissible as post-offence conduct or state of mind evidence, Mr. Turcotte's behaviour at the R.C.M.P. detachment, including his refusal to answer some of the police's questions, was, arguably, admissible as an inextricable part of the narrative. As previously indicated, no issue was raised about its admissibility either at trial or on appeal. But, having admitted his silence into evidence, the trial judge was obliged to tell the jury in the clearest of terms that it could not be used to support an inference of guilt in order to contradict an intuitive impulse to conclude that silence is incompatible with innocence. Where evidence of silence is admitted, juries must be instructed about the proper purpose for which the evidence was admitted, the impermissible inferences which must not be drawn from evidence of silence, the limited probative value of silence, and the dangers of relying on such evidence. The failure to give the jury this limiting instruction, particularly given the circumstantial nature of the Crown's case, was highly prejudicial.

Given the significance of the error, I agree with the Court of Appeal that the curative proviso is inapplicable and a new trial is required. I would dismiss the appeal.

At his new trial, Turcotte was convicted in a judge-alone trial. What seemed to satisfy the trial judge of Turcotte's guilt was his statement that no one would be in danger at the farm.[163]

After *Turcotte* it will be especially important to distinguish between the common law right to silence, on which the judgment turns, and the s. 7 *Charter* pre-trial right to silence recognized in *Hebert*. The Court decided that the common law right to silence applies whether or not the accused was cautioned as to the right to silence, prior to arrest or detention, and also that the doctrine of waiver applies. As to waiver, as you cannot waive something of which you are unaware, it would appear that the Court is asserting a common law right to be advised of the right to silence, although it never says this expressly. In contrast, limits imposed on the *Charter* right to silence recognized in *Hebert* include that the right is only triggered on detention and that the doctrine of waiver does not apply.

The gains in *Turcotte* are not all in favour of accused. The Court indicates that evidence of silence is admissible in limited circumstances with an appropriate warning where the Crown can establish a real relevance and a proper basis. Justice Abella offers six examples. The sixth is "inextricably bound up with the narrative or other evidence and cannot easily be extricated". No authority is provided for this new exception. Resort to language of "admissible as part of the narrative" is notorious as a device to avoid evidential rules and principles. In this case, Abella J. remarks that the evidence of how the accused refused to answer the police may "arguably be admissible as part of the narrative". This may suggest that the Court was not unanimous on this point. Justice Abella did say that

> juries must be instructed about the proper purpose for which the evidence was admitted, the impermissible inferences which must not be drawn from evidence of silence, the limited probative value of silence, and the dangers of relying on such evidence. [para. 58].

Could a jury ever not use such evidence to draw an adverse inference from silence or lack of cooperation? If this exception is widely applied, the right to silence may be illusory, which is what the Court set out to avoid.

(vii) *No Adverse Inference from Trial Silence*

Should adverse inferences be drawn from an accused's failure to testify? Should there be a distinction between inferences that might flow from silence during the investigative process and inferences from silence at trial? The appropriateness of drawing such inferences, the fairness, must be judged separately. Many protections available to an accused at trial are not present during police questioning. At trial the accused will normally be represented by counsel. The accused will then know the charge against him or her and will have listened to and been able to

---

[163]   See *R. v. Turcotte*, [2006] B.C.J. No. 3631 (B.C. S.C.).

challenge the evidence against him or her. The trial is in public and an impartial judge is present to ensure the accused's rights are safeguarded and the hearing is conducted according to the rules of natural justice. There are certain procedural safeguards in place as to how the accused may be questioned if he or she decides to take the stand. Before the accused is called on to answer the judge will have decided that there is a case to meet; the trial judge will have decided that there is evidence upon which a reasonable jury properly instructed could return a verdict of guilty. Finally, it is almost certain that judges and juries will draw adverse inferences from the accused's silence at trial as they personally witness the accused's silence in the face of accusation; there is no need for evidence to be led as to the accused's silence.

We have seen in *Turcotte* that the Supreme Court has determined that normally no adverse inference should be drawn from the accused remaining silent before trial. The Supreme Court in some early cases suggested that different considerations apply to silence at trial given that the accused is represented, the accused knows the case to meet due to disclosure, and there are rules regarding the admissibility of evidence. It appeared to be clear from various Supreme Court *dicta* that adverse inferences can be drawn against an accused for not testifying in some circumstances. What those circumstances are was far less clear. In *R. v. François*,[164] McLachlin J. wrote for the majority that:

> subject to the caveat that failure to testify cannot be used to shore up a Crown case which otherwise does not establish guilt beyond a reasonable doubt, a jury is permitted to draw an adverse inference from the failure of an accused person to testify.[165]

In *R. v. Lepage*,[166] the Supreme Court divided 3-2 as to whether the trial judge had drawn an adverse inference from the accused's failure to offer an explanation for the presence of his fingerprints but was in agreement that such an inference could be drawn "once the Crown had proved a *prima facie* case".[167] Chief Justice Lamer in *P. (M.B.)*,[168] in describing the "principle against self-incrimination" for the Court, stated the following:

> Once the Crown discharges its obligation to present a *prima facie* case, such that it cannot be non-suited by a motion for a directed verdict of acquittal, the accused can be expected to respond . . . and failure to do so may serve as the basis for drawing adverse inferences. [Once] there is a "case to meet" which, if believed, would result in conviction, the accused can no longer remain a passive participant in the prosecutorial process and becomes — in a broad sense — compellable. That is, the accused must answer the case against him or her, or face the possibility of conviction.[169]

---

[164]   (1994), 31 C.R. (4th) 201 (S.C.C.).
[165]   *Ibid.* at 210. La Forest J., Gonthier J. and Iacobucci J. concurred. Major J. (Sopinka J. and Cory J. concurring) dissented.
[166]   (1995), 36 C.R. (4th) 145 (S.C.C.).
[167]   Sopinka J. for the majority at 159, Major J. for the minority.
[168]   (1994), 29 C.R. (4th) 209 (S.C.C.).
[169]   *Ibid.* at 227-228.

It would appear at this point that the Supreme Court had no objections to adverse inferences based on the accused's failure to testify provided that there is otherwise enough evidence to go to the jury.

However in *Noble* a 5-4 majority abruptly changed course and decided that normally an adverse inference should not be drawn from trial silence.

R. v. NOBLE
[1997] 1 S.C.R. 874, 6 C.R. (5th) 1, 114 C.C.C. (3d) 385

The manager of an apartment building found two young men in the parking area of his building, one of whom appeared to be attempting to break into a car with a screwdriver. When the manager asked the man for identification, he handed over an expired driver's licence. The manager testified that he thought the photograph on the licence accurately depicted the man in front of him in the garage and told the man that he could retrieve the licence from the police. The accused was eventually charged with breaking and entering and having in his possession an instrument suitable for the purpose of breaking into a motor vehicle. At trial, neither the manager nor anyone else could identify the accused, but the trial judge concluded that he as the trier of fact could compare the picture in the driver's licence with the accused in the courtroom and conclude that the driver's licence accurately depicted the accused. He also was satisfied that the building manager would have carefully examined the licence at the time of the incident. The trial judge noted that the accused faced an overwhelming case to meet as a result of the licence, yet remained silent. In the trial judge's view, he could draw "almost an adverse inference" that "certainly may add to the weight of the Crown's case on the issue of identification". The accused was convicted on both counts. The Court of Appeal set aside the conviction and ordered a new trial. A 5-4 majority of the Supreme Court dismissed the Crown's appeal.

SOPINKA J. (L'HEUREUX-DUBÉ, CORY, IACOBUCCI and MAJOR JJ. concurring): —

. . .

The right to silence is based on society's distaste for compelling a person to incriminate him- or herself with his or her own words. Following this reasoning, in my view the use of silence to help establish guilt beyond a reasonable doubt is contrary to the rationale behind the right to silence. Just as a person's words should not be conscripted and used against him or her by the state, it is equally inimical to the dignity of the accused to use his or her silence to assist in grounding a belief in guilt beyond a reasonable doubt. To use silence in this manner is to treat it as communicative evidence of guilt. To illustrate this point, suppose an accused did commit the offence for which he was charged. If he testifies and is truthful, he will be found guilty as the result of what he said. If he does not testify and is found guilty in part because of his silence, he is found guilty because of what he did not say. No matter what the non-perjuring accused decides, communicative evidence emanating from the accused is used against him. The failure to testify tends to place the accused in the same position as if he had testified and admitted his guilt. In my view, this is tantamount to conscription of self-incriminating communicative evidence and is contrary to the underlying purpose of the right to silence. In order to respect the dignity of the accused, the silence of the accused should not be used as a piece of evidence against him or her.

The Presumption of Innocence

The presumption of innocence, enshrined at trial in s. 11(d) of the Charter, provides further support for the conclusion that silence of the accused at trial cannot be placed on the evidentiary scales against the accused. . . . If silence may be used against the accused in establishing guilt, part of the burden of proof has shifted to the accused. In a situation where the accused exercises his or her right to silence at trial, the Crown need only prove the case to some point short of beyond a reasonable doubt, and the failure to testify takes it over the threshold. The presumption of innocence, however, indicates that it is not incumbent on the accused to present any evidence at all, rather it is for the Crown to prove him or her guilty. Thus, in order for the burden of proof to remain with the Crown, as required by the Charter, the silence of the accused should not be used against him or her in building the case for guilt. Belief in guilt beyond a reasonable doubt must be grounded on the testimony and any other tangible or demonstrative evidence admitted during the trial.

Some reference to the silence of the accused by the trier of fact may not offend the Charter principles discussed above: where in a trial by judge alone the trial judge is convinced of the guilt of the accused beyond a reasonable doubt, the silence of the accused may be referred to as evidence of the absence of an explanation which could raise a reasonable doubt. If the Crown has proved the case beyond a reasonable doubt, the accused need not testify, but if he doesn't, the Crown's case prevails and the accused will be convicted. It is only in this sense that the accused "need respond" once the Crown has proved its case beyond a reasonable doubt. Another permissible reference to the silence of the accused was alluded to by the Court of Appeal in this case. In its view, such a reference is permitted by a judge trying a case alone to indicate that he need not speculate about possible defences that might have been offered by the accused had he or she testified. . . Such treatment of the silence of the accused does not offend either the right to silence or the presumption of innocence. If silence is simply taken as assuring the trier of fact that it need not speculate about unspoken explanations, then belief in guilt beyond a reasonable doubt is not in part grounded on the silence of the accused, but rather is grounded on the evidence against him or her. The right to silence and its underlying rationale are respected, in that the communication or absence of communication is not used to build the case against the accused. The silence of the accused is not used as inculpatory evidence, which would be contrary to the right to silence, but simply is not used as exculpatory evidence. Moreover, the presumption of innocence is respected, in that it is not incumbent on the accused to defend him- or herself or face the possibility of conviction on the basis of his or her silence. Thus, a trier of fact may refer to the silence of the accused simply as evidence of the absence of an explanation which it must consider in reaching a verdict. On the other hand, if there exists in evidence a rational explanation or inference that is capable of raising a reasonable doubt about guilt, silence cannot be used to reject this explanation.

. . .

The principles to which I have referred which derive from ss. 7 and 11(d) of the Charter find ample support in recent case law of this Court. While earlier cases on the appropriate use of silence by the trier of fact are admittedly ambiguous, recent decisions are clear: silence may not be used by the trier of fact as a piece of inculpatory evidence. . . In my view, these comments clearly indicate that it is not permissible to use the failure to testify as a piece of evidence contributing to a finding of guilt beyond a reasonable doubt where such a finding would not exist without considering the failure to testify. McLachlin J. stated that the failure to testify could not be used to "shore up a Crown case which otherwise does not establish guilt beyond a reasonable doubt". Major J. stated that "this lack of testimony cannot otherwise be used to strengthen the Crown's case where the Crown has fallen short of proving guilt". In my view, these statements indicate that silence cannot be used to take an unproven case to a proven case.

. . .

There may, however, be confusion over the use of the words "adverse inference" in the above cases. Professor R. J. Delisle, in an annotation to *R. v. François* (1994), 31 C.R. (4th) 203, asked that if an adverse inference is permitted, what inference is relevant if it can only be drawn after guilt beyond a reasonable doubt has been proved? He stated at p. 204:

> The essence of a criminal trial is whether the Crown has established its case beyond a reasonable doubt. If a jury cannot use the failure to testify to assist in its determination of whether they are satisfied beyond a reasonable doubt, then pray tell what the permissible adverse inference does? For what else can the jury use it?

As set out above, silence is not inculpatory evidence, but nor is it exculpatory evidence. Thus, as in *Lepage*, if the trier of fact reaches a belief in guilt beyond a reasonable doubt, silence may be treated by the trier of fact as confirmatory of guilt. Silence may indicate, for example, that there is no evidence to support speculative explanations of the Crown's evidence offered by defence counsel, or it may indicate that the accused has not put forward any evidence that would require that the Crown negative an affirmative defence. In this limited sense, silence may be used by the trier of fact. If, however, there is a rational explanation which is consistent with innocence and which may raise a reasonable doubt, the silence of the accused cannot be used to remove that doubt. Thus, there are permissible uses of silence by the trier of fact. However, Delisle is correct in stating that, since these permissible uses only arise after the trier of fact has reached a belief in guilt beyond a reasonable doubt, the uses may be superfluous. I would therefore conclude that courts should generally avoid using the potentially confusing term "inference" in discussing the silence of the accused. "Inference" could be taken to indicate that the trier of fact used silence to help establish the case for guilt beyond a reasonable doubt, which is not a permissible use of silence. Indeed, because of the potential for confusion, discussion of the silence of the accused should generally be avoided. However, where silence is mentioned by the trial judge as confirmatory of guilt given the totality of the evidence, but not as a "make-weight", there is no reversible error. *Lepage* provides an example of such a situation.

. . .

On a related point, I would add that nothing in s. 4(6) or in the analysis thus far prevents the trial judge from telling the jury that the evidence on a particular issue is uncontradicted. In such a circumstance, the judge is not instructing the jury to consider the failure of the accused to testify per se, but rather is simply instructing the jury to take note of the fact that no evidence had been led to contradict a particular point. Rather than inviting the jury to place the failure of the accused on the evidentiary scales, the judge is instructing the jury that it need not speculate about possible contradictory evidence which has not been led in evidence.

. . .

Alibi Cases

The appellant submitted that *Vézeau v. The Queen*, [1977] 2 S.C.R. 277, held that silence could be treated as a "make-weight". In *Vézeau*, this Court considered the significance of the failure to testify in the context of a defence of alibi. In that case, the defence was alibi, but the accused did not testify. In giving his instructions to the jury, the judge said that they could not draw any conclusion unfavourable to the accused from the fact that he had not testified. The majority of this Court held that, aside from the prohibition of comment on the failure of the accused to testify set out in the Canada Evidence Act, it was an error of law for the trial judge to instruct the jury that they could not consider the absence of testimony by the accused in assessing the alibi. Martland J. stated on behalf of the majority at p. 292 that:

> It was part of the appellant's defence to the charge that he could not have committed the offence because he was in Montreal when the murder occurred. Proof of this alibi was tendered by a witness who claimed to have been with the appellant in Montreal. The direction of the trial judge precluded the jury, when considering this defence, from taking into consideration the fact that the appellant had failed to support his alibi by his own testimony. The failure of an accused person, who relies upon an alibi, to testify and thus to submit himself to cross-examination is a matter of importance in considering the validity of that defence. The jury, in this case, was instructed that they could not take that fact into account in reaching their verdict.

In my view, *Vézeau* set out a narrow exception to the impermissibility of using silence to build the case against the accused at trial. It has clearly been recognized in other contexts that alibi defences create exceptions to the right to silence. . . In my view, there are two reasons supporting the alibi exception to the right to silence pre-trial which apply also to the right to silence at trial: the ease with which alibi evidence may be fabricated; and the diversion of the alibi inquiry from the central inquiry at trial. I am therefore sympathetic to the view expressed in *Vézeau* that in the limited case of alibi, the failure of the accused at trial to testify and expose him- or herself to cross-examination on the alibi defence may be used to draw an adverse inference about the credibility of the defence. A second reason to permit such a limited exception to the right to silence at trial is that the alibi defence is not directly related to the guilt of the accused; as Gooderson put it, "[a]libi evidence, by its very nature, takes the focus right away from the area of the main facts". Rejecting the alibi defence does not build the case for the Crown in the sense of proving the existence of the required elements of the offence in question, but rather negatives an affirmative defence actively put forward by the accused. Using silence to inform the trier of fact's assessment of the credibility of the accused's affirmative defence of alibi simply goes to the alibi defence itself.

. . .

On balance, it appears to me that the trial judge used the failure to testify as evidence going to identification which permitted him to reach a belief in guilt beyond a reasonable doubt. Indeed, he stated explicitly that the failure to testify "certainly may add to the weight of the Crown's case" and concluded by finding guilt on the basis of "those reasons", which appeared to include the discussion of the failure to testify. In light of these statements, when the trial judge stated that he "can be" satisfied on the identity issue prior to discussing the failure to testify, in my view he indicated that the evidence before him was consistent with proof of identity, and the failure to testify took belief in identity beyond a reasonable doubt.

. . . Given my conclusion that such reasoning constituted an error of law, I would dismiss the appeal and confirm the judgment of the Court of Appeal ordering a new trial.

LAMER C.J. (dissenting): —

According to Sopinka J. the silence of an accused can only be used by the trier of fact in two very limited senses. The accused's silence may: (1) confirm prior findings of guilt beyond a reasonable doubt; and (2) remind triers of fact that they need not speculate about unstated defences. With greatest respect, this misinterprets the case law. This Court and others have repeatedly held that when the Crown presents a case to meet that implicates the accused in a "strong and cogent network of inculpatory facts", the trier of fact is entitled to consider the accused's failure to testify in deciding whether it is in fact satisfied of his or her guilt beyond a reasonable doubt. . . None of these early cases suggests that the accused should be compelled to testify or that the accused is anything other than presumed innocent until proven guilty. They merely recognize that when an accused is implicated or "enveloped" in a case of unexplained inculpatory circumstances, there are consequences to silence that trial judges, juries, and appellate courts alike may consider in reaching a verdict. This does not happen in every case. A trier of fact is entitled to draw adverse inferences only where there is a "damning chain of evidence" or more aptly a "strong and cogent network of inculpatory facts".

In separate opinions LaForest, Gonthier and McLachlin JJ. agreed with Lamer C.J. in dissent.

English law takes a very different approach to the right to silence at trial. The *Criminal Justice and Public Order Act, 1994*[170] allows U.K. judges and juries to consider a defendant's failure to testify as evidence of his or her guilt. The Act extends to England and Wales the reforms accomplished in Northern Ireland in 1988. By s. 35, if the accused chooses not to give evidence or, having been sworn, refuses to answer questions, the judge or jury is entitled to draw such inferences as appear to them to be proper.

(viii) *Comments on Accused's Failure to Testify*

If triers of fact are not entitled to draw inferences tending to guilt should we talk about it openly? Should the judge, in his or her reasons or direction to the jury?

In *Griffin v. California*[171] the accused was convicted of murder. Both the judge and the prosecutor had commented to the jury on the accused's failure to testify. This was in accordance with the State's constitution. The United States Supreme Court, however, decided that this was violative of the Fifth Amendment to the *U.S. Constitution* as applicable to the states through the Fourteenth Amendment. The dissent argued:

> It is not at all apparent to me, on any realistic view of the trial process, that a defendant will be at more of a disadvantage under the California practice than he would be in a court which permitted no comment at all on his failure to take the witness stand. How can it be said that the inferences drawn by a jury will be more detrimental to a defendant under the limiting and carefully controlling language of the instruction here involved than would result if the jury were left to roam at large with only its untutored instincts to guide it, to draw from the defendant's silence broad inferences of guilt.[172]

The majority saw quite a difference:

> [Comment] is a penalty imposed by courts for exercising a constitutional privilege. It is said however that the inference of guilt from failure to testify as to facts peculiarly within the accused's knowledge is in any event natural and irresistible, and that comment on the failure does not magnify that inference into a penalty. What the jury may infer, given no help from the court, is one thing. What it may infer when the court solemnizes the silence of the accused into evidence is quite another.

The *Canada Evidence Act*[173] provides: "The failure of the person charged, or of the wife or husband of that person, to testify shall not be made the subject of comment by the judge or by counsel for the prosecution."

---

[170] The *Criminal Justice and Public Order Act* (Commencement No. 6) Order 1995 provided for the coming into force, on April 10, 1995, of the sections relating to inferences from the accused's silence.

[171] 380 U.S. 609 (1964).

[172] *Ibid.* at 621.

[173] R.S.C. 1985, c. C-5, s. 4(6).

The first thing to notice about the Canadian provision is that our courts have decided that the comment is only prohibited in cases of trial by jury and when the comment is made in the presence of the jury. In *R. v. Binder*[174] Roach, J. wrote:

> I had always understood that the comment there prohibited was one made by either the Judge or Crown counsel to or in the presence of the jury. I still think so. Counsel for the appellant was unable to refer to any case in which it was held otherwise.
>
> . . .
>
> It is impossible to think of any other reason for prohibiting such a comment than its improper effect upon a jury.[175]

Perhaps such reasoning was born of a belief that in trials by judge alone the accused's failure to testify could not be magnified out of its proper proportion, since a trial judge is able to place it in its proper perspective.

The next thing to notice is that comment by an accused on his or her co-accused's failure to take the stand is not foreclosed by the section.[176] In *R. v. Crawford*[177] the accused and another were charged with second degree murder. The accused Crawford made no statement to the police. He testified at trial and blamed the other. He was cross-examined by the other's counsel on his failure to make any statements to the police. The other accused Creighton did not testify at trial. His version of the events was set out in a videotaped statement to the police on his arrest. Crawford's lawyer said to the jury "an innocent man sitting in Creighton's seat would have gotten into that witness box and sworn that he was not guilty". Only Crawford appealed to the Supreme Court. The Supreme Court was then principally concerned with the extent to which one accused could use his co-accused's silence during the investigation to challenge the credibility of the co-accused's testimony in court. The language of the Court, however, appears to accept that comment by one accused on the other's failure to testify is permissible. The Court noted in passing that in *R. v. Naglik*[178] the Ontario Court of Appeal had held that neither s. 11(c) of the *Charter* nor s. 4(6) of the *Canada Evidence Act* prevented a co-accused's counsel from commenting on an accused's failure to testify. The Court of Appeal in *R. v. Creighton* concluded that: "[I]t was open to counsel for Crawford to comment upon the failure of Creighton to testify on his own behalf."[179]

---

[174]   (1948), 92 C.C.C. 20 (Ont. C.A.); followed in *Pratte v. Maher*, [1965] 1 C.C.C. 77 (Que. C.A.), *R. v. Bouchard*, [1970] 5 C.C.C. 95 (N.B. C.A.), and *Tilco Plastics Ltd. v. Skurjat*, [1967] 1 C.C.C. 131 (Ont. H.C.), affirmed [1967] 2 C.C.C. 196n (Ont. C.A.).

[175]   *Binder, supra* note 174 at 24-25.

[176]   This appears also to be the approach in England (see *R. v. Wickham* (1971), 55 Crim. App. R. 199 (C.A.)) but contrary to the approach in the United States (see *DeLuna v. U.S.*, 308 F.2d 140 (1962)).

[177]   [1995] 1 S.C.R. 858.

[178]   (1991), 65 C.C.C. (3d) 272.

[179]   *R. v. Creighton* (1993), 20 C.R. (4th) 331 (Ont. C.A.) at 348.

Does s. 4(6) of the *Canada Evidence Act* preclude a trial judge from instructing a jury not to draw an adverse inference from the accused's failure to testify?

R. v. PROKOFIEW
[2012] 2 S.C.R. 639, 290 C.C.C. (3d) 280, 96 C.R. (6th) 57 (S.C.C.)

The accused was charged with conspiracy to defraud. At trial, the Crown alleged that P and his co-accused, S, participated in a fraudulent scheme involving the fictitious sale of heavy equipment to generate harmonized sales tax that was then not remitted to the federal government as required. The fraudulent nature of the scheme was never challenged. The involvement of P and S in the scheme was also conceded. The question for the jury was whether either or both accused were aware of the fraudulent nature of the scheme. P did not testify, but was incriminated by S's testimony. In his closing address, S's counsel invited the jury to infer P's guilt from the latter's failure to testify. The trial judge, relying on *dicta* of Justice Sopinka for the Supreme Court in *Crawford* and *Noble*, concluded that s. 4(6) of the *Canada Evidence Act* prohibited him from telling the jury that it could not use the accused's silence at trial as evidence against him. The trial judge made it clear that, but for his understanding of the prohibition in s. 4(6), he would have given a remedial instruction. The jury convicted the appellant and his co-accused. The accused appealed, *inter alia*, arguing that s. 4(6) was unconstitutional.

The appeal was dismissed by Doherty J.A on behalf of a unanimous five- person panel of the Ontario Court of Appeal.[180] Justices Feldman, MacPherson, Blair and Juriansz concurred. The Court held that Justice Sopinka's comments were *obiter* and should not be followed given earlier pronouncements from the Supreme Court that s. 4(6) did not preclude comments not prejudicial to the accused and permitted a trial judge to tell a jury that an accused who does not testify is exercising his or her constitutional right and that no adverse inference can be drawn from that failure to testify. However, the Court held on consideration of the entirety of the instructions on the presumption of innocence and reasonable doubt that this was a case for the curative proviso under s. 686(1)(b)(iii). The jury would have to understand that guilt had to be established on the evidence and that the accused's silence at trial could not be used to infer the accused's guilt.

A 5-4 majority of the Supreme Court dismissed the further appeal.

Moldaver J. (Deschamps, Abella, Rothstein and Karakatsanis JJ. concurring):—

[1] Largely for the reasons given by Doherty J.A., I would dismiss Mr. Prokofiew's further appeal to this Court.

[2] I have had the benefit of reading the reasons of my colleague Justice Fish and I agree with much of his analysis. Where I disagree with him is in the

---

[180]   (2010), 256 C.C.C. (3d) 355, 77 C.R. (6th) 52 (Ont. C.A.).

result. I will explain our disagreement and why the appeal should be dismissed, but before doing so, I will address the matters on which my colleague and I agree — albeit with some additional observations.

I. *Matters of Agreement*

[3] My colleague and I agree that s. 4(6) of the *Canada Evidence Act*, R.S.C. 1985, c. C-5 ("*CEA*"), does not prohibit a trial judge from affirming an accused's right to silence. In so concluding, I should not be taken — nor do I understand my colleague to suggest — that such an instruction must be given in every case where an accused exercises his or her right to remain silent at trial. Rather, it will be for the trial judge, in the exercise of his or her discretion, to provide such an instruction where there is a realistic concern that the jury may place evidential value on an accused's decision not to testify.

[4] In cases where the jury is given an instruction on the accused's right to remain silent at trial, the trial judge should, in explaining the right, make it clear to the jury that an accused's silence is not evidence and that it cannot be used as a makeweight for the Crown in deciding whether the Crown has proved its case. In other words, if, after considering the whole of the evidence, the jury is not satisfied that the charge against the accused has been proven beyond a reasonable doubt, the jury cannot look to the accused's silence to remove that doubt and give the Crown's case the boost it needs to push it over the line.

[5] The case at hand provides an example of a situation where such an instruction would be warranted — cut-throat defences where one accused testifies and points the finger at the other, while the other exercises his right not to testify. My colleague and I agree that, in summing up to the jury, Mr. Solty's counsel could have relied on the fact that his client had testified to argue that Mr. Solty was innocent and had "nothing to hide". Moreover, he could have emphasized that Mr. Solty's testimony stood uncontradicted and that the jury could consider this in assessing whether they believed his evidence or whether it left them in a state of reasonable doubt.

[6] What Mr. Solty's counsel could not do is mislead the jury on a matter of law. He could not invite the jury to use Mr. Prokofiew's silence at trial as evidence, much less evidence of guilt.

[7] In cases where there is a risk of counsel misleading the jury on a co-accused's right to remain silent at trial, trial judges would do well to spell out the governing principles and ensure that counsel's remarks conform to those principles. That way, the potential harm can be prevented from occurring, thereby sparing the need for a remedial instruction.

[8] In the context of the charge as a whole, I think it might be helpful to explain how a jury may use a lack of contradictory evidence in deciding whether the Crown has proved its case beyond a reasonable doubt.

[9] Apart from a few notable exceptions — such as when an accused raises the defence of not criminally responsible on account of a mental disorder under s. 16 of the *Criminal Code*, R.S.C. 1985, c. C-46 — in every criminal trial, juries are instructed that an accused has no obligation to prove anything. The onus of proof rests upon the Crown from beginning to end and it never shifts.

[10] Juries are also told that in deciding whether the Crown has proved its case to the criminal standard, they are to look to the whole of the evidence — and, having done so, they may only convict if they are satisfied, on the basis of evidence they find to be both credible and reliable, that the Crown has established the accused's guilt beyond a reasonable doubt. In coming to that conclusion, a jury may not use an accused's silence at trial as evidence, much less evidence of guilt, and, where appropriate, the jury should be so instructed.

[11] That said, in assessing the credibility and reliability of evidence upon which the Crown can and does rely, a jury is entitled to take into account, among other things, the fact that the evidence stands uncontradicted, if that is the case — and the jury may be so instructed. Of course, the fact that evidence is uncontradicted does not mean that the jury must accept it, and an instruction to that effect should be given.

II. *Is a New Trial Required?*

A. *Failure to Instruct the Jury on the Appellant's Right to Silence*

[12] In the course of his closing address to the jury, which covered 23 pages of transcript, counsel for Mr. Solty incorporated the following rhetorical question into his remarks: "Did [Mr. Prokofiew] have something to hide or did he simply have no response that could help him since there is no point in trying to contradict the truth?" (A.R., vol. V, at p. 17). That comment was improper in that it implicitly invited the jury to treat Mr. Prokofiew's silence at trial as evidence of guilt. It should not have been made.

. . .

[26] In sum, while I agree that an explicit remedial instruction from the trial judge would have been preferable — and would have been warranted in these circumstances — I am satisfied that the instructions that were given in the instant case, when considered as a whole, were adequate. Like Doherty J.A., I am confident that the jury would have understood, in the context of the entirety of the instructions, that the Crown could prove Mr. Prokofiew's guilt only on the evidence and, as Mr. Prokofiew's silence at trial did not constitute evidence, it could not be used to prove his guilt. However, I do not fault the trial judge for concluding — wrongly but understandably — that he was prohibited by s. 4(6) of the *CEA* from making any reference at all to Mr. Prokofiew's failure to testify. My colleague has addressed that matter and it should not pose a problem in future cases.

Fish J. (McLachlin C.J. and LeBel and Cromwell jj. concurring) (dissenting).

[44] The Court of Appeal for Ontario, correctly in my view, held that s. 4(6) prohibits comments *prejudicial to the accused* — but not the remedial instruction requested by defence counsel and contemplated by the judge (2010 ONCA 423, 100 O.R. (3d) 401). The Court of Appeal held as well, again correctly, that the trial judge had erred in admitting hearsay evidence. It is undisputed in this Court that the hearsay evidence was inadmissible and ought to have been excluded.

[45] The Court of Appeal nonetheless dismissed Mr. Prokofiew's appeal on the ground that both errors were harmless. With respect, I am of a different view. For the reasons that follow, I would quash Mr. Prokofiew's conviction, allow the appeal and order a new trial.

. . .

[64] *Noble* establishes that a trier of fact may not draw an adverse inference from the accused's failure to testify and that the accused's silence at trial may not be treated as evidence of guilt. To do so would violate the presumption of innocence and the right to silence. It would to that extent and for that reason shift the burden of proof to the accused, turning the accused's constitutional right to silence into a "snare and a delusion" (*Noble*, at para. 72).

[65] We are now urged by the Crown to overrule *Noble*. Upon careful consideration of Crown counsel's full and able argument, and the helpful submissions of all counsel on this issue, I would decline to do so.

[66] I see no persuasive reason to overturn *Noble*. *Noble* is a recent and important precedent regarding a fundamental constitutional principle. The Court's decision in that case is constitutionally mandated and has not proven unworkable in practice. Nothing of significance has occurred since 1997 to cause the Court to reconsider its decision. And it is well established that the Court must exercise particular caution in contemplating the reversal of a precedent where the effect, as here, would be to diminish the protection of the *Canadian Charter of Rights and Freedoms*: *R. v. Henry*, 2005 SCC 76, [2005] 3 S.C.R. 609, at para. 44.

. . .

[79] In short, s. 4(6) of the *Canada Evidence Act* does not prohibit an affirmation by the trial judge of the accused's right to silence. And, in appropriate circumstances, an instruction that no adverse inference may be drawn from the silence of the accused at trial is not a prohibited "comment" on the accused's failure to testify within the meaning of that provision.

[80] I turn now to consider whether the trial judge in this case erred in failing to instruct the jury that no adverse inference could be drawn from the appellant's

failure to testify. Unlike the Court of Appeal, and with the greatest of respect, I believe that he did. And I believe as well that this error, though understandable in light of *Crawford* and *Noble*, is fatal to the jury's verdict.

. . .

[94] Trial judges must take care to ensure that the right to silence becomes neither a snare nor a delusion (*Noble*, at para. 72). To this end, whenever there is a "significant risk" — as the trial judge found in this case — that the jury will otherwise treat the silence of the accused as evidence of guilt, an appropriate remedial direction ought to be given to the jury. That was not done here.

[95] Standard instructions on the definition of evidence, the presumption of innocence, the Crown's burden of proof, and the reasonable doubt standard will not suffice. That is particularly true where, as here, counsel for one accused has suggested unmistakably to the jury that the guilt of a co-accused may be inferred from that person's failure to testify.

. . .

[104] We are urged by the Crown to apply the curative *proviso* of s. 686(1)(*b*)(iii) if we conclude, as I would, that the trial judge erred in law in failing to give the jury the remedial instruction requested by defence counsel and, again, in admitting the hearsay evidence that ought to have been excluded.

[105] It is now well established that the *proviso* may only be applied where the Crown satisfies the court that the evidence of the appellant's guilt is overwhelming or that the trial judge's errors of law were harmless because there is "no realistic possibility that a new trial would produce a different verdict" (*R. v. Jolivet*, 2000 SCC 29, [2000] 1 S.C.R. 751, at para. 46; *R. v. Sarrazin*, 2011 SCC 54, [2011] 3 S.C.R. 505, at paras. 23-24). I am not satisfied that the Crown has discharged its burden in this case.

Do you think the Supreme Court ought to have required a mandatory direction in every jury case where an accused does not testify that the jury should not draw an adverse inference where an accused has exercised his or her right to silence? Do you think that allowing instructions to the jury that Crown evidence was uncontradicted in fact allows indirect comments on the accused's failure to testify?[181]

2. MANNER OF QUESTIONING

The chief source of information for the trier of fact is oral testimony elicited from witnesses called by the parties. The fact that the witnesses are chosen by the parties and may be prepared in advance by them has led to different rules regarding their manner of questioning dependent on who is putting the questions. The witness description of the incident is first elicited

---

[181] See further Stuart, *Charter Justice in Canadian Criminal Law*, 7th ed. (2018) at 190-193.

by the party calling him or her in a process labelled examination-in-chief or direct examination. On the conclusion of direct examination, the adversary engages in cross-examination; the adversary is able to elicit further data concerning the incident from the witness and is also able to question the witness concerning his or her powers of perception and memory, to demand explicitness in his or her communication and to explore his or her sincerity, all in an attempt to challenge the accuracy of his or her first description. Following cross-examination the witness may be re-examined by the party who called him or her and permitted to explain or amplify answers given on cross-examination. Further opportunities to cross-examine and re-examine, all at the discretion of the trial judge, are possible.

(a) Leading Questions

A party calling a witness should not ask leading questions. One of the first instances of this rule's articulation provides a good illustrative characterization of the phrase "leading question", and at the same time demonstrates both the rule's justification as well as the frequent irretrievability of the harm done. In the *Trial of Thomas Rosewell*[182] the accused was indicted for High Treason. Witnesses against him had testified that in his preaching he had spoken against Charles I and Charles II as "two wicked Kings". The accused maintained that mention in his sermon of "two wicked Kings" was not concerning Charles I or his present majesty but rather was in reference to Kings referred to in the Book of Chronicles in the Old Testament (i.e., Ahab and his son Ahaziah, whose example he was using to expound on the 20th chapter of Genesis). To make his point the accused called a witness, Hudson, and the transcript reads:

L.C.J. Jeffries: Come, here is your witness, what say you to him? . . .

Rosewell: Pray Sir, as to the truth of the business; Did you hear me speak of two wicked Kings? That, my lord, came in, I say upon the second verse of the 20th of Genesis, which I then was expounding.

L.C.J.: Nay ask him in general what he heard you say; and whether he heard you say anything of two wicked kings, and what it was.

Rosewell: Ay, about Ahab, and Ahaziah his son —

L.C.J.: Nay, nay, I must have none of those things, we must have fair questions put; for, as you see we will not admit the king's counsel to put any questions to the witnesses, nor produce any witnesses against you, that are leading, or not proper, so nor must you. But if you have a mind to ask him any questions, what he heard concerning two wicked kings generally, do so.

Hudson: Upon the second verse he was then.

---

[182]   (1684), 10 Howell's State Trials 147 (K.B.).

L.C.J.:   Of what chapter?

Hudson: Of the 20th of Genesis.[183]

To describe the common law position it would be difficult to improve on the test of Mr. Justice Beck in *Maves v. Grand Trunk Pacific Railway Co.*[184]

I find the general subject of leading questions dealt with in a most satisfactory way in Best on Evidence, 11th ed., 624 *et seq.* I quote, italicising what I wish to emphasize: —

The chief rule of practice relative to the interrogation of witnesses is that which prohibits "*leading questions,*" *i.e.*, questions which directly or indirectly suggest to the witness the answer he is to give. The rule is, that *on material points* a party must not lead his own witnesses, but may lead those of his adversary; in other words, that leading questions are allowed in cross-examination, but not in examination-in-chief. This seems based on two reasons: first, and principally, on the supposition that the witness has a bias in favour of the party bringing him forward, and hostile to his opponent; secondly, that the party calling a witness has an advantage over his adversary, in knowing beforehand what the witness will prove, or, at least, is expected to prove; and that, consequently, if he were allowed to lead, he might interrogate in such a manner as to extract only so much of the knowledge of the witness as would be favourable to his side, or even put a false gloss upon the whole.

I think a third reason may be added, namely, that a witness, though intending to be entirely fair and honest may, owing, for example, to lack of education, of exactness of knowledge of the precise meaning of words or of appreciation at the moment of their precise meaning, or of alertness to see that what is implied in the question requires modification, honestly assent to a leading question which fails to express his real meaning, which he would probably have completely expressed if allowed to do so in his own words.

. . .

So that the *general* rule is that in examining one's own witness, not that no leading questions must be asked, but that *on material points* one must *not* lead his own witness but that on points that are *merely introductory and form no part of the substance* of the inquiry one *should* lead.

. . .

A case which not infrequently arises in practice is that of a witness who recounts a conversation and in doing so omits one or more statements which counsel examining him is instructed formed part of it. The common and proper practice is to ask the witness to repeat the conversation from the beginning. It is often found that in his repetition he gives the lacking statement — possibly omitting one given the first time. This method may be tried more than once, and as a matter of expediency — so as to have the advantage of getting the whole story on the witness' own unaided recollection — counsel might pass on to some other subject and later revert to the conversation, asking him to again state it. But when this method fails, the trial Judge undoubtedly ought to permit a question

---

[183] *Ibid.* at 190.
[184] (1913), 14 D.L.R. 70 (Alta. C.A.) at 73-77. And see Denroche, "Leading Questions" (1963-64), 6 Crim. L.Q. 21.

containing a reference to the subject-matter of the statement which it is supposed has been omitted by the witness. If this method fails, then and not till then — that is when his memory appears to be entirely exhausted, the trial Judge should allow a question to be put to him containing the supposedly omitted matter. It will be, of course, for the jury, or the Judge if there be no jury, to draw a conclusion as to the truthfulness of the witness; although the permitting of a question in a certain form is largely — though I think not wholly — in the discretion of the trial Judge. I should think that, with regard to the class of leading question I have been considering, they should, in every case, be permitted after all the steps which appear to shew the witness' memory to have been exhausted have been taken. If not permitted, great injustice may result. If permitted, the jury or Judge acting as a jury, may, of course, as I have said, disbelieve the answer elicited.

The third reason suggested by Justice Beck for prohibiting leading questions in chief highlights a different kind of leading question from that which directly suggests an answer: a question may be so phrased as to assume within it the truth of some fact, which remains controverted between the parties, and a witness not attuned to that fact may inadvertently agree to its existence. An example would be "when did the accused stop spanking her child?" Another example, "what was the deceased doing when the accused shot her?", in a prosecution where the issue is the identity of the assailant, is equally objectionable as leading, or "misleading", as the witness may unwittingly testify to a fact concerning which he or she has no knowledge or which he or she has no wish to concede.

The common law, then, prohibits leading questions but provides exceptions to the general rule. A list of exceptions would include:

a) for introductory, formal or undisputed matters;

b) for the purpose of identifying persons or things;

c) to allow one witness to contradict another regarding statements made by that other;

d) where the witness is either hostile to the questioner or unwilling to give evidence;

e) where it is seen, in the trial judge's discretion, to be necessary to refresh the witness' memory;

f) where the witness is having difficulty communicating on account of age, education, language or mental capacity;

g) where the matter is of a complicated nature and, in the opinion of the trial judge, the witness deserves some assistance to determine what subject the questioner is asking about.

In exercising his or her discretion to allow leading questions the trial judge should, however, keep in mind the reasons for the rule canvassed above, and rule not according to a grocery list of exceptions but in accord with the underlying philosophy. The evidence we seek is that of the witness and not that of the questioner. Stating the rule in this open way is preferable, as one could never close the list of exceptions and the matter must be left to the trial judge's discretion. In determining whether a question suggests an answer, much will depend on the character, mood and bias of the witness, and the manner and inflection of the questioner, all matters to be determined in the particular case.[185]

Justice Beck, though admitting that the authorities were not quite clear on the point, suggested that, given the underlying rationale of the rule, the trial judge has a discretion to restrain the cross-examining party from using leading questions when the witness appears to favour him or her. If the judge does not restrain such leading questions the form of the question may nevertheless detract from the weight of the answer; comment thereon to the jury might be made, and perhaps counsel might be warned of this effect.

R. v. ROSE
(2001), 42 C.R. (5th) 183, 153 C.C.C. (3d) 225 (Ont. C.A.)

The accused was charged with trafficking in cocaine and possession for the purpose of trafficking. The charges arose as a result of police surveillance observations of an alleged drug transaction between the accused and B. B was observed entering a motor vehicle driven by the accused. The motor vehicle was on the fringes of an area known to the police for its high level of crack cocaine selling activity. Shortly after B entered the motor vehicle, the police stopped it. The accused was arrested. After the arrest, money and crack cocaine were found inside the vehicle. B was initially charged jointly with the accused. However, on the first date set for trial, B agreed to give a statement to the police and testify against the accused. It was the Crown's theory that the accused, at the time of his arrest, had just finished selling drugs to B. B testified in accordance with this theory. The accused testified that B was the trafficker and that he was merely an accommodation buyer picking up some drugs for a friend. The trial judge rejected the accused's evidence and found that the accused was the owner of the drugs located in the motor vehicle and that he was the one selling drugs to B on the occasion in question. The accused was convicted. Most of the grounds of appeal related to Crown counsel's conduct of the trial.

CHARRON J.A. (FELDMAN and MACPHERSON JJ.A. concurring): —

1. Proof of the Crown's case through the use of leading questions

[9] A leading question is one that suggests the answer. It is trite law that the party who calls a witness is generally not permitted to ask the witness leading questions. The reason for the rule arises from a concern that the witness, who in many instances favours the party who calls him or her, will readily agree to the suggestions put in the form of a question rather than give his or her own answers to the questions. Of course, the degree of concern that may arise from

---

[185] See *Reference re R. v. Coffin*, [1956] S.C.R. 191 (S.C.C.) at 211 per Kellock, J.: "...while, as a general rule, a party may not either in direct or re-examination put leading questions, the court has a discretion, not open to review, to relax it whenever it is considered necessary in the interests of justice."

the use of leading questions will depend on the particular circumstances, and the rule is applied with some flexibility. For example, leading questions are routinely asked to elicit a witness' evidence on preliminary and non-contentious matters. This practice is adopted for the sake of expediency and generally gives rise to no concern. Leading questions are also permitted to the extent that they are necessary to direct the witness to a particular matter or field of inquiry. Apart from these specific examples, the trial judge has a general discretion to allow leading questions whenever it is considered necessary in the interests of justice: *Reference Re R. v. Coffin* (1956), 114 C.C.C. 1 at 22 (S.C.C.).

[10] The transcript in this case presents numerous transgressions of this rule by Crown counsel. The appellant relies mainly on the examination-in-chief of the Crown's main witness, Noel Beaudry. Several excerpts are reproduced below. The questions that are most offensive are highlighted.

> Q. All right, and do you recall when — when and how you first met Mr. Rose?
>
> A. No.
>
> Q. And what's your connection with Mr. Rose?
>
> A. What do you mean, connection?
>
> Q. Well, what do you do with Mr. Rose?
>
> A. I talk to him.
>
> Q. What else do you do with him?
>
> A. That's about it.
>
> *Q. Does he supply you with crack cocaine?*
>
> A. Sometimes.
>
> *Q. Now, my information is that the police had set up surveillance on yourself and on the 19th of August you got into a motor vehicle with Mr. Rose. The 21st of August you got into a motor vehicle with Mr. Rose.*

[11] At this point, defence counsel objected to the leading questions. Crown counsel maintained that his questions were not leading. His submission to the trial judge, in answer to defence counsel's objection, somewhat exemplifies the general approach Crown counsel adopted in questioning not only Beaudry, but all of the Crown witnesses:

> [Crown]: Well, this is information I have and I'm asking this witness to either confirm or deny it. If he confirms it, it will become a fact. If he denies it, it won't become a fact. I don't think it's leading at all. It's information I have and I'm asking him to confirm it or deny it. It's not suggesting the answer.

[12] The judge ruled that the question was still incomplete and not objectionable at that point in time. He invited defence counsel to renew his objection if he so wished after hearing the whole question. Crown counsel continued to question the witness much in the same fashion and defence

counsel did not renew his objection. Counsel for the appellant relies more particularly on the following excerpts from the examination-in-chief in support of his contention that Crown counsel proved his case through the use of leading questions:

> Q. Mr. Beaudry, I started advising you that my information is that the police were conducting surveillance and on the following dates they saw you get into a motor vehicle which Mr. Rose was driving and those dates were August 19, August 21, September 4, and September 5. Did you, in fact, meet Mr. Rose on those dates?
>
> A. If it's right there, I guess so. I don't mark it in a book, you know, it's just —
>
> Q. You didn't mark it. *How many times have you purchased crack cocaine from Mr. Rose?* You don't have to give me an exact number, give your best estimate or you can give me a range.
>
> A. Three, four times.
>
> Q. Three or four times, and do you recall when those three or four times would have been?
>
> A. No.
>
> Q. Now, on the 6th of September — or the 5th of September, you were in an automobile with Mr. Rose and the police stopped that automobile?
>
> A. Yeah.
>
> Q. You remember that?
>
> A. Yeah. I don't remember the date, but I remember when they stopped us.
>
> Q. And there were police cars in front and back of Mr. Rose's car?
>
> A. Something like that.
>
> Q. And do you recall what kind of automobile Mr. Rose was driving or drives?
>
> A. A black car.
>
> Q. You don't know the make?
>
> A. No.
>
> Q. The license number? Has it been — *all the times that you've purchased crack cocaine from Mr. Rose, has he been in the same motor vehicle?*
>
> A. Yeah.
>
> Q. And that's the black car you just indicated?
>
> A. Black car, yeah.
>
> Q. *Now, when the — on the 5th of September when the police officers stopped the motor vehicle, you were in Mr. Rose's automobile, were you not?*
>
> A. Yeah.
>
> Q. *Mr. Rose was in the automobile?*
>
> A. Yeah.
>
> Q. Correct, and who was driving the automobile?

A. Mr. Rose.

Q. Mr. Rose, and you were in which seat, *the front passenger seat?*

A. Yeah. The front seat.

Q. Was there anyone else in the car?

A. No.

Q. All right, and what was your purpose for being in that automobile on that date and time, why were you there?

A. To tell you the truth, I don't even know because it happened so fast. I didn't have time to say nothing or nothing, you know.

Q. *Well, were you going to purchase crack cocaine from Mr. Rose on that date?*

A. I guess I would have tried.

Q. Did you have money with you?

A. Yeah. Of course, it was my rent money, but . . .

Q. *Well, I — is it fair to say that every time you had gotten into Mr. Rose's automobile in the past you purchased crack cocaine from him?*

A. Maybe two out of three.

Q. Two out of three. Did you have any crack cocaine with you at that time when you got into Mr. Rose's car on the 5th of September?

A. No.

Q. You had money with you though?

A. Yeah.

Q. *Would you agree with me that it's — it seems that you were there to buy crack cocaine from him?*

A. I could have.

Q. Other than meeting Mr. Rose to buy crack cocaine from him, have you and Mr. Rose ever done anything else together? Do you go to movies together, go to see friends together?

A. No, we just went for coffee.

Q. *Coffee and when you go for coffee does that end up — is that when you have a conversation about whether —*

A. Sometimes.

Q. *—he has crack cocaine?*

A. Sometimes no. All depends.

Q. How often would you have gone for coffee with Mr. Rose?

A. I don't know. Four times, three times.

Q. *Okay, as many times as you've bought crack cocaine from him?*

A. Maybe a little bit less.

Q. Now, when the police stopped the automobile they found some crack cocaine in the automobile?

A. That's what they claim.

[13] In my view, Crown counsel's questions to Beaudry were clearly suggestive of the answers. Indeed the entire examination-in-chief reads more like the cross- examination of a witness. This was highly improper particularly in these circumstances where Beaudry, as the trial judge himself stated in his reasons, was "the primary Crown witness" and the questions concerned crucial and contentious matters. The impropriety of Crown counsel's approach is further heightened by the fact that Beaudry's testimony, obtained as it was in return for a stay of the charges against him, was already highly suspect. The manner in which his testimony was elicited could only further undermine its probative value.

[14] Consequently, I am of the view that the trial judge erred in ruling against the defence's initial objection and further erred in failing to intervene when Crown counsel continued in this fashion. I do not view defence counsel's failure to renew his objection as an impediment to raising this ground of appeal. In view of the trial judge's failure to appreciate that Crown counsel's questions were indeed leading at the time the objection was made, defence counsel may well have thought that any further objection would be futile.

[15] Virtually all of the incriminating evidence given by Beaudry was elicited through leading questions. Given the circumstances in which he agreed to testify against the appellant, this irregularity raises a real concern that the testimony was proffered, not for its truth, but for the purpose of meeting the expectations of the Crown and the police. The trial judge ultimately accepted some of Beaudry's evidence "as being cogent and vital". Consequently, the finding of guilt may be based, at least in part, on highly questionable evidence.

New trial ordered.

(b) Refreshing Memory/Past Recollection Recorded

R. v. WILKS
(2005), 35 C.R. (6th) 172, 201 C.C.C. (3d) 11 (Man. C.A.)

The accused was involved in a car accident and was receiving income replacement benefits from an insurer. The case manager for the insurer met the accused and talked to her on the phone on several occasions. He took notes that were summaries rather than verbatim accounts of what was said. The contents of those notes were subsequently entered into a computer and the notes were destroyed. The case manager became suspicious of the accused and subjected her to video surveillance. The tapes showed her reporting was at variance with her actual physical condition. She was charged with fraud.

At her trial, the trial judge permitted the case manager to refresh his memory from the computer notes. During his testimony he frequently relied on his notes rather than his memory. The trial judge convicted. She appealed.

PHILP and FREEDMAN JJ.A. (KROFT J.A. concurring): —

Because this issue seemed to the court one of potential significance, we requested, and received from counsel, supplementary submissions on the issue. These submissions effectively highlighted the relevant legal principles, which may be briefly explained in the following way.

Witnesses often forget, and so it is permissible to use aids to assist the witness. The use of these aids will fall into one of two categories. They will either i) assist the witness by reviving his or her memory so that the witness, whose memory has been jogged by the aid, now has a present memory of the fact ("present memory revived"), or ii) be a record of the fact, previously made and now attested to as an accurate record ("past recollection recorded"). The distinction has been explained this way in Professor Alan W. Mewett, Q.C. & Peter J. Sankoff, *Witnesses,* vol. 1, looseleaf (Toronto: Carswell, 2004) (at 13-3):

> True cases of "present memory revived" involve a witness who has actually had his or her memory refreshed. "Past recollection recorded" is probably best viewed as an exception to the hearsay rule, whereby evidence of which a witness has no current recall can nonetheless be admitted for the truth of its contents as it was recorded at a time when the witness was able to verify its accuracy.

In the case of present memory revived, the aid is not evidence, but is simply a facilitative mechanism which becomes irrelevant once the witness has had his or her present memory revived by the use of the aid. In the case of past recollection recorded, there is no present memory, so it is the evidence of the past recollection, recorded usually in the form of notes or the like, that is admitted.

i) *Present Memory Revived*

There are few restrictions on the nature and use of testimonial aids which are used to revive a witness's memory. Mewett and Sankoff state (at 13-3ff):

> Anything may, in fact, jog a person's memory - a smell, a sound, some association, or something the witness is reminded he or she said on a previous occasion. In principle, the use of something said on a previous occasion in order to jog a person's memory is no different from the use of anything else; nevertheless, this proposition has not always been accepted, likely because . . . the courts have confused true cases of present memory revived with past recollection recorded.

In cases where the aid genuinely revives the witness's memory, the nature of the aid, its contemporaneity with the event and other issues relating to it are not relevant to the admissibility of the evidence. If reviewing a note jogs the witness's memory, then it is the memory, now articulated in testimony, which becomes the evidence of the witness.

ii) Past Recollection Recorded

Here matters are entirely different. Out-of-court evidence, such as notes, are admitted because facts once remembered have been forgotten. Whether viewed as an exception to the hearsay rule or as a separate rule of evidence, where such evidence is admitted for its truth, the criteria of necessity and reliability must be satisfied. As Mewett and Sankoff write (at 13-12.1):

> There is certainly a strong argument to be made suggesting that the doctrine was not designed to allow for the wholesale admission of complex statements, but rather to allow persons to supplement their oral evidence with records preserving obscure or intricate details that a person would not ordinarily remember. In these situations, reliability is assured by the contemporaneous nature of the recording as well as by the nature of the information recorded. Where the recollection involves a licence plate number or other "technical" detail, there is less worry about a subjective interpretation of words that cross-examination is designed to explore . . . [Where, however, it is the admissibility of a complex statement which is at issue] it makes sense to examine the hearsay criteria (reliability and necessity) to ensure that the evidence is not overly prejudicial to the accused. The past recollection recorded doctrine should not be utilized to ignore very real hearsay dangers.

One of the most recent, and a very clear, exposition of the principles applicable to this type of evidence was in the decision of the Supreme Court of Canada in *R. v. Fliss*, [2002] 1 S.C.R. 535, 2002 SCC 16. In *Fliss*, the accused freely confessed to an undercover police officer that he had killed a woman. This conversation was recorded and the next day the officer reviewed and corrected the transcript. The trial judge declared the tape and transcript inadmissible for reasons not relevant here, but admitted the officer's viva voce evidence which was basically a recitation of the corrected transcript. At the Supreme Court, the issue related to "the indirect' reading of the excluded transcript into evidence" (at para. 18).

Binnie J. (writing for the majority) said that the jury was entitled to hear from the officer about the conversation because the officer had a present recollection of the "gist" of the important elements of the discussion (which related to graphic details of the murder).

Binnie J. explained why even inadmissible evidence could be used to refresh memory (at para. 45):

> There is also no doubt that the officer was entitled to refresh his memory by any means that would rekindle his recollection, whether or not the stimulus itself constituted admissible evidence. This is because it is his recollection, not the stimulus, that becomes evidence. The stimulus may be hearsay, it may itself be largely inaccurate, it may be nothing more than the sight of someone who had been present or hearing some music that had played in the background. If the recollection here had been stimulated by hearing a tape of his conversation with the accused, even if the tape was made without valid authorization, the officer's recollection — not the tape — would be admissible.

But the problem in the case was that what went into evidence went well beyond the officer's current recollection. For example, "[t]he account of the murder was put into evidence word for word from the excluded . . . transcript" (at para. 55). This, said Binnie J., should not have been permitted (at paras. 60-61):

> ... The officer was quite entitled to attempt to "refresh" his memory by an out-of-court review of the corrected transcript, but in the witness box his testimony had to be sourced in his "refreshed" memory, not the excluded transcript.

> In short, the problem with the corrected transcript as a stimulus to memory is not that it was itself inadmissible but that it failed to stimulate.

Futhermore, the testimony did not meet the standards applicable to "past recollection recorded" (at para. 63):

> Secondly, the officer's testimony does not qualify for admission as "past recollection recorded". This doctrine would apply only if the prosecutor could satisfy the four Wigmore criteria, usefully summarized by the Alberta Court of Appeal in *R. v. Meddoui* (1990), 61 C.C.C. (3d) 345, per Kerans J.A., at p. 352:

> > The basic rule *in Wigmore on Evidence* (Chadbourn rev. 1970), vol. 3, c. 28, s. 744 et seq. provided:

> > 1. The past recollection must have been recorded in some reliable way.

> > 2. At the time, it must have been sufficiently fresh and vivid to be probably accurate.

> > 3. The witness must be able now to assert that the record accurately represented his knowledge and recollection at the time. The usual phrase requires the witness to affirm that he "knew it to be true at the time".

> > 4. The original record itself must be used, if it is procurable.

And (at para. 64):

> ... The admission of past recollection recorded but no longer remembered is an exceptional procedure and the conditions precedent to its reception should be clearly satisfied.

iii) *The Importance of the Two Rules*

We refer again to Mewett and Sankoff (at 13-13):

> ... Failure to distinguish between a witness using something to refresh his or her present memory and a witness using something as a record of a past memory may result in a witness being refused permission to consult notes or other memory-jogging devices or, *conversely, being permitted to testify on the basis that his memory has been refreshed when it is clear that it is not the memory that is being refreshed, but an inadmissible record of past memory that is being introduced.* [Emphasis added]

It will be convenient to refer back (see paras. 9-10) to the ruling of the trial judge regarding the use by Unger of his notes. It is clear that they were to be used to jog Unger's memory, so that his present memory of the events at issue (i.e., his discussions with the accused) could be revived. The trial judge specifically rejected the applicability of the "past recollection recorded" principle. Yet, as is evident from the extracts of the transcript quoted earlier, Unger was, in respect of those matters at least, totally reliant on his notes. He had and demonstrated no present memory, and candidly said so. On these matters, he knew what was in his notes, and no more, only because they were in his notes. That is the classic situation of "past recollection recorded," as discussed in *Fliss*, yet that was not the basis on which Unger was permitted to refer to his notes. The present case illustrates clearly the differences in the two concepts. The failure to distinguish properly between them may result in the introduction of inadmissible evidence, which is an error of law. That is what happened here.

As noted above, before evidence which falls into the "past recollection recorded" category is admitted, the conditions precedent to its admission are to be clearly satisfied. When the notes do not revive memory, as here, the notes or the recitation of them become the evidence. The witness cannot be effectively cross-examined on his or her recollection, because he or she has no recollection of the event. That is why, for the notes or what is in them to become evidence, stringent rules apply.

On the other hand, as Professor David M. Paciocco & Professor Lee Stuesser, *The Law of Evidence*, 3rd ed. (Toronto: Irwin Law, 2002) explain, a witness whose past memory has been revived, say by notes, is subject to proper cross- examination on his testimony: "As original testimony, the information supplied by the witness can be cross-examined on as effectively as any other original testimony" (at p. 336).

The trial judge ruled that the notes were only to be used to refresh memory. However, if the circumstances relating to the notes and Unger's reliance on them did meet the rigorous standards for admissibility under the "past recollection recorded" rule, Unger's evidence as to what was in his notes would still have been admissible. For this to occur, however, each of the four rules outlined by Wigmore (see *Fliss*, above, at para. 27) must be satisfied. In our opinion, a review of the transcript discloses that the first and third rules were not met.

. . .

In summary, there is insufficient testimony regarding how and when the notes were made and the Crown did not ask if they were a complete and accurate record of the discussions which they purport to summarize. The Crown did not establish definitively that the witness's memory was fresh when he made the notes, although Unger does say that the notes were made as he was talking to the accused. Further, at no point did the witness say expressly that he was certain that the notes were accurate when he made them. The most he said was that he attempted to take accurate notes. Threshold reliability was not established.

The trial judge inadvertently erred by allowing into the record the contents of Unger's notes under the guise of present memory revived. In so doing, evidence was let in that amounted to an unacceptable past recollection recorded. If Unger truly did not remember the events and facts about which he testified, and that seems to have been the case here, then his recitation amounted to inadmissible past recollection.

D) Applicability of Principles to this Case

The notes did not revive Unger's memory on the many matters dealt with in the notes on which he testified. The foundation for the use of the notes, purportedly to refresh his memory, fell short of what was required for that purpose. Although no precise formula need be followed, the substance of what is dealt with in the following extract from Thomas A. Mauet, Donald G. Casswell & Gordon P. Macdonald, *Fundamentals of Trial Technique*, 2nd Canadian ed. (Boston: Little Brown and Co., 1984), must be discernible from the evidence (at pp. 102-3):

A certain litany must be followed to establish the foundation for refreshing recollection . . .

. . .

The following elements must be demonstrated to establish a foundation for refreshing the recollection of a witness who is on the witness stand:

1.   Witness knows the facts, but has a memory lapse on the stand.

2.   Witness knows his report or other writing will refresh his memory.

3.   Witness is given and reads the pertinent part of his report or other writing.

4.   Witness states his memory has now been refreshed.

5.   Witness now testifies what he knows, without further aid of the report or other writing.

None of these elements was established by the Crown's evidence. Moreover, at no time did Unger say (nor was he asked) that looking at his notes would jog his memory. He simply had carte blanche to refer to the notes, and it is obvious that in many respects he could do no more than read, or repeat, what was written. The problem in this case is that the notes did not refresh his memory. Unger's evidence reciting matters recorded in the notes was inadmissible.

The trial judge was clearly aware of the two legal principles. He noted that the weight and probative value of Unger's refreshed memory would be considered later. He did not do so. In his brief decision, he simply accepted Unger's evidence entirely, and effectively treated his recitation of his notes as evidence of the same quality as all the other evidence. With respect, he did not do what was nicely explained by Mewett and Sankoff (at 13-14):

. . . Ultimately, after his or her own observation of the witness and after assessing how the witness answers questions on oral examination and cross-examination, the trial judge will have to rule on whether the evidence of the witness can be received as present memory revived or rejected as an attempt to circumvent the rules relating to past recollection recorded.

So, in our opinion, the evidence derived from the notes should not have been admitted under the present memory revived principle. For the reasons given earlier, it also failed to meet the standards for admissibility under the present recollection recorded principle.

We conclude that what was in Unger's notes formed an essential part of the evidence warranting conviction. The notes were, therefore, critical to the Crown's case. Permitting the evidence to be part of the record was highly prejudicial to the accused. Without the notes, Unger's evidence would have been decidedly weaker and more equivocal. The evidence was critical because, by itself, the videotape was neutral. What was needed was the contrast provided by Unger's evidence.

The Crown referred to the failure by defence counsel to object to the use to which the notes were put, but the failure cannot make admissible evidence which is inadmissible. (*R. v. D. (L.E.)*, [1989] 2 S.C.R. 111, at 126-27; *R. v. D. C.B.* (1994), 95 Man. R. (2d) 220 (C.A.), at para. 14.)

Finally, the Crown suggested that "this might be a case where s. 686(1)(b)(iii) [of the *Criminal Code*] ought to be applied." Given what has been said above, it is not possible to conclude that, notwithstanding the error of law discussed above, no substantial wrong or miscarriage of justice has occurred.

The evidence of Unger could be no more probative if a new trial was held. In all the circumstances, we would allow the appeal and order the entry of a verdict of acquittal.

R. v. B. (K.G.)
(1998), 125 C.C.C. (3d) 61 (Ont. C.A.)

The accused was charged with second degree murder. At his first trial he was acquitted. The Crown's appeal to the Court of Appeal was dismissed. On the Crown's further appeal to the Supreme Court of Canada, the appeal was allowed and a new trial directed. At that trial he was convicted of the included offence of manslaughter. On appeal the accused argued that the trial judge erred in his consideration of the evidence of the mothers of two accomplices of the accused because, before testifying, they had refreshed their memories from statements each had given to the police some considerable time after the events about which they were testifying. The accused argued that the two mothers had little or no independent recollection of the subject events and that their evidence should have been given little or no weight. The mothers each acknowledged that they had refreshed their memories from statements that they had given to the police, two and one-half and three and one-half years after the meeting at which they said that the accused admitted killing the deceased. This is not a case where either witness drew a blank in the witness box and sought to refresh her memory from a previous statement. They refreshed their memories well before the trial.

OSBORNE J.A. (AUSTIN and GOUDGE JJ.A. concurring):—

. . .

The trial judge meticulously reviewed the testimony of both Mrs. D. and Mrs. McD. before he accepted it and relied on it. He concluded that the fact that both witnesses had refreshed their memories from statements that they had given to the police could affect the weight of their evidence. Nevertheless, he found as a fact that both witnesses had an independent recollection of the relevant events and that their evidence was reliable. The evidence of both witnesses supports this conclusion. In the end, the trial judge confronted the defence position concerning the weight to be given to Mrs. D.'s and Mrs. McD.'s evidence by stating in his reasons for conviction:

> It is the position of the defence that Mrs. D. and Mrs. McD. were honest but unreliable witnesses. The defence submits that Mrs. D. and Mrs. McD. should not have refreshed their memories from statements which were given to the police a substantial time, two and a half and three and a half years respectively, after the events. While I believe that it is permissible for a witness to refresh his or her memory out of court from notes which were not made contemporaneously with the events about which he or she is testifying it is equally clear that doing so can, and does, affect the weight to be given to the witness's evidence.

I see nothing wrong with either witness reviewing her police statement before testifying. There is also nothing wrong with a defence counsel attempting to determine in cross-examination whether Mrs. D. or Mrs. McD. had a present memory of events about which she testified. What triggers recollection is not significant. This was long ago made clear in 1814 in *Henry v. Lee* (1814), 2 Chitty 124, where Ellenborough L.C.J. said:

> If upon looking at any document he can so far refresh his memory as to recollect a circumstance, it is sufficient; and it makes no difference that the memorandum is not written by himself, for it is not the memorandum that is the evidence but the recollection of the witness.

There is a danger in allowing the phrase "refreshing memory" to apply to those cases where the witness has no present memory, but is able to state that she accurately recorded a past event. In such cases, the witness has no present memory. The evidence, to the extent there is any, is the past record. When a witness refreshes her memory from some external source or event, she has a present memory, albeit one that has been refreshed; how reliable and truthful her recollection is, will be determined by the trier of fact, as happened here.

. . .

I see nothing wrong with the trial judge's approach to the evidence of Mrs. D. and Mrs. McD. He was alert to all factors that might bear upon the reliability of their evidence, including the fact that both had refreshed their memories from earlier statements that were not made contemporaneously with the events referred to in them. Clearly, the evidence given by Mrs. D. and Mrs. McD. was not their previous statements but their current recollection of the appellant's admission, as refreshed by their earlier review of their statements. Refreshing memory may take place before trial, as happened here, or in some cases, at trial. I would not give effect to this ground of appeal.

R. v. MATTIS
(1998), 20 C.R. (5th) 93 (Ont. Prov. Div.)

The accused was charged with trafficking in cocaine. The trial judge considered the evidence of the Crown and of the defence as to what had been observed prior to the accused's arrest.

BIGELOW J.:—

. . .

Officers Peters and Berrill whose evidence was clearly crucial to the Crown's case both stated that they had made up their notes of the events separately. In cross-examination they both admitted that their notes with respect to that incident were identical save and except for some short forms of words used by Officer Peters in her notebook. Neither were able to provide any explanation for how this could have occurred.

. . .

Obviously credibility is a major factor in this case. Mr. Rusonik argues that there are significant concerns with respect to the credibility of the police witnesses. As well Ms. Mattis has given evidence on her own behalf contradicting that of the police witnesses.

The only reasonable inference which can be drawn from the fact that the notebooks were identical is that one of the officers copied the notes of the other. In the recent decision of *R. v. Green*, [1998] O.J. No. 3598 (Ont. Ct. Gen. Div.). Malloy, J. commented on the importance of police officers preparing their notes independently:

> There are important reasons for requiring that officers prepare their notes independently. The purpose of notes made by a police officer is to record the observations made by that officer. The notes themselves are not admissible as evidence for the truth of their contents. An officer with relevant evidence to offer may testify at trial as to the act or observations made by him or her. However, that officer is not permitted to testify as to the information received from other officers for the purpose of proving their truth. Such evidence [is] hearsay and inadmissible.
>
> An officer's notes perform a valuable function at trial. It is usually many months, sometimes years, from the time of an occurrence to the time that the officer is called upon to testify at trial. Without the assistance of notes to refresh his or her memory, the evidence of the officer at trial would inevitably be sketchy at best. If the officer's notes are prepared without any indication of which is the officer's independent recollection and which is somebody else's recollection, there is every likelihood that that officer at trial will be "refreshing" his or her own memory with observations made by someone else. In effect, the officer will be giving hearsay evidence as if it was his or her own recollection rather than the observations of somebody else written into the notes without attribution.

The concerns raised by Malloy, J. are particularly relevant in the present case where it was clear that neither Officer Peters nor Officer Birrell had a clear recollection of the events and both were relying heavily on notes in giving their evidence.

Malloy, J. went on to comment on the effect of collaboration in the making of notes would have on the credibility of the testimony of police officers:

> The fact that officers have collaborated on their notes will always cause a trier of fact to give careful consideration to the reliability of that officer's evidence. There will, however, be situations in which such collaboration, although not good police practice, will not undermine the testimony of the officers. The extent to which the

collaboration renders the evidence of the officers' unreliable will depend on the circumstances of each case and the explanation given by the officers.

In the present case no explanation was offered as to how the notebooks could be identical. The obvious fact that the notebooks were copied combined with the lack of any explanation as to how this occurred and the lack of specific recollection by both officers has a significant impact on the reliability of the evidence. Absent confirmation of that evidence in material particulars, it would be unsafe to base a conviction on it.

. . .

As indicated above absent confirming evidence, it would be dangerous to base of finding of guilt in this case on the evidence of Officers Peters and Birrell. . . Accordingly, all three charges are dismissed.

In *Schaeffer v. Wood*[186] the Supreme Court of Canada recognized the public duty of a police officer "to prepare accurate, detailed, and comprehensive notes as soon as practicable after an investigation".[187] To ensure that that public duty is not compromised by an officer's private interest where he or she is the subject of an SIU investigation,[188] the Supreme Court held that officers do not have the right to consult with a lawyer prior to preparing their notes.

There are ethical restraints on the ability of counsel to communicate with a witness during his or her testimony. For example, in Ontario, Rule 4 of the *Rules of Professional Conduct* provides:

4.04 COMMUNICATION WITH WITNESSES GIVING EVIDENCE

4.04 Subject to the direction of the tribunal, the lawyer shall observe the following rules respecting communication with witnesses giving evidence:

(a) during examination-in-chief, the examining lawyer may discuss with the witness any matter that has not been covered in the examination up to that point,

(b) during examination-in-chief by another legal practitioner of a witness who is unsympathetic to the lawyer's cause, the lawyer not conducting the examination- in-chief may discuss the evidence with the witness,

(c) between completion of examination-in-chief and commencement of cross- examination of the lawyer's own witness, the lawyer ought not to discuss the evidence given in chief or relating to any matter introduced or touched on during the examination-in-chief,

(d) during cross-examination by an opposing legal practitioner, the witness's own lawyer ought not to have any conversation with the witness about the witness's evidence or any issue in the proceeding,

(e) between completion of cross-examination and commencement of re-examination, the lawyer who is going to re-examine the witness ought

---

[186]   2013 SCC 71, [2013] 3 S.C.R. 1053, 304 C.C.C. (3d) 445, 7 C.R. (7th) 59 (S.C.C.).
[187]   *Ibid.* at para. 67.
[188]   The Special Investigations Unit (SIU) is an independent agency in Ontario that investigates incidents of death or serious injury involving the police.

not to have any discussion about evidence that will be dealt with on re-examination,

(f)   during cross-examination by the lawyer of a witness unsympathetic to the cross- examiner's cause, the lawyer may discuss the witness's evidence with the witness,

(g)   during cross-examination by the lawyer of a witness who is sympathetic to that lawyer's cause, any conversations ought to be restricted in the same way as communications during examination-in-chief of one's own witness, and

(h)   during re-examination of a witness called by an opposing legal practitioner, if the witness is sympathetic to the lawyer's cause the lawyer ought not to discuss the evidence to be given by that witness during re-examination. The lawyer may, however, properly discuss the evidence with a witness who is adverse in interest.

PROBLEMS

Problem 1

The defendant is being tried for the theft of a quantity of household goods, the property of Ms. Farid. The defendant had been hired to move these goods from Ms. Farid's former residence to her new address and Ms. Farid maintains that some of her things never arrived. Ms. Farid has testified that as her chattels were being taken out of her house she made longhand notes and later, in anticipation of the trial, she copied these notes on her typewriter. The witness is being examined by the prosecutor:

Q.:   When you look at that typewritten sheet, does that refresh your recollection as to the items therein mentioned?

A.:   It does.

Q.:   In what way?

A.:   Well, every item here — for instance: "2 Chinese vases octagonal shape Satsuma," I remember.

Q.:   You remember these items individually as packed?

A.:   Individually, each one. I lived with these things, your Honour, I know them.

The Court: You lived with them yourself?

A.:   I did.

The Court: So when you look at that paper, it does refresh your recollection?

A.:   Absolutely.

Prosecutor: Your Honour I tender in evidence as proof of the items removed from Ms. Farid's home this typewritten list.

Do you have any objection to make? Do you have any questions to ask? Suppose the typewritten copy had been made by the investigating officer from Ms. Farid's notes: any difference? See *R. v. Kearns,* [1945] 2 W.W.R. 477 (B.C. C.A.).

Problem 2

A witness to a hit-and-run collision recorded the licence number of the fleeing automobile. The witness advised the investigating officer, who made a notation in his notebook; the witness heard the officer correctly broadcast the licence number on the police radio but never looked at his notebook. At trial, the witness, having lost her own note, seeks to refresh her memory from the officer's notebook. **How would you rule?** Compare *R. v. Davey* (1969), 68 W.W.R. 142 (B.C. S.C.). See also *R. v. Hanaway* (1980), 63 C.C.C. (2d) 44 (Ont. Dist. Ct.) and *R. v. Lamb,* [2007] N.J. No. 239 (P.C.).

Problem 3

You are a Crown prosecuting a domestic violence case. Court ends for the day while you are still in the middle of your examination-in-chief of the complainant. That night, she is in your office for moral support. You would like to take the opportunity to discuss with her evidence that you have not yet covered. **Can you?**

Problem 4

Your client in a medical malpractice case is being examined for discovery by the defendant's lawyer. Before lunch, your client advises you that she would like to speak with you privately. **Can you meet with her?**

(c) Adoption

When does a witness adopt a statement given on an earlier occasion?

R. v. MCCARROLL
(2008) 238 C.C.C. (3d) 404, 61 C.R. (6th) 353 (Ont. C.A.)

The accused was charged with second degree murder. The victim was beaten to death with a baseball bat during a fight between two groups of friends. Kidd was part of the accused's group of friends. The issue at trial was who dealt the fatal blow. In a videotaped statement and at the accused's preliminary inquiry, Kidd put the accused in possession of a baseball bat. At trial, she did not remember these details. She did say, however, that she told the truth at the preliminary inquiry. The trial judge instructed the jury that Kidd had adopted her statements. The accused was convicted. On appeal, the conviction was overturned. The Court of Appeal held that the trial judge had erred.

EPSTEIN J.A. (for the Court):

Did Kidd adopt her previous statement?

38 I agree with the appellant's argument that the trial judge erred in instructing the jury that Kidd adopted the contents of her prior statement given she had no present recollection of the events it described.

39 Where a witness adopts a prior statement as true, the statement becomes part of that witness' evidence at trial and is admissible for its truth: *R. v. Deacon* (1947), 89 C.C.C. 1 (SCC), at p. 4. The question becomes whether the witness adopts the prior statement "as being the truth as she now sees it": *R. v. McInroy* (1979), 42 C.C.C. (2d) 481, at p. 498. As this court said in *R. v. Toten* (1993), 83 C.C.C. (3d) 5 (C.A.), at p. 23, in order for a prior statement to be incorporated into trial testimony, or adopted':

> The witness must be able to attest to the accuracy of the statement based on their present memory of the facts referred to in that statement. In this sense, adoption refers to both the witness's acknowledgment that he or she made the prior statement and the witness's assertion that his or her memory while testifying accords with the contents of the prior statement.

See *R. v. Tat* (1997) 117 C.C.C. (3d) 481 (Ont. C.A.), at para. 28, and *R. v. Atikian* (1990) 62 C.C.C. (3d) 357 (Ont. C.A.), at p. 364.

40 The determination of whether the witness adopts all or part of the statement must be made by the trier of fact, in this instance, the jury. However, as a condition of admissibility the trial judge must be satisfied that there is an evidentiary basis on which the trier of fact could conclude that the witness adopted the statement. The witness must acknowledge having made the statement and, based on present memory of the events referred to in the statement, verify the accuracy of its contents.

41 Kidd did acknowledge having made the statement and did say that she was likely telling the truth when she made it. However, given her selective memory of the events surrounding Prebtani's death, Kidd was, at best, only able to vouch for the accuracy of the statement based on circumstances surrounding its recording. She could not continue to assert the truth of its contents: see *Toten* at p. 24.

42 The trial judge committed two errors by directing the jury that Kidd had adopted her statement. First, there was no evidentiary basis for that conclusion. Adoption was simply not possible in these circumstances. Second, even if there was an evidentiary basis, it was a matter for the jury to decide whether or not Kidd adopted what she said in her interview with the police as part of her trial testimony and imprinted it with her trial oath. The trial judge usurped a function that was within the exclusive purview of the jury.

43 On appeal, the Crown advanced three arguments that were not advanced at trial. First, what Kidd said was tantamount to adoption. Second, the

statements could have been admitted under the hearsay exception for past recollections recorded. Third, under the principled approach to the admission of hearsay evidence the statement would have been admitted.

44 Before this court, the Crown submits that under an expanded notion of the concept of adoption, the portions of the videotaped statement were properly before the jury for the truth of their contents.

45 Relying on *R. v. C.C.F.* (1997) 120 C.C.C. (3d) 225 (SCC), the Crown argues that the application of the principled approach in cases involving prior videotaped statements where the witness is available for cross-examination has substantially modified the orthodoxy of the traditional cases.

46 While the principled approach to the law of evidence continues to cultivate changes in how the court receives evidence, particularly in relation to the reception of hearsay, I do not accept the Crown's submission that these changes have eliminated the need for an adult witness to have some recollection of the events contained in the statement.

47 At issue in *C.C.F.* were the requirements for the admissibility of a videotaped statement under s. 715.1 of the *Criminal Code*, R.S.C. 1985, c. C-46, a statutory exception to the hearsay rule that permits an out-of-court statement to be admitted at the trials of certain enumerated offences if the complainant is a child under the age of eighteen and if the video was made within a reasonable time following the alleged offences. The court held that the word "adopts" in s. 715.1 should be given a meaning that advances the dual purposes of the section; to create a record of what is likely to be the witness' best recollection of the events and to reduce the harm to a child of further participation in court proceedings.

48 To this end the legislators incorporated several factors into the section to provide the requisite reliability that traditionally comes from the witness' adopting the statement under oath. First, the statement must be made at a time reasonably proximate to the events in issue. Second, the statement must describe the acts complained of. Third, the child must be given the opportunity to attest to the fact that he or she was trying to tell the truth when the statement was recorded. As made clear in *C.C.F.*, the fact that a child does not have a present memory of the events described is not a barrier to the admission of the statement. In such circumstances, the trier of fact must have an opportunity to watch the entire videotaped statement — providing an opportunity to judge the child's demeanour.

49 The decision in *C.C.F.* does not affect the law as it applies to the adoption of out-of-court statements of adults. Quite the opposite. It reinforces the importance of adopting a statement under oath. Cory J. for the court makes it very clear that the traditional tests for adoption still apply outside the s. 715.1 context — the guarantees of reliability built into s. 715.1 make the strict

adoption test unnecessary in relation to the evidence of children: see *C.C.F.* at para. 40.

. . .

Appeal allowed and new trial ordered.

(d) Cross-examination

The purposes of cross-examination, its place in our adversarial system, its scope, and its control may perhaps best be appreciated by examining a few classic quotations:

Professor Wigmore:

> For two centuries past, the policy of the Anglo-American system of Evidence has been to regard the necessity of testing by cross-examination as a vital feature of the law. The belief that no safeguard for testing the value of human statements is comparable to that furnished by cross-examination, and the conviction that no statement (unless by special exception) should be used as testimony until it has been probed and sublimated by that test, has found increasing strength in lengthening experience.
>
> Not even the abuses, the mishandlings, and the puerilities which are so often found associated with cross-examination have availed to nullify its value. It may be that in more than one sense it takes the place in our system which torture occupied in the mediaeval system of the civilians. Nevertheless, it is beyond any doubt the greatest legal engine ever invented for the discovery of truth. . . If we omit political considerations of broader range, then cross-examination, not trial by jury, is the great and permanent contribution of the Anglo-American system of law to improved methods of trial-procedure.[189]

Professor McCormick:

> For two centuries, common law judges and lawyers have regarded the opportunity of cross-examination as an essential safeguard of the accuracy and completeness of testimony, and they have insisted that the opportunity is a right and not a mere privilege.[190]

Mr. Justice Dennistoun:

> Cross-examination is a powerful weapon of defence, and often its sole weapon. The denial of full opportunity to sift and probe the witnesses of the opposing side has always been regarded with extreme disfavour by British Courts of justice.
>
> Cross-examination may be insisted on for a number of purposes: First, to bring out facts as to which a witness has not been asked to testify, or is anxious to conceal; Second, to show that the witness is unworthy of belief; Third, to adduce facts in mitigation of sentence; Fourth, to adduce facts which in the case of a guilty person may minimize his offence and assist in the rehabilitation of his character.

. . .

---

[189] 5 Wigmore, *Evidence* (Chad. Rev.), s. 1367.
[190] McCormick, *Evidence*, 2nd ed. at 43.

> That full cross-examination of an opposite witness should be permitted by the trial Judge is well settled. The Judge may check cross-examination if it become irrelevant, or prolix, or insulting, but so long as it may fairly be applied to the issue, or touches the credibility of the witness it should not be excluded.[191]

Notice particularly that the cross-examiner is not confined to asking questions about matters in issue which arose in examination-in-chief. Notice as well that the trial judge has some discretion to control the questioning if it is unduly lengthy or insulting.[192] Aside from the trial judge's discretion there is an obligation on counsel as well to have concern for the limited time and resources available to the court and also to have some respect for the witness as a fellow human being. As Lord Sankey noted:

> It is right to make due allowance for the irritation caused by the strain and stress of a long and complicated case, but a protracted and irrelevant cross-examination not only adds to the cost of litigation, but is a waste of public time. Such a cross-examination becomes indefensible when it is conducted, as it was in this case, without restraint and without the courtesy and consideration which a witness is entitled to expect in a court of law. It is not sufficient for the due administration of justice to have a learned, patient and impartial judge. Equally with him, the solicitors who prepare the case and the counsel who present it to the court are taking part in the great task of doing justice between man and man.[193]

Well-prepared and competent counsel should always have a purpose in mind in cross-examining. Not all cross-examination is destructive where the major aim is to impeach (i.e., to seek to destroy credibility). In many cases the aim is merely to use cross-examination for another purpose such as to clarify, pin the witness down, or elicit other evidence. So, for example, counsel who called the witness elicits three things in chief. Opposing counsel seeks to elicit three other things the witness observed, which material supports opposing counsel's case.[194]

Is counsel entitled to put a question on cross-examination although he or she is not then in a position to prove the same by other evidence?

R. v. LYTTLE
(2004), 17 C.R. (6th) 1, 180 C.C.C. (3d) 476 (S.C.C.)

The accused was charged with robbery, assault, kidnapping and possession of a weapon. The victim was brutally beaten by five men with baseball bats. The victim said he was assaulted so that his assailants could recover a $7,000 chain that they thought he had stolen. The accused alleged that the victim was hurt during a drug deal gone awry and accused him in

---

[191]   *R. v. Anderson*, [1938] 3 D.L.R. 317 (Man. C.A.) at 319-320. And see *R. v. Roulette* (1972), 7 C.C.C. (2d) 244 (Man. Q.B.) and *R. v. Makow* (1973), 13 C.C.C. (2d) 167 (B.C. C.A.).

[192]   See *R. v. Shearing*, [2002] 3 S.C.R. 33.

[193]   *Mechanical & Gen. Inventions Co. v. Austin* (1935), 153 L.T. 153 (H.L.) at 157, cited with approval in *R. v. Rowbotham (No. 5)* (1977), 2 C.R. (3d) 293 (Ont. Co. Ct.).

[194]   See generally Younger, *The Art of Cross-examination* (Chicago: A.B.A., Litigation Section, 1976).

order to protect associates in a drug ring. Early on in the investigation, the police believed that the offences were committed against the victim in the context of a drug deal. The victim had a drug conviction record and certain features of the offence suggested "drug gangsterism". At trial, the Crown refused to call as its own witnesses the officers who formed the early theory. The trial judge did not permit defence counsel to put the drug transaction theory to witnesses, unless she was prepared to call evidence in support of that theory. Defence counsel undertook to call two officers, and was permitted to cross-examine other witnesses on the drug theory. After the cross-examinations, counsel sought to resile from the undertaking to call the two police officers, attempting to preserve the accused's right to address the jury last. The accused was forced to call the officers, who confirmed that the drug theory had been an initial operating theory. The accused was not permitted to address the jury last and was convicted. The Court of Appeal found that the trial judge unduly constrained defence counsel's cross-examination, but applied the curative proviso in s. 686(1)(b)(iii) of the *Criminal Code*. The appeal by the accused from his conviction was allowed and a new trial ordered.

MAJOR and FISH JJ. for the Court: —

. . .

The right of an accused to cross-examine prosecution witnesses without significant and unwarranted constraint is an essential component of the right to make a full answer and defence. Commensurate with its importance, the right to cross-examine is now recognized as being protected by ss. 7 and 11(d) of the Canadian Charter of Rights and Freedoms. The right of cross-examination must therefore be jealously protected and broadly construed. But it must not be abused. Counsel are bound by the rules of relevancy and barred from resorting to harassment, misrepresentation, repetitiousness or, more generally, from putting questions whose prejudicial effect outweighs their probative value. [Citations omitted.]

Just as the right of cross-examination itself is not absolute, so too are its limitations. Trial judges enjoy, in this as in other aspects of the conduct of a trial, a broad discretion to ensure fairness and to see that justice is done—and seen to be done. In the exercise of that discretion, they may sometimes think it right to relax the rules of relevancy somewhat, or to tolerate a degree of repetition that would in other circumstances be unacceptable.

. . .

This appeal concerns the constraint on cross-examination arising from the ethical and legal duties of counsel when they allude in their questions to disputed and unproven facts. Is a good faith basis sufficient or is counsel bound, as the trial judge held in this case, to provide an evidentiary foundation for the assertion?

Unlike the trial judge, and with respect, we believe that a question can be put to a witness in cross-examination regarding matters that need not be proved independently, provided that counsel has a good faith basis for putting the question. It is not uncommon for counsel to believe what is in fact true, without being able to prove it otherwise than by cross-examination; nor is it uncommon for reticent witnesses to concede suggested facts—in the mistaken belief that they are already known to the cross-examiner and will therefore, in any event, emerge.

In this context, a "good faith basis" is a function of the information available to the cross-examiner, his or her belief in its likely accuracy, and the purpose for which it is used. Information falling short of admissible evidence may be put to the witness. In fact, the information may be incomplete or uncertain, provided the cross-examiner does not put suggestions to the witness recklessly or that he or she knows to be false. The cross-examiner may pursue any hypothesis that is honestly advanced on the strength of reasonable inference, experience or intuition. The purpose of the question must be consistent with the lawyer's role as an officer of the court: to suggest what counsel genuinely thinks possible on known facts or reasonable assumptions is in our view permissible; to assert or to imply in a manner that is calculated to mislead is in our view improper and prohibited.

In *Bencardino*, Jessup J.A. applied the English rule to this effect:

> Whatever may be said about the forensic impropriety of the three incidents in cross- examination, I am unable to say any illegality was involved in them. As Lord Radcliffe said in *Fox v. General Medical Council*, [1960] 1 W.L.R. 1017 at p. 1023:
>
>> "An advocate is entitled to use his discretion as to whether to put questions in the course of cross- examination which are based on material which he is not in a position to prove directly. The penalty is that, if he gets a denial or some answer that does not suit him, the answer stands against him for what it is worth."

More recently, in *R. v. Shearing*, [2002] 3 S.C.R. 33, 2002 SCC 58, 165 C.C.C. (3d) 225, 214 D.L.R. (4th) 215, while recognizing the need for exceptional restraint in sexual assault cases, Binnie J. reaffirmed, at paras. 121-22, the general rule that "in most instances the adversarial process allows wide latitude to cross-examiners to resort to unproven assumptions and innuendo in an effort to crack the untruthful witness". As suggested at the outset, however, wide latitude does not mean unbridled licence, and cross-examination remains subject to the requirements of good faith, professional integrity and the other limitations set out above.

A trial judge must balance the rights of an accused to receive a fair trial with the need to prevent unethical cross-examination. There will thus be instances where a trial judge will want to ensure that "counsel [is] not merely taking a random shot at a reputation imprudently exposed or asking a groundless question to waft an unwarranted innuendo into the jury box". See *Michelson v. United States*, 335 U.S. 469 (1948) at p. 481, per Jackson J. Where a question implies the existence of a disputed factual predicate that is manifestly tenuous or suspect, a trial judge may properly take appropriate steps, by conducting a voir dire or otherwise, to seek and obtain counsel's assurance that a good faith basis exists for putting the question. If the judge is satisfied in this regard and the question is not otherwise prohibited, counsel should be permitted to put the question to the witness.

As long as counsel has a good faith basis for asking an otherwise permissible question in cross-examination, the question should be allowed. In our view, no distinction need be made between expert and lay witnesses within the broad scope of this general principle.

Lyttle is an important decision on the scope of cross-examination and control by trial judges on counsel who abuse their position as officers of the court. The Supreme Court has announced a revised regime. The Court declares that cross-examination is permissible on unproven facts without evidentiary foundation subject only to good faith assurance from counsel.

The Court revises its earlier decision in *R. v. Howard*,[195] where Lamer J., for a 3-1 majority of the Supreme Court, held that

> It is not open to the examiner or cross-examiner to put as a fact, or even a hypothetical fact, that which is not and will not become part of the case as admissible evidence.

The Court in *Lyttle* claimed that the ratio of *Howard* had been "misunderstood and misapplied". According to Major and Fish JJ., Lamer J.'s remarks only applied to cross-examination on evidence that was otherwise inadmissible. In *Howard*, the Crown sought to cross-examine an expert on the significance of an inadmissible guilty plea by a co-accused. There was, held the Supreme Court in *Lyttle*, a "crucial difference" between cross-examination on inadmissible evidence and cross-examination upon unproven facts (para. 61). The Court concluded that, as long as counsel has a good faith basis for the question, cross-examination should be allowed, and that no distinction is to be drawn between expert and lay witnesses within the broad scope of this general principle (para. 66).

Lyttle is a decision of enormous import for both civil and criminal trials. In seeking to balance the right to cross-examination and the need for judicial control against abuse by counsel, the Court clearly comes down on the side of favouring full cross-examination. It is of interest that the judgment is authored by two justices with substantial experience as trial counsel.

The Court could have been more forthright in its consideration of *Howard*. The Court essentially overruled *Howard* and should have said so. Justice Lamer's remarks were certainly clear and capable of broad application: see, for example, Proulx and Layton, *Ethics and Canadian Criminal Law*[196] and decisions referred to by the Supreme Court in *Lyttle*. *Howard* has been responsible for confusion and inconsistency.

Reasonable belief is the long-accepted standard for cross-examination in the U.K. and was adopted by the B.C. Court of Appeal in *R. v. Wilson*.[197] **Is the *Lyttle* test of "good faith" any different? Will it prove difficult for trial**

---

[195] [1989] 1 S.C.R. 1337.
[196] (Toronto: Irwin Law, 2001) at 677.
[197] (1983), 5 C.C.C. (3d) 61 (B.C. C.A.).

judges to police the good faith standard especially given that it can be based on intuition and counsel may mount claims of privilege? As a practical matter, most judicial control is still likely to be exercised by relying on the overriding discretion recognized in a line by the Supreme Court in *Lyttle* to exclude evidence where probative force is exceeded by prejudicial value. The Court does not say, as it did in *R. v. Shearing*,[198] that defence evidence should only be excluded where prejudicial effect substantially outweighs its probative value.

R. v. R. (A.J.).

(1994), 94 C.C.C. (3d) 168 (Ont. C.A.)

The accused was convicted of incest with his daughter and granddaughter, sexual assault and threatening. One of his grounds of appeal concerned the prejudicial effect of the cross-examination of the accused conducted by Crown counsel. He alleged Crown counsel had argued with and demeaned the accused in cross-examining him; inserted editorial comment and gave evidence while cross-examining him; called upon the accused to comment on the veracity of Crown witnesses; and conducted an improper attack on the accused's character.

DOHERTY J.A. (OSBORNE and LASKIN JJ.A. concurring):—

. . .

The Cross-examination of the Appellant

Counsel for the appellant submits that Crown counsel's cross-examination of the appellant resulted in a miscarriage of justice. He does not base this contention on any isolated feature of the cross-examination or any specific line of questioning, but contends that the overall conduct and tenor of the cross-examination was so improper and prejudicial to the appellant, that it rendered the trial unfair and resulted in a miscarriage of justice. This argument is becoming a familiar one in this court.

Crown counsel conducted an aggressive and exhaustive 141-page cross-examination of the appellant. She was well prepared and well armed for that cross-examination. Crown counsel is entitled, indeed in some cases expected, to conduct a vigorous cross-examination of an accused. Effective cross-examination of an accused serves the truth-finding function as much as does effective cross- examination of a complainant.

There are, however, well-established limits on cross-examination. Some apply to all witnesses, others only to the accused. Isolated transgressons of those limits may be of little consequence on appeal. Repeated improprieties during the cross-examination of an accused are, however, a very different matter. As the improprieties mount, the cross-examination may cross over the line from the aggressive to the abusive. When that line is crossed, the danger of a miscarriage of justice is very real. If improper cross-examination of an

---

[198]   (2002), 2 C.R. (6th) 213 (S.C.C.).

accused prejudices that accused in his defence or is so improper as to bring the administration of justice into disrepute, an appellate court must intervene.

After careful consideration of the entire cross-examination of the appellant in the context of the issues raised by his examination-in-chief and the conduct of the entire trial, I am satisfied that the cross-examination must be characterized as abusive and unfair.

From the outset of the cross-examination, Crown counsel adopted a sarcastic tone with the accused and repeatedly inserted editorial commentary into her questions. I count at least eight such comments in the first eight pages of the cross-examination. During that part of the cross-examination, Crown counsel referred to one answer given by the appellant as "incredible". She repeatedly asked the appellant if he "wanted the jury to believe that one too". When questioned as to how he met T., the appellant said he was told by a friend that a relative would be coming to see him, whereupon Crown counsel remarked "so I guess you were expecting some long lost cousin in the old country". After the appellant had described his reaction to being told by T. that she was his daughter, Crown counsel sarcastically said "gee, I guess everybody would react the way you did".

Crown counsel's approach from the very beginning of the cross-examination was calculated to demean and humiliate the appellant. She persisted in that approach throughout. For example, after the appellant said that he had allowed T. to move in with him shortly after they had met, Crown counsel said "you are just a really nice guy". At another point, she said, "tell me sir, do fathers usually have sexual intercourse with their daughters". Still later, after the appellant had testified that his girlfriend had left him but had told him that she wished to come back, Crown counsel said "you just have all these women running after you wanting to come back".

These are but a few of a great many instances where Crown counsel used the pretence of questioning the appellant to demonstrate her contempt for him and the evidence he was giving before the jury. No counsel can abuse any witness. This self-evident interdiction applies with particular force to Crown counsel engaged in the cross-examination of an accused.

The tone adopted by Crown counsel is not the only problem with her cross-examination. Crown counsel repeatedly gave evidence and stated her opinion during cross-examination. She also engaged in extensive argument with the appellant. For example, when the appellant gave contradictory explanations in the course of cross-examination, Crown counsel announced "you were lying", and when the appellant questioned Crown counsel's description of T. as "your victim" Crown counsel replied "certainly she is". Still later, after Crown counsel had very effectively cross-examined the appellant as to when he had learned that T. was his daughter, she proclaimed "you are playing games with me, with this jury". She followed that comment with the admonition "let's try and be honest". In several instances, the cross-examination degenerated into pure argument between the appellant and Crown counsel. After one lengthy exchange, Crown counsel announced: "It is hard to keep up with you sir because you keep changing your story".

Statements of counsel's personal opinion have no place in a cross-examination. Nor is cross-examination of the appellant the time or place for argument.

Crown counsel also repeatedly called upon the appellant to comment on the veracity of Crown witnesses and to explain why these witnesses had fabricated their evidence. Crown counsel pursued this line of questioning in relation to at least four Crown witnesses. With respect to some of the witnesses, the questions were repeated at different points in the cross-examination. For example, Crown counsel asked the appellant whether J. had "totally fabricated that evidence" and then asked him "why that little girl totally fabricated that evidence". After Crown counsel had put the appellant in the position of calling four of the Crown witnesses liars, the trial judge intervened and suggested that the questions were improper. Crown counsel returned to that form of questioning on at least one occasion following the trial judge's admonition.

The impropriety of these questions cannot be doubted and Crown counsel in this court acknowledged that they were improper. Crown counsel submitted that although the questions were improper, they caused no prejudice. She observed, quite accurately, that the defence implicitly involved an assertion that the Crown witnesses and, in particular, T., had concocted the allegations against the appellant.

The nature of the defence advanced will impact on the harm, if any, caused by this type of questioning. Despite the defence advanced, I cannot say that the repeated resort to this technique, whereby the appellant was placed in the position of accusing others, did not prejudice him in the eyes of the jury. By means of these improper questions, Crown counsel was able to paint the appellant as a callous accuser ready to charge virtually everyone, including a terrified, emotionally distraught young child, with deliberately fabricating evidence against him. These improper questions also forced the appellant to offer explanations for the allegedly false testimony offered by the Crown witnesses. In the case of J. and T., the explanations only served to open further fertile grounds for cross-examination.

I am also driven to the conclusion that at many points in the cross-examination, Crown counsel conducted what amounted to an improper and potentially prejudicial attack on the appellant's character and lifestyle. Given the allegations, it was inevitable and essential that the jury learn something of the appellant's sordid lifestyle and character to assess the charges before them properly. The appellant's decision to testify also meant that his lengthy criminal record would be placed before the jury. These conditions created a real danger that the jury could convict based on their assessment of the appellant as a despicable and evil man, rather than on a finding that the Crown had proven any or all of the charges beyond a reasonable doubt. Crown counsel's cross- examination significantly increased this danger.

There are numerous instances in the cross-examination when the questions went beyond the bounds of relevancy and legitimate credibility impeachment and became an attempt to highlight the appellant's bad character and deviant lifestyle. The appellant was cross-examined about whether he had filed income tax returns. He was also questioned about the criminal records of his associates and about his attitudes, as "a former drug dealer", to T.'s use of prescription pills. Still later, Crown counsel asked the appellant about his respect "for the law and court orders". Crown counsel also cross-examined the appellant to show that he was sexually promiscuous and had no sense of responsibility to any of the women with whom he had been involved during his lifetime. At another point in the cross- examination, she referred to the appellant as "a jailhouse lawyer".

The appellant was also cross-examined about the paternity of C., T.'s young son. He denied that he was the father. Crown counsel then gave evidence to the effect that C. could not be adopted because it was believed that he was the product of an incestuous relationship. She then asked the appellant why he did not submit to a blood test so that the question of C.'s paternity could be cleared up and C. could become eligible for adoption. None of this had anything to do with the allegations against the appellant and could only serve to inflame the jury further against the appellant. Defence counsel at trial objected to the question on the basis that it had no evidentiary foundation. The trial judge upheld the objection on the basis of relevancy, however, Crown counsel persisted, asking:

> If you knew you weren't the father of this child, why didn't you ask to take a blood test to show you weren't?

Cross-examination on this issue continued for several more questions. I can see only one purpose to these questions. Crown counsel wanted to demonstrate that the appellant did not have the decency to take the steps necessary to make C. eligible for adoption.

Defence counsel (not Mr. Campbell) did, at a recess, suggest that some of Crown counsel's questions were bringing out "discreditable conduct not covered by the indictment". He referred specifically to the questions about the income tax returns. Crown counsel responded that counsel should object when the questions were asked "not some two hours later". The trial judge made no ruling and when the jury returned Crown counsel continued her cross-examination in the same manner. Crown counsel also asked the appellant on more than one occasion about conversations he had had with his lawyer. These questions were improper in that they invited the appellant to disclose privileged communications or risk appearing non-responsive to the questions. The questions were also totally irrelevant. Defence counsel did eventually object to this type of questioning and Crown counsel did not pursue it. Crown counsel did, however, continue to ask the appellant questions about whether he intended to call certain persons as witnesses. Crown counsel would know full well that such decisions were for counsel and not the appellant. It was unfair to ask the appellant questions which Crown counsel knew he could not answer.

It must be acknowledged that the appellant was a difficult witness and to some extent contributed to the tone of the cross-examination through his own attitude and refusal on several occasions to answer directly the questions put to him. The vast majority of what I have characterized as improper cross-examination was not objected to at trial. Both of these considerations are relevant when deciding the propriety and potential prejudicial effect of a cross-examination. The failure of counsel to object does not, however, give Crown counsel carte blanche at trial or immunize the cross-examination from appellate scrutiny.

Cases like this, where the allegations are particularly sordid, the complainants particularly sympathetic and the accused particularly disreputable, provide a severe test of our criminal justice system. It is very difficult in such cases to hold the scales of justice in balance and to provide the accused with the fair trial to which he or she is entitled. By her cross-examination, Crown counsel skewed that delicate balance. The cross-examination, considered in its totality and in the context of the entire trial, prejudiced the appellant in his defence and significantly undermined the appearance of the fairness of the trial.

. . .

The cross-examination destroyed the necessary appearance of fairness in the trial and resulted in a miscarriage of justice. The strength of the Crown's case becomes irrelevant in determining the appropriate disposition and s. 686(1)(b)(iii) has no application. The miscarriage of justice lies in the conduct of the proceedings and not in the verdict arrived at by the jury. All of the convictions must be set aside and a new trial ordered on all of those charges.

In *R. v. T. (A.)*,[199] the accused was charged with attempted murder and conspiracy to commit murder after his three children, aged 11, 14 and 16 years, unsuccessfully attempted to drown their mother in a bathtub. The Crown's theory was that the accused was the mastermind behind the murder plot and that he used his religious beliefs to influence the children to kill their mother. The Crown's address to the jury included the following:

> I ask you to consider the Jonestown massacre, November 1978. Over 900 people, men, women and children, died in a mass suicide ... in Jonestown, Guyana ... at the instructions of cult leader Jim Jones.

> Consider the brutal murders committed by the members of the cult of Charles Manson in the late 1960's.

> Perhaps more timely, as as [defence counsel] himself alluded to, consider that since September 11th, 2001, and even before, on almost a daily occurrence we've heard of terrible suicide bombings where religious zealots strap on explosive vests and blow themselves up in an effort to kill innocent women and children.

> We can even reflect on a much broader scale to the involvement of the German people in the rise and support of the Nazis of the Third Reich who killed millions upon millions of innocent people in the war years and before.

The jury convicted the accused but the Ontario Court of Appeal allowed the appeal against conviction on the basis that the Crown's remarks, which were not addressed or corrected in the trial judge's charge to the jury, rendered the trial unfair.

---

[199]   2015 ONCA 65, 124 O.R. (3d) 161, 18 C.R. (7th) 420 (Ont. C.A.).

R. v. OSOLIN
[1993] 4 S.C.R. 595, 86 C.C.C. (3d) 481, 26 C.R. (4th) 1 (S.C.C.)

CORY J. —

A complainant should not be unduly harassed and pilloried to the extent of becoming a victim of an insensitive judicial system. Yet a fair balance must be achieved so that the limitations on the cross-examination of complainants in sexual assault cases do not interfere with the right of the accused to a fair trial.

. . .

The reasons in *Seaboyer* make it clear that eliciting evidence from a complainant for the purpose of encouraging inferences pertaining to consent or the credibility of rape victims which are based on groundless myths and fantasized stereotypes is improper. A number of rape myths have in the past improperly formed the background for considering evidentiary issues in sexual assault trials. These include the false concepts that: women cannot be raped against their will; only "bad girls" are raped; anyone not clearly of "good character" is more likely to have consented. (See C. A. MacKinnon, *Toward a Feminist Theory of the State* (1989), at p. 175; L. L. Holmstrom and A. W. Burgess, *The Victim of Rape: Institutional Reactions* (1983); and *Gender Equality in the Canadian Justice System, supra*, at p. 18.) In *Seaboyer, supra*, McLachlin J. observed that these myths were now discredited at p. 604:

> Evidence that the complainant had relations with the accused and others was routinely presented (and accepted by judges and juries) as tending to make it more likely that the complainant had consented to the alleged assault and as undermining her credibility generally. These inferences were based not on facts, but on the myths that unchaste women were more likely to consent to intercourse and in any event, were less worthy of belief. These twin myths are now discredited.

It might be helpful to summarize the principles that can be taken from *Seaboyer* with regard to the cross-examination of complainants. Generally, a complainant may be cross-examined for the purpose of eliciting evidence relating to consent and pertaining to credibility when the probative value of that evidence is not substantially outweighed by the danger of unfair prejudice which might flow from it. Cross-examination for the purposes of showing consent or impugning credibility which relies upon "rape myths" will always be more prejudicial than probative. Such evidence can fulfil no legitimate purpose and would therefore be inadmissible to go to consent or credibility. Cross-examination which has as its aim to elicit such evidence should not be permitted. It will be up to the trial judge to take into consideration all of the evidence presented at the *voir dire* and to then determine if there is a legitimate purpose for the proposed cross-examination.

In each case the trial judge must carefully balance the fundamentally important right of the accused to a fair trial against the need for reasonable protection of a complainant, particularly where the purpose of the cross-examination may be directed to "rape myths". In order to assure the fairness of the trial, where contentious issues arise as to the cross-examination of the complainant a *voir dire* should be held. In the *voir dire* it will be necessary to show either by way of submissions of counsel, affidavit or *viva voce* evidence that the proposed cross-examination is appropriate. If at the conclusion of the *voir dire* the cross-examination is permitted then the jury must be advised as to the proper use that can be made of the evidence derived from the cross-examination. As a general rule the trial of an accused on a charge of sexual assault need not and should not become an occasion for putting the complainant's lifestyle and reputation on trial. The exception to this rule will arise in those relatively rare cases where the complainant may be fraudulent, cruelly mischievous or maliciously mendacious.

R. v. MILLS
[1999] 3 S.C.R. 668, 139 C.C.C. (3d) 321, 28 C.R. (5th) 207 (S.C.C.)

MCLACHLIN and IACOBUCCI JJ. —

90 Equality concerns must also inform the contextual circumstances . . . of full answer and defence . . . In this respect, an appreciation of myths and stereotypes in the context of sexual violence is essential to delineate properly the boundaries of full answer and defence. As we have already discussed, the right to make full answer and defence does not include the right to information that would only distort the truth-seeking goal of the trial process. . . . The accused is not permitted to "whack the complainant" through the use of stereotypes regarding victims of sexual assault.

R. v. SHEARING
2002 SCC 58, [2002] 3 S.C.R. 33, 165 C.C.C. (3d) 225, 2 C.R. (6th) 213 (S.C.C.)

BINNIE J. —

76 It has been increasingly recognized in recent years, however, that cross-examination techniques in sexual assault cases that seek to put the complainant on trial rather than the accused are abusive and distort rather than enhance the search for truth. Various limitations have been imposed. One of these limits is the privacy interest of the complainant, which is not to be needlessly sacrificed.

. . .

121 While in most instances the adversarial process allows wide latitude to cross-examiners to resort to unproven assumptions and innuendo in an effort to crack the untruthful witness, sexual assault cases pose particular dangers. *Seaboyer, Osolin* and *Mills* all make the point that these cases should be decided without resort to folk tales about how abuse victims are expected by people who have never suffered abuse to react to the trauma: *Mills, supra*, at paras. 72, 117-19; *R. v. D.D.*, [2000] 2 S.C.R. 275, 2000 SCC 43 (CanLII), at para. 63.

122 This does not turn persons accused of sexual abuse into second-class litigants. It simply means that the defence has to work with facts rather than rely on innuendoes and wishful assumptions. This means, in turn, that the defence should not be prevented from getting at the facts. As L'Heureux-Dubé J. wrote in *O'Connor*, *supra*, at para. 124:

> Although the defence must be free to demonstrate, without resort to stereotypical lines of reasoning, that such information is actually relevant to a live issue at trial, it would mark the triumph of stereotype over logic if courts and lawyers were simply to assume such relevance to exist, without requiring any evidence to this effect whatsoever. [Emphasis in original.]

R. v. SCHMALTZ

2015 ABCA 4, 320 C.C.C. (3d) 159, 17 C.R. (7th) 278 (Alta. C.A.)

The accused was charged with sexual assault of the complainant in her daughter's home. He claimed that the sexual activity was consensual. During the course of the trial, the accused applied for a mistrial on the ground of a reasonable apprehension of bias. He alleged that the trial judge had pre-judged the credibility of the complainant and improperly interfered with cross-examination of her. The trial judge dismissed the application and convicted the accused. He appealed. A majority of the Alberta Court of Appeal allowed the appeal and ordered a new trial.

This decision is controversial.[200] **Who do you think got it right and why?**

BROWN J.A. (WAKELING J.A. concurring):

Interjections during Cross-Examination

19 In this case, where trial unfairness is said to arise in part from the trial judge's interventions in defence counsel's cross-examination of a witness, several principles ought to be borne in mind:

> (1) The right of an accused to present full answer and defence by challenging the Crown's witnesses on cross-examination flows from the presumption of innocence and the right of the innocent not to be convicted: *R v Seaboyer*, [1991] 2 SCR 577 at para 39, [1991] SC J No 62 (QL); *Osolin* at para 25. This is particularly so when credibility is the central issue in the trial: *Osolin* at para 27, citing *R v Giffin*, 1986 ABCA 107, 69 AR 158 at 159.

---

[200] See very different views expressed in the media and in C.R. comments by Janine Benedet, Don Stuart and Nathan Gorham. For views that defence counsel need to be further controlled in exercising their legal and ethical responsibilities in cross-examining sexual assault complainants see Elaine Craig, "The Ethical Obligations of Defence Counsel in Sexual assault Cases" (2014) 51 Osgoode Hall L.J. 427 and David Tanovich in "'Whack' No More: Infusing Equality into the Ethics of Defence Lawyering in Sexual Assault Cases" (2015) 45(3) Ottawa L. Rev. 495. Contrast *R. v. Rhayel*, 2015 ONCA 377, 324 C.C.C. (3d) 362, 22 C.R. (7th) 78 (Ont. C.A.), where the Court ordered a new trial because the trial judge relied too much on demeanour evidence and his credibility assessments unduly favoured the complainant.

(2) The trial judge may intervene in certain instances, including to clarify an unclear answer, to resolve misunderstanding of the evidence, or to correct inappropriate conduct by counsel or witnesses. This would extend to protecting complainant witnesses—especially complainants to a sexual assault—from questions tendered for an illegitimate and irrelevant purpose designed to demean, particularly where those questions are random shots at the complainant's reputation or groundless questions directed to discredited "rape myths" to the effect that the complainant's unchaste or aroused state made it more likely that she would have consented to the sexual activity in question: *Lyttle* at 208-09; *R v Valley*, (1986) 26 CCC (3d) 207 at para 53, 13 OAC 89, leave to appeal refused [1986] SCCA No 298 (QL) [*Valley*]; *R v Regan*, 2002 SCC 12 at para 85, [2002] 1 SCR 297; *R v Shearing*, 2002 SCC 58 at para 76), [2002] 3 SCR 33.

(3) When the trial judge does intervene, he or she must not do so in a manner which undermines the function of counsel, that frustrates counsel's strategy, or that otherwise makes it impossible for defence to present the defence or test the evidence of Crown witnesses: *Valley* at para 55; *R v Brouillard*, [1985] 1 SCR 39 at 44-47, 1985 CanLII 56; *R v Konelsky*, 98 AR 247 at 248, 68 Alta L R (2d) 187 (CA).

(4) If a trial judge "enters the fray" and appears to be acting as an advocate for one side this may create the appearance of an unfair trial: *R v Switzer*, 2014 ABCA 129 at para 7, 572 AR 311 [*Switzer*].

(5) In determining whether the trial judge's interventions deprived the accused of a fair trial, those interventions should not be considered separately and in isolation from each other, but cumulatively: *R v Khan*, 2001 SCC 86 at para 77, [2001] 3 SCR 823 [*Khan*]; *R v Stucky*, 2009 ONCA 151 at para 72, 303 DLR (4th) 1, *R v Watson* (2004), 191 CCC (3d) 144 at para 14, 192 OAC 263. The concern here is that incidents which, considered in isolation, might be viewed as insignificant might combine to lead a reasonably minded person to consider that the accused had not had a fair trial: *Khan* at para 76; *R v Stewart* (1991), 62 CCC (3d) 289 at para 46, 1991 CarswellOnt 1317 (CA) [*Stewart*].

. . .

25 [The]. . . appellant argues the trial judge's interventions during defence counsel's cross-examination of the complainant created trial unfairness because he impaired the defence strategy of demonstrating inconsistencies as among the complainant's statement to the police, her testimony at the preliminary inquiry, and her trial testimony. In short, he says the trial judge unfairly disrupted the defence's strategy of testing the complainant's credibility. He points in particular to interjections during cross-examination of the complainant on whether she smoked marijuana, whether she had flirted with the appellant, whether she was wearing a bra when the incident occurred, and her sobriety.

26 Conversely, the Crown says that the trial judge's interventions were appropriate in the circumstances and fell within his discretion to control the trial process.

. . .

Flirting

33 The appellant. . .argues that the trial judge interfered in defence counsel's cross-examination of the complainant about flirting with the appellant. The complainant testified in chief as follows: Transcript, 43/15-16:

> Q Had there been any flirting going on —
>
> A No.

34 During cross-examination, defence counsel drew the complainant's attention to her previous statement to the police where she answered "Yeah. Yeah, he's a young guy" when asked if there was flirting going on: Transcript, 86/27-35:

> Q At any time in the evening, did you flirt with Mr. Schmaltz?
>
> A No.
>
> Q And I'm reading from page 13 of 22, that's from the statement to the police, and Constable Guerard asked, "All right. And was, um — was there flirting happening?", to which you respond, line 310, "Was there what?" Constable Guerard says, "Flirting?". You indicate, at line 312, "Yeah. Yeah, he's a young guy."

35 Defence counsel tried to cross-examine the complainant on this prior statement to explore a potential contradiction as to whether she had been flirting with the appellant. The trial judge intervened, stating that the police statement "clearly" meant that the appellant, and not the complainant, had been flirting: Transcript, 87/25-30. The trial judge asserted there was no contradiction between the complainant's testimony that she had not flirted with the appellant, and her statement to the police that the appellant had flirted with her. Defence counsel stated that the police statement answer was not so clear to her, but moved on from that line of questioning: Transcript, 88/12-38.

36 This intervention was. . .inappropriate. The passive language adopted by the questioning in chief and by the police ("[h]ad there been any flirting?" and "[w]as there flirting happening?") left open the question of who was flirting — the complainant, the appellant, or both. The trial judge asserted an interpretation that the appellant was the only one flirting, leaving defence counsel little choice but to abandon that line of questioning.

37 What happened next illustrates the sort of difficulty that can arise when trial judges enter the fray during cross-examination by, in this case, asserting one particular interpretation of a statement that is capable of supporting more than one interpretation. The Crown revisited the statement during re-examination of the complainant, receiving from the complainant the very answers which the trial judge had suggested during his earlier interjection: Transcript, 99/41-100/5, 100/11-19, 100/36-39, 101/14-15:

Q The police statement, or the statement to police in August 2008, pages 13 and 14, there was a discussion about flirting.

A OK.

Q So defence counsel have read into the record the questions from Constable Guerard to you about, "Was there any flirting happening?"

. . .

And you said "Yeah. Yeah, he's a young guy." It had been read into the end, "did he say anything?"

"No, not—not in the way of—he said, oh well, you know, You're pretty cool. You're a pretty cool mom, stuff like that."

In that reference, ... who were you talking about was doing the flirting?

A See, I didn't really take it as flirting. I mean, he's a young guy but it was Josh talking to me.

. . .

Q Okay. So I—but I'm going even basic—more basic than that. When you said "Yeah" to Guerard's question of, "Was there any flirting?", who did you mean was flirting?

A Josh flirting with me.

. . .

Q Was there any flirting going on by you?

A No.

38 The intervention of the trial judge here not only effectively shut down cross-examination by defence counsel on a potentially critical ambiguity in the complainant's statement to police, it suggested a resolution to that ambiguity that Crown counsel was able to exploit. This. . .tends to support a finding of trial unfairness.

. . .

Trial Fairness Conclusion

47 It bears emphasizing that, in sexual assault cases, trial judges must be alert to their important role of protecting complainants from questions tendered for the purpose of demeaning and pointing to discredited, illegitimate and irrelevant factors personal to the complainant. The trial judge clearly understood this role, and took it seriously. His concern was not without foundation, since at least one line of defence counsel's questioning of the complainant was in this regard highly objectionable (Transcript, 85/21-23 and 31-32) although, for reasons I cannot discern from the transcript, during that line of questioning the trial judge remained silent. He did, however, correctly suggest in his reasons for judgment that it was improper, and further observed that it did not operate to discredit the complainant or to otherwise prove consent: ARD F005/36-F006/30. In any event, and as he explained in his ruling on the mistrial application, his concern about such questioning motivated some of his interjections (Transcript, 187/41 and 188/1-25), including those on whether she was wearing a bra and on her alcohol consumption. The difficulty however is that, while these issues may have been irrelevant to whether the complainant consented *per se*, defence counsel's strategy was to show inconsistencies between the complainant's trial testimony on these topics and her earlier statements. On these lines of questioning, defence counsel was not propagating rape myths. They were directed not to the issue of consent, but to the issue of credibility, which was central to the accused's defence.

48 The trial judge frustrated this strategy by interjecting and preventing defence counsel from forming questions to probe these potential inconsistencies. During defence counsel's questions about flirting, consumption of marijuana, and disclosing alcohol consumption in the police report, he appeared to enter the fray. In more than one instance, he interjected to ask leading questions or to suggest the most favourable interpretation to the complainant before she had a chance to answer the question. He also demonstrated that he was not listening to or understanding some of the inconsistencies presented by defence counsel. The cumulative effect of the trial judge's interventions was that he frustrated, to a significant and unwarranted degree, defence counsel's strategy to test the complainant's credibility. This would lead a reasonable, well-informed and right- minded observer to conclude that the appellant was not able to make full answer and defence. The interventions therefore led to trial unfairness.

. . .

[The majority went on to rule that there was, however, no reasonable apprehension of bias.]

Conclusion

60 The appeal is allowed. Regrettably, and mindful of the further imposition this result imposes upon all concerned including the complainant, my conclusion regarding the trial judge's interventions having created the appearance of an unfair trial necessitates a new trial. An unfair trial is a miscarriage of justice (*Khan* at para 27; *R v Karas*, 2007 ABCA 362 at para 53, 422 AR 344; *R v Pompeo*, 2014 BCCA 317 at para 80, 13 CR (7th) 420), and the curative proviso in section 686(1)(b) of the *Criminal Code* has no application here.

61 M.S. PAPERNY J.A. (dissenting):— I have had the benefit of reviewing my colleagues draft judgment in this appeal. I agree with his disposition regarding reasonable apprehension of bias. I am unable, however, to reach the conclusion that the interventions of the trial judge during the complainant's cross-examination resulted in trial unfairness warranting this court's intervention.

The law

62 I agree generally with the law on trial fairness as stated by my colleague. Where I take issue with his analysis is in the application of that law. The law is clear that a trial must not only be fair but appear to be fair in the mind of the reasonably informed observer. However, in my view, that observer, and likewise an appellate court reviewing trial conduct, must look beyond mere appearances and consider whether, in fact and in law, interventions by the trial judge deprived the appellant of his right to make full answer and defence.

63 The right to make full answer and defence is fundamental to our criminal justice system and, as has been pointed out, "the right of an accused to cross-examine prosecution witnesses without significant and unwarranted constraint is an essential component of the right to make a full answer and defence": *R v Lyttle*, [2004] 1 SCR 193, 2004 SCC 5 at para 41. The right to cross-examine is not, however, absolute. Its parameters are governed by the rules of evidence and rules of criminal law and procedure. The Supreme Court in *Lyttle* discussed some of those restrictions, noting that "[c]ounsel are bound by the rules of relevancy and barred from resorting to harassment, misrepresentation, repetitiousness or, more generally, from putting questions whose prejudicial effect outweighs their probative value.": *Lyttle* at para 44; see also *R v Meddoui*, [1991] 3 SCR 320; *R v McLaughlin*, [1974] 2 OR (2d) 514, 15 CCC (2d) 562 (CA). With respect specifically to charges of sexual assault, the accused's right to cross-examine a complainant is circumscribed by common law rules and by provisions of the *Criminal Code*, which prohibit evidence of, among other things, a complainant's sexual history, reputation, and irrelevant questions directed to discredited "rape myths".

. . .

65 Moreover, there is always a strong presumption of impartiality and a presumption that a trial judge has not unduly intervened in a trial: *R v Hamilton*, 2011 ONCA 399 at para 29. The Ontario Court of Appeal has referred to three situations where interventions by a trial judge have been found to lead to an unfair trial:

1.   Questioning an accused or defence witness to such an extent or in such a manner that it conveys the impression that the trial judge has placed his authority on the side of the prosecution;

2.   Interventions that effectively made it impossible for defence counsel to advance the defence; and

3.   Interventions that effectively preclude the accused from telling his or her story in his or her own way. See *Hamilton* at para 31; *R v Stucky* (2009), 240 CCC (3d) 141 (ONCA); *R v Valley* (1986), 26 CCC (3d) 207 (ONCA).

Application of the law to these facts

67 The complainant testified at trial that she had been sexually assaulted by the appellant in her daughter's home. The appellant did not deny the sexual activity, but testified that the complainant consented to it. Thus, the core issue at trial was whether the appellant's testimony was accepted and, if not, whether it nevertheless raised a reasonable doubt, or whether on the whole of the evidence that was accepted a reasonable doubt as to the appellant's guilt was raised. In this judge alone trial, the trial judge was clearly aware that his role was to assess the evidence in its entirety. The complainant's credibility was front and centre in that assessment.

68 As my colleague fairly acknowledges, the trial judge was alert to the unique challenges faced by complainants in sexual assault cases. In some instances, vigorous cross-examination may have the impact of re-victimizing the witness and adversely affecting personal integrity. It falls upon trial judges to ensure that witnesses are treated fairly, and that cross-examination does not go beyond the scope permissible in law. In my view, this is not a matter of balancing the rights of the accused to make full answer and defence against proper treatment of a witness, but rather of ensuring a fair trial. Sometimes interventions by a trial judge accrue to the benefit of the accused, sometimes not. The test is not who benefits, but what impact the intervention has on the trial.

The appellant's specific complaints

69 The appellant submits that the trial judge's interventions at various points during the cross-examination of the complainant created trial unfairness because they prevented defence counsel from demonstrating inconsistencies that went to the complainant's credibility. The assessment of the specific complaints, taken individually and together, is twofold: were the interventions proper, and if not, did they thwart the defence strategy of demonstrating inconsistencies in the complainant's testimony and deprive the appellant of his right to make full answer and defence?

. . .

Flirting

79 The appellant's. . .complaint is that the trial judge improperly interfered in defence counsel's cross-examination of the complainant regarding whether she and the appellant had been flirting earlier in the day. The Crown submits that the trial judge's intervention on this point was proper and done to allay any confusion.

80 The complainant testified that she did not flirt with the appellant. Defence counsel then put an interview transcript with the police to the complainant to allege a contradiction. The transcript stated that "flirting happened". The trial judge expressed concern that the contradiction counsel was attempting to put to the complainant was not necessarily a contradiction at all, positing that the transcript said that the appellant, but not the complainant, had been flirting. This, says the appellant, deprived him of an important line of questioning. I disagree. First, defence counsel could have continued her cross-examination to make clear whether the complainant herself had been flirting with the appellant. Indeed, she did so later in her cross-examination, at which time the complainant denied flirting with the appellant. Defence counsel could have, at that later point, confronted the complainant with the alleged contradictory statement to the police. She did not do so.

81 In his testimony, the appellant testified that the complainant was flirting with him. The transcript read as a whole makes clear that the he was able to put forward his story that the complainant was flirting with him, and that she may have given a somewhat different version at trial compared to what she earlier said to police.

82 My colleagues disagree and conclude that the intervention shut down cross-examination on a potentially critical ambiguity in the complainant's statement to police. This assumes two things: that there was an ambiguity and that the ambiguity could have been important. Neither assumption is borne out by the record. But, assuming that the cross-examination was improperly limited, the question of materiality must be considered. Could it be considered material to the appellant's case whether or not the complainant had been "flirting" with him? It does not go to the ultimate issue at trial, namely whether the complainant consented to being digitally penetrated by the appellant, and could not serve as a defence or as a fact to bolster a defence of consent. It could only tangentially go to the complainant's credibility - did she give a somewhat different version of their interaction to the police. In my view, the "ambiguity" was collateral at best and irrelevant on the ultimate issue of consent.

. . .

Conclusion

86 Judicial intervention in cross-examination of a complainant by definition interrupts the flow of defence counsel's cross examination. But judicial intervention in cross-examination does not rise to the level of injustice warranting a new trial where the interventions were proper, or even if improper, immaterial. In this case there are examples of both. There were many interventions by this trial judge. Some were a response to defence counsel's inappropriate approach to cross-examination. Others were less helpful and sometimes inappropriate. However, it cannot be said that they deprived the appellant of his right to make full answer and defence. The defence case was clear: he maintained that the complainant was a liar, a possible drug user, was drunk at the time of the assault, and consented to the sexual activity. All elements of his defence were clearly put forward. There is no suggestion that the accused himself was prevented by the trial judge from setting out his side of the story in his own way.

87 In all the circumstances, the high threshold required to establish an injustice warranting a new trial has not been met. I would dismiss the appeal.

(e) Duty to Cross-examine (Rule in *Browne v. Dunn*)

Aside from counsel's right to cross-examine there may at times be a duty to cross-examine.

R. v. McNEILL
(2000), 33 C.R. (5th) 390, 144 C.C.C. (3d) 551 (Ont. C.A.)

The accused was charged with numerous offences arising out of an alleged abduction of one C. One of the people involved in the abduction, B, testified as Crown witness that he was retained by the accused to collect a drug debt from the victim, that he and the accused went to the victim's motel room for that purpose. The appellant testified and denied any involvement in the abduction.

MOLDAVER J.A. (McMURTRY C.J.O., and GOUDGE J.A. concurring): —

. . .

Cross-examination of the Appellant on Defence Counsel's Failure to Pose Specific Questions to the Crown witness Bonello

In his examination-in-chief of the appellant, defence counsel asked whether the appellant had spoken to Bonello after the Cudney incident. The appellant answered in the affirmative and the following series of questions and answers ensued, without objection from Crown counsel:

Q. And what did Mr. Bonello say about it?

A. I was — I was probably a little aggressive with him at first, and he became aggressive right back saying that . . . you know . . . I told him that Bob Cudney — you did this for me; and he said: No, no, no, no. This was done for "killer". It had nothing to do with you.

Q. For who?

A. "Killer". I know that sounds a little bit cliché, but . . . as you heard other people testify . . . this is actually somebody's name.

Q. Did you force the issue with Bonello?

A. I wouldn't force any issue with Bonello. He just told me that it was Cud — or "killer's" beef and it had nothing to do with me.

For reasons unknown, defence counsel did not question Bonello about this conversation. He was obliged to do so under s. 11 of the Canada Evidence Act, R.S.C. 1985, c. C-5, if it was his intention to lead evidence of a prior statement inconsistent with Bonello's testimony. Had Crown counsel raised the appropriate objection, it would have been for the trial judge to decide whether the appellant should be permitted to testify about the purported conversation (see *R. v. P. (G.)* (1996), 112 C.C.C. (3d) 263 at pp. 278-87 (Ont. C.A.)).

Defence counsel's failure to question Bonello about the conversation did not go unnoticed by the Crown. No doubt, she was concerned that Bonello had not been given the opportunity to confirm, deny or explain it. To the extent she felt the matter was worth pursuing, in my view, the proper procedure would have been to raise the issue with the trial judge in the absence of the jury. That way, the trial judge could have determined whether her concern was valid and if so, what steps should be taken to remedy the situation. Regrettably, Crown counsel did not pursue this course. Instead, she chose to confront the appellant with the fact that defence counsel had not questioned Bonello about the purported conversation either at the preliminary hearing or at trial:

> Q. The gentlemen that you named . . . that you said Bonello named as having been the whole cause of the Cudney incident; you said his name was "killer"?
>
> A. He said it was "killer's gig", that he was involved with Cudney over, not me; "killer's gig".
>
> Q. You were present at the preliminary hearing as well as at the trial of this matter, isn't that true?
>
> A. Absolutely.
>
> Q. You never heard Mr. Bolnello asked if it was "killer's gig" did you?
>
> A. I never heard him . . . ?
>
> Q. Anybody ask Bonello anything about "killer's gig", or if he said that to you?
>
> A. No. I believe "killer" was mentioned somewhere in this. I think by Bob Cudney. I don't believe Bonello ever used his name. He may have but I don't recall off the top of my head.
>
> Q. That was my point sir. You're telling us about a conversation that you had with Mr. Bonello, but no one ever suggested to Bonello that that conversation occurred, correct?

In my view, this line of questioning was improper because it was capable of leaving the jury with the impression that the appellant should be held responsible for what may have been a tactical decision or mere oversight on the part of defence counsel. As explained, defence counsel's failure to question Bonello about the purported conversation involved a breach of s. 11 of the Canada Evidence Act. That, however, is not the way the issue was presented to us. Rather, it was framed as a breach of the rule in *Browne v. Dunn* (1893), 6 R. 67 (H.L.). Accordingly, I propose to address that rule, primarily with a view to considering the options available when it is breached.

The rule in *Browne v. Dunn* was succinctly stated by Labrosse J.A. in *R. v. Henderson, supra*:

> This well-known rule stands for the proposition that if counsel is going to challenge the credibility of a witness by calling contradictory evidence, the witness must be given the chance to address the contradictory evidence in cross-examination while he or she is in the witness-box.

In *R. v. Verney* (1993), 87 C.C.C. (3d) 363 at p. 376 (Ont. C.A.), Finlayson J.A. outlined the purpose and ambit of the rule:

> *Browne v. Dunn* is a rule of fairness that prevents the "ambush" of a witness by not giving him an opportunity to state his position with respect to later evidence which contradicts him on an essential matter. It is not, however, an absolute rule

and counsel must not feel obliged to slog through a witness's evidence-in-chief, putting him on notice of every detail that the defence does not accept. Defence counsel must be free to use his own judgment about how to cross-examine a hostile witness. Having the witness repeat in cross-examination, everything he said in chief, is rarely the tactic of choice. For a fuller discussion on this point, see *Palmer and Palmer v. The Queen* (1979), 50 C.C.C. (2d) 193 at pp. 209-10, [1980] 1 S.C.R. 759, 14 C.R. (3d) 22 (S.C.C.).

While these decisions explain the rule and its underlying purpose, they do not address the options available to a party who feels aggrieved by the failure of his or her opponent to adhere to it. To that end, I offer these suggestions. In cases such as this, where the concern lies in a witness's inability to present his or her side of the story, it seems to me that the first option worth exploring is whether the witness is available for recall. If so, then assuming the trial judge is otherwise satisfied, after weighing the pros and cons, that recall is appropriate, the aggrieved party can either take up the opportunity or decline it. If the opportunity is declined, then, in my view, no special instruction to the jury is required beyond the normal instruction that the jury is entitled to believe all, part or none of a witness's evidence, regardless of whether the evidence is uncontradicted.

The mechanics of when the witness should be recalled and by whom should be left to the discretion of the trial judge.

In those cases where it is impossible or highly impracticable to have the witness recalled or where the trial judge otherwise determines that recall is inappropriate, it should be left to the trial judge to decide whether a special instruction should be given to the jury. If one is warranted, the jury should be told that in assessing the weight to be given to the uncontradicted evidence, they may properly take into account the fact that the opposing witness was not questioned about it. The jury should also be told that they may take this into account in assessing the credibility of the opposing witness. Depending on the circumstances, there may be other permissible ways of rectifying the problem. The two options that I have mentioned are not meant to be exhaustive. As a rule, however, I am of the view that they will generally prove to be the fairest and most effective solutions.

Returning to the issue at hand, Ms. Fairburn does not attempt to justify the impugned line of questioning. Instead, she submits that the trial judge's instructions to the jury were sufficient to overcome any prejudice occasioned to the appellant. The trial judge dealt with this issue in general terms as follows:

> The procedure of cross-examination is a procedure I regard as one of fairness; a rule of professional practice. It is applicable where it is intended to suggest the witness is not speaking the truth on a particular point. The question, by the suggestion made, often sets the stage, as I have tried to indicate, for defence evidence to be led in support of the suggestion. If put to a witness in cross-examination, the witness has the opportunity to explain. If not put to the witness in cross-examination, but put later to other witnesses, the suggestion is then perhaps impossible to explain, and triers of fact can be left with the inference that the witness's story is untrue and the witness unworthy of credit . . . believability.

There is therefore the practice of cross-examining counsel to put to the witness all significant matters upon which they seek to contradict. I emphasize the words "all significant matters", as some matters may be so obvious as not to be of significance, and likewise some matters may be so insignificant or interrelated with other matters so as not to require a singling out, and the use of time that might be involved in that singling out.

It is for you to decide if there were any significant matters upon which crown witnesses were not cross-examined, which matters were put forward by other witnesses with a view to suggesting the particular crown witness was not worthy of belief. It is for you to decide if there were any such lapses or failure to cross-examine, and if so, what weight to be given to the particular evidence to be called for which there was no opportunity to explain.

In my view, these instructions were deficient in two respects. First, to the extent the jury understood them to relate to defence counsel's failure to question Bonello about the purported conversation, the trial judge left the jury with the impression that Bonello (and inferentially the Crown), was left in the impossible position of being unable to explain the conversation. With respect, that was both inaccurate and misleading. Had Crown counsel wished to have Bonello's explanation before the jury, she could have sought permission to have him recalled. There was nothing to suggest that Bonello was unavailable or that his recall would have posed any difficulty. As it is, she made no effort to do so. Accordingly, it was wrong to leave the jury with the impression that defence counsel's failure to question Bonello rendered it impossible for him to offer an explanation.

Second, although the jury was instructed on the use that could be made of defence counsel's failure to question Bonello, they were not told that the appellant should not be held responsible for what may have been a tactical decision or mere oversight on the part of his counsel.

New trial ordered for this and other errors.

The existence of the *Browne v. Dunn* issue was recognized by the Supreme Court in *Lyttle.* The Court decided it did not arise for decision in that case.

In recent years it has been increasingly clear that Canadian judges have wide discretion as to how to apply the so-called rule in *Browne v. Dunn.* There is now significant agreement that its application in criminal trials is a matter of discretion for trial judges. There is consensus that its application should be reserved for serious matters and that discretionary remedies include the possibility of recall (see Moldaver J.A. in *McNeill*, above) and careful judicial direction, although the courts emphasize there is no hard and fast legal rule.[201] As to judicial direction, Justice Borins, speaking for the Ontario Court of Appeal, in *R. v. Marshall*,[202] confirmed that this should not

---

[201]   See *R. v. Giroux* (2006), 207 C.C.C. (3d) 512 (Ont. C.A.) at 529 and *R. v. Carter*, (2005) 32 C.R. (6th) 1 (B.C. C.A.). See now *R. v. Wapass*, 2014 SKCA 76, 314 C.C.C. (3d) 561, 12 C.R. (7th) 373 (Sask. C.A.), *R. v. Quansah*, 2015 ONCA 237, 323 C.C.C. (3d) 191, 19 C.R. (7th) 33 (Ont. C.A.) and *R. v. Gill*, 2017 BCCA 67, 346 C.C.C. (3d) 212 (B.C. C.A.).

be in the nature of a special instruction, should not invite the drawing of an adverse inference and should not involve comments on counsel deficiencies. According to Borins J.A.:

> I think much of the detail in the judge's charge should have been limited to a simple direction that the failure to cross- examine...on the matters in issue could be considered in weighing the [accused's] evidence and did not necessitate an adverse inference in respect of the [accused's] testimony.[203]

Some courts have voiced concern that the rule's application in criminal trials may unduly jeopardize the presumption of innocence. In *R. v. Carter*,[204] the Court ordered a new trial where the trial judge did not attempt to rectify the Crown's error in asking the jury to draw an adverse inference against the defence for not properly confronting the complainants. The Court left open the question of whether such an error could ever be cured by a judge's direction. Judge Allen of the Alberta Provincial Court in *R. v. Melnick*[205] went further. He broke new ground in deciding that although there was a failure to confront on a significant matter, the breach was not so egregious as to require any judicial response. It may be that it is time for our courts to abandon a contentious rule derived from a civil case in the House of Lords more than a century ago.

A high-profile context to consider the rule in *Browne v. Dunn* and the collateral fact rule is the 1995 O.J. Simpson case. One of the theories of the defence was that the lead detective planted the "bloody glove" at Simpson's estate. The defence suggested that he was motivated to do so by a racist intent. F. Lee Bailey pointedly asked Detective Fuhrman whether he had ever used the "n" word to describe African-Americans. He answered that he had never used the word in the past 10 years. The defence then called Laura McKinney, an aspiring screenwriter, who had interviewed Fuhrman for her screenplay about female police officers. In an audiotaped conversation, Fuhrman repeatedly used the "n" word and bragged about beating and torturing African-Americans. When Fuhrman was later asked at the trial whether he had planted or manufactured evidence in the Simpson case, he invoked his privilege against self-incrimination. **Did *Browne v. Dunn* require these questions be put to Fuhrman? Assuming the questions were not asked, would a judicial comment on the fact that the defence did not ask Fuhrman really add anything of value? Was the question about his use of the "n" word a collateral issue?**

(f) Collateral Facts Rule

Counsel is entitled in cross-examination to ask questions about matters relevant to the material issues in the case but is also entitled to ask questions about other matters that may be relevant to the witness' credibility. These

---

202 (2005), 201 O.A.C. 154, 200 C.C.C. (3d) 179 (Ont. C.A.).
203 *Ibid.* at para. 67.
204 (2005), 32 C.R. (6th) 1, 199 C.C.C. (3d) 74 (B.C. C.A.).
205 (2005), 32 C.R. (6th) 18 (Alta. Prov. Ct).

questions are subject only to the discretion of the trial judge, who will take into account such considerations as time and fairness to the witness. The common law decided that considerations of economy of time, the danger of confusing the issues before the jury, and fairness to the witness who came prepared to testify to matters framed by the suit, demanded a rule which obliged the cross-examiner to be content with answers given to collateral matters.

The "collateral facts rule" is simple to state but often difficult in its application. The rule forbids the introduction of extrinsic evidence which contradicts a witness' testimonial assertion about collateral facts. A witness is summoned to court to testify concerning the material facts involved in the suit. In cross-examination the witness may be asked questions concerning the description given in chief, and may also be asked questions that impact solely on the witness' credibility. If the questions regarding credibility are collateral, the cross-examiner must accept the answers given, and cannot lead other witnesses to contradict the first witness on such matters.

The rule is difficult in its application because of the difficulty in determining what is "collateral". The *Hitchcock* case is the classic exposition.

In *Attorney General v. Hitchcock*[206] the defendant was tried for a violation of the revenue laws. The Crown witness, who had testified to having observed the violation, was asked in cross-examination whether he had not earlier made a statement that the officers of the Crown had offered him a bribe to give that evidence. The witness denied having said so and defence counsel proposed to call another witness to testify that in fact such a statement was made.

An objection that such evidence was *collateral* and the witness could not thereby be contradicted was allowed and the evidence excluded. It was held that the ruling at trial was correct. Had the evidence been that the witness had made a statement that he had *accepted* a bribe the ruling would have been different as that would have reflected the possibility of bias. The Court saw testimonial factors, bias, interest, corruption, capacity to observe and remember and so forth, as matters "directly in issue before the Court" on which the witness may then be contradicted. Evidence of such matters are proveable independently of the contradiction; they have relevance apart from the simple fact of contradiction. There are then *two* classes of facts which are not collateral: facts which are relevant to a material issue, and facts relevant to a testimonial factor.[207]

Baron Rolfe explained:

> If we lived for a thousand years instead of about sixty or seventy, and every case were of sufficient importance, it might be possible, and perhaps proper, to throw a light on matters in which every possible question might be suggested, for the purpose of seeing by such means whether the whole was unfounded, or what portion of it was not, and to raise every possible inquiry as to the truth of the

---

[206]   (1847), 154 E.R. 38 (Exch. Ct.).
[207]   See 3A Wigmore, *Evidence* (Chad. Rev.), ss. 1004-1005.

statements made. But I do not see how that could be; in fact, mankind find it to be impossible. Therefore some line must be drawn.[208]

R. v. R. (D.)
[1996] 2 S.C.R. 291, 107 C.C.C. (3d) 289, 48 C.R. (4th) 368 (S.C.C.)

MAJOR J.:

. . .

The appellants D.R. and H.R. are the natural parents of the complainants, Michael R., who as born in 1979, and Michelle R. and Kathleen (Kathy) R., twins who were born in 1982. The appellant D.W. is the boyfriend of H.R., now divorced from D.R. All the appellants are deaf; only D.W. is able to speak.

The appellants were jointly charged with several counts of sexual assault and gross indecency, and one count of assault, arising out of alleged incidents involving the children between January 1, 1983 and December 31, 1989. In this time period the children ranged in age from one to ten. D.R. and H.R. were also charged with incest and several additional counts of assault causing bodily harm.

. . .

C. Cross-Examination of Ms. Bunko-Ruys

Ms. Bunko-Ruys was the children's therapist. She was qualified as an expert in the behavioural, social and emotional characteristics of sexually abused children. Ms. Bunko-Ruys had been present during the videotaped interviews of the children conducted by Sergeant Dueck. The appellants sought to cross-examine Ms. Bunko-Ruys on the interview techniques employed during those interviews using unproved copies of the transcripts of those interviews. They were seeking to discredit the child witnesses, or prove that the children had been coached or manipulated. They did not seek to admit the transcripts into evidence, nor did they question Sergeant Dueck or Dr. Elterman about the interview techniques used. The trial judge refused to permit the use of the transcripts in the cross-examination of Ms. Bunko-Ruys. She was concerned that, if the evidence was to be used to show that there had been coaching or manipulation, it was collateral.

The test for whether an issue is collateral was set out by Pollock C.B. in *Attorney-General v. Hitchcock* (1847), 1 Ex. 91, 154 E.R. 38, at p. 42:

> . . . the test, whether the matter is collateral or not, is this: if the answer of a witness is a matter which you would be allowed on your part to prove in evidence — if it have such a connection with the issue, that you would be allowed to give it in evidence — then it is a matter on which you may contradict him.

---

[208]   *Hitchcock, supra* note 206 at 44-45.

The credibility of the children was at the heart of the case against the appellants. The appellants would have been entitled to lead evidence on the effect of the interview techniques on the memories of the children and accordingly, met the test in *Hitchcock*. Any evidence that might have cast doubt on the children's credibility, or that might show that the children had been subjected to coaching and manipulation, was evidence that would have been crucial to the appellants' case.

. . .

Thus, given the importance of the right to cross-examine witnesses, and the fact that the issue of the children's credibility was central to the allegations against the accused, the trial judge erred in restricting the cross-examination of Ms. Bunko-Ruys. Whether Ms. Bunko-Ruys was an expert on interview techniques is immaterial, as the scope of cross-examination of an expert is not restricted to his or her area of expertise. The fact that the appellants might have made other use of the transcripts, or introduced them into evidence, is irrelevant in determining whether the appellants were wrongly restricted in their cross-examination of Ms. Bunko-Ruys. The appellants should have been allowed to cross-examine Ms. Bunko-Ruys using the transcripts of the interviews.

According to Professor McCormick:

The classical approach is that facts which would have been independently provable regardless of the contradiction are not "collateral".[209]

McCormick goes on to describe three kinds of facts which meet this test. The first kind of facts which are independently provable are facts relevant to the substantive issues in the case. The second kind are not relevant to the substantive issues but are independently provable by extrinsic evidence to impeach the witness; among these facts are facts showing a bias or interest in the witness. The third kind of facts with respect to which the witness might be contradicted are facts about which the witness could not have been mistaken if he or she really saw what he or she claims to have seen; contradicting such a fact would "pull out the linchpin of the story".

Another approach is that of Professor Younger:

We struggled with the problem in law school; we read an English case called Attorney General Hitchcock. You may not recall it because you may not have understood it. If you went back and read it today, you would not understand it. If you read it every day of your life until you die, you would not understand it; there is no meaning to it. The case is important only because it states what seems to be the prevailing rule with respect to the collateral/not collateral distinction: if the witness denies the prior inconsistent statement, the issue may or may not be collateral. Sometimes you may call another witness to prove the prior statement; sometimes you will not be able to call him. The real question is, when will it be collateral, and when will it not be collateral? The answer is simple: when it is important, it is not collateral. When it is unimportant, it is collateral. Ten thousand cases add up to that.[210]

---

[209] McCormick, *Evidence*, 3rd ed. at 110.
[210] *The Art of Cross-Examination* (1976).

When judges use the word "collateral" or the "collateral facts rule" this may be historical jargon for a ruling that the evidence is irrelevant or to be excluded under the discretion to exclude where the probative value is found to be exceeded by the prejudicial effect on the fact-finding process.

Most courts and authors now acknowledge that applying the collateral facts rule requires a "discretionary and principled analysis within the probative value/prejudicial effect context": S. Casey Hill, David Tanovich and Louis Strezos, *McWilliams' Canadian Criminal Evidence*, 5th ed. (Toronto: Canada Law Book, 2013) at 6:30.

One of the most misunderstood aspects of the collateral fact rule is its application in the context of cross-examination. Consider the following cases.

R. v. MACISAAC
2017 ONCA 172, 347 C.C.C. (3d) 37, 36 C.R. (7th) 144 (Ont. C.A.)

TROTTER J.A.:

[1] David MacIsaac burned down his two-storey building in Espanola and then attempted to collect the insurance proceeds. He was convicted of arson under s. 433 and 434 of the *Criminal Code*, R.S.C. 1985, c. C-46. The case against him was formidable, and included evidence of motive, planning, preparation, as well as forensic evidence suggesting that he was involved in setting the fire. The Crown also relied upon the testimony of a disreputable witness, who was probably an accomplice.

. . .

[3] In the early morning hours of March 19, 2012, downtown Espanola was rocked by a number of explosions. The ensuing fire destroyed two buildings, one of which was owned by Mr. MacIsaac ("the appellant").

[4] It was the Crown's theory that the appellant, along with Craig Hunda ("Hunda"), conceived of a plan to burn down the appellant's building. Late at night, the two men went to the appellant's property at 128 Tudhope Street ("the building"), accompanied by the Crown's main witness, Jordan Leggat ("Leggat"), who was Hunda's girlfriend. The appellant and Hunda doused toilet paper rolls with ignitable fluid and set the place on fire.

[5] Shortly after the explosions, first responders arrived to find the appellant lying on the ground just outside of his building. Both of his legs and one of his arms were neatly bound by duct tape. The appellant had been beaten about the face and stabbed in the back. He told first responders that strangers attacked him and then set fire to his building. However, the evidence later showed that the appellant was complicit in burning down his own building and his story about being attacked was a ruse.

. . .

(3) The Collateral Fact Rule

[51] The appellant argues that the trial judge erred by improperly curtailing the cross-examination of Leggat. This issue has its roots in the criminal proceedings against Leggat for her role in the arson. As discussed above (at para. 27), Leggat pled guilty to being an accessory after the fact to arson.

[52] The record is not entirely clear on this point, but it would appear that a report prepared by a psychologist, Dr. Valiant, was introduced at Leggat's sentencing hearing. During her testimony at the appellant's trial, defence counsel (not Mr. Burgess) confronted her with this report. The following exchange took place:

> **Q.**: Okay. When you met with Dr. Valiant you reported that you have special mystical powers or a special mission in life that other people do not accept. Right?
>
> **A.**: I said I had mystical powers?
>
> **Q.**: Mn-hmm.
>
> **A.**: No.
>
> **Q.**: Would you like to — would it help . . .
>
> **A.**: Yeah, I do.
>
> **Q.**: . . . you refresh your memory to see . . .
>
> **A.**: Yeah.
>
> **Q.**: . . . the report?
>
> **A.**: I never said I had . . . what are mystical powers? I don't even know what that word means.

[53] The trial judge intervened to question the relevance of this evidence. Defence counsel advised that Leggat in fact "said" she had mystical powers, but quickly backtracked to suggest that Leggat had "endorsed" having these powers. Defence counsel argued that the line of questioning was relevant to Leggat's credibility and reliability.

[54] In response, the Crown at trial (not Mr. Harper) read an excerpt from the report that suggested that the psychologist's conclusions were not based on Leggat's self-reports, but on her responses to psychometric tests. The Crown quoted the following:

> According to her responses content . . . she feels quite lonely, misunderstood at times, she endorses a number of extremely bizarre thoughts, suggesting the presence of delusions or hallucination. She apparently believes that she has special mystical powers.

[55] The trial judge curtailed this line of questioning, providing the following reasons:

Well, we're not going down that road, that's a collateral fact and if we're gonna start having evidence about when a person may or may not have told the truth I'm afraid that the, I'm afraid that the actors are gonna take over the circus, so that, that's not going to happen.

. . .

We're not, we're not here to determine a host of those things, we are not here to determine first of all whether she said it, because she's giving [sic] you the answer and she said she never made the statement. And, and with the assistance of the information provided, even if I were inclined to go down that road, which I'm not, the report on its face doesn't say that she made that statement.

So that's my ruling, I'm not going to permit you, unless you can phrase some other questions you may wish to put to me now, I'm not going to let you go down, go down that road. You asked the question, you got the answer, "No, I never made the statement to him that I have mystical powers." So where, where do you wish to go from here?

[56] Defence counsel did not pursue the matter further. Nor did he elect to call any evidence.

[57] Addressing this ground of appeal is made more difficult because the psychological report in question was not filed as a lettered exhibit at trial. It should have been: see *1162740 Ontario Limited v. Pingue*, 2017 ONCA 52 (CanLII), [2017] O.J. No. 331, at paras. 35-36. Without reading the report, it is difficult to put the "mystical powers" comment in its proper context. Nevertheless, even on the limited record that is available, it is clear that defence counsel's proposed line of questioning was not barred by the collateral fact rule. But as discussed below, the cross-examination was problematic in other ways.

[58] The collateral fact rule does not curtail what is otherwise proper cross-examination of a witness; it potentially limits the manner in which answers given may be subsequently challenged by extrinsic evidence: see Sidney N. Lederman, Alan W. Bryant and Michelle K. Fuerst, *The Law of Evidence in Canada*, 4th ed. (Toronto: LexisNexis Canada Inc., 2014), at pp. 1195-1201. As is often said, if the questioner asks a question that bears on a collateral issue, he or she is "stuck" with the answer, in the sense of not being permitted to lead extrinsic evidence to contradict it. However, this does not prevent proper questions from being put in the first place: see *R. v. Krause*, 1986 CanLII 39 (SCC), [1986] 2 S.C.R. 466, at pp. 474-475 and *R. v. Khanna*, 2016 ONCA 39 (CanLII), 127 W.C.B. (2d) 613, at para. 9.

[59] The collateral fact rule is most often engaged when a cross-examiner attempts to challenge the credibility of a witness. Generally speaking, credibility is considered to be collateral, thereby barring the questioner from adducing extrinsic evidence that bears solely on this issue. However, the rule has developed in a manner that admits of a number of exceptions: See Earl J. Levy, *Examination of Witnesses in Criminal Cases*, 7th ed. (Toronto: Thomson Reuters, 2016), at pp. 509-511. The exception that might have applied in this

case is that medical evidence may be adduced to prove that, by virtue of a mental or physical condition, the witness is incapable of telling or is unlikely to tell the truth. In *Toohey v. Metropolitan Police Commissioner*, [1965] A.C. 595 (H.L.), at p. 608, Lord Pearce held: " . . . it must be allowable to call medical evidence of mental illness which makes a witness incapable of giving reliable evidence, whether through the existence of delusions or otherwise." See also *R. v. Dietrich*, 1970 CanLII 377 (ON CA), [1970] 3 O.R. 725 (C.A.), at pp. 742-744.

[60] If Leggat suffered from delusions and/or experienced hallucinations, it may have affected her credibility and reliability as a witness. Defence counsel should have been permitted to explore this issue in cross-examination. Moreover, and although it was never expressed, if defence counsel was contemplating leading the type of evidence considered in *Toohey*, fairness to Leggat required that she be confronted with this suggestion during her testimony: see *Browne v. Dunn* (1893), 1893 CanLII 65 (FOREP), 6 R. 67 (H.L.) and *R. v. Lyttle*, 2004 SCC 5 (CanLII), [2004] 1 S.C.R. 193, at para. 65.

[61] This legitimate line of inquiry was undermined by the manner in which counsel framed his questions. Given that the psychological report said that Leggat "apparently believes" she has special mystical powers, it was appropriate to ask her whether she told Dr. Valiant that she had mystical powers. Defence counsel asked the question and Leggat denied the suggestion. Moreover, there would have been nothing improper in asking Leggat whether she believed that she had mystical powers. It was not appropriate, however, to cross-examine Leggat on an assessment or diagnosis contained in the report. It would appear that this is where things were headed when the trial judge intervened. It may have been appropriate to attempt to refresh Leggat's memory by reference to the report, assuming that a proper foundation for doing so could be laid: *R. v. Fliss*, 2002 SCC 16 (CanLII), [2002] 1 S.C.R. 535, para. 45. However, it is not clear from the portion of the transcript reproduced at para. 52 above whether Leggat actually looked at the report before saying, "I never said I had . . . what are mystical powers? I don't even know what that word means."

[62] Even though the trial judge improperly curtailed the cross-examination of Leggat, he offered defence counsel an opportunity to approach the issue in a different manner. Defence counsel did not accept the invitation, did not bring any authorities to the trial judge's attention, nor did he attempt to adduce evidence of a mental disorder along the lines of *Toohey*.

[63] Leggat was thoroughly cross-examined on all aspects of her previous statements, evidence, character and lifestyle. As discussed earlier in these reasons, she was exposed as a witness whose evidence required confirmation. I am not persuaded that the manner in which the trial judge dealt with this issue, while somewhat problematic, resulted in an unfair trial. I would not give effect to this ground of appeal.

R. v. A.C.
2018 ONCA 333 (Ont. C.A.)

HOURIGAN J.A.

[46] I am of the view that the parties and trial judge below, and consequently the parties on appeal, have operated on a misunderstanding of what the collateral fact rule actually prohibits. This is unsurprising, given that the rule has historically suffered from confusion in its application. The rule operates to prevent a party from calling extrinsic contradictory evidence to undermine the credibility of an opposing party's witness in relation to a collateral issue. It does not operate to confine the scope of what is otherwise proper cross-examination . . . The rule is based in trial efficiency and seeks to avoid confusing the jury and eating up too much time with the sub-litigation of non-essential issues: David M. Paciocco & Lee Stuesser, *The Law of Evidence*, 7th ed. (Toronto: Irwin Law Inc., 2015), at p. 476.

R. v. D.S.
2017 ONCJ 682, 41 C.R. (7th) 180 (Ont. C.J.)

DOODY J.:

[65] The collateral fact rule is described in this way in *Watt's Manual of Criminal Evidence 2016* at p. 216:

> The collateral facts or collateral issues rule prohibits the introduction of evidence for the *sole* purpose of *contradicting* a witness' testimony concerning a collateral fact. The rule seeks to avoid confusion and proliferation of issues, wasting of time and introduction of evidence of negligible assistance to the trier of fact in determining the real issues of the case. It endeavours to ensure that the sideshow does not take over the circus. In general, matters that relate wholly and *exclusively* to the credibility of a non-accused witness are collateral, hence beyond the reach of contradictory evidence.
>
> A *collateral* fact is one that is *not* connected with the *issue* in the case. It is one that the party would not be entitled to prove as part of its case, because it lacks relevance or connection to it. A collateral fact, in other words, is one that is neither
>
> i. *Material*; nor
>
> ii. *Relevant* to a material fact.
>
> If the answer of a witness that a party seeks to contradict, is a matter that the opponent could prove in evidence as part of its case, *independent* of the contradiction, the matter is *not* collateral. Contradictory evidence may be elicited. [emphasis in original]

[66] In *R. v. C.F.*, 2017 ONCA 480 (CanLII), the Court of Appeal approved this summary of the rule. Huscroft J.A., however, writing on behalf of a panel of the Court which included Watt J.A., held that the collateral fact rule was not absolute and that, following the Supreme Court of Canada's decision in *R. v. R. (D.)*, 1996 CanLII 207 (SCC), [1996] 2 S.C.R. 291, "evidence that

undermines a witness' credibility may escape the exclusionary reach of the collateral fact rule if credibility is central to the case against the accused."

Sometimes, but not always, the evidence that counsel wishes to use to contradict amounts to proof of a statement by the witness that is inconsistent with his or her present testimony. Proof of previous inconsistent statements, we will see, is subject to the collateral facts rule.

PROBLEMS
Problem 1
In a civil suit for damages the plaintiff's witness has described the motor vehicle accident, which he attributed to the fault of the defendant, and is now being cross-examined:

Q.:   Sir, you've testified that you observed this accident which occurred on July 12, 1987. Can you tell us how you happened to be at that location?

A.:   Well, yes, as a matter of fact. The accident occurred near the Exhibition Stadium and I was on my way to see a ball game there.

Q.:   Who was playing?

A.:   The Blue Jays and the Red Sox.

Q.:   And this was on July 12, 1987.

A.:   Yes

Q.:   You're sure about that.

A.:   I'm sure.

Q.:   You're as sure about it as you are about all the rest of your evidence

A.:   Yes, I am!

Q.:   Would it surprise you to know that on July 12, 1987, the Jays were in the middle of a road trip to the West Coast and that night they were playing a game in Seattle?

A: It would surprise me very much. I'm certain the Jays were at Exhibition Stadium that night.

Q: You're right about everything.

A: This time I am. I saw the accident, your client was at fault and the Jays were in Toronto.

Counsel: Your honour, I have no more questions of this witness. I do feel obliged to alert the Court and my friend that in presenting my client's case I intend to call evidence that on the evening in question the Toronto Blue Jays were in Seattle.

Counsel for Plaintiff: Your honour, our position is that this matter of where the Blue Jays were playing is collateral to the real issue between the parties, which is who was at fault in the accident. Being collateral the rules of evidence preclude the calling of contradictory evidence. My friend must take the answer of the witness and live with it.

What is your ruling?

Problem 2

The accused was charged with fraud in connection with the operation of a travel agency. The accused gave evidence and was asked in cross-examination whether he had filed income tax returns over a period of years. The accused stated that he had done so except for two or three years when his books were under seizure by Crown authorities. The Crown proposes to call evidence to establish that the accused has not filed any income tax returns for a period of some 10 years. The accused objects. **How would you rule on the objection?** See *R. v. Rafael* (1972), 7 C.C.C. (2d) 325 (Ont. C.A.). **Would it affect your ruling if the accused's evidence had come out in examination-in-chief?**

3. IMPEACHMENT

Professor McCormick has provided the outline for this section of the chapter:

> There are five main lines of attack upon the credibility of a witness. The first, and probably the most effective and most frequently employed, is an attack by proof that the witness on a previous occasion has made statements inconsistent with his present testimony. The second is an attack by a showing that the witness is biased on account of emotional influences such as kinship for one party or hostility to another, or motives of pecuniary interest, whether legitimate or corrupt. The third is an attack upon the character of the witness. The fourth is an attack by showing a defect of capacity in the witness to observe, remember or recount the matters testified about. The fifth is proof by other witnesses that material facts are otherwise than as testified to by the witness under attack.[211]

(a) Prior Inconsistent Statements

Proof that the witness made an earlier inconsistent statement may be gained during cross-examination out of the mouth of the witness himself or herself or, should the witness deny making the statement, by proof from other witnesses. Should the latter mode of contradiction prove necessary, the common law developed some limitations.

---

[211] McCormick, *Evidence*, 2nd ed. at 66.

The common law limitation with respect to collateral facts was legislated in England, with respect to statements, in the mid nineteenth century and that legislation was copied in all common law jurisdictions in Canada. For example, the *Canada Evidence Act*[212] provides:

> 10. (1) On any trial a witness may be cross-examined as to previous statements that the witness made in writing, or that have been reduced to writing, or recorded on audio tape or video tape or otherwise, relative to the subject- matter of the case, without the writing being shown to the witness or the witness being given the opportunity to listen to the audio tape or view the video tape or otherwise take cognizance of the statements, but, if it is intended to contradict the witness, the witness' attention must, before the contradictory proof can be given, be called to those parts of the statement that are to be used for the purpose of so contradicting the witness, and the judge, at any time during the trial, may require the production of the writing or tape or other medium for inspection, and thereupon make such use of it for the purposes of the trial as the judge thinks fit.
>
> (2) A deposition of the witness, purporting to have been taken before a justice on the investigation of a criminal charge and to be signed by the witness and the justice, returned to and produced from the custody of the proper officer shall be presumed, in the absence of evidence to the contrary, to have been signed by the witness.
>
> 11. Where a witness, on cross-examination as to a former statement made by him relative to the subject-matter of the case and inconsistent with his present testimony, does not distinctly admit that he did make the statement, proof may be given that he did in fact make it; but before that proof can be given the circumstances of the supposed statement, sufficient to designate the particular occasion, shall be mentioned to the witness, and he shall be asked whether or not he did make the statement.

Cross-examination on a prior inconsistent statement can be a highly effective strategy to attack credibility. However it should be attempted with preparation and care. Most advocacy texts (see e.g. Lee Stuesser)[213] identify four separate steps:

1. Anchor the contradiction by first confirming with some precision the witnesses's evidence in chief (e.g., "You testified this morning that the car was black. Is that correct"?)

2. Confront the witness with the fact that he or she made an earlier statement (e.g., "Do you recall speaking to the officer on the day of the accident and giving a signed statement?") If the witness denies making any statement it would have to be proved by calling the officer.

3. Highlight the contradiction (e.g., "In the statement you said the lighting was bad and you could not see the colour of the vehicle." Or have the witness read that passage out loud.)

---

[212] R.S.C. 1985, c. C-5, ss. 10 and 11; 1994, c. 44, s. 86.
[213] *An Advocacy Primer*, 3rd. ed. (2005) at 293-297.

4. Decide on a strategy:

>   (i)   explore the contradiction to show this witness cannot be believed,
>
>   (ii) leave that argument to counsel's final address or
>
>   (iii) get the earlier statement admitted as the truth, either by getting the witness to adopt it as the truth or by making a successful *B. (K.G.)* application (considered under Hearsay in Chapter 4). Only in (iii) can the statement be entered as an exhibit.

Section 10 is concerned with written statements and s. 11 with oral; contradictory proof is limited, as it was by the common law, to previous statements which are "relative to the subject-matter of the case".

(i) Impeaching One's Own Witness

By a common law rule obscure in its origin,[214] a party was not permitted to impeach his or her own witness by attacks on the witness' character. The rule may have been a lingering effect of the older form of trial by wager of law in which issues were decided by parties calling the requisite number of oath-helpers; these were partisan witnesses chosen by the party and it was unseemly for the party to later attack them should they disappoint him or her. As witnesses changed into their modern form the policy against impeachment was expressed in terms that a party calling a witness vouched for or guaranteed his or her credit. Another, and perhaps better, theory advanced was that it was wrong to permit a party to coerce a certain story from his or her witness by holding, to the sure knowledge of the witness, ammunition in reserve for the destruction of the witness's character should the witness deviate. Buller J. wrote in the eighteenth century:

> A party never shall be permitted to produce general evidence to discredit his own witness; for that would be to enable him to destroy the witness if he spoke against him, and to make him a good witness if he spoke for him, with the means in his hands of destroying his credit if he spoke against him. But if a witness prove facts in a cause which make against the party who called him, yet the party may call other witnesses to prove that those facts were otherwise; for such facts are evidence in the cause, and the other witnesses are not called directly to discredit the first witness, but the impeachment of his credit is incidental and consequential only.[215]

An exception to the common law rule prohibiting impeachment or cross-examination at large arises where the witness is declared hostile. In *Reference Re R. v. Coffin*[216] the Supreme Court held that hostile means "not

---

[214] See 3A Wigmore, *Evidence* (Chad. Rev.), s. 896; Ladd, "Impeachment of One's Own Witness" (1936-37) 4 U. Chi. L. Rev. 69; and Bryant, "The Common Law Rule Against Impeaching One's Own Witness" (1982) 32 U.T. L.J. 412.

[215] Buller's *Nisi Prius* at 297, quoted in *Wright v. Beckett* (1833), 174 E.R. 143 (C.C.P.) at 144.

[216] [1956] S.C.R. 191.

giving her evidence fairly and with a desire to tell the truth because of a hostile animus toward the prosecution".

Consider the approach to hostility taken by the following civil case.

ANDERSON v. FLYING SAUCER DRIVE-IN LTD.
(2009), 82 C.P.C. (6th) 184 (Ont. S.C.J.)

The plaintiff was a cook who worked in the defendant's restaurant in Niagara Falls. The plaintiff and other employees were offered the opportunity to enrol in a benefits plan provided by the defendant. The plaintiff signed a blank form that was then completed by the defendant's insurance agent, Kenneth Cunningham. Ten months later the plaintiff became disabled. Her benefits were calculated based on what Cunningham had written in the form as her income. He wrote $10,000 instead of $23,000, which was her salary. The plaintiff sued the defendant for misstatement of her income on the form. The defendant's theory was that the workers made a conscious decision to under-report their income to lower the cost of the insurance premiums.

J.W. QUINN J.:—

Introduction

1 In the midst of conducting his direct examination of a witness in the trial of this matter, counsel for the plaintiff moved to have the witness declared hostile. The motion did not rely on a prior inconsistent statement but, instead, invoked what counsel submitted was the common-law jurisdiction of the court to declare a witness to be hostile on the grounds that the witness: held animosity toward, and feared prosecution by, the plaintiff; was loyal to the defendant; and, was testifying in a vague and unresponsive manner. The object of the motion was to permit counsel to cross-examine the witness, contrary to the near-antiquitous common-law rule prohibiting a party from impeaching his or her own witness.

. . .

17 The next testimony came from Mr. Cunningham (who had been summonsed by the plaintiff). He entered the witness box and, upon being sworn, read a prepared statement:

> As the plaintiff, on January 26, 2001, threatened to sue me, I seek protection afforded to me by s. 9(2) of the Ontario Evidence Act [R.S.O. 1990, c. E.23, as am.], s. 5(2) of the Canada Evidence Act [R.S.C. 1985, Chap. C-5, as am.] and s. 13 of the [Canadian] Charter of Rights and Freedoms. Thank you, Your Honour.

. . .

21 When the trial resumed at 10:00 a.m. the next day, Mr. Richard made an oral motion requesting that I declare Mr. Cunningham a hostile witness so as to permit cross-examination.

Discussion

22 The motion presumably was prompted by answers given by Mr. Cunningham that contradict the evidence of the plaintiff (for example, he testified that the plaintiff provided him with the figure of $10,000 for the enrolment form and that he queried her about its accuracy).

23 Every reported decision that counsel could unearth for their submissions dealt with declaring a witness adverse, under either s. 9(1) of the *Canada Evidence Act* or s. 23 of the *Ontario Evidence Act*, in the face of a prior inconsistent statement.[217]

24 Mr. Richard argued that: (1) Mr. Cunningham harboured animosity toward the plaintiff; (2) claiming the protection of the statutes shows, in the mind of Mr, Cunningham at least, a fear of prosecution; (3) Mr. Cunningham was still the insurance agent for the defendant and, therefore, had a disqualifying loyalty to the defendant; (4) the nature of Mr. Cunningham's testimony so far in the trial was vague and unresponsive so as to betray a bias against the plaintiff and it reflected a lack of reliability.

25 As part of the inherent jurisdiction to control its own process, and in those situations not involving the prior-inconsistent-statement provisions of the federal and provincial evidence acts, the court has the discretion to permit counsel to cross-examine his or her own witness (either as to a specific topic or in general) where it would be unfair not to do so. However, such unfairness must rise to the level of a failure of justice before the discretion should be exercised. To say that this would be a rare occurrence is borne out by the fact that neither Mr. Richard nor Mr. Argiropoulos could find a supporting case.

26 The reality of litigation is that sometimes a witness will be called to prove or corroborate a matter of evidence where it is known or suspected that the witness will also give damaging testimony on another point. For counsel, litigation is all about choices. Mr. Richard knew that Mr. Cunningham had also been summonsed by the defendant and that Mr. Argiropoulos, counsel for the defendant, had undertaken to call him as part of the defence (neither counsel had interviewed Mr. Cunningham). Yet, the choice was made to call Mr. Cunningham as part of the plaintiff's case. Associated with that choice was the foreseeable risk that Mr. Cunningham would give evidence contrary to the position of the plaintiff.

27 Where counsel has reason to believe that a witness will be hostile, the proper procedure is to hold a voir dire. Where the hostility arises, without warning, in the course of the testimony of the witness the court will consider the testimony

---

[217] Although it is not entirely clear to me, I think that the term "adverse" should be restricted to situations falling within the two Evidence Acts, whereas "hostile" describes instances arising under the common law. The terms are not synonymous. A witness may be "adverse" without being "hostile."Here, we do not have such a statement.

already given by the witness, and, perhaps, slip into a voir dire for additional evidence. However, before doing any of these things, counsel requesting the finding of hostility must meet a threshold. Certainly, the mere fact that a witness seeks the protection of the two evidence acts and the Charter, by itself, is insufficient to declare a witness to be hostile. Neither is the fact that a witness may give, or gives, testimony unfavourable to the case of the summonsing party. Also, it is not enough to show that the witness has a business connection to the opposing party . . . Such a connection would go to the weight of the testimony. Finally, I respectfully disagree with the submission made by Mr. Richard that the testimony of Mr. Cunningham so far has been vague and unresponsive. The witness brought his file and seems to have made an effort to ensure that it was complete and he answered the questions put to him in an unremarkable manner. Mr. Cunningham has not shown, by his demeanour in the witness box or by his testimony, that he is being uncooperative, that he has a disregard for the trial process or that he is blatantly lying to thwart the plaintiff or at all.

Conclusion

28 The plaintiff has not met the evidentiary threshold needed to trigger the exercise of the common-law discretion permitting the impeachment of one's own witness. The motion is dismissed.

R. v. MALIK

(2003), 194 C.C.C. (3d) 572 (B.C. S.C.)

This application arose in the "Air India" bombing trial in British Columbia.

JOSEPHSON J.: —

Overview

The Crown applies for a declaration at common law that its witness, Inderjit Singh Reyat, is hostile, thus entitling it to cross-examine him. Mr. Reyat was previously charged with the offences contained in the indictment before the Court. On February 10, 2003, Mr. Reyat pleaded guilty to manslaughter and was sentenced.

The Crown does not rely on the statutory provisions set out in ss. 9(1) and 9(2) of the Canada Evidence Act, R.S.C. 1985, c. C-5 (the "Act").

The Position of the Crown

The Crown submits that a witness can be declared hostile at common law where it is shown that he does not give his "evidence fairly and with a desire to tell the truth because of a hostile animus toward the prosecution": *R. v. Coffin* (1956), 114 C.C.C. 1 (S.C.C.) at 24. Relying on *R. v. Cassibo* (1982), 70 C.C.C. (2d) 498 (Ont. C.A.), and *R. v. Haughton* (1983), 38 O.R. (2d) 536 (Ont. Co. Ct.), the Crown submits that the right to cross-examine one's own witness at common law exists independently of, and has not been abrogated by, s. 9 of the Act.

The Crown submits that Mr. Reyat demonstrated a consistent failure to tell the truth during his evidence in chief. While not pointing to any prior inconsistent statements, the Crown says his evidence is manifestly untrue, reflecting an intention to obfuscate, rather than impart, the truth. It submits that Mr. Reyat's lack of veracity was patently obvious with respect to a number of issues including the identity of "Mr. X", the particulars of the request by Talwinder Singh Parmar that he construct an explosive device, the nature of the device he constructed, the testing of this device, and his failure to question Mr. Parmar about his (Mr. Reyat's) own role in the events of June 22, 1985.

The Crown attributes Mr. Reyat's unwillingness to tell the truth to predisposition antithetical to the Crown based on both his identification with the perpetrators of the offences at issue and his perception that he has been victimized by the Crown over the past 15 years, as reflected in Mr. Reyat's application earlier in this trial to declare the Crown's actions an abuse of process.

Position of Mr. Malik and Mr. Bagri

Mr. Malik and Mr. Bagri characterize the Crown's application under the common law as novel and unprecedented. They submit that it is not grounded in either of the traditional bases; a prior inconsistent statement by the witness or a hostile demeanour or attitude in the witness stand. Mr. Reyat's evidence in chief was consistent with his previous statements to the police and the facts upon which the Crown accepted his guilty plea to the lesser charge of manslaughter. As such, it would be premature and inappropriate for the Court to make a finding with respect to Mr. Reyat's credibility without reference to the remainder of the evidence to be led at the trial.

They also submit that it is not open to the Crown to rely on the common law in this regard since it has been superseded by the statutory procedure set out in s. 9 of the Act: *R. v. T. (T.E.)* (1991), 3 B.C.A.C. 29 (B.C. C.A.); *R. v. Soobrian* (1994), 96 C.C.C. (3d) 208 (Ont. C.A.).

They submit that under either s. 9 of the Act or at common law, findings of adversity or hostility have been justified as necessary to neutralize or discredit unfavourable evidence that has taken the party calling the witness by surprise. Here, the witness testified in a manner consistent with what could reasonably be expected. Thus, there is no principled basis upon which to depart from ordinary rules of procedure.

Finally, while Mr. Malik recognizes the enormous public interest in determining who is responsible for the events of June 22, 1985, he submits that this trial is not the forum for a public inquiry or an investigative hearing.

Conclusion

The Crown, in urging the Court to sidestep s. 9 of the Act and go directly to the common law rule regarding hostile witnesses, points to the origins of that section as a mere procedural step in the common law process. While s. 9(1) does not expressly confer a right of cross-examination, that right has been judicially grafted onto it, not without some controversy.

The Crown could not identify any recent cases which have granted this common law declaration without reference to and reliance on s. 9. Only one case has been identified (*R. v. Haughton*, supra) which made this common law declaration, but that was over twenty years ago when the right to cross-examine under s. 9(1) may not have been clear and even then only subsequent to a cross- examination under s. 9(2). However, the common law rule, while appearing to have been completely abandoned, has not been issued a judicial or legislative death certificate.

Nonetheless, courts should exercise caution before leapfrogging legislation designed (as judicially interpreted) to set the boundaries of this right and embrace the pre-existing common law rule. Assuming the common law rule remains alive, I would nonetheless decline to grant the application. The Crown must establish that the withholding of the truth flows from a hostile animus to the Crown. While not necessarily the only route, in nearly every case where such animus has been established, it has been accomplished by demonstrating that the witness' evidence is inconsistent with a prior statement. In other cases, the manner and demeanour of the witness in giving evidence has also been a factor.

In this case, Mr. Reyat's evidence is generally consistent with his statement to police upon his arrest in 1985. It is not significantly inconsistent with the Crown theory advanced in the 1990 trial and conviction of Mr. Reyat for the offence of manslaughter. It also formed the basis of the Crown's acceptance of Mr. Reyat's plea of guilty to manslaughter in the course of this trial. Further, it has not been suggested that the Crown was misled or had any misapprehensions regarding the general nature of what Mr. Reyat's evidence would be.

The Crown submits that the improbabilities contained in Mr. Reyat's evidence mount so high that his untruthfulness is manifest. Assuming that to be the case, under the common law rule, the Crown must also demonstrate that this untruthful evidence flows from a hostile animus towards the Crown. That, the Crown submits, can be inferred from various factors including his affiliation with certain cultural and religious groups.

Hostile animus is more than an interest at variance with that of the Crown. Mr. Reyat's manner and demeanour in the witness box displayed no such animus. Keeping in mind that Mr. Reyat's version of events has been roughly consistent since his arrest in 1985, a more reasonable inference is that his evidence flows from a desire for self-preservation by minimizing his criminal conduct and a desire to protect his companions in crime. If these motives were to be regarded as sufficient to infer a hostile animus to the Crown, that inference would follow in nearly every case where a witness offers evidence which can be demonstrated to be untruthful.

I respectfully decline to declare Mr. Reyat a hostile witness at common law.

R. v. OSAE
2010 ONSC 3108 (Ont. S.C.J.)

The accused was charged with second degree murder. During the trial, the Crown applied to have its witness, Jordan Cromwell, declared a hostile witness. The vehicle used in the shooting was located in a parking garage where Cromwell lived. Cromwell was a friend of the accused who had also taken possession of the gun used in the shooting.

A.J. O'MARRA J.:—

. . .

Hostility

13 There is recognition in the case law that there is a difference in the meaning of a witness who is "hostile" at common law and a witness found to be "adverse" pursuant to s. 9(1) of the Canada Evidence Act. Further, different rights flow to the party that called the witness from the determination of whether a witness is hostile or adverse: (see Wawanesa Mutual Insurance Company v. Hanes, [1963] 1 C.C.C. 176 (OCA); R. v. Cassibo (1982), 70 C.C.C. (2d) 498 and R. v. Vivar, [2004] O.J. No. 9 (SCJ)).

14 In R. v. Coffin, [1956] S.C.R. 191, Kellock J. stated that a "hostile" witness is one who does not give "her evidence fairly and with a desire to tell the truth because of a hostile animus toward the prosecution". In Wawanesa v. Hanes, supra the seminal case in this area MacKay J.A. at para. 135 concluded that "hostile" means that such a witness must possess "hostility of the mind". Further, the determination of whether a person is hostile in mind to the party who called the witness is a question of fact. MacKay J.A. provided helpful guidance as to what should be considered in making the assessment:

> To determine this collateral issue a trial judge should hear all and any evidence relevant to that issue. The fact that a witness has made a previous contradictory statement is relevant, admissible and most cogent evidence on that issue and that evidence alone may be accepted by the judge as sufficient proof of the hostility of the witness irrespective of the demeanor and manner of the witness in the witness box. (It is also, of course, open to a trial judge to rule that a witness is hostile solely by reason of his manner of giving evidence and demeanor in the witness box.)

15 What is of importance in the determination is whether the inconsistency of a prior statement with his present testimony is on a vital matter and/or his demeanor as a witness displays a hostility of the mind. The trial judge must be satisfied by the evidence of inconsistency and/or demeanor the witness has not given his or her evidence fairly with a desire to tell the truth because of a hostile animus toward the prosecution.

16 If the court is so satisfied, as noted by MacKay J.A. in Wawanesa, supra, at para. 108 and 127 the consequences of a finding of hostility under the common law rule counsel is not limited to cross-examination only on the prior inconsistent statement, but may cross-examination the witness generally as to

all matters in issue. Where a witness called by a party is declared hostile the judge may grant leave to that party to cross-examine its own witness at large.

. . .

31 Jordan Cromwell has acknowledged he lied at the preliminary May 27, 2008, he lied in the videotaped statement May 29, 2008 when he had a chance to come clean, and he has lied on this trial. He has readily changed his evidence in material respects. He is prepared to be untruthful until confronted with information that contradicts what he has said. Oaths and affirmations are meaningless to him. His lack of veracity is palpable.

32 I have no doubt that some of his willingness to be untruthful flows from a sense of self-preservation through trying to minimize his conduct and involvement as an accessory after the fact to a murder by having helped to conceal the Mazda and its broken window, and by taking possession of the firearm used in a murder. He may well have concern about being seen as a "rat" and possible repercussions for breaking the code of silence and snitching on his friend. However, in my view, his untruthfulness also flows directly from a hostile animus toward the Crown to weaken the case against the defendant, his friend and an attempt to tailor his evidence to focus on Owusu, a virtual stranger to him.

33 Also, I consider Cromwell to be a hostile witness with animus toward the Crown based on his demeanor in response to questions asked of him by the Crown during examination-in-chief. Cromwell acknowledged that he had lied throughout the first day of the preliminary inquiry and when asked as to why, he stated it was because he was scared for his life. Later in questioning, when he reciled from that position, on being reminded of what he had stated earlier that he lied because he felt "scared" for his life, he responded angrily that the Crown had confused him. There were a number of instances when he retorted with questions to the Crown's questions in a confrontational tone. In other instances, he attempted to speak over the Crown's questions in an attempt to cut them off. Further, I accept the Crown's representation that at the end of the day after testifying here as he departed the court room and passed Crown counsel he hissed at her.

34 I do not accept that Mr. Cromwell testified in the manner he did on trial because he was confused or tired as suggested by defence counsel. Quite to the contrary, he did not display any lassitude during the day he testified before the jury. He claimed confusion only in an instance of obvious falsity and he attempted to blame the Crown because of the questions he was being asked. There was nothing in the manner of questioning to have caused confusion.

35 I find Jordan Cromwell to be a hostile witness to the prosecution based on the substantial inconsistencies between his prior statements, testimony on the preliminary inquiry and his testimony thus far on the trial, the numerous untruths both admitted and obvious, as well as his manner of giving evidence

and his demeanor in the witness stand toward the Crown. In my assessment of all of the circumstances, he has not given his evidence fairly with any desire to tell the truth because of a hostile animus toward the prosecution.

. . .

37 In holding that Jordan Cromwell is hostile witness the Crown shall be permitted to cross-examine generally to impeach the witness.

38 Accordingly, I shall instruct the jury that insofar as the prior statements may be used during the continuing examination of the witness the contents may be considered only for the purpose of assessing the credibility of the witness and not for the truth of the contents; unless they are satisfied he has accepted it as true while testifying.

(ii) *Canada Evidence Act, s. 9(1)*

Section 9(1) reads:

Adverse witnesses

9. (1) A party producing a witness shall not be allowed to impeach his credit by general evidence of bad character, but if the witness, in the opinion of the court, proves adverse, the party may contradict him by other evidence, or, by leave of the court, may prove that the witness made at other times a statement inconsistent with his present testimony, but before the last mentioned proof can be given the circumstances of the supposed statement, sufficient to designate the particular occasion, shall be mentioned to the witness, and he shall be asked whether or not he did make the statement.

The issues that have arisen under s. 9(1) include (i) the meaning of adverse (i.e., is it the same as hostile or is it broader to include unfavourable?); and (ii) what follows from a finding of adverse (i.e., does it permit cross-examination at large?). Only on the prior inconsistent statement? Or only proof that the earlier statement was made? These issues are addressed in the following case.

R. v. FIGLIOLA
2011 ONCA 457, 272 C.C.C. (3d) 518 (Ont. C.A.)

The appellant was convicted of first degree murder. The theory of the Crown at trial was that the appellant hired her co-accused (Di Trapani) to kill her husband. At trial, the Crown called Teresa Pignatelli to testify about the relationships between the appellant, her co-accused, the deceased, and a person the appellant was having an affair with. As well, Ms. Pignatelli had seen Di Trapani in an area on the night of the murder not far from the scene of the murder. One of the grounds of appeal was the Crown's cross-examination of its own witness.

By The Court:

[47] The Crown cannot be faulted for seeking an adversity ruling under s. 9(1), nor do we think there is any basis for interfering with the trial judge's discretionary decision to grant that order in the circumstances. He concluded after a voir dire—correctly, in our view—that Ms. Pignatelli had made a number of prior statements to the police and at the preliminary hearing that were inconsistent with her testimony at trial; that she adopted a position in her testimony opposite to the Crown's position; and that she had a motive to protect her friends. There was ample support on the record for those findings and for the decision based on them.

[48] The Crown sought an order under s. 9(1) declaring Ms. Pignatelli an adverse witness. The trial judge made an order declaring Ms. Pignatelli an adverse witness. The Crown did not seek, nor did the trial judge grant, an order declaring her a hostile witness, and, contrary to Ms. Pignatelli's submission, the trial judge did not make an order granting the Crown leave to cross-examine Ms. Pignatelli at large. Perilously, though, everyone appears to have assumed that such an order had been made. The Crown proceeded to cross-examine the witness forcefully in a wide-ranging fashion—and with considerable success—with no intervention by the trial judge and no objection from defence counsel (not counsel on the appeal) or request for a limiting instruction to the jury.

[49] However, this seamless move to a cross-examination at large was misguided. In Ontario, a ruling that a witness is "adverse" pursuant to s. 9(1) of the *Canada Evidence Act* is not the equivalent of a common law declaration of "hostility" entitling the beneficiary of the ruling to cross-examine the witness at large. This court has held that adversity and hostility are not synonymous for these purposes: *Wawanesa Mutual Insurance Co. v. Hanes*, [1961] O.R. 495, [1961] O.J. No. 562 (C.A.); *R. v. Cassibo* (1982), 39 O.R. (2d) 288, [1982] O.J. No. 3511 (C.A.). See, also, *R. v. Vivar*, [2004] O.J. No. 9, [2004] O.T.C. 5 (S.C.J.), at paras. 11-12; *R. v. S. (S.W.)*, [2005] O.J. No. 4958, [2005] O.T.C. 1004 (S.C.J.); *R. v. Osae*, [2010] O.J. No. 2285, 2010 ONSC 3108; *R. v. Gushue (No. 4)*, [1975] O.J. No. 2211 (Co. Ct.); and *R. v. Cronshaw*, [1976] O.J. No. 2466, 33 C.C.C. (2d) 183 (Prov. Ct.).

[50] This jurisprudence confirms that an "adverse" witness is one who is opposed in interest or unfavourable in the sense of opposite in position to the party calling that witness, whereas a "hostile" witness is one who demonstrates an antagonistic attitude or hostile mind toward the party calling him or her. In *R. v. Coffin*, [1956] S.C.R. 191, [1956] S.C.J. No. 1, 114 C.C.C. 1, at p. 213 S.C.R., p. 24 C.C.C., Kellock J. described a hostile witness as one who does not give his or her evidence fairly and with a desire to tell the truth because of a hostile animus towards the prosecution.

[51] The common law right of a party to cross-examine his or her own witness at large with leave of the trial judge, if in the judge's opinion the witness is "hostile", is not affected by s. 9(1) of the *Canada Evidence Act*: *Cassibo*, per Martin J.A., at p. 302 O.R. Section 9 makes no reference to a witness "proving hostile" and contains no suggestion of a right to cross-examine at large. As Porter C.J.O. pointed out in *Wawanesa*, a declaration of hostility and its consequences are something that arise "in addition [to]" a finding of adversity. At pp. 507-508 O.R., after reviewing the steps to be taken by a judge in deciding whether to make a declaration of adversity and the factors to be considered, he stated that "[t]he Judge, if he declared the witness hostile, might, in addition permit him to be cross-examined" (emphasis added). It follows that a declaration of adversity pursuant to s. 9(1) was not, itself, sufficient to trigger a right in the Crown to cross-examine Ms. Pignatelli generally as to all matters in issue.

[52] Ill-advisedly, however, that is what happened. The Crown cross-examined the witness about inconsistencies between her evidence at trial and statements she had made to the police during interviews on three occasions (October 2, 2002, January 14, 2003 and January 22, 2003) as well as between her evidence at trial and at the preliminary hearing. These inconsistencies related to such things as when she knew [that] Ms. Figliola was in a relationship with Mr. Gonsalves (at trial she acknowledged suspecting they were involved at the time of the murder, but in October she told the police she did not know); the amount of money Ms. Figliola had given her; and a number of details about the evening of August 6, 2001 (in her October statement she did not tell the police she had seen Mr. Di Trapani that night; in both January statements she said she twice saw Mr. Di Trapani and Mr. Latorre drive by her shop, where she was having an ice cream with Ms. Figliola's cousin, Bruna; at trial she said they drove by once).

[53] As Ms. Pignatelli's cross-examination by the Crown developed, however, it is apparent that these questions were simply a springboard to a much broader attack on her credibility.

. . .

[62] Following the s. 9(1) ruling, the Crown should have been restricted to cross- examining on the prior inconsistent statements and the circumstances surrounding them.... The jurors needed to understand clearly that if they found Ms. Pignatelli not to be credible, they could not use that finding to conclude that either or both of the appellants were not credible either. Nor could they use such a finding to so support a conclusion that either or both of the appellants were guilty . . .

[63] In our view, a specific instruction relating to Ms. Pignatelli was required in these circumstances. . . .

[65] We would therefore allow the appeal, set aside Ms. Figliola's conviction and order a new trial.

(iii) *Canada Evidence Act, s. 9(2)*

In 1969, s. 9 of the *Canada Evidence Act* was amended to include subsection (2):

> (2) Where the party producing a witness alleges that the witness made at other times a statement in writing, reduced to writing, or recorded on audio tape or video tape or otherwise, inconsistent with the witness' present testimony, the court may, without proof that the witness is adverse, grant leave to that party to cross-examine the witness as to the statement and the court may consider the cross-examination in determining whether in the opinion of the court the witness is adverse.[218]

The legislation was designed to allow the adversity, demanded by s. 9(1), to be demonstrated not only by the witness demeanour or bearing but also by cross-examination on an alleged prior contradictory statement. Notice that s. 9(2) is confined to written statements or statements reduced to writing or recorded in some way.[219] The new legislation was interpreted,[220] however, as if it created a new and independent method for impeachment of one's own witness. The cross-examination mentioned in s. 9(2) was intended to be in the absence of the jury since its purpose was to enable the court to determine whether the witness was adverse for the purposes of s. 9(1). But given the judicial interpretation, it was noted:

> The cross-examination provided for in s. 9(2) must be in the presence of the jury. The purpose of that cross-examination is to attack the credibility of the witness in respect to the evidence already given. As the jury are the judges of credibility, it is obvious the cross-examination would be meaningless if conducted in their absence.[221]

R. v. S. (C.L.)

(2011), 266 C.C.C. (3d) 360 (Man. Q.B.)

Three accused (C.L.S., C.A.C.D. and E.A.D.M.) were charged with second degree murder. At their trial, the Crown called C.G., who had given a videotaped statement to the police implicating two of the accused in the killing. At trial, he testified that he did not remember the events that he had discussed in his videotaped statement. The Crown brought an application pursuant to s. 9(2) to cross-examine its witness on his videotaped statement.

---

[218]   Now R.S.C. 1985, c. C-5; 1994, c. 44, s. 85. See David Paciocco, "Confronting Disappointing, Hostile and Adverse Witnesses in Criminal Cases" (2012) 59 C.L.Q. 302.

[219]   See *R. v. Carpenter* (1983), 31 C.R. (3d) 261 (Ont. C.A.) at 266. See also *R. v. Daniels*, [1984] N.W.T.R. 311 (S.C.), finding that a transcript of a taped interview is not a statement reduced to writing.

[220]   *R. v. Milgaard* (1971), 2 C.C.C. (2d) 206 (Sask. C.A.). The *Milgaard* view was specifically approved by the Supreme Court of Canada in *McInroy and Rouse v. R.* (1978), 42 C.C.C. (2d) 481.

[221]   *Milgaard, ibid.* at 222, per Culliton, C.J.S.

One of the issues raised by the defence was whether the Crown had to prove that the out-of-court statement was voluntary before it could be used to cross-examine the witness. Another issue was whether "I don't remember" constituted an "inconsistency".

BEARD J.A.:—

9 The leading decision regarding the procedure to be followed in an application under s. 9(2) is that of the Saskatchewan Court of Appeal in *R. v. Milgaard* (1971), 2 C.C.C. (2d) 206 (leave to appeal refused (1971), 4 C.C.C. (2d) 566n (S.C.C.). In that decision, the court set out the following procedure (at pp. 221-22):

(1) Counsel should advise the Court that he desires to make an application under s. 9(2) of the Canada Evidence Act.

(2) When the Court is so advised, the Court should direct the jury to retire.

(3) Upon retirement of the jury, counsel should advise the learned trial Judge of the particulars of the application and produce for him the alleged statement in writing, or the writing to which the statement has been reduced.

(4) The learned trial Judge should read the statement, or writing, and determine whether, in fact, there is an inconsistency between such statement or writing and the evidence the witness has given the Court. If the learned trial Judge decides there is no inconsistency, then that ends the matter. If he finds there is an inconsistency, he should call upon counsel to prove the statement or writing.

(5) Counsel should then prove the statement, or writing. This may be done by producing the statement or writing to the witness. If the witness admits the statement, or the statement reduced to writing, such proof would be sufficient. If the witness does not so admit, counsel then could provide the necessary proof by other evidence.

(6) If the witness admits making the statement, counsel for the opposing party should have the right to cross-examine as to the circumstances under which the statement was made. A similar right to cross-examine should be granted if the statement is proved by other witnesses. It may be that he will be able to establish that there were circumstances which would render it improper for the learned trial Judge to permit the cross- examination, notwithstanding the apparent inconsistencies. The opposing counsel, too, should have the right to call evidence as to factors relevant to obtaining the statement, for the purpose of attempting to show that cross-examination should not be permitted.

(7) The learned trial Judge should then decide whether or not he will permit the cross-examination. If so, the jury should be recalled.

10 The application of the procedure to the facts of this case raises two legal issues:

(i)   whether an inconsistency can arise where a witness claims to have forgotten the events in the statement; and

(ii)   the test and burden of proof to be applied in determining whether to permit the cross-examination.

(*i*)   *inconsistency*

11 In this case, the witness has not testified to facts that are different from those in his prior statement. In that statement, he related a conversation that he had had with E.A.D.M. in which E.A.D.M. spoke of his involvement in the beating, and another conversation in a similar vein with C.L.K. in which E.A.D.M. participated. In court, C.G. did not deny that those conversations took place; rather, he claimed to have forgotten what was said to him.

12 This is exactly the situation that was dealt with in *The Queen v. McInroy et al.*, [1979] 1 S.C.R. 588, wherein the witness swore that she could not recall what had been said to her in a conversation that took place with the accused despite her earlier written statement describing that conversation. On the question of whether that constituted an inconsistency, the court, which was unanimous on this point, found as follows (at p. 604):

> ... It was quite open to [the trial judge] to conclude that she was lying about her recollection and to form his own conclusions as to why she was refusing to testify as to her true recollection. Chief Justice Farris says in terms that "the trial judge clearly did not believe her when she said she had a lack of recall". This being so there was evidence of an inconsistency between what she said at the trial, i.e. that she had no recollection of a conversation, and what was contained in her written statement, i.e. a detailed recollection of it. (emphasis added)

13 Thus, a claim that a witness has no recollection of events that he or she related in an earlier statement can constitute an inconsistency within s. 9(2) of the CEA.

(*ii*)   *the test and burden of proof to be applied in determining whether to permit the cross-examination*

14 While the *Milgaard* decision sets out the procedure to be followed in determining whether to permit a cross-examination under s. 9(2), it does not set out the test to be applied in making that determination once there is a finding that the witness did, in fact, make a prior inconsistent statement, or who has the burden of proof. On the test to be met, step 6 refers to "circumstances which would render it improper for the judge to permit the cross-examination". As to which party bears the burden of proof, it appears that the counsel applying to cross-examine must establish the inconsistency, while step 6 states that "It may be that [the opposing party] will be able to establish that there were circumstances . . . ." From this it appears that the party calling the witness must show that there was an inconsistency between the prior statement and the in-court testimony, and then the burden shifts to the party opposing the cross-

examination to establish that there were circumstances that would render it improper for the judge to permit the cross-examination. This second issue could be important in determining how the voir dire should be conducted, but was not addressed in any of the precedents that I have reviewed.

15 In *McInroy*, the court approved the *Milgaard* procedure, but did not deal with either the nature of the test or which party bears the burden of proof. The court said only (at p. 605):

> The granting of the Crown's application was a matter for the sole discretion of the trial judge and in my view he had adequate ground for exercising in that discretion as he did.

16 The question of the test to be applied by the trial judge was addressed by the Ontario Court of Appeal in *R. v. Carpenter (No. 2)* (1982), 1 C.C.C. (3d) 149, wherein Grange J.A., for the court, stated as follows (at p. 155):

> . . . I do not, of course, mean that cross-examination should automatically have been permitted. The subsection is clearly permissive and the trial judge might well have refused permission in view of the circumstances of the taking of the statements and his opinion of its reliability. The test as put by Porter C.J.O. in [*Wawanessa Mutual Insurance Co. v. Hanes*, [1961] O.R. 495] at p. 508 is whether "the ends of justice would be best attained by admitting it. The section does not contemplate the indiscriminate admission of statements of this kind".

17 *Carpenter* proposed that the reliability of the statement was a factor to be considered in the test for determining whether to permit or refuse the application to cross-examine on the statement, although it is not clear whether the reference to reliability relates to the accuracy of the recording of the prior statement, the effect on reliability caused by the circumstances in which the statement was taken, the reliability of the contents of the statement, or all three.

18 The rational for the traditional rule permitting cross-examination is ably set out by Smith P.J. in *R. v. K. (R.J.)*, 2001 CarswellMan 215, wherein she states as follows (at para. 67):

> When it is established that a witness made a prior inconsistent statement with the testimony given in court, particularly on matters related to the central issues relevant to the proceeding, it will usually be in the interests of justice to permit cross- examination under Section 9(2). The ultimate objective of the trial process in which the preliminary hearing plays an important role is ascertaining the truth. Cross- examination is a technique that our system of justice accepts as a very effective tool in the pursuit of truth. It is unsettling when a witness tells one account in court and then apparently another outside court. It raises obvious concerns and question about the veracity of the witness' testimony. These concerns are best addressed by permitting cross-examination.

. . .

25 The test in *Carpenter* has recently been adopted and reinforced by the Manitoba Court of Appeal in *R. v. Aitkenhead (R.G.)*, 2001 MBCA 60, 156

Man.R. (2d) 86. In that case, the witness was a co-accused who had pled guilty. While he, himself, was an accused, he had given a statement to the police that Aitkenhead had committed the offence, but when he testified at the Aitkenhead's trial, he said that he, alone, was responsible. There was evidence that that statement was tainted by police inducements, threats and the denial of legal counsel, and as a result, the trial judge ruled that the statement could not be tendered as substantive evidence. He did, however, permit the statement to be used to cross-examine the witness, it being relevant to his credibility. On the appeal, the defence counsel argued that, where there was police intimidation, inducements, and a denial of prompt access to legal counsel, the court was bound to exercise the discretion under s. 9(2) against allowing cross-examination.

26 On the exercise of judicial discretion under s. 9(2), Huband J.A., for the court, stated as follows (at paras. 23-25 and 27-28):

> It is true that the statement would not have been admissible in court in a prosecution of Steve Stroppa himself, but there is a vast difference between interrogating an accused on a prior inconsistent statement and interrogating a Crown witness on a prior inconsistent statement. In the first instance, it would indeed bring the administration of justice into disrepute. In the second case, the liberty of the witness is not of immediate concern, but what is in issue is the truth of his assertions made at trial.

> In *R. v. Carpenter (No. 2)* (1982), 1 C.C.C. (3d) 149, the Ontario Court of Appeal, in reasons by Grange J.A., had occasion to consider the issue of cross-examination upon a previous statement. It was held that the right to cross-examine was by no means automatic. The court adopted the test of whether the ends of justice would best be attained by allowing cross-examination. It is clear that the trial judge in the present case was of the view that the ends of justice would best be attained by permitting Crown counsel to cross-examine Steve Stroppa. I am unable to say that he was wrong.

> Crown counsel rightly points out that cross-examination having taken place, defence counsel is also entitled to cross-examine the witness and did so. It is open to defence counsel to elicit the circumstances under which the prior statements were obtained and thus blunt the Crown's subsequent submission to the jury that the witness's trial testimony should be disbelieved.

> . . .

> In my opinion, no basis for appellate court interference with the discretion exercised by the trial judge under s. 9(2) has been established. This court should not substitute its discretion for that of the trial judge unless the case for doing so is plain.

> There may well be cases where to allow a cross-examination of one's own witness under s. 9(2) would indeed bring the administration of justice into disrepute. The circumstances must be considered on a case-by-case basis. In the present matter, the trial judge considered the circumstances and came to a rational conclusion and dealt with the matter appropriately in his subsequent charge to the jury.

> . . .

28 . . . I would suggest that the original *Milgaard* test has been redefined by *Carpenter* and *Aitkenhead*, and is now expanded to that of "whether the ends of justice would best be attained by allowing the cross-examination," which puts added emphasis on the importance of giving the jury the full opportunity to evaluate the credit of the witness in order to ascertain the truth of his or her assertions made at trial.

. . .

40 The application of s. 9(2) has been considered in the following additional cases: *R. v. Smith*, [1989] M.J. No. 394 (P.C.) (QL); *R. v. Morgan*, [1997] M.J. No. 5481 (Ont. Gen. Div.); *R. v. Fraser* (1990), 55 C.C.C. (3d) 551 (B.C. C.A.); *R. v. Soobrian* (1994), 96 C.C.C. (3d) 208 (Ont. C.A.); *R. v. A.M.*, 2005 ABPC 316, 392 A.R. 195; *R. v. Crossley*, 2005 BCSC 989, appeal dismissed on other grounds 2007 BCCA 333; and *R. v. Williams*, [2005] O.J. No. 4983 (Ont. Sup. Ct. J.) (QL), appeal dismissed on other grounds 2008 ONCA 413, 236 O.A.C. 251. These cases, and those mentioned earlier, give examples of some factors that judges can take into account on an application to permit cross-examination under s. 9(2): the actions of the police officers who had contact with the witness prior to the statement being made and the failure of the calling counsel to call on those police officers; the nature of the police questioning; the reason given to the witness for the need for a statement; whether the witness was detained or under arrest at the time of the statement or believed themselves to be so; whether there was any duress, coercion or inducement by the police; whether police "trickery" was used and its nature; any mistreatment of the witness; the length of time taken leading up to the statement-taking; the state of mind of the witness at the time of the statement; the demeanour of the witness when the statement was taken; whether the witness was impaired by alcohol or drugs or a non-operating mind; whether the statement was simple yes/no answers to question or a narrative; and the witness's demeanour while giving his testimony about the circumstances surrounding the taking of the statement.

. . .

42 From these cases, the following conclusions can be drawn:

-   the right to cross-examine under s. 9(2) is not automatic;
-   the test is whether, on a balance of probabilities, the ends of justice would best be attained by allowing or refusing the cross-examination;
-   one must look at all of the circumstances, including those of the taking of the statement, in deciding whether to permit the cross-examination, which circumstances are to be considered on a case-by-case basis;
-   even where the statement of a recanting witness (other than the accused) was taken under threats, promises and denial of the right to legal counsel (if such right existed at the time of the statement) such that the statement could not be admitted as substantive evidence, those circumstances may not be sufficient to deny the right to cross-examine on the statement;

- one must consider whether there are any circumstances such that allowing the cross-examination would bring the administration of justice into disrepute; and

- the circumstances under which cross-examination will be refused will be relatively rare.

Crown counsel often have to resort to ss. 9(1) and (2) in domestic assault prosecutions where the unfortunate reality is that principal witnesses often recant in whole or in part from previous incriminating statements. The current practice is to first try and coax the witness back by asking the witness to refresh his or her memory by reading his or her prior statement. If he or she persists in contradiction the usual practice is to use the above *Milgaard* procedure for a s. 9(2) application. If that is granted, many judges now allow cross-examination at large.[222] However some would require a further s. 9(1) application[223] and some even a declaration of hostility at common law before such cross-examination is permitted. The effect of such applications is that the Crown is granted permission to cross-examine its own witness on a prior inconsistent statement. The procedure is similar to any cross-examination under ss. 10 and 11 but the strategy here is not to destroy credibility but rather to try to get the witness to adopt the earlier statement as the truth. A new option is to make a *B. (K.G.)* application: see Chapter 4 under Hearsay, which turns on criteria of necessity and reliability.

The B.C. Court of Appeal decided in *R. v. Glowatski*[224] that the s. 9(2) procedure may be bypassed in a trial before judge alone in favour of a *B. (K.G.)* application.[225]

PROBLEM

You are a Crown counsel prosecuting a serious domestic assault case before judge and jury. The committal to trial after a preliminary inquiry was on consent of the defence counsel. No evidence was heard. A week before the trial you interviewed the complainant, Jane. She confirmed that on the day in question she was with the accused, Bob, in her apartment where the assault was alleged to have occurred. She admitted to having been in a common law relationship with him. Apart from that she was totally uncooperative and begged you to drop the charges as she is still with him and loves him. After a couple of minutes she walked out of the interview. You see this as a classic domestic assault case and wish to try for a conviction.

The arresting officer will testify that he answered a 911 call and arrived at the apartment to hear the sound of a fight, breaking glass and shouts. He broke the door down to find the complainant sobbing, clutching her side and

---

[222]   See *R. v. Boyce*, 2014 ONCA 150, 307 C.C.C. (3d) 275, 10 C.R. (7th) 136 (Ont. C.A.) and *R. v. Dayes*, 2013 ONCA 614, 301 C.C.C. (3d) 337, 6 C.R. (7th) 372 (Ont. C.A.).

[223]   See Watt J.A. in *R. v. Taylor*, 2015 ONCA 448, 325 C.C.C. (3d) 413 (Ont. C.A.) at 425 [C.C.C.].

[224]   (2001), 160 C.C.C. (3d) 525, 47 C.R. (5th) 230 (B.C. C.A.).

[225]   See too *R. v. Fleet* (2001), 48 C.R. (5th) 28 (N.S. C.A.).

with blood streaming down her face. The accused was sort of crouching over her and took a run at the officer. He was arrested but refused to answer any questions then or later. Another officer arrived on the scene and took Jane to hospital where she was treated for cracked ribs and received 10 stitches for a wound on her cheek. On her release from hospital she gave a signed statement to the second officer.

There were two earlier statements:

(a) an oral statement by Jane to the arresting officer on his entry to the apartment, "Please go easy on Bob. I love him and he did not mean to hit me that hard".

(b) a written statement signed by Jane to the second officer at the hospital in which Jane stated: "He got jealous when I spoke to another guy at a bar. When he is drunk he often gets moody. When we got back to the apartment he immediately picked up a large purple vase and smashed it over my head. He shouted at me "You bitch" and kicked me in the side. I am glad you guys rescued me. I am tired and I want to go to my mother's house".

You expect Jane to fully or partly recant both statements at trial. Leaving aside the possibility of a *B. (K.G.)* application, **plan your strategy in dealing with her as a witness in as much detail as you can.**

(b) Bias

Witnesses are no longer barred from testifying because of some interest they may have in the outcome of the litigation. Feelings for or against a party, though making testimony less than impartial, are not grounds for exclusion. These matters, however, are fruitful areas of exploration for impeachment purposes. The types of facts from which partiality or hostility may be inferred are infinitely varied and little is to be gained by exploring those judicially recognized in the reports. The inference may be made from the witness' circumstances, for example a family or employment relationship with the party, or from acts done by the witness, for example offering a bribe to another witness to testify falsely. Since such feelings betray emotional partiality which may impair the witness' testimonial qualifications, evidence of the same is not collateral and may be elicited in cross-examination of the witness *or* by extrinsic proof.[226]

If it is intended to impeach the witness by evidence of his or her prior conduct illustrating bias, it should be preceded by a cross-examination of the witness concerning the same.[227] If the witness admits his or her bias, that should be the end of it.

---

[226] See *Attorney General v. Hitchcock* (1847), 154 E.R. 38 (Exch. Ct.). See an application of this in *R. v. Finnessey* (1906), 11 O.L.R. 338 (C.A.) and cases there cited.

[227] Compare 3A Wigmore, *Evidence* (Chad. Rev.), s. 953 and McCormick, *Evidence*, 2nd ed. at 80. In the case of *Hitchcock, ibid*, Baron Alderson stated: "In [that case] it was held to be competent for the prisoner to shew that the witness had a spite against him. It was material to shew that the mind of the witness was not in a state of impartiality or equality towards the

In *General Films Ltd. v. McElroy* [228] the Saskatchewan Court of Appeal noted:

> . . . it is . . . only when the witness had denied his bias or partiality that counsel is entitled to adduce evidence to contradict him. In this case the witness deVries had admitted enough upon his cross-examination to show that he was adversely affected towards the plaintiff. Thus he had acknowledged that he was acting for a rival concern, that he was doing all he could to take business away from the plaintiff, and that he was interested in the result of the case . . . Having thus sufficiently established the state of de Vries' mind and feelings towards the litigation, I do not think that plaintiff's counsel should have been allowed to question Widdifield about what de Vries had said at their interview. Such evidence was objectionable . . . because it raised collateral issues which tend to unduly complicate and prolong trials without adequate reason.

A recent recognition of our courts' preference for admitting the possibility of bias affecting credibility rather than a blanket exclusion occurred in *R. v. Dikah*.[229] In that case the accused were charged with trafficking in cocaine. All charges involved alleged sales of cocaine to a paid police agent identified as Agent 21. The accused sought a stay alleging that the terms of Agent 21's agreement with the RCMP rendered any proceedings based on his alleged purchases of cocaine from the accused an abuse of process or a breach of the accused's rights under s. 7 of the *Charter*. The agreement provided that the agent could not anticipate full payment of his fees unless the RCMP were able, through the agent's assistance, to successfully investigate some or all of the subjects identified. The trial judge decided that this paragraph of the agreement invited corruption and prejudiced the informant from the beginning by inviting him to put a spin on his evidence and fabricate it so that charges could be laid and he could pocket more money. The trial judge stayed the proceedings, relying on s. 24(1) of the *Charter*. The Crown appealed successfully. Justice Labrosse wrote:

> To the extent that agents are paid to gather evidence, their testimony must be viewed by the trier of fact with a certain degree of suspicion. While an expectation of financial advantage may reduce the weight of a witness' testimony, it does not render such evidence inadmissible without more.
>
> . . .
>
> The testimony of some paid agents may be untrustworthy but it cannot be said that, as a category, all paid agents cannot be trusted to tell the truth. To paraphrase Dickson J. [in *Vetrovec*], the construction of a universal rule singling out the testimony of paid police agents as unreliable would reduce the law of evidence to blind and empty formalism.[230]

---

prisoner. The witness was asked the question in the first instance; but in that case I do not know that it might not have been proved independently of the question having been put to him, although, as I have before said, it is only just and reasonable that the question should be put."

[228]   [1939] 4 D.L.R. 543 (Sask. C.A.) at 549.

[229]   (1994), 31 C.R. (4th) 105 (Ont. C.A.), affirmed (*sub nom. R. v. Naoufal*), [1994] 3 S.C.R. 1020.

[230]   *Ibid.* at 113-114 [(C.A.)].

R. v. GHORVEI

(1999), 29 C.R. (5th) 102, 138 C.C.C. (3d) 340 (Ont. C.A.)

The accused was charged with trafficking in heroin, possession of heroin and breach of recognizance. A police officer testified that he saw the accused drive a third party to a location where the third party conducted a drug transaction. The charge of possession of heroin related to drugs found in the accused's possession when arrested. On his appeal from conviction, the accused sought to introduce fresh evidence relating to the police officer's credibility in the form of the transcript of an unrelated trial involving another accused person in which the trial judge, upon hearing the police officer testify for the Crown on the accused's application to exclude evidence, rejected the police officer's testimony as false and concluded that the officer was a compulsive liar. The appeal was dismissed.

CHARRON J.A.:—

. . .

In *Pappageorge*, Constable Nielsen testified for the Crown on the accused's application to exclude evidence under s. 24(2) of the Charter. At the conclusion of the hearing, the trial judge granted the accused's application and excluded the evidence. In his reasons, the trial judge indicated that he was not impressed with Constable Nielsen. He rejected his testimony as being "false" and concluded:

"I find that this officer is a compulsive liar. I do not believe his evidence at all."

Counsel for the appellant submits that the trial judge in *Pappageorge* made a clear finding that Constable Nielsen had lied under oath and that, if that finding had been available at the appellant's trial for the purpose of cross-examining Constable Nielsen, it could reasonably be expected to have affected the result. Consequently, the appellant seeks to admit this fresh evidence on his appeal and seeks an order directing a new trial on the basis of that evidence. The authority to admit fresh evidence on appeal is found in s. 683(1) of the Criminal Code. This court can admit fresh evidence "where it considers it in the interests of justice" to do so. The criteria for the admission of fresh evidence are set out in the often cited case of *Palmer v. The Queen*.

The determining issue is whether the evidence could reasonably be expected to have affected the result at trial. Of course, it could only have had any effect on the result if it could have been used at trial to impeach Constable Nielsen's credibility. The question then becomes whether a witness can be cross-examined on a prior judicial finding that he has lied under oath. If the prior judicial finding that Constable Nielsen lied under oath had formed the basis of a conviction of perjury or of giving contradictory evidence, it is clear that he could have been subjected to cross-examination on that conviction and on its underlying facts. See s. 12 of the Canada Evidence Act. Constable Nielsen, as an ordinary witness and unlike an accused person, would also be subject to cross-examination on relevant discreditable conduct even if the conduct has not resulted in a charge being laid or in a conviction. See *R. v. Gonzague* (1983), 4 C.C.C. (3d) 505 (Ont. C.A.). In this case, the judicial finding in *Pappageorge* that Constable Nielsen's testimony was "false" and that he was "a compulsive liar" was not made in the context of proceedings concerning the truth or falsity of the testimony in question. Had the finding been made in the context of a prosecution for perjury or for the giving of contradictory testimony, Constable Nielsen would have been given an opportunity to respond to the accusation that he had lied under oath and the trial judge's finding would have been subject to the criminal standard of proof beyond a reasonable doubt. As the matter stands, the judicial finding in question is nothing more than a rejection of Constable Nielsen's testimony, albeit in very strong terms.

In my view, it is not proper to cross-examine a witness on the fact that his or her testimony has been rejected or disbelieved in a prior case. That fact, in and of itself, does not constitute discreditable conduct. I do not think it would be useful to allow cross-examination of a witness on what is, in essence, no more than an opinion on the credibility of unrelated testimony given by this witness in the context of another case. The triers of fact who would witness this cross- examination would not be able to assess the value of that opinion and the effect, if any, on the witness's credibility without also being provided with the factual foundation for the opinion. This case, in fact, provides a good example of the difficulties that would arise if such cross-examination were permitted because, in my view, once the finding is examined in the context of the whole record in *Pappageorge*, it becomes apparent that it is essentially unfounded and hence can provide no assistance in determining Constable Nielsen's credibility.

Upon considering the full transcript in *Pappageorge*, I am unable to find support for the trial judge's finding that Constable Nielsen is "a compulsive liar". I can only surmise that this statement is either the unfortunate result of judicial intemperance or that the trial judge's conclusion is based on extraneous considerations not properly before the court. I make the first supposition on the basis that the transcript reveals that the trial judge made a number of premature expressions of incredulity with respect to Constable Nielsen's testimony while he was testifying and before hearing the whole evidence. I make the latter supposition based on the fact that the trial judge stated in his reasons that he has "known [the officer] for years". It may well be that the trial judge was not impressed with this witness but his finding must nonetheless be based on evidence properly before him.

Further, the trial judge's finding that the officer's testimony was "false" does not appear to be reasonable on the basis of the record before him. I note in this regard that the trial judge also disbelieved most of Mr. Pappageorge's testimony, yet, in the end analysis, it is on the basis of that testimony that he finds Constable Nielsen's evidence to be "false." While it was certainly open to the trial judge on the evidence to reject the officer's evidence, I find little support for any clear and express finding that the officer's testimony was "false", or, in other words, that he has lied under oath.[231]

---

[231] See comment by Addario & Pratt, "The Ontario Court of Appeal Polishes Up Some Bad Apples" (1999), 29 C.R. (5th) 102. *Ghorvei* was applied in *R. v. Karaibrahimovic* (2002), 164 C.C.C. (3d) 431, 3 C.R. (6th) 153 (Alta. C.A.) involving the prior testimony of an expert.

Do you find Justice Charron's reasoning persuasive? In light of the recent judicial acknowledgement of the systemic problem of police perjury, do you think the decision would be decided the same way today?[232]

(i) *Motives of Accused and Complainants*

R. v. JACKSON
[1995] O.J. No. 2471 (Ont. C.A.)

THE COURT:—

The absence of any motive to fabricate an allegation is a proper matter for consideration in the course of the fact finding process. The trial judge's reasons indicate no more than that he did consider the absence of any motive to fabricate as one feature of the case. The reasons do not suggest that the trial judge placed any onus on the appellant to prove a motive to fabricate. Nor do we accept that, because the trial judge's finding that the appellant's story had no ring of truth followed directly upon his reference to the absence of a motive to fabricate, the former was the exclusive product of the latter.

In sexual assault cases or cases involving police violence, there is sometimes a civil lawsuit filed after criminal charges are laid. Courts often take this into account in assessing credibility.[233] **Is there an argument that using civil remedies as a motive to lie in these contexts is unfair? How would you articulate it?**

R. v. D.S.
2017 ONCJ 682, 41 C.R. (7th) 180 (Ont. C.J.)

DOODY J:

(c) Complainant's motive to fabricate

[28] Defence counsel submitted that the complainant had a motive to fabricate the charges because she was hoping to get compensation — either from the defendant in a civil lawsuit, or from the Criminal Injuries Compensation Board. The complainant had been off work since late December 2013 or early January 2014 as a result of an incident in December. During that time, she was receiving money from the Employment Insurance program, during the waiting period before she was eligible for payments from the disability insurance she had from her government employer. Counsel noted that EI payments for being unable to work due to illness lasted only 15 weeks, a period which ended very close in time to April 7, 2014, the first date she reported the attacks to the

---

[232] See Tanovich, "Judicial and Prosecutorial Control of Lying by the Police" (2013), 100 C.R. (6th) 322-334.

[233] See e.g. *R. v. McClure*, 2001 SCC 14, [2001] 1 S.C.R. 445, 151 C.C.C. (3d) 321, 40 C.R. (5th) 1 (S.C.C.), discussed in Chapter 4 under Privilege.

police. The EI payments were less than her pay had been before the leave. She was not assured of being accepted as disabled by the disability insurer, and so she was financially stressed when she reported to the police.

[29] Counsel also referred to a posting by the complainant in an online forum in January, 2015 in which she had written:

> I am back at work, have been for 4 months and the leave was granted after an attack last December. Complete with police reports and very slow police investigation. I mean snails pace, don't think they've done anything in six months. I keep fighting but it's more than I can handle . . . I'm barely well enough to go to work, I returned early so I wouldn't lose my house. I have another option of suing my attacker but the police is being so slow with their investigation I'm drowning in payments.

[30] Later in the same forum, someone wrote "you may be eligible for compensation from the Criminal Injuries Compensation Board. Not much, but it might help." The complainant responded "I've already done half the paperwork with them. They require more steps and the detective asked me to wait before completing the application."

. . .

[32] When confronted with these posts in cross-examination, the complainant testified that she never had any intention of suing the defendant, and she had merely written that doing so was an option, not one she would pursue. She said she first went to the police in April 2014 in order to get advice about assistance she could access, both in terms of counselling and any financial assistance to which they could direct her. The police suggested both the Criminal Injuries Compensation Board and the Ottawa Rape Crisis Centre, and she was grateful for that. She did not ask the police to pursue the investigation until she returned and gave a video statement in August 2014. She admitted that the detective in charge of the investigation had suggested she should wait until the criminal case was complete before pursuing the Criminal Injuries Compensation Board, and said she was still considering whether to make that application. She also testified that her financial situation in January 2015 was more dire than it had been in April 2014 when she first went to the police.

[33] She also testified that even though she did successfully come to an agreement with her creditors in 2015 after making them a proposal under the Bankruptcy and Insolvency Act, and lost her condominium as a result, her finances were now in very good shape. She had been retroactively accepted as disabled, receiving significant back pay. Her brother, tragically, died and she received significant money from a life insurance policy. And she was now back at work in a better job than she had been doing. She has significant funds in the bank.

[34] The complainant was in financial stress at the time she went to the police in April 2014 and when she decided to ask them to pursue the investigation in

August 2014. She knew that suing the defendant was one of her options. She also knew that making an application to the Criminal Injuries Compensation Board was one of her options.

[35] This prevents me from concluding that the complainant had no motive to fabricate these allegations, as judges sometimes do when justifying credibility assessments. But it does not, in my view, make it more likely that the complainant is intentionally fabricating. Every person who suffers a criminal or civil wrong is entitled to pursue whatever remedies they see fit. If the defendant did what he is alleged to have done, the complainant is perfectly justified in suing him. If doing so made her evidence less credible, the same could be said for anyone who chooses to exercise his or her rights to seek compensation in the courts for wrongs done to them. That would not be right.

R. v. ELLARD
(2003), 172 C.C.C. (3d) 28, 10 C.R. (6th) 189 (B.C. C.A.)

Ellard was convicted of second degree murder in the beating and drowning death of Reena Virk. A number of witnesses testified that Ellard admitted her involvement in the deceased's death. In her testimony, Ellard admitted being involved in the swarming of the deceased but not her killing. She further denied admitting such to the witnesses. Credibility was the central issue at trial. The Crown cross-examined Ellard and asked her to provide a reason the witnesses would lie about the admissions. It was a prominent feature of her cross-examination. Ellard appealed on the grounds that this cross-examination was unfair. A new trial was ordered.

· · ·

DONALD J.A. (LAMBERT and ROWLES JJ.A. concurring): —

Asking the accused about the veracity of a Crown witness has long been considered improper. The accused's opinion is irrelevant and the questioning could prejudice her and render the trial unfair.

· · ·

The potential prejudice arising from this form of questioning is that it tends to shift the burden of proof from the Crown to the accused. It could induce a jury to analyze the case on the reasoning that if an accused cannot say why a witness would give false evidence against her, the witness's testimony may be true. The risk of such a course of reasoning undermines the presumption of innocence and the doctrine of reasonable doubt. The mind of the trier of fact must remain firmly fixed on whether the Crown proved its case on the requisite standard and not be diverted by the question whether the accused provided a motive for a witness to lie. I refer in this regard to the words of Finlayson J.A. giving judgment for the Ontario Court of Appeal in *R. v. W.S.* (1994), 90 C.C.C. (3d) 242 (Ont. C.A.) at 252-54, leave to appeal to S.C.C. refused 93 C.C.C. (3d) vi:

The Crown on appeal conceded that it was improper for the Crown at trial to demand an explanation from the appellant as to why the complainant would make up what counsel referred to as "this horrendous lie". There is no onus on an accused person to explain away the complaints against him or her. The trial judge should have resolutely rejected this approach. Instead he implicitly adopted it. He was favourably impressed with the complainant and the manner in which she testified and, consequently, he believed her. He then subtly shifted the onus to the appellant, as accused, to give some explanation as to why the complainant would lie. Why would she bring all this grief upon herself and risk jeopardizing the close relationship between the two families if it were not true? He also accepted that M. was necessarily lying to support her father. In this manner, the trial judge failed to properly apply the presumption of innocence, and to adequately found the conviction on the whole of the evidence. . . .

The trial judge in the present case gave full reasons and he recited the evidence accurately. He also referred to the appropriate authorities. I cannot say that he misdirected himself in a material way. His overall approach to this particular case, however, was wrong. Instead of questioning the veracity and accuracy of the witnesses who, because of the nature of the charge, were called to support a negative, he should have been more critical of the complainant who put forward the affirmative that the offences took place: see *R. v. Norman*, [(1993), 87 C.C.C. (3d) 153 (Ont. C.A.)], at pp. 172-3. This is another example of the way the trial judge shifted the onus to the appellant in spite of the Crown's burden to prove all elements of the crime beyond a reasonable doubt. [Emphasis added.]

R. v. LABOUCAN
[2010] 1 S.C.R. 397, 253 C.C.C. (3d) 129, 73 C.R. (6th) 235 (S.C.C.)

CHARRON J.:—

1. Introduction

1 Following his trial by judge alone, the respondent Joseph Wesley Laboucan was convicted of kidnapping, aggravated sexual assault, and first degree murder: 2007 ABQB 196, 413 A.R. 53 (sub nom. R. v. Briscoe). This appeal as of right raises the sole issue of whether the trial judge erred in law by rejecting Mr. Laboucan's testimony, in part, on the basis of his motive to lie because of his interest in securing an acquittal. The Alberta Court of Appeal was divided on this question (2009 ABCA 7, 1 Alta. L.R. (5th) 264), with the majority finding that the trial judge's reference to Mr. Laboucan's "very great motive to be untruthful" presumed his guilt, thereby revealing a fatal flaw which necessitated a new trial. Rowbotham J.A. dissented. In her view, the impugned passage, when read in context, did not constitute error.

2 I would allow the appeal. While the language used by the trial judge in referring to the accused's motive undoubtedly raises concern, it cannot be considered in isolation. When considered in context, I am satisfied that the reasons were responsive to the issues raised in this joint trial, where the testimony of every principal witness was challenged by Mr. Laboucan on the

ground that he or she had a motive to fabricate the evidence against him. When the trial judge's reasons are read as a whole, I am satisfied that, on the crucial question of Mr. Laboucan's credibility, he did not proceed on the basis of the impermissible assumption that the accused, because of his status as an accused, would lie to secure an acquittal.

2. The Facts and Judicial History

3 For the purposes of this appeal, a brief account of the facts will suffice. Shortly after midnight on April 3, 2005, 13-year-old Nina Courtepatte and her friend, Ms. K.B., were lured from West Edmonton Mall on the false promise of being taken to a party. The two young girls got into a car with five individuals: Mr. Laboucan, his co-accused Michael Erin Briscoe, and three youths, Mr. M.W., Ms. S.B. and Ms. D.T. Mr. Briscoe drove the group to an isolated golf course. While they were walking down a gravel path and onto a fairway, Ms. S.B. hit Nina with a wrench, causing her to fall. Nina was then held down, sexually assaulted by Mr. Laboucan and Mr. M.W., and beaten to death. Nina's friend, Ms. K.B., was not assaulted.

4 All five individuals whom Nina and her friend joined that fateful night were charged with kidnapping, aggravated sexual assault, and first degree murder. The two adults in the group, Mr. Laboucan and Mr. Briscoe, were jointly charged and tried together in this proceeding by a judge sitting without a jury. The three youths, Mr. M.W., Ms. S.B., and Ms. D.T., were charged separately. At the time of the joint trial, Mr. M.W. had pleaded guilty and was awaiting sentencing. The other youths were yet to be tried. Except for Mr. Briscoe, all charged individuals testified at the trial, as did Ms. K.B., giving various accounts of the tragic events.

5 During his testimony at trial, Mr. Laboucan admitted that he was present when the victim was kidnapped, sexually assaulted and murdered, but denied participating in any of those crimes. It was his position that the testimony of the other witnesses inculpating him had been fabricated for reasons of "jealousy, a desire for revenge, and a desire to avoid responsibility for their own actions" (trial judgment, at para. 201).

6 DNA and other forensic evidence was not conclusive insofar as it related to the two accused before the court. Credibility of the witnesses, including Mr. Laboucan, was, therefore, of central importance in the trial.

7 The trial judge provided lengthy and detailed reasons for judgment. In this appeal, we are concerned solely with the assessment of Mr. Laboucan's credibility and the role it played in arriving at a verdict of guilt. After outlining the approach set out in R. v. W. (D.), [1991] 1 S.C.R. 742, the trial judge concluded at the first stage of the W. (D.) analysis, that he disbelieved Mr. Laboucan. In giving his reasons for disbelieving him, the trial judge made reference to Mr. Laboucan's motive to lie in these terms:

I summarized Mr. Laboucan's testimony in paragraphs [100] to [132] above. Having carefully considered it, I have concluded that I do not believe Mr. Laboucan. My reasons for this conclusion are:

. . .

d) The fact that he has a very great motive to be untruthful given the consequences of being convicted of the offences charged.

e) The fact that in many respects his evidence is radically inconsistent with the evidence of other witnesses who have no, or at least less, reason to be untruthful about the particular point on which their respective evidence is inconsistent, or whose evidence on the point tends to implicate themselves as well as Mr. Laboucan. [Emphasis added; para. 202.]

8 For the same reasons, the trial judge concluded that Mr. Laboucan's evidence did not leave him in a reasonable doubt about his involvement in the crimes with which he was charged (para. 203). He proceeded to determine which evidence he did believe. Based on that evidence, the trial judge was satisfied beyond a reasonable doubt that the Crown had proven each element of the offences charged. He therefore convicted Mr. Laboucan on all charges.

. . .

3. Analysis

11 The fact that a witness has an interest in the outcome of the proceedings is, as a matter of common sense, a relevant factor, among others, to take into account when assessing the credibility of the witness's testimony. A trier of fact, however, should not place undue weight on the status of a person in the proceedings as a factor going to credibility. For example, it would be improper to base a finding of credibility regarding a parent's or a spouse's testimony solely on the basis of the witness's relationship to the complainant or to the accused. Regard should be given to all relevant factors in assessing credibility.

12 The common sense proposition that a witness's interest in the proceedings may have an impact on credibility also applies to an accused person who testifies in his or her defence. The fact that the witness is the accused, however, raises a specific concern. The concern arises from the fact that both innocent and guilty accused have an interest in not being convicted. Indeed, the innocent accused has a greater interest in securing an acquittal. Therefore, any assumption that an accused will lie to secure his or her acquittal flies in the face of the presumption of innocence, as an innocent person, presumably, need only tell the truth to achieve this outcome. In R. v. B. (L.) (1993), 13 O.R. (3d) 796 (C.A.), Arbour J.A. (as she then was) succinctly described the inherent danger in considering the accused's motive arising from his or her interest in the outcome of the trial. In an often-quoted passage, she stated as follows (at pp. 798-99):

It falls into the impermissible assumption that the accused will lie to secure his acquittal, simply because, as an accused, his interest in the outcome dictates that course of action. This flies in the face of the presumption of innocence and creates an almost insurmountable disadvantage for the accused. The accused is obviously interested in being acquitted. In order to achieve that result he may have to testify to answer the case put forward by the prosecution. However, it cannot be assumed that the accused must lie in order to be acquitted, unless his guilt is no longer an open question. If the trial judge comes to the conclusion that the accused did not tell the truth in his evidence, the accused's interest in securing his acquittal may be the most plausible explanation for the lie. The explanation for a lie, however, cannot be turned into an assumption that one will occur.

13 Counsel for Mr. Laboucan argues that it is inherently wrong in every case to consider an accused's interest in the outcome of the trial, as no useful inference can be drawn from that fact. She therefore urges the Court to adopt an absolute prohibition against considering the accused's motive to lie in assessing his or her credibility as a witness.

14 In most cases, I would agree with counsel that this factor is simply unhelpful and, as a general rule, triers of fact would be well advised to avoid that path altogether, lest they unwittingly err by making the impermissible assumption that the accused will lie to secure an acquittal. However, I would not adopt an absolute rule as proposed, for the following reasons.

15 An absolute rule prohibiting the trier of fact from considering that an accused may have a motive to lie in order to secure an acquittal, regardless of the circumstances, would artificially immunize the accused in a manner inconsistent with other rules of evidence that provide special protection to the accused. Courts have consistently rejected prohibitive rules that would result in a trier of fact acting upon a misleading view of a case. For example, there is a general rule prohibiting the Crown from introducing evidence about the accused's bad character. However, in McMillan v. The Queen, [1977] 2 S.C.R. 824, where the accused called evidence that his wife was psychopathic, making her the likely killer of an infant, the Court held that the Crown could adduce evidence of the accused's similar disposition. Otherwise the jury would have been left with an entirely distorted picture. Similarly, in R. v. Corbett, [1988] 1 S.C.R. 670, where the defence had vigorously attacked the credibility of the Crown witnesses, making much of their criminal records, Dickson C.J. held that "a serious imbalance would have arisen" had the jury not been apprised of the accused's criminal record (p. 690). This opened up the opportunity for a more extensive cross-examination on the accused's criminal record that might otherwise be viewed as unduly prejudicial. Therefore, whether or not it is appropriate for the trier of fact to consider that the accused may have a motive to lie because of his or her interest in the trial will depend on the evidence and the issues raised at trial.

16 An absolute rule as proposed would also be contrary to established principles of appellate review. It should now be regarded as trite law that a trial judge's reasons should be read as a whole, in the context of the evidence, the issues and the arguments at trial, together with "an appreciation of the purposes or functions for which they are delivered": R. v. R.E.M., 2008 SCC 51, [2008] 3 S.C.R. 3, at para. 16. Consistent with this approach, courts have

not held that the trial judge commits an error of law simply by making reference to or taking account of an accused's motive to lie. It all depends on the context . . .

17 In reviewing a trial judge's reasons for disbelieving the accused, a court should also be mindful of the useful distinction drawn by Doherty J.A. in *R. v. Morrissey* (1995), 97 C.C.C. (3d) 193 (Ont. C.A.), where he cautioned against reading a trial judge's reasons as if they were an instruction to a jury. The Court has repeatedly endorsed his observations (at p. 204):

> A trial judge's reasons cannot be read or analyzed as if they were an instruction to a jury. Instructions provide a road-map to direct lay jurors on their journey toward a verdict. Reasons for judgment are given after a trial judge has reached the end of that journey and explain why he or she arrived at a particular conclusion. They are not intended to be, and should not be read as a verbalization of the entire process engaged in by the trial judge in reaching a verdict.

. . .

18 It follows from these principles that the trial judge's consideration of Mr. Laboucan's "very great motive to be untruthful" must be placed within the context of the trial and the reasons as a whole. At the end of the day, the determining question is whether the trial judge's comments undermined the presumption of innocence. The majority in the Court of Appeal concluded that they did. I disagree. In my respectful view, the majority erred by effectively considering the impugned statement in isolation. As I read their reasons, the fact that "[t]he motivation was described as a motivation to be untruthful, not simply a motivation to be acquitted" (para. 22) effectively drove their conclusion. It mattered not what the trial judge wrote elsewhere in his reasons or in what context the words were chosen. In their view, the reference to the accused's motivation to be untruthful, as opposed to his motivation to secure an acquittal, was irreconcilable with the teachings in W. (D.) and "constituted a material flaw in the assessment of credibility bearing upon the substance of the judgment" (para. 31).

19 As I indicated at the outset, I agree with Rowbotham J.A.'s conclusion that the trial judge committed no error. I am also in substantial agreement with her analysis. In my view, she considered the impugned comments in their appropriate context. In the "road-map" part of the judgment where the trial judge instructed himself on the law, she noted that he correctly instructed himself as to the applicable W. (D.) principles and the burden of proof. Therefore, this is not a situation where the reviewing court has to rely on the presumption that the trial judge knows the law on credibility. His reasons make it clear that he did. The trial judge then faithfully followed the principles he had set out in analysing the evidence.

20 Rowbotham J.A. then reviewed at some length the numerous reasons given by the trial judge for disbelieving the accused's testimony, at paras. 50-58. I need not repeat those reasons here. They are numerous and well founded in the

evidence. They include: material inconsistencies between Mr. Laboucan's evidence at trial and his evidence given at a preliminary inquiry; further inconsistencies between his evidence at trial and that given in statements to police; his admission that he had made up an elaborate fiction concerning a murder he had witnessed, where he implicated real people even though they had no involvement whatsoever in the actual murder at which he was present; the fact that there was no medical evidence to support his claim that he entered into a state of shock which prevented him from responding to the events at the scene; and the stark conflict between his evidence and the evidence of every other witness present at the scene.

21 Finally, Rowbotham J.A. held that the comparison to the motivations of the witnesses in para. 202(e) was entirely appropriate in this case, given the defence position at trial. In my view, the defence position is a very important contextual factor that explains the language used by the trial judge. Central to this trial was the fact that the credibility of each of the main witnesses was challenged by Mr. Laboucan on the basis that they had a motive to lie and fabricate evidence against him, either to exculpate themselves in other proceedings or to minimize their participation in the crime. The trial judge was appropriately mindful of the defence position throughout his review of their evidence.

22 In these circumstances, where the defence theory rested on the contention that each witness who implicated Mr. Laboucan lied out of self-interest, it was entirely appropriate for the trial judge to consider that the witnesses would have had no, or less reason, to be untruthful on particular points of evidence in respect of which Mr. Laboucan provided radically inconsistent testimony. The trial judge's careful and detailed review of the evidence belies any contention that Mr. Laboucan's testimony was inappropriately isolated and subjected to greater scrutiny than the other witnesses on the basis of his status as an accused. Further, Mr. Laboucan's testimony and position regarding the witnesses had implications for the co- accused, Mr. Briscoe. Therefore, unlike Rowbotham J.A. who concluded that the impugned comments were "unnecessary and harmless" (para. 64), it is my view that, within the context of this trial, it was a crucial and unavoidable aspect of determining the credibility issues that the trial judge consider Mr. Laboucan's own motives.

23 As stated at the outset, while some of the language used by the trial judge in his reasons may give cause for concern when viewed in isolation, when the reasons are read in their entirety and in the light of the context of the trial as a whole, they reveal that the trial judge properly assessed and weighed the evidence of all the witnesses, including the accused, without undermining the presumption of innocence or the burden of proof.

4. Disposition

24 For these reasons, I would allow the appeal, set aside the order for a new trial, and restore the convictions.

Appeal allowed.

(c) Character of Witness

(i) *Extrinsic Evidence*

R. v. CLARKE

(1998), 18 C.R. (5th) 219, 129 C.C.C. (3d) 1 (Ont. C.A.)

On charges of forcible seizure, assault with a weapon, and possession of a weapon for the purpose of committing forcible seizure, defence counsel proposed to call five witnesses to testify about the reputation of the accused and the complainant, who were members of the small Caribbean community in Trenton. The trial judge held that the witnesses would be permitted to give their opinions as to the reputation of the accused and the complainant in the community of Trenton. Further, defence counsel could impeach the credibility of the complainant by asking questions of the character witnesses. The trial judge gave instructions as to the use of the character evidence in the charge to the jury.

ROSENBERG J.A.: —

The rules of evidence respecting the admissibility of character evidence are not always logical or founded in good policy. In this Crown appeal, the court is invited to reconsider the rationality of one of the more anomalous rules.

In *R. v. Gonzague* (1983), 4 C.C.C. (3d) 505, this court held that established authority permits the following line of inquiry of a witness called by the defence to give evidence about the character of a Crown witness:

1. Do you know the reputation of the witness as to truth and veracity in the community in which the witness resides?

    If the answer is "yes" the questioning proceeds.

2. Is that reputation good or bad?

    If the answer is "bad" a final question is permitted.

3. From that reputation, would you believe the witness on oath?

On behalf of the Crown, Mr. Shaw submits that the rule permitting the third question should be abrogated. He also urges this court to reassess whether the defence should automatically be entitled to ask the first two questions without an assessment of the probative value of the proffered testimony. Finally, Mr. Shaw argues that in any event the charge to the jury in this case as to the use of the evidence was inadequate.

I agree with Mr. Shaw that it is time to reassess this rule. I would hold that a judge has a limited discretion to prevent counsel from asking the first two questions of a witness called to attack the credibility of another witness.

I would also hold that only rarely should the third question be permitted.

. . .

Although evidence has some probative value, it is not necessarily admissible. Even if the evidence is not subject to some exclusionary rule, such as the hearsay rule, it may still be held to be inadmissible having regard to the particular circumstances of the case. Relevance cannot be determined in a vacuum but only on the basis of the particular issues raised in the trial. Thus, evidence that may be relevant to one issue may be irrelevant to another or may actually mislead the trier of fact on the second issue. The law of evidence therefore gives to the trial judge the task of balancing the value of the evidence against its potential prejudice. In a proper case, the judge has the power to exclude otherwise relevant evidence because the prejudicial effect of admitting the evidence outweighs its value. In *Seaboyer*, McLachlin J. clarified the test for exclusion of otherwise relevant evidence. She held that the judge has the power to exclude relevant evidence tendered by the Crown on the basis simply that its prejudicial effect outweighs its probative value. The power to exclude relevant defence evidence, however, is narrower and constrained by the fundamental tenet that an innocent person not be convicted, a tenet which now has constitutional protection.

. . .

In my view, the prejudicial effect of the answer to the third question will almost invariably substantially outweigh its probative value. The form in which the evidence is presented tends to usurp the function of the jury and engages what I have referred to as the fifth counter-balancing factor. . . While the defence witnesses may know the Crown witness' reputation for telling the truth in everyday affairs, for the reasons expressed earlier, their ability to predict the witness' behaviour in court is limited and entitled to no special deference. Where the outcome of the case depends upon the evidence of a single witness, an expression of opinion as to that witness' veracity is a comment on the ultimate issue. There is the risk that in some cases the jury will simply defer to the opinion of the character witness rather than embarking on the difficult task of examining the evidence and measuring it against the standard of proof beyond a reasonable doubt, on the theory that the character witness obviously knows the Crown witness and is in a much better position to determine the outcome of the case. Put another way, the ability of a character witness, who has not heard the evidence in the case, to predict whether another witness has told the truth under oath is very limited. The jury may, however, overvalue that opinion because the character witness knows the witness.

Accordingly, I would hold that the accused does not have the absolute right to ask the third question and that in most cases the trial judge would be justified in refusing to permit that question to be asked. I would adopt the holding by Cumming J.A. in *Masztalar v. Wiens* (1992), 10 B.C.A.C. 19 at 23 to the effect that while the rule need not be absolutely abolished it should be retained "to be sparingly applied only in the rare case where the interests of justice require it". To the extent that the decisions of this court in *Gonzague* and *Taylor* hold to the contrary, they should no longer be followed. There may be unusual circumstances where the reputation of the Crown witness is such that it is possible to more accurately predict the likelihood that the witness would lie under oath. In those cases, the answer to the third question may provide the jury with useful information. With a careful jury instruction the danger that this testimony will usurp the jury's function can be minimized.

With respect to the first two questions, in my view, the trial judge also has a discretion to exclude witnesses that would provide that evidence where the prejudicial effect would substantially outweigh its probative value. I should say, however, that in my view it would be an extremely rare case where a trial judge would be warranted in excluding the evidence. Unlike the third question, the first two questions do not invite answers that would have the tendency to usurp the jury's function. The reputation evidence is simply another piece of circumstantial evidence that the jury can use to assess the credibility of the Crown witness' story. I also do not think that this evidence has the same tendency to distract the jury from the main issue in the case, nor is it likely to create side issues.

The only serious problem about this defence evidence is whether the evidence will consume an undue amount of time. It seems to me that a trial judge has the discretion to limit the number of reputation witnesses called by the defence where the judge is satisfied that the prejudicial effect of calling an endless series of witnesses testifying to essentially the same fact substantially outweighs the probative value of this additional evidence. The judge will, however, wish to keep in mind that the Supreme Court in *Seaboyer* has held that the discretion to exclude relevant evidence must be exercised with extreme caution and that in most cases the better course would be to permit the defence to call all of those witnesses.

(ii) *Evidence Elicited on Cross-examination*

While extrinsic evidence of specific instances of misconduct was excluded the common law permitted cross-examination of the witness himself regarding the same. The reasons forbidding extrinsic evidence were seen to be not applicable; confusion was minimal as it ended with the question and answer and the witness was not unfairly surprised as he needn't meet other witnesses.[234] In 1746 the Lord Chancellor noted:

> The other party is at liberty to cross-examine him either to the matter of fact concerning which he had been examined, *or any other matter whatsoever* that shall tend to impeach his credit or weaken his testimony.[235]

The only limitation appears to be counsel's imagination, the restraint of ethical considerations and the trial judge's discretion to protect a witness from

---

[234]   3A Wigmore, *Evidence* (Chad. Rev.), s. 981.
[235]   Hardwicke, L.C. in *Lord Lovat's Trial*, 18 Howell's State Trials 529 at 651.

harassment when the relevance of the questioning is regarded as minimal.[236] Recall as well the discussion of the Supreme Court in *Lyttle*.

Protection for two particular classes of witnesses deserves closer examination: accused persons and complainants in sexual assault cases (rape shield law) (see Chapter 4, Character Evidence).

(iii) *Accused as Witness*

The accused was rendered a competent witness in Canada in 1893. The statute which accomplished this contained no language which would afford him or her any protection from cross-examination over and above that available to the ordinary witness.[237] This was early recognized in the cases. In Quebec in 1893 Wurtele J.A. stated:

> When a person on trial claims the right to give evidence on his own behalf, he comes under the ordinary rule as to cross-examination in criminal cases. He may be asked all questions pertinent to the issue, and cannot refuse to answer those which may implicate him. Under the new law, which protects him from the effect of his evidence in proceedings subsequently brought, but does not do so in the case in which the evidence is given, he may be convicted out of his own mouth. He cannot be compelled to testify, but when he offers and gives his evidence he has to take the consequences.[238]

In Ontario in 1902, Osler J.A. noted:

> The right, and if such it can be called, the privilege, of the accused now is to tender himself as a witness. When he does so he puts himself forward as a credible person, and except in so far as he may be shielded by some statutory protection, he is in the same situation as any other witness, as regards liability to and extent of cross-examination.[239]

Nevertheless, after some uncertainty,[240] some courts have recognized that the accused who chooses to become a witness exposes himself or herself to a greater possibility of prejudice than the ordinary witness. In *R. v. Davison*,[241] Martin J.A. described the accused's position:

> An accused who gives evidence has a dual character. As an accused he is protected by an underlying policy rule against the introduction of evidence by the

---

[236]   See e.g. the protection for a complainant in a rape prosecution in *Laliberte v. R.* (1877), 1 S.C.R. 117. Compare *R. v. Bradbury* (1973), 23 C.R.N.S. 293 (Ont. C.A.). See generally Stephen, *History of the Criminal Law* (1883), vol. 1 at 433. Observe the breadth of cross-examination permitted in *R. v. Titus* (1983), 33 C.R. (3d) 17 (S.C.C.); *R. v. Gonzague* (1983), 34 C.R. (3d) 169 (Ont. C.A.) and *A.G. Que. v. Charron* (1984), 43 C.R. (3d) 240 (Que. S.C.).

[237]   Compare the *Criminal Evidence Act*, 1898, 61 & 62 Vict., c. 36, s. 1(f) in England which forbade cross-examination of the accused regarding his or her record unless it was admissible as relevant to a fact in issue, the accused led evidence of his or her own good character or sought to impugn the character of the prosecutor or his or her witnesses or he or she has given evidence against a co-accused.

[238]   *R. v. Connors* (1893), 5 C.C.C. 70 (Que. Q.B.) at 72.

[239]   *R. v. D'Aoust* (1902), 5 C.C.C. 407 (Ont. C.A.) at 411.

[240]   See e.g. the judgment of Spence, J. in *Colpitts v. R.*, [1965] S.C.R. 739; and compare *Koufis v. R.*, [1941] S.C.R. 481 and *R. v. McLaughlan* (1974), 20 C.C.C. (2d) 59 (Ont. C.A.).

[241]   (1974), 20 C.C.C. (2d) 424 (Ont. C.A.). But compare *R. v. Bird* (1973), 13 C.C.C. (2d) 73 (Sask. C.A.).

prosecution tending to show that he is a person of bad character, subject, of course, to the recognized exceptions to that rule. As a witness, however, his credibility is subject to attack. If the position of an accused who gives evidence is assimilated in every respect to that of an ordinary witness he is not protected against cross- examination with respect to discreditable conduct and associations.

If an accused could in every case be cross-examined with a view to showing that he is a professional criminal under the guise of an attack upon his credibility as a witness it would be virtually impossible for him to receive a fair trial on the specific charge upon which he is being tried. It is not realistic to assume that, ordinarily, the jury will be able to limit the effect of such a cross-examination to the issue of credibility in arriving at a verdict.

In my view the policy rule which protects an accused against an attack upon his character lest it divert the jury from the issue which they are called upon to decide, namely, the guilt or innocence of the accused on the specific charge before the Court, is not wholly subordinated to the rule which permits an accused who elects to give evidence to be cross-examined on the issue of his credibility. In this area of the law, as in so many areas, a balance has been struck between competing interests, which endeavours so far as possible to recognize the purpose of both rules and does not give effect to one to the total exclusion of the other.

Consequently, limitations are imposed with respect to the cross-examination of an accused which do not apply in the case of an ordinary witness.[242]

Accordingly it was held that while witnesses generally are open to cross-examination at large as to credit, an accused, aside from questions regarding previous convictions, should not be cross-examined with regard to previous misconduct or discreditable associations unrelated to the charge for the purpose of impeachment.

One exception to this general rule is the statutory rule making the criminal record of a witness, even the accused, admissible to go to credibility. Section 12 of the *Canada Evidence Act* provides:

12. (1) A witness may be questioned as to whether the witness has been convicted of any offence, excluding any offence designated as a contravention under the Contraventions Act, but including such an offence where the conviction was entered after a trial on an indictment.

---

[242]   *Davison, ibid.* at 441-442. This excerpt from *Davison* was quoted and applied in *R. v. Lawrence* (1989), 52 C.C.C. (3d) 452 (Ont. C.A.); the Court allowed the accused's appeal from conviction of manslaughter arising out of the death of a child where the Crown had cross-examined the accused to show that he was a "biker", drug dealer and welfare cheat. And see *R. v. Geddes* (1979), 52 C.C.C. (2d) 230 (Man. C.A.):.

> The accused was convicted on a charge of criminal fraud. At trial the accused testified on his own behalf. In the course of the cross-examination the accused was asked questions regarding previous convictions of fraud and particularly was asked whether he had testified on his own behalf in the trial resulting in the seven convictions of fraud. The Court of Appeal held that the latter questions were improper because the jury was being invited to conclude that if the accused was not believed by the judge in the prior case, he ought not to be believed by the jury in this case. Huband J.A. said (at 238):
>
> > The question went beyond what is authorized by s. 12, and into an area which could only reflect on the character, rather than the credit of the accused. Crown counsel was attempting to convey the impression that, since the accused had not been believed at that trial, he should not be believed by the jury in the instant case.

(1.1) If the witness either denies the fact or refuses to answer, the opposite party may prove the conviction.

(2) The conviction may be proved by producing

> (a) a certificate containing the substance and effect only, omitting the formal part, of the indictment and conviction, if it is for an indictable offence, or a copy of the summary conviction, if for an offence punishable on summary conviction, purporting to be signed by the clerk of the court or other officer having the custody of the records of the court in which the conviction, if on indictment, was had, or to which the conviction, if summary, was returned; and
>
> (b) proof of identity.[243]

The precursor of s. 12 was first enacted at a time when the accused was not a competent witness at his or her trial. When the accused was made a competent witness in England, in 1898, it was recognized that the earlier legislation could affect him or her very differently than other witnesses. A jury would find it difficult to confine their use of the previous record to credibility and, despite any limiting instructions from the judge, the jury might use the fact of the previous conviction as indicative of the accused's character and as directly relevant to whether he or she did the deed alleged at his or her present trial. That use was prohibited by the rule of evidence which forbade the introduction of the accused's character save in particularly limited instances. The possibility of this prejudicial impact increased dramatically, of course, if the previous conviction resembled the matter at hand. The legislation which made the accused a competent witness in England addressed this concern and provided that an accused who chose to become a witness could not be asked as to his or her previous record unless the accused had led evidence of his or her own good character or attacked the character of the prosecution's witnesses.[244] When Canada made the accused a competent witness at his or her trial,[245] the legislators displayed no similar foresight and no such modification of the existing law occurred.

In Chapter 3 we saw the Supreme Court of Canada recognize in the *Corbett* decision that there was a discretion. The exercise of the discretion has been uneven and many, if not most, trial judges, unfortunately, will not exclude such questioning but there have been exceptions.

In *R. v. Bailey*,[246] the defence applied for an order to prohibit cross-examination of the accused on his record. Specifically the defence wanted the word "sexual" deleted from any reference to the accused's previous conviction for sexual assault with a weapon. Justice Zelinski granted the application as a matter of common sense. He wrote:

> If I were about to enter into a transaction . . . the first thing that I would like to know, referable to the person I was dealing with, is whether or not that person

---

[243] First enacted in 1869: *An Act Respecting Procedure in Criminal Cases, 1869*, S.C. 32 & 33 Vict., c. 29, s. 65.
[244] *Criminal Evidence Act*, 1898, 61 & 62 Vict., c. 36, s. 1.
[245] *Canada Evidence Act*, S.C. 1892, c. 31, s. 4.
[246] (1993), 22 C.R. (4th) 65 (Ont. Gen. Div.).

had engaged in the very type of activity I was concerned about. This, of course, identifies as propensity. I think even more than wanting to know whether someone has passed a bad cheque or cheated in cards, one would like to know whether or not that person has done something of the very nature as the matter you are concerned with, again, propensity.

. . .

Of course, in the exercise of discretion as indicated by La Forest J., the more similar the offence is to the subject matter of the charge, the better the reason, on principles of fairness, for excluding it. As he indicated, while it is commonplace to suggest that jurors are capable of understanding a direction that they must only use a prior conviction on issues of credibility, the likelihood is, based on the studies that he referred to, that this will not be the case and this should be realized.

. . .

I specifically challenged [the Crown] on the fact that her objection to the deletion of the word "sexual" is nothing more than a desire on the part of the Crown to save that word because of its potential identification with the offence before the jury (notwithstanding the charge I must give them, that evidence that a person who has done this or similar, previously, as proven by a conviction, cannot be used as evidence that he is likely to be at it again).[247]

In *R. v. Saroya*[248] the accused appealed from his conviction of assault. He admitted hitting the victim on the head with a bottle of wine but he testified that he did so in order to break up a fight between the victim and another man. One of the issues was with respect to the disclosure of his criminal record which included a conviction for attempted murder. The trial judge, in refusing the accused's request for protection against cross-examination on his criminal record, decided:

In the case at bar the accused has one prior conviction in 1988 for attempt murder. A man wears the chains he forges in life. A conviction is part of the accused's persona that he puts before the jury when he chooses to testify. I have considered all the factors pertaining to the exercise of discretion as set out in *Corbett*. In my view the accused would not be prejudiced by the admission of the prior conviction and in the interests of justice it should be admitted in evidence.[249]

The Court of Appeal decided:

The balancing exercise is a particularly difficult one in this case. The relevant factors point to both probative value and prejudice. The accused's prior record discloses a conviction for attempted murder in 1988, some four years prior to the trial at issue here. That was his only prior conviction. A conviction for attempted murder cannot be dismissed as having little probative value on the credibility of a witness. Although it is not a so-called offence of dishonesty, which may be probative of deception, attempted murder is such a serious offence that, in itself, it may be taken to indicate that the prospect of a conviction for perjury is unlikely to keep the witness in line. More significantly, it would be open to a jury to find, on

---

247   *Ibid.* at 67-68.
248   (1992), 18 C.R. (4th) 198 (Ont. Gen. Div.); affirmed (1994), 76 O.A.C. 25 (Ont. C.A.).
249   *Ibid.* at 201 [(Gen. Div.)].

all the relevant evidence, that the witness is unlikely to have more respect for the truth than he has shown for human life.

On the other hand, of course, a conviction for attempted murder shows a capacity for violence against the person, and, on a charge of aggravated assault and assault causing bodily harm invites an inference of guilt through disposition. Not only is the offence for which the appellant was previously convicted very similar to the one that he was facing at trial, but, being of a more serious nature, it would logically support an inference that if the appellant once attempted to kill someone, he would not likely hesitate to commit the types of assaults that he was alleged to have committed.

. . .

In the end, guidance comes from the *Corbett* decision. In that case, the majority of the Supreme Court ruled in favour of inclusion, in conformity with s. 12 of the *Canada Evidence Act*, of a prior murder conviction when the accused was facing a charge of first degree murder. Although the potential for prejudice was recognized as significant, the Supreme Court held that the potential prejudice could be displaced by a proper instruction to the jury about the impermissible use of the prior record. It is conceded that such proper instruction was given in the present case. As in *Corbett*, we are of the opinion that the deletion of the appellant's record would leave the jury with incomplete and therefore incorrect information about his credibility as a witness. To deprive the jury of that information in the present case, would hinder the jury's ability to correctly appreciate the facts. On balance, we think that the probative value of the appellant's criminal record of the question of his credibility as a witness outweighs the potential risk that the jury might use that prior conviction as evidence that the appellant is the type of person likely to have committed the offences with which he was charged.[250]

In *R. v. Brand* [251] the accused appealed from his conviction by a jury on a charge of trafficking in cocaine. The accused had made a *Corbett* application, submitting that the trial judge should edit the accused's record of criminal convictions. The accused had a very lengthy record which included convictions for crimes of dishonesty but concluded with three convictions for trafficking in narcotics. The trial judge declined to edit the record holding that such was an exceptional departure from the general rule which should only be invoked when there is some exceptional unfairness. The Court of Appeal decided:

> He was obliged to weigh and balance the risks for and against exclusion, bearing in mind the evidentiary value of previous convictions admitted pursuant to s. 12, and the fair trial of the accused. The three convictions in question had no probative value with respect to the appellant's credibility but were highly prejudicial. On the other hand, the balance of the record included offences that reflected on credibility. Viewed in this way, we think on the facts, this was a proper case to exclude the three convictions for trafficking. To do so would ensure that the jury had sufficiently complete and correct information about the appellant's credibility as a witness and would effectively remove the possibility of any unfairness by the introduction of the evidence in issue.[252]

---

[250]   *Ibid.* at 28 [(C.A.)].
[251]   (1995), 40 C.R. (4th) 137 (Ont. C.A.).

In *R. v. Charland*,[253] the Supreme Court in a brief oral judgment refused to overturn the conviction of sexual assault where the Crown had been permitted to cross-examine the accused as to prior sexual convictions. This was a discretionary decision, held Cory J., and the jury had been charged as to the very limited use they could make of the evidence.

Despite *Charland* there has been a recent trend to exclude, particularly in the Ontario Court of Appeal. Consider, for example,[254] that Court's decision in *McFadyen*.

R. v. McFADYEN
(2002), 2 C.R. (6th) 344, 161 C.C.C. (3d) 252 (Ont. C.A.)

The accused was convicted by a jury on a charge of sexual assault. The sole ground of appeal was that the trial judge erred by dismissing the accused's *Corbett* application and permitting the Crown to cross-examine him on his criminal record. That record included a conviction for indecent assault in 1981 and convictions for sexual assault in 1984 and 1986. His defence at trial was that the sexual intercourse had been consensual. Credibility had been the central issue.

Per GOUDGE J.A. (ROSENBERG and FELDMAN JJ.A. concurring): —

. . .

I recognize that the decision made on a Corbett application is a matter of discretion and that absent a clear error in the exercise of that discretion this court should not interfere in order to substitute its own view of how that discretion should have been exercised. See *R. v. P. (G.F.)* (1994),18 O.R. (3d) 1 at 5 (Ont. C.A.).

In my view, in this case the trial judge did make such an error. In essence, he admitted the appellant's record simply on the basis that the credibility of the complainant and the appellant would be a central issue at the trial. The Corbett

---

[252]   *Ibid.* at 140.

[253]   (1997), 12 C.R. (5th) 226 (S.C.C.). See criticism of P. Sankoff, "A Lost Opportunity to Clarify *Corbett* and the Use of an Accused's Criminal Record" (1997), 12 C.R. (5th) 228.

[254]   New trials were ordered on the basis that *Corbett* applications should have been allowed where the criminal record involved the very type of offence charged: *R. v. Brown* (2002), 6 C.R. (6th) 380, 166 C.C.C. (3d) 570 (Ont. C.A.) (drug trafficking) and *R. v. Madrusan* (2005), 35 C.R. (6th) 220, 203 C.C.C. (3d) 513 (B.C. C.A.) (robbery). A new trial was ordered in a manslaughter case where the accused had been cross-examined on a prior record for which he had been pardoned: *R. v. Bruha* (2006), 39 C.R. (6th) 384 (C.A.). In *R. v. Farrell* (2011) 89 C.R. (6th) 157 (Ont. C.A.) (see C.R. annotation by Lisa Dufraimont) a new aggravated assault trial was ordered where the trial judge invited the jury to consider the accused's prior assault convictions in determining whether the accused or the victim was the aggressor. This went to culpability not credibility, and was highly prejudicial. For arguments that the *Corbett* discretion is insufficiently protective of accused, see Peter Sankoff, "*Corbett*, Crimes of Dishonesty and the Credibility Contest: Challenging the Accepted Wisdom on What Makes a Prior Conviction Probative" (2006) 10 Can. Crim. L. Rev. 215 and "*Corbett* Revisited: A Fairer Approach to the Admission of an Accused's Prior Criminal Record in Cross-examination" (2006) 51 Crim. L.Q. 400. See further Sankoff, "The Search for a Better Understanding of Discretionary Power in Evidence Law" (2007) 32 Queen's L.J. 487. In *R. v. Lambert* (2010), 74 C.R. (6th) 181 (N.B. Q.B.), the Court reviewed the Sankoff position but held that, despite serious divisions in courts of appeal, *Corbett* was clear in its instructions to allow cross-examination on the criminal record of the accused "except in unusual circumstances".

process rather requires a weighing of the factors relevant to the prejudicial effect and the probative value of the previous convictions, against the backdrop that the general course of preference is to give the jury all the information, but at the same time give a clear direction as to the limited use they are to make of such information.

In this case the balancing of these factors requires that the appellant's record be excluded because of its very significant prejudicial effect and its minimal probative value. In *R. v. Batte* (2000), 145 C.C.C. (3d) 498 at 516 (Ont. C.A.) Rosenberg J.A. said this:

> In *Corbett*, while Dickson C.J.C. disagreed with La Forest J. as to whether the record should be admitted, he accepted the factors that should be taken into account in the exercise of the judge's discretion. Among the most important factors enumerated by La Forest J. at pp. 740-44 are: the nature of the previous conviction, the remoteness or nearness of the conviction to the present charge, whether it is a conviction for a similar offence (in which case there is a greater risk of prejudice to a fair trial), and the nature of the defence attack on the Crown witnesses.

The previous convictions were all at least 14 years old at the time of the appellant's trial. The fact that since his convictions the appellant has apparently led a legally blameless life for a long period of time substantially diminishes the relevance these convictions may have for his credibility. Moreover, the prior convictions were for offences similar to the one for which the appellant was on trial. The Crown does not advance them as similar acts. The prejudicial effect of the appellant's record is markedly greater given that the convictions were for offences of a similar kind. Finally, the appellant's attack on the complainant's credibility was not based on any assertion that she had a bad character or a criminal record of her own. There was no need on this score to balance the picture for the jury as there was in Corbett. Thus, all of these factors weigh against the admission of the prior convictions. . . I would therefore allow the appeal, set aside the conviction and order a new trial.[255]

In *R. v. Laing*[256] a *Corbett* application was dismissed where the defence allegation that the police planted the evidence amounted to a serious attack on the character of the police. Cross-examination was allowed on the full criminal record which included a prior conviction for firearms offence for which the accused was again charged. In a comment on *Laing* entitled "Two Major Steps Backwards on *Corbett* Applications",[257] Professor Peter Sankoff suggests that *Corbett* rulings have become "perhaps the most erratic discretionary application in the law of evidence" and that the ruling in Laing will add to the unpredictability. He regards the conclusion reached in *Laing*, that suggesting evidence was planted engages the credibility contest rationale for allowing cross-examination of the accused's record, as "highly contestable". He also suggests that the ruling that the appropriateness of the

---

[255] See generally Owen Rees, "The Jury's Propensity for Prohibited Reasoning: *Corbett* Revisited" (2002) 7 Can. Crim. L. Rev. 333.

[256] 2016 ONCA 184, 33 C.R. (7th) 48 (Ont. C.A.).

[257] (2016), 33 C.R. (7th) 63.

exercise of a trial judge's discretion in one set of circumstances is not determinative of how another trial judge must exercise his or her discretion in another makes a *Corbett* discretion virtually unreviewable on appeal. Sankoff discusses a growing body of social science research pointing to the need to treat this category of "bad character evidence but admissible only for credibility" with greater vigilance and argues that after 30 years the *Corbett* decision should be revisited.

The ruling in *Laing* does appear to significantly diminish the importance of the following long-accepted ruling of Goudge J.A. in *R. v. Brown*:

> While the cross-examination attacked both the reliability and the honesty of the police officers, it did so on the basis of matters which were directly connected with the offence and which were raised in an attempt by the defence to meet the prosecution's evidence. This in unlike Corbett where the attack on the credibility of the Crown witnesses was based on their character, especially as disclosed in the criminal record, rather than arising out of the events surrounding the offence.[258]

The *Laing* Court is at pains to distinguish *Brown* on the facts. However *Brown* also concerned an allegation the police had planted the evidence.

HUTTON v. WAY
(1997), 105 O.A.C. 361 (Ont. C.A.)

This was an appeal from an award of damages rendered by a jury. The appellant Hutton argued that the trial judge erred by admitting his criminal record into evidence. Hutton's record included convictions for sexual assault and possession of marijuana. The evidence was admitted as going to the credibility of Hutton's claim that he was unable to return to his employment as a counsellor at a treatment centre of adolescent boys due to the injuries he suffered. The defence argued that he did not return because he would have been dismissed due to his record. Hutton was not given any award for future loss of income and his wife and child received nothing on their *Family Law Act* claims.

Per FINLAYSON J.A. (CATZMAN and AUSTIN JJ.A. concurring): —

In my opinion, the trial judge erred in admitting into evidence the record of convictions for criminal offences committed by the appellant when he was a teenager. The convictions were for sexual assault on a female in 1976 and for dangerous driving and possession of marihuana in 1978. It is to be noted that none was for an offence of dishonesty or perjury. In aggravation of this criminal record was the evidence of a more recent charge for sexual assault on a female, a charge for which he was acquitted, when the evidence at trial demonstrated that he was not the assailant and was in fact innocent.

The basis of the admission of this evidence of a criminal record which is highly prejudicial was that the appellant, at the time of the accident, was employed at Bayfield House, a private residential treatment centre for problem

---

[258]   (2002), 166 C.C.C. (3d) 570, 6 C.R. (6th) 380 (Ont. C.A.) at 576 [C.C.C.].

adolescent boys. The appellant had undergone special training to equip himself for this job. On application, he was never asked if he had a criminal record and did not volunteer the fact. However, it was stated in evidence that a ministry initiative called for a review of all criminal records of employees in institutions such as Bayfield and that the disclosure of the fact of this criminal record would mean that he would have a remote chance of maintaining employment.

To justify the admissibility of the criminal record and this unsubstantiated accusation, it was said that the credibility of the appellant was in issue when he testified that he was unable to resume his employment at Bayfield after the accident because of his injuries. The respondent suggested that he resigned because he knew that his criminal record and the then outstanding charges would become known to Bayfield and his employment would be terminated.

In my opinion, the fact that the appellant might be terminated for reasons that had nothing to do with his qualifications or work record is not only speculative but irrelevant in a civil action for personal injuries. The nature and extent of his injuries had nothing to do with his early criminal record or his current charges for an offence of which he was innocent. The only result of this evidence was to paint the appellant as a sex offender and create a hostile environment for his claim.

As indicated, the stale dated criminal record of the appellant did not relate to offences involving fraud or dishonesty. While prima facie admissible under the Ontario Evidence Act, these convictions should have been excluded on the Corbett application brought by the appellant. The fact of an outstanding charge is not admissible under the Evidence Act under any circumstances and the grounds advanced at common law, while remotely relevant, are so prejudicial so as to outweigh what limited probative value the evidence had.

The verdict reflects a certain meanness of spirit. The appellant received general damages for his injuries which were at the lower end of the scale. He received no award for future loss of income although the verdict reflected past loss of income from the accident to trial (a period of four and one half years) and may have reflected future disability by awarding future rehabilitation expenses covering a six month period. The wife and child of the marriage received nothing under the Family Law Act despite the evidence concerning them that supported such claims.

The improper admission of the evidence as to the criminal record and the charge of sexual assault may well have coloured the quantum of the above awards. The relief would ordinarily be a new trial but, understandably, that is not the relief the appellant seeks. He relies strongly upon the inconsistencies in the answers given to the questions asked by the jury and submits that this court, "if it considers it just", should exercise its powers under s. 119 of the Courts of Justice Act, R.S.O. 1990, Ch. C. 43 and substitute its own assessment of the damages.

I think we should do just that with respect of those areas where inexplicably the jury made no award. Having in mind that the jury was inclined to award figures throughout which were at the lower end of the scale, I would amend the judgment to award the following damages:

(i)	future loss of income for six months	$12,500
(ii)	FLA claim of Leisa Hutton	5,000
(iii)	FLA claim of Caleb Hutton	1,000

Section 22 of the *Ontario Evidence Act* provides:

Proof of previous conviction of a witness

22. (1) A witness may be asked whether he or she has been convicted of any crime, and upon being so asked, if the witness either denies the fact or refuses to answer, the conviction may be proved, and a certificate containing the substance and effect only, omitting the formal part, of the charge and of the conviction, purporting to be signed by the officer having the custody of the records of the court at which the offender was convicted, or by the deputy of the officer, is, upon proof of the identity of the witness as such convict, sufficient evidence of the conviction, without proof of the signature or of the official character of the person appearing to have signed the certificate. R.S.O. 1990, c. E.23, s. 22 (1).

R. v. UNDERWOOD
[1998] 1 S.C.R. 77, 12 C.R. (5th) 241, 121 C.C.C. (3d) 117

The accused was charged with first degree murder. After the Crown closed its case, his counsel made a *Corbett* application to have the accused's lengthy criminal record excluded. The trial judge did not make a ruling at that time, but rather indicated that he would prefer to wait until the accused had given his testimony in chief. The accused elected not to testify. He was later convicted and his conviction was upheld by the Court of Appeal. On further appeal a new trial was ordered.

LAMER C.J.C.:—

. . .

The question which the Court must answer in this case is whether it is an error of law to refuse to make a ruling on a *Corbett* application before the accused has elected to testify and been examined in chief. On the one hand, it would be very undesirable to force the trial judge to make a decision without all the relevant information. On the other hand, the accused must have an opportunity to make an informed decision whether to testify and, accordingly, should know as much as possible about the consequences of that decision in advance of having to make it. A balance must be struck between these two necessities. However, the balance must reflect that the ultimate goal of the procedural and substantive protections in the criminal justice system are to ensure that trials are scrupulously fair. Our criminal process is based upon the principle that before the accused calls evidence in his own defence, he must have knowledge of the case to be met. The extent to which his criminal record will be admissible against him will encompass part of that case. In this context, the case-to-meet principle suggests that the accused should have a right to make a Corbett application, and to know its outcome at the close of the Crown's case. It would be manifestly unfair to force an accused to engage in what the appellant describes as "russian roulette", or what Professor Delisle, in an annotation to *R. v. Hoffman* (1994), 32 C.R. (4th) 396, at p. 398, calls "blind man's bluff".

Although fairness requires that the ruling be made no later than the close of the Crown's case, there is always the possibility that the defence evidence will influence that trial judge's prior evaluation of the probative value and prejudicial effect of the criminal record. There are various ways of dealing with this problem. One is the possibility of making a preliminary ruling, subject to reconsideration if necessary. [But] imagine the possible unfairness that would arise if the accused takes the stand in reliance on a ruling that some or all of his prior convictions will be excluded, and that ruling is subsequently reversed.

In my view, the situation can be resolved by holding a voir dire before the defence opens its case. In this voir dire, the defence will reveal the evidence which it intends to call, either through calling witnesses, or through agreed statements of fact. The trial judge can then consider the factors set out in Corbett (the nature of the previous convictions, the time since the previous convictions, and any attacks made on the credibility of Crown witnesses) in the context of the defence evidence, and make a final ruling on the Corbett application.

I would emphasize that the purpose of this voir dire is not "defence disclosure". It creates no independent rights in the Crown, and, therefore should not be treated as an excuse for the Crown to deeply probe the case for the defence, as the defence is entitled to do to the Crown's case at a preliminary inquiry. The point to to provide the trial judge with the information he or she needs to make an informed decision, but the Crown has no right to require more than that. There may even be cases in which the trial judge believes he or she has sufficient information to make a decision without such disclosure, such as where the nature of the defence is fairly clear or has otherwise been disclosed (e.g. an alibi), or where the outcome of the application is readily apparent without this information. In those cases, disclosure need not be given.

. . .

In summary, a *Corbett* application should be made after the close of the Crown's case. If the trial judge believes it to be necessary, a voir dire should be held in which the defence discloses what evidence it intends to call, so he or she can make a fully informed ruling on the application. This ruling may be subject to modification if the defence evidence departs significantly from what was disclosed. In this case, the trial judge refused to rule until after the appellant had testified, and in so doing, he erred.

In *Hewson v. R.*,[259] the Court decided, 5-4, that an accused could be questioned as to a previous conviction though at the time of the questioning the conviction was subject to a pending appeal. In *R. v. Titus*,[260] the accused had been convicted of murder. The court granted him a new trial because the

---

[259]   [1979] 2 S.C.R. 82.
[260]   [1983] 1 S.C.R. 259.

trial judge had precluded cross-examination by the defence of a Crown witness with respect to an outstanding murder charge preferred against that witness by the same police department that had laid the murder charge against the accused. The Court decided that cross-examination of a Crown witness concerning an outstanding indictment against that witness was proper and admissible for the purpose of showing a possible motivation to seek favour with the prosecution.

In *R. v. Danson*,[261] the Crown cross-examined the accused as to an incident where he was found guilty of assault and given a conditional discharge. The trial judge treated the discharge as a conviction. The conviction was quashed. The Court noted that an accused, unlike an ordinary witness, cannot be cross-examined with respect to discreditable acts unrelated to the charge on the issue of credibility unless he or she puts his or her character in issue or is examined pursuant to s. 12; an adjudication of guilt followed by the granting of a discharge is not a conviction.

In *R. v. Morris*,[262] the accused was found guilty on a charge of breaking and entering with intent. He appealed on the ground that the trial judge erred by allowing cross-examination of the accused as to his having been found guilty, under the *Juvenile Delinquents Act*, of offences, under the *Criminal Code*. The Supreme Court, 5-4, dismissed his appeal, saying the word "offence" as used in s. 12 includes a delinquency consisting of a violation of the *Criminal Code* enforceable under the *Juvenile Delinquents Act,* and a finding of delinquency under that Act was equivalent to a conviction within the meaning of s. 12. There are now conflicting authorities on whether a youth can be cross-examined on his or her youth record under s. 12.[263] **Which approach do you think is most consistent with the underlying protections given to young offenders under the *Youth Criminal Justice Act*?**

(d) Defects in Capacity of Witness

The cross-examiner is always entitled, subject to the trial judge's discretion, to attempt impeachment by questioning the witness' general capacity to observe, recollect and communicate, and his or her particular ability in the case under review. At times the witness may confess the possibility of error. In other instances the very incredibility of a fact deposed to on cross-examination will disclose such obvious error on one point as to cast doubt on the rest of his or her evidence. The witness' capacities may also be tested in front of the trier of fact by means of an experiment.

May extrinsic evidence by introduced to prove the incapacity alleged?

If the witness testifies that he or she observed the incident under review clearly because there was then a full moon, then obviously his or her opponent should be able to introduce contradictory evidence of the moon's

---

[261]   (1982), 35 O.R. (2d) 777 (C.A.). See also *R. v. Sark* (2004), 182 C.C.C. (3d) 530 (N.B. C.A.).

[262]   [1979] 1 S.C.R. 405.

[263]   See *R. v. Sheik-Qasim* (2007), 230 C.C.C. (3d) 531 (S.C.J.) (not allowed); and *R. v. U. (D.A.)*, 239 C.C.C. (3d) 409 (N.S. S.C.) (permitted).

illumination on the evening in question to demonstrate that the witness' opportunity for observation was less than full. But if the extrinsic evidence is previous specific instances of error by the witness, should we analogize to specific instances of misconduct and foreclose, or to evidence of bias and receive? If we seek to test the memory of the witness by asking him or her questions concerning matters which occurred at the same time as the material event, though unconnected with it, can we lead extrinsic evidence to contradict? May we seek to establish by extrinsic evidence that the witness misperceived other matters at other times unconnected with the material issue? Can we enunciate a clear rule or can we do more than simply rest the decision with the discretion of the trial judge who can weigh the probative value towards impeachment against consumption of time, confusion of issues and fairness to the witness?

Is the situation different when the extrinsic evidence on capacity is medical evidence? May a medical witness give his or her opinion on veracity and state the reasons for his or her belief ? In *R. v. Toohey* [264] the House of Lords analyzing that problem noted:

> This unreliability may have two aspects either separate from one another or acting jointly to create confusion. The witness may, through his mental trouble, derive a fanciful or untrue picture from events while they are actually occurring, or he may have a fanciful or untrue recollection of them which distorts his evidence at the time when he is giving it.
>
> The only general principles which can be derived from the older cases are these. On the one hand, the courts have sought to prevent juries from being beguiled by the evidence of witnesses who could be shown to be, through defect of character, wholly unworthy of belief. On the other hand, however, they have sought to prevent the trial of a case becoming clogged with a number of side issues, such as might arise if there could be an investigation of matters which had no relevance to the issue save in so far as they tended to show the veracity or falsity of the witness who was giving evidence which *was* relevant to the issue. Many controversies which might thus obliquely throw some light on the issues must in practice be discarded because there is not an infinity of time, money and mental comprehension available to make use of them.

and concluded:

> Human evidence shares the frailties of those who give it. It is subject to many cross-currents such as partiality, prejudice, self-interest and, above all, imagination and inaccuracy. Those are matters with which the jury, helped by cross-examination and common sense, must do their best. But when a witness through physical (in which I include mental) disease or abnormality is not capable of giving a true or reliable account to the jury, it must surely be allowable for medical science to reveal this vital hidden fact to them. If a witness purported to give evidence of something which he believed that he had seen at a distance of 50 yards, it must surely be possible to call the evidence of an oculist to the effect that the witness could not possibly see anything at a greater distance than 20 yards, or the evidence of a surgeon who had removed a cataract from which the witness was suffering at the material time and which would have prevented him

---

[264]   [1965] A.C. 595, (H.L.) at 607-608, per Lord Pearce.

from seeing what he thought he saw. So, too, must it be allowable to call medical evidence of mental illness which makes a witness incapable of giving reliable evidence, whether through the existence of delusions or otherwise.

4. SUPPORTING OR REHABILITATING CREDIBILITY

(a) General Rule

Speaking generally, evidence in support of credibility is not receivable unless and until credibility has been attacked. When the witness's character for truthfulness has been impeached by evidence of general reputation, opinion or specific instances of misconduct, the witness may be rehabilitated by evidence of good character, but not before.[265]

The first Supreme Court of Canada case to address the common law rule against oath-helping involved the use of the polygraph. The Court also set out the general prohibition against leading prior consistent statements.

R. v. BÉLAND

[1987] 2 S.C.R. 398, 36 C.C.C. (3d) 481, 60 C.R. (3d) 1

1 McIntyre J. (Dickson C.J., Beetz and Le Dain JJ concurring):—

This appeal involves the question of the admissibility in evidence in a criminal trial of the results of a polygraph examination of an accused person.

2 The respondents, Beland and Phillips, were charged with conspiracy to commit a robbery. The Crown led evidence to the effect that the respondents had conspired with one Grenier and one Filippone to rob an armoured truck. No robbery took place because Grenier disclosed the conspiracy to the police. He later gave evidence for the Crown and his testimony was the only evidence which directly implicated the respondents in the conspiracy. The respondents gave evidence on their own behalf, denying any participation in the conspiracy and saying that the evidence of Grenier was false. Each respondent during his testimony said that he was prepared to undergo a polygraph examination. After completion of the evidence at trial the respondents made an application to the trial judge to reopen their defence, in order to permit each of them to take a polygraph examination and submit the results in evidence. This motion was refused by the trial judge who held that the results of such an examination were inadmissible in evidence, in accordance with *Phillion v. The Queen*, [1978] 1 S.C.R. 18. The respondents were convicted. An appeal to the Court of Appeal by the respondents succeeded. By a majority, the Court of Appeal granted an order reopening the trial and directing that the results of the polygraph examination be submitted to the trial judge, for a ruling as to their admissibility in light of all the circumstances revealed in the evidence: [1984] C.A. 443, 15 D.L.R. (4th) 89, 16 C.C.C. (3d) 462, 40 C.R. (3d) 193. The Crown appeals to this Court as of right under s. 621(1)(a) of the Criminal Code. The

---

[265] See *R. v. Kyselka* (1962), 133 C.C.C. 103 (Ont. C.A.) rejecting psychiatric opinion in support of credibility. See also *R. v. Burkart*, [1965] 3 C.C.C. 210 (Sask. C.A.).

parties agree that the sole issue in this appeal is whether evidence of the results of a polygraph examination is admissible in light of the particular facts of this case.

. . .

5 The leading case in this Court concerning the admissibility of polygraph evidence is *Phillion v. The Queen, supra*, in which it was held that such evidence should be rejected. Speaking for the majority, Ritchie J. expressed the view that such evidence offended the hearsay rule. . ... Spence J., with whom Laskin C.J. concurred, wrote separate reasons in which he agreed that the evidence should be rejected, but he left open the question of whether in other circumstances the polygraph evidence might be admissible.

6 It was the suggestion of the possibility of a different result in other circumstances which was relied upon by the majority of the Court of Appeal to distinguish the *Phillion* case. As has been noted, *Phillion* did not give evidence himself but sought to rely on the evidence of the polygraph operator to place his story before the jury and lend it credibility. In the case at bar the two respondents each gave evidence at trial and now seek to invoke that of the polygraph operator to support their credibility.

General Rule Against Oath-helping

7 The Crown appellant argues that the admission of polygraph evidence offends the rule which prohibits a party from presenting evidence which has, as its sole purpose, the bolstering of the credibility of that party's own witnesses. This is sometimes referred to in the earlier cases as oath-helping. There does not appear to be any decision of this Court which has dealt specifically with the rule, but there is other substantial authority supporting it. The leading decision on this point in Canada is *R. v. Kyselka, s*upra. In that case, the three accused were charged with the rape of a mentally retarded 16-year-old girl. The trial judge permitted the Crown to call a psychiatrist, who gave evidence that because of her low mental age the complainant lacked sufficient imagination to concoct a story. It was therefore likely that she would tell the truth in court. The accused were convicted. On appeal, Porter C.J.O., speaking for the court (Porter C.J.O., Kelly and McLennan JJ.A.), held that the evidence of the psychiatrist should not have been admitted as its sole purpose was to suggest that the complainant, because of her mental classification, was likely to be a truthful witness. He said, at pp. 107-8:

> While the credit of any witness may be impeached by the opposite party, *R. v. Gunewardene*, [1951] 2 All E.R. 290 at p. 294, there is no warrant or authority for such oath-helping as occurred in the circumstances of this case, reminiscent as it is of the method before the Norman Conquest by which a defendant in a civil suit or an accused person proved his case by calling witnesses to swear that the oath of the party was true. If this sort of evidence were admissible in the case of either party no limit could be placed on the number of witnesses who could be called to testify about the credibility of witnesses as to facts. It would tend to produce, regardless

of the number of such character witnesses who were called, undue confusion in the minds of the jury by directing their attention away from the real issues and the controversy would become so intricate that truth would be more likely to remain hidden than be discovered. For these reasons this evidence was not admissible.

. . .

9 From the foregoing comments, it will be seen that the rule against oath-helping, that is, adducing evidence solely for the purpose of bolstering a witness's credibility, is well-grounded in authority. It is apparent that since the evidence of the polygraph examination has no other purpose, its admission would offend the well-established rule.

Rule Against Past Consistent Statements

. . .

11 The rule is generally expressed in relation to past consistent statements. In the case at bar, evidence would be given of statements made subsequent to the evidence given by the respondents at trial. In my view, however, this leads to no difference in principle. The concern is with consistent statements made out of court. The fact that they may be made after evidence has been given at trial would not change their probative value or reliability. In my view, the rule against admission of consistent out-of-court statements is soundly based and particularly apposite to questions raised in connection with the use of the polygraph. Polygraph evidence when tendered would be entirely self-serving and would shed no light on the real issues before the court. Assuming, as in the case at bar, that the evidence sought to be adduced would not fall within any of the well recognized exceptions to the operation of the rule—where it is permitted to rebut the allegation of a recent fabrication or to show physical, mental or emotional condition—it should be rejected. To do otherwise is to open the trial process to the time-consuming and confusing consideration of collateral issues and to deflect the focus of the proceedings from their fundamental issue of guilt or innocence. . .

12 It is therefore my opinion that evidence of the results of a polygraph examination would clearly offend the rule against the admission of past or out-of-court statements by a witness. All of the considerations upon which the rule is based are as applicable to polygraph evidence as to other statements. The repetition of statements by another witness adds nothing to their weight and reliability. The ultimate decision as to the truth or falsity of the evidence of a witness must rest upon the exercise of the judgment of the trier of fact. This is as true of evidence of polygraph tests as of any other evidence. In the last analysis, the trier of fact must reach its conclusion on the basis of the evidence given by a human being in court. The evidence of the polygraph operator if heard by the trier of fact adds nothing to the earlier statement of the witness which is sought to be supported.

. . .

18 In conclusion, it is my opinion, based upon a consideration of rules of evidence long established and applied in our courts, that the polygraph has no place in the judicial process where it is employed as a tool to determine or to test the credibility of witnesses. It is frequently argued that the polygraph represents an application of modern scientific knowledge and experience to the task of determining the veracity of human utterances. It is said that the courts should welcome this device and not cling to the imperfect methods of the past in such an important task. This argument has a superficial appeal but, in my view, it cannot prevail in the face of the realities of court procedures.

19 I would say at once that this view is not based on a fear of the inaccuracies of the polygraph. On that question we were not supplied with sufficient evidence to reach a conclusion. However, it may be said that even the finding of a significant percentage of errors in its results would not, by itself, be sufficient ground to exclude it as an instrument for use in the courts. Error is inherent in human affairs, scientific or unscientific. It exists within our established court procedures and must always be guarded against. The compelling reason, in my view, for the exclusion of the evidence of polygraph results in judicial proceedings is two-fold. First, the admission of polygraph evidence would run counter to the well established rules of evidence which have been referred to. Second, while there is no reason why the rules of evidence should not be modified where improvement will result, it is my view that the admission of polygraph evidence will serve no purpose which is not already served. It will disrupt proceedings, cause delays, and lead to numerous complications which will result in no greater degree of certainty in the process than that which already exists.

20 Since litigation replaced trial by combat, the determination of fact, including the veracity of parties and their witnesses, has been the duty of judges or juries upon an evaluation of the statements of witnesses. This approach has led to the development of a body of rules relating to the giving and reception of evidence and we have developed methods which have served well and have gained a wide measure of approval. They have facilitated the orderly conduct of judicial proceedings and are designed to keep the focus of the proceedings on the principal issue, in a criminal case, the guilt or innocence of the accused. What would be served by the introduction of evidence of polygraph readings into the judicial process? To begin with, it must be remembered that however scientific it may be, its use in court depends on the human intervention of the operator. Whatever results are recorded by the polygraph instrument, their nature and significance reach the trier of fact through the mouth of the operator. Human fallibility is therefore present as before, but now it may be said to be fortified with the mystique of science. Then, it may be asked, what does it do? It provides evidence on the issue of the credibility of a witness. This has always been a collateral issue and one to be decided by the trier of fact. Is the trier of fact assisted by hearing, firstly from witness "A" that he was not present at the scene of the crime, and then from witness "B", a polygraph operator, that "A" was probably truthful? What would the result be, one may

ask, if the polygraph operator concluded from his test that witness "A" was lying? Would such evidence be admissible, could it be excluded by witness "A", could it be introduced by the Crown? These are serious questions and they lead to others. Would it be open to the opponent of the person relying upon the polygraph to have a second polygraph examination taken for his purposes? If the results differed, which would prevail, and what right would there be for compelling the production of polygraph evidence in the possession of a reluctant party? It is this fear of turmoil in the courts which leads me to reject the polygraph. Like Porter C.J.O. in *Kyselka*, I would not wish to see a return to the method of pre-Norman trials where parties relied heavily upon oath-helpers who swore to their veracity. For a description of the role of the oath-helper in early times, see W.S. Holdsworth, *A History of English Law* (7th ed. 1956), vol. 1, at pp. 305-8, and W.F. Walsh, *Outlines of the History of English and American Law* (1926), at pp. 99-100 (footnote II). I would seek to preserve the principle that in the resolution of disputes in litigation, issues of credibility will be decided by human triers of fact, using their experience of human affairs and basing judgment upon their assessment of the witness and on consideration of how an individual's evidence fits into the general picture revealed on a consideration of the whole of the case.

21 For the above reasons, and following *Phillion, supra*, I would allow the Crown's appeal. I would set aside the order of the Court of Appeal and confirm the conviction recorded at trial.

La Forest J. (concurred).

WILSON J. (LAMER J. concurring) (dissenting):—

I must respectfully disagree . . . that these rules present a basis for excluding the polygraph evidence and I will comment briefly on each.

(1) *The Rule Against Oath-helping*

Oath-helping or compurgation was, as I understand it, a method used to prove one's case in pre-Norman England. The accused in a criminal case or the defendant in a civil case could prove his innocence by providing a certain number of compurgators who would swear to the truth of his oath. The compurgators swore a set oath. If they departed from it in the slightest, the "oath burst" and the opposing party won. The practice fell into desuetude in the 13th Century.

The connection between oath-helping and the admissibility of polygraph evidence seems to me to be very tenuous. Oath-helpers were not required to have any knowledge material to the innocence or guilt of the accused. They merely recited a particular oath and their oaths were not subject to rebuttal. The polygraph operator, on the other hand, has subjected the accused to a number of tests. He reports on the results of these tests and gives his expert opinion as to whether the physiological reactions of the accused are similar to those of someone telling the truth. He is open to cross-examination on his technique, his assumptions, his interpretation of the data and the accuracy of the device. His evidence is only one of the many factors the jury will consider when assessing the credibility of the accused.

In what sense then can polygraph evidence be said to be similar to the medieval device by which the accused was guaranteed an acquittal if he could muster a sufficient number of compurgators? Any suggestion of similarity would, it seems to me, have to be based on the assumption that, despite the cross- examination of the polygraph operator, the calling of other operators to challenge erroneous statements by the original operator, and the delivery of a proper charge to the jury, the jury would automatically base its decision on the polygraph operator's testimony. I think this is an unwarranted assumption. I do not think we can make it even if my colleague's concern about the heightened weight that might be given to polygraph evidence because of the "mystique of science" has some validity. For reasons which will be given later I doubt that this concern is a valid one.

My own view would be that the rule against oath-helping is a curious point of legal history that has little bearing on the issue of polygraph admissibility. Oath-helping was a method of proving one's case that ante-dated the modern concept of trial by evidence. Polygraph evidence, on the other hand, fits squarely within the modern trial theory whereby witnesses are examined to ascertain the truth.

It is suggested, however, that oath-helping is the antecedent of a "well-established rule" against the admissibility of evidence adduced solely for the purpose of bolstering the credibility of one's own witness. A number of authorities are cited in support of the proposition that evidence may not be given in chief to bolster the credit of one's own witnesses but, if evidence is given to impeach their credit, rebuttal evidence may be given on that issue. It is noted, however, that the Canadian cases relied on in support of the rule are all cases in which the Crown was attempting to lead evidence-in-chief to bolster the credibility of a Crown witness. No Canadian case was cited where an accused was denied permission to do this. I have some concern, therefore, as to the scope of the "well-established rule" in Canada. I believe it would require an extension of the rule in this case to apply it to the respondents. Perhaps it should be applied to Crown and defence alike but this is not self-evident. Analogies certainly can be drawn from other areas of criminal evidence law to support a more permissive approach to evidence led by an accused. For example, in *R. v. Miller* (1952), 36 Cr. App. R. 169, an accused was permitted to call evidence against a co-accused which would have been inadmissible if called by the Crown. . .

I am very mindful of the fact that the respondents in this case took the stand in order to deny their involvement in the conspiracy and that the only direct evidence implicating them was that of Grenier, a self-confessed conspirator. The Crown, through Grenier, was impugning the credibility of the respondents by saying that they were lying under oath. It was his word against theirs. The respondents were, in effect, responding to an attack on their credibility by the Crown by offering to take a lie detector test. Indeed, the

Crown's whole case was that the respondents were lying and that the informer Grenier was telling the truth.

Section 577(3) of the *Criminal Code* provides that an accused is entitled, after the close of the prosecution's case, to make full answer and defence. It might be said that this is precisely what the respondents were attempting to do through the introduction of the polygraph evidence. . .

(2) *The Rule Against Past Consistent Statements*

The second ground for exclusion of the polygraph evidence is that it infringes the rule against the admission of past consistent statements. The cases and authorities make it clear that these statements are excluded because they are at best irrelevant and at worst fabricated and self-serving. The irrelevance rationale has, it seems to me, little applicability to polygraph evidence. The argument that the mere repetition of a story has no bearing on the truth of the story is, of course, a convincing one. Polygraph evidence, however, is not merely evidence that the accused has said the same thing twice. It is expert evidence on how closely his physiological responses during the test correspond to those of someone telling the truth. It is, in my opinion, clearly relevant.

Nor am I persuaded that the evidence should be excluded on the ground that by "examiner shopping" and by engaging in practice tests the accused may be able to increase the likelihood of a "successful" test. Unless it can be established that polygraph tests are *per se* without probative value (and I do not think this has been or could be established), it would seem to me that the possibility of abuse should be a factor going to weight rather than to admissibility.

In 2009, Romeo Phillion's 1972 conviction for murder was set aside by the Ontario Court of Appeal[266] pursuant to a miscarriage of justice review under s. 696.3 of the *Criminal Code*. The Court of Appeal concluded that his initial trial was unfair because his counsel was unaware of evidence establishing an alibi for the offence.

In *R. v. Murphy*,[267] a new trial was ordered by the Yukon Territorial Court of Appeal where the trial judge was held to have wrongly admitted evidence of police impressions of witnesses and crime scenes where the sole purpose was to bolster the credibility of the Crown's case.

R. v. TASH
2013 ONCA 380, 306 O.A.C. 173 (Ont. C.A.)

WATT J.A.:

[1] Shortly after hearing a radio report of gunshots fired in the hallway of a high-rise apartment building, three police officers noticed two men walking away from the building where the shots had been reported.

---

[266]   See *R. v. Phillion* (2009), 241 C.C.C. (3d) 193, 65 C.R. (6th) 255 (Ont. C.A.).
[267]   2014 YKCA 7, 311 C.C.C. (3d) 401, 12 C.R. (7th) 210 (Y.T. C.A.).

[2] What attracted the officers' attention was the pace at which both men were walking, and the way in which one of the men, Ezekiel Tash (the appellant), held his right arm and hand by the waist area of his pants. Did the man have a gun in his pants? Had he been wounded in a shooting?

[3] The officers, dressed casually and driving an unmarked vehicle, approached the two men. When one of the officers in the car identified himself as a police officer, both pedestrians bolted. The first officer out of the vehicle ran after the appellant. The other two officers followed. No one pursued the other man.

[4] The foot chase was brief and ended in a physical altercation by a car parked near another apartment building. Outnumbered by his original pursuers and reinforcements, the appellant was overpowered, handcuffed, arrested, and ultimately charged with three firearms offences and two counts of assaulting police officers in the execution of their duty.

[5] A jury heard widely divergent accounts of the events that began with the police query and ended with the appellant's arrest. Based upon their verdict, finding guilt established on the firearms charges but not on the assault counts, it would seem clear that the jury did not unqualifiedly accept either of the conflicting accounts of the episode.

. . .

Ground #1: The Admissibility and Use of "oath-helping" Evidence

[28] This ground of appeal relates to the admissibility and use of evidence adduced by the trial Crown in re-examination of Sgt. Matys, the senior officer involved in the apprehension and arrest of the appellant.

The Additional Background

[29] Trial counsel for the appellant cross-examined Sgt. Matys, as well as the other two arresting officers, Jamison and Patel, on a version of events alleging that the officers had falsely accused the appellant of possession of the Glock handgun. Counsel suggested that Sgt. Matys was the last officer to arrive at the place of arrest because he had picked up the gun dropped by Richardson where the chase began, brought the gun with him to the place of arrest, and dropped it there so that the appellant could be charged with possession of it. Counsel further alleged that Sgt. Matys fabricated his notes and his evidence because he had a complete disregard for the appellant whom he considered "a piece of shit".

[30] Sgt. Matys denied counsel's suggestions.

[31] In re-examination, the trial Crown asked Sgt. Matys whether he had ever been charged with or cited for misconduct. After defence counsel objected to the question and the trial judge ruled in his favour, the trial Crown persuaded the judge to permit the question. Sgt. Matys denied any misconduct. He

testified that his police (disciplinary) records would confirm his denial. The trial Crown also elicited evidence from Sgt. Matys that he had been promoted since the appellant's arrest.

The Closing Addresses

[32] In their closing addresses, each counsel made passing reference to the evidence adduced in re-examination of Sgt. Matys. Defence counsel pointed out that Matys' evidence referred only to "documented" complaints. The trial Crown contended that Matys' promotion put paid to the appellant's claim of a police conspiracy.

. . .

The Governing Principles

[35] The issues raised in connection with this ground of appeal have to do with the credibility of witnesses. Particularly, this ground of appeal concerns the techniques an opponent may use to attack or impeach a witness' credibility, on the one hand, and the means available to the witness' proponent to rehabilitate the witness' credibility after impeachment, on the other. The issues can be resolved by the application of general principles.

[36] Credibility rules are of three types.

[37] The first type concerns attempts by the witness' proponent to bolster the witness' credibility even *before* it has been impeached. As a general rule, we do not permit the witness' proponent to elicit bolstering evidence in direct examination. The rule against "oath-helping" excludes it.

[38] The second group of credibility rules involves the techniques an opponent may invoke to attack or impeach a witness' credibility.

[39] The third set of rules governs the method that the witness' proponent may use to rehabilitate the witness' credibility after impeachment, in essence, to undo the damage done by the impeachment.

[40] Despite the hostility of the common law towards bolstering evidence, we liberally admit impeaching evidence. Among the modes of attack on a witness' credibility are attacks that show bias or corruption, and those that attack the witness' character. A witness may also be impeached by specific contradiction, in other words, by proof through other witnesses that material facts are otherwise than as described by the witness being impeached.

[41] We recognize that a witness' emotions or feelings towards the parties, or the witness' self-interest in the outcome of the case, may have a powerful distorting effect on human testimony. And so it is that we recognize that bias, or any conduct, relationships, or motives reasonably likely to produce it, may be established to impeach credibility. The disparate and varied kinds of sources

of partiality defy exhaustive listing, but doubtless include hostility or attitude towards an accused.

[42] A witness' character for truthfulness or mendacity is relevant circumstantial evidence on the question of the truthfulness of the witness' testimony. Evidence of a witness' previous deception tends to demonstrate a character for untruthfulness. In turn, the existence of such a character trait increases, at least slightly, the probability that the witness has lied under oath. Proof of a witness' character trait for untruthfulness can be accomplished in several ways including proof of prior untruthful conduct, the witness' associations, and prior history. Any other acts offered to establish character should have a significant relation to credibility.

[43] Our adversary system requires that the proponent of a witness be afforded an opportunity to meet attacks on the credibility of the witness by presenting evidence rehabilitating the witness. But the bolstering evidence must be responsive to the nature of the attack and not exceed permissible limits. For example, supportive evidence of good character for honesty of a witness impeached by evidence of "bad" character for untruthfulness or dishonesty is permissible. Proof of prior consistent statements to rebut impeachment on grounds of recent fabrication is also permissible. At root, the admissibility of rehabilitative evidence should depend on whether what is proposed is logically relevant to rebut the impeaching fact. The rehabilitating facts should meet the impeachment with relative directness. The wall, attacked at one point, may not be fortified at a distinctly separate point: *1 McCormick on Evidence* (7th ed., 2013, Thomson Reuters: Westlaw), at § 47, pp. 307-308.

The Principles Applied

[44] I would give effect to this ground of appeal, but defer consideration of its impact on the integrity of the jury's verdict and the fairness of the appellant's trial until the remaining grounds of appeal have been considered.

[45] Trial counsel for the appellant impeached each of the officers who pursued and arrested the appellant on the ground that, in this case, they fabricated their evidence about the circumstances in which they found the gun they attributed to the appellant. The principal motivating factor was their contempt for the appellant who fled when they wanted to speak to them, assaulted them when apprehended, and accused them of gratuitously beating him to the point of significant injuries.

[46] The rehabilitative evidence related only to Sgt. Matys, the officer which defence counsel alleged found the gun at the outset of the chase, picked it up, and planted it by the vehicle where the appellant was arrested so that possession of it could be attributed to the appellant.

[47] The rehabilitative evidence, that Sgt. Matys had no disciplinary record and had been promoted to his rank at trial after these events, lacked any probative

value on the issue to which it was directed. The rehabilitative evidence was not a response in kind to the particular basis on which the witness was impeached. The impeachment here was not an attack on each witness' character for truthfulness or integrity, but rather a case-specific allegation of fabrication based on a specific motive.

(b) Exceptions

To the general rule excluding previous consistent statements, the common law recognized certain exceptions.

(i) *To Rebut Allegation of Recent Fabrication*

R. v. STIRLING
[2008] 1 S.C.R. 272, 54 C.R. (6th) 228, 229 C.C.C. (3d) 257 (S.C.C.)

The judgment of the Court was delivered by:

1 BASTARACHE J.:— The appellant, Mr. Stirling, appeals his convictions on two counts of criminal negligence causing death and one count of criminal negligence causing bodily harm. The convictions arose out of a single-vehicle accident in which two of the car's occupants were killed and two others, including Mr. Stirling, were seriously injured. The primary issue before the trial judge was whether the Crown had established that the appellant, and not the other survivor of the accident, Mr. Harding, was driving the vehicle when the crash occurred. The trial judge ultimately concluded that Mr. Stirling was the driver. He based this finding on a number of pieces of evidence, including the testimony of Mr. Harding, who stated that Mr. Stirling had been driving.

2 During the cross-examination of Mr. Harding, counsel for the appellant questioned the witness about a pending civil claim he had launched against Mr. Stirling as the driver of the vehicle and about several drug-related charges against Mr. Harding which had recently been dropped. All parties agreed that this line of questioning raised the possibility that Mr. Harding had motive to fabricate his testimony and, following a voir dire, the judge admitted several prior consistent statements which served to rebut that suggestion.

3 The appellant argues on appeal that although the trial judge was correct in admitting the prior consistent statements for the purpose of refuting the suggestion of recent fabrication, he erroneously considered them for the truth of their contents. . .

4 In my view, this appeal ought to be dismissed. Although the passages above contain some ambiguous comments about the use the trial judge made of the prior consistent statements, these remarks must be read in the context of the reasons as a whole. It is clear from this judgment that the trial judge was very

aware of the limited use of the prior consistent statements, and he correctly instructed himself on this point repeatedly.

Analysis

5 It is well established that prior consistent statements are generally inadmissible (*R. v. Evans*, [1993] 2 S.C.R. 629; *R. v. Simpson*, [1988] 1 S.C.R. 3; *R. v. Béland*, [1987] 2 S.C.R. 398). This is because such statements are usually viewed as lacking probative value and being self-serving (*Evans*, at p. 643). There are, however, several exceptions to this general exclusionary rule, and one of these exceptions is that prior consistent statements can be admitted where it has been suggested that a witness has recently fabricated portions of his or her evidence (Evans, at p. 643; *Simpson*, at pp. 22-23). Admission on the basis of this exception does not require that an allegation of recent fabrication be expressly made—it is sufficient that the circumstances of the case reveal that the "apparent position of the opposing party is that there has been a prior contrivance" (*Evans*, at p. 643). It is also not necessary that a fabrication be particularly "recent", as the issue is not the recency of the fabrication but rather whether the witness made up a false story at some point after the event that is the subject of his or her testimony actually occurred (*R. v. O'Connor* (1995), 100 C.C.C. (3d) 285 (Ont. C.A.), at pp. 294-95). Prior consistent statements have probative value in this context where they can illustrate that the witness's story was the same even before a motivation to fabricate arose.

6 In this case, the parties do not dispute that the trial judge was correct to admit Mr. Harding's prior consistent statements. The cross-examination of this witness included questions about both a civil lawsuit he had pending against Mr. Stirling as the driver of the vehicle and the relationship between his testimony and criminal charges against him which had recently been dropped. Given these questions, it was appropriate for the judge to admit statements made prior to the launching of the civil suit and prior to the dropping of the charges because these statements, if consistent with the in-court testimony, could demonstrate that Mr. Harding's evidence was not motivated by either of these factors.

7 However, a prior consistent statement that is admitted to rebut the suggestion of recent fabrication continues to lack any probative value beyond showing that the witness's story did not change as a result of a new motive to fabricate. Importantly, it is impermissible to assume that because a witness has made the same statement in the past, he or she is more likely to be telling the truth, and any admitted prior consistent statements should not be assessed for the truth of their contents. As was noted in *R. v. Divitaris* (2004), 188 C.C.C. (3d) 390 (Ont. C.A.), at para. 28, "a concocted statement, repeated on more than one occasion, remains concocted"; see also J. Sopinka, S. N. Lederman and A. W. Bryant, *The Law of Evidence in Canada* (2nd ed. 1999), at p. 313. This case illustrates the importance of this point. The fact that Mr. Harding reported that the appellant was driving on the night of the crash before he launched the civil suit or had charges against him dropped does not in any way

confirm that that evidence is not fabricated. All it tells us is that it wasn't fabricated as a result of the civil suit or the dropping of the criminal charges. There thus remains the very real possibility that the evidence was fabricated immediately after the accident when, as the trial judge found, "any reasonable person would recognize there was huge liability facing the driver" (Ruling on voir dire, June 21, 2005, at para. 24). The reality is that even when Mr. Harding made his very first comments about who was driving when the accident occurred, he already had a visible motive to fabricate — to avoid the clear consequences which faced the driver of the vehicle — and this potential motive is not in any way rebutted by the consistency of his story. It was therefore necessary for the trial judge to avoid using Mr. Harding's prior statements for the truth of their contents.

8 It is clear from the reasons of the trial judge that he was aware of the limited value of Mr. Harding's prior statements. Not only did he acknowledge that this witness had a motive to fabricate immediately after the accident occurred (and thus before any statements were made about who was driving), but he also stated explicitly, on several occasions, that he had not considered the statements for the truth of their contents . . .

. . .

10 . . . [P]rior consistent statements have the impact of removing a potential motive to lie, and the trial judge is entitled to consider removal of this motive when assessing the witness's credibility.

11 Courts and scholars in this country have used a variety of language to describe the way prior consistent statements may impact on a witness's credibility where they refute suggestion of an improper motive. Both the Nova Scotia Court of Appeal and the Alberta Court of Appeal refer to the "bolstering" of the witness's credibility (*R. v. Schofield* (1996), 148 N.S.R. (2d) 175, at para. 23; *R. v. R. (J.)* (2000), 84 Alta. L.R. (3d) 92, 2000 ABCA 196, at para. 8), a term which is also used in the leading text of Sopinka, Lederman and Bryant, at p. 314. The Ontario Court of Appeal recently found that these statements are capable of "strengthening" credibility (R. v. *Zebedee* (2006), 211 C.C.C. (3d) 199, at para. 117), while the British Columbia Court of Appeal has referred to their ability to "rehabilitate" credibility (*R. v. Aksidan* (2006), 209 C.C.C. (3d) 423, 2006 BCCA 258, at para. 21). This Court has found that the statements can be admitted "in support of" the witness's credibility (*Evans*, at p. 643). What is clear from all of these sources is that credibility is necessarily impacted — in a positive way — where admission of prior consistent statements removes a motive for fabrication. Although it would clearly be flawed reasoning to conclude that removal of this motive leads to a conclusion that the witness is telling the truth, it is permissible for this factor to be taken into account as part of the larger assessment of credibility.

12 It is therefore not entirely accurate to submit, as the appellant contends, that prior consistent statements cannot be used to "bolster" or "support" the credibility of a witness generally. This argument attempts to insulate the

impact of the prior consistent statements from the remainder of the credibility analysis and suggests that "general" credibility can somehow be hived off from the specific credibility question to which the statements relate. Such a fine parsing of the notion of credibility is impractical and artificial. Further, while it would clearly be an error to conclude that because someone has been saying the same thing repeatedly their evidence is more likely to be correct, there is no error in finding that because there is no evidence that an individual has a motive to lie, their evidence is more likely to be honest.

. . .

Appeal dismissed.

R. v. ELLARD

(2009), [2009] 2 S.C.R. 19, 67 C.R. (6th) 78, 245 C.C.C. (3d) 183 (S.C.C.)

ABELLA J. (for the Court):—

. . .

32 Certain exceptions have nevertheless developed in the jurisprudence. In particular, where a party has made an allegation of recent fabrication, the opposing party can rebut the allegation by introducing prior statements made before the alleged fabrication arose, that are consistent with the testimony at trial. The allegation need not be express. It is enough if "in light of the circumstances of the case and the conduct of the trial, the apparent position of the opposing party is that there has been a prior contrivance" (*Evans*, at p. 643; see also *R. v. Simpson*, [1988] 1 S.C.R. 3, at p. 24).

33 To be "recent", the fabrication need only have been made after the event testified about (*Stirling*, at para. 5). A mere contradiction in the evidence is not enough to engage the recent fabrication exception. However, a "fabrication" can include being influenced by outside sources (*R. v. B. (A.J.)*, [1995] 2 S.C.R. 413). To rebut an allegation of recent fabrication, it is necessary to identify statements made prior to the existence of a motive or of circumstances leading to fabrication. In all cases, the timing of the prior consistent statements will be central to whether they are admissible.

. . .

42 As previously noted, because there is a danger that the repetition of prior consistent statements may bolster a witness's reliability, a limiting instruction will almost always be required where such statements are admitted. The purpose of such an instruction is to tell the jury that consistency is not the same as accuracy, and that the statements can only be used to rebut the allegation of recent fabrication, not to support the fact at issue or the general reliability of the witness. (See *R. v. Rockey*, [1996] 3 S.C.R. 829, per McLachlin J.; *R. v. Fair* (1993), 16 O.R. (3d) 1 (C.A.), at pp. 20-21; *R. v. Divitaris* (2004), 188 C.C.C. (3d) 390 (Ont. C.A.), at para. 31; *R. v. A. (J.)* (1996), 112 C.C.C. (3d) 528 (Ont. C.A.), at p. 533; and *R. v. Codina* (1995), 95 C.C.C. (3d) 311 (Ont. C.A.), at p. 330.)

43 Delineated exceptions to the generally stringent rule have emerged, some of which were canvassed in *R. v. Demetrius* (2003), 179 C.C.C. (3d) 26 (Ont. C.A.), at para. 22. These include situations where the defence itself relies on the prior statement, *R. v. S. (P.)* (2000), 144 C.C.C. (3d) 120 (Ont. C.A.), at paras. 62-63; where the prior statement was not offered as proof of the underlying fact, *R. v. G.M.*, [2000] O.J. No. 5007 (QL) (C.A.); or where the concern over self- corroboration and thereby bolstering the witness's reliability is not present, *R. v. Clark* (1995), 87 O.A.C. 178. (See also David M. Paciocco and Lee Stuesser, The Law of Evidence (5th ed. 2008), at p. 501.)

The full Supreme Court, over the sole dissent of Fish J., held that in the circumstances of *Ellard* no limiting instruction was required as the prior statements did not address the defence theory. The majority of the B.C. Court of Appeal had erred in ordering a fourth trial. By the time of the third trial eight years had elapsed since the murder.

(ii) *Prior Identification*

When a witness at trial is asked to identify a person in the courtroom the surrounding circumstances may seriously weaken the weight of the identification. In a criminal trial for assault the identification as the assailant of the person in the prisoner's dock would have little force, as the trier of fact might naturally theorize that the witness is not giving his or her present recollection of the incident but rather that the witness is concluding from the accused's location that the police have arrested the proper person. As in the previous section, the circumstances of the case may cast doubt on the witness' statement and we therefore receive evidence of any prior identification made when such circumstances were not present; a close examination of the earlier circumstances will enhance or detract from the cogency of the present identification.

R. v. TAT
(1997), 14 C.R. (5th) 116, 117 C.C.C. (3d) 481 (Ont. C.A.)

DOHERTY J.A.:

36 Clearly, the evidence of the prior descriptions given and the prior identifications made by the identifying witness constitute prior consistent statements made by that witness. Generally speaking, evidence that a witness made prior consistent statements is excluded as irrelevant and self-serving. However, where identification evidence is involved, it is the in-court identification of the accused which has little or no probative value standing alone. The probative force of identification evidence is best measured by a consideration of the entire identification process which culminates with an in-court identification: e.g. *R. v. Langille, supra*, at 555; *DiCarlo v. The U.S.*, 6 F. (2d) 364 at 369, per Hough J., concurring, (2d cir. 1925); *Clemons v. The U.S.*, 408 F. (2d) 1230 at 1243 (D.C. cir. 1968). The central importance of the pre-trial identification process in the assessment of the weight to be given to identification evidence is apparent upon a review of cases which have

considered the reasonableness of verdicts based upon identification evidence: e.g. see *R. v. Miaponoose* (1996), 110 C.C.C. (3d) 445 (Ont. C.A.).

37 If a witness identifies an accused at trial, evidence of previous identifications made and descriptions given is admissible to allow the trier of fact to make an informed determination of the probative value of the purported identification. The trier of fact will consider the entirety of the identification process as revealed by the evidence before deciding what weight should be given to the identification made by the identifying witness. Evidence of the circumstances surrounding any prior identifications and the details of prior descriptions given will be central to that assessment.

(iii) *Part of Narrative*

R. v. DINARDO
[2008] 1 S.C.R. 788, 231 C.C.C. (3d) 177, 57 C.R. (6th) 48 (S.C.C.)

The accused was charged with sexual assault and sexual exploitation of a person with a disability. The complainant was a 22-year-old woman who suffered from a mild mental disability. The accused was a taxi driver who picked up the complainant at a home for mentally challenged persons and drove her to another facility about 15 minutes away. The complainant alleged that the accused sexually assaulted her during the drive. The complainant spontaneously recounted these allegations to a teacher and several others on the day of the alleged assault.

The trial judge ruled the complainant competent to testify on a promise to tell the truth. The complainant's trial testimony was essentially consistent on the central parts of her allegations, but she gave confused and contradictory testimony on many points, including whether she knew what it meant to invent a story and whether she had in fact invented the allegations. The accused testified and denied the allegations.

The trial judge convicted the accused on both counts. In his reasons for judgment, the trial judge held that the contradictions in the complainant's testimony were not on important facts but only on details too unimportant to affect her credibility. He found that the complainant's testimony was corroborated by her repeated, consistent statements about the event. A majority of the Quebec Court of Appeal dismissed the appeal against conviction, and the accused appealed to the Supreme Court of Canada.

CHARRON J.A. (for the Court):—

. . .

36 As a general rule, prior consistent statements are inadmissible (*R. v. Stirling*, [2008] 1 S.C.R 272, 2008 SCC 10). There are two primary justifications for the exclusion of such statements: first, they lack probative value (*Stirling*, at para. 5), and second, they constitute hearsay when adduced for the truth of their contents.

37 In some circumstances, prior consistent statements may be admissible as part of the narrative. Once admitted, the statements may be used for the limited purpose of helping the trier of fact to understand how the complainant's story was initially disclosed. The challenge is to distinguish between "using narrative evidence for the impermissible purpose of 'confirm[ing] the truthfulness of the sworn allegation'" and "using narrative evidence for the permissible purpose of showing the fact and timing of a complaint, which may then *assist the trier of fact in the assessment of truthfulness or credibility*" McWilliams' *Canadian Criminal Evidence* (4th ed. (loose-leaf)), at pp. 11-44 and 11-45 (emphasis in original); see also *R. v. F. (J.E.)* (1993), 85 C.C.C. (3d) 457 (Ont. C.A.), at p. 476).

38 In *R. v. G.C.*, [2006] O.J. No. 2245 (QL), the Ontario Court of Appeal noted that the prior consistent statements of a complainant may assist the court in assessing the complainant's likely truthfulness, particularly in cases involving allegations of sexual assault against children. As Rouleau J.A. explained, for a unanimous court:

> Although properly admitted at trial, the evidence of prior complaint cannot be used as a form of self-corroboration to prove that the incident in fact occurred. It cannot be used as evidence of the truth of its contents. However, the evidence can "be supportive of the central allegation in the sense of creating a logical framework for its presentation", as set out above, and can be used in assessing the truthfulness of the complainant. As set out in *R. v. F. (J.E.)* at p. 476:
>
>> The fact that the statements were made is admissible to assist the jury as to the sequence of events from the alleged offence to the prosecution so that they can understand the conduct of the complainant and assess her truthfulness. However, the jury must be instructed that they are not to look to the content of the statements as proof that a crime has been committed.
>
> The trial judge understood the limited use that could be made of this evidence as appears from his reasons:
>
>> [I]t certainly struck me while the fact that you go and tell somebody that you were molested doesn't confirm the fact that you were molested. I'm struck by the manner or the way it came out, tends to confirm [the complainant's] story — how they were reading this book, and how the thing came up about child sexual abuse.
>
> In cases involving sexual assault on young children, the courts recognize the difficulty in the victim providing a full account of events. In appropriate cases, the way the complaint comes forth can, by adding or detracting from the logical cogency of the child's evidence, be a useful tool in assisting the trial judge in the assessment of the child's truthfulness. This was such a case. [Emphasis added; paras. 20-22.]

39 The Ontario Court of Appeal's reasoning in *G.C.* applies equally to the facts of this case. The complainant's prior consistent statements were not admissible under any of the traditional hearsay exceptions. Thus, the statements could not be used to confirm her in-court testimony. However, in light of the evidence that the complainant had difficulty situating events in time, was easily

confused, and lied on occasion, the spontaneous nature of the initial complaint and the complainant's repetition of the essential elements of the allegations provide important context for assessing her credibility.

40 The Court of Appeal correctly concluded that the trial judge erred when he considered the contents of the complainant's prior consistent statements to corroborate her testimony at trial, noting in his judgment that [TRANSLATION] "there is a form of corroboration in the facts and statements of the victim, who never contradicted herself" (para. 68). I am unable to agree with the majority, however, that the accused suffered no prejudice from the trial judge's improper use of the statements. The trial judge relied heavily on the corroborative value of the complainant's prior statements in convicting Mr. Dinardo. He was clearly of the view that the complainant's consistency in recounting the allegations made her story more credible. Accordingly, I would also allow the appeal on this basis.

The appeal was allowed and a new trial ordered.

R. v. CURTO
(2008), 230 C.C.C. (3d) 145, 54 C.R. (6th) 237 (Ont. C.A.)

ROSENBERG J.A. (for the Court):—

. . .

31 The admissibility of prior consistent statements under the narrative exception to the general exclusionary rule has been discussed in a number of cases, usually in the context of admission of prior statements by child complainants and often in respect of historical assaults. See for example: *R. v. Ay* (1994), 93 C.C.C. (3d) 456 (B.C. C.A.); *R. v. B. (D.C.)* (1994), 91 C.C.C. (3d) 357 (Man. C.A.); *R. v. C. (G.)* (1997), 8 C.R. (5th) 61 (Ont. S.C.J.); *R. v. F. (J.E.)* (1993), 85 C.C.C. (3d) 457 (Ont. C.A.); and *R. v. B. (O.)* (1995), 103 C.C.C. (3d) 531 (N.S. C.A.). To determine whether the trial judge misused the evidence in this case, it is necessary to briefly consider the basis for admitting evidence of prior consistent statements.

32 As Hill J. explains in *R. v. C. (G.)* at para. 44, evidence of prior consistent statements by any witness is excluded as a general rule because the evidence is irrelevant and lacking in probative value. The evidence is "self-serving, self-corroborative and superfluous". Put simply, the fact that a witness has on prior occasions said the same thing does not generally make his or her testimony any more truthful or reliable. However, there are exceptions to the rule against admission of prior consistent statements because in some circumstances, the evidence of prior consistent statements may in fact be probative of some issue in the case. One example is to rebut an allegation of recent fabrication. See *R. v. Evans* (1993), 82 C.C.C. (3d) 338 (S.C.C.).

33 Another example is what the cases describe as narrative. The narrative exception is, in my view, essentially a convenient label for instances falling

outside the traditional exceptions where the fact that the witness has made prior statements about the incident has some probative value. Finlayson J.A. considered the issue in *R. v. F. (J.E.)* at p. 472 in the context of the evidence of children:

> It seems to me that the court should look to narrative as an exception to the rule against the admission of previous consistent statements for a more hopeful approach to this vexing problem of the evidence of children in sexual assault cases. It must be a part of the narrative in the sense that it advances the story from offence to prosecution or explains why so little was done to terminate the abuse or bring the perpetrator to justice. Specifically, it appears to me to be part of the narrative of a complainant's testimony when she recounts the assaults, how they came to be terminated, and how the matter came to the attention of the police. [Emphasis added.]

34 The admissibility of prior consistent statements as part of the narrative will depend on the circumstances of each case. In *R. v. F. (J.E.)*, Finlayson J.A. stressed at p. 474 that the evidence was admissible only if it was necessary, for example, "to provide chronological cohesion and eliminate gaps". It will not always be necessary to know why or how the case came to the attention of the police and it will not always be necessary to fill in every gap in the chronology to understand the story and properly assess the witness's credibility.

35 The cases make it clear, however, that when prior consistent statements are admitted, the contents of those statements are not admissible for their truth. This limitation on the use of the prior statements helps to balance the probative value and prejudicial effect of the evidence. The probative value lies in the fact that the statement was made. The contents of the statement itself do not add to the probative value because, as I have said, mere repetition of a story on a prior occasion does not generally make the in-court description of the events any more credible or reliable. This limit on the use of prior consistent statements has been applied with particular rigour in jury trials, where it has been held to be reversible error for a trial judge not to warn the jury on the limited use of narrative statements. See *R. v. F. (J.E.)* at p. 476, *R. v. B. (O.)* at p. 542, and *R. v. Ay* at p. 473.

New trials have often been ordered where there was no warning given as to the use of evidence of prior consistent statements.[268]

In her Criminal Reports annotations on *Stirling and Dinardo*, Professor Lisa Dufraimont suggests that the distinction between prior consistent statements to support the witness's credibility but not the truth of the contents is difficult to apply and problematic.[269] **Do you agree with this criticism?**

---

[268]   See *R. v. T. (P.)*, 2014 NLCA 6, 308 C.C.C. (3d) 395, 9 C.R. (7th) 136 (N.L. C.A.) and *R. v. Warren*, 2016 ONCA 104, 26 C.R. (7th) 390 (Ont. C.A.).

[269]   See also concerns and suggestions of David Paciocco, "The Perils and Potential of Prior Consistent Statements: Let's Get It Right" (2013) 17 Can. Crim. L. Rev. 182. In *R. v. Khan*, 2017 ONCA 114, 345 C.C.C. (3d) 419, 37 C.R. (7th) 157 (Ont. C.A.) Justice Doherty in a concurring opinion acknowledged that prior consistent statements have to this point been

Wood J.A., in *R. v. Ay*,[270] held that where prior consistent statements are admissible only the fact the statement was made is admissible, not the "specific contents". Similarly, MacPherson J.A., in *R. v. R. (A.E.)*,[271] held that "prior consistent statements should only be described in general terms and should not contain much detail". **Do these approaches make any sense?**

(iv) *Exculpatory Arrest Statement*

R. v. EDGAR
78 C.R. (6th) 106, 260 C.C.C. (3d) 1 (Ont. C.A.)

1 SHARPE J.A.:— The appellant was convicted in 1996 of second degree murder in the stabbing death of his girlfriend, Tracey Kelsh. In January 2000, this court allowed his appeal from that conviction and ordered a new trial: (2000), 142 C.C.C. (3d) 401. In October 2001, after a three-week jury trial, the appellant was acquitted of murder but convicted of manslaughter. The Crown initiated a dangerous offender proceeding and, after a lengthy hearing, the trial judge designated the appellant a dangerous offender and sentenced him to indeterminate custody.

2 The appellant appeals both the conviction and the dangerous offender designation. The central issue on the appeal from conviction is whether the trial judge erred by refusing to admit, in their entirety, out-of-court statements made by the appellant shortly after his arrest. . . .

Factual Overview

3 The appellant and the deceased were involved in a short-term romantic relationship. Both were heavy users of cocaine and alcohol. The deceased had a lengthy history of mental illness and a pattern of impulsive, violent behaviour.

4 On October 8, 1994, and into the next day, the appellant and the deceased were partying and consuming cocaine and alcohol. After a violent struggle in the bathroom of the appellant's apartment, the deceased suffered multiple stab wounds and other injuries. The most serious and fatal wound she sustained was a deep cut slitting her throat.

5 The appellant testified that the deceased came after him, wielding two kitchen knives. She backed him into the bathroom and shouted bizarre statements about bikers and levelled accusations against him. A violent struggle ensued in the bathroom. The appellant testified that it was pitch dark, he was terrified

---

governed by a traditional common law model of a general exclusionary rule subject to stipulated exceptions, but urged the adoption of a new principled approach centred on broader considerations of relevance and probative value (para. 59).

[270]   (1994), 93 C.C.C. (3d) 456 (B.C. C.A.).
[271]   (2001), 156 C.C.C. (3d) 335, 43 C.R. (5th) 340 (Ont. C.A.).

and he feared for his life. He attempted to take the knives from the deceased, managed to seize one and recalled stabbing her in the arm.

6 Neighbours living immediately above the appellant's apartment heard the appellant yelling "shut up" several times and heard a female voice moaning in pain. They called the police who arrived quickly. The appellant and the deceased were still in the bathroom when the policed arrived. The appellant resisted their entrance into the bathroom. The police heard the appellant say "I'm going to stab/kill you", "I'm going to stab her", "I'm going to cut/slit her throat". The police heard no female voice. They eventually managed to force their way into the bathroom before proceeding to subdue and handcuff the appellant.

7 Shortly after his arrest and later during the morning, the appellant made three statements to the police that are the subject of the main ground of appeal. The first two statements were made very shortly after the appellant's arrest. The third statement was made about four hours after his arrest. The first two statements were partially exculpatory, but largely aberrant and incoherent. The third statement was coherent and entirely exculpatory.

9 At the trial which is the subject of this appeal, the appellant urged the trial judge to admit all three of his post-arrest statements in their entirety. The trial judge refused to do so and admitted only the edited versions of the statements found to be admissible by this court on the appeal from the first trial.

. . .

24 For the following reasons, I conclude that the spontaneous exculpatory statements made by an accused person upon or shortly after arrest may be admitted as an exception to the general rule excluding prior consistent statements for the purpose of showing the reaction of the accused when first confronted with the accusation, provided the accused testifies and thereby exposes himself or herself to cross-examination.

(d) Rationale for the traditional exclusionary rule

25 An inculpatory statement of an accused person made outside of court is admissible against the accused as a confession (an admission against interest), provided that that it is compliant with the Canadian Charter of Rights and Freedoms and voluntary when made to a person in authority.

26 Conversely, exculpatory out-of-court statements made by an accused person are generally considered inadmissible, although this rule is subject to many exceptions.

. . .

(e) Exceptions to the traditional rule

35 It is well recognized, however, that the prior consistent statements of an accused are not always excluded. Two established exceptions have already been mentioned. First, where an accused's prior consistent statement is relevant to his or her state of mind at the time the offence was committed, it may be admitted. Second, where the Crown alleges recent fabrication, the accused may adduce evidence of a prior consistent statement to rebut the allegation. A third exception is made for "mixed" statements that are partly inculpatory and partly exculpatory. Where the Crown seeks to adduce evidence of such a statement, the inculpatory portion is admissible as an admission against interest and, as a matter of fairness to the accused, the Crown is required to tender the entire statement, with the exculpatory portion being substantively admissible in favour of the accused: Rojas, at para. 37. A fourth exception is that the prior statement will be admitted where it forms part of the res gestae, in other words, where the statement itself forms part of the incident that gives rise to the charge: see Graham; *R. v. Risby*, [1978] 2 S.C.R. 139.

36 This list of exceptions is not exhaustive. In Simpson, the Supreme Court of Canada stated, at p. 22, that general exclusion of the prior consistent statements of an accused person is "not an inflexible rule, and in proper circumstances such statements may be admissible".

. . .

59 Canadian text writers are divided on the point but most favour admissibility. David M. Paciocco and Lee Stuesser, The Law of Evidence, 5th ed. (Toronto: Irwin Law, 2008), at pp. 496-98, concede that the question is unsettled, point to the authorities favouring it, but suggest that "the denial of guilt on arrest has only a modicum or relevance" and that other steps could be taken to ensure that juries do not infer guilt when left in the dark about what an accused did or said when arrested.

60 However, the preponderance of opinion emanating from commentators favours admitting a prior consistent statement made by the accused at the time of arrest, especially where that individual takes the stand and is thus exposed to cross-examination. Alan W. Bryant, Sidney N. Lederman & Michelle K. Fuerst, Sopinka, Lederman & Bryant: The Law of Evidence in Canada, 3rd ed. (Markham: LexisNexis, 2009), note that while the case law is not consistent, the Supreme Court's decision in *Lucas* stands for the proposition that an accused can offer such evidence. On this point, the authors provide the following rationale (which, as I have noted at para. 53 of these reasons, was quoted with apparent approval by this court in Toten), at p. 409:

> "In essence, the prior exculpatory statement is tendered to rebut any inference of [the accused's] guilt arising from any silence on his part at the time of arrest. Although such an inference cannot be drawn as a matter of law by reason of the right to remain silent, it might be drawn in fact. The accused can adduce the exculpatory statement as a matter of good tactics.

61 S. Casey Hill et al., in McWilliams' Canadian Criminal Evidence, vol. 1, 4th ed., looseleaf (Aurora, Ont.: Canada Law Book, 2003), provides an extended discussion of the issue that I have drawn upon liberally in the preparation of these reasons. The authors conclude, at para. 11:40.40, that "a close review of the case law reveals that there is no categorical prohibition against such evidence provided that its probative value outweighs any prejudicial effect" and strongly support the explicit recognition of an exception for statements made upon arrest.

62 In The Commission on Proceedings Involving Guy Paul Morin: Report, vol. 2 (Toronto: Ontario Ministry of the Attorney General, 1998), at pp. 1151-57, the Honourable Fred Kaufman, a retired judge, criminal law expert and evidence author, reviews the law and concludes the following, at p. 1157:

> In my view, there are policy considerations that arguably support the exclusion of the accused's exculpatory statements tendered at the instance of the defence, where the accused does not testify. However, there are compelling policy considerations, outlined above, for a reconsideration of the rule in circumstances where the accused is prepared to testify.

63 In this regard, the Kaufman Report found the following factors persuasive:

> "Juries are likely to draw an adverse inference from the absence of evidence about what an accused said upon arrest;

> "An early exculpatory statement may be important to rebut the suggestion or potential inference that the accused tailored his or her evidence based upon pre-trial disclosure, or having heard the Crown's evidence in advance of testifying; and

> "Admitting such statements would encourage counsel to be more receptive to clients making statements upon arrest.

64 Kaufman notes that recorded evidence may paint a compelling picture and, at p. 1156, agrees with the contention that: "if the jury had heard [Guy Paul Morin's] repeated and emphatic protestations of innocence throughout a long and tiring interrogation, it may have made the difference between conviction and acquittal."

. . .

65 The English authorities make a persuasive case that such statements will very often have significant probative value. While probative value will depend upon the facts and circumstances of each case, I agree with the English authorities that an accused person's spontaneous reaction to an accusation may be of "vital relevance" and "one of the best pieces of evidence that an innocent man can produce is his reaction to an accusation of a crime".

66 If a statement has probative value, it should only be excluded if there are sound reasons of law or policy to do so. In my view, the various rationales offered for exclusion simply do not warrant the imposition of a blanket exclusionary rule.

67 The rule against oath-helping does no more than re-state the need for evidence to have probative value. If evidence fails to add anything new, repetition is less than helpful. However, where an accused makes a spontaneous statement in the face of an accusation or arrest for a crime, something is added. The reaction of the accused in such circumstances may yield persuasive evidence of innocence, which has quite a different quality than the accused's testimony given months or years later in the formal proceedings of the courtroom.

68 I find the cases cited above entirely persuasive on the point that the hearsay rationale for exclusion of a prior consistent statement evaporates where the accused takes the stand and exposes himself or herself to cross-examination.

69 I am also of the opinion that too much is easily made of the risk of fabrication. To assert blindly that all statements made by an accused person upon arrest are fatally tainted with self-interest and the motivation to lie assumes guilt and runs counter to the presumption of innocence: see James H. Chadbourn, Wigmore on Evidence, vol. 2, rev. ed. (Toronto: Little, Brown & Co., 1979), at s. 293, cited in S. Casey Hill et al., at paras. 11:40.40.30. As discussed below at para. 97 of these reasons, this assertion is also contrary to the discouragement of jury directions counselling caution with respect to the evidence of an accused because of self-interest and motivation to say what it takes to secure an acquittal. The risk of fabrication can be dealt with more directly and precisely through cross- examination and by looking to the degree of spontaneity the proffered statement exhibits. Statements that are lacking in spontaneity may be either excluded or, in the case of doubt, made the subject of an instruction to the jury as to weight by the trial judge.

70 Trial efficiency is an important factor generally but rarely, if ever, will it justify the exclusion of relevant, probative evidence that could lead the trier of fact to acquit.

71 In my view, it is time to abandon what David Tanovich has described as the "myth" that exculpatory statements made upon arrest are inadmissible except to the extent that they bear upon state of mind or rebut an allegation of recent fabrication: "In the Name of Innocence: Using Supreme Court of Canada Evidence Jurisprudence to Protect Against Wrongful Convictions" (Paper presented to the Ontario Criminal Lawyers' Association Criminal Law in a Changing World Conference, Toronto, 8 November 2003) [unpublished].

72 I conclude, therefore, that it is open to a trial judge to admit an accused's spontaneous out-of-court statements made upon arrest or when first confronted with an accusation as an exception to the general rule excluding prior consistent statements as evidence of the reaction of the accused to the accusation and as proof of consistency, provided the accused takes the stand and exposes himself or herself to cross-examination. As the English cases cited above hold, the statement of the accused is not strictly evidence of the truth of

what was said (subject to being admissible under the principled approach to hearsay evidence) but is evidence of the reaction of the accused, which is relevant to the credibility of the accused and as circumstantial evidence that may have a bearing on guilt or innocence.

In *R. v. Badhwar*,[272] the Court of Appeal held that the accused's statement did not fall within the *Edgar* exception because there was a lack of spontaneity and an opportunity to "think things out". The accused had been involved in a high-speed accident. Five hours after the accident and following a call from the police, the accused turned himself in and gave an exculpatory statement.

(v) *Recent Complaint*

Until the beginning of the nineteenth century complaints of rape were received in evidence with little discussion of the underlying principles, their reception apparently justified simply by a tradition that had its roots in the early procedural requirement of the "hue and cry". In the thirteenth century the hazards of trial were great and it was adjudged that not every complaint would be sufficient to put the antagonist to his proof. Complaint witnesses, suitors, were demanded who would vouch for the plaintiff's cause:[273]

> It is not enough that the plaintiff should tell his tale: he must offer to prove its truth . . . No one is entitled to an answer if he offers nothing but his bare assertion, his *nude parole*. The procedure in the Appeal of Felony is no real exception to this rule. The appellor alleges, and can be called upon to prove, fresh "suit" with hue and cry, so that the neighbourhood . . . is witness to his prompt action, to the wounds of a wounded man, to the torn garments of a ravished woman. It should not escape us that in this case, as in other cases, what the plaintiff relies on as support for his word is "suit." This suggests that the suitors . . . whom the plaintiff produces in a civil action have been, at least in theory, men who along with him have pursued the defendant.[274]

During the nineteenth century, we see the courts enunciating principles to explain the reception of this evidence which violated the then-crystallized rule against previous consistent statements, and the most common principle announced is akin to the principle underlying the first two exceptions above discussed: the circumstances of a case may cast doubt on the witness's present description of the incident. If a woman had been raped it was assumed that it would be a very natural thing for her to then speak out, and the failure so to do would act to contradict her present accusation. If nothing was said at trial about the fact of an earlier complaint, the trier might then assume there was none and so reject her present testimony. Accordingly, if there was a complaint, evidence of it could be led to counter this assumption;[275] this might be done in chief without the necessity of any

---

[272] (2011), 270 C.C.C. (3d) 129 (Ont. C.A.).
[273] See Thayer, *Preliminary Treatise on Evidence at the Common Law* (1898) at 10-16.
[274] Pollock & Maitland, *History of English Law*, 2nd ed. (1898), vol. 2 at 605-606.

allegation of recent invention in cross-examination. During the nineteenth century the prosecutor was confined to proving the fact of the complaint, but in 1896, in *R. v. Lillyman*,[276] it was decided that the details of the complaint were also receivable:

> In reality, affirmative answers to such stereotyped questions as these, "Did the prosecutrix make a complaint" (a very leading question, by the way) "of something done to herself?" "Did she mention a name?" amount to nothing to which any weight ought to be attached; they tend rather to embarrass than assist a thoughtful jury, for they are consistent either with there having been a complaint or no complaint of the prisoner's conduct. To limit the evidence of the complaint to such questions and answers is to ask the jury to draw important inferences from imperfect materials, perfect materials being at hand and in the cognizance of the witness in the box. In our opinion, nothing ought unnecessarily to be left to speculation or surmise.

Although the details may be received, the complaint was not receivable for the purpose of proving its truth but solely to counter the influence of the assumption that might otherwise flow from silence and so confirm, by the victim's conduct, her present testimony.[277]

Belying its origins, the exception during the nineteenth century was confined to complaints of rape by female complainants. In the twentieth century the courts have extended the exception to cover the prosecution of other sexual offences,[278] whether the complainant was male or female.

In *Kribs v. R.*[279] Fauteux J. explained:

> The principle is one of necessity. It is founded on factual presumptions which, in the normal course of events, naturally attach to the subsequent conduct of the prosecutrix shortly after the occurrence of the alleged acts of violence. One of these presumptions is that she is expected to complain upon the first reasonable opportunity, and the other, consequential thereto, is that if she fails to do so, her silence may naturally be taken as a virtual self-contradiction of her story.
>
> . . .
>
> . . . by giving evidence of her conduct shortly after the alleged occurrence, the prosecutrix does not, in a sense, enhance or confirm her story any more than she does in reciting all that she did in resistance to the assault, but she rebuts a presumption and, in doing so, adds, for all practical purposes, a virtually essential complement to her story.

---

[275] See generally 4 Wigmore, *Evidence* (Chad. Rev.), s. 1134-1139, discussing this principle and others.

[276] [1896] 2 Q.B. 167 (C.C.R.) at 177-178. Accord, *R. v. Thomas*, [1952] 2 S.C.R. 344 (S.C.C.).

[277] See Hawkins, J. in *Lillyman, ibid.* at 170. See the difficulty experienced by Fauteux J. in *Kribs v. R.*, [1960] S.C.R. 400, seeking to distinguish these two uses. See also in *R. v. Thomas*, [1952] 2 S.C.R. 344, the Court allowing the statement to be used to show consistency but denying its use as corroboration. If the complainant doesn't testify the complaint is naturally inadmissible: see *R. v. Cook* (1979), 9 C.R. (3d) 85 (Ont. C.A.) and *R. v. Brasier* (1779), 168 E.R. 202 (Crown Cases).

[278] See the history of this development canvassed in *R. v. Lebrun* (1951), 100 C.C.C. 1 (Ont. C.A.). And see *R. v. Christenson*, [1923] 2 D.L.R. 379 (Alta. C.A.) per Beck J. suggesting the exception should operate in all crimes of violence, sexual or non-sexual.

[279] [1960] S.C.R. 400 (S.C.C.) at 405-406. And see *R. v. Boyce* (1975), 23 C.C.C. (2d) 16 (Ont. C.A.) at 33.

The courts held that if there was an absence of complaint at the first reasonable opportunity, the trial judge should charge the jury regarding the adverse inference they may draw against the complainant's credibility.[280]

In 1983 the *Criminal Code* was amended[281] to provide:

> 275. The rules relating to evidence of recent complaint in sexual assault cases are hereby abrogated.

To describe the provision as ambiguous is understatement. **Does it mean that evidence of recent complaint cannot be given?**[282]

R. v. O'CONNOR
(1995), 100 C.C.C. (3d) 285 (Ont. C.A.)

The accused was charged with touching for a sexual purpose a young girl who was a member of a church group of which he was the leader. The accused was tried by a judge sitting without a jury. The defence was that the allegations of sexual activity were fabricated. The Crown asked the complainant during examination-in-chief if she had told anyone of her relationship with the accused and received the answer that she had told a camp counsellor and her best friend. Defence counsel objected and stated that no allegation of recent fabrication had been made. The trial judge gave effect to that objection. In cross-examination, defence counsel asked the complainant whether she had told certain persons within a specified time frame about the sexual acts. The complainant replied that she had not. The trial judge later allowed the camp counsellor to testify as to a complaint to her within three days of the time frame relied on by the defence to support an adverse inference, and the complainant's stepmother and older sister were permitted to testify that the complainant had told them about the sexual relationship and that they agreed that the stepmother would inform the police.

The accused was convicted and appealed.

FINLAYSON J.A.:—

. . .

The position of the defence that emerges from the record at trial and the argument on appeal is that the testimony of the complainant, to the extent that it recounted sexual abuse, had been made up out of whole cloth. The fabrication was said to be in no sense recent, but defence counsel did not designate its origin as being at any specific time. Put simply, the position is that since the defence had never alleged *recent* fabrication (as opposed to fabrication *ab initio*), the Crown was not entitled to lead any evidence under the rubric of recent fabrication, because no such allegation had been made. Therefore (the submission went) while it was permissible for the defence to demand of the complainant why she had not complained of these assaults to

---

[280]   See *Boyce, ibid.* at 33.
[281]   S.C. 1980-81-82-83, c. 125, s. 19. See now R.S.C. 1985, c. C-46, s. 275.
[282]   See Elaine Craig, "The Relevance of Delayed Disclosure to Complainant Credibility in Cases of Sexual Offence" (2011) 36 Queen's L.J. 551.

her sister Kelly on a particular day, the Crown was not entitled to bring out in reply, or at all, that she had complained three days later to her camp counsellor and still later to her sister and her stepmother.

In my opinion, this is being too clever by half. "Recent" fabrication is by definition a subset of fabrication generally. One may escape this implication by asserting a challenge to the complainant's credibility based on an allegation of fabrication *simpliciter*, but not when it is coupled with a charge that she had not divulged the fact of the sexual conduct to a person to whom the trier of fact would expect her to complain, *i.e.*, an absence of recent complaint. The law does not require that an allegation of recent fabrication be made explicitly: the court can look at all the circumstances of the case. . .

In this case the whole thrust of the cross-examination relating to Jenny Lamb and the sister Kelly was structured so as to establish the lack of an early complaint to someone whom the trial judge would expect a complaint to be made under the circumstances. The questions as to why no complaints were made were restricted as to person and to time but with the object of leaving the impression that there were no complaints whatsoever. As such, the questioning was designed to give rise to an inference that the complaint was formulated subsequent to the event recounted in her testimony at trial. It clearly implied what is, by any other name, an allegation of recent fabrication.

I am of the view that an allegation of recent fabrication is no more than an allegation that the complainant has made up a false story to meet the exigencies of the case. The word "recent" means that the complainant's evidence has been invented or fabricated after the events in question and thus is a "recent" invention or fabrication. . .

. . .

I conclude that the rulings of the trial judge were correct and his use of the statements elicited were in accordance with the principle that he could only rely on the facts of the complaints, not the truth of their contents, in assessing the credibility of the complaint.

. . .

GOODMAN J.A.:—

. . . In my opinion, the evidence of the complaints made by the complainant to her sister Kelly, Cynthia Collins and Tanya Kronschnabl, in the circumstances of this case, was not admissible on the basis of the exception to the rule against prior consistent statements resulting from an allegation of recent fabrication but rather on the basis hereinafter set forth.

Prior to the 1983 amendment to the *Criminal Code* . . . , purporting to abrogate the rules relating to evidence of recent complaint . . . , the prosecution was permitted to elicit from the complainant evidence of a complaint of a sexual assault, made at the first reasonable opportunity, to support the credibility of the victim. After the 1983 amendment, the prosecution was no longer permitted to do so.

In my opinion, however, the amendment does not prevent defence counsel from cross-examining a complainant about the lack of recent complaint, but in doing so the door is opened to permit the Crown to adduce evidence of a prior complaint in order to rebut any adverse inference which might be drawn by the fact-finder from the silence alleged by the defence and to rebut the attack on the credibility of the complainant based on the lack of recent complaint.

In Sopinka, Lederman and Bryant, *The Law of Evidence in Canada*, 1992, it is stated at p. 317:

> It appears that the effect of the statutory amendment is that recent complaint evidence may not be led in anticipation of the adverse inference drawn from silence. However, defence counsel are not precluded from cross-examining a complainant about the lack of a prior complaint. If they do, they take the risk that the Crown may adduce a prior complaint to rebut the allegation.

And further at p. 318:

> . . . the ability of the defence to question a complainant on the absence or untimeliness of a complaint has had nothing to do in the past with the doctrine of recent complaint. One of the most common means of suggesting that a witness's testimony is fabricated is to allege failure to speak when it would have been expected, and this has always been recognized.

In the case at bar, defence counsel cross-examined the complainant in a manner which might leave the impression that she had never made a prior complaint or at the very least had not made a timely complaint to a person or persons to whom it was reasonable to expect that she would have complained. In that circumstance it was, in my opinion, permissible for the Crown to re-examine the complainant with respect to the reasons for the lack of complaint to the persons referred to by defence counsel in his cross-examination and to adduce evidence with respect to the prior complaints which had allegedly been made by the complainant prior to the complaint to the police.

. . .

WEILER, J.A.:— I am in agreement with Finlayson J.A. that the effect of the cross-examination which was conducted by counsel for the defence gave rise to the inference that the complainant had fabricated her evidence after the events in question and, in addition, suggested that there was an absence of any complaint concerning the alleged assault prior to the complaint being made to the police. In these circumstances, I agree with him that it was appropriate for the trial judge to hear evidence of the complainant's meeting with her sister Kelly and the social worker, Cynthia Collins, as well as her complaint to Tanya Kronschnabl. I also agree with Goodman J.A. that the impression resulting from the cross-examination, that there was no complaint made of any sexual assault prior to the complaint to the police, would have made the complainant's evidence of her complaint to Kelly, Cynthia Collins, and Tanya Kronschnabl admissible, quite apart from any suggestion of recent fabrication.

5. DEMEANOUR AS GUIDE TO CREDIBILITY

Lord Devlin, recognized by all as a great trial judge, wrote:

The great virtue of the English trial is said to be the opportunity it gives to the judge to tell from the demeanour of the witness whether or not he is telling the truth. I think that this is overrated. I would adopt in their entirety the words of Mr. Justice MacKenna:

> I question whether the respect given to our findings of fact based on the demeanour of the witness is always deserved. I doubt my own ability and sometimes that of other judges, to discern from a witness's demeanour, or the tone of voice whether he is telling the truth. He speaks hesitantly. Is that the mark of a cautious man, whose statements are for that reason to be respected or is he taking time to fabricate? Is the emphatic witness putting on an act to deceive me, or is he speaking from the fullness of his heart, knowing that he is right? Is he likely to be more truthful if he looks me straight in the face than if he casts his eyes on the ground perhaps from shyness or a natural timidity? For my part I rely on these considerations as little as I can help.[283]

Empirical studies conducted by psychologists confirm Lord Devlin's point.[284] They usually stress that bodily movements and the sound of the voice are better indicators than facial demeanour, but then only if the observer is acquainted with the normal mannerisms of the witness. Professor Ekman's empirical studies indicated that U.S. Secret Service agents scored very well in accurately picking out liars, but judges, trial lawyers, police, forensic psychiatrists and the FBI achieved at a level no better than chance![285]

And yet, the frailty of using demeanour as indicative of credibility, as accepted by Lord Devlin and seemingly established by the psychologists, is certainly at odds with *dicta* from most trial judges who in their reasons frequently use the same as indicating their acceptance or rejection of the testimony of witnesses. It is also at odds with the deference often paid by appellate courts who frequently say that although they have a transcript of what was said at trial they are disadvantaged in their assessment of the worth of testimonial evidence because they were not present when the testimony was given.

---

[283] Lord Devlin, *The Judge* (1979) at 63.
[284] See e.g. Ekman & Fresein, "Detecting Deception from the Body or Face" (1974) 29 J. of Personality & Social Psychology 288; Ekman, *Telling Lies: Clues to Deceit in the Marketplace, Politics and Marriage*, Norton, (U.S. 1991), esp. at 287-292; Blumenthal, "A Wipe of the Hands, A Lick of the Lips: The Validity of Demeanour Evidence in Assessing Witness Credibility" (1993) 172 Nebraska L. Rev. 1157; Stone, "Instant Lie Detection? Demeanour and Credibility in Criminal Trials" (1991), Crim. L. Rev. 821; and Loretta Re, "Oral v. Written Evidence: The Myth of the Impressive Witness" (1983) Aus. L.J. 679.
[285] Hunter & Cronin, *Evidence, Advocacy and Ethical Practice* (Butterworths, 1995) at 329.

R. v. NORMAN
(1993), 26 C.R. (4th) 256, 87 C.C.C. (3d) 153 (Ont. C.A.)

The accused was charged with raping the complainant, then 13 years old, in 1973. The complainant alleged that she had forgotten the rape, and remembered it in fragments in the course of therapy sessions. The accused testified and denied any sexual contact with the complainant. The trial judge found that the complainant was a credible witness and the accused was convicted.

The judgment of the court was delivered by FINLAYSON J.A.:—

. . .

The trial judge in this case seems to have determined credibility solely on the basis of the demeanour of the complainant and Mrs. Goebel. He said that he was impressed with the manner in which the complainant testified: she was straightforward and stood up well in cross-examination, and it appeared to him that she was not being vindictive. As for Mrs. Goebel, he said that she testified in an assured and straightforward manner and impressed him as a credible witness.

In *White v. R.*, [1947] S.C.R. 268 at p. 272, the senior Mr. Justice Estey discussed the issue of credibility. He said it is one of fact and cannot be determined by following a set of rules. He stated in part:

> It is a matter in which so many human characteristics, both the strong and the weak, must be taken into consideration. The general integrity and intelligence of the witness, his powers to observe, his capacity to remember and his accuracy in statement are important. It is also important to determine whether he is honestly endeavouring to tell the truth, whether he is sincere and frank or whether he is biased, reticent and evasive. All these questions and others may be answered from the observation of the witness' general conduct and demeanour in determining the question of credibility.

I do not think that an assessment of credibility based on demeanour alone is good enough in a case where there are so many significant inconsistencies. The issue is not merely whether the complainant sincerely believes her evidence to be true; it is also whether this evidence is reliable. Accordingly, her demeanour and credibility are not the only issues. The reliability of the evidence is what is paramount. So far as Mrs. Goebel is concerned, her evidence is inherently hard to credit, and should have been subjected to closer analysis. For the purposes of this case, I adopt what was said by O'Halloran J.A., speaking for the British Columbia Court of Appeal in *Faryna v. Chorny* (1951), 4 W.W.R. (N.S.) 171 at p. 174:

> The credibility of interested witnesses, particularly in cases of conflict of evidence, cannot be gauged solely by the test of whether the personal demeanour of the particular witness carried conviction of the truth. The test must reasonably subject his story to an examination of its consistency with the probabilities that surround the currently existing conditions. In short, the real test of the truth of the story of a witness in such a case must be its harmony with the preponderance of the probabilities which a practical and informed person would readily recognize as reasonable in that place and in those conditions.

O'Halloran J.A. pointed out later at page 175 that "[t]he law does not clothe the trial judge with a divine insight into the hearts and minds of the witnesses".

In *R. v. S. (W.)*[286] Justice Finlayson repeated the thought and explained:

I am not satisfied that a positive finding of credibility on the part of the complainant is sufficient to support a conviction in a case of this nature where there is significant evidence which contradicts the complainant's allegations. We all know from our personal experiences as trial lawyers and judges that honest witnesses, whether they are adults or children, may convince themselves that inaccurate versions of a given event are correct and they can be very persuasive. The issue, however, is not the sincerity of the witness but the reliability of the witness' testimony. Demeanour alone should not suffice to found a conviction where there are significant inconsistencies and conflicting evidence on the record.[287]

Moreover as Justice Saunders recognized in *R. v. P. (S.H.)*:[288]

Reasons of intelligence, upbringing, education, race, culture, social status and a host of other factors may adversely affect a witness's demeanour and yet may have little bearing on that person's truthfulness.[289]

The clear recent trend is to order new trials where there has been too much reliance on the demeanour of the witness in assessing credibility.[290]

R. v. S. (N.)
2012 SCC 72, [2012] 3 S.C.R. 726, 290 C.C.C. (3d) 404, 98 C.R. (6th) 1 (S.C.C.)

The Supreme Court of Canada considered the significance of demeanour in connection with the question of whether a witness may testify wearing a religious face veil. N.S. was the complainant in a sexual assault case, and she was called by the Crown as a witness at the preliminary inquiry. She expressed a desire to testify while wearing a niqab, a veil that covers her whole face except her eyes. The preliminary inquiry judge held a *voir dire*, in which N.S. testified while wearing her niqab. N.S. testified that her religious beliefs as a Muslim required her to wear the niqab in public where men other than certain close family members might see her. She admitted that she had removed her niqab so a female photographer could take the photo on her driver's license and that she would also remove it, if

---

[286] (1994), 29 C.R. (4th) 143 (Ont. C. A.).
[287] *Ibid.* at 149-150.
[288] (2003), 176 C.C.C. (3d) 281 (N.S. C.A.).
[289] See also S.L. Johnson, "The Colour of Truth: Race and the Assessment of Credibility" (1996) 1 Mich. J. of Race & Law 261 and D. Opekokew, "A Review of Ethnocentric Bias Facing Indian Witnesses" in R. Goose et al., eds., *Continuing Poundmaker and Riel's Quest* (Purich Publishing: Saskatoon, 1994).
[290] *R. v. Rhayel*, 2015 ONCA 377, 324 C.C.C. (3d) 362, 22 C.R. (7th) 78 (Ont. C.A.); *R. v. Giroux*, 2017 ABCA 270, 355 C.C.C. (3d) 275, 40 C.R. (7th) 198 (Alta. C.A.); *R. v. F. (J.)* (2003), 177 C.C.C. (3d) 1 (Ont. C.A.); *R. v. DeHaan* (2002), 155 O.A.C. 358 (Ont. C.A.); *R. v. Owen*, [2001] O.J. No. 4257 (Ont. C.A.); *R. v. A. (R.H.)* (2000), 34 O.A.C. 186 (Ont. C.A.); *R. v. Gostick* (1999), 137 C.C.C. (3d) 53 (Ont. C.A.); and *R. v. G. (G.)* (1997), 115 C.C.C. (3d) 1 (Ont. C.A.).

required, for a security check at a border crossing. The judge concluded that N.S.'s religious belief was not that strong and ordered her to remove her niqab, but N.S. objected and the preliminary inquiry was adjourned. The case went to the Supreme Court on the question of whether N.S. could be permitted to testify wearing her niqab.

The Supreme Court remitted the matter to the preliminary inquiry judge for decision. In its reasons, the Court split three ways, with the majority holding that whether a witness may testify while wearing a niqab must be decided in the particular circumstances of each case. Two *Charter* rights are engaged: the witness' right to religious freedom and the fair trial rights of the accused. Writing for the majority, McLachlin C.J. (Deschamps, Fish and Cromwell JJ., concurring) held that these rights should be accommodated where possible and subjected to a contextual balancing test when they conflict. The Chief Justice explained:

[16] M—d S. argues that allowing N.S. to testify with her face covered by a niqab denies his fair trial rights in two ways: first, by preventing effective cross-examination; and second, by interfering with the ability of the trier of fact (judge or jury) to assess N.S.'s credibility.

[17] We have no expert evidence in this case on the importance of seeing a witness's face to effective cross-examination and accurate assessment of a witness's credibility. All we have are arguments and several legal and social science articles submitted by the parties as authorities.

[18] M—d S. and the Crown argue that the link is clear. Communication involves not only words, but facial cues. A facial gesture may reveal uncertainty or deception. The cross-examiner may pick up on non-verbal cues and use them to uncover the truth. Credibility assessment is equally dependent not only on what a witness says, but on how she says it. Effective cross-examination and accurate credibility assessment are central to a fair trial. It follows, they argue, that permitting a witness to wear a niqab while testifying may deny an accused's fair trial rights.

[19] N.S. and supporting interveners, on the other hand, argue that the importance of seeing a witness's face has been greatly exaggerated. They submit that untrained individuals cannot use facial expressions to detect deception. Moreover, to the extent that non-verbal cues are useful at all, a niqab-wearing witness's eyes, tone of voice and cadence of speech remain available to the cross-examiner and trier of fact.

[20] The record sheds little light on the question of whether seeing a witness's face is important to effective cross-examination and credibility assessment and hence to trial fairness. The only evidence in the record is a four-page unpublished review article suggesting that untrained individuals cannot accurately detect lies based on the speaker's facial cues. This material was not tendered through an expert available for cross-examination. Interveners have submitted articles arguing for and against a connection, but they are not

part of the record and not supported by expert witnesses, and so are more rhetorical than factual.

[21] This much, however, can be said. The common law, supported by provisions of the *Criminal Code*, R.S.C. 1985, c. C-46, and judicial pronouncements, proceeds on the basis that the ability to see a witness's face is an important feature of a fair trial. While not conclusive, in the absence of negating evidence this common law assumption cannot be disregarded lightly.

[22] As a general rule, witnesses in common law criminal courts are required to testify in open court, with their faces visible to counsel, the judge and the jury. Face-to-face confrontation is the norm, although not an independent constitutional right: *R. v. Levogiannis* (1990), 1 O.R. (3d) 351 (C.A.), at pp. 366-67, aff'd [1993] 4 S.C.R. 475. To be sure, long-standing assumptions of the common law can be displaced, if shown to be erroneous or based on groundless prejudice — thus the reforms to eliminate the many myths that once skewed the law of sexual assault. But the record before us has not shown the long-standing assumptions of the common law regarding the importance of a witness's facial expressions to cross-examination and credibility assessment to be unfounded or erroneous.

. . .

[27] On the record before us, I conclude that there is a strong connection between the ability to see the face of a witness and a fair trial. Being able to see the face of a witness is not the only — or indeed perhaps the most important — factor in cross-examination or accurate credibility assessment. But its importance is too deeply rooted in our criminal justice system to be set aside absent compelling evidence.

. . .

[33] When the matter returns to the preliminary inquiry judge, the parties should be able to place before the court evidence relating to possible options for accommodation of the potentially conflicting claims. This is the first step in the reconciliation process. The question is whether there is a reasonably available alternative that would conform to the witness's religious convictions while still preventing a serious risk to trial fairness. On the facts of this case, it may be that no accommodation is possible; excluding men from the courtroom would have implications for the open court principle, the right of the accused to be present at his trial, and potentially his right to counsel of his choice. Testifying without the niqab via closed-circuit television or behind a one-way screen may not satisfy N.S.'s religious obligations. However, when this case is reheard, the preliminary inquiry judge must consider the possibility of accommodation based on the evidence presented by the parties.

[34] If there is no reasonably available alternative that would avoid a serious risk to trial fairness while conforming to the witness's religious belief,. . .the next. . .question is whether the salutary effects of requiring the witness to

remove the niqab, including the effects on trial fairness, outweigh the deleterious effects of doing so, including the effects on freedom of religion

. . .

[36] In terms of the deleterious effects of requiring the witness to remove her niqab while testifying, the judge must look at the harm that would be done by limiting the sincerely held religious practice. . .

[37] The judge should also consider the broader societal harms of requiring a witness to remove the niqab in order to testify. N.S. and supporting interveners argue that if niqab-wearing women are required to remove the niqab while testifying against their sincere religious belief they will be reluctant to report offences and pursue their prosecution, or to otherwise participate in the justice system. The wrongs done to them will remain unredressed. They will effectively be denied justice. The perpetrators of crimes against them will go unpunished, immune from legal consequences. These considerations may be especially weighty in a sexual assault case such as this one. In recent decades the justice system, recognizing the seriousness of sexual assault and the extent to which it is under-reported, has vigorously pursued those who commit this crime. Laws have been changed to encourage women and children to come forward to testify. Myths that once stood in the way of conviction have been set aside.

[38] Having considered the deleterious effects of requiring the witness to remove the niqab, the judge must also consider the salutary effects of doing so. These include preventing harm to the fair trial interest of the accused and safeguarding the repute of the administration of justice. An important consideration will be the extent to which effective cross-examination and credibility assessment on this witness's testimony is central to the case. On an individual level, the cost of an unfair trial is severe. The right to a fair trial is a fundamental pillar without which the edifice of the rule of law would crumble. No less is at stake than an individual's liberty — his right to live in freedom unless the state proves beyond a reasonable doubt that he committed a crime meriting imprisonment. This is of critical importance not only to the individual on trial, but to public confidence in the justice system.

. . .

[44] These are but some of the factors that may be relevant to determining whether the party seeking removal of the niqab has established that the salutary effects of doing so outweigh the deleterious effects. Future cases will doubtless raise other factors, and scientific exploration of the importance of seeing a witness's face to cross-examination and credibility assessment may enhance or diminish the force of the arguments made in this case. At this point, however, it may be ventured that where the liberty of the accused is at stake, the witness's evidence is central to the case and her credibility vital, the possibility of a wrongful conviction must weigh heavily in the balance, favouring removal of the niqab.

In a concurring judgment, LeBel J. (Rothstein J. concurring) concluded that a witness in Canadian courts should not be allowed to wear a niqab. Justice LeBel reasoned:

[67] . . .[T]he Canadian criminal trial process remains faithful in its core aspects to an adversarial model. This process developed in the common law. Some of its features are now part of the constitutional order. . . [T]he criminal process itself is also designed to ensure that the accused is given a fair trial, to safeguard the constitutional presumption of innocence and, hopefully, to avert wrongful convictions. The adversarial model is based on interaction between the prosecution, the plaintiff, counsel for the parties, witnesses and, finally, the judge and, where applicable, the jurors. This model of justice imposes a significant personal burden on witnesses and parties. This burden cannot be lifted entirely. The price might very well be reading the most basic rights of the accused out of the criminal law and of the Charter.

. . .

[78] A clear rule that niqabs may not be worn would be consistent with the principle of openness of the trial process and would safeguard the integrity of that process as one of communication. It would also be consistent with the tradition that justice is public and open to all in our democratic society. This rule should apply at all stages of the criminal trial, at the preliminary inquiry as well as at the trial itself. . .

In sole dissent, Abella J. concluded that N.S. should be allowed to testify wearing her niqab. Justice Abella took the view that, with very limited exceptions, as where the identity of the witness is in issue, a witness who wears a niqab should not be required to remove it in order to testify in court. She explained:

[82] I concede without reservation that seeing more of a witness' facial expressions is better than seeing less. What I am not willing to concede, however, is that seeing less is so impairing of a judge's or an accused's ability to assess the credibility of a witness, that the complainant will have to choose between her religious rights and her ability to bear witness against an alleged aggressor. . .The court system has many examples of accepting evidence from witnesses who are unable to testify under ideal circumstances because of visual, oral, or aural impediments. I am unable to see why witnesses who wear niqabs should be treated any differently.

. . .

[93] A number of interests are engaged when a witness is not permitted to wear her niqab while testifying. First, she is prevented from being able to act in accordance with her religious beliefs. As noted by Martha C. Nussbaum, religious requirements are experienced as "obligatory and nonoptional", that is, as not providing a genuine choice to the religious believer. . .:

[94] This has the effect of forcing a witness to choose between her religious beliefs and her ability to participate in the justice system: Natasha Bakht,

"Objection, Your Honour! Accommodating Niqab-Wearing Women in Courtrooms", in Ralph Grillo et al., eds., Legal Practice and Cultural Diversity (2009), 115, at p. 128. As a result, as the majority notes, complainants who sincerely believe that their religion requires them to wear the niqab in public, may choose not to bring charges for crimes they allege have been committed against them, or, more generally, may resist being a witness in someone else's trial. It is worth pointing out as well that where the witness is the accused, she will be unable to give evidence in her own defence. To those affected, this is like hanging a sign over the courtroom door saying "Religious minorities not welcome".

. . .

[97] This brings us to the extent to which N.S., by exercising her freedom of religion in wearing a niqab, harms the accused's fair trial rights. The right to a fair trial is crucial to the presumption of innocence and maintaining confidence in the criminal justice system. While I agree that witnesses generally and ideally testify with their faces uncovered in open court, abridgements of this "ideal" often occur in practice yet are almost always tolerated.

[98] "Demeanour" has been broadly described as "every visible or audible form of self-expression manifested by a witness whether fixed or variable, voluntary or involuntary, simple or complex": Barry R. Morrison, Laura L. Porter and Ian H. Fraser, "The Role of Demeanour in Assessing the Credibility of Witnesses" (2007), 33 *Advocates' Q.* 170, at p. 179. Trial judges often rely on many indicators *other than* facial cues in finding a witness credible, including

> certitude in speaking, dignity while on the stand, exhibition of disability, exhibition of anger, exhibition of frustration, articulate speaking, thoughtful presentation, enthusiastic language, direct non-evasive answering, non-glib answering, exhibition of modesty, exhibition of flexibility, normal (as in as expected) body movement, cheerful attitude, kind manner, normal exhalation, normal inhalation. . . .

(Morrison, at p. 189)

[99] Moreover, while the ability to assess a witness' demeanour is an important component of trial fairness, many courts have noted its limitations for drawing accurate inferences about credibility. . .

. . .

[101] The Canadian Judicial Council's model jury instructions also acknowledge the inherent limitations in relying on demeanour:

> What was the witness's manner when he or she testified? Do not jump to conclusions, however, based entirely on the witness's manner. Looks can be deceiving. Giving evidence in a trial is not a common experience for many witnesses. People react and appear differently. Witnesses come from different backgrounds. They have different intellects, abilities, values, and life experiences. There are simply too many variables to make the manner in which a witness testifies the only or the most important factor in your decision.

(Model Jury Instructions, Part I, Preliminary Instructions, 4.11 Assessing Testimony (online))

[102] And courts regularly accept the testimony of witnesses whose demeanour can only be partially observed. . . .

[103] A witness may also have physical or medical limitations that affect a judge's or lawyer's ability to assess demeanour. A stroke may interfere with facial expressions; an illness may affect body movements; and a speech impairment may affect the manner of speaking. All of these are departures from the demeanour ideal, yet none has ever been held to disqualify the witness from giving his or her evidence on the grounds that the accused's fair trial rights are thereby impaired.

[104] There are other situations where we accept a witness' evidence without being able to assess demeanour at all. The *Criminal Code*, R.S.C. 1985, c. C-46, permits a judge to order and admit a transcript of evidence by a witness who is unable to attend the trial because of a disability, even when the accused's counsel is not present for the taking of the evidence: ss. 709 and 713 . Courts also allow witnesses, including material witnesses, to give evidence and be cross-examined by telephone: *Criminal Code*, s. 714.3; see also *R. v. Chapdelaine*, 2004 ABQB 39 (CanLII); *R. v. Butt* (2008), 280 Nfld. & P.E.I.R. 129 (N.L. Prov. Ct.).

[105] Exceptions to hearsay evidence are another example where the trier of fact is completely unable to assess the demeanour of the person whose statement is being admitted as evidence. . . .

[106] Wearing a niqab presents only a partial obstacle to the assessment of demeanour. A witness wearing a niqab may still express herself through her eyes, body language, and gestures. Moreover, the niqab has no effect on the witness' verbal testimony, including the tone and inflection of her voice, the cadence of her speech, or, most significantly, the substance of the answers she gives. Unlike out-of-court statements, defence counsel still has the opportunity to rigorously cross-examine N.S. on the witness stand.

. . .

[109] In my view, therefore, the harmful effects of requiring a witness to remove her niqab, with the result that she will likely not testify, bring charges in the first place, or, if she is the accused, be unable to testify in her own defence, is a significantly more harmful consequence than not being able to see a witness' whole face.

With whom do you agree?[291]

---

[291]   See Amna M. Qureshi, "Relying on Deneanour Evidence to Assess Credibility during Trial: A Critical Examination" (2014) 61 Crim. L.Q. 236 and Ranjan K. Agarwal & Carlo Di Carlo, "The Re-emergence of a Clash of Rights: A Critical Analysis of the Supreme Court of Canada's

R. v. SANTHOSH
2016 ONCA 731, 342 C.C.C. (3d) 41, 32 C.R. (7th) 197 (Ont. C.A.); C.R.
comment by Lisa Dufraimont

The accused, a physiotherapy assistant, was charged with sexually assaulting a female patient by touching her breast during a treatment. The accused testified and denied any sexual contact with the complainant, but claimed that, on the day in question and on previous occasions, the complainant made suggestive remarks and acted in a sexually provocative manner toward him. In convicting the accused, the trial judge gave several reasons for finding the complainant's allegation credible. These included that the complainant (who repeatedly invoked God as her witness) presented as a God-fearing person, and that her manner of dress was not provocative. The Ontario Court of Appeal held that these factors had no legitimate bearing on the assessment of the complainant's credibility.

JURIANSZ J.A. (CRONK and WATT JJ.A. concurring):

16 The manner of a witness' appearance in court is irrelevant to assessing the witness' creditworthiness. This court has held that how a witness dresses in court is no indicator of his or her credibility: R. v. Minuskin (2003), 68 O.R. (3d) 577, at para. 31. The conservative nature of a witness' in-court apparel, like flamboyant or provocative in-court dress by a witness, offers no assurance of the veracity of the witness' testimony. Both are immaterial to the creditworthiness of the witness' testimony.

17 There is no principled basis on which to conclude that a complainant in a sexual assault case who is modestly or "demurely" dressed in court is more likely to tell the truth than a complainant who is provocatively dressed. To conclude otherwise runs the risk of engaging in prohibited stereotypical reasoning. See, by analogy, R. v. Ewanchuk, [1999] 1 S.C.R. 330, at paras. 82, 88-89, per L'Heureux-Dubé J., concurring. A complainant's manner of dress in a sexual assault case simply has no probative value in assessing the truthfulness and reliability of his or her testimony.

. . .

40 . . . [Similarly,] evidence of a witness's religious beliefs is not admissible for the purposes of enhancing or impeaching his or her credibility, nor can it be relied upon for those purposes. I reach this conclusion for three reasons.

41 First, evidence of a witness' religious beliefs is simply not useful in assessing credibility . . . .

. . .

Decision in R. v. S. (N.)" (2013) 53 Supreme Court L. Rev. 143. In the Fall of 2011 the case was heard again by the preliminary inquiry judge who applied the approach of the majority of the Supreme Court. It was held that the complainant had a sincere religious belief but since no accommodation was possible she was ordered to remove her niqab. See R. v. S. (M.), 2013 ONCJ 209, 3 C.R. (7th) 214 (Ont. C.J.) and C.R. annotation by Lisa Dufraimont.

43 . . . [T]he bare fact of membership in a particular faith group does nothing to establish such a tendency or disposition. Rosenberg J.A. said in Minuskin, at paras. 30-31, that a witness's attendance at a religious school and wearing of a yarmulke in court were "no indicia of his credibility". To hold otherwise would require the court to accept the spurious premise that members of religions are more likely than non-members to act morally or honestly.

44 Evidence that merely establishes a witness holds religious beliefs does not establish a "tendency or disposition" to tell the truth or to lie. Courts, generally, seem to recognize this. This court was not referred to any previous authority in which a judge used evidence of a witness' religious beliefs, in and of themselves, as a basis for determining that he or she was more or less likely to tell the truth. There are people of all religious beliefs — and of no religious beliefs — who lie, just as there are those who are truthful.

. . .

46 Second, and relatedly, the risk of prejudice associated with using evidence of a witness' religious beliefs for credibility purposes is extremely high, far outstripping any possible probative value. There is a risk of both moral and reasoning prejudice, concepts described by Binnie J. in *R. v. Handy*, 2002 SCC 56, 164 C.C.C. (3d) 481, at paras. 139-147; see also *R. v. Pollock* (2004), 187 C.C.C. (3d) 213 (Ont. C.A.), at paras. 99-111.

47 Evidence of a witness' religious beliefs may distract the trier of fact from the core issues and lead them to draw improper inferences based on prejudice or stereotyping. This is particularly true in cases where a witness holds minority religious views that are poorly understood, or even disliked, by the majority in society. Of course, the converse is also of serious concern: there is a risk that the witness who holds more mainstream, popularly understood beliefs is more likely to be held credible.

48 And there is one final risk. In comparing two witnesses, one religious and one not, the religious witness may all too often benefit from the easy, ready-made inference of credibility that adherence to religious principles provides. No such ready-made inference is available to the non-believer, merely because her personal ethics may not fit within an easily understood or articulable archetype. . . .

49 Third, public policy concerns militate against using evidence of a witness' religious beliefs for credibility purposes. In s. 14 of the *Canada Evidence Act*, R.S.C. 1985, c. C-5, Parliament has made clear that an oath and affirmation are equivalent. This legislative policy reflects the Charter values of freedom of conscience and religion and of equality. This policy would be undermined by permitting or encouraging inquiry into the religious beliefs of witnesses in our courts for the purposes of assessing credibility. While there are some very limited circumstances in which inquiry into the degree to which an oath or affirmation binds a witness' conscience is permissible, these are restricted to

where there is reason to believe that the witness' oath or affirmation is not genuine. Such an inquiry is primarily a question of testimonial competence as opposed to credibility. See for example: *R. v. T.R.J.*, 2013 BCCA 449, 6 C.R. (7th) 207, at para. 4; *R. v. A.K.H.*, 2011 ONSC 5510, 97 W.C.B. (2d) 413, at paras. 27-28; *R. v. Bell*, 2011 ONSC 1218, [2011] O.J. No. 803, at para. 57.

50 It would be inappropriate to permit any more invasive inquiry. If religious beliefs (or the absence thereof) were to be considered relevant to bolstering a witness' credibility, then surely they would also be relevant to impeaching credibility. Under this approach, witness testimony could easily devolve into a roving inquiry into collateral facts relating to the religious beliefs of witnesses. The efficient and fair functioning of our courts would not be well served by such a development.

. . .

54 . . . It is an error of law to consider evidence of a witness' religious beliefs in assessing his or her credibility. This is true whether the issue is framed in relation to the significance of the oath for the witness, or in some other manner.

6. CORROBORATION

(a) When Required?

The ecclesiastical and civil law systems of proof provided that a verdict could not be had on the strength of one witness' evidence. For most issues two witnesses were sufficient but in other cases a higher number might be required. In addition, particular witnesses, according to their inherent quality or weakness, would be assigned a particular numerical value, perhaps a quarter or half of a regular witness. The common law generally resisted attempts at any quantitative measurement of the evidence necessary to a finding and the testimony of a single witness was sufficient. The common law was interested then in the quality of the witnesses tendered and not their number. The judge was entitled to express his opinion regarding that quality, but it was always for the jury, on the basis of their assessment, to accept or reject the testimony. As Greenshields J. expressed it:

> On questions of fact the presiding Judge is entitled to express an opinion as to the value of testimony offered; he is entitled to give his opinion as to the credibility of any particular witness, always, however, making it reasonably clear to the Jury that it is not bound to accept his opinion with respect to the facts; that it is the province of the Jury, irrespective of the guiding opinion of the Judge, to find upon the facts, particularly to pass upon the guilt or innocence of the accused. The extent to which the trial Judge should dwell upon the facts is largely discretionary, and that discretion rests with the Judge, and will not, if fairly and judicially exercised, be interfered with by an Appellate Court.[292]

---

[292]   *R. v. Gouin* (1926), 41 Que. K.B. 157 (C.A.). However see the criticism by O'Halloran, J.A. in *R. v. Pavlukoff* (1953), 10 W.W.R. 26 (B.C. C.A.) at 40-44.

The one common law exception to the general rule was the crime of perjury. The crime of perjury had been normally prosecuted in the Court of Star Chamber and that court followed ecclesiastical procedures wherein two witnesses were required. When the Court of Star Chamber was abolished in 1641 the prosecution of perjury in the common law courts incorporated the long-established practice of requiring two witnesses as an exception to its normal process. This practice is now reflected in Canada in s. 133 of the *Criminal Code*, which forbids a conviction of perjury "on the evidence of only one witness unless the evidence of that witness is corroborated in a material particular by evidence that implicates the accused".[293] A number of other statutory exceptions to the general rule have been created dependent either on the issue being litigated or on the kind of witness tendered. In some instances corroboration is required for a verdict while in others a warning is required that it is unsafe to convict without corroboration but open to the trier to do so.

(i) *Treason*

By the *Criminal Code*[294] the offence of treason requires corroboration. The roots of this requirement can be traced to a statute of Edward VI in 1547[295] requiring two witnesses in treason trials. The legislators, mindful of the excesses of Henry VIII, apparently saw this as a device to protect themselves against future regal uses of the law of treason. Wigmore wrote:

> The object of the rule requiring two witnesses in treason is plain enough. It is, as Sir William Blackstone said, to "secure the subject from being sacrificed to fictitious conspiracies, which have been the engines of profligate and crafty politicians in all ages.[296]

(ii) *Forgery*

The *Criminal Code* provided that corroboration was required to convict of forgery.[297] The requirement was an historical accident. This requirement was initially imposed in the *Forgery Act* of 1869,[298] when it was decided to allow witnesses to testify in such matters though they were interested in the outcome of the litigation.[299] It was, then, an exhibit of the legislators' caution in moving in that direction. Notice that the requirement of corroboration was limited to cases of those witnesses who were interested persons. When the *Criminal Code* was enacted in 1892 that limitation was abandoned and corroboration was required regardless of the character of the witness. No

---

[293] See *R. v. Doz* (1984), 12 C.C.C. (3d) 200 (Alta. C.A.) and *R. v. Predy* (1983), 17 C.C.C. (3d) 379 (Alta. C.A.).

[294] R.S.C. 1985, c. C-46, s. 47(2).

[295] 1 Edw. VI, c. 12, s. 22, discussed in 7 Wigmore, *Evidence* (3rd ed.), s. 2036.

[296] 7 Wigmore, *Evidence* (3rd ed.), s. 2037.

[297] R.S.C. 1985, c. C-46, s. 367(2). See *R. v. Esposito* (1985), 24 C.C.C. (3d) 88 (Ont. C.A.)

[298] 32 & 33 Vict., c. 19, s. 54.

[299] Parties could not testify until 1869: see the *Evidence Act*, S.O., 33 Vict., c. 13.

intelligent reason can presently be advanced for the requirement and the section was repealed in 1994.[300]

(iii) *Accomplices*

It is well-recognized that an accomplice who testifies for the prosecution may be purchasing immunity for himself or herself and this particular weakness in his or her testimony may need to be pointed out to the trier. During the nineteenth century it became a rule of practice. Lord Abinger wrote in 1837:

> It is a practice which deserves all the reverence of law, that judges have uniformly told juries that they ought not to pay any respect to the testimony of an accomplice, unless the accomplice is corroborated in some material circumstance. . . The danger is, that when a man is fixed, and knows that his own guilt is detected, he purchases impunity by falsely accusing others.[301]

This rule of practice became a rule of law in the twentieth century,[302] and the judge was required

> to warn the jury of the danger of convicting a prisoner on the uncorroborated testimony of an accomplice or accomplices, and, in the discretion of the judge, to advise them not to convict upon such evidence; but the judge should point out to the jury that it is within their legal province to convict upon such unconfirmed evidence.[303]

Failure to warn would result in the conviction being overturned. The classic definition of corroboration, accepted as gospel by the Canadian courts, was given by Lord Reading in *R. v. Baskerville*:

> We must hold that evidence in corroboration must be independent testimony which affects the accused by connecting or tending to connect him with the crime. In other words it must be evidence which implicates him, that is, which confirms in some material particular not only the evidence that the crime has been committed, but also that the prisoner committed it.[304]

Some courts required the trial judge to also indicate to the jury what evidence in the case was capable of constituting corroboration and to confine the jury to a consideration of those matters when determining if corroboration existed.[305] The law in this area grew into a complexity[306] which belied its humble beginnings as an admirable practice of caution.

---

[300]   *Criminal Law Amendment Act*, S.C. 1994, c. 44, s. 24.

[301]   *R. v. Farler* (1837), 173 E.R. 418 at 419.

[302]   See *R. v. Baskerville*, [1916] 2 K.B. 658 (C.C.A.); *Davies v. D.P.P.*, [1954] A.C. 378 (H.L.). And see in Canada *R. v. Gouin*, [1926] S.C.R. 539 accepting the *Baskerville* direction as a rule of law.

[303]   *Baskerville*, *ibid.* at 663. See *R. v. Chayko* (1984), 12 C.C.C. (3d) 157 (Alta. C.A.).

[304]   *Baskerville*, *ibid.* at 667.

[305]   See *R. v. Racine* (1977), 32 C.C.C. (2d) 468 (Ont. C.A.). The Supreme Court of Canada left this point open: see *Kirsch v. R.* (1982), 62 C.C.C. (2d) 86 (S.C.C.).

[306]   To see how complex see Branca, *Corroboration in Studies in Canadian Criminal Evidence* (1972), ed. by Salhany & Carter; and Maloney, *Corroboration Revisited, Studies in Criminal Law and Procedure* (1973, C.B.A). See also the book by Wakeling, *Corroboration in Canadian Law* (1977).

VETROVEC v. R.

[1982] 1 S.C.R. 811, 67 C.C.C. (2d) 1, 27 C.R. (3d) 304

The accused were two of several persons charged with conspiring to traffic in heroin. The principal evidence against the accused was given by an accomplice who testified that he met the accused in Hong Kong and that they supplied him with six pounds of heroin which he then brought into the United States where he again met with the accused, and then into Canada where he again met them. The trial judge directed the jury that it was dangerous to act on the uncorroborated evidence of the accomplice but that certain pieces of evidence indicating that the accused were in Hong Kong at the relevant time and other pieces of evidence referring to subsequent events and indicating that the accused were involved in drug trafficking were all capable of corroborating the accomplice. The accused were convicted. The appeal by the accused was dismissed.

DICKSON J.: —

. . .

I would like to review and reassess general principles relating to the law of corroboration of accomplices. This is one of the most complicated and technical areas of the law of evidence. It is also in need of reform. Both the Law Reform Commission of Canada (Report on Evidence, s. 88(b) of the proposed Code) and the English Criminal Law Revision Committee (11th Report on Evidence 1972, Cmnd 4991, paras. 183-5), have recently recommended a drastic overhaul of the law of corroboration. The Evidence Code proposed by the Law Reform Commission of Canada would contain the following provision:

> 88. For greater certainty it is hereby provided that:
>
> . . .
>
> > (b) Every rule of law that requires the corroboration of evidence as a basis for a conviction or that requires that the jury be warned of the danger of convicting on the basis of uncorroborated evidence is abrogated.
>
> . . .

In the case of a jury charge in which a witness who might be regarded as an accomplice testifies, it has become not merely a rule of practice but a rule of law for the trial judge to warn the jury that it is dangerous to found a conviction on the evidence of an accomplice unless that evidence is corroborated in a material particular implicating the accused. The jury may convict in such circumstances but it is dangerous to do so. The judge must determine as a matter of law whether the witness might be an accomplice for the purposes of the rule. The jury must then decide whether he is in fact an accomplice. The judge explains the legal definition of "corroboration" with heavy reliance upon what was said by Lord Reading in *R. v. Baskerville*. The judge lists for the jury the pieces of evidence which are in his view capable of amounting to corroboration. Finally, they are told that it is for the jury to decide whether the evidence to which their attention has been directed does amount to corroboration, As the study paper of the Law Reform Commission of Canada "Evidence: Paper Study 11, Corroboration" dryly observes an "enormous superstructure ... has been erected on the original basic proposition that the evidence of some witnesses should be approached with caution".

The accused is in the unhappy position of hearing the judge draw particular attention to the evidence which tends to confirm the testimony the accomplice has given. Cogent prejudicial testimony is thus repeated and highlighted. For the jury this part of the charge can only be, in the words of Lord Diplock in *Director of Public Prosecutions v. Hester*, [1972] 3 All E.R. 1056 at p. 1075, "a frequent source of bewilderment". The task of a trial judge seeking to identify the evidence capable of amounting to corroboration is unenviable. Lord Reading in the Baskerville case said that it would be in high degree dangerous to attempt to formulate the kind of evidence which could be regarded as corroboration. It is also often a difficult and dangerous exercise identifying what pieces of evidence are capable of being corroborative.

. . .

In evaluating the adequacy of the law in this area, the first question which must be answered is a basic one: why have a special rule for accomplices at all? Credibility of witnesses and the weight of the evidence is, in general, a matter for the trier of fact. Identification evidence, for example, is notoriously weak, and yet the trial judge is not automatically required, as a matter of law, to instruct the jury on this point. Similarly, the trial judge is not required in all cases to warn the jury with respect to testimony of other witnesses with disreputable and untrustworthy backgrounds. Why, then, should we automatically require a warning when an accomplice takes the stand.

. . .

Since the judge's instructions on this issue involve questions of law, numerous technical appeals are taken on the issue of whether a particular item of evidence is "capable" of constituting corroboration. The body of case-law is so complex that it has in turn produced a massive periodical literature. Moreover, the cases are difficult to reconcile. The Law Reform Commission of Canada has described the case-law in the area as full of "subtleties, variations, inconsistencies and great complexities": study paper 11, at p. 7. The result is that what was originally a simple, common-sense proposition — an accomplice's testimony should be viewed with caution — becomes transformed into a difficult and highly technical area of law. Whether this "enormous superstructure" (to use the description of the Law Reform Commission) has any meaningful relationship with the task performed by the jury is unknown.

. . .

The law of corroboration is unduly and unnecessarily complex and technical. I would hold that there is no special category for "accomplices". An accomplice is to be treated like any other witness testifying at a criminal trial and the judge's conduct, if he chooses to give his opinion, is governed by the general rules. I would only like to add one or two observations concerning the proper practice to be followed in the trial court where as a matter of common sense something in the nature of confirmatory evidence should be found before the finder of fact relies upon the evidence of a witness whose testimony occupies a central position in the purported demonstration of guilt and yet may be suspect by reason of the witness being an accomplice or complainant or of disreputable character. There are great advantages to be gained by simplifying the instruction to juries on the question as to when a prudent juror will seek some confirmation of the story of such a witness, before concluding that the story is true and adopting it in the process of finding guilt in the accused as charged. It does not, however, always follow that the presiding justice may always simply turn the jury loose upon the evidence without any assisting analysis as to whether or not a prudent finder of fact can find confirmation somewhere in the mass of evidence of the evidence of a witness.

Because of the infinite range of circumstance which will arise in the criminal trial process it is not sensible to attempt to compress into a rule, a formula or a direction the concept of the need for prudent scrutiny of the testimony of any witness. What may be appropriate, however, in some circumstances, is a clear and sharp warning to attract the attention of the juror to the risks of adopting, without more, the evidence of the witness. There is no magic in the word corroboration, or indeed in any other comparable expression such as confirmation and support. The idea implied in those words may, however, in an appropriate case, be effectively and efficiently transmitted to the mind of the trier of fact. This may entail some illustration from the evidence of the particular case of the type of evidence, documentary or testimonial, which might be drawn upon by the juror in confirmation of the witness's testimony or some important part thereof. I do not wish to be taken as saying that such illustration must be carried to exhaustion. However, there is, in some circumstances, particularly in lengthy trials, the need for helpful direction on the question of sifting the evidence where guilt or innocence might, and probably will, turn on the acceptance or rejection, belief or disbelief, of the evidence of one or more witnesses. All of this applies equally in the case of an accomplice, or a disreputable witness of demonstrated moral lack, as, for example, a witness with a record of perjury. All this takes one back to the beginning and that is the search for the impossible: a rule which embodies and codifies common sense in the realm of the process of determining guilt or innocence of an accused on the basis of a record which includes evidence from potentially unreliable sources such as an accomplice.

[The Court, in the result, decided that in this case it would have been sufficient for the trial judge simply to have instructed the jury that they should view the testimony of the accomplice with great caution and that it would be wise to look for other supporting evidence before convicting the accused. However, since the trial judge did outline for the jury items of evidence he considered capable of corroborating the accomplice's testimony, the court examined this evidence to ensure that the accused were not prejudiced by the instruction. The Court decided that the evidence referred to by the trial judge was capable of corroborating the accomplice. In the result, the instructions by the trial judge did not prejudice the accused.]

R. v. KHELA
[2009] 1 S.C.R. 104, 62 C.R. (6th) 197, 238 C.C.C. (3d) 489 (S.C.C.)

The two accused, K and S, were tried jointly on charges of first degree murder. It was alleged that K paid two shooters to murder the victim, and that S helped to organize the killing. The case against K rested primarily on testimony from two members of a prison-based gang that K had hired the two shooters. Several women associates of these unsavoury witnesses also testified against K. The case against S rested mainly on the testimony of W, S's girlfriend at the time of the shooting, who claimed to have witnessed various incriminating acts and statements by S before and after the killing.

The two prison gang members were the subject of a *Vetrovec* warning. The trial judge stated that, given these witnesses' criminal backgrounds, it would be dangerous to convict on their evidence unless it was confirmed or supported by other evidence. The trial judge instructed the jury to look for some confirmation from somebody or something other than what the unsavoury witnesses had to say before relying on their testimony to convict. The trial judge noted that the jury might find some confirmatory evidence in the case, and that they should consider the evidence of the female associates in that regard, while remembering that the defence had labelled the female associates as liars. The female witnesses were not the subjects of a *Vetrovec* warning.

The issue before the Supreme Court was the adequacy of this unsavoury witness warning.

FISH J. (BINNIE, LEBEL, FISH, ABELLA, CHARRON, ROTHSTEIN JJ. concurring):

[11] The central purpose of a *Vetrovec* warning is to alert the jury to the danger of relying on the unsupported evidence of unsavoury witnesses and to explain the reasons for special scrutiny of their testimony. In appropriate cases, the trial judge should also draw the attention of the jurors to evidence capable of confirming or supporting the material parts of the otherwise untrustworthy evidence.

[12] Since the decision of this Court in *Vetrovec*, the very real dangers of relying in criminal prosecutions on the unsupported evidence of unsavoury witnesses, particularly "jailhouse informers", has been highlighted more than once by commissions of inquiry into wrongful convictions (see, for example, *The Commission on Proceedings Involving Guy Paul Morin: Report* (1998) and *The Inquiry Regarding Thomas Sophonow* (2001)). The danger of a miscarriage of justice is to be borne in mind in crafting and in evaluating the adequacy of a caution.

[13] The crafting of a caution appropriate to the circumstances of the case is best left to the judge who has conducted the trial. No particular set of words is mandatory. In evaluating its adequacy, appellate courts will focus on the content of the instruction and not on its form. Intervention on appeal will not be warranted unless a cautionary instruction should have been given but was

not, or the cautionary instruction that was given failed to serve its intended purpose.

[14] No single formula can be expected to produce an appropriate instruction for every foreseeable — let alone *unforeseeable* — situation at trial. That is why we vest in trial judges the discretion they must have in fashioning cautionary instructions responsive to the circumstances of the case. Trial judges nonetheless seek, and are entitled to expect, guidance from this Court as to the general characteristics of a sufficient warning. I shall later outline in broad brushstrokes a proposed template which, while not at all mandatory, will in my view be of assistance to trial judges without unduly fettering their discretion, and will reduce the number of appeals attributable to the present uncertainty regarding the governing principles.

[15] Read as a whole, and in the context of the trial, the charge to the jury in this case was adequate. Any shortcomings in the *Vetrovec* caution itself were compensated for in the remainder of the charge. I am satisfied that the jury would have understood that it could not convict the appellants on the basis of the evidence of the impugned witnesses unless they found elsewhere in the evidence sufficient comfort that those witnesses were telling the truth.

[16] Accordingly, I would dismiss the appeals.

. . .

[31] This Court, in *Vetrovec*, changed the law in relation to unsavoury witness warnings in two important ways. First, the Court held that trial judges, rather than attempting to "pigeonhole" witnesses as an "accomplices", ought instead to consider all of the factors that might impair their credibility and decide on that basis whether a special instruction is necessary. Second, the Court relieved triers of fact from applying the technical definition of corroboration and directed them instead simply to determine whether the "evidence properly weighed overcame its suspicious roots" (*Brooks*, at para. 69). Dickson J. held that there was no magic in the word corroboration, "or indeed in any other comparable expression such as confirmation and support" (*Vetrovec*, at p. 831).

[32] Dickson J. adopted this "common sense" approach having found the law of corroboration "unduly and unnecessarily complex and technical" (p. 830). This approach, while unburdening judges and juries of the technical requirements of corroboration, was not meant to imply that any and all evidence is capable of confirming the testimony of a potentially untrustworthy witness. As Major J. noted in *Brooks*,

> [t]his new approach, while a change, was not intended to prejudice the accused. It would not lessen the protection afforded the accused when faced with unsavoury witnesses. Equally, it was intended that the jury could view that evidence with more ease but not less scepticism than previously required. [para. 69]

[33] The relaxation of the corroboration rules in *Vetrovec* was not a signal that juries should be set "loose upon the evidence without any assisting analysis as to whether or not a prudent finder of fact can find confirmation somewhere in the mass of evidence" (*Vetrovec*, at p. 831). The trial judge retains the role of providing the jury with "the proper framework within which that credibility can be evaluated" (*Brooks*, at para. 130, *per* Binnie J.).

[34] Since *Vetrovec*, this Court and several appellate courts have provided guidance on the appropriate form and content of the "clear, sharp warning". In *Brooks*, Justice Major wrote (at para. 94) that while no particular language is required, "[a]t a minimum", the caution must focus the jury's attention specifically on the inherently unreliable evidence. It should refer to the characteristics of the witness that bring the credibility of his or her evidence into serious question. It should plainly emphasize the dangers inherent in convicting an accused on the basis of such evidence unless confirmed by independent evidence.

[35] Speaking for himself and Justices Iacobucci and Arbour, Major J. also cited with approval (at para. 79) this passage from a commentary by Marc Rosenberg (now Rosenberg J.A.) on *Vetrovec* and its progeny:

> The judge should first in an objective way determine whether there is a reason to suspect the credibility of the witness according to the traditional means by which such determinations are made. This would include a review of the evidence to determine whether there are factors which have properly led the courts to be wary of accepting a witness's evidence. Factors might include involvement of criminal activities, a motive to lie by reason of connection to the crime or to the authorities, unexplained delay in coming forward with the story, providing different accounts on other occasions, lies told under oath, and similar considerations. It is not then whether the trial judge personally finds the witness trustworthy but whether there are factors which experience teaches that the witness's story be approached with caution. Second, the trial judge must assess the importance of the witness to the Crown's case. If the witness plays a relatively minor role in the proof of guilt it is probably unnecessary to burden the jury with a special caution and then review the confirmatory evidence. However, the more important the witness the greater the duty on the judge to give the caution. At some point, as where the witness plays a central role in the proof of guilt, the warning is mandatory. This, in my view, flows from the duty imposed on the trial judge in criminal cases to review the evidence and relate the evidence to the issues. ("Developments in the Law of Evidence: The 1992-93 Term — Applying the Rules" (1994), 5 *S.C.L.R.* (2d) 421, at p. 463)

[36] Though he arrived at a different result, Binnie J. agreed in *Brooks* (at para. 130) that what matters, in determining the need for a clear and sharp warning, is not the judge's personal opinion as to the trustworthiness of the witness, but whether there are factors which experience shows us as requiring "that the witness's story be approached with caution".

[37] In *Sauvé*, at para. 82, the Ontario Court of Appeal set out a principled framework that will assist trial judges in constructing *Vetrovec* warnings

appropriate to the circumstances of each case. That proposed framework, which I adopt and amplify here, is composed of four main foundation elements: (1) drawing the attention of the jury to the testimonial evidence requiring special scrutiny; (2) explaining *why* this evidence is subject to special scrutiny; (3) cautioning the jury that it is dangerous to convict on unconfirmed evidence of this sort, though the jury is entitled to do so if satisfied that the evidence is true; and (4) that the jury, in determining the veracity of the suspect evidence, should look for evidence from another source tending to show that the untrustworthy witness is telling the truth as to the guilt of the accused (*R. v. Kehler*, 2004 SCC 11, [2004] 1 S.C.R. 328, at paras. 17-19).

[38] While this summary should not be applied in a rigid and formulaic fashion, it accurately captures the elements that should guide trial judges in crafting their instructions on potentially untrustworthy witnesses. The fourth component, of particular interest on this appeal, provides guidance on the kind of evidence that is capable of confirming the suspect testimony of an impugned witness.

[39] Common sense dictates that not all evidence presented at trial is capable of confirming the testimony of an impugned witness. The attribute of independence defines the kind of evidence that can provide comfort to the trier of fact that the witness is telling the truth. Where evidence is "tainted" by connection to the *Vetrovec* witness it can not serve to confirm his or her testimony (N. Harris, "*Vetrovec* Cautions and Confirmatory Evidence: A Necessarily Complex Relationship" (2005), 31 C.R. (6th) 216, at p. 225; *R. v. Sanderson*, 2003 MBCA 109, 180 C.C.C. (3d) 53, at para. 61).

[40] Materiality is a more difficult concept. In *Vetrovec*, the Court did away with the requirement that corroborating evidence implicate the accused. As Dickson J. noted, such evidence is not the only type capable of convincing a jury that a witness is telling the truth. In *Kehler*, the Court confirmed that evidence, to be considered confirmatory, does not have to implicate the accused. We maintain that position here.

[41] Individual items of confirmatory evidence need not implicate the accused. As Dickson J. explained in *Vetrovec*:

> The reason for requiring corroboration is that we believe the witness has good reason to lie. We therefore want some other piece of evidence which tends to convince us that he is telling the truth. Evidence which implicates the accused does indeed serve to accomplish that purpose but it cannot be said that this is the only sort of evidence which will accredit the accomplice. [p. 826]

[42] However, when looked at in the context of the case as a whole, the items of confirmatory evidence should give comfort to the jury that the witness can be trusted in his or her assertion that the accused is the person who committed the offence.

Deschamps J. dissented in part on the basis that the majority's opinion was part of a regrettable incremental return to the former formalism of the former law of corroboration.[307]

(iv) *Informers*

R. v. BROOKS
[2000] 1 S.C.R. 237, 30 C.R. (5th) 201, 141 C.C.C. (3d) 321

A 19-month-old child was found murdered in her crib wrapped in a green comforter. Only the accused and the child's mother had access to her on the night of the murder. The Crown led evidence from two jailhouse informants, King and Balogh, who testified that the accused, while incarcerated, had admitted that he had killed the child to stop her crying. Both informants had lengthy criminal records of dishonesty. One unsuccessfully sought a lighter sentence in return for his testimony and had testified as an informant in a prior trial. The other had a history of substance abuse and a psychiatric history highlighted by suicide attempts, paranoia, deep depression and a belief in clairvoyant ability. Both had histories of offering to testify in criminal trials. The trial judge's jury charge did not provide a *Vetrovec* warning to the jury about the danger of relying on the informants' testimonies. Neither counsel requested a warning nor objected to the lack of a warning. The accused was convicted of first degree murder. The Court of Appeal set aside the conviction and ordered a new trial.

BASTARACHE J. (GONTHIER, and MCLACHLIN JJ. concurring): —

. . .

It is my opinion that the decision not to give a *Vetrovec* warning was within the discretion of the trial judge and that the exercise of this discretion should not have been interfered with on appeal. I have reached this conclusion for the reasons I set out below.

In *Vetrovec*, Dickson J. held that a trial judge has the discretion, and not the duty, to give a clear and sharp warning to the jury with respect to the testimony of certain "unsavoury" witnesses. Dickson J. followed what he referred to as the "common sense" approach, moving away from "blind and empty formalism" and "ritualistic incantations".... This Court in *Vetrovec* deliberately chose not to formulate a fixed and invariable rule where "clear and sharp" warnings would be required as a matter of course regarding the testimony of certain categories of witnesses. Rather, where a witness occupies a central position in the determination of guilt and, yet, may be suspect because of a disreputable or untrustworthy character, a clear and sharp warning may be appropriate to alert the jury to the risks of adopting the evidence "without more". It is therefore within the trial judge's discretion to give a *Vetrovec* caution. . . In exercising his or her discretion to warn the jury regarding certain evidence, the trial judge may consider, *inter alia*, the credibility of the witness and the importance of the evidence to the Crown's case. These factors affect

---

[307]   For comments on *Khela* see C.R. annotations by Lisa Dufraimont and Michael Plaxton.

whether the *Vetrovec* warning is required. In other words, the greater the concern over the credibility of the witness and the more important the evidence, the more likely the *Vetrovec* caution will be mandatory. Where the evidence of so called "unsavoury witnesses" represents the whole of the evidence against the accused, a "clear and sharp" *Vetrovec* warning may be warranted. Where, however, there is strong evidence to support the conviction in the absence of the potentially "unsavoury" evidence, and less reason to doubt the witness's credibility, the *Vetrovec* warning would not be required, and a lesser instruction would be justified. The trial judge's instruction with respect to the evidence of jailhouse informants must therefore be commensurate with the particular circumstances of the case. For example, the trial judge is not required to give a "clear and sharp" warning on the dangers of convicting on the impugned evidence where, in the circumstances, the trial judge believes that there is no such danger. Similarly, the trial judge may properly decline to give a warning if the warning may prejudice the accused's case rather than assist it. Provided there is a foundation for the trial judge's exercise of discretion, appellate courts should not interfere. Here, that foundation was established having regard to the credibility of the witnesses, the importance of their evidence and the failure to request a warning.

. . .

To find that the trial judge's failure to provide a "clear and sharp" *Vetrovec* warning in the circumstances of this case amounts to an error of law runs counter to the spirit of *Vetrovec*, which affirmed a judicial discretion to provide warnings only in appropriate circumstances. Provided there is a foundation for the judge's exercise of discretion, appellate courts should not interfere. Here that foundation existed. For these reasons, I am unable to conclude that the failure of the trial judge to give a "clear and sharp" *Vetrovec* warning amounted to an error of law. I would allow the appeal accordingly and restore the conviction entered by the trial judge.

MAJOR J. (IACOBUCCI and ARBOUR JJ. concurring): —

. . .

In my opinion, the trial judge ought to have given a *Vetrovec* warning. In its absence the charge was not the equivalent nor was it adequate. In the result it cannot be said that the verdict would necessarily have been the same and accordingly the appeal should be dismissed.

. . .

In summary, two main factors are relevant when deciding whether a *Vetrovec* warning is necessary: the witness's credibility, and the importance of the witness's testimony to the Crown's case. No specific threshold need be met on either factor before a warning becomes necessary. Instead, where the witness is absolutely essential to the Crown's case, more moderate credibility problems will warrant a warning. Where the witness has overwhelming credibility problems, a warning may be necessary even if the Crown's case is a strong one without the witness's evidence. In short, the factors should not be looked to independently of one another but in combination.

Recommendations of the Kaufman Report

Since the decisions of this Court in *Vetrovec* and *Bevan*, the extreme dangers of relying on the use of "jailhouse informers" as witnesses in criminal prosecutions has been highlighted in the *Report of The Commission on Proceedings Involving Guy Paul Morin* (the "Kaufman Report") released in 1998 where the Honourable Fred Kaufman, C.M., Q.C., stated at p. 602:

> In-custody informers are almost invariably motivated by self-interest. They often have little or no respect for the truth or their testimonial oath or affirmation. Accordingly, they may lie or tell the truth, depending only upon where their perceived self-interest lies. In-custody confessions are often easy to allege and difficult, if not impossible, to disprove.

and at p. 638:

> The evidence at this Inquiry demonstrates the inherent unreliability of in-custody informer testimony, its contribution to miscarriages of justice and the substantial risk that the dangers may not be fully appreciated by the jury. In my view, the present law has developed to the point that a cautionary instruction is virtually mandated in cases where the in-custody informer's testimony is contested.

Since the release of the Kaufman Report, the Ministry of the Attorne_timesy General of Ontario has revised its internal policies to reflect many of the Report's recommendations. New policies include the establishment of an "In-Custody Informer Committee", the function of which is to review the use of all in-custody informers in criminal trials to determine whether their use as a witness is in the public interest. The Ministry has also adopted into its Policy Manual the Kaufman Report's recommended list of factors to be considered in assessing an informer's reliability or lack thereof. The factors also serve as a useful guide to a trial judge when determining whether a *Vetrovec* warning is necessary.

. . .

In my opinion the failure of the trial judge to give a *Vetrovec* warning was a misdirection of law. The question is then whether in light of all the evidence the test in *Bevan* is met. Would the result have necessarily been the same?

[Major J. then examined the other evidence in the case and concluded.]

There was evidence that implicated the accused but with a proper instruction regarding the testimony of the jailhouse informants it is difficult for me to preclude the possibility of a different result. I agree with the Court of Appeal and would dismiss the appeal and confirm the order for a new trial.

BINNIE J.: —

I agree with the result reached by Justice Bastarache, but I reach that conclusion by a different route. In my view, the evidence of the "jailhouse informants" in this case was tainted by a combination of some of the more notorious badges of testimonial unreliability, including the opportunity to lie for personal benefit, and the jury ought to have been given a clear and sharp warning to that effect. The trial judge erred in law in failing to give such a warning, as found by Justice Major and a majority of the Ontario Court of Appeal. At the same time, I differ, with respect, from the conclusion that this error of law requires a new trial. Given the other evidence against the respondent that was necessarily accepted by the jury in reaching their verdict of first degree murder, I think, with great respect to those of the opposite view, that there is no reasonable possibility that the verdict would have been different had the error of law not been made.

. . .

[Binnie J. then reviewed the evidence and concluded.]

For these reasons, I conclude that the failure of the trial judge to give a *Vetrovec* warning was an error of law, but that there is no reasonable possibility the jury would have rendered a different verdict had the proper warning been given. The Crown bears a heavy onus in seeking the application of the curative provision of s. 686(1)(*b*)(iii) but, for the reasons given, it is my view that justice does not require a new trial on the particular facts of this case. The appeal should therefore be allowed and the respondent's conviction and sentence restored.

(v) *Primary Witnesses in Sex Cases*

In the early common law the testimony of the victim in the trial of a sexual offence was sufficient to support a conviction. In Hale, *Pleas of the Crown,* we read:

> The party ravished may give evidence upon oath and is in law a competent witness; but the credibility of her testimony, and how far forth she is to be believed, must be left to the jury, and is more or less credible according to the circumstances of fact that concur in that testimony. . . It is one thing whether a witness be admissible to be heard; another thing, whether they are to be believed when heard. It is true, rape is a most detestable crime, and therefore ought severely and impartially to be punished with death; but it must be remembered that it is an accusation easily to be made and hard to be proved; and harder to be defended by the party accused, tho never so innocent.[308]

By 1925, however, the common law had come to demand a similar warning about the evidence of primary witnesses in sex cases as they had required respecting the evidence of accomplices. Hewart L.C.J. in *R. v. Jones* wrote:

> The proper direction in such a case [where the offence charged is a sexual offence] is that it is not safe to convict upon the uncorroborated testimony of the prosecutrix, but that the jury, if they are satisfied of the truth of her evidence, may, after paying attention to that warning, nevertheless convict.[309]

In Canada the *Criminal Code* was amended in 1954 to provide that with regard to five sexual offences (rape, attempted rape, sexual intercourse with

---

[308]   1680, Hale, L.C.J., *Pleas of the Crown* at 1, 633, 635 quoted in 7 Wigmore, *Evidence,* 3rd ed., s. 2061.

[309]   (1925), 19 Cr. App. R. 40 at 41.

a female under 14, sexual intercourse with a female between 14 and 16, and indecent assault on a female):

> . . . the judge shall, if the only evidence that implicates the accused is the evidence, given under oath, of the female person in respect of whom the offence is alleged to have been committed and that evidence is not corroborated in a material particular by evidence that implicates the accused, instruct the jury that it is not safe to find the accused guilty in the absence of such corroboration, but that they are entitled to find the accused guilty if they are satisfied beyond a reasonable doubt that her evidence is true.[310]

Glanville Williams sought to justify the instruction:

> There is sound reason for this, because sexual cases are particularly subject to the danger of deliberately false charges, resulting from sexual neurosis, fantasy, jealousy, spite, or simply a girl's refusal to admit that she consented to an act of which she is now ashamed. Of these various possibilities, the most subtle are those connected with mental complexes.[311]

In 1975 the *Criminal Code* provision was repealed and, after a period of uncertainty, it now seems settled that the common law requirement of a warning was not thereby revived.[312]

The *Criminal Code* continued to require corroboration prior to conviction for a number of other sexual offences: per s. 139, sexual intercourse with the feeble-minded, incest, seduction of a female between 16 and 18 years of age, seduction under the promise of marriage, sexual intercourse with a step-daughter, seduction of female passengers on vessels, parent or guardian of female person procuring her defilement; per s. 195, procuring;[313] per s. 253, communicating venereal disease to another person;[314] per s. 256, procuring a feigned marriage.[315] Wigmore described statutory requirements of corroboration in sex cases:

> The fact is that, in the light of modern psychology, this technical rule of corroboration seems but a crude and childish measure, if it be relied upon as an adequate means for determining the credibility of the complaining witness in such charges. The problem of estimating the veracity of feminine testimony in complaints against masculine offenders is baffling enough to the experienced psychologist. This statutory rule is unfortunate in that it tends to produce reliance upon a rule of thumb. Better to inculcate the resort to an expert scientific analysis of the particular witness' mentality, as the true measure of enlightenment.[316]

---

[310] See R.S.C. 1970, c. 34, s. 142.

[311] "Corroboration — Sexual Cases" [1962] Crim. L. Rev. 662.

[312] See *R. v. Camp* (1977), 36 C.C.C. (2d) 511 (Ont. C.A.) and *R. v. Firkins* (1977), 37 C.C.C. (2d) 227 (B.C. C.A.). But compare *R. v. Riley* (1978), 42 C.C.C. (2d) 437 (Ont. C.A.) and *R. v. Curtis*, [1989] N.J. No. 84 (C.A.), regarding the need for caution when relying solely on the evidence of the complainant in a sexual assault case. In *R. v. Fatunmbi*, 2014 MBCA 53, 310 C.C.C. (3d) 93, 12 C.R. (7th) 146 (Man. C.A.) the Court held that a trial judge should warn the jury where the complainant's evidence is central to guilt and the inconsistencies are significant. See strong criticism of Janine Benedet that this wrongly reintroduces a corroboration requirement.

[313] See now R.S.C. 1985, c. C-46, s. 212.

[314] *Ibid.*, s. 289.

[315] *Ibid.*, s. 292.

[316] 7 Wigmore, *Evidence* (3rd ed.), s. 2061 at 354. For a good critical note calling for the repeal of such statutory provisions see "The Rape Corroboration Requirement: Repeal Not Reform"

Notice that the requirements here imposed *forbade conviction* even if the trier of fact was satisfied of the accused's guilt beyond a reasonable doubt.

The neanderthal ideas and attitudes above described in this section have now been largely overcome, at least in our legislative provisions. In 1982 s. 139 was repealed and s. 246.4 enacted. Section 246.4 was later enlarged in 1988 and the counterpart section now provides:

> 274. If an accused is charged with an offence under section 151, 152, 153, 153.1, 155, 159, 160, 170, 171, 172, 173, 212, 271, 272 or 273, no corroboration is required for a conviction and the judge shall not instruct the jury that it is unsafe to find the accused guilty in the absence of corroboration.

R. v. S. (F.)

(1997), 116 C.C.C. (3d) 435 (Ont. C.A.)

The accused was charged with sexual assault causing bodily harm.

FINLAYSON J.A. (WEILER and LASKIN JJ.A. concurring):—

The complainant's testimony was central to the case for the Crown. However, with the exception of her evidence with respect to the incidents at the motel, her testimony was unsupported by any independent confirmatory evidence. In my opinion this case did call for a "clear and sharp warning" in relation to the testimony of the complainant as called for in *Vetrovec*. Apart from the highly suspect account she gave of the Lake Wilcox incident, the complainant had a lengthy psychiatric history, the details of which were before the jury, and which included "flashback" recollections of certain events. Her past conduct also revealed a pattern of false statements of fact to her doctors.

(vi) *Unsworn Evidence of Children*

If a child is sworn as a witness the judge is directed to warn the jury to treat his or her evidence with caution much as he or she would warn them with respect to the testimony of accomplices. In *R. v. Kendall*,[317] Judson J. explained:

> The basis for the rule of practice which requires the Judge to warn the jury of the danger of convicting on the evidence of a child, even when sworn as a witness, is the mental immaturity of the child. The difficulty is fourfold: 1. His capacity of observation. 2. His capacity of recollection. 3. His capacity to understand questions put and frame intelligent answers. 4. His moral responsibility.

Section 586 of the *Criminal Code* forbade conviction "upon the unsworn evidence of a child unless the evidence of the child is corroborated in a material particular by evidence that implicated the accused". Provisions in the *Canada Evidence Act* and in most of the provincial Evidence Acts mirrored

---

(1972) 81 Yale L.J. 1365. See also Bienen, "A Question of Credibility: John Henry Wigmore's Use of Scientific Authority" (1983) 19 Cal. Western L. Rev. 235.

[317] (1962), 132 C.C.C. 216 (S.C.C.) at 220.

this requirement.[318] Notice again that findings were *prohibited* though the trier is satisfied beyond a reasonable doubt.

In 1988 s. 586 (659) of the *Criminal Code*[319] and s. 16(2) of the *Canada Evidence Act*[320] were repealed. While the requirement of corroboration for the unsworn testimony of children was dispensed with, the legislation did not, unlike the new s. 246.4, say anything forbidding a cautionary warning. For many, unfortunately, the "wisdom" of *Kendall* will cause many judges and lawyers to continue to be distrustful of the evidence of children. The common sense displayed in *Vetrovec* mandates that we ought not to automatically characterize a witness's capacity for truth-telling depending on whether they belong to a particular class of people. No one should assume that all children are inherently suspect. The child witness should be treated like other witnesses, as an individual with whatever individual shortcomings or individual attributes that are there to be observed. Rather than parroting such phrases as "Out of the mouths of babes can only come truth . . .", or "It is well known that children fantasize (have poor memories, lack perceptual abilities) . . ." we, as lawyers, need to become more aware of the social science literature and the empirical studies that have been done.

(vii) *Miscellaneous Provisions*

A number of statutory provisions exist in provincial legislation which require corroboration for a finding. For example, provisions in a number of Evidence Acts demand corroboration in actions against estates of deceased persons,[321] and in actions by or against the mentally ill.[322]

(b) What is Corroboration?

The classic definition of corroboration given by Lord Reading in *R. v. Baskerville*[323] requires that the corroborative evidence be independent of the principal witness and implicate the accused, that is "confirms in some material particular not only the evidence that the crime has been committed, but also that the prisoner committed it". Many of the statutory provisions requiring corroboration have similar language: "upon the evidence of only one witness, unless the evidence of that witness is corroborated in a material particular by evidence that implicates the accused". It is in the application of this definition to the evidence in the particular case that trial judges have had great difficulty and it "probably has given rise to more new trials being ordered by appellate courts than any other branch of the law of evidence".[324] It is difficult, if not impossible, to reconcile all the reported decisions on the

---

[318]   See *Canada Evidence Act*, s. 16(2); *Ontario Evidence Act*, s. 18(2).
[319]   1987, c. 24, s. 15; see now R.S.C. 1985, c. C-46, s. 659; 1993, c. 45, s. 9.
[320]   1987, c. 24, s. 18.
[321]   See e.g. R.S.O. 1980, c. 145, s. 13; R.S.A. 1980, c. A-21, s. 12.
[322]   See e.g. R.S.O. 1980, c. 145, s. 14; R.S.N. 1970, c. 115, s. 15.
[323]   [1916] 2 K.B. 658 (C.C.A.).
[324]   *Task Force Report on Uniform Rules of Evidence* (1981) at 428.

application of the definition but the Supreme Court has recently sought to explain.

R. v. B. (G.)
[1990] 2 S.C.R. 3, 77 C.R. (3d) 327, 56 C.C.C. (3d) 161

The accused was charged with committing an aggravated sexual assault on the complainant, a kindergarten student who was five years old at the time of the alleged offence. The complainant gave unsworn testimony at the trial. There was, then, a need for corroboration, pursuant to the legislation then in existence.

WILSON J. (L'HEUREUX-DUBÉ, GONTHIER, CORY and MCLACHLIN JJ., concurring):—

. . .

Any review of the case law dealing with corroboration must begin with a discussion of *Baskerville*. . .

It is the interpretation of [*Baskerville*] which seems to have caused confusion in recent years. . .

[The Crown] submits that the *Baskerville* rule is open to two interpretations. The first, or narrow rule, sees corroborative evidence as independent evidence that itself implicates the accused. The second, and considerably broader interpretation, is that if the witness identifies the accused and the evidence of the witness is confirmed in some material particular, then there is corroboration in law of that witness's evidence. The Crown advocates the broader interpretation. However, in my view, support for the broader interpretation is not to be found in Lord Reading's judgment. He made it abundantly clear throughout his reasons that there had to be corroborative evidence as to a material circumstance of the crime <u>and</u> as to the identity of the accused in relation to that crime. In *Vetrovec*, Dickson J. shared this view, stating at p. 826:

> Prior to the judgment of Lord Reading, there had been controversy over whether corroborative evidence must implicate the accused, or whether it was sufficient if it simply strengthened the credibility of the accomplice. Lord Reading settled the controversy in favour of the former view.

In the years following *Baskerville* the narrow interpretation of the rule was approved in numerous decisions of this Court. One text writer has commented that this Court acted upon the narrow interpretation of the rule on at least fifteen occasions over a period of sixty years: see Schiff, *Evidence in the Litigation Process* (1988), vol. 1, at p. 613. . . .

The Court [in *Vetrovec*] expressed a preference for a common sense approach rather than the overly technical approach in *Baskerville*. It found at least three problems with *Baskerville*. The first was that it confuses the reason behind the accomplice warning and prompts the courts to determine whether the corroborative evidence fits the definition rather than deciding whether there is evidence that bolsters the credibility of the accomplice. Secondly, because corroboration became a legal term of art the law in the area became increasingly complex and technical. Thirdly, and most importantly, the Court was of the view that the definition was unsound in principle. Dickson J. stated at p. 826:

> With great respect, on principle Lord Reading's approach seems perhaps over-cautious. The reason for requiring corroboration is that we believe the witness has good reason to lie. We therefore want some other piece of evidence which tends to convince us that he is telling the truth. Evidence which implicates the accused does indeed serve to accomplish that purpose but it cannot be said that this is the only sort of evidence which will accredit the accomplice.
>
> . . .

It seems to me, therefore, that this Court has clearly rejected an ultra technical approach to corroboration and has returned to a common sense approach which reflects the original rationale for the rule and allows cases to be determined on their merits. . .

I am, accordingly, in agreement with the Crown's position.

. . .

Also in favour of the liberal interpretation [of the legislation requiring corroboration] are the presumptions that the law does not require the impossible and the legislator intends only what is just and reasonable. Since the only evidence implicating the accused in many sexual offences against children will be the evidence of the child, imposing too restrictive a standard on their testimony may permit serious offences to go unpunished and perhaps to continue. Moreover, it is reasonable to assume that the legislator did not intend an accused to benefit from the youthful age of his victim by placing unnecessary impediments in the way of prosecuting offences against small children.[325]

---

[325]   See further regarding what counts as corroborative evidence *R. v. Dhillon* (2002), 166 C.C.C. (3d) 262 (Ont. C.A.) and *R. v. Kehler* (2004), 19 C.R. (6th) 49 (S.C.C.).

TABLE OF CASES

INDEX